CoreEconomics: Resources for the Contemporary Classroom

By Eric P. Chiang, Florida Atlantic University

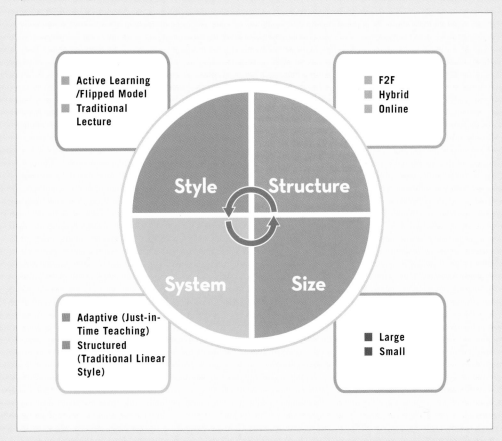

We have taken the best from the **CoreMedia** suite of resources and identified highly-regarded materials from contributors to **Open Educational Resources** to provide a guide for instructors looking to re-shape or re-vitalize their classroom. This includes face-to-face, hybrid, and online courses, matching the best resources with each approach. Resources include:

- **LaunchPad for Eric Chiang, CoreEconomics, 3e** including book-specific assignment and question banks, LearningCurve adaptive quizzing, e-book resources, dynamic and traditional PowerPoint slides, and student tutorials. Website: worthpublishers.com/LaunchPad

- **Resources for Instructors Looking to Develop an Active Learning Classroom** including sites run by pioneers in active learning (Eric Mazur), studies on "flipping the classroom," and blog-sites devoted to effective teaching practices (Agile Learning and the Eberly Center). Website: worthpublishers.com/activeecon

- **Resources to Add Content to Active Learning Classrooms** including in-class and online experiments from vEconLab, polling and clicker software and strategies, problem-solving and problem-based learning exercises. Website: worthpublishers.com/activeecon

- **Resources for Teaching with iPad and Tablet Computers** including apps and programs like iAnnotate, Notability, Haiku Deck, OmniGraphSketcher as well as content from EconWise, The World in Figures, FRED and the IMF Library. Website: worthpublishers.com/activeecon

Website: **worthpublishers.com/activeecon**

nomics Resources	Open Educational Resources (OER)	Notes
ıs signments essment	■ Present Data and Images ■ Additional Examples for Lecture ■ More OER examples at: worthpublishers.com/activeecon	This category represents a wide variance in teaching techniques depending on the experience and creativity of instructors. It is a common format in schools with a committee-designed curriculum.
blus… Chiang	■ Experiments from vEconLab ■ Blogs and Podcasts ■ More OER examples at: worthpublishers.com/activeecon	Many schools offer economic principles courses online, with lecture capture technologies growing in popularity. Online courses require greater emphasis on self-reinforcement tools that facilitate learning when classroom interaction is not available.
blus… onse Questions quizzing (including Instructor Lecture Topics) mework onomist	■ ii>clicker questions in class adapt the lecture to student needs. ■ Data from pre-lecture assessments can influence lecture discussions ■ More OER examples at: worthpublishers.com/activeecon	This format is common in honors courses, which would cover the core content and then cover additional topics based on the abilities and interests of students.
Chiang (with student response essment	■ Prezi and other presentation software can present many topics at varying depth for students ■ More OER examples at: worthpublishers.com/activeecon	This type of course is popular in vocational institutions, in which courses are offered online to the non-traditional student, such as working adults. Instructors must therefore adapt to the experiences and abilities of students as the course progresses.
blus… edded i>clicker Questions rPoints d Handouts Chiang	■ Add experiments from vEconLab or other sources ■ Use up-to-date FRED data from the St. Louis FED ■ More OER examples at: worthpublishers.com/activeecon	This is an increasingly popular method of teaching, especially in small classrooms, but can also be accomplished in large classes with preparation. Instructors must incentivize students to study course content before attending class.
Chiang ssessment scussion Boards essment	■ Prezi and other presentation software can present many topics at varying depth for students ■ Use up-to-date FRED data from the St. Louis FED ■ More OER examples at: worthpublishers.com/activeecon	Instructors pursuing this type of active learning online course would require various levels of student interaction. In some cases, students are asked to conduct presentations by uploading a recording of their presentation to YouTube or similar website.
esentations with embedded short quizzes rPoints quizzing (including instructor feedback ics) Chiang ssessment	■ Use polling software to determine comprehension ■ Prezi and other presentation software can present many topics at varying depth for students ■ Add experiments from vEconLab or other sources ■ More OER examples at: worthpublishers.com/activeecon	This method of instruction has gained acclaim for its demonstrated effectiveness, especially in physics. In-class activities like problems, policy debates and current events become the centerpiece of student learning.
quizzing (including instructor feedback ics) Chiang (with student response questions) esentations with embedded ssessment	■ Use discussion boards to drive questioning and comprehension ■ More OER examples at: worthpublishers.com/activeecon	Online classes with non-traditional students would benefit most from this instructional method, because it gives instructors the freedom to target the interests and abilities of their students.

Style	Structure	System	Description	CoreEc◆
Traditional	Face-to-Face/ Hybrid	Structured	A standard lecture-style classroom (both small and large) in which the instructor teaches course topics and students reinforce knowledge through post-lecture assignments and assessment. The outline of course topics (e.g., one chapter per week) is pre-determined.	■ PowerPoint Presentatio ■ LaunchPad Pre-Built A ■ Student Tutorials ■ Video Tutorials and Ass
Traditional	Online	Structured	Online courses can be distance-education (in which students read books and view slides without formal lectures) or lecture capture (in which students view pre-recorded lectures). The course outline is pre-determined and students are given assignments to reinforce lecture content.	■ F2F/Hybrid Structured ■ Video Lectures by Eric ■ Video Tutorials
Traditional	Face-to-Face/ Hybrid	Adaptive	This category can be considered the purest form of teaching, in which instructors lecture in a classroom but do not follow a pre-determined course outline. The level and breadth of instruction is determined as the term progresses based on student performance.	■ F2F/Hybrid Structured ■ i>clicker: Student Resp ■ LearningCurve adaptive Feedback for choosing ■ LaunchPad Practice Ho ■ RSS Feed from The Ec◆
Traditional	Online	Adaptive	A form of online teaching in which instructors tailor the course based on the experiences of students and their performance on each assessment. Instructors then increase or decrease the level and coverage of topics to meet student needs.	■ Online Structured plus ■ Video Lectures by Eric questions) ■ Video Tutorials and Ass
Active	Face-to-Face/ Hybrid	Structured	Active classrooms encourage students to read and prepare topics before class (often aided by online tutorials), thereby utilizing class time for activities such as peer-based learning, classroom experiments, and topical debates and discussions. The outline of topics in the course is pre-determined.	■ Traditional F2F/Hybrid ■ Dynamic PowerPoint Presentations with emb and short quizzes ■ Standard i>clicker Pow ■ Classroom Activities an ■ Video Lectures by Eric
Active	Online	Structured	Active online classrooms encourage students to read and prepare topics independently, and then engage in online discussion boards or chat sessions. Students share their knowledge and perspectives to the benefit of others in the class. The outline of topics in the course is pre-determined.	■ Video Lectures by Eric ■ Student Tutorials and A ■ Issues debates using D ■ Video Tutorials and Ass
Active	Face-to-Face/ Hybrid	Adaptive	This category represents a very open-ended form of class. Students are expected to read and prepare material before class, and engage in various activities such as peer-learning, classroom experiments, and debates. Instructors allow students to influence the time spent on each topic.	■ Dynamic PowerPoint Pr i>clicker Questions and ■ Standard i>clicker Pow ■ Classroom Activities ■ LearningCurve adaptive for choosing lecture top ■ Video Lectures by Eric ■ Student Tutorials and A
Active	Online	Adaptive	Flexible active online classrooms encourage students to read and prepare materials, and then participate in online discussion boards and chat rooms. Instructors would monitor the progress of the class based on active learning activities, and then tailor the course to fit student needs.	■ LearningCurve adaptive for choosing lecture top ■ Video Lectures by Eric ■ Dynamic PowerPoint Pr i>clicker Questions ■ Student Tutorials and A

Dear Colleague:

I am pleased that you are considering CoreEconomics, 3rd edition for your principles of economics course. Like many instructors, I share a common teaching philosophy that courses must adapt to the changing needs of students, particularly in today's technology-driven world. Textbooks also need to adapt to the new ways in which students learn and instructors teach.

Many college students today are part of the post-millennial generation. They have been "connected" their entire lives. As more courses implement online learning components such as homework management software, and as more institutions offer hybrid or fully-online courses, teaching methods must adapt as well. Therefore, the accompanying resource list provides a guide to using resources effectively in various types of learning environments, including face-to-face versus online, traditional lectures versus active learning, and structured versus adaptive instruction. The changing learning environment means more than just updating course content; it means updating its delivery as well.

However, one must be careful that teaching methods are revised to adapt to a new generation of students without sacrificing the integrity and quality of the principles of economics course. We cannot just fill our courses with flashy images and pop culture multimedia. Once the core fundamentals and pedagogy are in place, then the subsequent goal is to convey these concepts in the most interesting way so that students can learn, retain, and apply knowledge.

My coauthor, Gerald Stone, considered himself—first and foremost—a teacher. So am I. Jerry taught principles of economics for over 30 years. In my 13 year teaching career to date, I have taught every term and in nearly every type of classroom setting (traditional small class, large auditorium, distance education, lecture capture, and honors classes). Further, I have used most resources available today, from course and homework management software, i>clickers, text-based polling, to social media tools. Like Jerry, I believe that the best textbooks are written by authors who are invested in their students' learning experience.

Lastly, a growing concern is how the changes in teaching methods affect accreditation. In addition to being an instructor, I am also an administrator, serving as the Director of Instructional Technology which oversees our college's online course offerings that serve nearly 5,000 students per term. One of my roles is to work with faculty to ensure that course content, resources, and assessment are designed to meet common objectives in accreditation reviews, including those of AACSB (for business schools) and regional accreditation standards. I kept accreditation standards in mind as I developed *CoreEconomics,* ensuring that every chapter contains strong learning objectives, applied examples, reinforcement mechanisms, and assessment activities.

The goal of *CoreEconomics* is to create a better learning experience for students and a broader teaching experience for instructors. Please contact me to share your own ideas or to let me know how I can continue to improve what is offered here.

Eric P. Chiang

Eric P. Chiang

CoreEconomics
Third Edition

Eric P. Chiang
Florida Atlantic University

Gerald W. Stone
Metropolitan State University of Denver

Worth Publishers
A Macmillan Higher Education Company

Senior Vice President, Editorial and Production: Catherine Woods
Publisher: Charles Linsmeier
Marketing Manager: Tom Digiano
Marketing Assistant: Tess Sanders
Senior Development Editor: Bruce Kaplan
Associate Development Editor: Mary Walsh
Editorial Consultant: Paul Shensa
Associate Media Editor: Lindsay Neff
Director of Market Research and Development: Steven Rigolosi
Director of Print and Digital Development: Tracey Kuehn
Associate Managing Editor: Lisa Kinne
Senior Project Editor: Georgia Lee Hadler
Copy Editor: Martha Solonche
Art Director: Babs Reingold
Senior Designer: Kevin Kall
Interior Designer: Amanda Kavanagh
Cover Designers: Amanda Kavanagh/Kevin Kall
Photo Editor: Christine Buese
Photo Researcher: Julie Tesser
Production Manager: Barbara Anne Seixas
Supplements Production Manager: Stacey Alexander
Supplements Project Editor: Edgar Bonilla
Layout Designer and Illustrations: TSI Graphics
Composition: TSI Graphics
Printing and Binding: Quad/Graphics
Cover Photo: Tatiana Nikolaevna Kalashinikova/Getty Images

Credits for chapter opening photographs can be found on page CR-1, which is an extension
of this copyright page.

ISBN-13: 978-1-4292-7846-1
ISBN-10: 1-4292-7846-3

Library of Congress Control Number: 2013951179

Worth Publishers
41 Madison Avenue
New York, NY 10010
www.worthpublishers.com

To John and Tina Chiang, my parents,
who instilled in me a work ethic
that allowed me to pursue endless
opportunities

Memorial to Jerry Stone

Worth Publishers regrets to inform you that Jerry Stone passed away after a difficult battle with cancer at the end of August 2010. Jerry Stone had a remarkable career as a longtime teacher at Metropolitan State University of Denver and as an author of two successful principles of economics textbooks. Those who knew Jerry miss his steadfast commitment to the teaching of economics, a legacy that lives on in each new edition of *CoreEconomics.* Jerry Stone long-believed that the best principles of economics textbooks are authored by people invested in their students' classroom experience. The decisions made in the shaping of the second edition were educated by Jerry's thirty-plus years in the classroom and by the team of instructors that contributed to every aspect of the media and supplements package. The second edition was Jerry's accomplishment: a book envisioned, designed, and executed to be the principles of economics book that teaches better than any other textbook on the market.

About the Author

Eric P. Chiang received his bachelor's degree in economics from the University of Nevada Las Vegas, and his master's and doctorate in economics from the University of Florida. His first academic position was at New Mexico State University. Currently, Eric is an associate professor and graduate director of the Department of Economics at Florida Atlantic University. Eric also serves as the director of instructional technology for the College of Business.

In 2009, Eric was recipient of Florida Atlantic University's highest teaching award, the Distinguished Teacher of the Year. He also received the Stewart Distinguished Professorship awarded by the College of Business among numerous other teaching awards. He has published twenty-five articles in peer-reviewed journals on a range of subjects including technology spillovers, intellectual property rights, telecommunications, and health care. His research has appeared in leading journals, including the *Review of Economics and Statistics*, the *Journal of Technology Transfer*, and the *Southern Economic Journal*. He has presented papers at all major economics conferences and at universities across the country and around the world.

As an instructor who teaches both face-to-face and online courses, Eric uses a variety of technological tools including clickers, text-response systems, and homework management systems to complement his active learning style lectures. As an administrator in the College of Business, Eric's role as director of instructional technology involves assisting instructors with effectively implementing classroom technologies. In this position, Eric also ensures that the quality of online courses meets accreditation standards including those set by AACSB.

In addition to his dedication to teaching economic principles and his administrative duties, Eric devotes time to new research in economic education. His current research agenda focuses on the effects of online versus face-to-face courses and the power of visual learning. The third edition of *CoreEconomics* embodies Eric's devotion to economic education and the benefits of adapting to the new, often creative ways in which students learn and instructors teach.

In his spare time, Eric enjoys studying cultures and languages, and travels frequently. He has visited all fifty U.S. states, many of them to run half-marathons, and over seventy countries, and enjoys long jogs and walks when he travels in order to experience local life to the fullest.

Brief Contents

Contents

6 Consumer Choice and Demand

11 The Labor Market

12 Land, Capital Markets, and Innovation

13 Externalities and Public Goods

14 Network Goods

15 Poverty and Income Distribution

16 Introduction to Macroeconomics

17   Measuring Inflation and Unemployment

21 Fiscal Policy and Debt

22 Saving, Investment, and the Financial System

23   Money Creation and the Federal Reserve

26 International Trade

27 Open Economy Macroeconomics

Preface

Every instructor faces the same problem, every day, with every class: How many students can we reach today? Can we reach each one?

Every time I teach principles of economics, I keep in mind that many of my students are learning about economics for the first time, and how they perceive *my* course may influence their perceptions of economics for a long time. I take this challenge seriously each time I enter a classroom.

I have taught over 10,000 students since 2001—in small classrooms, large auditoriums, online classes, day classes, and evening classes. The diversity of my students has provided abundant examples of learning by experience. Each setting provides a laboratory for using innovative teaching techniques to motivate students to appreciate the endless possibilities that thinking like an economist can provide.

The challenge, of course, is reaching each and every student. This challenge has been compounded by the increasing number of ways in which students learn.

A critical component of a positive first experience in economics is a good textbook. The best textbooks fascinate students by conveying interesting and intuitive examples while providing a guide to understanding difficult and often frustrating concepts in a principles course. Therefore, in my search for a textbook, I desired a book that was written by an author who shared a similar teaching philosophy, one who loves teaching and has spent her or his career in the classroom. I believe that the best principles of economics textbooks are authored by people invested in their students' classroom experience.

I found that author in Gerald Stone, a lifelong teacher, and his text *CoreEconomics*. The concept was novel: Based on a comprehensive survey of what instructors actually had time to cover in their classes, the text covered the core chapters that all instructors taught. Additional material was kept to a minimum. This had several benefits. First, no longer would students be overwhelmed by a huge tome that gave the impression that economics was all about topic after topic—after topic after topic. Second, because *CoreEconomics* was shorter than the standard text, it offered a corresponding price break. My students were grateful that they paid only for chapters taught in the course. Third, once relieved of the pressure to cover most of a text, I could devote more time to enriching the learning experience of my students. Since I began using *CoreEconomics*, I have been afforded the time to discuss more current events, to engage my students with more applications of key concepts, and to devote classroom time to active learning exercises.

➔ The Story of *CoreEconomics* Transformed

Intrigued by the promise of *CoreEconomics*, I became involved in the development of the text as an accuracy checker for the first edition, then on the technology side with the development of *EconPortal*, an online homework and course management system that became a standard offering with the second edition. Hired as a faculty editor in 2009, I saw firsthand how the many parts of the textbook were all linked, from the author-written *CourseTutor*, Test Bank, and PowerPoint slides, to the multimedia and graphing tools created for *EconPortal*.

In early 2010, Gerald Stone was diagnosed with cancer, and could not continue authorship of *CoreEconomics*. In May 2010, he invited me to Littleton, Colorado, where we shared a long discussion about our teaching experiences. Like a teacher bestowing wisdom to a pupil but with the relaxed nature of lifelong friends, he shared words of advice and encouragement. I was pleased to discover that Jerry looked beyond the textbook to the entire learning experience of students and to the teaching experience of fellow instructors, as demonstrated by his close involvement with the supplements. After all, Jerry was one of the creators of the first computerized test bank. His holistic approach to learning and teaching, which I will explain in more detail later in this preface, mirrored my own. As a result of this meeting and further discussions, he asked me to take over the authorship of *CoreEconomics* with the third edition, with the expectation that I would carry *CoreEconomics* forward to a new generation of students and instructors with new needs. Sadly, Jerry passed away a few months after our meeting in Littleton.

My expectations were rather modest at that time. I had inherited a fantastic legacy. I knew that I could bring some innovations to the textbook on the pedagogical side based on what I had discovered teaching large numbers of students every semester. I assumed that my contributions on the content side of the textbook would be greater than the often cursory revisions of other texts that I examined (revisions often limited to changing some boxes and updating data), but I thought that my additions would be minimal. As for the broader learning experience, I assumed that I would continue enhancing the content in *EconPortal* (now renamed *LaunchPad*) as the importance of technology resources increase in higher education. Was I surprised!

Looking back at that time and evaluating what I have done, I am astounded at the amount of effort I chose to devote to the third edition to reach this generation of students and to assist this generation of teachers. The textbook and its learning and teaching package have been more than just revised. It is more appropriate to think of this as a transformation, from a high-quality textbook by a great educator to a textbook and its related course materials that engage and accommodate the changing nature of the classroom for today's instructors and students alike. Here's why this new edition is a transformation.

➲ The Textbook: Innovations in Pedagogy

I knew I could use my classroom experience to bring pedagogical innovations to the text to reach students better. I developed three key pedagogical innovations.

Visual Chapter Summaries

Chapter summaries in nearly all principles of economics textbooks are text-based. Some use bullet points to highlight key points, while others summarize each section of the chapter into a paragraph or two. Surveys of students have found that many students tend to skip the chapter summaries, or at best skim through them. Although chapter summaries contain the main points from each chapter, they often do little to help students *retain and understand* information other than reiterating the content in an abridged manner.

I took a different approach in creating each chapter summary. People are naturally visual learners. Numerous studies have shown that adding a picture to a concept's description significantly improves the retention of that concept. Therefore, the chapter summaries contain multiple visual elements, such as pictures, graphs, and other contextually rich features to help aid in the review and retention of chapter content. The chapter summaries also are inspired by the use of concept maps common in textbooks in other disciplines, such as psychology, in which concepts are linked to one another in a logical manner. In this book, each chapter summary appears as a colorful two-page spread, with concepts and features flowing naturally from one section to another.

Each visual chapter summary complements the traditional text-based section reviews called Checkpoints, which appear at the end of each major section of a chapter. Each Checkpoint contains bullet points of the main concepts discussed within each section followed by a critical thinking question. In sum, the combination of text- and visual-based summaries provides students with more than one approach to reviewing and retaining concepts from each chapter.

A Greater Visual Dimension

As with the chapter summaries, so with the chapter text preceding it. I brought in more photos, again to help students retain key concepts. I tried to make these photos directly recognizable to students and their way of life. Other texts have photos: I would like to think that the ones used here are more interesting and better utilized to portray concepts.

The Data Dimension

Students today are bombarded with data and data graphs in the popular press and online. Students need to become good consumers of data to make sound decisions. Students who are equipped with skills to analyze the abundance of data that accompanies their lives tend to make better decisions when it comes to seeking a career, deciding where to live, or even whom to marry. The presence of data has become a common component of the choices we make, and this textbook reinforces this skill with the By the Numbers feature.

The previous edition introduced the By the Numbers feature in a limited number of chapters. By the Numbers aims to provide students with a practical connection between economic concepts and empirical data. Now, By the Numbers appears in every chapter, always on the third page, presenting data, data graphs, and pictures focused around a theme based on the content contained in the chapter. Students are not expected to have read the chapter prior to examining the feature, although doing so may provide a deeper understanding of what the data convey.

Our goal is for students to become more comfortable examining and evaluating data. Viewing data in By the Numbers is not effective if comprehension is not achieved. To assess a student's understanding of the data, each chapter now contains two Using the Numbers questions based on data appearing in By the Numbers. Each question requires students to read data from various data graphs, compare trends, and to make conclusions about what the data convey. The questions can be assigned, used for in-class discussion, or used as a starting point for students to explore a topic in further depth. The data sources have been gathered at the back of the book in Sources for By the Numbers. This way they can be used if desired without getting in the way.

All of these pedagogical innovations should help students understand and retain information, whether they are comfortable with old text-heavy ways or the more visual and data-driven ways we see more frequently today.

The Textbook: Innovations in Content

In taking over the authorship of *CoreEconomics*, I had assumed I would improve the text but thought this would be a straightforward task. I was surprised by the extent of the content changes I made to transform this text into something compelling to my students. These changes came about mainly due to three factors: changes in approach and emphasis in economic theory because of the need to explain pressing problems such as the recent financial crisis and its jobless recovery, the natural progression of economics research, and changes in the student body.

Microeconomics

It may be useful to present key changes in microeconomics in three ways.

1. *Chapters that provided a strong foundation.* I found that there was a group of chapters that provided a very strong foundation for learning topics. For example, Chapter 4, Markets and Government, presents expanded coverage of consumer surplus and producer surplus at the beginning of the chapter to emphasize the importance of these welfare measures in economic analysis. Chapter 6, Consumer Choice and Demand, begins with an analysis of budget lines and consumer choice, leading to a section on marginal utility analysis. These chapters underwent greater changes than other chapters, such as Chapter 8, Perfect Competition, which in the second edition presented the perfect competition model so clearly and revealed its use as a benchmark so concisely that I did not want to tamper with it too much.

I added "Five Steps to Profit Maximization," a pedagogical device for understanding market structure figures in Chapters 8–10.

2. *Chapters that changed because of the progression of economic research.*
I discovered that while all of microeconomics has been affected by the rapid pace of economic research, three chapters were changed significantly.

  a. *Behavioral Economics.* Chapter 6, Consumer Choice and Demand, now contains a new section on behavioral economics. My students are fascinated by topics such as framing and the perils of overconfidence. This section follows the material on budget lines, consumer choice, and marginal analysis, giving students a fuller understanding of decision-making theory.

  b. *Game Theory.* The previous edition contained a section on game theory in Chapter 10, Monopolistic Competition, Oligopoly, and Game Theory. Now, game theory is presented in two sections: The first focuses on strategic thinking and Nash equilibrium, and the second focuses on applications of game theory, including the analysis of games that fall under the categories of Prisoner's Dilemma, repeated games, leadership, and chicken games. This has the benefit of adding new applications for instructors who want to enhance their coverage of game theory, while letting other instructors concentrate on the rudiments of game theory in the first section.

  c. *New Chapter: Network Goods.* Research on networks and network goods has exploded in recent years as networks such as Facebook have become crucial in the lives of many people. My students appreciate studying them. I thought it best to include a brand new chapter (Chapter 14, Network Goods) to give these goods the analysis they deserve, rather than trying to shoehorn them into another chapter.

3. *Chapters that changed because of changes in the student body.* I realized that some material in the second edition was just too tough for my students as currently presented. I reworked Chapter 4, now entitled Markets and Government. My students need to know early in the course that market failure exists, but an in-depth treatment needs to wait until they have a more solid grounding in standard micro building blocks such as costs, profit maximization, and market power. Trimming back the early market failure material substantially let me add some material on using consumer and producer surplus. I moved the analysis of price ceilings and price floors from Chapter 3 to Chapter 4 to incorporate the effects of welfare measures on consumer and producer welfare.

Macroeconomics

It may be useful to present key changes in macroeconomics in three ways.

1. *Chapters already a standard in the market.* I found that there was a group of chapters that provided a strong foundation and that were superior to those in other books. Chapter 19, Aggregate Expenditures, was to me the best and clearest account of the Keynesian model that I have ever seen in a textbook. Also, it fit nicely with the ensuing chapter, Aggregate Demand and Supply. I emphasized how spending by one creates income for others and trimmed a bit, while leaving the basic presentation intact.

2. *Chapters that changed because of the aftermath of the financial crisis.* I discovered that the aftermath of the financial crisis and its jobless recovery affected the macro part to a great extent.

  a. *Unemployment measurement.* The aftermath of the financial crisis affected a seemingly straightforward chapter (Chapter 17, Measuring Inflation and Unemployment). How do unemployment statistics account for discouraged workers who have dropped out of the labor force? What do we mean by jobless recoveries? These topics needed more attention.

  b. *Fiscal policy.* The financial crisis put the spotlight on fiscal policy. I took the second edition chapter on debt and deficits and combined it with fiscal policy. How successful was fiscal policy in dealing with the crisis? What are the ramifications of fiscal policy measures (e.g., stimulus spending and tax cuts) on the national debt? The combined chapter (Chapter 21, Fiscal Policy and Debt) provides a more direct link to the role that fiscal policy plays in the economy and how it affects the federal budget.

  c. *Three-chapter reorganization of money, banking, and monetary policy.* A big benefit of presenting deficits with fiscal policy and the ensuing elimination of one chapter is that it freed up an additional chapter for the coverage of money and monetary policy. Now, the coverage of money is presented in three chapters, not two chapters as formerly. This let me add coverage on money leakages and on a comparison of how the Federal Reserve and the European Central Bank responded to the financial crisis. It also let me add an introductory section on what we really mean when we say that the Fed is following an expansionary or a contractionary monetary policy, terms students are often presented with in news and online media outlets. My students, like many others, needed some foundation material before studying the theory in the monetary policy chapter.

3. *Chapters that changed because of changes in the student body.* I realized that for my students, macroeconomic events and theory needed firm grounding from a broader perspective. I completely rewrote Chapter 18, Economic Growth, with this in mind. The chapter now starts with a focus on the BRIC (Brazil, Russia, India, and China) countries and includes a section on government's role in fostering growth. There is a discussion of the more than 1 billion people in the world still living in poverty, and the prospects of economic growth lifting them out. Economic growth is a crucial idea; it takes center stage in macroeconomics. Finally, more and more instructors want their students to benefit from a higher degree of financial literacy. A new section in Chapter 22 focuses on financial tools for a better future, giving students some practical guidance to finance and their own lives.

This is just a brief summary of the key changes in the textbook. Every chapter was changed to some degree, some to a great extent, others to a lesser extent. The chapter-by-chapter explanations later in this preface define the wide range of changes to the content of the text.

The Text: Vivid Examples for Students

Another way I have transformed this textbook has been to replace just about all of the Issues. Each chapter now has two Issues that appeal to the diverse body of students studying economics. Here are some of my favorites:

  Chapter 1: Have Smartphones and Social Media Made Life Easier?
  Chapter 2: Will Renewable Energy Be the Next Innovative Breakthrough?
  Chapter 4: Are Price-Gouging Laws Good for Consumers?
  Chapter 5: Are Sales Taxes Fair to Low-Income Households?
  Chapter 7: How Large Are Fixed Costs? A Look at the Pharmaceutical and Software Industries
  Chapter 9: Is Flexible Ticket Pricing the New Form of Price Discrimination?
  Chapter 11: Reality TV and the Labor Market for Entertainers
  Chapter 12: The Role of Educational Systems in Human Capital Accumulation
  Chapter 16: The End of the Recession . . . It Does Not Feel Like It
  Chapter 17: Why Do Unemployment Rates Differ So Much Within the United States?
  Chapter 18: Can Economic Growth Bring a Billion People Out of Poverty?
  Chapter 22: Did the 2007–2009 Stock Market Crash Affect Long-Term Savings?
  Chapter 23: What Can the Fed Do When Interest Rates Reach 0%?
  Chapter 25: The Bernanke Inflation Jump—When?

A Holistic Approach to Learning and Teaching

Earlier I mentioned that Jerry Stone and I shared a holistic approach to teaching principles of economics. By holistic, I refer to how all elements of a course, including lectures, discussions, online assignments and resources, and assessment tools are connected to one another in a logical and cohesive manner that facilitates both the learning process by students and the teaching process by instructors. Unlike other books on the market, I did not want to create a bunch of supplements merely to accompany the text. Instead, the resources produced for this third edition of *CoreEconomics* were created to complement a suite of learning and teaching approaches used in higher education today, including the increased presence of online, hybrid, and active learning classrooms in addition to the traditional lecture- and discussion-based classes.

A Suite of Learning and Teaching Approaches

I was pleased to discover that transforming the text with my current students in mind actually freed up time to consider active learning methodologies for them. Instructors often encourage or even require students to read their textbook prior to the related lecture. When students do, class time can be used more effectively to refine the knowledge learned through independent study and to engage in activities that apply that knowledge. In order to facilitate the active learning approach to the classroom, a textbook must be approachable to a student seeing a concept for the first time.

This edition was written with this active learning objective in mind. Each chapter contains a wealth of vivid examples, intuitive explanations that build on one's natural instincts and innate knowledge. Further, the expanded use of photos and other visuals where appropriate helps to convey a concept or aid in the retention of an important lesson or key point.

Like a majority of instructors who utilize technological resources, I use a homework management system. I find that providing a seamless connection between technology resources and the textbook is a vital element for learning. Many publishers provide homework management systems that are generic in the sense that they are used in conjunction with *any* textbook. The disadvantage of this approach is that the content may not always reflect the style and content presented in the textbook. Therefore, it is important to me that I use a homework management system for which all content was created for *CoreEconomics*; *LaunchPad* is the answer. Because *LaunchPad* corresponds directly with the textbook, I was able to contribute to its content and oversee all of the elements to ensure that the user experience of students and teachers is a positive one. Further, *LaunchPad* is compatible with most LMS systems (such as Blackboard) used by colleges and universities, allowing students to complete assignments and view grades without having to log into a separate system.

Outline of the Book and Changes in the Third Edition

Chapter 1: Exploring Economics

- Chapter opener changed from focus on growth to economics as a decision-making discipline.
- The ten Key Ideas of Section 2 have been trimmed to seven Key Principles. (Several of the more obscure ones have been dropped so that students will not have to struggle with things such as the money supply in the first chapter, something they will have little to no understanding of at the start of the course.)
- New Issue: Have Smartphones and Social Media Made Life Easier?
- New Issue: Do Economists Ever Agree on Anything?

Chapter 2: Production, Economic Growth, and Trade

- New Figure 1: From Factors of Production to Output.
- New steps added on calculating opportunity costs in the comparative advantage section, with a new Table 1 summarizing the opportunity costs.
- New Issue: Will Renewable Energy Be the Next Innovative Breakthrough?
- New Issue: Do We Really Specialize in That? Comparative Advantage in the United States and China.

Chapter 3: Supply and Demand

- To explain where demand curves come from, a new section (and Figure 1) has been added on willingness-to-pay.

- The section on price ceilings and floors has been moved to Chapter 4.
- New Issue: Do Markets Exist for Everyone, Including Dogs and Cats?
- Figure 8, a summary figure, has been simplified.

Chapter 4: Markets and Government [title change]

- Second edition chapter had a long, tough section on market failure, and a history of the U.S. economy over the past 150 years. New third edition chapter prunes down the market failure material to approximately 1 page. The history section has been moved to the Web site.
- The chapter introduces consumer and producer surplus as tools to measure economic efficiency, then applies these concepts to show what happens when price is greater than or less than equilibrium, then covers price ceilings and floors. This is much more mainstream than the second edition.
- The consumer/producer surplus material starts by using willingness-to-pay (introduced in Chapter 3) and willingness-to-sell.
- New Issue: Can Markets Accurately Predict the Future?
- New Issue: Are Price-Gouging Laws Good for Consumers?

Chapter 5: Elasticity

- New separate section: Total Revenue and Other Measures of Elasticity.
- Cross elasticity is covered before income elasticity.
- New descriptive material (1½ pages) added to tax section.
- New Issue: Using Loss Leaders to Generate Higher Total Revenue.
- New Issue: Are Sales Taxes Fair to Low-Income Households?

Chapter 6: Consumer Choice and Demand

- New first section on budget lines and choices. Now covers how budget lines change based on prices or income.
- Second section on marginal utility analysis now combines parts of the first two sections in the second edition. The consumer surplus material has been removed because it is now discussed fully in Chapter 4.
- New third section on behavioral economics.
- New Issue: Smaller Cars and Larger Homes: A Permanent Trend?
- Appendix streamlined by dropping the long Issue on terrorism.

Chapter 7: Production and Costs

- Additional material makes the distinction between accounting and economic profits clearer, and emphasizes the fact that "zero economic profits" can still be a large accounting profit, depending on the opportunity costs of the firm.
- Focus on the AVC, ATC, and MC curves, with de-emphasis on the AFC curve.
- New Issue: The Vast World of Corporate Offshoring and Profits.
- New Issue: How Large Are Fixed Costs? A Look at the Pharmaceutical and Software Industries.

Chapter 8: Perfect Competition [title change]

- Chapter title changed to better capture what is covered in the chapter.
- New coverage of "Five Steps to Profit Maximization"—a method that will work for all market structures.
- Tables trimmed back.

Chapter 9: Monopoly

- Section 1 of the second edition divided into two sections: (1) Monopoly Markets, and (2) Comparing Monopoly and Competition.
- New coverage of "Five Steps to Profit Maximization"
- Section 2: New subsection on the benefits and costs of monopoly.
- New section combines regulation with antitrust, and trims some of the legal material in the antitrust coverage.

A Unified Pedagogical Approach

Every chapter is structured around a common set of features including visual elements, applications, and end of chapter material unique to *CoreEconomics*.

Chapter 3

After studying this chapter you should be able to:

- Describe the nature and purposes of markets.
- Describe the nature of demand, demand curves, and the law of demand.
- Describe the determinants of demand and be able to forecast how a change in one or more of these determinants will change demand.
- Explain the difference between a change in demand and a change in quantity demanded.

- Determine market equilibrium price and output.
- Determine and predict how price and output will change given changes to supply and demand in the market.

LEARNING OBJECTIVES

Each chapter begins with a set of learning objectives which instructors can use for assessment and students can rely on to determine their depth of knowledge of economic concepts in the chapter.

What $60 billion global industry sells a product that many people typically can obtain easily from another source free of charge? The bottled water industry! This industry began its meteoric rise in the early 1990s, and today, the ubiquitous bottle of water has changed the way we live. It also has created new concerns regarding the environmental impact of the billions of plastic bottles used and discarded.

The bottled water industry took off as consumers changed their hydration habits, spurred by greater awareness of the health benefits of drinking water, including weight loss, illness prevention, and overall health maintenance. As water consumption increased, people started wanting something more than just ordinary water from the tap. They desired water that was purer, more consistent in taste, or infused with flavor or minerals. Plus, consumers wanted water that was easy to carry. Bottle[...]sumers wanted, and the market was willing to provide it.

Bottled water comes from many sources, both domes[...]of either spring water (from natural springs underneath[...](ordinary tap water that undergoes a complex purificati[...]grew, new varieties of water were made available. Water t[...]springs, vitamin-infused water, flavored water, and carbo[...]choices consumers were given. The total amount of water p[...]industry continued to increase as long as there were cust[...]the market.

In the late 2000s, falling incomes from a deteriorating gl[...]the harmful effects of discarded plastic bottles on the enviro[...]water purification devices, and even some laws against the[...]ally halted the market's growth. The economy has since im[...]industry responded to the environmental concerns by usin[...]plastic or by using new technologies to reduce the plastic [...]responding to the desires of consumers. As a result, sales in[...]

Consumers have many choices of what water to buy an[...]bottled water market is one in which prices vary considera[...]of purchase. A single bottle of water of[...]$0.99 at a convenience store, $1.25 fro[...]and $3.00 or more at a theme park, sp[...]product be sold in different places at s[...]

Supply and Demand

3

This chapter analyzes the various [...]different settings and circumstances. V[...]tives into account in determining wha[...]what prices to charge. The interaction [...]determines the prices we pay.

In any given market, prices are d[...]factors determine what the market will[...]the marketplace cause prices to chang[...]to supply and demand analysis. The ba[...]chapter will let you determine why pr[...]in, and how many goods will be offere[...]ketplace. Later chapters use this same [...]wages are set and how personal incom[...]

This chapter introduces some of t[...]understand how the forces of supply a[...]the law of demand, demand curves, the[...]curves, the determinants of supply, an[...]

THE INTERACTION OF TEXT AND VISUALS THROUGHOUT

Research into how the mind processes information emphasizes the importance of pairing different mediums together to increase comprehension. Throughout the chapter, images and text are paired together: in the chapter opening story and chapter opening image; the By The Numbers visual display of data; the use of photographs and text to illustrate economic concepts; the pairing of figures and tables with relevant description; and the Visual Summaries that conclude each chapter.

➡ Markets

A **market** is an institution that enables buyers and sellers to interact and transact with one another. A lemonade stand is a market because it allows people to exchange money for a product, in this case lemonade. Ticket scalping, which remains illegal or

markets Institutions that bring buyers and sellers together so they can interact and transact with each other.

BY THE NUMBERS

The outset of each chapter includes a By The Numbers—a visual display of data. By The Numbers emphasize the importance of data, helping students to become better consumers of data in their daily lives.

BY THE NUMBERS

The World of Markets

Markets form the foundation of all economic transactions. As various factors affect the supply and demand for goods and services, prices adjust upward or downward correspondingly to reach equilibrium.

The legalization of casinos in many states has resulted in dramatic growth in the industry. Top gaming revenues by state in 2011:

In Millions of U.S. Dollars

Nevada, New Jersey, Pennsylvania, Indiana, Louisiana, Mississippi, Missouri, Illinois, Michigan, Iowa

0 2,000 4,000 6,000 8,000 10,000 12,000

age fotostock/SuperStock

PjrStudio/Alamy

Prices for precious metals vary widely due to their relative demand and supply.

7,300,000,000

Total value (in U.S. dollars) of the worldwide virtual goods market associated with online gaming in 2012.

72,800,000,000

Total number of half-liter water bottles consumed in the United States in 2012 (over 220 bottles per person).

Millions of U.S. Dollars

12,000 / 10,000 / 8,000 / 6,000 / 4,000 / 2,000 / 0

1982   1992   2002   2012

Total sales of bottled water in the United States took off in the 1990s and continued to grow steadily since.

ZUMA Wire Service/Alamy

University of Phoenix is the largest for-profit university with nearly 500,000 students.

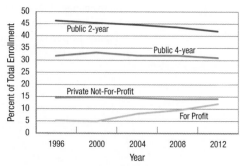

Percent of Total Enrollment

50 / 45 / 40 / 35 / 30 / 25 / 20 / 15 / 10 / 5 / 0

Public 2-year

Public 4-year

Private Not-For-Profit

For Profit

1996   2000   2004   2008   2012

Year

Enrollment at for-profit universities grew significantly over the past 16 years compared to not-for-profit institutions.

ISSUE

Features items from our economic world written for the third edition students in mind. Each Issue is kept to less than half a page to incentivize students to explore the world of economics around us.

 ISSUE

Two-Buck Chuck: Will People Drink $2-a-Bottle Wine?

The great California wines of the 1990s put California vineyards on the map. Demand, prices, and exports grew rapidly. Overplanting of new grapevines was a result. When driving along Interstate 5 or Highway 101 north of Los Angeles, one can see vineyards extending for miles, and most were planted in the mid- to late 1990s. The 2001 recession reduced the demand for California wine, and a rising dollar made imported wine relatively cheaper. The result was a sharp drop in demand for California wine and a huge surplus of grapes.

Bronco Wine Company president Fred Franzia made an exclusive deal with Trader Joe's, an unusual supermarket that features exotic food and wine products. He bought the excess grapes at distressed prices, and in his company's modern plant produced inex-

pensive wines—chardonnay, merlot, cabernet sauvignon, shiraz, and sauvignon blanc—under the Charles Shaw label. Consumers flocked to Trader Joe's for wine costing $1.99 a bottle and literally hauled cases of wine out by the carload. In less than a decade, 400 million bottles of Two-Buck Chuck, as it is known, have been sold. This is not rotgut: The 2002 shiraz beat out 2,300 other wines to win a double gold medal at the 28th Annual International Eastern Wine Competition in 2004. Still, to many Napa Valley vintners it is known as Two-Buck Upchuck.

Two-Buck Chuck was such a hit that other supermarkets were forced to offer their own discount wines. This good, low-priced wine has had the effect of opening up markets. People who previously avoided wine because of the cost have begun

joel zatz/Alamy

drinking more. However, the influence of Two-Buck Chuck, which sold 60 million bottles in 2012, may be waning. In January 2013, Trader Joe's announced an increase in the price of the Two-Buck Chuck from $1.99 to $2.49 due to a poor grape harvest that raised the cost of producing the wine. Although the new price is still a bargain, the product that changed the wine industry may soon need another name.

Predicting the New Equilibrium When Both Curves Shift When both supply and demand change, things get tricky. We can predict what will happen with price in some cases and output in other cases, but not what will happen with both.

Figure 12 portrays an increase in both demand and supply. Consider the market for corn. Suppose t̶   causes de̶   d for corn

● CHECKPOINT

MARKETS

- Markets are institutions that enable buyers and sellers to interact and transact business.
- Markets differ in geographical location, products offered, and size.
- Prices contain a wealth of information for both buyers and sellers.
- Through their purchases, consumers signal their willingness to exchange money for particular products at particular prices. These signals help businesses decide what to produce, and how much of it to produce.
- The market economy is also called the price system.

QUESTION: What are the important differences between the markets for financial securities such as the New York Stock Exchange and your local farmer's market?

Answers to the Checkpoint question can be found at the end of this chapter.

CHECKPOINT

Every section concludes with a set of review bullets that identify the key takeaways from that section of the chapter. Each CHECKPOINT also includes an open-ended critical thinking question. The answer can be found at the end of the chapter.

Demand

...ever you purchase a product, you are voting with your money. You are selecting one ...ct out of many and supporting one firm out of many, both of which signal to the ...ss community what sorts of products satisfy your wants as a consumer. ...onomists typically focus on wants rather than needs because it is so difficult to deter... ...what we truly need. Theoretically, you could survive on tofu and vitamin pills, living ... ...to made of cardboar...

GRAPHS

Use Numbers not Symbols

Graphs use numbers on the horizontal and vertical axes whenever possible. This minimizes the level of abstraction that a student needs to understand economic models.

Panel A
Demand

Determinants of Demand		Determinants of Supply	
Decrease in Demand	**Increase in Demand**	**Decrease in Supply**	**Increase in Supply**
Tastes and preferences fall	Tastes and preferences rise	Technology falls	Technology rises
Income falls (for normal goods)	Income rises (for normal goods)	Resource costs rise	Resource costs fall
Price of substitutes falls	Price of substitutes...	...product ...stit...	Price of production substitute

VISUAL SUMMARY

Each chapter concludes with a two-page visual flow-chart of key concepts in the chapter. Instead of the traditional method of brief paragraphs of text (which are often read instead of the chapter text), the visual summaries pair images from the chapter with text to provide students with a deeper understanding of the relationship between terms and concepts in the chapter.

72

chapter summary

Section 1: **Markets**

A **market** is an institution that enables buyers and sellers to interact and transact with one another.

Stars and Stripes/Alamy

Corbis/SuperStock

Markets can be as simple as a lemonade stand, as large as an automobile lot, as valuable as the stock market, as virtual as an Internet shopping site, or as illegal as a ticket scalping operation.

Buyers and sellers communicate their desires in a market through the prices at which goods and services are bought and sold. Hence, a market economy is called a **price system.**

Robert Harding World Imagery/Corbis

Section 2: **Demand**

Demand refers to the goods and services people are willing and able to buy during a period of time. It is a horizontal summation of individual demand curves in a defined market.

Price

D

Alan Schein Photography/Corbis

Roller coasters are a lot of fun, but riding the same one over and over gives less satisfaction with each ride; therefore, willingness-to-pay falls with each ride.

...nents ...d... Demand Curves Shift

Section 3: Supply

Supply analysis works the same way as demand, but looking at the market from the firm's point of view.

The **law of supply** states that as prices increase, firms want to supply more, and vice versa. It leads to an upward-sloping supply curve.

Philip Gostelow/Aurora Photos/Corbis

Determinants of Supply: How Supply Curves Shift

- ↑ Production technology: Supply shifts right.
- ↑ Cost of resources: Supply shifts left.
- ↑ Price of other commodities: Supply shifts left.
- ↑ Price expectations: Supply shifts left.
- ↑ Number of sellers: Supply shifts right.
- ↑ Taxes: Supply shifts left.
- ↑ Subsidies: Supply shifts right.

Section 4: Market Equilibrium

Market equilibrium occurs at the price at which the quantity supplied is equal to quantity demanded; in other words, where demand intersects supply.

How does equilibrium change?

Which curve slopes up and which slopes down? Two tricks to aid in memory:

- S"up"ply contains the word "up" for upward-sloping.
- Only the fingers on your right hand can make a "d" for demand. Hold that hand up in front of you!

A shift in demand or supply will change equilibrium price and quantity.

- Enhanced reliance on the concept of market power.
- New Issue: "But Wait . . . There's More!" The Success and Failure of Infomercials.
- New Issue: Is Flexible Ticket Pricing the New Form of Price Discrimination?

Chapter 10: Monopolistic Competition, Oligopoly, and Game Theory

- The major change is taking the section on game theory in the second edition and dividing it into two sections. Section 3, the first game theory section, now provides the introductory material, including the Nash equilibrium, and two examples. Section 4, the second game theory section, provides applications of game theory, with an emphasis on the Prisoner's Dilemma, repeated games, leadership, and chicken games.
- The first section on monopolistic competition now has more coverage of advertising.
- The section on oligopoly now has a fuller discussion of cartels and the incentive to cheat (with a new figure).
- New Issue: Mission Impossible: The Power of Focal Points in a Simulated Mission.

Chapter 11: The Labor Market [new as a separate chapter]

- Major change: In the second edition, Chapter 11 included all of the factors including labor, and Chapter 12 included additional labor market issues. Thus, labor markets were divided over two chapters. In the third edition, all of labor is covered in Chapter 11, and the other factors are covered in Chapter 12.
- Labor market monopoly and monopsony are now covered in the chapter appendix, not the chapter body.
- New Issue: Reality TV and the Labor Market for Entertainers.
- New Issue: Will Public Unions Become an Endangered Species?

Chapter 12: Land, Capital Markets, and Innovation [new as a separate chapter]

- Land, capital, and innovation are now covered in a separate chapter, without labor.
- More coverage of land than in the previous edition.
- Financial capital section enhanced.
- New Issue: Venture Capital: A Few Success Stories and One Big Missed Opportunity.
- New Issue: The Role of Educational Systems on Human Capital Accumulation.

Chapter 13: Externalities and Public Goods

- Started the chapter with externalities rather than public goods because students typically find externalities easier to understand.
- Sections made more flexible so that instructors can cover externalities and public goods, and then skip environmental policy and climate change, if they wish.
- New Issue: Cap-and-Trade: The Day Liberal Environmentalists and Free-Market Conservatives Agreed.

Chapter 14: Network Goods [new chapter]

- Network goods are contemporary and of interest to students. Some network goods covered are software, wireless devices, and social networks such as Facebook.
- Network goods often have very large fixed costs but marginal costs close to zero.
- The demand curve for network goods is unlike the demand curves previously covered in the book because it slopes up initially and then slopes down.
- Full coverage of pricing strategies to attract and to lock in users.
- Issue: The Broadband Effect: Virtuous and Vicious Cycles in Network Goods.
- Issue: Do Exclusive Marketing Deals Lock In Customers?

Chapter 15: Poverty and Income Distribution

- New coverage of the 1% and the 99%.
- New subsection on the causes of poverty.
- Mobility of poor families moved from an Issue in the second edition into the chapter body. (The figure has been removed.)
- New Issue: What Is Considered "Poor" Around the World?

Chapter 16: Introduction to Macroeconomics

- New chapter opener on the jobless recovery.
- New By the Numbers: The Slow Macroeconomic Recovery.
- New Figure 1: Markets and Institutions in the Macroeconomy.
- First section changed from The Scope of Macroeconomics to Business Cycles. Leading Economic Index added.
- GDP and Our Standard of Living, a secondary-level head in the second edition within the GDP Measurement section, becomes a primary-level head. Additional material on GDP and environmental quality.
- New Issue: The End of the Recession . . . It Does Not Feel Like It.
- New Issue: How Should Environmental Quality Be Incorporated into GDP Measures?

Chapter 17: Measuring Inflation and Unemployment

- New equation showing how to calculate price changes from two CPI numbers.
- Personal consumption expenditures index no longer covered, in line with other texts.
- New subsection on employment trends. Coverage of the Weekly Jobs Report added.
- Enhanced coverage of underemployment and discouraged workers.
- New figure on the unemployment rate versus the NAIRU from 1960 to 2012 to illustrate cyclical unemployment and the duration of jobless recoveries (how they flatten the downward sloping portions of the curve).
- New Issue: The Consequences of Counterfeit Money on Inflation.
- New Issue: Why Do Unemployment Rates Differ So Much Within the United States?

Chapter 18: Economic Growth [heavily revised]

- New chapter opener on China (comparing the 1980s with today) and the BRIC (Brazil, Russia, India, China) countries, discussing their relatively high growth rates.
- New Section 1. This section in the second edition focused on the classical model. In the third edition, this material has been shortened and moved to the introduction to Chapter 16. The new section in this chapter concentrates on why economic growth is important, highlights the significance of compounding growth (using the Rule of 70 as an estimation tool), and brings in measurement issues.
- Section 2 in the second edition covered long-run growth: productivity. In the third edition, this section has been split into two. New Section 2 covers the basics of the production function and adds material comparing short-run with long-run growth (using PPF diagrams). New Section 3 applies the production function by looking at sources of growth.
- Section 3 in the second edition covered infrastructure and economic growth. In the third edition, this section is refocused on government's role in promoting growth.
- New Issue: Can Economic Growth Bring a Billion People Out of Poverty?
- New Issue: The Role of Social Media in Promoting Economic Growth.

Chapter 19: Aggregate Expenditures [new title]

- Aggregate expenditures model still linked to the Keynesian model.
- New chapter opener on the recent recession and government expenditures in Maine.
- Stronger emphasis on the importance of how spending by one creates income to others.
- Discussion of the contrast between classical and Keynesian policies.
- New Issue: Do High Savings Rates Increase the Risk of a Long Recession?

Chapter 20: Aggregate Demand and Supply

- New chapter opener explains aggregates in the face of varying levels of performance by different industries and different areas of the country.
- New Issue: Did the Collapse of the Housing Market Affect Aggregate Demand?
- New Issue: Why Didn't Recent Stimulus Measures Lead to Inflation?

Chapter 21: Fiscal Policy and Debt [significantly revised]

- Two chapters from the second edition—Chapter 20 on fiscal policy and Chapter 21 on debt—are combined into one.
- Added new subsection on the bias toward borrowing rather than taxing.

- New subsection on the future: the effect of Social Security and Medicare on fiscal sustainability.
- New Issue: How Big Was the Stimulus Multiplier, Really?
- New Issue: How Big Is the Economic Burden of Interest Rates on the National Debt?

Chapter 22: Saving, Investment, and the Financial System [new three-chapter organization]

- Major change: Three chapters now cover money, banking, and monetary policy.
- This chapter has four sections: (1) What Is Money? (2) The Market for Loanable Funds, (3) The Financial System, and (4) Financial Tools for a Better Future.
- The Financial System section covers intermediaries and types of financial assets.
- The fourth section, on financial tools, is new. It focuses on some personal finance decisions and emphasizes compounding, risk assessment, and incentives for saving.
- New Issue: Did the 2007–2009 Stock Market Crash Affect Long-Term Savings?

Chapter 23: Money Creation and the Federal Reserve [new three-chapter organization]

- The second of the three money chapters has four sections: (1) How Banks Create Money, (2) The Money Multiplier and Its Leakages, (3) The Federal Reserve System, and (4) Federal Reserve: Tools, Targets, and Policy Lags.
- More on money leakages.
- New Issue: Did Tighter Lending Practices Reduce the Money Multiplier?
- New Issue: What Can the Fed Do When Interest Rates Reach 0%?

Chapter 24: Monetary Policy [new three-chapter organization]

- New opening section—What Is Monetary Policy?—introduces policy by looking at the importance of interest rates and comparing expansionary with contractionary policy.
- Section 2, which includes monetary theories, simplified by focusing more on the effectiveness of policy. Note that some of the figures have been combined, which shortens what was a tough section in the second edition.
- The second edition ending section on the financial crisis of 2008–2009 has been replaced with a new Section 4 on monetary policy challenges facing the Fed and the European Central Bank now. The Fed part focuses on extraordinary actions by the Fed to deal with the financial crisis. The ECB part focuses on member-country problems and the threat to the euro. This is very timely euro coverage.
- New Issue: The Challenges of Monetary Policy with Regional Differences in Economic Performance.

Chapter 25: Macroeconomic Policy: Challenges in a Global Economy [new title]

- Section 1 is new to this chapter. It is a combination of the last sections of second edition Chapters 23 and 24. Covers the Great Recession and the factors leading up to it (such as the housing bubble), with a policy aspect at the end.
- The second edition sections on the Phillips curve and rational expectations have been combined. Both are trimmed, especially coverage of the Phillips curve, to cut out some of the historical material. All equations have been removed.
- New third section on current problems and the future. Three problems identified: jobless recoveries, debt and long-run inflation, and globalization and economic growth.
- New Issue: The Bernanke Inflation Jump—When?
- New Issue: Inflating Our Way Out of Debt: Is This an Effective Approach?

Chapter 26: International Trade

- Added discussion of three main reasons why nations trade: (1) Countries cannot produce everything they want (interindustry trade), (2) consumers desire variety (intraindustry trade), and (3) specialization increases total production and consumption (gains from trade).
- New Issue: The Challenge of Measuring Imports and Exports in a Global Economy.
- New Issue: Do Foreign Trade Zones Help or Hurt American Consumers and Workers?

Chapter 27: Open Economy Macroeconomics

- New subsection, Pegging Exchange Rates Under a Flexible Exchange Rate System, focuses on countries that peg their currency to the dollar or the euro.

- New Issue: Would a Stronger Chinese Yuan Be Good for Americans?
- New Issue: Would Flexible Exchange Rates in OPEC Nations Affect Oil Markets?

CoreMedia Learning Suite: Transformed to Support Today's Students and Instructors

The CoreMedia Learning Suite establishes a new methodology behind creating great support materials for instructors and students. CoreMedia includes new and adapted resources engineered to match new approaches to classroom teaching and learning. Education research guides our decisions from the value of active learning classrooms to supporting hybrid and online education; each resource was crafted to support instructors and students understanding that no two classrooms are exactly the same. For more information on how each of the following resources supports different teaching and learning approaches, from traditional lectures to "flipped classrooms" or lecture capture to online or hybrid courses, please visit: www.coreecon.com.

➡ For Instructors

Teaching Manual and Suggested Answers to Problems

⭐ **Best Classroom Use:** Traditional/Face-to-Face or Active-Learning/Face-to-Face

The Teaching Manual (TM) prepared by Mary H. Lesser (Lenoir-Rhyne University) is an ideal resource for many classroom teaching styles. The Teaching Manual focuses on expanding and enlivening classroom lectures by highlighting varied ways to bring real-world examples into the classroom. Portions of the Teaching Manual have been designed for use as student handouts. Every chapter of the Teaching Manual includes:

- *Chapter Overview*: A brief summary of the main topics in each chapter.
- *Ideas for Capturing Your Classroom Audience*: Written with experienced and novice instructors in mind, suggestions can be used for in-class demonstrations or enrichment assignments in on-site, hybrid, and online course formats.
- *Debate the Issues in the Chapter*: The TM reproduces the issues used in the chapter to spur student debate.
- *Examples Used in the End-of-Chapter Questions*: The TM provides the instructor with a succinct overview of those questions that refer to specific articles from major news sources that can be used to develop more in-depth analysis of current events.
- *For Further Analysis*: Each TM contains an additional extended example that can be used as a formatted, one-page handout, or posted online. It is designed for in-class group work or individual assignment. Learning objectives are specified and a one-page answer key is also available for reference or distribution.
- *Web-Based Exercises*: Each TM chapter includes a web-based example that requires students to obtain information from a Web site and use it to answer a set of questions. As an in-class group exercise or an individual assignment, it can help students become better consumers of information and stronger evaluators of online data and research.
- *Tips from a Colleague*: Each chapter of the TM concludes with "tips," which share ideas about classroom presentation, use of other resources, and insights about topics that students typically find difficult to master.

Test Bank

⭐ **Best Classroom Use:** All Approaches
Coordinators: Jane Himarios (University of Texas at Arlington) and Eric Chiang (Florida Atlantic University)

Contributors and Accuracy Checkers: Dixie Button (Embry-Riddle Aeronautical University), Michael Fenick (Broward College), Scott Hegerty (Northeastern Illinois University), Fred May (Trident Technical College), Janet Wolcutt (Wichita State University), Sarah Jenyk (Youngstown State University), and Michael Dale (Trident Technical College).

Because technology should never get in the way

At Macmillan Higher Education, we are committed to providing online instructional materials that meet the needs of instructors and students in powerful, yet simple ways— powerful enough to dramatically enhance teaching and learning, yet simple enough to use right away.

We've taken what we've learned from thousands of instructors and the hundreds of thousands of students to create a new generation of Macmillan Higher Education technology—featuring **LaunchPad**. **LaunchPad** offers our acclaimed content curated and organized for easy assignability in a breakthrough user interface in which power and simplicity go hand in hand.

LaunchPad Units

Curated LaunchPad Units make class prep a whole lot easier. Combining a curated collection of video, simulations, animations, multimedia assignments, and e-book content, LaunchPad's interactive units give you a building block to use as-is, or as a starting point for your own learning units. An entire unit's worth of work can be assigned in seconds, drastically saving the amount of time it takes for you to have your course up and running.

- **Give students LearningCurve**—and get them more engaged with what they're learning. Powerful adaptive quizzing, a game-like format, direct links to the e-Book, instant feedback, and the promise of better grades make using LearningCurve a no-brainer. Customized quizzing tailored to each text adapts to student responses and provides material at different difficulty levels and topics based on student performance. Students love the simple yet powerful system and instructors can access class reports to help refine lecture content.

LEARNINGCurve 　　　　　　　　　　　　3.2.2 Understanding Shifts of the Demand Curve

Suppose that clothes from the thrift store are inferior goods. If incomes decrease

- ○ demand will decrease.
- ○ demand will increase.
- ○ demand will decrease and then shift back to its original level.
- ◉ ~~demand will remain the same.~~

Whoops. The correct answer is not:

demand will remain the same.

→ *If incomes decrease, demand for inferior goods will increase.*

Try again, check the e-book, GET A HINT, or click SHOW ME to see the answer and try another question.

- Index:1/1
- Topic: Test Questions
- Level: 2
- Answer: demand will increase.
- edit item

? ≡ Get a Hint 　　　👁 Show Me

- **Everything is Assignable.** You can customize the LaunchPad Units by adding quizzes and other activities from our vast wealth of resources. You can also add a discussion board, a dropbox, and RSS feed, with a few clicks. LaunchPad allows you to customize your students' experience as much or as little as you'd like.

- **Useful Analytics.** The gradebook quickly and easily allows you to look up performance metrics for your whole class, for individual students and for individual assignments. Having ready access to this information can help in both lecture prep and in making office hours more productive and efficient.

- **An e-Book that delivers more than content.** Every LaunchPad e-Book comes with powerful study tools for students, video and multimedia content, and easy customization for instructors. Students can search, highlight, and bookmark, making it easier to study and access key content. And teachers can make sure their class gets just the book they want to deliver: customize and rearrange chapters, add and share notes and discussions, and link to quizzes, activities, and other resources.

- **Intuitive interface and design.** Students can be in only two places – either viewing the home page with their assigned content, or working to complete their assignments. Students' navigation options and expectations are clearly laid out in front of them at all times ensuring they can never get lost in the system.

- **Electronically graded graphing problems** replicate the paper and pencil experience better than any program on the market. Students are asked to draw their response and label each curve. The software automatically grades each response, providing feedback options at the instructor's discretion, including partial credit for incomplete, but not entirely incorrect, responses. Graphing questions are tagged to appropriate textbook sections and range in difficulty level and skill.

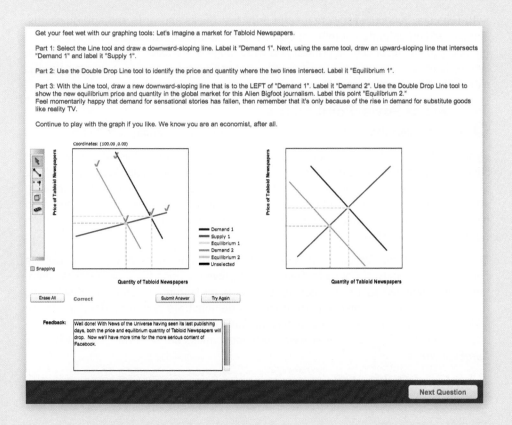

The test bank contains nearly 7,000 carefully constructed, thoroughly edited and revised, and comprehensively accuracy checked questions. Each question was thoroughly reviewed by Jane Himarios and Eric Chiang; in fact, no component of the learning suite received as much scrutiny as the revision of the test bank.

- *New to this edition:* Each chapter features a set of *anchor questions* carefully selected by Eric Chiang as foundation questions around which a quiz, homework assignment, or test can be built.
- Each question has *skill descriptors* based on Bloom's Taxonomy and a *degree of difficulty* (easy, moderate, or difficult). *Easy* questions require students to recognize concepts and definitions; *moderate* questions require some analysis, including distinguishing between related concepts; and *difficult* questions usually require more detailed analysis.
- To further aid instructors in building tests, each question is referenced by the specific heading in the textbook. Questions are presented in the order in which concepts are presented in the book.
- The test bank includes questions with tables that students must analyze to solve for numerical answers. It contains questions based on graphs that appear in the book and require students to interpret information presented in the graph.

Computerized Test Bank

⭐ **Best Classroom Use:** Online and Hybrid Course Formats | Building Tests for Face-to-Face Instruction

Diploma was the first software for PCs that integrated a test-generation program with grade-book software and online testing system. Diploma is now in its fifth generation. The Test Banks are available for both Windows and Macintosh users.

With Diploma, you can easily create and print test banks and write and edit questions. You can add an unlimited number of questions, scramble questions and distractors, and include figures. Tests can be printed in a wide range of formats. The software's unique synthesis of flexible word-processing and database features creates a program that is extremely intuitive and capable.

Two Sets of PowerPoint Slides

⭐ **Best Classroom Use:** Traditional/Face-to-Face or Active Learning/Face-to-Face

Dynamic PowerPoint Presentation by Eric Levy (Florida Atlantic University): PowerPoint slides designed with front-of-the-classroom presentation and visual learning in mind. This set of PowerPoint slides contains fully animated graphs, visual learning images, additional examples, links, and embedded questions. These slides may be customized by instructors and accessed via the catalog page at www.wortheconomics.com or within *LaunchPad* for *CoreEconomics.*

Lecture PowerPoint Presentation consists of PowerPoint slides designed by Debbie Evercloud (University of Colorado, Denver) that provide graphs from the textbook, data, tables, and bulleted lists of key concepts suitable for lecture presentation. Key figures from the text are replicated and animated to demonstrate how they develop. These slides may be customized by instructors to suit individual needs. These files may be accessed on the catalog page at www.wortheconomics.com or within *LaunchPad* for *CoreEconomics.*

Additional Online Offerings

www.saplinglearning.com
Sapling Learning provides interactive learning experiences for economics that significantly improve student comprehension, retention, and problem-solving skills.

Sapling Learning's system delivers unmatched benefits and capabilities including:

- **Proven Results**. Independent university studies have shown Sapling Learning improves student performance by 0.75 to a full letter grade.
- **Industry-Leading Support**. We match instructors with a Technology TA—PhD and master's-level subject experts—to provide software and course support throughout the semester.
- **Instant Student Feedback**. Our easy-to-use online homework assignments provide instant feedback and tutorials tailored to students' responses.
- **Performance Tracking**. Sapling Learning grades assignments, tracks student participation and progress, and compiles performance analytics—helping instructors save time and tailor assignments to address student needs.

www.aplia.com/worth

Worth/Aplia courses are all available with digital textbooks, interactive assignments, and detailed feedback. With Aplia, you retain complete control of and flexibility for your course. You choose the content you want students to cover, and you decide how to organize it. You decide whether online activities are practice (ungraded or graded).

- **Extra problem sets** (derived from in-chapter questions in the book) suitable for homework and keyed to specific topics from each chapter
- **Regularly updated news analyses**
- **Interactive tutorials** to assist with math and graphing
- **Instant online reports** that allow instructors to target student trouble areas more efficiently

Further Resources Offered

CourseTutor

CourseTutor, revised by Albert J. Sumell (Youngstown State University) and Gregory Rose (Sacramento City College) is more than a traditional study guide. It originated as a study aid crafted by Gerald Stone to help students in his Saturday sections at Metropolitan State University of Denver.

Each chapter of the *CourseTutor* is divided into two basic sections: a six-step detailed walk-through of the material to help each student check his or her individual progress, followed by a section with standard study material such as fill-in, true/false, multiple-choice, and short essay questions. Both sections are designed for interactivity and many of these features can be found in a digital format within *LaunchPad* for *CoreEconomics* including:

- *Solved Problems*: developed by Irina Pritchett (North Carolina State University), the solved problems are designed for the online environment using a graphing and assessment engine. Students receive detailed feedback and guidance on where to go for further review.

Students learn by many different methods and *CourseTutor* provides a buffet of learning choices. Students select those methods that best help them learn. In this way, the *CourseTutor* was a precursor to the many adaptive methodologies at work in online learning software, including those found in *LaunchPad* for *CoreEconomics*.

CourseSmart e-Books

www.coursesmart.com

CourseSmart e-books offer the complete book in PDF format. Students can save money—up to 60% off the price of the printed textbook. In CourseSmart, students have the ability to take notes, highlight, print pages, and more. It is great alternative to renting a textbook and it is compatible with most mobile platforms.

i>clicker

Developed by a team of University of Illinois physicists, i>clicker is the most flexible and reliable classroom response system available. It is the only solution created *for educators, by educators*—with continuous product improvements made through direct classroom testing and faculty feedback. You'll love i>clicker, no matter your level of technical expertise, because the focus is on your teaching, not the technology. To learn more about packaging i>clicker with this textbook, please contact your local sales representative or visit www.iclicker.com.

LMS Integration

LaunchPad for *CoreEconomics* can be fully integrated with any campus LMS including such features as single sign-on for students revisiting the site, gradebook integration for all activities completed in *LaunchPad*, as well as integration of assignments within the campus LMS for certain products. For more information on LMS integration, please contact your local publisher's representative.

➔ Acknowledgments

No project of this scope is accomplished alone. *CoreEconomics* and its suite of learning resources came together as a result of the dedication of many individuals who devoted incredible amounts of time to the project. These include reviewers of manuscript chapters, focus group participants, accuracy reviewers, supplements contributors, project specialists, and the production and editorial staff at Worth Publishers.

I want to thank those reviewers of the third edition who read through chapters in manuscript and offered many important suggestions that have been incorporated into this project. They include:

Bill Adamson, University of South Dakota
Stephen Bannister, University of Utah
Robert Burrus, University of North Carolina-Wilmington
Suparna Chakraborty, University of San Francisco
AnaMaria Conley, Regis University
Dale DeBoer, University of Colorado, Colorado Springs
Erwin Erhardt III, University of Cincinnati
Scott Gilbert, Southern Illinois University
Ross J. Hallren, University of Oklahoma
Moon Moon Haque, University of Memphis
Michael G. Heslop, Northern Virginia Community College
Ryan Herzog, Gonzaga University
Scott Hunt, Columbus State Community College
Sarah Jenyk, Youngstown State University
Janis Y. F. Kea, West Valley College
Barry Kotlove, Edmonds Community College

Larry Landrum, Virginia Western Community College
Jim Lee, Texas A&M University Corpus Christi
Sang H. Lee, Southeastern Louisiana University
Fred May, Trident Technical College
Robert McKizzie, Tarrant County College Southeast
Randy Methenitis, Richland College
Stan Mitchell, McLennan Community College
Douglas Orr, City College of San Francisco
Tomy Ovaska, Youngstown State University
Martin Sabo, Community College of Denver
Ravi Samitamana, Daytona State College
Albert J. Sumell, Youngstown State University
Deborah Thorsen, Palm Beach State College
Jane A. Treptow, Broward College
Christine Walthen, Middlesex County College
Wendy Wysocki, Monroe County Community College

I would like to thank those focus group participants who devoted a lot of time and effort to discussing the proposed revisions to the third edition and how this edition of *CoreEconomics* can facilitate a broad range of learning and teaching approaches. Their suggestions (and criticisms) contributed immensely to the development of this project. They include:

Nelson Altamirano, National University
Dennis Avola, Framingham State University
Kristie Briggs, Creighton University
Bruce Brown, California Polytechnic University, Pomona
Parama Chaudhury, University College London
Salvador Contreras, University of Texas Pan American

Brent Evans, Mississippi State University
Virginia Fierro-Renoy, Keiser University
Melanie Fox, Austin College
Lisa Gloege, Grand Rapids Community College
Oskar Harmon, University of Connecticut
Ryan Herzog, Gonzaga University

Jennifer Imazeki, San Diego State University

Ahmed Kader, University of Nevada Las Vegas

Hossein Kazemi, Stonehill College

Steven Levkoff, University of California San Diego

Eric Levy, Florida Atlantic University

Rotua Lumbantobing, Westminster College

Shakun Mago, University of Richmond

Diego Mendez-Carbajo, Illinois Wesleyan University

Evelina Mengova, California State University Fullerton

Rebecca Moryl, Emmanuel College

James Murray, University of Wisconsin, La Crosse

Robert Pennington, University of Central Florida

Robert Rebelein, Vassar College

Matthew Rousu, Susquehanna University

Rochelle Ruffer, Nazareth College

Scott Simkins, North Carolina A&T University

Jim Wollscheid, University of Arkansas, Fort Smith

Madelyn Young, Converse College

I would like to thank my current and former student assistants who helped with data collection and shared ideas for examples that would click with college students today. These students include Alan Jagessar, Eileen Schneider, Phil Esterman, Enrique Valdes, Kevin Brady, Thomas Thornton, Brett Block, and Craig Haberstumpf. I also thank all of the students who have taken my principles courses. Their comments, body language, and facial expressions provided cues to whether my concept explanations and applications were clear and provided guidance on how to approach these topics in the book.

I would like to thank Jose Vazquez of the University of Illinois at Urbana-Champaign and Rochelle Ruffer of Nazareth College for their willingness to use the preliminary version of the third edition in their classes. The feedback I received from their experience as well as from their students allowed me to improve the textbook prior to its publication.

I am extremely grateful to Jane Himarios of the University of Texas at Arlington who not only oversaw the complete revision of the Test Bank but also took on the role of an expert accuracy checker. Further, Jane provided constant moral support throughout the project.

I want to thank James Watson for his tireless examination of the page proofs to ensure accuracy. Despite dozens of eyes that have read through manuscript and proofs, James still managed to catch errors that none of us want to see in the final product.

A huge debt of gratitude is owed to Lindsay Neff and the supplements authors. Lindsay did a remarkable job to get the best people to author the supplements. They include Jane Himarios of the University of Texas at Arlington who managed the revision of the Test Bank, Albert J. Sumell of Youngstown State University and Gregory Rose of Sacramento City College who revised the *CourseTutor*, Eric Levy of Florida Atlantic University who created the dynamic PowerPoint slides, and Solina Lindahl of California Polytechnic University–San Luis Obispo for coordinating the pedagogical resources available to instructors. I would also like to thank Ting Levy of Florida Atlantic University, Tamika Steward, James Watson and Brett Block for the development of materials for *LaunchPad* for *CoreEconomics*. *CoreEconomics* and the *CoreMedia* came together into a cohesive set of instructor and student resources because of their efforts.

I owe a significant debt to the team of technology specialists who created many fascinating digital resources for *CoreEconomics*. I thank Tom Acox for his instrumental role in the development and management of the online resources, especially *LaunchPad*. There has been more than one occasion when a crisis situation with my class required immediate attention, and Tom was always available, day and night, to resolve the problem. He truly exemplifies his title as digital solutions manager.

I am truly indebted to Jeremy Brown, who over the years has taught me the tools and tricks of digital technology that have become indispensable in today's media-driven world. These tools include video editing, animation, and other visual effects, creating a professional Web site, and maximizing the effectiveness of social media. Whenever I have a technology-related question, I can count on Jeremy for an answer. His influence has given me the confidence to use cutting-edge technology to its maximum potential to the benefit of the *CoreEconomics* suite of resources.

Several persons have provided inspiration for various teaching pedagogies as well as a willingness to lend an ear. These individuals include Gregory Rose of Sacramento City College, Djeto Assane of the University of Nevada Las Vegas, Yoram Bauman (Stand-up

Economist), Janice Hauge of the University of North Texas, Marc Cannon, and William Bosshardt of Florida Atlantic University.

The production team at Worth is truly the best in the industry. My heartfelt thanks go to the entire team, including Kevin Kall, senior designer, for creating a fantastic set of interior and cover designs; Georgia Lee Hadler, senior project editor, for skillfully managing the copyediting and proofing of the book; Martha Solonche for her superb copyediting; Christine Buese and Julie Tesser for their immense efforts at finding and obtaining rights to the hundreds of photos used in the book; Mary Walsh for her meticulous work in preparing manuscripts for production; Tracey Kuehn, Barbara Seixas, and production specialists Susie Bothwell, Lisa Hankins, and Christina Welker. Each of these individuals made sure each part of the production process went smoothly. Thank you very much for a job well done.

I want to thank Charles Linsmeier, publisher of economics, for recruiting me for this project and making this collaboration with Jerry Stone a reality. Not only did Chuck sign me to Worth, he also has provided dedicated support throughout the entire process. I also thank Paul Shensa for this support from the beginning of the project to its completion. From his ideas on editorial changes to marketing, Paul is an indispensable resource for any author.

There is no one person I can thank more than Bruce Kaplan, senior development editor, who has guided me on the revision of *CoreEconomics* from start to finish. Bruce had a long working relationship with Jerry Stone on his first two editions and was able to provide the continuity into the third edition without Jerry's presence. In fact, in my last conversation with Jerry Stone, he told me to "stick with Bruce; he's the best and will take you far." Jerry's words ring true each time I work with Bruce, who is the best editor and mentor an author can have.

You couldn't ask for a better marketing team than that at Worth. In the early stages of this edition, I had the pleasure of working with Scott Guile, whose enthusiasm is infectious and his efforts tireless. Scott's promotion left big shoes to fill, but the arrival of Tom Digiano as marketing manager provided a flawless transition. Tom's expertise in online homework systems and social media marketing is inspiring, and has encouraged me to push the boundaries to create wonderful marketing pieces that I am proud to put my name on. I thank Tom Kling for his role in motivating the sales reps to the benefits of this project, and for always making me feel at home during sales meetings. I thank the entire sales force, which devotes its time, effort, and passion to showcasing *CoreEconomics* in a way that truly exemplifies its value to economics education.

I wish to thank Sarah Dorger, for without her efforts, my authoring role would not have happened. I thank Sharon Balbos, whose abundance of experience with textbook-related projects prior to *CoreEconomics* helped me to develop a keen eye for detail that is vital to an author. I thank Craig Bleyer, who for many years encouraged me to become an author before I finally did. And I thank Catherine Woods and Elizabeth Widdicombe for supporting me as an author.

Finally, I thank Jerry Stone, a true friend and colleague who put his full trust in me when he offered me the opportunity to take over authorship of *CoreEconomics* in 2010 and carry the book forward to a new generation of students and instructors with new needs. I wish Jerry were still here to collaborate on the textbook he created so successfully in the first two editions. I will never cease my efforts to make *CoreEconomics* a long-lasting legacy of Jerry's brilliance and dedication to students and instructors.

Eric P. Chiang

Eric P. Chiang

Exploring Economics

1

After studying this chapter you should be able to:

- Explain how economic analysis can be used in decision making.

- Differentiate between microeconomics and macroeconomics.

- Describe how economists use models.

- Describe the *ceteris paribus* assumption.

- Discuss the difference between efficiency and equity.

- Describe the key principles in economics.

- Apply the key principles to situations faced in your daily routine.

P erched high atop the 3,000-foot vertical monolith known as El Capitan, a climber gazes out upon a perfect view of Yosemite National Park. Holding onto the wall *with no rope,* one tiny slip of the foot will lead to certain death. Welcome to the sport of free soloing, an extreme form of rock climbing done *without* ropes or harnesses. Does this sound thrilling? Or perhaps crazy? Or even irrational? These are common thoughts that come to mind when people talk about the new wave of risky adventure sports. Would you think that whether or not to participate in such an activity is an economic question?

Most people probably wouldn't. But this example resembles an economic problem in many ways. Free soloing involves a challenge, one with a *benefit* (a sense of accomplishment) and a *cost* (both monetary and physical risks). It involves *tradeoffs*—the thousands of hours spent practicing and perfecting the climbing techniques needed to be successful. And it involves societal beliefs about whether such activities should be *regulated* or even banned. Benefits, costs, tradeoffs, regulation: These are the foundations for making a decision using the tools of economic thinking, as we will see. Nearly all decisions made by individuals, firms, and governments in pursuit of an objective or goal can be understood using these economic concepts.

By the end of this course, you will come to understand that economics involves all types of decisions, from small everyday decisions on how to manage one's time to world-changing decisions made by the president of the United States. Consumers make decisions about what clothes to buy and what foods to eat. Businesses must decide what products to make and how much of each product to stock on store shelves. Indeed, one cannot escape making decisions, and the outcomes of these decisions affect not only our own lives but those of entire societies and countries.

You still might be asking yourself: Why should I study economics? First, you will spend roughly the next 40 years working in an economic environment: paying taxes, experiencing ups and downs in the overall economy, investing money, and voting on various economic issues. It will benefit you to know how the economy works. More important, economic analysis gives you a structure from which you can make decisions in a more rational manner. Economics teaches you how to make better and wiser decisions given your limited resources. This course may well change the way you look at the world. It can open your eyes to how you make everyday decisions from what to buy to where you choose to live.

Like our opening example, economic analysis involves decisions that are not just "economic" in the general sense of the term. Certainly economic thinking may change your views on spending and saving, on how you feel about government debt, and on your opinion of environmental policies or globalization. But you also may develop a different perspective on how much time to study for each of your courses this term, or where you might go for Spring Break this year. Such is the wide scope of economic analysis.

In this introductory chapter, we take a broad look at economics. We take a brief look at a key method of economic analysis: model building. Economists use stylized facts and the technique of holding some variables constant to develop testable theories about how consumers, businesses, and governments make decisions. Then we turn to a short discussion of some key principles of economics to give you a sense of the guiding concepts you will come across in this book.

This introductory chapter will give you a sense of what economics is, what concepts it uses, and what it finds to be important. Do not go into this chapter thinking you have to memorize these concepts. Rather, use this chapter to get a sense of the broad scope of economics. You will be given many opportunities to understand and use these concepts throughout this course. Return to this chapter at the end of the course and see if everything has now become crystal clear.

What Is Economics About?

Economics is a very broad subject. It often seems that economics has something important to say about almost everything.

To boil it down to a simple definition, **economics** is about making choices. Economics studies how individuals, firms, and societies make decisions to maximize

economics The study of how individuals, firms, and society make decisions to allocate limited resources to many competing wants.

BY THE NUMBERS

Economic Issues Are All Around Us

Economics is one of the most popular college majors in the country. This is because so much of what we do, the decisions we face, and the issues we confront involve economics.

　　Each chapter in this book includes a By the Numbers box. It has two purposes. First, items in the feature preview some of the topics covered in the chapter. We hope these topics motivate you to read on. Second, the data explosion affecting our understanding of the world will only continue to accelerate. Numerical literacy will grow in importance. This By the Numbers box seeks to encourage a nonthreatening familiarity with data and numbers. At the end of each chapter, there are two Using the Numbers questions to test how well you understood the numbers.

Total Number of Bachelor's Degrees
(in thousands) Granted by Major in 2011

Business majors represented the largest number of college graduates in terms of the total number of bachelor's degrees granted in 2011. Economics majors represented the sixth most popular degree granted.

Technology Company CEO Majors:	Fortune 100 Company CEO Majors:
1. Economics (22%)	1. Engineering (17%)
2. Computer Science (20%)	2. Economics (12%)
3. Engineering (17%)	3. Business Administration (12%)

41%
Percent of Fortune 500 Companies (America's largest companies by revenue) founded by immigrants or their children.

$94,700
The median salary of workers with economics degrees after 15 years of work experience.

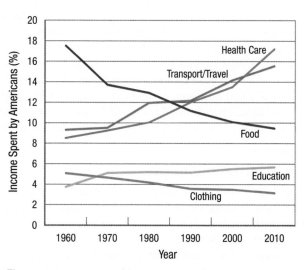

The average percentage of income Americans spent on food and clothing has fallen since 1960, but the percentage of income spent on travel, education, and health care has increased.

Median Salaries (in thousands)

What do economists do? Common jobs held by economists with bachelor's degrees and their median salaries.

scarcity Our unlimited wants clash with limited resources, leading to scarcity. Everyone (rich and poor) faces scarcity because, at a minimum, our time on earth is limited. Economics focuses on the allocation of scarce resources to satisfy unlimited wants.

their well-being given limitations. In other words, economics attempts to address the problem of having too many wants but too few resources to achieve them all, an important concept called **scarcity.** Note that scarcity is not the same thing as something being *scarce*. Although all resources are scarce, certain goods are less scarce than others. For example, cars are not very scarce—there are car dealerships around the country chock-full of cars ready to be sold, but that doesn't mean you can go out tonight and buy three. Scarcity refers to the fact that one must make choices given the resource limitations she or he faces.

What kind of limitations are we referring to here? It could be money, but money is not the only resource that allows us to achieve the life we want. It's also our time, our knowledge, our work ethic, and anything else that can be used to achieve our goals. It is this broad notion of economics being the study of how people make decisions to allocate scarce resources to competing wants that allows the subject to be applied to so many topics and applications.

Why Should One Study Economics?

The first answer that might come to mind as to why you are taking this course is "because you have to." Although economics is a required course for many college students, economics should be thought of as something much, much more. For example, studying economics can prepare you for many types of careers in major industries and government. Studying economics also is a great launching pad for pursuing a graduate degree in law, business, or other fields. More practically speaking, economics helps you to think more clearly about the decisions you make every day and to understand better how the economy functions and why certain things happen the way they do.

For example, economics has some important things to say about the environment. Most people care about the environment to some degree, and do their part by recycling, not littering, and turning off the lights when leaving a room. But not all people make decisions in the same way: Some might do much more to conserve resources, such as driving less or driving a more fuel efficient car, joining a local organization to plant trees, or even writing to policymakers to support sustainability legislation. The extent to which people participate in environmental activities depends on the benefit they perceive when pursuing such actions compared to the costs, which can include monetary costs, time and effort, and forgone opportunities such as driving a larger, more comfortable car. Economics looks at all of these factors to determine how people make decisions that affect the environment, which affects us all. Economics is a way of thinking about an issue, not just a discipline that has money as its chief focus.

incentives The factors that motivate individuals and firms to make decisions in their best interest.

Economists tend to have a rational take on nearly everything. Now all of this "analysis/speculation" may bring only limited insight in some cases, but it gives you some idea of how economists think. We look for rational responses to **incentives.** Incentives are the factors, both good and bad, that influence how people make decisions. For example, tough admissions requirements for graduate school provide an incentive for students to study harder in college, while lucrative commissions push car salespeople to sell even the ugliest or most unreliable car. Economics is all about how people respond to incentives. We begin most questions by considering how rational people would respond to the incentives that specific situations provide. Sometimes (maybe even often) this analysis leads us down an unexpected path.

Microeconomics Versus Macroeconomics

microeconomics The decision making by individuals, businesses, industries, and governments.

Economics is split into two broad categories: microeconomics and macroeconomics. **Microeconomics** deals with decision making by individuals, businesses, industries, and governments. It is concerned with issues such as which orange juice to buy, which job to take, and where to go on vacation, as well as which items a business should produce and what price it should charge, and whether a market should be left on its own or be regulated.

Microeconomics looks at how markets are structured. Some markets are very competitive, where many firms offer similar products; while other markets have only one or two large firms, offering little choice. What decisions do businesses make under different market structures? Microeconomics also extends to such topics as labor laws, environmental policy, and health care policy. How can we use the tools of microeconomics to analyze the costs and benefits of differing policies?

Macroeconomics, on the other hand, focuses on the broader issues we face as a nation. Most of us don't care whether an individual buys Nike or Merrell shoes. We *do* care whether prices of *all* goods and services rise. Inflation—a general increase in prices economy-wide—affects all of us. So does unemployment (virtually every person will at some point in their life be unemployed, even if it's just for a short time when switching from one job to another) and economic growth. What decisions do governments make to deal with macroeconomic problems such as inflation and recessions?

Macroeconomics uses microeconomic tools to answer some questions, but its main focus is on the broad aggregate variables of the economy. Macroeconomics has its own terms and topics, such as business cycles, recession, and unemployment. Macroeconomics looks at policies that increase economic growth, the impact of government spending and taxation, the effect of monetary policy on the economy, and inflation. It also looks closely at theories of international trade and international finance. All of these topics have broad impacts on our economy and our standard of living.

Still not clear? Here's an easy way to remember the difference between microeconomics and macroeconomics. Only one letter separates the two terms, so just remember that the "i" in microeconomics refers to "individual" entities (such as a person or a firm), while the "a" in macroeconomics refers to "aggregate" entities (such as cities or a nation as a whole).

Economics is a social science that uses many facts and figures to develop and express ideas. This inevitably involves numbers. For macroeconomics, this means getting used to talking and thinking in huge numbers: billions (nine zeros) and trillions (twelve zeros). Today we are talking about a federal government budget approaching $4 trillion. To wrap your mind around such a huge number, consider how long it would take to spend a trillion dollars if you spent a dollar every second, or $86,400 per day. To spend $1 trillion would require over 31,000 years. And the federal government now spends nearly 4 times this much in one year.

Although we break economics into microeconomics and macroeconomics, there is considerable overlap in the analysis. Both involve the analysis of how individuals, firms, and governments make decisions that affect the lives of people. We use simple supply and demand analysis to understand *both* individual markets and the general economy as a whole. You will find yourself using concepts from microeconomics to understand fluctuations in the macroeconomy.

Economic Theories and Reality

If you flip through any economics text, you'll likely see a multitude of graphs, charts, and equations. This book is no exception. The good news is that all of the graphs and charts become relatively easy to understand since they all basically read the same way. The few equations in this book stem from elementary algebra. Once you get through one equation, the rest are similar.

Graphs, charts, and equations are often the simplest and most efficient ways to express data and ideas. Equations are used to express relationships between two variables. Complex and wordy discussions can often be reduced to a simple graph or figure. These are efficient techniques for expressing economic ideas.

Model Building As you study economics this term, you will encounter stylized approaches to a number of issues. By *stylized,* we mean that economists boil down facts to their basic relevant elements and use assumptions to develop a stylized (simple) model to analyze the issue. There are always situations that lie outside these models, but they are the exception. Economists generalize about economic behavior and reach broadly applicable results.

We begin with relatively simple models, then gradually build to more difficult ones. For example, in the next chapter we introduce one of the simplest models in economics,

macroeconomics The broader issues in the economy such as inflation, unemployment, and national output of goods and services.

ceteris paribus Assumption used in economics (and other disciplines as well), where other relevant factors or variables are held constant.

efficiency How well resources are used and allocated. Do people get the goods and services they want at the lowest possible resource cost? This is the chief focus of efficiency.

equity The fairness of various issues and policies.

the production possibilities frontier that illustrates the limits of economic activity. This model has profound implications for the issue of economic growth. We can add in more dimensions and make the model more complex, but often this complexity does not provide any greater insight than the simple model.

Ceteris Paribus: All Else Held Constant To aid in our model building, economists use the *ceteris paribus* assumption: "Holding all other things equal." That means we will hold some important variables constant. For example, to determine how many songs you might be willing to download from iTunes in any given month, we would hold your monthly income constant. We then would change song prices to see the impact on the number purchased (again holding your monthly income constant).

Though model building can lead to surprising insights into how economic actors and economies behave, it is not the end of the story. Economic insights lead to economic theories, but these theories must then be tested. In some cases, such as the extent to which a housing bubble could lead to a financial crisis, economic predictions turned out to be false. Thus, model building is a *process*—models are created and then tested. If models fail to explain reality, new models are constructed.

ISSUE

Have Smartphones and Social Media Made Life Easier?

Maxx-Studio/Shutterstock

Two decades ago, if your professor wanted to convey an important announcement about an upcoming class, she or he would have to wait until the next class period, or if more urgent, make a phone call to each student. Similarly, if you worked for a company, communications with your boss generally ended when you left the office for the day.

Today, we live in a society in which nearly everybody uses online technologies, whether it be for keeping up with friends on Facebook, writing a recommendation for a friend on LinkedIn, or completing homework using classroom management software. Further, we live in a world in which computers and phones are no longer fixed; instead, we carry miniature versions of them with us at all times. According to a Nielsen survey, over 55% of all American adults own a smartphone, and over 75% of those between the ages of 18 and 24 do. So how do these technologies affect our lives?

We can analyze this question using the standard economic benefit versus cost approach. On the benefit side, Internet and mobile technologies have clearly improved the speed and ease of communications, whether staying in touch with family and friends, or trying to locate a loved one

at the mall (no more preplanned meeting locations required).

In addition to benefits, there are also costs. For example, greater ease of communications often comes with greater expectations. Several survey studies found that over 95% of Americans answer at least one work-related email or business phone call while on vacation. Students are expected to respond quickly to emails from professors. And even your friends might expect you to respond instantly to text messages and to "like" their latest posts on a social media site. Indeed, sometimes being too connected adds new pressures in life.

Each individual is unique and weighs the benefits and costs of technology differently. How you value these benefits and costs will ultimately determine how you choose to adapt to new and existing technologies. Economics involves all sorts of decisions, including how well connected we choose to be in life.

Efficiency Versus Equity

Efficiency deals with how well resources are used and allocated. No one likes waste. Much of economic analysis is directed toward ensuring that the most efficient outcomes result from public policy. *Production efficiency* occurs when goods are produced at the lowest possible cost, and *allocative efficiency* occurs when individuals who desire a product the most get those goods and services. As an example, it would not make sense for society to allocate to me a large amount of cranberry sauce—I would not eat it. Efficient policies are generally good policies.

The other side of the coin is **equity,** or fairness. Is it fair that the CEOs of large companies make hundreds of times more money than rank-and-file workers? Many think not. Is it fair that some have so much and others have so little? Again, many think not. There are many divergent views about fairness until we get to extreme cases. When just a few people earn nearly all of the income and control nearly all of a society's wealth, most people agree that this is unfair.

Throughout this course you will see instances where efficiency and equity collide. You may agree that a specific policy is efficient, but think it is unfair to some group of people. This will be especially evident when you consider tax policy and its impact on income distribution. Fairness, or equity, is a subjective concept, and each of us has different ideas about what is just and fair. When it comes to public policy issues, economics will help you see the tradeoffs between equity and efficiency, but you will ultimately have to make up your own mind about the wisdom of the policy given these tradeoffs.

Positive Versus Normative Questions

Returning to the example in the chapter opener, we ask ourselves many questions whenever a decision needs to be made or an issue is debated. Some questions involve the understanding of basic facts, such as how risky a particular sport is, or how much enjoyment one gets from participating in the sport. Economists call these types of questions **positive questions.** Positive questions (which need not be positive or upbeat in the literal sense) are questions that can be answered one way or another as long as the information is available. This does not mean that people will always agree on an answer, because facts and information can differ.

positive question A question that can be answered using available information or facts.

Another type of question that arises is how something ought to be, such as whether extreme sports should be banned or whether additional safety measures should be required. Economists call these types of questions **normative questions.** Normative questions involve societal beliefs on what should or should not be done; differing opinions on an issue can sometimes make normative questions difficult to resolve.

normative question A question that is based on societal beliefs on what should or should not take place.

Throughout this book, positive and normative questions will arise, which will play an important role in how individuals and firms make decisions, and how governments form policy proposals that may or may not become law. Indeed, economics encompasses many ideas and questions that affect everyone.

 CHECKPOINT

WHAT IS ECONOMICS ABOUT?

- Economics is about making decisions under scarcity, in which wants are unlimited but resources are limited.
- Economics is separated into two broad categories: microeconomics and macroeconomics.
- *Microeconomics* deals with individuals, firms, and industries and how they make decisions.
- *Macroeconomics* focuses on broader economic issues such as inflation, employment and unemployment, and economic growth.
- Economics uses a stylized approach, creating simple models that hold all other relevant factors constant (*ceteris paribus*).
- Economists and policymakers often face a tradeoff between efficiency and equity.
- Positive questions can be answered with facts and information, while normative questions ask how something should or ought to be.

QUESTION: In each of the following situations, determine whether it is a microeconomic or macroeconomic issue.

1. Hewlett-Packard announces that it is lowering the price of its printers by 15%.

2. The president proposes a tax cut.

3. You decide to look for a new job.

4. The economy is in a recession, and the job market is bad.

5. The Federal Reserve announces that it is raising interest rates because it fears inflation.

6. You get a nice raise.

7. Average wages grew by 2% last year.

Answers to the Checkpoint questions can be found at the end of this chapter.

➜ Key Principles of Economics

Economics has a set of key principles that show up continually in economic analysis. Some are more restricted to specific issues, but most apply universally. These principles should give you a sense of what you will learn in this course. In the following, we summarize seven key principles that will be applied throughout the entire book. By the end of this course, these principles should be crystal clear and you will likely find yourself using these principles throughout your life, even if you never take another economics course.

Principle 1: Economics Is Concerned with Making Choices with Limited Resources

Economics deals with nearly every type of decision we face every day. But when a typical person is asked what economics is about, the most common answer is "money." Why is economics commonly misconceived as dealing only with money? This may be due in part to how economics is portrayed in the news—dealing with financial issues, jobs and wages, and the cost of living, among other money matters. While money matters are indeed an important issue studied in economics, you now know that economics involves much, much more.

Economics is about making decisions on allocating limited resources to maximize an individual or society's well-being. Money is just one source of well-being, assuming that more money makes a person happier, all else equal. But other factors also improve a person's well-being, such as receiving a day off from work with pay. Even if one does not have a lot of money or free time, satisfaction can come from other activities or events, such as participating in a fun activity with friends or family, or watching one's favorite team win.

In sum, many aspects of life contribute to the well-being of individuals and of society. Unfortunately, often these are limited by various resource constraints. Therefore, one must think of economics in a broad sense of determining how best to manage all of society's resources (not just money) in order to maximize well-being. This involves tradeoffs and opportunity costs, which we consider next.

Principle 2: When Making Decisions, One Must Take Into Account Tradeoffs and Opportunity Costs

Tony Avelar/Bloomberg via Getty Images

Wouldn't it be great if we all had the resources of Mark Zuckerberg (the founder of Facebook) and could buy just about any material possession one could possibly want? Most likely we won't, so back to reality.

We all have limited resources. Some of us are more limited than others, but each of us, even Mark Zuckerberg, faces limitations (and not because Mark chooses to wear a $30 shirt instead of a $3,000 Brioni suit). For example, we all face time limitations: There are only 24 hours in a day, and some of that must be spent sleeping. The fact that we have many wants but limited resources (scarcity) means that we must make tradeoffs in nearly everything we do. In other words, we have to decide between alternatives, which always exist whenever we make a decision.

How is this accomplished? What factors determine whether you buy a nicer car or use the extra money to pay down debt? Or whether you should spend the weekend at a local music festival or use the time to study for an exam? Economists use an important term to help weigh the benefits and costs of every decision we make, and that term is **opportunity cost**. In fact, economics is often categorized as the discipline that always weighs benefits against costs.

At its very core, opportunity cost is determined by asking yourself, in any situation, "What could I be doing right now if I wasn't _____ (fill in the activity)?" or "What could I have bought if I didn't buy this _____ (fill in the last good or service you bought)?" In other words, opportunity cost measures the value of the next best alternative use of your time or money, or what you *give up* when you make an economic decision. And since there are always alternatives, one cannot avoid opportunity costs.

A common mistake that people make is that they sometimes do not fully take their opportunity costs into account. Have you ever camped out overnight in order to get tickets for a concert? Was it even worth going to the concert? Opportunity cost includes the value

opportunity cost The value of the next best alternative; what you give up to do something or purchase something.

of everything you give up in order to attend the concert, including the cost of the tickets and transportation, and the time spent buying tickets, traveling to and from the venue, and of course attending the concert. The sum of all opportunity costs can sometimes outweigh the benefits.

Another example of miscalculating opportunity costs occurs when a student spends a copious amount of time to dispute a $15 parking ticket. Like the previous example, the opportunity cost (time and effort disputing the ticket which can be used for some other activity) may exceed the $15 savings if successful and certainly if the attempt to dispute the ticket fails.

In other cases, individuals do respond to opportunity costs. Why do many people choose a paper towel over a hand dryer in a public restroom when given the choice? It's because the opportunity cost of using the hand dryer is higher than using a paper towel.

Every activity involves opportunity costs. Sleeping, eating, studying, partying, running, hiking, and so on, all require that we spend resources that could be used on another activity. Opportunity cost varies from person to person. A company president rushing from meeting to meeting has a higher opportunity cost than a retired senior citizen, and therefore is more likely to choose the quickest option to accomplish day-to-day activities.

Opportunity costs apply to us as individuals and to societies as a whole. For example, if a country chooses to spend more on environmental conservation, it must use resources that could be used to promote other objectives, such as education and health care.

Principle 3: Specialization Leads to Gains for All Involved

Whenever we pursue an activity or a task, we use time that could be used for other activities or tasks. However, sometimes these other tasks are best left to others to perform. Life would be much more difficult if we all had to grow our own food. This highlights the idea that tradeoffs (especially with one's time) can lead to better outcomes if one is able to specialize in activities in which she or he is more proficient.

Suppose you and your roommate can each cook your own dinner and clean your own rooms. Alternatively, you might have your roommate clean both rooms (he's better at it than you) in exchange for you preparing dinner for two (you're a better cook). Using this arrangement, both tasks are completed in less time since each of you are specializing in the activity you're better at, plus both of you will benefit from a cleaner apartment and a tastier dinner.

Therefore, specialization in tasks in which one is more proficient can lead to gains for all parties as long as exchange is possible and those involved trade in a mutually beneficial manner. Each person is acting on the opportunity to improve his or her well-being, an example of how incentives affect people's lives.

Principle 4: People Respond to Incentives, Both Good and Bad

Each time an individual or a firm makes a decision, that person or firm is acting on an incentive that drives the individual or firm to choose an action. These incentives often occur naturally. For example, we choose to eat every day because we face an incentive to survive, and we study and work hard because we face an incentive to be successful in our careers. However, incentives also can be formed by policies set by government to encourage individuals and firms to act in certain ways, and by businesses to encourage consumers to change their consumption habits.

For example, tax policy rests on the idea that people follow their incentives. Do we want to encourage people to save for their retirement? Then let them deduct a certain amount that they can put into a tax-deferred retirement account. Do we want businesses to spend more to stimulate the economy? Then give them tax credits for new investment. Do we want people to go to college? Then give them tax advantages for setting up education savings accounts.

Tax policy is an obvious example in which people follow incentives. But this principle can be seen in action wherever you look. Want to encourage people to fly during the slow travel season? Offer price discounts or bonus frequent flyer miles for flying during that time. Want to spread out the dining time at restaurants? Give early-bird discounts to those willing to eat at 5:00 P.M. rather than at 7:30 P.M.

Note that in saying that people follow incentives, economists do not claim that everyone follows each incentive every time. Though you may not want to eat dinner at 5:00 P.M., there might be other people who are willing to eat earlier in return for a price discount.

If not properly constructed, incentives might lead to harmful outcomes. During the 2008 financial crisis, it became clear that the way incentives for traders and executives were set up by Wall Street investment banks was misguided. Traders and executives were paid bonuses based on short-term profits. This encouraged them to take extreme risks to generate quick profits and high bonuses with little regard for the long-term viability of the bank. The bank may be gone tomorrow, but these people still have those huge bonuses.

Would you pick it up? Who wouldn't?

Responding to badly designed incentives is often described as greed, but they are not always the same. If you found a $20 bill on the sidewalk, would you pick it up? Of course, but would that make you a greedy person? The stranger who accidentally dropped the bill an hour ago might think so, but you are just responding to an incentive to pick up the money before the next lucky person does. Could incentives ever be designed to prevent people from picking up money they find? It may surprise you that one industry has: In many casinos, it is prohibited to keep chips or money you find on the floor.

The natural tendency for society to respond to incentives leads individuals and firms to work hard and generate ideas that increase productivity, a measure of a society's capacity to produce that determines our standard of living. A worker who can do twice as much as another is likely to earn a higher salary, because productivity and pay tend to go together. The same is true for nations. Countries with the highest standards of living are also the most productive.

Principle 5: Rational Behavior Requires Thinking on the Margin

Have you ever noticed that when you eat at an all-you-can-eat buffet, you always go away fuller than when you order and eat at a non-buffet restaurant? Is this phenomenon unique to you, or is there something more fundamental? Remember, economists look at facts to find incentives to economic behavior.

In this case, people are just rationally responding to the price of *additional* food. They are thinking on the margin. In a non-buffet restaurant, dessert costs extra, and you make a decision as to whether the enjoyment you receive from the dessert (the marginal benefit) is worth the extra cost (the marginal cost). At the buffet, dessert is free, which means the marginal cost is zero. Even so, you still must ask yourself if dessert will give you satisfaction. If the dessert tastes terrible or adds unwanted calories to your diet, then you might pass on dessert even if it is free. But the fact that one is more likely to have dessert at a buffet than at a menu-based restaurant highlights the notion that people tend to think on the margin.

The idea of thinking on the margin applies to a society as well. Like asking ourselves whether we want another serving of dessert, a society must ask itself whether it wants a little bit more or a little bit less of something, and policymakers and/or citizens vote on such policy proposals. An example of society thinking on the margin is whether taxes should be raised a little to pay for other projects, or whether a country should send up another space exploration craft to study other planets.

Throughout this book, we will see examples of thinking on the margin. A business uses marginal analysis to determine how much of its products it is willing to supply to the market. Individuals use marginal analysis to determine how many hours to exercise or study. And governments use marginal analysis to determine how much pollution should be permitted.

Principle 6: Markets Are Generally Efficient; When They Aren't, Government Can Sometimes Correct the Failure

Individuals and firms make decisions that maximize their well-being, and markets bring buyers and sellers together. Private markets and the incentives they provide are the best mechanisms known today for providing products and services. There is no government food board that makes sure that bread, cereal, coffee, and all the other food products you demand are on your plate during the day. The vast majority of products we consume are privately provided.

Competition for the consumer dollar forces firms to provide products at the lowest possible price, or some other firm will undercut their high price. New products enter the market and old products die out. Such is the dynamic characteristic of markets.

What drives and disciplines markets? Prices and profits are the keys. Profits drive entrepreneurs to provide new products (think of Apple) or existing products at lower prices (think of Wal-Mart). When prices and profits get too high in any market, new firms jump in with lower prices to grab away customers. This competition, or sometimes even the threat of competition, keeps markets from exploiting consumers.

Individuals and firms respond to prices in markets by altering the choices and quantities of goods they purchase and sell, respectively. These actions highlight the ability of markets to provide an efficient outcome for all. Markets can achieve this efficiency without a central planner telling what people should buy or what firms should sell. This phenomenon that markets promote efficiency through the incentives faced by individuals and firms (as if they were guided by an omnipotent force) is referred to as the *invisible hand*, a term coined by Adam Smith, long considered the father of economics.

As efficient as markets usually are, society does not desire a market for everything. For example, markets for hard drugs or child pornography are largely deemed undesirable. In other cases, a market does not provide enough of a good or service, such as public parks or public education. For these products and services, markets can fail to provide an optimal outcome.

But when markets do fail, they tend to do so in predictable ways. Where consumers have no choice but to buy from one firm (such as a local water company), the market will fail to provide the best solution, and government regulation is often used to protect consumers. Another example is pollution: Left unregulated, companies often will pollute the air and water. Governments then intervene to deal with this market failure. Finally, people rely on information to make rational decisions. When information is not readily available or is known only to one side of the market, markets again can fail to produce the socially desirable outcome.

Oriental Touch/Robert Harding

Markets can be crowded and chaotic, but they generally promote an efficient outcome by bringing buyers and sellers together.

We also can extend the idea of market efficiency to the greater economy. The market forces of supply and demand generally keep the economy in equilibrium. But occasionally fluctuations in the macroeconomy will occur, and markets take time to readjust on their own. In some cases, the economy becomes stuck in a severe downturn. In these instances, government can smooth the fluctuations in the overall economy by using policies such as government spending or tax cuts. But remember, just because the government *can* successfully intervene does not mean it *always* successfully intervenes. The macroeconomy is not a simple machine. Successful policy-making is a tough task.

Principle 7: Institutions and Human Creativity Help Explain the Wealth of Nations

We have seen how individuals and firms make decisions to maximize their well-being, and how tradeoffs, specialization, incentives, and marginal analysis play an important role. We then saw how markets bring buyers and sellers together to promote better outcomes, and that governments sometimes step in when markets fail to produce the best outcome. But how does all of this affect the overall wealth of a nation? Two important factors influencing

ADAM SMITH (1723–1790)

When Adam Smith was four years old, he was kidnapped and held for ransom. Had his captors not taken fright and returned the boy unharmed, the history of economics might well have turned out differently.

Born in Kirkaldy, Scotland, in 1723, Smith graduated from the University of Glasgow at age 17 and was awarded a scholarship to Oxford. Smith considered his time at Oxford to be largely wasted. Returning to Scotland in 1751, Smith was named Professor of Moral Philosophy at the University of Glasgow.

After 12 years at Glasgow, Smith began tutoring the son of a wealthy Scottish nobleman. This job provided him with the opportunity to spend several years touring the European continent with his young charge. In Paris, Smith met some of the leading French economists of the day, which helped stoke his own interest in political economy. While there, he wrote a friend, "I have begun to write a book in order to pass the time."

Returning to Kirkaldy in 1766, Smith spent the next decade finishing *An Inquiry Into the Nature and Causes of the Wealth of Nations.* Before publication in 1776, he read sections of the text to Benjamin Franklin. Smith's genius was in taking the existing forms of economic analysis available at the time and putting them together in a systematic fashion to make sense of the national economy as a whole. Smith demonstrated how individuals left free to pursue their own economic interests end up acting in ways that enhance the welfare of all. This is Smith's famous "invisible hand." In Smith's words: "By directing that industry in such a manner as its produce may be of the greatest value, he intends only his own gain, and he is in this, as in many other cases, led by an invisible hand to promote an end which was no part of his intention."

How important was Adam Smith? He has been called the "father of political economy." Many of the foundations of economic analysis we use today are still based on Adam Smith's writings of several centuries ago.

Sources: Howard Marshall, *The Great Economists: A History of Economic Thought* (New York: Pitman Publishing, 1967; Paul Strathern, *A Brief History of Economic Genius* (New York: Texere), 2002; Ian Ross, *The Life of Adam Smith* (Oxford: Clarendon Press), 1995.

the wealth of nations are good institutions and human creativity.

Institutions include a legal system to enforce contracts and laws and to protect the rights of citizens and the ideas they create, a legislative process to develop laws and policies that provide incentives to individuals and firms to work hard, a government free of corruption, and a strong monetary system.

Equally as important as institutions is the ability of societies to create ideas. Ideas change civilizations. Ideas are the basis for creating new products and finding new ways to improve upon existing goods and services. Human creativity starts with a strong educational system, and builds with proper incentives that allow innovation and creativity to flourish into marketable outcomes to improve the lives of all.

Summing It All Up: Economics Is All Around Us

The examples presented in these key principles should have convinced you that economic decisions are a part of our everyday lives. Anytime we make a decision involving a purchase, or decide what we plan to eat, study, or do with our day, we are making economic decisions. Just keep in mind that economics is broader than an exclusive concern with money, despite the great emphasis placed on money in our everyday economic discussions.

Instead, economics is about making decisions when we can't have everything we want, and how we interact with others to maximize our well-being given limitations. The existence of well-functioning markets allows individuals and firms to come together to achieve good outcomes, and government institutions and policies provide incentives that can lead to a better standard of living for all residents.

The key principles discussed in this chapter will be repeated throughout this book, and you will learn more about these important principles as the term progresses. For now, realize that economics rests on the foundation of a limited number of important principles. Once you fully grasp these basic ideas, the study of economics will be both rewarding and exciting, because after this course you will discover and appreciate how much more you understand the world around you.

ISSUE

Do Economists Ever Agree on Anything?

Give me a one-handed economist! All my economists say, "on one hand . . . on the other."

Harry S Truman

President Truman once exclaimed that the country needed more *one-handed economists*. What did he mean by that? He was saying that anytime an economist talks about a solution to an economic problem, the economist will often follow that statement by saying "on the other hand . . .".

This story highlights the point that every issue can be viewed from different perspectives, so much so that economists seemingly disagree with one another on everything. Solutions often depend on how benefits and costs are measured. For example, suppose we debate whether gasoline taxes are too high. *On the one hand*, higher gasoline taxes will reduce oil consump-

tion, reduce pollution, reduce traffic congestion, and generate money to promote public transportation such as buses, subways, and high-speed trains. *On the other hand*, higher gasoline taxes result in higher prices for most consumer goods due to higher transportation costs, and higher prices for gas and consumer goods affect lower-income households more since they spend a greater share of their money on such goods.

Different opinions about the relative weights of benefits and costs make economic policymaking challenging. Economic conditions are always changing. This is why economists rely so much on models and assumptions in order to prescribe a solution based on the conditions facing the economy.

But despite differences and frequent disagreements in economic policy, a recent survey of the IGM Economic

Experts Panel, consisting of forty-one prominent economists from all different schools of thought, found that economists do agree on many things. First, most economists agree that specialization in activities leads to gains to all parties involved. Second, most economists agree that markets and competition promote efficiency. Third, most economists believe that stimulus programs and bailout packages do reduce unemployment (though not all believe such measures are worth their costs). Fourth, most economists believe flexible exchange rates are ideal. And finally, most economists believe that individuals and firms respond to incentives.

In sum, despite the constant bickering one often hears in economic policy debates, economists agree on a number of issues, and these are typically grounded in the key economic principles described in this chapter.

 CHECKPOINT

KEY PRINCIPLES OF ECONOMICS

- Economics is concerned with making choices with limited resources.
- When making decisions, one must take into account tradeoffs and opportunity costs.
- Specialization leads to gains for all involved.
- People respond to incentives, both good and bad.
- Rational behavior requires thinking on the margin.
- Markets are generally efficient; when they aren't, government can sometimes correct the failure.
- Institutions and human creativity help explain the wealth of nations.

QUESTION: McDonald's introduced a premium blend of coffee that sells for more than its standard coffee. How does this represent thinking at the margin?

Answers to the Checkpoint question can be found at the end of this chapter.

chapter summary

Section 1: **What Is Economics About?**

Economics is the study of how individuals, firms, and societies make decisions to improve their well-being given limitations.

Scarcity is the idea that people have unlimited wants but limited resources. Resources can be money, time, ability, work ethic, or anything that can be used to generate productive outcomes.

Scarce versus scarcity: Large uncut diamonds are scarce—only a few are found in the world each year—and are sold for millions of dollars each. A car, on the other hand, is less scarce, as car dealerships around the country have lots full of them. But both large diamonds and cars are subject to scarcity—many people want them, but can only buy what they can afford.

What Is the Difference Between Microeconomics and Macroeconomics?

- M"i"croeconomics deals with individual entities, such as individuals, firms, and industries (Remember "i" = "individual")

- M"a"croeconomics deals with aggregate entities, such as cities or the nation (Remember "a" = "aggregate" or "all")

How governments deal with pollution is an important problem that can be addressed using economic analysis.

Efficiency   Equity

Economists and policymakers often confront the tradeoff between efficiency and equity. Efficiency reflects how well resources are used and allocated. Equity (or fairness) of an outcome is a subjective matter, where differences of opinion exist.

Economic analysis uses a stylized approach, where models boil issues and facts down to their basic relevant elements. To build models means that we make use of the *ceteris paribus* assumption and hold some important variables constant. This useful device often provides surprising insights about economic behavior.

Section 2: **Key Principles of Economics**

1. Economics Is Concerned with Making Choices with Limited Resources

Economics involves making decisions to maximize one's well-being, which can come from many sources, including money, time, happiness, or a fortuitous event.

"We should have done something different this weekend . . .".

2. When Making Decisions, One Must Take Into Account Tradeoffs and Opportunity Costs

Choice and scarcity force tradeoffs because we face unlimited wants but limited resources. We must make tradeoffs in nearly everything we do. Opportunity costs are resources (e.g., time and money) that could be used in another activity. Everything we do involves opportunity costs, the value of the next best alternative use of our resources.

3. Specialization Leads to Gains for All Involved

Specializing in tasks in which one is comparatively better at doing than another allows individuals to achieve productivity gains as long as the work is shared in a mutually beneficial manner.

4. People Respond to Incentives, Both Good and Bad

Incentives encourage people to work hard and be more productive.

Rewarding the top salesperson in the company creates a valuable incentive to work hard.

Maximizing your food intake at a buffet is not thinking at the margin if you end up bloated from overeating.

5. Rational Behavior Requires Thinking on the Margin

When making a decision involving benefits and costs, one should continue to consume or produce as long as the marginal (additional) benefit exceeds the marginal (additional) cost.

6. Markets Are Generally Efficient; When They Aren't, Government Can Sometimes Correct the Failure

Markets bring buyers and sellers together. Competition forces firms to provide products at the lowest possible price. New products are introduced to the market and old products disappear. This dynamism makes markets efficient. In some instances though, markets might fail, such as in dealing with pollution, leading governments to intervene. During extended economic downturns, government can smooth fluctuations in the overall economy.

Market equilibrium often is achieved by letting market participants make decisions freely.

7. Institutions and Human Creativity Help Explain the Wealth of Nations

Institutions include the legal system, laws and policies, a government free of corruption, and a strong monetary system. Ideas and innovation lead to new products and improve on existing ones, raising the standard of living of all residents.

economics, p. 2
scarcity, p. 4
incentives, p. 4
microeconomics, p. 4

macroeconomics, p. 5
ceteris paribus, p. 6
efficiency, p. 6
equity, p. 6

positive question, p. 7
normative question, p. 7
opportunity costs, p. 8

QUESTIONS AND PROBLEMS

Check Your Understanding

1. What is wrong with the statement "Economics is everything to do with money"?

2. Does your going to college have anything to do with expanding choices or reducing scarcity? Explain.

3. What is the difference between a positive question and a normative question?

4. You normally stay at home on Wednesday nights and study. Next Wednesday night, your best friend is having his big 21st birthday party. What is the opportunity cost of going to the party?

5. What is the incentive to spend four years of one's life and tens of thousands of dollars to earn a college degree?

6. Why do markets typically lead to an efficient outcome for buyers and sellers?

Apply the Concepts

7. In contrasting equity and efficiency, why do high-tech firms seem to treat their employees better (better wages, benefits, working environments, vacations, etc.) compared to how landscaping or fast-food franchises treat their employees? Is this fair? Is it efficient?

8. Stores sometimes offer "mail-in rebates" to customers who purchase certain goods to get a portion of the purchase price refunded. Typically, a mail-in rebate requires proof of purchase (like a UPC from the actual product along with a store receipt) and a completed form to be mailed in for processing, with the rebate being mailed in the form of a check or a prepaid debit card six to eight weeks later. Why would some customers, but not all, take advantage of mail-in rebates?

9. The black rhinoceros is extremely endangered. Its horn is considered a powerful aphrodisiac in many Asian countries, and a single horn fetches many thousands of dollars on the black market, creating a great incentive for poachers. Unlike other stories of endangered species, this one might have a simple solution. Conservationists could simply capture as many rhinos as possible and remove their horns, reducing the incentive to poach. Do you think this will help reduce poaching? Why or why not?

10. Most amusement parks in the United States charge a fixed price for admission, which includes unlimited roller coaster rides for the day. Some people attempt to ride the roller coasters as often as possible in order to maximize the value of their admission. Why is riding a roller coaster at an amusement park over and over to "get your money's worth" not considered *thinking on the margin*?

11. With higher gasoline prices, the U.S. government wants people to buy more hybrid cars that use much less gasoline. Unfortunately, hybrids are approximately $4,000 to $5,000 more expensive to purchase than comparable cars. Because people follow incentives, what can the government do to encourage the purchase of hybrids?

12. Some colleges and universities charge tuition by the credit hour, while others charge tuition by the term, allowing students to take as many classes as they desire. How do these tuition structures affect the incentives students face when deciding how many

classes to take? Provide an example of a beneficial effect and an example of a potentially harmful effect resulting from the incentives created with each system. How does marginal analysis affect the incentives with each system?

In the News

13. *The New York Times* reported on January 18, 2012, in an article titled "What the Top 1% of Earners Majored In," that 8.2% of Americans who majored in economics for their undergraduate degree are in the top 1% of salary earners. Only those who majored in pre-med had a higher percentage in the top 1%. What might be some reasons why economics majors have done well in the job market?

14. Ticketmaster, the largest event ticket seller in the country, recently expanded its use of paperless tickets that requires buyers to pick up tickets on the day of the event and show identification (*Reuters,* "Paperless Tickets: Is Ticketmaster Hurting Consumers?," March 29, 2011) rather than mailing paper tickets weeks before the event. What are some reasons Ticketmaster is expanding this method of ticket delivery? How does this change the incentives in the secondary (resale) market?

Solving Problems

15. Suppose your favorite band is on tour and coming to your area. Tickets are $100, and you take a day off from work for which you could have earned $60. What is your opportunity cost of going to the concert?

16. Suppose you pay $10 to watch a movie at the local multiplex cinema, and then afterward sneak into the next theater to watch a second movie without paying. What would be your marginal cost of watching the second movie?

USING THE NUMBERS

17. According to By the Numbers, the average percentage of income spent on various items has changed since 1960.

   a. What percent of income did Food represent in 1960? In 2010? This represents a drop of approximately what percent? (Hint: it is *not* 8%.)

   b. What percent of income did Health Care represent in 1960? In 2010? This represents an increase of approximately what percent? (Hint: it is *not* 9%.)

18. According to By the Numbers, about how many economics degrees were awarded to college graduates in 2011? How does this number compare to the number of nursing degrees? Communications degrees?

ANSWERS TO QUESTIONS IN CHECKPOINTS

Checkpoint: What Is Economics About?

(1) microeconomics, (2) macroeconomics, (3) microeconomics, (4) macroeconomics, (5) macroeconomics, (6) microeconomics, (7) macroeconomics.

Checkpoint: Key Principles of Economics

McDonald's is adding one more product (premium coffee) to its line. Thinking at the margin entails thinking about how you can improve an operation (or increase profits) by adding to your existing product line or reducing costs.

After studying this appendix you should be able to:

- Describe the four simple forms of data graphs.
- Make use of a straightforward approach to reading graphs.
- Read linear and nonlinear graphs and know how to compute their slopes.
- Use simple linear equations to describe a line and a shift in the line.
- Explain why correlation is not the same as causation.

Appendix
Working with Graphs and Formulas

You can't watch the news on television or read a newspaper without seeing a graph of some sort. If you have flipped through this book, you have seen a large number of graphs, charts, and tables, and a few simple equations. This is the language of economics. Economists deal with data for all types of issues. Just looking at data in tables often doesn't help you discern the trends or relationships in the data.

Economists develop theories and models to explain economic behavior and levels of economic activity. These theories or models are simplified representations of real-world activity. Models are designed to distill the most important relationships between variables, and then these relationships are used to predict future behavior of individuals, firms, and industries, or to predict the future course of the overall economy.

In this short section, we will explore the different types of graphs you are likely to see in this course (and in the media) and then turn to an examination of how graphs are used to develop and illustrate models. This second topic leads us into a discussion of modeling relationships between data and how to represent these relationships with simple graphs and equations.

Graphs and Data

The main forms of graphs of data are time series, scatter plots, pie charts, and bar charts. Time series, as the name suggests, plots data over time. Most of the figures you will encounter in publications are time series graphs.

Time Series

Time series graphs involve plotting time (minutes, hours, days, months, quarters, or years) on the horizontal axis and the value of some variable on the vertical axis. Figure APX-1 illustrates a time series plot for civilian employment of those 16 years and older. Notice that since the early 1990s, employment has grown by almost 25 million for this group. The vertical strips in the figure designate the last three recessions. Notice that in cases when the recession hit, employment fell, then rebounded after the recession ended.

Scatter Plots

Scatter plots are graphs in which two variables (neither variable is time) are plotted against each other. Scatter plots often give us a hint if the two variables are related to each other in some consistent way. Figure APX-2 plots one variable, median household income, against another variable, percentage of Americans holding a college degree.

Two things can be seen in this figure. First, these two variables appear to be related to each other in a positive way. A rising percentage of college graduates leads to a higher median household income. It is not surprising that college degrees and earnings are related, because increased education leads to a more productive workforce, which translates into more income. Second, given that the years for the data are listed next to the dots, we can see that the percentage of the population with college degrees has risen significantly over the last half-century. From this simple scatter plot, we get a lot of information and ideas about how the two variables are related.

FIGURE APX-1

Civilian Employment, 16 Years and Older

This time series graph shows the number of civilians 16 years and older employed in the United States since 1990. Employment has grown steadily over this period, except in times of recession, indicated by the vertical strips. Note that employment fell during the recession, and then bounced back after each recession ended.

Pie Charts

Pie charts are simple graphs that show data that can be split into percentage parts that combined make up the whole. A simple pie chart for the relative importance of components in the consumer price index (CPI) is shown in Figure APX-3 on the next page. It reveals how the typical urban household budget is allocated. By looking at each slice of the pie, we get a picture of how typical families spend their income.

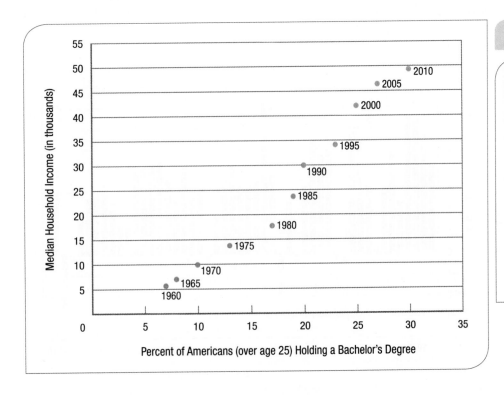

FIGURE APX-2

The Relationship Between the Median Household Income and the Percentage of Americans Holding a College Degree

This scatter diagram plots the relationship between median household income and the percentage of Americans holding a college degree. Median household income increased as a greater proportion of Americans earn college degrees. Note that the percentage of Americans earning college degrees has increased significantly in the last half-century.

Relative Importance of Consumer Price Index (CPI) Components (2011)

This pie chart shows the relative importance of the components of the consumer price index, showing how typical urban households spend their income.

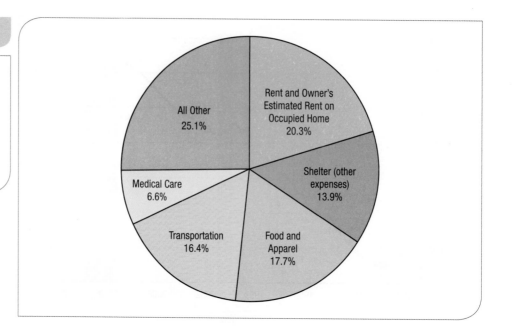

Bar Charts

Bar charts use bars to show the value of specific data points. Figure APX-4 is a bar chart showing the annual changes in real (adjusted for inflation) gross domestic product (GDP). Notice that over the last 50 years the United States has had only 7 years when GDP declined.

Simple Graphs Can Pack In a Lot of Information   It is not unusual for graphs and figures to have several things going on at once. Look at Figure APX-5, illustrating the number of social media users as a percent of each age group. On the horizontal axis are the age groups in years. On the vertical axis is the percent of each age group that regularly used social media. Figure APX-5 shows the relationship between age and social media

Percent Change in Real (Inflation Adjusted) GDP

This bar chart shows the annual percent change in real (adjusted for inflation) gross domestic product (GDP) over the last 50 years. Over this period, GDP has declined only seven times.

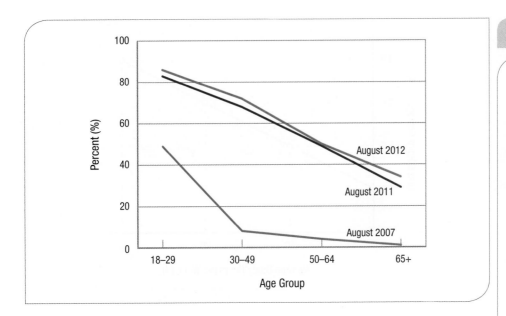

Social Media Usage Across Age Groups

These curves show the percentage of Americans using a social media site by age. The curves slope downward because older Americans are less likely to use social media than younger Americans. However, over time, more Americans in all age groups are using social media as evident by each point on the August 2011 curve being higher than the corresponding point on the August 2007 curve, and each point on the August 2012 curve being higher than the corresponding point on the August 2011 curve.

penetration for different periods. They include the most recent period shown (August 2012), a year previous (August 2011), and five years ago (August 2007).

You should notice two things in this figure. First, the relationship between the variables slopes downward. This means that older Americans are less likely to use social media than younger Americans. Second, use of social media has increased across all ages over the three periods studied (from August 2007 to August 2011 to August 2012) as shown by the position of the curves. Each point on the August 2007 curve is below the corresponding point on the August 2011 curve, which is subsequently below each point on the August 2012 curve.

A Few Simple Rules for Reading Graphs Looking at graphs of data is relatively easy if you follow a few simple rules. First, read the title of the figure to get a sense of what is being presented. Second, look at the label for the horizontal axis (*x* axis) to see how the data are being presented. Make sure you know how the data are being measured. Is it months or years, hours worked or hundreds of hours worked? Third, examine the label for the vertical axis (*y* axis). This is the value of the variable being plotted on that axis; make sure you know what it is. Fourth, look at the graph itself to see if it makes logical sense. Are the curves (bars, dots) going in the right direction?

Look the graph over and see if you notice something interesting going on. This is really the fun part of looking closely at figures both in this text and in other books, magazines, and newspapers. Often simple data graphs can reveal surprising relationships between variables. Keep this in mind as you examine graphs throughout this course.

One more thing. Graphs in this book are always accompanied by explanatory captions. Examine the graph first, making your preliminary assessment of what is going on. Then carefully read the caption, making sure it accurately reflects what is shown in the graph. If the caption refers to movement between points, follow this movement in the graph. If you think there is a discrepancy between the caption and the graph, reexamine the graph to make sure you have not missed anything.

Graphs and Models

Let's now take a brief look at how economists use graphs and models, also looking at how they are constructed. Economists use what are called *stylized graphs* to represent relationships between variables. These graphs are a form of modeling to help us simplify our analysis and focus on those relationships that matter. Figure APX-6 on the next page is one such model.

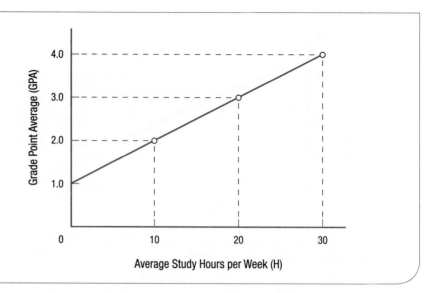

FIGURE APX-6

Studying and Your GPA

This figure shows a hypothetical linear relationship between average study hours and GPA. Without studying, a D average results, and with 10 hours of studying, a C average is obtained, and so on.

Linear Relationships

Figure APX-6 shows a linear relationship between average study hours and grade point average (GPA), indicating a higher GPA the more you study. By a linear relationship, we mean that the "curve" is a straight line. In this case, if you don't study at all, we assume you are capable of making Ds and your GPA will equal 1.0, not enough to keep you in school for long. If you hit the books for an average of 10 hours a week, your GPA rises to 2.0, a C average. Studying for additional hours raises your GPA up to its maximum of 4.0.

The important point here is that the curve is linear; any hour of studying yields the same increase in GPA. All hours of studying provide equal yields from beginning to end. This is what makes linear relationships unique.

Computing the Slope of a Linear Line

Looking at the line in Figure APX-6, we can see two things: The line is straight, so the slope is constant, and the slope is positive. As average hours of studying increase, GPA increases. Computing the slope of the line tells us how much GPA increases for every hour of additional studying. Computing the slope of a linear line is relatively easy and is shown in Figure APX-7.

FIGURE APX-7

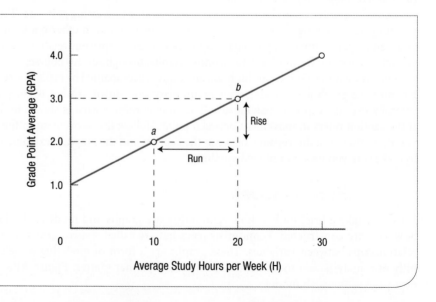

Computing Slope for a Linear Line

Computing the slope is based on a simple rule: rise over run (rise divided by run). In the case of this straight line, the slope is equal to 0.1 because every 10 additional hours of studying yields a 1.0 increase in GPA.

The simple rule for computing slope is: Slope is equal to rise over run (or rise ÷ run). Since the slope is constant along a linear line, we can select any two points and determine the slope for the entire curve. In Figure APX-7 we have selected points a and b where GPA moves from 2.0 to 3.0 when studying increases from 10 to 20 hours per week.

Your GPA increases by 1.0 for an additional 10 hours of study. This means that the slope is equal to 0.1 (1.0 ÷ 10 = 0.1). So for every additional hour of studying you add each week, your GPA will rise by 0.1. Thus, if you would like to improve your grade point average from 3.0 to 3.5, you would have to study five more hours per week.

Computing slope for negative relations that are linear is done exactly the same way, except that when computing the changes from one point to another, one of the values will be negative, making the relationship negative.

● Nonlinear Relationships

It would be nice for model builders if all relationships were linear, but that is not the case. It is probably not really the case with the amount of studying and GPA either. Figure APX-8 depicts a more realistic nonlinear and positive relationship between studying and GPA. Again, we assume that one can get a D average (1.0) without studying and reach a maximum of straight As (4.0) with 30 hours per week.

Figure APX-8 suggests that the first few hours of study per week are more important to raising GPA than are the others. The first 10 hours of studying yields more than the last 10 hours: One goes from 1.0 to 3.3 (a gain of 2.3), as opposed to going only from 3.8 to 4.0 (a gain of only 0.2). This curve exhibits what economists call diminishing returns. Just as the first bite of pizza tastes better than the 100th, so the first 5 hours of studying brings a bigger jump in GPA than the 25th to 30th hours.

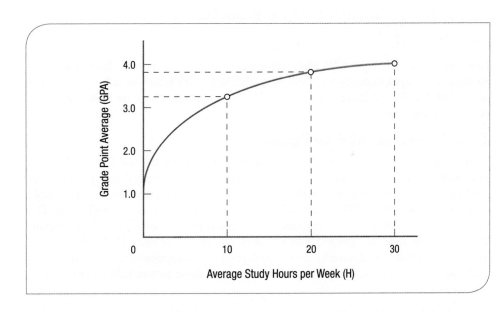

FIGURE APX-8

Studying and Your GPA (Nonlinear)

This nonlinear graph of study hours and GPA is probably more typical than the one shown in Figures APX-6 and APX-7. Like many other things, studying exhibits diminishing returns. The first hours of studying result in greater improvements to GPAs than further hours of studying.

Computing the Slope of a Nonlinear Curve

As you might suspect, computing the slope of a nonlinear curve is a little more complex than for a linear line. But it is not that much more difficult. In fact, we use essentially the same rise over run approach that is used for lines.

Looking at the curve in Figure APX-8, it should be clear that the slope varies for each point on the curve. It starts out very steep, then begins to level out above 20 hours of studying. Figure APX-9 on the next page shows how to compute the slope at any point on the curve.

Computing the slope at point a requires drawing a line tangent to that point, then computing the slope of that line. For point a, the slope of the line tangent to it is found by

Computing Slope for a Nonlinear Curve

Computing the slope of a nonlinear curve requires that you compute the slope of each point on the curve. This is done by computing the slope of a tangent to each point.

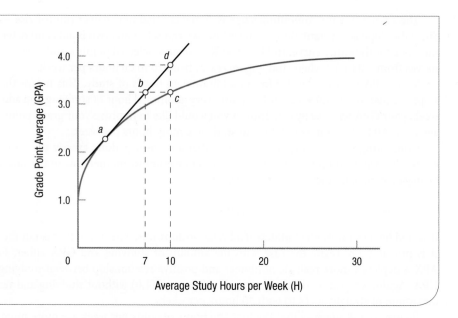

computing rise over run again. In this case, it is length $dc \div bc$ or $[(3.8 - 3.3) \div (10 - 7)] = 0.5 \div 3 = 0.167$. Notice that this slope is significantly larger than the original linear relationship of 0.1. If we were to compute the slope near 30 hours of studying, it would approach zero (the slope of a horizontal line is zero).

Ceteris Paribus, Simple Equations, and Shifting Curves

Hold on while we beat this GPA and studying example into the ground. Inevitably, when we simplify analysis to develop a graph or model, important factors or influences must be controlled. We do not ignore them, we hold them constant. These are known as *ceteris paribus* assumptions.

Ceteris Paribus: All Else Equal

By *ceteris paribus* we mean other things being equal or all other relevant factors, elements, or influences are held constant. When economists define your demand for a product, they want to know how much or how many units you will buy at different prices. For example, to determine how many DVDs you will buy at various prices (your demand for DVDs), we hold your income and the price of movie tickets and online movie downloads constant. If your income suddenly jumped, you would be willing to buy more DVDs at all prices, but this is a whole new demand curve. *Ceteris paribus* assumptions are a way to simplify analysis; then the analysis can be extended to include those factors held constant, as we will see next.

Simple Linear Equations

Simple linear equations can be expressed as: $Y = a + bX$. This is read as, Y equals a plus b times X, where Y is the variable plotted on the y axis and a is a constant (unchanging), and b is a different constant that is multiplied by X, the value on the x axis. The formula for our studying and GPA example introduced in Figure APX-6 is shown in Figure APX-10.

The constant a is known as the vertical intercept because it is the value of GPA when study hours (X) is zero, and therefore it cuts (intercepts) the vertical axis at the value of 1.0 (D average). Now each time you study another hour on average, your GPA rises by 0.1, so the constant b (the slope of the line) is equal to 0.1. Letting H represent hours of studying, the final equation is: GPA = $1.0 + 0.1H$. You start with a D average without

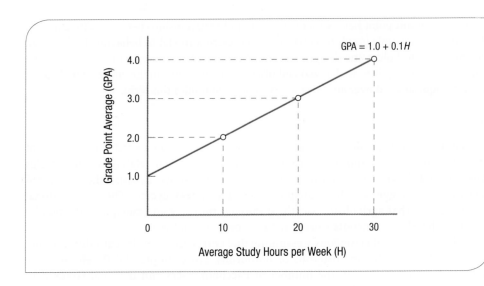

FIGURE APX-10

Studying and Your GPA: A Simple Equation

The formula for a linear relationship is $Y = a + bX$, where Y is the y axis variable, X is the x axis variable, and a and b are constants. For the original relationship between study hours and GPA, this equation is $Y = 1.0 + 0.1X$.

studying and as your hours of studying increase, your GPA goes up by 0.1 times the hours of studying. If we plug in 20 hours of studying into the equation, the answer is a GPA of 3.0 $[1.0 + (0.1 \times 20) = 1.0 + 2.0 = 3.0]$.

Shifting Curves

Now let's introduce a couple of factors that we have been holding constant (the *ceteris paribus* assumption). These two elements are tutoring and partying. So, our new equation now becomes $GPA = 1.0 + 0.1H + Z$, where Z is our variable indicating whether you have a tutor or whether you are excessively partying. When you have a tutor, $Z = 1$, and when you party too much, $Z = -1$. Tutoring adds to the productivity of your studying (hence $Z = 1$), while excessive late-night partying reduces the effectiveness of studying because you are always tired (hence $Z = -1$). Figure APX-11 shows the impact of adding these factors to the original relationship.

With tutoring, your GPA-studying curve has moved upward and to the left. Now, because $Z = 1$, you begin with a C average (2.0), and with just 20 hours of studying (because of tutoring) you can reach a 4.0 GPA (point a). Alternatively, when you don't have tutoring and you party every night, your GPA–studying relationship has worsened (shifted downward and to the right). Now you must study 40 hours (point c) to accomplish a 4.0 GPA. Note that you begin with failing grades.

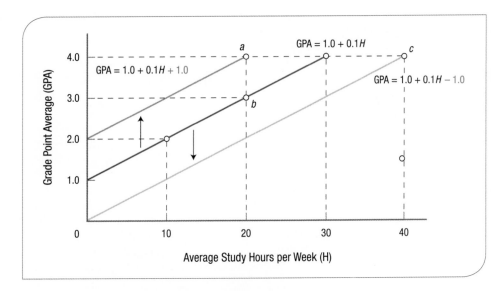

FIGURE APX-11

The Impact of Tutoring and Partying on Your GPA

The effect of tutoring and partying on our simple model of studying and GPA is shown. Partying harms your academic efforts and shifts the relationship to the right, making it harder to maintain your previous average (you now have to study more hours). Tutoring, on the other hand, improves the relationship (shifts the curve to the left).

The important point here is that we can simplify relationships between different variables and use a simple graph or equation to represent a model of behavior. In doing so, we often have to hold some things constant. When we allow those factors to change, the original relationship is now changed and often results in a shift in the curves. You will see this technique applied over and over as you study economics this term.

Correlation Is Not Causation

Just because two variables seem related or appear related on a scatter plot does not mean that one causes another. Economists 100 years ago correlated business cycles (the ups and downs of the entire economy) with sunspots. Because they appeared related, some suggested that sunspots caused business cycles. The only rational argument was that agriculture was the dominant industry and sunspots affected the weather; therefore, sunspots caused the economy to fluctuate.

Other examples of erroneously assuming that correlation implies causality abound, some of which can be preposterous or humorous. For example, did Facebook cause the Greek debt crisis? Both the number of Facebook users and the total Greek debt skyrocketed between the years of 2005 and 2011. Just because two variables appear to be related does not mean that one causes the other to change.

Understanding graphs and using simple equations is a key part of learning economics. Practice helps.

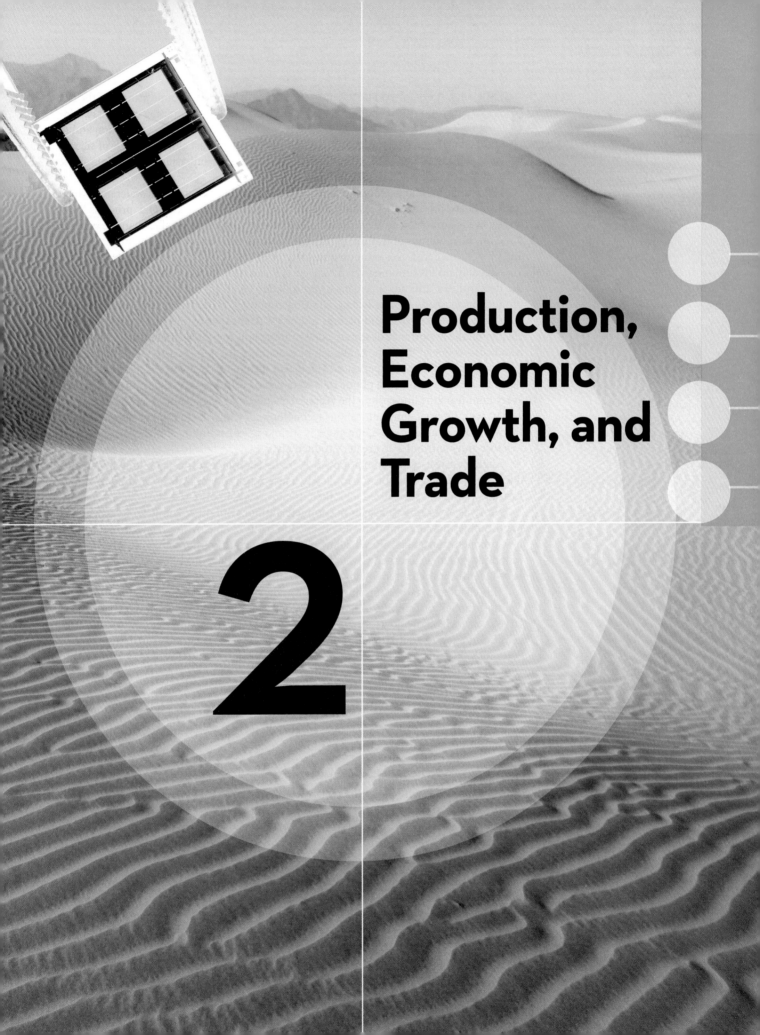

Production, Economic Growth, and Trade

2

Can a speck of sand be the most significant driver of economic growth of the last generation? Just about every piece of electronic and computing equipment contains a microchip, a tiny piece of circuitry that allows devices to function and to store immense amounts of data and multimedia. Most chips are made of silicon, which is nothing more than a basic element found in sand, and aside from oxygen is the most abundant element in the Earth's crust.

Extracting the silicon from the sand, melting it, and creating silicon wafers on which transistors are produced to create a functioning microchip is a complex process. More impressive is how efficient the process has become. A single chip smaller than the size of a dime can hold billions of transistors, enough to store and display all of the music, videos, and photos you could ever want on a single device.

Arguably no invention has transformed the economy more in the past 30 years than the development and advancement of the silicon chip. Technological change has made production methods more efficient, allowing countries to produce more goods and services using fewer physical and natural resources. And as we emphasized in the previous chapter on the importance of scarcity, determining how to achieve more using less—fewer resources—is one of the important goals of economics.

An industry that has experienced significant technological change is telecommunications. In 1950, long distance phone calls were placed with the assistance of live operators, every minute on the line costing the average consumer the equivalent of several hours pay. Today, with Internet communications technology allowing one to call virtually anyone in the world for pennies or less, the globe is shrinking as communications brings us closer together and contributes to greater productivity.

Another driver of economic growth is trade. Several centuries ago, individuals produced most of what they consumed. Today, most of us produce little of what we consume. Instead, we work at specialized jobs, then use our wages to purchase the goods we need.

Nearly every country engages in commercial trade with other countries to expand the opportunities for consumption and production by its people. As products are consumed, new products must be produced, allowing increased consumption in one country to spur economic growth in another. Given the ability of global trade to open economic doors and raise incomes, it is vital for economic growth in all nations.

This chapter gives you a framework for understanding economic growth. It provides a simple model for thinking about production, then applies this model to economies at large so you will know how to think about economic growth and its determinants. It then goes on to analyze international trade as a special case of economic growth. By the time you finish this chapter, you should understand the importance of economic growth and what drives it.

Basic Economic Questions and Production

Regardless of the country, its circumstances, or its precise economic structure, every economy must answer three basic questions.

Basic Economic Questions

The three basic economic questions that each society must answer are:

- What goods and services are to be produced?
- How are these goods and services to be produced?
- Who will receive these goods and services?

The response an economy makes to the first question—What goods and services should it produce?—depends on the goods and services a society wants. In a communist state, the government decides what a society wants, but in a capitalist economy, consumers signal what products they want by way of their demands for specific commodities. In the next chapter, we investigate how consumer demand for individual products is determined and how markets meet these demands. For now, we assume that consumers, individually and as a society, are able to decide on the mix of goods and services they most want, and that producers supply these items at acceptable prices.

BY THE NUMBERS

Growth, Productivity, and Trade Are Key to Our Prosperity

Over the last century, investment in education, infrastructure, and technology development, along with increased international trade, has resulted in increased productivity and growth, leading to higher incomes and standards of living around the world.

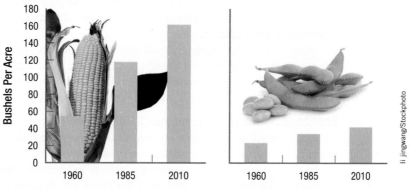

Farm productivity has dramatically increased since 1960 as a result of modern agricultural machinery and new seeds and fertilizers, resulting in higher yields per acre of crops such as corn and soybeans.

4–7%

Increase in a nation's economic output from increasing the average years of schooling by 1 year.

17

Number of countries in which the United States has a free trade agreement with as of 2012.

Weeks of Pay Required to Fire a Worker

Firing workers can be costly in some countries. Firing a full-time worker with 20 years at the company costs roughly 70 weeks pay in Germany, but it is even more costly in China.

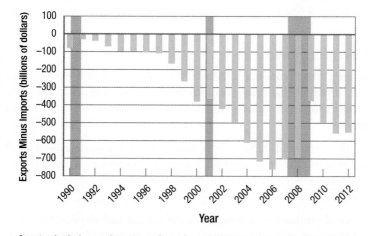

Our trade balance (exports minus imports) has grown steadily negative over the last two decades. During each of the last three recessions (shaded areas), our purchases of imports fell, improving our trade balance.

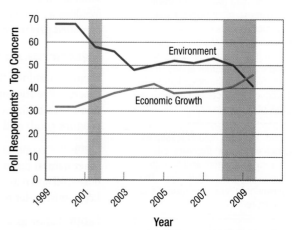

American attitudes about concerns for the environment or a preference for economic growth vary based on the state of the economy. As the economy enters a recession (shaded areas), the desire for economic growth increases while concern for the environment ebbs.

Once we know what goods a society wants, the next question its economic system must answer is, How are these goods and services to be produced? In the end, this problem comes down to the simple question of how land, labor, and capital should be combined to produce the desired products. If a society demands a huge amount of corn, for example, we can expect its use of land, labor, and capital will be different from a society that demands digital equipment. But even an economy devoted to corn production could be organized in different ways, perhaps relying on extensive use of human labor, or perhaps relying on automated capital equipment.

Once an economy has determined what goods and services to produce and how to produce them, it is faced with the distribution question: Who will get the resulting products? *Distribution* refers to the way an economy allocates to consumers the goods and services it produces. How this is done depends on how the economy is organized.

Economic Systems All economies have to answer the three basic economic questions. How that is done depends on who owns the factors of production (land, labor, capital, and entrepreneurship) and how decisions are made to coordinate production and distribution.

In *capitalist* or *market* economies, private individuals and firms own most of the resources. The what, how, and who decisions are determined by individual desires for products and profit-making decisions by firms. Product prices are the principal mechanism for communicating information in the system. Based on prices, consumers decide whether to buy or not, and firms decide how to employ their resources and what production technology to use. This competition between many buyers and sellers leads to highly efficient production of goods and services. Producers are free to survive or perish based on their efficiency and the quality of their products. The government's primary roles are protecting property rights, enforcing contracts between private parties, providing public goods such as national defense, and establishing and ensuring the appropriate operating environment for competitive markets. Today the U.S. economy is not a pure *laissez-faire* ("leave it alone," or minimal government role) market economy but more of a mixed economy with many regulations and an extended role for government.

In contrast, *planned* economies (socialist and communist) are systems in which most of the productive resources are owned by the state and most economic decisions are made by central governments. Big sweeping decisions for the economy, often called "five-year plans," are centrally made and focus productive resources on these priorities. Both the former Soviet Union and China (until quite recently) were highly centrally planned, and virtually all resources were government owned. Although Russia and China have moved toward market economies, a large portion of each country's resources is still owned by the state. Socialist countries (e.g., the Scandinavian nations of Europe) enjoy a high degree of freedom with a big role both for government services paid for by high taxes, and for highly regulated private businesses.

Resources and Production

Having examined the three basic economic questions, let's take a look at the production process. **Production** involves turning **resources** into products and services that people want. Let's begin our discussion of this process by examining the scarce resources used to produce goods and services.

Land For economists, the term **land** includes both land in the usual sense as well as all other natural resources that are used in production. Natural resources such as mineral deposits, oil and natural gas, and water are all included by economists in the definition of land. Economists refer to the payment to land as *rent.*

Labor **Labor** as a factor of production includes both the mental and physical talents of people. Few goods and services can be produced without labor resources. Improvement to labor capabilities from training, education, and apprenticeship programs—typically called human capital—all add to labor's productivity and ultimately to a higher standard of living. Labor is paid *wages.*

---

production The process of converting resources (factors of production)—land, labor, capital, and entrepreneurial ability—into goods and services.

---

resources Productive resources include land (land and natural resources), labor (mental and physical talents of people), capital (manufactured products used to produce other products), and entrepreneurial ability (the combining of the other factors to produce products and assume the risk of the business).

---

land Includes natural resources such as mineral deposits, oil, natural gas, water, and land in the usual sense of the word. The payment to land as a resource is called rent.

---

labor Includes the mental and physical talents of individuals who produce products and services. The payment to labor is called wages.

Capital Capital includes all manufactured products that are used to produce other goods and services. This includes equipment such as drill presses, blast furnaces for making steel, and other tools used in the production process. It also includes trucks and automobiles used by businesses, as well as office equipment such as copiers, computers, and telephones. Any manufactured product that is used to produce other products is included in the category of capital. Capital earns *interest*.

Note that the term *capital* as used by economists refers to real (or physical) capital—actual manufactured products used in the production process—not money or financial capital. Money and financial capital are important in that they are used to purchase the real capital that is used to produce products.

Entrepreneurial Ability Entrepreneurs *combine* land, labor, and capital to produce goods and services, and they assume the *risks* associated with running a business. Entrepreneurs combine and manage the inputs of production, and manage the day-to-day marketing, finance, and production decisions. Today, the risks of running a business are huge, as the many bankruptcies and failures testify. Globalization has opened many opportunities as well as risks. For undertaking these activities and assuming the risks associated with business, entrepreneurs earn *profits*.

Production and Efficiency

Production turns *resources*—land, labor, capital, and entrepreneurial ability—into products and services. The necessary production factors vary for different products. To produce corn, for instance, one needs arable land, seed, fertilizer, water, farm equipment, and the workers to operate that equipment. Farmers looking to produce corn would need to devote hundreds of acres of open land to this crop, plow the land, plant and nurture the corn, and finally harvest the crop. Producing digital equipment, in contrast, requires less land but more capital and more highly skilled labor.

As we have seen, every country has to decide what to produce, how to produce it, and decide who receives the output. Countries desire to do the first two as efficiently as possible by choosing the production method that results in the greatest output using the least amount of resources. Figure 1 shows how factors of production enter into a production method to generate goods and services. Determining the production method is the role of a manager, who must decide how factors of production are best used. Economists refer to this actual choice as the production function, a concept that will be discussed in greater detail in a later chapter. For now, just understand that *how* resources are used is as important as the amount of resources available.

Productivity is a measure of efficiency determined by the amount of output produced given the amount of inputs used. But economists also use specific concepts to describe two different aspects of efficiency: production efficiency and allocative efficiency.

Production efficiency occurs when the mix of goods is produced at the lowest possible resource or opportunity cost. Alternatively, production efficiency occurs when as much output as possible is produced with a given amount of resources. Firms use the best technology available and combine the other resources to create products at the lowest cost to society.

---

capital Includes manufactured products such as tractors, welding equipment, and computers that are used to produce other goods and services. The payment to capital is referred to as interest.

entrepreneurs Entrepreneurs combine land, labor, and capital to produce goods and services. They absorb the risk of being in business, including the risk of bankruptcy and other liabilities associated with doing business. Entrepreneurs receive profits for this effort.

production efficiency Goods and services are produced at their lowest resource (opportunity) cost.

Factors of Production (Inputs)

Land, Labor, Capital, Entrepreneurial Ability → Production Method → Output (Goods and Services)

FIGURE 1

From Factors of Production to Output

Each of the four factors of production is employed in a production method in order to generate goods and services. The ability to use factors of production efficiently within a production method increases the amount of output given an amount of inputs used.

allocative efficiency The mix of goods and services produced is just what the society desires.

Allocative efficiency occurs when the mix of goods and services produced is the most desired by society. In capitalist countries, this is determined by consumers and businesses and their interaction through markets. The next chapter explores this interaction in some detail. Needless to say, it would be inefficient (a waste of resources) to be producing cassette tapes in the age of digital music players. Allocative efficiency requires that the right mix of goods be produced at the lowest cost.

Every economy faces constraints or limitations. Land, labor, capital, and entrepreneurship are all limited. No country has an infinite supply of available workers or the space and machinery that would be needed to put them all to work efficiently. No country can break free of these natural restraints. Such limits are known as production possibilities frontiers, and they are the focus of the next section.

⬤ CHECKPOINT

BASIC ECONOMIC QUESTIONS AND PRODUCTION

- Every economy must decide what to produce, how to produce it, and who will get what is produced.

- Production is the process of converting factors of production (resources)—land, labor, capital, and entrepreneurial ability—into goods and services.

- To the economist, land includes both land and natural resources. Labor includes the mental and physical resources of humans. Capital includes all manufactured products used to produce other goods and services. Entrepreneurs combine resources to manufacture products, and they assume the risk of doing business.

- Production efficiency requires that products be produced at the lowest cost. Allocative efficiency occurs when the mix of goods and services produced is just what society wants.

QUESTION: The one element that really seems to differentiate entrepreneurship from the other resources is the fact that entrepreneurs shoulder the *risk* of the failure of the enterprise. Is this important? Explain.

Answers to the Checkpoint question can be found at the end of this chapter.

➡ Production Possibilities and Economic Growth

As we discovered in the previous section, all countries and all economies face constraints on their production capabilities. Production can be limited by the quantity of the various factors of production in the country and its current technology. Technology includes such considerations as the country's infrastructure, its transportation and education systems, and the economic freedom it allows. Although perhaps going beyond the everyday meaning of the word *technology,* for simplicity, we will assume that all of these factors help determine the state of a country's technology.

To further simplify matters, production possibilities analysis assumes that the quantity of resources available and the technology of the economy remain constant, and that the economy produces only two products. Although a two-product world sounds far-fetched, this simplification allows us to analyze many important concepts regarding production and tradeoffs. Further, the conclusions drawn from this simple model will not differ fundamentally from a more complex model of the real world.

Production Possibilities

Assume that our simple economy produces backpacks and tablet computers. Figure 2 with its accompanying table shows the production possibilities frontier for this economy. The table shows seven possible production levels (*a–g*). These seven possibilities, which range from 12,000 backpacks and zero tablets to zero backpacks and 6,000 tablets, are graphed in Figure 2.

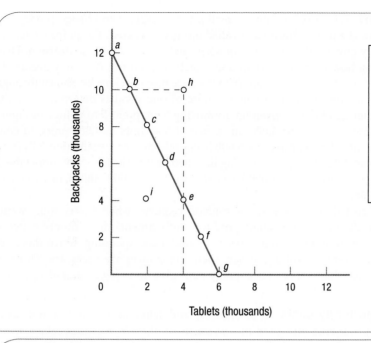

Possibility	Backpacks	Tablets
a	12,000	0
b	10,000	1,000
c	8,000	2,000
d	6,000	3,000
e	4,000	4,000
f	2,000	5,000
g	0	6,000

Production Possibilities Frontier

Using all of its resources, this stylized economy can produce many different mixes of backpacks and tablets. Production levels on, or to the left of, the resulting PPF are attainable for this economy. Production levels to the right of the PPF are unattainable.

FIGURE 2

When we connect the seven production possibilities, we delineate the **production possibilities frontier (PPF)** for this economy (some economists refer to this curve as the production possibilities curve). All points on the PPF are considered *attainable* by our economy. Everything to the left of the PPF is also attainable, but is an inefficient use of resources—the economy can always do better. Everything to the right of the curve is considered *unattainable.* Therefore, the PPF maps out the economy's limits; it is impossible for the economy to produce at levels beyond the PPF without an increase in resources or technology.

What the PPF in Figure 2 shows is that, given an efficient use of limited resources and taking technology into account, this economy can produce any of the seven combinations of tablets and backpacks listed, each of which represents a point of maximum output for the economy. If society wants to produce 1,000 tablets, it will only be able to produce 10,000 backpacks, as shown by point *b* on the PPF. Should the society decide that mobile Internet access is important, it might decide to produce 4,000 tablets, which would force it to cut backpack production down to 4,000, shown by point *e*. At each of these points, resources are fully employed in the economy, and therefore increasing production of one good requires giving up some production of the other. Also, the economy can produce any combination of the two products on or within the PPF, but not any combinations beyond it.

Contrast points *c* and *e* with production at point *i*. At point *i* the economy is only producing 2,000 tablets and 4,000 backpacks. Clearly, some resources are not being used. When fully employed, the economy's resources could produce more of both goods (point *d*).

Because the PPF represents a maximum output, the economy could not produce 4,000 tablets and still produce 10,000 backpacks. This situation, shown by point *h,* lies to the right of the PPF and hence outside the realm of possibility. Anything to the right of the PPF is impossible for our economy to attain.

production possibilities frontier (PPF) Shows the combinations of two goods that are possible for a society to produce at full employment. Points on or inside the PPF are attainable, and those outside of the frontier are unattainable.

opportunity cost The cost paid for one product in terms of the output (or consumption) of another product that must be forgone.

Opportunity Cost Whenever a country reallocates resources to change production patterns, it does so at a price. This price is called **opportunity cost.** Recall from Chapter 1 that opportunity cost is what you *give up* when making an economic decision. Here society is deciding how many backpacks and tablets to produce. If society decides to produce more tablets, it gives up the ability to produce more backpacks. Shown through the PPF, the opportunity cost of producing more of one good is determined by the amount of the other good that is given up. In moving from point *b* to point *e* in Figure 2, tablet production increases by 3,000 units, from 1,000 units to 4,000 units. In contrast, the country must forgo producing 6,000 backpacks because production falls from 10,000 backpacks to 4,000 backpacks. Giving up 6,000 backpacks for 3,000 more tablets represents an opportunity cost of 6,000 backpacks for these 3,000 tablets, or two backpacks for each tablet.

Opportunity cost thus represents the tradeoff required when an economy wants to increase its production of any single product. Governments must choose between guns and butter, or between military spending and social spending. Since there are limits to what taxpayers are willing to pay, spending choices are necessary. Think of opportunity costs as what you or the economy must give up to have more of a product or service.

Increasing Opportunity Costs In most cases, land, labor, and capital cannot easily be shifted from producing one good or service to another. You cannot take a semi-trailer and use it to plow a field, even though the semi and a top-of-the-line tractor cost about the same. The fact is that some resources are suited to specific sorts of production, just as some people seem to be better suited to performing one activity over another. Some people have a talent for music or art, and they would be miserable—and inefficient— working as accountants or computer programmers. Some people find they are more comfortable working outside, while others require the amenities of an environmentally controlled, ergonomically designed office.

A magician might be perfect for a birthday party entertainer, but is probably less adept at baking the perfect birthday cake.

© Lawrence Manning/Corbis

Thus, a more realistic production possibilities frontier is shown in Figure 3. This PPF is concave to (or bowed away from) the origin, because opportunity costs rise as more factors are used to produce increasing quantities of one product. Another way of saying this is that resources are subject to diminishing returns as more resources are devoted to the production of one product. Let's consider why this is so.

Let's begin at a point at which the economy's resources are strictly devoted to backpack production (point *a*). Now assume that society decides to produce 3,200 tablets. This will require a move from point *a* to point *b*. As we can see, 2,000 backpacks must be given up to get the added 3,200 tablets. This means the opportunity cost of 1 tablet is 0.625 backpacks (2,000 ÷ 3,200 = 0.625). This is a low opportunity cost, because those resources that are better suited to producing tablets will be the first ones shifted into this industry.

But what happens when this society decides to produce an additional 2,000 tablets, or moves from point *b* to point *c* on the graph? As Figure 3 illustrates, each additional tablet costs 2 backpacks because producing 2,000 more tablets requires the society to sacrifice 4,000 backpacks. Thus, the opportunity cost of tablets has more than tripled due to diminishing returns on the tablet side, which arise from the unsuitability of these new resources as more resources are shifted to tablets.

To describe what has happened in plain terms, when the economy was producing 12,000 backpacks, all its resources went into backpack production. Those members of the labor force who are engineers and electronic assemblers were probably not well suited to producing backpacks. As the economy reduces backpack production to start

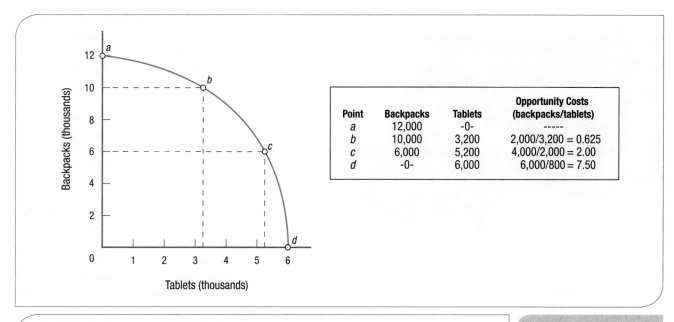

Production Possibilities Frontier (Increasing Opportunity Costs)

This figure shows a more realistic production possibilities frontier for an economy. This PPF is bowed out from the origin since opportunity costs rise as more factors are used to produce increasing quantities of one product or the other.

FIGURE 3

producing tablets, the opportunity cost of tablets was low, because the resources first shifted, including workers, were likely to be the ones most suited to tablet production and least suited to backpack manufacture. Eventually, however, as tablets became the dominant product, manufacturing more tablets required shifting workers skilled in backpack production to the tablet industry. Employing these less suitable resources drives up the opportunity costs of tablets.

You may be wondering which point along the PPF is the best for society. Economists have no grounds for stating unequivocally which mixture of goods and services would be ideal. The perfect mixture of goods depends on the tastes and preferences of the members of society. In a capitalist economy, resource allocation is determined largely by individual choices and the workings of private markets. We consider these markets and their operations in the next chapter.

Economic Growth

We have seen that PPFs map out the maximum that an economy can produce: Points to the right of the PPF are unattainable. But what if the PPF can be shifted to the right? This shift would give economies new maximum frontiers. In fact, we will see that economic growth can be viewed as a shift in the PPF outward. In this section, we use the production possibilities model to determine some of the major reasons for economic growth. Understanding these reasons for growth will enable us to suggest some broad economic policies that could lead to expanded growth.

The production possibilities model holds resources and technology constant to derive the PPF. These assumptions suggest that economic growth has two basic determinants: expanding resources and improving technologies. The expansion of resources allows producers to increase their production of all goods and services in an economy. Specific technological improvements, however, often affect only one industry directly. The development of a new color printing process, for instance, will directly affect only the printing industry.

"Beaming" objects might not be restricted to *Star Trek* fantasy with the development of 3D printers capable of reproducing objects. Could this be the next big technological advancement in printing?

Nevertheless, the ripples from technological improvements can spread out through an entire economy, just like ripples in a pond. Specifically, improvements in technology can lead to new products, improved goods and services, and increased productivity.

Sometimes technological improvements in one industry allow other industries to increase their production with existing resources. This means producers can increase output without using added labor or other resources. Alternatively, they can get the same production levels as before by using fewer resources than before. This frees up resources in the economy for use in other industries.

When the electric lightbulb was invented, it not only created a new industry (someone had to produce lightbulbs), but it also revolutionized other industries. Factories could stay open longer since they no longer had to rely on the sun for light. Workers could see better, thus improving the quality of their work. The result was that resources operated more efficiently throughout the entire economy.

The modern-day equivalent of the lightbulb might be the smartphone. Widespread use of these mobile devices enables people all across the world to produce goods and services more efficiently. Insurance agents can file claims instantly from disaster sites, deals can be closed while one is stuck in traffic, and communications have been revolutionized. Thus, this new technology has ultimately expanded time, the most finite of our resources. A similar argument could be made for the Internet. It has profoundly changed how many products are bought, sold, and delivered, and has expanded communications and the flow of information.

Expanding Resources The PPF represents the constraints on an economy at a specific time. But economies are constantly changing, and so are PPFs. Capital and labor are the principal resources that can be changed through government action. Land and entrepreneurial talent are important factors of production, but neither is easy to change by government policies. The government can make owning a business easier or more profitable by reducing regulations, or by offering low-interest loans or favorable tax treatment to small businesses. However, it is difficult to turn people into risk takers through government policy.

Increasing Labor and Human Capital A clear increase in population, the number of households, or the size of the labor force shifts the PPF outward, as shown in Figure 4. With added labor, the production possibilities available to the economy expand from PPF_0 to PPF_1. Such a labor increase can be caused by higher birthrates, increased immigration, or an increased willingness of people to enter the labor force. This last type of increase has occurred over the past several decades as more women have entered the labor force on a permanent basis. America's high level of immigration (both legal and illegal) fuels a strong rate of economic growth.

Rather than simply increasing the number of people working, however, the labor factor can also be increased by improving workers' skills. Economists refer to this as *investment in human capital*. Education, on-the-job training, and other professional training fit into this category. Improving human capital means people are more productive, resulting in higher wages, a higher standard of living, and an expanded PPF for society.

Capital Accumulation Increasing the capital used throughout the economy, usually brought about by investment, similarly shifts the PPF outward, as shown in Figure 4. Additional capital makes each unit of labor more productive and thus results in higher possible production throughout the economy. Adding robotics and computer-controlled machines to production lines, for example, means each unit of labor produces many more units of output.

The production possibilities model and the economic growth associated with capital accumulation suggest a tradeoff. Figure 5 illustrates the tradeoff all nations face between current consumption and capital accumulation.

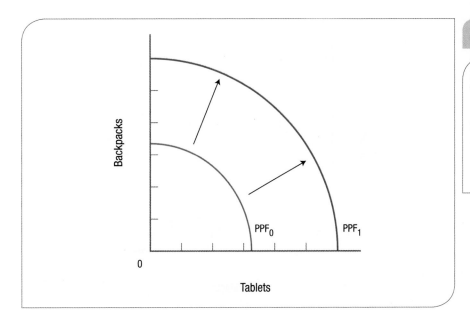

FIGURE 4

Economic Growth by Expanding Resources

A clear increase in population, the number of households, or the size of the labor force shifts the PPF outward. In this figure, a rising supply of labor expands the economy's production possibilities from PPF_0 to PPF_1.

Let's first assume that a nation selects a product mix in which the bulk of goods produced are consumption goods—that is, goods that are immediately consumable and have short life spans, such as food and entertainment. This product mix is represented by point *b* in Figure 5. Consuming most of what it produces, a decade later the economy is at PPF_b. Little growth has occurred, because the economy has done little to improve its productive capacity—the present generation has essentially decided to consume rather than to invest in the economy's future.

Contrast this decision with one in which the country at first decides to produce at point *a*. In this case, more capital goods such as machinery and tools are produced, while fewer consumption goods are used to satisfy current needs. Selecting this product mix results in the much larger PPF a decade later (PPF_a), because the economy steadily built up its productive capacity during those 10 years.

Technological Change Figure 6 on the next page illustrates what happens when an economy experiences a technological change in one of its industries, in this case the tablet industry. As the figure shows, the economy's potential output of tablets expands greatly, although its maximum production of backpacks remains unchanged. The area between the two curves

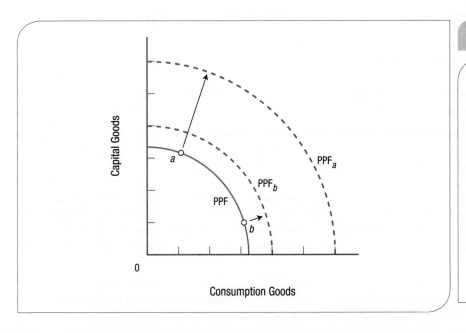

FIGURE 5

Consumption Goods and Capital Goods and the Expansion of the Production Possibilities Frontier

If a nation selects a product mix in which the bulk of goods produced are consumption goods, it will initially produce at point *b*. The small investment made in capital goods has the effect of expanding the nation's productive capacity only to PPF_b over the following decade. If the country decides to produce at point *a*, however, devoting more resources to producing capital goods, its productive capacity will expand much more rapidly, pushing the PPF out to PPF_a over the following decade.

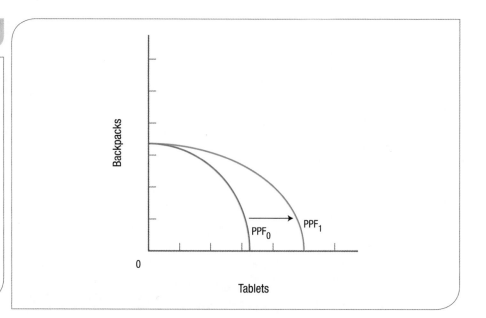

FIGURE 6

Technological Change and Expansion of the Production Possibilities Frontier

In this figure, an economy's potential output of tablets has expanded greatly, while its maximum production of backpacks has remained unchanged. The area between the two curves represents an improvement in the society's standard of living, since more of both goods can be produced and consumed than before. Some of the resources once used for tablet production can be diverted to backpack production, even as the number of tablets produced increases.

represents an improvement in the society's standard of living. People can produce and consume more of both goods than before: more tablets because of the technological advancement, and more backpacks because some of the resources once devoted to tablet production can be shifted to backpack production, even as the economy is turning out more tablets than before.

This example reflects the United States today, where the computer industry is exploding with new technologies. Companies such as Apple and Intel lead the way by relentlessly developing newer, faster, and more powerful products. Consequently, consumers have seen home computers go from clunky conversation pieces to powerful, fast, indispensable machines. Today's computers are more powerful than the mainframe supercomputers of just a few decades ago. And the latest developments in smartphones allow them to do what powerful computers did a decade ago.

Besides new products, technology has dramatically reduced the cost of producing tablets and other high-tech items, allowing countries to produce and consume more of other products, expanding the entire PPF outward. However, the effect of technology on an economy also depends on how well its important trade centers are linked together. If a country has mostly dirt paths rather than paved highways, you can imagine how this deficiency would affect its economy: Distribution will be slow, and industries will be slow to react to changes in demand. In such a case, improving the roads might be the best way to stimulate economic growth.

As you can see, there are many ways to stimulate economic growth. A society can expand its output by using more resources, perhaps by encouraging more people to enter the workforce or raising educational levels of workers. The government can encourage people to invest more, as opposed to devoting their earnings to immediate consumption. The public sector can spur technological advances by providing incentives to private firms to do research and development or underwrite research investments of its own.

Summarizing the Sources of Economic Growth Economic growth is driven by many factors, as we have seen. A study by the Organisation for Economic Co-operation and Development (OECD)[1] focused on what has been driving economic growth in twenty-one nations over the last several decades. The study first looked at contributions to economic growth from the macroeconomic perspective of added resources and technological improvements as we have been discussing in this chapter. It then looked at some benefits from good government policies that stimulate growth, and finally examined the industry and individual firm level for clues to the microeconomic sources of growth. The study showed

---

[1] *The Sources of Economic Growth in the OECD Countries* (Paris: Organisation for Economic Co-operation and Development), 2003.

ISSUE

Will Renewable Energy Be the Next Innovative Breakthrough?

For much of modern history, economic growth has relied on the innovative abilities of humans to generate new ideas that translate into productive inputs and valued goods and services. The Industrial Revolution of the 19th century brought us innovations such as the telegraph, steel production, and railways. In the early 1900s, the automobile was invented, along with electricity and telecommunications. In the mid-1900s, commercial air travel and television were introduced. In the latter part of the 20th century, the invention of personal computing led to dramatic gains in productivity. And at the turn of the 21st century, the creation of the Internet once again changed the way we live.

These "waves of innovation," as described by economist William Baumol, contribute much of the economic growth we have seen over the past century. But to sustain such growth, innovation must not slow down. Instead, pressure to innovate has become more

intense as the Earth's population grows and its resources diminish.

Hence, much attention has been placed on resource scarcity by focusing on expanding renewable resources, particularly energy sources such as those from the sun, wind, and water. Although the renewable energy industry is still developing, substantial strides have been made to increase investment in renewable energy.

The drawbacks of renewable energies are evident in the near term, as expensive solar panels, wind turbines, and hydroelectric dams cost much more to produce than traditional sources of energy such as coal mines and fossil fuels, let alone the often unsightly views such infrastructures create. But these obstacles are changing.

Today, countries around the world are finding innovative ways to incorporate renewable energy sources into their infrastructure, dramatically reducing the use of traditional energy. It may just be a matter

The Bahrain World Trade Center incorporates wind turbines into the structure that provide much of the building's energy.

of time before innovation finds ways to allow everybody to use the sun, wind, and rain to sustain our energy needs. Succeeding in this endeavor would be an innovative breakthrough that would add to the remarkable list of innovations in our history.

that some of the policies that have led to growth and subsequently higher standards of living in these countries include:

- Increasing business investment (physical capital).
- Increasing average education levels (human capital).
- Increasing research and development.
- Reducing both the level and variability of inflation.
- Reducing the tax burden.
- Increasing the level of international trade.

One important point to take away from this discussion is that our simple stylized model of the economy using only two goods gives a good first framework upon which to judge proposed policies for the economy. While not overly complex, this simple analysis is still quite powerful.

 CHECKPOINT

PRODUCTION POSSIBILITIES AND ECONOMIC GROWTH

- A production possibilities frontier (PPF) depicts the different combinations of goods that a fully employed economy can produce, given its available resources and current technology (both assumed fixed in the short run).
- Production levels inside and on the frontier are possible, but production mixes outside the curve are unattainable.

- Because production on the frontier represents the maximum output attainable when all resources are fully employed, reallocating production from one product to another involves *opportunity costs*: The output of one product must be reduced to get the added output of the other. The more of one product that is desired, the higher its opportunity costs because of diminishing returns and the unsuitability of some resources for producing some products.

- The PPF model suggests that economic growth can arise from an expansion in resources or improvements in technology. Economic growth is an outward shift of the PPF.

QUESTION: Taiwan is a small mountainous island with 23 million inhabitants, little arable land, and few natural resources, while Nigeria is a much larger country with 7 times the population, 40 times more arable land, and tremendous deposits of oil. Given Nigeria's sizable resource advantage, why is Nigeria's total annual production only half the size of Taiwan's?

Answers to the Checkpoint question can be found at the end of this chapter.

Specialization, Comparative Advantage, and Trade

As we have seen, economics is all about voluntary production and exchange. People and nations do business with one another because all expect to gain from the transactions. Centuries ago, European merchants ventured to the Far East to ply the lucrative spice trade. These days, American consumers buy wines from Italy, cars from Japan, electronics from Korea, and millions of other products from countries around the world.

Many people assume that trade between nations is a zero-sum game—a game in which, for one party to gain, another party must lose. This is how poker works. If one player walks away from the table a winner, someone else must have lost. But this is not how voluntary trade works. Voluntary trade is a positive-sum game: Both parties to a transaction score positive gains. After all, who would voluntarily enter into an exchange if he or she did not believe there was some gain from it? To understand how all parties to an exchange (whether individuals or nations) can gain from it, we need to consider the concept of comparative advantage developed by David Ricardo roughly 200 years ago, and how this concept differs from the concept of absolute advantage.

Absolute and Comparative Advantage

Figure 7 shows hypothetical production possibilities curves for the United States and Mexico. To simplify the analysis, we assume that opportunity costs are constant (PPFs are straight lines); however, the same analysis applies to PPFs with increasing opportunity costs. Both countries are assumed to produce only crude oil and silicon chips. Given

DAVID RICARDO (1772–1823)

David Ricardo's rigorous, dispassionate evaluation of economic principles influenced generations of theorists, including such vastly different thinkers as John Stuart Mill and Karl Marx. Ricardo was born in London as the third of 17 children. At age 14 he joined his father's trading business on the London Stock Exchange. At 21, he started his own brokerage and within five years had amassed a small fortune.

While vacationing in Bath, England, he chanced upon a copy of Adam Smith's *The Wealth of Nations,* and decided to devote his energies to studying economics and writing. He once wrote to his lifelong friend Thomas Malthus (another prominent economist of the time) that he was "thankful for the miserable English climate because it kept him at his desk writing." Ricardo and Malthus corresponded on a regular basis, and their exchanges led to the development of many economic concepts still used today.

Later, as a member of the British Parliament, Ricardo was an outspoken critic of the 1815 Corn Laws, which placed high tariffs on imported grain to protect British landowners. Ricardo was a strong advocate of free trade, and his writings reflected this view. His theory of "comparative advantage" suggested that countries would mutually benefit from trade by specializing in export goods they could produce at a lower opportunity cost than another country. His classic example was trade in cloth and wine between Britain and Portugal.

Ricardo died in 1823 of an ear infection, leaving an enduring legacy of classical (pre-1930s) economic analysis.

Sources: E. Ray Canterbery, *A Brief History of Economics* (New Jersey: World Scientific), 2001; Howard Marshall, *The Great Economists: A History of Economic Thought* (New York: Pitman Publishing), 1967; Steven Pressman, *Fifty Major Economists, 2nd ed.,* (New York: Routledge), 2006.

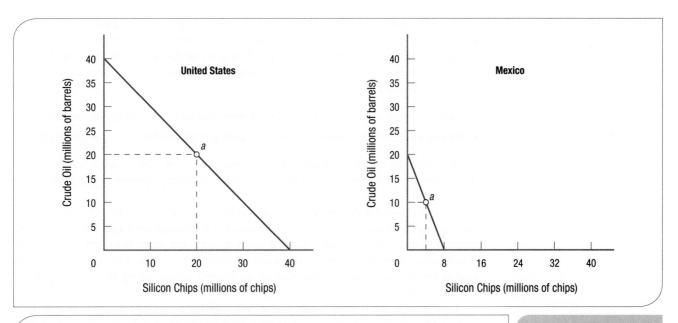

Production Possibilities for the United States and Mexico

One country has an absolute advantage if it can produce more of a good than another country. In this case, the United States has an absolute advantage over Mexico in producing both silicon chips and crude oil—it can produce more of both goods than Mexico can. Even so, Mexico has a comparative advantage over the United States in producing oil, since it can increase its output of oil at a lower opportunity cost than can the United States. This comparative advantage leads to gains for both countries from specialization and trade.

FIGURE 7

the PPFs in Figure 7, the United States has an **absolute advantage** over Mexico in producing both products. An absolute advantage exists when one country can produce more of a good than another country. In this instance, the United States can produce 2 times more oil (40 million versus 20 million barrels) and 5 times as many silicon chips (40 million versus 8 million chips) as Mexico.

At first glance you might wonder why the United States would even consider trading with Mexico. The United States has so much more production capacity than Mexico, so why wouldn't it just produce all of its own crude oil and silicon chips? The answer lies in comparative advantage.

One country has a **comparative advantage** in producing a good if its opportunity cost to produce that good is lower than the other country's. We can calculate each country's opportunity cost for each good using the production possibility frontiers in Figure 7.

If the United States uses all of its resources efficiently, it can produce a maximum of 40 million barrels of oil *or* 40 million silicon chips. It can also produce some of both goods, though clearly not 40 million of each, because in order to produce more of one good, it must reduce production of another (its opportunity cost). Because the PPF is linear, the tradeoff between oil and chips is constant. For the United States, it can substitute 1 million barrels of oil for 1 million silicon chips, which means it can produce 20 million barrels of oil and 20 million silicon chips. The opportunity cost for each good is summarized as follows:

- For every barrel of oil the United States produces, it must give up producing one silicon chip.

- For every silicon chip the United States produces, it must give up producing one barrel of oil.

absolute advantage One country can produce more of a good than another country.

comparative advantage One country has a lower opportunity cost of producing a good than another country.

Now let's look at Mexico. If it uses its resources efficiently, it can produce a maximum of 20 million barrels of oil *or* 8 million silicon chips. For Mexico, although the tradeoff between goods also is constant, the tradeoff is not one-for-one as in the United States. Because Mexico is better at producing oil than silicon chips, its opportunity cost for each good is as follows:

- For every barrel of oil Mexico produces, it must give up producing 0.4 silicon chips.
- For every silicon chip Mexico produces, it must give up producing 2.5 barrels of oil.

Note that the values of 0.4 and 2.5 are inverses of one another. In other words, $1/0.4 = 2.5$, and $1/2.5 = 0.4$. This relationship exists when calculating opportunity costs in a two-product economy.

Now that we have determined the opportunity cost of each good in both countries, we can conclude that Mexico has a comparative advantage over the United States in producing oil. This is because Mexico gives up only 0.4 chips for every barrel of oil it produces, while the United States must give up 1 chip. Thus, Mexico's opportunity cost of producing oil is less than that of the United States, giving Mexico a comparative advantage.

Conversely, the United States has a comparative advantage over Mexico in producing silicon chips: Producing a silicon chip in the United States costs one barrel of oil, whereas the same chip in Mexico costs two-and-a-half barrels of oil. Table 1 summarizes the opportunity costs of each good and which country has the comparative advantage.

TABLE 1	Comparing Opportunity Costs for Oil and Chip Production		
	U.S. Opportunity Cost	**Mexico Opportunity Cost**	**Comparative Advantage**
Oil Production	1 chip	0.4 chips	Mexico
Chip Production	1 barrel of oil	2.5 barrels of oil	United States

Note that each country has a comparative advantage in one good, even though the United States has an absolute advantage in both goods. However, it is comparative advantage that generates gains from trade. These relative costs suggest that the United States should pour its resources into producing silicon chips, while Mexico specializes in crude oil. The two countries can then engage in trade to their mutual benefit. As long as relative production costs differ between countries, specialization and trade can be mutually beneficial, allowing all countries to consume more.

The same idea applies to individuals. Although we have focused on trade between countries, the concept of comparative advantage explains why individuals specialize in a few tasks and then trade with one another. For example, if you are relatively better at understanding economics than your roommate who is on the golf team, you might offer to tutor economics in exchange for golf lessons. Comparative advantage explains all trade: between individuals as well as between countries.

The Gains from Trade

To see how specialization and trade can benefit all trading partners, let's return to our example in which the United States has the ability to produce more of both goods than Mexico. Assume that each country is at first (before trade) operating at point *a*

ISSUE

Do We Really Specialize in That? Comparative Advantage in the United States and China

What do tofu, edamame, ink, soy sauce, livestock feed, and soy milk have in common? They are all important products commonly made from soybeans. Although direct human consumption of soybeans in the United States is often confined to health food products and food in Asian restaurants, soybeans are much more important to the U.S. economy than most people think. The United States has a comparative advantage in soybean production. It produces and sells more soybeans than any other country, with much of it being sold to China.

How can a rich, technologically advanced country like the United States end up with a comparative advantage in an agricultural good like soybeans? Several factors play a role. First, the United States has an abundance of farmland ideal in climate and soil for soybean production. Second, modern fertilizers and seed technologies have made soybean production a much more innovative industry than in the past, allowing farms to increase soybean yields per acre of land. And third, a strong appetite for soy-based products, particularly in China, has made soybeans a very lucrative industry.

China is the second largest trading partner to the United States after Canada, trading $539 billion worth of goods between the countries in 2011. Yet, the top five U.S. export goods (items sold) and import goods (items bought) with China, listed below, may be surprising.

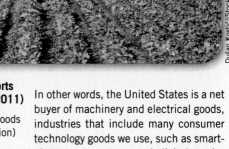

DuŠan Kostić/iStockphoto

Top Five Exports to China (2011)

1. Machinery ($12.2 billion)
2. Soybeans ($10.7 billion)
3. Electrical goods ($10.1 billion)
4. Automobiles ($6.8 billion)
5. Aircraft ($6.4 billion)

Top Five Imports from China (2011)

1. Electrical goods ($98.7 billion)
2. Machinery ($94.9 billion)
3. Toys/sporting goods ($22.6 billion)
4. Furniture ($20.5 billion)
5. Footwear ($16.7 billion)

Although the United States sells a lot of machines and electrical goods to China (mostly specialized machinery and electronics used in factories and research labs), it buys significantly greater amounts of these products *from* China.

In other words, the United States is a net buyer of machinery and electrical goods, industries that include many consumer technology goods we use, such as smartphones, computers, and digital equipment. Besides soybeans, paper pulp and copper are two other resource industries (not listed above) that constitute a large portion of U.S. sales *to* China.

In sum, specialization and trade are not as simple as they used to be. Products such as computers and electronics that once were the purview of "rich" countries such as the United States are now being manufactured in China and other countries, while improved technology in the agricultural and natural resource industries has given the United States a new form of specialization that would have been unheard of 50 years ago.

in Figure 7. At this point, both countries are producing and consuming only their own output; the United States produces and consumes 20 million barrels of oil and 20 million silicon chips; Mexico, 10 million barrels of oil and 4 million chips. Table 2 summarizes these initial conditions.

Initial Consumption-Production Pattern			TABLE 2
	United States	**Mexico**	**Total**
Oil	20	10	30
Chips	20	4	24

Now assume that Mexico focuses on oil, producing the maximum it can: 20 million barrels. We also assume both countries want to continue consuming 30 million barrels of oil between them. Therefore the United States only needs to produce 10 million barrels of oil because Mexico is now producing 20 million barrels. For the United States, this frees up some resources that can be diverted to producing silicon chips. Because each barrel of oil in the United States costs one chip, reducing oil output by 10 million barrels means that 10 million more chips can be produced.

TABLE 3	Production After Mexico Specializes in Producing Crude Oil		
	United States	Mexico	Total
Oil	10	20	30
Chips	30	0	30

Table 3 shows each country's production after Mexico has begun specializing in oil production.

Notice that the combined production of crude oil has remained constant, but the total output of silicon chips has risen by 6 million chips. Assuming that the two countries agree to share the added 6 million chips between them equally, Mexico will now ship 10 million barrels of oil to the United States in exchange for 7 million chips. From the 10 million additional chips the United States produces, Mexico will receive 4 million (its original production) plus 3 million for a total of 7 million, leaving 3 million additional chips for U.S. consumption. The resulting mix of products consumed in each country is shown in Table 4. Clearly, both countries are better off, having engaged in specialized production and trade.

TABLE 4	Final Consumption Patterns after Trade		
	United States	Mexico	Total
Oil	20	10	30
Chips	23	7	30

The important point to remember here is that even when one country has an absolute advantage over another, both countries still benefit from trading with one another. In our example, the gains were small, but such gains can grow. As two economies become more equal in size, the benefits of their comparative advantages grow.

Practical Constraints on Trade

Before leaving the subject of international trade and how it contributes to growth in both countries, we should take a moment to note some practical constraints on trade. First, every transaction involves costs, including transportation, communications, and the general costs of doing business. Even so, over the last several decades, transportation and communication costs have been declining all over the world, resulting in growing global trade.

Second, the production possibilities curves for nations are not linear, but rather governed by increasing costs and diminishing returns. Therefore, it is difficult for countries to specialize in producing one product. Complete specialization would be risky, moreover, because the market for a product can always decline, perhaps because the product becomes technologically obsolete. Alternatively, changing weather patterns can wreak havoc on specialized agricultural products, adding further instability to incomes and exports in developing countries.

Finally, although two countries may benefit from trading with one another, expanding this trade may well hurt some industries and individuals within each country. Notably, industries finding themselves at a comparative disadvantage may be forced to scale back production and lay off workers. In such instances, government may need to provide workers with retraining, relocation, and other help to ensure a smooth transition to the new production mix.

When the United States signed the North American Free Trade Agreement (NAFTA) with Canada and Mexico, many people experienced what we have just been discussing. Some U.S. jobs went south to Mexico because of low production costs. By opening up more markets for U.S. products, however, NAFTA did stimulate economic growth, such that retrained workers may end up with new and better jobs.

 CHECKPOINT

SPECIALIZATION, COMPARATIVE ADVANTAGE, AND TRADE

- An absolute advantage exists when one country can produce more of some good than another.

- A comparative advantage exists if one country has lower opportunity costs of producing a good than another country. Both countries gain from trade if each focuses on producing those goods with which it has a comparative advantage.

- Voluntary trade is a positive-sum game, because both countries benefit from it.

QUESTION: Why do Hollywood stars (and many other rich individuals)—unlike most people—have full-time personal assistants who manage their personal affairs?

Answers to the Checkpoint question can be found at the end of this chapter.

chapter summary

Section 1: Basic Economic Questions and Production

Every economy must decide:

1. What to produce.
2. How to produce it.
3. Who will get the goods produced.

Rainer Plendl/Dreamstime.com

Factors of Production (Inputs)

Land
Labor
Capital
Entrepreneurial Ability

Production Method

Output (Goods and Services)

Using scarce resources productively leads to:

Production efficiency: Goods and services are produced at their lowest possible resource cost.

Allocative efficiency: Goods are produced according to what society desires.

Section 2: Production Possibilities and Economic Growth

The **production possibilities frontier (PPF)** shows the different combinations of goods that a fully employed economy can produce, given its available resources and current technology.

Constant Opportunity Cost

Pizza

Unattainable

Attainable but inefficient

Tablets

Increasing Opportunity Cost

Pizza

Unattainable

Attainable but inefficient

Tablets

Production possibilities frontiers (PPFs) illustrate tradeoffs—if an economy operates at full employment (on the PPF), producing more of one good requires producing less of the other. A concave PPF shows how opportunity costs rise due to diminishing returns.

47

Some pizza makers were never meant to produce computers and some computer workers were never meant to produce pizza, increasing the opportunity cost of production as more of one good is produced.

The production possibilities model shows how economic growth can arise from an expansion in resources or from improvements in technology.

Changes in the PPF: From PPF$_A$ to PPF$_B$: An increase in productivity in the production of one good (for example, an increase in the number of students studying computer engineering).

From PPF$_A$ to PPF$_C$: An increase in productive capacity of both goods (for example, an increase in overall technology, or an increase in labor or capital resources).

Section 3: Specialization, Comparative Advantage, and Trade

An **absolute advantage** exists when one country can produce more of some good than another.

A **comparative advantage** exists when one country can produce a good at a lower opportunity cost than another.

Gains from trade result when a country specializes in the production of goods in which it has a comparative advantage, and trades these goods with another country. Trade is a positive-sum game. Both countries can benefit even if one country has an absolute advantage in both goods.

Calculating Opportunity Costs Using Production Numbers (units produced per day per worker)

	Australia	New Zealand
Boomerangs	20	8
Kiwi	12	16

- Opportunity cost of 1 boomerang in:
  Australia: 12 kiwi/20 boomerangs = 0.6 kiwi per boomerang
  New Zealand: 16 kiwi/8 boomerangs = 2 kiwi per boomerang
  Australia has a lower opportunity cost producing boomerangs

- Opportunity cost of 1 kiwi in:
  Australia: 20 boomerangs/12 kiwi = 1.7 boomerangs per kiwi
  New Zealand: 8 boomerangs/16 kiwi = 0.5 boomerangs per kiwi
  New Zealand has a lower opportunity cost producing kiwi

Countries export goods for which they have a comparative advantage, and import goods for which they do not, leading to gains from trade to both countries.

KEY CONCEPTS

production, p. 30
resources, p. 30
land, p. 30
labor, p. 30
capital, p. 31

entrepreneurs, p. 31
production efficiency, p. 31
allocative efficiency, p. 32
production possibilities frontier
  (PPF), p. 33

opportunity cost, p. 34
absolute advantage, p. 41
comparative advantage, p. 41

QUESTIONS AND PROBLEMS

Check Your Understanding

1. When can an economy increase the production of one good without reducing the output of another?

2. In which of the three basic questions facing any society does technology play the greatest role?

3. Explain the important difference between a straight line PPF and the PPF that is concave to (bowed away from) the origin.

4. How would unemployment be shown on the PPF?

5. List three factors that can contribute to an economy's growth.

6. How can a country that does not have an absolute advantage in producing goods still benefit from trade?

Apply the Concepts

7. China has experienced levels of economic growth in the last decade that have been about 5 times that of the United States (10% versus 2% per year in the United States). Has China's high growth rate eliminated scarcity in China?

8. Describe how a country producing more capital goods rather than consumption goods ends up in the future with a PPF that is larger than a country that produces more consumption goods and fewer capital goods.

9. The United States has an absolute advantage in making many goods, such as short-sleeved cotton golf shirts. Why do Indonesia and Bangladesh make these shirts and export them to the United States?

10. Why is it that America uses heavy street cleaning machines driven by one person to clean the streets, while China and India use many people with brooms to do the same job?

11. If specialization and trade as discussed in this chapter lead to a win-win situation in which both countries gain, why is there often opposition to trade agreements and globalization?

12. American attitudes about the tradeoff between the environment and economic growth shown in By the Numbers at the beginning of the chapter changed significantly when the economy entered a recession. However, during the recession in 2009, Americans were roughly equally split between their concerns for the environment and economic growth. What would you expect to find in a similar survey in a relatively poor developing nation?

In the News

13. According to a March 8, 2012, *New York Times* report, the 2011 earthquake in Japan that triggered a devastating tsunami led to a near complete shutdown of Japan's nuclear

energy industry, which generates one-third of the country's total electricity. The resulting energy crisis caused severe supply disruptions in nearly all industries. How do natural disasters such as the tsunami in Japan affect a country's ability to achieve economic growth? Illustrate your answer using a PPF.

14. The recession of 2007–2009 and the slow recovery led to severe budget cuts in state governments across the United States. Public colleges and universities, which are highly subsidized by state governments, saw dramatic cuts in their budgets, making it more difficult for students to attend school and/or complete their degrees. The *Chronicle of Higher Education* of January 17, 2012, argued that cuts to higher education will "imperil competitiveness" in America. How might the cost savings from reduced educational spending end up costing states even more in the future?

Solving Problems

15. Political commentators often make the argument that growth in another country (most notably China) is detrimental to the economic interests of the United States. Look back at Tables 2 to 4 in the Gains from Trade section of the chapter. Then, assume that Mexico doubles in size, and make those changes to Table 2. Reconstruct Tables 3 and 4 given Mexico's greater capacity. Has the United States benefited by Mexico being able to produce more?

16. The table below shows the potential output combinations of oranges and jars of prickly pear jelly (from the flower of the prickly pear cactus) for Florida and Arizona.

    a. Compute the opportunity cost for Florida of oranges in terms of jars of prickly pear jelly. Do the same for prickly pear jelly in terms of oranges.

    b. Compute the opportunity cost for Arizona of oranges in terms of jars of prickly pear jelly. Do the same for prickly pear jelly in terms of oranges.

    c. Would it make sense for Florida to specialize in producing oranges and for Arizona to specialize in producing prickly pear jelly and then trade? Why or why not?

Florida		Arizona	
Oranges	**Prickly Pear Jelly**	**Oranges**	**Prickly Pear Jelly**
0	10	0	500
50	8	20	400
100	6	40	300
150	4	60	200
200	2	80	100
250	0	100	0

USING THE NUMBERS

17. According to By the Numbers, in which period (1960 to 1985 or 1985 to 2010) did corn and soybean production increase faster in terms of yield per acre?

18. According to By the Numbers, in the period between 1990 and 2012, in how many years did the U.S. trade balance improve from the previous year and in how many years did the trade balance deteriorate (assume the trade balance deteriorated from 1989 [not shown in the figure] to 1990)?

ANSWERS TO QUESTIONS IN CHECKPOINTS

Checkpoint: Basic Economic Questions and Production

Typically, entrepreneurs put not only their time and effort into a business but also their money, often pledging private assets as collateral for loans. Should the business fail, they stand to lose more than their jobs, rent from the land, or interest on capital loaned to the firm. Workers can get other jobs, landowners can rent to others, and capital can be used in other enterprises. The entrepreneur must suffer the loss of personal assets and move on.

Checkpoint: Production Possibilities and Economic Growth

Although Nigeria has significantly more natural resources and labor (two important factors of production) than Taiwan, these resources alone do not guarantee a higher ability to produce goods and services. Factors of production also include physical capital (machinery), human capital (education), and technology (research and development), all of which Taiwan has in great abundance. Thus, despite the lack of land, labor, and natural resources, Taiwan is able to use its resources efficiently and expand its production possibilities well beyond that of Nigeria.

Checkpoint: Specialization, Comparative Advantage, and Trade

For Hollywood stars and other rich people, the opportunity cost of their time is high. As a result, they hire people at lower cost to do the mundane chores that each of us is accustomed to doing because our time is relatively less valuable.

Supply and Demand

3

What $60 billion global industry sells a product that many people typically can obtain easily from another source free of charge? The bottled water industry! This industry began its meteoric rise in the early 1990s, and today, the ubiquitous bottle of water has changed the way we live. It also has created new concerns regarding the environmental impact of the billions of plastic bottles used and discarded.

The bottled water industry took off as consumers changed their hydration habits, spurred by greater awareness of the health benefits of drinking water, including weight loss, illness prevention, and overall health maintenance. As water consumption increased, people started wanting something more than just ordinary water from the tap. They desired water that was purer, more consistent in taste, or infused with flavor or minerals. Plus, consumers wanted water that was easy to carry. Bottled water was the product consumers wanted, and the market was willing to provide it.

Bottled water comes from many sources, both domestic and foreign, and consists of either spring water (from natural springs underneath the earth) or purified water (ordinary tap water that undergoes a complex purification process). As the industry grew, new varieties of water were made available. Water that came from exotic faraway springs, vitamin-infused water, flavored water, and carbonated water were some of the choices consumers were given. The total amount of water produced for the bottled water industry continued to increase as long as there were customers willing to pay for it in the market.

In the late 2000s, falling incomes from a deteriorating global economy, concerns about the harmful effects of discarded plastic bottles on the environment, increased use of home water purification devices, and even some laws against the use of bottled water eventually halted the market's growth. The economy has since improved, and the bottled water industry responded to the environmental concerns by using bottles made from recycled plastic or by using new technologies to reduce the plastic content in water bottles, again responding to the desires of consumers. As a result, sales increased again in 2011.

Consumers have many choices of what water to buy and where to buy it. Even so, the bottled water market is one in which prices vary considerably depending on the location of purchase. A single bottle of water of the same brand might cost $0.69 at a grocery store, $0.99 at a convenience store, $1.25 from a vending machine, $1.49 at a local coffee shop, and $3.00 or more at a theme park, sports stadium, or movie theater. How can the same product be sold in different places at so many different prices?

This chapter analyzes the various factors influencing how consumers value goods in different settings and circumstances. We also study how producers take costs and incentives into account in determining what products to produce, how much to produce, and what prices to charge. The interaction between consumers and producers within a market determines the prices we pay.

In any given market, prices are determined by "what the market will bear." Which factors determine what the market will bear, and what happens when events that occur in the marketplace cause prices to change? For answers to these questions, economists turn to supply and demand analysis. The basic model of supply and demand presented in this chapter will let you determine why product sales rise and fall, what direction prices move in, and how many goods will be offered for sale when certain events happen in the marketplace. Later chapters use this same model to explain complex phenomena such as how wages are set and how personal income is distributed.

This chapter introduces some of the basic economic concepts you need to know to understand how the forces of supply and demand work. These concepts include markets, the law of demand, demand curves, the determinants of demand, the law of supply, supply curves, the determinants of supply, and market equilibrium.

⬢ Markets

A **market** is an institution that enables buyers and sellers to interact and transact with one another. A lemonade stand is a market because it allows people to exchange money for a product, in this case lemonade. Ticket scalping, which remains illegal or

markets Institutions that bring buyers and sellers together so they can interact and transact with each other.

The World of Markets

Markets form the foundation of all economic transactions. As various factors affect the supply and demand for goods and services, prices adjust upward or downward correspondingly to reach equilibrium.

The legalization of casinos in many states has resulted in dramatic growth in the industry. Top gaming revenues by state in 2011:

Nevada
New Jersey
Pennsylvania
Indiana
Louisiana
Mississippi
Missouri
Illinois
Michigan
Iowa

0   2,000 4,000 6,000 8,000 10,000 12,000
In Millions of U.S. Dollars

age fotostock/SuperStock

PjrStudio/Alamy

Prices for precious metals vary widely due to their relative demand and supply.

7,300,000,000

Total value (in U.S. dollars) of the worldwide virtual goods market associated with online gaming in 2012.

72,800,000,000

Total number of half-liter water bottles consumed in the United States in 2012 (over 220 bottles per person).

Millions of U.S. Dollars

12,000
10,000
8,000
6,000
4,000
2,000
0

1982   1992   2002   2012

Total sales of bottled water in the United States took off in the 1990s and continued to grow steadily since.

ZUMA Wire Service /Alamy

University of Phoenix

University of Phoenix is the largest for-profit university with nearly 500,000 students.

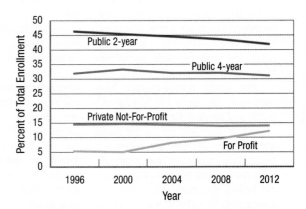

Percent of Total Enrollment

50
45
40
35
30
25
20
15
10
5
0

Public 2-year

Public 4-year

Private Not-For-Profit

For Profit

1996   2000   2004   2008   2012
Year

Enrollment at for-profit universities grew significantly over the past 16 years compared to not-for-profit institutions.

price system A name given to the market economy because prices provide considerable information to both buyers and sellers.

highly restricted in some states, similarly represents market activity since it leads to the exchange of money for tickets, whether it takes place in person outside the stadium or online.

The Internet, without a physical location, has dramatically expanded the notion of markets. Online market sites such as eBay permit firms and individuals to sell a large number of low-volume products, ranging from rare collectible items to an extra box of unused diapers, and still make money. This includes students who resell their textbooks on Amazon.com and Half.com. The Internet also has launched markets for virtual goods. For example, buying virtual tools, cash, and animals in online games has become an important part of social media sites.

Even though all markets have the same basic component—the transaction—they can differ in a number of ways. Some markets are quite limited because of their geographical location, or because they offer only a few different products for sale. The New York Stock Exchange serves as a market for just a single type of financial instrument, stocks, but it facilitates exchanges worth billions of dollars daily. Compare this to the neighborhood flea market, which is much smaller and may operate only on weekends, but offers everything from food and crafts to T-shirts and electronics. Cement manufacturers are typically restricted to local markets due to high transportation costs, whereas Internet firms can easily do business with customers around the world.

ISSUE

Do Markets Exist for Everyone, Including Dogs and Cats?

Over 78 million dogs and 86 million cats call the United States home, with many times more finding homes around the world. Over four in ten U.S. households include at least one pet, which is often treated as a beloved member of the family. The expenses associated with pet ownership often extend beyond the basic necessities of food and vet checkups.

Jefferson Graham

Total spending on pet-related products in the United States has increased every year since 2001, surpassing $50 billion in 2011. Even during the depths of the last economic downturn, spending on pets continued to increase. The seeming immunity of the pet goods market to economic hardships raises an interesting question of who the market is geared toward: the pets or their sometimes fanatical owners?

Pet goods manufacturers have increased the types of "consumer" goods and services for pets. These include a greater selection of pet foods and toys, but increasingly sellers are being more creative in their offerings. For example, the number of pet spas, pet hotels, and even pet airlines, allowing pets to bathe in luxury as they or their owners travel, has boomed over the past decade.

Pet consumerism has even gone high-tech. Since the introduction of tablets, programmers have introduced new tablet apps designed for cats, including games that are played feline versus human. Such apps highlight the ability of businesses to turn pets into consumers, whose desires (even if imagined by their owners) turn into actual purchases.

The power of consumer decisions extending beyond the wants of humans demonstrates the broad reach of markets. Because humans share a deep connection with their furry loved ones, they will often incorporate their pets' desires into real consumption choices. And based on the growth of this market, it's likely that dogs and cats will continue to be avid consumers in this market.

The Price System

When buyers and sellers exchange money for goods and services, accepting some offers and rejecting others, they are also doing something else: They are communicating their individual desires. Much of this communication is accomplished through the prices of items. If buyers value a particular item sufficiently, they will quickly pay its asking price. If they do not buy it, they are indicating they do not believe the item to be worth its asking price.

Prices also give buyers an easy means of comparing goods that can substitute for each other. If the price of margarine falls to half the price of butter, this will suggest to many consumers that margarine is a better deal. Similarly, sellers can determine what goods to sell by comparing their prices. When prices rise for tennis rackets, this tells sporting goods store operators that the public wants more tennis rackets, leading the store operators to order more. Prices, therefore, contain a huge amount of useful information for both consumers and sellers. For this reason, economists often call our market economy the **price system.**

CHECKPOINT

> **MARKETS**
>
> ■ Markets are institutions that enable buyers and sellers to interact and transact business.
>
> ■ Markets differ in geographical location, products offered, and size.
>
> ■ Prices contain a wealth of information for both buyers and sellers.
>
> ■ Through their purchases, consumers signal their willingness to exchange money for particular products at particular prices. These signals help businesses decide what to produce, and how much of it to produce.
>
> ■ The market economy is also called the price system.
>
> QUESTION: What are the important differences between the markets for financial securities such as the New York Stock Exchange and your local farmer's market?
>
> Answers to the Checkpoint question can be found at the end of this chapter.

Demand

Whenever you purchase a product, you are voting with your money. You are selecting one product out of many and supporting one firm out of many, both of which signal to the business community what sorts of products satisfy your wants as a consumer.

Economists typically focus on wants rather than needs because it is so difficult to determine what we truly need. Theoretically, you could survive on tofu and vitamin pills, living in a lean-to made of cardboard and buying all your clothes from thrift stores. Most people in our society, however, choose not to live in such austere fashion. Rather, they want something more, and in most cases they are willing and able to pay for more.

Willingness-to-Pay: The Building Block of Market Demand

Imagine sitting in your economics class around mealtime. In your rush to class, you did not have a chance to make a sandwich at home or to stop at the cafeteria on your way to class. You think about foods that sound appealing to you (just about anything at this point), and plan to go to the cafeteria immediately after class and buy a sandwich. Given your growling stomach, you think more about what you want on your sandwich and less about how much the sandwich will cost. In your mind, your **willingness-to-pay** for that sandwich can be quite high, say $10 or even more.

Economists refer to willingness-to-pay as the maximum amount one would be willing to pay for a good or service, which represents the highest value that a consumer believes the good or service is worth. Of course, one always hopes that the actual price would be much lower. In your case, willingness-to-pay is the cutoff from buying a sandwich and not buying a sandwich.

Willingness-to-pay varies from person to person, from the circumstances each person is in to the number of sandwiches one chooses to buy. Suppose your classmate ate a full meal before she came to class. Her willingness-to-pay for a sandwich would be much lower than yours because she isn't hungry at that moment. Similarly, after you buy and consume your first sandwich, your willingness-to-pay for a second sandwich would decrease because you would be less hungry. The desires consumers have for goods and services that are expressed through their purchases are known as demands in the market.

Figure 1 on the next page illustrates how individuals' willingness-to-pay (WTP) is used to derive market demand curves. Suppose you are willing to pay up to $10 for the first sandwich and $4 for the second sandwich (shown in panel A), while Jane, your less-hungry classmate, would pay up to $6 for her first sandwich and only $2 for her second sandwich (shown in panel B). If we take the WTP for your two sandwiches and the WTP of Jane's two sandwiches and place all four values in order from highest to lowest, a two-person market for sandwiches is created as shown in panel C. Notice how the distance between steps becomes smaller in the two-person market. Now suppose we combine the WTPs for

willingness-to-pay An individual's valuation of a good or service, equal to the most an individual is willing and able to pay.

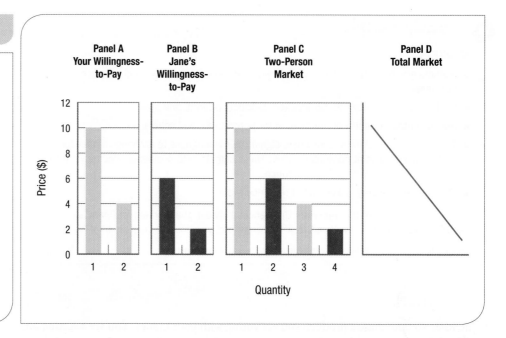

FIGURE 1

From Individual Willingness-to-Pay to Market Demand

In panel A, you would be willing to pay up to $10 for your first sandwich and $4 for the second. Jane, however, is only willing to pay up to $6 for her first sandwich and $2 for a second (panel B). Placing the WTP for sandwiches by you and Jane in order from the highest to lowest value, we generate a market with two consumers shown in panel C. As more and more individuals are added to the market, the demand for sandwiches becomes a smooth downward-sloping line, shown in panel D.

demand The maximum amount of a product that buyers are willing and able to purchase over some time period at various prices, holding all other relevant factors constant (the *ceteris paribus* condition).

law of demand Holding all other relevant factors constant, as price increases, quantity demanded falls, and as price decreases, quantity demanded rises.

everybody in the class (or for an entire city or country) into a single market. What would that diagram look like? In large markets, the difference in WTP between each unit of a good becomes so small that it becomes a straight line, as shown in panel D.

These illustrations show how ordinary demand curves, which we will discuss in detail in the remainder of this section, are developed from the perceptions of what individual consumers believe a good or service is worth to them (their willingness-to-pay). Let's now discuss an important characteristic of market demand.

The Law of Demand: The Relationship Between Quantity Demanded and Price

Demand refers to the goods and services people are willing and able to buy during a certain period of time at various prices, holding all other relevant factors constant (the *ceteris paribus* condition). Typically, when the price of a good or service increases (say your favorite café raises its prices), the quantity demanded will decrease because fewer and fewer people will be willing and able to spend their money on such things. However, when prices of goods or services decrease (think of sales offered the day after Thanksgiving), the quantity demanded increases.

In a market economy, there is a negative relationship between price and quantity demanded. This relationship, in its most basic form, states that as price increases, the quantity demanded falls, and conversely, as prices fall, the quantity demanded increases.

This principle, when all other factors are held constant, is known as the **law of demand.** The law of demand states that the lower a product's price, the more of that product consumers will purchase during a given time period. This straightforward, commonsense notion happens because, as a product's price drops, consumers will substitute the now cheaper product for other, more expensive products. Conversely, if the product's price rises, consumers will find other, less expensive products to substitute for it.

To illustrate, when videocassette recorders first came on the market 30 years ago, they cost $3,000, and few homes had one. As VCRs became less and less expensive, however, more people bought them, and others found more uses for them. Today, DVD players and digital video recorders (DVRs) are everywhere, and VCRs are essentially consigned to museums.

The day after Thanksgiving, dubbed "Black Friday," is when stores offer steep discounts to jumpstart the holiday shopping season. This leads to massive quantities of goods sold, in an example of the law of demand.

Digital music players have altered the structure of the music business, and digital cameras have essentially replaced cameras that use film.

Time is an important component in the demand for many products. Consuming many products—watching a movie, eating a pizza, playing tennis—takes some time. Thus, the price of these goods includes not only their monetary cost, but also the opportunity cost of the time needed to consume them. It follows that, all other things being equal, including the cost of a ticket, we would expect more consumers to attend a two-hour movie than a four-hour movie. The shorter movie simply requires less of a time investment.

The Demand Curve

The law of demand states that as price decreases, quantity demanded increases. When we translate demand information into a graph, we create a **demand curve.** This demand curve, which slopes down and to the right, graphically illustrates the law of demand. A demand curve shows both the willingness-to-pay for any given quantity and what the quantity demanded will be at any given price. In Figure 1, we saw how individual demands (measured by willingness-to-pay) can be combined to represent market demand, which can consist of many consumers. For simplicity, from this point we will assume that all demand curves, including those for individuals, are linear (straight lines).

Suppose Abe and Betty are the only two consumers in the market for computer games. Figure 2 shows each of their annual demands using a demand schedule and a demand curve. A **demand schedule** is a table indicating the quantities consumers are willing to purchase at each price. Looking at the demand schedule, we can see that both Abe and Betty are willing to buy more computer games as the price decreases. When the price is $100, Abe is willing to buy 10 games while Betty buys none. When the price falls to $80, Abe is willing to buy 15 games and Betty would buy 5.

We can take the values from the demand schedule in the table and graph them in a figure, with price shown on the vertical axis and computer games on the horizontal axis, following the convention in economics of always placing price on the vertical axis and quantity demanded on the horizontal axis. By doing so, we can create a demand curve for both Abe and Betty. Both the table and the graph convey the same information. They also both portray the law of demand. As the price decreases, Abe and Betty demand more computer games.

Although individual demand curves are interesting, market demand curves are far more important to economists, as they can be used to predict changes in product price

demand curve A graphical illustration of the law of demand, which shows the relationship between the price of a good and the quantity demanded.

demand schedule A table that shows the quantity of a good a consumer purchases at each price.

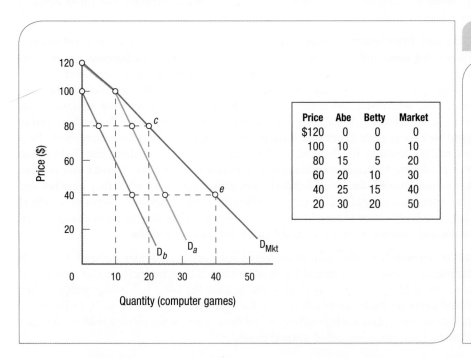

Price	Abe	Betty	Market
$120	0	0	0
100	10	0	10
80	15	5	20
60	20	10	30
40	25	15	40
20	30	20	50

FIGURE 2

Market Demand: Horizontal Summation of Individual Demand Curves

Abe and Betty's demand schedules (the table) and their individual demand curves (the graph) for computer games are shown. Abe will purchase 15 computer games when the price is $80, buy 25 games when the price falls to $40, and buy more as prices continue to fall. Betty will purchase 5 computer games when the price is $80 and buy 15 when the price falls to $40. The individual demand curves for Abe and Betty are shown as D_a and D_b, respectively, and are horizontally summed to get market demand, D_{Mkt}. Horizontal summation involves adding together the quantities demanded by each individual at each possible price.

and quantity. Further, one can observe what happens to a product's price and quantity and infer what changes have occurred in the market. Market demand is the sum of individual demands. To calculate market demand, economists simply add together how many units of a product all consumers will purchase at each price. This process is known as **horizontal summation.**

Turning to the demand curves in Figure 2, two individual demand curves for Abe and Betty, D_a and D_b, are shown. For simplicity, let's assume they represent the entire market, but recognize that this process would work for any larger number of people. Note that at a price of $100 a game, Betty will not buy any, although Abe is willing to buy 10 games at $100 each. Above $100, therefore, the market demand is equal to Abe's demand. At $100 and below, however, we add both Abe's and Betty's demands at each price to obtain market demand. Thus, at $80, individual demand is 15 for Abe and 5 for Betty, therefore the market demand is equal to 20 (point *c*). When the price is $40 a game, Abe buys 25 and Betty buys 15, for a total of 40 games (point *e*). The heavier curve, labeled D_{Mkt}, represents this market demand; it is a horizontal summation of the two individual demand curves.

This all sounds simple in theory, but in the real world estimating market demand curves is a tricky business, given that many markets contain millions of consumers. Economic analysts and marketing professionals use sophisticated statistical techniques to estimate the market demand for particular goods and services in the industries they represent.

The market demand curve shows the maximum amount of a product consumers are willing and able to purchase during a given time period at various prices, all other relevant factors being held constant. Economists use the term determinants of demand to refer to these other, nonprice factors that are held constant. This is another example of the use of *ceteris paribus:* holding all other relevant factors constant.

Determinants of Demand

Up to this point, we have discussed only how price affects the quantity demanded. When prices fall, consumers purchase more of a product, thus quantity demanded rises. When prices rise, consumers purchase less of a product, thus quantity demanded falls. But several other factors besides price also affect demand, including what people like, what their income is, and how much related products cost. More specifically, there are five key **determinants of demand:** (1) tastes and preferences; (2) income; (3) prices of related goods; (4) the number of buyers; and (5) expectations regarding future prices, income, and product availability. When one of these determinants changes, the *entire* demand curve changes. Let's see why.

Tastes and Preferences We all have preferences for certain products over others, easily perceiving subtle differences in styling and quality. Automobiles, fashions, phones, and music are just a few of the products that are subject to the whims of the consumer.

Remember Crocs, those brightly colored rubber sandals with the little air holes that moms, kids, waitresses, and many others favored recently? They were an instant hit. Initially, demand was D_0 in Figure 3. They then became such a fad that demand jumped to D_1 and for a short while Crocs were hard to find. Eventually Crocs were everywhere. Fads come and go, and now the demand for them settled back to something like D_2, less than the original level. Notice an important distinction here: More Crocs weren't sold because the *price* was lowered; the entire demand curve shifted rightward when they were hot and more Crocs could be sold at *all* prices. Now that the fad has subsided, fewer can be sold at all prices. It is important to keep in mind that when one of the determinants changes, such as tastes and preferences in this case, the *entire* demand curve shifts.

Income Income is another important factor influencing consumer demand. Generally speaking, as income rises, demand for most goods will likewise increase. Get a raise, and you are more likely to buy more clothes and acquire the latest technology gadgets. Your demand curve for these goods will shift to the right (such as from D_0 to D_1 in Figure 3). Products for which demand is positively linked to income—when income rises, demand for the product also rises—are called **normal goods.**

horizontal summation Market demand and supply curves are found by adding together how many units of the product will be purchased or supplied at each price.

determinants of demand Nonprice factors that affect demand, including tastes and preferences, income, prices of related goods, number of buyers, and expectations.

normal good A good for which an increase in income results in rising demand.

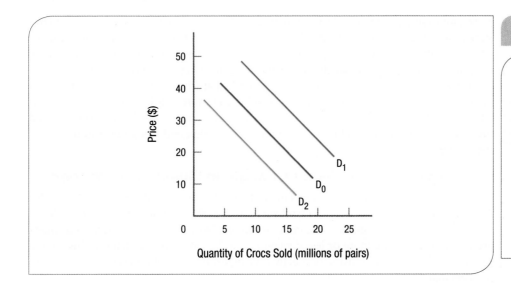

FIGURE 3

Shifts in the Demand Curve
The demand for Crocs originally was D_0. When they became a fad, demand shifted to D_1 as consumers were willing to purchase more at *all* prices. Once the fad cooled off, demand fell (shifted leftward) to D_2 as consumers wanted less at each price. When a determinant such as tastes and preferences changes, the *entire* demand curve shifts.

There are also some products for which demand declines as income rises, and the demand curve shifts to the left. Economists call these products **inferior goods.** As income grows, for instance, the consumption of discount clothing and cheap motel stays will likely fall as individuals upgrade their wardrobes and stay in more comfortable hotels when traveling. Similarly, when you graduate from college and your income rises, your consumption of ramen noodles will fall as you begin to cook tastier dinners and eat out more frequently.

inferior good A good for which an increase in income results in declining demand.

Prices of Related Goods The prices of related commodities also affect consumer decisions. You may be an avid concertgoer, but with concert ticket prices often topping $100, further rises in the price of concert tickets may entice you to see more movies and fewer concerts. Movies, concerts, plays, and sporting events are good examples of **substitute goods,** because consumers can substitute one for another depending on their respective prices. When the *price* of concerts rises, your *demand* for movies increases, and vice versa. These are substitute goods.

substitute goods Goods consumers will substitute for one another depending on their relative prices. When the *price* of one good rises and the *demand* for another good increases, they are substitute goods, and vice versa.

Movies and popcorn, on the other hand, are examples of **complementary goods.** These are goods that are generally consumed together, such that an increase or decrease in the consumption of one will similarly result in an increase or decrease in the consumption of the other—see fewer movies, and your consumption of popcorn will decline. Other complementary goods include cars and gasoline, hot dogs and hot dog buns, and ski lift tickets and ski rentals. Thus, when the *price* of lift tickets increases, the quantity of lift tickets demanded falls, which causes your *demand* for ski rentals to fall as well (shifts to the left), and vice versa.

complementary goods Goods that are typically consumed together. When the *price* of a complementary good rises, the *demand* for the other good declines, and vice versa.

The Number of Buyers Another factor influencing market demand for a product is the number of potential buyers in the market. Clearly, the more consumers there are who would be likely to buy a particular product, the higher its market demand will be (the demand curve will shift rightward). As our average life span steadily rises, the demands for medical services and retirement communities likewise increase. As more people than ever enter universities and graduate schools, demand for textbooks and backpacks increases.

Expectations About Future Prices, Incomes, and Product Availability The final factor influencing demand involves consumer expectations. If consumers expect shortages of certain products or increases in their prices in the near future, they tend to rush out and buy these products immediately, thereby increasing the present demand for the products. The demand curve shifts to the right. During the Florida hurricane season, when a large storm forms and begins moving toward the coast, the demand for plywood, nails, bottled water, and batteries quickly rises.

The expectation of a rise in income, meanwhile, can lead consumers to take advantage of credit in order to increase their present consumption. Department stores and furniture stores, for example, often run "no payments until next year" sales designed to attract consumers who want to "buy now, pay later." These consumers expect to have more money later, when they can pay, so they go ahead and buy what they want now, thereby increasing the present demand for the sale items. Again, the demand curve shifts to the right.

The key point to remember from this section is that when one of the determinants of demand changes, the *entire* demand curve shifts rightward (an increase in demand) or leftward (a decline in demand). A quick look back at Figure 3 shows that when demand increases, consumers are willing to buy more at all prices, and when demand decreases, they will buy less at all prices.

Changes in Demand Versus Changes in Quantity Demanded

When the price of a product rises, consumers simply buy fewer units of that product. This is a movement along an existing demand curve. However, when one or more of the determinants change, the entire demand curve is altered. Now at any given price, consumers are willing to purchase more or less depending on the nature of the change. This section focuses on this important distinction between *changes in demand* versus *changes in quantity demanded.*

change in demand Occurs when one or more of the determinants of demand changes, shown as a shift in the entire demand curve.

Changes in demand occur whenever one or more of the determinants of demand change and demand curves shift. When demand changes, the demand curve shifts either to the right or to the left. Let's look at each shift in turn.

Demand increases when the entire demand curve shifts to the right. At all prices, consumers are willing to purchase more of the product in question. Figure 4 shows an increase in demand for computer games; the demand curve shifts from D_0 to D_1. Notice that more computer games are purchased at all prices along D_1 as compared to D_0.

Now look at a decrease in demand, when the entire demand curve shifts to the left. At all prices, consumers are willing to purchase less of the product in question. A drop in consumer income is normally associated with a decrease in demand (the demand curve shifts to the left, as from D_0 to D_2 in Figure 4).

change in quantity demanded Occurs when the price of the product changes, shown as a movement along an existing demand curve.

Whereas a change in demand can be brought about by many different factors, a **change in quantity demanded** can be caused by only one thing: *a change in product price.* This is shown in Figure 4 as a reduction in price from \$80 to \$40, resulting in sales (quantity demanded) increasing from 20 (point *a*) to 40 (point *c*) games. This distinction between a change in demand and a change in quantity demanded is important. Reducing price to increase sales is different from spending a few million dollars on Super Bowl advertising to increase sales at all prices.

These concepts are so important that a quick summary is in order. As Figure 4 illustrates, given the initial demand D_0, increasing sales from 20 to 40 games can occur in

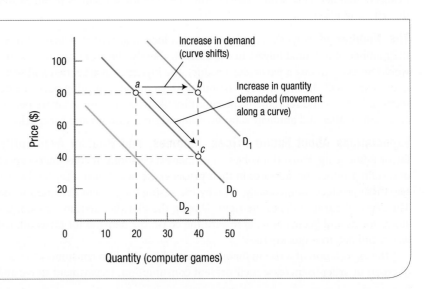

FIGURE 4

Changes in Demand Versus Changes in Quantity Demanded

A shift in the demand curve from D_0 to D_1 represents an *increase in demand,* and consumers will buy more of the product at each price. A shift from D_0 to D_2 reflects a *decrease in demand.* Movement along D_0 from point *a* to point *c* indicates an *increase in quantity demanded;* this type of movement can only be caused by a change in the price of the product.

either of two ways. First, changing a determinant (say, increasing advertising) could shift the demand curve to D_1 so that 40 games would be sold at $80 (point *b*). Alternatively, 40 games could be sold by reducing the price to $40 (point *c*). Selling more by increasing advertising causes an increase in demand, or a shift in the entire demand curve. Simply reducing the price, on the other hand, causes an increase in quantity demanded, or a movement along the existing demand curve, D_0, from point *a* to point *c*.

 CHECKPOINT

DEMAND

- A person's willingness-to-pay is the maximum amount she or he values a good to be worth at a particular moment in time and is the building block for demand.

- Demand refers to the quantity of products people are willing and able to purchase at various prices during some specific time period, all other relevant factors being held constant.

- The law of demand states that price and quantity demanded have an inverse (negative) relation: As price rises, consumers buy fewer units; as price falls, consumers buy more units. It is depicted as a downward-sloping demand curve.

- Demand curves shift when one or more of the determinants of demand change.

- The determinants of demand are consumer tastes and preferences, income, prices of substitutes and complements, the number of buyers in a market, and expectations about future prices, incomes, and product availability.

- A shift of a demand curve is a *change in demand*, and occurs when a determinant of demand changes.

- A *change in quantity demanded* occurs only when the price of a product changes, leading consumers to adjust their purchases along the existing demand curve.

QUESTIONS: Sales of electric plug-in hybrid cars are on the rise. The Chevrolet Volt is selling well, despite being priced almost double that of similar-sized gasoline-only cars in Chevrolet's line. Other manufacturers are adding plug-in hybrids to their lines at an astonishing pace. What has been the cause of the rising sales of plug-in hybrids? Is this an increase in demand or an increase in quantity demanded?

Answers to the Checkpoint questions can be found at the end of this chapter.

Supply

The analysis of a market economy rests on two foundations: supply and demand. So far, we've covered the demand side of the market. Let's focus now on the decisions businesses make regarding production numbers and sales. These decisions cause variations in product supply.

The Relationship Between Quantity Supplied and Price

Supply is the maximum amount of a product that producers are willing and able to offer for sale at various prices, all other relevant factors being held constant. The quantity supplied will vary according to the price of the product.

What explains this relationship? As we saw in the previous chapter, businesses inevitably encounter rising opportunity costs as they attempt to produce more and more of a product. This is due in part to diminishing returns from available resources, and in part to the fact that when producers increase production, they must either have existing workers put in overtime (at a higher hourly pay rate) or hire additional workers away from other industries (again at premium pay).

Producing more units, therefore, makes it more expensive to produce each individual unit. These increasing costs give rise to the positive relationship between product price and quantity supplied to the market.

supply The maximum amount of a product that sellers are willing and able to provide for sale over some time period at various prices, holding all other relevant factors constant (the *ceteris paribus* condition).

The Law of Supply

law of supply Holding all other relevant factors constant, as price increases, quantity supplied will rise, and as price declines, quantity supplied will fall.

Unfortunately for producers, they can rarely charge whatever they would like for their products; they must charge whatever the market will permit. But producers can decide how much of their product to produce and offer for sale. The **law of supply** states that higher prices will lead producers to offer more of their products for sale during a given period. Conversely, if prices fall, producers will offer fewer products to the market. The explanation is simple: The higher the price, the greater the potential for higher profits and thus the greater the incentive for businesses to produce and sell more products. Also, given the rising opportunity costs associated with increasing production, producers need to charge these higher prices to increase the quantity supplied profitably.

The Supply Curve

supply curve A graphical illustration of the law of supply, which shows the relationship between the price of a good and the quantity supplied.

Just as demand curves graphically display the law of demand, **supply curves** provide a graphical representation of the law of supply. The supply curve shows the maximum amounts of a product a producer will furnish at various prices during a given period of time. While the demand curve slopes *down* and to the right, the supply curve slopes *up* and to the right.[1] This illustrates the positive relationship between price and quantity supplied: the higher the price, the greater the quantity supplied.

Market Supply Curves

As with demand, economists are more interested in market supply than in the supplies offered by individual firms. To compute market supply, use the same method used to calculate market demand, horizontally summing the supplies of individual producers. A hypothetical market supply curve for computer games is depicted in Figure 5. The quantity of computer games that producers will offer for sale increases as the price of computer games rises. The opposite would happen if the price of computer games falls.

FIGURE 5

Supply of Computer Games

This supply curve graphs the supply schedule and shows the maximum quantity of computer games that producers will offer for sale over some defined period of time. The supply curve is positively sloped, reflecting the law of supply. In other words, as prices rise, quantity supplied increases; as prices fall, quantity supplied falls.

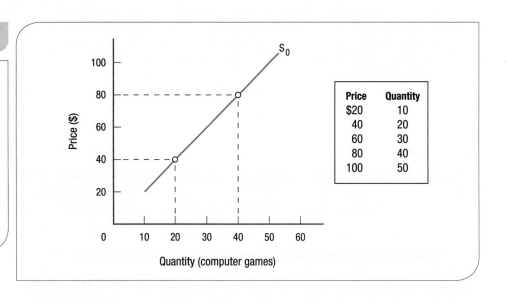

Price	Quantity
$20	10
40	20
60	30
80	40
100	50

Determinants of Supply

determinants of supply Nonprice factors that affect supply, including production technology, costs of resources, prices of other commodities, expectations, number of sellers, and taxes and subsidies.

Like demand, several nonprice factors help to determine the supply of a product. Specifically, there are six **determinants of supply:** (1) production technology, (2) costs of resources, (3) prices of other commodities, (4) expectations, (5) the number of sellers (producers) in the market, and (6) taxes and subsidies.

---

[1] There are some exceptions to positively sloping supply curves. But for our purposes, we will ignore them for now.

Production Technology Technology determines how much output can be produced from given quantities of resources. If a factory's equipment is old and can turn out only 50 units of output per hour, then no matter how many other resources are employed, those 50 units are the most the factory can produce in an hour. If the factory is outfitted with newer, more advanced equipment capable of turning out 100 units per hour, the firm can supply more of its product at the same price as before, or even at a lower price. In Figure 6, this would be represented by a shift in the supply curve from S_0 to S_1. At every single price, more would be supplied.

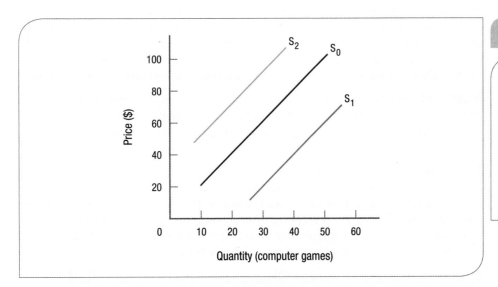

FIGURE 6

Shifts in the Supply Curve
The supply of computer games originally is S_0. If supply shifts to S_1, producers are willing to sell more at *all* prices. If supply falls, supply shifts leftward to S_2. Now firms are willing to sell less at each price. When a determinant of supply changes, the *entire* supply curve shifts.

Technology further determines the nature of products that can be supplied to the market. A hundred years ago, the supply of computers on the market was zero because computers did not yet exist. More recent advances in microprocessing and miniaturization brought a wide array of products to the market that were not available just a few years ago, including mini-tablets, auto engines that go 100,000 miles between tune-ups, and constant-monitoring insulin pumps that automatically keep a diabetic patient's glucose levels under control.

Costs of Resources Resource costs clearly affect production costs and supply. If resources such as raw materials or labor become more expensive, production costs will rise and supply will be reduced (the supply curve shifts to the left, from S_0 to S_2 in Figure 6). The reverse is true if resource costs drop (the supply curve shifts to the right, from S_0 to S_1). The growing power of microchips along with their falling cost has resulted in cheap and plentiful electronics and computers. Nanotechnology—manufacturing processes that fashion new products through the combination of individual atoms—may soon usher in a whole new generation of inexpensive products.

On the other hand, if the cost of petroleum goes up, the cost of products using petroleum in their manufacture will go up, leading to the supply being reduced (the supply curve shifts leftward). If labor costs rise because immigration is restricted, this drives up production costs of California vegetables (fewer farmworkers) and software in Silicon Valley (fewer software engineers from abroad) and leads to a shift in the supply curve to the left in Figure 6.

Prices of Other Commodities Most firms have some flexibility in the portfolio of goods they produce. A vegetable farmer, for example, might be able to grow celery or radishes, or some combination of the two. Given this flexibility, a change in the price of one item may influence the quantity of other items brought to market. If the price of celery should rise, for instance, most farmers will start growing more celery. And since they all have a limited amount of land on which to grow vegetables, this reduces the quantity of radishes they can produce. Hence, in this case, the rise in the price of celery may well cause a reduction in the supply of radishes (the supply curve for radishes shifts leftward).

Expectations The effects of future expectations on market supplies can be confusing, but it need not be. When sellers expect prices of a good to rise in the future, they are likely to restrict their supply in the current period in anticipation of receiving higher prices in some future period. Examples include homes and stocks—if you believe prices are going up, you'd be less likely to sell today, which decreases the supply of such goods (supply shifts to the left). Similarly, expectations of price reductions can increase supply as sellers try to sell off their inventories before prices drop (supply shifts to the right).

Eventually, if prices do rise in the next period, producers would increase the quantity supplied of the good; however, this would be due to the law of supply, not due to a shift of the supply curve. In other words, rising prices result in a movement along the supply curve. Only when producers anticipate a change in a future price, causing a reaction now, does supply shift.

Number of Sellers Everything else being held constant, if the number of sellers in a particular market increases, the market supply of their product increases. It is no great mystery why: Ten dim sum chefs can produce more dumplings in a given period than five dim sum chefs.

Taxes and Subsidies For businesses, taxes and subsidies affect costs. An increase in taxes (property, excise, or other fees) will shift supply to the left and reduce it. Subsidies are the opposite of taxes. If the government subsidizes the production of a product, supply will shift to the right and rise. A proposed new tax on expensive health care insurance plans may reduce supply (the tax is equivalent to an increase in production costs), while today's subsidies to ethanol producers expand ethanol production.

Changes in Supply Versus Changes in Quantity Supplied

A **change in supply** results from a change in one or more of the determinants of supply; it causes the entire supply curve to shift. An increase in supply of a product, perhaps because advancing technology has made it cheaper to produce, means that more of the commodity will be offered for sale at every price. This causes the supply curve to shift to the right, as illustrated in Figure 7 by the shift from S_0 to S_1. A decrease in supply, conversely, shifts the supply curve to the left, since fewer units of the product are offered at every price. Such a decrease in supply is here represented by the shift from S_0 to S_2.

A change in supply involves a shift of the entire supply curve. In contrast, the supply curve does not move when there is a **change in quantity supplied.** Only a change in the price of a product can cause a change in the quantity supplied; hence, it involves a

change in supply Occurs when one or more of the determinants of supply change, shown as a shift in the entire supply curve.

change in quantity supplied Occurs when the price of the product changes, shown as a movement along an existing supply curve.

FIGURE 7

Changes in Supply Versus Changes in Quantity Supplied

A shift in the supply curve from S_0 to S_1 represents an *increase in supply,* because businesses are willing to offer more of the product to consumers at *all* prices. A shift from S_0 to S_2 reflects a decrease in supply. A movement along S_0 from point *a* to point *c* represents an *increase in quantity supplied;* it results from an increase in the product's market price from $40 to $80.

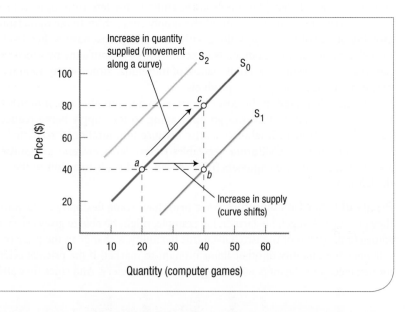

movement along an existing supply curve rather than a shift to an entirely different curve. In Figure 7, for example, an increase in price from $40 to $80 results in an increase in quantity supplied from 20 to 40 games, represented by the movement from point *a* to point *c* along S_0.

In summary, a change in supply is represented in Figure 7 by the shift from S_0 to S_1 or S_2, which involves a shift in the entire supply curve. For example, an increase in supply from S_0 to S_1 results in an increase in supply from 20 computer games (point *a*) to 40 (point *b*) provided at a price of $40. More games are provided at the same price. In contrast, a change in quantity supplied is shown in Figure 7 as a movement along an existing supply curve, S_0, from point *a* to point *c* caused by an increase in the price of the product from $40 to $80.

As on the demand side, this distinction between changes in supply and changes in quantity supplied is crucial. It means that when a product's price changes, only quantity supplied changes—the supply curve does not move. A summary of the determinants for both supply and demand is shown in Figure 8.

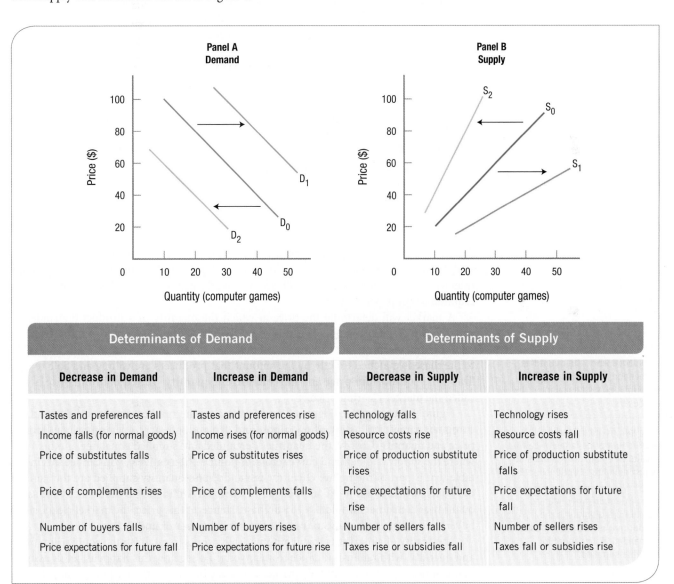

Determinants of Demand		Determinants of Supply	
Decrease in Demand	**Increase in Demand**	**Decrease in Supply**	**Increase in Supply**
Tastes and preferences fall	Tastes and preferences rise	Technology falls	Technology rises
Income falls (for normal goods)	Income rises (for normal goods)	Resource costs rise	Resource costs fall
Price of substitutes falls	Price of substitutes rises	Price of production substitute rises	Price of production substitute falls
Price of complements rises	Price of complements falls	Price expectations for future rise	Price expectations for future fall
Number of buyers falls	Number of buyers rises	Number of sellers falls	Number of sellers rises
Price expectations for future fall	Price expectations for future rise	Taxes rise or subsidies fall	Taxes fall or subsidies rise

Summary of Changes in Demand and Supply and Their Determinants

Various factors cause a market demand curve to shift to the left (decrease in demand) or shift to the right (increase in demand) in panel A. Similarly, various factors cause a market supply curve to shift to the left (decrease in supply) or shift to the right (increase in supply) in panel B. The table summarizes the factors influencing demand and supply shifts.

FIGURE 8

● CHECKPOINT

SUPPLY

- Supply is the quantity of a product producers are willing and able to put on the market at various prices, all other relevant factors being held constant.
- The law of supply reflects the positive relationship between price and quantity supplied: the higher the market price, the more goods supplied, and the lower the market price, the fewer goods supplied.
- As with demand, market supply is arrived at by horizontally summing the individual supplies of all of the firms in the market.
- A change in supply occurs when one or more of the determinants of supply change.
- The determinants of supply are production technology, the cost of resources, prices of other commodities, expectations, the numbers of sellers or producers in the market, and taxes and subsidies.
- A *change in supply* is a shift in the supply curve. A shift to the right reflects an increase in supply, while a shift to the left represents a decrease in supply.
- A *change in quantity supplied* is only caused by a change in the price of the product; it results in a movement along the existing supply curve.

QUESTIONS: At the end of the term, bookstores often increase the prices offered to students for their used textbooks in order to stock their shelves for the following term. Would an increase in the buyback price affect the supply or the quantity supplied of used textbooks? Suppose an unusually difficult professor leads to many students having to retake the course the next term. How might this affect the supply for used textbooks?

Answers to the Checkpoint questions can be found at the end of this chapter.

➡ Market Equilibrium

Supply and demand together determine the prices and quantities of goods bought and sold. Neither factor alone is sufficient to determine price and quantity. It is through their interaction that supply and demand do their work, just as two blades of a scissors are required to cut paper.

A market will determine the price at which the quantity of a product demanded is equal to the quantity supplied. At this price, the market is said to be cleared or to be in **equilibrium,** meaning that the amount of the product that consumers are willing and able to purchase is matched exactly by the amount that producers are willing and able to sell. This is the **equilibrium price** and the **equilibrium quantity.** The equilibrium price is also called the market-clearing price.

Figure 9 puts together Figures 2 and 5, showing the market supply and demand for computer games. It illustrates how supply and demand interact to determine equilibrium price and quantity. Clearly, the quantities demanded and supplied equal one another only where the supply and demand curves cross, at point *e.* Alternatively, you can see this in the table that is part of the figure: Quantity demanded and quantity supplied are the same at only one particular point. At $60 per game, sellers are willing to provide exactly the same quantity as consumers would like to purchase. Hence, at this price, the market clears, since buyers and sellers both want to transact the same number of units.

The beauty of a market is that it automatically works to establish the equilibrium price and quantity, without any guidance from anyone. To see how this happens, let us assume that computer games are initially priced at $80, a price above their equilibrium price. As we can see by comparing points *a* and *b,* sellers are willing to supply more games at this price than consumers are willing to buy. Economists characterize such a situation as one of excess supply, or **surplus.** In this case, at $80, sellers supply 40 games to the market (point *b*), yet buyers want to purchase only 20 (point *a*). This leaves an excess of 20 games overhanging the market; these unsold games ultimately become surplus inventories.

---

equilibrium Market forces are in balance when the quantities demanded by consumers just equal the quantities supplied by producers.

equilibrium price Market equilibrium price is the price that results when quantity demanded is just equal to quantity supplied.

equilibrium quantity Market equilibrium quantity is the output that results when quantity demanded is just equal to quantity supplied.

surplus Occurs when the price is above market equilibrium, and quantity supplied exceeds quantity demanded.

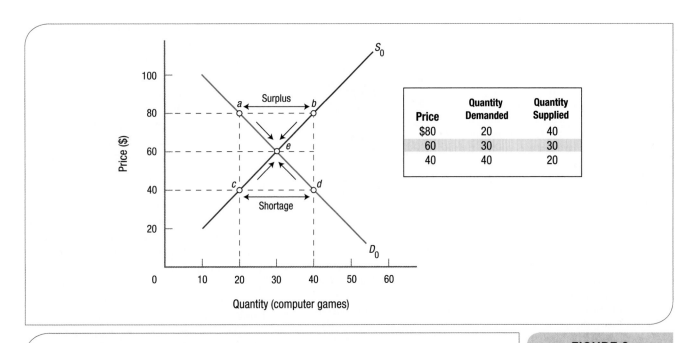

Equilibrium Price and Quantity of Computer Games

Market equilibrium is achieved when quantity demanded and quantity supplied are equal. In this graph, that equilibrium occurs at point e, at an equilibrium price of $60 and an equilibrium output of 30. If the market price is above equilibrium ($80), a surplus of 20 computer games will result (b − a), and market forces would drive the price back down to $60. When the market price is too low ($40), a shortage of 20 computer games will result (d − c), and businesses will raise the offering prices until equilibrium is again restored.

FIGURE 9

Here is where the market kicks in to restore equilibrium. As inventories rise, most firms cut production. Some firms, moreover, start reducing their prices to increase sales. Other firms must then cut their own prices to remain competitive. This process continues, with firms cutting their prices and production, until most firms have managed to exhaust their surplus inventories. This happens when prices reach $60 and quantity supplied equals 30, because consumers are once again willing to buy up the entire quantity supplied at this price, and the market is restored to equilibrium.

In general, therefore, when prices are set too high, surpluses result, which drive prices back down to their equilibrium levels. If, conversely, a price is initially set too low, say at $40, a **shortage** results. In this case, buyers want to purchase 40 games (point d), but sellers are only providing 20 (point c), creating a shortage of 20 games. Because consumers are willing to pay more than $40 to obtain the few games available on the market, they will start bidding up the price of computer games. Sensing an opportunity to make some money, firms will start raising their prices and increasing production once again until equilibrium is restored. Hence, in general, excess demand causes firms to raise prices and increase production.

When there is a shortage in a market, economists speak of a tight market or a seller's market. Under these conditions, producers have no difficulty selling off all their output. When a surplus of goods floods the market, this gives rise to a buyer's market, because buyers can buy all the goods they want at attractive prices.

We have now seen how changing prices naturally works to clear up shortages and surpluses, thereby returning markets to equilibrium. Some markets, once disturbed, will return to equilibrium quickly. Examples include the stock, bond, and money markets, where trading is nearly instantaneous and extensive information abounds. Other markets react very slowly. Consider the labor market, for instance. When workers lose their jobs due to a plant closing, most will search for new jobs that pay at least as much as that at their previous jobs. Some

shortage Occurs when the price is below market equilibrium, and quantity demanded exceeds quantity supplied.

ALFRED MARSHALL (1842-1924)

British economist Alfred Marshall is considered the father of the modern theory of supply and demand—that price and output are determined by both supply *and* demand. He noted that the two go together like the blades of a scissors that cross at equilibrium. He assumed that changes in quantity demanded were only affected by changes in price, and that all other factors remained constant. Marshall also is credited with developing the ideas of the laws of demand and supply, and the concepts of consumer surplus and producer surplus—concepts we will study in the next chapter.

With financial help from this uncle, Marshall attended St. John's College, Cambridge, to study mathematics and physics. However after long walks through the poorest sections of several European cities and seeing their horrible conditions, he decided to focus his attention on political economy.

In 1890, he published *Principles of Economics*. In it he introduced many new ideas, though he would never boast about them as being novel. In hopes of appealing to the general public, Marshall buried his diagrams in footnotes. And, although he is credited with many economic theories, he would always clarify them with various exceptions and qualifications. He expected future economists to flesh out his ideas.

Above all, Marshall loved teaching and his students. His lectures were known to never be orderly or systematic because he tried to get students to think *with* him and ultimately think for themselves. At one point near the turn of the twentieth century, essentially all of the leading economists in England had been his students. More than anyone else, Marshall is given credit for establishing economics as a discipline of study. He died in 1924.

Sources: E. Ray Canterbery *A Brief History of Economics: Artful Approaches to the Dismal Science* (Hackensack, New Jersey: World Scientific), 2001; Robert Skidelsky, *John Maynard Keynes: Volume 2, The Economist as Saviour 1920–1937* (New York: Penguin Press), 1992; and John Maynard Keynes, *Essays in Biography* (New York: Norton), 1951.

will be successful, while others might struggle, having to settle for a lower paying position after a long job search. Similarly, real estate markets can be slow to adjust because sellers will often refuse to accept a price below what they are asking, until the lack of sales over time convinces sellers to adjust the price downward.

These automatic market adjustments can make some buyers and sellers feel uncomfortable: It seems as if prices and quantities are being set by forces beyond anyone's control. In fact, this phenomenon is precisely what makes market economies function so efficiently. Without anyone needing to be in control, prices and quantities naturally gravitate toward equilibrium levels. Adam Smith was so impressed by the workings of the market that he suggested that it is almost as if an "invisible hand" guides the market to equilibrium.

Given the self-correcting nature of the market, long-term shortages or surpluses are almost always the result of government intervention, as we will see in the next chapter. First, however, we turn to a discussion of how the market responds to changes in supply and demand, or to shifts of the supply and demand curves.

Moving to a New Equilibrium: Changes in Supply and Demand

Once a market is in equilibrium and the forces of supply and demand balance one another out, the market will remain there unless an external factor changes. But when the supply curve or demand curve shifts (some determinant changes), equilibrium also shifts, resulting in a new equilibrium price and/or output. The ability to predict new equilibrium points is one of the most useful aspects of supply and demand analysis.

Predicting the New Equilibrium When One Curve Shifts When only supply or only demand changes, the change in equilibrium price and equilibrium output can be predicted. We begin with changes in supply.

Changes in Supply Figure 10 shows what happens when supply changes. Equilibrium initially is at point *e*, with equilibrium price and quantity at $9 and 30, respectively. But let us assume that a rise in wages or the bankruptcy of a key business in the market (the number of sellers falls) causes a decrease in supply. When supply declines (the supply curve shifts from S_0 to S_2), equilibrium price rises to $12, while equilibrium output falls to 20 (point *a*).

If, on the other hand, supply increases (the supply curve shifts from S_0 to S_1), equilibrium price falls to $6, while equilibrium output rises to 40 (point *b*). This is what has happened in the electronics industry: Falling production costs have resulted in more electronic products being sold at lower prices.

We can predict how equilibrium price and quantity will change when supply changes. When supply increases, equilibrium price will fall and output will rise; when supply decreases, equilibrium price will rise and output will fall.

Changes in Demand The effects of demand changes are shown in Figure 11. Again, equilibrium is initially at point *e,* with equilibrium price and quantity at $9 and 30, respectively. But let us assume that the economy then enters a recession and incomes

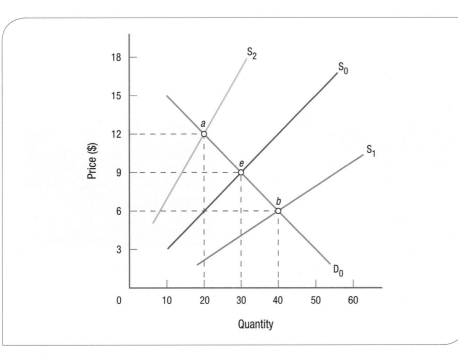

FIGURE 10

Equilibrium Price, Output, and Shifts in Supply

When supply alone shifts, the effects on both equilibrium price and output can be predicted. When supply grows (S_0 to S_1), equilibrium price will fall and output will rise. When supply declines (S_0 to S_2), the opposite happens: Equilibrium price will rise and output will fall.

sink, or perhaps the price of some complementary good soars; in either case, demand falls. As demand decreases (the demand curve shifts from D_0 to D_2), equilibrium price falls to $6, while equilibrium output falls to 20 (point *a*).

During the same recession just described, the demand for inferior goods (beans and bologna) will rise, as falling incomes force people to switch to less expensive substitutes. For these products, as demand increases (shifting the demand curve from D_0 to D_1), equilibrium price rises to $12, and equilibrium output grows to 40 (point *b*).

Like changes in supply, we can predict how equilibrium price and quantity will change when demand changes. When demand increases, both equilibrium price and output will rise; when demand decreases, both equilibrium price and output will fall.

Sergey Kashkin/iStockphoto

Truffles, a mushroom-like delicacy, can easily fetch over a $1,000 per pound, due to their scarce supply. Truffles grow in the wild and generally are found using trained dogs. But along with limited supply, demand for truffles has increased among foodies, putting upward pressure on their prices.

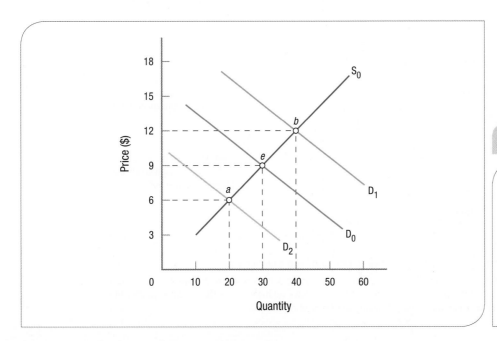

FIGURE 11

Equilibrium Price, Output, and Shifts in Demand

When demand alone changes, the effects on both equilibrium price and output can again be determined. When demand grows (D_0 to D_1), both price and output rise. Conversely, when demand falls (D_0 to D_2), both price and output fall.

ISSUE

Two-Buck Chuck: Will People Drink $2-a-Bottle Wine?

The great California wines of the 1990s put California vineyards on the map. Demand, prices, and exports grew rapidly. Overplanting of new grapevines was a result. When driving along Interstate 5 or Highway 101 north of Los Angeles, one can see vineyards extending for miles, and most were planted in the mid- to late 1990s. The 2001 recession reduced the demand for California wine, and a rising dollar made imported wine relatively cheaper. The result was a sharp drop in demand for California wine and a huge surplus of grapes.

Bronco Wine Company president Fred Franzia made an exclusive deal with Trader Joe's, an unusual supermarket that features exotic food and wine products. He bought the excess grapes at distressed prices, and in his company's modern plant produced inex-

pensive wines—chardonnay, merlot, cabernet sauvignon, shiraz, and sauvignon blanc—under the Charles Shaw label. Consumers flocked to Trader Joe's for wine costing $1.99 a bottle and literally hauled cases of wine out by the carload. In less than a decade, 400 million bottles of Two-Buck Chuck, as it is known, have been sold. This is not rotgut: The 2002 shiraz beat out 2,300 other wines to win a double gold medal at the 28th Annual International Eastern Wine Competition in 2004. Still, to many Napa Valley vintners it is known as Two-Buck Upchuck.

Two-Buck Chuck was such a hit that other supermarkets were forced to offer their own discount wines. This good, low-priced wine has had the effect of opening up markets. People who previously avoided wine because of the cost have begun

drinking more. However, the influence of Two-Buck Chuck, which sold 60 million bottles in 2012, may be waning. In January 2013, Trader Joe's announced an increase in the price of the Two-Buck Chuck from $1.99 to $2.49 due to a poor grape harvest that raised the cost of producing the wine. Although the new price is still a bargain, the product that changed the wine industry may soon need another name.

Predicting the New Equilibrium When Both Curves Shift When both supply and demand change, things get tricky. We can predict what will happen with price in some cases and output in other cases, but not what will happen with both.

Figure 12 portrays an increase in both demand and supply. Consider the market for corn. Suppose that an increase in corn-based ethanol production causes demand for corn

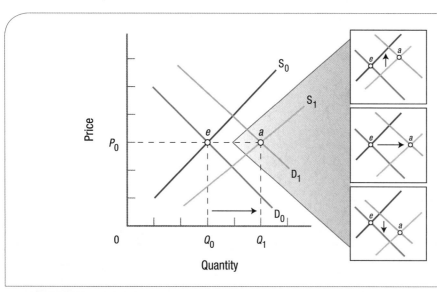

	Price increases because the increase in demand exceeds the increase in supply.
	Price remains the same because the increase in demand is the same as the increase in supply.
	Price decreases because the increase in demand is less than the increase in supply.

FIGURE 12

Increase in Supply, Increase in Demand, and Equilibrium

When both demand and supply increase, output will clearly rise, but what happens to the new equilibrium price is uncertain. If demand grows relatively more than supply, price will rise, but if supply grows relatively more than demand, price will fall.

The Effect of Changes in Demand or Supply on Equilibrium Prices and Quantities				TABLE 1
	Change in Demand	**Change in Supply**	**Change in Equilibrium Price**	**Change in Equilibrium Quantity**
One Curve Shifting	No change	Increase	Decrease	Increase
	No change	Decrease	Increase	Decrease
	Increase	No change	Increase	Increase
	Decrease	No change	Decrease	Decrease
Both Curves Shifting	Increase	Increase	Indeterminate	Increase
	Decrease	Decrease	Indeterminate	Decrease
	Increase	Decrease	Increase	Indeterminate
	Decrease	Increase	Decrease	Indeterminate

to increase. Meanwhile, suppose that bioengineering results in a new corn hybrid that uses less fertilizer and generates 50% higher yields, causing supply to also increase. When demand increases from D_0 to D_1 and supply increases from S_0 to S_1, output grows to Q_1 as shown in the left panel.

But what happens to the price of corn is not so clear. If demand and supply grow the same, output increases but price remains at P_0 (also captured in the middle panel to the right). If demand grows relatively more than supply, the new equilibrium price will be higher (top panel on the right). Conversely, if demand grows relatively less than supply, the new equilibrium price will be lower (bottom panel on the right). Figure 12 is just one of the four possibilities when both supply and demand change. The other three possibilities are shown in Table 1 along with the four possibilities when just one curve shifts. When only one curve shifts, the direction of change in equilibrium price and quantity is certain. But when both curves shift, the direction of change in either the equilibrium price or quantity will be indeterminate.

CHECKPOINT

MARKET EQUILIBRIUM

- Together, supply and demand determine market equilibrium, which occurs when the quantity supplied exactly equals quantity demanded.

- The equilibrium price is also called the market-clearing price.

- When quantity demanded exceeds quantity supplied, a shortage occurs and prices are bid up toward equilibrium. When quantity supplied exceeds quantity demanded, a surplus occurs and prices are pushed down toward equilibrium.

- When supply and demand change, equilibrium price and output change.

- When only one curve shifts, the resulting changes in equilibrium price and quantity can be predicted.

- When both curves shift, we can predict the change in equilibrium price in some cases or the change in equilibrium quantity in others, but never both. We have to determine the relative magnitudes of the shifts before we can predict both equilibrium price and quantity.

QUESTIONS: As China and India (both with huge populations and rapidly growing economies) continue to develop, what do you think will happen to their demand for energy, and specifically oil? What will suppliers of oil do in the face of this demand? Will this have an impact on world energy (oil) prices? What sort of policies or events could alter your forecast about the future price of oil?

Answers to the Checkpoint questions can be found at the end of this chapter.

chapter summary

Section 1: **Markets**

A **market** is an institution that enables buyers and sellers to interact and transact with one another.

Corbis/SuperStock

Stars and Stripes/Alamy

Markets can be as simple as a lemonade stand, as large as an automobile lot, as valuable as the stock market, as virtual as an Internet shopping site, or as illegal as a ticket scalping operation.

Buyers and sellers communicate their desires in a market through the prices at which goods and services are bought and sold. Hence, a market economy is called a **price system.**

Robert Harding World Imagery/Corbis

Section 2: **Demand**

Demand refers to the goods and services people are willing and able to buy during a period of time. It is a horizontal summation of individual demand curves in a defined market.

Price / Quantity

D

The **law of demand** states that as prices increase, quantity demanded falls, and vice versa, resulting in downward-sloping demand.

A Common Confusion in Terminology:

A "change in demand" is a shift of the entire demand curve and is caused by a change in a nonprice demand factor.

A "change in quantity demanded" is a movement from one point to another on the same demand curve, and is caused only by a change in price.

Price / Quantity

Price / Quantity

Alan Schein Photography/Corbis

Roller coasters are a lot of fun, but riding the same one over and over gives less satisfaction with each ride; therefore, willingness-to-pay falls with each ride.

Determinants of Demand: How Demand Curves Shift

- ↑ Tastes and preferences: Demand shifts right.
- ↑ Income: Demand for normal goods shifts right, while demand for inferior goods shifts left.
- ↑ Price of substitutes: Demand shifts right.
- ↑ Price of complements: Demand shifts left.
- ↑ Number of buyers: Demand shifts right.
- ↑ Price expectations: Demand shifts right.

Bryan Smith/ZUMA Press/Newscom

When investors expect stock prices to increase, demand for stock increases.

Section 3: Supply

Supply analysis works the same way as demand, but looking at the market from the firm's point of view.

Philip Gostelow/Aurora Photos/Corbis

The **law of supply** states that as prices increase, firms want to supply more, and vice versa. It leads to an upward-sloping supply curve.

Determinants of Supply: How Supply Curves Shift

- ↑ Production technology: Supply shifts right.
- ↑ Cost of resources: Supply shifts left.
- ↑ Price of other commodities: Supply shifts left.
- ↑ Price expectations: Supply shifts left.
- ↑ Number of sellers: Supply shifts right.
- ↑ Taxes: Supply shifts left.
- ↑ Subsidies: Supply shifts right.

Section 4: Market Equilibrium

Market equilibrium occurs at the price at which the quantity supplied is equal to quantity demanded; in other words, where demand intersects supply.

 How does equilibrium change?

A shift in demand or supply will change equilibrium price and quantity.

Which curve slopes up and which slopes down? Two tricks to aid in memory:

- S"up"ply contains the word "up" for upward-sloping.
- Only the fingers on your right hand can make a "d" for demand. Hold that hand up in front of you!

Neil Emmerson/Robert Harding World Imagery/Corbis

Higher oil prices raise the cost of resins used to produce surfboards.

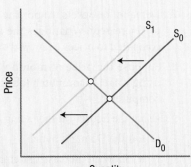

Summary of Demand and Supply Shifts on Equilibrium Price and Quantity:

D shifts right: P↑ Q↑
D shifts left: P↓ Q↓
S shifts right: P↓ Q↑
S shifts left: P↑ Q↓

Supply of surfboards shifts left, raising equilibrium price and lowering equilibrium quantity.

KEY CONCEPTS

QUESTIONS AND PROBLEMS

Check Your Understanding

1. Product prices give consumers and businesses a lot of information besides just the price. What kinds of information?

2. Describe the determinants of demand. Why are they important?

3. As the world population ages, will the demand for cholesterol drugs increase, decrease, or remain the same? Assume there is a positive relationship between aging and cholesterol levels. Would this cause a change in demand or a change in quantity demanded?

4. Describe some of the reasons why supply changes. Improved technology typically results in lower prices for most products. Why do you think this is true? Describe the difference between a change in supply and a change in quantity supplied.

5. If a strong economic recovery boosts average incomes, what would happen to the equilibrium price and quantity for a normal good? How about an inferior good?

6. Suppose the market for tomatoes is in equilibrium, and events occur that simultaneously shift both the demand and supply curves to the right. Is it possible to determine how the equilibrium price and/or quantity would change?

Apply the Concepts

7. Demand for tickets to sporting events such as the Super Bowl has increased. Has supply increased? What does the answer to this tell you about the price of these tickets compared to prices a few years ago?

8. Suppose the price of monthly data plans required to access the Internet anywhere using a tablet computer falls in price. How would this affect the market for tablet computers?

9. Using the figures on the facing page, answer the following questions:

   a. On the Demand panel:

      - Show an increase in demand and label it D_1.
      - Show a decrease in demand and label it D_2.
      - Show an increase in quantity demanded.

- Show a decrease in quantity demanded.
- What causes demand to change?
- What causes quantity demanded to change?

b. On the Supply panel:
- Show an increase in supply and label it S_1.
- Show a decrease in supply and label it S_2.
- Show an increase in quantity supplied.
- Show a decrease in quantity supplied.
- What causes supply to change?
- What causes quantity supplied to change?

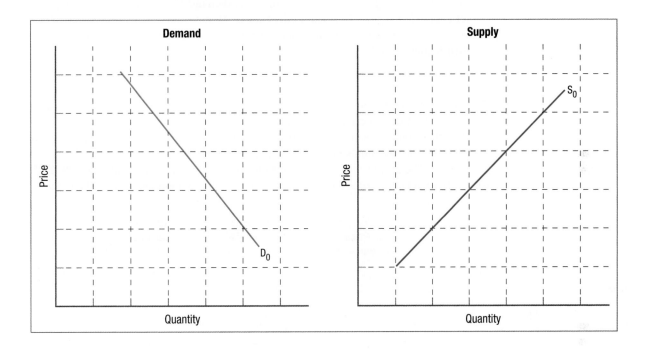

10. Several medical studies have shown that drinking red wine in moderation is good for the heart. How would such a study affect the public's demand for wine? Would it have an impact on the type of grapes planted in new vineyards?

11. Assume initially that the demand and supply for premium coffees (one-pound bags) are in equilibrium. Now assume Starbucks introduces the world to premium blends, and so demand rises substantially. Describe what will happen in this market as it moves to a new equilibrium. If a hard freeze eliminates Brazil's premium coffee crop, what will happen to the price of premium coffee?

12. Over the past decade, cruise ship companies have dramatically increased the number of mega-ships (those that carry 3,000 passengers or more), increasing the supply of cruises. At the same time, the popularity of cruising has increased among consumers, increasing demand. Explain how these two effects can coincide with a decrease in the average price of cruise travel.

In the News

13. In China, a small but increasing number of people are choosing to work as professional queuers, and exactly as it sounds, they are paid to wait in line for others. An NPR story in July 25, 2011, tells the story of a few professional queuers who earn about $3 an hour to wait in line, a wage that is about double that of the typical factory worker in China. Given that one can easily pay someone else to wait, what do you think will happen in the market for goods and services most prone to long waiting times, such as for concert tickets, the latest technology gadget, or low-cost apartments?

14. An August 12, 2011, article in *Time Magazine*, "As Regular Malls Struggle, Outlet Malls Are Booming," analyzed trends in how consumers shop, and found that more and more consumers are visiting outlet malls as a way to save money on name brand clothing and housewares. Given that most stores offer an outlet option, why would anyone choose to pay more at regular malls? Use supply and demand analysis to explain why prices differ between regular stores and outlet stores. Why would outlet stores be a strategic way for businesses to sell their unsold (surplus) goods instead of just offering a sale at their regular stores?

Solving Problems

15. The table below represents the world supply and demand for natural vanilla in thousands of pounds. A large portion of natural vanilla is grown in Madagascar and comes from orchids that require a lot of time to cultivate. The sequence of events described below actually happened, but the numbers have been altered to make the calculations easier. (See James Altucher, "Supply, Demand, and Edible Orchids," *Financial Times*, September 20, 2005, p. 12.) Assume the original supply and demand curves are represented in the table below.

Price ($/pound)	Quantity Demanded (thousands)	Quantity Supplied (thousands)
0	20	0
10	16	6
20	12	12
30	8	18
40	4	24
50	0	30

a. Graph both the supply (S_0) and demand (D_0) curves. What is the current equilibrium price? Label that point *a*.

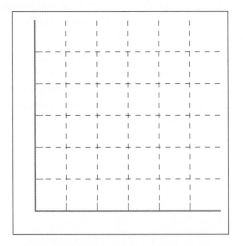

b. Assume that Madagascar is hit by a hurricane (which actually did happen in 2000), and the world's supply of vanilla is reduced by five-sixths, or 83%. Label the new supply curve (S_1). What will be the new equilibrium price in the market? Label that point *b*.

c. Now assume that Coca-Cola announces plans to introduce a new "Vanilla Coke," and this increases the demand for natural vanilla by 25%. Label the new demand curve (D_1). What will be the new equilibrium price? Label this new equilibrium point *c*. Remember that the supply of natural vanilla was reduced by the hurricane earlier.

d. Growing the orchids that produce natural vanilla requires a climate with roughly 80% humidity, and the possible grower countries generally fall within 20° north or south of the equator. A doubling of prices encouraged several other countries (e.g., Uganda and Indonesia) to begin growing orchids or increase their current production. Within several years, supply was back to normal (S_0), but by then, synthetic vanilla had replaced 80% of the original demand (D_0). Label this new demand curve (D_2). What is the new equilibrium price and output?

16. The following figure shows the supply and demand for strawberries. Answer the questions that follow.

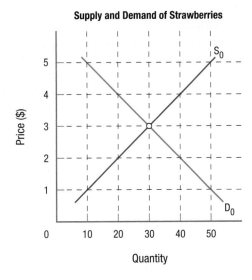

Supply and Demand of Strawberries

a. Indicate the equilibrium price and equilibrium quantity.

b. Suppose sellers try to sell strawberries at $4. How much of a shortage or a surplus of strawberries would result?

c. Now suppose that the demand for strawberries falls by ten units at every price. Draw the new demand curve in the figure, and estimate what the new equilibrium price and equilibrium quantity would be.

d. If sellers still try to sell strawberries at $4, would the shortage or the surplus increase or decrease?

USING THE NUMBERS

17. According to By the Numbers, about how many times larger is the bottled water market in the United States in the year 2012 compared to 1982?

18. According to By the Numbers, which of the following categories of college/university enrollment have risen from 1996 to 2012: public two year, public four year, private not-for-profit, private for-profit? Which of these categories have fallen in enrollment from 1996 to 2012?

Checkpoint: Markets

The market for financial securities is a huge, well-organized, and regulated market compared to local farmer's markets. Trillions of dollars change hands each week in the financial markets, and products are standardized.

Checkpoint: Demand

Rising gasoline prices, a general rise in environmental consciousness, and incentives (such as preferred parking and reduced tolls offered by some states) have caused the demand for plug-in hybrids to swell. This is a change in demand, because factors other than the price of the car itself have led to an increase in demand for such cars.

Checkpoint: Supply

A higher textbook buyback price would entice more students to sell their textbooks instead of keeping them. Because the price of the offer has increased, it results in an increase in the quantity supplied of used textbooks. If, however, many students are forced to retake a class, they would likely not sell their textbooks, hence the supply of used textbooks would shift to the left.

Checkpoint: Market Equilibrium

Demand for both energy and oil will increase. Suppliers of oil will attempt to move up their supply curve and provide more to the market. Because all of the easy (cheap) oil has already been found, costs to add to supplies will rise, and oil prices will gradually rise; in the longer term, alternatives will become more attractive, keeping oil prices from rising too rapidly.

Markets and Government

4

After studying this chapter you should be able to:

- Define the concepts of consumer surplus and producer surplus and explain how they are used to measure the benefits and costs of market transactions.

- Use consumer surplus and producer surplus to describe the gains from trade.

- Explain the causes of deadweight loss and how markets can mitigate them.

- Understand why markets sometimes fail to provide an optimal outcome.

- Describe what an effective price ceiling or price floor does to a market and how it creates shortages or surpluses.

- Determine the winners and losers when price ceilings and price floors are used.

Hamachi, Unagi, Ikura, Maguro, Toro. . . . Fish from an ocean halfway around the world to a dinner plate in a rural inland town highlights the ability of efficient markets to provide what consumers want.

Once an exotic food from the orient eaten by few outside Asia, sushi has become part of the American diet in all parts of the country, available in sushi bars, cafés, buffets, and even grocery stores. The popularity of sushi stems largely from the known health benefits of eating fish, providing omega-3-rich, low-fat, and low-calorie meals. But to have sushi, one must have access to fresh fish, not easy for those not living near a coastline. Or is it?

To provide fresh sushi to inland consumers, fish must be caught, flash frozen (to kill bacteria), then flown to destinations in a short period of time in order to maintain the fish's freshness. In some cases, fish is flown around the world to meet the demand. At the Tsukiji fish market in Tokyo, Japan, the largest fish market in the world, over 6 million pounds of fish are auctioned off *each morning* and then flown to wholesalers and restaurants around the globe.

Why would fishermen, fish markets, wholesalers, and restaurants go through so much trouble just to provide fresh sushi to customers in faraway places whom they will never meet? Because the market provides incentives for each person to do so. Every person in the supply chain for sushi acts in his or her own best interest by supplying what the market wants (as determined by the prices received for their goods), and that leads to an efficiently functioning market. Adam Smith's notion of the *invisible hand* works to ensure that, in a market society, consumers get what they want.

Everywhere we look in the world there are markets, and not just the big markets for fish or other major industries. Countless smaller markets dot our local landscapes, and many new virtual markets are springing up on the Internet. All play a similar role in terms of providing what consumers want, using prices as a way to signal the values placed on goods and services.

The previous chapter considered how supply and demand work together to determine the quantities of various products sold and the equilibrium prices consumers must pay for them in a market economy. The markets we have studied thus far have been stylized versions of competitive markets: They have featured many buyers and sellers, a uniform product, consumers and sellers who have complete information about the market, and few barriers to market entry or exit.

In this chapter, we start with this stylized competitive market and introduce tools for measuring the efficiency of competitive markets. We then apply these tools to reveal the gains from trade. We briefly consider some of the complexities inherent to most markets. The typical market does not meet all the criteria of a truly competitive market. That does not mean that the supply and demand analysis you just absorbed will not be useful in analyzing

BY THE NUMBERS

Price Controls and Supports in the Economy Today

Efficient markets are an essential part of modern societies. However, sometimes governments intervene in markets to address equity concerns. The use of price controls and price supports is a common way of intervening in markets, as the following illustrates.

Average difference between rent-controlled housing prices and market prices:

1. New York City—43%
2. San Francisco—41%
3. Washington, D.C.—30%
4. Los Angeles—26%

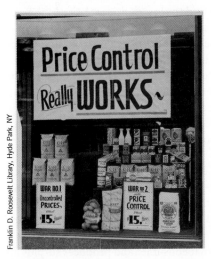

Franklin D. Roosevelt Library, Hyde Park, NY

World War II price controls.

States receiving the most federal telephone support in 2011:

1. Alaska: $280 million
2. Oklahoma: $235 million
3. Mississippi: $232 million
4. Louisiana: $152 million
5. Kansas: $142 million

States paying the most federal telephone support in 2011:

1. California: $326 million
2. Florida: $290 million
3. New York: $230 million
4. New Jersey: $175 million
5. Pennsylvania: $169 million

image100/SuperStock

Prices for telephone landlines in rural communities are capped below their cost, with the shortfall in revenues compensated for by a government program funded by all U.S. states, resulting in some states paying more than they receive in support and some states receiving more than they pay.

$7.25
The U.S. federal minimum wage (price floor) for workers over age 16 in 2013.

$11,176,000,000
Spending by the U.S. government in 2012 to maintain agricultural price floors.

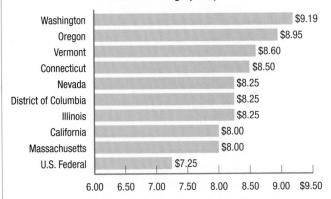

Minimum Wage (2013)

State	Wage
Washington	$9.19
Oregon	$8.95
Vermont	$8.60
Connecticut	$8.50
Nevada	$8.25
District of Columbia	$8.25
Illinois	$8.25
California	$8.00
Massachusetts	$8.00
U.S. Federal	$7.25

6.00 6.50 7.00 7.50 8.00 8.50 9.00 $9.50

Nine U.S. states have a statewide minimum wage of $8.00 per hour or more, significantly higher than the federal minimum wage of $7.25 per hour.

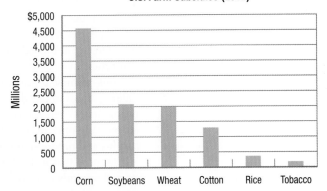

U.S. Farm Subsidies (2012)

Millions (y-axis: $5,000 / 4,500 / 4,000 / 3,500 / 3,000 / 2,500 / 2,000 / 1,500 / 1,000 / 500 / 0)

Corn Soybeans Wheat Cotton Rice Tobacco

Certain agricultural crops are protected by price supports (price floors), with the difference from their market prices paid by the U.S. government.

economic events. Often, however, you will need to temper your analysis to fit the specific conditions of the markets you study. Finally, we will look at what happens when government intervenes in markets.

Consumer and Producer Surplus: A Tool for Measuring Economic Efficiency

Suppose you find a rare comic book on eBay that you believe is worth $100, and start putting in bids hoping to buy it. After a week, you get the comic book with the winning bid of $80. You are happy because not only will you get the comic book you've been looking for, but you have paid a price lower than what you were willing to pay. However, you're likely not the only one who is happy. The person who sold you that comic book found it in her granddad's old trunk that she inherited, and had hoped to get at least $60 for it. In fact she ended up receiving more money than the minimum amount she had hoped to receive. In this situation, the transaction took place, and both the buyer and seller are better off.

When consumers go about their everyday shopping or when they seek out their next major purchase, their objective typically is to find the lowest price relative to the perceived value of the product. It is the reason why consumers compare prices, shop online, or bargain with sellers. In other words, the general goal of consumers is to find the product at a price no greater than their willingness-to-pay (perceived value); if the price is less, consumers benefit more. These "savings," so to speak, are referred to as **consumer surplus,** and are a measure of the net benefits consumers receive in the market.

Producers also have a corresponding objective. When an entrepreneur opens up a new business, her intention is to maximize its success by getting the highest price for a product relative to its cost for as large a quantity as possible. Sometimes this is achieved by selling fewer units at a higher markup (such as rare art), while other times it is achieved through the sale of mass quantities of products at relatively small markups (such as goods sold at Walmart). Regardless of the strategy used, the general goal of producers is to obtain a price at least equal to their willingness-to-sell; if the price is higher, producers benefit more. These gains are called **producer surplus,** and are a measure of the net benefits producers receive in the market.

Now that you have an intuitive sense of what consumer and producer surplus are, let's look more carefully into how they are measured. We begin with a single case of a buyer and a seller at a car dealership. Suppose you are the buyer, and you find a car that interests you. Let's assume that the most you would be willing to pay for that car is $20,000. In other words, you find the car to be worth $20,000, but paying that price would be the worst case scenario other than not buying the car at all. You would rather get a better deal by negotiating with the sales manager. But now let's look at the other side: Assume that the sales manager has a minimum price of $15,000 at which he is willing to sell the car. Selling the car at this price would be his worst case scenario other than not selling the car.

We have now determined a potential "gain" of $5,000 that can be shared by the buyer and seller depending on the final negotiated price for this car. Figure 1 shows this gain as the difference between the buyer's willingness-to-pay (WTP) and the seller's willingness-to-sell (WTS). Assume that the final negotiated price of the car is $17,200. We can now use this information to calculate consumer surplus (WTP − P = $20,000 − $17,200 = $2,800) and producer surplus (P − WTS = $17,200 − $15,000 = $2,200).

This example is unique in that the price of the car is negotiated between the buyer and seller. In most of our daily transactions, however, the prices of goods and services are not negotiated. When you go to the grocery store, all of the prices are fixed. You don't negotiate over the price of milk, bread, or chicken. Nonetheless, the measurements of consumer surplus and producer surplus remain the same when prices are fixed.

Suppose that instead of just one buyer and one seller, the market contains dozens or even thousands of buyers and sellers. What would change? Let's look at the market for Frisbees used in the popular intramural sport of Ultimate. First, each of the many buyers would have a different WTP, which would be represented as a downward-sloping demand curve (by definition, demand is just a collection of WTP of all consumers in a market).

consumer surplus The difference between market price and what consumers (as individuals or the market) would be willing to pay. It is equal to the area above market price and below the demand curve.

producer surplus The difference between market price and the price at which firms are willing to supply the product. It is equal to the area below market price and above the supply curve.

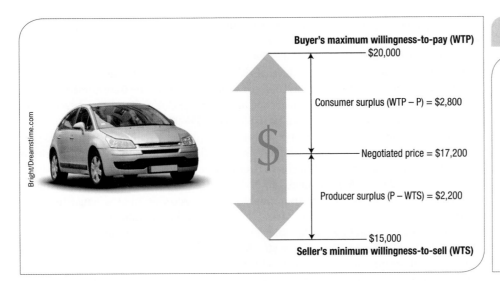

Buyer's maximum willingness-to-pay (WTP)
— $20,000

Consumer surplus (WTP – P) = $2,800

Negotiated price = $17,200

Producer surplus (P – WTS) = $2,200

— $15,000
Seller's minimum willingness-to-sell (WTS)

FIGURE 1

Willingness-to-Pay and Willingness-to-Sell

In a transaction with a single buyer and a single seller, consumer surplus ($2,800) is the difference between the maximum amount the buyer was willing to pay ($20,000) and the actual price paid ($17,200). Producer surplus ($2,200) is the difference between the actual price ($17,200) and the minimum amount the seller was willing to accept ($15,000).

Second, each of the many sellers would have a different WTS, which would be represented as an upward-sloping supply curve. But the definition of consumer surplus (WTP – P) and producer surplus (P – WTS) remains the same, except that now we apply it to the entire market. Figure 2 illustrates how consumer and producer surplus is determined in a small market for Frisbees with specific consumers and firms and for the overall market.

Panel A in Figure 2 represents a small market with 6 individual buyers and 6 individual sellers, with an equilibrium price of $6 (point *e*) at which 6 units of output are sold. In this market, Alanna has the highest willingness to pay, because she values a Frisbee to be worth $11. Because the market determines that $6 is the price everyone pays, Alanna clearly gets a

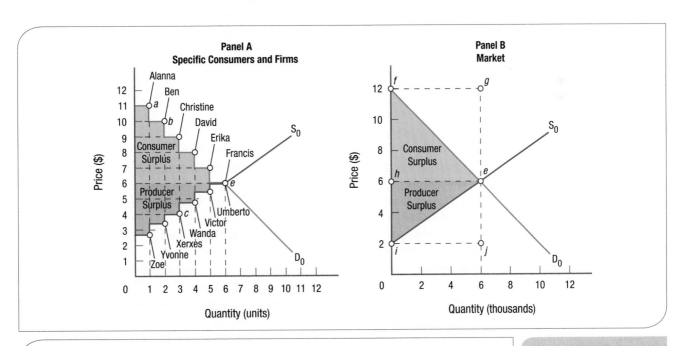

Consumer and Producer Surplus

Panel B shows a market consisting of many more of the specific consumers and firms shown in panel A. This market determines equilibrium price to be $6 (point *e*), and total sales for the market is 6,000 units. Consumer surplus is equal to the area under the demand curve but above the equilibrium price of $6. Producer surplus is the area under the equilibrium price but above the supply curve.

FIGURE 2

bargain by purchasing the unit and receiving a consumer surplus equal to $5 ($11 − $6). Ben, however, values a Frisbee a little less at $10, but still receives a consumer surplus of $4 ($10 − $6). And so on for Christine, David, and Erika, who receive a consumer surplus of $3, $2, and $1, respectively. Only Francis, who values a Frisbee to be worth exactly the same amount as the price, earns no consumer surplus. Total consumer surplus for the 6 consumers in panel A is found by adding all of the individual consumer surpluses for each unit purchased. Thus, total consumer surplus in panel A is equal to $5 + $4 + $3 + $2 + $1 + $0 = $15.

In a similar way, assume that each point on the supply curve represents a specific seller, each with a Frisbee to sell but each with a different willingness to sell. Equilibrium price is still $6, therefore Zoe, who is willing to sell her Frisbee for just $2.67, receives a producer surplus of $3.33 ($6 − $2.67). Yvonne, Xerxes, Wanda, and Victor, who each have a higher willingness-to-sell, receive a correspondingly smaller producer surplus equal to $2.67, $2.00, $1.33, and $0.67, respectively. And Umberto, who had a willingness-to-sell of $6, receives no producer surplus for his sale. Total producer surplus in panel A is equal to $3.33 + $2.67 + $2.00 + $1.33 + $0.67 + $0 = $10.

Panel B illustrates consumer and producer surplus for an entire market. For convenience we have assumed that the market is 1,000 times larger than that shown in panel A, so the *x* axis is output in thousands. Whereas in panel A we had discrete buyers and sellers, we now have one big market, therefore consumer surplus is equal to the area under the demand curve and above equilibrium price, or the area of the shaded triangle labeled "consumer surplus."

To put a number to the consumer surplus triangle (*feh*) in panel B, we can compute the value of the rectangle *fgeh* and divide it in half. Thus, total market consumer surplus in panel B is [($12 − $6) × 6,000] ÷ 2 = ($6 × 6,000) ÷ 2 = $18,000. The shaded triangle labeled "producer surplus" (area *hei*) is found in the same way by computing the value of the rectangle *heji* and dividing it in half. Producer surplus is equal to [($6 − $2) × 6,000] ÷ 2 = ($4 × 6,000) ÷ 2 = $12,000.

Although we simplify the calculation of consumer and producer surplus using the area of the triangle, remember that it is still the sum of the consumer and producer surpluses of many individual buyers and sellers. It is merely the fact that markets have thousands of buyers and sellers that the steps in panel A of Figure 2 become very small, thus resulting in smooth demand and supply curves in panel B.

We have now defined consumer surplus and producer surplus for individuals and for markets. But how do we know whether the market leads to an ideal outcome for consumers and producers? The next section goes on to reveal the efficiency of markets.

 CHECKPOINT

CONSUMER AND PRODUCER SURPLUS: A TOOL FOR MEASURING ECONOMIC EFFICIENCY

- Consumers and producers both attempt to maximize their well-being by achieving the greatest gains in their market transactions.

- Consumer surplus occurs when consumers would have been willing to pay more for a good or service than the actual price paid. It represents a form of savings to consumers.

- Producer surplus occurs when businesses would have been willing to provide a good or service at prices lower than the going price. It represents a form of earnings to producers.

QUESTION: At the end of the semester, four college students list their economics textbooks for sale on the bulletin board in the student union. The minimum price Alex is willing to accept is $20, Caroline wants at least $25, Kira wants at least $30, and Will wants at least $35. Now assume that four college students taking an economics class next semester are searching for a deal on the textbook. Cole wishes to pay no more than $50, Jacqueline no more than $55, Sienna no more than $60, and Tessa no more than $65. Suppose that the actual sales price for each of the four textbooks is $40. What is the total consumer surplus received by the four buyers and the total producer surplus received by the four sellers?

Answers to the Checkpoint question can be found at the end of the chapter.

→ Using Consumer and Producer Surplus: The Gains from Trade

Markets are efficient when they generate the largest possible amount of net benefits to all parties involved. When transactions between a buyer and a seller take place, each party is better off than before the transaction, leading to gains from trade. We had previously looked at gains from trade in an earlier chapter from the perspectives of individuals, firms, and countries specializing in activities and engaging in mutually beneficial transactions. This is no different than our present market examples, in which buyers and sellers mutually gain from transacting with one another.

At the equilibrium price, shortages and surpluses are nonexistent, and all consumers wanting to buy a good at that price are able to find a seller willing to sell at that price. The market efficiency that results maximizes the sum of consumer surplus and producer surplus, referred to as **total surplus,** gained in the market. Total surplus is a measure of the total net benefits a society achieves when both consumers and producers are valued components of an economy.

To see why markets are efficient at equilibrium, we need to analyze what happens to total surplus when markets deviate from equilibrium.

total surplus The sum of consumer surplus and producer surplus, and a measure of the overall net benefit gained from a market.

The Consequences of Deviating from Market Equilibrium

The market mechanism ensures that goods and services get to where they are most needed, because consumers desiring them bid up the price, while suppliers eager to make money supply them. Adam Smith termed this process the *invisible hand* to describe how resources are allocated efficiently through individual decisions made in markets.

But not all markets end up in equilibrium, especially if buyers or sellers hold inadequate information about products, or if buyers or sellers hold unrealistic or inaccurate expectations about market prices and behavior. Let's examine two scenarios in the market for video game consoles in which prices deviate from the equilibrium price.

When Prices Exceed Equilibrium Figure 3 illustrates a market for video game consoles with an equilibrium price of $300. Suppose that due to unrealistic expectations of demand, prices for video game consoles are set at $400, above the equilibrium price. We know from the previous chapter that a price above equilibrium leads to excess supply, because consumers only demand 10 thousand units while producers desire to sell 30 thousand units. Our tools of consumer surplus and producer surplus allow us to evaluate the effects on buyers and sellers in this market.

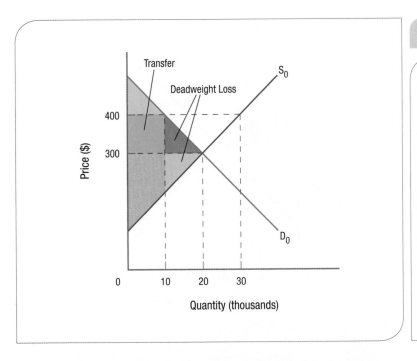

FIGURE 3

Consumer and Producer Surplus When Prices Exceed Equilibrium

Compared to the equilibrium price, a price of $400 would prevent some consumers from purchasing the product. A loss of consumer surplus equal to the blue region occurs. Further, consumers who still purchase the product pay $100 more than the equilibrium price, causing an additional loss of consumer surplus equal to the pink area. Producers, meanwhile, lose producer surplus equal to the yellow area resulting from the units that consumers no longer buy, but earn additional producer surplus equal to the pink area as a result of the higher price. Total lost surplus, called deadweight loss, is the blue and yellow areas (no one gets this because some trades are not made now). The pink area is surplus transferred from consumers to producers because of the higher price.

When prices are above equilibrium, consumer surplus shrinks due to two effects: First, a price of $400 causes some consumers to not make a purchase, because these consumers were only willing to pay between $300 and $400. The area shown in blue represents the lost consumer surplus from these forgone purchases. Second, the consumers who still are willing and able to purchase a unit pay $100 more, which represents a loss in consumer surplus equal to the pink area. In sum, the pink and blue regions represent the total reduction in consumer surplus from the higher price.

Producers, on the other hand, may or may not benefit from the higher price because of two opposing effects. First, the fact that the higher price causes some consumers to not purchase a unit causes a loss in producer surplus equal to the area shaded in yellow. However, this is offset by the additional money earned from the consumers who buy the unit at the higher price, which is represented by the pink area.

deadweight loss The reduction in total surplus that results from the inefficiency of a market not in equilibrium.

Therefore, the pink area represents a transfer of surplus from consumers to producers. The blue and yellow areas represent **deadweight loss,** the loss of consumer surplus and producer surplus caused by the inefficiency of a market not operating at equilibrium. Nobody gets the blue and yellow areas. Deadweight loss represents a loss in total surplus, because both buyers and sellers would have benefited from these transactions.

When Prices Fall Below Equilibrium
When prices are below equilibrium, the opposite effects happen as a result of a shortage. Figure 4 shows the market for video game consoles in which the price of $200 is below the equilibrium price. At that price, sellers provide 10 thousand units for sale, while buyers demand 30 thousand units, causing a shortage.

At a price of $200, producers are clearly worse off. Some producers are unable to sell at that low price, causing a loss of producer surplus equal to the yellow area, while those who still sell the product earn $100 less per unit, resulting in a loss of producer surplus equal to the pink area.

At first, you might believe consumers are better off with the lower price, and some in fact are. But these gains, shown by the pink area, are limited to consumers lucky enough to purchase the good. The rest of the consumers who are affected by the shortage are worse off, because consumer surplus equal to the blue area is lost because of trades never made. In sum, deadweight loss equal to the blue and yellow areas results.

The two scenarios shown in Figures 3 and 4 demonstrate that whenever prices deviate from equilibrium, total surplus as measured by the sum of consumer surplus and producer surplus falls, resulting in a deadweight loss from mutually beneficial transactions between

---

FIGURE 4

Consumer and Producer Surplus When Prices are Below Equilibrium

Compared to the equilibrium price, a price of $200 causes some producers to not sell the product, resulting in a loss of producer surplus equal to the yellow area. Further, producers who still sell the product earn $100 less than before, causing an additional loss of producer surplus equal to the pink area. Consumers, meanwhile, lose consumer surplus equal to the blue area resulting from the shortage of units, but receive additional consumer surplus equal to the pink area as a result of the lower price for those lucky enough to find units for sale. Once again, deadweight loss is the blue and yellow areas, and the pink area is surplus transferred.

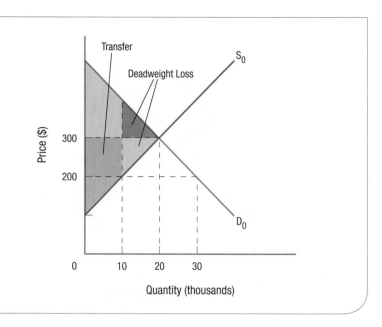

buyers and sellers not taking place. But why would markets not achieve equilibrium? Sometimes a market will fail to achieve equilibrium because it is prevented from doing so on its own.

Market Failure

Markets are inherently efficient mechanisms for allocating resources because of the incentives that drive consumers and firms to act in their own best interests. But like all things, exceptions occur when circumstances prevent the market from achieving the socially desirable outcome. When freely functioning markets fail to provide an optimal amount of goods and services, a **market failure** occurs.

There are four major reasons why markets fail: a lack of competition, a mismatch of information, external benefits or costs, and the existence of public goods, each of which causes total surplus to fall, resulting in deadweight loss.

Lack of Competition When a market has many buyers and sellers, no one seller has the ability to raise its price above that of its competitors. But when a market lacks competition, a firm can raise its price in the market without worrying that other firms will undercut its price. The local water provider is an example of a firm in a market that lacks competition, which can lead to inefficient production and higher prices unless the market failure is corrected using government regulation.

Information Is Not Shared by All Parties Adequate information about products by buyers and sellers is an important condition for efficient markets. Sometimes, one party knows more about a product than the other, a situation known as **asymmetric information.** For example, a seller of a used car knows more about the true condition of the car than a potential buyer. Conversely, an art or antique buyer may know more about the value of items than the seller at an estate sale. In these cases, a mismatch of information may lead to prices being set too high or too low.

The Existence of External Benefits or Costs When you drive your car on a crowded highway, you inflict external costs on other drivers by adding to congestion. When you receive a flu shot, you confer external benefits on the rest of us by reducing the chances of spreading an illness. Markets rarely produce the socially optimal output when external costs or benefits are present. When deciding whether to drive or obtain a flu shot, you tend not to think of the costs and benefits you impose on others. As a result, more people drive and fewer people receive flu shots than would be ideal to achieve the socially optimal outcome.

market failure Occurs when a free market does not lead to a socially desirable outcome.

asymmetric information Occurs when one party to a transaction has significantly better information than another party.

NOBEL PRIZE
PAUL A. SAMUELSON (1915–2009)

In 1970, Paul Samuelson became the first American to win the Nobel Prize in Economics. One could say that Paul Samuelson literally wrote the book on economics. In 1948, when he was a young professor at the Massachusetts Institute of Technology, the university asked him to write a text for the junior year course in economics. Sixty years later more than 4 million copies of his textbook, *Economics,* have been sold.

Samuelson's interests were wide ranging, and his contributions include everything from the highly technical and mathematical to a popular column for *Newsweek* magazine. He made breakthrough contributions to virtually all areas of economics.

Born in Gary, Indiana, in 1915, Samuelson attended the University of Chicago. He received the university's Social Science Medal and was awarded a graduate fellowship, which he used at Harvard, where he published eleven papers while in the graduate program.

He wanted to remain at Harvard, but was only offered an instructor's position. However, MIT soon made a better offer and, as he describes it, "On a fine October day in 1940 an *enfant terrible emeritus* packed up his pencil and moved three miles down the Charles River, where he lived happily ever after." He often remarked that a pencil was all he needed to theorize. Seven years later, he published his Ph.D. dissertation, *Foundations of Economic Analysis,* a major contribution to the area of mathematical economics. Robert Lucas, another Nobel winner, declared, "Here was a graduate student in his twenties reorganizing all of economics in four or five chapters right before your eyes . . ."

Harvard made several attempts to lure him back, but he spent his entire career at MIT and is often credited with developing a department as good as or better than Harvard's. Samuelson was an informal advisor to President John F. Kennedy. A prolific writer, he averaged one technical paper each month during his active career, and often said "a day spent in committee meetings [is] for me a day lost." He wrote that he "has always been incredibly lucky, throughout his lifetime overpaid and underworked." Quite a modest statement for a man whose *Collected Works* takes up five volumes and includes more than 350 articles. He was an active economist until his death in 2009 at the age of 93. As you read through this book, keep in mind that in virtually every chapter, Paul Samuelson has created or added to the analysis in substantial ways.

Sources: David Warsh, *Knowledge and the Wealth of Nations: A Story of Economic Discovery* (New York: Norton), 2006; Paul Samuelson, "Economics in My Time," in William Breit and Roger Spencer, *Lives of the Laureates: Seven Nobel Economists* (Cambridge, MA: The MIT Press), 1986.

ISSUE

Can Markets Accurately Predict the Future?

Can an online market predict the outcomes of political elections, wars, and other world events? A growing number of online betting exchanges think they can. These simple online markets have predicted major events and elections over the past decade with precision.

Traditionally, polls and other surveys are used to make predictions about the likelihood of future events. Although no one can truly predict the future, predictions markets gained significant attention by allowing real people to wager real money.

The first major online predictions market was the Iowa Electronic Markets established by the University of Iowa in 1988, allowing any individual to buy "shares" of various events ranging in price from $0.00 (0% probability of occurring) to $1.00 (100% probability of occurring). The value of these shares fluctuates as the perceived probability of the event occurring changes, allowing individuals to buy and sell shares at the current price until the event actually occurs (or not occurs).

The efficiency of this market lies in (1) the perpetual trading of shares and (2) the fact that people are motivated to make accurate predictions based on monetary incentives rather

than personal opinions. For example, if one buys shares at $0.60 and something increases the perceived likelihood of the event occurring to 70% (or $0.70 a share), the shareholder can sell her shares at the new price, earning $0.10 per share without incurring any further risk.

The accuracy of predictions markets has been impressive. Intrade, one of the most popular predictions markets (established in 1999), accurately predicted the winner of the last four U.S. presidential elections, and with three exceptions it predicted the candidate winning the most votes in every state, even when various news polls showed opposing outcomes.

Although the power of predictions markets is potent, its legal status is not as certain. Intrade was shut down in 2013 after facing legal issues regarding its status as either an unregulated market exchange or an online betting site. To avoid legal troubles, other companies have found ways to harness the predictive power of markets by using incentives other than money, such as game points and prizes. Regardless of the incentives used, predictions markets remain a powerful tool that illustrates the efficiency of markets.

The Existence of Public Goods

Most goods we buy are private goods, such as meals and concert tickets; once we buy them, no one else can benefit from them. Public goods, however, are goods that one person can consume without diminishing what is left for others. Public television, for example, is a public good that illustrates nonrivalry (my watching of PBS does not mean there is less PBS for you to watch) and nonexclusivity (once a good is provided, others cannot be excluded from enjoying it). Because of these characteristics, public goods are difficult to provide in the private market.

Market Efficiency Versus Equity

Overcoming market failure is an important goal of government, which can enact policies to address markets in which private transactions do not lead to the optimal outcome. But the role of government extends beyond that of achieving social efficiency. It is also tasked with the goal of achieving equity in markets. For example, if a policy creates considerable unfairness, while spurring only a small gain in efficiency, some other policy might be better. One tool used by government to balance efficiency with equity is the use of price controls, which we turn to next.

 CHECKPOINT

USING CONSUMER AND PRODUCER SURPLUS: THE GAINS FROM TRADE

- The sum of consumer surplus and producer surplus is total surplus, a measure of the overall net benefits for an economy.
- Markets are efficient when all buyers and all sellers willing to buy and sell at a market price are able to do so.
- When buyers and sellers engage in a market transaction, gains from trade are created from consumer surplus and producer surplus.
- Total surplus is maximized at a market equilibrium.
- When markets deviate from equilibrium, deadweight loss is created, an inefficiency caused by the loss of total surplus.
- Markets are typically efficient, although sometimes they can fail by not providing the socially optimal amount of goods and services.
- Market failure is caused by a lack of competition, mismatched information, external costs and external benefits, and the existence of public goods.

QUESTION: Waiting for an organ transplant is an ordeal for patients. Some wait years for an available donor organ that is compatible. Some economists have suggested that offering monetary compensation to organ donors would increase the supply of available organs. Would such a system lead to gains from trade? Why are such incentives difficult to implement?

Answers to the Checkpoint questions can be found at the end of this chapter.

Price Ceilings and Price Floors

To this point, we have assumed that competitive markets are allowed to operate freely, without any government intervention. Economists refer to freely functioning markets as **laissez-faire,** a French term meaning "let it be." The justification for this type of economic policy is that when competitive markets are left to determine equilibrium price and output, they clear. Businesses provide consumers with the quantity of goods they want to purchase at the established prices; there are no shortages or surpluses. Consumer and producer surplus together, or total surplus, is maximized.

laissez-faire A market that is allowed to function without any government intervention.

However, as we saw at the end of the previous section, sometimes freely functioning markets fail to achieve the optimal quantity of goods and services. This is an equilibrium price in a free market that leads to what many people consider an unfair price. Because of these economic (*efficiency*) or political (*equity*) reasons, governments will sometimes intervene in the market by setting limits on the prices of various goods and services. Governments use price ceilings and price floors to keep prices below or above market equilibrium. What really happens when government sets prices below or above market equilibrium? The previous section hinted at the answer. Let's look at price ceilings and floors more closely.

Price Ceilings

When the government sets a **price ceiling,** it is legally mandating the maximum price that can be charged for a product or service. This is a legal maximum; regardless of market forces, price cannot exceed this level. An historical example of a price ceiling is the establishment of rent-controlled apartment buildings in New York City during World War II, many of which still exist today. However, more common examples of price ceilings include limits on what insurance companies can charge customers, price caps on telecommunications and electric services to customers in rural or remote locations, and limits on tuition hikes at state public universities.

price ceiling A government-set maximum price that can be charged for a product or service. When the price ceiling is set below equilibrium, it leads to shortages.

Panel A in Figure 5 on the next page shows an *effective* price ceiling, or one in which the ceiling price is set below the equilibrium price. In this case, equilibrium price is at P_e, but the government has set a price ceiling at P_c. Quantity supplied at the ceiling price is Q_1, whereas consumers want Q_2, therefore the result is a shortage of $Q_2 - Q_1$ units of the product. As we saw in the previous section, setting a price below equilibrium alters consumer and producer surplus and results in a deadweight loss indicated by the shaded area. If the price ceiling is raised toward equilibrium, the shortage is reduced along with the deadweight loss. If the price ceiling is set above P_e (as shown in panel B), the market simply settles at P_e, and the price ceiling has no impact; it is nonbinding, and no deadweight loss occurs. A price ceiling can also *become* nonbinding if market factors cause supply to rise or demand to fall, pushing the equilibrium price below the ceiling.

A common mistake when analyzing the effect of price ceilings is assuming that effective price ceilings appear above the market equilibrium, because the word *ceiling* refers to something *above you.* Instead, think of ceilings as something that keep you from moving higher. Suppose you build a makeshift skateboarding ramp in your apartment hallway, and tempt your friends to test it out. If the ceiling is too low, some of your friends might end up with a severe headache. In other words, an effective (binding) ceiling is one that is kept lower than normal. If the ceiling can be raised by 5 feet, then all of your friends would achieve their jumps without bumping their heads. In sum, price ceilings have their strongest effects when kept very low; as the ceiling is

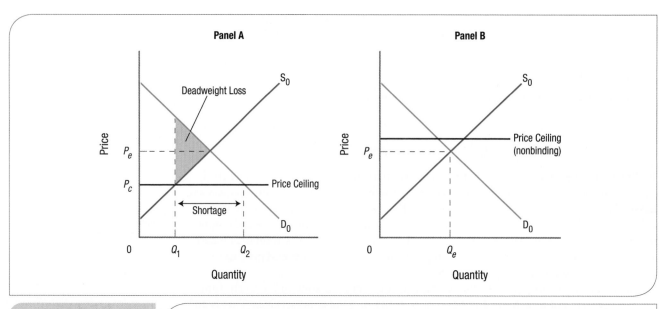

Panel A

Price

Deadweight Loss

S_0

P_e

P_c — Price Ceiling

Shortage

D_0

0   Q_1 Q_2

Quantity

Panel B

Price

S_0

Price Ceiling (nonbinding)

P_e

D_0

0   Q_e

Quantity

FIGURE 5

A Price Ceiling Below Equilibrium Creates Shortages

When the government enacts a price ceiling below equilibrium (panel A), consumers will demand Q_2 and businesses will supply only Q_1, creating a shortage equal to $Q_2 - Q_1$, and causing deadweight loss equal to the shaded area. If the price ceiling is set above equilibrium (panel B), the price ceiling has no effect, and the market price and quantity prevail with no deadweight loss created.

raised, the effect of the policy goes away, and becomes nonbinding once it reaches the equilibrium price.

Given the price ceiling, one might argue that although shortages might exist, at least prices will be kept lower and therefore more "fair." The question is, fairer to whom? Suppose your university places a new price ceiling on the rents of all existing apartments located on campus, one that is below the rents of similar apartments off campus. This might sound like a great idea, but often what sounds like a great idea comes with costs.

A price ceiling creates a much higher demand for on-campus apartments than the available supply, creating a shortage. Those lucky enough to obtain an on-campus

Low ceilings have a greater impact than high ceilings; similarly, price ceilings below equilibrium (rather than above equilibrium) lead to shortages in the market.

apartment benefit from the lower rents. But what about those who couldn't? Because some students who really could have benefited from lower rents (those with lower incomes or without cars) cannot find an on-campus apartment, while other students who could have easily afforded a higher priced off-campus apartment managed to snatch one up, this creates a **misallocation of resources.** Further, when on-campus apartments do open up, students eager to obtain one might spend a lot of time and resources trying. These resources (an opportunity cost) end up offsetting some or all of the savings from finding an on-campus apartment.

Besides the misallocation of resources and potential opportunity costs of long waits and search costs, price ceilings also lead to some unintended long-term consequences. For example, if a landlord owns some apartments on campus (where rents are controlled) and some apartments off campus (where rents are higher), on which apartments is she likely to spend more money for upgrades and/or maintenance? The quality of goods and services subjected to price ceilings tends to deteriorate over time, as the incentives shift toward products with higher prices. Further, when it comes time to invest in new apartments, where do you think they are likely to be built—on campus or off?

The key point to remember here is that price ceilings are intended to keep the price of a product below its market or equilibrium level. When this happens, consumer surplus increases for those able to purchase the good, while producer surplus falls. The ultimate effect of a price ceiling, however, is that the quantity of the product demanded exceeds the quantity supplied, thereby producing a shortage of the product in the market. When shortages occur, deadweight losses are created because some mutually beneficial transactions do not take place, causing a reduction in total surplus.

misallocation of resources Occurs when a good or service is not consumed by the person who values it the most, and typically results when a price ceiling creates an artificial shortage in the market.

Price Floors

A **price floor** is a government-mandated minimum price that can be charged for a product or service. Regardless of market forces, product price cannot legally fall below this level.

Figure 6 shows the economic impact of price floors. In panel A, the price floor, P_f, is set above equilibrium, P_e, resulting in a surplus of $Q_2 - Q_1$ units. At price P_f, businesses

price floor A government-set minimum price that can be charged for a product or service. When the price floor is set above equilibrium, it leads to surpluses.

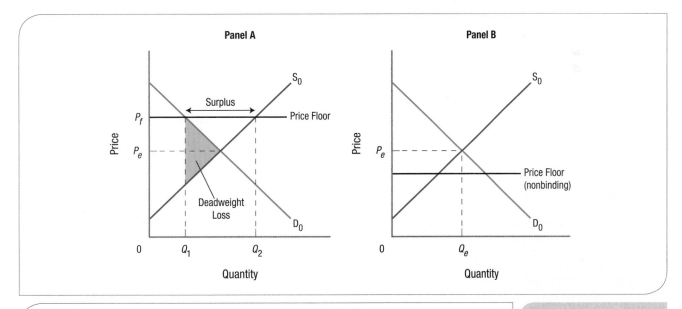

A Price Floor Above Equilibrium Creates Surpluses

When the government sets a price floor above equilibrium (panel A), businesses try to sell Q_2 at a price of P_f, but consumers are willing to purchase only Q_1 at that price, resulting in a surplus equal to $Q_2 - Q_1$, and causing deadweight loss equal to the shaded area. If the price floor is set below equilibrium (panel B), the price floor has no effect, and the market price and quantity prevail with no deadweight loss created.

FIGURE 6

want to supply more of the product (Q_2) than consumers are willing to buy (Q_1), thus generating a surplus. Because only Q_1 is transacted in the market, a deadweight loss equal to the shaded area is created. If the price floor is set below equilibrium (as shown in panel B), the market will move toward the equilibrium price, P_e. Therefore, a price floor set below P_e has no impact on the market and no deadweight loss occurs. Likewise, a price floor can *become* nonbinding if market factors push the equilibrium price above the price floor.

Throughout much of the past century, the U.S. government has used agricultural price supports (price floors) in order to smooth out the income of farmers, which often fluctuates due to wide annual variations in crop prices. This approach is not limited to the United States. Many developed countries, including members of the European Union and Japan, have long protected their agricultural industries by ensuring a minimum price level for many types of crops.

ISSUE

Are Price Gouging Laws Good for Consumers?

During the summer hurricane season, residents along the Atlantic and Gulf Coasts brace for hurricanes that can wreak havoc on the unprepared. The routine is well known: buy plywood and shutters to protect windows; fill up gas tanks in cars and buy extra gas for generators; and stock up on batteries, bottled water, and nonperishable foods. Because of the huge spike in demand, numerous states have introduced price gouging laws, which prevent stores from raising prices above the average price of the past 30 days. Penalties for violating such laws are severe.

Price gouging laws generally pass with huge majority votes from both major political parties. The logic seems clear—to prevent businesses from exploiting a bad situation to their benefit by raising prices. Passing such laws always appears to be a victory for the consumer. But is it really?

Price gouging laws are price ceilings placed at the price last existing when times were normal. But during a natural disaster, the market is far from normal—demand is higher, and supplies are often restricted due to plant closures. The figure shows what happens when these two effects come together—the market price spikes upward. But price goug-

The inside of a jumbo jet cargo plane, a spacious solution to supply shortages, as long as an incentive exists to use that plane for this purpose.

ing laws require that prices remain at the *original* level, resulting in a shortage when demand increases to D_1 and supply falls to S_1.

What happens during a shortage? Huge lines form at home improvement stores, gas stations, and grocery stores. Time spent waiting in line is time that can be spent completing other tasks in

preparation for the storm. What might be a better solution?

Instead of capping prices and causing a shortage, efforts can be made to provide incentives to businesses to generate more supply. If supply shifts enough to the right to compensate for the increase in demand, then prices need not increase, regardless of the price ceiling. But the question is, How do we incentivize supply? Subsidies to offset increased transportation costs might be an example. Imagine how many supplies could be flown in on a single jumbo jet cargo plane from a non–hurricane-prone area. Quite a bit, but firms aren't willing to spend that money. If the incentive is provided, supply will increase, reducing shortages and costs to everyone.

These price supports act very much as they are intended. By ensuring a minimum price for a crop, farmers have an incentive to grow more of these crops relative to crops that aren't protected by price supports. Further, because the price supports typically are above market equilibrium prices, resulting in higher prices for consumers, demand for such crops is less than what it would be without the supports.

Thus, with greater supply and smaller demand, price supports lead to surpluses of crops. What happens to these surpluses? Because the government guarantees the price levels of the crops, it must purchase the excess supply, which is typically stored for use in the event of future shortages. But surpluses eventually rot, which means government must find other ways to use the surplus before it goes bad. One common use of surplus foods is in public school lunches, leading to some criticism that the types of foods being provided (wheat, grains, and corn) are not the most nutritious foods for children to eat.

Surplus foods resulting from government price floors are often given away to public schools to be used in school lunches.

Another criticism of agricultural price supports comes from developing countries that depend on agricultural exports for their economic output. These countries claim that price supports hamper their economic development by preventing them from selling goods in which they have a comparative advantage. In other words, agricultural price supports restrict gains from trade.

Despite their questionable economic justification, political pressures have ensured that agricultural price supports and related programs still command a sizable share of the discretionary domestic federal budget.

Price floors are also used in regard to the minimum wage. To the extent that the minimum wage is set above the equilibrium wage, unemployment—a surplus of labor—may result if jobs go uncreated when employers are forced to pay the higher minimum wage. However, the minimum wage offers a potential positive effect of reducing income inequality by raising earnings among low-wage workers. This effect is stronger if increasing the minimum wage subsequently leads to higher wages for workers who are already earning slightly more than the minimum wage.

In sum, price ceilings and price floors often are policies aimed at promoting equity or fairness in a society, such as preventing rapid price increases for consumers or ensuring fair wages for workers. Still, governments must be careful when setting price ceilings and price floors to avoid meddling with markets.

◉ CHECKPOINT

PRICE CEILINGS AND PRICE FLOORS

- Governments use price floors and price ceilings to intervene in markets.
- A price ceiling is a maximum legal price that can be charged for a product. Price ceilings set below equilibrium result in shortages.
- A price floor is the minimum legal price that can be charged for a product. Price floors set above market equilibrium result in surpluses.

QUESTION: The day after Thanksgiving, also known as *Black Friday*, is a day on which retailers advertise very steep discounts on selected items such as televisions or laptops. Assuming the number of units available at the discounted price is limited, in what ways are the effects of this pricing strategy similar to a price ceiling set by the government? In what ways do they differ?

Answers to the Checkpoint questions can be found at the end of the chapter.

chapter summary

Section 1: Consumer and Producer Surplus: A Tool for Measuring Economic Efficiency

Paul Bradbury/Getty Images

Economic efficiency is measured by the gains that consumers and producers achieve when engaging in an economic transaction.

Consumer surplus is the difference between a person's willingness-to-pay and the price paid. For a market, consumer surplus is the area between the demand curve and the market price. In the figure, consumer surplus equals $1,250.

Producer surplus is the difference between the price a seller receives and its marginal cost. For a market, producer surplus is the area between the market price and the supply curve. In the figure, producer surplus equals $1,000.

Section 2: Using Consumer and Producer Surplus: The Gains from Trade

Markets exhibit efficiency when every buyer and every seller eager to buy and sell goods is able to do so, resulting in **gains from trade.** Gains from trade are measured by the **total surplus,** or the sum of consumer and producer surplus in a market. Total surplus is maximized when a market is at equilibrium.

Suppose the price of a good rises above equilibrium to $75. The higher price causes two effects on consumer surplus and two effects on producer surplus:

1. Consumers who are priced out of the market lose consumer surplus equal to the blue area.

2. Consumers who continue to buy the good pay more, and lose consumer surplus equal to the pink area.

3. Producers who want to sell more at $75 but cannot lose producer surplus equal to the yellow area.

4. Producers who do sell units earn $25 more per unit, equal to the pink area.

Deadweight loss occurs when prices deviate from equilibrium. In the above example, deadweight loss is shown by the blue and yellow areas.

Markets can sometimes fail to produce the socially optimal output. Reasons for **market failure** include:

Lack of competition

When a firm faces little to no competition, it has an incentive to raise prices.

Existence of external benefits or costs

Markets tend to provide too little of products that have external benefits, and too much of products with external costs.

Planting trees creates external benefits.

Talking loudly on your phone creates external costs.

A mismatch of information

Asymmetric information occurs when either a buyer or a seller knows more about a product than the other.

Existence of public goods

Public goods are nonrival and nonexclusive. This means:

- My consumption does not diminish your ability to consume.
- Once a good is provided for one person, others cannot be excluded from enjoying it.

Ecological conservation is a public good. Once people devote time and resources to saving the environment, everybody benefits from it, even if one does not contribute to the costs of maintaining it.

Section 3: Price Ceilings and Price Floors

A **price floor** is a minimum price for a good. A binding price floor appears above equilibrium and causes a surplus.

A **price ceiling** is a maximum price for a good. A binding price ceiling appears below equilibrium and causes a shortage.

Prices cannot go below the floor

S

Price Floor

Price

Price Ceiling

Prices cannot go above the ceiling

D

Quantity

A literal mountain of surplus corn caused by agricultural price floors.

consumer surplus, p. 82
producer surplus, p. 82
total surplus, p. 85
deadweight loss, p. 86

market failure, p. 87
asymmetric information, p. 87
laissez-faire, p. 89
price ceiling, p. 89

misallocation of resources, p. 91
price floor, p. 91

QUESTIONS AND PROBLEMS

Check Your Understanding

1. Describe how consumer surplus and producer surplus are measured.

2. Using the graph below, show what happens to consumer surplus when a new technology reduces the cost of production.

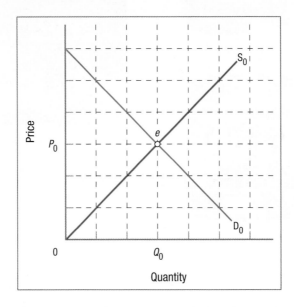

3. Explain why deadweight loss can occur with a price below equilibrium even when some consumers benefit from it.

4. Provide three examples of activities that generate external benefits and three activities that generate external costs.

5. Why does an effective price ceiling appear below the equilibrium rather than above it?

6. If a price floor is reduced toward equilibrium but not below it, does the surplus and deadweight loss in this market increase or decrease?

Apply the Concepts

7. An increasing number of charities have turned to online auctions as a way to raise money by selling unique experiences donated by celebrities (such as a *meet-and-greet* with a celebrity before a concert or a walk-on role on a television show). Why would the use of auctions lead to a better outcome for the charity as opposed to just setting a fixed price? Explain using the concepts of consumer surplus and producer surplus.

8. Luigi's is the only pizzeria in a small town in northern Alaska. It is constantly busy but there is never a wait for a table. One of Luigi's friends suggests that he would earn much more money if he raises his menu prices by 25%, because no one is likely to open a new pizzeria in the near future. If Luigi follows his friend's advice, what would happen to consumer and producer surplus, and efficiency, in this market?

9. "If millions of people are desperate to buy and millions more desperate to sell, the trades will happen, whether we like it or not." This quote from Martin Wolf[1] refers to trades in illicit goods such as narcotics, knockoffs (counterfeit goods), slaves, organs, and other goods we generally refer to as "bads." Wolf suggests that the only way to eliminate traffic in these illicit goods is to eliminate their profitability. Do you agree? Why or why not?

10. Academic studies suggest that the amount people tip in restaurants is only slightly related to the quality of service, and that tips are poor measures of how happy people are with the service. Is this another example of market failure? What might account for this situation?

11. In the 1940s, rent controls were widely used in New York City, and to this day, tenants in rent-controlled apartments continue to pay low rents as long as they do not move. As a result, some of New York's prime real estate is renting for a fraction of the true market value. Explain how the existence of rent controls affects the market prices for non-rent-controlled apartments. How are incentives by New York landlords affected in terms of maintaining rent-controlled and non-rent-controlled apartments?

12. The U.S. Department of Labor reports that of the roughly 155 million people employed, just over half are paid by the hour, but fewer than 5% earn the minimum wage or less; 95% of wage earners earn more. And of those earning the minimum wage or less, 25% are teenagers living at home. If so few people are affected by the minimum wage, why does it often seem to be such a contentious political issue?

In the News

13. In 2009, the Hershey Company of Pennsylvania became the latest company to open a candy factory in Mexico (*USA Today,* February 13, 2009), joining other American candy companies including Brach's Confections and Ferrara Pan Candy, which had opened plants there earlier. The reason for Hershey's move was more than just lower wages; it was also because of lower sugar prices. Sugar prices in the United States have for many decades been supported in order to protect the American sugar industry and the thousands of farmers it employs. Using the tools of consumer and producer surplus, explain how the events described may have resulted from price supports for sugar.

14. Professor Donald Boudreaux wrote (*Wall Street Journal,* August 23, 2006, p. A11) that "there are heaps of bad arguments for raising the minimum wage. Perhaps the worst . . . is that a minimum wage increase is justified if a full-time worker earning the current minimum wage cannot afford to live in a city such as Chicago." He then asked, "why settle for enabling workers to live only in the likes of Chicago? Why not raise the minimum wage so that everyone can afford to live in, say, Nantucket, Hyannis Port or Beverly Hills, within walking distance of Rodeo Drive?" Should the minimum wage be a "living wage," so a full-time worker can live comfortably in a given locale? What would be the impact if minimum wages were structured this way?

---

[1] Martin Wolf, "The Profit Motive May Be Universal but Virtue Is Not," *Financial Times,* November 16, 2005, p. 13.

Solving Problems

15. Consider the market shown in the graph below.

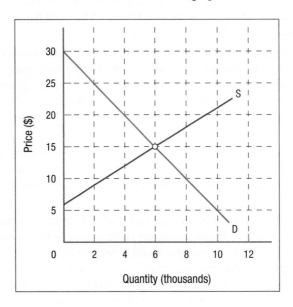

a. Compute the consumer surplus.

b. Compute the producer surplus.

Now assume that government puts a price floor on this product at $20 a unit.

c. Compute the new consumer surplus.

d. Compute the new producer surplus.

e. What group would tend to have their advocates or lobbyists support price floors?

16. Suppose the U.S. government places a price ceiling on the sale of gasoline at $3 per gallon in the figure below.

a. How much of a shortage or surplus of gasoline would result?

b. Calculate the effects of this policy in terms of the changes in consumer surplus and producer surplus.

c. How much deadweight loss is created?

d. What would happen if the price ceiling is raised to $6 per gallon?

⊕ USING THE NUMBERS

17. According to By the Numbers, how much would you earn in one year if you worked 2,000 hours (50 weeks × 40 hours) at the federal minimum wage? How much more would you earn per year if you worked at the minimum wage rate in Washington state?

18. According to By the Numbers, which state received the highest average federal telephone support per capita in 2011? Approximately how much support did this state receive per resident? (Hint: search for the population of each state online to calculate the average support per person.)

ANSWERS TO QUESTIONS IN CHECKPOINTS

Checkpoint: Consumer and Producer Surplus: A Tool for Measuring Economic Efficiency

Cole's consumer surplus is ($50 − $40) = $10, Jacqueline's is ($55 − $40) = $15, Sienna's is ($60 − $40) = $20, and Tessa's is ($65 − $40) = $25. Total consumer surplus is $10 + $15 + $20 + $25 = $70. Alex's producer surplus is ($40 − $20) = $20, Caroline's is ($40 − $25) = $15, Kira's is ($40 − $30) = $10, and Will's is ($40 − $35) = $5. Total producer surplus is $20 + $15 + $10 + $5 = $50.

Checkpoint: Using Consumer and Producer Surplus: The Gains from Trade

Although many people voluntarily become organ donors because of the goodwill they feel knowing that their actions can potentially save a life, still many others choose not to become organ donors because they do not see any monetary benefit from doing so. Compensating individuals for becoming organ donors, thereby raising the "price" of organs, would be a way to increase the supply of organs, allowing the shortage to dissipate until equilibrium is reached. In doing so, organ donors and recipients both benefit, resulting in gains from trade. However, moral objections to selling body parts have led to many laws preventing organ donors from being compensated. As a result, shortages continue to be a problem.

Checkpoint: Price Ceilings and Price Floors

Black Friday specials are typically deeply discounted in order to attract customers into the store, which is why such specials are prominently shown on the first page of sales circulars. Like a price ceiling that is set below the equilibrium price, the quantity demanded for the discounted good increases, while stores limit the number of units available for sale, creating a shortage. Some buyers will be fortunate to find units available to purchase, while subsequent shoppers will find that the product has sold out. Deadweight loss is generated because some customers who would have been willing to pay a little more are unable to purchase the good. However, unlike with a price ceiling, stores strategically choose to advertise goods with many alternatives, such as different brands of televisions and laptops, so that when the discounted product sells out, customers may consider buying a nondiscounted product. Therefore, the pricing strategy leads to a strategic shortage that is designed to attract customers into the store to buy goods in addition to those that are advertised.

Elasticity

5

From gas guzzlers to gas misers, auto manufacturers make what customers demand, which is influenced by the price of gasoline.

At the start of the new millennium, the price of gasoline hovered around $1.50 per gallon—a veritable bargain—with a tankful costing roughly $20. Encouraged by low gas prices and a healthy economy, consumer appetites for bigger vehicles grew, leading to a rapid increase in the market for sport utility vehicles (SUVs) and trucks. Not only did the quantity of large vehicles increase, but the size of SUVs and trucks grew as well. The Hummer H2, Ford Excursion, and Chevy Suburban were all designed for consumers who wanted cars with plenty of space and who were not too concerned about gas prices.

Over the decade that followed, the market for oil and gasoline changed dramatically. Increased tensions in the Middle East along with a huge spike in oil demand from emerging markets such as China and India pushed the prices of a gallon of gas in 2010 to over double what they were a decade ago, and prices have since remained elevated. How did consumers respond to the 100% increase in the average price of gasoline? They reduced consumption by driving less, carpooling, and using public transportation. But by *how much* did the quantity of gasoline demanded fall?

The rising price of oil not only reduced the amount of gasoline consumers demanded, consumers also changed their preferences for cars. SUVs and trucks became less desirable, while small cars, hybrids, and flex-fuel vehicles became popular. How responsive were consumers in terms of changing their vehicle preferences? Not only did consumers change their buying habits as a result of higher gasoline prices, but producers responded. As prices for oil rose, more companies found it worthwhile to drill for oil, leading countries in Africa, Northern Europe, and even the United States, Canada, and Mexico to increase production. By *how much* did oil producers respond?

Lastly, as demand for SUVs and trucks fell in response to higher gas prices, car manufacturers responded by reducing the quantity of SUVs and trucks produced. Hummers and Ford Excursions were phased out completely. Producers of vehicles that use gas inefficiently responded as well, but by *how much*?

We learned in Chapter 3 that consumers respond to higher prices by buying less, while producers respond to higher prices by producing more. We also know that as prices rise, demand for complements falls while demand for substitutes rises. However, we have not yet measured the extent of such responses. In other words, how responsive are consumers and producers to changes in prices in terms of what is purchased and what is produced?

We answer the important "how responsive" question in this chapter by studying how consumers and producers respond to changes in the price of goods and services.

Elasticity—the responsiveness of one variable to changes in another—is the term economists use to measure this change. In our example above, we know that the price of gasoline is one variable and the quantity of gasoline demanded is the other variable. The concept of elasticity lets us measure the relative change in quantity demanded corresponding to various changes in the price of gasoline.

But as our example shows, elasticity can be measured for many different items. If the price of gasoline changes, how will this affect sales of large cars? Small cars? How would demand for train and bus tickets change? And we not need limit our analysis to prices either. For example, income elasticity measures changes in consumer demand

BY THE NUMBERS

Elasticity: How Markets React to Price Changes

Elasticity varies across goods and services, largely due to factors involving the price of the good, availability of substitutes, and whether a good is a necessity. Elasticity also varies across consumer groups and by country.

Salt (0.1)

Movies (0.9)

Foreign Travel (4.0)

Inelastic   **Unitary Inelastic**   **Elastic**

Prescription Medicine (0.3)

Fast Food (1.3)

Diamonds (4.2)

Note: The numbers in parentheses refer to the price elasticity of demand.

Food is necessary for survival, and thus an inelastic good. Yet, elasticity varies by country; when the price of food rises, poorer countries reduce consumption more than rich countries.

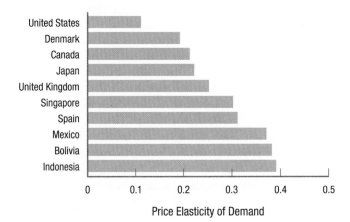

United States
Denmark
Canada
Japan
United Kingdom
Singapore
Spain
Mexico
Bolivia
Indonesia

0   0.1   0.2   0.3   0.4   0.5

Price Elasticity of Demand

2% 1%
8%
19%
70%

■ Gas   ■ Flex Fuel   ■ Hybrid   ■ Diesel   ■ Electric

Alternative-fuel cars are growing in popularity. In 2012 they represented 30% of new vehicle sales.

Don't like paying for parking? You're not alone. When the price of downtown parking in major cities increased 10%, people on average:

- Used that parking lot 5.4% less.
- Used farther parking lots 8.3% more.
- Used park & ride 3.6% more.
- Rode public transit 2.9% more.
- Reduced the number of trips downtown 4.6%.

71%
Average rise in public university tuition (a highly inelastic good) from 2000–2010.

68%
Average fall in international calling rates (a highly elastic good) from 2000–2010.

in response to changes in income. As incomes rise with a growing economy, will purchases of cars and trucks pick up? By how much? This is information automakers want to know.

Elasticity is a simple economic concept that nonetheless contains a tremendous amount of information about demand for specific products. If a firm raises its price by 50 cents, will it end up with more in revenue, or will the increase in price lead to a drop in quantity demanded that more than offsets the price increase? Knowing a product's price elasticity allows economists to predict the amount by which quantity demanded will drop in response to a price increase, or grow in response to a price decrease. The concept of elasticity helps you to put supply and demand concepts to work.

Elasticity of Demand

We know by the law of demand that as prices rise, quantity demanded falls. The important question is, *How much* will sales decline? If a small price increase results in *all* of your customers switching to your competitors, it is clearly not a good idea to raise the price; you will be out of business. And if a small price increase still results in a large reduction in quantity sold, then raising prices probably is not a good idea. However, if a large price increase elicits only a small loss in sales, then raising prices may make sense. As we shall see, the concept of elasticity and the impact of changing price on a firm's sales revenue help to determine the answer.

price elasticity of demand A measure of the responsiveness of quantity demanded to a change in price, equal to the percentage change in quantity demanded divided by the percentage change in price.

Price elasticity of demand (E_d) is a measure of how responsive quantity demanded is to a change in price and is defined as

$$E_d = \frac{\text{Percentage Change in Quantity Demanded}}{\text{Percentage Change in Price}}$$

For example, if prices of strawberries rise by 5% and sales fall by 10%, then the price elasticity of demand for strawberries is

$$E_d = \frac{-10\%}{+5\%} = -2$$

Alternatively, if a 5% reduction in strawberry prices results in a 10% gain in sales, the price elasticity of demand also is −2 ($E_d = 10 \div [-5] = -2$).

Often we are not given percentage changes. Rather, we are given numerical values and have to convert them into percentage changes. For example, to compute a change in price, take the new price (P_{new}) and subtract the old price (P_{old}), then divide this result by the old price (P_{old}). This approach to calculating percentage changes is known as the *base method.* Finally, to put this ratio in percentage terms, multiply by 100. In equation form:

$$\text{Percentage Change} = \frac{(P_{new} - P_{old})}{P_{old}} \times 100$$

For example, if the old price of gasoline (P_{old}) was $2.00 per gallon and the new price goes up by $1.00 to $3.00 per gallon, then the percentage change is

$$\text{Percentage Change} = \frac{\$3.00 - \$2.00}{\$2.00} = \frac{\$1.00}{\$2.00} = 0.50 \times 100 = 50\%$$

Price Elasticity of Demand as an Absolute Value

The price elasticity of demand is always a negative number. This reflects the fact that the demand curve's slope is negative: As prices increase, quantity demanded falls. Price and quantity demanded stand in an inverse relationship to one another, resulting in a negative value for price elasticity. Economists nevertheless frequently refer to price elasticity of demand in positive terms. They simply use the *absolute value* of the computed price elasticity of demand. Recalling our examples, where $E_d = -2$, we can take the absolute value of -2, written as $|-2|$, and refer to E_d as 2. For most comparisons, we can use the absolute value of elasticity and ignore the minus sign.

What does this elasticity value of 2 tell us? Quite simply, that for every 1% increase in price, quantity demanded will decline by 2%. Conversely, for every 1% decline in price, quantity demanded will increase by 2%.

Measuring Elasticity with Percentages

Measuring elasticity in percentage terms rather than specific units enables economists to compare the characteristics of various unrelated products. Comparing price and sales changes for houses, cars, and hamburgers in dollar amounts would be so complex as to be meaningless. Because a dollar increase in the price of gasoline is different from a dollar increase in the price of a BMW, by using percentage change we can compare the sensitivity of demand curves of different products. Percentages allow us to compare changes in prices and sales for any two products, no matter how dissimilar they are; a 100% increase is the same percentage change for any product.

We have seen how to compute the elasticity of demand, and we have seen why working with percentage changes is so important. Elasticity is a relative measure giving us a way to compare products with widely different prices and output measures.

Elastic and Inelastic Demand

All products have some price elasticity of demand. When prices go up, quantity demanded will fall. That is the basis of the negative slope of the demand curve. But people are more responsive to changes in the prices of some products than others. Economists label goods as being *elastic, inelastic,* or *unitary elastic.*

Elastic When the absolute value of the computed price elasticity of demand is greater than 1, economists refer to this as **elastic demand.** An elastic demand curve is one that is responsive to price changes. At the extreme is the *perfectly elastic* demand curve shown in panel A of Figure 1 on the next page. Notice that it is horizontal, showing that the slightest increase in price will result in zero output being sold.

In reality, no branded product—Coca-Cola, Apple iPhone, or Toyota Prius—ever has a perfectly elastic demand curve. Still, products with many close substitutes face highly elastic demand curves. One recent study of several brands of bath tissue found the price elasticities of demand for Scott, Kleenex, Charmin, Quilted Northern, and other brands ranged from 2.0 to 4.5—highly elastic.[1] Raise the price of Charmin, and watch how quickly sales fall as people switch to Quilted Northern or Scott. Canned peaches, nuts and bolts, cereal, and bottled water are all examples of products facing highly elastic demands. If one bottled water company were to raise its price by much, many consumers would switch to other brands, because all bottled water tastes pretty much the same. Demand curves for elastic goods are relatively flat, as shown in panel B in Figure 1.

Inelastic At the other extreme, what about products that see little change in sales even when prices change dramatically? The opposite of the perfectly elastic demand curve is the curve showing no response to changes in price. Economists call this a *perfectly inelastic* demand curve. An example appears in panel E of Figure 1. This curve is vertical, not horizontal as in panel A. For products with perfectly inelastic demands, quantity demanded does not change when price changes.

elastic demand The absolute value of the price elasticity of demand is greater than 1. Elastic demands are very responsive to changes in price. The percentage change in quantity demanded is greater than the percentage change in price.

---

[1] Lawrence Wu, "Two Methods of Determining Elasticities of Demand and Their Use in Merger Simulation," in Lawrence Wu, Ed., *Economics of Antitrust: New Issues, Questions, and Insights* (New York: National Economic Research Associates), 2004, pp. 21–33.

FIGURE 1

The Shape and Elasticity of Demand Curves

The horizontal demand curve in panel A represents perfectly elastic demand because when price increases, quantity demanded drops to zero. Panel E, on the other hand, illustrates a perfectly inelastic demand curve where quantity demanded does not change when the price changes. Panel B shows an elastic demand curve, which is relatively flat, and Panel D shows an inelastic demand curve, which is relatively steep. Panel C shows that if elasticity of demand is unitary, then a 1% increase in price will result in a 1% decrease in quantity demanded. Note that the unitary elastic demand curve is not a straight line.

inelastic demand The absolute value of the price elasticity of demand is less than 1. Inelastic demands are not very responsive to changes in price. The percentage change in quantity demanded is less than the percentage change in price.

What products might be inelastically demanded? Consider products that are immensely important to our lives but have few substitutes—for example, drugs that ameliorate life-threatening illnesses such as heart disease or stroke, and insulin for diabetics. If people who need these products have the money, they will buy them, no matter how high the price. Some products that are relatively, though not perfectly, inelastic include gasoline, tobacco, and most spices. If gasoline prices rise too sharply, some consumers will curtail their driving. Still, it takes a fairly drastic rise in gasoline prices before most people curtail their driving significantly. Doubling the price of cinnamon will probably not reduce our demand because it is such a small fraction of our overall food budget. Economists define **inelastic demand** as demand curves with elasticity coefficients that are less than 1. These demand curves are relatively steep, as shown in panel D in Figure 1.

Note that the demand for gasoline is inelastic, but the demand for specific brands of gasoline is elastic. Brand preferences for commodities that are nearly identical to one another, such as gasoline, are weak, and many different outlets exist for buying gas. If your local Shell station raises gasoline prices by a significant amount, you will probably go to the Exxon station down the street. Giving up using gasoline altogether, on the other hand, is much harder. Over time, public transportation or electric cars may be possible substitutes for gas-powered cars, but few people will be able to adopt these substitutes in the short run. On the contrary, many people are highly dependent on their gas-powered cars, therefore gas purchases do not drop substantially when prices rise. Thus, demand for a particular brand of gas (Exxon, Shell) is elastic, while the demand for gasoline as a commodity is inelastic.

unitary elasticity of demand
The absolute value of the price elasticity of demand is equal to 1. The percentage change in quantity demanded is just equal to the percentage change in price.

Unitary Elasticity Elastic demand curves have an elasticity coefficient that is greater than 1, while inelastic demand curves have a coefficient of less than 1. That leaves those products with an elasticity coefficient just equal to 1. This condition is called **unitary elasticity of demand.** It means the percentage change in quantity demanded is precisely equal to the percentage change in price. Panel C of Figure 1 shows a demand curve where price elasticity equals 1. Note that this demand curve is not a straight line. The reasons for this will become clear in our discussion later in the chapter.

Determinants of Elasticity

Price elasticity of demand measures how sensitive sales are to price changes. But what determines elasticity itself? The four basic determinants of a product's elasticity of demand are (1) the availability of substitute products, (2) the percentage of income or household budget spent on the product, (3) the difference between luxuries and necessities, and (4) the time period being examined.

Substitutability The more close substitutes, or possible alternatives, a product has, the easier it is for consumers to switch to a competing product and the more elastic the demand. For many people, beef and chicken are substitutes, as are competing brands of cola, such as Coke and Pepsi. All have relatively elastic demands. Conversely, if a product has few close substitutes, such as insulin for diabetics or tobacco for heavy smokers, its elasticity of demand tends to be lower.

Proportion of Income Spent on a Product A second determinant of elasticity is the proportion (percentage) of household income spent on a product. In general, the smaller the percent of household income spent on a product, the lower the elasticity of demand. For example, you probably spend little of your income on salt, or on cinnamon or other spices. As a result, a hefty increase in the price of salt, say 25%, would not affect your salt consumption because the impact on your budget would be tiny. But if a product represents a significant part of household spending, elasticity of demand tends to be greater, or more elastic. A 10% increase in your rent upon renewing your lease, for example, would put a large dent in your budget, significantly reducing your purchasing power for many other products. Such a rent increase would likely lead you to look around earnestly for a less expensive apartment.

Luxuries Versus Necessities The third determinant of elasticity is whether the good is considered a luxury or a necessity. Luxuries tend to have demands that are more elastic than those of necessities. Necessities such as food, electricity, and health care are more important to everyday living, and quantity demanded does not change significantly when prices rise. Luxuries such as trips to Hawaii, yachts, and designer watches, on the other hand, can be given up when prices rise.

Time Period The fourth determinant of elasticity is the time period under consideration. When consumers have some time to adjust their consumption patterns, the elasticity of demand becomes more elastic. When they have little time to adjust, the elasticity of demand tends to be more inelastic. Thus, as we saw earlier, when gasoline prices rise suddenly, most consumers cannot immediately change their transportation patterns, therefore gasoline sales do not drop significantly. However, as gas prices continue to remain high, we see shifts in consumer behavior, to which automakers respond by producing smaller, more fuel-efficient cars.

Table 1 provides a sampling of estimates of elasticities for specific products. As we might expect, medical prescriptions and taxi service have relatively inelastic price elasticities of demand, while foreign travel and restaurant meals have relatively elastic demands.

Selected Estimates of Price Elasticities of Demand					TABLE 1
Inelastic		**Roughly Unitary Elastic**		**Elastic**	
Salt	0.1	Movies	0.9	Shrimp	1.3
Gasoline (short run)	0.2	Shoes	0.9	Furniture	1.5
Cigarettes	0.2	Tires	1.0	Commuter rail service (long run)	1.6
Medical care	0.3	Private education	1.1	Restaurant meals	2.3
Medical prescriptions	0.3	Automobiles	1.2	Air travel	2.4
Pesticides	0.4			Fresh vegetables	2.5
Taxi service	0.6			Foreign travel	4.0

Source: Compiled from numerous studies reporting estimates for price elasticity of demand.

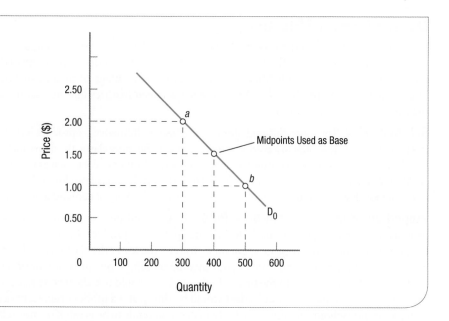

Computing Price Elasticities

When elasticity is computed between two points, the calculated value will differ depending on whether price is increasing or decreasing. For example, in Figure 2, if the price *increases* from $1.00 to $2.00, elasticity is equal to

$$E_d = \frac{300 - 500}{500} \div \frac{2.00 - 1.00}{1.00}$$

$$= \frac{-200}{500} \div \frac{1.00}{1.00}$$

$$= -0.4 \div 1$$

$$= |{-0.4}|$$

$$= 0.4$$

But when price *decreases* from $2.00 to $1.00, elasticity is equal to

$$E_d = \frac{500 - 300}{300} \div \frac{1.00 - 2.00}{2.00}$$

$$= \frac{200}{300} \div \frac{-1.00}{2.00}$$

$$= 0.67 \div -0.5$$

$$= |{-1.33}|$$

$$= 1.33$$

Using Midpoints to Compute Elasticity To avoid getting different results computing elasticity from different directions, economists compute price elasticity using the midpoints of price $[(P_0 + P_1)/2]$ and the midpoints of quantity demanded $[(Q_0 + Q_1)/2]$ as the base. This approach to calculating percentage changes is referred to as the *midpoint method*.

Therefore, the *price elasticity of demand* formula (assuming price falls from P_0 to P_1 and quantity demanded rises from Q_0 to Q_1) is

$$E_d = \frac{Q_1 - Q_0}{(Q_0 + Q_1)/2} \div \frac{P_1 - P_0}{(P_0 + P_1)/2}$$

Using the midpoints of price and quantity to compute the relevant percentage changes essentially gives us the average elasticity between point *a* and point *b*. Price elasticity of demand is the difference in quantity over the sum of the two quantities divided by 2, divided by the difference in price over the sum of the two prices divided by 2. In Figure 2, the price elasticity of demand between points *a* and *b* would equal

$$E_d = \frac{500 - 300}{(300 + 500)/2} \div \frac{1.00 - 2.00}{(2.00 + 1.00)/2}$$

$$= \frac{200}{400} \div \frac{-1.00}{1.50}$$

$$= 0.50 \div -0.67$$

$$= |-0.75|$$

$$= 0.75$$

Check for yourself to see that this elasticity formula yields the same results whether you compute elasticity for a price increase from $1.00 to $2.00 or for a price decrease from $2.00 to $1.00.

Now that we have seen what price elasticity of demand is and how to calculate it, let's put this knowledge to work by looking at how elasticity affects total revenue.

 # CHECKPOINT

ELASTICITY OF DEMAND

- Elasticity summarizes how responsive one variable is to a change in another variable.
- Price elasticity of demand summarizes how responsive quantity demanded is to changes in price.
- Price elasticity of demand is defined as the percentage change in quantity demanded divided by the percentage change in price.
- Inelastic demands are relatively unresponsive to changes in price, while quantity demanded is more responsive with elastic demands.
- Elasticity is determined by a product's substitutability, its proportion of the budget, whether it is a luxury or a necessity, and the time period considered.
- Economists use midpoints to derive consistent estimates whether price rises or falls.

QUESTION: Using your knowledge of the determinants of elasticity, why is gasoline inelastic in the short-term but elastic in the long-term? Explain why automobiles tend to have the opposite effect, being elastic in the short-term but inelastic in the long-term?

Answers to the Checkpoint questions can be found at the end of this chapter.

⊙ Total Revenue and Other Measures of Elasticity

Elasticity is important to firms because elasticity measures the responsiveness of quantity sold to changes in price, which provides valuable information to firms in deciding whether to increase or decrease prices. Owners of a restaurant that is completely full each evening might ponder raising its prices, but only if it can retain most of its customers. Another restaurant, which has few customers, might wish to lower its prices to generate more business, but only if it generates enough business to offset the lower prices it charges.

Elasticity is also important because it allows firms to determine how a change in the price of one product might affect the demand for other items, or how changes in economic conditions might affect the market for their goods. If a supermarket discounts the price of sirloin steaks, how would this affect the demand for other cuts of beef, or other meats? Would it increase sales of steak sauce and potatoes? These are questions we address in this section using other measures of elasticity.

Elasticity and Total Revenue

The elasticity of demand, which we learned about in the previous section, has an important effect on the total revenues of the firm. **Total revenue** (*TR*) is equal to the number of units sold (*Q*) times the price of each unit (*P*), or

$$TR = Q \times P$$

The sensitivity of output sold to price changes greatly influences how much total revenue changes when price changes.

Inelastic Demand   When consumers are so loyal to a product or so few substitutes exist that consumers continue to buy the product even when its price goes up, the product is inelastically demanded. Panel A of Figure 3 shows the impact such a price increase has on total revenue when the demand for a product is inelastic. Price rises from $2.00 to $4.00, and sales decline from 600 to 500 units. In this case, total revenue *rises*. We know this because the revenue gained from the price hike [($4.00 − $2.00) × 500 = $1,000] is greater than the revenue lost [($2.00 × (600 − 500) = $200]. We can see this by comparing the size of the area labeled "Revenue Gained" with the area labeled "Revenue Lost" in the figure. What has happened here? The price hike has driven off only a few customers, but the firm's many remaining customers are paying a much higher price, thus driving up the firm's total revenue.

This may suggest that firms would always want the demand for their products to be inelastic. Unfortunately for them, inelastic demand has a flip side. Specifically, if supply increases (due to a technical advance, say), sales will rise only moderately, even as prices fall dramatically. This leads to a drop in total revenue: Consumers indeed buy more of the product at its new lower price, but not enough to offset the lower price per unit received by firms.

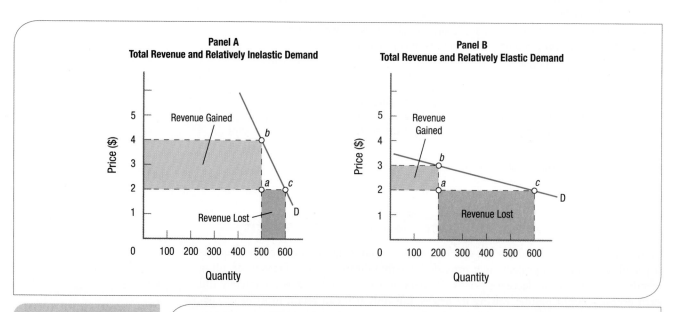

Panel A
Total Revenue and Relatively Inelastic Demand

Panel B
Total Revenue and Relatively Elastic Demand

FIGURE 3

Total Revenue and Elasticity of Demand

Given inelastic demand in panel A, when price rises from $2 to $4, revenue rises because the revenue gained from the price hike ($1,000) is greater than the revenue lost from fewer sales ($200). The price hike may have driven off a few customers, but the firm's many remaining customers are paying a much higher price, thus increasing the firm's revenue. When products have elastic demands as shown in panel B, usually because many substitutes are available, firms feel a greater impact from changes in price. A small rise in price causes sales to fall off dramatically.

Elastic Demand Elastic demand is the opposite of inelastic demand. Firms with elastically demanded products will see their sales change dramatically in response to small price changes. Panel B of Figure 3 shows what happens to total revenue when a firm increases the price of a product with elastic demand. Although price does not increase much, sales fall significantly. Revenue lost greatly exceeds the revenue gained from the price increase, thus total revenue falls.

The opposite occurs when prices fall and demand is elastic. The high elasticity of demand faced by restaurants helps explain why so many of them offer "Happy Hour" specials and other discounts. As prices fall, sales have the potential to expand rapidly, thus increasing revenue.

Unitary Elasticity We have looked at the impact of changing prices on revenue when demand is elastic and inelastic. When the elasticity of demand is unitary ($E_d = 1$), a 10% increase in price results in a 10% reduction in quantity demanded. As a result, total revenue is unaffected.

Table 2 summarizes the effects price changes have on total revenue for different price elasticities of demand.

Total Revenue, Price Changes, and Price Elasticity of Demand			TABLE 2
	Elasticity		
Price Change	**Inelastic**	**Elastic**	**Unitary Elastic**
Price increases	TR increases	TR decreases	No change in TR
Price decreases	TR decreases	TR increases	No change in TR

Elasticity and Total Revenue Along a Straight-Line (Linear) Demand Curve Elasticity varies along a straight-line demand curve. Figure 4 on the next page shows a linear demand curve in panel A and graphs the corresponding total revenue points in panel B. In panel A, the elastic part of the curve is that portion above point *e*. Notice that when price falls from $11 to $10, the revenue gained ($100) is much larger than the revenue lost ($10), and thus total revenue rises. This is shown in panel B, where total revenue rises when output grows from 10 to 20 units.

As we move down the demand curve, elasticity will eventually equal 1 (at point *e*) where elasticity is unitary. Price was falling up to this point, while total revenue kept rising until the last price reduction just before $6, where revenue did not change. Revenue is at its maximum at point *e* or a price of $6 in both panels.

As price continues to fall below $6, the demand curve moves into an inelastic range because the percentage change in quantity demanded is less than the percentage change in price. Therefore, when price falls from $3 to $2, revenue declines. The revenue gained ($20) is less than the revenue lost ($90). This decline in revenue is shown in panel B, as total revenue falls as output rises from 90 to 100 units sold.

To summarize, elasticity changes along a negatively sloped linear demand curve because the *percentage* change in price and quantity varies along the curve. When the price of a product is low, a 1-unit change in price is a large percentage change while the percentage change in quantity demanded is small. When the price is high, a 1-unit change in price is a small percentage change but the percentage change in quantity is large.

FIGURE 4

Price Elasticity and Total Revenue Along a Straight Line (Linear) Demand Curve

Price elasticity varies along a straight line demand curve. In panel A, the elastic part of the curve lies above point *e*. Thus, when price falls from $11 to $10, revenue rises, as shown in panel B. As we move down the demand curve, elasticity equals 1 (at point *e*) where elasticity is unitary. Revenue is maximized at this point. As price continues to fall below $6, demand moves into an inelastic range. When price falls from $3 to $2, revenue declines, as shown in panel B.

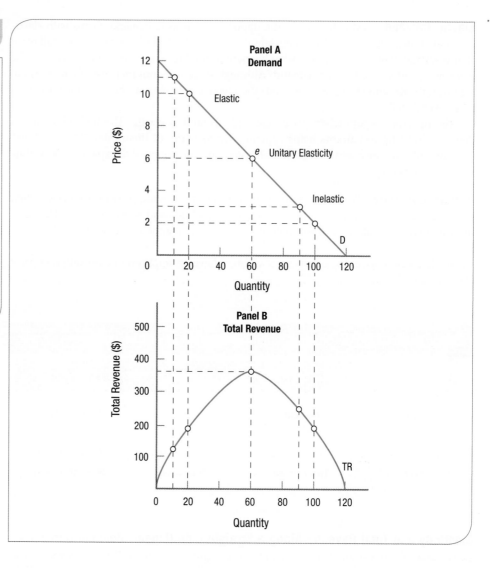

Other Elasticities of Demand

Besides the price elasticity of demand, two other elasticities of demand are important. The first, *cross elasticity of demand*, measures how changes in the price of one good affect the demand for other related goods. If Toyota is planning a price reduction, what impact will this have on the sale of Fords? Ford will want to estimate this to decide whether to ignore Toyota or lower its own automobile prices.

Another type of elasticity measures how responsive quantity demanded is to changes in income. This is called *income elasticity of demand*. Incomes vary as the economy expands and contracts. To plan their future employment and production, many industries want to know how the demand for their products will be affected when the economy changes. How much will airline travel be affected if the economy moves into a recession? What will happen to sales of lattes at Starbucks? Each business faces a different situation.

Let's consider these two elasticities of demand more closely, beginning with cross elasticity of demand.

Cross Elasticity of Demand   **Cross elasticity of demand** (E_{ab}) measures how responsive the quantity demanded of one good (product a) is to changes in the price of another (product b):

cross elasticity of demand
Measures how responsive the quantity demanded of one good is to changes in the price of another good. Substitute goods have positive cross elasticities: An increase in the price of one good leads consumers to substitute (buy more of) the other good whose price has not changed. Complementary goods have negative cross elasticities: An increase in the price of a complement leads to a reduction in sales of the other good whose price has not changed.

$$E_{ab} = \frac{\text{Percentage Change in Quantity Demanded of Product a}}{\text{Percentage Change in Price of Product b}}$$

Using cross elasticity of demand, we can classify goods in two ways. Products a and b are **substitutes** if their cross elasticity of demand is positive ($E_{ab} > 0$). Common sense tells us that chicken and turkey are substitutes. Therefore, if the price of turkey rises, people will substitute away from turkey and toward chicken, thus the quantity demanded for chicken will grow. This illustrates a positive cross elasticity. Similar relationships exist between Toyota and Honda cars, wireless services provided by AT&T and Verizon, and the price of gas and public transportation.

Second, products a and b are **complements** if their cross elasticity of demand is negative ($E_{ab} < 0$). This is an instance in which a minus sign conveys important information. Complementary products are those goods and services that are consumed together, such as lift tickets and snowboard rentals. When the price of lift tickets rises, the result is that the quantity demanded for snowboard rentals falls as fewer people head to the mountains. Other complementary goods include coffee and cream, hamburgers and french fries, and hot dogs and hot dog buns. Finally, two goods are *not related* if a cross elasticity of demand is zero, or near zero.

Income Elasticity of Demand The **income elasticity of demand** (E_Y) measures how responsive quantity demanded is to changes in consumer income. We define the income elasticity of demand as

$$E_Y = \frac{\text{Percentage Change in Quantity Demanded}}{\text{Percentage Change in Income}}$$

Depending on the value of the income elasticity of demand, we can classify goods in three ways. First, a **normal good** is one whose income elasticity is positive, but less than 1 ($0 < E_Y < 1$). As income rises, quantity demanded rises as well, but not as fast as the rise in income. Most products are normal goods. If your income doubles, you will probably buy more sporting equipment and restaurant meals, but not twice as many.

A second category, *income superior goods* or **luxury goods,** includes products with an income elasticity greater than 1 ($E_Y > 1$). As income rises, quantity demanded grows faster than income. Goods and services such as Mercedes automobiles, caviar, fine wine, and visits to European spas are luxury or income superior goods.

Finally, **inferior goods** are those goods for which income elasticity is negative ($E_Y < 0$). When income rises, the quantity demanded for these goods falls. Inferior goods include potatoes, beans, cheap motels, and nosebleed section concert tickets. Get yourself a nice raise, and you will probably buy concert tickets that let you see the band up close and personal.

Keep in mind that inferior goods are not necessarily poor in quality; they simply describe goods that one buys fewer of as income increases, and vice versa. Therefore, inferior goods can vary from person to person. Nosebleed seats might be an inferior good for an avid concertgoer, but can be a normal good to a person who rarely goes to concerts.

Understanding how product sales are affected by changing incomes and economic conditions can help firms to diversify their product lines so that sales and employment can be stabilized to some extent over time. For example, firms that produce all three types of goods can try to switch production toward the good that current economic conditions favor: In boom times, production is shifted more toward the making of luxury goods. Chevrolet will produce more Corvettes in boom times, and more Chevy Sparks during economic slowdowns.

This is a good place to stop and reflect on what we have discovered so far. We have seen that elasticity measures the responsiveness of one variable to changes in another. Elasticity measures changes in percentage terms so that products of different magnitudes—a bottle of soda and an airplane—can be compared. Products that have a price elasticity of demand greater than 1 are elastic; products with price elasticity of demand less than 1 are inelastic; and products with a price elasticity

substitutes Goods consumers substitute for one another depending on their relative prices, such as coffee and tea. Substitutes have a positive cross elasticity of demand.

complements Goods that are typically consumed together, such as coffee and sugar. Complements have a negative cross elasticity of demand.

income elasticity of demand Measures how responsive quantity demanded is to changes in consumer income.

normal goods Goods that have positive income elasticities of less than 1. When consumer income grows, quantity demanded rises for normal goods, but less than the rise in income.

luxury goods Goods that have income elasticities greater than 1. When consumer income grows, quantity demanded of luxury goods rises more than the rise in income.

inferior goods Goods that have income elasticities that are negative. When consumer income grows, quantity demanded falls for inferior goods.

Ocean/Corbis

After college, incomes rise, which means fewer packed lunches on the lawn and more fancy lunches at the local bistro.

ISSUE

Using Loss Leaders to Generate Higher Total Revenue

At the start of each school year, office supply stores will often advertise items for as low as one cent. These items typically are essential school supplies such as paper, pencils, and folders that parents need to buy for their children. Because school supplies are necessities and generally low-priced, they are relatively inelastic goods. Why, then, would stores choose to reduce their prices, knowing that such actions would lead to a fall in total revenue?

The answer lies not in how prices for school supplies affect total revenue, but instead the effect that those remarkably low prices, known as *loss leaders*, has on the cross elasticity of demand for more pricier items, such as laptops, color printers, and office furniture, sold at the store. In other words, the practically free school supplies are used as an incentive to attract parents into the store.

Wouldn't some parents just buy the school supplies on sale and nothing else? Some actually do. However, most stores place limits on the quantity of the discounted items that can be purchased. Further, the inelastic nature of school supplies means that parents are not likely to hoard large quantities of school supplies because of the reduction in prices. More important, the potential gain from just one customer choosing to buy a high-priced computer or printer would offset the lost revenue from the loss leaders many times over. And because the start of the school year is when many high-priced school items are purchased, few parents end up buying just the advertised items.

Loss leaders are an effective advertising tool to increase total revenues from the sale of higher priced related goods. And loss leaders are not limited to office supply stores. Other examples of loss

Barbara Helgason/Dreamstime.com

leaders include convenience stores advertising a free soda or coffee on large banners visible to potential customers at the gas pump, fast-food restaurants featuring a 99 cent sandwich special on their marquee, or a campus sporting goods store offering a free T-shirt just for stopping by. In each case, stores are betting on consumers making decisions beyond that of the loss leader, thus illustrating the importance of cross elasticity of demand in business decisions.

of demand equal to 1 are unitary elastic. We saw how total revenue increases when price rises for an inelastic good but decreases when price rises for an elastic good. Finally, we saw that elasticity can be used to measure the effects of related goods using cross elasticity of demand, as well as changes in income using income elasticity of demand.

 CHECKPOINT

TOTAL REVENUE AND OTHER MEASURES OF ELASTICITY

- When demand is inelastic and prices rise, total revenue rises. When demand is inelastic and prices fall, total revenue falls.
- When demand is elastic and prices rise, total revenue falls. When demand is elastic and prices fall, total revenue rises.
- Straight line demand curves have elastic (at higher prices) and inelastic (at lower prices) ranges.
- Cross elasticity of demand measures how responsive the quantity demanded of one product is to price changes of another. Substitutes have positive cross elasticities while complements have negative cross elasticities.
- Income elasticity of demand is a measure of how responsive quantity demanded is to changes in income. This determines whether a good is a luxury, normal, or inferior good.

QUESTION: Two clothing stores located in the same shopping center have a big sale: 20% off on everything in the store. After the sale, store 1 finds that its total revenue has increased, while store 2 finds that total revenue has decreased. What does this tell you about the price elasticity of demand for the clothes in stores 1 and 2?

Answers to the Checkpoint question can be found at the end of this chapter.

Elasticity of Supply

So far, we have looked at the consumer when we looked at the elasticity of demand. Now let us turn our attention to the producer, and look at elasticity of supply.

Price elasticity of supply (E_s) measures the responsiveness of quantity supplied to changes in the price of the product. Price elasticity of supply is defined as

$$E_s = \frac{\text{Percentage Change in Quantity Supplied}}{\text{Percentage Change in Price}}$$

Note that because the slope of the supply curve is positive, the price elasticity of supply will always be a positive number. Economists classify price elasticity of supply in the same way that they classify price elasticity of demand. Classification is based on whether the percentage change in quantity supplied is greater than, less than, or equal to the percentage change in price. When price rises just a little and quantity increases by much more, supply is elastic, and vice versa. The output of many commodities such as gold and seasonal vegetables cannot be quickly increased if their price increases, so they are inelastic. In summary:

> **Elastic supply:** $E_s > 1$
> **Inelastic supply:** $E_s < 1$
> **Unitary elastic supply:** $E_s = 1$

Looking at the three supply curves in Figure 5, we can easily determine which curve is inelastic, which is elastic, and which is unitary elastic. First, note that all three curves go through point *a*. As we increase the price from P_0 to P_1, we see that the response in quantity supplied is different for all three curves. Consider supply curve S_1 first. When price changes to P_1 (point *b*), the change in output (Q_0 to Q_1) is the smallest for the three curves. Most important, the percentage change in quantity supplied is smaller than the percentage change in price, therefore S_1 is an inelastic supply curve.

Contrast this with S_3. In this case, when price rises to P_1 (point *d*), output climbs from Q_0 all the way to Q_3. Because the percentage change in output is larger than the percentage change in price, S_3 is elastic. And finally, curve S_2 is a unitary elastic curve because the percentage change in output is the same as the percentage change in price.

price elasticity of supply A measure of the responsiveness of quantity supplied to changes in price. An elastic supply curve has elasticity greater than 1, whereas inelastic supplies have elasticities less than 1. Time is the most important determinant of the elasticity of supply.

elastic supply Price elasticity of supply is greater than 1. The percentage change in quantity supplied is greater than the percentage change in price.

inelastic supply Price elasticity of supply is less than 1. The percentage change in quantity supplied is less than the percentage change in price.

unitary elastic supply Price elasticity of supply is equal to 1. The percentage change in quantity supplied is equal to the percentage change in price.

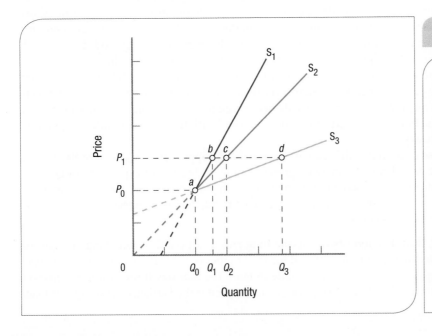

FIGURE 5

Price Elasticity of Supply

All three supply curves in this figure run through point *a*, but they respond differently when price changes from P_0 to P_1. Considering supply curve S_1 first, when price changes, the percentage change in quantity supplied is smaller than the percentage change in price, thus S_1 is an inelastic supply curve. Curve S_2 is a unitary elastic supply curve, because the percentage change in output is the same as the percentage change in price. For supply curve S_3, the percentage change in output is greater than the percentage change in price, so S_3 is elastic. Elastic linear supply curves cross the price axis, inelastic linear supply curves cross the quantity axis, and unitary elastic linear supply curves go through the origin.

Here is a simple rule of thumb. When the supply curve is linear, like those shown in Figure 5, you can always determine if the supply curve is elastic, inelastic, or unitary elastic by extending the curve to the axis and applying the following rules:

- Elastic supply curves always cross the price axis, as does curve S_3.
- Inelastic supply curves always cross the quantity axis, as does curve S_1.
- Unitary elastic supply curves always cross through the origin, as does curve S_2.

Time and Price Elasticity of Supply

The primary determinant of price elasticity of supply is time. To adjust output in response to changes in market prices, firms require time. Firms have both variable inputs, such as labor, and fixed inputs, such as plant capacity. To increase their labor force, firms must recruit, interview, and hire more workers. This can take as little time as a few hours—a call to a temp agency—or as long as a few months. On the other hand, building another plant or expanding the existing plant to increase output involves considerably more time and resources. In some instances, such as building a new oil refinery or computer chip plant, it can take as long as a decade, with environmental clearance alone often requiring years of study and costing millions of dollars. Finally, in some markets, such as that for original Rembrandt paintings, new supply will never be created (assuming that the dead cannot return). Economists typically distinguish among three types of time periods: the market period, the short run, and the long run.

market period Time period so short that the output and the number of firms are fixed. Agricultural products at harvest time face market periods. Products that unexpectedly become instant hits face market periods (there is a lag between when the firm realizes it has a hit on its hands and when inventory can be replaced).

The Market Period The **market period** is so short that the output and the number of firms in an industry are fixed; firms have no time to change their production levels in response to changes in product price. Consider a raspberry market in the summer. Even if consumers flock to the market, their tastes having shifted in favor of fresh raspberries, farmers can do little to increase the supply of raspberries until the next year. Figure 6 shows a market period supply curve (S_{MP}) for agricultural products such as raspberries. During the market period, the quantity of product available to the market is fixed at Q_0. If demand changes (shifting from D_0 to D_1), the only impact is on the price of the product. In Figure 6, price moves from P_0 (point e) to P_1 (point a). In summary, if demand grows over the market period, price will rise, and vice versa.

Changes in demand over the market period can be devastating for firms selling perishable goods. If demand falls, cantaloupes cannot be kept until demand grows; they must either be sold at a discount or trashed.

short run Time period when plant capacity and the number of firms in the industry cannot change. Firms can employ more people, have existing employees work overtime, or hire part-time employees to produce more, but this is done in an existing plant.

The Short Run The **short run** is defined as a period of time during which plant capacity and the number of firms in the industry cannot change. Firms can, however, change the amount of labor, raw materials, and other variable inputs they employ in the short run to adjust their output to changes in the market. Note that the short run does not imply a specific number of weeks, months, or years. It simply means a period short enough that firms cannot adjust their plant capacity, but long enough for them to hire more labor to increase their production. A restaurant with an outdoor seating area can hire additional staff and open this area in a relatively short timeframe when the weather gets warm, but manufacturing firms usually need more time to hire and train new people for their production lines. Clearly, the time associated with the short run differs depending on the industry.

This also is illustrated in Figure 6. The short-run supply curve, S_{SR}, is more elastic than the market period curve. If demand grows from D_0 to D_1, output expands from Q_0 to Q_2 and price increases to P_2 as equilibrium moves from point e to point b. Because output can expand in the short run in response to rising demand, the price increase is not as drastic as it was in the market period.

long run Time period long enough for firms to alter their plant capacities and for the number of firms in the industry to change. Existing firms can expand or build new plants, or firms can enter or exit the industry.

The Long Run Economists define the **long run** as a period of time long enough for firms to alter their plant capacity and for the number of firms in the industry to change. In the long run, some firms may decide to leave the industry if they think the market will be unfavorable. Alternatively, new firms may enter the market, or existing firms can

FIGURE 6

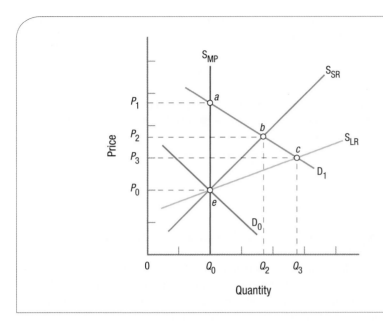

Time and Price Elasticity of Supply

During the market period, the quantity of output available to the market is fixed and the only impact will be on the price of the product, which will rise from P_0 to P_1 if demand increases. Over the short run, firms can change the amount of inputs they employ to adjust their output to market changes. Thus, the short-run supply curve (S_{SR}) is more elastic than the market period curve; and price increases are more moderate. In the long run, firms can change their plant capacity and enter or exit an industry. Long-run supply curve S_{LR} is elastic, and a rise in demand leads to only a small increase in price.

alter their production capacity. Because all these conceivable changes are possible in the long run, the long-run supply curve is more elastic, as illustrated in Figure 6 by supply curve S_{LR}. In this case, a rise in demand from D_0 to D_1 gives rise to a small increase in the price of the product, while generating a major increase in output, from Q_0 to Q_3 (point c).

In giving the long-run supply curve S_{LR} a small but positive slope, we are assuming that an industry's costs will increase slightly as it increases its output. Firms must compete with other industries to expand production. Wages and other input prices rise in the industry as firms attempt to draw resources away from their immediate competitors and other industries.

Some industries may not face added costs as they expand. Fast-food chains, copy centers, and coffee shops seem to be able to reproduce at will without incurring increasing costs. Therefore, their long-run supply curves may be nearly horizontal.

At this point, we have seen how elasticity measures the responsiveness of demand to a change in price and how total revenue is affected by different demand elasticities. We have also seen that supply elasticities are mainly a function of the time needed to adjust to price change signals. Next, let's apply our findings about elasticity to a subject that concerns all of us: taxes.

Eastphoto/age fotostock

A crowded restaurant might encourage its owner to expand. In the market period (i.e., same day), little can be done to accommodate more diners. In the short run, the restaurant can rearrange tables and hire more waitstaff. In the long run, it can expand the restaurant or open a second location.

CHECKPOINT

ELASTICITY OF SUPPLY

- Elasticity of supply measures the responsiveness of quantity supplied to changes in price.
- Elastic supplies are very responsive to price changes. With inelastic supply, quantity supplied is not very responsive to changing prices.

- Supplies are highly inelastic in the market period, but can expand (become more elastic) in the short run because firms can hire additional resources to raise output levels.

- In the long run, supplies are relatively elastic because firms can enter or exit the industry, and existing firms can expand their plant capacity.

QUESTION: A number of products are made in preparation for the annual flu season, although the types of goods vary in terms of their elasticity of supply. Rank the following goods from most elastic to least elastic: (a) over-the-counter flu remedies, (b) flu shots, (c) chicken soup, and (d) boxes of tissue.

Answers to the Checkpoint question can be found at the end of this chapter.

Taxes and Elasticity

On average, families pay more than 40% of their income in taxes, including income, property, estate, sales, and excise taxes. (An excise tax is a sales tax applied to a specific product, such as gasoline or tobacco.) Add to this the taxes that are embedded into the goods and services we buy, such as tariffs (taxes) on imports, tourism taxes, and airport security taxes, and it's no wonder that taxes are a perennial issue of debate among policymakers and their constituents.

Nobody likes paying taxes, but they are necessary to provide many of the public goods and services (such as roads, national defense, police protection, public education, clean air, and parks) from which everybody receives some benefit. The questions economists deal with are how to determine the efficient level of taxation and what is the most efficient way to reach that level?

Taxes can be separated into two general categories: taxes on income sources and taxes on spending. We now study how the economic burden of both categories of taxes can vary depending on how the tax policy is designed (in the case of income) and on the elasticity of the good or service being purchased (in the case of spending).

We begin by studying the various ways taxes are collected on income.

Taxes on Income Sources and Their Economic Burden

progressive tax A tax that rises in percentage of income as income increases.

flat tax A tax that is a constant proportion of one's income.

regressive tax A tax that falls in percentage of income as income increases.

lump-sum tax A fixed amount of tax regardless of income, and is a type of regressive tax.

Taxes on income sources constitute the largest source of revenues for the federal government and many state governments. The most common types of taxes include individual income tax, payroll tax (i.e., Social Security tax), corporate income tax, dividend tax (taxes on earnings from financial assets), and capital gains tax (taxes on the rising values of assets such as property and financial instruments when sold).

Much of the debate on the economic burden of income taxes focuses on whether taxes are progressive, flat, or regressive with respect to income earned. **Progressive taxes** are those that rise in burden as income increases. **Flat taxes** take a constant percentage of one's income. **Regressive taxes** fall in burden as income increases, which means that individuals with lower incomes pay a greater percentage of their income in taxes than individuals with higher incomes. A type of regressive tax is called a **lump-sum tax,** which takes a fixed amount of tax regardless of income earned, and therefore falls in percentage as income rises. Table 3 lists the three categories of taxes and provides an example of an actual tax that falls within each category.

TABLE 3	Types of Taxes and Their Economic Burden	
Type of Tax	**Example**	**Description of Tax Burden**
Progressive	Individual income tax	As income rises, income is taxed at a higher percentage rate when a higher tax bracket is reached.
Flat	Medicare tax	Medicare tax is 2.9% of all income earned (half of which is paid by employees and half paid by employers).
Regressive	Payroll tax	Payroll taxes are a flat tax of 6.2% paid by both employees and employers up to an income cap. Therefore, those earning above the cap will pay a lower overall percentage of income in payroll taxes.

Taxes on Spending and the Incidence of Taxation

The typical household pays a substantial amount of taxes on goods and services. Almost everybody pays sales taxes on goods and services purchased, homeowners pay property taxes each year on the value of their homes, and all sorts of excise taxes exist on everything from car rentals and hotel stays to gasoline purchases.

Although income taxes typically represent the largest burden on most households, taxes on spending are sometimes larger for certain groups of people. For example, households with very low incomes often pay little to no income taxes, but pay a sizeable portion of their income in sales and excise taxes. Similarly, wealthy households often receive most of their income by way of investment earnings, which are taxed at a lower rate than traditional income earnings; for these households, taxes paid on property (often on multiple homes) and luxury taxes (on yachts and other expensive toys) may constitute a larger portion of their tax burden.

In sum, taxes on spending are not trivial, and elasticity plays an important role in determining the impact of these various taxes on individuals, families, and businesses. Economists studying taxes are interested in the **incidence of taxation** and in *shifts* in the tax burden. The incidence of a tax refers to who bears its economic burden. Statutes determine what is taxed, who must pay various taxes, and what agencies are responsible for collecting taxes and remitting the revenue collected. Even so, the individuals, firms, or groups paying a tax may not be the ones bearing its economic burden. This burden can be shifted onto others. Considering the elasticities of demand and supply will help us determine the incidence of various taxes—who really bears the tax burden—and thus the ultimate impact of various tax policies.

incidence of taxation Refers to who bears the economic burden of a tax. The economic entity bearing the burden of a particular tax will depend on the price elasticities of demand and supply.

Let's now analyze how the elasticity of a good or service can affect the incidence of taxation. To simplify the analysis, we will focus on excise taxes for the remainder of this section.

Elasticity of Demand and Tax Burdens

Let us consider what happens when an excise tax is levied on a product with elastic demand, such as strawberries. Panel A of Figure 7 shows the market before an excise tax is imposed. The initial supply curve (S_0) is supply before the tax and demand curve D_0 reflects

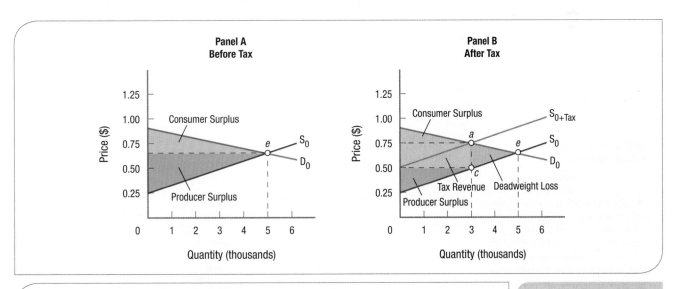

Tax Burden with Relatively Elastic Demand

S_0 is the initial supply curve for a product with elastic demand (panel A). When a 25 cent excise tax is placed on the product, the supply curve shifts upward by the amount of the tax, S_{0+Tax} (panel B). With demand remaining constant at D_0, equilibrium moves to point *a* (3,000 units). In this case, output falls substantially when the tax is imposed because elastic demand means extreme price sensitivity. As a result, sellers end up bearing most of the burden of this tax, and the deadweight loss is relatively large (area *cae*).

FIGURE 7

demand. Originally, the market is in equilibrium at point *e*, at which 5,000 baskets are sold for 65 cents each.

In panel B, we now add a per unit tax—say, 25 cents a basket—paid by the grower. This, in effect, adds 25 cents to the cost for each basket and adds a wedge between what consumers pay and what growers receive. Supply curve S_0 therefore shifts upward by this amount, to S_{0+Tax}. The new supply curve runs parallel to S_0, with the distance the curve has shifted (*ac*) equaling the 25 cent tax per basket collected by the government.

Assuming demand remains constant at D_0, the new equilibrium is at point *a*, with 3,000 baskets sold for a price of 75 cents each. The producer receives 75 cents per basket, of which it must send 25 cents to the government, keeping 50 cents for itself. Keep in mind that, because this demand is elastic, many consumers are not really willing to pay a higher price for the product; this is why output declines so much and why sellers bear most of the burden of this tax.

Before the tax, both consumer and producer surplus (discussed in Chapter 4) in panel A were substantial. After the tax, the government collects revenue equal to the tax (25 cents) times the number of baskets sold (3,000), or $750 (the blue area), consumer surplus now equals the area above the blue section, and producer surplus equals the area below it. Note that consumers and producers lose surplus equal not only to the revenue gained by the government but also to area *cae*, which represents a deadweight loss. Although this area is lost to society as a result of the tax, how the tax revenues are used to benefit society determines whether society is better or worse off with the tax.

Contrast this situation with the impact of an excise tax when the demand is inelastic (e.g., cigarettes), as in Figure 8. Initially, 23,000 packs are sold at $3.00 per pack. With a $1.25 tax, supply shifts to S_{0+Tax}, market equilibrium moves to point *g*, price increases from $3.00 to $4.00 per pack, and output declines from 23,000 to 20,000. Inelastic demands are price insensitive, therefore output declines much less when this tax is imposed. The $1.25 tax in this case is *gh*, with consumers paying *gi* (a dollar), sellers paying *ih* (25 cents), and a deadweight loss equal to area *hge*. In general, deadweight losses are small when demand is inelastic. A small quantity reduction given a higher price means that nearly all the excise tax is shifted forward to consumers. In this case, consumers pay an additional $1.00 for each unit, but manufacturers end up bearing only a small burden (25 cents).

We can generalize about the effects of elasticity of demand on the tax burden. For a given supply of some product, the greater the price elasticity of demand, the lower the share of the total tax burden shifted to consumers and the greater the share borne by sellers, and vice versa.

FIGURE 8

Tax Burden with Relatively Inelastic Demand

S_0 is the initial supply curve for a product with inelastic demand. When a $1.25 excise tax is placed on the product, the supply curve shifts upward by the amount of the tax, to S_{0+Tax}. Assuming demand remains constant at D_0, the new equilibrium will be at point *g*. Because this demand curve is inelastic, consumers are willing to pay a higher price for the product, and bear nearly all the burden of the tax. The deadweight loss (area *hge*) is relatively small when demand is inelastic.

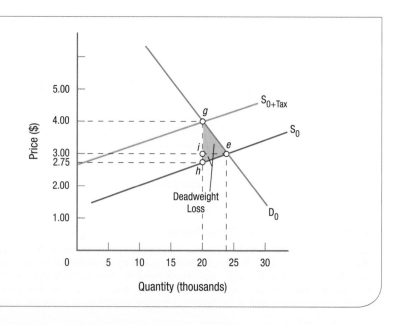

This analysis shows why proposals to raise excise taxes usually focus on such inelastically demanded commodities as tobacco, gasoline, and alcohol. For products with inelastic demands, the reduction in output is lower when prices rise because of the tax—most smokers keep smoking even when the tobacco tax goes up. Therefore, these taxes generate more revenue than would excise taxes on elastically demanded products. Proposals to raise excise taxes are often cloaked in public health and welfare rhetoric, politicians finding it easier to sell the idea of taxes that punish "sins" such as smoking and drinking. However, if the products in question did not have inelastic demands, the tax revenues generated by such taxes would be small. Because consumers substantially reduce their purchases when demand is elastic, many workers in the industries with such elastically demanded products would become unemployed. As a result, such taxes are rarely enacted on products with elastic demands.

Elasticity of Supply and Tax Burdens

In a similar way, the elasticity of supply is an important determinant of who bears the ultimate burden of taxation. In panel A of Figure 9, demand is held constant at D_0 and equilibrium is initially at point e. Supply curve S_0 is perfectly elastic, or horizontal. When a per unit tax is added to the product, supply shifts vertically to S_{0+Tax} and the new market equilibrium moves to point d, with Q_1 units sold at price P_1. Notice that in this limiting situation of perfectly elastic supply, the full monetary burden of the tax $(P_1 - P_0)$ is borne by consumers in the form of higher prices, although industry bears an indirect burden of reduced output and employment. The deadweight loss, area cde, is relatively large with elastically supplied products.

Now consider the case in which the supply curve is inelastic, as with S_0 in panel B of Figure 9. When we add the same tax as before to this supply curve, market equilibrium

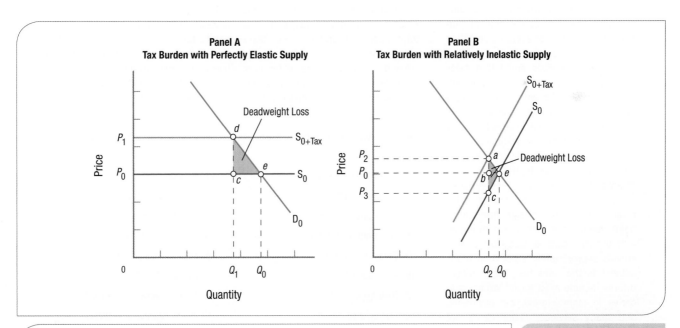

Panel A
Tax Burden with Perfectly Elastic Supply

Panel B
Tax Burden with Relatively Inelastic Supply

Tax Burden and Supply Elasticities

When supply curve S_0 is perfectly elastic as shown in panel A, a per unit excise tax added to the product shifts supply vertically to S_{0+Tax}. In this limiting case of perfectly elastic supply, the full burden of the tax $(P_1 - P_0)$ is borne by consumers through higher prices. The deadweight loss is relatively large with elastic supply curves and equal to area cde. When supply is inelastic as in panel B, with the same excise tax (ac in panel B = cd in panel A), price increases are less, and the reduction in output is also less than before. Consumers pay only part of the tax, ab, and the deadweight loss to society is equal to area cae, less than with the elastic supply shown in panel A.

FIGURE 9

moves to point *a*. Price increases less than before (P_2 in panel B is lower than P_1 in panel A) and the reduction in output is also less than before ($Q_0 - Q_2$ in panel B is less than $Q_0 - Q_1$ in panel A). Consumers pay only part of the tax, *ab*, while sellers must absorb *bc*, and the deadweight loss *cae* is relatively small.

Note what happens in all of these tax cases. Figures 7 to 9 show that whenever a tax is added, the tax moves the market away from its equilibrium point, regardless of whether the tax is borne by consumers, producers, or both. All taxes generate a tax wedge, resulting in a deadweight loss to society. The more elastic the demand or supply, the greater this deadweight loss. Table 4 summarizes these general results.

 ISSUE

Are Sales Taxes Fair to Low-Income Households?

With few exceptions, sales taxes are added to the price of nearly everything we buy. Sales taxes vary by state, and can also vary by cities or counties within states. Unlike income taxes, for which the tax rate changes as income rises, sales taxes are a fixed percentage of one's total purchase. For example, in the state of New Jersey, with a sales tax rate of 7%, you would pay $3.50 in sales tax if you bought a watch that sells for $50. Because of this fixed percentage, sales taxes are often referred to as a flat (or proportional) tax, because the tax rate remains constant regardless of the amount purchased. But is this an accurate depiction of the economic burden of sales taxes?

Many economists argue that sales taxes are *regressive* in nature, meaning that households with lower incomes pay a greater share of their income in sales taxes than households with higher incomes. Such claims have led some economists to vehemently oppose legislation that proposes higher sales taxes as a way to increase state tax revenues.

To measure the burden of sales taxes, one must first analyze how households spend their money. For example, a household earning $25,000 a year spends approximately $5,500 on items subject to the sales tax. These expenditures include most goods (except groceries in many states), car payments, and many services. Major items not subjected to sales taxes include rent and mortgage payments, tuition payments, and most financial instruments. Using an average sales tax rate of 7%, this household would spend $385 a year on sales taxes, or 1.54% of total

income. A household earning $100,000 a year, however, spends approximately $18,000 on taxable items. This amounts to $1,260 a year in sales tax, or 1.26% of total income. Therefore, sales taxes *are* regressive.

How do states compare in terms of the average sales tax rate? The following table shows the ten states with the highest

average sales tax rate and the ten states with the lowest. Surprisingly, a number of states with the highest sales tax rates are those with lower average incomes, such as Tennessee, Louisiana, Arkansas, and Alabama. This creates a double whammy—income tends to be lower in these states, and being poor takes an even greater toll with high sales taxes.

In sum, when municipalities and states need to raise revenue, the sales tax is the type of tax that hurts the poor the most. Therefore, a few states have opted not to use sales taxes at all, and instead rely on state income taxes, corporate taxes, or property taxes that are *progressive*, meaning that those with higher incomes pay a greater percentage in taxes. But for most states, sales taxes remain an important source of revenues.

Highest Average Sales Tax Rate	Lowest Average Sales Tax Rate
1. Tennessee (9.44%)	41. Wisconsin (5.43%)
2. Arizona (9.16%)	42. Wyoming (5.34%)
3. Louisiana (8.87%)	43 (tied). Virginia (5.00%)
4. Washington (8.86%)	43 (tied). Maine (5.00%)
5. Oklahoma (8.67%)	45. Hawaii (4.35%)
6. Arkansas (8.61%)	46. Alaska (1.69%)
7. New York (8.48%)	47 (tied). Delaware (0.00%)
8. Alabama (8.45%)	47 (tied). Montana (0.00%)
9. Kansas (8.38%)	47 (tied). New Hampshire (0.00%)
10. Illinois (8.25%)	47 (tied). Oregon (0.00%)

Source: Tax Foundation, 2013. (Percentages are state sales tax rate + average local sales tax rate.)

Image Source/Getty Images

| Summary of Elasticity and Taxes | | | | | **TABLE 4** |
| Elasticity | | Tax Burdens | | | |
Demand	**Supply**	**On Consumers**	**Businesses**	**Deadweight Loss**	**Figure Where Shown**
Elastic	No change	Lower	Higher	Large	7
Inelastic	No change	Higher	Lower	Small	8
No change	Elastic	Higher	Lower	Large	9A
No change	Inelastic	Lower	Higher	Small	9B

These last three chapters have given us the powerful tools of supply and demand analysis. Elasticity is important because it encapsulates the complex relationships among prices, quantity demanded, and total revenues in just two words: elastic and inelastic. When demands are inelastic and some incident marginally reduces supply, policymakers (and now you) know that price will go up substantially, although consumers will continue to purchase the product. Again, this is what happens when gasoline prices rise—consumers continue to purchase roughly the same amount as before, thus oil industry revenue and profits rise substantially in the short run.

If, however, demand is elastic and the same incident reduces supply, prices will rise, but by a smaller amount, and output and employment will fall a lot more. If weather conditions in California and Florida ruin the orange crop, reducing the supply and increasing the price of orange juice, consumers will readily substitute other juices. As a result, output, employment, revenues, and profits will decline in the orange industry.

 CHECKPOINT

TAXES AND ELASTICITY

- Taxes on income can be progressive, flat, or regressive based on the percentage of income that becomes taxes. Most income taxes are progressive, but certain forms of flat and regressive taxes exist.

- When price elasticity of demand is elastic, consumers bear a smaller burden of taxes while more is borne by sellers. When demands are inelastic, a higher share of the total tax burden is shifted to consumers.

- When the price elasticity of supply is elastic, buyers bear a larger burden of taxes. Elastic supplies also lead to a larger deadweight loss. When supply is inelastic, more of the tax burden is shifted to sellers, but the deadweight loss is lower.

QUESTION: Excise taxes were the principal taxes levied in the United States for the first 100 years or so after the Revolutionary War. Today, excise taxes fall mainly on cigarettes, liquor, luxury cars and boats, telephones, gasoline, diesel fuel, aviation fuel, gas-guzzling vehicles, and vaccines. What do all of these products seem to have in common?

Answers to the Checkpoint question can be found at the end of this chapter.

chapter summary

Section 1: **Elasticity of Demand**

The **price elasticity of demand** measures how sensitive consumers are to changes in price.

What Do the E_D Numbers Mean?

$E_D > 1$: Elastic Demand (many substitutes, high-priced goods, longer time horizon, luxury goods)

$E_D < 1$: Inelastic Demand (few substitutes, low-priced goods, shorter time horizon, necessities)

$E_D = 1$: Unitary Elastic Demand (a change in price results in an equal % change in quantity demanded)

Your textbook is an **inelastic** good because few alternatives to it exist for your class and it may be required (a necessity).

A Spring Break trip is **elastic** because many choices of destinations exist, it is expensive, and it is not really a necessity.

The formula for price elasticity of demand is:

E_D = % change in quantity demanded / % change in price

Since all E_D must be negative according to the law of demand, the convention is to drop the negative sign.

Calculating % changes: **base method** versus **midpoint method**

base method: % Δ in P = Δ in P/old P

The base method is simple because it is how one normally calculates percentages in everyday life, such as for store discounts or restaurant tips. For example, adding a 15% tip to a $20 bill is $3, or taking 25% off of a $40 shirt makes the shirt $30 using the base method.

midpoint method: % Δ in P = Δ in P/[(old P + new P)/2]

The midpoint method is slightly more difficult to calculate; however, the advantage is that the percentage change stays the same whether a value increases or decreases. For example, using the midpoint method, going from 10 to 20 or from 20 to 10 is a 66.7% change in either direction.

How Do You Remember Which Diagram Is Elastic?

Think of a pair of shorts: You can easily pull them **side-to-side** because the waistband is very elastic!

| Panel A Perfectly Elastic $E_d = \infty$ | Panel B Elastic $1 < E_d < \infty$ | Panel C Unitary Elastic $E_d = 1$ | Panel D Inelastic $0 < E_d < 1$ | Panel E Perfectly Inelastic $E_d = 0$ |

The flatter the demand curve, the more elastic the good or service; the steeper the demand curve, the more inelastic the good or service. Because elasticity changes along a linear demand curve, unitary elastic demand has a curved shape.

Section 2: Total Revenue and Other Measures of Elasticity

Total revenue is calculated as price × quantity demanded.

Total revenue increases when price rises on an inelastic good or is lowered on an elastic good.

Total revenue decreases when price rises on an elastic good or is lowered on an inelastic good.

Elasticity and total revenue vary along a straight-line demand curve. Total revenue is maximized at the point where demand is unitary elastic.

When competition is nearly nonexistent, sellers can raise prices and increase total revenue because the good is inelastic.

Cross elasticity of demand measures how responsive quantity demand for one good is to a change in the price of another good: $E_{ab} = \%\Delta Q_a / \%\Delta P_b$

$E_{ab} > 0$: Goods a and b are substitutes

$E_{ab} < 0$: Goods a and b are complements

$E_{ab} = 0$: Goods a and b are unrelated

Income elasticity of demand measures how quantity demand responds to changes in income: $E_Y = \%\Delta Q / \%\Delta Income$

$0 < E_Y < 1$: normal good

$E_Y > 1$: luxury good

$E_Y < 0$: inferior good

Section 3: Elasticity of Supply

The **elasticity of supply** measures the extent to which businesses react to price changes.

The **elasticity of supply** formula is virtually identical to that of demand:

$E_S = \%\Delta Quantity Supplied / \%\Delta Price$

The base and midpoint methods both are still used to calculate % changes.

The **time horizon** affects the elasticity of supply: the longer the period, the more a firm is able to adjust to changing prices, and therefore the more elastic the good.

Short run: a time period in which plant capacity is fixed and the number of firms in an industry does not change.

Long run: a time period long enough for firms to alter their plant capacity or for firms to enter or leave the industry.

Section 4: Taxes and Elasticity

The **incidence of taxation** refers to who bears the economic burden of a tax.

The more elastic the demand or inelastic the supply, the greater the incidence of a tax on sellers. The more inelastic the demand or elastic the supply, the greater the incidence of a tax on consumers.

A new tax collected on sellers shifts the supply curve to the left. The intersection of S_{+tax} and D is the price consumers pay, P_C. P_S is the price sellers receive. The difference between P_C and P_S is the tax per unit.

The tax created a deadweight loss shown in gray, along with a reduction in consumer surplus (CS) and producer surplus (PS). The government collects tax revenue shown as the area in blue.

price elasticity of demand, p. 104
elastic demand, p. 105
inelastic demand, p. 106
unitary elasticity of demand, p. 106
total revenue, p. 110
cross elasticity of demand, p. 112
substitutes, p. 113
complements, p. 113

income elasticity of demand, p. 113
normal goods, p. 113
luxury goods, p. 113
inferior goods, p. 113
price elasticity of supply, p. 115
elastic supply, p. 115
inelastic supply, p. 115
unitary elastic supply, p. 115

market period, p. 116
short run, p. 116
long run, p. 116
progressive tax, p. 118
flat tax, p. 118
regressive tax, p. 118
lump-sum tax, p. 118
incidence of taxation, p. 119

QUESTIONS AND PROBLEMS

Check Your Understanding

1. When the demand curve is relatively inelastic and the price falls, what happens to total revenue? If the demand is relatively elastic and price rises, what happens to total revenue?

2. Why is the demand for gasoline relatively inelastic, while the demand for Exxon's gasoline is relatively elastic?

3. Describe cross elasticity of demand. Why do substitutes have positive cross elasticities? Describe income elasticity of demand. What is the difference between normal and inferior goods?

4. Describe the impact of time on the price elasticity of supply.

5. Why would the demand for business airline travel be less elastic than the demand for vacation airline travel by retirees?

6. Would an excise tax placed on cereal be more likely or less likely to be passed on to consumers than an excise tax on wireless phone and data services? Why or why not?

Apply the Concepts

7. One major rationale for farm price supports is that rapidly improving technology, better crop strains, improved fertilizer, and better farming methods increased supply so significantly that farm incomes were severely depressed. Explain how the elasticity of demand for these crops influences this rationale.

8. If the price of chicken rises by 15% and the sales of turkey breasts expand by 10%, what is the cross elasticity of demand for these two products? Are they complements or substitutes?

9. For which of the following pairs of goods and services would the cross elasticity of demand be negative: (a) iPods and songs downloaded from iTunes, (b) digital satellite service and digital video recorders, (c) recreational vehicles and camping tents, (d) bowling and co-ed softball, (e) textbooks and study guides.

10. Consider chip plants: potato and computer. Assume there is a large rise in the demand for computer chips and potato chips.

    a. How responsive to demand is each in the market period?

    b. Describe what a manufacturer of each product might do in the short run to increase production.

    c. How does the long run differ for these products?

11. If one automobile brand has an income elasticity of demand of 1.5 and another has an income elasticity equal to −0.3, what would account for the difference? Give an example of a specific brand for each type of car.

12. Suppose you estimated the cross elasticities of demand for three pairs of products and came up with the following three values: 2.3, 0.1, −1.7. What could you conclude about these three pairs of products? If you wanted to know if two products from two different firms competed with each other in the marketplace, what would you look for?

In The News

13. A February 24, 2012, *New York Times* article titled "Access to the Car Pool Lane Can Be Yours, for a Price" describes the growing number of cities implementing express toll lanes alongside free lanes, allowing drivers to pay to avoid traffic (with higher tolls during times of greater traffic). However, when Atlanta introduced its express tolls lanes in October 2011, hardly anyone used them, causing even greater gridlock on the free lanes. Within a week and after much criticism, Governor Nathan Deal slashed the maximum toll from $5.50 to $3.05. When the express toll lanes were put in, what did the policymakers in Atlanta believe about the elasticity of demand for using the express toll lanes? Given the evidence, were they correct? By reducing the maximum toll, how would total revenues change given the elasticity of demand of Atlanta motorists?

14. According to a report from the Federal Trade Commission (FTC), in the first three weeks of August 2003, gas prices in Phoenix, Arizona, jumped from $1.52 to $2.11 a gallon, roughly a 40% increase, due to a ruptured pipeline between Tucson and Phoenix. The pipeline normally brought 30% of Phoenix's fuel from a Texas refinery. During this period, Phoenix gas stations were able to buy gas from West Coast refineries at higher prices. By the end of the month, the rupture was repaired and prices returned to normal. During this three-week period of supply disruption, gasoline sales fell by 8%. What was the approximate price elasticity of demand for gasoline during this period? If the gas stations were unable to get additional gas from the West Coast and supplies fell by the full 30%, how high might have prices risen during that three-week period?

Solving Problems

15. Rising world wholesale fair-trade coffee bean prices force the local Dunkin' Donuts franchise to raise its price of coffee from 89 cents to 99 cents a cup. As a result, management notices that donut sales fall from 950 to 850 a day. Shortly after the coffee price spike, the local Cinnabon franchise reduced its price on cinnamon rolls from $1.89 to $1.69. This resulted in a further decline in Dunkin' Donuts donut sales to 750 a day.

    a. What is the cross elasticity of demand for coffee and donuts? Are these two products complements or substitutes?

    b. What is the cross elasticity of demand for Dunkin' Donuts donuts and Cinnabon cinnamon rolls? Are these two products complements or substitutes?

16. Suppose the demand and supply for imported Kobe beef is as shown in the figure below. Now assume that the U.S. government imposes an import tax of $10 per pound on Kobe beef.

a. How does the market price change with the imposition of the $10 per pound tax?
b. Do the buyers or the sellers of Kobe beef bear the greater burden of the tax?
c. How much tax revenue does the government collect from this market?
d. Calculate the approximate value of deadweight loss created in this market from the tax.

USING THE NUMBERS

17. According to By the Numbers, how much greater is the elasticity of demand for food in Canada than in the United States? How about Mexico compared to the United States?

18. According to By the Numbers, what type of alternative-fuel car generated the highest sales in the year 2012? Which type of alternative-fuel car generated the second highest sales?

ANSWERS TO QUESTIONS IN CHECKPOINTS

Checkpoint: Elasticity of Demand

Gasoline is inelastic in the short-term because it is difficult to switch quickly to more fuel-efficient options. In the long-term, one can buy a more fuel-efficient car or move closer to work or to public transportation, allowing one to be more responsive to prices. Automobiles, however, tend to have the opposite effect. When prices of cars increase, consumers might keep their existing cars longer (an elastic response). In the long-term, however, older cars become more costly to maintain, and consumers would more likely buy a new car despite the higher prices (an inelastic response).

Checkpoint: Total Revenue and Other Measures of Elasticity

Store 1 has an elastic demand for its clothes, while store 2 faces an inelastic demand. Look back at Table 2.

Checkpoint: Elasticity of Supply

Although these rankings can be subjective, the most likely rank from most elastic to least elastic is: chicken soup, boxes of tissue, over-the-counter flu remedies, flu shots (generally requires over six months to produce, giving it the least flexibility in response to a price change for the current flu season).

Checkpoint: Taxes and Elasticity

They all appear to have relatively inelastic demands. This reduces the impact of taxes on the industries and leads to higher tax revenues.

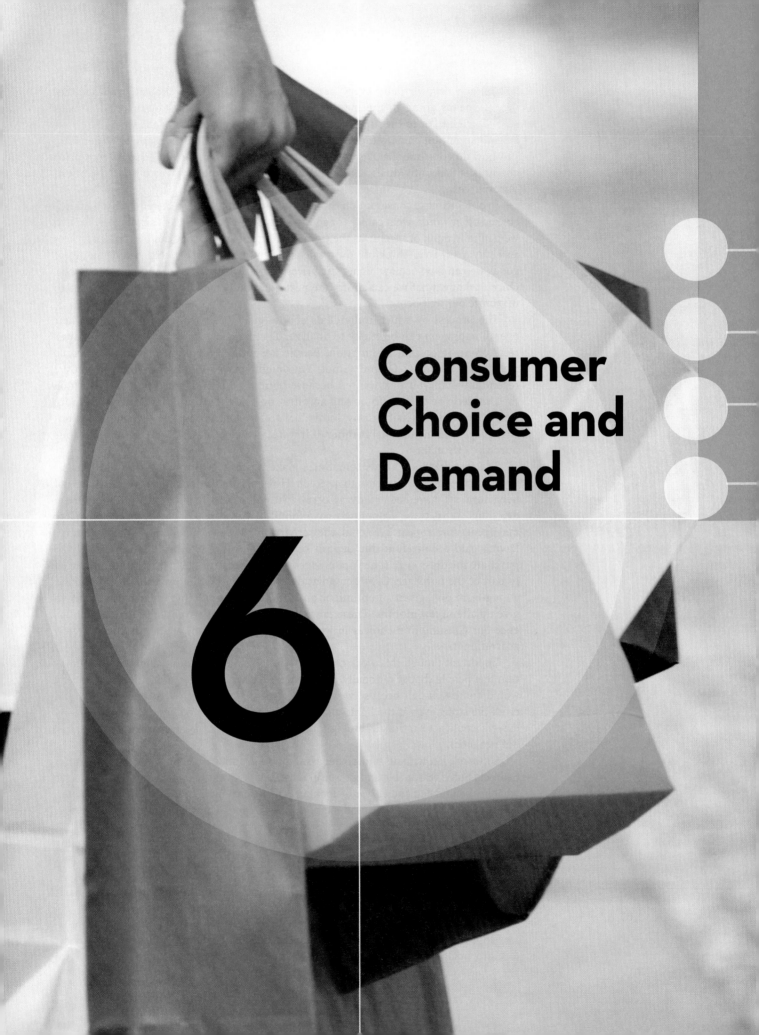

Consumer Choice and Demand

6

Each day, virtually every person makes consumption choices, whether that means going to the mall to buy a new outfit, to a restaurant to dine with friends, or to the supermarket to stock up on groceries for the week. The consumption choices that people make form what we have described as demand. But how do consumers make these choices? One of the important lessons from prior chapters is that individuals aim to maximize their well-being given a limited amount of resources.

In order to make consumption choices, individuals must first determine what is affordable; in other words, what choices of goods and services one's budget can afford. Although we naturally think of income as the primary determinant of what can be afforded, prices also play a key role. Think of how a sale at a department store increases the amount of goods we can buy, or how higher gas prices restrict what we can spend on other goods. Once we know what we can afford, the next question is then how to allocate budgets to maximize our well-being.

The process by which individuals choose goods and services to maximize their overall happiness can be tricky to analyze. The main reason is that demand analysis rests on an important assumption: People are rational decision makers. Do people always act rationally? Of course not. You might spend more money at an expensive restaurant than you had wanted because your friends convinced you to go, which then caused you to give up buying an outfit on sale that would have given you more satisfaction. In these situations, individuals often come to realize that money is not always spent in the optimal manner; if it were, we would never regret the spontaneous purchases we make.

The fact that individuals sometimes make irrational decisions makes the analysis of consumer choice difficult to predict. However, a number of economists, called behavioralists, have been studying certain situations in which people make irrational decisions. What these economists have found is that although the decisions we make may sometimes appear irrational, they are irrational in *predictable* ways. For example, having paid a nonrefundable deposit on a wedding dress, a bride is more likely to purchase the dress even if her preferences change, because she had already committed to part of the purchase. Or, a person attempting to start a diet program may purchase a long-term plan given an optimistic anticipation of completing the program, only to give up after a few months. These examples illustrate how psychological factors influence our consumption choices in ways that lead to decisions economists would view as irrational.

Important though this work on the irrational is, it does not invalidate the assumption that people choose rationally. If there were a preponderance of irrationality, society would come to a halt because we could not predict anything. What pedestrian would cross the street even if the light said "walk" if there was a modicum of fear that many drivers would act irrationally and ignore a red light? People *do* miss or ignore red lights, but not often.

So we are left with an underlying assumption of rational decision making that is not bedrock, but is reasonable and powerful nonetheless. In this chapter, we are going to see what lies behind demand curves by looking at how consumers choose. In the next chapter, we will examine what lies behind supply curves by looking at how producers choose to produce what they do.

There are two major ways to approach consumer choice. The first theory explaining what people choose to buy, given their limited incomes, is known as *utility theory* or *utilitarianism*, and owes its roots to the work of 18th century philosopher Jeremy Bentham. This theory holds that rational consumers will allocate their limited incomes so as to maximize their happiness or satisfaction.

The second approach, *indifference curve analysis,* is covered in the Appendix. Developed by Francis Ysidro Edgeworth in the late 19th century, it added analytical rigor to utility analysis by developing *indifference curves,* which portray combinations of two

BY THE NUMBERS

How Do We Decide What to Buy?

Each day, we make economic decisions on what to buy, what to eat, and how to allocate our limited time. Although marginal utility analysis can guide us into making rational decisions, behavioral economic factors play an important role as well.

The average distribution of U.S. household budgets on various expenditure components in 2011, along with trends in selected components from 2009 to 2011.

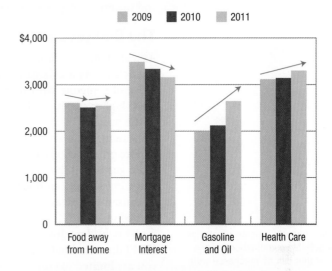

254,212,610
Total number of passenger vehicles registered in the United States in 2011 (1 car for every 1.2 persons).

$346,170,000,000
Total amount of charitable giving by Americans in 2011 (over $1,100 per person).

As preferences for organic foods increase, more supermarket chains respond, leading to rising sales of organic foods.

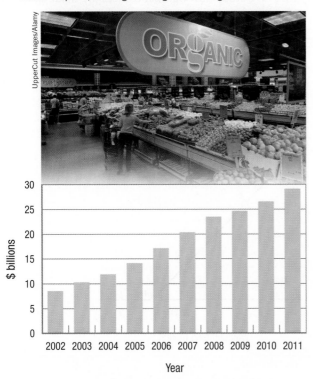

Player jerseys represent the largest component of the $3 billion annual NBA product market. The top selling jerseys in the 2011–2012 season were:
1. Derrick Rose, Chicago Bulls
2. Jeremy Lin, New York Knicks
3. Kobe Bryant, Los Angeles Lakers
4. LeBron James, Miami Heat
5. Carmelo Anthony, New York Knicks

goods of equal total utility. Edgeworth, a shy man who studied in public libraries because he saw material possessions as a burden, brought the precision of mathematics to bear on utility theory.

The Budget Line and Choices

To begin an analysis of consumption choices, we first must consider how a limited income and the prices of goods and services put constraints on our choices.

The Budget Line

As a student, you came to college to improve your life not only intellectually but also financially. As a college graduate, you can expect your lifetime earnings to be triple those of someone with only a high school education. Even once you have achieved these higher earnings, there will be limits on what you can buy. But first, let us return to the present.

Assume you have $50 a week to spend on pizza and wall climbing. This is a proxy for a more general choice between food and entertainment. We could use different goods or more goods, but the principle would still be the same. In our specific example, if pizzas cost $10 each and an hour of wall climbing costs $20, you can climb walls for 2.5 hours or consume 5 pizzas each week, or do some combination of these two. Your options are plotted in Figure 1.

This **budget line** (constraint) is a lot like the production possibilities frontier (PPF) discussed in Chapter 2. Although you might prefer to have more of both goods, you are limited to consumption choices lying on the budget line, or inside the budget line if you want to save any part of your $50 weekly budget. As with the PPF curve, however, any points to the right of the line are unattainable for you—they exceed your available income.

In this example, the budget line makes clear that many different combinations of wall climbing and pizzas will exhaust your $50 budget. But which of these possible combinations will you select? That depends on your personal preferences. If you love pizza, you will probably make different choices than if you are a fitness fanatic who rarely consumes fatty foods. Your own preferences determine how much pleasure you can expect to get from the various possible options. We study how optimal choices are made in the next section of this chapter.

budget line Graphically illustrates the possible combinations of two goods that can be purchased with a given income, given the prices of both goods.

FIGURE 1

The Budget Constraint or Line

When pizzas cost $10 each, wall climbing costs $20 per hour, and you have $50 a week to spend, you could buy 5 pizzas per week, 2.5 hours of wall climbing, or some combination of the two. The budget line makes clear all of the possible purchasing combinations of two products on a particular budget.

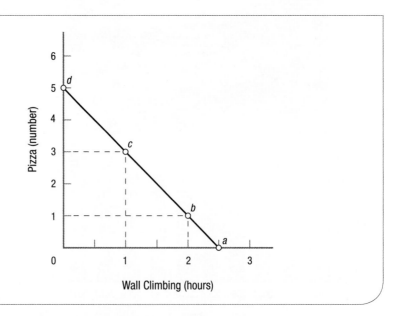

Changes to the Budget Line

The budget line, like most money matters, is subject to changes in the prices of goods or changes in income. When the price of a good or income changes, the combinations of goods that become affordable change as well. Let's look at how the budget line changes.

Changes to the Price of a Good Suppose the wall-climbing establishment offers a half-price discount to college students, reducing the price of wall climbing from $20 to $10 per hour. Figure 2 illustrates what happens when the price of wall climbing changes as the price of pizza stays the same. Notice that the vertical intercept remains at 5 pizzas; because the price of pizza did not change, the total number of pizzas that can be purchased for $50 is still 5. However, the reduction in the price of wall climbing allows the total number of hours that can be purchased to increase from 2.5 to 5. In Figure 2, the budget line pivots outward to budget line *b*, which opens up many more combinations of pizza and wall climbing that previously were unaffordable.

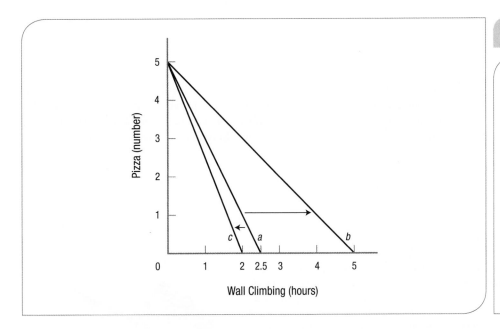

FIGURE 2

Changes in Price on a Budget Line

Budget line *a* shows the consumption choices available with a budget of $50 and prices of pizza and wall climbing at $10 and $20, respectively. When the price of wall climbing decreases to $10, the budget line pivots outward to budget line *b*. The combinations of pizza and wall climbing that can be purchased increases. When the price of wall climbing increases to $25, the budget line pivots inward to budget line *c*, reducing the amounts that can be purchased.

Notice that in this case it is possible for a person to actually consume *more* of both pizza and wall climbing, even though the price of pizza did not change, nor did the income of $50. Suppose that originally you would spend the entire $50 on wall climbing, purchasing 2.5 hours. Because the price is now $10, the new cost of maintaining the same purchase of 2.5 hours is $25, leaving $25 to use on *either* more wall climbing or pizza, or both. By virtue of the price of wall climbing decreasing to $10, what this income can buy increases, even though the actual income stays the same. This is true for any point along the original budget line except for the one point at which the entire budget was spent on pizza. Only in this case does the fall in price of wall climbing not increase the number of pizzas that can be purchased.

Now suppose that instead of a discount on wall climbing, the gym decides to raise the price to $25. How would this affect the budget line? It pivots inward. In Figure 2, budget line *c* shows the maximum quantity of wall climbing decreasing to two hours. The increase in price reduces the combinations of both pizza and wall climbing that can be purchased with $50.

Changes to Income We now know that changes in the price of a good will pivot the budget line inward or outward along the axis for that good. But what if income itself changes? Suppose that prices of pizza and wall climbing remain at $10 and $20, respectively, but you are given extra money by your parents, allowing you to increase your

FIGURE 3

Changes in Income on a Budget Line

Budget line *a* shows the consumption choices available with a budget of $50 and prices of pizza and wall climbing at $10 and $20, respectively. When the budget increases to $100, the budget line shifts parallel outward to budget line *b*, doubling the quantities that can be purchased. When the budget falls to $20, the budget line shifts inward to budget line *c*, reducing the amounts that can be purchased.

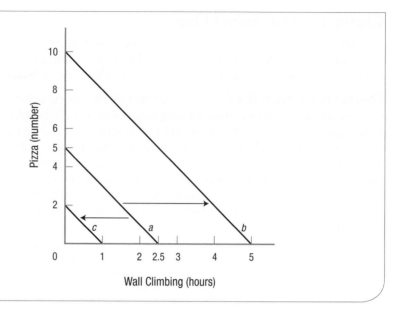

entertainment budget to $100 per week. Figure 3 illustrates how an increase in income shifts your budget line outward to budget line *b* in a parallel fashion. Because $100 is double the original income, you can now afford twice as many pizzas and wall climbing hours as before as long as prices do not change. Budget line *b* shows that the maximum

 ISSUE

Smaller Cars and Larger Homes: A Permanent Trend?

Housing and auto transportation are the two largest monthly expenditures of a typical American household. As the prices of homes and cars change, along with the costs associated with their maintenance, the types of homes and cars consumers buy change as well.

The average home price in the United States fell by nearly 20% from 2006 to 2012, while the average price of a new car rose by nearly 20% over this same period. Although the effect of these price changes on consumption is predictable, other factors influence consumption patterns as well.

Unlike most consumer goods, individuals rarely buy homes and cars outright, but instead lease them or borrow money to pay them off over time. Therefore, an important factor influencing how homes and autos affect one's budget is the interest rate for borrowing. Further, maintaining a house or a car is not lim-

ited to the monthly payment. Complementary items, such as property taxes, utility bills, and furniture expenses affect the cost of home ownership, while gas prices and auto insurance premiums affect auto purchases.

Has there been a change in the costs of home and auto ownership?

From 2006 to 2012, mortgage interest rates declined significantly, from an average of 6% to 3%. As mortgage interest rates fell, housing payments fell, allowing people to seek larger homes that are now affordable with the same budget. The opposite occurred in the auto industry, as gas prices rose from an average of $2.50 per gallon in 2006 to $3.60 per gallon in 2012. As gasoline prices increased, transportation costs rose significantly, causing people to seek smaller and more fuel-efficient cars.

Changes in the costs of home and automobile ownership lead individu-

als to adjust their consumption habits as their budgets adjust. As a result, smaller cars and larger homes have been a trend for much of the past decade. Whether this trend continues depends on how prices, which play a critical role in the budget line, adjust in the future.

Kimimasa Mayama/Bloomberg via Getty Images

quantity of pizza that can be purchased increases to 10 and the maximum quantity of climbing hours increases to 5.

Like prices, we can analyze the effect of a decrease in income on the budget line as well. Suppose increased expenses elsewhere force you to cut back on entertainment spending from $50 to $20 per week. Figure 3 shows how the reduced income shifts the budget line parallel inward to budget line *c*.

Now that we have analyzed how budget lines determine what we can afford, we must now answer the important question of what combination of goods and services achieves the highest satisfaction. One approach is to use marginal utility analysis, which we turn to next.

A decrease in the price of a good that you typically buy has the same effect as an increase in income. In both cases, your budget line expands outward, allowing for more consumption choices.

CHECKPOINT

THE BUDGET LINE AND CHOICES

- The budget line graphically illustrates the limits on purchases for a given income (budget).
- Changes in the price of a good cause the budget line to pivot inward or outward, affecting the combinations of goods that can be afforded.
- When the price of one good decreases, perceived income increases, allowing one to purchase more of both goods.
- Changes in income (budget) cause a parallel shift in the budget line.

QUESTION: Suppose that each week you eat ten meals on campus at $7.50 each and five meals off campus at $15 each. What is your total spending on meals? Suppose the price of off-campus meals decreases to $10. Explain how you can eat more meals in both locations (on campus and off campus), even though the price of on-campus meals stayed the same.

Answers to the Checkpoint question can be found at the end of this chapter.

Marginal Utility Analysis

The previous section showed how our choices of goods and services are limited to what we can afford given a budget. Similar to how PPFs showed the maximum output an economy can produce, budget lines show the maximum quantity of goods (in various combinations) that can be purchased. And like PPF analysis, an individual is able to select a point on the budget line that would maximize one's satisfaction. But which point would accomplish this goal?

To answer this question, we need to determine which combination of goods and services results in the highest level of satisfaction. Solving this riddle of consumer behavior can be accomplished using **marginal utility analysis.** Let's begin by defining preferences and utility, and then discuss how marginal utility analysis allows a person to maximize his or her well-being.

Preferences and Utility

Utility is a hypothetical measure of consumer satisfaction. It was introduced by early economists attempting to explain how consumers make decisions. The utilitarian theory of consumer behavior assumes, first of all, that utility is something that *can* be

marginal utility analysis A theoretical framework underlying consumer decision making. This approach assumes that satisfaction can be measured and that consumers maximize satisfaction when the marginal utilities per dollar are equal for all products and services.

utility A hypothetical measure of consumer satisfaction.

JEREMY BENTHAM (1748–1832)

Jeremy Bentham was a social philosopher, legal reformer, and writer who founded the philosophy known as utilitarianism. As an economic theorist, his most valuable contribution was the idea of *utility,* which explained consumer choices in terms of maximizing pleasure and minimizing pain.

Born in 1748, Bentham was the son of a wealthy lawyer. At age 12 he entered Oxford University, then studied for the bar although he decided not to practice law. Instead, he pursued a life of writing and thinking, with his primary contribution analyzing the notion of utility as a driving force in social and economic behavior. Bentham believed that the aim of society and government should be to maximize utility or to promote the "greatest happiness for the greatest number." In 1789, he published his most famous work, *Introduction to the Principles of Morals,* which laid out his utilitarian philosophy. Bentham believed it was possible to derive a "Felicific Calculus" to compare the various pleasures or pains.

Although modern economists have cast doubt on the notion that utility could be measured or calculated, Bentham had many ideas that were ahead of his time, including the notion of cost-benefit analysis, which logically followed from his utilitarian views on government policies. Bentham also formulated the contemporary notion of marginal utility. After reading this chapter, it will be hard for you to avoid thinking in Bentham's terms about your own consumption choices, and you'll find yourself asking questions such as, "Do I really get $12 worth of satisfaction out of a Coke and popcorn at the movies, or do I have better alternatives for that money?"

measured. Returning to our example from the previous section, the theory assumes that we can quantifiably determine how much utility (satisfaction) you derive from consuming one or more pizzas, and how much utility you derive from spending one or more hours on the climbing wall. Table 1 provides estimates of the utility you derive from both pizzas and wall climbing, measured in *utils,* hypothetical units of satisfaction or utility. Compare columns (1) and (2) with columns (4) and (5).

At first glance, it might seem that if you wanted to maximize your utility given your $50 budget, you would simply go wall climbing for 2.5 hours, thereby maximizing your total utility at 270 utils. If you spent a little time analyzing the table, you would notice that combinations give you more total utility. If you went wall climbing for 2 hours and had 1 pizza (again spending your entire $50 budget), your total utility would be 330 utils (260 + 70 = 330), much more than concentrating on one item alone.

Other than trial and error, how do we determine the best combination? Before we can see just which combination of these two goods would actually bring you the most happiness, we need to distinguish between *total utility* and *marginal utility.*

total utility The total satisfaction that a person receives from consuming a given amount of goods and services.

Total and Marginal Utility **Total utility** is the total satisfaction that a person receives from consuming a given quantity of goods and services. In Table 1, for example, the total utility received from consuming 3 pizzas is 180 utils, whereas the total utility from 4 pizzas is 220 utils. Marginal utility is something different.

TABLE 1	Total and Marginal Utility from Pizzas and Wall Climbing					
	Pizza			Wall Climbing		
(1) Quantity	(2) Total Utility	(3) Marginal Utility	(4) Quantity	(5) Total Utility	(6) Marginal Utility	
0	0	0	0.0	0	0	
1	70	70	0.5	90	90	
2	130	60	1.0	170	80	
3	180	50	1.5	230	60	
4	220	40	2.0	260	30	
5	250	30	2.5	270	10	

Marginal utility is the satisfaction derived from consuming an *additional* unit of a given product or service. It is determined by taking the difference between the total utility derived from, say, consuming 4 pizzas and consuming 3 pizzas. The total utility derived from 4 pizzas is 220 utils, and that from 3 pizzas is 180 utils. Therefore, consuming the fourth pizza yields only an additional 40 utils of satisfaction (220 − 180 = 40 utils).

The marginal utility for both pizza eating and wall climbing is listed in Table 1. Notice that as we move from one quantity of pizza to the next, total utility rises by an amount exactly equal to marginal utility. This is no coincidence. Marginal utility is nothing but the change in total utility obtained from consuming one more pizza (the marginal pizza), therefore as pizza eating increases by 1 pizza, total utility will rise by the amount of additional satisfaction derived from consuming that additional pizza. Also note that, for both pizzas and wall climbing, marginal utility declines the more a particular product or activity is consumed.

marginal utility The satisfaction received from consuming an additional unit of a given product or service.

The Law of Diminishing Marginal Utility Why does marginal utility decline as the consumption of one product or activity increases? No matter our personal tastes and preferences, we eventually become sated once we have consumed a certain amount of any given commodity. Most of us love ice cream. As youngsters, some of us imagined a world in which meals consisted of nothing but ice cream—no casseroles, no vegetables, just ice cream. To children this might sound heavenly, but as adults, we recognize that we would quickly grow sick of ice cream. Human beings simply crave diversity; we quickly tire of the same product or service if we consume it day after day.

law of diminishing marginal utility As we consume more of a given product, the added satisfaction we get from consuming an additional unit declines.

This fact of human nature led early economists to formulate the **law of diminishing marginal utility.** This law states that as we consume more of a product, the rate at which our total satisfaction increases with the consumption of each additional unit will decline. And if we continue to consume still more of the product after that, our total satisfaction will eventually begin to decline.

This principle is illustrated by Figure 4 on the next page, which graphs the total utility and marginal utility for pizza eating, as listed in Table 1. Notice that total utility, charted in panel A, rises continually as we move from 1 pizza per week to 5 pizzas. Nevertheless, the rate of this increase declines as more pizzas are consumed. Accordingly, panel B shows that marginal utility declines with more pizzas eaten. On your student budget, you could not afford any more than 5 pizzas a week, but we can imagine that if you were to keep eating pizzas—20 pizzas in a week—your total utility would actually start to drop with each additional pizza. At some point, it simply hurts to stuff down any more pizzas.

Mega buffets in Las Vegas draw millions of diners each year. Diminishing marginal utility from each additional plate of food keeps the amount of food consumed by each diner at a reasonable level.

It is one thing to grasp the obvious fact that consumers have limited budgets and that the products they can choose among provide them increasing satisfaction but are subject to diminishing marginal utility. It is another thing to figure out exactly how consumers allocate their limited funds so as to maximize their total level of satisfaction or utility. We now turn our attention to how early economists solved the problem of maximizing utility and the analytic methods that flowed out of their work.

Maximizing Utility Let's take a moment to review everything we need to know to plot the budget line in Figure 1: your total income and the prices of all the products you could purchase. In our example, the weekly budget is $50, pizzas cost $10 apiece, and wall climbing is $20 per hour or $10 per half-hour. This is enough information to plot all of the options open to you.

Given these options, how do individuals maximize the total utility from the various combinations of goods? Knowing the marginal utility of each unit of a good consumed is

FIGURE 4

Total and Marginal Utility for Pizza

Total utility, charted in panel A, rises continually as we move from 1 pizza per week to 5. Nevertheless, the rate of this increase declines as more pizzas are consumed. Accordingly, panel B shows that marginal utility declines with more pizzas eaten.

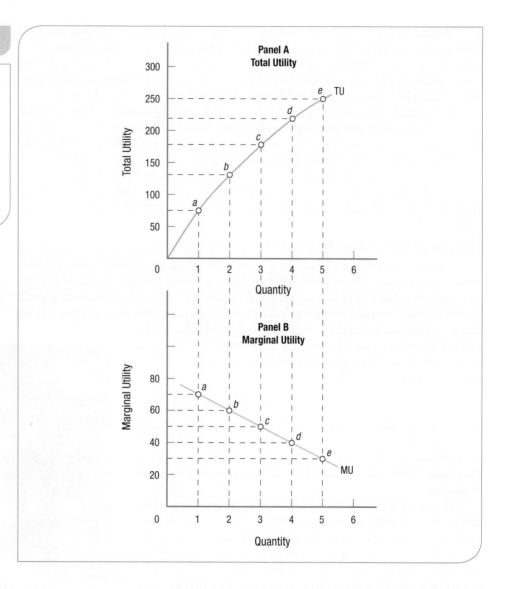

not enough. Surely the marginal utility of a new car is greater than the marginal utility of a cup of coffee. But the price of the car is also much greater than the price of coffee. The ability to maximize utility given a fixed budget requires us to compare the marginal utilities *per dollar* spent on each good.

Take a look at columns (4) and (8) of Table 2. These two columns express the marginal utilities of pizzas and wall climbing, respectively, in terms of marginal utility per dollar; these amounts are computed by dividing the marginal utility of each product by the product's price.

To see the importance of computing marginal utility per dollar, consider the following. Given the figures in columns (4) and (8), and assuming you want to get the most for your money, on which activity would you spend the first $10 of your weekly budget? You can spend the first $10 on a pizza or on a half-hour of wall climbing. A pizza returns 70 utils of satisfaction, whereas a half-hour of wall climbing yields 90 utils. Since 90 is greater than 70, clearly the first $10 would be better spent on wall climbing.

Now, for the sake of simplicity, let's keep your spending increments constant. On what will you spend your next $10—pizza or climbing? Look again at the table. Your first pizza still gives you 70 utils, while the second half-hour of wall climbing returns 80 utils. Wall climbing again is the obvious choice. If your total budget had only been $20 per week, you would have been inclined to give up pizzas completely.

Total and Marginal Utility per Dollar from Pizzas and Wall Climbing — TABLE 2

	Pizza				Wall Climbing		
(1) Quantity (units of pizza)	(2) Total Utility	(3) Marginal Utility	(4) Marginal Utility per Dollar (price = $10)	(5) Quantity (hours of wall climbing)	(6) Total Utility	(7) Marginal Utility	(8) Marginal Utility per Dollar (price = $10 per half-hour)
0	0	0	0	0.0	0	0	0
1	70	70	7	0.5	90	90	9
2	130	60	6	1.0	170	80	8
3	180	50	5	1.5	230	60	6
4	220	40	4	2.0	260	30	3
5	250	30	3	2.5	270	10	1

Proceeding in the same way, using your third $10 to buy your first pizza will yield an additional 70 utils of satisfaction, whereas using this money to purchase a third half-hour of wall climbing will bring only 60 utils. (Wall climbing is starting to get a bit boring.) Thus, because 70 is greater than 60, with your third $10 you buy your first pizza.

The next $10 provides the same amount of utility (60 utils) regardless of whether you buy another pizza or another half-hour of wall climbing. Therefore, you split the remaining $20 of your budget evenly between these two activities. When the consumption of additional units of two products provides equal satisfaction, economists say consumers are *indifferent* to which product they consume first.

By following this incremental process, therefore, we have determined that you will spend your $50 on 2 pizzas ($20) and 1.5 hours of wall climbing ($30). This results in a total utility of 360 utils (130 for pizza and 230 for wall climbing). *No other combination of pizzas and wall climbing will result in total satisfaction this high,* as you can prove to yourself by trying to spend the $50 differently.

Note also that for the last two units of each product consumed, the marginal utilities per dollar were equal at 6. This result is to be expected. Simple logic tells us that if one activity yields more satisfaction per dollar than some other, you will continue to pursue the activity with the higher satisfaction per dollar until some other activity starts yielding more satisfaction. This observation leads to a simple rule for maximizing utility: You should allocate your budget so that the marginal utilities per dollar are equal for the last units of the products consumed. This **utility maximizing rule,** in turn, leads to the following equation, where MU = marginal utility and P = price.

$$\frac{MU_{Pizza}}{P_{Pizza}} = \frac{MU_{Wall\ Climbing}}{P_{Wall\ Climbing}}$$

This equation and the analyses described earlier can be generalized to cover numerous goods and services. For all goods and services $a, b, \ldots n$:

$$\frac{MU_a}{P_a} = \frac{MU_b}{P_b} = \ldots = \frac{MU_n}{P_n}$$

utility maximizing rule Utility is maximized where the marginal utility per dollar is equal for all products, or $MU_a/P_a = MU_b/P_b = \ldots = MU_n/P_n$.

The important point to remember is that, according to this theory of consumer behavior, consumers approach every purchase by asking themselves which of all possible additional acts of consumption would bring them the most satisfaction per dollar.

You have seen how the marginal utility analysis of consumer behavior works when we assume that satisfaction or well-being can be measured directly (in utils). We can now use this theory of consumer behavior to derive the demand curve for wall climbing.

Deriving Demand Curves

We know that consumers will maximize their utility by spending each dollar of their limited budgets on the goods and services yielding the highest marginal utility per dollar. In our previous example, with pizzas costing $10 each and an hour of wall climbing costing $20, this meant you bought 2 pizzas and 1.5 hours of wall climbing. Would your consumption choices change if these prices changed? Let us consider what happens when the cost of wall climbing rises to $30 per hour.

Now that wall climbing costs $30 per hour or $15 per half-hour, column (8) of Table 3 has been altered to reflect this new rate for wall climbing. The first half-hour of climbing yields 90 utils and now costs $15, so each dollar yields 6 utils. Now your first $10 will be spent on a pizza ($MU/P = 7$ for pizza versus $MU/P = 6$ for wall climbing).

TABLE 3	Total and Marginal Utility per Dollar from Pizzas and Wall Climbing (Price of Wall Climbing Increases to $30 per Hour or $15 per Half-Hour)						
	Pizza			Wall Climbing			
(1) Quantity (units of pizza)	(2) Total Utility	(3) Marginal Utility	(4) Marginal Utility per Dollar (price = $10)	(5) Quantity (hours of wall climbing)	(6) Total Utility	(7) Marginal Utility	(8) Marginal Utility per Dollar (price = $15 per half-hour)
0	0	0	0	0.0	0	0	0.00
1	70	70	7	0.5	90	90	6.00
2	130	60	6	1.0	170	80	5.33
3	180	50	5	1.5	230	60	4.00
4	220	40	4	2.0	260	30	2.00
5	250	30	3	2.5	270	10	0.67

The next $25 is split between another pizza and a half-hour of wall climbing because $MU/P = 6$ for both. Your final $15 is spent on wall climbing because its marginal utility per dollar (5.33) is higher than for a third pizza (5).

Thus, your final allocation is 2 pizzas and 1 hour of wall climbing. Clearly, consumer choices respond to changes in product prices. With wall climbing at $20 per hour, you consumed 1.5 hours of climbing and 2 pizzas. When the price of wall climbing rose to $30 per hour you altered your consumption. Now, instead of 1.5 hours and 2 pizzas, you consume 1 hour and 2 pizzas. This new level is shown in the shaded row of Table 3.

Figure 5 plots both your budget constraint and your demand for wall climbing based on the results of Tables 2 and 3. Panel A shows the effect of increasing the

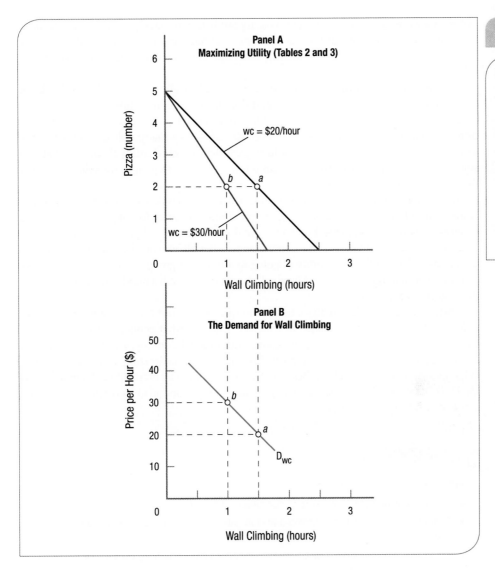

FIGURE 5

Deriving the Demand for Wall Climbing Using Marginal Utility Analysis

With the price of wall climbing at $20 per hour, you climb for 1.5 hours (point *a* in both panels). When the price increases to $30 per hour, you reduce your consumption of wall climbing to 1 hour (point *b* in both panels). Connecting these points in panel B yields the demand curve for wall climbing.

price of wall climbing from $20 to $30 per hour. At the increased price of wall climbing, if you were to spend your entire budget on this activity, you could only climb for 1.67 hours ($50/$30 = 1.67). This price increase rotates the budget line leftward, reducing your consumption opportunities, as the figure illustrates.

When the price of wall climbing was $20 per hour, you climbed for 1.5 hours (points *a* in both panels of Figure 5). When the price was increased to $30 per hour, marginal utility analysis led you to reduce your consumption of wall climbing to 1 hour (point *b* in both panels). Connecting these points in panel B of Figure 5 yields the demand curve for wall climbing.

Thus, the marginal utility theory of consumer behavior helps explain both how consumers allocate their income according to their personal preferences and the law of demand. Remember that the law of demand posited an inverse (negative) relationship between price and quantity demanded. This negative relationship is shown in panel B.

Limitations of Marginal Utility Analysis

Marginal utility analysis explains not only how consumers purchase goods and services but also how all household choices are made. We can analyze the decision of whether or not to get a job, for example, by comparing the marginal utility of work versus the marginal utility of leisure. As a college student, you are familiar with having many demands made on your time. More work means more money but less time for leisure, and vice versa. Marginal utility theory helps us to identify that point at which work and leisure (and hopefully study) balance out.

Although marginal utility theory is an elegant and logically consistent theory that helps us to understand how consumers behave, it does have some limitations. First, it assumes that consumers are able to measure the utility they derive from various sorts of consumption. Yet, this is virtually impossible in everyday life—how many utils do you get out of eating a bowl of ice cream? This is not to suggest that marginal utility theory is invalid. It simply requires one very restrictive assumption, namely, that people are able to measure their satisfaction for every purchase.

Others have argued that it is absurd to think that we could carry out the mental calculus required to compare the ratios of marginal utility to price for all possible goods and services. This is no doubt true, but even if we do not compare all possible goods and services in this way, we do draw some comparisons. After all, we somehow need to be able to distinguish between the desirability of going to a movie or going to a concert, because we cannot do both at the same time. Marginal utility theory is still a good way of approaching this choice, in a general way.

Lastly, marginal utility analysis has been criticized for not fully explaining why individuals sometimes act irrationally, at least according to what economic models predict. Indeed, human psychology often plays games with rational thinking, leading individuals to make decisions that would seem to go against the goal of maximizing utility. This topic of behavioral economics, which studies how human psychology enters into economic behavior, is one that has become increasingly popular among economists in recent decades, and is the focus of the next section.

CHECKPOINT

MARGINAL UTILITY ANALYSIS

- Utility is a hypothetical measure of consumer satisfaction.
- Total utility is the total satisfaction a person gets from consuming a certain amount of goods.
- Marginal utility is the additional satisfaction a consumer gets from consuming one more unit of the good or service.
- The law of diminishing marginal utility states that as consumption of a specific good increases, the increase in total satisfaction will decline.
- Consumers maximize satisfaction by purchasing goods up to the point at which the marginal utility per dollar is equal for all goods.
- Demand curves for products can be derived from marginal utility analysis by changing the price of one good and plotting the resulting changes in consumption.

QUESTIONS: Even though convenience stores have significantly higher prices than normal grocery stores such as Safeway, they seem to do well, judging by their numbers. Why are people willing to pay these higher prices? If a Safeway began to operate 24/7, would this affect the sales of a nearby convenience store?

Answers to the Checkpoint questions can be found at the end of this chapter.

Behavioral Economics

Up to this point, we generally have assumed that individuals make rational decisions that maximize their well-being. Yet, an increasing number of economists have devoted their attention to studying situations in which individuals *do not* appear to follow rational economic thinking, at least the behavior that economic models predict will result. This section turns our attention to the study of behavioral economics. **Behavioral economics** is the study of how human psychology enters into economic behavior as a way to explain why individuals sometimes act counter to how economic models predict.

All individuals from time to time make irrational decisions; that is part of human nature. An important point to keep in mind is that we are not analyzing random behavior. Instead, behavioral economics looks at situations in which people act irrationally in *predictable* ways. This could be a big deal because it challenges the notion of economic rationality that we have assumed in our models. The fact that irrational behavior can occur in predictable ways means that clever people try to take advantage of this behavior. What psychological factors influence irrational behavior, and how do these factors translate into clever opportunism?

This section presents five important psychological factors influencing economic behavior: (1) sunk cost fallacy, (2) framing bias, (3) overconfidence, (4) overvaluing the present relative to the future, and (5) altruism. Each of these factors influences decisions we make every day. In fact, marketers of goods and services often exploit these factors in order to attract consumers to make purchases they otherwise might not make. Let's look at each factor and some common examples illustrating each concept.

Sunk Cost Fallacy

Suppose a few months ago you had paid a nonrefundable registration fee of $200 to attend your favorite annual collector's convention in town to be held this weekend. The fee is not refundable or transferable to another person. Therefore, the $200 fee you paid is a **sunk cost,** a cost that has been paid and cannot be recovered. As the weekend approaches, you realize that you are extremely behind in your studies, so much so that going to the convention would likely take away the last bit of time to prepare for upcoming midterm exams.

You think to yourself, "If I would have known I'd be so busy with school, I wouldn't have paid $200 to register for the convention. But since I've already paid it, I'm certainly not going to let my money go to waste, so I'm going to go despite the potential consequences to my grades." Does this seem logical?

According to economic theory, it does not. Sunk costs are costs that cannot be undone. Therefore, the decision whether to attend should not hinge upon past payments, because the registration fee has already been paid. By incorporating sunk costs into present and future decisions, a **sunk cost fallacy** occurs as people make decisions based on how much was already spent rather than how the decision might affect their current well-being. In this case, because going to the convention may have consequences on your grades, the wise decision would be to forgo the convention. Either way, the money is already gone.

The sunk cost fallacy often appears in situations in which people feel that they have invested too much time or money into a project to quit. Another common example is the tuition paid for school, a sunk cost. Often, students who fail the midterm and have little hope of raising their grades are reluctant to withdraw from a class because they are unwilling to give up a class that is already paid for, instead hoping for a miracle (or a sympathetic professor) that the final grade will be a passing one. But often the result is a failing grade, which means not only do they need to retake the class (and pay for it once more), but worse, a failing grade appears on their transcript.

Framing Bias

Does a price of $9.99 seem a lot different from $10.00? It really shouldn't, given the difference is one-tenth of 1%. Even more startling are prices displayed at most gas stations, which often show prices in tenths of a cent, such as 3.99^9 (the next time you pass by a gas

behavioral economics The study of how human psychology enters into economic behavior as a way to explain why individuals sometimes act in predictable ways counter to economic models.

sunk cost A cost that has been paid and cannot be recovered; therefore, it should not enter into decision making affecting the present or future.

sunk cost fallacy Occurs when people make decisions based on how much was already spent rather than how the decision might affect their current well-being.

The not-so-noticeable nine-tenths of a cent added to the price of a gallon of gasoline adds up to over $1 billion in revenue for gas stations each year.

fred hall/iStockphoto

framing bias Describes when individuals are steered into making one decision over another or are convinced they are receiving a higher value for a product than what was paid for it.

station, notice the extra nine-tenths of a cent). Compared to $4.00, $3.99⁹ is a difference of just one-fortieth of 1%. Finally, does "Buy One Get One Half-Off" sound like a better deal than "25% off"? It might; however, if you buy two items with the same price, the total cost is the same under each deal.

In each of the above examples, the percentage difference between the two prices is zero or virtually zero. Yet, consumers tend to react differently to these prices, with the former being interpreted as a lower price than the latter, enough to influence buying decisions. This ability to influence consumer decisions by how prices are displayed is an example of a **framing bias,** which occurs when individuals are steered toward one choice over another by how those choices are portrayed. Framing techniques are used by marketers to increase sales of products without actually lowering the price.

Framing biases are not limited to pricing strategies. Much in the same way that firms steer consumers toward buying products using prices, a broad range of framing effects can be used to steer individuals toward one political candidate or one political issue over another, toward one product over another in advertising campaigns, and toward one policy over another in legislative debates.

Framing biases also occur when firms convince buyers that what they purchased is worth much more than what they paid. This type of strategy attempts to alter the perceptions of buyers into believing they are always receiving a great deal. Ever notice that some stores perpetually have sales of 10% to 20% off everything, or give money back in the form of gift cards for future visits? Wouldn't it be the same if a store just marks down the sticker prices of everything? Perhaps, but consumers tend to respond more positively to sales and other seemingly good offers.

Overconfidence

Feeling confident about one's abilities, attractiveness, or intellectual capacity is a trait often instilled from one's childhood. No doubt self-esteem plays an important role in the success of many people. But overconfidence in one's abilities can have the opposite effect.

Watch the auditions of any reality talent show, and notice the pitchy, off-key singers who belt their hearts out as if they were on stage at the Grammy Awards, only to be brought back to reality by the harsh criticism of the judges. Being overconfident can lead to decisions that have consequences, such as picking the wrong stock in which to invest, spending too much time and effort applying to only the very top graduate school or law school, or turning down potential respectable boyfriends or girlfriends in hopes of a dream mate.

Wanting to feel confident about one's abilities and choices sometimes leads to decisions that run counter to economic theory, and marketers often take advantage of this factor. One- and two-year gym memberships offered for an attractive upfront prepaid price is a great deal for someone eager to lose weight and get in shape. But often such ambitions fall short, leading many gym memberships to go unused (with the money comfortably in the gym's bank account).

Overvaluing the Present Relative to the Future

It is often difficult to plan for the future. Money saved today can earn interest, and money invested in financial instruments and assets can increase in value over time. Despite the higher value of money in the future, it is still money one must give up using *today*. Therefore, people sometimes are reluctant to save for the future despite lucrative incentives such as retirement fund matching programs offered by employers.

The same is true for paying off debt. Paying the minimum payment on credit card balances seems easy, but accruing finance charges of 15% or more can put a severe crunch on finances in the future. Although differences in time preferences themselves are not irrational per se, because the future often appears so distant, it can blur the reasoning behind sound economic decisions. For example, a society's unwillingness to fully tackle climate change results from overvaluing present benefits relative to future costs.

Altruism

The last factor to be discussed is **altruism,** or actions undertaken merely out of goodwill or generosity. Buying a sandwich for a homeless person you will likely not see again, donating money to a charitable organization, or helping a tourist find his or her way to a hotel all are friendly gestures that do not provide any reward except for the positive feeling one gets from helping others.

altruism Actions undertaken merely out of goodwill or generosity.

 ISSUE

Tipping and Consumer Behavior

If consumers maximize their utility with a given (limited) budget, why would they ever tip? Consider that tips come at the end of a meal. How can tips affect the quality of service already given?

Many reasons might explain tipping. First, if it is a restaurant you frequent, tips might assure better service in the future. Second, you might consider tips to be rewards for higher quality service. Third, tipping is a custom and is part of the income for several dozen occupations.

What would happen if many people refused or neglected to tip? Would people in various occupations seek to make tipping legally binding? It is likely this would be the result, if a recent case in New York is any guide.

If you have ever gone to a restaurant with a large party, you will notice that menus and bills often state that a set tip will be added for large parties. One large party gave a very small tip after what they considered to be inadequate service. The restaurant sued, claiming that an 18% tip was mandatory. The

court's decision for the tipper turned on the phrasing in the menu. This could be viewed as a first shot: If too many people refuse to tip or tip poorly, we can expect legal redress.

We can establish, then, that tipping is a custom that leads to better service, and so is followed even though the tip comes after the service is performed. In this way, it seems to run counter to the idea of people tipping based on a calculation of marginal utility. And how much we tip raises questions about how we calculate marginal utility.

Economists have found only a weak statistical link between quality of service and size of the tip. Tipping also appears to be unrelated to the number of courses in the meal, and whether or not people intend to return to the restaurant. The accompanying table shows some of the things that do affect the size of the tip.

Obviously, a waiter or waitress cannot do all of these things and expect to see tips increase by the sum of all the percentages, but we all have experienced many of these techniques in restaurants. Interestingly, if a waitress draws a smiley face on the bill, her tips go up, but if a waiter does the same, his tips go down. Suggestive selling raises the tip because people tend to tip based on the size of the bill. After having read about this study, you probably will find yourself being a little cynical when some of these techniques are used the next time you dine out.

Percentage Increase in Tips from Specific Behavior by Waitstaff	
Tip Enhancing Action	**Change in Tip**
Wearing a flower in hair	17%
Introducing yourself by name	53%
Squatting down next to the table	20%–25%
Repeat order back to customers	100%
Suggestive selling	23%
Touching customer	22%–42%
Using tip trays with credit card insignia	22%–25%
Waitress drawing a smiley face on check	18%
Writing "thank you" on the check	13%

See Michael Lynn, *Mega Tips: Scientifically Tested Techniques to Increase Your Tips,* 2004, p. 25.

Source: Based on Raj Persaud, "What's the tipping point?" *Financial Times,* April 9, 2005, p. w3.

Helping the community by volunteering one's time provides satisfaction that is not measured by monetary gains.

Thus, altruistic behavior provides utility in the sense of feeling good about one's actions, even though the actions may cost money, time, and effort, resources that will reduce one's ability to consume other items. Although altruism is generally not viewed as a *mistake,* it nonetheless represents a limitation of the rational choice model. And because altruistic behavior is so commonplace (such as the generosity of individuals in times of natural disasters, both within the country and abroad), economic models need to account for the utility gained from being generous. Yet, such feelings of goodwill are difficult to measure in economic models, which makes it a factor left to behavioral economists to take into account.

Each of the five factors described in this section add to the discussion in the previous section that marginal utility analysis does not capture all circumstances of individual economic behavior. But it is important to note that these limitations and the behavioral factors are the exceptions to the rule; marginal utility analysis still plays an important role in how we live our daily lives.

Recognizing the validity of these criticisms, economists have tried to limit themselves to working with the sorts of data they can collect, in this case purchases by individuals. By formulating hypotheses about what consumers purchase and what this says about their preferences, economists have managed to develop a theory of consumer behavior that does not require that utility be measured. This more modern approach to analyzing consumer behavior that reaches the same conclusions as marginal utility theory is known as *indifference curve analysis.* Because indifference curve analysis extends the discussion of consumer behavior beyond the principles of consumer choice, it is discussed in the Appendix.

 CHECKPOINT

BEHAVIORAL ECONOMICS

- Behavioral economics involves incorporating human psychology into economic decision making to explain why individuals sometimes do not act according to what economic models predict.

- Behavioral economics studies *predictable* deviations from rational behavior.

- The sunk cost fallacy is a common mistake when individuals feel obligated to take sunk cost expenditures into account when making present and future decisions.

- Framing biases occur when marketers present prices in a way that makes them appear lower than what they actually are.

- Overconfidence, overvaluing the present relative to the future, and altruistic actions are other factors influencing economic behavior.

QUESTIONS: A common practice in some supermarkets is to hang signs in the soup section that read "limit 12 per customer." Would our previous economic models predict that consumer behavior would change at all? How about behavioral economics? If it did, what deviation would this be?

Answers to the Checkpoint questions can be found at the end of this chapter.

chapter summary

Section 1: **The Budget Line and Choices**

A **budget line** shows all the combinations of two goods that can be purchased with a given income and given the prices of each good.

Example: Monthly workout budget = $100; price per wall climbing session = $20; price per racquetball session = $10.

Changes in Prices and Income (initial budget = $30; initial price of movie ticket and cover charge = $10 each)

If the cover charge falls by 50% and the price of movie tickets stays the same, the budget line pivots outward.

If the prices stay the same, but the budget doubles, the budget line shifts outward, expanding consumption choices.

Section 2: **Marginal Utility Analysis**

Utility is a hypothetical measure of satisfaction.

Total utility is the satisfaction a person receives from consuming a quantity of a good, while **marginal utility** is the satisfaction received from consuming *one more unit* of a good.

Where should one consume on the budget?

The budget line shows what combinations are affordable, but not which point maximizes utility. This is determined using the **utility maximization rule,** which says that utility is maximized when the marginal utility per dollar is equal across all goods.

Wall climbing is fun, but climbing the same rock wall every time might make the experience less exciting over time due to the **law of diminishing marginal utility.**

Section 2: Marginal Utility Analysis (continued)

The **utility maximization rule** states that total utility is maximized when the marginal utility per dollar is equal for all products purchased:

$$\frac{MU_a}{P_a} = \frac{MU_b}{P_b} = \ldots = \frac{MU_n}{P_n}$$

When this rule is not met, one should consume fewer goods providing smaller marginal utility per dollar and more goods providing larger marginal utility per dollar.

Lucas Tange/cultura/Corbis

Watching a boring movie is likely to provide very little utility, resulting in even smaller marginal utility per dollar spent at the cinema. Money in this case ought to have been spent on an activity providing greater marginal utility per dollar in order to maximize total utility.

Section 3: Behavioral Economics

Behavioral economics is the incorporation of human psychology into economic decision making to explain why individuals sometimes act differently from what economic models predict.

Psychological Factors Influencing Economic Decisions

- **Sunk cost fallacy:** occurs when individuals take sunk costs into account when making decisions about the present or future.

- **Framing bias:** occurs when individuals are steered toward making one decision over another, or when individuals are led to believe that they are getting a better deal than they actually are.

- **Overconfidence:** occurs when strong feelings of one's abilities lead to irrational decisions.

- **Overvaluing the present relative to the future:** occurs when future decisions appear too distant to be concerned about in the present, leading to irrational decisions.

- **Altruism:** occurs when feelings of goodwill lead individuals to make decisions that benefit others at the expense of their own consumption.

Image Source/Corbis

Overconfidence in one's ability to select stocks may cause some to lose significant sums of money. Further, once losses in the stock market occur, traders are often reluctant to sell, and instead hold onto stocks as they potentially fall further in price, an example of the sunk cost fallacy.

KEY CONCEPTS

budget line, p. 134
marginal utility analysis, p. 137
utility, p. 137
total utility, p. 138
marginal utility, p. 139

law of diminishing marginal utility,
  p. 139
utility maximizing rule, p. 141
behavioral economics, p. 145
sunk cost, p. 145

sunk cost fallacy, p. 145
framing bias, p. 146
altruism, p. 147

QUESTIONS AND PROBLEMS

Check Your Understanding

1. Using a budget line, why does a decrease in the price of a good allow one to potentially consume more of both goods?

2. Why do price changes cause a budget line to pivot while income changes cause a budget line to shift in a parallel manner?

3. Describe the utility-maximizing condition in words. Explain why it makes sense.

4. What conditions are necessary for total utility to be positive while marginal utility is negative?

5. Why should sunk costs not be taken into consideration when making decisions about the present or the future?

6. Why do the prices of many goods and services end in 99 cents? Why don't businesses just round to the nearest whole dollar?

Apply the Concepts

7. Scruffie the cat has $15 to spend each month on cat toys, which cost $3 each, and cat treats, which cost $1.50 each. Draw a budget line to show the combinations of each good that Scruffie can afford if she spends her entire budget. Now suppose that cat treats go on sale for $1 each. How does this change in price affect the budget line (show on a graph)?

8. Eric enjoys having sushi and sashimi for lunch every day. Suppose the marginal utility of the last sushi roll Eric eats is 40 and the marginal utility of the last piece of sashimi Eric eats is 20. If the price of a roll of sushi is $8 and the price per piece of sashimi is $2, did Eric maximize his utility? Explain.

9. One luxury goods manufacturer noted that, "Our customers do not want to pay less. If we halved the price of all our products, we would double our sales for six months, and then we would sell nothing." Is there something about luxury goods that suggests consumers are irrational? Do luxury goods not follow the law of demand?

10. Advertisements on television both inform consumers and persuade them to purchase products in differing proportions, depending on the ad. But today, because digital video recorders can be found in virtually all households, much of what these households watch is recorded, and the vast bulk of the ads are skipped. If this trend continues, where will consumers find out about new products?

11. Critics of marginal utility analysis argue that it is unrealistic to assume that people make the mental calculus of marginal utility per dollar for large numbers of products. But when you are making a decision to either go to a first-run movie or to buy a used DVD of last summer's blockbuster, does this analysis seem so complex? Is it a reasonable representation of your thought process?

12. A common practice at many supermarkets is to show the customer's total "savings" on their purchase at the bottom of the receipt. Such savings include the total discounts from goods purchased along with savings from coupons used. How would listing the total savings on a receipt influence an individual's consumption habits? Of what type of behavioral factor does this strategy take advantage?

In the News

13. Richard Layard, in his book *Happiness: Lessons from a New Science,* states that once a country's annual income exceeds $20,000 per capita, there is little relationship between happiness and income. But if you are poor, more money does make you happier. Does this fact suggest that the marginal utility from more income above $20,000 per capita is small?

14. In the summer of 2009, Chrysler announced that beginning with its 2010 models it was dropping the current lifetime powertrain (engine and transmission parts) warranty and replacing it with a five-year, 100,000-mile guarantee. *The Wall Street Journal* (August 20, 2009) reported that "Chrysler spokesman Rick Deneau said that the decision was driven by market research that showed customers prefer warranties with a fixed time period." The new five-year warranty was transferable if the vehicle was sold, while the prior lifetime warranty applied only to the original owner.

    Given marginal utility analysis, does it seem reasonable that consumers really prefer a five-year, 100,000-mile warranty to a lifetime warranty? What customers actually benefit from this new warranty?

Solving Problems

15. Assume a consumer has $20 to spend and for both products the marginal utilities are shown in the table below:

Quantity	MU_A	MU_B
1	20	30
2	10	10
3	5	2

Assume that each product sells for $5 per unit.

a. How many units of each product will the consumer purchase?

b. Assume the price of product B rises to $10 per unit. How will this consumer allocate her budget now?

c. If the prices of both products rise to $10 per unit, what will be the budget allocation?

16. Answer the questions following the table below.

First-Run Movies			Bottles of Wine		
Quantity	Total Utility	Marginal Utility	Quantity	Total Utility	Marginal Utility
0	0	—	0	0	—
1	140	_____	1	180	_____
2	260	_____	2	340	_____
3	360	_____	3	460	_____
4	440	_____	4	510	_____
5	500	_____	5	540	_____

a. Complete the table.

b. Assume that you have $50 a month to devote to entertainment (column labeled First-Run Movies) and wine with dinner (column labeled Bottles of Wine). What will be your equilibrium allocation if the price to see a movie is $10 and a bottle of wine cost $10 as well?

c. A grape glut in California results in Napa Valley wine dropping in price to $5 per bottle, and you view this wine as a perfect substitute for what you were drinking earlier. Now what will be your equilibrium allocation between movies and wine?

d. Given this data, calculate your elasticity of demand for wine over these two prices (see the midpoint method in Chapter 5).

USING THE NUMBERS

17. Using By the Numbers, list the top five categories that the average American household spent their incomes on in the year 2011 (start with the largest expenditure and proceed downward in terms of percentage of household budget).

18. According to By the Numbers, what category or categories of goods and services have increased in price (on average) every year from 2009 to 2011? What category or categories have fallen in price every year from 2009 to 2011?

ANSWERS TO QUESTIONS IN CHECKPOINTS

Checkpoint: The Budget Line and Choices

The total amount spent on meals each week is $(10 \times \$7.50) + (5 \times \$15) = \$150$. If the price of off-campus meals decreases to $10, the cost of maintaining the same routine as before (10 meals on campus and 5 meals off campus) falls to $125, leaving $25 left over. This extra money (savings from the price decrease) can be used to purchase more meals at either location, including more meals on campus.

Checkpoint: Marginal Utility Analysis

Convenience stores offer a small set of products at high prices nearer to home and have extended hours of operation. They also provide quicker service in that customers are in and out of the store quickly with what they need. The marginal utility of convenience overcomes the higher prices, thus people shop there because time is money. A 24/7 Safeway would have an impact on convenience store sales. At off-hours, supermarkets might be as fast as convenience stores, but cheaper.

Checkpoint: Behavioral Economics

According to marginal utility analysis, putting up a sign indicating a limit of 12 cans of soup per customer should not affect buying behavior, unless the shopper actually planned to buy more than 12 cans, in which case the sign puts a restriction on the purchase. However, in behavioral economics, putting up this sign represents a framing technique: by putting a limit of 12 cans, the supermarket is implying that the soup is so good that customers have a habit of buying large quantities (which may not be likely at all). By suggesting the soup is "popular," it draws customers into buying the soup that they otherwise might overlook, creating a framing bias.

Appendix
Indifference Curve Analysis

After studying this Appendix you should be able to:

- Understand the properties of indifference curves and preference maps.

- Use indifference curves to derive demand curves and measure income and substitution effects.

Marginal utility analysis provides a good theoretical glimpse into the consumer decision-making process, yet it requires that utility be measured and that marginal utility per dollar be computed for innumerable possible consumption choices. In reality, measuring utility is impossible, as is mentally computing the marginal utility of thousands of products. To get around these difficulties, economists have developed a modern explanation of consumer decisions that does not require measuring utility. The foundation of this analysis is the indifference curve.

Indifference Curves and Consumer Preferences

If consumers cannot precisely measure the exact satisfaction they receive from specific products, economists reason that people can distinguish between different bundles of goods and decide whether they prefer one bundle over another. This analysis eliminates the idea of measuring consumer satisfaction. It instead assumes that consumers will either be able to choose between any two bundles, or else be *indifferent* to which bundle is chosen. An **indifference curve** shows all points at which consumers' choices are indifferent—points at which consumers express no preference between combinations of two products.

indifference curve Shows all the combinations of two goods where the consumer is indifferent (gets the same level of satisfaction).

To illustrate how an indifference curve works, let us return to our original example of pizzas and wall climbing, now graphed in Figure APX-1. Compare the combination represented by point *b* (2 pizzas and 1.5 hours of climbing) and the combination at point *e* (2 pizzas and 0.5 hour of wall climbing). Which would you prefer, assuming you enjoy both of these? Clearly, the combination at point *b* is preferable to the combination at point *e* because you get the same amount of pizza but more wall climbing. By the same logic, bundle *f* is preferable to bundle *b* because you get the same amount of climbing, but 3 more pizzas.

These choices have all been easy enough to make. But now assume you are offered bundles *d* and *b*. Bundle *d* contains more pizzas than bundle *b*, but bundle *b* has more climbing time. Given this choice, you may well conclude that you do not care which

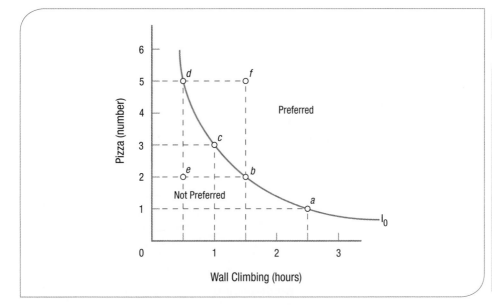

FIGURE APX-1

An Indifference Curve

All of the different possible combinations lying on the indifference curve I_0 represent bundles of goods to which you are indifferent—you would just as soon have any one of these combinations as any other. But compare the combination represented by point *b* and the combination at point *e*. Which would you prefer? Point *b*, of course, because you get more. All points upward and to the right are preferred to all points on indifference curve I_0.

bundle you get—you are indifferent. In fact, all of the different possible combinations lying on the indifference curve I_0 represent bundles to which you are indifferent, such that you would just as soon have any one of these combinations as any other. And this tells us what an indifference curve is: It identifies all possible combinations of two products that offer consumers the same level of satisfaction or utility. Notice that this mode of analysis does not require us to consider the precise quantity of utility that various bundles yield, but only whether one bundle would be preferable to another.

Properties of Indifference Curves

Indifference curves have negative slopes and are convex to the origin; they bow inward, that is. They have negative slopes because we assume consumers will generally prefer to have more, rather than less, of each product. Yet, to obtain more of one product and maintain the same level of satisfaction, consumers must give up some quantity of the other product. Hence, the negative slope.

Indifference curves are bowed inward toward the origin because of the law of diminishing marginal utility discussed earlier. When you have a lot of pizzas (point d in Figure APX-1), you are willing to give up 2 pizzas to obtain another half-hour of climbing (moving from point d to point c). But once you have plenty of wall time, yet few pizzas (point b), you are unwilling to give up as many pizzas to get more climbing time. This is the law of diminishing marginal utility at work: As we consume more of any particular product, the satisfaction we derive from consuming additional units of this product falls.

Indifference (or Preference) Maps

indifference map An infinite set of indifference curves in which each curve represents a different level of utility or satisfaction.

An indifference curve is a curve that represents a set of product bundles to which a consumer is indifferent. An **indifference map,** or *preference map,* is an infinite set of indifference curves, each representing a different level of satisfaction. Three possible indifference curves, forming part of a preference map, are shown in Figure APX-2.

Indifference curve I_0 is the same curve shown in Figure APX-1. Indifference curve I_1 provides consumers with greater satisfaction than I_0 because it is located farther from the origin. In general, utility rises as curves move outward from the origin, because these curves represent larger quantities of both goods. Conversely, indifference curve I_2 offers consumers less total satisfaction because it is located closer to the origin and represents smaller amounts of both products than I_0.

To confirm the observations just made, compare point a on indifference curve I_2 with point b on indifference curve I_0. Points a and b contain the same amount of pizza, but point b contains more climbing time. Hence, point b offers a higher level of satisfaction than

FIGURE APX-2

Three Indifference Curves for Pizza and Wall Climbing (An Indifference Map)

An indifference map, or preference map, contains an infinite set of indifference curves, each representing a different level of satisfaction. Three possible indifference curves for pizzas and wall climbing, forming part of a preference map, are shown here.

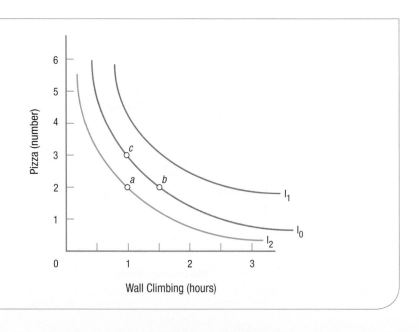

point *a*. An analysis of points *a* and *c* yields a similar conclusion. Because both points *c* and *b* on indifference curve I_0 are preferred to point *a* on I_2, indifference curve I_0 must generally offer higher levels of satisfaction than the points on indifference curve I_2.

This result leads us to one final property of indifference curves: They do not intersect. Because all of the points on any indifference curve represent bundles of goods to which consumers are indifferent, if two indifference curves were to cross, this would mean that some of the bundles they represent offered the same level of satisfaction (where the curves meet), but others did not (where the curves do not touch). Yet, this is a logical impossibility, because each indifference curve is defined as a set of bundles offering exactly the same level of satisfaction.

We now turn to the question of how consumers use such preference maps to optimize their satisfaction within their budget constraints.

⊙ Optimal Consumer Choice

Figure APX-3 superimposes a budget line of $50 per week onto a preference map that assumes pizzas cost $10 each and wall climbing costs $20 per hour. Maximizing your satisfaction on your limited income requires that you purchase some bundle of goods on the highest possible indifference curve. In this example, the best you can do is indicated by point *b*: 2 pizzas and 1.5 hours of wall climbing. Clearly, if you were to pick any other point on the budget line, your satisfaction would be diminished because you would end up on a lower indifference curve (points *a* or *c* in Figure APX-3). It follows that the indifference curve running tangent to the budget line identifies your best option, in this case the indifference curve that just touches the budget line at point *b*.

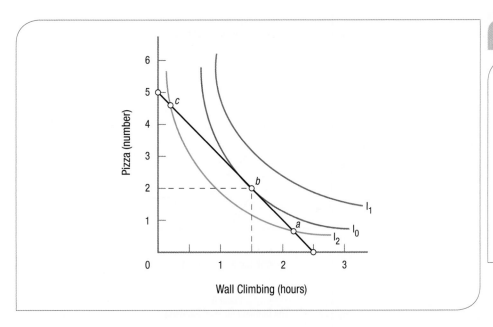

Optimal Consumer Choice
Maximizing your satisfaction on your limited income requires purchasing some bundle of goods on the highest possible indifference curve. The best you can do in this situation is indicated by point *b*: 2 pizzas and 1.5 hours of wall climbing. Indifference curve I_0 is the highest indifference curve that can be reached with the budget line shown.

Of course, this is the same result we reached earlier using marginal utility analysis, specifically in Table 2. Notice, however, that using indifference curve analysis, we did not have to assume that utility can be measured. We were able to understand how you would allocate your budget between two goods so as to achieve the highest possible level of satisfaction, even without knowing exactly how high that level might be.

⊙ Using Indifference Curves

Indifference curves are a useful device to help us understand consumer demand. Economists use indifference curves, for instance, to shed light on the impact of changes in consumer income and product substitution resulting from a change in product price. Indifference curve analysis, moreover, provides some insight into how households determine their supply of labor (this analysis, however, is left to a later chapter). Before we move on to applications of indifference curve analysis, however, we first need to derive a demand curve from an indifference map.

Deriving Demand Curves

We derive the demand curve using indifference curve analysis in much the same way we did using marginal utility analysis. Panel A of Figure APX-4 restates the results of Figure APX-3: When you have a budget of $50 per week, the price of pizza is $10, and climbing is $20 per hour, your optimal choice is found at point *a*. In panel B, we want to plot the demand curve for wall climbing. We know that when wall climbing costs $20 per hour, you will climb for 1.5 hours, so let us indicate this on panel B by marking point *a*.

To fill out the demand curve, let us now increase the price of wall climbing to $30 per hour. This produces a new budget line, *cd*. (Point *d* is located at 1.67 hours because $50/$30 = 1.67 hours of possible wall climbing.) This shift in the budget line yields a new optimal choice at point *b* on indifference curve I₂, now indicating the highest level of satisfaction you can attain. As panel A shows, the ultimate result of this hike in the price of wall climbing to $30 an hour is a reduction in your climbing to 1 hour per week. Transferring this result to panel B, we mark point *b* where price = $30 and climbing hours = 1. Now connecting points *a* and *b* in panel B, we are left with the demand curve for wall climbing.

Once again, therefore, we arrive at the same conclusion using indifference curve analysis as we did earlier using marginal utility analysis. Both approaches are logical and elegant,

FIGURE APX-4

Deriving the Demand for Wall Climbing Using Indifference Curve Analysis

In panel A, when wall climbing costs $20 per hour, your optimal choice is found at point *a*. When the price of wall climbing rises to $30 per hour, this produces a new budget line, *cd*, shifting the optimal choice to point *b*. Transferring points *a* and *b* down to panel B and connecting the points generates the demand curve for wall climbing.

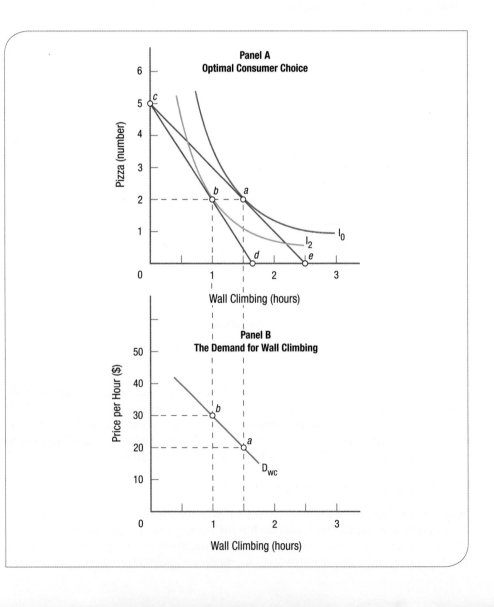

and both approaches tell us something about the thought processes consumers must use as they make their spending decisions. Indifference curve analysis, however, arrives at its conclusion without requiring that utility be measurable or that consumers perform complex arithmetic computations.

Income and Substitution Effects

Another way economists use indifference curves is to separate income and substitution effects when product prices change. First we need to distinguish between these two effects.

When the price of some product you regularly purchase goes up, your spendable income is thereby essentially reduced. If you always buy a latte a day, for instance, and you continue to do so even when the price of lattes goes up, you must then reduce your consumption of other goods. This essentially amounts to a reduction in your income. And we know that when income falls, the consumption of normal goods likewise declines. Hence, when higher prices essentially reduce consumer incomes, the quantity demanded for normal goods generally falls. Economists call this the **income effect.**

When the price of a particular good rises, meanwhile, the quantity demanded of that good will fall simply because consumers substitute lower priced goods for it. This is called the **substitution effect.** Thus, when the price of wall climbing rises from $20 to $30, you cut back on your climbing, in part because you decide to dedicate more of your money to pizza eating. The challenge for us now is to determine just how much of this reduction in your climbing is due to the substitution effect (more pizzas mean less climbing) and how much is due to the income effect (the rise in price effectively leaves you with less money to spend).

Figure APX-5 reproduces panel A of Figure APX-4, adding one line (*gh*) to divide the total change in purchases into the income and substitution effects. To see how this line is derived, let us begin by reviewing what has happened thus far. At point *a* you split your $50 budget into 2 pizzas at $10 each and 1.5 hours of wall climbing at $20 per hour. When the price of wall climbing rose to $30 per hour, you reduced your climbing time to 1 hour.

Consider now what happens when we evaluate what you are getting for your *current* allocation of money, but using the *old* price of wall climbing ($20 per hour). You are now getting 2 pizzas, worth $10 apiece, plus 1 hour of wall climbing, formerly valued at $20. This means that your budget has effectively been cut to $40. The ultimate effect of the rise in the price of climbing, in other words, has been to reduce your income by $10. In Figure APX-5, the hypothetical budget line *gh* represents this new budget of $40, though again reflecting the old price of climbing.

income effect When higher prices essentially reduce consumer income, the quantity demanded for normal goods falls.

---

substitution effect When the price of one good rises, consumers will substitute other goods for that good, therefore the quantity demanded for the higher priced good falls.

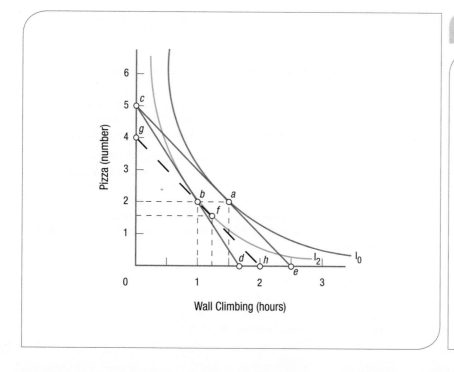

Income and Substitution Effects

Panel A of Figure APX-4 is reproduced in this figure. The price of climbing having risen to $30 per hour, this effectively reduces your budget to $40 per week, assuming you continue climbing as much as you did before. Line *gh* represents a new budget of $40, though reflecting the old price of climbing. This new budget line *gh* allows us to divide the total change in purchases into the income and substitution effects. Increasing the price of wall climbing from $20 to $30 an hour would mean a reduction in wall climbing (holding income constant at $40) from point *f* to point *b*. This is the substitution effect. The income effect is thus the reduction in consumption from point *a* to point *f*. Adding both effects together yields the total reduction.

Compare the original equilibrium point *a* on budget line *ce* with the new equilibrium point *f* on budget line *gh*. This new budget line *gh* reflects a budget of $40 with the old price of climbing ($20 per hour). Had your income previously been $40, you would have reduced your climbing by 15 minutes (to point *f*). This is the *income effect* associated with the rise in the price of wall climbing from $20 to $30 per hour. The rising price essentially reduced your income, causing you to consume 15 minutes less of wall climbing and 0.5 fewer pizzas due to this income reduction alone.

The change in price is the only thing that differentiates equilibrium point *b* from point *f*, income having been held constant. This difference of 15 minutes between point *f* and point *b* therefore represents a *substitution effect*. By changing the price of climbing while holding income constant, you consume 0.5 more pizza and 15 minutes less wall climbing.

Combined, the substitution and income effects constitute the entire change in quantity demanded when the price of wall climbing rises by $10 per hour. The income effect (movement from point *a* to point *f*) is a movement from one budget line to another. The substitution effect (movement from point *f* to point *b*) is a movement along the new budget line. Together, they represent the total change in quantity demanded. In this case the income and substitution effects were the same, 15 minutes, but this will not always be the case.

This chapter examined how consumers and households make decisions. Households attempt to maximize their well-being or satisfaction within the constraints of limited incomes. We have seen that the analysis of consumer decisions can be approached in two different ways, using marginal utility analysis or indifference curve analysis.

Marginal utility analysis assumes that consumers can readily measure utility and make complex calculations regarding the utility of various possible consumption choices. Both of these assumptions are empirically rather dubious. This does not, however, invalidate marginal utility analysis; it just makes it difficult to use and test in an empirical context. Indifference curve analysis gives us a more powerful set of analytical tools without these restrictive assumptions.

 CHECKPOINT

INDIFFERENCE CURVE ANALYSIS

- Indifference curve analysis does not require utility measurement. All it requires is that consumers can choose between different bundles of goods.

- An indifference curve shows all the combinations of two goods where the consumer has the same level of satisfaction.

- Indifference curves have negative slopes, are convex to the origin due to the law of diminishing marginal utility, and do not intersect with one another.

- An indifference map is an infinite set of indifference curves.

- Consumer equilibrium occurs where the budget line is tangent to the highest indifference curve.

- When the price of one product rises, not only will your consumption of that product fall (the substitution effect), but also your relative income will be reduced as well, and for normal goods you will consume less (the income effect). The opposite occurs when price falls.

QUESTION: Consumers face a set of goods called "credence goods." Consumers of such goods must "take it on faith that the supplier has given them what they need and no more."[1] Examples include surgeons, auto mechanics, and taxi drivers. These experts tell us what medical procedures, repairs, and routes we require to satisfy our needs, and very often we don't know the price until the work is done. If we do not know the price and cannot establish whether we actually need some of these goods, how does this square with our indifference curve analysis?

Answers to the Checkpoint question can be found at the end of this chapter.

---

[1] "Economic Focus: Sawbones, Cowboys and Cheats," *Economist*, April 15, 2006.

APPENDIX KEY CONCEPTS

indifference curve, p. 155   income effect, p. 159   substitution effect, p. 159
indifference map, p. 156

APPENDIX QUESTIONS AND PROBLEMS

Check Your Understanding

1. Indifference curves cannot intersect. Why not?

2. Explain why the following bundles of apples (A) and bananas (B) cannot be on the same indifference curve: (4A, 2B); (1A, 5B); (4A, 3B).

3. Answer the following questions using the figure below:

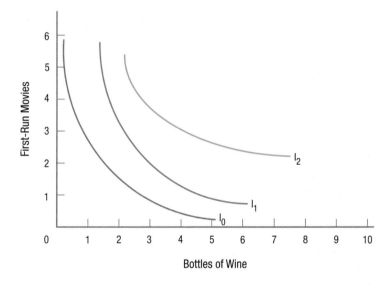

a. Assume that you have $50 a month to devote to entertainment (First-Run Movies) and wine with dinner (Bottles of Wine). What will be your equilibrium allocation if the price to see a movie or buy a bottle of wine is $10? Graph the equilibrium on the figure and label it point *a*.

b. A grape glut in California results in Napa Valley wine dropping in price to $5 a bottle, and you view this wine as a perfect substitute for what you were drinking. Now what will be your equilibrium allocation between movies and wine? Graph that on the figure and label the new equilibrium as point *b*.

4. Research by Walter Enders and Todd Sandler, *The Political Economy of Terrorism* (New York: Cambridge University Press), 2006, and David Wessel, "Princeton Economist Says Lack of Civil Liberties, Not Poverty, Breeds Terrorism," *Wall Street Journal*, July 5, 2007, p. A2, suggests that terrorists are not spurred by poverty, but rather often are educated individuals who live in countries with a lack of civil liberties. These researchers treat terrorists as rational actors who maximize a set of goals subject to constrained resources.

Assume that terrorists can choose between nonviolent acts and violent acts. Draw a budget line and indifference curves that show where a utility maximizing combination of these activities would occur. Now suppose that the U.S. government can choose between two types of antiterrorism policies: (1) a defensive approach such as increased airport screenings, and (2) a proactive approach, which includes activities such as infiltrating terrorist cells and freezing bank assets. Analyze how these policies affect the budget line of terrorists and how it affects the utility-maximizing combination of terrorist activities.

ANSWERS TO APPENDIX CHECKPOINT QUESTION

Checkpoint: Indifference Curve Analysis

Not very well. They are largely a problem of incomplete information and a challenging problem for consumers. If doctors make more money performing complex operations, they will be inclined to prescribe them more often. One study found that doctors elect surgery for themselves less often than nondoctors. As long as consumers are aware of the incentive structure of these transactions, they can build this into the decision calculus, but ultimately, information asymmetries are not adequately represented in this model.

Production and Costs

7

Twenty years ago, most people did not think much about what they could do with sustainable products. Energy and gas prices were low, and the problem of climate change was not very prominent in everyday discussions and news reports. This has changed, and many people today do think about the impact their consumption habits have on the environment. This has led to a rise in demand for energy-efficient products to address not only climate change issues but also wallet issues as rising energy costs take a greater share of a household's budget.

In the automobile industry, the use of sustainable energy resources such as ethanol remains expensive. However, in the mid-1990s manufacturers foresaw an opportunity to satisfy consumer demand for cars that achieve much greater fuel efficiency, resulting in a similar effect as using sustainable energy. In 1997, Toyota unveiled the Prius, the first well-selling car to use hybrid electric technology.

Creating a new type of car, especially one that runs on a new source of energy, is not like creating a new type of pizza. It costs much more to develop, design, and produce the very first car. Toyota invested over $1 billion to develop the Prius, a great deal of money for a new compact car in an untested market. What motivated Toyota to undertake such an expensive investment? The answer is profits.

Profits are one of the most important goals of firms. To determine profits, a firm must calculate its revenues from sales and subtract all of its costs. How does a firm measure these costs, and what do these costs include?

In this chapter, we look at what motivates firms to do what they do—profits. We then look at the production and cost part of the profit equation. We discuss the concept of profit as properly understood by economists. Unlike an accountant or agents of the Internal Revenue Service, economists use a different measure of profit, one that takes into account explicit (out-of-pocket) costs and then adds the opportunity costs (the value of forgone opportunities) of a business decision. We then go on to discuss the production process and how output is determined based on the amount of inputs used. Finally, we take a look at the measurement of costs. Specifically, economists break down costs into different categories in order to create decision rules that firms follow to maximize profits. In subsequent chapters, we add in the revenue part to the production part. In this way, we will discover what lies behind supply curves.

⊙ Firms, Profits, and Economic Costs

We just read that Toyota had to make a decision about producing a product. Who makes such decisions? It's the firms and entrepreneurs who choose to take on the risk and effort to launch a new product. They are motivated by the profits that can be earned if the investment proves successful. But how do we measure profits, as properly understood by economists?

This section highlights the important role that firms and entrepreneurs play in producing the goods and services we enjoy as consumers. No matter how the organizational structure is set up, firms and entrepreneurs hold profits as their motivating force. To achieve profits, both revenues and costs must be considered. As we will see, profits can be measured using an accounting approach or an economics approach. These approaches differ in the way costs are measured.

Firms

A **firm** is an economic institution that transforms inputs, or factors of production, into outputs, or products. Most firms begin as family enterprises or small partnerships. When successful, these firms can evolve into corporations of considerable size.

In the process of producing goods and services, firms must make numerous decisions. First, they have to determine a market need. Then, most broadly, firms must decide what quantity of output to produce, how to produce it, and what inputs to employ. The latter two decisions depend on the production technology that the firm selects.

Any given product can typically be produced in a wide variety of ways. Some businesses, like McDonald's franchises and Dunkin' Donuts shops, use considerable amounts of capital equipment, whereas others, such as T-shirt shops and small eateries, require very little. Even among similar firms, the quality and quantity of resources available often

---

After studying this chapter you should be able to:

- Describe the nature of firms and markets.

- Explain the difference between accounting and economic costs and how they affect the determination of profits.

- Differentiate between the short run and long run.

- Describe the nature of short-run production, total product, marginal product, and average product.

- Differentiate among increasing, constant, and decreasing returns.

- Describe and compare the differences among fixed costs, variable costs, marginal costs, and average costs.

- Explain the importance of marginal costs in a firm's production decision.

- Use graphs to show the relationships among short-run average variable cost, average total cost, and marginal cost curves.

- Describe long-run costs.

- Describe the reasons for economies and diseconomies of scale.

firm An economic institution that transforms resources (factors of production) into outputs.

BY THE NUMBERS

Innovation, Productivity, and Costs Rule Business

To remain in business, firms must innovate not only by improving the products they make but also by controlling their costs. Controlling costs is done by introducing new technologies in production and increasing productivity. This holds for the service sector as well.

The cost of industrial robots has fallen over 70% since 1992.

Christopher Honeywell/Alamy

Productivity has risen over 50% since 1992.

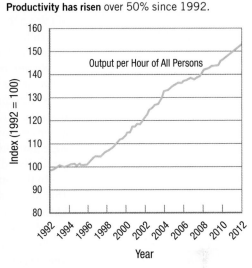

$9,000,000,000
Annual revenue needed to support a new semiconductor fabrication plant.

9.17 hours
Time spent by the average American on government paperwork each year.

"We've found the key to productivity. It's Fred, down in the shop. He makes the stuff."
From The Wall Street Journal, Permission Cartoon Features Syndicate

Cost Breakdown for an iPad

Retail Price	$399
Costs	
Touch display screen	85
Hard drive	52
Battery	22
Apps Processor	14
Misc. components	56
Assembly	10
Distribution costs	70
Profit for Apple	90

Businesses face a relentless need to lower costs, which has changed the way we live and travel. The percentage of travelers purchasing airline tickets and checking in online highlights this trend.

Online Flight Bookings

iStockphoto

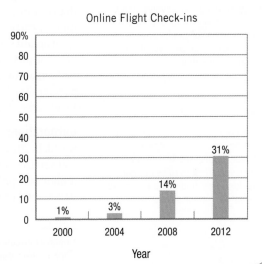

Online Flight Check-ins

determine what technologies are used. Firms located in areas with an abundance of low-cost labor tend to use low-technology, labor-intensive production methods. In areas in which high-skill, high-wage labor is the norm, production is more often done using high-technology, capital-intensive processes.

Entrepreneurs

If a product or service is to be provided to the market, someone must first assume the risk of raising the required capital, assembling workers and raw materials, producing the product, and, finally, offering it for sale. Markets provide incentives and signals, but it is entrepreneurs who provide products and services by taking risks in the hopes of earning profits.

Recent research in neuroscience has shown that entrepreneurs' brains were more active in the region responsible for making risky or "hot" decisions.[1] The research compared entrepreneurs who had founded at least two high-tech firms with senior managers from the private and public sectors. When the decisions were "emotionally neutral," the groups performed the same, but when the decisions were "hot" or risky, the entrepreneurs were more impulsive and more mentally flexible. It is this willingness to take risk to earn profits that distinguishes entrepreneurs from the rest of us.

In the United States, 12% of people ages 18 to 64 classify themselves as entrepreneurs. This means they are running start-up businesses or businesses less than 42 months old. Entrepreneurial rates in Europe are only half the American rate, and Japanese entrepreneurship is less than 2%.[2]

Entrepreneurs can be divided into three basic business structures: sole proprietorships (one owner), partnerships (two or more owners), and corporations (many stockholders). The United States has more than 25 million businesses, over 70% of them sole proprietorships or small businesses. Only 20% of American businesses are corporations. Nevertheless, corporations sell nearly 90% of all products and services in the United States. Likewise, around the world, the corporate form of business has become the dominant form. To see why, we must first take a brief look at the advantages and disadvantages of each business structure.

sole proprietorship A type of business structure composed of a single owner who supervises and manages the business and is subject to unlimited liability.

Sole Proprietors
The **sole proprietorship** represents the most basic form of business organization. A proprietorship is composed of one owner, who usually supervises the business operation. Local restaurants, dry cleaning businesses, and auto repair shops are often sole proprietorships. A sole proprietorship is easy to establish and manage, having much less paperwork associated with it than other forms of business organization. But the sole proprietorship has disadvantages. Single owners are often limited in their ability to raise capital. In many instances, all management responsibilities fall on this single individual. And most important, the personal assets of the owner are subject to unlimited liability. If you own a pizza shop as a sole proprietor and someone slips on the floor, he or she can sue you and you could lose your house and your life savings if you do not have sufficient insurance coverage.

partnership Similar to a sole proprietorship, but involves more than one owner who share the management of the business. Partnerships are also subject to unlimited liability.

Partnerships
Partnerships are similar to sole proprietorships except that they have more than one owner. Establishing a partnership usually requires signing a legal partnership document. Partnerships find it easier to raise capital and spread around the management responsibilities. Like sole proprietors, however, partners are subject to unlimited liability, not only for their share of the business, but for the entire business. If your partner takes off for Bermuda, you are left to pay all the bills, even those your partner incurred. The death of one partner dissolves a partnership, unless other arrangements have been made ahead of time. In any case, the death of a partner often creates problems for the continuity of the business.

corporation A business structure that has most of the legal rights of individuals, and in addition, can issue stock to raise capital. Stockholders' liability is limited to the value of their stock.

Corporations
The **corporation** is the premier form of business organization in most of the world. In 2012, roughly 5 million American corporations sold over $27 trillion worth of goods and services worldwide. This is an amazing statistic when you consider that the country's 23 million sole proprietorships had sales totaling just over $1.3 trillion. Clearly, corporations are structured in a way that enhances growth and efficiency.

---

[1] Andrew Lawrence et al., "The Innovative Brain," *Nature,* November 13, 2008, pp. 168–169.
[2] *Global Entrepreneurship Monitor,* "2011 Extended Report: Entrepreneurs and Entrepreneurial Employees Across the Globe," 2012.

Corporations have most of the legal rights of individuals; in addition, they are able to issue stock to raise capital, and most significant, the liability of individual owners (i.e., stockholders) is limited to the amount they have invested in (or paid for) the stock. This is what distinguishes corporations from the other forms of business organization: the ability to raise large amounts of capital because of limited liability.

Some scholars argue that corporations are the greatest engines of economic prosperity ever known.[3] Daniel Akst writes:

> When I worked for a big company, there was a miracle in the office every couple of weeks, just like clockwork. It happened every payday, when sizable checks were distributed to a small army of employees who also enjoyed health and retirement benefits. Few of us could have made as much on our own, and somehow there was always money left over for the shareholders as well.[4]

Without the corporate umbrella, most of the jobs we hold would not exist; most of the products we use would not have been invented; and our standard of living would be a fraction of what it is today.

What is it that motivates business owners of all types to take on the risks of creating a product? Profits.

Steve Wozniak (right) and Steve Jobs began their computer business in the Jobs family garage as a partnership before turning it into a public company, Apple, in 1980. Today, Apple is one of the largest companies in the world by market value.

 ISSUE

The Vast World of Corporate Offshoring and Profits

Most Americans are aware of the fact that corporations, particularly in manufacturing industries, often relocate factories to developing countries to take advantage of lower costs for labor and raw materials (in a process called offshoring) and to gain access to emerging markets for their products. Yet, another incentive exists for why companies choose to place important offices, even headquarters, abroad, and that is to avoid U.S. regulations and taxes.

One common example of corporate offshoring occurs in the cruise ship industry. Despite many cruise ships starting and ending trips at U.S. ports, virtually all large cruise vessels are registered outside of the United States, allowing cruise lines to circumvent, for example, U.S. labor laws (ever wonder how a room steward is able to legally work seven days a week, day and night, at less than minimum wage?).

The more egregious examples of offshoring occur when companies relocate headquarters to certain countries to take advantage of lower tax rates. And by relocating, this often does not mean moving to a shiny new skyscraper in a major European or Asian capital. On the contrary, it sometimes involves merely having a mailbox in an obscure town or island serving as the headquarters for a multimillion dollar enterprise.

Recent media attention exposing the abuse of corporate offshoring has led to new reforms being proposed in the United States and the European Union. Various proposed legislation, such as the 2011 Stop Tax Haven Abuse Act, aimed at curbing the use of corporate offshoring when the sole purpose is to avoid taxes (as opposed to traditional offshoring to take advantage of less expensive inputs of production). But like all new policies,

At its height in 2011, Zug, Switzerland, was home to 30,000 corporate headquarters from around the world. Impressive for a quiet lakeside town with just 26,000 residents.

tradeoffs exist, as companies affected by the new legislation claim such rules would reduce competition and raise consumer prices. The costs and benefits of any new policy are likely to be debated extensively before becoming law.

---

[3] John Micklethwait and Adrian Wooldridge, *The Company: A Short History of a Revolutionary Idea* (New York: The Modern Library), 2003.
[4] Daniel Akst, "Where Those Paychecks Come From," *Wall Street Journal*, February 3, 2004.

Profits

Entrepreneurs and firms employ resources and turn out products with the goal of making profits. This is not to say that firms put profit above all else (i.e., that they would do something immoral or socially irresponsible to increase profits), but instead that firms do not intentionally make decisions that would knowingly result in lower profit. **Profit** is the difference between total revenue and total cost.

Total revenue is the amount of money a firm receives from the sales of its products. It is equal to the price per unit times the number of units sold ($TR = p \times q$). Note that we use lower case p and q when we are dealing with an individual firm and use upper case when describing a market. **Total cost** includes both out-of-pocket expenses and opportunity costs; we will discuss this concept shortly.

Economists explicitly assume that firms proceed rationally and have the maximization of profits as their primary objective. Alternative behavioral assumptions for firms have been tested, including sales maximization, various goals for market share, and customer satisfaction. Although these more complex assumptions for firm behavior often predict different outcomes, economists have not been persuaded that any of them yield results superior to those of the profit maximization approach. Profit maximization has stood the test of time, and thus we will assume it is the primary economic goal of firms.

Economic Costs

When economists say "profit," they mean profits properly understood. Economists approach business costs and profits from the opportunity cost perspective discussed in Chapter 2. They separate costs into explicit costs, or out-of-pocket expenses, and implicit costs, or opportunity costs. **Economic costs** are the sum of explicit and implicit costs.

Explicit costs are those expenses paid directly to some other economic entity. These costs include wages, lease payments, expenditures for raw materials, taxes, utilities, and so on. A company can easily determine its explicit costs by summing all of the checks it has written during the normal course of doing business.

Implicit costs refer to all of the opportunity costs of using resources that belong to the firm. Recall that opportunity cost measures the value of the next best alternative use of resources, including that of time and capital. Implicit costs include depreciation, the depletion of business assets, and the opportunity cost of a firm's capital.

In any business, some assets are depleted over time. Machines, cars, and office equipment depreciate with use and time. Finite oil or mineral deposits are depleted as they are mined or pumped. Even though firms do not actually pay any cash as these assets are worn down or used up, these costs nonetheless represent real expenses to the firm.

Another major component of implicit costs is the capital firms have invested. Even small firms incur large implicit costs from their capital investment. Small entrepreneurs, for example, must invest both their own capital and labor into their businesses. Such people could normally be working for someone else, so their "lost salary" must be treated as an implicit cost when determining the true profitability of their businesses. Similarly, any capital invested in a business enterprise could just as well be earning interest in a bank account or returning dividends and capital gains through the purchase and sale of stock in other enterprises. Though not directly paid out as expenses, these forgone earnings nonetheless represent implicit costs for the firm.

Sunk Costs

The previous chapter introduced the concept of **sunk costs,** which are costs that have already been incurred and *cannot* be recovered. For example, should you leave in the middle of a movie because it stinks? The cost of admission has been paid, and staying until the end might add to the anguish of an already bad situation. Similarly, tuition is a sunk cost. Most colleges and universities do not provide refunds for dropped courses beyond the first week or two of the term. Because sunk costs are not recoverable, future decisions, such as whether to drop a course one is failing, should not depend on them. To a business, the decision to advertise a product in a new magazine depends on the benefits and costs of that advertising, not on how much has been spent on television ads in the past. You will hear the phrase that "sunk costs are sunk," meaning ignore them, they are gone.

profit Equal to the difference between total revenue and total cost.

total revenue Equal to price per unit times quantity sold.

total cost The sum of all costs to run a business. To an economist, this includes out-of-pocket expenses and opportunity costs.

economic costs The sum of explicit (out-of-pocket) and implicit (opportunity) costs.

explicit costs Those expenses paid directly to another economic entity, including wages, lease payments, taxes, and utilities.

implicit costs The opportunity costs of using resources that belong to the firm, including depreciation, depletion of business assets, and the opportunity cost of the firm's capital employed in the business.

sunk costs Those costs that have been incurred and cannot be recovered, including, for example, funds spent on existing technology that has become obsolete and past advertising that has run in the media.

Economic and Normal Profits

The primary goal of any firm is to earn a profit. However, how the Internal Revenue Service (IRS) measures profit for tax purposes is different from how an economist determines profit. Suppose that after graduating, you decide to open a new billiards hall on campus. After a year, counting all the revenues and subtracting all explicit costs (costs that you actually pay out), you end up with a profit of $20,000. Is your business a success? The IRS certainly thinks so, as it will collect taxes on these profits. And you might brag to friends that you turned a profit in your first year. But then you start thinking of all the time you spent on the business and the missed opportunities, such as the $40,000 a year job offer you turned down, and the money you could have earned had you invested your savings in stocks or bonds rather than in your business. Now, your business doesn't feel successful.

Economists include both explicit and implicit costs in their analysis of business profits. An **accounting profit** is calculated by including only explicit costs, while an **economic profit** is calculated using both explicit and implicit costs. Therefore, when a firm is earning economic profits, it is generating profits in excess of zero once implicit costs are factored in. This brings us to an important benchmark called **normal profits,** which occurs when economic profit equals zero. Economists refer to this level of profit as a *normal rate of return* on capital, a return just sufficient to keep investors satisfied and to keep capital in the business over the long run. If a firm's rate of return on capital falls below this rate, investors will put their capital to use elsewhere.

Although earning zero economic profit might sound dismal, this simply means that the firm is earning the same profit it would have earned had it chosen its next best alternative use of its capital, which can be quite substantial in terms of accounting profit. For example, if Mark Zuckerberg left Facebook and opened a new business, his new business (assuming he uses the same amount of capital and labor) would have to earn billions of dollars a year just to achieve normal profits. Not bad for *zero* economic profit. In other words, any profit less than what would be earned at Facebook under his leadership would be considered an *economic loss*. A firm earning normal profits means that it is earning just enough to cover the opportunity cost of its capital. Therefore, a firm may be earning *accounting profits* as defined by the IRS for tax purposes, yet still be suffering economic losses, because taxable income does not reflect all implicit costs.

Let's look at the difference between accounting profits and economic profits further in Table 1 on the next page, using our example of the billiards hall. Suppose your annual total revenue is $120,000. After subtracting out-of-pocket (explicit) costs of $100,000, you end up with an accounting profit of $20,000. However, if you could have earned $40,000 working elsewhere and $10,000 more by putting your savings into a stock or bond investment rather than into your business, you would incur a $30,000 economic loss.

Economists designate normal profits as economic profits equal to zero. To achieve normal profits, you would need to be just as well off operating the billiard hall as you would if you instead took another job and invested your savings elsewhere, which means earning $50,000 in accounting profits. Because you earned only $20,000 (or $30,000 less than the alternative), this results in an economic loss of $30,000. Normal profits are the profits necessary to keep a firm in business over the long run. This brings us to an important economic distinction, between the short run and the long run.

Short Run Versus Long Run

Although the short and the long run generally differ in their temporal spans, they are *not* defined in terms of time. Rather, economists define these periods by the ability of firms to adjust the quantities of various resources that they are employing.

As discussed in a previous chapter, the **short run** is a period of time over which at least one factor of production is fixed, or cannot be changed. For the sake of simplicity, economists typically assume that plant capacity is fixed in the short run. Output from a fixed plant can still vary depending on how much labor the firm employs. Firms can, for instance, hire more people, have existing employees work overtime, or run additional shifts. For discussion purposes, we focus here on labor as the variable factor, but changes in the raw materials used can also result in output changes.

The **long run,** conversely, is a period of time sufficient for a firm to adjust all factors of production, including plant capacity. Since all factors can be altered in the long run,

accounting profit The difference between total revenue and explicit costs. These are the profits that are taxed by the government.

economic profit Profit in excess of normal profits. These are profits in excess of both explicit and implicit costs.

normal profits The return on capital necessary to keep investors satisfied and keep capital in the business over the long run.

short run A period of time over which at least one factor of production (resource) is fixed, or cannot be changed.

long run A period of time sufficient for firms to adjust all factors of production, including plant capacity.

TABLE 1	Comparing Accounting Versus Economic Profits from Operating a Business		

Fancy Collection/SuperStock

Item	Accountant	Economist
Annual revenue	$120,000	$120,000
less **explicit costs**		
Wages	–$50,000	–$50,000
Lease payments	–$20,000	–$20,000
Cost of goods sold	–$15,000	–$15,000
Utilities	–$5,000	–$5,000
Insurance	–$5,000	–$5,000
Office supplies	–$5,000	–$5,000
Accounting Profit	**+$20,000**	
less **implicit costs**		
Forgone earnings from job offer	—	–$40,000
Forgone earnings from money invested	—	–$10,000
Economic Profit		**–$30,000**

existing firms can even close and leave the industry, and new firms can build new plants and enter the market.

In the short run, therefore, with plant capacity and the number of firms in an industry being fixed, output varies only as a result of changes in employment. In the long run, as plant capacity and other factors are made variable, the industry may grow or shrink as firms enter or leave the business, or some firms alter their plant capacity.

Because all industries are unique, the time required for long-run adjustment varies by industry. Family-owned restaurants, lawn-mowing services, and roofing firms can come and go fairly rapidly. High-capital industries on the other hand, such as the chemical, petroleum, and semiconductor industries, face obstacles to change that require a long time to overcome, whether these be strenuous environmental regulation, immense research and development requirements, or huge capital costs for plant construction. Adding plant capacity in one of these industries can take a decade or more and cost billions of dollars.

The important point to note from this section is that firms seek economic profits and determine profits by first calculating their costs. These costs may differ over the short run versus the long run. Therefore, we look first at production basics, then consider costs in both the short run and the long run.

 CHECKPOINT

FIRMS, PROFITS, AND ECONOMIC COSTS

- Firms are economic institutions that convert inputs (factors of production) into products and services.
- Entrepreneurs provide goods and services to markets. Entrepreneurs can be organized into three basic business structures: sole proprietorships, partnerships, and corporations.
- Corporations are the premier form of business organization because they give owners (shareholders) limited liability, unlike sole proprietorships and partnerships.
- Profit is the difference between total revenues and total costs.

- Explicit costs are those expenses, such as rent and the cost of raw materials, paid directly to some other economic entity. Implicit costs represent the opportunity costs of doing business, including depreciation and the firm's capital costs.

- Normal profits (or normal rates of return) are equal to zero economic profit. The firm is earning just enough to keep capital in the firm over the long run. Economic profits are those in *excess* of normal profits.

- The short run is a period of time during which one factor of production (usually plant capacity) is fixed. In the long run all factors can vary and the firm can enter or exit the industry.

QUESTION: Assume for a moment that you want to go into business for yourself and that you have a good idea. What are the pros and cons of setting up your company as a corporation as opposed to keeping it as a sole proprietorship?

Answers to the Checkpoint question can be found at the end of this chapter.

➡ Production in the Short Run

Production is the process of turning inputs into outputs. Most products can be made using a variety of different technologies. As discussed earlier, these can be either capital-intensive or labor-intensive. The type of technology a firm chooses will depend on many things, including ease of implementation and the relative cost of each input into the process.

production The process of turning inputs into outputs.

Again, in the simplified model we are working with, firms can vary their output in the short run only by altering the amount of labor they employ, because plant capacity is fixed in the short run. The extent to which output will change from adding labor depends on the ability to specialize in tasks and use other resources efficiently. But like all resources, labor is eventually subject to diminishing returns. Therefore, an individual firm's production possibilities will follow the same general pattern as the production function for the entire economy introduced in Chapter 2. In the short run, output for an existing plant will vary by the amount of labor employed. This output is referred to as *total product*.

Total Product

Let's examine some production basics by assuming that you start your own firm. Imagine that you decide to begin manufacturing windsurfing sails in an old warehouse that you rent. Your physical plant is constrained in the short run by the size of the manufacturing facility. Table 2 lists your firm's total output (total product) as you hire more workers.

Panel A of Figure 1 on the next page displays your total product curve for windsurfing equipment, based on the data in columns (1) and (2) of Table 2. Output of sails varies with

Production Data for Windsurfing Sail Firm			TABLE 2
(1) **L** (labor)	**(2)** **Q** (total product)	**(3)** **MP** (marginal product)	**(4)** **AP** (average product)
0	0		—
		3	
1	3		3.00
		5	
2	8		4.00
		8	
3	16		5.33
		6	
4	22		5.50
		4	
5	26		5.20
		2	
6	28		4.67
		-2	
7	26		3.71
		-3	
8	23		2.88

FIGURE 1

Total Product Curve, Marginal Product, and Average Product

These two panels show the relationship between additional labor and productivity. Panel A shows how increasing labor increases productivity, up to a point. Panel B shows marginal and average product. Marginal product reaches its maximum as the third worker is hired, after which marginal product starts decreasing. Total product keeps increasing, however, until you hit 6 employees. At that point, marginal product becomes negative, meaning that each additional employee actually reduces production.

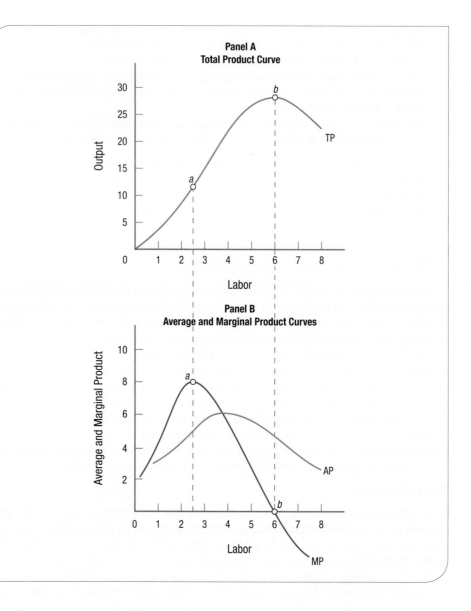

the number of people you employ. Output rises from 0 to 16 when 3 people are working to a maximum of 28 when 6 people are employed (point *b*). As you continue to hire employees beyond 6, you encounter *negative returns*. Total output actually begins to fall, possibly because the workplace has become overly crowded, confusing, hazardous, or noisy. Clearly, hiring any more than 6 employees would be counterproductive, because output falls but costs (such as the total wages of all the employees) rise.

Marginal and Average Product

marginal product The change in output that results from a change in labor (ΔQ/ΔL).

Marginal product [column (3) in Table 2] is the change in output that results from a change in labor input. Marginal product is computed by dividing the change in output (ΔQ) by the change in labor (ΔL). The delta (Δ) symbol is used to denote "change in." Thus, marginal product (MP) is equal to ΔQ/ΔL; it is the change in output that results from adding additional workers.

Notice that when employment rises from 2 workers to 3 workers, output grows from 8 to 16 sails. Marginal product is therefore 8 sails at this point (point *a* in panel B of Figure 1). This is shown graphically with a point placed between the second and third worker, because this represents the change in output going from 2 workers to 3 workers. Contrast this with a change in employment when 6 people are already employed. Adding another employee actually reduces the total output of windsurfing sails from 28 to 26, therefore marginal product is −2 from the sixth to the seventh worker.

Average product (AP) or output per worker is found by dividing total output by the number of workers employed to produce that output (Q/L). Average product is shown in panel B of Figure 1. When employment is 3 people and output is 16, for instance, average product is 5.33.

Increasing and Diminishing Returns

In our example, each of the first three workers adds more to output than the previous worker hired. Therefore, the marginal product going from zero to one worker, one to two workers, and two to three workers increases. This is called the **increasing marginal returns** portion of the curve. In this range, output grows faster as you employ additional labor.

However, after you have employed three people, *marginal productivity* begins to trail off. Between three and six workers, you face **diminishing marginal returns** because each additional worker adds to total output, but at a diminishing rate.

Finally, once you have hired six employees, if you hire any more, this will result in negative marginal returns. Therefore, the marginal product curve crosses the horizontal axis at the sixth worker, which corresponds to the highest point on the total product curve (point *b* in Figure 1). Hiring additional people will actually reduce output, therefore rational firms never operate in this range.

Meanwhile, the average product curve follows a similar path as the marginal product curve, although there isn't as dramatic a change as each worker is added. Average product gives you a sense of the overall productivity of a firm. The relationship between marginal product and average product is an important one. When marginal product exceeds average product—when a new worker adds more to output than the average of the previous workers—hiring an additional worker increases average productivity. This might be because hiring more people allows you to establish more of a production line, thereby increasing specialization and raising productivity. The marginal product curve always crosses the average product curve at its highest point, because once marginal product falls below the average product, the average product must fall as well.

Firms hire workers to produce output based on available resources, many of which are fixed in the short run. By adding more workers, firms can increase productivity by allowing workers to specialize in tasks for which they are more suited. As more workers are hired, diminishing or even negative returns can set in. The typical production curves shown in Figure 1 embody the *law of diminishing returns*. All firms eventually face diminishing marginal returns, but this does not mean production should be avoided as long as the value of the additional output produced exceeds the additional costs.

This analysis is important because it shows how much output is generated based on the number of workers hired, which will eventually translate into revenues for the firm once the output is sold. Therefore, production is an important component of profits, but not enough to determine the optimal production output. To maximize profits, we must also evaluate the costs of production, to which we turn next.

average product Output per worker, found by dividing total output by the number of workers employed to produce that output (Q/L).

increasing marginal returns A new worker hired adds more to total output than the previous worker hired, so that both average and marginal products are rising.

diminishing marginal returns An additional worker adds to total output, but at a diminishing rate.

● CHECKPOINT

PRODUCTION IN THE SHORT RUN

- Production is the process of turning inputs into outputs.
- Total product is the total output produced by the production process.
- Marginal product (MP) is the change in output that results from a change in labor input and is equal to $\Delta Q/\Delta L$.
- Average product (AP) is output per worker and is equal to Q/L.
- Increasing marginal returns occur when adding a worker adds *more* to output than the previous worker hired.

- Diminishing marginal returns occur when adding a worker adds *less* to output than the previous worker hired.

- Negative marginal returns occur when adding a worker actually leads to less *total* output than with the previous worker hired.

- In most production processes, firms experience both increasing and then diminishing marginal returns to labor as workers are added.

QUESTION: Suppose a company has a policy to hire workers only when each additional worker hired is more productive than the previous worker hired. Using what you know about labor productivity, would this be a good policy?

Answers to the Checkpoint question can be found at the end of this chapter.

Costs of Production

Production tells only part of the story. We have to calculate how much it costs to produce this output in order to figure out if it is profitable to do so. Let's now bring resource prices, including labor costs, into our analysis to develop the typical cost curves for the firm, both in the short run and the long run.

Short-Run Costs

In a very straightforward way, production costs are determined by the productivity of workers. Ignoring all costs except wages, if you, by yourself, were to produce ten pizzas an hour and you were paid $8 an hour, then each pizza would cost an average of 80 cents to produce—the cost of your labor. Yet, to ignore any other costs would be to neglect a significant portion of business expenses known as *overhead*.

To begin developing the concept of overhead specifically, and production costs more generally, remember that production periods are split into the short run and the long run. In the short run, at least one factor is fixed, whereas in the long run, all factors are variable. This has led economists to define costs as fixed and variable.

fixed costs Costs that do not change as a firm's output expands or contracts, often called overhead. These include items such as lease payments, administrative expenses, property taxes, and insurance premiums.

variable costs Costs that vary with output fluctuations, including expenses such as labor and material costs.

Fixed and Variable Costs **Fixed costs,** or overhead, are those costs that do not change as a firm's output expands or contracts. Lease or rental payments, administrative overhead, and insurance premiums are examples of fixed costs—they do not rise or fall as a firm alters production to meet market demands. **Variable costs,** on the other hand, do fluctuate as output changes. Labor and material costs are examples of variable costs, because making more products requires hiring more workers and purchasing more raw materials.

Certain costs don't always fall so neatly into these two categories. For example, a new wireless communications tower can serve thousands of customers at the same cost as serving one (and resembles a fixed cost), but once capacity is reached, a new tower is needed (and resembles a variable cost). These types of costs are known as *incremental costs*. To

A cruise ship can cost hundreds of millions of dollars, a fixed cost that is spent regardless of how many passengers cruise. Food for meals, however, is a variable cost because it varies based on how many passengers are on board.

keep things simple, however, we will assume that all costs fit into either the fixed or variable cost categories, such that total cost (TC) is equal to total fixed cost (FC) plus total variable cost (VC), or

$$TC = FC + VC$$

Marginal Cost Although measuring total cost is important in determining the overall profitability of a business, the decision of whether to increase or decrease production largely depends on how total costs change when one increases or decreases the quantity produced. If the additional cost of producing one more unit of a good is greater than the additional revenue earned from that unit, then this unit would not be worth producing. Therefore, it is important to measure the change in costs with each additional unit of output produced.

Let's return to the windsurfing sail business example. Suppose your firm has orders for ten windsurfing sails this month, and you get an order for one more sail at the last minute. Just how much would this additional windsurfing sail cost to produce? Or, in the language of economics, what is the *marginal cost* of the next sail produced?

Marginal cost is the change in total cost arising from the production of additional units of output. Marginal cost (MC) is equal to the change in total cost (ΔTC) divided by the change in output (ΔQ), or

$$MC = \Delta TC/\Delta Q = \Delta FC/\Delta Q + \Delta VC/\Delta Q$$

Note that, for simplicity, we have been discussing changes of one unit of output, but we can calculate MC for a change in output of any amount by plugging in the appropriate value for ΔQ. And because fixed costs do not vary with changes in output, ΔFC/ΔQ = 0, and thus marginal cost is also equal to just ΔVC/ΔQ.

Table 3 provides us with more complete cost data for your windsurfing sail business. Assuming that you pay $1,000 per month in rent for the warehouse, fixed costs equal $1,000 [column (2)]. Your variable costs (the wages you pay your employees plus the price of raw materials) vary depending on the number of sails produced, and is shown in column (3). The total cost, therefore, is the sum of fixed and variable cost and is shown in column (4). Marginal cost measures the change in total (or variable) cost with each additional sail produced, and is given in column (5).

Let's go through one row so that you can be sure of how we arrived at the numbers in columns (2) to (5). Looking at the row showing 4 sails, the fixed cost is $1,000 because this does not change based on the number of sails produced. Variable cost does change, because more work hours are needed to produce more sails; to produce 4 sails,

marginal cost The change in total costs arising from the production of additional units of output (ΔTC/ΔQ). Because fixed costs do not change with output, marginal costs are the change in variable costs associated with additional production (ΔVC/ΔQ).

Cost Data for Windsurfing Sail Firm **TABLE 3**

(1) Q	(2) FC	(3) VC	(4) TC	(5) MC	(6) AFC	(7) AVC	(8) ATC
0	$1,000	$0	$1,000		—	—	—
				$500			
1	$1,000	$500	$1,500		$1,000.00	$500.00	$1,500.00
				$300			
2	$1,000	$800	$1,800		$500.00	$400.00	$900.00
				$200			
3	$1,000	$1,000	$2,000		$333.33	$333.33	$666.67
				$400			
4	$1,000	$1,400	$2,400		$250.00	$350.00	$600.00
				$500			
5	$1,000	$1,900	$2,900		$200.00	$380.00	$580.00
				$700			
6	$1,000	$2,600	$3,600		$166.67	$433.33	$600.00
				$1,000			
7	$1,000	$3,600	$4,600		$142.86	$514.29	$657.14

the variable cost is $1,400. Total cost is simply fixed cost plus variable cost, or $2,400 for 4 sails. Finally, the marginal cost of the fourth sail is the change in total cost from producing 3 sails ($2,000) to producing 4 sails ($2,400). Therefore, the marginal cost of the fourth sail is the change from $2,000 to $2,400, or $400, and is shown in column (5) between the third and fourth units. It is common for marginal costs to first fall and then rise, which gives the marginal cost curve the distinct shape, which we will see later.

Average Costs When a firm produces a product or service, it typically wants a breakdown of how much labor, raw material, plant overhead, and sales costs are imbedded in each unit of the product. Modern accounting systems permit a detailed breakdown of costs for each unit of production. For our purposes, however, that level of detail is not necessary. For us, cost per unit of output (or *average cost*), average fixed cost, and average variable cost are sufficient.

If we divide the total cost equation (TC) by total output Q, we get

$$TC/Q = FC/Q + VC/Q$$

average fixed cost Equal to total fixed cost divided by output (FC/Q).

---

average variable cost Equal to total variable cost divided by output (VC/Q).

---

average total cost Equal to total cost divided by output (TC/Q). Average total cost is also equal to AFC + AVC.

Economists refer to total fixed costs divided by output (FC/Q) as **average fixed cost** (AFC). This represents the average amount of overhead for each unit of output. Total variable costs divided by output is known as **average variable cost** (AVC). It represents the labor and raw materials expenses that go into each unit of output. Adding AFC and AVC together results in **average total cost** (ATC), and thus the equation above can be rewritten as

$$ATC = AFC + AVC$$

Hence, average cost per unit (ATC) is the sum of average fixed cost (AFC) and average variable cost (AVC).

Average total cost is an important piece of information for firms. Specifically, it provides a general measurement of productivity—how cost-efficient a firm is in producing a specified number of units. Further, it provides the firm guidance as to whether it is earning a profit or whether it should shut down the business and leave the industry altogether.

Returning to Table 3, columns (6), (7), and (8) provide the average fixed cost, average variable cost, and average total cost, respectively, for each quantity of windsurfing sails produced. Let's calculate the average costs of producing 4 sails. The average fixed cost is calculated by taking the fixed cost of $1,000 and dividing it by 4 to equal $250. Average variable cost takes the variable cost of $1,400 and divides by 4 to equal $350 in AVC. We can calculate average total cost in two ways. First, we can take total cost of $2,400 and divide by 4 sails to equal $600 in ATC. Second, we know that ATC = AFC + AVC, so if we know that AFC is $250 and AVC is $350, then $250 + $350 = $600.

Notice a few trends in the average cost data. First, the average fixed cost falls continuously as more output is produced; this is because your overhead expenses are getting spread out over more and more units of output (this is known as the *spreading effect*). Figure 2 shows the average fixed cost curve using the data from Table 3. If 2 sails are produced, the average fixed cost is $1,000 / 2 = $500 (point *a* on the AFC curve); if 4 sails are produced, the average fixed cost is $1,000 / 4 = $250 (point *b* on the AFC curve). Average fixed costs are important to entrepreneurs, who often seek out new businesses with low fixed costs, allowing them to recover these expenses quickly.

Second, average variable costs and average total costs typically fall initially before rising, just like marginal costs. In the short run, these costs initially fall as the costs of procuring variable inputs fall and due to the *spreading effect* (which affects the average total cost curve), but these costs eventually rise with greater output as access to available resources dries up, leading to diminishing returns (resulting in a *diminishing returns effect*). Finally, average variable cost will always be smaller than the average total cost according to the ATC = AFC + AVC equation. These trends will be important as we make greater use of average cost in the next three chapters.

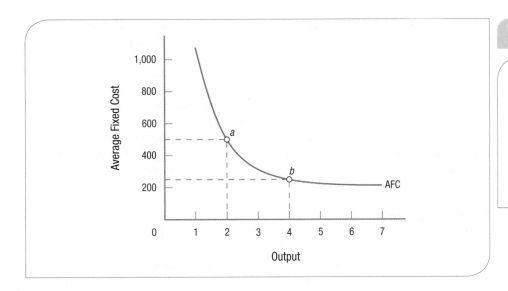

FIGURE 2

The Average Fixed Cost Curve

The average fixed cost (AFC) curve always decreases as production increases. This is because, in the short run, total fixed costs do not change, so that increasing production spreads the fixed costs over more units of output (the *spreading effect*).

Short-Run Cost Curves for Profit-Maximizing Decisions

Table 3 provides the numerical values for costs. Although all of the costs are important in their own way, we focus on three costs that will provide guidance to firms in their need to maximize profits. These are average variable cost, average total cost, and marginal cost. Let us now translate these costs into figures to make their analysis simpler. Figure 3 shows the three cost measures in graphical form, drawn using the data from Table 3.

Average Variable Cost (AVC) The AVC and ATC curves are U-shaped. At relatively low levels of output, the curves slope downward, reflecting an increase in returns as average costs drop. As production levels rise, however, diminishing returns set in, and average costs start to climb back up. We get some sense of this by examining Table 3, in which the numbers for AVC and ATC fall and then rise, but the figure makes it far easier to see.

In Figure 3, the average variable cost curve reaches its minimum where 3 sails are produced (point c). Since $AVC = VC/Q$, then $VC = AVC \times Q$. Thus, at point c, VC is equal to the rectangular area 0ace, or $1,000 ($333.33 \times 3$).

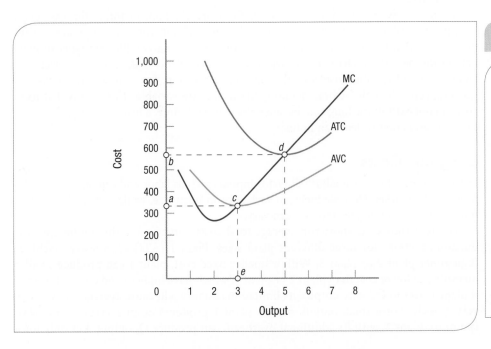

FIGURE 3

Average Total Cost, Average Variable Cost, and Marginal Cost

The average variable cost (AVC), average total cost (ATC), and marginal cost (MC) curves are shown. The bowl shape of the AVC and ATC curves demonstrates the law of diminishing returns: Beyond a certain level of output, average costs increase. Marginal costs represent the added cost of producing one more unit of output. Note that the marginal cost curve passes through the minimum points on both the AVC and ATC curves.

Average Total Cost (ATC) Average total cost equals total costs divided by output ($ATC = TC/Q$), or average fixed costs plus average variable cost ($ATC = AFC + AVC$). In Figure 3, the average total cost reaches its minimum where 5 sails are produced (point *d*). At this point, the average total cost is $580. As in the previous example, we can calculate the total cost of the firm at any point along the average total cost curve by multiplying the average total cost by the output produced. For example, the total cost of 5 sails would be $580 \times 5 = \$2,900$, exactly as shown in Table 3.

Therefore, the use of cost curves allows us to determine both the total and average costs for a firm, which again is an important component in determining profits. Still, we cannot proceed until we examine marginal costs, a key determinant in whether firms should produce more or less output.

Marginal Cost (MC) Drawing our discussion of short-run costs to a close, Figure 3 plots the marginal cost curve, adding it to the AVC and ATC curves we have plotted already.

Notice that the marginal cost curve intersects the minimum points of both the AVC and ATC curves. This is not a coincidence. Marginal cost is the cost necessary to produce another unit of a given product. When the cost to produce another unit is *less* than the average of the previous units produced, average costs will *fall*. For the AVC curve in Figure 3, this happens at all output levels less than 3 units (*point c*); for the ATC curve, it happens at all output levels less than 5 units (*point d*). But when the cost to produce another unit *exceeds* the average cost for all previous output, average costs will *rise*.

In Figure 3, this happens at output levels greater than 3 units (point *c*) for AVC and greater than 5 units (point *d*) for ATC. Over these ranges, marginal cost exceeds AVC and ATC, respectively, and thus the two curves rise. At points *c* and *d*, marginal cost is precisely equal to average variable cost and average total cost, respectively, and thus the AVC and ATC curves are at their minimum values (where the slopes are zero).

The average variable cost, average total cost, and marginal cost curves will help us analyze the profit-maximizing equilibrium for each market structure in the next three chapters. We will see how marginal cost provides guidance to firms on the quantity of output to produce, and how average variable cost and average total cost inform firms whether to maintain or expand operations, shut down, or leave the industry.

We have now examined short-run costs for firms when one factor, in this case plant size, is fixed. When this occurs, firms face decisions about whether to operate or shut down given that the fixed costs are paid up front. As we analyze different types of markets in the next three chapters, we will examine how firms make short-run decisions when fixed and variable costs are taken into consideration. Let us now turn to costs in the long run, when all factors, including plant size, are variable. This means that fixed costs do not exist in the long run, because given enough time, a firm can expand or close its plant, and enter or leave an industry.

Long-Run Costs

In the long run, firms can adjust all factor inputs (such as labor and capital) to meet the needs of the market. Here we focus on variations in plant size, while recognizing that all other factors, including technology, can vary.

Figure 4 shows the short-run average total costs curves using three different production functions for three different plant sizes. Plant 1 (ATC_1) has fewer machines than either plant 2 or plant 3. With a smaller fixed cost, plant 1 can produce smaller quantities at lower cost than plant 2 or plant 3, which have higher fixed costs. However, if plant 1 tries to increase output, its limited machinery will cause average costs to rise very quickly. For a small output, say Q_0, plant 1 produces at an average cost of AC_0 (point *b*). Plant 2, with its additional overhead, can produce Q_0 output, but only for a

FIGURE 4

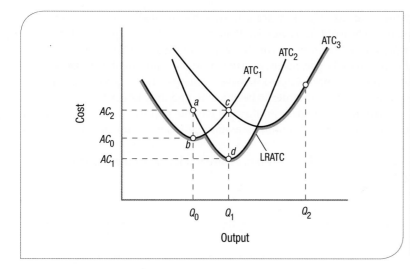

Various Short-Run Average Cost Curves and the Long-Run Average Total Cost Curve
This figure shows the average total cost curve for three plants of different sizes. The larger plants have relatively high average total costs at lower levels of output, but much lower average total costs at higher output levels. Firms are free to adjust plant size in the long run, therefore they can switch from one plant type to the next to minimize their costs at each production level. The green envelope curve represents the firm's lowest cost to produce any given output in the long run and represents the LRATC curve.

higher average cost of AC_2 (point a). And plant 3's average cost of producing Q_0 would be even higher.

Therefore, at lower levels of production, plant 1 is able to achieve the lowest average cost. However, plant 2 and plant 3 achieve greater cost savings at higher levels of production. Once output rises to Q_1, plant 2 begins to enjoy the benefits of a lower average cost of production. The additional machines mean that plant 2 can produce Q_1 for AC_1 (point d), whereas the machines in plant 1 become overwhelmed at this level of output, resulting in an average cost of AC_2 (point c). Similarly, if a firm expects market demand eventually to reach Q_2, it would want to build plant 3 because plant 1 and plant 2 are too small to accommodate that level of production efficiently.

Long-Run Average Total Cost The **long-run average total cost** (LRATC) curve represents the lowest unit cost at which any specific output can be produced in the long run, when a firm is able to adjust the size of its plant. In Figure 4, the LRATC curve is indicated by the green segments of the various short-run cost curves; these are the segments of each curve at which output can be produced at the lowest per unit cost (also known as the *envelope* curve, named after its telltale shape). In short, the LRATC assumes that, in the long run, firms will build plants of the size best fitting the levels of output they wish to produce.

Although the LRATC curve in Figure 4 is relatively bumpy, it will tend to smooth out as more plant size options are considered. In some industries, such as agriculture and food service, the options for plant size and production methods are virtually unlimited. In other industries, such as semiconductors, however, sophisticated plants may cost several billion dollars to build and require being run at near capacity to be cost-effective.

These huge, sophisticated plants are so complex that Intel Corporation has dedicated teams of engineers that build new plants and operate them exactly as all others. These teams ensure that any new plant is a virtual clone of the firm's other operating facilities. Even small deviations from this standard have proven disastrous to cost control in the past.

Economies and Diseconomies of Scale As a firm's output increases, its LRATC tends to decrease. This is because, as the firm grows in size, **economies of scale** result from such items as specialization of labor and management, better use of capital, and increased possibilities for making several products that utilize complementary production techniques.

A larger firm's ability to have workers specialize in particular tasks reduces the costs associated with shifting workers from one task to another. Similarly, management

long-run average total cost In the long run, firms can adjust their plant sizes so that LRATC is the lowest unit cost at which any particular output can be produced in the long run.

economies of scale As a firm's output increases, its LRATC tends to decline. This results from specialization of labor and management, and potentially a better use of capital and complementary production techniques.

in larger operations can use technologies not available to smaller firms, for example computers to supervise workers remotely. It is true that today's powerful personal computer networks have begun to narrow the gap in this arena. Larger firms, though, can still afford to purchase larger, more specialized capital equipment, whereas smaller firms must often rely on more labor-intensive methods. This equipment typically requires large production runs in order to be efficient, and only larger firms can generate the sales necessary to satisfy these production volume requirements. Finally, larger firms are better able to engage in complementary production and use by-products more effectively.

The area for *economies of scale* is shown in Figure 5 at levels of output below Q_0 (average costs are falling).

FIGURE 5

Economies, Diseconomies, and Constant Returns to Scale

The curve in this figure shows how increasing production affects long-run average total cost (LRATC). Up to Q_0, economies of scale reduce LRATC as production increases. Over the range Q_0 to Q_1, the firm enjoys constant returns to scale, meaning that it can expand without affecting LRATC. Past Q_1, however, diseconomies of scale kick in, such that any further expansion causes an increase in LRATC.

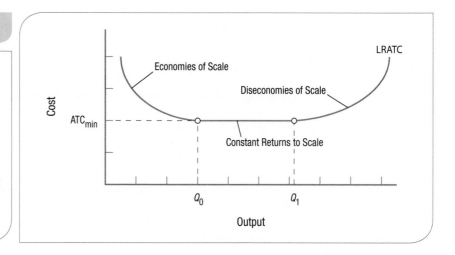

In many industries, there is a wide range of output wherein average total costs are relatively constant. Examples include fast-food restaurants, family restaurants such as Outback Steakhouse, and automotive service operations such as Jiffy Lube. Such businesses tend to have steady average costs because the cost to replicate their business in any community is relatively constant. Constructing and running a Dairy Queen franchise, for example, costs roughly the same no matter where it is operated. In Figure 5, this area of **constant returns to scale** is represented by output levels between Q_0 and Q_1.

As firms continue to grow, they eventually encounter **diseconomies of scale**. At some point, the firm gets so big that management is unable to control its operations efficiently. Some firms become so big that they get bogged down in bureaucracy and cannot make decisions quickly. In the late 1980s, Apple fell into this trap—slow to react to changing market conditions for computers and software, the company was left behind by sleeker competition from Dell and Microsoft. Only through downsizing, reorganizing, refocusing, and a management change did Apple get back on track in the late 1990s. Diseconomies of scale—where increased output increases costs disproportionately—are shown at outputs above Q_1 in Figure 5.

Economies of Scope When firms produce a number of products, it is often cheaper for them to produce another product when the production processes are interdependent. These economies are called **economies of scope.** For example, once a company has established a marketing department, it can take on the campaign of a new product at a lower cost. It has already developed the expertise and contacts necessary to sell the product. Book publishers can introduce a new book into the market more quickly and cheaply, and with more success than can a new firm starting in the business.

constant returns to scale A range of output where average total costs are relatively constant. The expansion of fast-food restaurant franchises and movie theaters, which are essentially replications of existing franchises and theaters, reflect this.

diseconomies of scale A range of output where average total costs tend to increase. Firms often become so big that management becomes bureaucratic and unable to control its operations efficiently.

economies of scope By producing a number of products that are interdependent, firms are able to produce and market these goods at lower costs.

Some firms generate ideas for products, then send the production overseas. After they have been through this process, they become more efficient at it. Economists refer to this as *learning by doing.* Economies of scope often play a role in mergers as firms look for other firms with complementary products and skills.

Procter & Gamble makes hundreds of household products, taking advantage of large economies of scope by producing many products that use the same inputs and equipment. For example, some of the chemicals used to produce Tide detergent are also used to produce Cascade dishwasher tablets.

Role of Technology We know that technology creates products that were the domain of science fiction writers of the past. Dick Tracy's wrist radio, first introduced in the comics of 1940s, has now morphed into the many wireless products we see today.

But we should mention in passing the role technology plays in altering the shape of the LRATC curve. The output level at which diseconomies of scale are reached has significantly and continuously expanded since the beginning of the industrial revolution.

Enhanced production techniques, instantaneous global communication, and the use of computers in accounting and cost control are just a few recent examples of ways in which technology has permitted firms to increase their scale beyond what anyone had imagined possible 50 years earlier. Who would have imagined a century ago that one firm could have millions

Eric Chiang

Procter & Gamble makes hundreds of household products, taking advantage of large economies of scope by producing many products that use the same inputs and equipment.

 ISSUE

How Large Are Fixed Costs? A Look at the Pharmaceutical and Software Industries

We show in this chapter that certain input costs are fixed in the short run, leading to U-shaped average variable and average total cost curves as economies of scale are realized and then exhausted. For most goods and services, economies of scale eventually disappear due to diminishing returns to production, causing average variable and average total costs to rise.

For certain industries, however, fixed costs represent the majority of the total cost of production. Consider the pharmaceutical industry: The cost of developing a successful new drug typically ranges from $100 million to over $1 billion, while the marginal cost of reproducing each pill costs just pennies. The same is true for the software industry; thousands of software engineers spend years writing code, costing the software company

millions of dollars to produce the original copy, while the cost of disseminating the software to customers is virtually nothing (if purchased and downloaded online) or a few dollars if nicely packaged on a disc.

In both cases, the fixed cost of producing a new product far outweighs its variable cost, leading to marginal and average cost curves that differ from the typical U-shaped curves we have seen thus far. Because the marginal cost of reproduction is virtually nothing in these industries, the marginal cost curve for these goods will be horizontal and close to $0. As a result, the average total cost curve will be nearly identical to the average fixed cost curve, which slopes downward as more units are produced.

From this, we see that some products do not follow the typical shape of cost curves. However, these are the exceptions to the rule. Most products continue to show U-shaped marginal and average total cost curves, which are representative of goods that have both fixed and nonnegligible variable costs in their production.

of employees and billions of dollars in annual sales? Today, Wal-Mart has more than two million employees and annual sales of over $500 billion.

What spurs firms and entrepreneurs to develop new technologies and bring new products to market? Three things: profits, profits, and profits. In this chapter, we analyzed where profits come from by looking at what firms do, how they measure profits, and how they determine production and costs. In the next chapter, we will look at revenues, as well as examine how firms can maximize their profits by adjusting output to market demand.

 CHECKPOINT

COSTS OF PRODUCTION

- Fixed costs (overhead) are those costs that do not vary with output, including lease payments and insurance. Fixed costs occur in the short run—in the long run, firms can change plant size or even exit an industry.

- Variable costs rise and fall as a firm produces more or less output. These variable costs include raw materials, labor, and utilities.

- Total cost equals fixed cost plus variable cost (TC = FC + VC).

- Average fixed cost, average variable cost, and average total cost provide a general measure of efficiency when looking at the total amount of output produced.

- Marginal cost is the change in total cost divided by the change in output (MC = $\Delta TC/\Delta Q$). Marginal cost provides important information to firms deciding whether to produce more or less output.

- The long-run average total cost curve (LRATC) represents the lowest unit cost at which specific output can be produced in the long run.

- As a firm grows in size, economies of scale result from specialization of labor and better use of capital, while diseconomies of scale occur because a firm gets so big that management loses control of its operations and the firm becomes bogged down in bureaucracy.

- Economies of scope result when firms produce a number of interdependent products, so it is cheaper for them to add another product to the line.

- Modern communications and computers have permitted firms to become huge before diseconomies are reached.

QUESTION: In the late 1990s, Boeing reported that it took roughly 12 years and $15 billion to bring a new aircraft from the design stage to a test flight. Boeing signed a 20-year exclusive agreement to supply aircraft to Delta, American, and Continental (now United) Airlines. The rationale for the agreement was that every time production of the plane doubled, the average production cost per plane would fall by about 20%.[5] Why would doubling production cut costs per unit by 20%?

Answers to the Checkpoint question can be found at the end of this chapter.

---

[5] "Peace in Our Time," *The Economist,* July 26, 1997.

chapter summary

Section 1: **Firms, Profits, and Economic Costs**

Firms are economic institutions that transform inputs (factors of production) into outputs (products and services).

© Rick Barrentine/Corbis

Nearly half of all businesses in the United States close within five years as new businesses take their place.

Types of Businesses

Sole proprietorship: unlimited liability, full control

Partnership: unlimited liability, shared control

Corporation: limited liability, ability to issue stock

Profit = Total Revenue − Total Cost

Accounting Costs	vs.	Economic Costs
Includes only explicit (out-of-pocket) costs		Includes explicit and implicit (opportunity) costs

Economic profit = total revenue − economic costs

Normal profit is an economic profit of $0.

Short run: period of time during which at least one factor of production is fixed.

Long run: a period long enough that firms can vary all factors, as well as leave and enter industries.

Section 2: **Production in the Short Run**

Total product is the quantity of output produced using a certain amount of labor inputs.

Marginal product is the change in output associated with hiring one additional worker, or $\Delta Q/\Delta L$.

Increasing Versus Decreasing Returns to Labor

When *increasing returns* are present, each additional worker adds more to total output than previous workers.

Eventually, all production is subject to the *law of diminishing returns*, causing decreasing returns from adding more workers.

EIGHTFISH/Alamy

Having extra workers is very productive at first, but eventually everyone gets in each other's way, leading to decreasing returns to labor.

Section 3: **Costs of Production**

Short-Run Costs

In the short run, firms have **fixed costs** (FC) that do not vary with output and **variable costs** (VC) that do vary.

Total cost (TC) = fixed cost + variable cost

Marginal cost (MC) = change in total cost from producing one more unit

Average fixed cost (AFC) = fixed cost / quantity

Average variable cost (AVC) = variable cost / quantity

Average total cost (ATC) = total cost / quantity

Opening a personal training business involves fixed costs (equipment or gym membership) and variable costs (time spent with each client).

Abbreviated Cost Table for a Firm in the Short Run

Q	FC	VC	TC	MC	ATC
0	20	0	20	25	—
1	20	25	45	15	45
2	20	40	60	45	30
3	20	85	105		35

Why Does MC Cross ATC at Its Minimum Point?

When the next unit costs less than the average (MC < ATC), ATC falls. When the next unit costs more than the average (MC > ATC), ATC rises. For example, suppose your current course grade is 85%. If your grade on your next exam is 90%, your marginal exam score is greater than your average score, therefore your average rises. However, if your next exam grade (marginal score) is 70%, your average falls.

Long-Run Average Total Cost

In the long run, all factors of production are variable, and firms can enter or leave the industry. The **long-run average total cost** (LRATC) curve is the lowest unit cost for any specific output level in the long run.

Economies of scale occur when the average cost of production falls as a firm grows and cost savings from specialization in labor and management occur.

Eventually, **diseconomies of scale** occur when a firm's size becomes so large that efficient management becomes impossible.

Economies of scope are cost savings resulting from the ability of firms to produce many interdependent products.

Advanced computer and communications technologies have radically increased the size of firms that can be efficiently managed. IKEA, for example, operates over 350 mega stores in 40 countries.

KEY CONCEPTS

firm, p. 164
sole proprietorship, p. 166
partnership, p. 166
corporation, p. 166
profit, p. 168
total revenue, p. 168
total cost, p. 168
economic costs, p. 168
explicit costs, p. 168
implicit costs, p. 168
sunk costs, p. 168

accounting profit, p. 169
economic profit, p. 169
normal profits, p. 169
short run, p. 169
long run, p. 169
production, p. 171
marginal product, p. 172
average product, p. 173
increasing marginal returns, p. 173
diminishing marginal returns, p. 173
fixed costs, p. 174

variable costs, p. 174
marginal cost, p. 175
average fixed cost, p. 176
average variable cost, p. 176
average total cost, p. 176
long-run average total cost, p. 179
economies of scale, p. 179
constant returns to scale, p. 180
diseconomies of scale, p. 180
economies of scope, p. 180

QUESTIONS AND PROBLEMS

Check Your Understanding

1. What is the difference between explicit and implicit costs? What is the difference between economic and accounting profits? Are these four concepts related? How?

2. Why should sunk costs be ignored for decision making?

3. How does the short run differ from the long run? Is the long run the same for all industries? Why or why not?

4. Why should a firm never hire a worker when negative marginal returns set in?

5. Why is the average fixed cost curve not U-shaped? Why does it not turn up as the average variable cost and average total cost curves do?

6. What is the difference between marginal cost and average total cost?

Apply the Concepts

7. If you work hard building your business and end up earning zero economic profit for the year, would this be considered a failed business to an economist? Why or why not?

8. In order to take this class, you had to pay tuition, buy the textbook, and buy a new laptop. Which of these items (if any) would be considered a sunk cost? Explain your reasoning.

9. Skype, the Internet phone company, uses peer-to-peer network principles to enable people to make free phone calls over the Internet to anywhere in the world. Skype forwards calls through users' computers without having any central infrastructure. Users agree to let their computer's excess capacity be used as transfer nodes. In this way, Skype does not have to invest in more infrastructure as it adds users, and the system is highly robust and scalable. What is the marginal cost to Skype to add another user to its system?

10. List some of the reasons why the long-run average total cost curve has sort of a flat bowl shape. It declines early on, then is rather flat over a portion, and finally slopes upward.

11. The Finger Lakes region in New York State produces wine. The climate favors white wines, but reds have been produced successfully in the past 15 years. Categorize the following costs incurred by one winery as either fixed or variable:

    a. the capital used to buy 60 acres of land on Lake Seneca

    b. the machine used to pick some varieties of grapes at the end of August and the beginning of September

    c. the salary of the chief vintner, who is employed year-round

    d. the wages paid to workers who bind the grape plants, usually in April, and usually over a period of three to four days

    e. the wages paid to the same workers who pick the grapes at the end of August or early September

    f. the costs of the chemicals sprayed on the grapes in July

    g. the wages of the wine expert who blends the wine in August and September, after the grapes have been picked

    h. the cost of the building where wine tastings take place from April to October

    i. the cost of the wine used in the wine tasting

12. If marginal cost is less than average total cost, are average total costs rising or falling? Alternatively, if marginal cost is more than average total cost, are average total costs rising or falling? Explain how this example might apply to a basketball player attempting to achieve a high average *points per game*.

In The News

13. Twenty-five years ago, coffee was a commodity product. Coffee brands such as Maxwell House ("good to the last drop") and Folger's advertised on television, but the difference between the brands was minimal. Not very satisfying, but no great pressure for change, either. In the 1990s, after touring coffeehouses in Rome, Howard Schultz brought the concept of upscale coffee to the United States and Starbucks was born ("Starbucks to Open 1,500 More Cafes in the U.S.," *The Seattle Times*, December 5, 2012). In 2012, over 13,000 Starbucks existed in the United States alone. How could a company such as Starbucks make any money in a highly competitive market like coffee? What factors did Howard Schultz need to consider before venturing into this business?

14. When J. P. Morgan Chase, one of the largest banks in the world, admitted to an embarrassing $9 billion trading loss in 2012, policymakers rushed to propose new regulations to prevent banks from taking risky bets ("J. P. Morgan Loss Spurs Scrutiny of Fed Governance," *Wall Street Journal*, May 14, 2012). Clearly, memories of bank bailouts by taxpayers in 2008 made the sentiment stronger. How do new regulations affect the costs of doing business? Do regulations represent a fixed or variable cost?

Solving Problems

15. Suppose you pay $10 to watch a movie at the local cineplex, and afterward you sneak into the next theater to watch a second movie without paying. What is your marginal cost of watching the second movie? What is the average cost of watching the two movies? After the movies, you go to the batting cages and stand in for two rounds of pitches, each round costing $2. What is your marginal cost of batting the second round? What is the average cost of batting two rounds?

16. Using the table below, answer the following questions.

Labor	Output	Marginal Product	Average Product
0	0		—
1	7	_____	_____
2	15	_____	_____
3	25	_____	_____
4	33	_____	_____
5	40	_____	_____
6	45	_____	_____

a. Complete the table, filling in the answers for marginal and average products.

b. Over how many workers is the firm enjoying increasing returns?

c. At what number of workers do diminishing returns set in?

d. Are negative returns shown in the table?

USING THE NUMBERS

17. According to By the Numbers, explain why a correlation exists between the costs of industrial robots and the productivity rate over the last 20 years.

18. According to By the Numbers, between which four years from 2000 to 2012 did Internet flight bookings increase the most (by percentage of overall sales)? Between which four years from 2000 to 2012 did Internet flight check-ins increase the most (by percentage of overall check-ins)?

ANSWERS TO QUESTIONS IN CHECKPOINTS

Checkpoint: Firms, Profits, and Economic Costs

Setting up your firm as a corporation has its benefits and its costs. One benefit of a corporation is limited liability, which means that if your company fails, the company can declare bankruptcy without it affecting your personal assets or credit. Another benefit is the ability to raise capital by issuing bonds or stocks. The downside of setting up a corporation is that profits are potentially shared by many shareholders. Also, corporations involve much more paperwork (such as setting up the firm and filing tax returns) than a sole proprietorship, which is much easier to set up and manage.

Checkpoint: Production in the Short Run

By hiring a worker only when she or he is more productive than the last worker hired means that a company insists on maintaining increasing marginal returns to labor. However, this generally occurs only for a limited number of workers. Eventually, all firms face diminishing marginal returns. This doesn't mean a firm should stop hiring, because the additional workers may still provide valuable productivity relative to their cost.

Checkpoint: Costs of Production

This immense $15 billion development cost is spread over more planes, and rising volume creates economies. Producing commercial aircraft has huge economies of scale and scope.

Perfect
Competition

8

Visit your local farmer's market on a weekend morning, and you'll find dozens of individual stands offering the freshest fruits and vegetables, many of which are grown locally and delivered to the market directly by the grower. As you meander through the market you notice that the prices for any one type of fruit or vegetable are virtually the same from one stand to another. Further, the prices at the farmer's market often aren't much different from those that you might find in your grocery store's produce section.

With prices being nearly identical, shoppers are then left with the challenge of selecting the fruits and vegetables that look, feel, smell—and sometimes taste, if samples are available—the best, which for a food connoisseur is one of the pleasures of visiting a farmer's market. The rest of us, who do not have the skill to select the juiciest watermelon or peach, are often left to rely on our instincts. Even so, the difference in quality of the fruit across the various sellers is likely to be so small (because all are grown in the same area with the same climate) that typically one need not worry about making a bad choice.

This is the essence of a purely competitive market—the quality of a product is mostly indistinguishable, and hence the prices tend to be the same across sellers. In fact, each individual seller, being just one among thousands of sellers of fruit and vegetables, has little control over prices, another characteristic of a highly competitive market which forces sellers to be efficient. It's an example of the classic "survival of the fittest" problem—either produce high-quality produce at the lowest prices, or be sent packing.

The nature of intense competition extends well beyond farming, of course. Much of the goods we consume each day are produced in massive factories, often in Asia, where thousands of workers toil diligently in an often dreary environment to provide what we desire at the lowest cost. Before we debate the merits of whether this is good or bad for the factory workers, let's look at why many companies are using this form of production to stay competitive.

A firm's production function describes the manner in which inputs (resources such as labor and capital) are turned into outputs (goods). Since the cost of a set amount of inputs is fixed, being able to manufacture *more* with those inputs reduces the cost of production and increases productivity.

How does a firm increase productivity? First, it can hire better workers or offer training to make each worker more productive. Second, it can utilize better machinery (capital). And third, it can design the factory in a way to maximize the production given the workers and capital available. Choosing the production method by which inputs such as labor and capital are used is critical to productivity and the success of a firm. This is the role of the manager. If a firm uses inputs inefficiently, more efficient firms will drive it out of business.

The goal of any firm is to maximize profits given the market structure in which it exists. This is easier in some markets than in others. For example, if a company is the industry leader and has few competitors, earning profits is easier than it is for a struggling company facing intense competition.

This chapter focuses on market structure and the purest form of competition, which we call perfect competition. We explore some of the implications competition has for markets and consider why the competitive market structure is so central to the thinking of economists. When Adam Smith wrote his classic book, *The Wealth of Nations,* he wrote of a "hidden hand" that guides businesses in their pursuit of self-interest, or profits, allowing only the efficient to survive. Some observers have noted similarities between Smith's work, written in 1776, and Charles Darwin's *Origin of Species,* published in 1872. The late biologist and zoologist Stephen Jay Gould commented that "the theory of natural selection is, in essence, Adam Smith's economics transferred to nature."[1] Clearly, the notions of competition and the competitive market have played a prominent role in the history of ideas.

In this and the next two chapters, keep in mind the profitability equation developed in the previous chapter. Profits equal total revenues minus total costs. Total revenues equal

---

[1] Stephen Jay Gould, *The Structure of Evolutionary Theory* (Cambridge, MA: Belknap Press of Harvard University Press), 2002, pp. 121–125.

BY THE NUMBERS

Perfect Competition and Efficiency

Cost efficiency plays an important role in the survival of firms in perfectly competitive industries. Because each firm represents just one of many firms in the market, the actions of one firm do not affect any other firm.

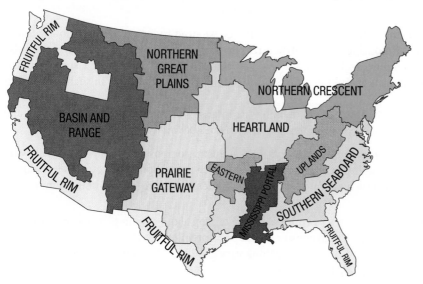

The world's top tea producers:

- Rest of World 25.3%
- China 32.5%
- Turkey 5.2%
- Sri Lanka 6.2%
- Kenya 8.8%
- India 21.9%

The United States Department of Agriculture divides the nation into regions for agricultural economic analysis. The number of farm workers varies significantly by region.

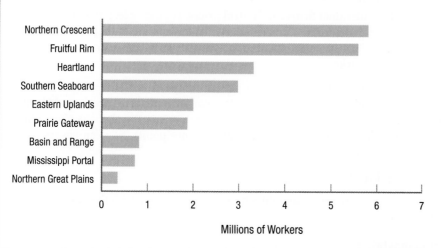

Millions of Workers

- Northern Crescent
- Fruitful Rim
- Heartland
- Southern Seaboard
- Eastern Uplands
- Prairie Gateway
- Basin and Range
- Mississippi Portal
- Northern Great Plains

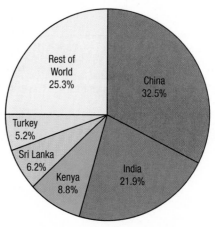

epa European Pressphoto Agency creative account/Alamy

9,980,823,315
Total world production of tea (in pounds) in 2012.

19,536,321,570
Total world production of coffee (in pounds) in 2012.

The legalization of marijuana in certain states has dramatically increased the number of growers in a highly competitive market, despite risk of federal prosecution.

The average price per bushel of soybeans, wheat, and corn increased significantly in the past decade.

Soybeans

Wheat

Corn

Year

AP Photo/Jeff Barnard, File

price times quantity sold. Keep in mind the three items that determine profitability: price, quantity, and cost. We will see how firms try to control each one of these. What you learn in this chapter will give you a benchmark to use when we consider the other market structures in the following chapters.

Market Structure Analysis

market structure analysis By observing a few industry characteristics such as number of firms in the industry or the level of barriers to entry, economists can use this information to predict pricing and output behavior of the firm in the industry.

To appreciate intensely competitive markets, we need to look at competition within the full range of possible market structures. Economists use **market structure analysis** to categorize industries based on a few key characteristics. By knowing simple industry facts, economists can predict the behavior of firms in that industry in such areas as pricing and sales.

Below are the four factors defining the intensity of competition in an industry and a few questions to give you some sense of the issues behind each one of these factors.

- **Number of firms in the industry:** Is the industry composed of many firms, each with limited or no ability to set the market price, such as local pizza places, or is it dominated by a large firm such as Wal-Mart that can influence price regardless of the number of other firms?
- **Nature of the industry's product:** Are we talking about a homogeneous product such as salt, for which no consumer will pay a premium or are we considering leather handbags, which consumers may think vary greatly, in that some firms (Coach, Gucci) produce better goods than others?
- **Barriers to entry:** Does the industry require low start-up and maintenance costs such as found at a roadside fruit and vegetable stand, or is it a computer-chip business that may require $1 billion to build a new chip plant?
- **Extent to which individual firms can control prices:** For example, pharmaceutical companies can set prices for new medicines, at least for a period of time, because of patent protection. Farmers and copper producers have virtually no control and get their prices from world markets.

Possible market structures range from perfect competition, characterized by many firms, to monopoly, where an industry is made up of only one firm. These market structures will make more sense to you as we consider each one in the chapters ahead. Right now, use this list and the descriptions below as reference points. You can always return here and put the discussion in context.

Primary Market Structures

The primary market structures economists have identified, along with their key characteristics, are as follows:

Perfect Competition

- Many buyers and sellers
- Homogeneous (standardized) products
- No barriers to market entry or exit
- No long-run economic profit
- No control over price

Monopolistic Competition

- Many buyers and sellers
- Differentiated products
- No barriers to market entry or exit
- No long-run economic profit
- Some control over price

Oligopoly

- Fewer firms (such as the auto industry)
- Mutually interdependent decisions
- Substantial barriers to market entry
- Potential for long-run economic profit
- Shared market power and considerable control over price

Monopoly

- One firm
- No close substitutes for product
- Nearly insuperable barriers to entry
- Potential for long-run economic profit
- Substantial market power and control over price

Putting off discussion of the other market structures for later chapters, we turn to an extended examination of the requirements for a perfectly competitive market. In the remainder of this chapter, we explore short-run pricing and output decisions, and also the importance of entry and exit in the long run. Moreover, we use the conditions of perfect competition to establish a benchmark for efficiency as we turn to evaluate other market structures in the following chapters.

Defining Perfectly Competitive Markets

The theory of **perfect competition** rests on the following assumptions:

1. Perfectly competitive markets have many buyers and sellers, each of them so small that none can individually influence product price.
2. Firms in the industry produce a homogeneous or standardized product.
3. Buyers and sellers have all the information about prices and product quality they need to make informed decisions.
4. Barriers to entry or exit are nonexistent in the long run; new firms are free to enter the industry if so doing appears profitable, while firms are free to exit if they anticipate losses.

perfect competition A market structure with many relatively small buyers and sellers who take the price as given, a standardized product, full information to both buyers and sellers, and no barriers to entry or exit.

One implication of these assumptions is that perfectly competitive firms are **price takers.** Market prices are determined by market forces beyond the control of individual firms. That is, firms must take what they can get for their products. Paper for copy machines, most agricultural products, basic computer memory chips, and many other goods are produced in highly competitive markets. The buyers or sellers in these markets are so small that their ability to influence market price is nonexistent. These firms must accept whatever price the market determines, leaving them to decide only how much of the product to produce or buy.

price taker Individual firms in perfectly competitive markets get their prices from the market because they are so small they cannot influence market price. For this reason, perfectly competitive firms are price takers and can produce and sell all the output they produce at market-determined prices.

Panel A of Figure 1 on the next page portrays the supply and demand for windsurfing sails in a perfectly competitive market; the market is in equilibrium at a price of $200 per sail and industry output Q_e. Remember that this product is a standardized sail (similar to 2×4 lumber, corn, or crude oil) and that the market contains many buyers and sellers, who collectively set the product price at $200.

Panel B shows the demand for a seller's products in this market. The firm can sell all it wants at $200 or below. Yet, what firm would set its price below $200 when it can sell everything it produces at $200? Were the firm to set its price above $200, however, it would sell nothing. What consumer, after all, would purchase a standardized sail at a higher price when it can be obtained elsewhere for $200? The individual firm's demand curve is horizontal at $200. The firm can still determine how much of its product to produce and sell, but this is the only choice it has. The firm cannot set its own price, therefore it is a *price taker*.

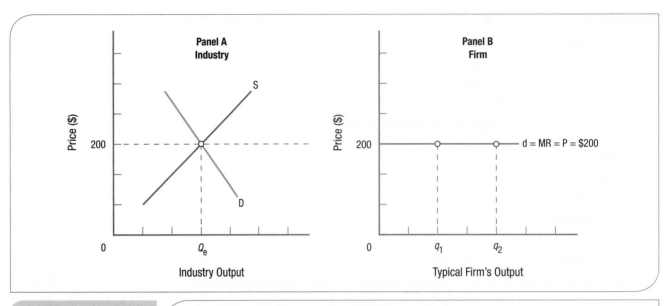

The Market for Competitive Products with an Equilibrium Price of $200

Panel A shows a market for standardized windsurfing sails in equilibrium at a price of $200 and industry output Q_e. This price is determined by the market's many buyers and sellers. Panel B illustrates product demand for an individual seller. The individual firm can sell all it wants to at $200 and has no reason to set its price below that. If it tries to sell at prices higher than $200, it sells nothing. The demand curve for the individual firm is horizontal at $200.

Recall the profitability equation. Profit equals total revenue minus total cost. Total revenue equals price times quantity sold. In perfectly competitive markets, a firm's profitability is based on a given market price, quantity sold, and its costs. So how does it determine how much to sell?

The Short Run and the Long Run (A Reminder)

Before turning to a more detailed examination of how firms decide how much output to produce in a perfectly competitive market, we need to recall a distinction introduced in the last chapter between the *short run* and the *long run*.

In the *short run,* one factor of production is fixed, usually the firm's plant size, and firms cannot enter or leave an industry. Thus, in the short run, the number of firms in a market is fixed. Firms may earn economic profits, break even, or suffer losses, but still they cannot exit the industry, nor can new firms enter.

In the *long run,* all factors are variable, and thus the level of profits induces entry or exit. When losses prevail, some firms will leave the industry and invest their capital elsewhere. When economic profits are positive, new firms will enter the industry. The long run is far more dynamic than the short run.

 CHECKPOINT

MARKET STRUCTURE ANALYSIS

- Market structure analysis allows economists to categorize industries based on a few characteristics and use this analysis to predict pricing and output behavior.

- The intensity of competition is defined by the number of firms in the industry, the nature of the industry's product, the level of barriers to entry, and how much firms can control prices.

- Market structures range from perfect competition (many buyers and sellers), to monopolistic competition (differentiated product), to oligopoly (only a few firms that are interdependent), to monopoly (a one-firm industry).

- Perfect competition is defined by four attributes: Many buyers and sellers who are so small that none individually can influence price, firms that produce and sell a homogeneous (standardized) product, buyers and sellers who have all the information necessary to make informed decisions, and barriers to entry and exit that are nonexistent.

- Firms in perfectly competitive markets get the product price from national or global markets. In other words, firms are price takers.

- In the short run, one factor (usually plant size) is fixed. In the long run, all factors are variable, and firms can enter or leave the industry.

QUESTION: For the following firms, explain where in our market structure approach each firm best fits: Verizon (a wireless communications service provider), NFL (a professional football organization), Grandma's Southern Kitchen (a small café), Jack's Lumber (an independent lumber mill).

Answers to the Checkpoint question can be found at the end of this chapter.

Perfect Competition: Short-Run Decisions

Figure 1 in the previous section presented a perfectly competitive market with an equilibrium price of $200. This translates into a horizontal demand curve for individual firms at that price. Individual firms are price takers in this competitive situation: They can sell as many units of their product as they wish at $200 each.

Marginal Revenue

Economists define **marginal revenue** as the change in total revenue that results from the sale of one additional unit of a product. Marginal revenue (MR) is equal to the change in total revenue (ΔTR) divided by the change in quantity sold (Δq); thus,

$$MR = \Delta TR / \Delta q$$

Total revenue (TR), meanwhile, is equal to price per unit (p) times quantity sold (q); thus:

$$TR = p \times q$$

In a perfectly competitive market, we know that price will not change based on the output of any one firm. And because marginal revenue is defined as the change in revenue that comes from selling one more unit, marginal revenue is simply equal to price. To verify, suppose a firm sells ten units of a good at $200 each, earning a total revenue of $2,000. If the firm sells eleven units at $200 each, total revenue becomes $2,200. Using our marginal revenue equation, the added revenue a firm receives from selling the 11th unit is $200, which is equal to the product price. Thus determining marginal revenue in a perfectly competitive market is easy. As we will see in later chapters, this gets more complicated in market structures in which firms have some control over price.

Profit-Maximizing Output

Suppose that you own a windsurfing sail manufacturing firm in a perfectly competitive market. Figure 2 on the next page shows the price and marginal cost curve that your firm faces while it seeks to maximize profits. As the price and cost curve show, you can sell all you want at $200 a sail. Our first instinct might be to conclude that you will produce all that you can, but this is not the case. Given the marginal cost curve shown in Figure 2, if you produce 85 units, profit will be less than the maximum possible. This is because revenue from the sale is $200, but the 85th sail costs $210 to produce (point *b*). This means producing this last sail reduces profits by $10.

Suppose instead that you produce 84 sails. The revenue from selling the 84th unit (MR) is $200. This is precisely equal to the added cost (MC) of producing this unit, $200

marginal revenue The change in total revenue from selling an additional unit of output. Because competitive firms are price takers, P = MR for competitive firms.

FIGURE 2

Profit Maximization in the Short Run in Perfectly Competitive Markets

If the firm produces 85 standardized windsurfing sails, the marginal cost to produce the last sail exceeds the revenue from its sale, thus reducing the firm's profits. For the 84th unit produced, marginal cost and price are both equal to $200, therefore the firm earns a normal return from producing this unit. Producing only 83 units means relinquishing the normal return that could have been earned from the 84th sail. Hence, the firm maximizes profits at an output of 84 (point *e*), where MC = MR = P = $200.

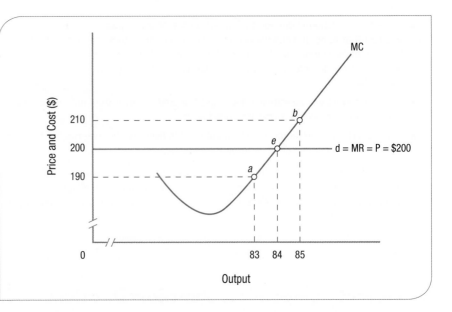

profit maximizing rule Firms maximize profit by producing output where MR = MC. No other level of output produces higher profits.

(point *e*). Therefore, your firm earns zero economic profit by producing and selling the 84th sail. Zero economic profit, or normal profits, mean that your firm is earning a normal return on its capital by selling this 84th sail. If you produce only 83 sails, however, the additional cost (point *a*) will be less than the price, and you will have to relinquish the normal return associated with the 84th sail. Profits from selling 83 sails will therefore be lower than if 84 sails are sold because the normal return on the 84th sail is lost.

These observations lead us to a **profit maximizing rule:** *A firm maximizes profit by continuing to produce and sell output until marginal revenue equals marginal cost (MR = MC).* As we will see in subsequent chapters, this rule applies to all firms, regardless of market structure.

Economic Profits

Continuing with the example of your windsurfing sail manufacturing firm, assume that the market has established a price of $200 for each sail. Your marginal revenue and cost curves are shown in Figure 3 (the MR and MC curves are the same as those shown in Figure 2).

Earlier, we found that profits are maximized when your firm is producing output such that MR = MC, in this case, 84 sails. Looking at Figure 3, we see that profits are maximized at point *a*, because this is where MR = MC at $200. We can compute the profit in this scenario by multiplying average profit (profit per unit) by output. Average profit equals price minus average total costs (P − ATC). In the figure, the average total cost of producing 84 sails is $180 (point *b*). Thus, when 84 sails are produced, average profit is the distance *ab* in Figure 3, or $200 − $180 = $20. Total profit, or average profit times output [(P − ATC) × Q], is $20 × 84 = $1,680; this is represented in the figure by area *cfab*. This area also is equivalent to total revenue minus total cost (TR − TC).

Note that there *is* a profit-maximizing point. The competitive firm cannot produce and produce—it has to take into consideration its costs. Therefore, for the price-taking competitive firm, its cost structure is crucial.

Five Steps to Maximizing Profit

Profit maximization is an important goal of any firm in any market structure. Yet, understanding revenue and cost curves can be frustrating given the many market structures and the different types of curves facing each market. Wouldn't it be useful to have a single approach when solving for a profit-maximizing outcome?

Let's review how we solved for the profit-maximizing equilibrium in the previous section, but this time using five simple steps that are illustrated in Figure 4.

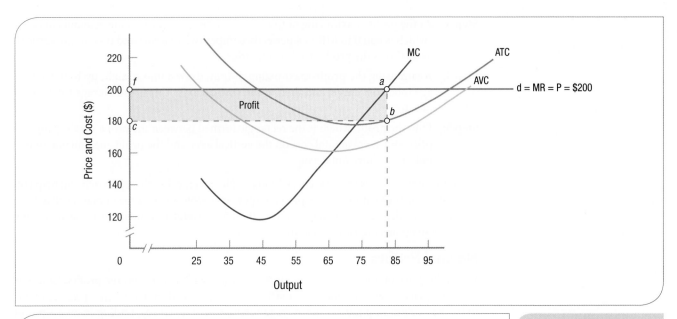

A Perfectly Competitive Firm Earning Economic Profits

Profits are maximized where marginal revenue equals marginal cost (MR = MC), or at an output of 84 and a price of $200. Price minus average total cost equals average profit per unit, represented by the distance *ab*. Average profit per unit times the number of units produced equals total profit; this is represented by area *cfab*.

FIGURE 3

Step 1: Find the point at which marginal revenue (MR) equals marginal cost (MC). Remember that in a perfectly competitive market, MR equals price.

Step 2: At the point at which MR = MC, find the corresponding point on the horizontal axis; this is the profit-maximizing output.

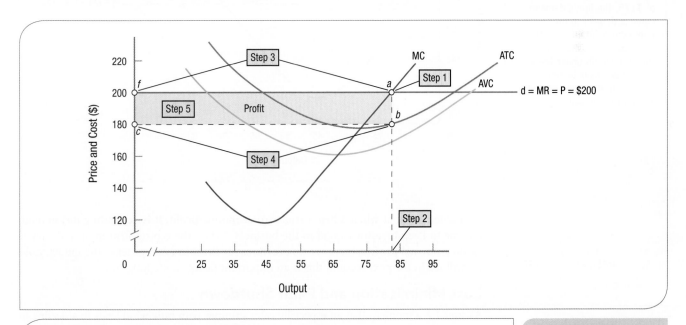

Five-Step Process to Determine Maximum Profit

The five steps shown provide a consistent approach to determining the profit-maximizing output and price and the area representing profit using revenue and cost curves in any market structure.

FIGURE 4

Step 3: At the profit-maximizing output, draw a line straight up to the demand curve (which is equal to MR in a perfectly competitive market) and then to the vertical axis. This is the profit-maximizing price.

Step 4: Again using the profit-maximizing output, draw a line straight up to the average total cost curve, and then to the vertical axis. This is the average total cost per unit.

Step 5: Find the profit, which is the rectangle formed between the profit-maximizing price and average total cost on the vertical axis, and the profit-maximizing output on the horizontal axis.

Some of these steps might seem redundant. However, using this approach will help you to identify the profit-maximizing price, output, and profit in any type of market structure, as we'll see in the next two chapters. It is therefore useful to remember these steps now when the diagrams are easier to follow.

Normal Profits

When the price of a windsurfing sail is $200, your firm earns economic profits. Consider what happens, however, when the market price falls to $175 a sail. This price happens to be the minimum point on the average total cost curve, corresponding to an output of 75 sails. Figure 5 shows that at the price of $175, the firm's demand curve is just tangent to the minimum point on the ATC curve (point *e*), which means that the distance between points *a* and *b* in Figure 3 has shrunk to zero. By producing 75 sails, your firm earns normal profits, or zero economic profit.

FIGURE 5

A Perfectly Competitive Firm Earning Normal Profits (Zero Economic Profit)

If the market sets a price of $175, the firm's demand curve is tangent to the minimum point on the ATC curve (point *e*). The best the firm can do under these circumstances is to earn normal profits on the sale of 75 windsurfing sails.

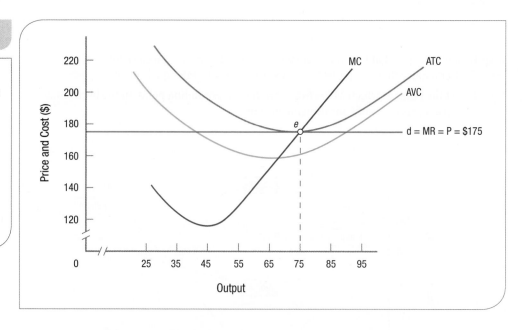

Remember that when a firm earns zero economic profit, it is generating just enough income to keep investor capital in the business. When the typical firm in an industry is earning **normal profits,** there are no pressures for firms to enter or leave the industry. As we will see in the next section, this is an important factor in the long run.

normal profits Equal to zero economic profits; where P = ATC.

Loss Minimization and Plant Shutdown

Assume for a moment that an especially calm summer with little wind leads to a decline in the demand for windsurfing sails. Assume also that, as a consequence, the price of windsurfing sails falls to $170. Figure 6 illustrates the impact on your firm. Market price has fallen below your average total cost of production (which takes into account the fixed cost, which in this case is $1,000, an amount determined in the previous chapter), but remains above your

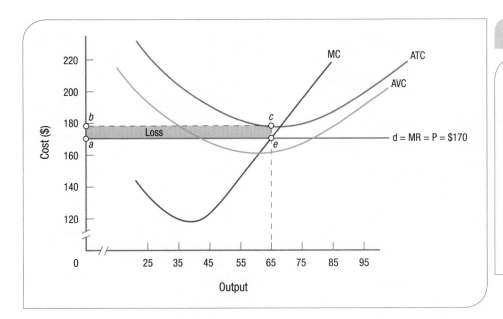

FIGURE 6

A Perfectly Competitive Firm Minimizing Losses

Assume that the price of windsurfing sails falls to $170 a sail. Loss minimization requires an output at which MR = MC, in this case at 65 units (point *e*). Average total cost is $178 (point *c*), therefore loss per unit is equal to $8. Total loss is equal to $8 × 65 = $520. Notice that this is less than the fixed costs ($1,000) that would have to be paid even if the plant was closed.

average variable cost. Profit maximization—or, in this case, *loss minimization*—requires that you produce output at the level at which MR = MC. That occurs at point *e,* where output falls to 65 units.

Using Figure 6, at 65 units the average total cost at this production level is $178, thus with a market price of $170, loss per unit is $8. The total loss on 65 units is $8 × 65 = $520, corresponding to area *abce*.

These results may look grim, but consider your alternatives. If you were to produce more or fewer sails, your losses would just mount. You could, for instance, furlough your employees. But you will still have to pay your fixed costs of $1,000. Without revenue, your losses would be $1,000. Therefore, it is better to produce and sell 65 sails, taking a loss of $520, thereby cutting your losses nearly in half.

But what happens if the price of windsurfing sails falls to $160? Such a scenario is shown in Figure 7. Your revenue from the sale of sails has fallen to a level just equal to variable costs. If you produce and sell 60 units of output (where MR = MC), you will be able to pay your employees their wages, but have nothing left over to pay your

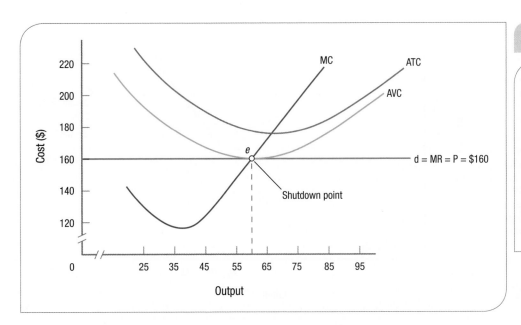

FIGURE 7

Plant Shutdown in a Perfectly Competitive Industry

When prices fall below $160, or below the minimum point of the AVC curve, losses begin to exceed fixed costs. The firm will close if price falls below this minimum point (point *e*); this is the firm's shutdown point.

NOBEL PRIZE
HERBERT SIMON (1916–2001)

When he was awarded the Nobel Prize for Economics in 1978, Herbert Simon (1916–2001) was an unusual choice on two fronts. First, he wasn't an economist by trade; he was a professor of computer science and psychology at the time of his award. Second, Simon's major contribution to economics was a direct challenge to one of the basic tenets of economics: Firms, in fact, do not always act to maximize profits.

In his book *Administrative Behavior,* Simon approached economics and the behavior of firms from his outsider's perspective. Simon thought real-world experience showed that firms are not always perfectly rational, in possession of perfect information, or striving to maximize profits. Rather, he proposed, as firms grow larger and larger, the access to perfect information becomes a fiction and that firms are run by individuals whose decisions are altered by their inability to remain perfectly and completely rational.

To Simon, the reality is not that firms tilt at the mythical windmill of maximizing profits, but that, as he said in his Nobel Prize acceptance speech, they recognize their limitations and instead try to come up with an "acceptable solution to acute problems" by setting realistic goals and making reasonable assessments of their successes or failures.

Simon's views provided a new approach to analyzing market structure models. Simon brought data, theories, and knowledge from other disciplines and paved the way for behavioral economics (discussed in Chapter 6) to eventually become a prominent field of economics by broadening its scope and applying more realistic conditions found in the marketplace.

overhead; thus your loss will be $1,000. Point *e* in Figure 7 represents a **shutdown point,** because your firm will be indifferent to whether it operates or shuts down—you lose $1,000 either way.

If prices continue to fall below $160 a sail, your losses will grow still further, because revenue will not even cover wages and other variable expenses. Once prices drop below the minimum point on the AVC curve (point *e* in Figure 7), losses will exceed total fixed costs and your loss minimizing strategy must be to close the plant. It follows that the greatest loss a firm is willing to suffer in the short term is equal to its total fixed costs. Remember that the firm cannot leave the industry at this point, because market participation is fixed in the short run, but it can shut down its plant and stop production.

How practical is it to shut down production? That depends on the size of the firm and whether short-run losses are temporary or indicative of a permanent trend. The owner of a small kiosk selling decorative baskets might shut down and lay off the staff if losses mount and prospects for future profits are grim, while the owner of a fishing boat might furlough her employees during the off-season, with the expectation of resuming operations later on when prices recover and profits return.

The Short-Run Supply Curve

A glance at Figure 8 will help to summarize what we have learned so far. As we have seen, when a competitive firm is presented with a market price of P_0, corresponding to the minimum point on the AVC curve, the firm will produce output of q_0. If prices

---

FIGURE 8

The Short-Run Supply Curve for a Perfectly Competitive Firm

If prices fall below P_0, the firm will shut its doors and produce nothing. For prices between P_0 and P_1, the firm will incur losses, but these losses will be less than fixed costs, thus the firm will remain in operation and produce where MR = MC. At a price of P_1, the firm earns a normal return. If price should rise above P_1 (e.g., to P_2), the firm will earn economic profits by selling an output of q_2. The portion of the MC curve above the minimum point on the AVC curve, here thickened, is the firm's short-run supply curve.

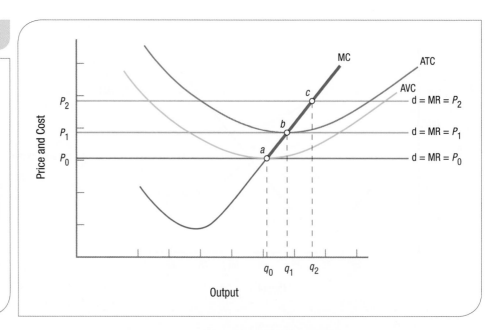

should fall below P_0, the firm will shut its doors and produce nothing. If, on the other hand, prices should rise to P_1, the firm will sell q_1 and earn normal profits (zero economic profits). And if prices continue climbing above P_1, say, to P_2, the firm will earn economic profits by selling q_2. In each instance, the firm produces and sells output where MR = MC.

From this quick summary, we can see that a firm's **short-run supply curve** is equivalent to the MC curve above the minimum point on the AVC curve. This curve, shown as the thickened portion of the MC curve in Figure 8, shows how much the firm will supply to the market at various prices, keeping in mind that it will supply no output at prices below the shutdown point.

Keep in mind also that the short-run supply curve for an industry is the horizontal summation of the supply curves of the industry's individual firms. To obtain industry supply, in other words, we add together the output of every firm at various price levels.

> **shutdown point** When price in the short run falls below the minimum point on the AVC curve, the firm will minimize losses by closing its doors and stopping production. Because P < AVC, the firm's variable costs are not covered, therefore by shutting the plant, losses are reduced to fixed costs only.
>
> **short-run supply curve** The marginal cost curve above the minimum point on the average variable cost curve.

 CHECKPOINT

PERFECT COMPETITION: SHORT-RUN DECISIONS

- Marginal revenue is the change in total revenue from selling an additional unit of a product.

- Perfectly competitive firms are price takers, getting their price from markets, enabling them to sell all they want at the going market price. As a result, their marginal revenue is equal to product price and the demand curve facing the perfectly competitive firm is a horizontal straight line at market price.

- Perfectly competitive firms maximize profit by producing that output where marginal revenue equals marginal cost (MR = MC).

- When price is greater than the minimum point of the average total cost curve, firms earn economic profits.

- When price is just equal to the minimum point of the average total cost curve, firms earn normal profits.

- When price is below the minimum point of the average total cost curve, but above the minimum point of the average variable cost curve, the firm continues to operate, but earns an economic loss.

- When price falls below the minimum point on the average variable cost curve, the firm will shut down and incur a loss equal to total fixed costs.

- The short-run supply curve of the firm is the marginal cost curve above the minimum point on the average variable cost curve.

QUESTION: Describe why profit-maximizing output occurs where MR = MC. Does this explain why perfectly competitive firms do not sell "all they can produce"?

Answers to the Checkpoint question can be found at the end of this chapter.

Perfect Competition: Long-Run Adjustments

We have seen that perfectly competitive firms can earn economic profits, normal profits, or losses in the short run because their plant size is fixed, and they cannot exit the industry. We now turn our attention to the long run. In the long run, firms can adjust all factors, even to the point of leaving an industry. And if the industry looks attractive, other firms can enter it in the long run. Why are some industries (such as medical marijuana) thriving while others (such as photo developing) declining? The answer is tied to economic profits and losses.

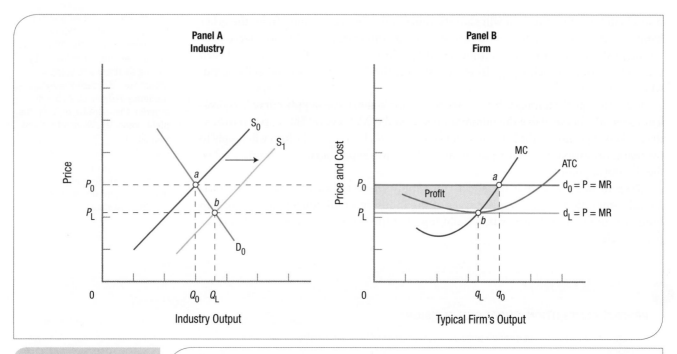

Long-Run Adjustment with Short-Run Economic Profits

Panel A shows a market initially in equilibrium at point *a*. Industry supply and demand equal S_0 and D_0, and equilibrium price is P_0. This equilibrium leads to the short-run economic profits shown in the shaded area in panel B. Short-run economic profits lead other firms to enter the industry, thus raising industry output to Q_L in panel A, while forcing prices down to P_L. The output for individual firms declines as the industry moves to long-run equilibrium at point *b*. In the long run, firms in perfectly competitive markets can earn only normal profits, as shown by point *b* in panel B.

Adjusting to Profits and Losses in the Short Run

If firms in the industry are earning short-run economic profits, new firms can be expected to enter the industry in the long run, or existing firms may increase the scale of their operations. Figure 9 illustrates one such possible adjustment path when the firms in an industry are earning short-run economic profits. To simplify the discussion, we will assume there are no economies of scale in the long run.

In panel A, the market is initially in equilibrium at point *a*, with industry supply and demand equal to S_0 and D_0, and equilibrium price equal to P_0. For the typical firm shown in panel B, this translates into a short-run equilibrium at point *a*. Notice that, at this price, the firm produces output exceeding the minimum point of the ATC curve. The shaded area represents economic profits.

These economic profits (sometimes called supernormal profits) will attract other firms into the industry. Remember that in a perfectly competitive market, entry and exit are easy in the long run; therefore, many firms decide to get in on the action when they see these profits. As a result, industry supply will shift to the right, to S_1, where equilibrium is at point *b*, resulting in a new long-run industry price of P_L. For each firm in the industry, output declines to q_L and is just tangent to the minimum point on the ATC curve. Thus, all firms are now earning normal profits and keeping their investors satisfied. There are no pressures at this point for more firms to enter or exit the industry.

Consider the opposite situation—that is, firms in an industry that are incurring economic losses. Figure 10 depicts such a scenario. In panel A, market supply and demand

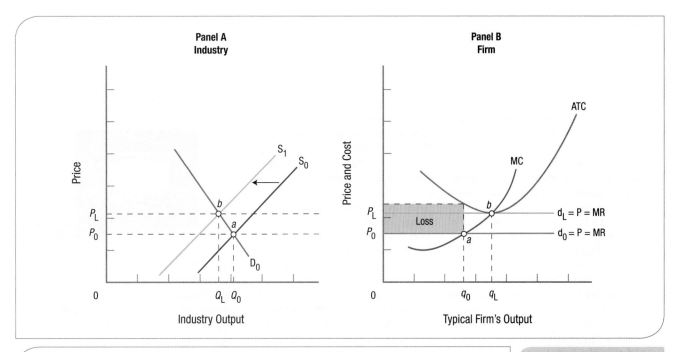

Long-Run Adjustment with Short-Run Losses

Panel A shows a market initially in equilibrium at point *a*. Industry supply and demand equal S_0 and D_0, and equilibrium price is P_0. This equilibrium leads to the short-run economic losses shown in the shaded area in panel B, thus inducing some firms to exit the industry. Industry output contracts to Q_L in panel A, raising prices to P_L and expanding output for the individual firms remaining in the industry, as the industry moves to long-run equilibrium at point *b*. Again, in the long run, firms in perfectly competitive markets will earn normal profits, as shown by point *b* in panel B.

FIGURE 10

are S_0 and D_0, with equilibrium price at P_0. In panel B, firms suffer economic losses equal to the shaded area. These losses cause some firms to reevaluate their situations and some decide to leave the industry, thus shifting the industry supply curve to S_1 in panel A, generating a new equilibrium price of P_L. This new price is just tangent to the minimum point of the ATC curve in panel B, expanding output for those individual firms remaining in the industry. Firms in the industry are now earning normal profits, therefore the pressures to leave the industry dissipate.

Notice that in Figures 9 and 10, the final equilibrium in the long run is the point at which industry price is just tangent to the minimum point on the ATC curve. At this point, there are no net incentives for firms to enter or leave the industry.

If industry price rises above this point, the economic profits being earned will induce other firms to enter the industry; the opposite is true if price falls below this point. A simple way to remember this is with the *elimination principle*: In a competitive industry in the long run with easy entry and exit, profits are eliminated by firm entry, and losses are eliminated by firm exit.

Competition and the Public Interest

Competitive processes dominate modern life. You and your friends compete for grades, concert tickets, spouses, jobs, and many other benefits. Competitive markets are simply an extension of the competition inherent in daily life. Figure 11 on page 205 illustrates the long-run equilibrium for a firm in a competitive market. Market price in the long run is P_{LR}; it is equal to the minimum point on both the short-run average total cost

ISSUE

Can Businesses Survive in an Open-Source World?

Open-source software can be downloaded free, used free, and altered by anyone, provided that any changes made can also be freely used and altered by anyone else. Open-source systems such as Linux and Apache server software are used to run many of the Internet's biggest sites. Other types of software, including word processing, spreadsheets, and photo manipulation programs, are now becoming open source. Digital formats allow the cost of downloading, using, and duplicating this software to approach zero. Making a profit selling open-source software, even with enhanced features, is therefore a difficult process.

But now there is a movement to open-source *hardware*: products and plans that are available free, which anyone can duplicate, alter if they wish, and sell. What happens when open-source software is followed by open-source hardware?

Cory Doctorow, in his novel *Makers*, imagines a world in which the "system makes it hard to sell anything above the marginal cost of goods unless you have a really innovative idea, which can't stay innovative for long, so you need continuous invention and reinvention, too." This sounds eerily similar

to the battles going on today with smart phones, televisions, video games, eBooks, and other high-tech products. As soon as one company presents a game-changing product (think iPod, iPhone, and iPad), other firms work feverishly to clone it and competition pushes prices and margins down to lower levels. Imagine what would happen if these products were both hardware and software open source.

Makers presents a world in which two engineers make three-dimensional (3D) desktop printers that can produce any product consumers want from inexpensive "goop." In *Makers*, the economy collapses, department stores vanish, and unemployment approaches depression levels of more than 20%. Coming up with a continuous stream of clever innovative ideas that initially make high short-run profits is the only way to stay ahead, because the transition to the long run happens so fast. Worse, people use their own 3D printers to duplicate products or designs for virtually nothing (just the cost of the goop).

Technology of the kind we are seeing now has the possibility of driving markets to these kinds of levels at which marginal cost and profit margins are

low. Many companies have thousands of employees that make products from toothbrushes to plasticware to nearly everything you see at dollar stores. If households had the capability to produce their own products from some inexpensive substance, many companies we know today would disappear. Cory Doctorow explores what happens when the printers can produce other printers and other open-source machines. Although *Makers* is science fiction, the prototypes of 3D printers available today suggest it is not so far-fetched.

Sources: Cory Doctorow, *Makers* (New York: Tom Doherty Associates), 2009; L. Gordon Crovitz, "Technology Is Stranger Than Fiction," *Wall Street Journal*, November 23, 2009, p. A19; and Justin Lahart, "Taking an Open-Source Approach to Hardware," *Wall Street Journal*, November 27, 2009, p. B8.

(SRATC) curve and the long-run average total cost (LRATC) curve. At point *e*, the following is true:

$$P = MR = MC = SRATC_{min} = LRATC_{min}$$

This equation illustrates why competitive markets are the standard (benchmark) by which all other market structures are evaluated. First, competitive markets exhibit *productive efficiency*. Products are produced and sold to consumers at their lowest possible opportunity cost. For consumers, this is an excellent situation: They pay no more than minimum production costs plus a profit sufficient to keep producers in business, and consumer surplus shown in panel A is maximized. When we look at monopoly firms in the next chapter, consumers do not get such a good deal.

Second, competitive markets demonstrate *allocative efficiency*. The price that consumers pay for a given product is equal to marginal cost. Because price represents the value consumers place on a product, and marginal cost represents the

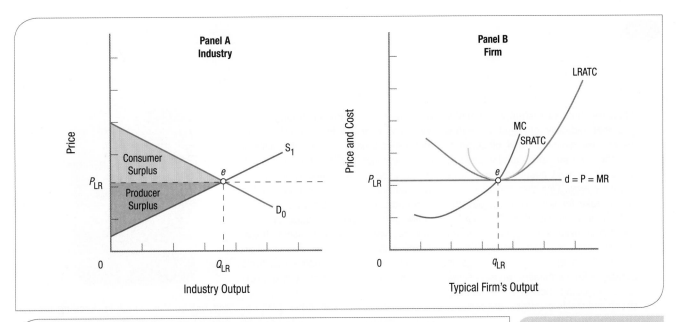

Long-Run Equilibrium for the Perfectly Competitive Firm

Market price in the long run is P_{LR}, corresponding to the minimum point on the SRATC and LRATC curves. At point e, $P = MR = MC = SRATC_{min} = LRATC_{min}$. This is why economists use perfectly competitive markets as the benchmark when comparing the performance of other market structures. With competition, consumers get just what they want because price reflects their desires, and they get these products at the lowest possible price ($LRATC_{min}$). Further, as panel A illustrates, the sum of consumer and producer surplus is maximized. Any reduction in output reduces the sum of consumer and producer surplus.

FIGURE 11

opportunity cost to society to produce that product, when these two values are equal, the market is allocating the production of various goods according to consumer wants.

The flip side of these observations is that if a market falls out of equilibrium, the public interest will suffer. If, for instance, output falls below equilibrium, marginal cost will be less than price. Therefore, consumers place a higher value on that product than it is costing firms to produce. Society would be better off if more of the product were put on the market. Conversely, if output rises above the equilibrium level, marginal cost will exceed price. This excess output costs firms more to produce than the value placed on it by consumers. We would be better off if those resources were used to produce another commodity more highly valued by society.

Long-Run Industry Supply

Economies or diseconomies of scale determine the shape of the long-run average total cost (LRATC) curve for individual firms. A firm that enjoys significant economies of scale will see its LRATC curve slope down for a wide range of output. Firms facing diseconomies of scale will see their average costs rise as output rises. The nature of these economies and diseconomies of scale determines the size of the competitive firm.

Long-run industry supply is related to the degree to which increases and decreases in industry output influence the prices firms must pay for resources. For example, when all firms in an industry expand or new firms enter the market, this new demand for raw materials and labor may push up the price of some inputs. When this happens, it gives rise to an **increasing cost industry** in the long run.

increasing cost industry An industry that, in the long run, faces higher prices and costs as industry output expands. Industry expansion puts upward pressure on resources (inputs), causing higher costs in the long run.

Globalization and "The Box"

When we think of disruptive technologies that radically changed an entire market, we typically think of computers, the Internet, and cellular phones. Competitors must adapt to the change or wither away. One disruptive technology we take for granted today, but one that changed our world, is "the box"—the standardized shipping container. As Dirk Steenken reported, "Today 60% of the world's deep-sea general cargo is transported in containers, whereas some routes, especially between economically strong and stable countries, are containerized up to 100%."

Before containers, shipping costs added about 25% to the cost of some goods and represented over 10% of U.S. exports. The process was cumbersome; hundreds of longshoremen would remove boxes of all sizes, dimensions, and weight from a ship and load them individually onto trucks (or from trucks to a ship if they were going the other way). This process took a lot of time, was subject to damage and theft, and was costly and inconvenient for business.

In 1955, Malcom McLean, a North Carolina trucking entrepreneur, got the idea to standardize shipping containers. He originally thought he would drive a truck right onto a ship, drop a trailer, and drive off. Realizing that the wheels would consume a lot of space, he soon settled on standard containers that would stack together, but would also load directly onto a truck trailer.

Containers are 20 or 40 feet long, 8 feet wide, and 8 or 8½ feet tall. This standardization greatly reduced the costs of handling cargo. McLean bought a small shipping company, called it Sea-Land, and converted some ships to handle the containers. In 1956 he converted an oil tanker and shipped 58 containers from Newark, New Jersey, to Houston, Texas. It took roughly a decade of union bargaining and capital investment by firms for containers to catch on, but the rest is history.

Longshoremen and other port operators thought he was nuts, but as the idea took hold, the West Coast longshoremen went on strike to prevent the introduction of containers. They received some concessions, but containerization was inevitable. Containerization was so cost effective that it could not be stopped. It set in motion the long-run adjustments we see in competitive markets. Ports that didn't adjust went out of business, and trucking firms that failed to add containers couldn't compete. The same was true for oceanic shipping companies.

Much of what we call globalization today can be traced to "the box." Firms producing products in foreign countries can fill a container, deliver it to a port, and send it directly to the customer or wholesaler in the United States. The efficiency, originally seen by McLean, was that the manufacturer and the customer would be the only ones to load

Youssouf Cader

and unload the container, keeping the product safer, more secure, and cutting huge chunks off the cost of shipping. Today, a 40-foot container with 32 tons of cargo shipped from China to the United States costs roughly $5,000 to ship, or 7 cents a pound! This efficient technology has facilitated the expansion of trade worldwide and increased the competitiveness of many industries.

Sources: Based on Tim Ferguson, "The Real Shipping News," *Wall Street Journal,* April 12, 2006, p. D12, and on Mark Levinson, *The Box* (Princeton, NJ: Princeton University Press), 2006. Dirk Steenken et al., "Container Terminal Operation and Operations Research," in Hans-Otto Gunther and Kap Hwan Kim, *Container Terminals and Automated Transport Systems* (New York: Springer), 2005, p. 4. Christian Caryl, "The Box Is King," *Newsweek International,* April 10–17, 2006. Larry Rather, "Shipping Costs Start to Crimp Globalization," *New York Times,* August 3, 2008, p. 10.

To illustrate, panel A of Figure 12 shows two sets of short-run supply and demand curves. Initially, demand and supply are D_0 and S_0, and equilibrium is at point *a*. Assume demand increases, shifting to D_1. In the short run, price and output will rise to point *b*. As we have seen earlier, economic profits will result and existing firms will expand or new firms will enter the industry, causing product supply to shift to S_1 in the long run. Note that at the new equilibrium (point *c*), prices are higher than at the initial equilibrium (point *a*). This is caused by the upward pressure on the prices of industry inputs, notably raw materials and labor that resulted from industry expansion. Industry output has expanded, but prices and costs are higher. This is an *increasing cost industry.*

Alternatively, an industry might enjoy economies of scale as it expands, as suggested by panel C of Figure 12. In this case, price and output initially rise as the short-run

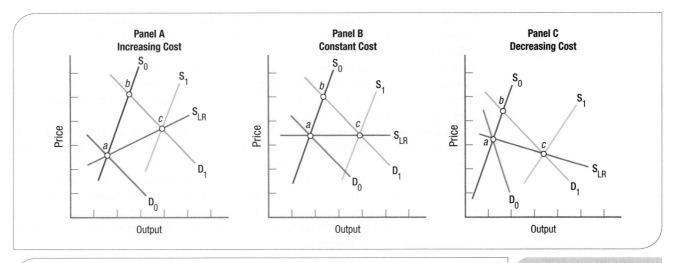

Long-Run Industry Supply Curves

Panel A shows an increasing cost industry. Demand and supply are initially D_0 and S_0, with equilibrium at point *a*. When demand increases, price and output rise in the short run to point *b*. As new firms enter the industry, they drive up the cost of resources. Supply increases in the long run to S_1 and the new equilibrium point *c* reflects these higher resource costs. In constant cost industries (panel B), firms can expand in the long run without economies or diseconomies, therefore costs remain constant in the long run. In decreasing cost industries (panel C), expansion leads to external economies and thus to a long-run equilibrium at point *c*, with lower prices and a higher output than before.

FIGURE 12

equilibrium moves to point *b*. Eventually, however, this industry expansion leads to lower prices; perhaps suppliers enjoy economies of scale as this industry's demand for their product increases. The semiconductor industry seems to fit this profile: As the demand for semiconductors has risen over the past few decades, their price has fallen dramatically. In the long run, therefore, a new equilibrium is established at point *c*, where prices are lower and output is higher than was initially the case. This illustrates what happens in a **decreasing cost industry.**

Finally, some industries seem to expand in the long run without significant change in average cost. These are known as **constant cost industries** and are shown in panel B in Figure 12. Some fast-food restaurants and retail stores, such as Wal-Mart, seem to be able to clone their operations from market to market without a noticeable rise in costs.

Summing Up

This chapter has focused on markets in which there is perfect competition—that is, in which industries contain many sellers and buyers, each so small that they ignore the others' behavior and sell a homogeneous product. Sellers are assumed to maximize the profits they earn through the sale of their products, and buyers are assumed to maximize the satisfaction they receive from the products they buy. Further, we assume that buyers and sellers have all the information necessary for informed transactions, and that sellers can sell as much of their products as they want at market equilibrium prices.

These assumptions allow us to reach some clear conclusions about how firms operate in competitive markets. In the long run, firms will produce the efficient level of output at which LRATC is minimized, and profits are enough to keep capital in the industry. This output level is efficient because it gives consumers just the goods they want and provides these goods at the lowest possible opportunity costs. Competitive market efficiency represents the benchmark for comparing other market structures.

Competitive markets as we have described them might seem to have such restrictive assumptions that this model only applies to a few industries, such as agriculture, minerals,

decreasing cost industry An industry that, in the long run, faces lower prices and costs as industry output expands. Some industries enjoy economies of scale as they expand in the long run, typically the result of technological advances.

constant cost industry An industry that, in the long run, faces roughly the same prices and costs as industry output expands. Some industries can virtually clone their operations in other areas without putting undue pressure on resource prices, resulting in constant operating costs as they expand in the long run.

and lumber. Most businesses you deal with don't look like the assumptions of these competitive markets. This is true, but most businesses you encounter, such as bars, restaurants, coffee shops, fast-food franchises, cleaners, grocery stores, and shoe and clothing stores, do share some of the characteristics of perfectly competitive markets such as earning normal profits over the long run. In the chapter after next, we examine those markets where consumers see products as differentiated and see how that industry's behavior is different from a perfectly competitive market.

Because perfect competition is so clearly in the public interest and is the benchmark for comparing other market structures, we can ponder the answer to the following question: Do firms seek the competitive market structure? The answer is: Generally, no. Why? Recall the profit equation. In perfectly competitive markets, firms are price takers. They can achieve economic profits in the short run but find it almost impossible to have long-run economic profits. Most firms instead want to achieve long-run economic profits. To do so, they must have some ability to control price. In the next chapter, we will see what firms do to achieve this market power.

CHECKPOINT

PERFECT COMPETITION: LONG-RUN ADJUSTMENTS

- When perfectly competitive firms are earning short-run economic profits, these profits attract firms into the industry. Supply increases and market price falls until firms are just earning normal profits.

- The opposite occurs when firms are making losses in the short run. Losses mean some firms will leave the industry. This reduces supply, thus increasing prices until profits return to normal.

- Competitive markets are efficient because products are produced at their lowest possible opportunity cost, and the sum of consumer and producer surplus is at a maximum.

- An industry in which prices rise as the industry grows is an increasing cost industry, and increased costs may be caused by rising prices of raw materials or labor as the industry expands.

- Decreasing cost industries see their prices fall as the industry expands, possibly due to huge economies of scale or rapidly improving technology.

- Constant cost industries seem to be able to expand without facing higher or lower prices.

QUESTION: Most of the markets and industries in the world are highly competitive, and presumably most CEOs of businesses know that competition will mean that they will only earn normal profits in the long run. Given this analysis, why do they bother to stay in business, when any economic profits will vanish in the long run?

Answers to the Checkpoint question can be found at the end of this chapter.

chapter summary

Section 1: **Market Structure Analysis**

A **market structure** describes an industry based on several characteristics, including the number of firms, nature of the industry's product, barriers to entry, and the extent to which individual firms can control prices.

Types of Market Structure

Perfect competition: Many price-taking firms producing a nearly identical product.

Monopolistic competition: Many firms producing a differentiated product.

Oligopoly: Few large firms producing a standardized product.

Monopoly: One firm producing a unique product protected by barriers to entry.

Soybeans are produced in a perfectly competitive market. Because each soybean farmer produces a small portion of total soybean production, each farmer has no influence on price, and is therefore a **price taker.**

In a perfectly competitive market, the price of a good is determined by ordinary industry supply and demand curves, and that price becomes the horizontal demand curve for the price-taking firm. Any shift in demand or supply (such as the demand shift from D_0 to D_1) causes price to change for the firm.

Section 2: Perfect Competition: Short-Run Decisions

Marginal revenue is the change in total revenue from producing one more unit, or $\Delta TR/\Delta Q$. In a perfectly competitive market, price does not change, therefore P = MR.

The **profit maximizing rule** says that firms maximize profit at an output where marginal revenue equals marginal cost.

When price (MR) > MC, the firm should increase production. When price (MR) < MC, the firm should decrease production.

Five Steps to Maximizing Profits in a Competitive Market:

1. Find MR = MC
2. Find optimal quantity where MR = MC
3. Find optimal price (Hint: It's already given!)
4. Find the average total cost at the optimal Q
5. Find the profit = $Q \times$ (P − ATC)

In the graph to the right, this competitive firm is earning economic profits equal to the blue shaded area.

Many shops in ski villages shut down during the summer when AVC cannot be covered due to fewer tourists.

Economic Versus Normal Profits

Economic profits take into account all explicit costs AND implicit costs such as the value of the next best use of time and money (opportunity cost).

Normal profits occur when economic profits are zero. But remember, zero economic profits can still represent substantial normal profits on paper.

The Short-Run Supply Curve for a Competitive Firm

When P < AVC: The firm shuts down immediately.

When AVC < P < ATC: The firm operates in the short run to minimize losses, but exits the industry in the long run. The MC curve above AVC equals the firm's short-run supply curve.

When P > ATC: The firm is earning economic profits. The MC curve above ATC equals the firm's long-run supply curve.

Section 3: Perfect Competition: Long-Run Adjustments

Firm Entry and Exit

Because perfectly competitive markets have no barriers to entry, short-run profits and losses are eliminated in the long run.

Short-run profits encourage new firms to enter, shifting supply right, lowering price until profits return to zero.
Short-run losses encourage inefficient firms to exit, shifting supply left, raising price until losses are eliminated.

Productive and Allocative Efficiency

In the long run, the price of goods in a perfectly competitive market equals the minimum point on the LRATC curve. This demonstrates productive efficiency (goods are produced at their lowest possible cost) and allocative efficiency (goods are produced according to what society desires).

A **long-run industry supply curve** is flatter than a short-run industry supply curve, and can slope upward (increasing cost industry), downward (decreasing cost industry), or can be horizontal (constant cost industry). Costs are determined by industry structure, technology, and economies of scale.

Technology goods are a decreasing cost industry. Over time, the cost of production falls due to economies of scale. Further, costs fall as new technologies enable firms to produce the product at a much lower cost.

QUESTIONS AND PROBLEMS

Check Your Understanding

1. Why must price cover average variable costs if the firm is to continue operating?

2. Why do perfectly competitive firms sell their products only at the market price? Why not try to raise prices to make more profit or lower them to garner more sales?

3. Describe the role that easy entry and exit play in competitive markets over the long run.

4. Why are marginal revenue and price equal for the perfectly competitive firm?

5. Why, if competitive firms are earning economic profits in the short run, are they unable to earn them in the long run?

6. Describe the reasons why an industry's costs might increase in the long run. Why might they decrease over the long run?

Apply the Concepts

7. When a sports team consistently struggles, one strategy is to replace the coach. But when this happens, the new coach initially has the same players (its primary input). How can a new coach improve the team's record when the players are mostly the same?

8. How is the short-run supply curve for the competitive firm determined?

9. Suppose you master the art of growing herbs in your garden and selling them for profit at the local farmer's market. Your neighbor sees your profitable business and decides to do the same, however with less experience he faces a much higher marginal cost curve. How is it possible for both you and your neighbor to sell herbs at the same price?

10. Assume a competitive industry is in long-run equilibrium and firms in the industry are earning normal profits. Now assume that production technology improves such that average total cost declines by $5 per unit. Describe the process this industry will go through as it moves to a new long-run equilibrium.

11. When a competitive firm is earning economic profits, is it also maximizing profit per unit? Why or why not?

12. In this chapter we suggested that whenever market price fell below average variable costs, the firm would shut down. At that point revenue is not covering its variable costs and the firm is losing more money than if it just shut down and lost fixed costs. Clearly, shutting the firm is more complicated than that. Under what circumstances might the firm continue to operate even though prices are below average variable costs?

In The News

13. A January 25, 2012, article in *The New York Times* describes how more states are attempting to pass legislation to collect sales tax on Internet sales (sometimes dubbed the *Amazon Tax*) even when the seller does not have a physical presence in that state. Given the intense competition between online retailers and physical (brick-and-mortar) stores, how would such laws affect competition? Would brick-and-mortar stores be better off? How about customers? Why or why not?

14. An April 19, 2012, article by Art Carden in *Forbes* entitled "Let's Be Blunt: It's Time to End the Drug War" argues that legalizing marijuana is a key solution to ending the drug war. He argues that turning the industry into a competitive market would force cost-inefficient drug cartels to exit the market. Using what you know about competitive markets and firm entry and exit, explain the economics behind the author's theory.

Solving Problems

15. Use the following figure for a firm in a perfectly competitive market.

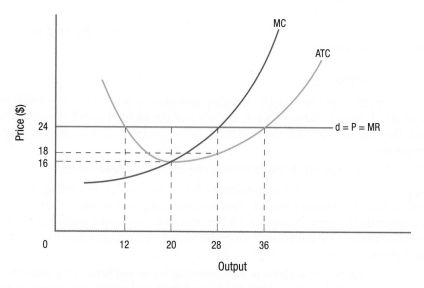

a. What is the output that maximizes the firm's profit?
b. At the profit-maximizing output, calculate total revenue and total cost.
c. If the firm maximizes profit, how much profit does it earn?
d. What will likely happen to market demand or market supply in the long run?
e. What will likely happen to the market price in the long run?

16. Use the figure below to answer the following true/false questions:
    a. If market price is $25, the firm earns economic profits.
    b. If market price is $20, the firm earns economic profit equal to roughly $100.
    c. If market price is $9, the firm produces roughly 55 units.
    d. If market price is $12.50, the firm produces roughly 70 units and makes an economic loss equal to roughly $210.
    e. Total fixed costs for this firm are roughly $100.
    f. If market price is $15, the firm sells 80 units and makes a normal profit.

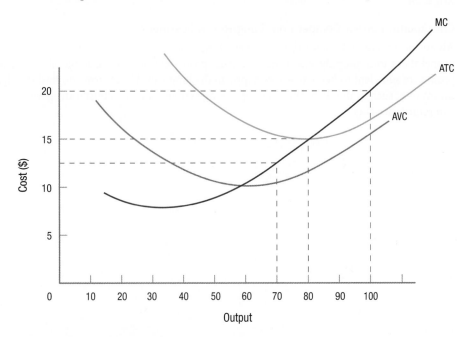

USING THE NUMBERS

17. According to By the Numbers, which two regions employ the highest number of people in the farm and farm-related industries? Approximately how many total persons are employed in the farm and farm-related industries in these two regions combined?

18. According to By the Numbers, in which year (since 1986) did the following crops reach their highest and lowest prices per bushel: corn, wheat, soybeans?

ANSWERS TO QUESTIONS IN CHECKPOINTS

Checkpoint: Market Structure Analysis

Verizon is one of a few major wireless providers in the U.S. market (others include AT&T, T-Mobile, and Sprint). The industry has considerable barriers to entry (e.g., the costs of cellular towers) and is therefore an oligopoly. The NFL is the only major organization for professional football teams, having complete control over all NFL teams nationwide. It also has exclusive contracts with advertisers and television networks. The NFL is best described as a monopoly. Grandma's Southern Kitchen is one of many restaurants serving southern food, and is differentiated by its location, menu, and quality of food. It is therefore a monopolistically competitive firm. Finally, Jack's Lumber is one of thousands of lumber mills across the country, each producing a standardized product. It is therefore in a perfectly competitive industry.

Checkpoint: Perfect Competition: Short-Run Decisions

Keep in mind that marginal cost is the additional cost to produce another unit of output, and price equals marginal revenue and is the additional revenue from selling one more unit of the product. If MR is greater than MC, the firm earns more revenue than cost by selling that next unit, therefore the firm will sell up to the point at which MR = MC. At that last unit at which MR = MC, the firm is earning a normal profit on that unit (a positive accounting profit). When MC > MR, the firm is spending more to produce that unit than it receives in revenue and is losing money on that last unit, lowering overall profits. Thus, firms will not produce and sell all they can produce: They will produce and sell up to the point at which MR = MC.

Checkpoint: Perfect Competition: Long-Run Adjustments

All businesses are looking for the "next new thing" that will generate economic profits and propel them to monopoly status. Even normal profits are not trivial. Remember, normal profits are sufficient to keep investors happy in the long run. When firms do find the right innovation, such as the iPad, Windows operating system, or a blockbuster drug, the short-run returns are huge.

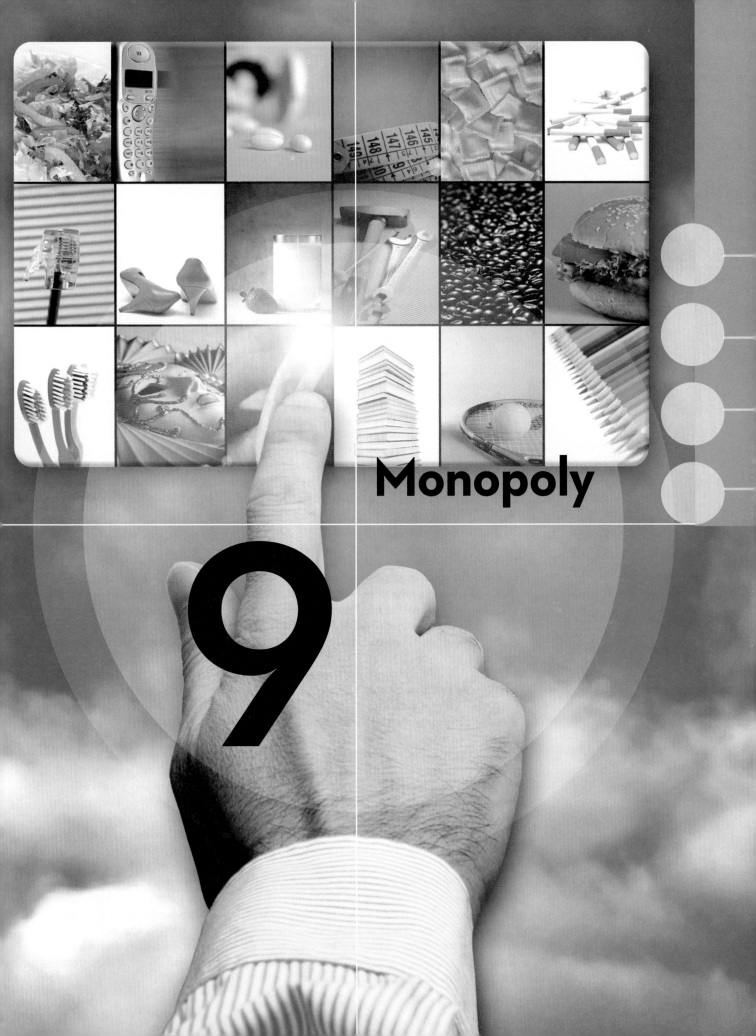

Monopoly

9

After studying this chapter you should be able to:

- Describe the characteristics of a monopoly and market power.

- Describe the ways in which firms maximize market power using barriers to entry.

- Use monopoly market analysis to determine the equilibrium level of output and price for a monopoly.

- Describe the differences between monopoly and competition.

- Describe the different forms of price discrimination.

- Describe the different approaches to regulating a natural monopoly.

- Relate the history and purpose of antitrust legislation to monopoly analysis.

- Apply concentration ratios and the Herfindahl-Hirschman index to analyze the likelihood of regulation in a given market.

- Describe the conditions of a contestable market and its significance.

When was the last time you used Google to search for information? How about YouTube, Gmail, Google+, Google Docs, Chrome, or any Android application (app)? If you have used any of these services within the past 24 hours, you're in the majority of Americans who rely on at least one of over one hundred Web-based services offered by Google. And the best part is . . . it's all free. Or is it?

Although Google users rarely pay to use any of its Web services, the market value of the company as of June 2013 was over $250 billion, or approximately the same total market value of McDonald's (with its 35,000 restaurants) and Coca-Cola (which sells 1.7 billion servings each day) combined. How can Google be worth so much if it doesn't *sell* any physical products?

The answer is that Google sells advertising services, and lots of them (over $35 billion in sales in 2012), to companies worldwide that pay to have their Web sites show up on the first page of Web search results, or along the top and sides of Google's "free" services. Incredibly, Google charges some companies as much as $50 every time someone clicks on their ad links, although the average price is closer to $1. But with over 1 billion Google users worldwide, it doesn't take much to bring in a significant amount of revenue.

How is Google so profitable? In the previous chapter, we constructed a model of perfectly competitive markets in which many sellers compete against one another for the business of many buyers. This model assumed that different firms sell almost identical products, produce at the point where price equals marginal cost, and face no barriers to entry, entering or exiting industries when they see profit opportunities. Keep in mind that firms in perfectly competitive markets have no pricing power. They are price takers, accepting the market price as given—they have no ability to change prices.

Although Google has competitors, such as Yahoo!, Bing, and others, Google commands a dominant share (over 70%) of the search engine market. Unlike perfectly competitive firms, Google has a lot of market power. By market power, we mean the ability to have some control over price.

In reality, most firms have some market power. You see this every day. The cleaners located at the train station is more convenient than the cleaners located in town, at least for those taking the train, and therefore can get away with charging a little more for cleaning and pressing shirts or skirts. A gas station located near a highway can charge a little more than a gas station a mile away.

As we move down the market structure spectrum from the perfectly competitive firms on one end to the monopolistically competitive firms, and then to the oligopolies, finally ending up with monopolies at the other end, we will see that firms obtain more and more market power. We will see why firms want to be monopolies.

What is a monopoly? When a single company is the only firm in the industry, the company is a pure monopoly. Google is not a pure monopoly because it has some competitors, but it is so dominant that it comes close. In both situations, the economic analysis is similar, and for simplicity we refer to these firms as monopolies, even if they are not in the purest sense.

This chapter studies the theory of monopoly, which is at the other market-structure extreme from the competitive model. Whereas the competitive model is in the public interest, we can guess at the outset that monopolies generally are not. We will see why monopolies exist and how they act. Then we will see what it means to have market power, the ability to set price, and why monopolies have maximum market power. After that, we will see what can be done to mitigate the powers of monopolies that must exist, and how the United States tries to prevent monopolies from arising in the first place.

We also study how monopolies can be beneficial. Some monopolies create economies of scale or provide product innovation and creativity. Many of today's new technologies and pharmaceuticals would never have been created if firms with complete market power did not exist. These products create benefits to users that offset some of the inefficiencies firms with market power pass on to consumers through higher prices. As with all economic analysis, costs and benefits must be weighed to determine the effect on consumers and producers, and the study of monopoly is no different.

BY THE NUMBERS

Monopoly and Market Power

Monopolies achieve market power by establishing barriers to entry preventing competition. These barriers include prohibitive fixed costs, control of a key resource, and government protection.

Professional sports leagues exhibit market power by establishing exclusive relationships with players, teams, and television networks. U.S. television viewers by championship series:

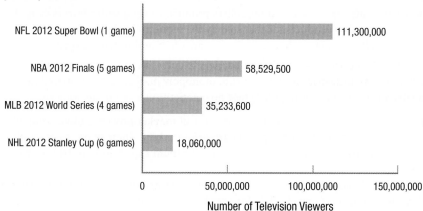

NFL 2012 Super Bowl (1 game) — 111,300,000

NBA 2012 Finals (5 games) — 58,529,500

MLB 2012 World Series (4 games) — 35,233,600

NHL 2012 Stanley Cup (6 games) — 18,060,000

0   50,000,000   100,000,000   150,000,000

Number of Television Viewers

Facebook maintains a dominant market share in social media despite attempts by competitors to wrestle this power away.

AP Photo/Paul Sakuma

Pharmaceutical companies spend billions of dollars developing successful drugs. Government patents allow companies to recoup their investment by preventing competition for a fixed period of time, allowing drugs to be priced high when they cost pennies to reproduce (marginal cost is very low). The world's most expensive drugs by annual cost of treatment:

1. Soliris (to treat a rare immune system disease): $409,500
2. Naglazyme (to treat a rare metabolic disorder): $365,000
3. Elaprase (to treat Hunter's syndrome): $350,000
4. Cynryze (to prevent dangerous face swelling): $350,000

Pictac/Dreamstime.com

$250,000
Published price (in 2013) for one ride on Virgin Galactic into space.

91.6%
Global desktop market share of Microsoft Windows in March 2013.

Many electric companies are natural monopolies protected from competition by the government. However, the annual percentage growth in electricity demand has fallen at the same time as competition from renewable energy increases.

John Kroetch/Dreamstime.com

12

10

8

6

4

2

0

-2

Percent Growth

1950 1953 1956 1959 1962 1965 1968 1971 1974 1977 1980 1983 1986 1989 1992 1995 1998 2001 2004 2007 2010 2013

Year

monopoly A one-firm industry with no close product substitutes and with substantial barriers to entry.

market power A firm's ability to set prices for goods and services in a market.

barriers to entry Any obstacle that makes it more difficult for a firm to enter an industry, and includes control of a key resource, prohibitive fixed costs, and government protection.

economies of scale As the firm expands in size, average total costs decline.

The NFL draft is an annual event at which the best players are offered multi-million dollar contracts. The exclusivity of the event gives the NFL maximum market power.

Monopoly Markets

The very word *monopoly* almost defines the subject matter: a market in which there is only one seller. For example, if you pay an electric bill every month, it's likely that you do not have a choice of which electric company services your apartment or house. Economists define a **monopoly** as a market sharing the following characteristics:

- The market has just one seller—one firm *is* the industry. This contrasts sharply with the competitive market, where many sellers comprise the industry.

- No close substitutes exist for the monopolist's product. Consequently, buyers cannot easily substitute other products for that sold by the monopolist. In the case of electricity, you could install solar panels, but such options are often prohibitively expensive.

- A monopolistic industry has significant barriers to entry. Though competitive firms can enter or leave industries in the long run, monopoly markets are considered nearly impossible to enter. Thus monopolists face no competition, even in the long run.

This gives pure monopolists what economists call **market power.** Unlike competitive firms, which are price takers, monopolists are *price makers.* Their market power allows monopolists to adjust their output in ways that give them significant control over product price.

As we noted already, nearly every firm has some market power, or some control over price. Your neighborhood dry cleaner, for instance, has some control over price because it is located close to you, and you are probably not going to want to drive 5 miles just to save a few cents. This control over price reaches its maximum in the case of monopolies, and becomes minor as markets approach more competitive conditions at the other end of the market structure spectrum.

Sources of Market Power

Monopoly is defined as one firm serving a market in which there are no close substitutes and entry is nearly impossible. Market power means that a firm has some control over price. As a market structure approaches monopoly, one firm gains the maximum market power possible for that industry. The key to the market power of monopolies is significant **barriers to entry.** These barriers can be of several forms.

Control Over a Significant Factor of Production If a firm owns or has control over an important input into the production process, that firm can keep potential rivals out of the market. This was the case with Alcoa Aluminum 70 years ago. Alcoa owned nearly all the world's bauxite ore, a key ingredient in aluminum production, before the company was eventually broken up by the government.

A contemporary example would be the National Football League (NFL), which has negotiated exclusive rights with colleges to draft top players (the most important input), along with exclusive rights with television networks and sponsors to broadcast games. Such control over key components of football entertainment makes entry into the industry very difficult.

Economies of Scale The **economies of scale** in an industry (when average total costs decline with increased production) give an existing firm a competitive advantage over potential entrants. By establishing economies of scale early, an existing firm has the ability to underprice new competitors, thereby discouraging their entry into the market. By doing so, a firm increases its market power.

In some industries, economies of scale can be so large that demand supports only one firm. Figure 1 illustrates this case. Here the long-run average total cost curve (LRATC) shows extremely large economies of scale. With industry demand at D_0, one firm can earn economic profits by producing between Q_0 and Q_1. If the industry were to contain two firms, however, demand for each would be D_1, and neither firm could remain in business without suffering losses. Economists refer to such cases as *natural monopolies.*

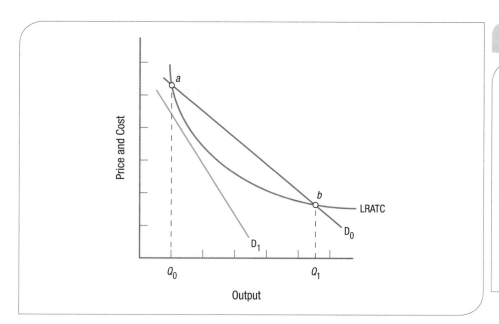

FIGURE 1

Economies of Scale Leading to Monopoly

The economies of scale in an industry can be so large that demand supports only one firm. In the industry portrayed here, one firm could earn economic profits (by producing output between Q_0 and Q_1 when faced with demand curve D_0). If the industry consisted of two firms, however, demand for each would be D_1, and neither firm could remain in business without suffering losses.

Utility industries have traditionally been considered natural monopolists because of the high fixed costs associated with power plants and the inefficiency of several different electric companies stringing their wires throughout a city. Recent technology, however, is slowly changing the utilities industry, as smaller plants, solar units, and wind generators permit a smaller yet efficient scale of operations. Smaller plants can be quickly turned on and off, and the energy from the sun and wind is beginning to be stored and transported to where it is needed in the system.

Government Franchises, Patents, and Copyrights The government is the source of some barriers to market entry. A government franchise grants a firm permission to provide specific goods or services, while prohibiting others from doing so, thereby eliminating potential competition. The United States Postal Service, for example, has an exclusive franchise for the delivery of mail to your mailbox. Similarly, water companies typically are granted special franchises by state or local governments.

Patents provide legal protection to individuals who invent new products and processes, allowing the patent holder to reap the benefits from the creation for a limited period, usually 20 years. Patents are immensely important to many industries, including pharmaceuticals, technology, and automobile manufacturing. Many firms in these industries spend huge sums of money each year on research and development—money they might not spend if they could not protect their investments through patenting. Similarly, a copyright protects ideas created by individuals or firms in the form of books, music, art, or software code, allowing these innovators to benefit from their creativity.

Some firms guard trade secrets to protect their assets for even longer periods than the limited timeframes provided by patents and copyrights. Only a handful of the top executives at Coca-Cola, for instance, know the secret to blending Coke.

Copyrights allow Matt Stone and Trey Parker, creators of *South Park,* to earn royalties on every episode (new and repeated) shown on television.

Monopoly Pricing and Output Decisions

Monopolies gain market power because of their barriers to entry. Shortly we will discuss some ways in which this power is maintained. First, however, let us consider the basics of monopoly pricing and output decisions. In the previous chapter, we saw that competitive firms maximize profits by producing at a level of output where MR = MC, selling this output at the established market price. The monopolist, however, *is* the market. It has the ability to set the price by adjusting output.

MR < P for Monopoly A monopolist faces a demand curve, just like a perfectly competitive firm. But there is a big difference. For the monopolist, marginal revenue is less than price (MR < P). To see why, look at Figure 2. Panel A shows the demand curve for a perfectly competitive firm. At a price of $10, the competitive firm can sell all it wants. For each unit sold, total revenue rises by $10. Recalling that marginal revenue is equal to the change in total revenue from selling an added unit of the product, marginal revenue is also $10.

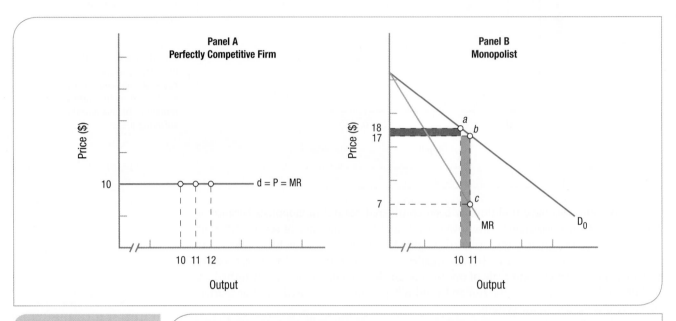

FIGURE 2

Marginal Revenue for Monopolies and Perfectly Competitive Firms

Panel A shows the demand curve for a perfectly competitive firm. At a price of $10, the competitive firm can sell all it wants. For each unit sold, revenue rises by $10; hence, marginal revenue is $10. Panel B shows the demand curve for a monopolist. Because the monopolist constitutes the entire industry, it faces a downward sloping demand curve (D_0). If the monopolist decides to sell 10 units at $18 each (point *a*), total revenue is $180. Alternatively, if the monopolist wants to sell 11 units, the price must be dropped to $17 (point *b*). This raises total revenue to $187 (11 × $17), but marginal revenue falls to $7 ($187 − $180, point *c*). Gaining the added $17 in revenue from the sale of the 11th unit requires the monopolist to give up $10 in additional revenue that would have come from selling the previous 10 units for an extra $1, or $18 each.

Contrast this with the situation of the monopolist in panel B. Because the monopolist constitutes the entire industry, it faces the downward sloping demand curve (D_0). If the monopolist decides to produce and sell 10 units, they can be sold in the market for the highest price the market would pay for 10 units (based on the demand curve), which is $18 each (point *a*), generating total revenue of $180. Alternatively, if the monopolist wants to sell 11 units, the price must be dropped to $17 (point *b*). This raises total revenue to $187 (11 × $17). Notice, however, that marginal revenue, or the revenue gained from selling this added unit, is only $7 ($187 − $180). In other words, the $17 in revenue (shown in green) gained from the sale of the 11th unit requires that the monopolist give up $10 in revenue (shown in red) that would have come from selling the previous 10 units for $1 more, or $18 each. Marginal revenue for the 11th unit is shown as $7 (point *c*) in panel B, which is also the difference between the green and red areas.

Notice that we are assuming that the monopolist cannot sell the 10th unit for $18 and then sell the 11th unit for $17; rather, the monopolist must offer to sell a given quantity to the market at a single price per unit. We are assuming, in other words, that there is no way for the monopolist to separate the market by specific individuals who are willing to pay different prices for the product. Later in this chapter, we will relax this assumption and discuss *price discrimination.*

In summary, we can see from panel B of Figure 2 that MR < P, and the marginal revenue curve is always plotted below the demand curve for the monopolist. This contrasts with the situation of the perfectly competitive firm, for which price and marginal revenue are always the same. We should also note that marginal revenue can be negative. In such an instance, total revenue falls as the monopolist tries to sell more output. However, no profit maximizing monopolist would knowingly produce in this range because costs are rising even as total revenue is declining, thus reducing profits.

Equilibrium Price and Output As noted earlier, product price is determined in a monopoly by how much the monopolist wishes to produce. This contrasts with the perfectly competitive firm that can sell all it wishes, but only at the *market-determined price.* Both types of firms wish to make profits. Finding the monopolist's profit maximizing price and output is a little more complicated, however, because competitive firms have only output to consider.

Like competitive firms, the profit maximizing output for the monopolist is found where MR = MC. Turning to Figure 3, we find that marginal revenue equals marginal cost at point *e,* where output is 120 units. Now we must determine how much the monopolist will charge for this output. This is done by looking to the demand curve. An output of 120 units can be sold for a price of $30 (point *a*).

Profit for each unit is equal to $8, the difference between price ($30) and average total cost ($22). Profit per unit times output equals total profit ($8 × 120 = $960), as indicated by the shaded area in Figure 3. Following the MR = MC rule, profits are maximized by selling 120 units of the product at $30 each.

Using the Five Steps to Maximizing Profit We can use the same five-step approach to analyzing equilibrium for a profit maximizing monopolist as we used for a perfectly competitive firm in the previous chapter. The main difference is that for a monopolist, the

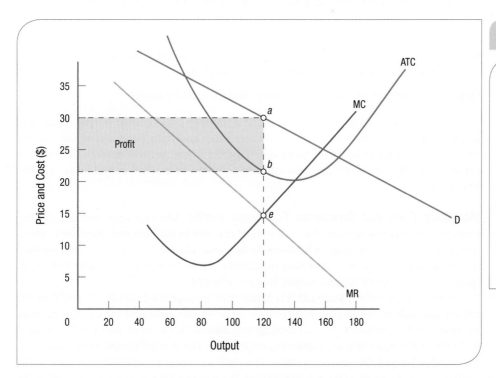

FIGURE 3

Monopolist Earning Economic Profits

Profit maximizing output is found for monopolists, as for competitive firms, at the point where MR = MC. In this figure, marginal revenue equals marginal cost at point *e,* where output is 120 units. These 120 units are sold for $30 each (point *a*). Profit is equal to average profit per unit times units sold: Profit = (P − ATC) × Q = ($30 − $22) × 120 = $8 × 120 = $960. The shaded area represents profit.

FIGURE 4

Five-Step Process to Determine a Monopolist's Optimal Output, Price, and Profit

The same five steps that were used to determine the profit maximizing output, price, and profit in a perfectly competitive market can be used in a monopoly market. The process begins by finding MR = MC, and then locating the optimal output and price, average total cost, and finally profit.

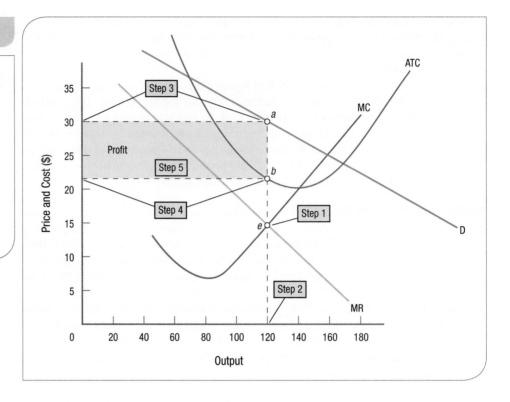

demand and marginal revenue curves are downward sloping, but that does not change the procedure, as shown in Figure 4.

Step 1: Find the point at which MR = MC.

Step 2: At that point, look down and determine the profit maximizing output on the horizontal axis.

Step 3: At this output, extend a vertical line upward to the demand curve and follow it to the left to determine the equilibrium price on the vertical axis.

Step 4: Using the same vertical line, find the point on the ATC curve to determine the average total cost per unit on the vertical axis.

Step 5: Find total profit by taking P − ATC, and multiply by output.

Using the five-step process to determine a monopolist's optimal output, price, and profit is a useful way to avoid making mistakes when analyzing revenue and cost curves. The same five steps can be used to analyze a perfectly competitive market, as shown in the previous chapter, and a monopolistically competitive market, as will be seen in the next chapter.

Monopoly Does Not Guarantee Economic Profits

We have seen that competitive firms may or may not be profitable in the short run, but in the long run, they must earn at least normal profits to remain in business. Is the same true for monopolists? Yes. Consider the monopolist in Figure 5. This firm maximizes profits by producing where MR = MC (point *e*) and selling 80 units of output for a price of $25.

In this case, however, price ($25) is lower than average total cost ($28), and thus the monopolist suffers the loss of $240 (−$3 × 80 = −$240) indicated by the shaded area. Because price nonetheless exceeds average variable costs, the monopolist will minimize its losses in the short run by continuing to produce. But if price should fall below AVC, the monopolist, just like any competitive firm, will minimize its losses at its fixed costs by shutting down its plant. If these losses persist, the monopolist will exit the industry in the long run.

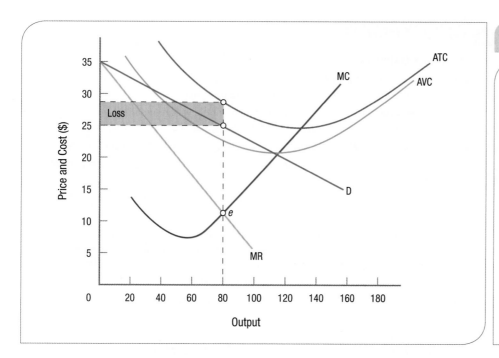

FIGURE 5

Monopolist Firm Making Economic Losses

Like perfectly competitive firms, monopolists may or may not be profitable in the short run, but in the long run, they must at least earn normal profits to remain in business. The monopolist shown here maximizes profits (minimizes losses) by producing at point *e*, selling 80 units of output at $25 each. Price is lower than average total cost, so the monopolist suffers the loss indicated by the shaded area. Because price still exceeds average variable cost (AVC), in the short run the monopolist will minimize its losses by continuing to produce.

This is an important point to remember. Being a monopolist does not automatically mean that there will be monopoly profits to haul in. Even monopolies face *some* cost and price pressures, and they face a demand curve, which ultimately limits their price making.

 ISSUE

"But Wait . . . There's More!" The Success and Failure of Infomercials

"But wait . . . there's more!" is a familiar phrase to anyone who has watched an infomercial selling unique products that generally are not sold in retail stores. The size of the infomercial industry is significant and growing. In 2012, infomercials generated over $150 billion in sales. What do infomercials sell? Why are they successful and why do many infomercial products fail?

Unlike regular television commercials, which air for 30 seconds or one minute during daytime and primetime shows, infomercials typically are longer, ranging from one minute to 30 minutes or longer. The longest infomercials typically air in the middle of the night when television advertising rates are much lower.

Infomercials typically sell newly invented products that are not well known. Most infomercial products fit the monopoly market structure because although the product may have similarities to other products, infomercials advertise them as one-of-a-kind products. Examples include new types of knives, towels, beauty products, and workout equipment. However, because not all infomercials are able to convince prospective buyers of the distinction from existing products, many infomercial products fail.

Infomercials focus on the product characteristics that make the product completely different from anything on the market. Because the target market of infomercials is consumers who buy on impulse, even in the middle of the night, they use various techniques to increase sales. First, many infomercials show a high "retail" price (such as $100) and then reduce it rapidly until it becomes $19.99. Second, infomercials will offer something extra with the tag line "But wait . . . there's more!" Third, many infomercials show a fixed time period in which to buy, often within hours, even

if the deadline is not actually enforced. And last, infomercials tend to offer return policies and often lifetime warranties (which is attractive but not that valuable if the company fails).

Some infomercials have become remarkably successful, with the product even becoming sold in stores. One example of a successful product that started from an infomercial is the Ped Egg, a cheese-grater-like device that removes dead skin from one's feet, which has sold over 50 million units and is now available through retailers such as Walgreens and Amazon.com.

CHECKPOINT

MONOPOLY MARKETS

- Monopoly is a market with no close substitutes, high barriers to entry, and one seller; the firm is the industry. Hence, monopolists are price makers.

- Monopolies gain maximum market power from control over an important input, economies of scale, or from government franchises, patents, and copyrights.

- For the monopolist, MR < P because the industry's demand is the monopolist's demand.

- Profit is maximized by producing that output where MR = MC and setting the price off the demand curve.

- Being a monopolist does not guarantee economic profits if demand is insufficient to cover costs.

QUESTIONS: When legendary country singer Dolly Parton goes on tour, sometimes she will perform in a relatively small (< 1,500 seats) venue when she could easily fill much larger arenas. Why would music artists intentionally choose a smaller venue? Wouldn't they make more money if they performed in a larger arena?

Answers to the Checkpoint questions can be found at the end of this chapter.

Comparing Monopoly and Competition

We have seen that perfectly competitive firms are price takers and produce as much as they can where MR = MC. In contrast, monopolies are price makers: They have the market power to set price and quantity, constrained only by their demand curve.

Would our economy be better off with more or fewer monopolies? This question almost answers itself. Who would want more monopolies—except the few lucky monopolists? The answer is, consumers are better off when competition is strong and monopolies are limited to certain industries. The reasons for this have to do with the losses associated with monopoly markets and market power. Losses directly attributed to monopolies include reduced output at higher prices, deadweight losses, rent-seeking behavior of monopolists, and x-inefficiency losses. But as we'll see later in this section, part (but not all) of these losses can be at least partially offset by some benefits that monopolies provide.

Higher Prices and Lower Output from Monopoly

Imagine for a moment that a competitive industry is monopolized, and the monopolist's marginal cost curve happens to be the same as the competitive industry's supply curve. Figure 6 illustrates such a scenario. In panel A, the competitive industry produces where supply equals demand, and thus where price and output are P_C and Q_C (point a). In panel B, monopoly price and output, as previously determined, are P_M and Q_M (point b).

Clearly, monopoly output is lower, and monopoly price is higher, than the corresponding values for competitive industries. How does this translate into the welfare of consumers and producers? Recall that we measure consumer surplus as the difference between market demand and price, as shown by the green areas in each panel. Producer surplus is the difference between price and market supply (marginal cost) as shown by the orange areas in each panel. The higher price charged by a monopolist results in part of the consumer surplus from Panel A being transferred into producer surplus in Panel B. Panel B shows a smaller consumer surplus and a larger producer surplus under a monopoly compared to a competitive market in Panel A. But this is not the end of the story.

Notice that at monopoly output Q_M, consumers value the Q_Mth unit of the product at P_M (point b), even though the cost to produce this last unit of output is considerably less (point c). This difference creates inefficiency because additional beneficial transactions could take place if output were expanded. The *deadweight loss,* otherwise known as the *welfare loss,* is comprised of consumer surplus and producer surplus that is lost from producing less than the efficient output. In panel B, deadweight loss from monopoly is

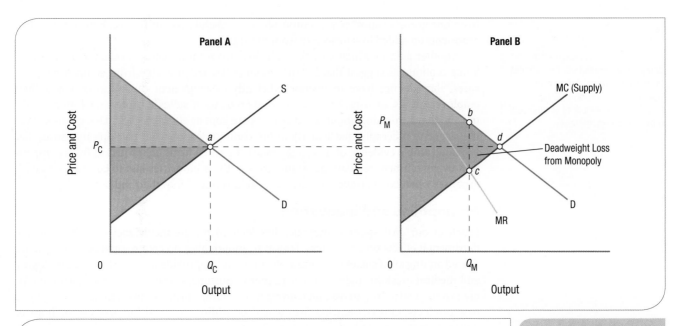

Monopoly Inefficiency

This figure shows what would happen if a competitive industry were monopolized and the new monopolist's marginal cost curve was the same as the competitive industry's supply curve. When the industry was competitive, it produced where S = D, and thus where price and output are P_C and Q_C (point *a* in panel A). Monopoly price and output, however, are P_M and Q_M (point *b* in panel B); output is lower and price is higher than the corresponding values for competitive firms. As a result, part of consumer surplus (shown in green) is transferred into producer surplus (shown in orange) in a monopoly, and in the process, inefficiency is created in the form of deadweight loss (shaded area *bcd*).

FIGURE 6

shown as the shaded area *bcd*. This area represents the deadweight loss to society from a monopoly market.

Even though deadweight loss derives partly from lost producer surplus, monopoly firms willingly forgo this portion of producer surplus in order to transfer a larger portion of consumer surplus into producer surplus (the orange rectangular area above the P_c line in Panel B). Therefore, monopoly firms use their market power to gain producer surplus at the expense of consumers and create inefficiency in the form of deadweight loss. But this is not the only source of inefficiency caused by firms with complete market power.

Rent Seeking and X-Inefficiency

Monopolies earn economic profits by producing less and charging more than competitive firms. Although these actions generate deadweight loss, monopolists are protective of the profits they earn. If barriers to entry to the market were eased, economic profit would evaporate as price falls, as it does in competitive markets. How, then, can a monopolist protect itself from potential competition? One way is to spend resources that could have been used to expand its production on efforts to protect its monopoly position.

Economists call this behavior **rent seeking**—behavior directed toward avoiding competition. Firms hire lawyers and other professionals to lobby governments, extend patents, and engage in a host of other activities intended solely to protect their monopoly position. For example, in order to pick up passengers on the street, taxis in New York City require a medallion registered with the Taxi and Limousine Commission; restricting the number of medallions drives up their price and gives medallion holders a further incentive to restrict the number of new medallions issued, by lobbying and other means. Many industries spend significant resources lobbying Congress for tariff protection to reduce foreign competition. All these activities are inefficient, in that they use resources and shift income

rent seeking Resources expended to protect a monopoly position. These are used for such activities as lobbying, extending patents, and restricting the number of licenses permitted.

from one group to another without producing a useful good or service. Rent seeking thus represents an added loss to society from monopoly.

x-inefficiency Protected from competitive pressures, monopolies do not have to act efficiently. Spending on corporate jets, travel, and other perks of business represents x-inefficiency.

Another area in which society might lose from monopolies is called **x-inefficiency.** Some economists suggest that because monopolies are protected from competitive pressures, they do not have to operate efficiently. Management can offer itself and their employees perks, such as elaborate corporate retreats or suites at professional sports stadiums, without worrying about whether costs are kept at efficient levels. Deregulation over the last several decades, particularly in the communications and trucking industries, has provided ample evidence of inefficiencies arising when firms are protected from competition by government regulations. Many firms in these industries had to cut back on lavish expenses when competitive pressures were reintroduced into their industries.

Monopolies and Innovation

Much of our analysis of monopolies has focused on the inefficiencies created and the detrimental effects on consumers. However, monopolies do create some benefits that are shared among all of society. For example, monopolies provide new products, technologies, and medical breakthroughs that benefit many consumers. The incentives to earn monopoly profits created by patents and copyrights encourage firms to invest in developing these new products. Otherwise, what firm would be willing to spend hundreds of millions of dollars inventing a product only to have it copied and sold by other firms?

Similarly, much of the entertainment industry, including music, television shows, books, and movies would not exist to such a great extent if copyrights did not provide singers, authors, and other media creators the monetary incentive to create such products for our enjoyment. Therefore, the ability to achieve market power through innovation provides an incentive to individuals and firms to invest time and money to create new products and other creative works that could generate substantial profits over time.

Benefits Versus Costs of Monopolies

Are there any other benefits to monopolies aside from innovation? The answer to this question is, "Possibly yes, though generally no." If the economies of scale associated with an industry are so large that many small competitors would face substantially higher marginal costs than a monopolist, a monopolist would produce and sell more output at a lower price than could competitive firms. This is the case of natural monopolies, and the justification for why monopolies are allowed to exist in industries such as the provision of water or electricity in many communities.

Although often criticized for inefficient operations, the U.S. Postal Service still offers the ability to send a letter to any address in the country, including far places such as Hawaii, Alaska, or Guam, for the price of a single stamp.

Imagine what might happen if a storm knocks out power to your neighborhood, and instead of one electric company restoring power to your street, each household needed to wait for its specific electricity provider to show up.

Larger firms, moreover, can allocate more resources to research and development than smaller firms, and the possibility of economic profits may be the incentive monopolists require to invest.

Still, economists tend to doubt that monopolies are beneficial enough to outweigh their disadvantages.

In actuality, pure monopolies are rare, in part because of public policy and antitrust laws—more about this later in this chapter—and in part because rapidly changing technologies limit most monopolies to short-run economic profits—witness the battle between Facebook and Google+ for domination of social media services, and Sony, Amazon.com, Apple, and several other firms to dominate the eBook market. Even so, firms seek to increase their market power by trying to become monopolies and gain the ability to influence price.

We have seen what monopolies are and how they arise. We also saw why a monopolist produces less than the socially optimal quantity at a higher than socially necessary price, and witnessed how monopoly compares unfavorably to the competitive model. Furthermore, we looked at an expensive drawback of monopolies: the amount of resources wasted in maintaining a monopolist's position. In the next section, we relax the assumption of one price, revealing what monopolies are always trying to do.

CHECKPOINT

COMPARING MONOPOLY AND COMPETITION

- Monopoly output is lower and price is higher when compared to competition, resulting in a deadweight loss.
- Monopolies are subject to rent-seeking behavior directed toward avoiding competition (lobbying and other activities to extend the monopoly).
- Because monopolies are protected from competitive pressures, they often engage in x-inefficiency behavior—extending perks to management and other inefficient activities.
- Monopolies can provide benefits in the form of economies of scale and incentives to innovate. However, these benefits are outweighed by the costs resulting from the lack of competition.

QUESTIONS: Google has over 70% of the search business on the Internet and generates a great deal of advertising revenue. Microsoft has 85% of the operating system business, 55% of the Internet browsers in use, and a growing search engine market. In late 2012, Microsoft accused Google of engaging in dishonest searches in the online shopping market (which Google denied) by listing search results based on how much merchants are willing to pay in ads. Microsoft even launched a Web site and campaign called "Scroogled" whose main purpose was to attack Google. Do these actions by Microsoft feel a little like monopolistic rent-seeking? Should the government step in, or is this just competition between giants?

Answers to the Checkpoint questions can be found at the end of this chapter.

Price Discrimination

When firms have some market power, they will try to charge different customers different prices for the same product. For example, senior citizens might pay less for a movie ticket than you do. This is called **price discrimination** and it is used to increase the firm's profits by converting part or all of consumer surplus into producer surplus. If a product costs $100 in a competitive market but you are willing to pay $150, a monopolist wants to grab as much of your $50 consumer surplus as possible.

price discrimination Charging different consumer groups different prices for the same product.

Remember that unlike monopolies, competitive firms cannot price discriminate because they get their prices from the market (they are price takers). Several conditions are required for successful price discrimination:

- Sellers must have some market power.
- Sellers must be able to separate the market into different consumer groups based on their elasticities of demand.
- Sellers must be able to prevent arbitrage; that is, it must be able to keep low-price buyers from reselling to higher-price buyers.

There are three major types of price discrimination. The first is known as **perfect (first-degree) price discrimination.** It involves charging each customer the *maximum price* each is willing to pay. Because firms cannot always determine individual willingness-to-pay, other forms of price discrimination exist. **Second-degree price discrimination** involves charging different customers different prices based on the *quantities* of the product they purchase. The final and most common form of price discrimination is **third-degree price discrimination,** which occurs when firms *charge different groups of people different prices.* This is an everyday occurrence with airline, bus, and movie theater tickets.

perfect (first-degree) price discrimination Charging each customer the maximum price each is willing to pay, thereby expropriating all consumer surplus.

second-degree price discrimination Charging different customers different prices based on the quantities of the product they purchase.

third-degree price discrimination Charging different groups of people different prices based on varying elasticities of demand.

Perfect (First-Degree) Price Discrimination

When perfect price discrimination can be employed, a firm will charge each customer the maximum price each is willing to pay. This type of price discrimination is perhaps best exemplified by an online auction, where buyers often bid up the price of a good to their maximum willingness to pay. Figure 7 on the next page portrays such a scenario for a market with constant cost conditions (assumed for simplicity) and where one unit of the good

FIGURE 7

Perfect Price Discrimination

With perfect price discrimination, firms charge each customer the maximum price each is willing to pay in order to extract all consumer surplus. Thus, every point on the demand curve in this figure represents a price. The first few customers—those who value the product most—are charged a high price. The next customers are charged a slightly lower price, and so on, until the last unit is sold for P_C (point b). As a result, a perfectly discriminating monopolist earns profits represented by the shaded area $P_C P_T b$. This is considerably more profit than the monopolist would earn by selling Q_M units at price P_M, represented by area $P_C P_M ac$.

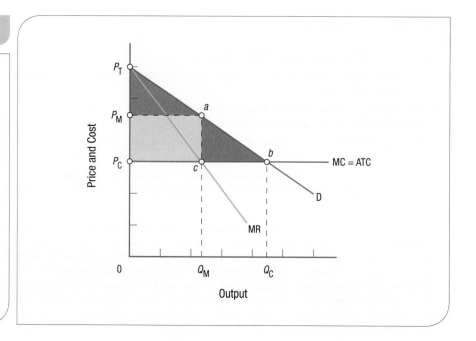

is offered to the highest bidder each day. Every point on the demand curve represents a price. The first few customers—those who value the product the most—are charged a high price. The next customers are charged slightly lower prices, the Q_Mth customer is charged P_M (point a), and so on, until the last unit is sold to the Q_Cth customer for P_C (point b). As a result, a perfectly discriminating monopolist earns profits equal to the shaded area $P_C P_T b$.

Figure 7 shows why firms would want to price discriminate. Typical monopoly profits in this case, assuming the monopolist sells Q_M units at price P_M, would be the rectangle area $P_C P_M ac$ (the lighter shaded area). This area is considerably smaller than the triangle $P_C P_T b$, earned by the perfectly price discriminating monopolist. That is why price discrimination exists—it is profitable. Note also that the *last* unit of the product sold by this monopolist is priced at P_C, the competitive price. In this limited sense, then, the monopolist who can perfectly price discriminate is as efficient as a competitive firm. Notice that perfectly price discriminating monopolists manage to expropriate the entire consumer surplus.

Second-Degree Price Discrimination

Second-degree price discrimination involves charging consumers different prices for different blocks of consumption. For example, by purchasing items in bulk (such as a pack of six tubes of toothpaste) at Costco or Sam's Club, the cost per unit is typically less than buying just one tube at the local store. Similarly, producers of electric, gas, and water utilities often incorporate block pricing. You pay one rate for the first so many kilowatt-hours of electricity and a lower rate for more, and so on.

The rationale for second-degree price discrimination is twofold. First, the cost of selling many units of a good to one customer is often less than that of selling a single unit to many customers due to overhead costs such as cashiers and accounting expenses. Second, if stores convince consumers to buy more than they had intended by offering discounts, profits can be earned as long as the discounted price exceeds marginal cost.

An illustration of second-degree price discrimination is shown in Figure 8 using the block pricing scheme example.

For the first Q_0 units of the product, consumers are charged P_0; between Q_0 and Q_1, the price falls to P_1; and after that, the price is reduced to P_C. This results in profit to the firm equal to the shaded area. The shaded profit area for the price discriminating monopolist is greater than that of the monopolist charging just one price P_M (area $P_C P_M ac$). The most common price discrimination scheme, however, is third-degree, in which *groups* of consumers are charged different prices.

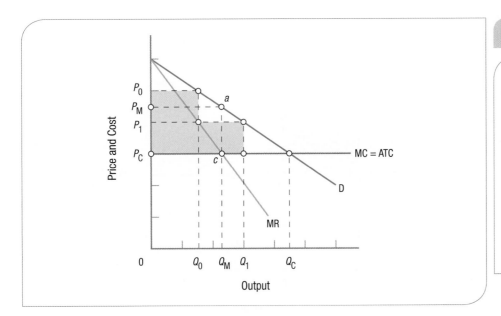

FIGURE 8

Second-Degree Price Discrimination

Second-degree price discrimination involves charging different customers different prices based on the quantities of the product they purchase. A single-price monopolist would earn economic profits equal to $P_C P_M ac$, but by charging three different prices—P_0, P_1, and P_C—profits increase, as shown by comparing the shaded area with area $P_C P_M ac$.

Third-Degree Price Discrimination

Third-degree, or imperfect, price discrimination involves charging different groups of people different prices. An obvious example would be the various fares charged for airline flights. Business travelers have much lower elasticities of demand for flights than do vacationers, therefore airlines place all sorts of restrictions on their tickets to separate people into distinct categories. Purchasing a ticket several weeks in advance, for instance—which vacationers can usually do, but businesspeople may not be able to—often results in a significantly lower fare. Arbitrage (the ability of low-price buyers to sell to higher-price buyers) is prevented, meanwhile, by rules stipulating that passengers can only travel on tickets purchased in their name. Other examples of third-degree price discrimination include different ticket prices for children, adults, and seniors at movie theaters; student discounts for many services; and even ladies' night at clubs.

Firms engage in third-degree price discrimination in order to increase their producer surplus from serving more customers. For example, if a software firm is restricted to offering their product at one price, it would choose the profit maximizing monopoly price, which means customers with lower willingness-to-pay would be priced out of a purchase. However, by offering a discounted price to these customers (and only these customers who otherwise would not have made a purchase), firms can gain more producer surplus as long as the discounted price exceeds the marginal cost of providing the extra units.

Third-degree price discrimination is illustrated in Figure 9 on the next page. The two demand curves, D_0 and D_1, represent two segments of a market with different demand elasticities. The less elastic market, D_1, is offered price P_1. This is higher than price P_0 offered to the more elastic market, D_0. Profits are maximized for both markets. For market D_0, profits are $P_C P_0 bc$, and for less elastic market D_1, they are $P_C P_1 ad$. Like the perfectly discriminating monopolist, the third-degree price-discriminating monopolist earns profits that exceed those that would come from a normal one-price policy.

We can look at price discrimination in an intuitive way by focusing on a restaurant. Most dinner customers frequent the restaurant after 6:30 P.M. However, the restaurant is still open from 4:30 to 6:30 P.M. and incurs costs (if workers start their shifts before the 6:30 rush). It is in the restaurant's interest to offer early bird specials, discounting dinners purchased before 6:30, as long as this policy attracts new customers and does not pull in too many of its later-appearing regular diners. In this way, the restaurant

Theme park pricing shows both second-degree price discrimination (the more days you buy, the lower the average price per day) and third-degree price discrimination (lower prices for guests under age 10).

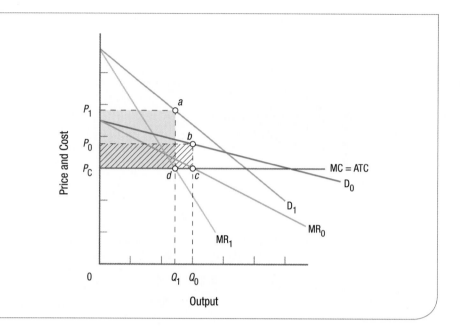

FIGURE 9

Third-Degree Price Discrimination

This figure illustrates third-degree price discrimination, in which firms segment markets based on consumers' willingness-to-pay in order to maximize producer surplus. The two demand curves, D_0 and D_1, represent two segments of a market with different demand elasticities. The less elastic market, D_1, is offered price P_1, which is higher than price P_0, offered to the more elastic market, D_0, thus maximizing the profits in both markets.

generates profits from two separate groups, while charging two separate prices. As long as the restaurant has some market power—it can offer these two prices without driving its regular customers from higher-priced meals to lower-priced meals—it makes sense for it to act this way. Therefore, we can conclude that firms with market power will always try to price discriminate.

 ISSUE

Is Flexible Ticket Pricing the New Form of Price Discrimination?

Ticketmaster has long held market power in the entertainment and sports ticket-selling industry. Although Ticketmaster faces competition from other ticket sellers, its market power stems from the exclusivity contracts it establishes with concert promoters, artists, and sports teams.

When an agreement is made with Ticketmaster, it becomes the only site through which consumers can purchase tickets other than the ticket resale market. This gives ticket sellers and the entertainers and shows they represent considerable market power to set prices.

In early 2010, concert promoter Live Nation merged with Ticketmaster, giving the new combined company (Live Nation) even more market power. This allowed the new company to implement new strategies to correct problems with their original pricing model. Specifically, Ticketmaster typically offered several ticket tiers with

different prices based on seating location. These prices, however, often are printed on the tickets and do not change.

However, setting prices too low results in a quick sellout, leading to a resale market in which tickets initially sold at one price are resold at much higher prices, with the profits going to the reseller instead of Ticketmaster. Setting prices too high, on the other hand, leaves many tickets unsold and results in many tickets being given away in radio promotions and other deals.

In 2011, Live Nation announced a new flexible pricing model (to be implemented in phases) that has been successfully used in the airline industry. With flexible pricing, concert tickets do not have a fixed price. Instead, ticket prices are set and changed based on demand—if tickets sell too fast, prices would rise; if tickets sell too slowly, pric-

es would fall. This form of price discrimination allows ticket sellers to reap more consumer surplus that otherwise might go to the resale market. This new approach to ticket sales is another example of how firms use strategies to maximize their market power.

In all three types of price discrimination, monopoly firms use their market power to increase their producer surplus. Although part of this increase in producer surplus comes from consumers in the form of higher prices, the rest comes from the reduction in deadweight loss. Unlike a single-price monopolist, efficiency is improved in multiple-price scenarios because more output is being produced, allowing more consumers to purchase the good. Still, all forms of monopoly pricing (single-price or multiple-price through price discrimination) create concerns about the welfare of consumers. Therefore, regulations and rules are sometimes used to reduce the market power firms exert. We turn to these topics in the next section.

 ## CHECKPOINT

PRICE DISCRIMINATION

- Firms with market power price discriminate to increase profits.

- To price discriminate, firms must have some market power (control over price) and must be able to separate the market into different consumer groups based on their elasticity of demand, and firms (sellers) must be able to prevent arbitrage.

- With perfect price discrimination the firm can charge each customer a different price and expropriate the entire consumer surplus for itself.

- Second-degree price discrimination involves charging customers different prices for different quantities of the product.

- Third-degree price discrimination (the most common) involves charging different groups of people different prices.

- Price discrimination may lead to higher prices for some consumers, but it also improves efficiency by allowing more consumers to purchase the good, reducing deadweight loss.

QUESTIONS: Researchers at Yale University and the University of California, Berkeley, found that minorities and women pay about $500 more on average for a car than white men when bargaining directly with car dealers. However, when minorities and women used online auto retailers such as Autobytel.com to purchase a car, the price discrimination disappeared. Is this price discrimination the same as that discussed in this section? Why or why not?

Answers to the Checkpoint questions can be found at the end of this chapter.

 ## Regulation and Antitrust

We have seen that monopolies have the ability to raise prices and restrict quantities, putting them at the other end of the spectrum from the competitive market price-taker ideal. Thus, monopolies are price makers. Also, we have just seen that firms use their market power to price discriminate, attempting to achieve as much producer surplus as they can even if it comes by way of reducing consumer surplus. In an attempt to mitigate the maximum market power of monopolies, government has used two approaches: regulation and antitrust.

Regulating the Natural Monopolist

As we saw when we discussed barriers to entry, there are some instances when natural monopolies occur. A **natural monopoly** exists when economies of scale are so large that the minimum efficient scale of operation is roughly equal to market demand. In this case, efficient production can only be accomplished if the industry lies in the hands of one firm—a monopolist. Public utilities and water departments are examples.

How can policymakers prevent natural monopolists from abusing their positions of market dominance? There are various approaches to dealing with natural monopolies: (1) They can be publicly owned, (2) they can be privately owned but subjected to price and quantity constraints, or (3) their right to operate could be auctioned to the firm agreeing to the most competitive price and quantity conditions.

natural monopoly An industry exhibiting large economies of scale such that the minimum efficient scale of operations is roughly equal to market demand.

A market representing a natural monopoly is shown in Figure 10. Notice that the average cost and marginal cost curves decline continually because of large economies of scale.

If the monopolist were a purely private firm, it would produce only output Q_M and sell this for price P_M (point *a*). Accordingly, the monopolist would earn economic or monopoly profits, and consumers would be harmed, receiving a lower output at a higher price. This is the major argument for regulation.

Marginal Cost Pricing Rule

Ideally, regulators would like to invoke the P = MC rule of competitive markets and force the firm to sell Q_C units for a price of P_C. This is the **marginal cost pricing rule** and would be the optimal resource allocation solution. Yet, because price P_C is below the average total cost of production for output Q_C, this would force the firm to sustain losses of *cd* per unit, ultimately driving it out of business. The public sector could subsidize the firm by an amount equal to area $P_C C_C dc$; this subsidy allows the firm to supply the socially optimal output at the socially optimal price, while earning a normal return. This approach has not been used often in the United States. Amtrak, with its history of heavy subsidies for maintaining rail service, may be the one major exception.

Average Cost Pricing Rule

The more common approach to regulation in the United States has been to insist on an **average cost pricing rule.** Such a rule requires that the monopolist produce and sell output where price equals average total costs. This is illustrated by point *b* in Figure 10, where the demand curve intersects the ATC curve and the firm produces output Q_R and sells it for price P_R. The result is that the firm earns a normal return. Consumers do lose something, in that they must pay a higher price for less output than they would under ideal competitive conditions. Still, the normal profits keep the firm in business, and the losses to consumers are significantly less than if the firm were left unregulated.

marginal cost pricing rule Regulators would prefer to have natural monopolists price where P = MC, but this would result in losses (long term) because ATC > MC. Thus, regulators often must use an average cost pricing rule.

average cost pricing rule Requires a regulated monopolist to produce and sell output where price equals average total cost. This permits the regulated monopolist to earn a normal return on investment over the long term and therefore remain in business.

FIGURE 10

Regulating a Natural Monopoly

A natural monopoly exists when economies of scale are so large that the minimum efficient scale of operation is roughly equal to market demand. In this case, efficient production can only be accomplished if the industry lies in the hands of one firm—a monopolist. Yet, if the monopolist is a purely private firm, it will produce only output Q_M, selling it for price P_M (point *a*). This is the principal rationale for regulating natural monopolies to produce output Q_R for a price of P_R (point *b*).

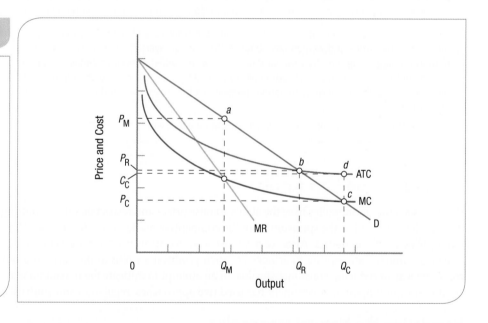

Regulation in Practice

America has a long history of public utility regulation. For most of this history, regulation has been accepted as the lesser of two evils. Monopolists have long been viewed with distrust, but regulators have just as often been portrayed as incompetent and ineffectual, if not lapdogs of the industries they regulate.[1] Although this characterization is probably unfair, a number of economists, including Nobel Prize–laureate George Stigler, viewed regulation with skepticism and proposed changes on improving the efficiency of regulation.

---

[1] See George Stigler, "The Theory of Economic Regulation," *Bell Journal of Economics*, 1971, pp. 3–21.

Regulating a large enterprise always presents immense difficulties and tradeoffs. For one thing, finding a point like *b* in Figure 10 is difficult in practice, given that estimating demand and cost curves is an inexact science, at best, and markets are always changing. In practice, regulators must often turn to *rate of return* or *price cap* regulation.

Rate of return regulation allows a firm to price its product in such a way that it can earn a normal return on capital invested. This leads to added regulations about the acceptable items that can be included in costs and capital expenditures. Can the country club memberships of top executives be counted as capital investments? Predictably, firms always want to include more expenses as legitimate business expenses, and regulators want to include fewer. Regulatory commissions and regulated firms often have large staffs to deal with such issues, and protracted court battles are not uncommon.

Alternatively, regulators can impose **price caps** on regulated firms, which place maximum limits on the prices firms can charge for products. These caps can be adjusted in response to changing cost conditions, including changes in labor costs, productivity, technology, and raw material prices. When a large part of a regulated firm's output is not self-produced but purchased on the open market, price caps can have disastrous results. This was seen in the California energy market, when wholesale prices for energy went through the roof, but price caps prevented private utilities from raising the retail price of electricity. Several firms had to file for bankruptcy.

NOBEL PRIZE
GEORGE STIGLER (1911–1991)

Few modern economists have broken ground in so many different areas as George Stigler, described by some admirers as the "ultimate empirical economist." His 1982 Nobel Prize cited seminal work in industrial structure, the functioning of markets, and the causes and effects of public regulation.

Born in 1911 in the Seattle suburb of Renton, Washington, Stigler attended graduate school at the University of Chicago with fellow students and eventual Nobel Prize winners Milton Friedman and Paul Samuelson. Stigler later became a professor at the University of Chicago where he stayed until his death in 1991.

Exploring the relationship between size and efficiency led him to the "Darwinian" conclusion that by observing competition in an industry, he could determine the most efficient sizes for firms, a method he called "the survivor technique." In the 1960s, Stigler studied the impacts of government regulation on the economy with skepticism, arguing that government interventions were often designed to optimize market conditions for producers instead of protecting the public interest. This work opened up a new field known as "regulation economics" and kindled greater interest in the relationship between law and economics.

Stigler considered his work on information theory his greatest contribution to economics. Conventional wisdom suggested that prices for perfectly competitive industries should be uniform, but in the real world, prices often varied. His research suggested that the variation could be explained by the costs of gathering and diffusing information about goods and prices. The Internet was supposed to bring a convergence of prices for nearly every product because the Internet's low information costs and competition would force firms to quickly meet the lowest seller's price. The fact that there are still widely varying prices for many products suggests that Stigler's insights are still important.

Today, the pace of technological change is so rapid that regulation has lost some of its earlier luster and is not used as often. Rather than regulate the few natural monopolies that do arise, government has sought to prevent monopolies and monopolistic practices from arising at all—what is called antitrust policy.

Antitrust Policy

Rather than regulatory tinkering, governments have tried a broader approach to deal with monopolies and their market power. The goal of **antitrust law** is to preserve competition and prevent monopolies with their maximum market power from arising in the first place.

The origin of antitrust policy came in the late 1800s, when many large trusts were established, which brought many firms under one organizational structure allowing them to act as monopolists. Massive wealth accumulations by such "robber barons" as John D. Rockefeller (Standard Oil) and Jay Gould (railroads and stock manipulation) sparked resentment and fear against trusts and the growing inequity of income and wealth. Trusts had become so powerful—and so hated—that Congress passed the first antitrust act, the Sherman Act, in 1890. Antitrust laws and policies thus had their origins in trust-busting activity. Many of these laws still are in existence today with their primary role of preventing the inefficiencies associated with monopoly behavior.

rate of return regulation Permits product pricing that allows the firm to earn a normal return on capital invested in the firm.

price caps Maximum price at which a regulated firm can sell its product. They are often flexible enough to allow for changing cost conditions.

antitrust law Laws designed to maintain competition and prevent monopolies from developing.

The Major Antitrust Laws

Several major statutes form the core of the country's antitrust laws. The most important provisions of these laws (as amended) are described in Table 1.

TABLE 1	Major Antitrust Laws

I. The Sherman Act (1890)

A. Activity in "restraint of trade" is made a felony.

B. Monopolization or attempt to monopolize is made a felony.

C. Conviction in either carries a fine of up to $10,000,000 for corporations and $350,000 for individuals, and/or a prison sentence of up to 3 years.

D. Congress purposefully left "restraint of trade" and "monopolization" undefined, thus requiring the courts to flesh them out.

II. The Clayton Act (1914)

A. Unlawful to price discriminate if such discrimination substantially lessons competition. This rule was strengthened by the Robinson-Patman Act in 1936, although today the federal government rarely enforces its provisions, viewing them as outdated.

B. Companies cannot acquire all or part of another where the effect may be to substantially lessen competition or create a monopoly. This rule was strengthened by the 1950 Celler-Kefauver Act by preventing mergers via asset acquisition and setting up elaborate premerger notification requirements for mergers exceeding a certain size.

III. The Federal Trade Commission Act (1914)

A. Unfair methods of competition and deceptive acts are made illegal.

B. Established an independent regulatory body, the Federal Trade Commission (FTC).

This Act is the centerpiece of federal consumer protection. The Supreme Court has given the FTC the power to enforce antitrust laws, except the Sherman Act.

The intensity of antitrust enforcement has varied over the past century, from an early focus on monopolies, then on mergers, and more recently on price fixing—conspiracies by firms to agree on industry prices to suppress or eliminate competition. Although price-fixing cases have been prominent, it is merger policy developed in the 1950s that has really stood the test of time. Economists and judges generally agree that the reason for antitrust enforcement is to prevent the inefficiencies associated with significant market power. Premerger notification for approval or challenge by the Department of Justice is designed to prevent mergers that have a reasonable likelihood of creating market power. This is easier said than done.

Defining the Relevant Market and Market Power

The first problem involves defining market power. What is the relevant product market? Some markets can be severely limited geographically, such as concrete, with its extremely high transport costs, and dry cleaning, limited by the unwillingness of consumers to travel far for this service. Other markets are national in scope, like airlines, breakfast cereals, and electronics. Still others extend beyond the borders of a country, with the forces of global competition increasingly reducing domestic market power.

The second problem is determining the proper measuring device of market power. As an industry moves from competition to monopoly, pricing power rises from zero to total. One of the challenges economists have faced is developing one measure that accurately reflects market power or concentration for all these market structures.

Industries that become more concentrated increase the losses to society. Therefore, any measure of concentration should accurately reflect the ability of firms to increase prices above that point which would prevail under competitive conditions.

Concentration Ratios The most widely used measure of industry concentration is the **concentration ratio.** The *n*-firm concentration ratio is the share of industry sales accounted for by the industry's *n* largest firms. Typically, four- and eight-firm concentration ratios (CR-4 and CR-8) are reported.

Although useful in giving a quick snapshot of an industry, concentration ratios express only one piece of the market power distribution picture: the market share enjoyed by the industry's four or eight largest firms. Table 2 shows the market shares of the four largest firms in two different industries. Industry 1 contains a dominant firm with 65% of the market, followed by a bunch of smaller firms. Industry 2 consists of four fairly equal-sized firms, followed by a bunch of smaller firms. In both industries, however, the four-firm concentration ratio is 85; that is, the top four firms control 85% of industry sales. But do the two industries exhibit the same level of monopoly power? Hardly! The second industry, whose top four firms are roughly equal in size, would be expected to be more competitive than the first, in which 65% of the market is controlled by one firm.

concentration ratio The share of industry shipments or sales accounted for by the top four or eight firms.

Four-firm Concentration Ratio	Industry 1	Industry 2
Firm 1's market share	65%	25%
Firm 2's market share	10%	20%
Firm 3's market share	5%	20%
Firm 4's market share	5%	20%
All other firms' market share combined	15%	15%
Four-firm concentration ratio	**85**	**85**

TABLE 2

Industry 1 is dominated by a large firm with 65% of market share, whereas Industry 2 contains four fairly equal-sized firms, with smaller firms making up the rest of both industries. The CR-4 is the same in both industries, although Industry 2 would be expected to be much more competitive.

Without more information about each industry, concentration ratios are not overly informative, except to point out extreme contrasts. If one industry's four-firm concentration ratio is 85, for instance, and another's is 15, the first industry has considerably more monopoly power than the second.

Economists and antitrust enforcers, however, need finer distinctions than concentration ratios permit. For this reason, the profession has developed the Herfindahl-Hirschman index.

Herfindahl-Hirschman Index The **Herfindahl-Hirschman index (HHI)** is the principal measure of concentration used by the Department of Justice to evaluate mergers and judge monopoly power. The HHI is defined by the equation:

$$HHI = (S_1)^2 + (S_2)^2 + (S_3)^2 + \ldots + (S_n)^2,$$

Herfindahl-Hirschman index (HHI) A way of measuring industry concentration, equal to the sum of the squares of market shares for all firms in the industry.

where $S_1, S_2, \ldots S_n$ are the percentage market shares of each firm in the industry. Thus, the HHI is the sum of the squares of each market share. In a five-firm industry, for instance, in which each firm enjoys a 20% market share, the HHI is

$$HHI = 20^2 + 20^2 + 20^2 + 20^2 + 20^2$$
$$= 400 + 400 + 400 + 400 + 400$$
$$= 2,000$$

The HHI ranges from roughly zero (a huge number of small firms) to 10,000 (a one-firm monopoly: $100^2 = 10,000$). By squaring market shares, the HHI gives greater weight to those firms with large market shares. Thus, a five-firm industry with market shares equal to 65, 15, 10, 5, and 5 would have an HHI equal to

$$HHI = 65^2 + 15^2 + 10^2 + 5^2 + 5^2$$
$$= 4{,}225 + 225 + 100 + 25 + 25$$
$$= 4{,}600$$

The HHI is consistent with our intuitive notion of market power. It seems clear that an industry with several competitors of roughly equal size will be more competitive than an industry in which one firm controls a substantial share of the market.

Applying the HHI The Hart-Scott-Rodino Act (1976) requires prenotification of large proposed mergers to the FTC and the antitrust division of the Department of Justice. Prenotification gives federal agencies a chance to review proposed mergers for anticompetitive impacts. This approach prevents some mergers from taking place that would ultimately have to be challenged by Sherman Act litigation, a far more costly alternative for the government and for the firms involved.

The Department of Justice and the FTC in 1992 issued merger guidelines based on the HHI. These guidelines classify industries as follows:

- HHI < 1,000: Industry is not concentrated.
- 1,000 < HHI < 1,800: Industry is moderately concentrated.
- HHI > 1,800: Industry is highly concentrated.

Mergers where the resulting HHI is below 1,000 will often be approved. Mergers with postmerger HHIs between 1,000 and 1,800 will be closely evaluated; they are often challenged if the proposed merger raises the HHI by 100 points or more. When the HHI for the industry exceeds 1,800, a postmerger rise in the HHI of 50 points is enough to spark a challenge.

These guidelines have worked well, giving businesses a good idea of when the government will challenge mergers. Most mergers are rapidly approved; the remainder often require only minor adjustments or more information to satisfy government agencies. In the end, only a few proposed mergers are seriously challenged.

Contestable Markets

contestable markets Markets that look monopolistic but where entry costs are so low that the sheer threat of entry keeps prices low.

Sometimes what looks like a monopolist does not act like a monopolist. Markets that are contestable fit this description. **Contestable markets** are those markets with entry costs so low that the sheer threat of entry keeps prices in contestable markets low. Potential competition constrains firm behavior. For example, Microsoft might charge more for its latest version of Windows if Linux were not nipping at its heels.

Another common example of a contestable market is the airline industry. Small regional carriers often fly unique routes from small airports to major tourist destinations such as Las Vegas and several spots in Florida. Although many of these routes are unique (in that only one airline serves the route), airlines tend to keep fares reasonable rather than exploit their market power for that route. Airlines realize that if fares are priced at the monopoly level, another airline might enter and compete. The ability to change airline service routes quickly forces airlines to keep prices at a competitive level, even if they are the only airline providing service between two cities.

The Future of Antitrust Policy

Today's economy differs from the old economy in many ways. The old economy was grounded in manufacturing and distributing physical goods such as steel, automobiles, appliances, and shoes. These old economy industries enjoyed economies of scale in production, often requiring huge capital requirements and modest rates of innovation.

Much of what new economy firms produce is intellectual property. In large measure, it is computer code of one form or another. Most of the costs to produce the programs are fixed, already sunk once the product is completed. To produce and distribute the product costs only a fraction of the product's value; if the Internet is used, distribution costs can approach zero. This means markups and profits are high, which creates a strong incentive to clone successful products. Monopolies, therefore, tend to be transitory in the new economy. The travails of Lotus 123, WordPerfect, MySpace, and Netscape all testify to the vulnerability of temporary monopolists in the media industry. All were industry leaders at one point, only to be rapidly displaced.

Antitrust laws and policy need to be adjusted to new market realities. In our global information and service economy, many of the old rules are irrelevant. One federal judge and economist, Richard Posner, argues that we should repeal all the old antitrust laws and replace them with a simple statute that prohibits "unreasonably anti-competitive practices."[2]

When a firm's market share approaches monopoly levels, turning to antitrust laws is the obvious response.

This and the last chapter looked at the polar opposites of market structures, competition and monopoly, with characteristics of each shown in Table 3. The next chapter looks at the market structures in the middle and also looks at a more modern approach to analyzing firm behavior, game theory.

Comparison Between Perfect Competition and Monopoly		TABLE 3
Perfect Competition	**Monopoly**	Perfectly competitive firms and monopoly firms differ in the number of firms in the industry, the ability to set prices, the barriers to enter the industry, the ability to earn long-run economic profits, and the likelihood of achieving a socially efficient output.
Many firms	One firm	
Price-taking	Price-making	
No barriers to entry	Significant barriers to entry	
Marginal revenue = Price	Marginal revenue < Price	
Zero economic profit in the long run	Potential economic profits in the long run	
No deadweight loss (efficiency)	Deadweight loss (inefficiency)	

⬤ CHECKPOINT

REGULATION AND ANTITRUST

- Regulating monopolies may involve a marginal cost pricing rule (have the monopolist set price equal to marginal cost) or an average cost pricing rule (have the monopolist set price equal to average total cost).

- In practice, regulation often involves setting an acceptable rate of return on capital or setting price caps on charges.

- The Sherman Act (1890) prohibited monopolization and attempts to monopolize.

- The Clayton Act (1914) prohibited price discrimination that lessened competition.

- The Federal Trade Commission Act (1914) prohibited unfair or deceptive business practices and established the Federal Trade Commission.

- Concentration ratios measure market concentration by looking at the share of industry sales accounted for by the top *n* firms.

- The Herfindahl-Hirschman index (HHI) measures concentration by computing the sum of the squares of market shares for all firms in the industry.

- The Department of Justice uses the HHI to set premerger guidelines.

- Contestable markets are markets with entry costs so low that the potential threat of entry keeps prices low.

QUESTION: In September 2011, AT&T attempted to buy one of its major competitors, T-Mobile, in a $39 billion acquisition that the U.S. Department of Justice eventually blocked. Explain why the Department of Justice would block such a merger from taking place. Assume that the wireless communications industry contains four equal-sized firms (AT&T, Verizon, Sprint, and T-Mobile); how would the HHI be used to justify the government's decision?

Answers to the Checkpoint question can be found at the end of this chapter.

---

[2] Richard A. Posner, *Antitrust Law*, 2nd ed. (Chicago: University of Chicago Press), 2001, p. 260.

chapter summary

Section 1: **Monopoly Markets**

A **monopoly** is a one-firm industry with no close product substitutes and with substantial barriers to entry.

Types of Barriers to Entry

Control over a significant factor of production: occurs when a company owns a significant share of its key ingredient or input in production

Economies of scale: occurs when firms must incur large fixed costs before production can begin

Government protection: patents and copyrights that provide an exclusive right to sell a product

5 Steps to Maximizing Profits for a Monopolist:

1. Find MR = MC
2. Find optimal quantity where MR = MC
3. Find optimal price where quantity meets the demand curve
4. Find average total cost at the optimal Q
5. Find the profit = $Q \times (P - ATC)$

Output

The firm's demand and supply curve is the same as the industry's demand and supply curve.

Marginal revenue is less than price for a monopoly: If a firm can sell 4 units at $10 but must drop price to $9 to sell 5 units, marginal revenue equals $5 because the seller loses a dollar from each of the previous 4 units (red area) but gains $9 from the sale (green area).

Output

Just because a monopolist has no competitors doesn't mean it always earns profits. Think of late-night infomercials selling, at times, bizarre products. Some are successful but others fail.

Eric Chiang

Mop slippers were a unique invention that really never took off. Not all monopolies are profitable.

Section 2: **Comparing Monopoly and Competition**

In a monopoly market, output is lower and price is higher compared to a competitive market due to the lack of competitors to the monopoly firm.

A firm with market power is more likely to engage in **rent-seeking** behavior (spending resources to protect market power) and **x-inefficiency** (wasting resources because competition doesn't exist).

Joe Robbins/Getty Images

Without competition from another football league, the NFL likely produces fewer games and charges higher prices than it would in a competitive market.

Section 3: **Price Discrimination**

Price discrimination is charging different prices for the same product in the attempt to grab more surplus from consumers.

Conditions for Price Discrimination to Work Best

1. Firm must have market power (i.e., cannot be a price taker).
2. Market can be segmented into different consumer groups.
3. Seller must be able to prevent arbitrage.

Three Forms of Price Discrimination

Perfect (first-degree) price discrimination: Seller charges exactly what consumers are willing to pay, and extracts all consumer surplus.

Second-degree price discrimination: Prices differ based on the quantity being purchased.

Third-degree price discrimination: Prices differ based on consumer characteristics, such as age (e.g., kids and senior discounts), status (e.g., student or military discounts), or flexibility (e.g., airline pricing).

Shopping at Costco might save you money, but you often need to buy in bulk, an example of second-degree price discrimination.

Section 4: **Regulation and Antitrust**

A **natural monopoly** has large economies of scale such that one firm is more efficient than multiple firms. The profit maximizing point occurs where MC (and ATC) is falling. To prevent exploitation of market power, natural monopolies are often regulated.

Ways to Measure Market Power

Concentration ratios: adding up the market shares of the 4 or 8 largest firms in an industry, and ranges from 0 to 100.

HHI index: sum of the square of market shares of all firms in an industry, and ranges from 0 (perfect competition) to 10,000 (monopoly). HHI values over 1,800 are concentrated industries where mergers are likely to be challenged.

Besides economies of scale, most people prefer just one electric company as a monopolist, rather than multiple electric companies each with its own power lines.

Antitrust laws are designed to promote competition and prevent monopolies from developing.

Two Major Antitrust Laws

Sherman Act of 1890: outlawed trusts and cartels—restraint of trade and monopolization.

Clayton Act of 1914: outlawed some forms of price discrimination and mergers that would significantly reduce competition.

A **contestable market** looks like a monopoly but does not act like one because the threat of entry keeps prices low. Low-fare airlines that serve unique routes still offer low prices if they fear new entrants.

monopoly, p. 218
market power, p. 218
barriers to entry, p. 218
economies of scale, p. 218
rent seeking, p. 225
x-inefficiency, p. 226
price discrimination, p. 227
perfect (first-degree) price
  discrimination, p. 227

second-degree price discrimination,
  p. 227
third-degree price discrimination,
  p. 227
natural monopoly, p. 231
marginal cost pricing rule, p. 232
average cost pricing rule, p. 232
rate of return regulation, p. 233
price caps, p. 233

antitrust law, p. 233
concentration ratio, p. 235
Herfindahl-Hirschman index (HHI),
  p. 235
contestable markets, p. 236

QUESTIONS AND PROBLEMS

Check Your Understanding

1. Are McDonald's and Starbucks monopolies? Why or why not?

2. Explain why MR < P for the monopolist, but MR = P for perfectly competitive firms.

3. What do economists mean when they call monopolies inefficient? What is the dead-weight loss of monopoly?

4. Why are monopoly firms able to earn long-run economic profits while perfectly competitive firms cannot?

5. Under what market conditions would a firm find it easier to engage in price discrimination?

6. What is a natural monopoly and why is such a monopoly often regulated by government?

Apply the Concepts

7. How important is the existence of a significant barrier to entry to maintaining a monopoly? What would be the result if a monopoly market could easily be entered? Why might a monopoly in a high-tech field such as computers, the Internet, and consumer electronics be rather short-lived?

8. My dentist recently recommended that I have a tooth replaced with a titanium pin inserted in my jaw and capped with a crown. I went to an oral surgeon to have the tooth removed and the pin inserted. The bill for the procedure was $300 to remove the tooth and $1,500 to insert the titanium pin. Removing the tooth and inserting the pin each took roughly the same amount of time. Because the cost of the pin is negligible and both parts of the procedure took the same amount of time, why would the oral surgeon charge 5 times as much to set the pin as to pull the tooth? (Hint: Market power and level of competition underlies the answer.)

9. The taxi industry in many large cities spends millions of dollars lobbying local policymakers not to build rail links connecting airports to the city center, even if such mass transportation infrastructure would benefit many consumers traveling to and from the airport. Explain why such actions by the taxi industry are taken. Then, explain why taxi owners in cities without airport rail links are less likely to invest in fuel-efficient cars and in-taxi technologies such as televisions and Internet access.

10. If the Miami Heat can sell five courtside seats for $2,000 each or six courtside seats if it reduces the price to $1,600 each, what is the marginal revenue of the sixth seat? Should the owner make this sixth seat available? If all six seats can be sold for $1,800 each, would this make the sixth seat worth selling? (Hint: What costs are involved with selling the sixth seat?)

11. Sally owns the only cake shop in town (she is a monopolist). At a quantity of five, the marginal cost of producing one more cake is $12, while the marginal revenue from selling one more cake is $10. In order for Sally to maximize profits, should she increase or decrease output? Should she increase or decrease prices? Explain.

12. Airlines that compete against one another have at times merged with each other to create a larger airline. What are some factors that would determine whether such a merger would constitute an uncompetitive environment according to antitrust law?

In the News

13. In July 2012, a court found several electronics manufacturers guilty of price-fixing LCD television and computer panels in one of the largest price-fixing cases in history ("What the $1.1 Billion LCD Price-Fixing Settlement Means for You," *CNN Money*, July 16, 2012). The alleged actions involved many major manufacturers, including Toshiba, Samsung, and Sharp. The total settlement that manufacturers paid to compensate victims of the scheme came to an astounding $1.12 billion. What potential benefits do companies gain by working together to fix prices on a good? Why do companies choose to engage in such unlawful behavior despite the risk of being caught and having to pay significant fines?

14. Being number one in any business attracts a lot of attention. As *The Economist* (December 17, 2005) noted,

> As soon as a firm climbs above the sharp elbows of its rivals, it starts getting pelted with the eggs of anti-business activities. People who hate big business aim high. So while big, bad Wal-Mart is pilloried, Target has in the past couple of years blithely cut the benefits of its non-union workers. And when was the last time you saw an anti-globalization mob destroy a Burger King outlet?

Describe some of the benefits of being number two in a large industry. In terms of total revenues (sales), name the number one and two firms in the following industries: major auto manufacturers, major drug manufacturers, and major integrated oil and gas.

Solving Problems

15. Using the figure for a monopoly firm below, answer the following questions.

    a. What will be the monopoly price, output, and profit for this firm?

    b. If this monopolist could perfectly price discriminate, what would profit equal?

    c. If this industry were competitive, what would be the price, output, and profit?

    d. How large (in dollars) is the deadweight loss from this monopolist?

16. Assume the following table represents the sales figures for the eight largest firms in the auto industry in the United States:

Company	Sales (billions of dollars)
General Motors	2.063
Toyota	1.77
Ford	1.616
Honda	1.151
Chrysler	0.931
Nissan	0.77
Hyundai	0.435
Mazda	0.208
Total	**8.944**

a. Compute the four-firm concentration ratio for the industry.

b. Compute the HHI for the industry (assuming the industry contains just these eight firms).

c. Assuming the industry is represented by these eight firms, if Toyota and Ford wanted to merge, and you were the head of the Department of Justice, would you permit the merger? Why or why not? (Hint: Calculate the new values from parts a and b assuming the merger takes place.) How about if Hyundai and Mazda wanted to merge?

USING THE NUMBERS

17. According to By the Numbers, assuming that the number of viewers for each of the five games in the 2012 NBA Finals were the same, approximately how many more people watched the 2012 Super Bowl than the final game of the 2012 NBA Finals?

18. According to By the Numbers, the annual growth in demand for electricity has fallen over the past half-century but remained positive nearly every year. In what years did actual electricity demand fall (negative growth in demand)?

ANSWERS TO QUESTIONS IN CHECKPOINTS

Checkpoint: Monopoly Markets

By performing in a smaller venue (such as a performing arts hall with 1,500 seats instead of an arena with 10,000 or more seats), the artist can target the core fans willing to pay high prices for tickets. With market power in pricing (there is only one Dolly Parton), nearly all seats would be sold at the high price, as opposed to having to offer much lower prices to fill a larger arena. If the costs of performing at a larger arena are significant, artists can do better by producing less (selling fewer tickets), charging a much higher price, and reducing the costs of putting on the concert.

Checkpoint: Comparing Monopoly and Competition

Although Microsoft's actions in this case do not involve lobbying for special privileges (the traditional definition of rent seeking), its tactics nonetheless resemble rent seeking in that costly (even wasteful) actions are being used to protect one's market share. Microsoft has a huge capital base and cash flow, and could compete with Google in the search market without the need to make accusations regarding its business practices.

Checkpoint: Price Discrimination

No, this is not the same type of price discrimination discussed in this section. This type of discrimination occurs because of information problems, gender discrimination, racism, or other factors. The authors conclude that a large part of the price differences between buying online and bargaining in the showroom comes from the fact that online consumers have better information. Price discrimination in this section of the chapter is based on consumers with different elasticities of demand, not information problems or racism. Examples include student, senior, and adult pricing in movie theaters.

Checkpoint: Regulation and Antitrust

The government aims to prevent powerful monopolies, which can restrict competition and lead to fewer choices and higher prices, from forming. The Sherman Antitrust Act of 1890 and the Clayton Act of 1914 provide the legal basis for such action. The government uses concentration ratios or the HHI as a gauge to determine whether a pending merger would harm competition. If each of four firms controls 25% of the market, the HHI is 2,500, already a very concentrated industry. By allowing AT&T and T-Mobile to merge, the HHI would increase from 2,500 to 3,750, making the industry even more concentrated.

Monopolistic Competition, Oligopoly, and Game Theory

10

After studying this chapter you should be able to:

- Describe product differentiation and its impact on the firm's demand curve, and how it determines the market power that a monopolistically competitive firm can exercise.

- Compare pricing and output decisions for monopolistically competitive firms in the short run and long run, and explain why firms earn only normal profits in the long run.

- Compare the efficiency of monopolistic competition to perfect competition.

- Describe cartels and the reasons for their instability.

- Describe the kinked demand curve model and why prices can be relatively stable in oligopoly industries.

- Describe the benefits of using game theory to understand oligopoly and strategic interdependence.

- Describe the basic components of a game and explain the difference between simultaneous-move and sequential-move games.

- Solve for Nash equilibria using a best-response analysis and understand their importance to economists.

- Recognize why Prisoner's Dilemma outcomes occur and provide real-life examples of such situations.

- Explain how firms can overcome the Prisoner's Dilemma using cooperative strategies and repeated actions.

A scientific calculator in the early 1970s was an expensive investment, about $400 at the time, which is over $2,000 in today's dollars.

Home computing made its debut in the early 1980s. At that time, a basic computer with a single-color monitor and disk drive (not for DVDs, but rather for 5¼-inch floppy disks—do you know what those are?) with less computing power than a basic cell phone today cost several thousand dollars. What changed over the past three decades? A combination of technology and innovation, driven by competition, spurred better products that could be produced at lower costs.

The previous two chapters studied perfect competition and monopoly, which are at the opposing extremes of market structures we typically see. Perfect competition assumes a homogeneous (identical) good, while a monopoly assumes a unique good produced by just one firm. In reality, over 90% of the goods and services we consume do not fall into either category. Most of the goods and services we consume are competitive in nature but are also differentiated (or branded) in some way.

Suppose you want a quick burger for lunch. Your choices include McDonald's, Wendy's, Burger King, Five Guys, and many other burger joints located in your town. The market for burgers is clearly not a monopoly. Yet, given the variety of burgers to choose from, it's not pure competition either, unless you think that all burgers are the same—but most people do not. This chapter looks at two market structures, monopolistic competition and oligopoly, in which firms face intense competition for market share. Important differences exist between these markets in terms of the number of firms and the types of pricing strategies used. But in both market structures, pressures to remain competitive and to gain market share are important factors in a firm's success.

These pressures limit the market power that can be exercised by monopolistically competitive and oligopolistic firms. We saw in the previous chapter that monopolies have the most market power, which is the ability to set price (and get away with it). We contrasted this with perfectly competitive firms, which are price takers: They have no ability to set price. In this chapter, we will see that monopolistically competitive firms have a very limited amount of market power. Oligopolies have more market power, but less than monopolies.

While market power is a downside of monopolistic competition and oligopoly, competitive pressures on them can result in benefits to all. Firms are constantly looking for ways to make their products better (to increase their value) or less expensive

BY THE NUMBERS

Product Differentiation and Market Share

For nearly all goods and services we buy, we are faced with numerous choices: brands, features, quality, style, and more. Product differentiation is a signature characteristic of monopolistically competitive markets, and to a lesser extent oligopoly markets.

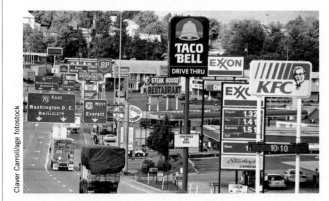

The largest fast-food chains in the United States (numbers of stores as of May 2012).

The wireless communications market is an oligopoly dominated by four large firms, controlling 93% of total market share.

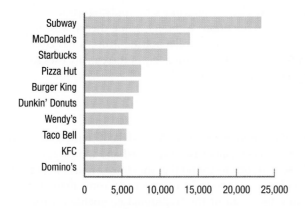

Subway
McDonald's
Starbucks
Pizza Hut
Burger King
Dunkin' Donuts
Wendy's
Taco Bell
KFC
Domino's

0   5,000   10,000   15,000   20,000   25,000

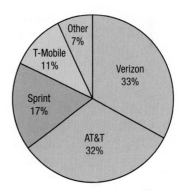

Other 7%
T-Mobile 11%
Verizon 33%
Sprint 17%
AT&T 32%

655
Total marathons in the United States in 2012 (differentiated by location, size, elevation change, and scenery).

1,500+
Total number of shoe models produced by Nike Corporation since 1972.

Colleges and universities are differentiated by size, location, athletic prowess, and academic reputation.

Largest Universities in the United States
(on a single campus in the Fall of 2012)
Arizona State University; Tempe, AZ: 60,169 students
University of Central Florida; Orlando, FL: 59,767
The Ohio State University; Columbus, OH: 56,387

Smallest Colleges in the United States
Alaska Bible College; Glennalen, AK: 38
Shimer College; Chicago, IL: 81
Sterling College; Craftsbury Common, VT: 105

to produce. By doing so, this has led to a number of important changes in the global competitive market:

1. Increase in technological development
2. Increase in variety of goods and services
3. Reduction in the price of inputs and resources (with economies of scale or offshoring of production)
4. Reduction in transportation costs
5. Reduction in trade barriers

Recall from Chapter 3 that when supply increases (shifts to the right), the market price falls and the market quantity rises. For each of the factors listed above, a corresponding increase in supply results, helping to explain why last year's computers and smartphones cost so much less than today's—even if the suppliers of computers and smartphones are oligopolies with some degree of market power.

The key to understanding monopolistic competition is product differentiation, as we saw in the burger example, and the key to understanding oligopolies is interdependence. By interdependence, economists mean that pricing and other decisions have to be made by taking into consideration what other firms might do. If Delta Airlines raises its prices, will United and American follow suit, or will they freeze their prices in the hope of luring Delta customers to their airlines?

To best explain interdependence, the chapter concludes by studying game theory, a modern way to examine strategy and competition. Although game theory was initially developed to analyze the behavior of interdependent oligopolistic firms, it has countless uses and applications in our daily lives. We will touch on a few of these many uses so that you can see the richness of taking a game theory approach.

➔ Monopolistic Competition

Until the 1920s, competition and monopoly were the only models of market structure that economists had in their toolbox. As consumerism expanded and more varieties of goods and services became available, economists found that these two models were inadequate to explain the vast markets for many goods. In other words, some markets were considered imperfect, or not fitting the mold of the traditional competitive structure. This led to the study of imperfect markets, which included monopolistic competition and oligopoly.

monopolistic competition A market structure with a large number of firms producing differentiated products. This differentiation is either real or imagined by consumers and involves innovations, advertising, location, or other ways of making one firm's product different from that of its competitors.

Monopolistic competition is nearer to the competitive end of the spectrum and is defined by the following:

- A large number of small firms. Similar to perfect competition, each firm has a very small share of the overall market. They and their competitors cannot appreciably affect the market and, therefore, mostly ignore the reactions of their rivals.

- Entry and exit are easy.

- Unlike perfect competition, products are different. Each firm produces a product that is different from its competitors or is perceived to be different by consumers. What distinguishes monopolistic competition from perfectly competitive markets is product differentiation.

Product Differentiation and the Firm's Demand Curve

Most firms sell products that are in some way differentiated from their competitors. For example, this differentiation can take the form of a superior location. Your local dry cleaner, restaurant, grocery, and gas station can have slightly higher prices, but you will not abandon them altogether. Other companies have branded products that give them some ability to increase price without losing all of their customers, as would happen under perfect competition.

FIGURE 1

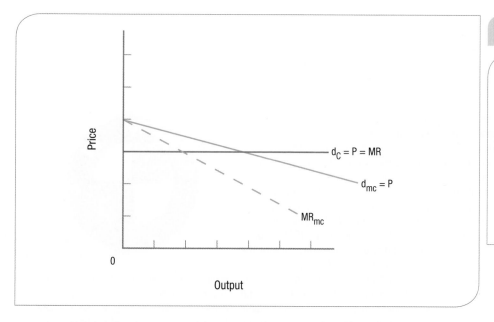

Product Differentiation and Demand

Product differentiation gives the firm some market power to raise prices. Demand curve d_{mc} is the demand curve for a monopolistically competitive firm with modest price-making ability. Marginal revenue curve MR_{mc} also slopes downward, reflecting the weak negative slope of the demand curve.

Product differentiation gives the firm some (however modest) control over prices (market power). This is illustrated in Figure 1. Demand curve d_c is the competitive demand curve, and d_{mc} is the demand faced by a monopolistic competitor. This is similar to the monopolist's demand, but the demand curve is considerably more elastic. Because a monopolistic competitor is small relative to the market, there are still a lot of substitutes. Thus, any increase in price is accompanied by a substantial decrease in output demanded. But unlike the perfectly competitive firm that faces a horizontal demand curve with no power to raise price, a monopolistically competitive firm has some market power with its not quite horizontal demand curve.

Like a monopolist, the monopolistically competitive firm faces a downward sloping marginal revenue curve, shown in Figure 1 as MR_{mc}.

Product differentiation can be the result of a superior product, a better location, superior service, clever packaging, or advertising. All of these factors are intended to increase demand or reduce the elasticity of demand and generate loyalty to the product or service. Therefore, the demand curve for monopolistically competitive firms can vary. Although demand curves tend to be elastic (flat), firms that are able to differentiate their products the most can achieve greater market power, which makes their demand curves steeper, allowing them to charge higher prices.

product differentiation One firm's product is distinguished from another's through advertising, innovation, location, and so on.

The Role of Advertising

An important way to differentiate products is through advertising. Economists generally classify advertising in two ways: informational and persuasive. The informational aspects of advertising let consumers know about products and reduce search costs. Advertising is a relatively inexpensive way to let customers know about the quality and price of a company's products. It can also enhance competition by making consumers aware of substitute or competitive products. Advertising also has the potential to reduce average costs by increasing sales, bringing about economies of scale.

But advertising does have a negative side as well. Because so much of advertising is persuasive (ads containing little informational content but designed to shift buyers among competitors of similar products), the result is that the cost of advertising drives up the price of many products. With all the advertising we see, a significant portion probably cancels each other out.

Advertising is another area in which technology has transformed the medium: Digital video recorders permit ad-skipping and have significantly reduced the impact of TV ads. A lot of advertising dollars are shifting away from conventional media (newspapers, magazines, and television) and moving to the Internet, where consumers can be targeted more inexpensively and efficiently.

Mikael Damkier/Dreamstime.com

Product differentiation counts. Although hundreds of brands of blue jeans compete in the same general market, product differentiation in style and comfort allows some brands to achieve substantial market power, resulting in higher prices.

ISSUE

Do Brands Really Represent Pricing Power?

What is a brand? All of us know brands through their names and logos. Nike has the swoosh, Intel has a logo and the four-note jingle that sounds whenever its processors are advertised, Coca-Cola has a distinctive way of spelling its name. Names and logos are communication devices, but brands are more than this. They are a promise of performance. A branded product or service raises expectations in a consumer's mind. If these expectations are met, consumers pay a price premium. If expectations are not met, the value of the brand falls as consumers seek alternatives.

Brand names start with the company that makes the product or provides the service. In the past, this meant that brand names came from a limited number of sources. Some companies were named after their founders, such as Walt Disney; some companies were named after what they supplied, such as IBM (International Business Machines); and some have also been named by their main product, such as the Coca-Cola Company. Sometimes the company name has a tenuous link with the product but is strong nevertheless, such as the Starbucks name for coffee products: Master Starbuck was first mate to Captain Ahab in *Moby-Dick* and

did drink coffee in the book, but who remembers that?

Whatever their origins, these brands have recognizable brand names, and they command price premiums. According to the annual BrandZ study by Millward Brown, Apple was the most valuable brand in 2012, valued at nearly $182 billion, followed by IBM, Google, McDonald's, and Microsoft. Nine of the top ten brands were American, with the only non-American brand being China Mobile, coming in at number ten and worth $47 billion. Brands this valuable must convey some considerable pricing power, or what we called market power in the previous chapter. Market power is what companies want.

In the auto industry, Toyota was knocked out of its position as the highest valued brand by BMW, whose brand is worth $25 billion. This was not the result of a lack of an efficient production system by Toyota, but rather a case of bad luck in recent years. First, in 2010, Toyota recalled over 7 million cars due to an accelerator issue that ultimately was determined to have been caused by driver error. Then, in 2011, an earthquake and tsunami in Japan caused severe supply disruptions to car manufacturers, which caused further deterioration of Toyota's

Peter Probst/Alamy

reputation. Despite these setbacks, Toyota maintained its concentration on consistent high quality, a commitment to customer service, and continuous improvement of the product line.

The Toyota brand has cachet: At the California plant that until 2009 Toyota shared with General Motors, *identical* cars came off the production line. Some were branded as GM cars, others Toyotas. When the cars were traded in, the Toyotas had a much higher trade-in value. The Toyota brand conveys quality, which gives Toyota its pricing power. As Toyota rebuilds its reputation from the recent setbacks, it may potentially re-emerge as the top auto brand.

Sources: BrandZ Top 100 Most Valuable Global Brands 2012, Millward Brown, WPP Companies.

All of these ways to differentiate their products give monopolistically competitive firms some control over price. This market power means that their profit maximizing decisions will be a little different from those of perfectly competitive firms.

Price and Output Under Monopolistic Competition

Profit maximization in the short run for the monopolistically competitive firm is a lot like that for a monopolist, but given the firm's size, profit will tend to be less. Short-run profit maximizing behavior is shown in Figure 2. The firm maximizes profit where MR = MC (point c) by selling output q_0 for a price of P_0. Total profits are the shaded area C_0P_0ab. All of this should look very familiar from the last chapter (review the five-step approach to maximizing profit). The difference is that the monopolistically competitive demand curve is quite elastic, and economic profits are diminished. The level of profits is dependent on the strength of demand, but in any event will be considerably lower than that of a monopolist.

This does not mean that profits are trivial. Many huge global firms sell their products in even larger global markets, and their profits are significant. They are large firms, but do not

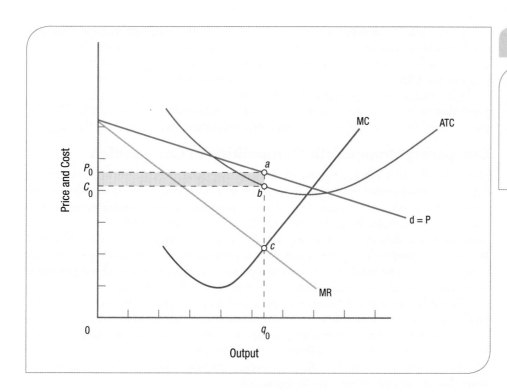

FIGURE 2

Short-Run Equilibrium for Monopolistic Competition

This monopolistically competitive firm will maximize profits in the short run by producing where MR = MC (point *c*). Profits are equal to the shaded area.

have significant market power. Many companies—such as Armani, Nike, and Sony—are all quite large but relative to their markets face daunting competition.

If firms in the industry are earning economic profits like those of the firm shown in Figure 2, new firms will want to enter. Since there are no restrictions on entry or exit, new firms will enter, soaking up some industry demand and reducing the demand to each firm in the market. Demand will continue to decline as long as economic profits exist. At equilibrium in the long run, the typical firm in the industry will look like the one shown in Figure 3.

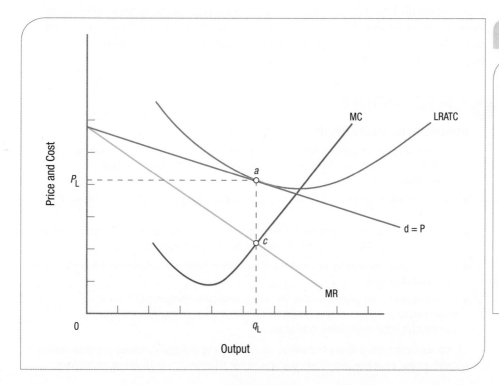

FIGURE 3

Long-Run Equilibrium for Monopolistic Competition

In the long run, easy entry and exit will adjust the demand for each firm so that the demand curve will be tangent (at point *a* in this case) to the long-run average total cost curve. This is long-run equilibrium because existing firms are earning normal profits and there is no incentive for further entry or exit. Compared to perfect competition, this long-run output does not minimize LRATC, which means prices are higher in a monopolistically competitive industry.

Notice that the demand curve is just tangent to the long-run average total cost (LRATC) curve, resulting in the firm earning normal profits in the long run. The firm produces and sells q_L output at a price of P_L (point a). Note that price P_L is not at the minimum point of the LRATC, which shows that prices in monopolistically competitive markets are higher than prices in perfectly competitive markets. Once the typical firm reaches this point, there is no longer any incentive for other firms to enter the industry. Like perfectly competitive firms, monopolistically competitive firms earn normal profits in the long run.

Comparing Monopolistic Competition to Competition

How does allocative efficiency compare for the two market structures? Because firms in both earn normal profits, you might think that both market structures are equally efficient. Unfortunately, this is not the case. Differentiated products create minimarkets within each industry. For example, Wrangler and True Religion are both brands of blue jeans, but each caters to a different set of customers, allowing True Religion to charge more than Wrangler. By differentiating products, economies of scale for monopolistically competitive firms are likely to be smaller compared to a perfectly competitive firm whose product is essentially identical, resulting in slightly higher prices and lower output.

These relatively small differences in price and output represent the costs we pay for product differentiation and innovation. To the extent that these differences are real, the costs are justified. When advertising provides accurate information that helps us select products, or if the products are sufficiently distinct that they provide real choices, then the additional costs can be worth it. Plus, competitive pressures will keep prices significantly lower than if a monopoly emerges in the market.

Firms differentiate their products through style and features that matter. Coca-Cola offers Cherry, Vanilla, and Black Cherry Vanilla Coke, as well as diet versions. Watches offer everything from the time and date to temperature, stopwatch capabilities, Global Positioning System (GPS) capability, altitude, and, most recently, Internet access. Product differentiation is important and for most of us valuable, but not free.

From this discussion, you might get some sense of the pressures firms face to differentiate their products. The more they can move away from the competitive model, the better chance they have of using their market power to make more profit. But because market power evaporates over the long run for monopolistically competitive firms, these firms have to try to sustain the value in the differentiated product. This is hard to do. The price premium charged by Hollister will not be paid when Hollister becomes less fashionable, or more like everyone else. Yet, it is in the firm's interest to product differentiate as long as it can. When you see firms trying to differentiate their products, ask yourself if the products really are so different after all.

 CHECKPOINT

MONOPOLISTIC COMPETITION

- Monopolistically competitive firms look like perfectly competitive firms (large number of small firms in a market in which entry and exit is unrestricted) but have differentiated products.

- Monopolistically competitive firms have downward-sloping demand curves and elastic demands.

- Short-run equilibrium output for the monopolistic competitor (like the monopolist) is at an output where MR = MC, and can result in positive or negative profits.

- In the long run, easy entry and exit result in monopolistically competitive firms earning only normal profits.

- Output is lower and price is higher for monopolistically competitive firms when compared to price and output for perfectly competitive firms. Monopolistically competitive firms have some market power.

QUESTION: At Disney World in Florida, you can stay at the Disney Grand Floridian Resort for $350/night or at the Disney All-Star Resort for $125/night. Both hotels are located within the park boundaries and are owned by Disney. How does product differentiation explain the significant price difference? Search and browse the hotels' Web sites to provide examples of product differentiation between the hotels.

Answers to the Checkpoint question can be found at the end of this chapter.

Oligopoly

Oligopoly markets are those in which a large market share is controlled by just a few firms. What constitutes a few firms controlling a large market share is not rigidly defined. Further, these firms can sell either a homogeneous product (e.g., gasoline, sugar) or a differentiated product (e.g., automobiles, pharmaceuticals).

Industries can be composed of a dominant firm with a few smaller firms making up the rest of the industry (e.g., computer operating systems), or the industry can be composed of a few similarly sized firms (e.g., automobiles, tobacco). The point of this discussion is that oligopoly models are numerous and varied, and we will explore only a few. Oligopoly models do, however, have several common characteristics.

Defining Oligopoly

All oligopoly models share several common assumptions:

- There are only a few large firms in the industry.
- Each firm recognizes that it must take into account the behavior of its competitors when it makes decisions. Economists refer to this as **mutual interdependence.**
- There are significant barriers to entry into the market.

Because there are only a few firms, each firm possesses substantial market power. However, because the products sold by oligopolists are similar to each other, the actions of one will affect the ability of the others to sell or price their output successfully. If one firm changes the specifications of its product or increases its advertising budget, this will have an impact on its rivals, and they can be expected to respond in kind. Thus, one firm cannot forecast its change in sales for a new promotion without first making some assumption about the reaction of its rivals.

In an industry composed of just a few firms, entry scale is often huge. Plus, with just a few firms, typically brand preferences are quite strong on the part of consumers, and a new firm may need a substantial marketing program just to get a foot in the door. For example, the investment in a plant for a new automaker is huge, and the marketing effort also must be large to get people to even consider a new auto brand.

Cartels: Joint Profit Maximization and the Instability of Oligopolies

Cartels are theft—usually by well-dressed thieves.

GRAEME SAMUEL, HEAD OF AUSTRALIA'S ANTITRUST OFFICE

The first oligopoly model we examine is *collusive* joint profit maximization, or a **cartel** model. Here we assume that a few firms collude (combine secretly) to operate like a monopoly, using maximum market power to set the monopoly price and output and share the monopoly profits. Cartels are illegal in the United States and in the European Union, although international laws do not ban them.

The most famous cartel operating today is OPEC, the Organization of Petroleum Exporting Countries. OPEC countries meet to establish an output level that each individual member can produce, thus pushing up prices and carving up shares of the profits. OPEC, formed principally of Middle Eastern countries in the early 1960s, really didn't become effective until 1973 when member countries took greater control of their domestic oil industries. Today, however, competition from non-OPEC countries in Africa, Northern Europe, and Canada is slowly reducing the power of OPEC.

oligopoly A market with just a few firms dominating the industry, where (1) each firm recognizes that it must consider its competitors' reactions when making its own decisions (mutual interdependence), and (2) there are significant barriers to entry into the market.

mutual interdependence When only a few firms constitute an industry, each firm must consider the reactions of its competitors to its decisions.

cartel An agreement between firms (or countries) in an industry to formally collude on price and output, then agree on the distribution of production.

FIGURE 4

Cartels and the Incentive to Cheat

A cartel consisting of five firms collectively agrees to restrict total output to the monopoly output of 100 units and charges $10 per unit. If one firm chooses to cheat by increasing its output by an additional 20 units, total output increases to 120 units and price falls to $8. This results in a loss of revenue of $200, which is shared equally among the five cartel members ($40 loss per member, equal to one share of the yellow area). However, the cheating member gains $160 from the additional 20 units sold at $8 each (green area). The marginal revenue for the cheating member is therefore $160 − $40 = $120.

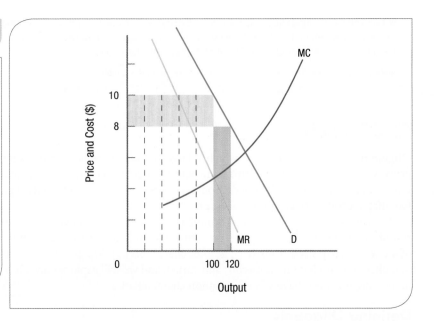

Figure 4 illustrates a hypothetical cartel consisting of five firms. By forming a cartel, these five firms agree to fix their overall output equal to the profit maximizing output of a monopolist, which is 100. At this restricted output, each cartel member produces its fixed quota of output (20 units per firm, assuming the cartel divides total output equally), and shares the resulting profit. Under this scenario, the cartel exhibits maximum market power equal to a single-firm monopolist.

However, cartels are inherently unstable because of the incentive to cheat by individual members. Although the cartel as a whole is maximizing profits, each individual member can potentially earn more profits by producing more than its output quota. As illustrated in Figure 4, if one firm exceeds its quota by doubling output from 20 to 40, the overall output of the cartel increases from 100 to 120 units. By expanding production, the market price falls from $10 to $8, causing revenues to fall by $200 ($2 × 100 units), shown as the yellow area. This reduction in revenues is *shared* by all five firms, with each firm losing $40 (or one share of the yellow area). Despite this loss, the cheating firm benefits because the extra 20 units it produces earns the firm $160 in additional revenue ($8 × 20 units), shown as the green area. The marginal revenue from cheating is therefore $160 − $40 = $120. As long as the marginal cost of producing the extra 20 units is less than $120, the firm benefits from cheating on the cartel agreement.

However, when one firm cheats, this often leads to other firms cheating. As more and more cartel members cheat, the price continues to fall toward the competitive price, greatly hurting the noncheating members. Over time, the cartel falls apart when all members increase their output, resulting in a competitive outcome. Therefore, market power in a cartel can range from the monopoly case (if all members adhere to their quotas) to the competitive case when cartels completely break down.

One reason that cartels are inherently unstable is because increasing output by one member can be undetected. However, once quotas are breached, the effects on all other members expand, increasing the likelihood of more cheating, especially if the marginal cost of production is low. For oil-producing countries, additional production is particularly profitable because a $100 barrel of oil may only cost $10 to $20 to produce. Each firm in the cartel faces these incentives, and if many attempt to sell additional output, the cartel agreement will break down. This analysis has led some economists to lose interest in cartels, because cartels are likely to fail in the long run.

Although cartels are inherently unstable, certain factors can enhance the likelihood of the cartel's survival. First, cartel stability is enhanced with fewer members with similar goals. With fewer members, any action that breaches the cartel agreement is more easily noticed and punishable. Second, stability is improved if the cartel is maintained with legal provisions (such as government protection). Third, stability is improved if firms are unable to differentiate their products (such as providing enhanced service or some other product as an inducement to purchase). Fourth, stability is improved when each firm's cost structure is similar, thereby not giving any firm a cost advantage over another. Finally, a cartel is more stable when there are significant barriers to entry preventing new firms from competing against existing cartel members.

These factors do not bode well for the future of the twelve member countries of OPEC. Although OPEC members produce a uniform product (crude oil) and have similar cost structures, enforcement of the quotas has at times been shaky with politically unstable countries. Further, OPEC's total share of world oil production has been surpassed by non-OPEC countries, led by Russia, the United States, Mexico, Canada, China, and Brazil. Maintaining an effective oil cartel will become more difficult as more countries enter the industry and as new alternative fuels are developed.

The Kinked Demand Curve Model and the Stability of Oligopolies

Oligopoly industries share a characteristic that prices tend to be stable for extended periods of time. For example, prices for wireless data plans are often $39.99 per month, and prices of unlimited texting plans are usually $19.99 per month. Why do these prices tend to stay the same when the underlying costs of providing the services change?

A study by Sweezy, Hall, and Hitch in the 1930s recognized that prices tended to be stable for extended periods in oligopolistic industries. It was in an effort to model this price stability that they settled on the idea of a kinked demand curve.

Demand curve d in Figure 5 represents the demand for one firm when all other firms in the industry *do not follow* its price changes. Demand curve D represents demand when all other firms raise or lower prices *in concert*. Demand curve d is relatively more elastic than demand curve D because when the firm raises prices and others do not follow, quantity demanded declines rapidly as customers substitute to the now lower priced products from competitors. Similarly, when one firm's prices fall and the others ignore this change, demand for the lower priced products grows rapidly. Hence, demand curve d is relatively elastic.

Demand curve D, on the other hand, is more like the industry demand. When all firms raise and lower their prices together, demand will be less elastic than demand curve d.

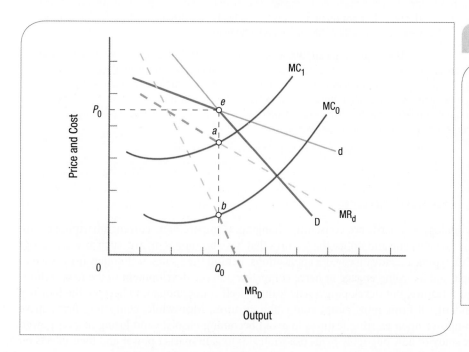

FIGURE 5

The Kinked Demand Curve Model of Oligopoly

The kinked demand curve model of oligopoly shows why oligopoly prices appear stable. The model assumes that if the firm raised its price, competitors will not react and raise their prices, but if the firm lowers its price, other firms will lower theirs in response. These reactions create a "kink" in the firm's demand curve at point e, and a discontinuity in the MR curve equal to the distance between points a and b. This discontinuity permits marginal costs to vary from MC_0 to MC_1 before the firm will change its price.

kinked demand curve An oligopoly model that assumes that if a firm raises its price, competitors will not raise theirs; but if the firm lowers its price, all of its competitors will lower their price to match the reduction. This leads to a kink in the demand curve and relatively stable market prices.

The **kinked demand curve** model assumes the following:

- If a firm raises prices for its products, its competitors will not react by raising prices, expecting to see their market share rise.

- If a firm lowers its prices, its competitors will meet the new prices with lower ones of their own to make sure that they do not lose market share.

As a result, the relevant demand curve facing the firm is the darkened portion of demand curves d and D that is kinked at point e. The relevant portion of the marginal revenue curve is the darkened dashed curve MR with the discontinuity between points a and b. Notice, we are just using the relevant portions of MR_d and MR_D. As shown, marginal cost crosses through the discontinuity, resulting in an equilibrium price and output of P_0 and Q_0.

It is, of course, the discontinuity in the MR curve that gives this model its price stability. The marginal cost curve can vary anywhere between points a and b before the firm will have any incentive to change prices to maximize profits.

The analysis of unstable and stable oligopoly models underscores the importance of the mutual interdependence of firms. How one firm reacts to a competitor's market strategy determines the nature of competition in the industry. These ideas led to game theory, which we consider in the next section.

◯ CHECKPOINT

OLIGOPOLY

- Oligopolies are markets (a) with only a few firms, (b) where each firm takes into account the reaction of rivals to its policies or firms recognize their mutual interdependence, and (c) where there are significant barriers to entry.

- The market power for an oligopoly can be substantial, although the ability of a firm to utilize its market power fully depends on its interdependence with competing firms.

- Cartels result when several firms collude to set market price and output. Cartels typically use their market power to act like monopolists and share the economic profits that result.

- Cartels are inherently unstable because individual firms can earn higher profits by selling more than their allotted quota. As more firms in the cartel cheat, prices fall, defeating the agreement.

- The observation that prices are stable in oligopoly industries (other than in cartels) gave rise to the kinked demand curve model. The model assumes that competitors will follow price reductions but not price increases. This leads to a discontinuity in MR, permitting cost to vary substantially before prices are changed.

QUESTION: The major drug cartels operating along the U.S.–Mexico border have become increasingly violent in recent years as cartels try to protect their trafficking routes to the U.S. market from competitors. But in addition to conflicts with external competition, cartel members have been murdered for exceeding their distribution quotas. Given the nature of how cartels function, explain why cartel leaders have become increasingly violent as a result of the above events.

Answers to the Checkpoint question can be found at the end of this chapter.

➲ Game Theory

Technology standards are constantly changing. Compare your current smartphone with your previous one and notice the features that have become standard, such as voice recognition typing and advanced GPS applications. Behind the scenes, technology firms such as Apple and Samsung engage in fierce competition in the development of the next technological feature. But developing a new feature itself is not enough; to become the industry standard, all firms must adopt compatible features. Meanwhile, competing firms strive to improve upon existing features to avoid becoming obsolete and losing market power. The study of how oligopoly firms use strategies to gain market power and their effects on competing firms and on consumers form the foundation of game theory.

game theory The study of how individuals and firms make strategic decisions to achieve their goals when other parties or factors can influence that outcome.

Reuters/CORBIS

Jacob Andrzejczak/Getty Images

Dan Kelly Photo/Corbis

What do Warren Buffett, Bill Gates, Annie Duke, and Mike McCarthy have in common? They are all experts in strategic thinking.

Game theory is the study of how individuals and firms make strategic decisions to achieve their goals when other parties or factors can influence that outcome. In short, it is the study of strategy and strategic behavior and is used in any situation in which one must predict the actions of others and respond by choosing among more than one strategy, each resulting in a potentially different outcome. Although game theory was first developed from the analysis of imperfect competition, particularly in explaining the actions of firms that are oligopolies, today it is used to study situations that extend well beyond the typical economic problems we have seen thus far in this book.

Real-life applications of game theory are abundant, and include situations common in sports coaching, business pricing, management, politics and elections, law and courtroom proceedings, military strategy, and even literal games such as poker. In 1995, Johnnie Cochran successfully defended O. J. Simpson against a murder charge when the evidence seemed to be stacked against him. In 2004, Annie Duke became the world's top female poker player by winning the World Series of Poker Tournament of Champions. In 2005, Bill Belichick took his New England Patriots to an unprecedented third Super Bowl win in four years. In 2008, Barack Obama surpassed favored Hillary Clinton to become his party's presidential nominee and eventually the president. As these events suggest, the importance of strategic thinking is a reason why game theory is an interdisciplinary topic that extends well beyond economics.

This section highlights key concepts of game theory, beginning with the important concept of a Nash equilibrium, named after famous mathematician-turned-economist and eventual Nobel Prize winner John Nash. In the next section, we extend this analysis to realistic cases and applications to illustrate how game theory is a part of our lives. We will show how game theory helps explain the actions of oligopolies.

NOBEL PRIZE
JOHN NASH

No person arguably has had more influence on strategic economic analysis than John Nash, a mathematician turned economist whose theories led to the development of modern game theory. Born in 1928 to well-educated parents in Bluefield, West Virginia, John Nash was encouraged to pursue educational interests at a young age. As his aptitude for math developed, he enrolled in advanced mathematics classes at a local college while still in high school.

At age 16, he attended the Carnegie Institute of Technology (now Carnegie Mellon University), where by age 20 he earned both his bachelor's and master's degrees in mathematics. His advisor wrote a one-line letter of recommendation for his graduate school applications: "This man is a genius." Nash continued his education at Princeton University where he earned his Ph.D. at age 22, completing what remains one of the shortest yet most influential dissertations: a 28-page study of noncooperative games whose conclusion would eventually be coined the Nash equilibrium.

John Nash worked as a professor at the Massachusetts Institute of Technology and also for the U.S. government as an expert code breaker. It was during these early adult years when mental illness began to set in, and he eventually was diagnosed with paranoid schizophrenia. His battles with severe disillusions consumed much of his life, and he was often seen talking to imaginary figures. Yet, his ability to make new contributions to game theory, a relatively new topic at the time, earned him a permanent faculty position at Princeton, where he remains a professor to this day.

In 1994, John Nash was recognized with the Nobel Prize in economics for his contributions to game theory. His life would be the subject of several books, including Sylvia Nasar's *A Beautiful Mind*, published in 1998. The book was adapted into the 2001 blockbuster movie by the same name, starring Russell Crowe, that would go on to win four Academy Awards, including Best Picture.

Basic Game Setup and Assumptions

A basic setup of a "game" requires players, information, strategies, outcomes, and payoffs. This game setup applies to virtually all situations in which strategy (game theory) is used to analyze a real-life scenario. Let's look at each component.

- **Players:** Players can be firms competing for customers, a plaintiff and a defendant in a courtroom, two or more countries at war, or actual *players* in the literal sense in a sporting match or card game.
- **Information:** Each player holds information that is either known to others or is private. Having private information changes the way in which a game is played and the outcomes it produces.
- **Strategies:** Players make choices based on strategies devised from the information they have and the information they suspect other players hold. Players use strategies to improve the likelihood of achieving their best outcome.
- **Outcomes:** Outcomes refer to all possibilities, good and bad, that can occur given the strategies employed by players. In zero-sum games, outcomes are a "win" or a "loss." In any given hand in poker, for example, one person wins the pot of money while everyone else loses. In other games, there may be no losers per se, but firms compete for market share, or job applicants compete for various types of jobs.
- **Payoffs:** The payoff is the value players attach to each outcome. Each player has his or her own perception of each outcome, because rarely do players in a game have exactly the same objective. Payoffs are what players ultimately try to maximize.

In addition to identifying the setup described above, analyses of situations involving game theory typically make two general assumptions:

1. *Preferences are clearly defined.* The objectives of each player must be known. For example, a firm's objective might be to maximize its profits, while a golfer's objective is to achieve a low score.

2. *Players rationally choose strategies to achieve objectives.* Players make consistent decisions that improve their chances of achieving their goals. Sometimes, however, people make decisions that seem irrational. Game theory does have something to say about irrational behavior, but this is beyond the scope of this section.

Simultaneous Versus Sequential-Move Games

simultaneous-move games Games in which players' actions occur at the same time, forcing players to make decisions without knowing how the other players will act. These games are analyzed using diagrams called game tables.

Game theory moves can be simultaneous or sequential. **Simultaneous-move games** involve actions by players that occur at the same time. Examples include sporting matches such as a soccer game with offensive and defensive players, and business pricing where firms must decide on prices to be placed in ads without knowing what prices their competitors will choose. **Sequential-move games** are situations in which one player at a time makes a move. Examples include games such as chess or tic-tac-toe, but also extend to examples such as negotiations (where offers are made back-and-forth), golf, or reality show competitions.

sequential-move games Games in which players make moves one at a time, allowing players to view the progression of the game and to make decisions based on previous moves.

The way in which simultaneous-move and sequential-move games are analyzed differs. We focus primarily on simultaneous-move games, leaving the discussion of sequential-move games to later in the chapter.

Simultaneous-Move Games

Figure 6 illustrates a two-player simultaneous-move game in a diagram called a game table (also known as a payoff matrix or normal form analysis). In our example, Lowe's and Home Depot must choose one of two policies: advertise in the local paper or don't advertise. Lowe's strategies are listed in rows, while Home Depot's strategies are listed in columns. Because players (firms) move at the same time, outcomes are determined by the interaction of strategies chosen by each player. In this case, four potential outcomes exist, with Lowe's payoff shown before Home Depot's in each outcome. The outcome depends on which strategy each player actually chooses.

Let's go through each outcome, to show you how to read the figure. If Lowe's and Home Depot both advertise, each will earn a profit of $100,000. The advertising will induce some customers to buy now, but won't much affect whether they will buy at Lowe's or at Home Depot. There is a cost to advertising, which is why profits are lower when both firms advertise than when both do not. When both do not advertise, each earns a profit of $200,000. Customers continue to go to Lowe's and Home Depot about equally, and both firms do not bear the cost of the advertising.

What happens if one advertises while the other does not? The one that advertises increases profits. If Lowe's advertises while Home Depot does not, it earns a profit of $300,000 compared to Home Depot's $50,000. Why this result? Lowe's has to pay the cost of advertising but more than makes up for it by taking customers away from Home Depot. By not advertising, Home Depot saves on this cost, but it does not make up for the lost customer sales. This result is the same, but reversed, if Lowe's does not advertise while Home Depot does: Home Depot sees $300,000 in profits while Lowe's profit is only $50,000.

FIGURE 6

Simultaneous-Move Game Illustrated in a Game Table

A simultaneous-move game between Lowe's and Home Depot is shown in which both firms must choose whether to advertise in the local paper or not, without knowing what the other will do. The choice made by each firm results in a different payoff for each.

Strategically, what is the best thing for each to do: advertise or not advertise? Let's first look at the best possible outcome for Lowe's. Its best outcome would be to advertise when Home Depot does not, allowing Lowe's to earn $300,000 while Home Depot ends up with $50,000, its worst outcome. Alternatively, the best collective outcome for Lowe's and Home Depot occurs when both do not advertise and each earns $200,000. Is either of these outcomes likely?

Let's approach this question by looking at the best response of one firm to the other's action. Suppose Home Depot strives for its highest possible outcome of $300,000 by advertising. What would be Lowe's best response? Clearly, Lowe's does not want to bear the minuscule profits of $50,000 if it does not advertise and Home Depot does advertise, therefore it advertises and earns $100,000. Therefore, choosing to advertise is a best response if competitors advertise. In Figure 6, this payoff is underlined.

Looking at it from Home Depot's point of view, it also advertises in response to Lowe's advertising, because it too would not want Lowe's to grab too many of its customers. Advertising is a best response for Home Depot because it results in a payoff of $100,000 (underlined) instead of $50,000. If both Lowe's and Home Depot act strategically by advertising to avoid the worst possible outcome, then the best case scenario of earning $300,000 is not possible.

If the best outcome is not possible, then how about the best collective outcome in which both firms choose not to advertise and each earns $200,000? Clearly, this outcome is better than if both firms advertise. But they cannot call each other up and say "I will not advertise if you do not advertise." This is collusion, prevented by law in the United States and in many other countries. Each firm has to make a decision without knowing what the other will do.

Again using the best-response approach, if Home Depot chooses not to advertise, Lowe's would still be better off advertising, because (1) it eliminates the worst-case outcome if Home Depot does in fact advertise, and (2) if Home Depot does not advertise, advertising would allow Lowe's to achieve its highest payoff of $300,000. Therefore, Lowe's best response to Home Depot not advertising is still to advertise (the corresponding payoff is underlined in Figure 6). From Home Depot's perspective, its best response if Lowe's does not advertise would be to advertise as well.

In sum, the best action each firm can take, *considering each of the possible actions the other might take*, is to bear the cost of advertising. This outcome is what economists call a Nash equilibrium.

Nash Equilibrium

Nash equilibrium An outcome that occurs when all players choose their optimal strategy in response to all other players' potential moves. At a Nash equilibrium, no player can be better off by unilaterally deviating from the noncooperative outcome.

A **Nash equilibrium** occurs when all players in a game use an optimal strategy in response to all other players' strategies. It is the outcome that maximizes all players' expected payoffs (the value of each potential outcome times the probability of that outcome occurring) given the information they have. In other words, aiming for the outcome with the highest payoff is not always prudent if the likelihood of achieving that outcome is small. Solving for Nash equilibrium is therefore valuable because it represents a player's best payoff taking into account the self-interested actions of all other players affecting the outcome. Once a Nash equilibrium is achieved, no individual player can do better by changing his or her mind.

For example, it is possible that Lowe's or Home Depot could see higher profits if it chose not to advertise, but there's a higher probability of it leading to lower profits. Nash equilibrium guides players to choose strategies that result in the best expected payoff. In the Lowe's–Home Depot example, the Nash equilibrium is for each to advertise when neither knows what the other will do.

An outcome is a Nash equilibrium if it results from all players acting strategically (using a best response) to each other's actions. In some cases, players choose the same action regardless of what others do, while in other cases, players choose different actions in response to other players' actions. In the Home Depot–Lowe's example, each firm's best response is to advertise regardless of what the other firm does, and is known as a dominant strategy. A **dominant strategy** occurs when one player chooses the same action regardless of what the other player chooses. When both players have a dominant strategy, a single Nash equilibrium will result. For Lowe's and Home Depot, both advertising is the Nash equilibrium. But not all Nash equilibria are the result of dominant strategies. In fact, games need not be limited to one Nash equilibrium. When dominant strategies do not exist, games can have no Nash equilibrium while others might have more than one, as we'll soon see.

dominant strategy Occurs when a player chooses the same strategy regardless of what his or her opponent chooses.

Also, a Nash equilibrium outcome is not always obvious. In Figure 6, it might seem that Lowe's and Home Depot not advertising would be a Nash equilibrium; besides, the profits for both are higher than the profits with advertising. But such a quick conclusion does not take into account the fact that one firm could do even better by advertising if the other does not. And because neither firm wishes to risk the worst-case scenario, they both engage in advertising as their best response action. Fortunately, not all Nash equilibrium outcomes are so pessimistic. In many cases, acting in response to another player's actions can lead to a good outcome for all players, as we'll see next.

Nash Equilibrium: A Personal Example Let's look at a personal example to make sure that the idea of a Nash equilibrium is clear. Suppose you are talking with a friend on the phone, and the line suddenly goes dead. Does this scenario sound familiar? Perhaps it is because it happens so often. This very moment often creates a quick but annoying dilemma: Do you immediately call your friend back, or do you wait for your friend to call you back?

For simplicity, assume you are given just one opportunity to make a decision. If both you and your friend immediately call each other back, chances are you might end up reaching each other's voicemail. If instead, you both wait for each other to call back, then you end up waiting anxiously wondering why your friend didn't call you back. In each situation, players did not accurately select the best response to the other player's action. Therefore, a Nash equilibrium occurs when one person calls and the other responds by waiting.

	Friend	
	Call back	Wait
You Call back	Voicemail	Connected call
Wait	Connected call	Silence

Tim Pannell/Corbis

FIGURE 7

Dropped Call Dilemma: Who Should Call Back First?

The two cases in which the call is successfully connected each represent a Nash equilibrium.

Figure 7 illustrates each of the four possible outcomes. Two outcomes meet the criteria for a Nash equilibrium, which is common for coordination-type games when players are attempting to achieve a mutually beneficial outcome. For each Nash equilibrium, both you and you friend used a best-response action that led to a completed call; in other words, if your friend calls, you wait. If your friend waits, you call.

To review, a Nash equilibrium describes any outcome when all players respond optimally to all possible actions by other players. At that outcome, no player would choose to deviate unilaterally from that outcome; this doesn't mean that a better outcome might prevail with some cooperation, but rather that no player would change her position by herself. Finding a Nash equilibrium is therefore useful because it represents the best outcome given the self-interested actions of all other players.

We have seen two situations with different Nash equilibrium outcomes. For Lowe's and Home Depot, the Nash equilibrium was an outcome that neither firm truly desired. In the next section, we will classify these outcomes as a Prisoner's Dilemma and show what can be done to overcome such outcomes. For the dropped call example, we found more than one Nash equilibrium in which both players would be happy. But we need not stop here. The next section will highlight other Nash equilibrium outcomes that can result depending on the circumstances facing each player.

ISSUE

Mission ~~Impossible~~: The Power of Focal Points in a Simulated Mission

Barry Nalebuff is a respected economist who has published several books on game theory, and is known for constructing unorthodox methods of using game theory to solve life's problems. In 2006, Barry Nalebuff teamed up with the show *PrimeTime* to create a unique game theory experiment dealing with Nash equilibria and focal points. They took six pairs of people who did not know one another and placed them in different locations in New York City's Manhattan. The objective of this game was to have at least one pair find one of the other five pairs within a day, not knowing where they would be or what they looked like. It's a true needle in a haystack problem trying to locate an unfamiliar person among millions in Manhattan. Sound impossible? Perhaps. But game theory teaches us to use clues effectively to solve such problems. In this case, when players have the same goal, strategies can be employed to maximize the chances of achieving it.

Recall the concepts of Nash equilibrium in the dropped call problem. Unlike that situation, which contained four potential outcomes and two Nash equilibria, the present example contains infinite outcomes and infinite Nash equilibria (since pairs could meet at any of millions of locations at any time of the day). When many possible solutions exist, players must use focal points to reach an equilibrium solution. Focal points are solutions that seem more obvious based on clues and past experience.

In the present example, focal points rely on three dimensions: where, when, and who. Where would pairs go to facilitate spotting others? Common answers might include Times Square, the Empire State Building, the Statue of Liberty, and Grand Central Terminal, among others. By listing these likely locations, we reduce the number of likely outcomes from millions of locations to fewer than a dozen. Next is the timing issue. Two pairs could be at the same location but at different times. Thus, a focal point in time is necessary; obvious times might be noon (the strongest focal point), 9 A.M., 3 P.M., or 5 P.M. Lastly, two pairs could be at the same location at the same time, but still not recognize one another. Thus, a focal point on recognizing another pair is necessary, and can be achieved through costumes, posters and signs, and noisemaking devices. Would the combination of each of the dimensions of focal points turn a seemingly impossible task into a successful one?

On the show, the six teams had resounding success. Three teams found each other at the top of the Empire State Building at noon wearing signs, while another three teams found each other in Times Square at noon also holding signs and using whistles and other noisemakers. Clearly, the use of game theory is a powerful and effective tool when confronted with some of life's biggest challenges.

Because the Nash equilibrium in each situation is not automatically obvious, it's important to use the best-response method to solve for Nash equilibrium to ensure that each player's expected payoff is maximized.

 ## CHECKPOINT

GAME THEORY

- Game theory uses sophisticated mathematical analysis to help explain the actions of oligopolies, as well as develop optimal strategies for life's everyday situations.
- Game theory characteristics include the number of players and strategies, information completeness, and the value of potential outcomes (payoffs).
- Simultaneous-move games occur when players make decisions without knowing what other players will choose, and are analyzed using diagrams called game tables.
- Nash equilibrium analysis describes outcomes in which all players respond optimally to all possible actions by other players to achieve the highest expected payoff.
- It is possible to have zero, one, two, or more Nash equilibria in a game.

QUESTION: In the dropped call example presented earlier, two Nash equilibria existed in which one person calls back and the other person waits. However, this does not completely resolve the situation because each player must still figure out what his or her role will be: to call back or to wait. Using your own personal experiences with this type of situation, what strategies would you use to determine who would call and who would wait? Assume that you have just one opportunity to choose (either to call or wait) and that you cannot communicate using any other method (such as texting).

Answers to the Checkpoint question can be found at the end of this chapter.

Applications of Game Theory

This section focuses on four common categories of games: Prisoner's Dilemma, repeated games, leadership games, and chicken games. In each of the examples within each category, we solve for a Nash equilibrium using the best-response method introduced in the previous section, and discuss the characteristics of these outcomes that are found in real-life examples. In doing this, you should get a sense of how game theory helps explain many oligopoly behaviors.

The Prisoner's Dilemma

Ever notice how competing stores pay very close attention to what their competitors do? When Office Depot offers back-to-school specials, Staples is sure to do the same. When one airline offers a summer fare sale, other airlines tend to follow. In our example of Lowe's and Home Depot in the previous section, each firm chooses to advertise even if it results in lower profits than if neither advertises. If you were a manager of one of these firms, shouldn't you immediately cease advertising? Not necessarily. Game theory helps to explain this seemingly counterintuitive outcome. In each of these situations, the Nash equilibrium that results is an outcome that is inferior to another outcome that can be achieved through cooperation, and is referred to as a **Prisoner's Dilemma.**

Given the similarities of products sold by monopolistically competitive and oligopoly firms, Prisoner's Dilemma outcomes occur frequently as firms compete for market share, such as AT&T and Verizon in wireless communications, Carnival and Royal Caribbean in cruise vacations, and Target and Wal-Mart in discount retailing.

For consumers, however, Prisoner's Dilemma outcomes are beneficial because they result in lower prices for goods. As competing firms lower their prices to gain market share, they earn a smaller profit from each customer. In some cases, competition becomes so intense that a competitor is forced out of business. Just ask Circuit City, Borders, Sharper Image, and Linens-N-Things, just to name a few. Why would firms compete to the

Prisoner's Dilemma A noncooperative game in which players cannot communicate or collaborate in making their decisions, which results in inferior outcomes for both players. Many oligopoly decisions can be framed as a Prisoner's Dilemma.

point of nearly zero profit margins? Wouldn't it make sense for competing firms to utilize their collective market power by all raising their prices to make more money?

Alas, here's the dilemma: Firms cannot openly collude to raise prices (that is illegal under antitrust laws). However, firms *can* silently collude by raising prices unilaterally and hoping that others will follow. But will the others follow?

Suppose two shoe stores operate near campus, Shoe Carnival and Shoe Festival. Assume, for simplicity, that each has two pricing strategies: a high markup and a low markup. If both stores choose the same strategy, they each attract the same number of customers. But if one store is less expensive than the other, it takes most of the customers and profits (despite earning less profit per customer at the lower price). Figure 8 shows a game table with presumed profits under the four outcomes.

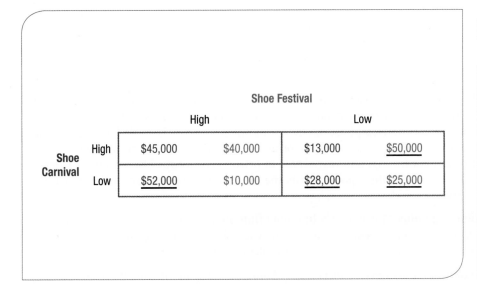

FIGURE 8

Prisoner's Dilemma Game Between Two Firms

Intense competition between Shoe Carnival and Shoe Festival results in both stores pricing their products low, resulting in a Nash equilibrium payoff of $28,000 for Shoe Carnival and $25,000 for Shoe Festival. However, another outcome provides a greater profit for *both* stores, that is, if both stores price high. But because the two stores cannot openly collude, and neither trusts the other to maintain high prices, both stores end up pricing their products low, resulting in lower profits.

Using the best-response method to solve for Nash equilibrium, Shoe Carnival's best response to a high price by Shoe Festival is to price low, thereby stealing most of Shoe Festival's customers and earning a higher profit. And to prevent the same from happening if Shoe Festival prices low, Shoe Carnival's best response is also to price low. Therefore, Shoe Carnival has a dominant strategy to keep its prices low regardless of what Shoe Festival does. In Figure 8, the strategies selected by Shoe Carnival in response to each strategy by Shoe Festival are underlined. If we conduct the same analysis for Shoe Festival, we also find that Shoe Festival has a dominant strategy to price low, resulting in a Nash equilibrium when both stores price low, resulting in a payoff of $28,000 for Shoe Carnival and $25,000 for Shoe Festival.

Does this equilibrium seem odd? It might because another outcome (where both stores price high) provides greater profit to *both* stores. Yet, that outcome is *not* a Nash equilibrium. A Prisoner's Dilemma therefore results because players are unable to cooperate effectively with one another. Why don't the stores just agree to price their products high? They can't do it by colluding; that is illegal. And if one store raises its prices unilaterally, there is no guarantee the other store will follow, thus risking a loss of customers and profit.

The Classic Prisoner's Dilemma How did the Prisoner's Dilemma get its name? Two criminal suspects (Matthew and Chris) are apprehended on a charge of robbery. They are separated, put in solitary confinement, and are unable to speak to each other. Each prisoner is offered the same bargain: Confess that you and your partner both committed the crime and you will go free while your non-confessing partner will go to prison for three years. If neither confesses, the state likely will convict them both on lesser charges resulting in a one-year sentence for each. Finally, if both confess, they each will go to prison for two years.

Figure 9 on the next page illustrates this game in which payoffs represent the number of years in prison. The prisoners must make a decision without knowing what the

FIGURE 9

The Classic Prisoner's Dilemma

Matthew and Chris are two suspects held in separate cells. Each is given an opportunity to confess to the crime, with the resulting jail sentences shown for each outcome. Under this payoff structure, the optimal response by each player is to confess, resulting in a single Nash equilibrium where each receives two years of jail time. This Nash equilibrium is a Prisoner's Dilemma because a better outcome (not confessing) exists for both players.

		Chris			
		Do not confess		Confess	
Matthew	Do not confess	1 year	1 year	3 years	0 years
	Confess	0 years	3 years	2 years	2 years

other chose, and decisions are irrevocable. Each prisoner is only concerned with his own welfare—minimizing his time in prison. Is there a unique solution?

Using the best-response method, Matthew and Chris both have a dominant strategy to confess! This outcome results despite the fact that both would be better off by not confessing: one year served in prison versus two. The Prisoner's Dilemma results because neither player trusts the other not to confess given the structure of the payoffs.

Other Examples of Prisoner's Dilemma Outcomes Now that you have an idea of what a Prisoner's Dilemma entails, particularly when oligopoly firms compete, let's mention a few other examples in which a Prisoner's Dilemma might occur.

- **Political Campaigns:** Politicians spend immense amounts of time, effort, and money to win elections. Some members of Congress in swing districts spend half of their two-year terms in office campaigning, leaving little time to get anything else done, like passing laws. If competing candidates have roughly equal amounts of time and money, the result is likely to be similar if the candidates agree not to campaign at all; but that requires each candidate to trust the other not to break that promise, which is not an easy proposition.

- **Legal Disputes:** When individuals or firms end up in litigation, plaintiffs and defendants often will spend large amounts of money in legal fees and for consultants merely to offset what the other side spends. For high-profile cases, add the costs of media coverage and the costs incurred by family, friends, and curious onlookers, and the outcome often is more costly for all parties involved.

- **Trade Disputes:** When one country restricts imported goods to protect domestic producers from foreign competition, other countries have an incentive to do the same, making it difficult for domestic producers to sell their goods abroad. When countries restrict trade against each other, a Prisoner's Dilemma outcome occurs because trade barriers cause a reduction in the gains from specialization and trade, harming all countries.

Resolving the Prisoner's Dilemma Prisoner's Dilemma type of situations are difficult to resolve in a noncooperative framework when the players are not able to coordinate their strategies, whether as a result of antitrust laws or an inability to retaliate against other players if the cooperative action is not played. Although Prisoner's Dilemma outcomes might be bad for firms in a pricing game or for litigants in a trial, they surely are beneficial to consumers who enjoy lower prices and for lawyers who might earn a lot of money in a high-profile case.

Let's consider a case of trade protection in which a Prisoner's Dilemma might be resolved successfully. A Prisoner's Dilemma occurs when countries enact trade barriers, causing the gains from trade to be restricted. Free trade agreements are a way for countries to overcome the Prisoner's Dilemma by agreeing to promote free trade among members. And unlike collusive agreements between firms, free trade agreements are legal and have been implemented extensively in recent decades.

Another way to overcome the Prisoner's Dilemma is by ensuring that the game is repeated over time. When games are played just once, players have an incentive to maximize their payoffs in the game without worrying about long-term consequences. However, when a game is repeated indefinitely, incentives change, and players worry about retaliation.

Repeated Games

Pick up a Sunday newspaper and notice the large selection of circulars included. Many retailers advertise their products using a Sunday ad without knowing what their competitors' ads look like. But because this game is repeated every Sunday, no firm would risk retaliation by advertising prices that are *too* low relative to other firms. Thus, repeated games provide a way for competing players to check how other players are behaving, and to provide a way of punishing unfair players.

Sunday ads: an example of a repeated game by retailers.

Games can be endlessly (infinitely) repeated or repeated for a specific number of rounds. In either case, repeating opens the game to different types of strategies that are unavailable for a game played only once. These strategies can take into account the past behavior of rivals. This section briefly explores these strategies and some of their implications for understanding oligopoly behavior.

One possibility is simply to cooperate or defect from the beginning. These strategies, however, leave you at the mercy of your opponent, or lead to unfavorable outcomes where both firms earn less or suffer losses. A more robust set of strategies are **trigger strategies:** action is taken contingent on your opponent's past decisions. Here are a few of them.

trigger strategies Action is taken contingent on your opponent's past decisions.

Grim Trigger Let's start by considering an industry that is earning oligopoly profits. Suppose that all of a sudden, one firm lowers its price, maybe because it is in financial trouble and wants to increase sales right away. Under the grim trigger rule, the other firms lower their prices—but they do not stop there. They permanently lower their prices, making the financial condition of the original firm that reduced prices even more severe.

The grim trigger rule, thus, is this: Any decision by your opponent to defect (choose an unfavorable outcome) is met by a permanent retaliatory decision forever. This is a harsh decision rule. Its negative aspect is that it is subject to misreading. For example, has your competition lowered its price in an attempt to gain market share at your expense, or has the market softened for the product in general? This strategy can quickly lead to the unfavorable Prisoner's Dilemma result. To avoid this problem, oligopoly firms might use other trigger strategies.

Trembling Hand Trigger A trembling hand trigger strategy allows for a mistake by your opponent before you retaliate. This gives your opponent a chance to make a mistake and reduces misreads that are a problem for the grim trigger strategy. This approach can be extended to accept two nonsequential defects, and so on, but they can be exploited by clever opponents who figure out that they can get away with a few "mistakes" before their opponent retaliates.

Tit-for-Tat A **tit-for-tat** strategy is one that repeats the prior move of competitors. If one firm lowers its price, its rivals follow suit one time. If the same firm offers rebates or special offers, rivals do exactly the same in the next time period. This strategy has the efficient qualities that it rewards cooperation and punishes defection.

tit-for-tat strategies A trigger strategy that rewards cooperation and punishes defections. If your opponent lowers its price, you do the same. If your opponent returns to a cooperative strategy, you do the same.

This short list of strategies illustrates the richness of repeated games. Strategies tend to be more successful if they are relatively simple and easy to understand by competitors, tend to foster cooperation, have some credible punishment to reduce defections, and provide for forgiveness to avoid the costly mistakes associated with misreading opponents.[1]

Using Sequential-Move Analysis to Model Repeated Games Because repeated games involve multiple iterations of the same game, it can be shown in sequential-move game diagrams called game trees, also called decision trees or extensive form analysis. In Figure 10, a game tree is shown between two hardware firms that advertise each week in the Sunday ads. To avoid the Prisoner's Dilemma, both firms must choose to advertise lightly. They continue to do so unless one firm chooses to advertise heavily, which would lead to a trigger strategy in the next stage. Suppose Tool Shack contemplates advertising heavily this week: Tool Kingdom can respond to this action by advertising heavily next week, or choose not to. In the figure, Tool Shack makes the first decision whether to advertise lightly or heavily. If Tool Shack chooses to advertise heavily, Tool Kingdom then chooses whether to respond.

FIGURE 10

Sequential-Move Game Illustrated in a Game Tree

A sequential-move game is illustrated between Tool Shack and Tool Kingdom. Tool Shack makes the first move by choosing whether to advertise heavily. After seeing Tool Shack's decision, Tool Kingdom responds by choosing to retaliate (by also advertising heavily) or not. For each possible outcome, a payoff results for each firm.

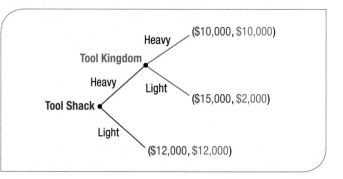

Looking at Tool Kingdom's payoffs, it is in its best interest to advertise heavily if Tool Shack chooses to advertise heavily. Tool Shack, knowing that advertising heavily would be Tool Kingdom's best response in the next stage, would likely choose to maintain its light advertising to avoid the Prisoner's Dilemma outcome. The sequential nature of game trees allows players to see the progression of moves across time from start to finish.

Resolving the Prisoner's Dilemma is an important outcome of cooperative strategies. But not all competitive games lead to a Prisoner's Dilemma to begin with. One example is called a leadership game, where an industry is dominated by a market leader.

Leadership Games

Facebook is the world's largest social media provider, which earns its revenues primarily through advertising and sets prices to maximize its profits. Yet, other smaller social networks also compete for revenues. Unlike earlier examples, in which competing firms are of similar size, Facebook's market dominance allows it to ignore the pricing actions of its smaller competitors. In other words, if Facebook loses a few advertisers due to lower prices on other networks, the loss in revenues is smaller than what it would lose if Facebook lowers its own prices.

---

[1] Nick Wilkinson, *Managerial Economics: A Problem Solving Approach* (Cambridge: Cambridge University Press), 2005, p. 373.

Another example of a leadership game occurs when a small low-fare airline competes against a larger airline. Frontier Airlines is a relatively small airline based in Denver; it competes on many routes that United Airlines serves. But because United is a significantly larger airline with greater market power, it does not always match Frontier's lower fares because United believes it would not lose many customers.

Chicken Games

Another category of game that does not result in a Prisoner's Dilemma can be seen if you belong to a union at work, or enjoy watching professional sports or television shows, situations where collective bargaining (organized labor) is powerful. Every once in a while, a labor dispute boils over to a point where a strike is either threatened or sometimes carried out. Although we discuss labor disputes in the next chapter, this is an example of an important class of games called chicken.

A chicken game is portrayed in the classic movie *Rebel Without a Cause*, in which James Dean's character is challenged by a rival to a stunt challenge. Both players race their cars toward a cliff, and the first person to jump out is the "chicken." The winner is the person who stays in the car longer. Of course, if neither player leaves his car, they both plunge to their deaths.

Chicken games describe games of holdouts or brinkmanship. Players involved in chicken games want to hold out as long as they can to win, trying to get the other side to give in. If neither side does, the worst outcome occurs. Examples of brinkmanship occur regularly in Congress. Neither Democrats nor Republicans wish to concede anything up to the very end, when some catastrophic consequence threatens the economy such as a government default (from failing to raise the debt ceiling) or a *fiscal cliff* of higher taxes and severe spending cuts (from failing to agree on a budget). Brinkmanship often ties one's hands.

Figure 11 illustrates a chicken game using the 2012 NHL labor dispute as an example. Suppose the players union and the team owners are in a dispute over salaries. Each side can remain tough, or loosen their position. The worst outcome occurs when both sides refuse to give in, resulting in a lockout or strike that is devastating to both sides, not to mention all the fans, who are not able to watch their favorite teams play.

FIGURE 11

A Chicken Game Between NHL players and NHL Owners

Neither side wishes to give in to the other side in a labor dispute, but if neither gives in, the worst outcome of 0, 0 results (i.e., a lockout or strike). In chicken games, two Nash equilibria exist, each with one player achieving his ideal result while the other side settles.

Using the best-response method, we find that chicken games have two Nash equilibria, where one side ultimately *gives in* to the other. Specifically, if NHL owners choose the tough strategy by refusing to compromise, the best response of players would be to loosen their position and earn a payoff of 1 instead of 0. If NHL owners are willing to compromise, the best response of players would be to maintain a tough position and earn a payoff of 4 instead of 2. The same best-response strategies can be determined by the NHL owners in response to the NHL players' strategies.

Thus, in a chicken game, one party is much happier with a Nash equilibrium result than the other. Yet, the *loser* still would not have wanted to change its strategy, for doing so unilaterally would result in an even worse outcome. Unfortunately for the NHL, a Nash equilibrium did not occur as both sides refused to give in, resulting in a lockout and a severely compromised 2012–2013 season. This is an outcome that occasionally occurs in chicken games, one that had clear consequences for both players and owners, not to mention many disappointed fans.

As seen in the many applications in this and the last section, game theory is a powerful tool to analyze market competition when firms each have the ability to influence price and the market share of their competitors. The ability to anticipate another player's actions and respond optimally is the key to achieving a Nash equilibrium. Nash equilibrium is the outcome that maximizes all players' expected payoffs. Recognizing such outcomes allows all players to achieve the best outcome given the self-interested motives of all other players involved. Game theory has applications that extend beyond oligopoly competition and economics in general.

Summary of Market Structures

In this and the previous two chapters, we have studied the four major market structures: perfect competition, monopolistic competition, oligopoly, and monopoly. As we move through this list, market power becomes greater, and the ability of the firm to earn economic profits in the long run grows.

Table 1 summarizes the important distinctions among these four market structures. Keep in mind that market structure analysis allows you to look at the overall characteristics of the market and predict the pricing and profit behavior of the firms. The outcomes for perfect competition and monopolistic competition are particularly attractive for consumers because firms price their products equal to average total costs and earn just enough to keep them in the business over the long haul.

TABLE 1	Summary of Market Structures			
	Perfect Competition	**Monopolistic Competition**	**Oligopoly**	**Monopoly**
Number of Firms	Many	Many	Few	One
Product	Homogeneous	Differentiated	Homogeneous or differentiated	Unique
Barriers to Entry or Exit?	No	No	Yes	Yes
Strategic Interdependence?	No	No	Yes	Not applicable
Market Power	None	Limited	Some	Absolute
Long-Run Price Decision	P = ATC	P = ATC	P > ATC	P > ATC
Long-Run Profits	Zero	Zero	Usually economic	Economic
Key Summary Characteristic	Price taker	Product differentiation	Mutual interdependence	One-firm industry

In contrast, the outcomes for oligopoly and monopoly industries are not as favorable to consumers. Concentrated markets have considerable market power, which shows up in pricing and output decisions. However, keep in mind that markets with market power (oligopolies) often involve giants competing with giants. Even though there is a mutual interdependence in their decisions and they may not always compete vigorously over prices, they often are innovative because of some competitive pressures. We see this today especially in the electronics and automobile markets.

CHECKPOINT

APPLICATIONS OF GAME THEORY

- The Prisoner's Dilemma is a noncooperative game in which players minimize their maximum prison time by both confessing, a strategy that neither would have taken had they been able to communicate with one another.

- Applications of Prisoner's Dilemma games extend well beyond criminal cases, and can involve firm pricing strategies, legal disputes, international trade protection, and political campaigns.

- Resolving the Prisoner's Dilemma is not easy because of antitrust laws preventing firms from colluding. However, when games are repeated, the threat of retaliation encourages players to use a cooperative strategy.

- Games that are repeated lead to more nuanced trigger strategies, including grim trigger, trembling hand trigger, and tit-for-tat.

- Leadership games describe competitive games in which one player is dominant in size relative to the rest of the players.

- Chicken games involve players who try to hold out for the optimal outcome; however, if neither side gives in, the worst outcome occurs. Labor disputes that often end up in strikes or lockouts are examples of chicken games.

QUESTIONS: Suppose your economics professor grades the class on a curve, such that exactly 25% of the class receives an A, 25% receives a B, 25% receives a C, and 25% receives a D, regardless of how the class actually performs. One of your classmates comes up with an idea: Instead of having the entire class study for hours and hours for each exam, everyone in the class agrees *not* to study, with the presumption that everyone would likely receive the same grade as if they did study given the grade distribution. Would this strategy work? Why or why not? What type of game does this best represent, a chicken game or a Prisoner's Dilemma? Explain.

Answers to the Checkpoint questions can be found at the end of this chapter.

chapter summary

Section 1: **Monopolistic Competition**

A **monopolistically competitive** industry has the following characteristics:

- Large number of firms with insignificant market share.
- No barriers to entry and exit.
- Products sold by firms are similar but differentiated (has a brand).
- Limited market power.

Short-run profit maximization for a monopolistically competitive industry looks identical to a monopoly. In the long run, however, the demand curve is tangent to the average total cost curve, signaling zero economic profit.

Because of product differentiation, a firm's demand curve is downward sloping. However, it is highly elastic due to the competitive nature of the industry.

A shopping mall offers dozens of stores at which to buy clothing, each of which is differentiated.

Types of Product Differentiation

Location

Quality

Style, Design, and Features

Advertising

Section 2: **Oligopoly**

Oligopoly industries are controlled by a few large firms. Barriers to entry are significant, the product is less differentiated than in monopolistically competitive industries, and pricing decisions by one firm directly impact other firms (mutual interdependence). Oligopoly firms possess market power but not as much as a monopoly.

Cartels are agreements to restrict output to push prices higher, but are inherently unstable because cheating is profitable.

A **kinked demand curve** occurs because firms are reluctant to match price increases but not price decreases. The kink creates a discontinuity in the marginal revenue curve, allowing marginal cost to vary (from MC_0 to MC_1) while prices remain stable.

Competing gas stations keep their prices close to one another's.

Section 3: Game Theory

Game theory is the study of strategic decision making when multiple players each act in their own interests.

Components of a Game

Players

Information

Strategy choices

Outcomes and payoffs

Golf is a sequential-move game, in which players take their shots one at a time.

Nash equilibrium is an outcome that results from all players responding optimally to all other players' actions to maximize their expected payoffs. In a Nash equilibrium, no player wishes to deviate unilaterally from that outcome.

Solving for a Nash equilibrium requires analyzing a game table for best responses to the other player's possible actions.

		Player 2	
		Left	Right
	Top	8 4	2 6
Player 1	Down	6 3	7 5

Player 1's best response to "Left" is "Top" = 8.

Player 1's best response to "Right" is "Down" = 7.

Player 2's best response to "Top" is "Right" = 6.

Player 2's best response to "Down" is "Right" = 5.

One Nash equilibrium = "Down", "Right" = (7, 5).

Section 4: Applications of Game Theory

A **Prisoner's Dilemma** occurs when optimal noncooperative play results in an outcome that is inferior to another for both players.

Ways to Overcome the Prisoner's Dilemma

Collusion: This is illegal in most cases, although international cartels exist, such as the OPEC oil cartel and the De Beers diamond cartel. Also, free trade agreements are a legal form of cooperation between countries.

Tacit collusion: Occurs when one player takes the lead, and everyone else follows. This strategy is more effective when games are repeated, allowing for the possibility of retaliation should other players not cooperate.

Trigger Strategies Used in Repeated Games

Grim trigger: When one player defects, the other refuses to cooperate again (no forgiveness).

American Airlines was the first major airline to charge for checked baggage. Almost all other airlines followed, allowing the airlines to achieve a mutually beneficial outcome.

Trembling hand trigger: Players forgive certain instances of defection as "mistakes" before retaliation is taken.

Tit-for-tat trigger: Essentially an eye-for-an-eye: If one player defects, the other player punishes this player until cooperation resumes.

Chicken games occur when opposing players have an incentive to maintain a tough stance; however, if neither player refuses to back down, the worst outcome for both players occurs.

QUESTIONS AND PROBLEMS

Check Your Understanding

1. How do monopolistically competitive markets differ from perfectly competitive markets? If monopolistically competitive firms are making economic profits in the short run, what happens in the long run?

2. How do monopolistically competitive firms exhibit market power? In what ways can a firm increase market power?

3. Explain what strategic interdependence means and how it applies to oligopoly markets.

4. Why is it difficult for cartels to maintain high prices effectively over the longer term?

5. Why would the use of repeated games make overcoming the Prisoner's Dilemma easier compared to a game that is played only once?

6. What is the difference between a tit-for-tat trigger strategy and a grim trigger strategy?

Apply the Concepts

7. "Monopolistic competition has a little of monopoly and a little of competition, hence its name." Do you agree? Why or why not?

8. We saw in the last chapter that the HHI (Herfindahl-Hirschman index) is used by the Department of Justice to measure industry concentration. Because domestically we have very few monopolies, some would argue that the HHI is really used to measure the degree of oligopoly. However, the HHI represents domestic concentration, and many of the products we purchase are made globally and sold in the United States by foreign firms. Has global competition made these HHI estimates less meaningful? Are old-line American oligopolies (autos, steel, and airlines) more like monopolistic competitors today? Why or why not?

9. In both competitive and monopolistically competitive markets, firms earn normal profits in the long run. What enables oligopoly firms to have the opportunity to earn economic profits in the long run?

10. Poker players are known to *bluff* once in a while, meaning that they will make a large bet despite holding bad cards in an effort to pressure other players to *fold* their hands. Would bluffing be considered a dominant strategy to be used in poker?

11. Suppose you choose to pledge for your top choice of sorority or fraternity at your university. Despite the tiny odds of getting accepted into your top choice, that does not deter you from spending all of rush week focusing on your top choice. Would this strategy coincide with a best-response strategy in a Nash equilibrium?

12. Suppose two competing stores each announce a "low price guarantee," meaning that each store would match the prices of the other store if they were lower. Does providing this guarantee make it easier or more difficult to overcome the Prisoner's Dilemma facing the two firms?

In the News

13. The *Wall Street Journal* reported on April 25, 2012, that Pakistan launched a test missile in response to India launching a missile of its own the previous week. Both countries want to prove that they are the dominant military power in South Asia. Explain how this ongoing game between nuclear powers represents a game of chicken, and what might happen if neither side chooses to back down.

14. "Bank of America Faces Outrage over Debit Card Charge" was the headline in the *Washington Post* on September 30, 2011. Bank of America attempted to institute a new fee on debit card accounts by charging its debit card users $5 per month, in hopes that other banks would follow its lead. However, no other major bank did, and Bank of America was pummeled in the media and by customers who closed their accounts until Bank of America relented and dropped the new fee. Explain how Bank of America was attempting to overcome the Prisoner's Dilemma. Provide reasons why this attempt was unsuccessful.

Solving Problems

15. Suppose each member of a diamond cartel consisting of five producers agrees to sell 100 carats of diamonds a day. With 500 total carats being sold, the market price is $1,000/carat, and each firm earns $100,000. Now assume that one producer cheats by producing 110 carats, causing the market price for 510 total carats to drop to $980/carat. How does this action affect the revenues of the cheating firm and the noncheating firms? Suppose the four noncheating firms change course and all produce 110 carats, and the market price for 550 total carats drops to $850/carat. How much does each firm earn now? How important is loyalty to maintaining an effective cartel?

16. The following shows a pricing game between JetBlue and Delta. Each airline has a choice between engaging in a fare sale or not. The resulting profits of each airline are provided, where the first number in each payoff box equals JetBlue's profit and the second number is Delta's profit.

		Delta			
		Fare sale		**No fare sale**	
JetBlue	**Fare sale**	80	500	200	800
	No fare sale	50	700	100	1200

What is the Nash equilibrium of this game? Does this game resemble a Prisoner's Dilemma? Explain.

#️⃣ USING THE NUMBERS

17. According to By the Numbers, in terms of number of restaurants, what percentage of all restaurants among the top ten chains is a Subway, McDonald's, or a Starbucks? (Hint: First calculate the total number of Subways, McDonald's, and Starbucks combined and compare with the total restaurants among all top ten chains.)

18. According to By the Numbers, if the third and fourth largest wireless providers merged into one new company, would the combined company surpass the market share of either of the largest two firms prior to the merge?

Checkpoint: Monopolistic Competition

Although both hotels are located on Disney property, the Grand Floridian Resort is much closer to the theme parks, and is located on the Monorail for easy transportation throughout the park. Also, the Grand Floridian is an upscale hotel with many fine restaurants and shops, and offers luxurious room amenities. The All-Star Resort, on the other hand, caters to budget conscious families that are willing to forgo some convenience and amenities in exchange for significant savings. Disney differentiates its hotels to cater to different groups of customers with varying willingness-to-pay. The result is a significant price difference between the two hotels.

Checkpoint: Oligopoly

A cartel functions best when its members adhere to the established quotas (which keep prices for drugs high) and also when no external competition exists (allowing the cartel to operate as if it were a monopoly). Competition from noncartel drug traffickers as well as cartel members exceeding their production quotas poses a threat to the cartel's existence, and hence cartels will often use violence to prevent those activities from occurring. When the drug trade is dominated by several large and powerful organizations, the actions of one organization have a significant effect on the others, an example of the mutual interdependence of firms in an oligopoly.

Checkpoint: Game Theory

This is a situation in which each player must develop a coordination strategy to achieve a Nash equilibrium (a connected call). No rule exists for coordination strategies. Instead, such strategies often are formed by experience. For example, the person who calls back might be the one who made the initial call, or the one who typically calls. Or, it might be the one who has more at stake in the call (such as a pesky friend asking to borrow money). With more experience, coordination strategies become easier to implement.

Checkpoint: Applications of Game Theory

This strategy might work in theory if everybody in the class is committed to it. Practically speaking, it's highly unlikely that everyone would stick to the agreement. For example, if you were someone destined to receive a C or a D, and you know that the A and B students promised not to study if you don't study, you would have a strong incentive to break your promise and study hard knowing that an A or a B is now within easier reach. At the same time, those destined for an A or a B might want to insure themselves against the plan by studying to secure the high grade. In the end, the cooperative agreement does not hold, because each player has a dominant strategy to study. This represents a Prisoner's Dilemma because, in the end, everyone studies and the scheme falls apart.

The Labor Market

11

Why are Kyle Blanks and Ramiro Peña making more than the president of the United States? Have you ever heard of these guys?

After studying this chapter you should be able to:

- Define and describe competitive labor markets.
- Derive a supply curve for labor.
- Describe the factors that can change labor supply.
- Describe the factors that can change labor demand.
- Determine the elasticity of demand for labor.
- Determine the competitive market equilibrium for labor.
- Describe Becker's theory of economic discrimination.
- Describe the concept of segmented labor markets and how they affect wage levels.
- Describe federal laws and policies regarding discrimination.
- Describe the history, costs, and benefits of trade unions.

Did you see where some baseball player just signed a contract for $50,000 a year just to play ball? It wouldn't surprise me if someday they'll be making more than the President.

QUOTE FROM 1955

Some professions, such as baseball, try to maintain their traditions, but salaries for Major League Baseball players certainly have not remained the same. The average professional athlete did not used to be a multimillionaire. In 1964, the average salary in Major League Baseball was a mere $14,000 (about $100,000 in current inflation-adjusted dollars), suggesting that professional athletes back then chose their careers for the love of the game rather than as a way to become rich. Today, the labor market for professional athletes has changed. With lucrative advertising revenue and broadcasting rights, professional sport has become big business. In 2012, companies spent $28.6 billion for advertising in all U.S. sports. The World Series between the San Francisco Giants and the Detroit Tigers alone generated over $150 million, impressive considering only four of seven games were played, as the Giants swept the series.

Because the labor market demand for athletes is so great, professional sports leagues need to pay much higher salaries than they did 50 years ago in order to encourage the very best athletes to seek a career in sports. The result of this increase in demand in the labor market is a dramatic rise in salaries. In 2012, the average salary for a Major League Baseball player was $3,440,000, with the top earning player, Alex Rodriguez, earning $29 million. Even relatively unknown players, such as Kyle Blanks and Ramiro Peña, made over $480,000, the minimum salary in Major League Baseball in 2012. The president of the United States makes $400,000 a year. Indeed, the prediction from 1955 came true . . . for every player in the major leagues!

This chapter and the next begin our analysis of input markets, also called factor markets. Up to this point in the book, we have focused on product markets, mentioning input markets only incidentally. Sitting behind the production of goods and services, however, are inputs: workers, machinery, and manufacturing plants. Few firms can operate without employees or capital. Similarly, few households could survive without the income that work provides. Fortunately, many of the tools we introduced for the product market, such as demand and supply analysis, apply the same way in input markets. The main difference, however, is that in input markets, firms demand inputs whereas in product markets, firms supply goods and services.

This chapter focuses on the analysis of labor markets. The first two sections look at competitive labor markets, where the participants—firms and employees—are price takers. We then take a closer look at several situations in which wages are not set by competitive markets: instances of economic discrimination, and the economic effects of labor unions.

BY THE NUMBERS

Your Wages and Your Job After College

College students face important career decisions once they graduate. Some choose to pursue a professional or graduate degree, while others choose to venture into the labor force. One of the key factors influencing this decision is the wages offered to college graduates.

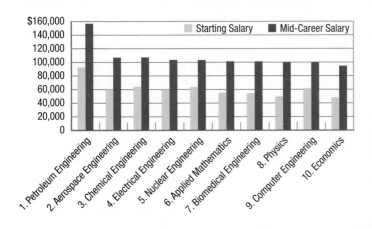

Legend: ▨ Starting Salary ■ Mid-Career Salary

(y-axis: $160,000 / 140,000 / 120,000 / 100,000 / 80,000 / 60,000 / 40,000 / 20,000 / 0)

(x-axis categories: 1. Petroleum Engineering, 2. Aerospace Engineering, 3. Chemical Engineering, 4. Electrical Engineering, 5. Nuclear Engineering, 6. Applied Mathematics, 7. Biomedical Engineering, 8. Physics, 9. Computer Engineering, 10. Economics)

Choosing the right major in college can lead to a higher paying job. Economics is among the top 10 highest earning undergraduate majors out of a total of 128 majors surveyed. Studying economics can be interesting *and* lucrative!

Randy Faris/Corbis

82.2%

Average salary for women as a percent of men's salaries for the same occupation in 2012.

41.3%

Average cost of full-time employee benefits (paid vacation, sick leave, health insurance, retirement benefits, and employer tax contributions) as a percent of wages.

Average Starting Salaries for Jobs Out-of-College in 2011.

Journalist:	$35,527
Counselor:	$37,392
Public school teacher:	$37,881
Architect:	$39,561
Marketing coordinator:	$43,628
Registered nurse:	$44,104
Hotel manager:	$46,106
Web designer:	$48,160
Accountant:	$50,708
Financial analyst:	$52,689
Computer technician:	$54,667
Electrical engineer:	$58,247

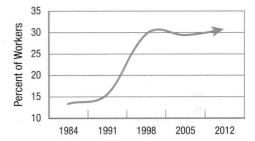

(y-axis: Percent of Workers — 35 / 30 / 25 / 20 / 15 / 10; x-axis: 1984 / 1991 / 1998 / 2005 / 2012)

Careers with flexible working hours ("flextime") increased in the 1980s and 1990s and have since leveled off. Today, three in ten full-time workers in the United States have flexible work schedules.

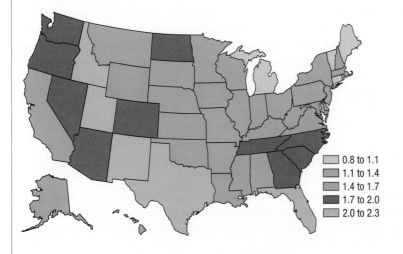

Legend:
▢ 0.8 to 1.1
▨ 1.1 to 1.4
▨ 1.4 to 1.7
■ 1.7 to 2.0
▨ 2.0 to 2.3

Projected annual job growth (in percent) through 2017 is shown by state. States with the highest projected job growth include Idaho, Texas, Utah, New Mexico, and Florida.

Competitive labor markets are similar to competitive product markets. We make several key assumptions. First, we assume that firms operate in competitive industries with many buyers and sellers, a homogeneous product, and easy entry and exit. A second assumption of competitive labor markets is that workers are regarded as equally productive, such that firms have no preference for one employee over another. Inhumane as it sounds, labor is treated as a homogeneous commodity. Third, a competitive labor market assumes that information in the industry is widely available and accurate. Everyone knows what the going wage rate is, therefore well-informed decisions about how much labor to supply are made by workers, and firms can wisely decide how many workers to hire.

A firm's demand for labor is a derived demand; it is derived from consumer demand for the firm's product and the productivity of labor. The labor supply, on the other hand, is determined by the individual preferences of potential workers for work or leisure. Like all competitive markets, supply and demand interact to determine equilibrium wages and employment.

Following the analysis of the competitive labor market, we then ask why some people make more than others. Although differences in occupation and skill levels play a dominant role in determining wages, how often are wage differences the result of discrimination against people of a certain race, ethnicity, or gender?

Another reason for differences in wages is the role of unions. Unions are legal associations of employees that bargain with employers over terms and conditions of work. Unions use strikes and the threat of strikes to achieve their goals. The Major League Baseball Players Association is a powerful union, which negotiates salaries and benefits on behalf of its members. Sometimes disputes between the players union and team owners have resulted in strikes. In 1994–1995, a long strike led to a very short baseball season. Without the union, today's baseball players might not all be making more than the president of the United States.

⊙ Competitive Labor Supply

Economists divide your activities into two categories: work and leisure. When you decide to work, you are giving up leisure, understood broadly as nonwork activity, in exchange for the income that work brings. Economists assume people prefer leisure activities to work. This may not be entirely true, as work can be a source of personal satisfaction and a network of social connections, as well as provide many other benefits. For our discussion, however, we follow the practice of economists in dividing individual or household time into just work and leisure. Note that the term *leisure* encompasses all activities that do not involve paid work, including caring for children, doing household chores, and activities that are truly leisurely.

Individual Labor Supply

supply of labor The amount of time an individual is willing to work at various wage rates.

The **supply of labor** represents the time an individual is willing to work—the labor the individual is willing to supply—at various wage rates. On a given day, the most a person can work is 24 hours, although clearly such a schedule could not be sustained for long, given that we all need rest and sleep. For high wages, you would probably be willing to work horrendous hours for a short time, whereas if wages were low enough, you might not be willing to work at all. Between these two extremes lies the normal supply of labor curve for most people.

Figure 1 shows a typical labor supply curve for individuals. This individual is willing to supply l_1 hours of work per day when the wage is W_1. What happens if the wage rate increases? Assume that wages increase to W_2: This individual now is willing to increase hours spent working from l_1 to l_2 (point b). But if the wage rate increases further to W_3, this individual reduces the hours spent working back to l_1 (point c). What determines how many hours a person is willing to work at each wage rate?

substitution effect Higher wages mean that the value of work has increased, and the opportunity costs of leisure are higher, hence work is substituted for leisure.

Substitution Effect When wages rise, people tend to substitute work for leisure because the opportunity cost of leisure grows. This is known as the **substitution effect.** The substitution effect for labor supply is always positive; it leads to more hours of work when the wage rate increases.

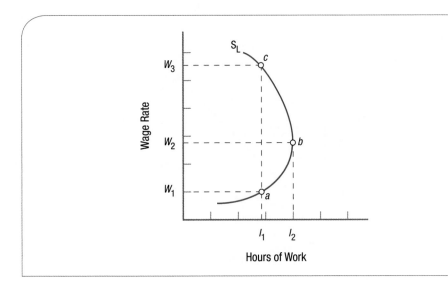

FIGURE 1

Individual Supply of Labor
When wages are W_1, this individual will work l_1 hours, but when the wage rate rises to W_2, her willingness to work rises to l_2. Over these two wage rates she is substituting work for leisure. Once the wage rises above W_2, the income effect begins to dominate, since she now has sufficient income that leisure is now more important and her labor supply curve is backward bending.

Note that this effect is similar to the substitution effect consumers experience when the price of a product declines. When the price of one product falls, consumers substitute that product for others. The substitution effect for consumer products, however, is negative (price falls and consumption rises), while it is always positive for labor (wages rise and the supply of labor increases).

Income Effect When wages rise, if you continue to work the same hours as before, your income will rise. As income rises, you have an ability to purchase more goods, *including leisure*. Thus, as wages rise to a level high enough to live the lifestyle you wish, you might desire to reduce the hours you work (besides, if you work too much you won't have time to enjoy spending the money you earned). This notion of working less (and consuming more leisure) as wages rise is known as the **income effect**. The income effect on labor supply is normally negative—higher wages and income lead to fewer hours worked as individuals desire more leisure. This effect counteracts the substitution effect, which encourages individuals to work more as wages rise.

Both the substitution and income effects are present for all individuals, but at varying levels. The individual supply of labor, therefore, depends on which effect is stronger at each wage rate, and the individual labor supply curve is *backward bending* as shown in Figure 1.

When the labor supply curve is positively sloped, as it is below W_2 in Figure 1, the substitution effect is stronger than the income effect; income is more important than leisure at these wage levels, thus, higher wages lead to more hours worked. Conversely, when the supply of labor curve bends backward, as it does above W_2, the income effect overpowers the substitution effect. In this case, higher wages mean fewer hours worked.

Backward bending labor supply curves have been observed empirically in developed and developing countries. Still, it takes rather high income levels before the income effect begins to overpower the substitution effect. People like to have incomes well beyond what is required to satisfy their basic needs before they select more leisure over work as wages rise.

Market Labor Supply Curves

The labor supply for any occupation or industry is upward sloping; higher wages for a job mean more inquiries and job applications. Thus, although an individual's labor supply curve may be backward bending, market labor supply curves are normally positively sloped as shown in Figure 2 on the next page. Note that this is true for all other inputs to the production process, including raw materials such as copper, steel, and silicon, as well as for capital and land: Higher prices mean higher quantities supplied.

income effect Higher wages mean that you can maintain the same standard of living by working fewer hours. The impact on labor supply is generally negative.

Market Labor Supply

Market labor supply is positively related to the wage rate. Increasing wages in one industry attract labor from other industries (a movement from point *d* to point *e* as the wage rises from W_1 to W_2). In contrast, market labor supply curves *shift* in response to demographic changes, changes in the nonwage benefits of jobs, wages paid in other occupations, and nonwage income.

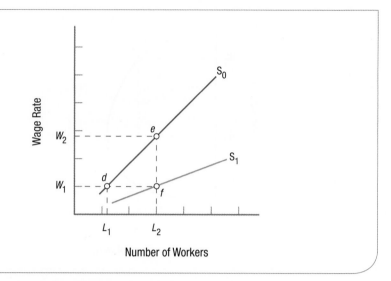

Changes in wage rates change the quantity of labor supplied. For example, increasing wages in one industry attract labor from other industries. This is a movement along the market labor supply curve, shown as a movement along S_0 from points *d* to *e* as wages (input prices) rise from W_1 to W_2.

Factors That Change Labor Supply

What factors will cause the entire market labor supply curve to shift from, say, S_0 to S_1 in Figure 2 so that L_2 workers are willing to work for a wage of W_1 (point *f*)? These include demographic changes, nonwage benefits of jobs, wages paid in other occupations, and nonwage income.

Demographic Changes Changes in population, immigration patterns, and labor force participation rates (the percentage of individuals in a group who enter the labor force) all change labor supplies by altering the number of qualified people available for work.

Over the past three decades, labor force participation rates among women have steadily risen, continually adding workers to the expanding American labor force; dual-earner households are increasingly the norm. Today, both parents work in about 60% of all married-couple households with children.

Another demographic change is the increasing portion of population growth in the United States resulting from immigration (both legal and illegal). Over 80% of net population growth over the next four decades will result from immigrants and their U.S.-born descendants.[1] This will have a significant effect on the labor supply.

Finally, other demographic changes have shifted the labor supply curve by modifying the labor–leisure preferences among workers. Health improvements, for example, have lengthened the typical working life, thereby increasing the supply of labor.

Nonmoney Aspects of Jobs Changes in the nonwage benefits of an occupation will similarly shift the supply of labor in that market. If employers can manage to increase the pleasantness, safety, or status of a job, labor supply will increase. Other nonmoney perks also help. The airline industry, for example, has greatly increased the number of people willing to work in mundane positions by allowing employees to fly anywhere free.

Wages in Alternative Jobs When worker skills in one industry are readily transferable to other jobs or industries, the wages paid in those other markets will affect wage rates and the labor supply in the first industry. For example, Web site designers and computer

---

[1] Jeffrey Passel and D'Vera Cohn, "Immigration to Play Lead Role in Future U.S. Growth," Pew Research Center Publications, February 11, 2008.

technicians are useful in all industries, and their wages in one industry affect all industries. Because at least some of the skills that all workers possess will benefit other employers, all labor markets have some influence over each other. Rising wages in growth industries will shrink the supply of labor available to firms in other industries.

Nonwage Income Changes in income from sources other than working (such as income from a trust) will change the supply of labor. As nonwage income rises, hours of work supplied declines. If you have enough income from nonwork sources, after all, the retirement urge will set in no matter what your age.

The key thing to remember here is that market labor supply curves are normally positively sloped, even though an individual's labor supply curve may be backward bending. In the next section, we put this together with the other blade of the scissors: the demand for labor in competitive labor markets.

 CHECKPOINT

COMPETITIVE LABOR SUPPLY

- Competitive labor markets assume that firms operate in competitive product markets and purchase homogeneous labor, and that information is widely available and accurate.

- The supply of labor represents the time an individual is willing to work.

- The substitution effect occurs when wages rise, as people tend to substitute work for leisure because the opportunity cost of leisure is higher, or vice versa when wages fall.

- When wages rise and you continue to work the same number of hours, your income rises. When wages rise high enough, an income effect occurs in which income is traded for leisure, and the supply of labor curve for individuals is backward bending.

- Industry or occupation labor supply curves are upward sloping.

- The labor supply curve shifts with demographic changes, changes in the nonwage aspects of an occupation, changes in the wages of alternative jobs, and changes in nonwage income.

QUESTIONS: Assume that you take a job with flexible hours, but initially your salary is based on a 40-hour week. Your salary begins at $15 an hour, or $30,000 a year. Assuming your salary rises, at what salary (hourly wage) would you begin to work fewer than 40 hours a week (remember, the job permits flexible hours)? If your rich aunt dies and leaves you $500,000, would this alter the wage rate at which you cut your work hours? Do you think this wage rate will be the same when you are 35 and have two children?

Answers to the Checkpoint questions can be found at the end of this chapter.

Competitive Labor Demand

The competitive firm's **demand for labor** is derived from the demand for the firm's product and the productive capabilities of a unit of labor.

Marginal Revenue Product

Assume that a firm wants to hire an additional worker, and that worker is able to produce 15 units of the firm's product. Further, assume that the product sells for $10 a unit, and labor is the only input cost (such as blackberry picking in Oregon), with this cost including a normal return on the investment. The last worker hired is therefore worth $150 to the firm ($15 \times \$10 = \$150$). If the cost of hiring this worker is $150 or less (remember, a normal profit is included in the wage), then the firm will hire this person. If the wage rate for labor exceeds $150, a competitive firm will not hire this marginal worker.

demand for labor Demand for labor is derived from the demand for the firm's product and the productivity of labor.

MRP differs from worker to worker. As we saw in Chapter 7, production is subject to diminishing marginal returns. In the example of blackberry picking, the first blackberry picker takes the nearest low-hanging fruit. The next picker takes low-hanging fruit farther away. The third has to do a little more work to harvest the same amount of fruit. Because each additional worker is able to pick less fruit per day, the MRP of each additional worker will correspondingly fall. This decrease in MRP represents the same diminishing marginal returns concept introduced in the product market.

To see how this works in greater detail, look at Table 1. The production function here is similar to the one used earlier in the chapter on production. Column (1) is labor input (L), column (2) is total output (Q), and column (3) is the **marginal physical product of labor** (MPP$_L$). This last value is the additional output a firm receives from employing an added unit of labor (MPP$_L$ = $\Delta Q \div \Delta L$). For example, adding a fourth worker raises output from 25 to 40 units, thus the marginal physical product of labor for this additional worker is 15 units.

marginal physical product of labor The additional output a firm receives from employing an added unit of labor (MPP$_L$ = $\Delta Q \div \Delta L$).

TABLE 1	Competitive Labor Market			
(1) L	(2) Q	(3) MPP$_L$	(4) MRP$_L$ (P = $10)	(5) W
0	0			$100
		7	$70	
1	7			$100
		8	$80	
2	15			$100
		10	$100	
3	25			$100
		15	$150	
4	40			$100
		14	$140	
5	54			$100
		11	$110	
6	65			$100
		10	$100	
7	75			$100
		9	$90	
8	84			$100
		6	$60	
9	90			$100
		5	$50	
10	95			$100

In this example, the firm is operating in a competitive market, therefore it can sell all the output it produces at the prevailing market price of $10. The value of another worker to the firm, called the **marginal revenue product** (MRP$_L$), is equal to the marginal physical product of labor times marginal revenue:

marginal revenue product The value of another worker to the firm is equal to the marginal physical product of labor (MPP$_L$) times marginal revenue (MR).

$$\text{MRP}_L = \text{MPP}_L \times \text{MR}$$

In our example, adding a fourth worker leads to a marginal revenue product of $150; we multiply the marginal physical product of labor of 15 units by the marginal revenue—or price in this competitive market—of $10 per unit.

A related term to marginal revenue product is the **value of the marginal product,** defined as VMP$_L$ = MPP$_L$ × P. Because competitive firms are price takers for whom marginal revenue is equal to the price of the product (MR = P), VMP$_L$ = MRP$_L$ in the competitive case.

value of the marginal product The value of the marginal product of labor (VMP$_L$) is equal to marginal physical product of labor times price, or MPP$_L$ × P.

Column (4) contains the firm's MRP$_L$. Additional workers add this value to the firm. Thus, the marginal revenue product curve is the firm's demand for labor, which is graphed

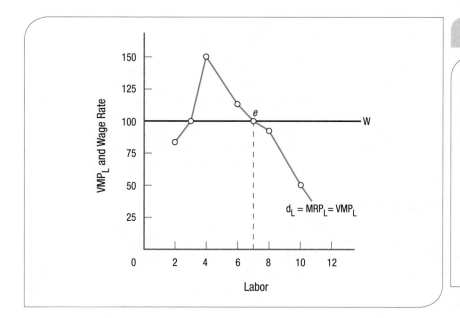

FIGURE 3

The Competitive Firm's Demand for Labor

This figure reflects the data from columns (4) and (5) of Table 1. In this example, the firm is operating in a competitive market, therefore it can sell all the output it produces at the prevailing market price. The value of the additional worker to the firm, the marginal revenue product (MRP_L), is equal to the marginal physical product of labor times marginal revenue (or price in this case). MRP_L is the competitive firm's demand for labor. If wages are equal to $100, the firm will hire 7 workers (point e).

in Figure 3. Note how the marginal revenue product reaches a maximum at 4 workers, as shown in column (4) of the table and in the figure.

Competitive firms hire labor from competitive labor markets. Because each firm is too small to affect the larger market, it can hire all the labor it wants at the market-determined wage.

Table 1 and Figure 3 assume that the going wage for labor (W) is $100. For our firm, this results in 7 workers being hired at $100 (point e), because this is the employment level at which $W = MRP_L$. Note that $W = MRP_L$ at 3 workers as well, but because the marginal revenue product is greater than the wage rate for workers 4 to 6, the firm would hire 7 workers, not 3, to maximize its gains. The value to the firm of hiring the seventh worker is just equal to what the firm must pay this worker. Profits are maximized for the competitive firm when workers are hired out to the point at which $MRP_L = W$.

However, if market wages were to fall to $90, the firm would hire an eighth worker to maximize profits, because with 8 employees, MRP_L is also equal to $90.

In a competitive labor market, the prevailing wage ($90 in this case) would be paid to each worker regardless of the actual MRP. Thus, firms maximize gains from hiring workers in the labor market similar to how consumers maximize consumer surplus when buying goods and services in the product market.

Factors That Change Labor Demand

The demand for labor is derived from product demand and labor productivity—how much people will pay for the product and how much each unit of labor can produce. It follows that changes in labor demand can arise from changes in either product demand or labor productivity. Because most production also requires other inputs, changes in the price of these other inputs also change the demand for labor.

Changes in Product Demand A decline in the demand for a firm's product will lead to lower market prices, reducing MRP_L, and vice versa. As MRP_L for all workers declines, labor demand will shift to the left. Anything that changes the price of the product in competitive markets will shift the firm's demand for labor.

A recent trend in the movie industry is for people to download movies directly to their computers or to order movies directly from their televisions. This has decreased demand for movies on DVDs, and subsequently led to a reduction in prices. As a result, labor demand by DVD movie manufacturers has shifted to the left.

Digital price tags, such as the one found in this European supermarket, make workers more productive.

Changes in Productivity Changes in worker productivity (usually increases) can come about from improving technology or because a firm uses more capital or land along with its workforce. For example, some supermarkets have introduced digital price tags on their store shelves, allowing prices to be changed remotely instead of having a store clerk physically replace each tag on the shelf as prices change. Such improvements in productivity raise MPP_L. The demand for the marginal worker rises, shifting the demand for labor to the right as firms are willing to pay higher wages. To be sure, the number of workers hired may fall due to digitalization, but the workers programming the price codes, as in any capital-intensive industry, are generally more highly skilled and hence earn higher wages.

Changes in the Prices of Other Inputs Changes in input prices can affect the demand for labor through their effect on capital prices. For example, rising steel and glass prices can dramatically raise the costs of equipment such that firms are unable to replace aging equipment. Without the ability to afford the rising costs of new capital equipment, firms are forced to substitute labor for capital in new projects, thus increasing the demand for labor. Relative costs of capital and labor will therefore affect the capital and labor mix firms choose for their production.

At this point, we know that more labor will be hired when wages fall, but how much more? The answer depends on the elasticity of demand for labor.

Elasticity of Demand for Labor

elasticity of demand for labor The percentage change in the quantity of labor demanded divided by the percentage change in the wage rate.

The **elasticity of demand for labor** (E_L) is the percentage change in the quantity of labor demanded (Q_L) divided by the percentage change in the wage rate (W). This elasticity is found the same way we calculated the price elasticity of demand for products, except that we substitute the wage rate for the price of the product:

$$E_L = \frac{\%\Delta Q_L}{\%\Delta W}$$

The elasticity of demand for labor measures how responsive the quantity of labor demanded is to changes in wages. An inelastic demand for labor is one in which the absolute value of the elasticity is less than 1. Conversely, an elastic curve's computed elasticity is greater than 1.

The time firms have to adjust to changing wages will affect elasticity. In the short run, when labor is the only truly variable factor of production, elasticity of demand for labor is more inelastic. In the long run, when all production factors can be adjusted, elasticity of demand for labor tends to be more elastic.

Factors That Affect the Elasticity of Demand for Labor

Although time affects elasticity, three other factors also affect the elasticity of demand for labor: elasticity of product demand, ease of substituting other inputs, and labor's share of the production costs. Let's briefly consider each of these.

Elasticity of Demand for the Product The more price elastic the demand for a product, the greater the elasticity of demand for labor. Higher wages result in higher product prices, and the more easily consumers can substitute away from the firm's product, the greater the number of workers who will become unemployed. An elastic demand for labor means that employment is more responsive to wage rates. The opposite is true for products with inelastic demands.

Ease of Input Substitutability The more difficult it is to substitute capital for labor, the more inelastic the demand for labor will be. At this point, computers cannot yet substitute for pilots in commercial airplanes, which results in an inelastic demand for pilots. As a result, pilots have been able to secure high wages from airlines. The easier it is to substitute capital for labor, the less bargaining power workers have, and labor demand tends to be more elastic.

Labor's Share of Total Production Costs The share of total costs associated with labor is another factor determining the elasticity of demand for labor. If labor's share of total costs is small, the demand for labor will tend to be rather inelastic. In the example of airline pilots, the percentage of costs going to pilot wages is small, perhaps 10%. Thus, a large increase in pilot wages would have a relatively small effect on ticket prices and demand, resulting in little change in demand for pilot labor. The opposite is true when labor's share of costs is large.

Competitive Labor Market Equilibrium

Generalized market equilibrium in competitive labor markets requires that we take into account the industry supply and demand for labor. The market supply for labor (S_L) is the horizontal sum of the individual labor supply curves in the market.

The market demand for labor, however, is not simply a summation of the demand for labor by all the firms in the market. When wages fall, for instance, this affects all firms—all want to hire more labor and produce more output. This added production reduces market prices for their output and negatively affects the demand for labor. For our purposes it is enough to be aware that market demands for labor are not the horizontal summation of individual firm demands.

Turning to Figure 4, we have put both sides of the market together. In panel A, the competitive labor market determines equilibrium wage ($100 per day) and employment (300 workers) based on market supply and demand. Individual firms, in light of their own situation, hire 6 workers at the point where this equilibrium wage is equal to marginal revenue product (MRP_L), point *e* in panel B. Much like the product markets we discussed in earlier chapters, the invisible hand of the marketplace sets wages and in the end determines employment.

To this point we have assumed that labor markets are competitive and that firms are able to hire as many workers as they desire at the prevailing wage rate. This analysis of competitive labor markets goes a long way but just as with product markets, it does not tell the whole story. We are going to look at two familiar cases in which the competitive

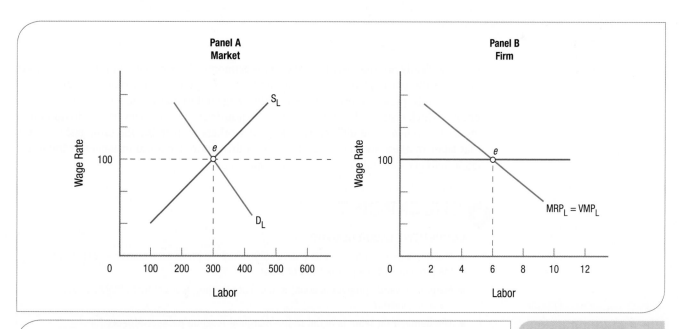

Competitive Labor Markets

In panel A, the competitive labor market determines equilibrium wages ($100 per day) and employment (300 workers). Individual firms hire 6 workers, where this equilibrium wage is equal to marginal revenue product (MRP_L), point *e* in panel B.

FIGURE 4

ISSUE

Reality TV and the Labor Market for Entertainers

Before the onslaught of reality shows that are today a ubiquitous presence on our television schedules, becoming a "TV star" was a much more arduous endeavor. One would need to find an agent and audition for specific roles, and then wait until a producer found an appropriate role for the aspiring actress or actor. The labor market for TV entertainment was considerably smaller at that time.

That all changed in 1992, when MTV debuted *The Real World* as an experiment bringing unknown people without any acting experience (but with unique personalities or traits) together to live in a house with cameras rolling. For the rest of the decade, *The Real World* continued to launch new seasons with new participants, but the idea of reality TV did not truly catch on until a major network, CBS, debuted *Survivor*, in 2000. Again produced as an experiment to fill a slow summer schedule, it became an instant hit.

Moreover, *Survivor* started a global phenomenon, which led to hundreds of reality shows including the top-rated series *The Amazing Race*, *The Apprentice*, and *Big Brother*, among others. Further, it led to the creation of new talent competitions including *American Idol* and *America's Got Talent*, which again turned unknowns into stars, even if just for one season.

How does reality TV affect the labor market for TV entertainers? With reality TV, almost anyone can audition for a show, with the eventual "star" being determined as the shows progress in front of television audiences. As a result, the supply of labor in the entertainment labor market has increased as more people seek to become the newest star.

But perhaps a greater effect is the new demand for labor. Traditional programs such as situation comedies and

The cast of the first season of *Survivor* started a global phenomenon of reality TV.

soap operas require networks to secure long-term contracts with their casts to ensure they return each season. Because reality TV stars generally appear for just one season, producers are constantly looking to cast new people each season. Although the success of reality TV has perhaps reduced the demand for traditional acting roles, it has created huge labor demand (opportunities), and subsequently higher wages, to the benefit of many aspiring entertainers.

model is clearly not the case. The first case is economic discrimination in the labor market in which the personal preferences of employers, employees, or consumers cause some workers to be preferred over others, creating wage differentials. The second case involves unions, which restrict labor supply in certain industries to raise wages relative to nonunion industries. When wage differentials exist for workers performing the same tasks, we say that labor markets are imperfect. There are other, more technical instances of imperfect labor markets—we hold these until the Appendix.

 CHECKPOINT

COMPETITIVE LABOR DEMAND

- The firm's demand for labor is a derived demand—derived from consumer demand for the product and the productivity of labor.

- Marginal revenue product is equal to the marginal physical product of labor times marginal revenue.

- The demand for labor is equal to the marginal revenue product of labor for competitive firms.

- The demand for labor curve will change if there is a change in the demand for the product, if there is a change in labor productivity, or if there is a change in the price of other inputs.

- The elasticity of demand for labor is equal to the percentage change in quantity of labor demanded divided by the percentage change in the wage rate.
- The elasticity of demand for labor will be *more* elastic the greater the elasticity of demand for the product, the easier it is to substitute other factors for labor, and the larger the share of total production costs attributed to labor.
- Market equilibrium occurs at the point at which the labor demand and supply curves intersect.

QUESTIONS: Individuals are different in terms of ability, attitude, and willingness to work. Given this fact, does it make sense to assume labor is homogeneous? Does this model better fit firms such as Wal-Mart that hire 800+ employees at each store at roughly standardized wages than, say, firms such as Google, which look for highly skilled computer geeks?

Answers to the Checkpoint questions can be found at the end of this chapter.

Economic Discrimination

We have seen that all workers are paid the same wage in competitive labor markets. This is seen in real life in low-skilled industries (such as fast-food restaurants) in which workers earn close to the minimum wage, or even in some occupations that require high-skilled workers whose wages are determined by contract based on market conditions. For example, public elementary school teachers in a district might all earn a starting salary set by a county school board. However, in industries in which managers are given discretion to set the wages of their employees, different wages may be given to employees doing the same work. Although these wage differentials may be due to differences in training or work experience, some differentials may be due to economic discrimination.

Economic discrimination takes place whenever workers of equal ability and productivity are paid different wages or are otherwise discriminated against in the workplace because of their race, color, religion, gender, age, national origin, sexual orientation, or disability. This can mean that one group is paid lower wages than another for doing the same job, or that members of different groups are segregated into occupations that pay different wages.

The U.S. Bureau of Labor Statistics (BLS) measures wages for persons of various races and ethnicities as well as by gender in the labor force. Each year, it collects data on the gender wage gap, the salary that women make as a percentage of what men earn in the same occupation. The trend has been a narrowing of the wage gap, indicating that gender discrimination has diminished over time. Less certain based on the data is whether discrimination based on race or ethnicity has seen similar improvements. Data from the BLS continue to show that African Americans and Latinos earn substantially less than Caucasians and Asians; however, these data are not separated by occupation, thus it is uncertain the extent these differences in earnings are due to discrimination as opposed to occupational choices.

Economic theories of discrimination generally take one of two approaches. The first, developed by Gary Becker, rests on the notion that bias is articulated in the *discriminatory tastes* of employers, workers, and consumers. The second approach, the *segmented markets approach,* maintains that labor markets are divided into segments based on race, gender, or some other category. This approach is often referred to as the *job crowding hypothesis,* or the *dual labor market hypothesis.*

economic discrimination When workers of equal ability are paid different wages or in any other way discriminated against because of race, color, religion, gender, age, national origin, or disability.

Becker's Theory of Economic Discrimination

Gary Becker's main contribution to economics is that he vastly broadened the issues that economists study. This was no small feat. Before Becker's influence, economists focused almost exclusively on the production and exchange of material goods and services. One early example shows the difficulties Becker faced in broadening this focus.

In 1955, Becker was asked to speak at Harvard about his dissertation on the economics of discrimination. Becker noted that his audience was perplexed. "They thought I

NOBEL PRIZE GARY BECKER

The 1992 winner of the Nobel Prize in Economic Sciences, Gary Becker, applied the theory of "rational choice" to areas of human behavior not ordinarily associated with economic analysis and research. He has offered provocative insights on a broad array of subjects, including family relations, racial discrimination, and the criminal justice system.

Born in Pottsville, Pennsylvania in 1930, Becker completed his undergraduate degree at Princeton before entering the University of Chicago, where he studied under economist Milton Friedman. In 1957, he published his dissertation, *The Economics of Discrimination,* an analysis of the effects of racial prejudice on earnings and employment among minorities.

In 1981, he published his book, *A Treatise on the Family.* According to his theory, rising wages led to changes in the family, including more women working outside the home instead of "specializing" in child care and housework. On questions of crime and punishment, Becker suggested that most criminals react in predictable ways to the costs and benefits of illegal activity; namely, that the probability of being caught and punished was a greater deterrent than the harsh nature of the punishment. On the question of race, Becker viewed discrimination as a "tax wedge" between social and private returns, concluding that prejudice tends to be economically detrimental to all parties concerned.

would discuss price discrimination"—that is, the analysis of why businesses charge different prices for the same goods. "No one conceived that an economist would talk about race discrimination in those days."[2]

Published in 1957, *The Economics of Discrimination* was not warmly received by the profession. Not until the mid-1960s, when the civil rights movement gained momentum, did the book receive the recognition it deserved. Surprisingly enough, Becker challenged the conventional view that discrimination benefits the person who discriminates. Let's see why he thought the conventional wisdom was wrong.

Becker argued that employers who discriminate against women will lose market share and profit opportunities, both because they do not always hire the best employees available, and because they must pay mostly high-wage male employees. Nondiscriminating firms, in contrast, will have lower labor costs, having more women earning lower wages on the payroll. Nondiscriminating firms will attract the most productive managers and employees, many of whom will be women. Profits for the nondiscriminating firm should therefore be higher. Becker concluded that the cost of wage differentials and the pressures of the marketplace should drive discrimination down to zero in the long run.

In practice, we know that wage discrimination still exists. According to the Bureau of Labor Statistics, women in 2012 earned 82.2% of what men earned in the same occupation. Why might competition fail to erase wage differentials? For one thing, the adjustment costs of firing unproductive workers, giving them severance pay, then recruiting and training new workers can be extremely high, especially considering the protections unions and the legal system offer workers. Second, women may be less mobile than men when it comes to work. They may be less willing to move to accommodate employer preferences, and thus be forced to accept lower wage positions. Third, if women continue to choose occupations with more flexible career paths that do not heavily penalize extended absences from the labor market, wage differentials between men and women may always exist. Note, however, that such differentials could also be caused by discrimination that precedes labor market entry, as when social norms direct girls toward lower-wage occupations such as elementary education or social work.

Segmented Labor Markets

segmented labor markets Labor markets split into separate parts. This leads to different wages paid to different sectors even though both markets are highly competitive.

Economists who advocate **segmented labor market** theories argue that discrimination does not arise due to a lack of competitive labor markets, but rather because these markets, although competitive, are segmented into a variety of constituent parts. And these different parts, while interacting, are noncompeting sectors. Segmented labor market theories have been developed along several different lines.

- The *dual labor market hypothesis* splits the labor market into primary and secondary sectors. The primary market consists of jobs that offer high wages, good working conditions, job stability, and advancement opportunities, while jobs in the secondary

[2] Peter Passell, "New Nobel Laureate Takes Economics Far Afield," *The New York Times,* October 14, 1992, p. D1.

market tend to have low wages and benefits, poor working conditions, high labor turnover, and little chance of advancement.

- The *job crowding hypothesis* breaks occupations into predominately male and female jobs. In 1922, Edgeworth recognized this problem when he wrote, "The pressure of male trade unions appears to be largely responsible for that crowding of women into a comparatively few occupations, which is universally recognized as a main factor in the depression of their wages."[3]

- The *insider-outsider theory* maintains that workers are segregated into those who belong to unions and those who are unemployed or are nonunion workers. Alternatively, economists have recognized that large firms use internal promotion and job security to inspire loyalty to the firm; however, such practices can also become an indirect method of segregating the labor market.

These hypotheses all predict that separate job markets will emerge for different groups. Figure 5 shows how segregated markets can lead to significant wage differentials, such as those we see for men and women.

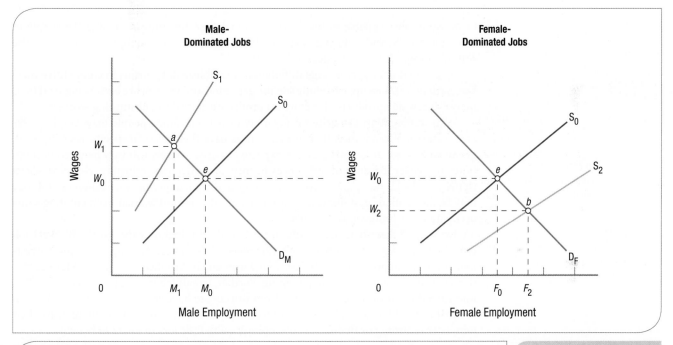

Job Crowding and a Dual Labor Market

Segregated markets can lead to significant wage differentials between men and women. Without discrimination, equilibrium wages will be W_0 for everyone, with total employment at $M_0 + F_0$. If, however, there is some form of discrimination in male-dominated jobs, the supply of labor to that segment will decline to S_1, wages will rise to W_1, and employment will fall to M_1 (point *a*). Those women who are excluded from jobs in this sector will have to move to available jobs in the female-dominated sector, thus increasing the labor supplied for these jobs to S_2, raising employment to F_2, but reducing wages to W_2 (point *b*). The result is a wage differential equal to $W_1 - W_2$.

FIGURE 5

In a world without discrimination, equilibrium wages for everyone would be W_0, with total employment at $M_0 + F_0$. If some form of discrimination in male-dominated jobs is present, labor supply to that segment will decline to S_1, wages will rise to W_1, and hiring will fall to M_1 (point *a*). Those women who are excluded from jobs in this sector will have

---

[3] F. Y. Edgeworth, "Equal Pay to Men and Women for Equal Work" (1922), p. 439, cited in Stephen Smith, *Labour Economics* (New York: Routledge), 1994, p. 102.

Traditional female-dominated and male-dominated professions are becoming less prevalent as gender discrimination and the gender wage gap continue to narrow.

to move to jobs available in the female-dominated sector, thus increasing the supply of labor there to S$_2$ and reducing wages to W_2, employment climbing to F_2 (point b). The result is a wage differential equal to $W_1 - W_2$.

Notice that once such a wage differential is established, the firms in competitive markets have no real incentive to eliminate the gap. Men and women are both being paid their marginal revenue products, therefore no profits are gained by substituting workers.

Wage differentials can arise for a variety of reasons. Some people may simply prefer one occupation to another. If such preferences have their roots in specific social groups, group-wide wage differentials can be expected to arise. Wages will vary between occupations, moreover, because of differences in their attractiveness, difficulty, riskiness, social status, and the human capital investments required. Still, lingering wage differentials today may be the result of past discriminatory practices that barred women from entering some occupations or professional schools.

Do wage differentials necessarily mean that discrimination exists in the market? Job crowding and wage differentials could just reflect different levels of human capital investment or different professional choices. Many women, for instance, may truly prefer occupations that are complementary to parenting. Further, female labor force participation is often interrupted when women take a break from working to have children. Therefore, jobs such as nursing, teaching, and administrative work may look attractive as women can leave their jobs, later returning or finding a new employer, with little loss in salary or benefits.

Public Policy to Combat Discrimination

For the first half of the last century, the inequities associated with various forms of discrimination were mostly accepted as a part of life in the United States. Gradually, however, a groundswell developed to end racial segregation and other forms of discrimination, culminating in passage of the Civil Rights Act in 1964. In what follows, we briefly outline the major acts and public policies that have been implemented with the goal of ending discrimination. Because of these policies, discrimination, wage differentials, and segmented labor markets have declined markedly over the past five decades.

The Equal Pay Act of 1963 The Equal Pay Act of 1963 amended the Fair Labor Standards Act of 1938. It requires that men and women receive equal pay for equal work. Equal work is defined as work performed under similar circumstances requiring equal effort, skill, and responsibility. Some argue that the Equal Pay Act was a hollow victory because occupational segregation forced women into specific occupations, causing them to earn less than men for essentially comparable work. Further, the law provided a limited time during which a worker must file a case against an employer for wage discrimination. This prevented many women from filing cases out of fear that they would lose their jobs.

In 2009, the Lily Ledbetter Fair Pay Act was signed into law, providing employees more flexibility to file cases asserting that they have been discriminated against with respect to pay. Specifically, it allowed the 180-day statute of limitations for filing a case to be reset with each discriminating paycheck received. Thus, a worker could file a case long after the discriminatory action began, as long as the worker had worked at the company within the last 180 days.

Civil Rights Act of 1964 Title VII of the Civil Rights Act of 1964 makes it unlawful to

> refuse to hire or to discharge any individual, or otherwise to discriminate against any individual with respect to his [her] compensation, terms, conditions, or privileges of employment, because of such individual's race, color, religion, sex, or national origin.

To date, most of the litigation brought under this statute has focused on the meaning of the phrase *to discriminate*, requiring a plaintiff to show that an employment practice inflicts a "disparate" or unequal impact on members of a minority group, as compared to its impact on others. Once this has been demonstrated, the burden shifts to the defendant (the employer) to show that its employment practices are related to employee performance or are otherwise a matter of "business necessity." Plaintiffs may sue for a full range of remedies, including back pay, reinstatement, court costs, attorney's fees, and punitive damages.

Executive Order 11246—Affirmative Action In 1965, President Lyndon Johnson issued Executive Order 11246. A key provision of this order required that firms doing at least $50,000 in business with the federal government submit an affirmative action program that includes a detailed analysis of their labor force.

Affirmative action programs have been controversial from the outset. Critics see such programs as "enforced quotas," whereas supporters see them as a way of breaking down discriminatory hiring barriers. Further, affirmative action has extended to other selection criteria such as college admissions.

In the summer of 2003, the U.S. Supreme Court ruled in the University of Michigan case (*Gratz v. Bollinger*) that adding a large specific numerical adjustment for minority group status to university admission criteria was unacceptable. The Law School at Michigan, on the other hand, simply took race into account in a nuanced approach to improving diversity of the class. The Supreme Court found this approach acceptable (*Grutter v. Bollinger*).

Age, Disabilities, and Sexual Orientation Two other acts were designed to reduce discrimination based on age and physical or mental disabilities. The Age Discrimination in Employment Act of 1967 protects workers over age 40 from discrimination based on age. The Americans with Disabilities Act of 1990 prohibits discrimination against people with a physical or mental disability who could still perform a job with reasonable accommodation by an employer. What constitutes "reasonable accommodation" has been a point of contention in many recent court cases. Lastly, the proposed Employment Non-Discrimination Act would prohibit discrimination against employees on the basis of sexual orientation or gender identity by civilian, nonreligious employers with at least 15 employees.

 CHECKPOINT

ECONOMIC DISCRIMINATION

- Economic discrimination occurs whenever workers of equal ability and productivity are paid different wages or otherwise discriminated against because of their race, color, religion, gender, age, national origin, sexual orientation, or disability.
- Becker's analysis of discrimination assumed that employers had a taste for discrimination, and he showed that both parties were harmed by discrimination.

- Segmented labor markets assume that separate markets lead to wage differentials that represent discrimination.
- Public policy to eliminate discrimination has included the Equal Pay Act of 1963, Civil Rights Act of 1964, Executive Order 11246 (Affirmative Action), Age Discrimination in Employment Act of 1967, Americans with Disabilities Act of 1990, and the Lily Ledbetter Fair Pay Act of 2009.

QUESTION: Some types of labor discrimination are more likely to be eroded by market forces than others. Provide an example of a type of discrimination that is likely to dissipate through the labor market and one that is likely to persist over time.

Answers to the Checkpoint question can be found at the end of this chapter.

Labor Unions and Collective Bargaining

Suppose Max, an engineer and project coordinator, has worked at a large construction company for eight years. He had been training new employees on various aspects of cost estimating and job specification, and he noticed that these new people were being hired at salaries approaching his own. He requested a raise several times, but was essentially ignored. Exasperated, he refused to go to work one day, informing his boss that he would not return without a raise. He did not quit; he simply staged a walkout and refused to return until given a raise. In other words, Max staged a one-man strike. He was out for two weeks before his supervisor called and asked him how much he wanted. They settled on a raise of over 20%.

This story is unique in that one-person strikes are rarely successful; more often they are career busters. In most instances, individual employees have little control over wages or job conditions, essentially being at the mercy of employers and the market. This is the primary reason that unions exist: Collective action is more powerful than the action of one individual. As individuals, we can easily be replaced (except in rare occasions like for Max in the story above). To replace an entire workforce, on the other hand, imposes serious costs to an employer.

This section looks at the role unions play in our economy, their history, and their effects on the labor market. We show how unions create wage differentials that work against the assumptions of the competitive labor market in which all workers earn the same wage. We will see that although unions have been successful in some industries, their influence has faded in other industries.

Types of Unions

Labor unions are legal associations of employees that bargain with employers over terms and conditions of work, including wages, benefits, and working conditions. They use strikes and threats of strikes, as well as other tactics, to try to achieve their goals.

Unions are usually defined by industry, or by craft or occupation. A *craft* union represents members of a specific craft or occupation, such as air traffic controllers (PATCO), truck drivers (Teamsters), and teachers (AFT). An *industrial* union represents all workers employed in a specific industry. Examples include auto workers (UAW) and public employees (AFSCME).

Benefits and Costs of Union Membership

Without a union, each individual employee would have to bargain with management over his or her own wages, benefits, and working conditions. Unions bring collective power to this bargaining arrangement. The source of this power is ultimately the willingness of the union to strike if no agreement is reached during negotiations. Collective bargaining often leads to a more equitable pay schedule than individual negotiation. It also provides workers with greater job security by protecting them against arbitrary or vindictive decisions by management.

Union membership, like everything else, has its price. First, union members must pay monthly dues. Then, if negotiations break down and a strike is called, wages are lost and the possibility exists, however remote, that management will refuse to settle with the union and replace the entire workforce. Finally, union workers must give up some individual flexibility because their work rules are more rigid.

Brief History of American Unionism

Labor unions date from the late 18th century in England. In the United States, public attitudes toward unions were highly unfavorable until the Great Depression. In the early part of the 20th century, employers could easily secure legal injunctions against union organization by arguing that unions behaved like monopolies, in violation of antitrust laws. Employers often required employees to sign enforceable *yellow dog contracts,* in which they agreed not to join a union as a condition of employment.

Figure 6 shows union membership as a percentage of total employment since 1930. Going into the 1930s, unions represented just over 7% of workers because of public attitudes and legal restrictions. With the onset of the Depression, attitudes about collective bargaining began to change. In 1932, Congress passed the Norris–LaGuardia Act, which outlawed yellow dog contracts and prohibited injunctions against union organizing. Then, in 1935, Congress enacted the Wagner Act, or the National Labor Relations Act (NLRA). It prohibited a variety of unfair labor practices by employers, including firing employees for engaging in union activities. The act also required employers to "bargain in good faith" with those unions that had won recognition through a majority vote of the firm's workers.

The NLRA also established the National Labor Relations Board (NLRB) to oversee union certification elections. These elections were to be held to determine which union, if any, would represent employees.

As Figure 6 illustrates, union membership grew dramatically from the mid-1930s until after World War II. Following the war, union membership covered over one-quarter of American workers. It was concentrated in a few major industries.

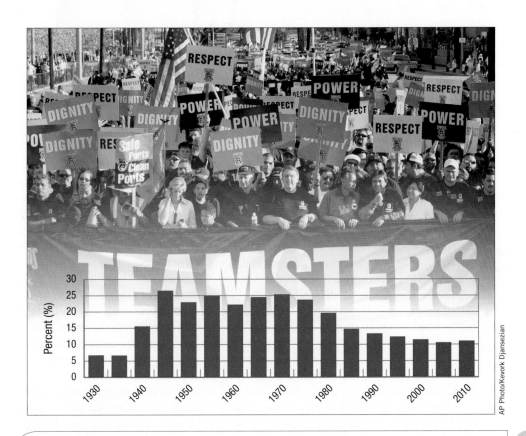

AP Photo/Kevork Djansezian

Union Membership as a Percent of Employment

Union membership grew dramatically from the mid-1930s until after World War II. Following the war, over one-quarter of American workers were unionized. Union membership has fallen because benefits obtained by unions for union members spread throughout the wider workforce, making the benefits of joining a union less valuable. Also, the changing economy led to faster growth in the service sector, which has traditionally been less unionized.

FIGURE 6

FIGURE 7

Work Stoppages (Strikes)

This figure shows work stoppages, or strikes, since 1950. In 1946, numerous strikes turned public opinion against unions. In 1947, Congress reacted by passing the Taft-Hartley Act, seeking a balance between unions and management. After this, the use of work stoppages by unions gradually began to decline.

closed shop Workers must belong to the union before they can be hired.

union shop Nonunion hires must join the union within a specified period of time.

agency shop Employees are not required to join the union, but must pay dues to compensate the union for its services.

right-to-work laws Laws created by the Taft-Hartley Act that permitted states to outlaw union shops.

Figure 7 shows work stoppages, or strikes, since 1950. In 1946 a rash of strikes turned public opinion against the unions; many people felt unions had become too powerful. Because of this swing in popular opinion, in 1947 Congress passed the Taft-Hartley Act, which prohibits some unfair labor practices by unions. Unions could no longer coerce or discriminate against workers who chose not to join the union, and unions were required to bargain in good faith, just like employers. With the passage of this act, the prolabor aspects of the 1935 Wagner Act were balanced.

Taft-Hartley changed the collective bargaining landscape dramatically by ending **closed shops,** workplaces in which workers are required to be union members before they can be hired. A **union shop** is one in which nonunion hires must join the union within a specified period, usually 30 days. In an **agency shop,** employees are not required to join the union, but they must pay union dues to compensate the union for its services. The Taft-Hartley Act outlawed closed shops outright, while permitting states to pass *right-to-work statutes* that prohibit union shops. Today, at least 24 states have **right-to-work laws.**

Until 1962, all collective bargaining statutes focused on the private sector; public employees were prohibited from organizing. In 1962, however, President John F. Kennedy signed Executive Order 10988, giving federal workers the right to bargain collectively. Still, public employees are not permitted to strike. Rather, when an impasse is reached, both sides must submit to binding arbitration in which a neutral arbitrator resolves the dispute. In 2011, the collective bargaining rights of public employees came to the forefront of public debate as many state legislatures considered bills to reverse these rights. This is discussed further in the Issue box on page 296.

Why has union membership declined as a percentage of wage and salary workers since World War II? The answer lies partly in the changes in labor laws just discussed, the country's changing economy—notably, a larger service sector—and ironically, the very success of labor at pushing its agenda of promoting rules that protect workers (such as minimum wage laws, antidiscrimination statues, and restrictions on firing employees) through Congress and the courts has resulted in union membership being a little less valuable. As a result, union membership may continue to shrink as a percentage of the workforce.

Union Versus Nonunion Wage Differentials

Why join a union? The primary benefit to unionization should be higher wages, given the union's collective bargaining power. The general theoretical argument for union–nonunion wage differentials is illustrated in Figure 8.

This figure shows how unions are able to increase the wages in their sectors by restricting entry into union jobs. The markets for both unionized and nonunion labor begin at equilibrium, at point e in both panels of Figure 8. Thus, union and nonunion wages are initially equal, at W_0. If the union successfully restricts supply to S_1 in panel A, union wages will rise to W_1, but employment will fall to L_1 (point a). Those workers who are released have no choice but to move over to the nonunion sector represented in panel B, thus shifting its supply to S_2. Equilibrium in the nonunion sector moves to point b, where more workers (L_2) are employed at lower wages (W_2). The resulting wage differential, $W_1 - W_2$, is caused by successful collective bargaining in the union sector. Notice that this analysis is substantially the same as that for discrimination in the segmented labor force described in Figure 5 earlier.

Union–nonunion wage differentials vary by the union, occupation, industry, and historical period. In general, average union wages are 10% to 20% higher than the average

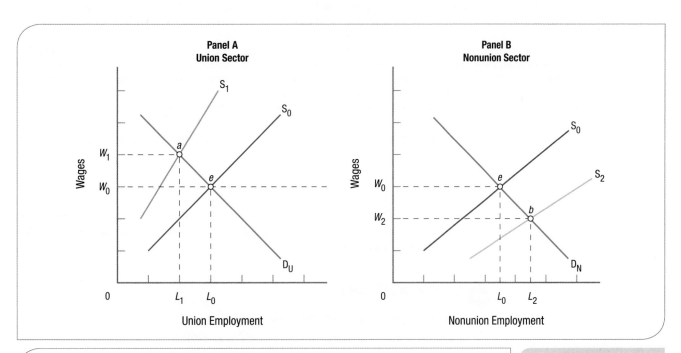

Union Versus Nonunion Wage Differentials

This figure illustrates the analysis of union–nonunion wage differentials. Unions increase wages in their sectors by restricting entry into union jobs. Assuming the markets for unionized and nonunionized jobs begin at equilibrium, at point e in both panels, union and nonunion wages are initially W_0. If the union successfully restricts supply to S_1 in panel A, union wages will rise to W_1, but employment will fall to L_1 (point a). Those workers released will have no choice but to move to the nonunion sector represented in panel B, thus increasing its supply to S_2. Equilibrium in the nonunion sector thus moves to point b, where more workers (L_2) are employed at a lower wage (W_2). The result is a wage differential equal to $W_1 - W_2$.

FIGURE 8

ISSUE

Will Public Unions Become an Endangered Species?

"I love teachers—I just can't stand your union."

—New Jersey Governor Chris Christie (Feb. 24, 2011, *New York Times* Magazine)

For nearly a month in February 2011, thousands of union workers staged a round-the-clock protest at the Wisconsin state capital as state legislators debated whether to prohibit collective bargaining among state employees including teachers, state agency employees, and others (though policemen and firemen were exempt from this legislation). The act effectively ended the long-standing ability of state workers to form unions within their professions.

As the quote from New Jersey Governor Christie suggests, Wisconsin was hardly alone. Attempts by other states to eliminate collective bargaining for public unions or otherwise reduce their powers subsequently arose. For example, Ohio passed a law abolishing collective bargaining for public unions; however, unlike Wisconsin, voters successfully overturned the law at the ballot box.

Still, why has there been hostility toward public unions? There is a simple answer: Public unions have an important difference from private unions such as

the automobile workers union or the steelworkers union.

Collective bargaining between private unions and private firms rests on three things. First, unions have the ability to strike. Second, while this threat of a strike can bring management to the negotiating table, management is constrained in what it can offer because of the need for the firm to generate profits. Third, the ultimate arbiter of what can be asked for by unions and acceded to by management is the market: The firm has to stay in business.

What is different about public unions? Many public unions are legally prevented from striking (teachers' unions are often an exception to this)—but this should make public unions more acceptable to state government, not less.

Public unions have a potent weapon that private unions do not have: the ballot box. Public unions can threaten state officeholders with something private unions cannot: votes, and getting out the votes to remove people from office. State officeholders have an incentive to placate large public unions if they want to keep their jobs.

Scott Olson/Getty Images

Critics of public unions say the result of this political power has been higher wages and benefits unseen in the private sector. For example, private businesses generally make workers contribute toward their health insurance premiums. Public union workers often do not have to make such contributions.

Who pays for these public union benefits? The taxpayers. What became particularly galling to harried taxpayers who had suffered through their own wage freezes or wage rollbacks were public unions that demanded large pay raises even during the depths of the last recession. Rather than just say no, politicians in some states sought more radical solutions such as abolishing collective bargaining for public unions.

---

nonunion wage. Union wage effects are most pronounced among blue-collar workers and service employees. These differentials suggest that unionization may tend to reduce the inequities inherent in labor markets.

 CHECKPOINT

LABOR UNIONS AND COLLECTIVE BARGAINING

- Unions are typically organized around a craft or an industry.
- Unions and the managers of firms must bargain "in good faith."
- In a closed shop, only union members are hired. This was outlawed by the Taft-Hartley Act. In a union shop, nonunion workers can be hired, but they must join the union within a specified period. An agency shop permits both union and nonunion workers, but the nonunion workers must pay union dues.
- Union wage differentials are between 10% and 20% higher.

QUESTION: Union negotiations always seem to run up against a "strike deadline." Are there incentives for both sides to put off a settlement until the very last moment?

Answers to the Checkpoint question can be found at the end of this chapter.

The Changing World of Work

Labor markets, like all other markets, change with time and the wishes of their participants. Over the last three decades, the entry of women into the labor force has been a major factor spurring economic growth. Over this same period, two-earner families increased so that today about 60% of all families with small children are two-earner households.

These demographic changes have shifted the focus of labor politics from union bargaining to issues such as telecommuting, family leave policies, affirmative action, and the question of how much employers should pay for medical benefits. As Social Security begins to look more fragile and the baby boomers begin flooding the retirement ranks, employer retirement packages will undoubtedly receive even more attention.

Immigration, legal and illegal, has caught the attention of labor economists. The United States has relatively open borders. Some argue that we need new immigrants to do the work that most Americans are unwilling to do. Other economists suggest that, in the absence of such inflows, salaries in these low-skill occupations would be high enough to attract the needed labor. This great tide of immigrants into lower wage jobs, together with the growth of high-skilled, high-wage jobs and the rise in dual-earner households, has resulted in a significant change in the types of jobs available today.

Jobs of the Past Versus the Present

Ask your parents or grandparents about the job opportunities they had when they completed school and you're likely to receive a description much different from the opportunities you have today. Prior to the Internet revolution and the globalization of manufacturing, the United States produced many of its own goods, including clothing, electronics, and household goods. As a result, work in factory plants was plentiful, and an individual with a high school diploma could find a well-paying job that led to a comfortable standard of living. What has changed over the past 25 to 50 years?

First, a shift from manufacturing to service industries occurred in the United States. Rather than producing physical products, considerable growth in the health care, computer programming, transportation, telecommunications, and technology industries led to greater production of services than goods. Service industries generally require a higher level of training as well as interpersonal and communications skills that one generally acquires with greater education.

Second, significant growth in international trade and foreign direct investment, components of globalization, changed labor demand. In addition to trading goods between countries, which reduces the need to produce certain goods in our own country, many industries have outsourced labor-intensive jobs to other countries, where wages are much lower than in the United States. At the same time, significant growth in high-skilled jobs in the United States has resulted from globalization, as the world demands better cell phone connectivity, health care services, and technology goods, which the United States is a leader in providing.

Third, the Internet has transformed the manufacturing process. With the ability to manage production in real time, many companies have moved away from producing and storing goods and now can source goods quickly from a variety of companies. For example, Amazon.com is a company that sells just about everything one can think of through their Web site, yet it hardly produces anything that it sells, but rather relies on thousands of individual manufacturers to provide ordered goods on demand. Similarly, for a small manufacturer, there are now thousands of Internet sites through which they can sell their goods. These changes have made the labor needs of firms much more flexible. Firms need not always rely on their own production to fill their customers' orders, and thus do not require an abundance of labor on their payrolls.

Future Jobs in the U.S. Economy

The future growth of jobs in the United States will likely continue to focus on those requiring increasingly higher levels of education and training, which we refer to as human capital and will be discussed in the next chapter. Growing professions such as health care professionals, financial services analysts, Web designers, social media managers, telecommunications technicians, and others will continue to exert increasing pressure to achieve greater levels of education. Projections from the Bureau of Labor Statistics *Occupational Outlook Handbook* show that the industries that are expected to generate the most new jobs over the next 10 years are health care, scientific and technical services, and education.

chapter summary

Section 1: **Competitive Labor Supply**

Work Versus Leisure: The Relationship Between Wages and Hours Worked

- Substitution effect: higher wages lead to more hours worked, and vice versa
- Income effect: higher wages lead to fewer hours worked, and vice versa

A strong **income effect** means that a worker chooses to work fewer hours as wages increase to pursue other activities (such as studying). This leads to a backward-bending *individual* labor supply curve.

Factors That Change Labor Supply

- Demographic changes (population growth, immigration, labor force participation)
- Nonmoney aspects of jobs
- Wages in alternative jobs
- Nonwage income

Market labor supply curves are upward sloping and can shift due to the factors listed above.

Section 2: **Competitive Labor Demand**

A firm's demand for labor is a derived demand: It depends on the productivity of labor and the demand for the good or service workers produce.

Factors That Change Labor Demand

- Change in product demand (affecting MR)
- Changes in productivity (affecting MPP_L)
- Changes in prices of other inputs

In a competitive labor market, wages are determined by the intersection of labor supply and labor demand. For an individual firm, they take wages as given (firms are price takers) and hire workers until its MRP equals the wage.

Marginal Revenue Product (MRP) $= MPP_L \times MR$

- MPP_L is the marginal physical product.
- MR is the marginal revenue from the product.
- MRP is the value provided by the last worker.
- Firms hire workers until MRP = wage.

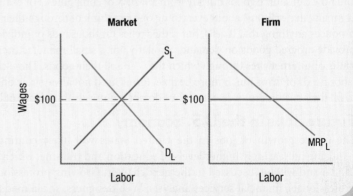

Section 3: **Economic Discrimination**

Economic discrimination occurs whenever workers of equal ability and productivity are paid different wages or otherwise discriminated against because of their:

- race or color
- religion
- gender
- age
- national origin
- sexual orientation
- disability

Laws Banning Labor Discrimination

- On gender: Equal Pay Act of 1963
- On race/ethnicity: Civil Rights Act of 1964
- On age: Age Discrimination in Employment Act of 1967
- On disabilities: Americans with Disabilities Act of 1990

Firms That Discriminate Must Pay More for Labor

- The supply of "preferred" workers decreases in a segmented market, increasing their wage.
- "Nonpreferred" workers enter a different market, increasing the labor supply and decreasing their wage.
- Firms that hire "nonpreferred" workers enjoy greater profits from a lower cost of labor.

Wavebreakmedia Ltd/Dreamstime.com

Employers choosing not to discriminate have access to a greater pool of talented labor.

Section 4: **Labor Unions and Collective Bargaining**

Labor unions are legal associations of employees formed to bargain collectively with employers over the terms and conditions of employment. They use:

- Strikes
- Threats of strikes
- Other tactics

Unions restrict labor supply, shifting the labor supply to the left, raising wages. Those not in the union are forced to find nonunion jobs, increasing the labor supply in those markets and lowering wages, creating a wage gap of $W_1 - W_2$.

Union Employment   Nonunion Employment

Major Laws Affecting Unions in the United States

- Wagner Act (National Labor Relations Act): protected union workers and their rights
- Taft-Hartley Act: Placed rules on unions to prevent them from becoming too powerful

Union membership has declined since the 1970s. Recent state laws banning collective bargaining among public workers may further reduce union membership.

Section 5: **The Changing World of Work**

Changes in the U.S. Labor Force

- Two-earner families: more women in labor force
- Immigration growth filling low-wage jobs
- Increase in flex-time workers: workers that are able to set their own work hours

Significant Changes in Careers in the Past 50 Years

- Shift from manufacturing to service industries
- Significant growth in international trade and foreign direct investment
- The introduction of the Internet, which has transformed the manufacturing process

KEY CONCEPTS

KEY CONCEPTS

supply of labor, p. 278
substitution effect, p. 278
income effect, p. 279
demand for labor, p. 281
marginal physical product of labor,
  p. 282

marginal revenue product, p. 282
value of the marginal product, p. 282
elasticity of demand for labor, p. 284
economic discrimination, p. 287
segmented labor markets, p. 288

closed shop, p. 294
union shop, p. 294
agency shop, p. 294
right-to-work laws, p. 294

QUESTIONS AND PROBLEMS

Check Your Understanding

1. Why are individual supply curves of labor potentially backward bending, but market and industry supply curves are always positively sloped?

2. What factors will increase the demand for labor?

3. When there is discrimination in the labor market, who loses? Why? Why is it harder to discriminate when both labor and product markets are competitive?

4. What are the important laws in place in the United States to prevent discrimination in the workplace based on race or gender?

5. How do unions exert their influence in the labor market?

6. What are some changes in the types of jobs available in the United States over the past 50 years and what are some trends for future labor employment?

Apply the Concepts

7. Some employees feel locked into their jobs because employer benefits, such as health insurance, are not transferrable to other companies. This "job lock" phenomenon is especially severe with health insurance coverage for employees if someone in their family has a severe pre-existing condition that prevents them from getting private health insurance at reasonable rates. What are the effects of this type of inflexibility on labor markets? What would be the impact if some form of health care reform eliminated the potential loss of health insurance for workers?

8. Why do college professors who usually spend five to seven years in graduate school and play such an important role in shaping our society make so much less than a Hollywood producer such as Jerry Bruckheimer, who is unknown to most people (he has produced over 40 films and a dozen TV shows)?

9. Why do we permit price discrimination with different ticket prices at movies based on age, or ladies' nights at bars (when women get in free or pay less for drinks), or insurance coverage, for which women sometimes pay more (health) or less (automobile), but we do not permit discrimination in wage rates?

10. Has globalization made it more difficult for unions to negotiate higher wages? Why or why not?

11. The airline pilots union has been very successful in negotiating six-figure salaries for pilots. The unions representing flight attendants have not been nearly as successful. What probably accounts for the difference?

12. Fifty years ago, married women ages 35 to 44 worked for pay only 10 hours per week on average; today they work over 26 hours on average. During the same period, the workweek for married men of the same age has been relatively constant, between 42 and 44 hours. Can you think of reasons why women's working hours have nearly tripled in the last half-century?

In the News

13. Tightened visa rules since September 11 have reduced the number of high-skill legal immigrants. Stiffer security rules and insufficient personnel have substantially increased the waiting time (and certainty) for visas. A *New York Times* article titled "Immigration and American Jobs" (October 19, 2012) reports a finding by economist Giovanni Peri that the wave of high-skilled legal immigrants from 1990 to 2007 increased the average wage of American workers by lifting the overall economy. Such findings have increased the pressure for immigration reform allowing more foreign graduates of American universities in the math, science, and technology fields to become permanent residents in the United States. Using the tools of labor demand and supply, evaluate the merits of the proposed immigration policy.

14. The National Bureau of Economic Research in December 2010 reported a study by Elizabeth Wilde, Lily Batchelder, and David Ellwood that a highly skilled woman loses anywhere from $230,000 to $349,000 in lifetime earnings by having children. What are the reasons that having children reduces women's earnings so much?

Solving Problems

15. Joe's Mechanic, which provides oil changes for $40 per car, decides to increase the number of mechanics on staff from four to five. As a result, the number of oil changes completed in a day increases from fifteen to seventeen. What is the marginal revenue product of the fifth worker?

16. In the following table, suppose the price of output is $10 per unit. What are the marginal physical product and the marginal revenue product of the sixth worker? If the wage of each worker is $150, should the sixth worker be hired?

Number of Workers	Units of Output
1	50
2	110
3	170
4	220
5	250
6	270

USING THE NUMBERS

17. According to By the Numbers, what is the average starting salary of workers with an undergraduate degree in economics? What is the average mid-career salary of workers with an undergraduate degree in economics?

18. According to By the Numbers, during which seven-year period did the percentage of Americans with flexible work schedules increase the most?

ANSWERS TO QUESTIONS IN CHECKPOINTS

Checkpoint: Competitive Labor Supply

Each person will have a different wage where their supply of labor curve bends backward. Getting a large inheritance will generate substantial nonwage income and typically lead to fewer hours worked. Having a family will probably raise the income required before you will cut your hours.

Checkpoint: Competitive Labor Demand

For many jobs, firms have standardized procedures that each employee follows. Therefore, the difference in productivity between individuals is relatively narrow. While homogeneous labor is a simplification, taking in everyone's difference would make analysis impractical. No, the model explains both since markets exist for each broad category of workers.

Checkpoint: Economic Discrimination

Discrimination in the workplace can be caused by preferences of employers, employees, or customers. If the discriminatory tastes are strictly due to employer preferences, then employers who discriminate will be forced to pay a higher wage for the "preferred" worker. Because employers who do not discriminate are able to hire an equally talented but less preferred worker at a lower wage, these employers will have a cost advantage in production. Over time, discriminating employers may need to reduce their discriminatory tastes or be forced out of business by lower cost competitors. Therefore, market forces tend to dissipate the extent of discrimination.

If the discriminatory tastes lie with the employees or customers, however, firms may be less able to reduce labor discrimination. For example, if employees refuse to work with a certain type of worker, or if customers refuse to buy goods and services from a particular type of worker, hiring these workers may negatively affect the firm's profit. Therefore, firms may choose to maintain segmented markets because the higher cost of labor is needed to prevent a potentially larger loss of revenues if their employees or customers act on their discriminatory tastes by refusing to work for or buy from the firm.

Checkpoint: Labor Unions and Collective Bargaining

Both sides work hard to get the best bargain for their constituents. There are incentives to continue negotiations up to the last moment to get the most and to appear to be driving a hard bargain. Strikes involve costs, and both sides use the threat of imposing these costs as a bargaining chip.

Appendix
Imperfect Labor Markets

In the world as we know it, markets are not perfectly competitive. Product markets and labor markets contain *monopolistic* and *oligopolistic* elements. In many product markets, a few firms control the bulk of market share. They may not be monopolies, but they do have some market power, through brand loyalty if nothing else.

Similarly, in most communities, there is only one government hiring firefighters and police officers. When the market contains only one buyer of a resource, economists refer to this lone buyer as a *monopsonist. Monopsony power,* meanwhile, is the control over input supply that the monopsonist enjoys. Before we look at the impact of **monopsony** on the labor market, let us first consider monopoly power in the product market.

→ Monopoly Power in Product Markets

monopsony A labor market with one employer.

As we know, firms that enjoy monopoly power in product markets are price makers, not price takers. Because $P > MR$, it follows that $VMP_L > MRP_L$. Figure APX-1 shows why. The firm depicted has monopoly power in the product market, but buys inputs in a competitive environment.

As Figure APX-1 shows, a competitive firm would equate the wage and the value of the marginal product (VMP_L), hiring L_C workers and paying the going wage of W_0 (point c). The firm with monopoly power, however, will equate the wage and marginal revenue product (MRP_L), thus hiring L_0 workers, though again paying the prevailing wage W_0 (point a). Therefore, although both firms hire workers at the same wage, the firm with monopoly power hires fewer workers.

This means that the value of the marginal product (VMP_L) of workers in the monopolistic firm is much higher than what they are paid. Their value to the firm

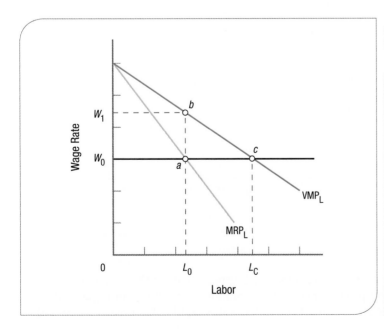

FIGURE APX-1

Monopoly Firm in Product Market Employing Labor from a Competitive Market

Firms with monopoly power in product markets are price makers. Because $P > MR$, it follows that $VMP_L > MRP_L$. A competitive firm would equate wages and value of the marginal product (VMP_L), hiring L_C workers and paying the going wage of W_0 (point c). A firm with monopoly power, however, will equate wages and marginal revenue product (MRP_L), thus hiring L_0 workers, although again paying the prevailing wage W_0 (point a). Hence, although both firms hire workers at the same wage, the firm with monopoly power hires fewer workers. Also, the value of the marginal product (VMP_L) of workers in the monopolistic firm is much higher than what they are paid; their value to the firm is W_1 (point b), although they are only paid W_0 (point a). This difference is called monopolistic exploitation of labor.

monopolistic exploitation of labor Occurs when workers are paid less than the value of their marginal product because the firm has monopoly power in the product market.

(point b) is W_1, even though they are only paid W_0. This difference is referred to as **monopolistic exploitation of labor.** The term is loaded, but what economists mean by it is that workers get paid less than the value of their marginal product when working for a monopolist. This is, as you might expect, a source of monopoly profits.

Monopsony

A monopsony is a market with one buyer or employer. The United States Postal Service, for instance, is the sole employer of mail carriers in this country, just as the armed forces are the only employers of military personnel. Single-employer towns used to dot the American landscape, and some occupations still face monopsony power regularly. Nurses and teachers, for example, often have only a few hospitals or local school districts for which they can work.

Because a monopsonist is the only buyer of some input, it will face a positively sloped supply curve for that input, such as supply curve S_L in Figure APX-2. This firm could hire 14 workers for $10 (point a), or it could increase wages to $11 and hire 15 workers (point b). Because the supply of labor is no longer flat, however, as it was in the competitive market, adding one more worker will cost the firm more than the new worker's higher wage. But just how much more?

marginal factor cost (MFC) The added cost associated with hiring one more unit of labor. For competitive firms, it is equal to the wage; but for monopsonists, it is higher than the new wage (W) because all existing workers must be paid this higher new wage, making MFC > W.

Marginal factor cost (MFC) is the added cost associated with hiring one more unit of labor. In Figure APX-2, assume that 14 workers earn $10 an hour (point a), and hiring the 15th worker requires paying $11 an hour (point b). Assume that you decide to go ahead and hire a 15th worker. When you employed 14 workers, total hourly wages were $140 ($10 × 14). But when 15 workers are employed at $11 an hour, all workers must be paid the higher hourly wage, and thus the total wage bill rises to $165 ($11 × 15). The total wage bill has risen by $25 an hour, not just the $11 hourly wage the 15th worker demanded. The marginal factor cost of hiring the 15th worker, in other words, is $25 per hour. This is shown as point c. Because the supply of labor curve is positively sloped, the MFC curve will always lie above the S_L curve.

FIGURE APX-2	

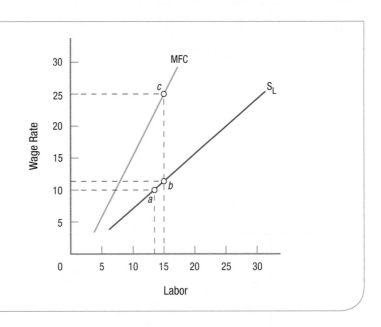

Marginal Factor Cost

This monopsonistic firm faces a positively sloped supply curve, S_L. The firm could hire 14 workers for $10 an hour (point a), or it could increase wages to $11 an hour and hire 15 workers (point b). Since the supply curve is positively sloped, however, adding one more worker will cost the firm more than the cost of a new worker. To hire an added worker requires a higher wage, and all current employees also must be paid the higher wage. Therefore, the total wage bill rises by more than just the added wages of the last worker hired. The marginal factor cost curve reflects these rising costs.

How does being a monopsonist in the labor market affect the hiring of a firm that is competitive in the product market? The monopsonist shown in Figure APX-3 is a competitor in the product market and has a demand for labor equal to its VMP_L.

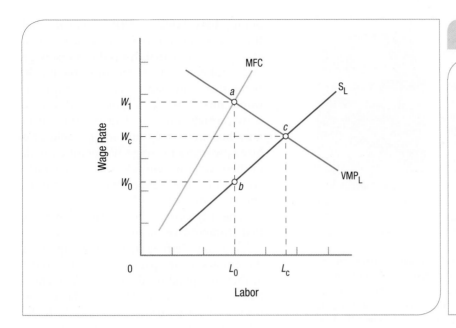

FIGURE APX-3

Competitive Firm in the Product Market That Is a Monopsonist in the Input Market

The monopsonist in this figure is a competitor in the product market and has a demand for labor equal to its VMP_L, while facing supply of labor, S_L. The firm will hire at the level where $MFC = VMP_L$ (point a), hiring L_0 workers at wage W_0 (point b). Note that these L_0 workers, although paid W_0, are worth W_1. This is called the monopsonistic exploitation of labor. Note also that the wages paid in this monopsony situation (W_0) are less than those paid under competitive conditions (W_c), and that monopsony employment (L_0) is lower than competitive employment (L_c).

This firm faces the supply of labor, S_L. It will hire at the level where $MFC = VMP_L$ (point a), thus hiring L_0 workers at wage W_0 (point b). Note that these L_0 workers, although paid W_0, are actually worth W_1. Economists refer to this disparity as the **monopsonistic exploitation of labor.** Again, the term is loaded, but to economists it describes a situation in which labor is paid less than the value of its marginal product.

Note that the wages paid in the monopsony situation (W_0) are less than those paid under competitive conditions (W_c), and that monopsony employment (L_0) is similarly lower than competitive hiring (L_c). As was the case with monopoly power, monopsony power leads to results that are less than ideal when compared to competitive markets.

To draw together what we have just discussed, Figure APX-4 portrays a firm with both monopoly and monopsony power. The firm's equilibrium hiring will be at the

monopsonistic exploitation of labor Occurs when workers are paid less than the value of their marginal product because the firm is a monopsonist in the labor market.

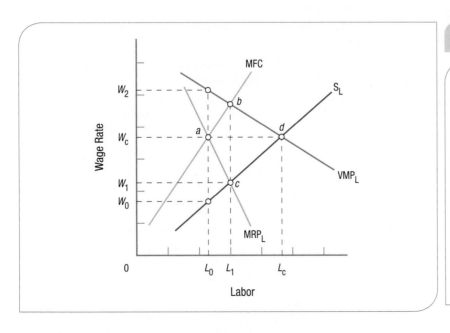

FIGURE APX-4

Monopolist Firm in the Product Market That Is a Monopsonist in the Input Market

This firm has both monopoly and monopsony power. The firm's equilibrium hiring will be at the point at which $MFC = MRP_L$ (point a), and thus the firm will hire L_0 workers, although at wage W_0. Note that this is the lowest wage and employment level shown in the graph. If the firm only had monopsony power, it would hire L_1 workers (point b) at a wage of W_1. If the firm only had monopoly power, it would also hire L_1 workers for wage W_1 (point c). Both of these employment levels and wage rates are less than the competitive outcome of L_c and W_c (point d).

KARL MARX (1818–1883)

"Working men of all countries unite!" With this exhortation, Karl Marx ended his seminal *Communist Manifesto,* neatly summing up both his philosophy and his view of the world.

Karl Marx was born in Germany in 1818, but spent much of his adult life in England. By the time of his death in 1883, Marx and Friedrich Engels had crafted the essence of communism—the last ideology to seriously challenge capitalism in the 20th century. In their two major works, *The Communist Manifesto* (1848) and *Das Kapital* (1867), Marx and Engels offered a severe critique of capitalism and extolled the virtues of proletariat rebellion.

To preserve their privileges, the ruling class had always striven to oppress the underclasses. Marx saw a struggle between the bourgeoisie (or property owners) and the proletariat (the working class). This exploitation—the essence of capitalism—not only kept the bourgeoisie in power, but it also alienated the proletariat from its own labor, which to Marx was the true essence of all economic value. The only prescription to cure the monopolistic and monopsonistic exploitation of labor was proletariat revolution.

point where MFC = MRP_L (point *a*), and thus the firm will hire L_0 workers, although at wage W_0. Note that this is the lowest wage and employment level shown in the graph. If the firm only had monopsony power, it would hire L_1 workers (point *b*) at a wage of W_1, which is higher than W_0. If the firm only had monopoly power, it would also hire L_1 workers for wage W_1 (point *c*). Both of these employment levels and wage rates are less than the competitive outcome of L_C and W_C (point *d*).

The key lesson to remember here is that competitive input (factor) markets are the most efficient, because inputs in these markets are paid precisely the value of their marginal products, and the highest employment results. This translates into the lowest prices for consumers at the highest output, assuming efficient production. Thus, just as competition is good for product markets, so too is it good for labor and other input markets.

 ## CHECKPOINT

IMPERFECT LABOR MARKETS

- When a firm is a monopolist in the product market and hires labor from competitive markets, the firm will hire labor at the point which the marginal revenue product is equal to the competitive wage.

- Monopolistic exploitation results because the monopolist pays less than the value of the marginal product of labor.

- Monopsony is a market with one employer. A monopsonist that sells its product in a competitive market hires labor at the point where the value of the marginal product is equal to the marginal factor cost.

- Monopsonistic exploitation occurs when the monopsonist pays labor less than the value of its marginal product.

QUESTIONS: Are public schools in rural areas a monopsony? Do they set wages in a way that is different from how wages are set in large urban areas?

Answers to the Checkpoint questions can be found at the end of this Appendix.

monopsony, p. 303
monopolistic exploitation of labor,
 p. 304

marginal factor cost (MFC), p. 304

monopsonistic exploitation of labor,
 p. 305

APPENDIX SUMMARY

Imperfect Labor Markets

If wages are determined in a competitive market, a firm will hire labor until $MRP_L = W$.
But if the firm enjoys some market power in the product market, marginal revenue product
will be less than the value of the marginal product because $MR < P$. The difference between
the value of the marginal product and marginal revenue product is known as monopolistic
exploitation of labor.

A monopsony is a market with a single buyer or employer. Marginal factor cost (MFC)
is the added cost associated with hiring one more unit of labor. For the monopsonist, the
MFC curve lies above the supply of labor curve because the firm must increase the wages
of all workers to attract added labor. A monopsonist, which is a competitor in the product
market, hires labor up to the point at which $VMP_L = MFC > W$. At this point, the value of
labor's marginal product exceeds the wage rate; economists refer to this as monopsonistic
exploitation of labor.

APPENDIX QUESTIONS AND PROBLEMS

1. The figure below shows the supply of labor, marginal factor costs, and the demand for
   labor for a firm that is large enough that it is essentially a monopsonist in the community in which it operates. Assume that all workers are paid the same wage and that they
   work 2,000 hours per year (40 hours a week for 50 weeks).

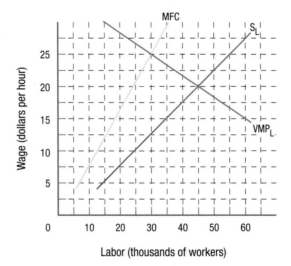

a. What is the total wage bill (total wages paid by the firm) for this monopsonistic
   firm?

b. If the firm was actually hiring from a competitive labor market, what would be the
   total wage bill for the firm?

    c. What is the total value of the monopsonistic exploitation of labor by this firm?

    d. Is the firm a competitor or a monopolist in the product market?

2. Would unions be more likely to organize successfully in highly competitive markets or in markets with monopsony power? Explain.

ANSWERS TO APPENDIX CHECKPOINT QUESTION

Checkpoint: Imperfect Labor Markets

Yes, they are monopsonists when it comes to hiring teachers. Generally, there is only one school district in rural areas. They probably act more like monopsonists when setting wages when compared to their urban counterparts, which have competition for teachers from other districts and private schools.

12

Land, Capital Markets, and Innovation

After studying this chapter you should be able to:

- Describe the impact of the supply of land on markets.
- Determine the present value of an investment.
- Compute the rate of return of an investment.
- Describe how businesses acquire financial capital.
- Understand how debt and equity instruments work and the differences between them.
- Describe the relationship between education and earnings.
- Know how market equilibrium levels for human capital are determined.
- Describe the different forms of on-the-job training and why both employers and employees benefit from it.
- Describe the impact of economic profits on entrepreneurs and markets.
- Explain the role of innovation in improving standards of living.

Patrick Smith www.askthepilot.com

Innovations in airplanes have made traveling more enjoyable. Korean Air's economy class seats feature a large personal video screen, satellite phone, USB charge port, cup holder, and coat hook.

Have you ever dreamed of venturing into space without having to undergo years of astronaut training? Richard Branson, the CEO of Virgin Group, wants to make that dream a reality with the launch of Virgin Galactic airlines. Already an innovator in the aerospace industry, Branson's new space travel service will take six passengers at a time on a 3.5-hour suborbital flight 65 miles above the Earth's surface, allowing passengers to experience several minutes of weightlessness before the spacecraft returns to Earth. How does a business like Virgin Galactic go about creating its service and what resources would it need?

In the previous chapter, we studied how businesses rely on labor markets to acquire the workers needed to produce their products. To build a technologically advanced product such as a space plane, much more than labor is needed. First, the firm must buy abundant amounts of capital inputs, such as aluminum, glass, and engines, in addition to the massive machinery required to put the plane together. Second, the firm must obtain the financial resources to fund the operation until the planes are built, placed into service, and generate revenue. Third, the firm must find labor that has the knowledge to build airplanes. For Virgin Galactic, it would seek workers who studied aerospace engineering in college or those who have acquired skills from previous jobs, such as serving in the Air Force. Last, the firm must have the overall vision to provide the market with what it wants—or what it thinks the market will want in the immediate future.

Although space travel might be just a dream for those unable to afford the expensive ride, examples of innovation abound in the aerospace industry. If you have recently flown on a commercial airliner, you may have noticed the technological innovations that are becoming more prevalent on airplanes. In some aircraft, you can now watch live TV, view movies on demand, and even browse the Internet. Such features are just some of the amenities airlines are offering to make airline travel more enjoyable. Further, innovations in aircraft operation, such as lighter composite materials used in new aircraft, will allow significant savings in fuel, the largest cost component of airlines. Developing a plane that provides customers with new amenities while cutting operating costs is a major goal of the aerospace industry.

The necessary inputs (also called factors) for the production of commercial spaceships and airplanes require firms to use other resource markets, such as those for land and capital, in addition to the labor market. Land markets are used to obtain actual land along with natural resources. Capital markets are used to obtain physical capital, financial capital, and human capital.

BY THE NUMBERS

Innovation Is the Cornerstone of Growth

Innovation is the use of ideas and knowledge to produce new goods and services that raise a country's standard of living. Human capital and financial capital are important drivers of innovation that lead to economic growth.

Human capital investment has grown over the past 35 years as the percent of high school graduates enrolling in college continues to increase. The percent of college graduates pursuing postgraduate degrees also has steadily increased.

253,155

Total number of patents granted in 2012 by the U.S. Patent and Trade Office.

66,170

Total number of patents granted in 1980 by the U.S. Patent and Trade Office.

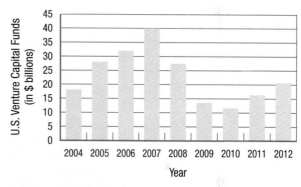

Venture capital firms provide financial capital to entrepreneurs to produce new products that lead to economic growth. The 2007–2009 recession dramatically reduced the amount of venture capital funds available.

Country	Length of High-Speed Rail in Kilometers
China	6,403
Japan	2,664
Spain	2,144
France	2,036
Germany	1,334
Italy	923
Turkey	447
South Korea	412
United States	362
Taiwan	345

The development of high-speed rail travel (defined as rail travel over 150 mph) is an innovation that saves time and costs in transporting passengers and freight. As of January 2013, China led the world in total length of high-speed rail in kilometers currently in operation as well as the amount of planned new railways over the next decade.

The Acela from Washington, D.C., to Boston is the only high-speed rail service currently in operation in the United States, with a top speed of 150 mph.

This chapter begins with an analysis of the land market, followed by a study of the three capital markets and the role that each plays in the economy. The chapter concludes with a discussion of entrepreneurship, the factor of production that brings all physical inputs together to generate profits and leads to innovation that increases economic growth.

⊙ Land and Physical Capital

In the previous chapter, we discussed the importance of labor in the production process. But certainly more is required than just workers to run a business and produce products. A business also needs land and physical capital.

Land

rent The return to land as a factor of production. Sometimes called economic rent.

For economists, the term *land* includes both land in the usual sense and other natural resources that are inelastically supplied. **Rent,** sometimes called *economic rent,* is any return or income that flows to land as a factor of production. This is a different meaning from when we speak of the rent on an apartment. Land is unique among the factors of production because of its inelasticity of supply.

In some instances, the supply of land is perfectly inelastic. Finding an empty lot on which to build in San Francisco is virtually impossible. The land available is fixed by the terrain; it cannot be added to nor moved from one place to another.

Figure 1 shows how rent is determined when the available supply of land is fixed. In this example, the number of acres of usable land is fixed at L_0 (or supply S_0). If the demand for land is D_0, the economic rent will be r_0 (point *a*). When demand rises to D_1, rent increases to r_1 (point *b*). Notice that because the supply of land in this example is perfectly inelastic, rent depends entirely on demand. If demand were to fall, rent would fall as well.

In a strict sense, land is not perfectly fixed in supply. Land can be improved. Land that is arid, like the deserts of Arizona, can be improved through irrigation. Jungles can be cleared, swamps can be drained, and mountains can be terraced, making land that was once worthless productive.

Even more ambitious are cities that have reclaimed land in the ocean by extending out from the coastline or creating new islands using large amounts of sand. Balboa Island off Newport Beach, California, and Star Island off Miami Beach, Florida, are examples of artificially made islands. Much larger projects are seen in Asia, where land is limited due to large populations and mountainous terrain. Still, even if the supply

---

FIGURE 1

Determination of Rent

This figure shows how rent is determined when the available supply of land is fixed. The acres of usable land are fixed at L_0 (supply S_0). If the demand for land is D_0, the economic rent is r_0 (point *a*). When demand rises to D_1, rent increases to r_1 (point *b*). Notice that because the supply of land in this example is perfectly inelastic, rent depends entirely on demand. If demand were to fall, rent would fall as well.

Reclaimed land was used to build Hong Kong Disneyland in 2005 in an area that used to be ocean. Although such methods have been used in coastal cities throughout the world, these expensive projects to increase the availability of land constitute a tiny portion of total land.

of land is not perfectly inelastic, it is quite inelastic when compared to other production inputs.

The price of land varies based on many factors, such as its terrain, its view, but most importantly, its location. Why are land prices so much higher in Manhattan and San Francisco than in Iowa? Land prices are driven by demand from households and firms choosing to build a home or a business. Because the supply of land in any single location is fixed (or the least inflexible), changes in demand will cause large fluctuations in land prices between more desirable and less desirable locations. But what determines a household or a firm's desire to locate in a particular place? The cost of land is an obvious factor, but other factors also influence a firm's potential profitability. For example, a business generally prefers to be close to its product market or its input suppliers.

Industrial agglomeration describes the geographical clusters of firms within an industry that choose to locate in close proximity with one another, such as Silicon Valley for the computer industry, Detroit for the auto industry, Dalton, Georgia, for the carpet industry, and Hollywood for the entertainment industry. By doing so, these firms benefit from external economies of scale. In a similar way, people of similar cultures sometimes choose to live near one another as well, leading to Chinatowns, Koreatowns, and Brazilian communities in various metropolitan areas throughout the country. Any time people choose a particular location for their home or business, demand for the land in that area increases, which will affect prices.

Physical Capital

Capital is the other important physical input in production. **Physical capital** includes all manufactured products that are used to produce goods and services. Examples of physical capital range from the massive cranes used to construct new skyscrapers to the espresso machine Starbucks uses to make your daily latte. Firms must determine what capital inputs are needed, and then calculate the value of adding additional capital to their production. When firms purchase capital inputs it is called investment. The investment decisions by firms involve calculating the marginal benefits and costs of each capital input.

In the previous chapter, we introduced the concept of the marginal revenue product of labor (MRP_L) and showed how firms choose to add additional units of labor if the cost of labor, or wage (W), is less than the MRP_L. In the capital market, we study a similar concept called the marginal revenue product of capital (MRP_K). Like MRP_L, MRP_K is downward

physical capital All manufactured products that are used to produce goods and services.

sloping, showing that the returns a firm earns on its investments diminish as more capital is invested.

When firms choose which capital inputs in which to invest, they clearly would make their most productive investments first. For a fast-food burger joint, for example, a working deep-fryer would be more valuable than an automatic soda dispenser. Firms continue to invest until the cost of capital is equal to the MRP_K.

The cost of capital is the price of an additional unit of capital. Because the price of actual capital inputs varies significantly, we simplify things by measuring the cost of capital by their opportunity cost, or interest rate (i). In other words, to buy another capital input, firms must either borrow money and pay interest, or use savings and forgo interest. Thus, the interest rate can be used to measure the cost of capital.

Financial resources to pay for capital inputs come from the savings of households and other firms. Suppliers of funds and the demanders of these funds interact through what is called the *loanable funds market.* As with competitive labor markets, in which the market determines wages and each individual firm determines how many workers to employ, the loanable funds market determines interest rates, leaving individual firms to calculate how much they should borrow.

Through their interactions in the loanable funds market, suppliers and demanders determine the interest rates to be charged for funds. Individual firms then evaluate their investment opportunities to determine their own investment levels. Figure 2 shows how this process works. The demand and supply of loanable funds is shown in panel A, where equilibrium interest rates equal i_0. Note that the demand for loanable funds looks just like a normal demand curve. Its downward slope shows that, as the price of funds declines—as interest rates go down—the quantity of funds demanded rises. The supply of funds is positively sloped because individuals will be willing to supply more funds to the market when their price (interest rate) is higher.

Once the market has determined an equilibrium rate of interest, an individual firm like the one shown in panel B will take this rate of interest, or cost of capital, and determine how much to invest.

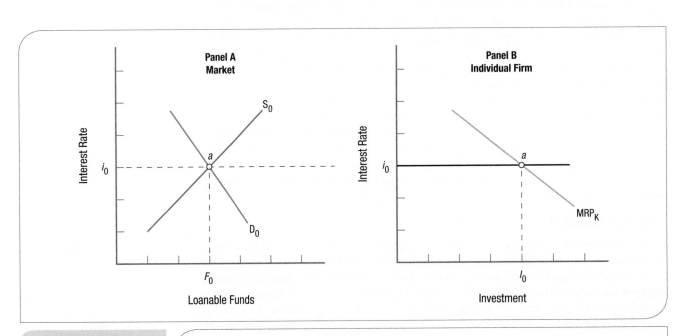

FIGURE 2

Loanable Funds Market and Individual Firm Investment

Panel A shows the market demand and supply of loanable funds, with equilibrium interest rates equal to i_0. Individual firms such as the one shown in panel B will take this rate of interest, or cost of capital, and determine how much to invest. Firms make their best investments first, and then continue investing (to I_0) until the cost of capital (i_0) is equal to the MRP_K.

This admittedly simplifies the investment process, but it is a good general model of investment decisions. Next, we turn to two more precise ways in which investment is determined, the present value approach and the rate of return approach.

Present Value Approach

When a firm considers upgrading its information system or purchasing a new piece of equipment, a building, or a manufacturing plant, it must evaluate the returns it can expect over time. Firms invest money today, but earn returns over years. To compare investments having different income streams and different levels of required investment, firms look at the *net* **present value** of the investment.

The sum of $100 *a year from now* is worth *less* than $100 *today*. This is illustrated by the fact that you could put less than $100 in the bank today, earn interest on this money over the next year, and still end up with $100 at year's end. Yet, exactly how much less than $100 would you be willing to give up today for $100 received a year from today? To answer this question, let us begin by looking at a simple form of financial assets, annuities.

An annuity is a financial instrument that pays the bearer a certain dollar amount in perpetuity, or generally for the life of the annuity holder. Assume that the market rate of interest is 5%, and you are offered an annuity that pays you or the holder of the annuity $1,000 a year indefinitely. How much would you be willing to pay for this annuity? If you want to follow the market in earning 5% a year, then the question you must ask is this: On what amount of money does $1,000 a year in income represent a 5% return? The answer is found through the formula:

$$PV = X/i$$

where PV is the present value of the investment (what you are willing to pay for the annuity today), X is the annual income ($1,000 in this case), and i is the market interest rate. In this case, you would be willing to pay $20,000 for this annuity, since $20,000 = $1,000 / 0.05. We have thus reduced an infinite stream of income to the finite amount you would pay today. You would pay $20,000, and the annuity would give you $1,000 a year, for an annual return on your investment of 5%.

What happens to the value of this annuity if the market interest rate should rise to 10%? You will still receive $1,000 a year, but if you want to sell the annuity to someone else, the buyer will only be willing to pay $10,000 for it ($10,000 = $1,000 / 0.10). Interest rates doubled, and the value of your annuity has been halved. Higher interest rates mean that income in future years is not worth as much today.

Valuing future income today by this process is known as *discounting*. This principle applies not only to annuities, but computing for years less than perpetuity requires a more complex formula. For example, assume that someone agrees to pay you $500 in two years, and that the going interest rate is 5%. What would you be willing to pay today for this future payment of $500? The answer is found using the following formula:

$$PV = X/(1 + i)^n$$

Again, PV is the present value of the future payment, X is the future payment of $500, i is the interest rate (5%), and n is the number of years into the future before the payment is made. In this case the calculations are

$$\begin{aligned} PV &= \$500/(1 + 0.05)^2 \\ &= \$500/[(1.05)(1.05)] \\ &= \$500 / 1.1025 \\ &= \$453.51 \end{aligned}$$

Hence, you would be willing to pay only $453.51 for this $500 payment coming two years in the future. Again, the higher the interest or discount rate, the lower your price.

present value The value of an investment (future stream of income) today. The higher the discount rate, the lower the present value today, and vice versa.

When only one future payment is at stake, computing the present value of that payment is fairly simple. When future streams of income are involved, however, things get more complicated. We must compute the present value of each individual future payment. The general formula looks nearly the same as before:

$$PV = \Sigma X_n/(1 + i)^n$$

Here, the Greek letter Σ (sigma) stands for "sum of," and X_n is the individual payment received at year n. Assume, then, that you are going to receive $500, $800, and $1,200 over the next three years, and that the interest rate is still 5%. The present value of this income stream is therefore

$$
\begin{aligned}
PV &= \$500 \:/\: (1.05)^1 + \$800 \:/\: (1.05)^2 + \$1,200 \:/\: (1.05)^3 \\
&= \$500 \:/\: (1.05) + \$800 \:/\: (1.1025) + \$1,200 \:/\: (1.1576) \\
&= \$476.19 + \$725.62 + \$1,036.63 \\
&= \$2,238.44
\end{aligned}
$$

Given the complexity of such computations, economists often use computers to solve for present value, especially when the annual income stream is complicated. When the annual income is constant, tables of discount factors are also available. In any case, the point to note is that payments to be made in the future are worth a lower dollar amount today.

Firms often use present value analysis to determine if potential investments are worthwhile. Turning back to our chapter opener, suppose that an airline is considering installing wireless Internet access in all of its planes. Assume that the service will yield a stream of income (from charging users a fee) exceeding operating costs over a given period. The present value of this income is then compared to the cost of installing the wireless Internet service. The service's *net present value* (NPV) is equal to the difference between the present value of the income stream and the cost of installing the service. If NPV is positive, the firm will invest; if it is negative, the firm will choose not to invest.

When interest rates are high, firms will find fewer investment opportunities where NPV is positive because the higher discount rate reduces the value of the income streams for investments. As interest rates fall, more investment is undertaken by firms.

Rate of Return Approach

An alternative approach to determining whether an investment is worthwhile involves computing the investment's rate of return. This rate of return is also known as a firm's *marginal efficiency of capital,* or its *internal* **rate of return.**

rate of return Uses the present value formula, but subtracts costs, then finds the interest rate (discount rate) at which this investment would break even.

Computing an investment's rate of return requires using essentially the same present value formula for income streams introduced above with a slight modification: You have to explicitly consider the cost of capital in the calculation. This new formula is

$$PV = [\Sigma X_n/(1 + i)^n] - C$$

where C represents the cost of capital. The question we must ask is: At what rate of interest (i) will the investment just break even? You would compute the present value of the income streams, then subtract the cost of the capital investment, and finally find the rate of interest (i) where the present value equals zero. This discount rate is the rate of return on the investment.

Suppose you find a rare vintage car for sale at $20,000 that you believe will be worth $25,000 next year. If you buy this car with the intention of selling it next year, the rate of return that would allow your investment to break even would be calculated as:

$$0 = [\$25,000 \:/\: (1 + i)^1] - \$20,000$$

Solving for i yields a rate of return of 25%.

The calculated rate of return can be compared to the firm's required rate of return on investments to determine whether the investment is worthwhile. The firm might require, say, a 20% yield on all projects based on the opportunity cost of the investment, in which case investments yielding returns of less than 20% are deemed not worthwhile. Risk in investment projects is usually managed by adding a risk premium to the required rate of return for risky projects. This risk premium can vary by project type or with the business cycle. Some investments, such as drilling for oil or researching innovative new drugs, are risky and require high rates of return if they are to be undertaken.

⬤ CHECKPOINT

LAND AND PHYSICAL CAPITAL

- Land includes both land and natural resources and is inelastically supplied. Returns on land are called rents (or economic rent).
- Because land is inelastically supplied, the rent on land is determined by demand.
- Firms weigh the benefits of investing in physical capital such as new buildings or machinery versus their costs.
- To compare investments with different investment streams over time, firms will use either the present value approach or the rate of return approach.

QUESTION: Suppose a good friend asks you to invest in some new equipment for her smoothie shop on campus in exchange for a share of the income earned at the end of the year. It will cost $10,000 to lease the new equipment for one year. What type of data and information would you be interested in estimating before you decide whether to pursue this investment?

Answers to the Checkpoint question can be found at the end of this chapter.

➡ Financial Capital

To this point, we have introduced various physical inputs needed to produce a product, including labor, land, and physical capital. But how does a firm pay for these inputs? Most new businesses start out small, using personal savings or help from family to come up with the money to lease business space and rent or buy equipment. In fact, the founders of Apple, Steve Wozniak and Steve Jobs, started out in the Jobs family garage, and Mark Zuckerberg started Facebook out of his college dorm room. How does a relatively new business expand? Sometimes a business can expand using the profits earned and saved from its initial operation. But eventually, most if not all businesses require larger sources of **financial capital,** which is money required to purchase inputs for production. Firms use capital markets to acquire financial capital.

In the previous section, we described generally how firms calculate the cost of capital using the interest rate determined in the *loanable funds market*. Firms use the cost of capital to determine how many inputs to employ in their production process. But the loanable funds market is a general description of all sources of capital funding, whether that be borrowing from banks, or using more complex instruments such as bonds, stocks, or venture capital. In this section, we describe the specific mechanisms that firms can use to acquire financial capital to build, operate, and expand their businesses.

financial capital The money required by businesses to purchase inputs for production and to run their operations.

Banks and Borrowing

Let's start with the simplest means of acquiring financial capital other than self-financing. Suppose you wish to open a new sporting goods store and estimate that you will need $100,000 in financial capital. One way to obtain this money is through your local bank. Banks and other financial institutions offer small business loans (called commercial and

collateral An asset used to secure a loan that can be sold if the borrower fails to repay a loan.

industrial loans) based on your credit history, the potential success of the business, and the ability to resell collateral used to secure the loan. **Collateral** is an asset, such as a home or building, that a bank can sell if a borrower is unable to repay a loan. If you buy a car and take out a loan to pay for it, the car is the collateral for the loan.

The ability to run a business with a bank loan is restricted to what the bank is willing to lend. This amount may not be enough to build a business and sustain its operation until a consistent cash flow is established to pay back the loan. Further, banks are more likely to address the inherent information problem between lenders and borrowers by scrutinizing the business plan and auditing files to ensure that a business is capable of paying back its loan. When bank borrowing is not feasible, the bond market may offer a more plentiful source of financial capital.

Bonds (Debt Capital)

Because bank loans are subject to credit restrictions and are usually limited in amount, it often is necessary for firms to borrow money by issuing bonds. A bond is an IOU certificate that promises to pay back a certain amount over time. The bond market offers firms an opportunity to acquire financial capital. The bond market is made up of firms that issue bonds and bondholders willing to invest by loaning money in exchange for an interest rate commensurate with the risk of that loan. Would you be willing to buy a bond issued by IBM or Coca-Cola? How about one issued by the Pep Boys—Manny, Moe, and Jack? This is an indication of what is meant by risk.

face value The value of a bond that is paid upon maturity. This value is fixed, and therefore not the same as the market value of a bond, which is influenced by changes in interest rates and risk.

There are three main components to a bond: its face value, its coupon rate, and its maturity date. The **face value** of a bond is the amount that must be repaid to the bondholder upon its maturity. A **coupon rate** is a periodic fixed payment made to a bondholder expressed as a percent of the face value; some bonds do not have coupon payments, and instead are repaid in a single payment (these bonds are called zero-coupon bonds or more generally, discount bonds). A **maturity** date is the date when the face value of a bond must be paid to the bondholder. Maturity dates vary, and the length of time to maturity can range from a few months to up to 30 years. Some bonds even have no maturity dates (called perpetuity bonds).

coupon rate A periodic fixed payment to the bond holder measured as an annual percent of the bond's face value.

Many types of bonds exist, including corporate bonds, Treasury bonds, and municipal bonds, in addition to the many bond choices within each category. Corporate bonds are most likely to be used by firms to purchase productive inputs. In most cases, corporate bonds can be bought and resold in a bond market between investors. Because the price of a bond will vary based on the coupon rate, current market interest rates, and risk factors at the time of the transaction, a bond's yield is an important value for investors. The **yield** is the current annual return to a bond measured as the coupon payment as a percentage of the current price of a bond.

maturity The date on which the face value of the bond must be repaid.

yield The annual return to a bond measured as the coupon payment as a percentage of the current price of a bond.

A bond's yield is positively related to its risk. In other words, the greater the risk that the company issuing the bond might default on its bond payments, the greater return an investor would demand for holding that bond. A bond's risk is measured by various bond agencies, including Moody's, Standard & Poor's (S&P), and Fitch. These agencies provide bond ratings that range from AAA (the safest bonds) to C (the riskiest rating by Moody's) or D (the riskiest by S&P and Fitch).

Figure 3 shows a corporate bond listing on January 2, 2013, showing the coupon rate, maturity date, bond ratings, the last price, and the yield. Looking at the first row, for JPMorgan Chase, this bond pays a coupon rate of 4.5% per year. However, because the bond's risk rating has improved since its initial issuance, the price has risen from its base price of 100 to 113.46. Because the face value of most corporate bonds is $1,000, this means one must pay $1,134.60 for this bond. Because the price exceeds the face value to earn the bond's fixed coupon payment, the yield falls to 2.809%, reflecting the reduced risk perceived by investors.

Looking at the last row, the Harrah's bond offers a coupon rate of 6.5%. In addition, you can buy the bond for $620 in January 2013, and cash this bond in for $1,000 at maturity in June 2016. The yield for this bond is significantly higher at 23.15%. Sounds like a

Issuer Name	Coupon	Maturity	Rating: Moody's/S&P/Fitch	Last Price	Yield
JPMorgan Chase	4.500%	Jan 2022	A2/A/A+	113.46	2.809
Microsoft	0.875%	Sept 2013	Aaa/AAA/AA+	100.48	0.228
IBM	7.125%	Dec 2096	Aa3/AA–/A+	159.80	4.415
Visant Corporation	10.000%	Oct 2017	Caa2/B–/___	90.50	12.709
Edison Mission Energy	7.000%	May 2017	Ca/D/C	53.25	20.357
Harrah's Operating Company, Inc.	6.500%	Jun 2016	Caa/CCC/C	62.00	23.150

FIGURE 3

Corporate Bond Listing in the *Wall Street Journal* on January 2, 2013

Corporate bond listings are shown with their current price in the "Last Price" column. Bond prices are standardized such that each bond is worth "100" percent of the $1,000 face value upon maturity. Bond prices higher than 100 means that the yield % is lower than the coupon %, which indicates that the bond is viewed as less risky relative to that suggested by the coupon rate. Conversely, bond prices lower than 100 suggest riskier bonds.

Data Source: FINRA and Wall Street Journal

great investment, but notice its risk rating of Caa/CCC/C, indicating a high likelihood of default. If Harrah's files for bankruptcy at any time up until June 2016, the expected 23.15% return will turn into a negative return after the bankruptcy filing. Indeed, high yields equal high risk.

Bonds provide advantages and disadvantages to acquiring financial capital compared to borrowing money from a bank. The benefits of bonds are that other investors share the risk of the business, and a business can generally raise more money through bonds by offering higher interest rates. The drawbacks are that bonds are a claim against a business, and the ability to issue future bonds depends on the ratings issued by ratings agencies and the overall demand and supply for its bonds in the market.

Although differences exist between bonds and bank loans, they still share similar characteristics. Both are IOUs to a lender, whether that be a bank or a bondholder. In both cases, the business maintains control over the management of the business. There is no risk of an outside investor or firm forcefully taking over the business, because the entire ownership is maintained by the company's owners. The disadvantage of relying on bonds and banks, however, is that the ability to raise large sums of capital may be difficult or expensive, and the burden of making debt payments may limit the performance of the business. An alternative approach is for a firm to acquire financial capital from the public in exchange for a share of ownership in the company. This involves stocks, which we discuss next.

Stocks (Equity Capital)

An alternative to using debt instruments such as a bank loan or the issuing of bonds to acquire financial capital is to offer partial ownership (also known as equity) in the company. The most common approach is to issue stock shares. Each **share of stock** issued represents one fraction (of the total shares issued) of ownership in the company, and subsequently one vote in shareholder meetings and one share of any dividends (periodic payments to shareholders).

When a firm issues stock, it receives money in exchange for ownership in the company. This is handled in what is known as an initial public offering, or IPO. Typically, the founders of the company will retain a significant portion of the shares for themselves. However, the more shares that are issued, the smaller the value that each share will be. Therefore, when firms increase the number of shares issued without justifying their value to existing shareholders through actual or potential earnings, it is likely that the price per share will fall.

share of stock A unit of ownership in a business that entitles the shareholder to one vote at shareholder meetings and one share of any dividends paid.

market cap The market value of a firm determined by the current price per share of its stock multiplied by the total number of shares issued.

The **market cap** of a firm is what a firm is estimated to be worth based on its stock value, calculated as the current price per share multiplied by the total number of shares issued. The price of a share of stock is determined by supply and demand just as in any other market, and for every buyer of a share of stock there must be a seller. Shares of stock generally are traded in stock exchanges (such as the New York Stock Exchange or NASDAQ).

An important point here is that firms receive money only once from issuing a share of stock. Once a share of stock is issued, the trading of that share among investors and the corresponding price fluctuations of that share do not provide any additional funds to the company, although company executives who hold significant number of shares clearly would benefit from a higher share price of their stock.

Like bonds, there are advantages and disadvantages to firms that raise financial capital from issuing stock. Advantages of issuing stock relative to bonds include the ability to raise substantial amounts of financial capital by sharing ownership in the business and its profits. In addition, businesses are not required to make repayments to stockholders, allowing them to reinvest their earnings as opposed to repaying lenders. Lastly, should the business fail, the losses are spread among all shareholders, not just to the business's founder, a concept known as *limited liability*. The main disadvantage of issuing stock is that partial ownership in the business is given up. In fact, with enough shareholder votes, an external investor can vote to replace a firm's management and/or board of directors, or even take over the company outright by buying all or a majority of the shares in the company.

From an investor's point of view, why would people find stocks an attractive investment given the real risks of businesses failing? Some companies do fail, and stockholders in these cases often lose their entire investment as opposed to bondholders, who are able to make claims on a firm's remaining assets before shareholders. However, historical data have shown that investing in stocks, despite the higher risk, generates a much higher return over the long run than investing in bonds, buying certificates of deposit (CDs), or keeping money in a savings account. In other words, by owning a share of stock, one is entitled to a share of the company's future value. For many businesses that do succeed, this can result in a very profitable return. In some cases, owning shares in certain businesses over time has made investors very wealthy.

Suppose that for your fifth birthday in 1998, instead of a shiny new bike, your parents bought you 50 shares of Apple Computer Inc. stock for $164 (each share of Apple stock was worth $3.28, adjusted for two stock splits, on January 1, 1998). Today, those 50 shares would be worth over $25,000. Would you rather have that bike or a brand new car today?

Kristoffer Tripplaar / Alamy

Venture Capital and Private Equity

An alternative approach to raising financial capital using equity instruments is to secure venture capital or private equity, both of which are large sums of money offered by financial investment firms eager to earn potentially large profits by investing a significant amount of money in a company.

The difference between venture capital firms and private equity firms lies primarily in the type of firms targeted. Venture capital firms typically invest in new start-up companies, providing seed money to entrepreneurs with potentially profitable ideas in exchange for a share of company ownership. Private equity firms typically target mature firms that are struggling to maximize profits or are on the verge of bankruptcy. By providing a substantial capital investment to a struggling firm in exchange for a large (often majority) share of company ownership, private equity firms can replace a firm's board of directors as well as management in an effort to turn a company's performance around.

How do venture capital and equity capital differ from financial capital acquired through the stock market? The key factors are timing, volume, and risk. A venture capital firm seeks out the next Fortune 500 company in its earliest stages, hoping to turn a relatively small amount of money into a huge return. Similarly, a private equity firm seeks large returns by reorganizing existing firms. In both cases, individual stock investors may be hesitant to invest, either because the company is too young (or has not established a product to generate revenues), or the company is nearing bankruptcy. By purchasing a large share of a company, venture capital and private equity firms take substantial risks in exchange for potential large returns to their own shareholders.

According to the National Venture Capital Association (NVCA), the largest trade association for venture capital firms, there were 526 venture capital investment firms in the United States in 2012. In 2012, a total of $20.6 billion in venture capital was invested in new businesses in many industries. According to the Private Equity Growth Capital Council, there were over 2,600 private equity firms in the United States in 2012. The amount of private equity investment is more difficult to measure, given the frequent buying and selling of shares in existing firms as opposed to the providing of start-up capital by venture capital firms, which is easier to measure.

Despite the year-to-year fluctuations in venture capital and private equity investments, these investments represent a large source of financial capital in the United States. While some investments have gone sour, some have turned into moneymaking machines. The following Issue box describes one of the most successful venture capital stories: Google. Yet, even today there are new firms that may potentially provide even bigger success stories, and investors are actively seeking these firms out.

ISSUE

Venture Capital: A Few Success Stories and One Big Missed Opportunity

Hardly a day goes by without most of us performing an Internet search using Google. Google has become one of the most successful Internet companies in history. How did Google get its start, and how did it find the financial capital to begin its remarkable climb to success? The story begins in 1996 with Larry Page and Sergey Brin.

Larry Page and Sergey Brin were Ph.D. candidates at Stanford University when in March 1996 they started a project called the Stanford Digital Library Project. It then became known as BackRub. Their first source of funding came in August 1998, when Andreas (Andy) von Bechtolsheim, co-founder of Sun Microsystems, and Professor David Cheriton of Stanford, provided $100,000 each in start-up capital in exchange for partial ownership of the still unincorporated company. The company was officially named Google as a play on the word *googol*, which is a number representing a 1 with 100 zeros after it.

The following year, in June of 1999, Google secured $25 million in venture capital from two venture capi-

tal firms (Sequoia Capital and Kleiner Perkins Caufield & Byers), which each received 10% ownership in the company. In the year prior to securing these funds, Page and Brin had made an offer to sell the entire company (albeit a much smaller company at the time) for as little as $750,000!

In 2004, Google made an initial public offering of stock shares, generating a huge infusion of cash, while Page, Brin, Bechtolsheim, Cheriton, the original venture capital firms, and Google's employees collectively retained nearly 90% of the shares for themselves. As of August 2013, Google was worth over $250 billion based on its stock value. For the venture capitalists who turned $12.5 million into $25 billion (10% ownership), that is a 200,000% return over 14 years. For Bechtolsheim and Cheriton, who each turned $100,000 into $2.5 billion, that is a 2,500,000% return over 15 years. Unfortunately, not all venture capitalists became billionaires. It was quite a missed opportunity for those who turned down Page and Brin's original offers.

CHECKPOINT

FINANCIAL CAPITAL

- Firms require financial capital to purchase inputs needed in their production.
- Financial capital can be obtained from bank loans, from the issuing of bonds or stock shares, or from venture capital or private equity firms.
- Bonds are IOU notes that provide a return based on their level of risk.
- Owning a share of stock entitles an investor to one share of ownership in a business, and can lead to substantial gains if the business is successful.
- Venture capital and private equity firms take on risk in exchange for potential large returns by investing in new or underperforming companies, respectively.

QUESTIONS: What is the difference between a bond and a share of stock? What are some advantages and disadvantages of acquiring financial capital by issuing bonds in the bond market instead of issuing shares in the stock market?

Answers to the Checkpoint questions can be found at the end of this chapter.

➡ Investment in Human Capital

In the previous chapter, we discussed some of the reasons why some people are paid more than others, including discrimination in the labor market and the role of unions. But even if we put these important considerations aside, other factors may lead to wage differences, such as how much education one has. Previously, we had treated labor as a homogeneous input to simplify our analysis. In this section, we look at labor that has been enriched by training or education and how it affects the productivity of firms.

Is there a relationship between your earnings and your education? Let us first consider the role education and on-the-job-training (OJT) play in determining wage levels in labor markets. Workers, students, and firms all invest in themselves or their employees to increase productivity. This is called **investment in human capital.** Workers invest by accepting lower wages while they undertake apprenticeships. Students invest by paying for tuition and books, and by forgoing job opportunities, to learn new skills. Firms invest in their workers through OJT and in-house training programs that involve workers being paid to attend classes. These investments entail costs in the current period that are borne in the interest of raising future productivity.

investment in human capital Investments such as education and on-the-job training that improve the productivity of labor.

Education and Earnings

One of the surest ways to advance in the job world and increase your income is by investing in education. The old saying, "To get ahead, get an education," still holds true. Table 1 shows the age/earnings profiles for all Americans between 25 and 64 for 2009. It provides strong evidence that education and earnings are related.

TABLE 1	Average Earnings by Highest Degree Earned, 2009				
Age Grouping	**No HS Diploma**	**HS Diploma**	**Some College**	**Bachelor's Degree**	**Professional**
25–34	$19,415	$27,511	$31,392	$45,692	$86,440
35–44	24,728	33,614	39,806	65,346	136,366
45–54	23,725	36,090	44,135	69,548	148,805
55–64	24,537	34,583	42,547	59,670	149,184

Source: U.S. Census Bureau, *Statistical Abstract of the United States, 2012* (Washington, DC: U.S. Government Printing Office), 2012, Table 232.

Average earnings for those without a high school diploma peaked at $24,728 a year, while those completing high school peaked at $36,090, a 45% increase. Getting a college degree bumped peak earnings up to $69,548, over a 180% rise. Going on to get a professional degree moved the peak all the way up to $149,184, over a 100% increase over a bachelor's degree alone. These figures represent average earnings. It is easy to see that earnings in all age groups were much higher for those with higher levels of education.

Table 1 suggests that education is a good investment. But like any investment, future earnings must be balanced against the cost of obtaining that education. The costs of education must be borne today, but the earnings benefits do not arrive until later. Making optimal educational decisions therefore requires some tools to help evaluate investments in human capital markets.

Education as Investment

To keep our analysis simple, we will focus on the decision to attend college for four years. The basic approach outlined in this section will nonetheless apply to other investments in education or training.

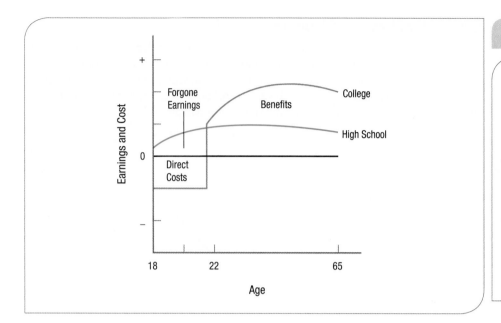

FIGURE 4

Benefits and Costs of a College Education

If an individual chooses not to go to college at age 18, he or she enters the labor market on leaving high school, and earnings rise and fall along the path labeled "High School." The college student incurs the direct costs of education, such as tuition and books, and the forgone earnings of not immediately entering the job market. The benefits of the college education show up as the difference in earnings from ages 22 to 65.

Figure 4 presents a stylized graph showing the benefits and costs of a college education. For simplicity, we will assume students go to college at age 18. If an individual chooses not to go to college, the high school earnings path applies: On leaving high school, the person enters the labor market immediately, and earnings begin rising along the path labeled "High School." Note that the earnings are positive throughout the individual's working life.

A college student immediately incurs costs in two forms. First, tuition, books, and other fees must be paid. These direct costs exclude living expenses, such as food and rent, because these must be paid whether one works or goes to college. Tuition varies substantially depending on whether one attends a private or public university.

Second, students give up earnings as they devote all their time to their studies (and to the occasional party). These costs can be substantial when compared to the direct costs of an education at a state-supported institution, because the average earnings for high school graduates range between $17,000 and $22,000 a year.

The benefits from a college degree show up as the difference in earnings from ages 22 to 65. If the return on a college degree is to be positive, this area must offset the direct costs of college and the forgone earnings. We must also keep in mind that a large part of the income high school and college graduates earn will not come until well into the future. For college graduates, this is especially important, because they will not see income for at least four years. How can we tell if this sacrifice is worth it? The fact that the median earnings of college graduates exceeded that of high school graduates by over 80% suggests a college education is worth it.[1]

An alternate way to decide which of the two career paths is best is by computing the rate of return on a college degree. If the annual return on a college education over the course of one's working life is 10% a year, the earnings of the college graduate in middle age will exceed those of the high school graduate by enough to generate a 10% return. A lower return would mean that the difference in earnings is smaller, while a higher return suggests the difference in earnings is greater. An extensive study[2] of rates of return to higher education in nearly 100 countries put the average return at nearly 20%. That is, college graduates around the world earn on average nearly 20% more per year over the course of their working lifetime than high school graduates, taking into consideration all of the costs of going to college.

[1] U.S. Census Bureau, *Statistical Abstract of the United States, 2012* (Washington D.C.: U.S. Government Printing Office), 2012.
[2] G. Psacharopoulos and H. Patrinos, "Returns to Investment in Education: A Further Update," *Education Economics*, 2004.

Equilibrium Levels of Human Capital

Each of us must decide how much to invest in ourselves. This decision, like so many in economics, ultimately depends on supply and demand, in this case, the supply of, and demand for, funds to be used for human capital investment. A hypothetical market for human capital is shown in Figure 5. In this scenario, "price" is the percentage rate of return on human capital investments and the interest cost of borrowing funds.

Equilibrium Levels of Investment in Human Capital

This graph portrays a hypothetical market for human capital; the percentage rates of return and the interest costs of borrowing funds are shown on the vertical axis. With demand D_0 and supply S_0, equilibrium will be at point e. If the supply of funds is reduced (S_1), interest rates and the cost of investment increase, resulting in less investment. Reduced demand for education (D_1) similarly reduces human capital investment.

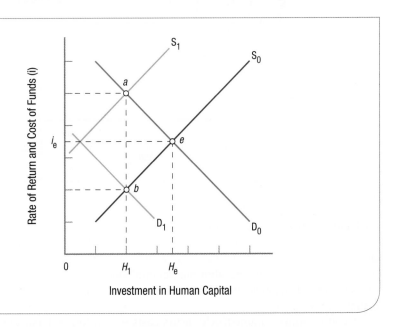

The demand for human capital investment slopes down and to the right, reflecting the diminishing returns of more education and that more time in school leaves you less time to earn back its costs. Students pursuing a Ph.D. or a medical degree are often into their thirties before they can begin paying back their student loans. As a result, they require higher salaries to bring their rates of return up above those of college-educated workers.

The supply of investable funds, meanwhile, is positively sloped, because students will use the lowest-cost funds first—mom and dad paying for college—then turn to government-subsidized funds, and finally use private market funds, if needed.

With demand (D_0) and supply (S_0), equilibrium in this market is at point e. Human capital investment is equal to H_e, with the rate of return equaling the interest rate (i_e). Notice that reducing the supply of funds, or shifting the supply curve to S_1, will increase interest rates and the cost of investment. This results in lower investments in education. Similarly, anything reducing the demand for funds, or shifting the demand curve to D_1, will result in reduced human capital investment. Let us briefly consider some of the factors that might cause these curves to shift.

The most important factor determining the supply of investable funds for students consists of family resources. Students from well-off families can draw on a pool of inexpensive funds, but students from poorer families must scratch together funds that are often expensive. At the aggregate level, reductions in federally subsidized low-interest student loans will result in a shift in the supply curve to S_1, meaning lower investments in human capital (H_1). Conversely, the GI Bills enacted after World War II and the Vietnam War, along with recent tax policies that allow certain individuals to deduct a portion of their tuition payments from their taxes, have made a college education easier to afford. These policies have shifted the supply curve to the right and have increased college enrollments and the stock of human capital in America.

Another factor influencing human capital investment is discrimination. Assume D_0 represents the demand for human capital investment for individuals facing no discrimination in the labor market. If these same people were to face a reduced wage in the market from wage discrimination, their demand for education would fall to D_1, reflecting the reduced return on investment in human capital. A similar decline in demand would result if the choice of jobs is limited by occupational discrimination.

The demand for human capital is also influenced by an individual's abilities and learning capacity: the more able the person, the larger the expected benefits of human capital investment.

Implications of Human Capital Theory

Individuals are more productive because of their investment in human capital, and thus they are capable of earning more during their working lives. Because younger people have longer earning horizons, they are more likely to invest in human capital and education. As workers get older and gain labor market experience and higher wages, their opportunity costs for attending college grow larger, while their potential post-college earning period shrinks. This explains why most students in college classrooms are young.

The greater the market earnings differential between high school and college graduates, the more people will attend college, because a higher earnings differential raises the return on college educations. Similarly, reductions in the cost of education lead to greater educational investment.

Further, the more an individual discounts the future—the more she or he values present earnings over future earnings—the less investment in human capital we would expect. People with high discount rates often are not willing to pursue doctoral or medical degrees because the time between the beginning of the training process and the point when earnings begin is simply too long.

Human Capital as Screening or Signaling

Human capital theorists see investments in human capital as improving the productivity of individuals. This higher productivity then translates into higher wages. There is another view of why higher educational levels lead to higher wages: Higher education acts as a **screening** or **signaling** device for employers.

Economists who advocate this view concede that some education will undoubtedly lead to higher productivity. But these economists argue that higher education is largely an indicator to employers that the college graduate is trainable, has discipline, and is intelligent. In their view, the job market is one big competition in which entry-level workers compete for on-the-job training. As a result, earning a college degree does little more than give the college graduate a leg up in this competition.

Most economists, however, doubt the theory that screening is the only purpose served by higher education. If it were, the high costs of college education and the higher wages employers must pay college graduates would create tremendous incentives for workers and employers to develop an alternative, less expensive screening device.

screening or **signaling** The use of higher education as a way to let employers know that the prospective employee is intelligent and trainable and potentially has the discipline to be a good employee.

On-the-Job Training

On-the-job training (OJT) is the investment by firms to increase the human capital of their workers, and can take many different forms. First, training can be as simple as receiving instructions from a supervisor on how to help customers, operate a machine, or retrieve items from inventory. Second, training can take place in a more formal setting away from the job, almost like a college course. Lastly, training can consist of a firm providing tuition reimbursement for college courses, professional certificates, or MBA degrees.

College internship programs are a good example of OJT that provide firms an extended look at potential employees while providing students with a look at several different firms and industries before graduating and entering the job market.

on-the-job training Training typically done by employers, ranging from suggestions at work to intensive workshops and seminars.

ISSUE

The Role of Educational Systems in Human Capital Accumulation

Countries use different strategies to promote human capital accumulation using their educational systems. For example, the educational system in the United States tends to emphasize a well-rounded curriculum by requiring most students to study subjects outside of their primary area of interest. Educational systems in Europe and Asia, however, tend to emphasize a more focused path of study, one in which students may select their area of study even before entering high school and take few courses outside of their major subject area. We can use anecdotal evidence to show how these differences translate into human capital outcomes.

For the United States, one can argue that emphasizing creativity and a diverse curriculum in the classroom has led to the development of world-renowned universities and research facilities, attracting students and researchers from around the world and leading to a huge boost in human capital. According to the annual *Times Higher Education's* World University Rankings, the United States is home to 15 of the top 20 universities in the world, and 47 of the top 100 universities in the world.

However, a tradeoff exists in that emphasizing one area means less em-phasis on others. For example, the U.S. primary and second-ary educational systems have lagged behind much of the de-veloped world in the subjects of math, science, and foreign language skills. According to the OECD Programme for Inter-national Student Assessment, in 2009 the United States ranked 25th out of thirty-four developed countries in math proficiency, while faring somewhat better (17th) in science. Finland and South Korea ranked at the top of most subject rankings.

What are other examples of policies aimed toward developing human capital through education? In Finland, which has one of the world's top primary education systems, teachers are highly paid and teaching is considered a prestigious job requiring many years of postgraduate education. Interestingly, the amount of time children spend in school is less than in most developed countries, using the philosophy that "less is more" by emphasizing quality over quantity.

Saudi Arabia offers all of its citizens the opportunity to study at any college

The United States consistently ranks first in the world in higher education, but lags behind most of the developed world in primary and secondary education.

in the world (based on acceptance at a college on the approved list) that is fully paid by the Saudi king (The King Abdullah Scholarship Program). Although there are no strings attached to the offer, a large majority of students graduating from foreign universities under this program returned to Saudi Arabia to work, a huge boost to human capital.

Regardless of how countries educate their citizens, investments in human capital lead to economic growth, making such investments among the most valuable in terms of the return on money spent.

Today, spending on OJT exceeds $100 billion a year, including training costs and the wages paid to employees during training. The costs of OJT are usually borne by employers, but workers may bear some of the costs through reduced wages throughout the training period. Firms benefit from OJT by gaining more productive workers, and workers gain by becoming more versatile, and thus more competitive, in labor markets. Because all OJT entails present costs meant to yield future benefits, firms choose to provide OJT if the returns from this investment compare favorably to other investment alternatives.

Investments in human capital go a long way toward explaining why people are paid different wages. Education and earnings are closely related. Human capital theorists believe that this is because education and productivity are closely related. For this reason, firms are willing to pay higher wages to individuals with greater amounts of human capital. For industries that require advanced skills, such as in computer programming, aerospace, and biotechnology (just to name a few), human capital is difficult if not impossible to replace with ordinary labor. Therefore, human capital is considered a capital input in the factors of production.

CHECKPOINT

INVESTMENT IN HUMAN CAPITAL

- Investment in human capital includes all investments in human beings such as education and on-the-job training.

- There is a positive relationship between education and earnings.

- The rate of return to education is computed by comparing the streams of income from two different levels of education.

- The greater the wage differential between two levels of education, the more people will pursue that next level of education.

- Higher education may just be a screening or signaling device telling potential employers that this individual is trainable, has discipline, and is intelligent.

- Firms are willing to provide on-the-job training when the future returns to human capital investment in terms of increased productivity to the firm exceed the costs of that training.

QUESTIONS: If the United States decided, as part of an immigration reform package, to restrict immigration only to those with college degrees, and thus decided to allow only 500,000 foreigners a year to enter, what would happen to the rate of return on college education? Alternatively, if, as part of a reform package, 500,000 low-skilled workers were permitted to enter the United States, what would happen to the rate of return on college education?

Answers to the Checkpoint questions can be found at the end of this chapter.

→ Entrepreneurship and Innovation

We have now addressed the basic requirements of production—acquiring land, labor, physical and human capital, and finding financial capital to pay for it. Is that all that is required to operate a business? Not quite. Recall from Chapter 2 that the factors of production are land, labor, capital, and entrepreneurship.

What is entrepreneurship? Entrepreneurship is the willingness to take risks and to use ideas to convert physical inputs into final products that are appealing to consumers. One can argue that entrepreneurship is the most essential factor of production—without a great idea on how to use resources, the final products will likely be of little value or may not even be produced.

Entrepreneurship

Profits are the rewards entrepreneurs receive for (1) combining land, labor, and capital to produce goods and services, and (2) assuming the risks associated with producing these goods and services. Entrepreneurs must combine and manage all the inputs of production; make day-to-day production, finance, and marketing decisions; innovate constantly if they hope to remain in business over the long run; and simultaneously bear the risks of failure and bankruptcy.

As we have seen over the past decade, large firms that have become household names can implode quickly. Lehman Brothers, Circuit City, Blockbuster Video, and Borders are a few companies that have either closed or filed for bankruptcy protection.

Even for large firms, business is risky. Bankruptcy or business failure, meanwhile, can be exceedingly painful for business owners, stockholders, employees, and communities. Still, a free economy requires such failures. If firms were guaranteed never to fail, perhaps through government subsidies (bailouts), they would have little incentive to be efficient or to innovate, or to worry about what consumers want from them.

When a firm earns economic profits—profits exceeding normal profits—this is a signal to other firms and entrepreneurs that consumers want more of the good or service the

intellectual property rights A set of exclusive rights granted to a creator of an invention or creative work, allowing the owner to earn profits over a fixed period of time. The types of protection include patents, copyrights, trademarks, and industrial designs.

profitable firm provides, and that they are willing to pay for it. Profit signals shift resources from areas of lower demand to the products and services consumers desire more highly. It is entrepreneurs who are attuned to the profit signals.

Innovation and the Global Economy

Innovation describes both entrepreneurship, when individuals and firms develop something new, and the constant retooling of existing products. Innovation arguably is the most productive input in the production process. Many countries, such as those in Africa, have abundant natural resources and labor, yet have not been able to convert those inputs into substantial outputs. Meanwhile, such countries as Japan, Germany, and Sweden, with more limited physical resources, have compensated by generating high levels of human capital and innovation, and subsequently generate a very high standard of living for their citizens.

An important issue is that to encourage innovation, those who innovate must be provided with incentives to make the money and effort invested worthwhile. For example, an individual's or a firm's innovations can be protected using **intellectual property rights,** including patents, copyrights, trademarks, and industrial designs, allowing innovators an exclusive right to earn profits from their investments for a fixed amount of time.

The importance of innovation as a driver of economic growth will continue to increase as the economy becomes more globalized. Specifically, deficiencies in physical capital can easily be resolved through trade and foreign direct investment. But deficiencies in human capital and innovation are a much more difficult obstacle to overcome.

Therefore, the future of a country's economic growth will depend on its ability to generate new ideas and find more productive uses of its limited resources. At the start of this chapter, we discussed the aerospace industry and its goals of developing planes that provide more comfort to passengers, and reduce operating costs. Both objectives increase the productive use of limited resources, which will allow the industry to grow as people demand more travel.

But advances in innovative technology cannot be limited to just a few industries. All industries must avoid falling behind the trend of increasing productivity throughout the world. Emerging countries have begun to invest significant sums to improve physical infrastructure and human capital. This had led to innovations in all industries and an improvement in the standards of living in these countries. In order for the United States to continue increasing its standard of living, it must maintain its position as a leader in innovation.

Visdia/Dreamstime.com

Investment in wind and solar energy technology has increased as more countries emphasize innovations in renewable energy.

◉ CHECKPOINT

ENTREPRENEURSHIP AND INNOVATION

- Entrepreneurs earn profits for combining other inputs to create products and for assuming the risks of producing goods and services.
- Innovation includes the efforts by entrepreneurs to produce new products as well as efforts by firms to make existing products better.
- Entrepreneurship and innovation is arguably the most productive of the factors of production, allowing countries to use limited resources to produce valuable outputs that lead to a higher standard of living.

QUESTIONS: Why is entrepreneurship considered a factor of production despite the fact that it does not exist in physical form? Suppose a country has abundant amounts of natural resources and labor, would this automatically translate into a highly productive economy?

Answers to the Checkpoint questions can be found at the end of this chapter.

chapter summary

Section 1: **Land and Physical Capital**

Land prices are driven by a fixed supply and by demand factors such as the terrain, attributes, view, and location.

Rent is the return or income that flows to land or physical capital as a factor of production.

MRP$_K$ is the additional value that a unit of capital brings to the firm. It represents the maximum a firm is willing to pay for capital.

MRP$_K$ slopes downward; where it crosses i is the amount a firm will invest.

Present Value Versus Rate of Return

- Present value measures the value today of money collected in the future.
- $PV = X/(1 + i)^n$, where i = discount rate and n = years.
- Rate of return is the interest rate that is required for a project to break even in the long run.
- Calculating the rate of return requires solving for the interest rate that makes the present value of all future income from a project equal to its cost of capital.

Section 2: **Financial Capital**

Banks: Offer loans based on credit history and ability to produce collateral in case of default; the amount borrowed is usually limited.

Bond market: Bonds are claims on a company's assets. A bond pays a fixed payment called a coupon rate and a face value upon maturity.

Four Sources of Financial Capital

Stock market: Stocks give partial ownership in a company, entitling owners (shareholders) to a vote in company matters and a share of dividends.

Venture capital: Provides seed money to new businesses in exchange for partial ownership in the company.

Section 3: Human Capital

Investment in human capital can come from

- Education
- On-the-job-training

The greater the wage differential between two levels of human capital investment, the more people will pursue that next level.

Is education just a signal or does it provide inherent productive value? Economists believe it's a little of both.

Average Earnings by Highest Degree Earned

Education is a good investment in terms of human capital accumulation, which translates to higher average salaries.

Section 4: Entrepreneurship and Innovation

Entrepreneurs assume the risk of using capital and labor markets to create new goods and services and to make existing products better.

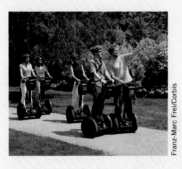

Success brings great rewards to entrepreneurs, many of whom have become very rich, such as the inventor of the Segway.

Failure is a part of free markets, as some innovations do not make it, such as Toshiba's HD DVD format.

Entrepreneurship is an important factor of production. It allows countries to turn limited resources into productive outputs and higher standards of living.

Intellectual property rights are needed to protect innovation and provide rewards for entrepreneurs. These include:

- Patents: to protect ideas and inventions
- Copyrights: to protect writings and artistic impression
- Trademarks: to protect names and symbols
- Industrial Designs: to protect product designs

KEY CONCEPTS

rent, p. 312
physical capital, p. 313
present value, p. 315
rate of return, p. 316
financial capital, p. 317
collateral, p. 318

face value, p. 318
coupon rate, p. 318
maturity, p. 318
yield, p. 318
share of stock, p. 319
market cap, p. 320

investment in human capital, p. 322
screening or signaling, p. 325
on-the-job training, p. 325
intellectual property rights, p. 328

QUESTIONS AND PROBLEMS

Check Your Understanding

1. What does the term *land* refer to in economics and why is it very inelastic in supply?

2. If the interest rate is 6% and you are offered a bond that will pay you $2,000 in two years, but no interest between now and then, what would you be willing to pay for this bond today?

3. What are the different ways in which businesses can acquire financial capital?

4. Why are colleges filled with young people rather than middle-aged individuals? If interest rates rose to over 10%, would this have any impact on the number of people attending college or its composition?

5. What is the difference between physical capital and human capital?

6. What do intellectual property rights protect and why is it important to entrepreneurship?

Apply the Concepts

7. How do times of growth in the general economy encourage capital investments? How do recessions discourage capital investments? What happens to the cost of capital in boom times when the economy is growing? What happens in recessionary times?

8. Cities such as London and Johannesburg spent billions in capital expenditures building new stadiums, roads, and public transportation to host the 2012 Summer Olympics and the 2010 World Cup, respectively, in hopes of generating a spike in future tourism and business investment. Explain how these cities would use a rate of return approach to determine whether the effort to host the sporting event was worthwhile.

9. Suppose you wish to purchase a corporate bond that offers a coupon rate of 10% in the bond market. On a particular day, you notice the price of the bond listed as greater than "100." Given this price, would the yield on this bond be greater than or less than 10%? List some possible reasons that would cause the price of the bond to exceed "100."

10. When a company uses resources to train staff or subsidize tuition for employees, it is clearly investing in human capital. However, this investment is treated as current spending (cost of selling or producing goods) rather than investment. Should these activities be treated as investments and be reflected in the investment statistics of the economy?

11. Does it seem reasonable that a certain portion of the benefits of a college education is essentially a way to show prospective employers that you are reasonably intelligent, trainable, and have a certain degree of discipline?

12. Some politicians during any election campaign offer proposals to make college more affordable by increasing subsidies through higher Pell grants and subsidizing reduced rate loans. If these policies come to pass, and college becomes less expensive, more people will attend college. What will this do to the rate of return on a college education?

In the News

13. A December 13, 2012, article in the *Los Angeles Times*, "Colorado River Water Supply to Fall Short of Demand . . . " highlighted the concern regarding the ability of the Colorado River, the primary source of water for the greater Los Angeles area residents, to fulfill the needs as the river continues to decrease in water flow. Using a market diagram, show what happens to water prices if the supply of water, a natural resource, is fixed each year while demand continues to increase due to population growth. If the article's predictions come true and the supply decreases, show what happens to the price of water.

14. Steve Wynn is a billionaire Las Vegas casino tycoon who built famous hotels such as the Mirage, Bellagio, Wynn, and Encore resorts. In 2012, he announced a plan to invest $4 billion to build his third hotel in Macao, a tiny former Portuguese colony near Hong Kong that has been returned to China ("Wynn Macao Plans to Invest $4 Billion for New Resort," Bloomberg.com, June 5, 2012). The size of the investment surprised analysts, because the gaming market in Macao, while still the world's largest in total revenue, has begun to slow in recent years. What are some market factors influencing the present value of Wynn's future earnings that might justify his decision to build such a lavish resort?

Solving Problems

15. Suppose you win the lottery and are given a choice to collect either the grand prize of $6 million in 20 annual installments of $300,000, or collect an immediate one-time payment of $4 million today. If the interest rate is 5% and that is what you use to discount future earnings, which option should you select to maximize the present value of the winnings?

16. The mayor of your city is considering building a new toll road to reduce congestion. The cost of the toll road is $10 million and is estimated to generate a profit (from tolls collected less expenses collecting the tolls and maintaining the road) of $1.5 million per year. If the discount rate is 10%, how many years would it take before the road is paid for? (Hint: Calculate the present value of the annual profit—for year 1, discount $1.5 million by 10%.)

USING THE NUMBERS

17. According to By the Numbers, in the year 2011 (the last year for which data are reported) approximately what percentage of high school graduates attended college? Approximately what percentage of college graduates attended a graduate program?

18. According to By the Numbers, by approximately what percentage did venture capital funding fall from its peak in 2007 to its lowest point in 2010?

ANSWERS TO QUESTIONS IN CHECKPOINTS

Checkpoint: Land and Physical Capital

To determine whether this investment is worthwhile, you would want to know how much income the store expects to generate over the year, as well as the current market interest rate. Using this information, you can estimate the net present value of the investment to determine whether it is a good idea or not. The higher the market interest rate, the greater the income stream you would require to invest.

Checkpoint: Financial Capital

Bonds are promises to pay back a lender (bondholder) a specific amount on a specific date, while stocks represent actual ownership (to the extent of the number of shares held) in a business. A bondholder does not own any part of the business, and therefore does not influence the day-to-day management of the firm.

An advantage of issuing bonds is that it allows a business to maintain control of its management. Another advantage is that the business is unlikely to be subjected to a forceful takeover by a large investor. A disadvantage of bonds is that a business must pay an interest rate that is sometimes high depending on how investors perceive their risk. Another disadvantage of bonds is that a business must make periodic coupon payments to bondholders, as well as pay back the bonds as they mature. This may restrict a business's ability to use available cash funds to invest in additional capital inputs.

Checkpoint: Investment in Human Capital

Letting in a large number of college-educated immigrants would drive the rate of return on college down as wages of college graduates would not grow very rapidly. The opposite would occur when unskilled immigrants enter, holding down the wages of those without college educations, leading to a growing gap between those with college degrees, increasing the rate of return to a college degree.

Checkpoint: Entrepreneurship and Innovation

Entrepreneurship is the idea and vision to turn physical inputs such as land, labor, and capital into valuable outputs that people demand. An economy cannot produce goods without someone willing and able to determine what the market wants. Therefore, entrepreneurship is a vital factor of production.

Although having abundant amounts of natural resources and labor may provide a country with an advantage in production, a country still requires entrepreneurship to turn those physical inputs into valuable products people desire. Thus, having abundant physical inputs does not automatically result in a productive economy. The reverse is also true—having few physical inputs does not preclude a country from being productive if it is able to use its limited resources effectively.

Externalities and Public Goods

13

A computerized visualization of the Arctic ice caps showing the extent to which the area covered by the thickest ice, known as *multiyear ice*, has diminished from 1980 to 2012.

After studying this chapter you should be able to:

- Describe the types of market failures.
- Describe the impact of negative and positive externalities on society.
- Describe the Coase theorem on social costs and the role transaction costs play in the optimal allocation of resources.
- Explain the nature of public goods and why they are difficult to provide in the market.
- Explain how common property resources can lead to resource degradation.
- Recognize the importance of the discount rate in assessing the costs and benefits of environmental policies.
- Use marginal analysis to determine the optimal level of pollution.
- Describe the differences between command and control policies and market-based approaches to environmental regulation.
- Understand the economic issues surrounding global climate change.

Each day, thousands of spectacular explosions occur in a process called calving, when ice breaks off from mountains of glaciers and falls into the ocean as icebergs, eventually melting away. The withering ice shelves and frozen tundra that constitute the vast wilderness of the arctic (and the Antarctic) have affected the landscape that hundreds of wildlife species, including the polar bear, call home.

According to a 2012 NASA study, the volume and area of the Arctic ice caps fluctuate from year to year based on atmospheric cycles, but the overall trend has been declining as average surface temperatures rise. Estimates show that the overall area covered by the thickest ice, known as multiyear ice, has been shrinking between 12% and 17% per decade over the last 30 years. Other ice caps and glaciers around the world are also melting, and the consequences extend beyond the wildlife affected. It also affects human lives as ocean levels rise. Despite widely varying estimates that ocean levels will rise between 7 inches and 63 inches by the end of the century, these statistics highlight the important idea that actions taken today, both positive and negative, will affect future generations.

The impact of human actions that contribute to global climate change is one that economic policy tries to address, although not without significant challenges and obstacles. An important issue is that the Earth's climate is shared: One country's efforts are not enough, while achieving consensus on environmental policy is difficult, if not impossible.

How environmental policies are set depends largely on the priorities placed by individual countries. For example, during much of the 20th century, the United States was a highly industrialized country; standards of living increased dramatically, but at the cost of greater pollution. However, many Americans now place a higher priority on maintaining a cleaner environment for future generations. This transformation from a polluting industrial society to a cleaner, energy-efficient society can be seen in many developed nations, such as the United States, the countries of the European Union, Japan, and Australia.

In contrast, much of the world remains very poor. In these poor countries, economic development to improve basic living conditions takes precedence over environmental concerns. In countries that have grown significantly in recent years, such as China and India, polluting factories are churning out goods as fast as they can, and consumers are buying more cars and air travel. China is now the largest market in the world for new cars. The ability of previously impoverished nations to experience economic prosperity often comes at the expense of the environment.

Because of differing environmental priorities among nations, it is difficult to achieve a consensus. In addition, any one country's efforts to improve the environment benefit the entire world, yet that country bears the full costs of these efforts. Meanwhile, other countries may exploit the environment for their economic gain, offsetting the environmental efforts made by others.

The actions affecting the environment extend beyond the national level. Individuals and firms make decisions that affect the environment, such as the type of cars we buy and

BY THE NUMBERS

The Environment and Sustainability

Having a sustainable economy will likely require a focus on energy other than fossil fuels, finding better methods to recycle waste, and developing methods to manage the natural environment.

Hybrid sales grew quickly from 2000 to 2007, then declined from 2008 to 2011 due to the last recession and slow economic recovery, before picking up again in 2012.

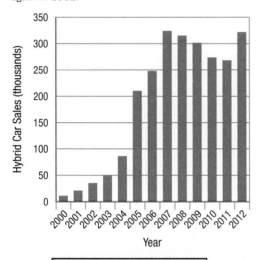

Millions of tons of solid waste fill landfills, while some is recovered and recycled. To be sustainable, the United States must recover more in the future.

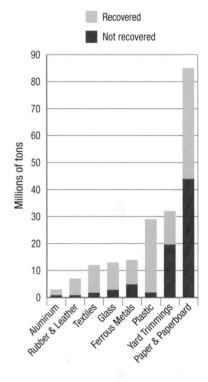

Legend:
- Recovered
- Not recovered

120 million
Number of electric bicycles in China.

301%
Increase in wind energy generated in the United States between 2007 and 2012.

$39
Annual savings from replacing five 60-watt bulbs with compact fluorescents.

1.4 (0.2)
Acres of arable land per person in the United States (and China).

Over 80,000 European fishing boats are fishing out Atlantic cod using advanced technology.

Jeff Rotman/Alamy

49¢
Average gasoline tax per gallon in the United States.

$4.85
Average gasoline tax per gallon in Britain.

Top 10 States in Wind Power Generation Capacity (megawatts)

Texas	10,648
Iowa	4,419
California	4,287
Illinois	2,852
Oregon	2,820
Minnesota	2,718
Washington	2,699
Oklahoma	2,039
Colorado	1,805
New York	1,418

Broker/Dreamstime.com

the production methods companies use. Each of these decisions affects not only the individual or company, but others who share the environment that is being affected.

On a brighter note, economic growth has led to increasing efficiencies in resource use. The growing popularity of hybrid and plug-in electric cars has improved fuel efficiency. Even new technologies in cow feed (such as the infusion of garlic) have reduced the level of harmful methane gases emitted by cows. Yet, clearly we still have many environmental problems that must be addressed, including global climate change, species extinction, overharvesting of fisheries, and overcrowding of highways and parks.

Still, global climate change seems to be an almost intractable problem. Beyond the obvious scientific issues of how to reduce our environmental footprints stands market failure, a concept introduced in Chapter 4. As we saw there, market failure describes how markets fail in specific ways to provide the socially optimal amount of goods and services. In the particular case of global climate change, what makes it so hard to deal with is that several specific market failures come together to make a solution tough to reach.

This chapter starts by examining market failures caused when actions taken by consumers or producers have effects on third parties (externalities), when certain types of goods called public goods provide poor incentives to market participants, and when specific resources are shared. After analyzing these market failures, the chapter then looks at the ways policy tries to solve them in the context of environmental issues. Finally, after you get your hands around market failures and various policies to resolve them, the chapter takes what you have learned and applies it to global climate change, which combines aspects of many market failures.

➡ Externalities

Actions by individuals and firms affect not only those involved, but also can create side effects for others in ways that can be either beneficial or costly. For example, suppose you share an apartment with a neat and organized person. Because your roommate always keeps the apartment clean and uncluttered, you reap the benefits of not having dishes piling up in the sink or potato chip crumbs all over the sofa. Clearly, you benefit from this situation. On the other hand, suppose the occupants of the apartment next door are members of an aspiring heavy metal band. They blast loud music all day, and occasionally have a jam session—and you're forced to hear everything they play. Unless you enjoy that music yourself, your neighbors' actions become a cost for you.

externalities The impact on third parties of some transaction between others in which the third parties are not involved. An external cost (or negative externality) harms the third parties, whereas external benefits (positive externalities) result in gains to them.

Externalities, often called *spillovers,* arise when actions or market transactions by an individual or a firm cause some other party not involved in the activity or transaction to benefit or be harmed. If the activity imposes costs on others, it is called a *negative externality* or an *external cost.* If the activity creates benefits to others, this is a *positive externality* or an *external benefit.* Negative externalities include air and water pollution, littering, and chemical runoff that affect fish stocks. Examples of activities that generate positive externalities include getting a flu shot, acquiring more education, landscaping, and maintaining beehives next to apple orchards.

Both producers and consumers can create externalities and can feel the effects of them. The matrix in Table 1 identifies the origin and impact of some common external effects.

Negative Externalities

When a market transaction harms people not involved in the transaction, negative externalities exist. Pollution of all sorts is the classic example. Firms and consumers rarely consider the impact their production or consumption will have on others. For simplicity, we focus on the pollution caused by production. Figure 1 shows a typical market.

Supply curve S_p represents the manufacturer's marginal private cost (MPC) of production. This supply curve ignores the external costs imposed on others from the pollution generated during production. These external costs might include toxic wastes dumped into lakes or streams, smokestack soot, or the clear-cutting associated with timber harvests. Ignoring these costs, market equilibrium is at point *e,* at which the product is priced at $6 and 30 units are sold.

Externalities by Origin and Impact

TABLE 1

Origin of Externality	Impact — Victims and Beneficiaries of Externality			
	Consumers		**Producers**	
	Positive	**Negative**	**Positive**	**Negative**
Consumers	• Private schools • Immunizations • Landscaping	• Auto pollution • Littering • Smoking	• Flu shot reducing sick days	• Private auto use that adds to road congestion slowing down commercial traffic
	Positive	**Negative**	**Positive**	**Negative**
Producers	• New factory leading to new shops and restaurants in town	• Factory air pollution on wilderness hikers • Pesticide runoff affecting trout fishing	• Honey bees improving apple orchards	• Pollution that harms commercial fishing

Recall from Chapter 4 that one way to measure the well-being of consumers and producers in a market is to measure the consumer surplus and producer surplus. Consumer surplus is the difference between what consumers are willing to pay for a good (shown by the demand curve) and the market price (equal to $6 in Figure 1). Therefore, consumer surplus is equal to $45 [(($9 − $6) × 30) / 2]. Producer surplus is the difference between the market price and the minimum amount at which sellers are willing to sell a product (shown by the supply curve), and is equal to $45 as well [(($6 − $3) × 30) / 2]. Summing up consumer surplus and producer surplus equals $90, which is shown as area *ace* in the figure.

Now let's assume that for every unit of the product produced, pollution costs (or effluent) equal to $2 is generated. Thus, at an output level of 30 units (point *e*), $60 in pollution

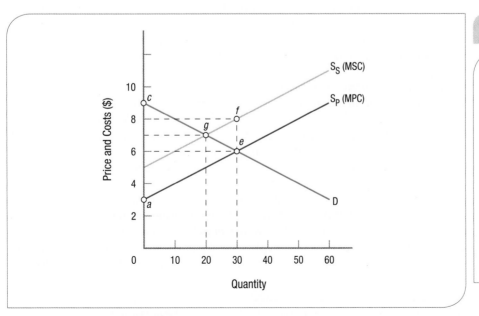

FIGURE 1

The Negative Externality Case

Supply curve S_P represents the manufacturer's supply when only its private costs are considered, ignoring the external costs imposed on others through pollution. Market equilibrium is 30 units sold at $6 each (point *e*). If each unit of production results in $2 in pollution costs, then supply curve S_S represents the marginal social costs (MSC) to manufacture the product. Socially optimal output is 20 units sold at $7 each (point *g*).

costs (or negative externalities) are generated. Subtracting this $60 in pollution from total consumer and producer surplus results in $30 of real social benefit from this output.

This means that the true marginal cost of producing the product, including pollution costs, is equal to supply curve S_S, representing the marginal social cost (MSC) of production. This new supply curve incorporates both the private and social costs of production, thus shifting supply upward by an amount equal to *ef,* or $2. Equilibrium moves to point *g,* at which 20 units of the product are sold at $7. This is the socially optimal production for this product given the pollution it creates.

So why is it better for society than when 30 units were produced? First, notice that when output is 20, the cost of the last unit produced—including the cost of pollution—is $7 (point *g*). This is just equal to the value society attributes to the product. Hence, consumers get just what they want when all costs are considered. Second, notice that consumer and producer surplus at an output of 20 units is $40 [(($9 − $5) × 20) / 2]. More important, it is now higher than the $30 of consumer and producer surplus minus the pollution costs when output was 30 units (point *e*).

Each unit of output produced beyond 20 costs more—taking both private and social costs into account—than its value to consumers.

Imagine a situation in which external costs exceed the consumer and producer surplus from consuming the good. Such a situation might arise when an extremely toxic substance is a by-product of production. Society is better off not permitting production of this good.

What has this analysis shown? First, when negative externalities are present, an unregulated market will produce too much of a good at too low a price. Second, optimal pollution levels are not zero, except in the case just mentioned of extremely toxic agents. In Figure 1, the socially optimal production is 20 units with total pollution costs of $40. Pollution reduction as a good has no price. Even so, we can infer a price, known as a shadow price, equal to the marginal damages—$2 per unit in this case. As we will see later, prices for the "right to pollute" will provide us with better approximations of the costs of pollution.

The Coase Theorem

Ronald Coase was awarded the Nobel Prize in Economics for his seminal paper, "The Problem of Social Cost." Coase has written few articles—less than a dozen—but, as economist Robert Cooter noted, although "most economists maximize the amount they write, Coase maximized the amount others wrote about his work."[1] Indeed, Coase's paper on social cost is one of the most cited works in economics.

Reducing output to the optimal level results in gains to "victims" because pollution is reduced. The reduction in output, however, causes losses to producers. The presence of losses and gains to two distinct parties, Coase argued, introduces the possibility of bargaining, provided that the parties are awarded the property rights necessary for negotiation.

The **Coase theorem** states that if transaction costs are minimal (near zero), the resulting bargain or allocation of resources will be efficient—output will decline to the optimal level—regardless of the initial allocation of property rights. The socially optimal level of production will be reached, that is, no matter whether polluters are given the right to pollute or victims are given the right to be free of pollution.

Even so, the distribution of benefits or income will be different in these two cases. If victims, for example, are assigned the property rights, their income will grow, but if polluters are assigned these rights, the income of victims will decline.

As Coase noted, for these efficient results to be achieved, transaction costs must approach zero. This means it must be possible for polluters and victims to determine their collective interests accurately, then negotiate and enforce an agreement. In many situations, however, this is simply not feasible. In cases involving air pollution, for instance,

Coase theorem If transaction costs are minimal (near zero), a bargain struck between beneficiaries and victims of externalities will be efficient from a resource allocation perspective. As a result, the socially optimal level of production will be reached.

---

[1] Peter Passell, "Economics Nobel to a Basic Thinker," *New York Times,* October 16, 1991, p. D6.

polluters and victims are so widely dispersed that negotiating is impracticable. In other cases, individuals may be both victims and polluters, making it difficult for an agreement to be reached and enforced.

Another problem associated with assigning rights to one party or another might be called *environmental mugging*. Polluters might at first threaten to pollute more than they anticipate, for instance, to increase their bargaining leverage and, ultimately, their income. Victims, in like manner, might assert exaggerated environmental concerns, again to bid up their compensation. Alternatively, if negotiations should prove to be unfruitful, polluters might start lobbying for legal relief, thus devoting their money to rent-seeking behaviors rather than buying pollution-abatement equipment.

Although the private negotiations Coase proposed have their limitations, his insights proved to be a turning point in environmental policy. Coase challenged the prevailing practice of assuming that victims had a right to be pollution-free. His analysis stressed that it does not matter who the rights are assigned to (the polluter or the pollution-victim, for example). No matter how property rights were assigned, if information was good and transaction costs were low, efficiency would result. Given the costs of pollution, affected parties have an incentive to work out efficient agreements.

This idea was so radical when Coase published "The Problem of Social Cost" in 1960 that another Nobel Prize winner, George Stigler, wondered "how so fine an economist could make such an obvious mistake." Coase was later invited to the University of Chicago to discuss his ideas; Stigler described what transpired[2]:

NOBEL PRIZE
RONALD COASE

University of Chicago professor Ronald Coase won the Nobel Prize in Economic Sciences in 1991 for "his discovery and clarification of the significance of transaction costs and property rights" in the institutional structure and functioning of the economy. According to his analysis, traditional microeconomic theory was incomplete because it neglected the costs of executing contracts and managing firms. To Coase, these "transaction costs" were the principal reason that firms existed. Economic actors found it cost efficient to create a more complex organization to minimize transaction costs.

Coase also analyzed the economy in terms of the *rights* to use goods and factors (inputs) of production rather than the actual goods and factors themselves. These "property rights" could be defined in different ways according to contracts and rules within organizations. Coase introduced the concept of property rights as an important element of economic analysis.

Born in 1910 in Willesden, a suburb of London, Coase attended the London School of Economics (LSE), where he earned a Bachelor of Commerce degree in 1932, and returned 15 years later and earned a Doctor of Science degree in economics in 1951. Becoming disillusioned with the future of British socialism and taking "a liking for life in America," he migrated to the United States in 1951 and taught at the University of Buffalo. Coase's 1960 article, "The Problem of Social Cost," questioned whether governments could efficiently allocate resources for social purposes through taxes and subsidies. He argued that arbitrarily assigning property rights and using markets to reach a solution was usually better than costly government regulation. This was instantly controversial and led to a lengthy exchange of papers in economics journals. In 1964, Coase joined the faculty at the University of Chicago and became editor of the *Journal of Law and Economics*. The journal was an important catalyst in developing the economic interpretation of legal issues.

We strongly objected to this heresy. Milton Friedman did most of the talking, as usual. He also did much of the thinking, as usual. In the course of two hours of argument the vote went from twenty against and one for Coase to twenty-one for Coase. What an exhilarating event! I lamented afterward that we had not had the clairvoyance to tape it.

The Coase theorem has changed the way economists look at many issues, not just environmental problems. In cases in which the costs of negotiation are negligible and the number of parties involved is small, economists and jurists have begun to look more closely at legal rules assigning liability.

Positive Externalities

When private market transactions generate benefits for others, a situation opposite to that just described results. Figure 2 on the next page illustrates a positive externality. Market supply curve S and private demand curve D_p (equal to the marginal private benefit, MPB,

---

[2] George Stigler, *Memoirs of an Unregulated Economist* (New York: Basic Books, 1988), p. 76.

FIGURE 2

The Positive Externality Case

Market supply curve S and private demand curve D_P represent the market for college education. Equilibrium is at point *e,* and the number of students enrolled is Q_e. Society would benefit, however, if more people would go to college. Demand curve D_S represents the marginal social benefit (MSB), which includes the private demand for college education plus the external benefits that flow from it. Socially optimal enrollment would be Q_1 (point *f*).

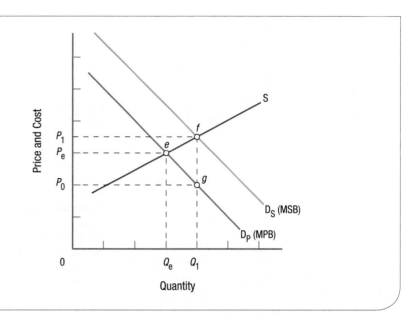

of consumption) represent the market for college education. Equilibrium is at point *e,* with Q_e students enrolling. Society would clearly benefit, however, if more people received a college education: Tax revenues would rise, crime rates would fall, and a better-informed electorate might produce a better-operating democracy.

Taking these considerations into account, social demand curve D_S is the private demand for college education plus the external benefits that flow from it. Socially optimal enrollment would be Q_1 (point *f*). How can society tweak the market so that more students will attend college? Students will demand Q_1 levels of enrollment only if its price is P_0 (point *g*). The public must therefore subsidize college education by *fg* to draw its price down to P_0.

The U.S. government recognizes that college education benefits society at large when it provides low-interest student loans, grants, and scholarships to students attending colleges and universities.

Limitations

Some caveats about our analysis of externalities need to be noted. First, producer and consumer surpluses are good measures of society's welfare if all incomes are weighted equally or the distribution of income is optimal. When income is unequally distributed, gross unfairness created throughout society swamps any improvements from efficiency. Thus, measures of efficiency such as consumer and producer surplus can become unconvincing for public policy. Because no one can agree on the correct distribution of income, economists generally ignore this question and focus on efficiency.

Second, the discussion has focused on the pollution that arises from production, not consumption. The results applied to congestion and littering, however, would be substantially the same.

Third, the examples presented here have assumed, moreover, that pollution has no cumulative effects. And, indeed, smaller amounts of pollution effluence may just flow into the ocean, for instance, with no lasting effects. But the same will not hold true for sustained higher pollution levels.

Fourth, for convenience, we have assumed that we can assign specific amounts to the damages resulting from pollution. In practice, this is not always easy to do.

Fifth, we have assumed that pollution can be reduced only by reducing output, but in real markets, there are other ways to reduce pollution.

Despite these limitations, the analysis presented here helps us focus our attention on ways of reducing the harm done to society by negative externalities.

In summary, the presence of externalities leads to overuse of resources and environmental degradation, causing a **market failure** to occur, when markets fail to provide the socially optimal level of goods and services. Another type of market failure occurs when resources are not privately owned, which we discuss in the next section.

CHECKPOINT

EXTERNALITIES

- Externalities arise when the production of one good generates benefits (positive externalities) or costs (negative externalities) for others not involved in the transaction.

- When negative externalities exist, overproduction is the result. When positive externalities are generated, underproduction of the good is the norm.

- The Coase theorem states that if transaction costs are minimal (near zero), no matter which party is provided the property rights to pollution (polluter or victim), the resulting bargain will result in the socially optimal level of pollution.

QUESTION: Compact fluorescent light (CFL) bulbs have grown in popularity as their quality improves and prices fall. But not all consumers are convinced of the benefits of CFL bulbs. Proponents point to the tremendous energy savings, because CFL bulbs require only about 20% of the energy used by incandescent light bulbs, and they last much longer as well. Critics point to the potential dangers of mercury contained in CFL bulbs, along with a less desirable light color emitted by CFL bulbs. In addition to these private benefits and costs, what are some external benefits and external costs that are created by the use of CFL bulbs?

Answers to the Checkpoint question can be found at the end of this chapter.

market failure When markets fail to provide the socially optimal level of output, and will provide output at too high or low a price.

 Public Goods

We saw in the previous section that externalities can lead to markets not providing the socially efficient amount of a good at the optimal price. Either too much or too little of the good is produced, or it is offered at too high or too low a price, leading to a market failure. The presence of externalities is one cause of market failure. This section looks at two other causes of market failure that arise when no individual or firm is able to claim ownership of a product. These goods and services are called *public goods* and *common property resources*.

What Are Public Goods?

Pure **public goods** are nonrival in consumption, and exhibit nonexcludability. **Nonrivalry** means that the consumption of a good or service by one person does not reduce the utility of that good or service to others. **Nonexcludability** means that it is not possible to exclude some consumers from using the good or service once it has been provided.

By way of contrast, a can of Coke is a rival product. When you drink a can of Coke, no one else can drink that same can. Airline flights exhibit excludability—one must either buy a ticket or obtain an award ticket to board the plane, even if empty seats are available. But consider a lighthouse. Once it is built and in operation, all ships can see the lighthouse and use the light to avoid obstacles. One captain's use of the lighthouse does not prevent another from using it, nor can a ship realistically be excluded from using the lighthouse's services. Hence, the lighthouse is a public good. Other examples of public goods include national defense, accumulated knowledge, standards such as a national currency, protection of property rights, vaccinations, mosquito spraying, and clean air. Table 2 on the next page provides a taxonomy of private and public goods.

Consumers cannot be excluded from a public good once it is provided, therefore they have little incentive to pay for the good in question. Instead, most will essentially be **free riders.** Think of the lighthouse again. If you have a ship and cannot be excluded from the benefits the lighthouse provides, why should you contribute anything to the lighthouse's

public goods Goods in which one person's consumption does not diminish the benefit to others from consuming the good (i.e., nonrivalry), and once provided, no one person can be excluded from consuming (i.e., nonexclusion).

nonrivalry The consumption of a good or service by one person does not reduce the utility of that good or service to others.

nonexcludability Once a good or service is provided, it is not possible to exclude others from enjoying that good or service.

free rider The ability of an individual to avoid paying for a public good because he or she cannot be excluded from enjoying the good once provided.

TABLE 2	Taxonomy of Private and Public Goods	
	Property Rights	
Characteristics of Goods	**Exclusive**	**Nonexclusive**
Rival	Pure private good • Airline seat • Ice cream bar	Common property resource • Ocean fishery • Highways
Nonrival	Public good with exclusion • Cable TV • Satellite radio	Pure public good • National defense • Public broadcasting

upkeep? But if everyone took this position, there would be no support for the lighthouse, and it would go into decline. With free riders, private producers cannot hope to sell many units of a good, and thus they have no incentive to produce it. Private markets will therefore fail to provide public goods, even if the goods are things everyone would like to see produced. This is why the government or special interest groups must get involved in the provision of products and services that have significant public good characteristics.

The Demand for Public Goods

Assessing the public's demand for public goods is clearly different from that of private goods where we found market demand by horizontally summing private demands. But the fact that once a public good is supplied, no one can be excluded from consuming it, and one person's consumption does not affect another's, plays a crucial role. Figure 3 provides a solution to finding the demand for public goods.

Figure 3 shows demand for a public good by two different consumers. Individual A wants none when the price is $40 and is willing and able to buy 40 units when the price approaches zero. Individual B wants none when the price is $60 and only is willing to buy 30 units when the price nears zero. Because each consumer can consume any given

FIGURE 3	

Demand for Public Goods: Vertical Summation of Individual Demand Curves

For public goods, exclusion is not possible, individuals can consume the good simultaneously, and market demand is found by summing vertically. Market demand for public goods is really a willingness-to-pay curve because the government will have to provide the good and levy taxes to pay the cost. The total demand for the public good is shown by the heavy line labeled $D_{Public\ Goods}$ and is the vertical summation of individual demands.

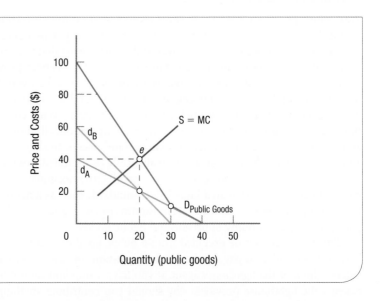

amount of a public good at the same time, the total demand for a public good is found by summing the individual demands *vertically*. To see why, consider when both individuals demand 20 units. This is the point at which the two demand curves cross, and both are willing to pay $20 for 20 units. Thus, total demand for 20 units is $40. The total demand for the public good in Figure 3 is shown by the heavy line labeled $D_{Public\ Goods}$ and is the vertical summation of individual demands.

Notice how this differs from our discussion of market demand curves for private goods. For private goods, others could be excluded from consuming any good we bought, therefore demands were horizontally summed. In contrast, with public goods, exclusion is not possible, therefore both individuals can consume the good simultaneously, and market demand is found by summing vertically. Market demand for public goods is really a *willingness-to-pay curve,* because the government will have to provide the good and levy taxes to pay the cost.

Optimal Provision of Public Goods

Providing the optimal amount of public goods is easy in theory and is illustrated in Figure 3. The supply of public goods is equal to the marginal cost curve (S = MC) shown in the figure. Just like the competitive market equilibrium we covered earlier, optimal allocation is where MC = P, and in this instance, it is 20 units of the good at a total price of $40 (point *e*). In this example, the taxes are split equally between individuals A and B. Determining how much tax each person should (or would be willing to) pay is hampered by the fact that once the public good is provided, no one can be excluded, therefore individuals will be unwilling to reveal their true preferences for the good because it might mean that they would have to pay a higher tax.

In reality, providing public goods such as national defense involves the political process. This means that politicians, bureaucrats, special interest groups, and many others generate the decisions on how much of any particular public good to provide. Since the demand for a public good represents the benefits to society and the supply curve represents society's costs, equating marginal benefits and marginal costs yields the optimal amount. But estimating the demand (benefits) from public goods and their costs can be a complex process. Most people desire the benefits of a strong military, but few enjoy paying the taxes required to pay for the cost. Because people cannot be excluded from the good, once provided, they have little incentive to reveal their true preferences, making this type of market failure difficult to overcome.

Common Property Resources

Commonly held resources are subject to nonexclusion but are rival in consumption. The market failure associated with such resources is often referred to as "the **tragedy of the commons.**"[3] The tragedy here is the tendency for commonly held resources to be overused and overexploited. Because the resource is held in common, individuals race to "get theirs" before others can grab it all.

One example of commonly held resources giving rise to problems involves oil fields. Oil reservoirs often span the surface property of many landowners. Because oil reservoirs are regarded as common property, each surface owner has an incentive to drill as many wells as possible and to pump out oil as rapidly as possible. Having too many wells pumping too quickly, however, reduces the oil field's water and gas pressure, thus reducing the total recoverable oil from the reservoir. Each owner's decision to drill a well therefore imposes an external cost on the other owners of land over the reservoir. At one point, this problem grew so severe that it resulted in passage of the 1935 Connally "Hot Oil" Act. This act restricted drilling, regulated the number and location of oil wells, and capped pumping rates.[4]

tragedy of the commons
Resources that are owned by the community at large (e.g., parks, ocean fish, and the atmosphere) and therefore tend to be overexploited because individuals have little incentive to use them in a sustainable fashion.

---

[3] Garrett Hardin, "The Tragedy of the Commons," *Science* 162, 1968, pp. 1243–1248.
[4] Daniel Yergin, *The Prize* (New York: Simon & Schuster), 1991.

ISSUE

Tragedy of the Commons: The Perfect Fish

Ocean fisheries are a good example of the problem of common property resources. Fish in the ocean were once in excess supply; there was no need to restrict the use of this resource. As global demand for fish rose, improved fishing technologies allowed fishing boats to increase their hauls. Because many of the world's fisheries are still unregulated, one species after another has been fished out in a clearly unsustainable situation.

The Patagonian toothfish, as it is known, lives up to 50 years and can weigh over 200 pounds. This big, ugly, gray-black fish lives in the cold deep waters of the Southern Ocean near Antarctica, and in the 1990s, it became the signature dish of top restaurants in the United States, Japan, and Europe. It became so popular that during the mid-1990s, the annual catch was estimated at 100,000 metric tons.

How did such an ugly fish with such an unappetizing name become so popular? In the late 1970s, Lee Lantz, a Los Angeles fish merchant, visited the docks in Valparaiso, Chile, and spotted a toothfish. He bought a sample and cooked it, but the oily flesh had little taste. Most fish have bladders that they inflate to adjust their buoyancy, reducing the energy it takes to move up and down in the water. Toothfish do not have bladders, but use oil (lighter than water) secreted to create buoyancy. Also, Patagonian toothfish are predators, waiting in ambush for prey. Thus, they do not need a lot of blood rushing through their system. As a result, toothfish meat is oily and white like cod. It is this oiliness—along with the fact that it absorbed any spice—that made the toothfish (now known as Chilean sea bass) a hit with restaurants.

As the reputation of the toothfish spread, so did the take in the ocean. Because this fish is found in the Southern Ocean where it is cold and where few venture, it was highly susceptible to poaching. A full hold of toothfish could fetch $1 million wholesale!

Soon it became clear to many that the species was being seriously overhar-

vested, and chefs began to notice that the filets were getting smaller. The tragedy of the commons was playing out again. Soon chefs from the best restaurants organized a boycott campaign called "Take a Pass on Chilean Sea Bass."

Today, limits are set on the catch, and Chilean sea bass is coming back from the brink of extinction. But as G. Bruce Knecht reported in his book *Hooked*, keeping pirates from poaching the toothfish is a dangerous job for the Australian Customs patrols. The toothfish's problem is that it is the perfect fish.

Source: G. Bruce Knecht, *Hooked: Pirates, Poaching, and the Perfect Fish* (Emmaus, PA: Rodale), 2006.

Road congestion is another illustration of the tragedy of the commons. Figure 4 shows a market for usage of a road that is fully used and is right at the tipping point before becoming congested. In Figure 4, demand for driving on this road is D_0, and

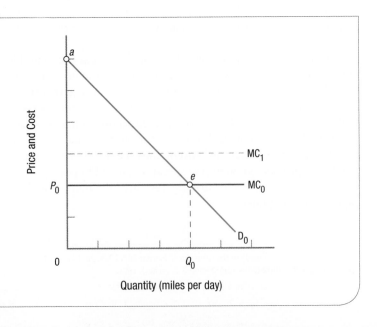

FIGURE 4

Road Congestion

Assume that this road is fully used and is right at the tipping point before becoming congested. Demand for driving on this road is D_0, and the marginal cost of using the road—gas, time, and auto expenses—is MC_0. Equilibrium is at point e, with Q_0 miles a day being driven. Consumer surplus is area P_0ae for the typical driver. When a new driver begins using the road, this increases the marginal cost of driving to MC_1 for everyone, because the tipping point has been passed, and the road is now congested. Consumer surplus shrinks because of overuse of this common good.

the marginal cost to use the road—gas, time, and auto expenses—is initially MC_0. Equilibrium is at point *e*, with Q_0 miles per day driven. Consumer surplus is area P_0ae for the typical driver.

Now assume that a new driver begins using the road. This increases the marginal costs of driving to MC_1 for everyone, because the tipping point has been passed, and the road is now congested. Consumer surplus shrinks because of overuse of the commons. Note that the new driver did not take these external costs into consideration; the driver assumed that the marginal cost would be equal to MC_0, not MC_1.

Possible solutions to common property resource problems can involve establishing private property rights, using government policy to restrict access to the resource, or informal organizations that restrict each user's benefits from the resource. Reduced congestion, for example, could be achieved by raising the tax on gasoline, subsidizing bus or rapid transit travel, or privatizing roads and allowing the owners to charge tolls.

Charles Smith/Corbis

A crowded public beach makes the experience less enjoyable.

The optimal provision of public goods, whether pure public goods or common property resources with significant public goods characteristics, is a significant challenge faced by society. Individuals tend to act in their self-interest when using public goods without contributing to their provision (free-riding) or overusing a resource without considering the impact of such use on others. An example of a public good that has risen to the forefront of policy debate is the environment, which we all share. We turn to environmental policy next.

CHECKPOINT

PUBLIC GOODS

- Pure public goods are nonrival in consumption, and once the good is provided, no one can be excluded from using it.

- The demand for public goods is found by vertically summing individual demand curves.

- Optimal provision of public goods is found where the marginal benefit of public goods (demand) is equal to the marginal cost of provision.

- Determining the optimal provision of public goods is easy in theory, but difficult in practice.

- Common property resources have the characteristics of nonexcludability but are rival. This typically leads to overuse and overexploitation.

QUESTIONS: On most college campuses, the use of the recreation center is open to all registered students without an additional fee. The cost of running the recreation center typically is paid for by an activity fee paid by all students, regardless of whether they use the facilities or not. In what ways does your campus recreation center resemble a public good? In what ways does it not?

Answers to the Checkpoint questions can be found at the end of this chapter.

Environmental Policy

We have seen that market failure can lead to excessive amounts of products that pollute or generate other negative externalities, or to overuse of commonly owned resources that result in environmental degradation. This section puts these market failures together by looking at environmental policy. First, we look at how government policies can fail to improve such situations if the incentives of politicians and policymakers are not aligned with the public interest. Then, we look at the actual policies used by government regulators to reduce pollution, ranging from direct intervention and control to the use of various market instruments. Policymakers also occasionally use publicity and moral suasion to encourage polluters to reduce emissions voluntarily.

Government Failure

Market failure is one reason why unregulated markets may produce inequitable or inefficient results. Government policies, however, do not always make things better. The terrible environmental record the Eastern Bloc countries accumulated during the Soviet era illustrates that, in environmental policy as elsewhere, governments—like markets—can fail.

Government failure occurs when (1) public policies do not bring about an optimal allocation of resources, and/or (2) the incentives of politicians and government bureaucrats are not in line with the public interest. As Nobel Prize–winner George Stigler has argued, economic regulation often benefits the group being regulated at the expense of the larger public. Government failures are often more acute in nondemocratic societies. Yet, even in the United States, public policy formation involves a struggle among interest groups, lobbyists, politicians, large corporate interests, and the public at large. The sausage calling itself "public policy" that results from this tug-of-war is often not pretty.

Government failure may result from the practical inability of policymakers to gather enough information to set good policies. Water pollution, for instance, is well understood, resulting in fairly obvious regulatory policies, but the same is not true for issues such as global climate change. Even if we all agree that the Earth is getting warmer and humans are partly to blame, controversy remains about the adequacy of public policy to address this problem. Although calls for government action—"there ought to be a law"—are often justified, we would do well to maintain a healthy skepticism about the ability of the public sector to solve our problems.

Intergenerational Questions

Should politicians consider the interests of voters whose great-grandparents have not yet been born? Environmental issues raise complex questions involving how resources are to be allocated across generations. Some resources, such as sunlight, are continual and renewable. Others, such as forests, fisheries, and the soil are renewable but exhaustible if overexploited. And some resources are nonrenewable, such as oil and coal. These resources are finite and cannot be renewed, but their available stock can be expanded through exploration or the use of new technologies that allow greater extraction or more efficient use.

When we develop environmental policies, we need to consider and evaluate different possible futures. Figure 5 is a reminder of the effects that discount rates have on the present

government failure The result when the incentives of politicians and government bureaucrats do not align with the public interest.

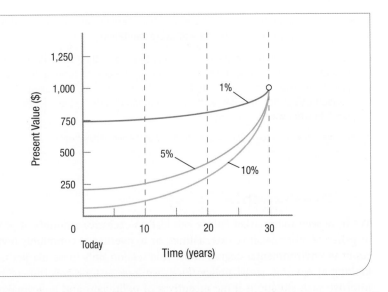

FIGURE 5

Present Value of $1,000 to Be Paid in 30 Years Discounted at 1%, 5%, and 10%

This figure is a reminder of the effects discount rates have on the present value of a fixed payment that will come due at a future date. A higher discount rate means that the value today of a future payment will be lower. The higher the discount rate we choose, the lower the value we place on the environmental damage to be suffered by future generations. The lower our discount rate, the more we are willing to protect the health of the future environment.

value of a fixed payment that will come due at some date in the future. For environmental policies, the discount rate we choose is crucially important.

A higher discount rate means that the value today of a future payment will be less. At a 10% discount, a payment of $1,000 in 30 years is worth only $42 today, whereas discounting the same $1,000 at 1% yields a present value of $748. The higher the discount rate we choose, the lower the value we place on the environmental damage to be suffered by future generations. The lower our discount rate, conversely, the more we are willing to protect the health of the future environment. As always, crafting good public policies requires striking a balance between the two.

Socially Efficient Levels of Pollution

We have already seen that some pollution is acceptable to society. To require that no one pollute, period, would bring most economic activity as we know it to a halt. Yet, pollution damages our environment. The harmful effects of pollution range from direct threats to our health coming from air and water pollution to reductions in species from deforestation.

The damages that come from pollution are a cost we incur for living: To be alive is to generate some pollution. Our focus is on marginal damage, which resembles the marginal cost curves we have studied earlier. The marginal damage (MD) curve in Figure 6 shows the change in damages that comes from a given change in emission levels. Notice that as emissions levels rise, the added damages rise.

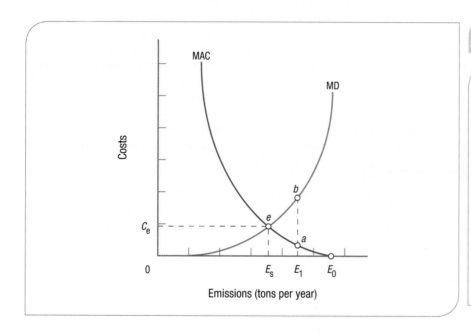

FIGURE 6

Marginal Damages and Marginal Abatement Costs

The marginal damage curve (MD) shows the *change* in damages that come from a given *change* in emission levels. The horizontal axis measures pollution. Note that E_0 is the maximum pollution that can occur without environmental cleanup. The vertical axis measures the environmental costs of this pollution. Marginal abatement costs curve (MAC) begins at zero at E_0, then rises as emission levels are reduced (moving leftward from E_0). Socially optimal pollution is E_s, at a cost to society of C_e (point e).

The horizontal axis of Figure 6 measures the tons of pollution emitted into the environment (tons per year). Note that E_0 represents the maximum pollution (no environmental cleanup at all). The vertical axis measures the environmental costs in dollars. These costs represent a dollar value for various environmental losses, including the physical costs of pollution (asthma attacks and other lung diseases), the aesthetic losses (visual impact of clear-cutting), and the losses associated with species reduction.

Abatement costs are the costs associated with reducing emissions. A utility plant dumping effluent into a river can treat the effluent before discharge, but this costs money. In Figure 6, marginal abatement costs (MAC) begin at zero at E_0, then rise as emission levels are reduced (moving leftward from E_0). The MAC curve in Figure 6 is a generalized abatement cost function, but in practice, the costs vary for different sources of pollution and the technologies available for reducing them. Chemical plants face different problems than utilities that release hot water into rivers. Cooling the water before release clearly requires a different technology—and is much easier—than eliminating toxic chemicals from effluent flow.

The socially optimal level of pollution in Figure 6 is E_S, at a cost to society of C_e (point e). To see why this is so, assume that we are at pollution level E_1. The cost to reduce another unit of emissions is equal to point a (measuring on the vertical axis), while the damage that would result from this pollution is shown at point b. Since $b > a$, society is better off if emissions are reduced. Once we begin reducing emissions below E_S, however, abatement costs overtake marginal damages, or the costs of cleanup begin to outweigh the benefits.

The total damage from pollution in Figure 6 is represented by the area beneath the marginal damages curve and to the left of E_S. Total abatement costs, meanwhile, are equal to the area beneath the marginal abatement costs curve and to the right of E_S. Combined, these two costs represent the total social costs from emissions. We turn now to consider how environmental policy can ensure that emissions approach this optimal level.

Overview of Environmental Policies

Over the years, many types of environmental policies have been developed in response to different problems, covering the spectrum from centralized control to decentralized economic incentives. To be effective, all environmental policies must be efficient, fair, and enforceable, and they must provide incentives for improvement in the environment.

As a general rule, the more centralized an environmental policy, the more likely it represents a **command and control** philosophy. This means that a centralized agency sets the rules for emissions, including levels of effluents allowed, usable technologies, and enforcement procedures. Command and control policies usually set standards of conduct that are enforced by the legal and regulatory system. Abatement costs at this point become compliance costs of meeting the standards. Standards are popular because they are simple, they treat all firms in an industry the same way, and they prevent competing firms from polluting.

At the other end of the spectrum are **market-based policies,** which use charges, taxes, subsidies, deposit-refund systems, or tradable emission permits to achieve the same ends. Examples of this approach include water effluent charges, user charges for water and wastewater management, glass and plastic bottle refund systems, and tradable permits for ozone reduction. We begin with a brief look at command and control policies, contrasting them with abatement taxes, then look at the case for tradable emission permits.

Command and Control Policies

Policymakers determine the pollution control or abatement that is best, then introduce the most efficient policies to achieve those ends. Figure 7 shows the supply and demand for pollution abatement. Demand curve $D_A = MB_A$ represents society's demand for abatement;

command and control policies
Environmental policies that set standards and issue regulations, which are then enforced by the legal and regulatory system.

market-based policies
Environmental policies that use charges, taxes, subsidies, deposit-refund systems, or tradable emission permits to achieve environmental goals.

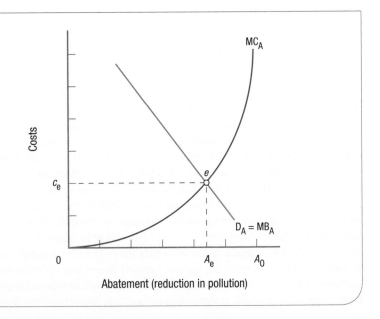

FIGURE 7

Marginal Cost of Abatement and Abatement Demand

Demand curve D_A represents society's demand for abatement. The marginal benefit from abatement (MB_A) declines as the environment becomes cleaner, because the gains from an ever cleaner environment become smaller and smaller (diminishing returns). The marginal costs of abatement are the costs of reducing pollution. These costs rise with abatement efforts and become high as zero pollution A_0 is approached (again, because of the law of diminishing returns, or increasing costs). Optimal abatement is A_e, costing c_e. This means optimal pollution, $A_0 - A_e$, is greater than zero.

it is a reflection of the marginal damage curve we looked at earlier. Note that the demand curve for abatement is negatively sloped because the *marginal benefit* from abatement declines as the environment becomes cleaner. The gains from an ever cleaner environment eventually become smaller and smaller because of the law of diminishing returns.

The marginal costs of abatement are the costs of cleaning up pollution. These costs rise with abatement efforts and become high as zero pollution, A_0, is approached. Optimal abatement comes at A_e, costing c_e. This means that optimal pollution, $A_0 - A_e$, is greater than zero. Command and control policies could set A_e as the abatement requirement and then set the right standards to meet this requirement. Aiming for abatement higher than A_e would be inefficient, because marginal costs would exceed marginal benefits.

Setting abatement requirements (or standards) equal to A_e in Figure 7 is a classic example of command and control policies. Again, command and control policies that set rigid standards for polluters have long been a favorite of policymakers. Yet, this approach can lead to inefficiencies, because different industries may emit the same (or equivalently dangerous) substances but face different technical problems and costs in reducing their pollution. To minimize the cost of reducing pollution, each source of pollution needs to be reduced to the point at which the marginal cost of abatement is equal for all sources. This can be achieved through market-based policies.

Market-Based Policies

Economists argue that market-oriented, or indirect, approaches to environmental policy are more efficient than command and control policies. Two of the most popular and effective of these indirect approaches are the use of emissions taxes and marketable or tradable permits.

Emissions Taxes An alternative to command and control policies is to enact an emissions tax on every unit of pollution produced to achieve the socially efficient outcome. Taxes of this sort are known as **Pigouvian taxes** (named after Arthur Pigou who developed the idea in 1920). Unlike command and control policies, polluting firms are not limited to a fixed amount of pollution. Instead, by forcing firms to pay for every unit of pollution created, firms would invest in pollution reduction measures up to the point at which the cost of abatement measures is no longer less than the tax. Such policies take into account the fact that some firms are able to reduce pollution at less cost than others. Therefore, it creates efficiencies by allowing firms with higher costs of pollution abatement to pollute more by paying more taxes, while encouraging firms with lower costs of pollution abatement to utilize such measures to reduce their tax burden.

Pigouvian tax A tax that is placed on an activity generating negative externalities in order to achieve a socially efficient outcome.

Returning to Figure 7, achieving the optimal level of pollution abatement, A_e, could be achieved by charging a tax equal to c_e per unit of pollution. Firms would adopt pollution controls up to A_e, because the costs to reduce pollution to this point are less than the tax. Firms would emit only $A_0 - A_e$ pollution. As a result, the same level of abatement is achieved using taxes as with using command and control policies; however, allowing the market to achieve this outcome through taxes allows for a more efficient outcome for the firms involved.

Marketable or Tradable Permits Another way that markets are used to limit pollution is through the use of marketable or tradable permits. Economists first proposed marketable or tradable permits when environmental laws were first being debated and enacted in the 1960s and 1970s. Environmental regulators essentially ignored this suggestion until the 1990s.

Today, tradable permits are used to reduce water effluents in the Fox River in Wisconsin, Tar-Pamlico River in North Carolina, and Dillon Reservoir in Colorado. One of the most successful uses of marketable permits for air pollution, described in the Issue in this section, has reduced the sulfur dioxide (SO_2) emissions in the Midwest that create acid rain in the East. Originally, the cost of this cleanup was expected to be significant, but technical advances steadily reduced abatement costs, causing the price of the permits to decline sharply.

Marketable permits require that a regulatory body set a maximum allowable quantity of effluents allowed, typically called the "cap," and issue permits granting the "right" to pollute a certain amount. These permits can be bought and sold, thus creating the property rights that permit transactions of the sort Coase advocated. Sales are normally between two polluters, with one polluter buying a permit from a more efficient operator. Polluters do not have to be the only purchasers: Victims or environmental groups could conceivably purchase pollution rights and hold them off the market, thereby reducing pollution below the established cap.

Figure 8 illustrates how such a market works. We assume that there are two firms in the market, each producing 10 tons of pollution, and that the government wishes to limit pollution to a total of 10 tons. Without restrictions, firms do zero abatement and total pollution is 20 tons. Setting a goal of 10 tons amounts to cutting pollution in half.

FIGURE 8

Tradable Permits

This figure illustrates how a market for tradable pollution permits works. Assume there are only two firms (X and Y) in the market and the government wishes to limit total pollution to 10 tons. Without restrictions, both firms do zero abatement and pollution is 20 tons. Setting a goal of 10 tons therefore amounts to cutting pollution in half. Assume that the government gives the permits to firm X. Demand curve D_Y represents firm Y's demand for these permits. Given a competitive market for permits, equilibrium will be at point e with a permit price equal to $300. Firm Y buys 7 permits and pollutes that amount, and firm X emits 3 tons of pollution.

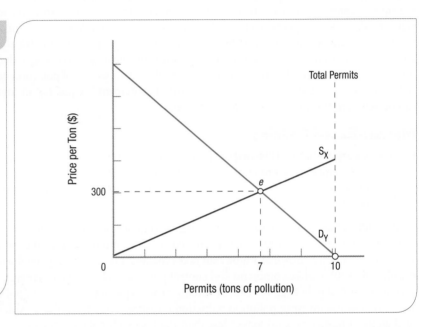

Assume, for simplicity, that the government at first gives the permits to firm X. (Remember that the Coase theorem suggests efficiency is not affected by who owns the rights to pollute.) Demand curve D_Y represents firm Y's demand for these permits. Assume that the market for permits is competitive, thus equilibrium will be at point e with a permit price equal to $300. Firm Y buys 7 permits and pollutes that amount, and firm X pollutes 3 tons.

Firm X pollutes less and sells 7 permits to firm Y because it can reduce more of its pollution before its marginal abatement costs reach $300. In this case, firm Y faces high clean-up costs that reach $300 a ton at 3 tons. Thus, it buys 7 tons of pollution rights from firm X. Firm X in this example ends up with the revenue from permit sales, while firm Y's income declines by the same amount ($2,100). Auctioning off the permits produces the same result, but the government receives the revenue.

Keep in mind that regulators could have set a $300 per ton tax on effluents and achieved the same result. One advantage of permits over taxes is that no knowledge of marginal abatement costs is needed to ensure that the tax rate is optimal. The market price of permits will adjust to variances in abatement costs. All the regulator must determine is how much to reduce pollution levels. If reducing pollution by a certain amount, regardless of the cost, is the goal, permits will achieve this goal.

Other Market-Based Policies We have looked at two of the most frequently used market-based policies, taxes and marketable permits. Emission taxes and charges have been used for water effluents, waste management, pesticide packaging, batteries, tires, and other products and processes. User charges are the most common way to finance wastewater treatment facilities.

ISSUE

Cap-and-Trade: The Day Liberal Environmentalists and Free-Market Conservatives Agreed

Environmental policies in recent decades have epitomized the battle between liberal environmentalists and free-market conservatives, with the former arguing for more limits on pollution while the latter want more market freedom. How then, could the two sides come to an agreement that would satisfy both of their primary objectives?

In the late 1980s, the problem of acid rain reached a boiling point, with heavy pollution from sulfur dioxide emissions causing health issues, polluted lakes and rivers, and reduced visibility. Further, it heightened tensions with Canada, which suffered negative externalities from the pollution from American power plants. With the environmental damage reaching front page news and a fierce political battle on how to fix it, it looked like a lost cause.

Then came a very unlikely alliance between Dan Dukek of the Environmental Defense Fund and Boyden Gray, a multimillionaire conservative who was appointed President Bush's White House counsel in 1988. Gray, a strong proponent of free-market principles, had long supported a method of allowing individuals and firms to buy and sell permits to pollute. The acid rain crisis allowed Dudek and Gray to propose an emissions permit trading program that placed significant caps on sulfur dioxide (placating environmentalists) while eliminating regulations and allowing the marketplace to determine permit prices (placating free-market proponents).

The program became law with the *Clean Air Act of 1990*. When the law, which became known as "cap-and-trade," took effect in 1995, emissions fell and led to significant external cost savings in what has been considered a resounding success in solving a major environmental program using a market-based approach as opposed to a command-and-control approach.

Today, much discussion centers on the proposed use of cap-and-trade to reduce carbon dioxide emissions. Such programs are law in the European Union and elsewhere, but proposals to pass cap-

and-trade legislation in the United States since 2008 have been held up, ironically, by the same market-based proponents who created the strategy that worked in the past. Opponents of cap-and-trade today argue that cap-and-trade still imposes harsh limits on the broader market, which they support. Yet, without cap-and-trade, resolutions to reduce global warming become less likely. It may take another unlikely alliance before the problem of global warming is solved.

Source: Richard Conniff, "The Political History of Cap and Trade," *Smithsonian*, August 2009.

Federal subsidies, the flip side of taxes or charges, are used when local communities do not have the resources for pollution control. Marketable permits have been most successful in programs to reduce air pollution, as well as those targeting acid rain and ozone reduction. Deposit-refund systems have been used mainly for recyclable products such as cans, bottles, tires, and batteries.

Over the years, most environmental policies have been of the command and control variety. The 1970 Clean Air Act focused on specific forms of air pollution—particulates, carbon monoxide, and so forth—and established air quality standards. Today, economic or market-based approaches to environmental policy are considered more efficient than command and control policies. Most environmental agencies, however, in this country and abroad, have not used these tools until recently.

One reason for this is probably that many people in the regulatory and environmental communities resist viewing environmental resources as commodities to be subjected to market forces of supply and demand. It is market failures, after all, that led to environmental decay in the first place. Why would we want to put the environment on the market? Many pollutants, moreover, are frequently mixed together and their individual impacts are difficult to determine. Consequently, setting the right tax rate or issuing the right number of allowable permits is difficult. Finally, some policymakers balk at giving corporations the right to pollute, even a limited amount.

CHECKPOINT

ENVIRONMENTAL POLICY

■ Government failure can occur when politicians and government do not have the right incentives to bring about an optimal allocation of resources.

■ The discount rate chosen for environmental policies determines the intergenerational impact of policy.

■ The socially optimal level of pollution occurs where the marginal damage is equal to the marginal abatement costs.

■ Policymakers determine the optimal pollution levels and then often use command and control policies to set the most efficient regulations or levels of abatement.

■ Tradable permits use market forces to bring pollution within limits set by regulators.

QUESTIONS: If a "cap-and-trade" program for carbon dioxide emissions is implemented in the United States, with the overall limit slowly reduced each year, what would happen to the price of permits if all production activity stays the same and the cost of pollution abatement remains unchanged? What would need to happen in order for the price of permits to fall over time?

Answers to the Checkpoint questions can be found at the end of this chapter.

Putting It All Together: An Analysis of Climate Change

Throughout this chapter, we saw how the market failures of externalities, public goods, and common property resources create markets that make it difficult to achieve a socially efficient outcome without some sort of intervention. As a result, governments often are tasked with establishing policies that attempt to incentivize individuals and firms to take actions that lead to a more efficient outcome. But how are such policies established? And how are the effects measured?

Many questions arise that require adequate measurement of how individuals value various objectives. For example, how do we account for the value of biodiversity? How much would we pay to keep certain species from going extinct? Or how much benefit must we obtain to endure living in a polluted city? The answers to these and other questions require the use of a consistent technique to ensure policies are well established to promote social efficiency.

A common approach taken to develop and debate policies is to use some form of **cost-benefit analysis.** Cost-benefit analysis provides a rational model for policy decisions, forces a focus on alternatives (opportunity costs), draws conclusions about the optimal *scale* of projects, makes the intergenerational aspects explicit through discounting, and takes into account the explicit preferences of individuals. In short, it takes all of the future benefits and costs of a proposed policy and discounts them to the present to determine whether it is worth implementing.

One of the major difficulties with cost-benefit analysis for big public projects and environmental programs is measuring nonmarket or intangible aspects of projects. To resolve these issues, economists use various methods to approximate the values of intangible items, such as how much people pay to avert harm, or even direct surveys among a small but representative portion of the population to determine how individuals value certain aspects of the environment.

Cost-benefit analysis, then, is a rational approach to valuing some things that are hard to put a price on. The issue of climate change is one topic that involves many such variables. Let's analyze in greater detail the issue of global warming, which often is characterized as the mother of all market failures.

cost-benefit analysis A methodology for decision making that looks at the discounted value of the costs and benefits of a given project.

Understanding Climate Change

There is growing scientific consensus that without a significant reduction in emissions, global warming from the buildup of greenhouse gases is likely to lead to irreversible damage to the climate, ecosystems, and coastlines.

A sense of urgency surrounds climate change because the state of climate science has advanced to the point where scientists can now put probability estimates on certain impacts of warming, some of which are catastrophic. Current levels of greenhouse gases are roughly 403 parts per million (ppm).[5] This compares to 280 ppm before the Industrial Revolution. Scientists predict that if greenhouse gases exceed 450 ppm, average global temperatures will have risen 2 degrees Celsius since the Industrial Revolution, a change that would lead to dramatic consequences. If the current trend continues, the 450 ppm threshold will be exceeded in less than 25 years.

What will happen as greenhouse gases increase and lead to global warming? Table 3 estimates these effects. The top part of the table shows a range of greenhouse gases from

Greenhouse Gases, Likely Temperature Changes, and Estimated Impacts	TABLE 3

	Greenhouse Gases (ppm)				
	400	**450**	**550**	**700**	**800**
	Eventual Temperature Change (relative to preindustrial)				
	1°C	**2°C**	**3°C**	**4°C**	**5°C**
Food	Rising crop yields in high-latitude developed countries	Rising number of people at risk from hunger	Falling crop yields in developing regions	Major decline in crop yields in all regions	?
Water	Small mountain glaciers disappear	Over a 30% drop in runoff in South Africa and the Mediterranean	Large numbers of people suffer water shortages	Billions of people affected by water shortages	Sea level rise threatens major cities, including New York, Hong Kong, and London
Ecosystems	Ocean coral reef systems damaged	Many ecosystems unable to maintain their current form	Part of Amazon rain forest begins to collapse	20% to 50% species extinction possible	?
Extreme Weather Events	Rising levels of storms, fires, droughts, floods, and heat waves →				
		Rising hurricane intensity →			
Major Irreversible Impacts	Risk of weakening the natural carbon absorption system →				
		Rising risk of large-scale shifts in climate system →			

Source: Nicholas Stern, *The Economics of Climate Change* (Cambridge: Cambridge University Press), 2007.

---

[5] European Environmental Agency, Atmospheric Greenhouse Gas Concentrations (CSI 013), January 8, 2013.

400 ppm to 800 ppm, with predicted effects on temperature below it. The bottom part estimates the impacts likely to arise with each increase in temperature. The estimated effects of a difference of just 1 or 2 degrees raise serious concerns.

Unique Timing Aspects

The global environment is essentially a common resource with many public goods aspects, and climate change is a huge global negative externality. But what makes analysis and decision making so difficult is the long time horizon that must be considered. Most cost-benefit studies do not look out 50 to 100 years and beyond. This extended time horizon adds a host of difficulties and uncertainties.

Air or water pollution is something that we can see on the horizon, can be measured, is typically localized, and can be altered in a short period of time by some of the approaches discussed earlier. Global warming, in contrast, is not something we can generally see; it is cumulative (this year's CO_2 adds to that from the past to raise concentrations in the future); and once it reaches a certain level, it may lead to extreme consequences that cannot be reversed.

Cleaning up pollution problems typically involves finding that level of abatement at which the marginal costs of abatement equal the marginal benefits from abatement and either taxing, assigning (or auctioning) marketable permits, or using command and control policies to require the optimal level of abatement. However, reducing global warming gases is not a short-term objective, but a cumulative process across many years. Yet, our short-run decisions will have immense impacts in the long run. Small changes in emissions today may have little effect on the current generation, but will have sizable effects many decades out. This aspect of the problem seriously complicates any policymaking and economic analysis.

Public Good Aspects

To compound the problem further, global climate change is a public good. Greenhouse gas emissions "are the purest example of a negative public good; nobody can have less of them because someone else has more; and nobody can be excluded from their malign consequences or the efforts of others to ameliorate them."[6]

One of the solutions is technical innovation that reduces our output of CO_2. But knowledge and technology have large public good aspects, therefore private firms will find it difficult to collect the full returns on their innovation investments that reduce greenhouse gases. Other firms and countries will to some extent be free riders on private innovation, thus society (and the world) may get less than the socially optimal level of innovation. This will mean that a substantial amount of climate change research and development will have to be financed by governments.

Equity Aspects

Why should I do anything for posterity? What has posterity ever done for me?

GROUCHO MARX

Much of what we do today to reduce global warming will have little immediate impact on our lives. The impacts will show up in the latter half of the century. Any action taken today principally benefits our great-grandchildren. Groucho Marx's joke not withstanding, this fact makes it more difficult to get a political consensus to act.

Also, rich countries will have to make the biggest sacrifices, yet they will not get the biggest benefits from efforts to reduce the impacts of global warming. Suppose that the United States reduces its dependence on carbon. What about China and India? They may decide that growth is worth more than a cleaner environment. At that point, the United States would have to be willing to pay China and India large sums to get them

---

[6] Martin Wolf, "Curbs on Emissions Will Take a Change of Political Climate," *Financial Times,* November 8, 2006, p. 15.

to decarbonize their economies. How well will that sell to American voters? Probably not well, but it may be what is ultimately necessary.

People in countries both rich and poor living along bodies of water will face floods if current climate forecasts come to pass. However, developing countries which are home to some of the world's poorest people will face the greatest challenge adapting to flooding given their severely limited resources. In addition, developing nations rely heavily on agriculture, one industry that will be hardest hit by the warming of the Earth.

Finding a Solution

Climate change is global, therefore it will take concerted international effort and cooperation to create price signals and markets for carbon, and to develop and promote new technologies, especially in developing countries.

Many economists argue that using fewer fossil fuels today will result in lower spending on environmental protection in the future, like a form of insurance to reduce future harm on the environment. This will require a transition to a low-carbon economy that will require actions such as establishing a worldwide price for carbon that includes its external costs. This can be done using carbon taxes or tradable permits. Initiatives such as the European Union Emissions Trade System (EU ETS), launched in 2005, have taken first steps toward capping emissions levels using tradable permits.

Robert Socolow of Princeton University has suggested that much of the technology

NOBEL PRIZE
ELINOR OSTROM (1933-2012)

When economists talk about common property resources, they typically discuss the tragedy of the commons and suggest a solution that involves privatization or central government takeover and management of the resource. Elinor Ostrom was awarded the 2009 Nobel Prize in Economic Sciences for challenging this conventional wisdom by showing how *user-managed* resources, where people cooperate to solve a resource issue, can be effective.

Born in 1933 during the depths of the Great Depression and completing her doctorate in political science in 1965, her dissertation looked at a case in which saltwater was seeping into western Los Angeles's water basin. A group of individuals formed a water association to solve the problem by creating rules and injected water along the coast. Their efforts saved the basin. This experience led her to look at other common resource problems from a new perspective.

She used field studies and thousands of case studies by other social scientists along with game theory to determine how these informal organizations evolved and what conditions make them successful.

Her work has determined the requirements for sustainable user-managed common resource property, including (a) rules must clearly define entitlement to the resource, (b) adequate conflict resolution measures must exist, (c) an individual's duty to maintain the resource must be in proportion to his or her benefits, (d) monitoring and sanctioning must be by users or accountable to users, (e) sanctions should be graduated—mild for a first violation and stricter as violations are repeated, (f) governance and decision processes must be democratic, and (g) self-organization is recognized by outside authorities. When these institutional conditions are met, user management of common pool resources typically is successful.

Professor Ostrom's insights and research have opened up an alternative to prevent the tragedy of the commons. Her work will be particularly important as nations begin working together to reduce the potential harm from global climate change, maybe our biggest common resource problem to date.

needed to reduce our carbon footprint is available today.[7] He and several colleagues suggest that carbon emissions can remain constant over the next 50 years if the following techniques are implemented:

- Use more efficient vehicles and reduce vehicle use in general.
- Build more efficient buildings.
- Capture CO_2 at power plants.
- Use nuclear power.
- Exchange biomass fuels for fossil fuels.
- Use wind and solar power.
- Reduce deforestation.

[7] Robert Socolow et al., "Solving the Climate Problem: Technologies Available to Curb CO_2 Emissions," *Environment,* December 2004, pp. 8–19.

Clearly, undertaking some policies to reduce our carbon footprint as a nation represents an insurance policy on the future. As new climate change information becomes available, policies can be adjusted to reduce the potential costs in the future.

To that end, carbon dioxide emissions are frequently placed on political agendas. However, a slow economic recovery makes it harder to focus people's attention on this issue. Furthermore, questions arise about the initial grant of permits in any cap-and-trade program. Do large established companies with huge capital resources get permits? What about smaller, possibly more innovative alternative energy companies? Do permits get auctioned off, and does this then favor the richer, more established companies? Political issues combine with economic issues to make this a thorny problem for the future.

As with climate change, each of the examples described in this chapter dealt with market failure in which externalities, public goods, or shared resources lead the market away from the socially desirable output. Resolving a market failure generally requires some policy tool, such as the assignment of property rights, regulation, or the creation of market incentives to achieve the ideal outcome. However, determining which policy tool to use often leads to intense debate, making issues of market failure a challenge that societies and their policymakers will continue to face.

 CHECKPOINT

PUTTING IT ALL TOGETHER: AN ANALYSIS OF CLIMATE CHANGE

- Global climate change is a huge negative externality with an extremely long time horizon.
- The public goods aspects of climate change make it a truly global problem.
- Balancing the current generation's costs and benefits against the potential harm to future generations raises difficult economic issues.
- Actions taken today to reduce a potential future calamity are a form of insurance.

QUESTION: One of the most difficult aspects of climate change policy is determining how much individuals are willing to sacrifice today for a better environment in the future. What are some factors that may influence whether a person holds a high or low discount rate on the future with regard to environmental policy?

Answers to the Checkpoint question can be found at the end of this chapter.

chapter summary

Section 1: **Externalities**

Externalities, or spillovers, arise when a transaction benefits or harms parties not involved in the transaction.

Externalities lead to **market failure** when external benefits or external costs push markets away from the socially optimal output.

Taking care of the front lawn creates an external benefit to the neighbors.

Factories spewing dirty smoke create an external cost to the area residents.

The **Coase theorem** suggests that when transactions costs are near zero, bargaining between parties will lead to an efficient allocation of resources no matter how property rights are allocated.

Example: If students have the right to party, the neighbors can pay the students to stay quiet. If neighbors have the right to a quiet environment, students can pay the neighbors for the right to party. Either way, those with the property rights can exercise their rights or accept payment to forgo the rights.

Section 2: **Public Goods**

Public goods exhibit two characteristics:

Nonrivalry: One person's consumption of a good does not reduce the availability of that good to others.

Nonexcludability: Once a good has been provided, no consumers can be excluded from consuming the product.

Public goods lead to market failure when individuals lack the incentive to pay for them, leading to such goods being underprovided.

Common property resources are owned by the community, and therefore individuals tend to overuse and overexploit them.

Section 3: Environmental Policy

Environmental policies depend on the discount rate chosen for how society values events in the future. A high discount rate places a significant burden on future generations, while a low discount rate places a greater burden on the current generation.

The optimal pollution level in a society is rarely zero. Instead, some pollution is acceptable if the cost of abatement exceeds its benefit. Therefore, optimal pollution levels are found where marginal abatement costs (MAC) equal the marginal damage caused by pollution. As long as the cleanup costs exceed damage, it would be optimal to allow pollution until MAC equals MD at E_s.

A surprising source of pollution is the methane and ammonia gases produced by cows through belching and flatulence, contributing approximately 14% of the world's greenhouse gases.

Environmental policy aimed at addressing market failure takes on several forms:

- Command and control: fixed standards for polluters that are enforced through inspections and legal action (does not always lead to optimal pollution levels).

- Effluent taxes: a fee that is paid to the government per unit of pollution emitted (can lead to optimal pollution levels if the fee is set appropriately).

- Pollution permits: also known as cap-and-trade, allows firms to buy, sell, and trade permits to pollute (can lead to optimal pollution levels).

Section 4: Putting It All Together: An Analysis of Climate Change

Global climate change is a huge global negative externality accompanied by public goods aspects and extremely long time horizons, making the inherent market failure difficult to address.

Equity issues arise when some countries (often developed) pay significantly more to reduce global climate change than developing countries.

Solutions to global pollution require cooperation between nations and global carbon pricing that is credible and covers the full costs of carbon-based products.

Crowded streets filled with polluting vehicles are a common scene in India, contributing to global pollution as the nation develops.

KEY CONCEPTS

externalities, p. 338
Coase theorem, p. 340
market failure, p. 343
public goods, p. 343
nonrivalry, p. 343

nonexcludability, p. 343
free rider, p. 343
tragedy of the commons, p. 345
government failure, p. 348
command and control policies, p. 350

market-based policies, p. 350
Pigouvian tax, p. 351
cost-benefit analysis, p. 354

QUESTIONS AND PROBLEMS

Check Your Understanding

1. When trying to estimate the external benefits of a college education, what kinds of specific benefits would you include?

2. How might the government use market forces to encourage recycling?

3. What makes public goods so different from private goods?

4. Why wouldn't a rural highway in Montana, Freeway 405 in Los Angeles, and the New Jersey Turnpike (toll) all be classified as public goods? Which would be most like a public good and which would be least?

5. Assume that you are convinced that if something isn't done now, global warming is going to create extensive problems and damage at the end of this century. If you were preparing a cost-benefit analysis of the impacts and had a 100-year horizon for your projections, would you use a 3% or an 8% discount rate?

6. What is the tragedy of the commons? How can it be solved?

Applying the Concepts

7. "Internalizing" the cost of negative externalities means that we try to set policies that require each product to include the full costs of its negative spillovers in its price. How do such policies affect product price and industry output and employment? Are these kinds of policies easy to implement in practice? How has globalization of production affected our ability to control pollution?

8. As a way to increase the funds for wildlife conservation, why don't we just auction off (say, on eBay) the right to name a new species when it is discovered? Why not do the same for existing species?

9. We can estimate the emissions caused in one year from automobile use. What can you do to offset these emissions? Buy a *green tag.* These voluntary purchases are akin to carbon offsets traded in Europe. For a small fee, individuals can purchase carbon offsets for their cars or SUVs, or companies can use them as a way to purchase wind power for their stores. Organizations selling the green tag (both for-profit and not-for-profit) provide a decal; most of the fee collected is provided to alternative energy producers as a subsidy, which then can lower their prices to the market to encourage use. Is this a public good being sold privately? Why would individuals or businesses buy a tag when they can free-ride?

10. Garbage dumps are a particular source of a potent global-warming gas, the methane that bubbles up as the garbage decomposes. Does it make sense for companies in the European Union to help Brazilian garbage dumps reduce their releases of methane as a way of meeting their Kyoto obligations?

11. The Presidio, previously a military base in San Francisco, is now a national park. It sits in the middle of San Francisco on some of the most valuable real estate in the United States. Congress, when it created the park, required that it rehabilitate the aging buildings and be self-sufficient within a decade or so, or the land would be sold off

to developers. The park appears to be well on its way to self-sufficiency by leasing the land to private firms—Lucas Films has built a large digital animation studio, and other firms have undertaken similar projects. These projects all must maintain the general character of the park and generate rent that will cover the park's expenses in the future. Would this privatization approach work with most of America's other national parks? Why or why not?

12. Nobel Prize–winner Simon Kuznets once suggested that poor nations tend to pollute more as they grow—until they reach a certain level of income per capita—after which they pollute less. Does this observation by Kuznets seem reasonable? Why or why not?

In the News

13. In 2009, the Cash for Clunkers program was initiated to encourage consumers to trade in their old inefficient cars for a credit to buy new fuel-efficient cars. What are some of the external benefits from such a policy?

14. One's home (whether a house or an apartment) is typically thought of as one's castle. But not so in the condominiums with homeowners associations (HOAs) in Jefferson County, Colorado. In an older four-unit condo, the HOA voted 3–1 to adopt a no-smoking rule (inside the individual condos) after smokers bought one of the units and smoke permeated the walls of the structure. In 2006, a district judge ruled that the HOA's adoption of no-smoking rules was a reasonable restriction on ownership rights, stating that the rules were designed to prevent the odor of cigarettes from penetrating the walls of neighboring condos.

Considering that there are a small number of people involved (three nonsmoking units, one smoking), you would think that transaction costs would be minimal. Why do you think the homeowners could not work out an agreement (à la Coase) and ended up in court? According to the Coase theorem, would it have made any difference if the judge had ruled against the HOA?

Solving Problems

15. Suppose the market demand and supply for flu shots is shown in the figure below. Not taking into account the external benefits from flu shots, what is the equilibrium price and quantity of flu shots? Now suppose that every flu shot generates $10 in external benefits (from others being less likely to get sick). Show how this positive externality affects the graph (draw in a new curve). Taking into account external benefits, what would be the new equilibrium price and quantity of flu shots?

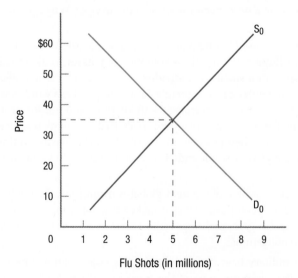

16. Suppose that the individual demand schedules for Al and Jane, the only two residents on a quiet city street, are shown in the table for speed bumps aimed at slowing cars passing through. In a single diagram, plot Al and Jane's individual demand curve, and then plot the total demand curve for each unit of the public good.

Al		Jane	
Quantity	Marginal benefit	Quantity	Marginal benefit
1	$50	1	$100
2	$25	2	$50
3	$10	3	$25
4	$5	4	$10

USING THE NUMBERS

17. According to By the Numbers, between which two years did total sales of hybrid cars increase the most? What factors might have led to this rise in hybrid sales?

18. According to By the Numbers, which two waste products are most recovered (recycled) by percentage, and which two waste products are least recovered?

ANSWERS TO QUESTIONS IN CHECKPOINTS

Checkpoint: Externalities

CFL bulbs create external benefits by reducing the overall use of energy, thus keeping energy prices lower for all consumers. The longer life of CFL bulbs also reduces waste and pollution. CFL bulbs can also create external costs. For example, careless disposal of CFL bulbs may allow mercury, a harmful toxin, to leak into landfills and into the environment, potentially harming all persons.

Checkpoint: Public Goods

If the recreation center on campus allows all students to use it without an additional fee, it resembles some of the characteristics of a public good. Although it can exclude nonstudents from the facility, it is open to all students. Therefore, it is partially nonexcludable. However, if too many students use it, it can become crowded, resembling more of a common property resource.

Checkpoint: Environmental Policy

If the "cap" on total carbon dioxide emissions is reduced each year while economic activity stays the same, permit prices would rise to encourage firms to produce less to meet the cap. In order for permit prices to fall, the costs of pollution abatement must fall due to technological advances, or new production methods (using clean energy) must be introduced to emit lesser carbon dioxide to begin with.

Checkpoint: Putting It All Together: An Analysis of Climate Change

Many answers are valid. But any factor that causes one to place greater emphasis on the future would result in a lower discount rate. Such factors might include having children or grandchildren, a greater desire to preserve Earth's natural beauty, having higher income or a business that relies on the availability of natural resources, or having empathy for future residents. Factors that might result in a high discount rate may include poverty, where emphasis is on improving one's current economic well-being in the future, or other difficult situations (wars and civil strife) that focus more attention on the present than on the future.

Network
Goods

14

Mom is calling. Is it this phone I pick up, or this one, or that one?

After studying this chapter you should be able to:

- Describe the similarities and differences among the three main types of networks.

- Explain what a network good is and how consuming a network good generates an external benefit.

- Describe the steps in deriving a demand curve for a network good.

- Describe how networks can rapidly expand or decline due to network effects.

- Describe the strategies firms use to compete in the market for network goods.

- Discuss the role of regulation in promoting network efficiency and competition.

- Explain how compatibility of industry standards can promote competition.

- Explain how interconnection promotes competition in industries with essential facilities.

W hen you use your AT&T cell phone to call your mother on her Verizon cell phone, do you ever consider what would happen if Verizon refused to connect your call from the AT&T network? Of course not—this just does not happen in the United States. But this is not always the case in other parts of the world. In Nigeria, for example, it is common for cell phone providers to ignore calls placed by callers using competing networks. The result? If you want to call your mom using a different network than hers, it might not work. In countries where customers using different networks are unable to place calls to one another reliably, people often carry multiple phones to make sure they can connect with their families and friends.

As this example illustrates, networks are an important part of our daily lives. In the United States, we often take networks for granted, failing to appreciate that without the efficient functioning of networks, we would be forced to endure a great deal of inconvenience and frustration. Where would you be without the word processing software you use to work collaboratively with others on group projects, or without the social networking site you use to stay in touch with friends?

This chapter studies the role of networks and network goods. Companies that provide network goods engage in competitive strategies to maintain the strength of their networks. Network industries tend to be volatile, and a market leader can quickly evaporate in this type of industry. Do you remember Friendster, AltaVista, Netscape, WordPerfect, and Sega Genesis? Each of these networks was once the market leader in its respective industry, but quickly lost its dominance when an opposing network became stronger.

Network goods are unique in economic analysis. Network goods have a different type of demand curve than we have previously seen, which makes them interesting to economists. More important, because of the nature of network industries, firms that provide network goods often become monopolies in their industries and devise strategies to maintain their monopoly status. However, these seemingly unbeatable monopolies are often short-lived, as was the case with the social networking company Myspace, which had gone from the world's most popular social network to one that is now struggling to reinvent itself as a niche social network. The fleeting nature of some network monopolies raises the question of where network goods fall in the market structure analysis we introduced in Chapters 8 to 10. Are they monopolies, oligopolies, fierce competitors, or somehow a

BY THE NUMBERS

How We Are Connected Today

The importance of networks in the global economy has led to dramatic growth in network goods over the past decade, especially those that use the Internet. As network capabilities continue to expand, industries and markets will transform and people everywhere will adjust to the new way of life.

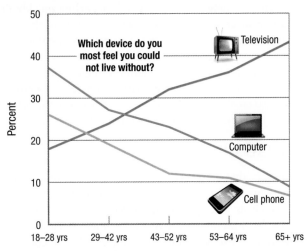

Which device can you not live without? The *New York Times* reported a study by Forrester Research that shows the device (television, computer, cell phone) people of different ages feel they are least able to live without. Older individuals still value the television the most, and younger individuals value computers and cell phones more.

The percentage of people using the Internet as of 2012 varied significantly around the world. However, developing regions are rapidly catching up. Over the past 10 years, while the number of Internet users has doubled in the developed world, it has increased 25-fold in Africa.

500 million
Number of Google Plus users worldwide in 2013.

VS.

1.15 billion
Number of Facebook users worldwide in 2013.

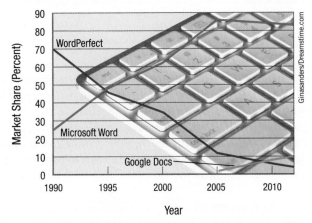

The powerful role of network effects can be seen in the rise and fall of market share for word processing software over the past two decades. In 1990, WordPerfect was the market leader, but saw its market share steadily decline as Microsoft Word became the dominant software provider. However, the recent introduction of Google Docs has begun to take some market share from Microsoft. Will we see another change in market leader in the next decade?

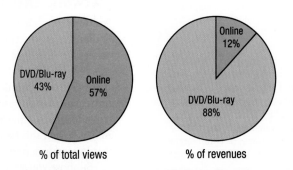

% of total views   % of revenues

The number of online movie downloads and streaming views surpassed total DVD and Blu-ray movie unit sales for the first time in 2012. However, DVD and Blu-ray sales still generated 88% of revenues in the home-viewing movie market.

network A structure that connects various entities with one another. A network can be physical, virtual, or social.

physical network A network connected by a physical structure such as fiber optics, transportation routes, or satellites.

virtual network A network connected by groups of people using the same type or brand of good.

mixture of these market structures? Also, the market for network goods exhibits externalities, a concept studied in the previous chapter, which influence how firms allocate their resources to maximize profits.

This chapter begins by defining three types of networks and discussing the importance of network effects, a concept related to externalities. We then describe how a network demand curve is derived based on network capacity. We go on to analyze equilibrium in the network industry, and explain how networks can expand or decline quickly due to network effects, which can lead to a successful or failed network. Because of the speed with which networks can expand or decline, firms engage in a variety of competitive strategies to promote and sustain their network. Finally, we look at the role of government regulation in network industries. One example of such regulation is the requirement that networks interconnect, which allows multiple networks, no matter the size, to coexist in a competitive market. But regulation also creates costs, and the tradeoff between the benefits and costs of a regulatory policy helps to determine whether such regulations are necessary.

What Is a Network Good?

A **network** is a type of structure that connects various entities with one another. There are three kinds of networks. First, there are **physical networks,** which are connected by fiber optics (such as a telephone network), transportation routes (such as an airline), satellites (such as a GPS network), or other physical connections. Second, there are **virtual networks,** which describe a network connected by groups of people using the same type or brand of good (such as mobile phone service, video game console, search engine, or software). Third, there are **social networks,** which combine elements of physical and virtual networks and describe groups of people using the same product or service who also are connected more directly (for business or entertainment purposes) within the network, such as through the use of "friends" on social networking sites and face-to-face networking in traditional business clubs, country clubs, or health clubs.

Physical networks include telecommunications cables laid across the ocean floor that connect the world. Physical networks are more expensive and less fluid than virtual or social networks.

Types of Network Goods

A **network good** describes a type of good or service that depends on the existence of a physical network, virtual network, or social network to exist. Although network goods have existed for centuries, the Internet created an immense rise in their importance, given the increased interaction between people and the information they share with one another. Today, network goods are ubiquitous and include but are not limited to smartphones, the Internet, satellite radio, software, digital music, MP3 players, 3D televisions, and social networking sites.

Network Effects

An important characteristic of a network good, whether connected physically or virtually, is that the production or consumption of that good creates a positive external benefit to others. For example, owning the newest Microsoft Xbox console capable of network play is not very useful if no one else owns the same system. As more people purchase the system, there are more people to play games with online, which encourages companies to develop more games. As a result, the value rises to those who already own the console and to those considering whether to purchase one. This rise in value is referred to as a **network externality.** When this benefit is taken into account in an individual or firm's decision making, it is known as a **network effect.**

social network A network that combines elements of physical and virtual networks by describing groups of people using the same product or service who also are connected more directly (for business or entertainment purposes) within the network.

network good A good or service that requires the existence of a physical, virtual, or social network to exist.

network externality An external benefit generated from the consumption of a network good.

Suppose you start a new social networking site for economics majors around the country to interact with one another. Initially, the value of such a network is limited to you and a few classmates who sign up. However, with each additional user, the potential benefit expands and generates spillovers to all users. Similarly, by subscribing to Facebook, you gain access to more than a billion potential "friends" (a clear benefit to you), while you provide an external benefit (albeit quite small unless you're famous) to all 1 billion existing users.

These examples highlight an important difference between a network externality and a positive externality as described in Chapter 13. As we saw in that chapter, a person generating

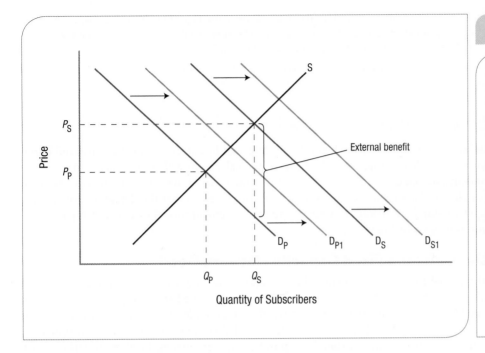

FIGURE 1

External Benefit of Consumption Pulls Private Demand Farther to the Right

Each consumer who joins a network generates an external benefit (the vertical distance between the private demand curve, D_P, and the social demand curve, D_S) enjoyed by all other people within the network. This in turn generates even more demand, shifting D_P and D_S farther to the right, to D_{P1} and D_{S1}, respectively. This effect on demand becomes smaller as more people join the network; a smaller effect is due to diminishing returns to the network externality. The same dynamic effect can work in reverse if a consumer chooses to leave the network.

a positive external benefit does not directly benefit from the externality he or she is creating. However, a network externality benefits all users, including the initial user and even potential users, because the external benefit increases the value of the overall network. This in turn generates even more demand for the network good.

Figure 1 illustrates the network effect described above. The consumer generates an external benefit equal to the vertical distance between the private demand curve, D_P, and the social demand curve, D_S. This external benefit increases the value of the overall network to its existing and potential users. The rise in the value of the network generates even more demand, as shown by the rightward shift of D_P and D_S to D_{P1} and D_{S1}, respectively. Although marginal benefit is not shown, it is important to note that external benefits are subject to diminishing returns. As a network becomes larger, an increase in demand generates fewer additional benefits to others. The benefit added by the 100th user in a new network is greater than the benefit added by the 100-millionth user.

Network effects also can work in reverse. When a consumer leaves a network, the value of the network is reduced to all remaining users, which may lead to a larger leftward shift in demand than is warranted by the loss of only one user. Note that this is not the same as a negative externality, which *imposes a cost* on others and causes the supply curve to shift to the left. In the present case, leaving a network *removes the external benefit* that had been provided to others. The dynamic nature of how network effects influence the demand for network goods affects how a network demand curve is derived.

network effect An external benefit generated from the consumption of a network good that is taken into account by individuals and firms in their decision making. It increases the value of a good as more people use or subscribe to a good.

CHECKPOINT

WHAT IS A NETWORK GOOD?

- Networks can be categorized into physical networks, virtual networks, and social networks.
- A network good is a good whose demand depends on the existence of a physical, virtual, or social network.
- Network externalities are generated when the consumption and/or production of a good leads to additional benefits to all existing users of a good. Taking away these externalities leads to diminished benefits but does not add a cost.
- When network externalities are taken into account in an individual or firm's decision making, they are referred to as network effects. Network effects can lead to a larger rise or a larger decline in demand than would occur in a nonnetwork industry.

QUESTION: Suppose your best friend purchases a new high-tech laptop that allows users to work simultaneously on the same software file. How might your friend's purchase lead to a network effect that generates additional demand?

Answers to the Checkpoint question can be found at the end of this chapter.

Demand Curve for a Network Good

Because the value of network goods is influenced by external benefits, a demand curve for a network good does not look like a typical downward-sloping demand curve. A **network demand curve** reflects the fact that the value of the good initially rises as more people purchase or subscribe to the good, which means that the demand curve has an upward-sloping portion at lower quantities. A general model of demand for network goods is described next.[1]

network demand curve A demand curve for a good or service that experiences a network effect, causing it to slope upward at lower quantities before sloping downward once the market matures.

Demand for a Fixed Capacity Network Good

The model for a network demand curve makes two important assumptions. First, the model assumes that the short-run supply curve is limited to the capacity of the firm's fixed investment, and therefore is vertical. For example, a new entrant in the airline industry starts off with just a few planes, and therefore the number of customers it can serve is fixed until it expands by purchasing more planes. Further, an airline must expand in large increments (that is, it must buy a new airplane that can serve hundreds of passengers a day), rather than by small increments, such as when a baker decides whether to make one more cake. Second, the model assumes that there is a short-run demand curve corresponding to each vertical supply curve that reflects the higher value of a larger network due to network externalities. These assumptions make the analysis easier but do not change the conclusions.

Figure 2 shows how a network market demand curve is developed. We start with a small network with a capacity of Q_0, where demand is small and price (P_0) is determined by the intersection of a vertical supply curve S_0 at Q_0 and demand D_0 for that capacity. As the network expands (supply shifts to the right by an increment to S_1), demand increases because the value to existing and new users increases. This is shown by the

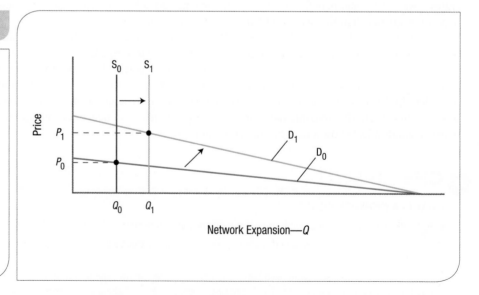

FIGURE 2

A Small Network with Fixed Capacity

A small network has a fixed capacity of Q_0, resulting in a vertical supply curve, S_0. The intersection of S_0 and D_0 results in an equilibrium price of P_0. As the network expands to S_1, the value to existing and new users increases due to network effects causing the demand curve to pivot to D_1. The intersection of S_1 and D_1 leads to a higher equilibrium price of P_1. This differs from a market for a nonnetwork good, in which an increase in supply leads to a lower price.

[1] This model is discussed in greater detail in Nicholas Economides, "The Economics of Networks," *International Journal of Industrial Organization*, 1996.

demand curve pivoting higher to D_1 (while intersecting the horizontal axis at the same point as D_0 to indicate a maximum demand for the network good) and reflecting a higher value to initial users and a higher market price at P_1. This differs from a market for a nonnetwork good, in which an increase in supply would not result in an increase in demand. For a nonnetwork good, the increase in supply would lead to a lower price on the demand curve.

Deriving the Full Network Demand Curve

Network effects are strongest in the early stages of a network good's development, as each additional consumer increases the marginal benefit to all consumers of the good. However, this network effect is always opposed by the law of demand we learned in Chapter 3: As price rises, quantity demanded falls. Which effect predominates?

When the quantity of a good provided on the market increases (without any change in demand), the price must fall in order for the market to clear. But the existence of network externalities causes demand to increase when a network expands, allowing prices to rise. Because the price effect and the network effect work in opposition to one another, the market price for a network good depends on which effect is stronger. For most network goods, the network effect dominates the price effect for small quantities, resulting in an upward-sloping portion of the network demand curve, as shown in Figure 3.

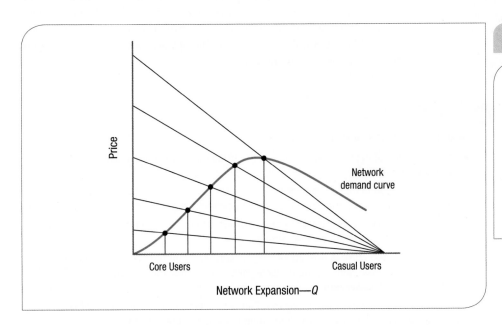

FIGURE 3

A Network Market Demand Curve

Network goods initially have an upward-sloping demand curve as core users build the network by attracting others to buy the good. Once the market matures, a network demand curve becomes downward-sloping as casual users buy the good when the price drops.

As the network expands along the upward-sloping portion of the network demand curve, the price increases as more **core users**—those who benefit most from consuming the good—purchase the good. The demand curve slopes upward as the network effect (which shifts demand to the right as quantity increases, increasing the price) dominates the price effect of an increase in quantity (which reduces the price).

As the market for a network good grows and reaches a critical number of consumers to support the network, additional consumers add fewer external benefits due to diminishing returns. These consumers who purchase the network good after it matures are called **casual users** (think of your grandmother buying an iPad only after everyone else in the family has one). Once a network good reaches this stage, the network demand curve slopes downward as the price effect (from the increase in supply due to lower production costs) dominates the network effect.

By connecting all of the intersections of demand and supply, a network demand curve is generated, which slopes upward from the origin as core users increase the value of the good and then slopes downward once the product matures and casual users buy the good.

core user A consumer who has a very high willingness to pay for a new product or service and is among the first to purchase it.

casual user A consumer who purchases a good only after the good has matured in the market and is more sensitive to price.

Examples of Network Demand Curve Pricing in Our Daily Lives

Justin Timberlake allowed his album, *The 20/20 Experience,* to stream online on numerous Web sites, including Spotify and Rdio, at no charge. The album generated a tremendous network effect that helped it sell nearly 1 million *paid* album downloads in its first week of official release in 2013.

What does the presence of a network demand curve mean for prices? It suggests that as a new network good is introduced, the price is kept low to attract new users. As the number of users increases, prices rise because people are willing to pay more for a network good used by more people. Prices continue to rise until the good matures, at which point prices must fall in order to sell a greater quantity.

Consider the following example: When Google launched in 1998, the search engine results displayed were quite bare—no ads, no preferred listings; the cost to use Google was essentially zero. However, as the number of users increased, Google began "charging" people to use the service by placing ads and suggested links alongside the search results. Although not a monetary cost, users pay an opportunity cost when viewing ads.

Another example of network demand curve pricing is a new rock band attempting to gain recognition by initially playing for nothing at local clubs, and/or offering their music free online. Once the band becomes better known, it begins charging for shows and for music downloads. Eventually, a downward-sloping demand curve will return, in which case lower prices are needed to increase quantity demanded. A similar effect can occur when an established musical artist prepares to release a new album. These examples demonstrate the upward- and downward-sloping nature of network demand curves.

CHECKPOINT

DEMAND CURVE FOR A NETWORK GOOD

- The production of network goods is typically carried out in large increments due to high fixed capital costs.
- The short-run equilibrium for a network good occurs at the intersection of a fixed capacity vertical supply curve and the demand curve for that quantity.
- As a network expands, the effect of network externalities is reduced due to diminishing returns as the price effect becomes stronger.
- A network demand curve is upward sloping for smaller quantities (when network effects are strong) and downward sloping for larger quantities (when the network good matures and network effects weaken).
- A network demand curve reflects the role that core users (represented on the upward-sloping portion of the curve) have in building the value of the network.

QUESTION: Why does a network demand curve slope upward for small quantities of a good, then slope downward for higher quantities?

Answers to the Checkpoint question can be found at the end of this chapter.

Market Equilibrium for a Network Good

tipping point (or **critical mass**) The quantity from which network effects are strong enough to support the network.

Now that we have learned how a network demand curve is developed, we can study how market equilibrium is reached in this type of industry. The market equilibrium for a network good occurs once most network effects are realized. Therefore, equilibrium generally is found on the downward-sloping portion of the network demand curve. However, not all network goods reach market equilibrium. As we will soon see, network goods can thrive or fail over a short period of time, making market equilibrium difficult both to achieve and to sustain.

Economies of Scale and Marginal Cost

An important characteristic of network goods is that they generally require a very large fixed cost to produce. Fixed costs can include the cost of writing and producing a new hit song, or the huge cost of building cell phone towers across the country. In Chapters 9 and 10, we saw how monopolies and oligopolies can form when industries exhibit high fixed costs and low marginal costs. Network goods are an excellent example of goods produced in such industries, for once a song is produced or a cell phone tower is built, the cost to serve customers (a firm's marginal cost) is minimal. An outcome from this type of industry is large economies of scale.

Finding an Equilibrium in the Market for Network Goods

Let's assume that the marginal cost of a network good is fixed at P_1, as shown in Figure 4. The equilibrium is point *d*, the intersection of the downward-sloping portion of the network demand curve and the marginal cost curve. To achieve equilibrium, the network for that good must expand from the origin to point *b*, which is called the **tipping point** (or **critical mass**), the quantity from which network effects are strong enough to continue building the network.

virtuous cycle The point at which a network good reaches its tipping point, when network effects cause demand for the good to increase on its own. As more people buy or subscribe to a good or service, it generates even more external benefits and more demand.

vicious cycle When a network good does not reach its tipping point, and therefore does not increase in value enough to retain its customers, customers leave the network, thereby further diminishing the value of the good until all customers leave the network.

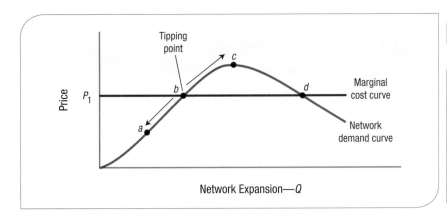

FIGURE 4

Equilibrium in a Market for Network Goods

Point *b* represents the tipping point—the point at which the network has achieved enough momentum to continue expanding until it reaches point *d* (an equilibrium created by a virtuous cycle). However, if a market fails to reach point *b*, a vicious cycle may result, leading to a collapse in market share.

Once a network reaches point *b*, the existence of network effects will continue to generate more demand, allowing the network to expand on its own until it reaches equilibrium at point *d*. This is referred to as a **virtuous cycle**, in which network effects push demand farther to the right, creating even more value for the network.

However, if a network good fails to reach point *b*, or if a new competing network good causes demand to move to a point left of point *b*, a **vicious cycle** can result. In a vicious cycle, people stop consuming a product or service, thereby reducing the value of the product to others, which causes even more people to avoid consuming the good. The result is typically a failed product, shown as a good at point *a* in Figure 4.

An example of a product entering a vicious cycle was the HD DVD format introduced by Toshiba in 2006. Toshiba competed vigorously for market share against Sony's Blu-ray format, but because Toshiba did not reach a critical mass, studios stopped offering their movies in HD DVD format, leading to a vicious cycle and the discontinuation of the format in 2008. Interestingly, several years later Blu-ray entered its own vicious cycle as online streaming of movies made physical media less relevant, leading to fewer movie offerings in Blu-ray format and a steep drop in sales.

Note how the network demand curve slopes upward to point *c*, then downward. What explains this change in slope? Point *c* represents the point of product maturity, when the network effect no longer dominates the price

A long line of core users waiting to buy a new product can propel a network good into a virtuous cycle.

effect. Remember that a demand curve slopes downward due to a price effect—it requires a lower price for people to consume more. However, network effects counter the price effect by raising the value of the good as consumers buy more. At point *c,* the network effect and price effect are equal in magnitude. Thus, the upward-sloping segment represents core users who are less price sensitive, and the downward-sloping segment represents casual users who are more price sensitive.

Networks Goods Can Face a Virtuous Cycle or a Vicious Cycle Very Quickly

The speed at which network effects can influence the success or failure of a product or service can be remarkably fast. As shown in Figure 4, once a firm enters a vicious cycle by moving down the network demand curve to the left of point *b,* it is often difficult to stop the cycle. Meanwhile, firms entering virtuous cycles enjoy what seems to be limitless growth over a very short period.

Table 1 provides examples of network goods that experienced a change in market leader at some point over the last two decades. In some cases the change was gradual (such as the transition from film to digital, because ardent film photographers took many years to make the switch to digital), whereas in other cases the change was almost instantaneous (such as that from the HP Mini to the Apple iPad).

TABLE 1   **Examples of Network Goods Facing Virtuous and Vicious Cycles**

Industry	Previous Market Leaders	Current Market Leader
Social networking	Friendster (2002–2004)	Facebook (2009–)
	Myspace (2005–2008)	
Internet search engines	AltaVista (1997–2002)	Google (2003–)
Word processing software	WordPerfect (1980–1996)	Microsoft Word (1997–)
Video game consoles	Sega Genesis (1990–1994)	Microsoft Xbox 360 (2012–)
	PlayStation 1 and 2 (1995–2007)	
	Nintendo Wii (2008–2011)	
Internet browsers	Netscape (1995–1998)	Internet Explorer (1999–)
Internet service providers	Prodigy (1991–1994)	AT&T DSL (2004–)
	America Online (1995–2003)	
Photography	Kodak (film) (1936–2004)	Canon (digital) (2005–)
Smartphones	Blackberry (2003–2010)	Apple iPhone (2011–)
Home printers	Epson (dot matrix) (1979–1995)	HP (inkjet/laser) (1996–)
Tablets/netbooks	HP Mini (2008–2009)	Apple iPad (2010–)

Interestingly, the quality of a network good is not always the most important factor in determining the market leader in a network industry. Because network effects are so powerful, consumers sometimes choose an inferior product that many people use over a superior product that fewer people use. For example, some video game enthusiasts claim that Sony's PlayStation 3 is superior in graphics and capabilities to Nintendo's Wii. Yet, the Wii system held its position as market leader for four years, partly due to its lower price but also due to a virtuous cycle it had enjoyed until Microsoft's Xbox 360 took over as the new market leader.

ISSUE

The Broadband Effect: Virtuous and Vicious Cycles in Network Goods

Most Americans rely on broadband Internet connections for work, school, or entertainment. Over 66% of U.S. households in 2012 had a broadband connection, up from just 11% in 2002. Part of this dramatic rise in broadband connectivity has been the result of government efforts to promote broadband usage in all areas of the country, especially in rural areas where it is costly to establish broadband connections.

In 2010, the U.S. Federal Communications Commission (FCC) established the Connect America Fund to promote the goal of ensuring that every household has access to broadband capability. This fund consists of fees collected from all broadband users nationwide and is used to subsidize service in high cost areas such as rural and mountainous communities. The FCC lists the social benefits of such an effort as including improved education, health care, public safety, and civic

engagement in rural areas. These ultimately benefit the entire nation.

No doubt, the near universal use of broadband has resulted in significant changes to network industries. For example, network services such as movie and live television streaming, online conferencing, worldwide telecommunications via Skype and other online providers, and instant music and software downloads were all either previously unavailable or excruciatingly time-consuming to use prior to broadband. These services experienced a virtuous cycle as more and more consumers gain access to faster Internet connections, leading to a validation of Metcalfe's Law, which states that the value of a telecommunications network increases exponentially with the number of users.

But not all industries fared well with the rise in broadband usage. Some markets faced a vicious cycle as consumers moved away from certain network goods. These include traditional international

calling, calling cards, and prepaid phones. Beyond telecommunications, broadband also contributed to the demise of most physical DVD and game rental stores, CD music stores, and software stores, as all of these services can now be obtained online.

Like all industries, goods come and go, and network goods are no different. What is remarkable is how quickly this transformation took place over the last decade. How today's network goods fare in the future will be an interesting question to examine as technological improvements continue to change the way we live.

Because of the speed at which market demand for network goods can occur, no firm is ever "safe" with its market share. Aware of this, businesses often engage in various competitive strategies to increase or secure their market shares. The next section describes some of these strategies.

 CHECKPOINT

MARKET EQUILIBRIUM FOR A NETWORK GOOD

- Network goods generally exhibit large economies of scale due to their high fixed costs and low marginal costs of production.
- A network good must reach its tipping point (or critical mass) to enter a virtuous cycle in which network effects generate additional demand until equilibrium is reached.
- Network goods that do not reach their tipping point enter into a vicious cycle, leading to a sharp decline in market share and likely failure of the good.
- Network goods can enter virtuous or vicious cycles in a very short period, such that no good is ever safe from rapid decline.

QUESTION: In 2003, Myspace entered the market and quickly became the world's most popular social networking site. In 2006, with more than 100 million subscribers, Myspace appeared destined to be a successful company over the long run. Enter Facebook, which had been introduced two years earlier as a niche social networking site for college students. Facebook quickly expanded beyond college students to target all consumer markets, and by 2009 Facebook surpassed Myspace, which has since seen a steady decline in subscribers. How does the network demand curve explain the speed at which Myspace rose to prominence and then fell to relative obscurity?

Answers to the Checkpoint question can be found at the end of this chapter.

➡ Competition and Market Structure for Network Goods

The network goods industry provides opportunities for firms to gain substantial market power. Such opportunities often lead to intense competition. A recent example of competition in network goods was the market for high-speed home Internet service between DSL providers (such as AT&T) and cable Internet providers (such as Comcast). With a majority of U.S. households having switched from dial-up Internet services to high-speed providers in the past decade, the race to become the dominant provider was critical to AT&T and Comcast.

AT&T focused on bundling strategies with their U-verse program that incorporates home phone, digital television, and high-speed Internet for one price. Comcast, in addition to their Xfinity program that bundles television, home phone, and Internet, invested heavily in television advertising featuring the Slowskys, a turtle couple that had an aversion to anything fast and was used as a metaphor for DSL-service speed.

This section describes some of the common strategies used to protect network goods from entering a vicious cycle or to increase the likelihood of entering a virtuous cycle. Undoubtedly, as a consumer, you encounter many of these marketing strategies when making decisions about which network goods to purchase. The goal of firms using these strategies is to attract you to their product and to keep you as a customer for a long time.

Competition and Pricing Strategies

teaser strategies Attractive up-front deals used as an incentive to entice new customers into a network.

switching cost A cost imposed on consumers when they change products or subscribe to a new network.

Network goods are characterized as having high fixed costs with low marginal costs. Further, network effects can cause some firms to flourish while causing others to fail, even when little or no quality differences exist between the firms' products. The determinant of market success is not always dependent on the quality of the good, but rather on competitive strategies to capture market share. Low marginal costs means it does not cost much to serve customers once they are committed to a product. Therefore, firms spend significant sums of money to gain new customers and use various strategies to keep existing customers. These strategies include teaser strategies, lock-in strategies, and market segmentation (such as product differentiation and price discrimination).

Capturing New Customers Using Teaser Strategies **Teaser strategies** are used by firms to gain new customers by offering various sign-up incentives and/or low prices for a short introductory period. Examples of teaser deals include wireless companies offering a free or highly discounted phone when purchasing a two-year wireless plan, cable companies offering six months of free cable or Internet service, banks offering 0% finance charges for a limited time when opening a new credit card account, online music companies offering new customers fifty free music downloads, and software companies allowing new users to sample their products with a 30-day free trial.

Why do companies offer such great deals to new customers? Unlike decisions for non-network goods, such as which brand of cereal to buy—a decision that is relatively easy to switch back and forth—purchasing a network good typically requires a long-term commitment. This can be due to a legal commitment, such as a one- or two-year contract, or it can be due to nonmonetary costs of switching from one product to another.

Have you ever had to switch from a software program that you have used for many years? Once you learn how to use a particular software program or once you are accustomed to a certain email program, it can be a hassle to switch to another. These **switching costs,** which

Zero percent interest lending rate deals abound to attract new customers, but beware, they do not last for long!

include monetary and nonmonetary costs of switching from one good to another, often are substantial for network goods. Therefore, to provide incentives for consumers to incur these costs to switch, firms must offer attractive up-front deals.

Retaining Existing Customers Using Lock-In Strategies In addition to offering teaser deals to entice new customers, firms also employ strategies to keep existing customers from leaving. **Lock-in strategies** occur after a customer adopts a product, and typically involve the firm engaging in strategies that raise the switching costs of consumers, thereby increasing the likelihood of retaining the customer.

Switching costs include the hassle of learning a new format and its features, dealing with the loss of other features one has become accustomed to, and so forth. In some cases, switching costs may be minimal or offset by benefits; for example, the excitement of purchasing the latest smartphone or computer may outweigh the switching costs of learning how to use it. But consumers generally do not like changing network goods once they are accustomed to one brand.

Common examples of lock-in strategies include the offering of loyalty programs, which reward consumers the more they use or the longer they stay with a company's products. Lock-in strategies also include preventing certain features from being transferred to another product, such as a phone's contact list or saved text messages.

Using Market Segmentation to Maximize Profits In Chapters 9 and 10, we saw how market power can reduce the elasticity of demand for a firm's product and increase potential profits of monopolies and monopolistically competitive firms. We draw from those analyses by studying how **market segmentation** strategies can be used to increase market share and profits in the market for network goods. Market segmentation is achieved when firms can differentiate their products in a way that allows similar goods to be priced differently to different groups of consumers. In other words, it allows firms to price discriminate, which increases producer surplus (as discussed in Chapter 9).

Because network goods generally have a low marginal cost of production, firms have greater flexibility in segmenting their products to allow for a greater range of prices, each targeting a different subset of the market. Market segmentation strategies in network goods include versioning, intertemporal pricing, peak-load pricing, and bundling strategies.

Versioning refers to pricing strategies that involve differentiating a good by way of packaging it into multiple products for people with different needs. A common

> **lock-in strategies** Techniques used by firms to raise the switching costs for its customers, making it less attractive to leave the network.
>
> **market segmentation** A strategy of making a single good in different versions to target different consumer markets with varying prices.
>
> **versioning** A pricing strategy that involves differentiating a good by way of packaging into multiple products for people with different demands.

ISSUE

Do Exclusive Marketing Deals Lock In Customers?

Competition among telecommunication providers has flourished since 1984, when the U.S. government forced AT&T, which at the time was the monopoly provider of about 80% of all telephone services, to break apart into seven regional companies and a long-distance company, and to allow competition in long-distance service. Almost immediately, long-distance companies MCI and Sprint began offering long-distance services equal to AT&T's services, and competing vigorously against AT&T for customers. In the 1990s, competition among these three carriers involved advertising in the form of nearly endless sales calls to people's homes, often during dinnertime, which eventually led to the creation of "Do Not Call" registries.

Today, competition among wireless carriers is as intense as competition among long-distance carriers was in the 1990s. But with limitations on advertising via sales calls, companies such as Verizon, AT&T, Sprint, and T-Mobile have turned to attractive teaser deals and exclusive phone arrangements with phone makers to offer the

Seemingly nonstop telemarketing calls, many from telephone service providers, led to the creation of "Do Not Call" registries and forced firms to find new sales strategies.

newest models of phones only with one wireless provider.

The use of teaser and lock-in strategies (such as preventing a person from keeping his or her phone when transferring wireless service to another provider) represents a new form of competition among network goods providers.

Is this competitive approach better than advertising? On the one hand, consumers today are not bombarded with telephone sales calls as they were in the 1990s, but on the other hand, the ability to switch from one provider to another has taken on additional switching costs.

example is the choice of a wireless plan. Do you choose an unlimited monthly plan, a fixed-minute monthly plan, or a prepaid plan? A single firm can offer each of these plans and price each plan to attract the appropriate subset of customers.

A similar but slightly different strategy is **intertemporal pricing.** Like versioning, a firm uses intertemporal pricing strategies to target different groups of consumers by differentiating their product, but in this case, by time. Specifically, they use the fact that some consumers are more impatient than others to buy a product. For example, new books often first appear in bookstores as expensive hardcover editions, then as less expensive paperbacks several months later, followed by the availability of the book for loan from public libraries at no cost for the most patient consumers.

intertemporal pricing A type of versioning in which goods are differentiated by the level of patience of consumers. Less patient consumers pay a higher price than more patient consumers.

Another example of intertemporal pricing shown in Table 2 is the release of a new movie. A new movie first appears in theaters, followed by on-demand or pay-per-view, then via paid online streaming or DVD rental, then on premium movie channels, and lastly on network TV. With each step, the price to view the movie generally decreases.

TABLE 2	Intertemporal Pricing of a New Movie	
Movie Format	**Average Wait Time from Movie Release**	**Approximate Cost to View**
Movie theater	Immediate	$10 per person
On-demand/pay-per-view	2 to 3 months	$10 per group of viewers
Paid streaming/DVD rental	6 to 9 months	$5 per group of viewers
Premium channels	6 months to 1 year	Cost of channel subscription
Network TV/Free streaming	1 year or longer	Free (basic TV or Internet access)

Firms that successfully use versioning and intertemporal pricing can price discriminate among consumers by charging less patient consumers, who have lower elasticities of demand, higher prices than those consumers with more patience and higher elasticities of demand. Once consumers with less elastic demand are served, the price is dropped to serve those with more elastic demand. The firm earns more profit by versioning products using time as the differentiating factor.

peak-load pricing A versioning strategy of pricing a product higher during periods of higher demand, and lower during periods of lower demand.

Peak-load pricing focuses less on differentiating a product than it does on charging higher prices when there is greater demand for the product. For example, ticket prices for evening movies and Broadway shows typically are higher than prices for matinees. Most wireless plans come with free or highly discounted evening and weekend usage. And airlines typically charge less for tickets on the nonpeak travel days of Tuesday, Wednesday, and Saturday. Similar to versioning and intertemporal pricing, the use of peak-load pricing attempts to segment the market into consumers with less flexible demand and those with more flexible demand.

Figure 5 illustrates a market with peak-load pricing, where P_P represents the higher prices charged during peak times when demand D_P is greater, whereas P_O is the lower price charged during off-peak times when demand D_O is lower.

bundling A strategy of packaging several products into a single product with a single price. Bundling allows firms to capture customers of related products by making it more attractive to use the same firm's products.

Finally, network industries engage in **bundling** strategies to increase demand for related products. Because network goods generally have low marginal costs to produce, it does not cost the firm much to package several products together. Customers who purchase one product are then more likely to use other products from the same company, thus supporting the firm's network and the value of all its goods. One example is Apple's strategy of bundling many types of software into its Mac operating system. Bundled programs such as Safari, iMovie, iPhoto, iTunes,

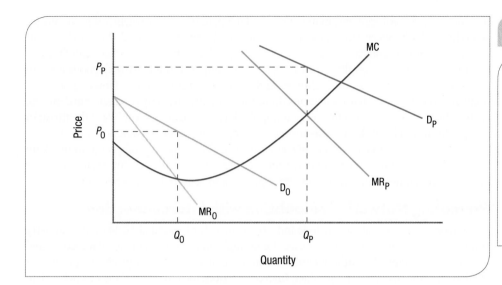

FIGURE 5

Peak-Load Pricing
Demand curve D_P represents a greater demand during peak periods, leading to an optimal price of P_P. During off-peak times, demand D_0 is much lower, leading to a lower price of P_0. Peak-load pricing can occur by time of day (telephone calls, live shows, movies), by day of the week (airline tickets), or by season (ski lift tickets).

and Garage Band provide users with convenient "free" options, thereby reducing the need to use other network providers (such as Adobe and Real), which sell competing media products.

 ## CHECKPOINT

COMPETITION AND MARKET STRUCTURE FOR NETWORK GOODS

- Competition for market share in network goods is often intense as firms attempt to avoid the vicious cycle of a failed network good.

- Teaser strategies include attractive up-front savings to customers willing to switch to another network good provider, while lock-in strategies are used to make it more costly to leave a network good provider.

- Market segmentation involves separating consumers based on their elasticity of demand, with less patient consumers (those with inelastic demands) paying more than patient consumers with elastic demands.

- Versioning is the practice of differentiating a good into multiple products from which consumers can choose. Versioning also can be done by time (intertemporal pricing) or by peak usage (peak-load pricing).

- Firms bundle their goods because the marginal cost of adding additional products is minimal and the benefit from network effects is high if consumers use the included products instead of purchasing them separately from competing firms.

QUESTIONS: Why would a firm selling a network good choose to segment its customers by charging different prices? Wouldn't it make more money by just charging everyone a high price?

Answers to the Checkpoint questions can be found at the end of this chapter.

Should Network Goods Be Regulated?

In a market where firms compete to become the dominant provider, whether as a monopolist or an oligopolist, firms use strategies to strengthen and maintain their market power. In such a market, government must assess the effects of these strategies on consumers. Unlike other firms with market power, those producing network goods face the continuing threat that a new network good might lead them into a vicious cycle. Therefore, competition can exist even when a network good is dominated by a single firm. This brings about the important question of whether or not government should regulate these firms.

Microsoft's market dominance with their Windows operating system, office-suite products (Office), and email and Internet programs (Outlook and Explorer), led the U.S. Department of

Justice, along with governments in the European Union, to investigate whether this dominance was achieved fairly. Specifically, some question Microsoft's bundling tactics, which make it convenient (perhaps too convenient) to adopt its related products once one product is purchased.

The government generally aims to ensure that competition for network goods leads to low prices for consumers, ample choices, and improvements in quality. However, government also must ensure that regulations do not impede productivity or create burdensome costs to firms. Just because a firm is a monopoly does not mean it doesn't face the threat of competition, which can keep firms from exploiting their market power.

One way to promote a competitive environment for network goods is not to break up monopolies, but rather to ensure that firms are prevented from securing exclusive access to a set of consumers. One such regulatory policy is to require interconnection.

Promoting Network Competition with Interconnection

industry standard A common format that is used, for example, in televisions, in digital recorders, or in software programs.

essential facility An input that is needed to produce a product or to allow a person to consume a product.

interconnection The physical linking of a network to another network's essential facilities. Interconnection promotes competition by ensuring that no firm has exclusive access to a set of customers.

Many types of network goods include industry standards or essential facilities. An **industry standard** is a common format that is used, for example, in televisions, in digital recorders, and in software programs. **Essential facilities** are inputs that are needed to produce a product or to allow a person to consume a product. **Interconnection,** the physical linking of a network to another network's essential facilities, helps to promote competition in situations in which firms are able to use their market power to block competitors from entering the industry. When interconnection is required, firms must allow competing providers access to their networks. As discussed in the chapter opener, a Verizon customer, for example, must be able to make a call to an AT&T customer in order for multiple networks to operate efficiently in the same market. For such calls to be possible, they must travel across networks owned by different firms.

Consider the incredible arrangement of networks required to make a telephone call to a friend in another country. To complete this call, parties must work together, starting with a wireless provider or local telephone provider (called a local exchange carrier), connecting to the distance call provider, then the network provider interconnecting to the foreign network operator, and finally connecting to the friend's local exchange carrier. Even more amazing is how the cost of this service has fallen dramatically over the years. How is this possible? We looked at the role of network effects, network competition, and interconnection to explain how competing networks are able to provide efficient and seamless service that in the past could only be possible via large natural monopolies. What is more important is the degree to which global markets are dependent on network technologies that did not exist 15 years ago—technologies that we often take for granted today.

An important role of regulation in network goods is to ensure that providers of essential facilities allow access to competing firms. The most common example of an essential facility is the phone line in your house. Prior to 1984, AT&T owned about 80% of all of these phone lines, and could effectively prevent any competitor from offering phone service because rival firms would not be able to complete a call without access to your (i.e., AT&T's) phone line. In 1984, the U.S. government forced AT&T to break up into smaller firms, and eventually forced these firms to open their networks to competition, paving the way for both land-based and wireless providers to enter the market. The effect on prices was substantial. If you watch an old TV show from the 1970s or early 1980s, you may catch some interesting scenes in which characters make a big deal about calling long distance. Today we don't think twice about calling long distance, or even making international calls. In fact, long-distance calling has lost its identity as a market, leading to the demise of many long-distance companies.

Industry Standards and Network Compatibility

A common issue with network goods is that firms tend to compete vigorously (leading to standards wars) to become the industry standard, thereby "owning" the network. A consequence of this competition is that firms spend large sums of money on marketing strategies to dominate the market (to become a monopoly) rather than to achieve productivity gains and cost reductions typical of more competitive markets. Network compatibility allows competing standards to coexist in a market by ensuring that media can be used on competing formats. For example, a spreadsheet can be shared by a person using a Windows computer and someone using a Mac computer. And the spreadsheet itself can be edited using either Microsoft Excel or Google Docs.

Does Interconnection Improve Efficiency in Network Industries?

A common theme throughout the market structure discussions in Chapters 8 through 10 is that competitive markets generate more consumer surplus than monopoly markets. Further, firms with market power generate deadweight loss. In network industries where monopolies can be created if network effects are strong, interconnection can bring about gains to society by facilitating competition and reducing deadweight loss.

In the long run, interconnection creates a more competitive environment that forces firms to be more efficient, leading to reduced costs. Yet, a more competitive market might limit the network effects and economies of scale that exist with fewer firms. Therefore, implementing regulation to promote competition involves a tradeoff between benefits and costs. In fact, the potential costs of regulation can even exceed the benefits.

Can Poor Regulation Be Worse Than No Regulation?

Throughout this section, it was argued that regulation can promote competition by preventing firms from exploiting their access to essential facilities. However, the benefits of network effects most likely contributed to a firm's dominance in the market. For example, although we enjoy having our choice of wireless carriers, which is a benefit from regulation, such choices do not come without cost.

As discussed in the Issue in the previous section, competition for exclusive contracts with phone makers has made it difficult to use certain providers with certain phones. A similar situation arises in sports broadcasting, in which television networks sign contracts with sports organizations to be the sole broadcaster of games to viewers (such as ESPN's exclusive right to broadcast *Monday Night Football*). Although these cases create minor burdens, other forms of regulation intended to protect consumers have led to major disasters.

The California electricity crisis of 2000–2001 is one such example of poor regulation of a network good. Although the initial objective of placing a price cap (a price ceiling) on electricity prices was to keep prices from rising too rapidly for consumers, it quickly led to strategic responses by producers. Because producers could not raise prices in California to compensate for rising input prices, many firms instead chose to reduce the quantity of electricity provided, creating a huge shortage of electricity. Ultimately, the price ceiling led to massive blackouts and much inconvenience to individuals and businesses for several months.

When determining whether network goods should be regulated or not, the benefits and costs of each policy must be evaluated to determine whether it would be best to implement the policy or to just leave the market alone. In many situations, such as with the California electricity price cap, life might have been brighter (pun intended) without regulation.

 CHECKPOINT

SHOULD NETWORK GOODS BE REGULATED?

- The purpose of regulatory policy is to promote a competitive market that will lead to more consumer choices and lower prices.
- One common form of regulation is requiring network providers to allow interconnection with their competitors—that is, allowing access to each other's network and essential facilities.
- Industry standards can lead to intense competition when competing firms attempt to become the dominant standard; however, network compatibility allows competing industry standards to coexist in a market.
- Interconnection facilitates competition and generally improves efficiency by forcing firms to be more productive and cost-effective.
- The costs of regulation, especially poor regulation, can be substantial and can exceed its potential benefits. Any regulatory policy should be evaluated based on the tradeoff between its benefits and costs.

QUESTIONS: The Apple iPod, iPhone, and iPad all serve as MP3 devices that allow individuals to play music that can be downloaded using Apple's iTunes music store and many other music providers. Why is an MP3 player considered an essential facility for playing music? Would regulatory policy ever be needed to prevent Apple from exploiting its essential facility?

Answers to the Checkpoint questions can be found at the end of this chapter.

chapter summary

Section 1: **What Is a Network Good?**

Networks can consist of physical, virtual, or social networks.

Network goods are either produced within a network or depend on a network for their existence.

Ajv123ajv/Dreamstime.com

Every new user of a social media app increases the value of the network to every existing user and potential user, generating a **network externality.** When these external benefits are taken into account in the decision making by individuals and firms, they are referred to as **network effects.**

Section 2: **Demand Curve for a Network Good**

Networks typically involve high fixed costs and therefore are produced in large increments, such as adding a new wireless tower that can serve many customers. This leads to a **network demand curve.**

A network demand curve has upward-sloping and downward-sloping segments:

- Upward-sloping segment: Shown where the network effect exceeds the price effect, and typically occurs when a network is relatively new. **Core users** of network goods are the target in this part of the network demand curve.

- Downward-sloping segment: Shown where the price effect exceeds the network effect, and typically occurs once a network matures. In this part of the network demand curve, **casual users** join the network.

Deriving a Network Demand Curve

A network begins with a vertical short-run supply curve that represents a fixed capacity (a maximum number of customers it can serve), and a corresponding demand curve. As the network expands, the vertical supply curve shifts to the right, and the corresponding demand curve increases due to a network effect.

Two Opposing Effects on Prices in a Network

- **Network effect:** puts upward pressure on prices as output increases
- **Price effect:** puts downward pressure on prices as output increases

Lisafx/Dreamstime.com

Even grandma and grandpa eventually fall in love with the newest technology gadget. However, older consumers are more likely to be casual users who buy network goods, such as tablet computers, after the goods have become common in society.

Section 3: Market Equilibrium for a Network Good

A network demand curve contains a **tipping point** (or **critical mass**), defined as the level of output that allows a network to expand further without significant effort by producers. When a tipping point is reached, the power of network effects propels the demand for a network good to a higher equilibrium point. This is referred to as a **virtuous cycle**. If a network good fails to reach its tipping point or falls below its tipping point, a vicious cycle can result as customers leave the network, further decreasing the value of the network to other users.

Goods can enter a virtuous cycle or a vicious cycle very quickly, especially if there is a competing network in the market.

Dropbox enjoyed a virtuous cycle in 2012 when over 50 million people signed up for this service that allows users to access and share files on any computer or mobile device.

Section 4: Competition and Market Structure for Network Goods

Firms engage in a variety of marketing strategies to increase the likelihood of entering a virtuous cycle or to avoid entering a vicious cycle. The pressure to gain and retain customers is enhanced by the low marginal cost of production, which makes customers more valuable the longer they use a firm's product.

Common strategies used by firms include:

- Teaser strategies
- Lock-in strategies
- Market segmentation by versioning (intertemporal pricing, peak-load pricing, and bundling)

Section 5: Should Network Goods Be Regulated?

Network effects allow successful firms to achieve significant market power, sometimes even a monopoly. To prevent firms from exploiting their market power, governments turn to regulation as a way to limit the abuse of market power.

Poor regulation can sometimes be worse than no regulation. Regulation is not always necessary when the costs of regulation exceed its benefits. The potential of competition itself can prevent monopolies from exploiting their market power.

Interconnection is a common requirement in the regulation of network industries, in which firms are required to give competitors access to each other's **essential facilities** such as telephone wires that allow for DSL broadband service.

KEY CONCEPTS

network, p. 368
physical network, p. 368
virtual network, p. 368
social network, p. 368
network good, p. 368
network externality, p. 368
network effect, p. 368
network demand curve, p. 370

core user, p. 371
casual user, p. 371
tipping point (critical mass), p. 373
virtuous cycle, p. 373
vicious cycle, p. 373
teaser strategies, p. 376
switching cost, p. 376
lock-in strategies, p. 377

market segmentation, p. 377
versioning, p. 377
intertemporal pricing, p. 378
peak-load pricing, p. 378
bundling, p. 378
industry standard, p. 380
essential facility, p. 380
interconnection, p. 380

QUESTIONS AND PROBLEMS

Check Your Understanding

1. What is a network externality and how does it differ from a typical externality?

2. Explain why a network demand curve slopes upward for small quantities.

3. List three strategies a firm can use to segment its market for a network good.

4. True or False: Once a firm's network good becomes the market leader, it is extremely unlikely for the firm to lose that position within a five-year period. Explain.

5. Why does the 3DTV industry exhibit large economies of scale? Would there also be network externalities in the consumption of 3DTVs? Explain.

6. If Matt wants to use his AT&T iPhone to call his girlfriend Sue, who uses a MyTouch from T-Mobile, why is interconnection necessary for the call to be completed?

Apply the Concepts

7. Suppose that two community organizations each plan their own public beach volleyball tournament on the same day at the same beach. Each organization wishes to have as many participants as possible. Further, a larger tournament is more fun for the participants. Suppose that a team consists of four players and at least four teams are required to hold a tournament. Explain what the tipping point would be and why a vicious cycle can develop if that number fails to be achieved.

8. If a person decides to unsubscribe from a popular social network, it decreases the value of the network to everyone else. Why wouldn't this action be considered a negative externality?

9. Suppose that expansion of the productive capacity of a firm producing a network good reduces the average cost due to economies of scale, but generates a very large increase in demand due to the network effect. Is this good likely to be on the upward-sloping or downward-sloping portion of the network demand curve? Explain.

10. Suppose that a new Harry Potter book called *The Untold Stories of Harry Potter* is released for sale, and fans line up for days to be the first to buy it. Are these fans core users or casual users in their demand for the new book? How could the book publisher maximize its profit using intertemporal pricing?

11. Suppose that your bank opens up a dozen more automatic teller machines (ATMs) throughout the city, making it much easier to find one. What happens to the demand and supply curves for this network as it expands?

12. Whenever a new car with satellite radio capability is purchased, the buyer is typically offered a free 90-day subscription to a satellite radio service such as SiriusXM. Explain why this offer would be considered a teaser strategy. Why wouldn't SiriusXM just charge a monthly subscription fee from the start?

In the News

13. The 2006 introduction of Google Docs, an online alternative but compatible software to Microsoft Office, forced Microsoft to develop new ideas to maintain its dominant market share. BBC News (May 12, 2010) reported that "Microsoft Takes Aim at Google Docs" by introducing a new online component with its Office 2010 product that offers the same features as Google Docs but with the familiarity of the Office software format. Why would the ability of Google Docs to read and edit a file created using Microsoft Office potentially cause the price of Microsoft Office software to fall?

14. Internet interconnection has become an important issue as countries improve their network infrastructure. According to the International Charging Arrangements for Internet Services (ICAIS) agreement, countries wishing to access U.S. Web sites or use U.S. backbones (Internet networks) must pay the full cost of interconnection (as opposed to, say, telephone interconnection, where each side shares the cost). Why would a country agree to this type of arrangement in the first place (in the 1990s), and what developments have taken place since then that would cause them to now oppose this arrangement?

Solving Problems

15. Suppose Ben values video game X at $100 and video game Y at $20, whereas Paul values video game X at $30 and video game Y at $80. The marginal cost to produce each game is $0. If a firm that produces both games decides to bundle X and Y, what price should it charge, and why is this bundling strategy more profitable than selling each game separately at a single price (assuming price discrimination is not possible)?

16. The accompanying figure shows two demand curves for ski lift tickets, one representing demand during February (peak season) and the other for April (low season). If the ski resort wishes to maximize its profit using peak-load pricing, what price should the ski resort set for lift tickets in February and what price should it set in April?

USING THE NUMBERS

17. According to By the Numbers, by what age category does the typical individual perceive television to be harder to live without than a mobile phone? By what age category does television become harder to live without than a computer?

18. According to By the Numbers, in what year did Microsoft Word surpass WordPerfect in terms of market share? In what year did Google Docs surpass WordPerfect? What are the current trends (up or down) for each software program in the last year reported?

Checkpoint: What Is a Network Good?

When your friend purchases a laptop capable of using newer, more elaborate software, it generates a benefit to anyone else (especially you) who would find it useful to collaborate on projects. As a result, your friend's laptop purchase increases the value of the laptop to you (a network effect), increasing the likelihood that you will purchase a similar laptop. And once you purchase the laptop, this will generate additional benefits to your other friends, potentially generating even more demand.

Checkpoint: Demand Curve for a Network Good

A network demand curve gains value based on the number of people who use it. For example, a network good with one consumer is virtually worthless. As more consumers buy the network good, its value rises and the network good becomes attractive to even more consumers. Once a good matures, the network effect weakens and additional consumers will buy the good only after the price drops. Hence, the demand curve slopes downward for higher quantities of the good.

Checkpoint: Market Equilibrium for a Network Good

The network demand curve shows how a good enters a virtuous cycle (where an increase in demand generates network externalities that lead to additional demand) and how it enters a vicious cycle (where a decline in demand reduces the value of the network that leads to further declines in demand). When Myspace was introduced in 2003, it provided new features that its competition (primarily Friendster) didn't offer, and quickly led to a virtuous cycle in which the growth in subscribers increased exponentially over several years. When Facebook entered the market and captured the attention of social networking users, it quickly entered a virtuous cycle as well. Once users began choosing Facebook over Myspace, the drop in Myspace subscriptions quickly led to a vicious cycle and a significant drop in market share.

Checkpoint: Competition and Market Structure for Network Goods

A network good generally has a low marginal cost of production; therefore, any revenue a firm collects, even at low prices, typically increases its profit. By segmenting the market, the firm is separating customers based on their elasticity of demand. Customers with lower elasticities of demand are willing to pay a higher price than customers with higher elasticities of demand. Firms can segment the market by versioning their products. Products can be differentiated by time, peak usage, or bundling to create different versions of the same good at different prices.

Checkpoint: Should Network Goods Be Regulated?

An MP3 player is needed to play digital music, and therefore is considered an essential facility. Because Apple produces its own MP3 player, it could potentially restrict its products to play only music downloaded from its iTunes music store. Doing so would prevent its customers from playing music downloaded from other music providers, restricting competition in the digital music market. If that were the case, then regulatory policy could be implemented to prevent producers of MP3 players from restricting sources from which music can be downloaded. But Apple is unlikely to make this restriction, because it benefits from the ability of people to play music downloaded from iTunes on non-Apple devices.

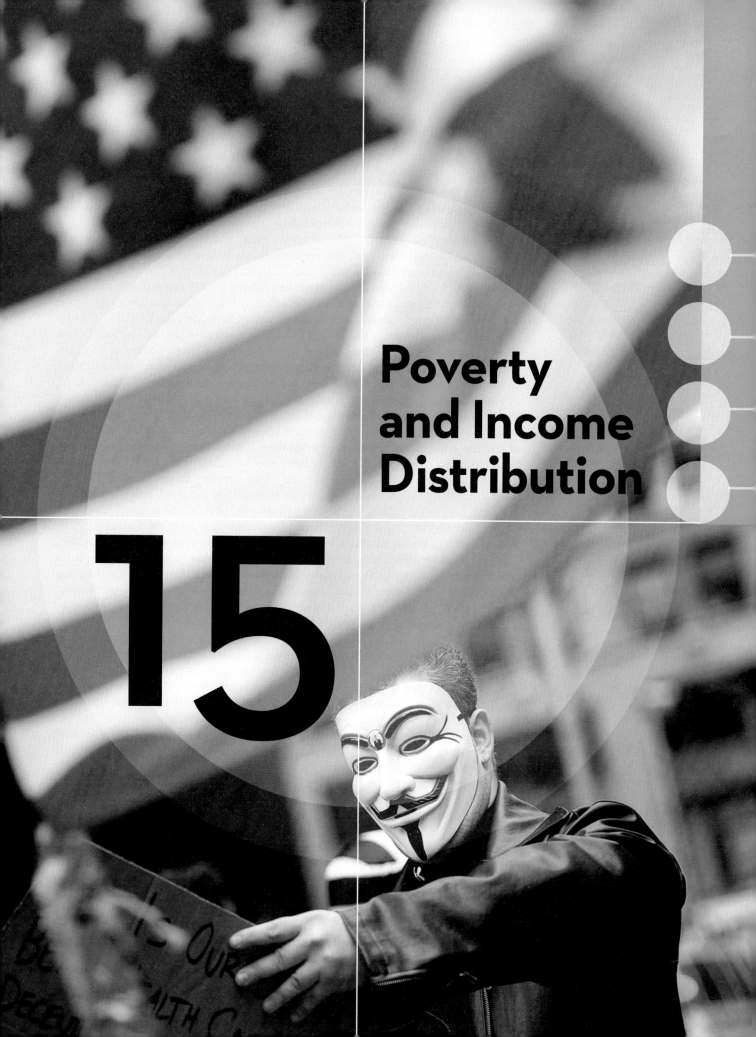

Poverty and Income Distribution

15

Craig Ruttle/Alamy

After studying this chapter you should be able to:

- Describe the difference between wealth and income.

- Describe the effects of life cycles on income.

- Analyze functional, personal, and family income distributions.

- Use a Lorenz curve and Gini coefficient to measure and describe the distribution of wealth and income.

- Describe the impact of income redistribution efforts.

- Describe the causes of income inequality.

- Describe the means for determining poverty thresholds.

- Describe the two measures for determining depth of poverty for families.

- Describe the prevailing theories on how to deal with poverty and income inequality.

On September 17, 2011, about 1000 protesters gathered in a small park near Wall Street in New York City to voice their concerns about social and economic inequality. What started as a local protest spurred by a social media campaign turned into a global movement known as Occupy.

The concerns raised by the Wall Street protesters and subsequently echoed by protesters in similar rallies in eighty-two countries on six continents dealt with a variety of issues relating to economic hardships that had been exacerbated during the recession of 2007–2009. Specifically, the Occupy movement claimed that the excessive influence of corporations on politics and the concentration of power by financial markets limited the opportunities of the majority of citizens in a democratic society. Supporters also lobbied for the right of citizens to have adequate access to health care, higher education, and a living wage. Above all, they are concerned about rising income inequality, which led to the coining of the slogan, "We are the 99%!" The slogan refers to the belief that economic prosperity has been unfairly concentrated among the richest 1% of the population, leaving the remaining 99% behind.

The issue of income inequality rose to the forefront in the United States as data showed that the richest 1% of the population earned nearly 20% of total income in 2012 and controlled over 40% of all wealth. This is a trend that is not slowing; inequality in the United States and around the world has expanded over the last three decades. Even during the last recession, when incomes of most Americans fell, the incomes of the richest Americans continued to rise.

What are the causes of income inequality? Two opposing theories exist. On the one hand, Occupy supporters claim that income inequality is the direct result of economic opportunities and tax policies that favor the wealthy few over the vast majority. The reductions in income and capital gains taxes on high-income earners in the United States are examples of how the tax structure became less progressive over time. On the other hand, others—including some prominent economists—believe that income inequality is the direct result of robust market incentives that reward entrepreneurial ability and success. These people do not believe income inequality is a result of some social injustice. Instead, they feel that wealth is the reward that comes from the opportunity for anyone to work hard, become successful, and be paid what they are worth to the economy.

Earlier, we saw that when input and product markets are competitive, wages are determined by worker productivity and the market value of output workers produce. This explains why some professional baseball players, who possess a unique ability to throw a 95-mph fastball and attract millions of fans, secure multimillion dollar contracts while teachers, who arguably perform a more valuable service but do so in a profession shared by millions of others with similar skills, earn salaries closer to the average.

Still, many people have trouble accepting that baseball pitchers earn millions, while teachers earn only thousands, and many others eke out subsistence wages. Income inequality is among the most contentious issues facing economists and other social scientists today.

Questions of fairness are normative. They can only be answered through individual value judgments. Economics has no right or wrong answers to offer in this area, but economists frequently contribute to these discussions.

Economic analysis gives us some insight into why income inequality exists. We have already seen how market power, unions, and discrimination can potentially skew income distribution. Even when public policy focuses on reducing these market imperfections, inequalities persist. Regardless of the causes of income inequality, addressing its effects requires special attention to those at the bottom of the income distribution: those who live in poverty.

This chapter looks at income inequality, its trends, its causes, and how it is measured. We then turn our attention to poverty, focusing on how poverty is traditionally measured, and the U.S. Census Bureau's new approach to measuring poverty. Finally, we look at current poverty trends and the causes of poverty. Throughout this chapter, we use economic analysis to provide a framework for analyzing income distribution, poverty, and the public policies used to combat poverty.

BY THE NUMBERS

Poverty and the Economy

Poverty is a problem facing people in virtually all countries, both rich and poor. Each country uses different methods to address poverty, including assistance for food, housing, health care, and education.

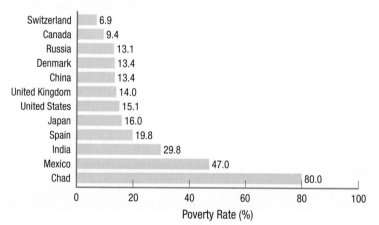

A single-parent working full time at the minimum wage is unable to keep a family out of poverty.

Jeff Greenberg/Alamy

The U.S. federal minimum wage is an example of government policy aimed at curbing poverty. In the 1960s and 1970s, one person working a full-time job at minimum wage was roughly able to keep a family of three out of poverty. Since the 1980s, the minimum wage has not kept up.

Poverty Rate (%)

Country	Poverty Rate (%)
Switzerland	6.9
Canada	9.4
Russia	13.1
Denmark	13.4
China	13.4
United Kingdom	14.0
United States	15.1
Japan	16.0
Spain	19.8
India	29.8
Mexico	47.0
Chad	80.0

56,000,000
Number of Medicaid (health care for low-income persons) recipients in 2012

$468
Average monthly U.S. government housing subsidy for a qualified household in 2012

Every country has its own measure of poverty, making a comparison of countries and their *official poverty rate* misleading. For example, Denmark and China both have an official poverty rate of 13.4%. In China, this means a family of four living on less than $1,400 a year; in Denmark, it means living on less than $45,000 a year plus having free health care, education, and retirement benefits.

Bob Daemmrich/The Image Works

The percentage of Americans receiving food stamps fluctuates with the economy. The last recession and slow recovery caused food stamp usage to rise.

Unlike food stamps of the past, food stamps today work like a debit card.

The Distribution of Income and Wealth

income A flow measure reflecting the funds received by individuals or households over a period of time, usually a week, month, or year.

Income is a *flow,* **wealth** is a *stock.* Income measures the receipt of funds by individuals or households over time, usually a week, month, or year. Income is a *flow of funds* measure. Wealth, in contrast, measures a family's assets and net liabilities at a given point in time. You may earn a certain income in 2014, but your net wealth is measured on a specific day, say, December 31, 2014. Many people were wealthy on January 1, 2007, but after suffering the ravages of a falling housing and stock market, they were considerably less wealthy on July 1, 2009.

wealth A stock measure of an individual's or family's assets, net of liabilities, at a given point in time.

You can be wealthy with low income if you do not work and your assets are in homes, stocks, and bonds that earn little to no interest or dividends. Alternatively, you can have little wealth, yet a high income, if you are like a rookie professional ballplayer who earns a seven-figure salary but has not yet accumulated assets.

Life Cycle Effects

Family and individual incomes vary significantly over the course of people's lives. Young people just starting their careers and their families often earn only modest incomes. Over their working careers, they become more experienced and their salaries increase, with income peaking roughly between the ages of 45 and 55. At some point between ages 45 and 60, family size begins to decline as the kids grow up and leave home. As people are approaching 60, income also begins declining, although household saving rises as they prepare for retirement. Incomes decline with retirement, but then again, so do family responsibilities.

One result of this economic life cycle is that a society that is growing older can expect to see changes in income distribution as greater numbers of households fall into lower income brackets. The life cycle also has implications for the economic effects of immigration. Newcomers to the United States often possess limited skills, therefore when the country admits more immigrants, it can expect more low-income households. The children of immigrants, however, move up the income distribution ladder.

The Distribution of Income

functional distribution of income The distribution of income for resources or factors of production (land, labor, capital, and entrepreneurial ability).

Income distribution can be considered from several different perspectives. First, we can look at the **functional distribution of income,** which splits income among the inputs (factors) of production. The functional distribution for the United States between 1929 and 2012 is shown in Table 1.

TABLE 1	Functional Distribution of Income (absolute dollars in billions, numbers in parentheses are percentages)

Year	Wages	Proprietor's Income	Rent	Corporate Profits	Net Interest
1929	51.1 (60.3)	14.9 (17.6)	4.9 (5.8)	9.2 (10.8)	4.7 (5.5)
1940	52.1 (65.4)	12.9 (16.2)	2.7 (3.4)	8.7 (10.9)	3.3 (4.1)
1950	154.8 (65.5)	38.4 (16.3)	7.1 (3.0)	33.7 (14.3)	2.3 (1.0)
1960	296.4 (69.4)	51.9 (12.1)	16.2 (3.8)	52.3 (12.2)	10.7 (2.5)
1970	617.2 (73.7)	79.8 (9.5)	20.3 (2.4)	81.6 (9.7)	38.4 (4.6)
1980	1651.7 (73.6)	177.6 (7.9)	31.3 (1.4)	198.5 (8.8)	183.9 (8.2)
1990	3351.7 (72.2)	381.0 (8.2)	49.1 (1.1)	408.6 (8.8)	452.4 (9.7)
2000	5715.2 (71.6)	715.0 (9.0)	141.6 (1.8)	876.4 (11.0)	532.7 (6.7)
2010	8093.9 (69.3)	1059.3 (9.1)	425.0 (3.6)	1435.1 (12.3)	661.9 (5.7)
2012	8795.5 (68.7)	1247.5 (9.7)	555.4 (4.3)	1629.1 (12.7)	583.3 (4.6)

Source: Bureau of Economic Analysis.

Labor's share of national income rose from 1929 to become relatively stable from the 1970s onward, but fell each decade after. The share of income going to small businesses, called "proprietor's income," has declined over this period but has stabilized at slightly under 10%. Rental income's share fell from 1960 to 1990, but has since grown back to over 4%. The share accruing to corporate profits has increased in recent years to over 12%.

As Table 1 illustrates, the biggest fluctuations in income share have been associated with income from interest earned by individuals and firms, and is caused largely by changes in interest rates. It declined into the 1960s, then rose in the 1980s and 1990s, before falling again in the last decade.

Personal or Family Distribution of Income

When most people use the term "the distribution of income," they typically mean **personal or family distribution of income.** This distributional measure is concerned with how much income, in percentage terms, goes to specific segments of the population.

To analyze personal and family income distribution, the Census Bureau essentially arrays households from the lowest incomes to the highest. It then splits these households into quintiles, or fifths, from the lowest 20% of households to the highest 20%. After totaling and averaging household incomes for each quintile, the Census Bureau computes the percentage of income flowing to each quintile.

Today, the United States contains approximately 120 million households. Therefore the 24 million households with the lowest incomes compose the bottom quintile, and the 24 million households with the highest incomes compose the upper quintile. Because much of the country's income is concentrated at the top, the Census Bureau breaks down the highest quintile further, showing the percentage of income flowing to the richest 10%, 5%, and 1% of the population.

Table 2 shows the official income distribution estimates for the United States since 1970. These estimates are based "solely on *money income before taxes* and do not include the value of noncash benefits, such as food stamps, Medicaid, public housing, or employer-provided fringe benefits."[1]

personal or family distribution of income The distribution of income to individuals or family groups (typically quintiles, or fifths, of the population).

Share of Aggregate Income Received by Each Household Quintile: 1970–2011 and the Gini Coefficient									TABLE 2
Year	Lowest	Second	Third	Fourth	Highest	Top 10%	Top 5%	Top 1%	Gini Coefficient
1970	4.1	10.8	17.4	24.5	43.3	32.5	19.9	8.5	0.394
1975	4.4	10.5	17.1	24.8	43.2	32.1	20.1	8.2	0.397
1980	4.3	10.3	16.9	24.9	43.7	30.0	20.2	8.8	0.403
1985	4.0	9.7	16.3	24.6	45.3	32.9	23.0	11.2	0.419
1990	3.9	9.6	15.9	24.0	46.6	33.8	23.9	11.9	0.428
1995	3.7	9.1	15.2	23.3	48.7	35.5	25.5	12.2	0.450
2000	3.6	8.9	14.9	23.0	49.6	39.8	30.0	17.3	0.462
2005	3.4	8.6	14.6	23.0	50.4	39.7	30.1	17.4	0.469
2011	3.2	8.4	14.3	23.0	51.1	40.2	31.4	18.7	0.477

Source: U.S. Census Bureau, Current Population Reports, P60-243, *Income, Poverty, and Health Insurance in the United States: 2011* (Washington, DC: U.S. Government Printing Office), 2012.

---

[1] U.S. Census Bureau, Current Population Reports, P60-243, *Income, Poverty, and Health Insurance in the United States: 2011* (Washington, DC: U.S. Government Printing Office), 2012, p. 3.

Note that if the income distribution were perfectly equal, all quintiles would receive 20% of aggregate income. A quick look at these income distributions over the past four decades suggests that our distribution of income has been growing more unequal. Specifically, the share of income received by the highest quintile has steadily risen since 1970, while the share of income received by each of the four other quintiles has steadily fallen since 1970. Even more notable is how the income flowing to the top 1% has increased the most, with the share of income more than doubling since 1970. Keep in mind that these numbers ignore taxes and transfers (direct payment to households such as welfare and food stamps) that temper income inequality somewhat.

Still, incomes of the richest Americans have fared best over the last generation, and one piece of evidence has been the meteoric rise in CEO salaries. Controlling for inflation, the average salary of a CEO increased eight-fold since 1978, while real wages for workers have barely changed. Such stark differences in worker compensation contributed to the growth of the Occupy movement in recent years and its claims against the power held by the richest 1%.

Compressing distribution data into quintiles allows us to see how distribution has evolved. Economists have developed two primary measures that allow comparisons to be drawn with ease across time and between countries. These measures are Lorenz curves and the Gini coefficient.

Lorenz Curves

Lorenz curves A graphical method of showing the income distribution by cumulating families of various income levels on the horizontal axis and relating this to their cumulative share of total income on the vertical axis.

Lorenz curves cumulate households of various income levels on the horizontal axis, relating this to their cumulated share of total income on the vertical axis. Figure 1, for simplicity, shows a two-person economy. Assume that both people earn 50% of the total income, or that income is divided evenly. Point *a* in Figure 1 marks out this point, resulting in equal distribution curve 0*ac*.

The second curve in Figure 1 shows a two-person economy where the low-income person earns 25% of the total income and the upper income person receives 75% (point *b*). This graph is skewed to the right (curve 0*bc*), indicating an unequal distribution. If this two-person income distribution were as unequal as possible (0% and 100%), the Lorenz curve would be equal to curve 0*dc*.

Figure 2 and its accompanying table offer more realistic Lorenz curves for income and wealth data for the United States in the year 2011. The quintile income distribution in the

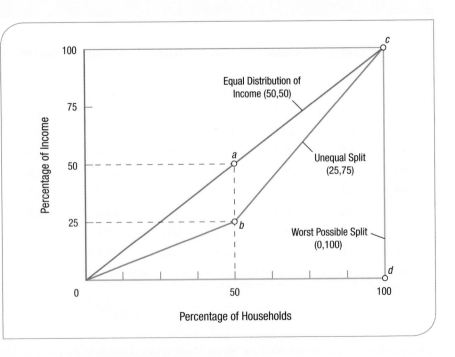

FIGURE 1

Lorenz Curves (Two-Person Economy)

If both people in this two-person economy earn 50% of the total income, income will be distributed perfectly equally, shown by the equal distribution curve 0*ac*. Curve 0*bc* represents the same economy in which the low-income person earns 25% of the total income and the upper income person earns 75%. This curve is skewed to the right, indicating an unequal distribution. The most extreme distribution between these two individuals (0% and 100%) is represented by the Lorenz curve 0*dc*.

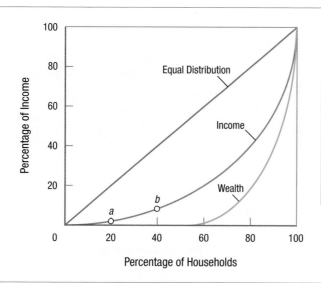

	Income		Wealth	
Quintile	**Income**	**Cum.**	**Wealth**	**Cum.**
Lowest	3.2	3.2	0.1	0.1
Second	8.4	11.6	0.2	0.3
Third	14.3	25.9	3.2	3.5
Fourth	23.0	48.9	7.6	11.1
Highest	51.1	100.0	88.9	100.0

Lorenz Curves

The graph shows the most recent Lorenz curves for income and wealth in the United States. The quintile distribution of income, found in the second column of the accompanying table, is cumulated in the third column and then plotted as a Lorenz curve. Notice how wealth is much more unequally distributed than income.

FIGURE 2

second column of the table is cumulated in the third column and plotted in Figure 2. (To *cumulate* a quintile means to add its percentage of income to the percentages earned by all lower quintiles.)

In Figure 2, for instance, the share of income received by the lowest fifth is 3.2%; it is plotted as point *a*. Next, the lowest two quintiles are summed (3.2 + 8.4 = 11.6) and plotted as point *b*. The process continues until all quintiles have been plotted to create the Lorenz curve.

Figure 2 also plots the Lorenz curve for wealth; it shows how wealth is much more unequally distributed than income. The wealthiest 20% of Americans control nearly 90% of wealth, even though they earn only half of all income.

Gini Coefficient

Lorenz curves give us a good graphical summation of income distributions, but they can be inconvenient to use when comparing distributions between different countries or across time. Economists would like one number that represents an economy's income inequality. The **Gini coefficient** provides such a number.

The Gini coefficient provides a precise method of measuring the position of the Lorenz curve. It is defined as the ratio of the area between the Lorenz curve and the equal distribution line, in the numerator, and the total area below the equal distribution line, in the denominator. In Figure 3 on the next page, the Gini coefficient is the ratio of area *A* to area (*A* + *B*).

If the distribution were equal, area *A* would disappear (equal zero), thus the Gini coefficient would be zero. If the distribution were as unequal as possible, with one individual or household earning all national income, area *B* would disappear, thus the Gini coefficient would be 1.

As a rule, the lower the coefficient, the more equal the distribution; the higher the coefficient, the more unequal. Looking back at the last column in Table 2, the Gini coefficient confirms that the basic income distribution has become more unequal since 1970. The Gini coefficient has risen from 0.394 in 1970 to 0.477 in 2011.

Gini coefficient A precise method of measuring the position of the Lorenz curve, defined as the area between the Lorenz curve and the equal distribution line divided by the total area below the equal distribution line.

FIGURE 3

The Gini Coefficient

The Gini coefficient is a precise method of measuring the position of the Lorenz curve. It is defined as the ratio of the area between the Lorenz curve and the equal distribution line, and the total area below the equal distribution line. Thus, the Gini coefficient is equal to the ratio between area A and area $(A + B)$. If distribution were equal, area A would be zero, and the Gini coefficient would equal zero. If distribution were as unequal as possible, area B would disappear, thus the Gini coefficient would be 1.

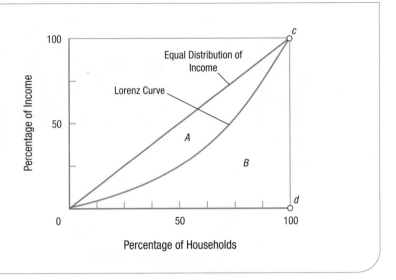

The Impact of Redistribution

In the United States, there is a vast array of income redistribution policies, including the progressive income tax (a tax that taxes higher incomes at a higher rate than lower incomes), housing subsidies, and other transfer payments such as Medicaid and Medicare, Social Security, and traditional welfare programs. Remember that the income distribution data in Table 2 *excluded* such government-provided cash and noncash benefits, and the effects of taxation.

Figure 4 provides an estimate of the impact progressive taxes and transfer payments (cash and in-kind) had on the income distribution in the United States. As we would expect, distribution became more equal: The Gini coefficient declined from 0.477 according to the official measure using gross income to 0.381 after adjusting for taxes and transfer payments.

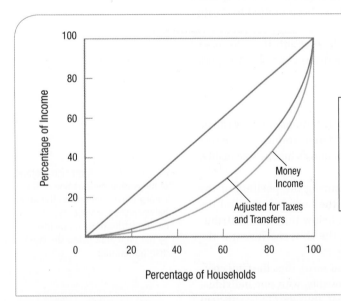

Quintile	Money Income Percent	Money Income Cum.	Adjusted Income Percent	Adjusted Income Cum.	Taxes Percent	Taxes Cum.
Lowest	3.2	3.2	6.2	6.2	0.4	0.4
Second	8.4	11.6	11.1	17.3	3.8	4.2
Third	14.3	25.9	15.8	33.1	9.5	13.7
Fourth	23.0	48.9	21.6	54.7	18.4	32.1
Highest	51.1	100.0	45.3	100.0	67.9	100.0

FIGURE 4

Lorenz Curves for the United States: Money Income and Income Adjusted for Taxes and Transfer Payments

These Lorenz curves provide an estimate of the impact progressive taxes and transfer payments (cash and in-kind) had on income distribution in the United States. As one would expect, distribution becomes more equal once taxes and transfer payments are taken into account. In this case, the Gini coefficient declined from 0.477 to 0.381.

Gini Coefficients for Various Countries, 2011 — TABLE 3

Country	Gini Coefficient	Country	Gini Coefficient
Australia	0.352	Italy	0.360
Bolivia	0.563	Japan	0.249
Brazil	0.547	Mexico	0.483
Canada	0.326	New Zealand	0.362
Chile	0.521	South Africa	0.631
China	0.425	Spain	0.347
Denmark	0.247	Sweden	0.250
France	0.327	United Kingdom	0.360
Israel	0.392	United States	0.477

Source: World Bank, *World Development Indicators* (Washington, DC: World Bank), 2012.

Table 3 provides some examples of how income distribution varies around the world. Income in European countries is generally more equally distributed than in the United States, while many South American countries have more unequal distributions.

Rio de Janeiro, Brazil, is one of the most beautiful cities in the world, but it also has some of the largest slums in the world.

Redistribution policies are the subject of intense debates. Those on the political right argue that differences in income are the natural result of a market system in which different individuals possess different personal endowments, schooling, and ambition. They believe, moreover, that the incentives of the marketplace are needed to encourage people to work and produce. The opportunities that markets provide mean that some people will be winners and others will lose. These analysts are unconcerned about the distribution of income unless it becomes so unequal that it discourages incentives and reduces efficiency.

Those on the political left argue that public policy should ultimately be guided by human needs. They see personal wealth as being the product of community effort as much as individual effort, and therefore they favor greater government taxation of income and wealth. By and large, European nations have found this argument more compelling than has the United States. This is reflected in the breadth of European social welfare policies. Because there is no correct answer (except possibly keeping distribution away from the extremes), this debate continues.

Causes of Income Inequality

Many factors contribute to income inequality in our society. First, as just mentioned, people are born into different circumstances with differing natural abilities. Families take varying interest in the well-being of their children, with some kids receiving immense inputs of family time and capital, while others receive little. These family choices largely fall outside the realm of public policy.

Human Capital The guarantee of a free public education through high school and huge subsidies to public colleges and universities for all Americans are designed to even out some of the economic differences among families. Still, public education does not eliminate the disparities. Some parents plan their children's education long before they are born, while other parents ignore education altogether.

Table 4 provides evidence of the impact investments in education have on earnings. Those without high school diplomas earned the least, roughly a third less than high school graduates. A college degree resulted in mean earnings nearly 3 times higher than what individuals without high school diplomas earned.

The U.S. economy has become more technologically complex. Manufacturing jobs have dwindled, reducing the demand for these workers, reducing their real wages. Several decades ago, people with low education levels could find highly productive work in manufacturing, with good wages and benefits. Globalization and increased capital mobility, however, have caused many of these jobs to migrate to lower wage countries. The result: Real wages have declined for Americans in many manufacturing occupations.

TABLE 4	Mean Earnings by Highest Degree Earned, 2009			
	Mean Earnings by Highest Degree			
	No High School Diploma	High School Graduate	College Graduate	Professional
All Persons	$20,241	$30,627	$56,665	$127,803
Male	23,036	35,468	69,479	150,310
Female	15,514	24,304	43,589	89,897
White	20,457	31,429	57,762	127,942
Black	18,936	26,970	47,799	102,328
Hispanic	19,916	25,998	49,017	79,228

Source: U.S. Census Bureau, Current Population Survey, *2012 Statistical Abstract of the United States*, Table 232.

Our economy is increasingly oriented toward service industries, making investments in human capital more important than ever. The service industry spans more than just burger flipping, maid service, and landscaping. The United States is still the world leader in the design and development of new products, basic scientific research and development, and other professional services. All these industries and occupations have one thing in common: the need for highly skilled and highly educated employees.

Other Factors In an earlier chapter, we saw that economic discrimination leads to an income distribution skewed against those subject to discrimination. Reduced wages then reduce an individual's incentive to invest in human capital because the returns are lower, perpetuating a vicious cycle.

Table 5 outlines some characteristics of households occupying two different income quintiles. By comparing the lowest quintile with the highest, we can see some of the reasons

Distribution of Households by Selected Characteristics within Income Quintiles, 2011		TABLE 5

Characteristic	Lowest Quintile	Highest Quintile
Type of Residence		
Inside metropolitan area	80.4%	90.5%
Inside central city	40.6	29.6
Outside central city	39.8	60.9
Outside metropolitan area	19.6	9.5
Type of Household		
Family households	40.1	86.8
Married-couple families	16.7	78.2
Nonfamily households	59.8	13.2
Householder living alone	56.0	6.6
Age of Householder		
15 to 34 years	23.7	14.6
35 to 54 years	26.9	51.0
55 to 64 years	17.4	22.7
65 years or older	31.9	11.6
Number of Earners		
No earners	61.7	2.9
One earner	33.8	22.2
Two or more earners	4.5	74.9
Work Experience of Householder		
Worked	32.3	87.1
Worked full-time, year-round	18.5	78.2
Worked part-time or part year	13.8	8.9
Did not work	67.7	12.9

Source: U.S. Census Bureau, Current Population Survey, Annual Social and Economic Supplement (Washington, DC: U.S. Government Printing Office), 2012.

for income inequality. As the Census Bureau summarizes these differences, "High-income households tended to be family households that included two or more earners, lived in the suburbs of a large city, and had a working householder between 35 and 54 years old. In contrast, low-income households tended to be in a city with an elderly householder who lived alone and did not work."

The rise in two-earner households over the last two decades accounts for a large part of the growing inequality in income. Note in Table 5 that only 4.5% of the lowest quintile households had two earners, while 74.9% of the highest quintile did. Also, only 2.9% of top quintile householders did not work, but 61.7% of those in the bottom quintile were not working.

It is hardly surprising that households with two people working should tend to have higher incomes than households with only one person or none working. In most households, whether one or two people work represents a choice. Today, clearly more couples are opting for two incomes. This is significant, given that rising income inequality is often cited as evidence that the United States needs to change its public policies to reduce inequalities. Yet, if the rise in inequality is due largely to changes in household attitudes toward work and income, with more couples choosing dual-career households, changes in public policy may not be needed. Rising inequality may simply be a reflection of the changing personal choices of many households.

This overview of income distribution and inequality provides a broad foundation for the remainder of the chapter, which focuses on poverty, its causes, and possible cures.

 ## CHECKPOINT

THE DISTRIBUTION OF INCOME AND WEALTH

- The functional distribution of income splits income among factors of production.
- The family or personal distribution of income typically splits income into quintiles.
- Lorenz curves cumulate households of various income levels on the horizontal axis and their cumulative share of income on the vertical axis.
- The Gini coefficient is the ratio of the area between the Lorenz curve and the equal distribution line to the total area below the equal distribution line. It is used to compare income distribution across time and between countries.
- Income redistribution activities such as progressive taxes, Medicare, Medicaid, and other transfer and welfare programs reduce the Gini coefficient and reduce the inequality in the distribution of income.
- Income inequality is caused by a number of factors, including individual investment in human capital, natural abilities, and discrimination.

QUESTIONS: Economist Charles Murray suggested doing away with all social insurance, including Social Security, Medicare, Medicaid, and other welfare programs, and instead simply giving $10,000 a year to every citizen of the United States over 21 years of age. His purpose was to reduce bureaucracy and the government's role in the decision making of families. Expand his idea slightly by eliminating the age restriction. Would this improve the income distribution in America? Why or why not?

Answers to the Checkpoint questions can be found at the end of this chapter.

 ## Poverty

Thus far, we have examined income distribution in general terms, looking at the spectrum from the top to the bottom. This section focuses on the bottom of the income spectrum—those who live in poverty. First, we look at poverty thresholds and how they are defined. Then we turn to the incidence of poverty and its trends. We then take a brief look at some experimental measures of poverty, considering their impact on measured rates of poverty. Lastly, we discuss the causes of poverty and how poverty can be reduced.

How difficult is life in poverty? A household of four in the United States that lived on less than $23,021 in the year 2011 was considered in poverty. That is equivalent to one wage earner working full-time as a maintenance worker at an apartment complex earning

$11.50 per hour, or about $1,900 per month before taxes. And this is a household living right at the poverty line; many households earn even less. Can a family get by on such meager income? In the United States, about 15% of all households do.

A household of four living on $1,900 per month can expect to have $1,675 after payroll and other taxes are deducted. Subtracting the rent on a modest subsidized apartment or a public housing apartment of $600 per month, $250 per month in utilities (electricity, gas, water, trash pickup, telephone, and basic Internet and cable), $250 per month toward a car payment, and $175 per month for fuel and auto insurance, this household has $400 left, or about $100 per week for everything else: food, clothing, school expenses, health care insurance, child care, and entertainment. Not to mention the occasional car repair, doctor and dentist co-payment, or parking ticket. And it certainly does not leave much to buy a $5 cup of coffee.

Living in poverty means that tough choices must be made to make ends meet. Some choose to give up their car and instead rely on public transportation. Others give up cable or the landline telephone. In more severe cases, some households are forced to cut back on food or health care. These choices are faced by one out of six persons in the United States. Why does the world's richest nation have so many poor citizens? Let's start to answer this by looking at how poverty is measured.

About one in six persons in the United States lives in poverty. For a family of four, this means living on less than $23,000 a year.

Measuring Poverty

Poverty thresholds were developed by Mollie Orshansky in the 1960s. They were based on the Department of Agriculture's Economy Food Plan, the least expensive plan by which a family could feed itself. The Department of Agriculture first surveyed the food-buying patterns of low-income households, using these data to determine the cost of a nutritionally balanced food plan on a low-income budget. Orshansky then extrapolated these costs to determine the cost of maintaining such a food plan for households of various compositions. Finally, to determine the official poverty threshold, Orshansky multiplied the cost of the food plan, adjusted for family size, by three. This multiplier was based on an earlier household survey that had shown the average family of three or more spends roughly a third of its income on food.[2]

Since the 1960s, the poverty thresholds have been updated every year for changes in inflation using the consumer price index (CPI). Table 6 shows the poverty

poverty thresholds Income levels for various household sizes, below which people are considered to be living in poverty.

U.S. Poverty Thresholds, 2011	TABLE 6
One person	$11,484
Two people	14,657
Three people	17,916
Four people	23,021
Five people	27,251
Six people	30,847
Seven people	35,085
Eight people	39,064
Nine people	46,572

Source: U.S. Census Bureau, Current Population Reports, P60-243, *Income, Poverty, and Health Insurance in the United States: 2011* (Washington, DC: U.S. Government Printing Office), 2012.

---

[2] See Constance F. Citro and Robert T. Michael, *Measuring Poverty: A New Approach* (Washington DC: National Academy Press), 1995, p. 13 and Chapter 2 for more detail on how thresholds are measured.

thresholds for 2011. If a family's income is less than the threshold, every person in the household is considered poor. Official thresholds do not vary geographically. "Income" includes all money income before taxes, including cash benefits, but not capital gains or noncash benefits such as public housing, food stamps, and Medicaid. Later, we will briefly look at some new alternative measures that do adjust for these factors.

The Incidence of Poverty

Poverty rates for the United States since 1960 are shown in Figure 5. Poverty fell rapidly between 1960 and 1975 but has remained roughly stable ever since, fluctuating with the business cycle: rising around recessions (the shaded vertical bars) and falling when times are good.

Poverty rates vary considerably along racial and ethnic lines. Figure 6 charts the poverty rate since 1970. Over most of this time, the poverty rate for blacks and Hispanics was roughly twice the rate for whites. Both of these minority groups benefited, however, from the strong economic growth of the 1990s, their poverty rates dropping from around 30% at the beginning of the decade to around 25% today. White poverty remained fairly steady over the 1990s, fluctuating between 10% and 11%. However, the recession in 2007–2009 and the slow economic recovery pushed the poverty rate for whites above 12%.

These data suggest that robust economic growth is a major force for reducing poverty. The expression "a rising tide floats all boats" would appear to have something to it.

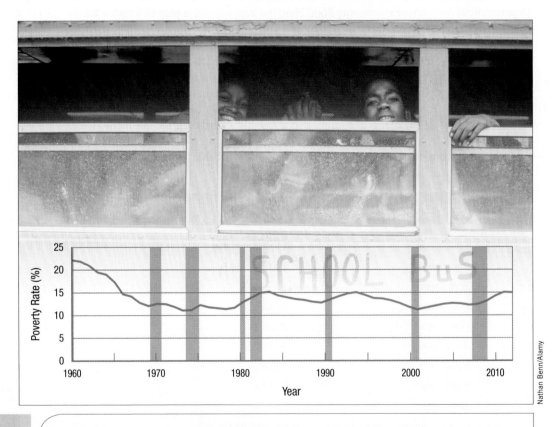

FIGURE 5

Poverty Rates in the United States, 1960–2011

Poverty fell rapidly between 1960 and 1975 but has remained roughly stable ever since.

Source: U.S. Census Bureau, Current Population Reports, P60-243, *Income, Poverty, and Health Insurance in the United States: 2011* (Washington, DC: U.S. Government Printing Office), 2012.

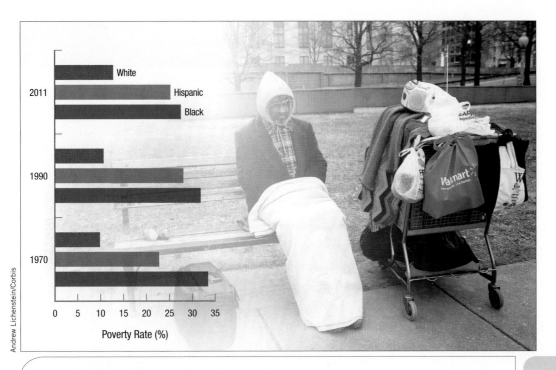

Poverty Rates by Race and Ethnic Origin, 1970–2011

Poverty rates vary considerably along racial and ethnic lines. Over most of this period, the poverty rate for blacks and Hispanics was roughly twice the rate for whites. Both of these minority groups benefited, however, from the strong economic growth of the 1990s, their poverty rates dropping from around 30% at the beginning of the decade to around 25% today. White poverty remained fairly steady over the 1990s, fluctuating between 10% and 11%, but rose above 12% after the 2007–2009 recession.

Source: U.S. Census Bureau, Current Population Reports, P60-243, *Income, Poverty, and Health Insurance in the United States: 2011* (Washington, DC: U.S. Government Printing Office), 2012.

FIGURE 6

Andrew Lichtenstein/Corbis

Table 7 on the next page shows other characteristics that contribute to poverty. Single parent households have 2 to 5 times the poverty rate of married couples. Not surprisingly, working part-time or not working at all leads to higher poverty rates. And, as we saw in Figure 6, black and Hispanic poverty rates are roughly twice that of whites.

Depth of Poverty

It is one thing to say that a certain percentage of the population is poor. It is another to determine just how poor they are. The poverty threshold for a family of four today is over $23,000. If most poor families have incomes approaching this threshold, we could be confident that poverty was just a transitory stage—one phase of the life cycle—and that many people who are poor today would have higher incomes tomorrow.

But if, conversely, many poor families have incomes below $10,000, our view of poverty would be different, and our public policies aimed at reducing poverty would need to be considerably more robust.

To gain a view of the broad spectrum of poverty, economists have developed two *depth of poverty* measures that describe the economic well-being of lower income families. One measure, the **income deficit,** tells us how far below the poverty threshold a family's income lies. In 2011, the income deficit for families living in poverty averaged $9,576. Using the poverty threshold for a family of four, the average income for a family living in poverty was $13,445.

The second measure of poverty, the one we will focus on, is the **ratio of income to poverty.** It compares family income to the poverty threshold and expresses this comparison as a ratio. Thus, the ratio for families with incomes equal to the poverty threshold equals 1.0;

income deficit The difference between the poverty threshold and a family's income.

ratio of income to poverty The ratio of family income to the poverty threshold. Families with ratios below 0.5 are considered severely poor, families with ratios between 0.5 and 1.0 are considered poor, and those families with ratios between 1.0 and 1.25 are considered near poor.

TABLE 7	People and Families in Poverty by Selected Characteristics, 2011

Characteristic	Poverty Rate
Type of Household	
Married-couple households	6.2%
Female households (no husband)	31.2
Male households (no wife)	16.1
Work Experience	
Worked full time, year round	2.8
Worked part-time, year round	16.3
Did not work	32.9
Race	
White	12.8
Black	27.6
Asian	12.3
Hispanic	25.3

Source: U.S. Census Bureau, Current Population Reports, P60-243, *Income, Poverty, and Health Insurance in the United States: 2011* (Washington, DC: U.S. Government Printing Office), 2012.

the ratio for those living at half the threshold income is 0.5. The Census Bureau considers people who live in families with ratios below 0.5 to be "severely or desperately poor." Those with ratios between 0.5 and 1.0 are "poor," and people with ratios above 1.0 but less than 1.25 (less than 25% above the poverty threshold) are considered to be "near poor."

Of the 46 million poor people in 2011, over 20 million of them were desperately poor, and an additional 15 million were categorized as near poor. These measures (income deficit and the ratio of income to poverty) provide us with a more nuanced picture of poverty.

Alternative Measures of Poverty Many researchers have questioned the relevance of the current method for determining poverty thresholds. The National Academy of Sciences studied the official approach to poverty thresholds and concluded that the measure is flawed because "[it]counts taxes as income, [and] is flawed in the adjustments to the households for different family circumstances."[3]

The study further concluded that the current poverty measure does not distinguish well among working parents, workers generally, nonworkers, or people with higher versus lower health care needs and costs. Finally, noting that the current threshold is just the threshold from "1963 updated for price changes," the panel questioned the value of such a simplistic approach, given how much the U.S. standard of living has changed.

Given the Academy's findings, the Census Bureau developed some new ways of measuring poverty. These alternative measures of poverty differ from the old in basing their estimates on after-tax income plus capital gains and counting as income such noncash benefits as food stamps and housing subsidies plus imputed return on home equity (that

---

[3] Citro and Michael, *Measuring Poverty,* pp. 97–98.

is, the savings from owning a home versus paying rent each month).

The Census Bureau derived its new estimates of income thresholds from a survey of expenditures on food, clothing, housing, utilities, and other necessities for the typical family of four (two adults and two kids). These figures were then adjusted to reflect differences in family composition and size, given that children consume less than adults, some household economies are associated with larger families, and the first child in a one-adult family costs more to support than the first child in a two-adult family. Under these measures, poverty rates fell by roughly a quarter.

Causes of Poverty

The reasons why poverty persists are wide-ranging. Traditional causes of poverty include a lack of human capital, mental or physical disabilities, and drug addictions that inhibit persons from achieving gainful employment. Reasons also include an unwillingness to work or an apathy toward work that leads to frequent terminations. Another reason for poverty is that some people refuse to relocate for work, despite having the skills and work ethic to escape poverty. This last reason explains why many communities in rural Appalachian states continue to experience high poverty rates: As industries moved out and jobs disappeared, residents chose to remain, seeking jobs that pay meager wages.

ISSUE

Why Do We Use an Outdated Measure of Poverty?

Why does the United States still define poverty as 3 times the cost of a *1963* low-income food budget adjusted for inflation? You might think that government policymakers could design a measure that reflects a family's well-being by looking at more than just money income based on some old formula a half-century old.

Based on this measure, poverty rates have fluctuated between 10% and 15% over the last four decades. But in that time, antipoverty programs were generously increased to include reduced tax burdens on the poor, as well as the expansion of food stamp and housing programs, the earned income tax credit, and Medicare, Medicaid, and other programs that have undoubtedly helped the poor. But the measure doesn't reflect this success and as a result provides little guidance to solving poverty. As Professor Rebecca Blank at the University of Michigan observes, "In a very fundamental way, our poverty statistics failed us and made it easy to claim that public spending on the poor had little effect."

Why has the Census Bureau failed to update our poverty measure in the same way that employment, unemployment, consumer prices, national income accounts, and many other economic statistics have been improved? The answer is straightforward and surprising. Through a historical accident, the Executive Office of the President is in charge of the measure. The decision rests with the Office of Management and Budget (OMB), and the president must ultimately approve any change. To date, no White House has been willing to approve any change. If a change in measurement results in falling poverty rates, some will claim manipulation. If a change results in higher poverty rates, the administration risks being seen as a failure on this front. Ultimately, we will probably not see improvement until Congress gives the Census Bureau responsibility for the statistic.

Source: Rebecca Blank, "Presidential Address: How to Improve Poverty Measurement in the United States," *Journal of Policy Analysis and Management*, 2008, pp. 233–254.

As economic and social change took place in recent decades, new factors have contributed to the rise in poverty. First, wages generally have not kept up with rising costs; specifically, a single parent working at the minimum wage cannot escape poverty today, when 40 years ago it was possible. Second, technological changes and globalization have changed employment opportunities and led to unemployment in certain industries that forced people into poverty. Third, rising health costs have led some to give up work to care for an ill family member, forgoing earnings. And finally, changes in family structure, particularly an increase in single parenthood, have made it more difficult to avoid a life of poverty. These reasons and others have encouraged policymakers to rethink approaches to eliminating poverty.

Eliminating Poverty

Poverty can be a relative or an absolute measure. As we saw earlier, the official measure of poverty in the United States is based on an absolute number, the poverty threshold. Some researchers, however, think a relative measure would be more useful, such as labeling the bottom 20% of American households as "poor."

ISSUE

What Is Considered "Poor" Around the World?

Every country uses its own definition of what constitutes being poor. In the United States, the official poverty threshold is calculated as an absolute measure. This means a family of four making $23,000 or less in the year 2011 was considered poor. However, a family of four making $23,000 a year in China or India would be considered quite wealthy in their countries. Compared to many developing countries, being poor in America still allows for a relatively comfortable life.

What is considered poor in America, such as living in a small old house in a rural community, might be considered rich elsewhere, such as in undeveloped areas of Africa where residents do not have access to running water and electricity.

Many countries in the European Union, however, use a relative measure of poverty. In Denmark, a family is considered poor if it earns less than 60% of the median income. With the median household income being over $75,000 a year, this means a family earning less than $45,000 a year is considered poor. In addition, Denmark offers full health care coverage to every citizen and free college tuition. Certainly an American family earning $45,000 a year and receiving free health care and college educations for its children would not be considered poor.

The main culprits for the difficulty in defining and comparing poverty rates between countries involve differences in the cost of living, the role of gov-ernment, and overall economic development. In rich countries, the cost of living is higher, governments often provide more services, and citizens have a higher expectation of what is considered necessary for survival. In poor countries, the cost of living is low, governments often cannot provide much assistance, and citizens are merely surviving.

To provide a better comparison of poverty across the world, various organizations have devised methods to compare living standards and poverty rates across countries. The United Nations publishes the *Human Development Index* each year, which provides an overall picture of a country's living standard based on factors such as access to education, running water and sanitation, health care, and communications. However, it does not provide a percentage of the country being poor. The World Bank uses an absolute measure with thresholds ranging from $1.25 a day (extreme poverty) to $2 a day, adjusted to the cost of living, to estimate the number of poor in mostly developing countries. Finally, the Organisation for Economic Cooperation and Development (OECD) publishes comparisons of poverty rates among mostly developed countries based on a fixed percentage of median incomes.

The availability of these statistics allows us to compare poverty rates around the world better. Still, difficulties remain when cultural differences influence what is considered vital for survival in each country.

If we decide to use such a measure, poverty will never be eliminated, no matter how wealthy our country might become. A relative measure obscures the fact that poverty in the United States means something different than it does in the developing world. In the United States, being poor might mean scraping by paycheck to paycheck and having to give up such things as cable television or eating out. In some developing countries, being poor might mean literally starving.

The official U.S. poverty threshold for an individual is an income of roughly $30 a day. In the developing world, by contrast, the World Bank and other agencies define poverty as incomes of less than $2 a day. By World Bank standards, poverty has already been eradicated in the United States.

Reducing Income Inequality Regardless of how poverty is defined, the question of how to reduce it is controversial. The political left views income and wealth redistribution as the chief means of reducing poverty. Social justice, they argue, requires that the government provide an extensive safety net for the poor. In their view, services that the government already provides, including public education, housing subsidies, Medicaid, and unemployment compensation, should be greatly expanded.

They say these policies should be supplemented, moreover, by increasing the progressivity of the tax system. This would reduce the inequalities in wealth and income. By increasing the tax burden on the well-to-do, people of modest incomes could lead more meaningful and just lives. It may also reduce acts of desperation, such as shoplifting and home burglaries, representing an external benefit from reducing poverty.

Increasing Economic Growth The opposite side of the political spectrum argues that such programs, when allowed to become too expansive, can be disastrous. Welfare significantly reduces the incentive to work and produce, thereby reducing the economy's output. A vibrant market economy accommodates the wishes of those who want full-time, upwardly mobile careers as well as those who only want just enough work to pursue other goals.

Because wages provide nearly 70% of all income, those on the political right note that there inevitably will be some inequality in a market system. Some people, after all, make bad choices and fail to invest enough in their education or job skills. Yet, the possibility of failure itself provides an incentive to work hard and invest, and the political right sees this sort of efficiency in the economy as being more important than equity or fairness. The best way to cure poverty, they argue, is by implementing policies that increase the economic pie shared by all, not just by splitting up the pie more evenly.

This political dispute has fueled a controversy in economics. One group of economists argues that economic growth raises low incomes at a rate similar to that of average incomes, such that the poor benefit from growth just as much as anyone else. Other economists reply that the shift toward freer markets around the world, combined with the resulting economic growth, has widened inequalities, causing the poor to fall further behind.

Who is right? Jagdish Bhagwati, a well-known development economist, argued that economic growth creates gainful employment, lifting people out of poverty. Further, economic growth increases government revenue, allowing for greater spending on health and education for the poor. He argues that

in economic terms, growth [is] an instrument, not a target—the means by which the true targets, like poverty reduction and the social advancement of the masses, would be achieved.

He adds a caveat, however, that

the political sustainability of the growth-first model requires both symbolic and material efforts. While growth does benefit the poor, the rich often benefit disproportionately. So to keep the poor committed to the system as their economic aspirations are aroused, the wealthy would be well advised to indulge less in conspicuous consumption.[4]

In sum, Bhagwati states that economic growth raises all incomes in absolute terms, including the poor, which reduces poverty. However, relative incomes may continue to suffer, as income inequality can widen with economic growth.

Rawls and Nozick Unfortunately, there is no unified theory of income distribution that takes the various issues we have discussed into account. Earlier chapters suggested that income depends on productivity—in competitive markets, each input (factor) is paid the value of its marginal product.

Human capital analysis adds that as people invest in themselves, their productivity and income rise. Analysis of imperfect input markets, however, shows that income distribution advantages accrue more to those with market power.

Our analysis of economic discrimination suggested several more reasons why incomes may be skewed in favor of some groups rather than others. The bargaining strength of labor unions is yet another factor that can skew income distribution, in this case in favor of union members.

---

[4] Jagdish Bhagwati, "Does Redistributing Income Reduce Poverty?" Project Syndicate, October 27, 2011.

These analyses have focused, in one way or another, on whether certain patterns of income distribution are economically efficient. Yet, how do we know whether various income distributions are equitable or fair? Is there anywhere to turn for theoretical help in addressing this question? The answer is a qualified "yes." Two philosophers, John Rawls and Robert Nozick, published competing views on this subject in the early 1970s.[5]

John Rawls proposed the "maximin principle," in which he argued that society should maximize the welfare of the least well-off individual. He asks us to conduct a thought experiment: Assume that you must decide on the income distribution for your society, without knowing where in the distribution you will end up. Because chance could lead to you being the least well-off individual in the society, Rawls suggests people would favor significant income redistribution under these circumstances.

Robert Nozick argued that it is "illegitimate to use the coercive power of the state to make some better off at the expense of others." To Nozick, justice requires protecting property rights "legitimately acquired or legitimately transferred."[6] Using Nozick's argument, a small group of friends in Finland who developed a game called *Angry Birds* that became a worldwide addiction, and subsequently became wealthy because millions willingly bought premium game subscriptions, cannot be considered unjust. Instead, Nozick would argue it would be unjust if the creators were not rewarded for their innovation that has provided countless hours of fun for so many people.

This debate highlights the perennial tradeoff in economic policy between equity and efficiency, a tradeoff that serves as a bone of contention in nearly every discussion of economic and public policy. Although microeconomics is sometimes beset by controversy, at its best it provides us with a dispassionate framework for analyzing and discussing many issues.

Mobility: Are Poor Families Poor Forever? The poverty rates and income distribution data provide a snapshot in time. How about over time? What is the human side to this? Do people start in poverty or fall into poverty and then stay there, or is there movement out of poverty?

A study by the U.S. Census Bureau tracking over 43,000 American households from 2004 to 2006 provides an answer. The study found that of the households that were living in poverty at the start of 2004, 42% were no longer living in poverty by the end of 2006.[7] Of these households, about half were living just above the poverty line, while the other half did much better and were earning incomes well above the poverty line. The results indicate that mobility between income groups is possible, and that not all who are in poverty stay there forever.

However, additional data from the Census Bureau tells the other side of the story. Although millions of households pull themselves out of poverty each year, millions more find themselves falling into poverty. During the last economic recession and the slow economic recovery that followed, millions of households fell into poverty for the first time, causing the poverty rate to rise above 15% in 2010. The fortunate news is that many of these households will remain in poverty only temporarily as new jobs are created with continued economic growth.

The movements of households in and out of poverty mirror the findings of the University of Michigan's Panel Study of Income Dynamics, which has followed 18,000 individuals since 1968. It shows how fluid the income distribution really is. Data from this

---

[5] John Rawls, *A Theory of Justice* (Oxford: Clarendon), 1972; Robert Nozick, *Anarchy, State and Utopia* (Oxford: Blackwell), 1974.

[6] John Kay, *The Truth about Markets: Their Genius, Their Limits, Their Follies* (London: Penguin Books), 2003, p. 187.

[7] U.S. Census Bureau, Current Population Reports, P70-123, *Dynamics of Economic Well-Being: Poverty, 2004–2006* (Washington, DC: U.S. Government Printing Office), 2011.

study show that within a 10-year period, over half of individuals in the poorest income quintile moved up the income distribution ladder. Surprisingly, the same pattern of mobility appears in the richest quintile: Roughly half were replaced by households from other quintiles. Overall, only one-third to one-half of all households remained in the original quintile after a decade.

Chris Tilly, director of UCLA's Institute for Research on Labor and Employment, states that "poverty is dynamic; not everybody stays in poverty long term. We've always known that people move in and out of poverty, [but] there are people who tend to get stuck."[8] Households that remain in poverty over time, although a relatively small percentage of the population, are the most worrisome. Research by Richard B. Freeman of Harvard tells us that there is a core of poor people who stay poor. This core has physical disabilities, suffers from substance abuse, or is unable to work for a host of other reasons.

These findings suggest that poverty will never be totally eradicated. They also suggest that policies to deal with core poverty should be different from policies that deal with people who start or who have fallen into poverty but are highly likely to escape.

 CHECKPOINT

POVERTY

- Poverty thresholds were developed in the 1960s based on a food budget, adjusted for family size, then multiplied by 3.
- Economic growth has been a major force in reducing poverty in the United States.
- The income deficit measures how far below the poverty threshold a family's income lies.
- The other depth of poverty measure is the ratio of income to poverty. If the ratio is below 0.5, the family is considered "severely or desperately poor." A ratio greater than 1.0 but less than 1.25 indicates the family is "near poor."
- The Census Bureau has introduced new measures of poverty that consider health care costs, transportation needs, and child care costs.
- The controversy surrounding reducing poverty centers on whether reducing income inequality or increasing economic growth is the best approach.
- Philosopher John Rawls proposed a "maximin principle" that suggests society should maximize the welfare of the least well-off individual.
- Robert Nozick argued that the state should not use its coercive power to make some people better off at the expense of others.
- Income mobility is quite robust in the United States, with more than half of all families moving up and down the income distribution ladder in any decade.

QUESTIONS: Return to the suggestion by economist Charles Murray that the United States should eliminate all social insurance, including Social Security, Medicare, Medicaid, and other welfare programs, and instead give $10,000 each year to each citizen over 21 years of age. Again, expand his idea by eliminating the age restriction. Would this eliminate poverty in America? Would this satisfy those on the left who wish to reduce inequality in income distribution? What do you think would be the response to such an idea by those on the political right?

Answers to the Checkpoint questions can be found at the end of this chapter.

---

[8] Ari Bloomekatz, "Poverty Often a Temporary State, U.S. Census Study Finds," *The Los Angeles Times*, March 28, 2011.

chapter summary

Section 1: **The Distribution of Income and Wealth**

Income: A flow of funds by individuals or households over time.

Wealth: A stock of assets less liabilities at a given point in time.

A household can have considerable wealth without much income, such as this retired couple who saved over their working careers.

Types of Income Distribution

Functional distribution of income: the distribution of inputs (factors) of production. Wages constitute nearly 70% of income using this approach.

Personal or family distribution of income: the percentage of income flowing to specific segments of the population. Quintiles (20% of the population) are used by the U.S. Census Bureau to measure income distribution.

Income inequality is measured either by constructing a Lorenz curve or by calculating a Gini coefficient for a specific population.

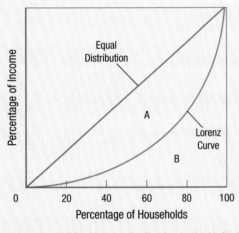

Lorenz curve: shows the cumulative income earned by each segment of the population. The farther the curve is from the 45 degree line, the more unequal the distribution of income.

Gini coefficient: is measured as the ratio between A (area of income inequity) and $A + B$ (total area below equal distribution line). The larger the Gini coefficient, the more unequal the distribution of income.

Since the 1970s, income distribution in the United States has become more unequal. Causes include:

- Differing educational levels
- Economic discrimination
- Market power
- Increase in the number of two-earner households

Redistribution policies are designed to reduce income inequality. Three common policies are:

1. Progressive taxation: higher tax rates as income increases
2. In-kind transfers: unemployment benefits, welfare, Pell Grants (for college)
3. Noncash benefits: Subsidized or public housing, Medicaid, food stamps

Section 2: **Poverty**

Poverty is defined differently by each country and by organizations such as the World Bank.

The poverty rate according to the U.S. Census Bureau is the percentage of persons with income below the poverty rate threshold. This includes all money income (before taxes are deducted) and cash benefits and excludes capital gains and noncash benefits.

The poverty rate in the United States dropped in the 1960s and 1970s, and has stabilized since, with minor drops during economic expansion and minor rises during recessions.

New Method of Measuring Poverty

- includes after-tax money income
- includes noncash benefits (such as food stamps and housing subsidies)
- deducts work-related expenditures (such as transportation and child care) and out-of-pocket medical expenditures

Stuart Key/Dreamstime.com

Rawls: Rawlsian theory states that a society's well-being is only as good as its least fortunate citizen. Therefore, to reduce poverty it advocates for the least amount of income inequality.

Nozick: This theory is based on the argument that property rights (including income) must be protected to provide incentives for growth, which will reduce poverty.

Hongqi Zhang (aka Michael Zhang)/ Dreamstime.com

The depth (or severity) of poverty can be measured using one of two approaches:

Income deficit: How far (in dollars) below the poverty threshold.

Ratio of income to poverty: Measured as the ratio of income compared to the poverty threshold.

0.00–0.50: severely poor (about 6% of Americans)

0.51–1.00: poor

1.01–1.25: near poor

Two Solutions to Reduce Poverty

1. Expand welfare and redistribution programs, and make taxes more progressive.

2. Increase incentives to promote economic growth, which benefits all people, including the poor.

Joel Stettenheim/CORBIS

Considerable movement occurs between income groups (quintiles). About half of all households in a quintile move to a different quintile each decade.

income, p. 390
wealth, p. 390
functional distribution of income,
  p. 390

personal or family distribution of
  income, p. 391
Lorenz curves, p. 392
Gini coefficient, p. 393

poverty thresholds, p. 399
income deficit, p. 401
ratio of income to poverty, p. 401

QUESTIONS AND PROBLEMS

Check Your Understanding

1. If you look at income distribution over the life cycle of a family, would it be more equally distributed than for one specific year?

2. List some of the reasons why household incomes differ.

3. How does the Gini coefficient differ from the Lorenz curve?

4. Currently the poverty threshold for a family of four is just over $23,000 a year. What does this amount take into account and not take into account?

5. Are the poor in year 2014 just as poor as the poor in 1954? What has changed in 60 years to make poverty different today?

6. What are the primary factors that lead to poverty?

Apply the Concepts

7. Is there an efficiency-equity tradeoff when income is redistributed from the rich to the poor? Explain.

8. What do you think has been the impact on the distribution of income in the United States from the combined impact of the large number of unskilled illegal immigrants and the growing number of dual-earner households?

9. It is probably fair to say that when we classify people as rich or poor at any given moment in time, we are simply describing similar people at different stages in life. Does this life cycle of income and wealth make the income distribution concerns a little less relevant? Why or why not?

10. What would be the change in the distribution of income (Gini coefficient) if the United States decided to permit 10 million new immigrants into the United States who were highly skilled doctors, engineers, executives of large foreign firms, and wealthy foreigners who just want to migrate to the United States? How would the Gini coefficient change if, instead, the United States decided to permit 10 million unskilled foreign workers to enter?

11. Roughly half of all marriages in the United States end in divorce. What is the impact of this divorce rate on the distribution of income and poverty?

12. Poverty rates have declined for blacks and have been relatively stable for everyone else over the last 40 years. But the poverty rate still hovers around 15%. What makes it so difficult to reduce poverty below 10% to 15% of the population?

In the News

13. In 2006, the Nobel Peace Prize went to economist Muhammad Yunus and the Grameen Bank "for their efforts to create economic and social development from below." Yunus led the development of micro loans to poor people without financial security: loans of under $200 to people so poor they could not provide collateral, to use for purchasing basic tools or other basic implements of work. This helped to pull millions of people out of poverty. Discuss how economic prosperity and security for everyone can result in a more peaceful planet.

14. According to the U.S. Department of the Treasury, people in the top income quintile (20%) pay roughly 70% of all federal income taxes, with the remaining 80% paying less than 30%. Further, the bottom half of the population pays less than 10% of all taxes. Many politicians often assert that they want to bring tax relief (presumably with the idea of redistributing income) to "middle- and lower-income" families. Given this distribution of income tax payments, what would middle- and lower-income tax relief look like?

Solving Problems

15. Use the two different distributions of income in the table below to answer the questions that follow.

Quintile	A	B
Poorest	11.2	10.5
Second	12.0	11.6
Middle	21.2	20.3
Fourth	26.0	25.7
Richest	29.6	31.9

a. Use the grid below and graph the two Lorenz curves.

b. Which curve has a more equal distribution?

c. Are these distributions more or less equal than that for the United States today?

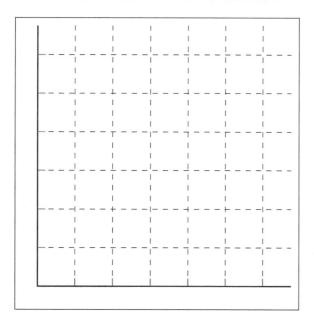

16. The following households each have four persons. Their annual incomes are as follows:

The Aikens:	$25,600
The Browns:	$21,800
The Carlyles:	$18,500
The Donaldsons:	$11,300

Assume that the poverty threshold for a household of four is $23,000. Calculate the income deficit and the income-to-poverty ratio for each family. Classify each family as either not poor, near poor, poor, or severely poor.

USING THE NUMBERS

17. According to By the Numbers, over what period of time did the gap between the full-time minimum wage earnings and the poverty threshold expand the most?

18. According to By the Numbers, about how many Americans used food stamps (now known as SNAP benefits) in the year 2000? How about in the year 2012? (Hint: Use the approximate U.S. population of 300 million to calculate the answers for both years.)

ANSWERS TO QUESTIONS IN CHECKPOINTS

Checkpoint: The Distribution of Income and Wealth

It would clearly improve (make more equal) the before-tax and benefits distribution of income. The impact on the distribution of income after adjusting for current benefits of such a policy would depend on the explicit value of current benefits. Murray suggested that his proposal would cost more for a decade and then begin saving money.

Checkpoint: Poverty

Based on the poverty thresholds, poverty would almost be eliminated by this proposal. In general, the political left would welcome this redistribution except for the elimination of the social safety net. Some people would make bad decisions and not save for retirement or purchase health care coverage, and the political left would still want these services to exist, defeating the idea of the proposal. The political right would worry that once the redistribution scheme is introduced, enough people would reduce their working hours to harm economic growth. Further, the political right would worry that after the redistribution, the safety net would creep back into existence, eroding the benefits of the original idea.

Introduction to Macroeconomics

16

Thousands of people lined up near Times Square in New York City early in the morning on April 30, 2010 . . . not for an audition, not for tickets to a popular concert, not to catch a glimpse of the newest fashion designs, but instead for a job. And not a high-paying job even. These people were seeking a service job at a new hotel that was opening later that summer. Among the over 2,500 applicants, only 300 were hired in a job market that reached the most desperate of conditions in many decades. This was not the Great Depression of the 1930s, but rather the aftermath of the most recent economic downturn of 2007–2009, dubbed the Great Recession.

Although the recession of 2007–2009 was the worst economic downturn in the United States in generations, recessions are not anything new. Over the last 150 years, the U.S. economy has endured more than thirty-three recessions—on average one every four to five years. What made the most recent recession particularly difficult for so many people was its significant impact on employment.

At the height of the recession, one in ten Americans was unemployed. Even more troubling was that as the economy began to recover in the summer of 2009, the unemployment rate did not fall by much. In fact, two years after the end of the recession, the unemployment rate still hovered above 9%; in 2013, four years later, the unemployment rate still exceeded 7%. When an economic recovery produces too few jobs to reduce the unemployment rate significantly, it is known as a *jobless recovery*.

This jobless recovery had macroeconomists stumped. That was not supposed to happen. Macroeconomics, as a discipline separate from microeconomics, was born out of the need to explain the Great Depression. John Maynard Keynes explained the causes and set forth a framework upon which to develop policies to avoid future severe macroeconomic downturns.

Unemployment was supposed to improve in a recovery. From the 1940s to the 1980s, the recovery from every recession coincided with a sharp increase in job growth and a reduction in the unemployment rate. That changed in the past two decades. The recessions of 1990–1991 and 2001 raised doubts about the resiliency of job growth following a recession. These recent recessions introduced the persistent unemployment associated with jobless recoveries. The recession of 2007–2009 was deeper and had even greater persistent unemployment.

Why did the unemployment rate stay high for so long after the recovery? The answer lies in the many factors affecting labor, capital, product, and financial markets that came together to make the unemployment rate worse during the recession and persistent during the recovery. Furthermore, structural changes in the macroeconomy contributed to the jobless recoveries after the last three recessions.

In the labor market, the collapse of the housing market in 2006 drove construction workers, real estate agents, and mortgage brokers out of work. Those who lost their jobs looked for employment in different industries. But those industries faced difficulties too. The ripple effect of the housing collapse quickly affected financial markets, which then affected capital and product markets, causing unemployment to spread.

In the financial market, when unprecedented numbers of people defaulted on their mortgages, banking institutions faced a crisis. These institutions restricted their lending practices, making it difficult for individuals and firms to borrow money to buy homes and build businesses that would generate jobs. The caution of the banking industry along with new government regulations made the borrowing process more cumbersome.

Businesses create jobs when they predict it will be profitable to do so. They depend on the sales of products and services. However, sales fell as people lost their jobs or faced wage cuts. People in general became pessimistic—even scared—and cut back on their consumption even after the recession ended. Because consumption by individuals represents the largest portion of all spending in the economy, the lack of consumer confidence spilled over to businesses, which in turn became reluctant to hire.

Lastly, high unemployment, lower consumption, and reduced investment by businesses led to decreased income, sales, and property tax revenues for the government. This reduction in tax revenues, coupled with increased government spending, led to large deficits. State and local governments felt the greatest brunt of the deficits, forced to make tough budget cuts that led to massive layoffs in public sector jobs including teaching, law enforcement, and firefighting.

BY THE NUMBERS

The Slow Macroeconomic Recovery

The 2007–2009 recession was the most severe economic downturn to face the United States in over 70 years. Although this recession officially lasted only 18 months, after 48 months of recovery the economy still had not returned to the level of employment and growth seen prior to the recession.

Savings rates have steadily fallen over the last three decades. However, high unemployment and income anxiety, especially during economic downturns, led consumers to tighten their belts and increase savings.

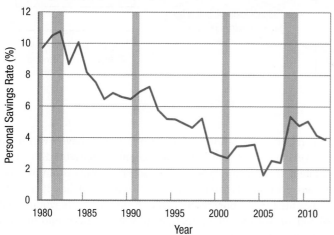

$16,420,300,000,000

United States gross domestic product (GDP) in 2012.

$69,970,000,000,000

Gross world product
(sum of GDP from every country in the world) in 2012.

Housing prices rose quickly from 2001 to 2006, then fell dramatically from 2006 to 2010. Prices stabilized in 2010 and have begun to rebound since.

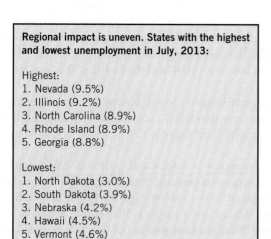

Regional impact is uneven. States with the highest and lowest unemployment in July, 2013:

Highest:
1. Nevada (9.5%)
2. Illinois (9.2%)
3. North Carolina (8.9%)
4. Rhode Island (8.9%)
5. Georgia (8.8%)

Lowest:
1. North Dakota (3.0%)
2. South Dakota (3.9%)
3. Nebraska (4.2%)
4. Hawaii (4.5%)
5. Vermont (4.6%)

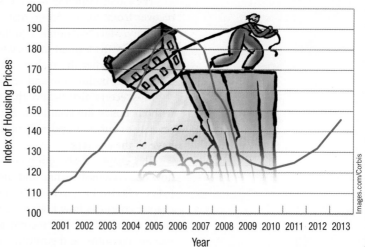

The reasons described thus far explain much of—but not the entire—story of jobless recoveries. Additional changes in the macroeconomy over the past two decades contributed to slower job growth. First, the world became much more connected. Recessions tend to spread from one country to another. Competition for jobs intensified due to greater immigration and more companies seeking lower costs by moving production facilities overseas. Second, population growth means more jobs were needed for a country just to stay at its same employment level. Third, pressures to earn profits in a competitive global economy forced businesses to find more efficient means of production, including the use of automation, leading to some job loss as workers are replaced by machines.

It is hard to imagine that such a difficult economic downturn and slow recovery could occur. The Internet boom of the late 1990s and the housing boom of the early 2000s led to low unemployment, rising incomes, and reductions in government deficits. Yet, such ups and downs of the economy are precisely what macroeconomics aims to study.

Macroeconomics describes how individuals, businesses, financial institutions, and government institutions interact to achieve the goals of job growth, low inflation, and economic growth. It is not just the conditions of one industry or group of workers that influence macroeconomic outcomes, but rather the conditions of all. Figure 1 illustrates how different markets and institutions come together to influence macroeconomic outcomes such as the unemployment rate.

FIGURE 1

Markets and Institutions in the Macroeconomy

Labor, capital, and product markets, along with financial and government institutions, come together to influence macroeconomic outcomes such as the unemployment rate.

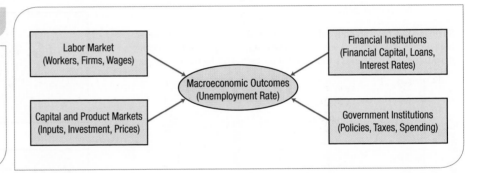

We have come a long way in our understanding of recessions, but we have a way to go yet. These jobless recoveries reveal that much about the macroeconomy remains difficult to understand. Market forces of demand and supply generally lead prices and output to equilibrium. One hundred years ago, economists thought the same to be true when it came to the overall economy. It was assumed that labor, capital, and product markets would keep the economy near full employment, with small fluctuations in wages, prices, and interest rates helping the economy adjust to disruptions.

The Great Depression, a recession that lasted four years and took nearly a decade to recover from, forced economists to reconsider this earlier way of looking at the macroeconomy. Macroeconomic equilibrium occurs over time through the course of the natural ups and downs termed the *business cycle*. The development of macroeconomics as a discipline came after the realization of such business cycles and the fact that they can vary significantly in duration and severity.

Most economists believe that the macroeconomy is too complex to function efficiently without policy interventions. Economists have developed many tools for managing the severity of business cycles. Persistent unemployment suggests that economists still do not have all the answers.

This chapter deals with how the macroeconomy is defined and measured. For example, how do economists define and measure business fluctuations? And what are the major statistics collected by government to keep track of the macroeconomy? The first section of this chapter considers how business cycles are defined and measured. The second section looks at the system of national income accounts. These accounts give us our primary measures of income, consumer and government spending, business investment, and foreign transactions, including exports and imports. The last section raises the question of how well the national income accounts measure our standard of living. We look at alternative measures of standard of living, nonmarket transactions, and the effect of environmental degradation and conservation. The foundation established in this chapter will apply to topics covered throughout the course.

Business Cycles

Macroeconomics is concerned with **business cycles,** those short-run fluctuations in the macroeconomy known also as booms and busts. Business cycles are a common feature of industrialized economies, and are important to study because they emphasize the idea that markets are intertwined with one another. What happens in one market is not usually independent from other markets, as we saw with the persistent unemployment during the recession of 2007–2009.

business cycles Alternating increases and decreases in economic activity that are typically punctuated by periods of recession and recovery.

Defining Business Cycles

Business cycles are defined as alternating increases and decreases in economic activity. As economists Arthur Burns and Wesley Mitchell wrote,

> Business cycles are a type of fluctuation found in the aggregate economic activity of nations that organize their work mainly in business enterprises: a cycle consists of expansions occurring at about the same time in many economic activities, followed by similarly general recession, contractions and revivals which merge into the expansion phase of the next cycle.[1]

Figure 2 shows the four phases of the business cycle. These phases, around an upward trend, include the peak (sometimes called a boom), followed by a recession (often referred to as a downturn or contraction), leading to the trough or bottom of the cycle, finally followed by a recovery or an expansion to another peak.

A peak in the business cycle usually means that the economy is operating at its capacity. Peaks are followed by downturns or recessions. This change can happen simply because the boom runs out of steam and business investment begins to decline, thereby throwing the economy into a tailspin.

Once a recession is under way, businesses react by curtailing hiring and perhaps even laying off workers, thus adding to the recession's depth. Eventually, however, a trough is reached, and economic activity begins to pick up as businesses and consumers become

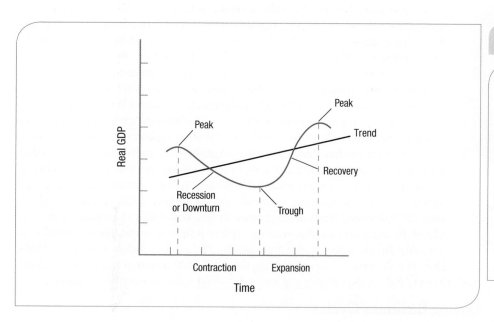

FIGURE 2

Typical Business Cycle

The four phases of the business cycle are the peak or boom, followed by a recession (often called a downturn or contraction), leading to the trough or bottom of the cycle, followed by a recovery or an expansion leading to another peak. Note that although this diagram suggests business cycles have regular movements, in reality the various phases of the cycle vary widely in duration and intensity.

---

[1] Arthur Burns and Wesley Mitchell, *Measuring Business Cycles* (New York: National Bureau of Economic Research), 1946, p. 3.

more enthusiastic about the economy. Often, the federal government or the Federal Reserve Bank institutes fiscal or monetary policies to help reverse the recession. We will look at government actions in future chapters.

Figure 2 suggests that business cycles are fairly regular, but in fact the various phases of the cycle can vary dramatically in duration and intensity. As Table 1 shows, the recessions of the last half-century have lasted anywhere from 6 months to 18 months. Expansions or recoveries have varied even more, lasting from 1 year to as many as 10 years. Some recessions, moreover, have been truly intense, bringing about major declines in income, while others have been little more than potholes in the road, causing no declines in real income.

TABLE 1	Selected Data for U.S. Business Cycles Since 1950						
Years	Peak	Trough	Recession Length (months)	Expansion Length (months)	Percentage Change in Real GDP	Maximum Unemployment Rate (%)
1953–1954	July 1953	May 1954	10	39	−2.2	5.9
1957–1958	Aug. 1957	April 1958	8	24	−3.6	7.4
1960–1961	April 1960	Feb. 1961	10	106	−0.6	7.1
1969–1970	Dec. 1969	Nov. 1970	11	36	+0.2	6.1
1973–1975	Nov. 1973	March 1975	16	58	−1.8	9.0
1980	Jan. 1980	July 1980	6	12	−2.3	7.8
1981–1982	July 1981	Nov. 1982	16	92	−2.2	10.8
1990–1991	July 1990	March 1991	8	120	−1.0	6.9
2001	March 2001	Nov. 2001	8	73	+0.5	5.8
2007–2009	Dec. 2007	June 2009	18	—	−4.1	10.0

Business cycles resemble roller coasters—some are higher, faster, or longer than others, but all are similar in terms of the up-and-down nature of the ride.

A good metaphor for the wide variation in business cycles is a roller coaster. Some roller coasters rise higher than others, fall faster than others, or climb slower than others. Some roller coasters have one large dip followed by a series of smaller ups and downs, while others may have a large dip followed by another large dip. This is true with business cycles—some business cycles are higher, faster, or longer than others, but all have the same four phases described earlier. An important difference between a business cycle and a roller coaster, however, is that a roller coaster typically ends at the same level as it starts, while business cycles tend to have an upward long-run trend in most countries, indicating a growing economy over time.

Unemployment has shown a similar variability: The more severe the recession, the higher the unemployment rate goes. In the recessions of 1990–1991 and 2001, the economy as a whole showed remarkable resiliency, but the recoveries were termed *jobless recoveries* because the economic growth following the recessions did not coincide with strong levels of job growth. In fact, sometimes an economy's recovery falls short and enters another recession before it fully recovers; this is referred to as a **double-dip recession.** The last double-dip recession occurred in the early 1980s. However, the slow recovery following the 2007–2009 recession caused many economists to worry that another double-dip recession would occur. Fortunately, it did not.

Dating Business Cycles

double-dip recession A recession that begins after only a short period of economic recovery from the previous recession.

Business cycles are officially dated by the National Bureau of Economic Research (NBER), a nonprofit research organization founded in 1920. The NBER assigns a committee of economists the task of dating "turning points"—times at which the economy switches from peak to downturn or from trough to recovery. The committee looks for clusters of aggregate data pointing either up or down. Committee members date turning points when they reach a consensus that the economy has switched directions.

The committee's work has met with some criticism because the decisions rest on the consensus of six eminent economists, who often bring different methodologies to the table. The committee's deliberations, moreover, are not public; the committee announces only its final decision. Finally, the NBER dates peaks and troughs only after the fact: Their decisions appear several months after the turning points have been reached.[2] By waiting, the panel can use updated or revised data to avoid premature judgments. But some argue that the long lag renders the NBER's decisions less useful to policymakers.

Nonetheless, the work of the NBER in dating the turning points is important for investors and businesses alike, as they help form expectations of how the economy might perform based on the phase of the business cycle it has reached. Businesses are more likely to invest during a time of expansion, and they don't want to be investing in greater production capacity at a time of recession when sales might fall.

Alternative Measures of the Business Cycle

Because the NBER focuses on historical data to date phases of the business cycle *after* they occur, economists have developed tools to analyze trends in an effort to predict phases of the business cycle *before* they occur. The following are three examples of methods used to predict business cycle movements.

National Activity Index The National Activity Index, developed by the Federal Reserve Bank of Chicago, is a weighted average of 85 indicators of national economic activity. These indicators are drawn from a huge swath of economic activity including production, income, employment, unemployment, hours worked, personal consumption, housing, sales, orders, and inventories.

Figure 3 shows the index since 1985. When the index has a zero value, the economy is growing at its historical trend rate of growth. Negative values mean that the

The Federal Reserve Bank of Chicago's National Activity Index

The National Activity Index is a weighted average of 85 indicators of economic activity in the economy. When the index moves below −0.70 (dashed line), the economy is probably moving into a recession. This index appears to track the official NBER peak turning points.

FIGURE 3

---

[2] Marcelle Chauvet and Jeremy Piger, "Identifying Business Cycle Turning Points in Real Time," *Review* (St. Louis: The Federal Reserve Bank of St. Louis), March/April 2003, pp. 47–61.

economy is growing slower and positive rates imply it's growing faster than its long-term trend. When the index moves below −0.70 following a period of expansion, this suggests a high likelihood that the economy has moved into recession. The index has done a remarkable job in pinpointing the signs of recession in a reasonably current time frame.

Leading Economic Index The Leading Economic Index (or LEI) established by The Conference Board, an independent business and research association, is another index that economists look to when predicting movements in the business cycle. The LEI uses ten important leading indicators to produce a weighted index. Because each indicator is a predictor of how the economy should perform in the near future, any change in the LEI index today is supposed to reflect how the economy will change tomorrow.

Indicators in the LEI Index
Average weekly hours, manufacturing
Average weekly initial claims for unemployment insurance
Manufacturers' new orders, consumer goods and materials
Index of supplier deliveries—vendor performance
Manufacturers' new orders, nondefense capital goods
Building permits, new private housing units
Stock prices, 500 common stocks
Money supply, M2
Interest rate spread, 10-year Treasury bonds less federal funds
Index of consumer expectations

The LEI predicts a recession whenever the index falls for three months in a row (compared to the same month the previous year). In fact, it has successfully predicted the last seven recessions since 1969, although critics point to the fact that it has also provided some false warnings of recessions (a funny adage shared among economists is that forecasters have predicted ten of the last seven recessions).

Yield Curve Perhaps the simplest, and surprisingly accurate, predictor of changes in the business cycle is the yield curve. A **yield curve** shows the interest rates for bonds (shown on the vertical axis) with different maturity rates (shown on the horizontal axis). For example, it would show the difference in interest rates between a 3-month Treasury bill and a 30-year Treasury bond (a "bill" is a type of bond with a maturity of less than one year).

One approach economists have used to predict recessions, shown in Figure 4, is to take the interest rate of a long-term 10-year bond and subtract the interest rate on a short-term 3-month bill. Whenever this value turns negative (in other words, interest

yield curve Shows the relationship between the interest rate earned on a bond (measured on the vertical axis) and the length of time until the bond's maturity date (shown on the horizontal axis).

FIGURE 4

Treasury Spread

The 10-year bond rate minus 3-month bill rate (monthly average). Shaded bars indicate recessions. In all but one recession since 1960, the difference in rates turned negative prior to the recession.

Source: New York Federal Reserve: http://www.newyorkfed.org/research/capital_markets/Prob_Rec.pdf.

ISSUE

The End of the Recession... It Does Not Feel Like It

According to the National Bureau of Economic Research, the most recent U.S. recession officially ended in June 2009. But ask most people (besides economists) at the time or even a year later whether they thought the recession was over and you would have likely been laughed at. Indeed, in June 2009, the economy was not in good shape: The unemployment rate was 9.5%, GDP was over 4% below its peak, and the stock market was nearly 40% below its high two years prior. Why would such dismal economic conditions signal the end of the recession?

Part of the explanation is how economists date the business cycle. The NBER looks at "turning points" when the economy goes from a peak to a downturn or from a trough to a recovery. A recession officially ends when the economy is at the trough, which occurs when the economy is at its worst (or near worst) condition. In fact, the NBER generally waits until evidence of two quarters of GDP growth is found before declaring the recession over. Therefore, some recovery may already have occurred when a recession ends.

Looking at the lives of everyday people, the beginning of a recovery is sometimes a more difficult time to live through than the recession itself. This brings about the other part of the explanation—how economists define each phase of the business cycle. A recession describes a decrease in the growth of the economy from its peak, while a recovery describes an increase in the growth of the economy from its trough. Therefore, although a recession may have officially begun, life is still good (for the time being), and people subsequently believe that the economy is still strong. Contrast this with the start of a recovery, in which life is dismal (for the time being) and people subsequently believe the economy is still in recession. The following tables provide a comparison.

To many people, life at the start of a recession was much better than life at the start of the recovery. In fact, the most recent recession had such a slow recovery period that even after two years from the official end of the recession, the unemployment rate stood at 9.1%, much higher than the 6.2% unemployment rate during the middle of the recession in 2008.

In sum, how economists date recessions and recoveries is based largely on

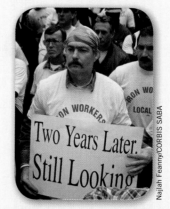

To these unemployed workers, the recession did not seem to have ended in 2009.

the turning points of the business cycle, which as shown may not always reflect what everyday people experience.

Start of Recession (December 2007)	Start of Recovery (June 2009)
Unemployment Rate = 5.0%	Unemployment Rate = 9.5%
GDP (2005 dollars) = $13.4 trillion	GDP (2005 dollars) = $12.8 trillion
Stock Market (Dow) = 13,500	Stock Market (Dow) = 8,800

Middle of Recession (September 2008)	Two Years of Recovery (June 2011)
Unemployment Rate = 6.2%	Unemployment Rate = 9.1%
GDP (2005 dollars) = $13.2 trillion	GDP (2005 dollars) = $13.4 trillion
Stock Market (Dow) = 11,200	Stock Market (Dow) = 12,000

rates on short-term bills exceed those on long-term bonds), a recession is likely to occur. Why? When investors believe an economic slowdown may occur, they buy long-term bonds to lock in interest rates, pushing interest rates on long-term bonds lower. This has been true for seven of the last eight recessions. However, some economists remain skeptical, pointing to several false warnings that the yield curve has given which did not result in actual recessions.

Each of the three indices is one of the many methods economists use to predict the movements of the business cycle. Although a perfect predictor of booms and busts is not possible, many people follow these indices because of the importance of the business cycle in the macroeconomy.

The duration and intensity of business cycles are measured using data collected by the Bureau of Economic Analysis and U.S. Department of Labor. These data for aggregate income and output come from the national income and product accounts. We turn in a moment to see how these data are collected and analyzed and consider how well they measure our standard of living. Keep in mind that these data are the key ingredients economists use to determine the state of the macroeconomy.

 CHECKPOINT

BUSINESS CYCLES

- Business cycles are alternating increases and decreases in economic activity.
- The four phases of the business cycle include the peak, recession (or contraction), trough, and recovery (or expansion).
- Business cycles vary in intensity, duration, and speed.
- Business cycles are dated by the National Bureau of Economic Research (NBER). Business cycles are usually dated some time after the trough and peak have been reached.
- Economists have developed different methods to predict movements in the business cycle, including the National Activity Index, the Leading Economic Index, and the yield curve method.

QUESTION: Do you think that the business cycle has a bigger impact on automobile and capital goods manufacturers or on grocery stores?

Answers to the Checkpoint question can be found at the end of this chapter.

National Income Accounting

The national income and product accounts (NIPA) let economists judge our nation's economic performance, compare American income and output to that of other nations, and track the economy's condition over the course of the business cycle. Many economists would say that these accounts represent one of the greatest inventions of the 20th century.[3]

Before World War I, estimating the output of various sectors of the economy—and to some extent the output of the economy as a whole—was a task left to individual scholars. Government agencies tried to measure various sorts of economic activity, but little came of these efforts. When the Great Depression struck, the lack of reliable economic data made it difficult for the administration and Congress to design timely and appropriate policy responses. Much of the information that was available at the time was anecdotal: newspaper reports of plant shutdowns, stories of home and farm foreclosures, and observations of the rapid meltdown of the stock market.

In 1933, Congress directed the Department of Commerce (DOC) to develop estimates of "total national income for the United States for each of the calendar years 1929, 1930, and 1931, including estimates of the portions of national income originating from [different sectors] and estimates of the distribution of the national income in the form of wages, rents, royalties, dividends, profits and other types of payments." This directive was the beginning of the NIPA.

In 1934, a small group of economists working under the leadership of Simon Kuznets and in collaboration with the NBER produced a report for the Senate. The report defined many standard economic aggregates still in use today, including gross national product, gross domestic product, consumer spending, and investment spending. Kuznets was later awarded a Nobel Prize for his lifetime of work in this area.

---

[3] William Nordhaus and Edward Kokkelenberg (eds.), *Nature's Numbers: Expanding the National Economic Accounts to Include the Environment* (Washington, DC: National Academy Press), 1999, p. 12.

Work continued on the NIPA through World War II, and by 1947 the basic components of the present day income and product accounts were in place. Over the years, the DOC has modified, improved, and updated the data it collects. These data are released on a quarterly basis, with preliminary data being put out in the middle of the month following a given quarter. By the end of a given quarter, the DOC will have collected about two-thirds of the survey data it needs, allowing it to estimate the remaining data to generate preliminary figures.

The Core of the NIPA

The major components of the NIPA can be found in either of two ways: by adding up the income in the economy or by adding up spending. A simple circular flow diagram of the economy shows why either approach can be used to determine the economy's level of economic activity.

NOBEL PRIZE
SIMON KUZNETS (1901–1985)

Simon Kuznets was awarded the Nobel Prize in 1971 for devising systematic approaches to the compilation and analysis of national economic data. Kuznets is credited with developing gross national product as a measurement of economic output.

Kuznets developed methods for calculating the size and changes in national income known as the national income and product accounts (NIPA). Caring little for abstract models, he sought to define concepts that could be observed empirically and measured statistically. Thanks to Kuznets, economists have had a large amount of data with which to test their economic theories.

The Circular Flow Diagram Figure 5 is a simple **circular flow diagram** that shows how businesses and households interact through the product and resource markets.

Let us first follow the arrows that point in a clockwise direction. Begin at the bottom of the diagram with households. Households supply labor (and other inputs or factors of production) to the resource market; that is, they become employees of businesses. Businesses use this labor (and other inputs) to produce goods and services that are supplied to the product markets. Such products in the end find their way back into households through consumer purchases. The arrows pointing clockwise show the flow of real items: hours worked, goods and services produced and purchased.

The arrows pointing counterclockwise, in contrast, represent flows of money. Businesses pay for inputs (factors) of production: land, labor, capital, and entrepreneurship. Factors are paid rents, wages, interest, and profits. These payments become income for the economy's households, which use these funds to purchase goods and services in the product market. This spending for goods and services becomes sales revenues for the business sector.

circular flow diagram Illustrates how households and firms interact through product and resource markets and shows that economic aggregates can be determined by either examining spending flows or income flows to households.

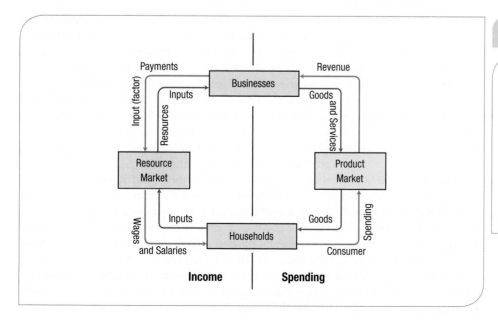

FIGURE 5

A Simple Circular Flow Diagram

This circular flow diagram illustrates why the economic aggregates in our economy can be determined in either of two ways. Spending flows through the right side of the diagram, while the left side of the diagram shows incomes flowing to households. Note that one person's spending is another person's income.

Spending and Income: Looking at GDP in Two Ways The circular flow diagram illustrates why economic aggregates in our economy can be determined in either of two ways. The spending in the economy accrues on the right side of the diagram. In this simple diagram, all spending is assumed to be consumer spending for goods and services. We know, however, that businesses spend money on investment goods such as equipment, plants, factories, and specialized vehicles to increase their productivity. Also, government buys goods and services, as do foreigners. This spending shows up in the NIPA, although it is not included in our simple circular flow diagram.

Second, similar income is generated equal to the spending in the product market. This is shown on the left side of the diagram. Wages and salaries constitute the bulk of income in our economy (roughly two-thirds of it), with rents, interest, and profits comprising the rest. Everything that is spent on the right side represents income on the left side; all spending must equal input (factor) incomes.

The main idea of a circular flow diagram is that every dollar spent in an economy becomes a dollar of income to someone else. For example, suppose you spend $5 on a smoothie, and suppose this $5 goes to the following:

$1 to rent and equipment = income to landlord and equipment makers
$1 to fruits and juices = income to farmers
$1 to wages for store workers and managers = income to labor
$1 to taxes = income to government
$1 to profit = income to investors

Therefore, regardless of whether economic activity is measured by the $5 in spending by the consumer or the $5 in income generated to various parties, the resulting measurement is the same.

Gross Domestic Product

Eric Chiang

gross domestic product (GDP) A measure of the economy's total output; it is the most widely reported value in the national income and product accounts (NIPA) and is equal to the total market value of all final goods and services produced by resources in a given year.

Gross domestic product (GDP) is a measure of the economy's total output; it is the most widely reported value in the NIPA. Technically, the nation's *GDP is equal to the total market value of all final goods and services produced by resources in the United States in a given year.* A few points about this definition need to be noted.

First, GDP reflects the *final* value of goods and services produced. Therefore, measurements of GDP do not include the value of intermediate goods used to produce other products. This distinction helps prevent what economists call "double counting," because a good's final value includes the intermediate values going into its production.

To illustrate, consider a box of toothpicks. The firm producing these toothpicks must first purchase a supply of cottonwood, let's say for $0.22 a box. The firm then mills this wood into toothpicks, which it puts into a small box purchased from another company at $0.08 apiece. The completed box is sold to a grocery store wholesale for $0.65. After a markup, the grocery retails the box of toothpicks for $0.89. The sale raises GDP by $0.89, *not* by $1.84 (0.22 + 0.08 + 0.65 + 0.89), because the values of the cottonwood, the box, and the grocery store's services are already included in the final sales price of a box of toothpicks. Thus, by including only final prices in GDP, double counting is avoided.

A second point to note is that, as the term gross *domestic* product implies, GDP is a measure of the output produced by resources in the United States. It does not matter whether the producers are American citizens or foreign nationals as long as the production takes place within the country's borders. GDP does not include goods or services produced abroad, even if the producers are American citizens or companies.

In contrast to GDP is *gross national product* (GNP), the standard measure of output the Department of Commerce used until the early 1990s. GNP reflects the market value of all goods and services produced domestically and abroad using resources supplied by U.S. citizens, while excluding the value of goods and services produced in the United States by foreign-owned businesses. The difference between GDP and GNP is small. The main reason the DOC switched its measurements was to ensure that its data were more directly comparable to that collected by the rest of the world. Also, in an increasingly globalized world, foreign-owned businesses contribute significantly to our economy in terms of jobs and domestic investment; GDP takes these contributions into account.

Third, whenever possible, the NIPA uses market values, or the prices paid for products, to compute GDP. Therefore, even if a firm must sell its product at a loss, the product's final sales price is what figures into GDP, not the firm's production costs.

Fourth, the NIPA accounts focus on market-produced goods and services. The major exceptions to this approach include substituting payroll costs for the value of government services and estimating (imputing) the rental value of owner-occupied housing. This focus on market values has been criticized on the grounds that child-care services, for instance, when provided by a nanny, are figured into GDP, while the values for these same services when performed by parents are not.

The Expenditures (Spending) Approach to Calculating GDP

Again, GDP can be measured using either spending or income. With the expenditures approach, all spending on final goods and services is added together. The four major categories of spending are personal consumption expenditures, gross private domestic investment (GPDI), government spending, and net exports (exports minus imports).

Personal Consumption Expenditures Personal consumption expenditures are goods and services purchased by residents and businesses of the United States. Goods and services are divided into three main categories: durable goods, nondurable goods, and services. Durable goods are products that have an average useful life of at least three years. Automobiles, major appliances, books, DVDs, and musical instruments are all examples of durable goods. Nondurable goods include all other tangible goods, such as canned soft drinks, frozen pizza, toothbrushes, and underwear (all of which should be thrown out before they are three years old). Services are commodities that cannot be stored and are consumed at the time and place of purchase, for example, legal, barber, and repair services. Table 2 gives a detailed account

personal consumption expenditures Goods and services purchased by residents of the United States, whether individuals or businesses; they include durable goods, nondurable goods, and services.

The Expenditures Approach to GDP (2012)   TABLE 2

Category	Billions of $	% of GDP
Personal Consumption Expenditures	**11,285.5**	**68.7**
Durable goods	1,230.7	7.5
Nondurable goods	2,595.4	15.8
Services	7,459.4	45.4
Gross Private Domestic Investment	**2,499.9**	**15.2**
Fixed nonresidential	2,018.2	12.2
Fixed residential	468.8	2.9
Change in inventories	13.0	0.1
Government Purchases of Goods and Services	**3,150.7**	**19.2**
Federal	1,275.2	7.8
State and local	1,875.4	11.4
Net Exports	**−515.8**	**−3.1**
Exports	2,213.7	13.5
Imports	2,729.5	16.6
Gross Domestic Product	**16,420.3**	**100.0**

Source: U.S. Department of Commerce, Bureau of Economic Analysis, www.bea.gov.

of U.S. personal consumption spending in 2012. Notice that personal consumption is almost 70% of GDP, far and away the most important part of GDP, and services are two-thirds of personal consumption.

Gross Private Domestic Investment

gross private domestic investment (GPDI) Investments in such things as structures (residential and nonresidential), equipment, and software, and changes in private business inventories.

Gross Private Domestic Investment The second major aggregate listed in Table 2 is **gross private domestic investment (GPDI),** which at about 15% of GDP, refers to *fixed investments,* or investments in such things as structures (residential and nonresidential), equipment, and software. It also includes changes in private inventories.

Residential housing represents about one-fifth of GPDI, and nonresidential structures make up the rest because inventory changes are small. Nonresidential structures include such diverse structures as hotels and motels, manufacturing plants, mine shafts, oil wells, and fast-food restaurants. Improvements to existing business structures and new construction are counted as fixed investments.

A "change in inventories" refers to a change in the physical volume of the inventory a private business owns, valued at the average prices over the period. If a business increases its inventories (whether intentionally or unintentionally due to weak sales volumes), this change is treated as an investment because the business is adding to the stock of products it has ready for sale. This type of investment is generally the least desirable, because excess inventory does not increase productivity and could fall in value if the goods become outdated or if the market price falls.

Private investment is a key factor driving economic growth and an important determinant of swings in the business cycle. Figure 6 tracks GPDI as a percentage of GDP since 1980. Recessions are represented by vertical shaded areas. Notice that during each recession, GPDI turns down, and when the recession ends, GPDI turns up. Investment is, therefore, an important factor shaping the turning points of the business cycle, especially at the troughs, and an important determinant of how severe recessions will be.

government spending Includes the wages and salaries of government employees (federal, state, and local); the purchase of products and services from private businesses and the rest of the world; and government purchases of new structures and equipment.

Government Purchases The government component of GDP measures the impact that **government spending** has on final demand in the economy. As Figure 7 illustrates, at nearly 20% of GDP, government spending is a relatively large component of GDP.

FIGURE 6

Gross Private Domestic Investment (GPDI) as a Percent of GDP

Private investment is a key factor driving economic growth and an important determinant of swings in the business cycle. This graph tracks GPDI as a percentage of GDP since 1980.

Government Spending as a Percent of GDP

Government spending as a percent of GDP mostly fell in the 1990s but has risen since, peaking in 2009.

FIGURE 7

It includes the wages and salaries of government employees (federal, state, and local) and the purchase of products and services from private businesses and the rest of the world. Government spending also includes the purchase of new structures and equipment.

Net Exports of Goods and Services   **Net exports** of goods and services are equal to exports minus imports for the current period. Exports include all the items we sell overseas, such as agricultural products, movies, pharmaceutical drugs, and military equipment. Our imports are all those items we bring into the country, including vegetables from Mexico, clothing from South Asia, and cars from Japan. Most years our imports exceed our exports, and therefore net exports are a negative percentage of GDP.

Summing Aggregate Expenditures   The four categories just described are commonly abbreviated as C (consumption), I (investment), G (government), and X − M (net exports; exports minus imports). Together, these four variables constitute GDP. We often summarize this by the following equation:

$$GDP = C + I + G + (X - M)$$

Using the information from Table 2, we can calculate GDP for 2012 (in billions of dollars) as

$$16,420.3 = 11,285.5 + 2,499.9 + 3,150.7 + (-515.8)$$

The Income Approach to Calculating GDP

As we have already seen, spending that contributes to GDP provides an income for one of the economy's various inputs (factors) of production. And in theory, this is how this process works. In practice, however, the national income accounts need to be adjusted to fully account for GDP when we switch from the expenditures to the income approach. Let's work our way through the income side of the NIPA, which Table 3 on the next page summarizes.

net exports Exports minus imports for the current period. Exports include all the items we sell overseas such as agricultural products, movies, and technology products. Imports are all those items we bring into the country, such as vegetables from Mexico, wine from Italy, and cars from Germany.

TABLE 3	The Income Approach to GDP (2012)		
Category		**Billions of $**	**% of GDP**
Compensation of Employees		8,795.5	53.6
Wages and salaries		7,094.6	43.2
Supplements to wages and salaries		1,700.9	10.4
Proprietors' Income		1,247.5	7.6
Corporate Profits		1,629.1	9.9
Rental Income		555.4	3.4
Net Interest		583.3	3.5
Miscellaneous Adjustments		1,136.2	6.9
National Income		13,947.0	84.9
Adjustments to National Income		2,473.3	15.1
Consumption of fixed capital		2,575.0	15.7
Statistical discrepancy		−101.7	−0.6
Gross Domestic Product		16,420.3	100.0

Source: U.S. Department of Commerce, Bureau of Economic Analysis, www.bea.gov.

Compensation of Employees Compensation to employees refers to payments for work done, including wages, salaries, and benefits. Benefits include the social insurance payments made by employers to various government programs, such as Social Security, Medicare, and workers' compensation and unemployment insurance. Some other benefits that count as labor income are employer-provided pensions, profit-sharing plans, group health insurance, and in-kind benefits such as day care services. Employee compensation is nearly 54% of GDP.

Proprietors' Income Proprietors' income represents the current income of all sole proprietorships, partnerships, and tax-exempt cooperatives in the country. It includes the imputed (estimated) rental income of owner-occupied farmhouses. Proprietors' income is adjusted by a capital consumption allowance to account for depreciating equipment (equipment that is used up while producing goods and services). Although there are a lot of proprietorships in the United States, their combined income is less than 8% of GDP.

Corporate Profits Corporate profits are defined as the income that flows to corporations, adjusted for inventory valuation and capital consumption allowances. Most corporations are private enterprises, although this category also includes mutual financial institutions, Federal Reserve banks, and nonprofit institutions that mainly serve businesses. Despite the huge profit figures reported in the news media, corporate profits are less than 10% of GDP.

Rental Income Rental income, at 3.4% of GDP, is the income that flows to individuals engaged in renting real property (calculated as rent collected less depreciation, property taxes, maintenance and repairs, and mortgage interest). It does not include the income of real estate agents or brokers, but it does include the imputed rental value of homes occupied by their owners (again, less depreciation, taxes, repairs, and mortgage interest), along with royalties from patents, copyrights, and rights to natural resources.

Net Interest Net interest is the interest paid by businesses less the interest they receive, from this country and abroad, and is 3.5% of GDP. Interest expense is the payment for the use of capital. Interest income includes payments from home mortgages, home improvement loans, and home equity loans.

Miscellaneous Adjustments Both indirect business taxes (sales and excise taxes) and foreign income earned in the United States are part of GDP, but must be backed out of payments to factors of production in this country. Neither is paid to U.S. factors of production, and therefore appears in a separate category for measurement purposes.

National Income National income is all income, including wages, salaries, and benefits; profits (for sole proprietors, partnerships, and corporations); rental income; and interest. Pay to employees represents nearly two-thirds of national income, whereas corporate profits comprise about 12%, with rental income and interest making up the rest.

national income All income, including wages, salaries and benefits, profits (for sole proprietors, partnerships, and corporations), rental income, and interest.

From National Income to GDP National income is the income that accrues to U.S.–supplied resources, whether at home or abroad. Getting from national income to GDP requires a few adjustments. Specifically, one major item (and some minor ones that we will ignore) plus a statistical discrepancy must be added to national income to arrive at the GDP figures listed at the bottom of Table 3.

An allowance for the depreciation (or consumption) of fixed capital is added back, because gross domestic product is gross of depreciation to fixed capital.

This adjusted sum is known as *gross domestic income.* Once a small statistical discrepancy has been corrected, it is equal to GDP. When these adjustments are completed, GDP is the same whether it is derived from spending or income.

Net Domestic Product As firms and individuals generate GDP, they use up some capital, which must be replaced if future production is to continue at similar levels. A more realistic measure of sustainable output, **net domestic product,** is defined as GDP minus depreciation, or the capital consumption allowance. Equipment wears out as output is produced. Road graders, cranes, trucks, and automobiles do not last forever. Therefore, net domestic product represents the output the economy produced after adjusting for capital used up in the process.

net domestic product Gross domestic product minus depreciation, or the capital consumption allowance.

Personal Income and Disposable Personal Income Personal income includes all income—wages, salaries, and other labor income; proprietors' income; rental income; personal interest and dividend income; and transfer payments (welfare and Social Security payments) received, with personal contributions for social insurance subtracted out.

People can do three things with the money they receive as personal income: pay taxes, spend the money (engage in consumption), or put the money into savings. **Disposable personal income** is defined as personal income minus taxes. Disposable income (Y) can be either spent (C) or saved (S); thus,

personal income All income, including wages, salaries, and other labor income; proprietors' income; rental income; personal interest and dividend income; and transfer payments (welfare and Social Security payments) received, with personal contributions for social insurance subtracted out.

$$Y = C + S$$

disposable personal income Personal income minus taxes.

This simple equation, which you will see again, led John Maynard Keynes to some powerful ideas about the workings of our economy.

We have seen how the national income and product accounts determine the major macroeconomic aggregates. But what does the NIPA tell us about our economy? When GDP rises, are we better off as a nation? Do increases in GDP correlate with a rising standard of living? What impact does rising GDP have on the environment and the quality of life? We conclude this chapter with a brief look at some of these questions.

CHECKPOINT

NATIONAL INCOME ACCOUNTING

- The circular flow diagram shows how households and firms interact through product and resource markets.
- GDP can be computed as spending or as income.
- GDP is equal to the total market value of all final goods and services produced by labor and property in an economy in a given year.
- Personal consumption expenditures are goods and services purchased by individual and business residents of the United States.

- Gross private domestic investment (GPDI) refers to fixed investments such as structures, equipment, and software.

- GDP is equal to consumer expenditures, investment expenditures, government purchases, and exports minus imports. In equation form, GDP = C + I + G + (X − M).

- GDP can also be computed by adding all of the payments to factors of production. This includes compensation to employees, proprietors' income, rental income, corporate profits, and net interest, along with some statistical adjustments.

QUESTIONS: Each individual has a sense of how the macroeconomy is doing. Is it a mistake to extrapolate from one's own experience what may be happening in the aggregate? How might individual experiences lead one astray in thinking about the macroeconomy? How might it help?

Answers to the Checkpoint questions can be found at the end of this chapter.

GDP and Our Standard of Living

GDP data provides us with one way of comparing the productivity of different nations. But it doesn't necessarily give us an accurate picture of the standard of living in each country. For example, China, India, and Brazil each have a GDP that places them among the top ten largest economies in the world. But clearly one would not describe the average citizen in these countries as wealthy. This section describes some of the factors that do not get measured in GDP and a few alternative measures of standard of living.

Population and GDP Per Capita

GDP per capita A country's GDP divided by its population. GDP per capita provides a useful measure of a country's relative standard of living.

How can GDP measures better reflect a country's population? The most common approach is to divide GDP by a country's population, resulting in a statistic known as **GDP per capita.** GDP per capita is a useful measure of the relative standard of living of citizens in different countries. However, by simply dividing GDP by population, GDP per capita does not take into account the differences in wealth between rich and poor within a country, and therefore might not fully reflect the standard of living of the typical citizen. For example, U.S. GDP per capita is about $50,000 per person, but certainly the typical American family of four does not earn $200,000 a year. Yet, GDP per capita data is fairly easy to measure, and thus is a useful measure of relative wealth between countries.

An alternative measure of the standard of living is median household income. Being the median household means that half of all households make less income and the other half make more. Using this statistic reduces the effect of outliers (that is, the very destitute or the superrich) skewing the averages. The U.S. median household income in 2013 was about $55,000, an amount that is closer to what middle-income households make.

Environmental Quality

People around the globe have become increasingly concerned with the impact economic activity has on the natural world. These days, it is difficult to watch a nightly newscast without seeing a report about some ecological disaster or looming environmental problem. Government, consumers, and businesses in the United States spend hundreds of billions of dollars annually to protect the environment at home and abroad. Surprisingly, however, our national income and production statistics do little to account for the environmental benefits or harmful impacts of economic activity.

In 1992, the Bureau of Economic Analysis decided to develop an experimental set of economic accounts known as the Integrated Environmental and Economic Satellite Accounts. Preliminary versions of these green GDP accounts were published in 1994, and later Congress directed the DOC to set up an outside panel of experts to study this issue in greater depth. The DOC asked the National Academy of Sciences to look at green economic accounting, which it did, appointing a select panel.

Roberto Candia/Associated Press

Santiago, Chile, is one of the richest cities in Latin America, but also one of the most polluted. Should the negative effects of pollution be reflected in Chile's GDP?

ISSUE

How Should Environmental Quality Be Incorporated into GDP Measures?

Would you rather live in a poor country with a pristine environment or a rich country with a filthy, polluted environment? If you're wishing for a third choice somewhere in between, you likely share the opinion of the majority. Most of us enjoy the benefits that a clean environment provides, which contribute to our standard of living.

But creating a measure of GDP that incorporates the productive value of a clean environment is not easy. In fact, it can be downright arbitrary. How does an economy accurately measure the economic impact a clean environment provides? Economists can make a rough estimate of the costs of pollution from the increase in medical costs. But placing a value on the ability to take walks in the fresh air or view a landscape void of smog is much more difficult. How then does an economist measure the value of a clean environment?

One clue might be the extent to which countries spend resources to reach a target level of environmental quality. For example, many countries have environmental regulations that limit the amount of carbon emissions or provide tradable permits forcing companies to pay for the pollution they cause. But because countries have varying environmental goals, a measure of GDP that includes the external value of carbon offsets would not be comparable across countries.

What we do know is that wealthier countries tend to place greater value on the environment compared to developing countries, which might view environmental quality as a luxury compared to necessities such as food, health care, and education.

Countries often undergo environmental degradation when transitioning from agricultural to manufacturing-based industries. However, as countries develop, they tend to spend more resources to improve environmental quality. The growth of investment in green technologies and even "green cities" throughout the world is proof of the increasing value people are placing on the environment once the resources are available to do so.

But investments in green technologies are not fully reflected in the NIPA. Although GDP measurements include the costs of cleaning up pollution and the jobs created from the development of renewable energy sources and environmental friendly technologies, GDP does not measure the human value placed on environmental quality.

Efforts have begun to find a replacement for traditional GDP measures. The World Resource Institute states that a macroeconomic indicator that values natural resources must include (1) genuine economic welfare, not just economic activity, and (2) an indicator of the sustainability of that welfare over time. For example, clearing the rainforests generates economic activity as defined in traditional GDP measures; however, the deleterious effects of such activities on future generations must also be taken into account.

Some progress has been made. Calculations are being made to determine what is "sustainable." Carbon footprints are being measured. And recent efforts have gained momentum in creating

A neighborhood in Lingang, China, with solar panels on rooftops. China currently leads the world in spending on green technologies. Although these efforts are monetarily expensive, people place value on healthy living and clean environments.

measures of economic progress that include environmental quality. One such measure is the Genuine Progress Indicator (GPI), which includes economic activity in GDP but also the costs of generating that activity, including resource depletion, crime, and pollution. For example, countries that experience strong economic growth but do so in an unsustainable manner would see a reduction in their GPI.

But difficulties remain in establishing an alternative measure to GDP. For example, GDP is "value neutral," meaning that it measures what is produced, not what should be produced or how it should be produced. Because people place different values on the environment and have different ideas on what constitutes a society's well-being, any alternative measure is not likely to be widely adopted until a consensus is achieved on what a benchmark level of environmental quality should entail.

The DOC panel concluded that "extending the U.S. NIPA to include assets and production activities associated with natural resources and the environment is an important goal."[4] In terms of natural resources, these include the flow of services that are produced by environmental capital such as forests, national parks, and ocean fisheries.

---

[4] Nordhaus and Kokkelenberg, *Nature's Numbers*, pp. 2–3.

But from a consumer's perspective, a cleaner environment also provides value. The ability to hike in parks, to suntan on clean beaches, and to swim in lakes and rivers all depend on a level of environmental quality that does not show up in our national accounts.

Nonmarket Activities and the Informal Economy

In addition to addressing such concerns as environmental impacts and the value of nonmarket natural resources, the DOC panel's recommendations highlight some of the broader shortcomings of the NIPA. For example, the national accounts ignore nonmarket transactions, investments in human capital, and the use of people's time.

Nonmarket transactions are an important part of our everyday lives. If a maid cleans your apartment, GDP rises, but if you did the same job yourself, GDP is unaffected. The same is true for babysitting, lawn care, and car maintenance. There is one exception—NIPA already imputes (estimates) the rental value, less expenses, of owner-occupied homes and adds this to GDP.

Many people believe that the NIPA should be an index of the well-being found within our economy. In that case, it would ideally need to take into account the implications of economic activity the DOC panel noted and more, perhaps including data on life expectancy; business spending on research and development; the stock of human capital, including education and health; greenhouse gas emissions; income distribution; poverty rates; and unemployment rates.

informal economy Includes all transactions that are conducted but are not licensed and/or generate income that is not reported to the government (for tax collection).

The **informal economy** (the underground or black market) is a large unmeasured component of our economy. The informal economy can be as simple as the money earned from a garage sale or from items sold on eBay that are not reported to the IRS. It also includes transactions dealing with illegal goods and services, such as drugs, prostitution, or unlicensed gambling. Finally, the informal economy includes the income earned by undocumented residents—those working on farms, factories, or restaurants for cash, or workers hired for housekeeping or babysitting services who are easily paid *under the table*. The size of the informal economy in the United States is estimated at around 10% of GDP. This is relatively small compared to many developing countries that can have an informal economy valued at as much as 50% of their GDP.

The effects of the informal economy can be positive and negative. On the upside, people working in the informal economy are generating and spending income, contributing to national economic activity. Countries with large informal markets have total output that is significantly larger than what is officially reported in their GDP statistics. On the downside, those working in the informal economy do not pay much if any taxes, placing a greater tax burden on the rest of society. Also, the informal economy is less regulated, which increases the probability of corruption and crime.

Despite these shortcomings in the NIPA measurements, it is important to keep the NIPA's original purpose in mind. As the DOC panel noted,

The informal market ranges from casual tutoring students do in their spare time for cash to the multimillion dollar online poker industry.

Ocean/Corbis

The modern national income and product accounts are among the great inventions of the twentieth century. Among other things, they are used to judge economic performance over time, to compare the economies of different nations, to measure a nation's saving and investment, and to track the business cycle. Much as satellites in space can show the weather across an entire continent, the national accounts can give an overall picture of the state of the economy.[5]

The NIPA has served us well. Still, making adjustments to account for various environmental and other nonmarket considerations might provide us with an even better picture of the health of our economy. But we must keep in mind that an aggregate measure of the economy cannot be all things to all people. As we add complexity to an already complex undertaking, the NIPA may lose some effectiveness as a measure of economic activity, as pointed out earlier in the discussion of environmental quality. This is a difficult balancing act facing policymakers.

The NIPA allow us to track business cycles, compare the domestic economy with that of other nations, and take a crude measure of our standard of living. In the next chapter, we will see how two other important policy variables, unemployment and inflation, are measured.

The next several chapters will focus on developing explanations of short-term movements in the business cycle and long-term economic growth (the trend line in Figure 2). If we can understand why upturns and downturns occur, we may be able to devise policies that reduce the severity of business cycle swings while promoting economic growth. These investigations and policy objectives form the essence of modern macroeconomic analysis.

 CHECKPOINT

GDP AND OUR STANDARD OF LIVING

- GDP per capita divides GDP by population, providing a useful measure of a country's relative standard of living.
- GDP does not include most of the benefits and costs from environmental and natural resources.
- GDP does not include nonmarket activities or the informal economy.
- Despite the shortcomings of the GDP measure, GDP provides a simple and consistent way of measuring the overall economic activity in an economy.

QUESTIONS: Each summer, many of the campsites at America's favorite national parks sell out months in advance due to their limited supply, low prices, and prime locations and views. This has led entrepreneurial individuals to reserve these campsites well in advance and then sell the reservations for a high premium on sites such as Craigslist. Does the money earned by these campsite scalpers appear in GDP? Why or why not? Suppose the government cracks down on campsite scalping by doubling the price of campsites. Would this affect GDP? Explain.

Answers to the Checkpoint questions can be found at the end of this chapter.

---

[5] Nordhaus and Kokkelenberg, *Nature's Numbers*, p. 12.

chapter summary

Section 1: Business Cycles

Business cycles are the alternating increases and decreases in economic activity typical of market economies.

Business cycles can vary in duration and intensity, just like a roller coaster. These fluctuations take place around a long-run growth trend.

Business cycles are officially dated by the National Bureau of Economic Research, which assigns a committee of economists to determine "turning points" when the economy switches from peak to recession or from trough to recovery. They do this using past data, which means announcements take place after the turning points occur.

(graph: Real GDP vs Time, showing Peak, Trend, Recovery, Recession or Downturn, Trough, Peak; Contraction, Expansion)

Four Phases of the Business Cycle

- **Peak:** The economy is operating at its capacity.
- **Recession:** Occurs when the economy runs out of steam and business investment falls.
- **Trough:** The economy reaches the depth of the recession.
- **Recovery:** Economic activity picks up and the economy grows.

Alternative Measures of Business Cycles

- National Activity Index
- Leading Economic Index
- Yield Curve

Section 2: National Income Accounting

The national income and product accounts (NIPA) allow economists to judge our nation's economic performance, compare income and output to that of other nations, and track the economy's condition over the course of the business cycle.

Gross domestic product (GDP) is the total market value of all final goods and services produced in a year within a country's borders, regardless of a firm's nationality. *Gross national product (GNP)* measures goods produced by a country's firms, regardless of where they are produced.

Caterpillar Tractor
U.S. firm; made in USA
Part of U.S. GDP and GNP

Toyota Avalon
Japanese firm; made in USA
Part of U.S. GDP, not GNP

Brooks Running Shoes
U.S. firm; made in China
Part of U.S. GNP, not GDP

The circular flow diagram shows how businesses and households interact through the resource and product markets. It shows spending as well as income.

The major components of the NIPA can be constructed in either of two ways: by summing the spending of the economy or by summing income. Likewise, GDP can be measured by adding together either spending or income.

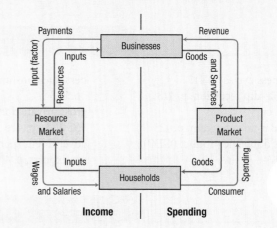

Calculating GDP Using Expenditures (% U.S. GDP)

Personal Consumption Expenditures (C):	69%
Gross Private Domestic Investment (I):	15%
Government Purchases (G):	19%
Net Exports (X – M):	–3%

Calculating GDP Using Income (% U.S. GDP)

Compensation of Employees:	54%
Proprietors' Income:	8%
Corporate Profits:	10%
Rental Income:	3%
Net Interest:	4%
Other/Adjustments:	21%

Section 3: GDP and Our Standard of Living

GDP per capita is measured as GDP divided by the population. It provides a rough measure of a country's standard of living relative to other countries. However, it does not reflect differences in wealth within a country.

Countries are placing greater emphasis on protecting the environment. The economic benefits from a clean environment, however, are mostly unmeasured in GDP statistics. This is changing as new measures are introduced to take environmental quality and degradation into account.

Liechtenstein: Small GDP but many rich citizens.

India: Large GDP but many poor citizens.

The popularity of poker has created many underground tournaments, which are part of the informal economy.

The **informal economy** includes all market transactions that are not officially reported and hence are not included in GDP measures; it creates both positive and negative effects:

- Positive: Transactions in an informal economy create jobs and contribute to overall economic activity

- Negative: Taxes are rarely paid on income in the informal economy, putting a greater tax burden on others. Also, the informal economy is less regulated, which can lead to unsafe products or risky job conditions.

QUESTIONS AND PROBLEMS

Check Your Understanding

1. How are business cycles defined? Describe the four phases of business cycles.

2. What is a key problem with the way the NBER dates recessions and recoveries?

3. Describe the circular flow diagram. Why must all income equal spending in the economy?

4. Why does GDP accounting include only the final value of goods and services produced? What would be the problem if intermediate products were included?

5. Describe why GDP can be computed using either expenditures or income.

6. What does GDP per capita measure? Why is it not a precise measure of a typical person's standard of living in a country?

Apply the Concepts

7. Explain how it is possible for an economy in the recovery phase of the business cycle to have a lower GDP and a higher unemployment rate than when it was in the recession phase of the business cycle.

8. Assume the federal government runs huge budget deficits today to finance, say, Social Security, Medicare, and other programs for the elderly, and finances these deficits by selling bonds, which raises interest rates. Because businesses often borrow money to invest, and interest is the cost of borrowing, these higher interest rates will reduce investment. Describe why this scenario is likely to be bad for the macroeconomy.

9. Critics argue that the NIPA are outdated and fail to account for "intangibles" in our new knowledge economy. For example, many firms create copyrighted materials (movies, books, etc.) that when completed are much more valuable than just the value of the marketplace inputs that went into their production. What might be some of the problems associated with trying to include these intangibles in the NIPA?

10. Gross domestic product and its related statistics are published quarterly and are often revised in the following quarter. Do you think quarterly publication and revision in the next quarter would present problems for policymakers trying to control the business cycle? Why or why not?

11. Gross private domestic investment (GPDI) includes new residential construction as investment. Why is new housing included? Isn't this just another consumer purchase of housing services? How would the sale of an existing house be treated in the GDP accounts?

12. Assume that we are able to account for environmental degradation in the NIPA accurately. Rank the following countries by the percent reduction to their GDP (from least to most percentage reduction): the United States, China, and Norway.

In the News

13. A headline in the January 27, 2012, *USA Today* read "Economists See Growth Slowing, Recession Risk Falling," highlighting government statistics that showed economic growth slowing to a 2.2% rate for the year, below previous estimates. If economic growth is slowing, wouldn't this suggest that another recession is likely to occur soon? Explain why the headline would suggest the opposite.

14. According to the *Happy Planet Index*, an annual survey conducted by the New Economics Foundation, Costa Rica ranks as the happiest country on Earth ("Take a Trip to the Happiest Country on Earth," *Forbes*, October 1, 2012). The index takes into account a number of factors including the quality of life and life expectancy, but most important the index values the sustainability of the environment, which it argues "establishes an undeniable link between happiness and the environment or nature." The World Bank estimates that Costa Rica's GDP per capita in 2012 was approximately $8,800, about one-fifth that of the United States. Explain why GDP per capita does not always correlate well with a country's standard of living.

Solving Problems

15. The table below lists gross domestic product (GDP), consumption (C), gross private domestic investment (I), government spending (G), and net exports (X – M). Compute each as a percent of GDP for the five years presented.

Year	GDP	C	I	G	X – M	C (%)	I (%)	G (%)	X – M (%)
1965	719.1	443.8	118.2	151.5	5.6				
1975	1638.3	1034.4	230.2	357.7	16				
1985	4220.3	2720.3	736.2	879	–115.2				
1995	7397.7	4975.8	1144	1369.2	–91.4				
2005	12455.8	8742.4	2057.4	2372.8	–716.7				

a. Which component of GDP is the most stable? Look for the smallest change from the year with the smallest contribution to GDP to the year with the largest contribution.

b. Which is the most volatile as a percent of GDP?

c. Ignoring net exports, which component has grown the fastest as a percent of GDP since 1965?

16. Using the data below (given in millions of $U.S.), compute GDP, national income, and net domestic product.

Corporate profits	1,200
Gross private domestic investment	2,000
Consumption of nondurable goods	3,000
Exports	1,200
Proprietors' income	900
Taxes, imports, and miscellaneous adjustments	800
Consumption of services	4,000
Net interest	550
Compensation of employees	7,000
Change in inventories	80
Imports	1,800
Rental income	150
Government spending	2,000
Consumption of durable goods	1,000
Capital consumption allowance	1,500

USING THE NUMBERS

17. According to By the Numbers, in what year since 2005 was the difference between the unemployment rate and the real GDP growth rate the largest? What phase of the business cycle would this year best represent?

18. According to By the Numbers, has the personal savings rate trended upward or downward during the last five economic recessions? Why does this trend occur?

ANSWERS TO QUESTIONS IN CHECKPOINTS

Checkpoint: Business Cycles

Big-ticket (high-priced, high-margin) items such as automobiles are affected by a recession more than grocery stores, where the margins are smaller and prices are lower. When the economy turns downward, investment falls, therefore the capital goods industry is one of the first to feel the pinch.

Checkpoint: National Income Accounting

In general, it is probably a bad idea to extrapolate how the aggregate economy is doing by using your personal situation. Just because you are having trouble finding a job does not mean that everyone else is. Downsizing by Bank of America and Citigroup in 2012 meant that bank workers had problems, even though the rest of the economy may have been growing steadily. There might be times when your situation (such as a layoff in an important industry) may be a leading indicator of what is coming for the economy as a whole. In general, anecdotal evidence is not particularly helpful in forecasting where the aggregate economy is going. When times are uncertain, anecdotal evidence may mislead. Even in recessions, some firms do well, therefore anecdotal evidence is suspect. This is why the NIPA was created.

Checkpoint: GDP and Our Standard of Living

The money earned by the scalpers is not counted in GDP because scalpers are not likely to report this income on their tax returns, and thus this is considered part of the informal economy. The revenues earned by Craigslist, a legitimate enterprise, for the transaction would count toward GDP.

If the government doubles the price of campsites and they continue to sell out, then GDP would increase because money paid to the National Parks is part of consumption spending in GDP.

17

Measuring Inflation and Unemployment

GAS 13 $\frac{8}{10}$

TAX 4 ¢

17 $\frac{8}{10}$

Fifty years ago, a single dollar bought a lot. A gallon of gasoline cost less than 30 cents, a movie theater ticket cost about 75 cents, and a meal at a relatively new restaurant chain called McDonald's cost about 50 cents.

Today, none of these items can be purchased for a dollar. The general rise in prices in the economy is referred to as inflation. Inflation has fluctuated each year, ranging from less than 5% in the 1960s, to nearly 15% in the 1970s, to less than 2% in recent years. Inflation reduces the ability of consumers to purchase goods and services: Your dollar just does not go as far. Inflation is a macroeconomic issue because it reduces the value of both income and savings over time.

Another macroeconomic concern facing the economy is unemployment, which measures the number of workers without a job but who are actively seeking one. Like the inflation rate, the unemployment rate fluctuates from year to year, falling below 5% during the Internet boom of the late 1990s and the housing bubble in the early 2000s, and reaching 10% during the early 1980s and late 2000s. Unemployment is a concern because not only does it force unemployed people to cut back on consumption and to use up their savings, it also influences the employed to cut back on their consumption as well. Unemployment puts considerable strain on the government when it results in lower tax revenues but higher spending on assistance programs for the unemployed.

Because inflation and unemployment can have such bad macroeconomic effects, they have been called the "twin evils" of the modern macroeconomy. Each alone is bad. Together, they amplify each other, making things worse.

In the 1960s, macroeconomists thought they had these twin evils beaten. Historical data led them to believe that inflation and unemployment were linked in an inverse fashion; when unemployment went up, inflation would go down, and vice versa. Macroeconomists thought policymakers faced a menu of choices. Pick an unemployment rate from column A and get a corresponding inflation rate from column B. Better yet, the rates at issue were thought to be relatively low: An inflation rate of 3% to 4% was thought to be needed to keep unemployment under 4%. For those unemployed in the recent recession when unemployment reached 10%, an unemployment rate less than 4% would seem like a dream. Is a 3% to 4% inflation rate so bad, considering?

Unfortunately, the data amassed in the 1960s gave a false reading, as the high unemployment *and* high inflation rates of the 1970s proved. According to the 1960s macroeconomic model, the macroeconomy was just not supposed to witness the twin evils together.

Jump ahead to 2013. This macroeconomy performed as the 1960s macroeconomists supposed. Falling but persistently high unemployment was at least met by very low inflation. However, that does not mean that the two together won't raise their ugly heads in the near future. Government policies instituted to counter the last recession might lead to rising inflation at a time when high unemployment is still an issue. We might have to confront the twin evils together again.

By now, you might be wondering: What is the big deal about inflation? You have a visceral sense that unemployment is bad. Inflation is less tangible. Thus, this chapter will start with inflation, what it is, how it is measured, why it is bad. It will then turn to unemployment. How does the government define the unemployment rate? A cab driver with a Ph.D. is employed, but is he or she really underemployed? Is someone who has given up looking for a job considered unemployed? You may be surprised at the answers.

The chapter then will categorize the types of unemployment, revealing which type can be moderated by government policies and which cannot. Finally, we will return to a key concern from the last chapter: jobless recoveries.

Inflation

Suppose that 20 years ago, your parents put aside $12,000 each for your and your twin sister's college education, almost enough money to have paid for four years of tuition at many public universities at that time. Your money was placed into a savings account that earned 1.5% interest per year on average, and your sister's money was placed into a Treasury Inflation-Protected Security (TIPS) bond, which pays a fixed interest rate but whose value also changes with the inflation rate. Now you and your sister withdraw the money to pay

BY THE NUMBERS

The Twin Evils of Inflation and Unemployment

Inflation and unemployment are two variables that governments monitor carefully. Nearly every country has experienced periods of very high unemployment or inflation at some point in its past, and government policies used to correct these problems vary significantly.

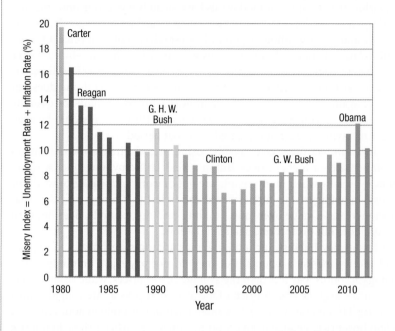

Do Unemployment and Inflation Measure Our Misery?

The **Misery Index** was created by economist Arthur Okun, an adviser to President Lyndon Johnson. It is the *sum* of the unemployment and inflation rates. The higher the number, the more misery the economy is suffering. Running against Gerald Ford for the presidency in 1976, Jimmy Carter made an issue of the Misery Index: It was 13%. He argued that no one should be reelected as president when the Misery Index is that high. When Carter sought reelection in 1980, the Misery Index approached 20%; he lost to Ronald Reagan.

$94 billion

Total amount spent by state and federal governments on unemployment benefits in 2012.

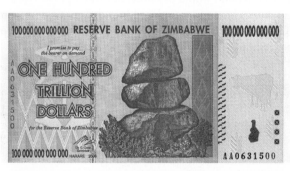

The Zimbabwean $100 trillion bill was one of the largest denominations of currency ever printed. It became nearly worthless just months after it was printed.

McDonald's menu in 1955.

The cost of tuition at public and private colleges and universities has risen faster than the consumer price index for all goods and services since 2001. (Index = 100 in year 2001.)

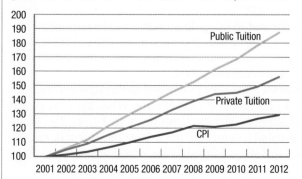

The social costs of unemployment: For every 1% rise in the national unemployment rate:

- $30 billion more is spent by the government on unemployment benefits per year.
- $6 billion more is spent on food stamps (SNAP benefits) per year.
- $12 billion less is collected in federal and state income tax revenues per year.

In addition, rising unemployment causes:

- More people to be underemployed
- An increase in alcoholism and depression
- A general increase in crime
- Greater calls for protectionist trade policies

for college. Big problem: The cost of tuition has more than doubled in the 20 years since your parents put the money into your accounts. Do you both still have enough to pay your tuition bill? Your sister perhaps does, but not you. Your account has $16,162 in it, and your sister's account has $26,250. Looks like your sister got the better deal.

Prices are constantly changing for the goods and services we buy. Prices for items such as concert tickets, airline tickets, and fast food meals have steadily risen over time, making every dollar earned worth a little less in terms of how much it can buy. Some goods, such as smartphones, laptops, and other technology goods, however, have fallen in price. Overall, the prices of a typical "basket" of goods and services we buy rise each year—by 43% over the last 15 years, and 660% over the last 50 years. This gradual rise in prices each year is known as **inflation.** Over time, the effects of inflation can be substantial if one does not take action to protect against rising prices. For example, paying $4 a gallon for gasoline today is much harder than paying $1.25 a gallon was back in 1998. But it would be even harder if your wages or savings have not increased over that period.

How do individuals protect themselves against rising prices? First, workers demand higher wages to compensate for higher prices. But in a weak economy, wage increases are not always possible, especially when many people are out of work and willing to work for lower wages. Second, individuals with money saved can invest that money in assets that earn interest or can increase in value over time. Holding cash, for example, does not earn interest and therefore does not protect one against inflation.

Many forms of assets pay interest, including savings accounts, certificates of deposit (CDs), bonds, and money market accounts. But they do not pay equal amounts—safer assets, such as savings accounts, pay less than the average rise in prices, while riskier assets might pay more than the average rise in prices. One asset that pays a rate roughly equal to the rise in prices are TIPS bonds, which pay a small fixed interest rate in addition to an adjustment based on how prices change in an economy. Therefore, when prices do not rise much, a TIPS bond would pay little, but when prices rise a lot, a TIPS bond will pay a lot. Table 1 shows how $12,000 placed into different assets would have grown over 20 years. The TIPS bond better ensures that when you take money out after 20 years, you will be more able to pay for college at the higher prices.

inflation A measure of changes in the cost of living. A general rise in prices throughout the economy.

TABLE 1	A Comparison of Two Investments	1993	2013
Average price of 4 years tuition at a public college or university		$12,600	$28,500
Value of $12,000 held in cash		$12,000	$12,000
Value of $12,000 held in a savings account		$12,000	$16,162
Value of $12,000 in a TIPS bond		$12,000	$26,250

What Causes Inflation?

Inflation is a measure of changes in the cost of living. In an economy like ours, prices are constantly changing. Some go up as others go down, and some prices rise and fall seasonally. Inflation is caused by many different factors, but the primary reasons can be attributed to demand factors, supply shocks, and government policy.

First, prices for goods and services are influenced by demand factors such as consumer confidence, income, or wealth. Think of a busy mall or restaurant. When there are plenty of customers, businesses are not pressured to offer discounts to attract buyers. This keeps prices higher than when consumer demand is depressed. For this reason, economic growth tends to coincide with inflation as a result of the demand for goods and services that higher incomes produce.

Second, prices are affected by supply shocks, caused by fluctuations in the price of inputs such as oil and natural resources. Less than a decade ago, the average price of a gallon of gasoline was under $2. But over the past decade, tremendous growth in China and India has led to a huge increase in demand for oil, which increased the price of gasoline. Rapidly rising oil prices directly raise the cost of living for individuals, but also, oil is an important input used in the production of electricity and plastics, and also to transport goods once produced. Higher oil prices therefore raise the costs of doing business, which get passed on to consumers in the form of higher prices.

Lastly, inflation can result from specific government actions. Government has a great power that no one individual has—the power to print money. No doubt you have heard that the federal government runs a budget deficit: It spends more than it receives in tax revenues. How does it get the money to overspend? It borrows by issuing Treasury bonds. When the bonds come due and the government does not have the money to buy them back, it can, in essence, run the printing presses and print up new dollars. As more new money is printed, a surplus of dollars is generated in relation to the supply of goods and services. When too much money chases a fixed quantity of goods and services, prices are bid up, which leads to inflation. Governments, like everyone else, have to obey the laws of supply and demand by limiting the growth of the money supply to prevent rampant inflation from occurring.

Gas prices from 1993, 2003, and 2013 show the rise in gas prices over the past 20 years. Rising gas prices contribute to inflation because individuals and businesses depend heavily on gas consumption.

Now that we have described the main causes of inflation, let's discuss how inflation is measured.

Measuring Inflation: Consumer Price Index, Producer Price Index, and GDP Deflator

Each month, the U.S. Department of Labor, through its Bureau of Labor Statistics (BLS), reports several important statistics that provide us with our principal measure of inflation. It does so by reporting changes in the average level of prices over the previous month in terms of the price level. The **price level** is the absolute level of a price index, whether this is the CPI (retail prices), the producer price index (PPI; wholesale prices), or the GDP deflator (average price of all items in GDP). The percentage increase in prices over a 12-month period is referred to as the *rate of inflation.*

Because inflation rates fluctuate up and down, the term **disinflation** is used to describe a reduction in the rate of inflation. Note that an economy going through disinflation still experiences rising prices, just at a slower pace. This was the case from the mid-1980s throughout the 1990s. However, if overall prices in an economy actually fall, this is referred to as **deflation.** Cases of deflation are rare, but did occur in the early 1930s.

Measuring consumer spending and inflation is one of the oldest data-collection functions of the BLS. According to the *BLS Handbook of Methods,* "The first nationwide expenditure survey was conducted in 1888–91 to study workers' spending patterns as elements of production costs . . . it emphasized the worker's role as a producer rather than as a consumer."[1] During World War I, surveys of consumer spending were conducted to compute one of the first cost-of-living indices. During the Great Depression, extensive consumer surveys were used to study the welfare of selected groups, notably farmers, rural families,

price level The absolute level of a price index, whether the consumer price index (CPI; retail prices), the producer price index (PPI; wholesale prices), or the GDP deflator (average price of all items in GDP).

disinflation A reduction in the rate of inflation. An economy going through disinflation typically is still facing inflation, but at a declining rate.

deflation A decline in overall prices throughout the economy. This is the opposite of inflation.

[1] U.S. Department of Labor, Bureau of Labor Statistics, *BLS Handbook of Methods,* 1997. Available at the www.bls.gov.

and urban families. The BLS began regular reports of the modern CPI in the late 1930s. Today, the CPI is the measure of inflation most Americans are familiar with, although the producer price index and the GDP deflator also are widely followed.

consumer price index (CPI) A measure of the average change in prices paid by urban consumers for a typical market basket of consumer goods and services.

The Consumer Price Index The **consumer price index (CPI)** measures the average change in prices paid by urban consumers (CPI-U) and urban wage earners (CPI-W) for a market basket of consumer goods and services. The CPI-U covers roughly 87% of the population.

The CPI is often referred to as a "cost-of-living" index, but the current CPI differs from a true cost-of-living measure. A cost-of-living index compares the cost of maintaining the same standard of living in the current and base periods. A cost-of-goods index, in contrast, merely measures the cost of a fixed bundle of goods and services from one period to the next.

Why does CPI use a fixed bundle of goods and services? First, this avoids having to measure how consumers react to price changes; for example, if the price of beef rises, people might buy more chicken. Second, because it is difficult to follow every decision made by consumers, the government measures how prices change for a fixed basket of goods that an average consumer would buy.

The CPI is calculated by dividing the market basket's cost in the current period by its cost in the base period. The current CPI is a cost-of-goods index because it measures changes in the price of a fixed basket of goods. The reference or base period used today for the CPI is 1982–1984, but any base year would work just as well.

How the Bureau of Labor Statistics Measures Changes in Consumer Prices Measuring consumer prices requires the work of many people. Data collectors record about 80,000 prices in 87 urban areas each month from selected department stores, supermarkets, service stations, doctors' offices, rental offices, and more. Yet, the BLS does not have enough resources to price all goods and services in all retail outlets; therefore, it uses three sample groups to approximate the spending behavior of all urban consumers. These include a *Consumer Expenditure Survey* tracking the spending habits of over 30,000 families nationwide used to construct the market basket of goods and services, a *Point-of-Purchase Survey* that identifies where households purchase goods and services, and census data to select the urban areas where prices are collected.

Goods and services are divided into more than 200 categories, with each category specifying over 200 items for monthly price collection. Data from the three surveys are combined, weighted, and used to compute the cost in the current period required to purchase the fixed market basket of goods. This cost is then compared to the base period to calculate the CPI using the following formula:

$$CPI = (\text{Cost in Current Period} \div \text{Cost in Base Period}) \times 100$$

For example, assume that the market basket of goods cost $5,000 in 2008 and that the same basket of goods now costs $5,750. The CPI for today, using 2008 for the base year, is:

$$115.0 = (\$5,750 \div \$5,000) \times 100.$$

Therefore, the cost of goods has risen by 15% over this time period because the index in the base year (2008 in this case) is always 100. Again, the choice of base year does not matter as long as the CPI for each year is calculated relative to the cost in the selected base year. In fact, one can use CPI data as reported by the BLS to calculate price changes between any two years, neither of which is the base year, using the following formula:

$$\% \text{ Change in Price} = [(\text{CPI in Current Year} / \text{CPI in Original Year}) \times 100] - 100$$

For example, if the CPI in 2013 was 233.8 and the CPI in 2008 was 215.3, the average change in prices over this five-year period was:

$$8.6\% = [(233.8 / 215.3) \times 100] - 100.$$

We now take a quick look at some of the problems inherent in the current approach to measuring the CPI.

Problems in Measuring Consumer Prices The CPI is a *conditional* cost-of-goods index in that it measures only private goods and services; public goods (such as national defense spending) are excluded. Other background environmental factors, meanwhile, are held constant. The current CPI, for instance, does not take into account such issues as the state of the environment, homeland security, life expectancy, crime rates, climate change, or other conditions affecting the quality of life. For these reasons alone, the CPI will probably never be a true cost-of-living index.

But even if we ignore the environmental factors and public services, the CPI still tends to overstate inflation for three key reasons: product substitution, quality improvements, and the introduction of new products.

The CPI uses a fixed market basket determined by consumer expenditure surveys that often are three to five years old. The CPI assumes that consumers continue to purchase the same basket of goods from one year to the next. We know, however, that when the price of one good rises, consumers substitute other goods that have fallen in price, or at least did not rise as much.

Also, in any given year, about 30% of the products in the market basket will disappear from store shelves.[2] Data collectors can directly substitute other products for roughly two-thirds of these dropped products, which means that about 10% of the original market basket must be replaced by products that have been improved or modified in some important way. These quality improvements affect standards of living although they are not fully accounted for in CPI measurements.

Another problem for CPI is the introduction of new products. Not too long ago, digital streaming of books, music, and movies did not exist. Neither did iPads and other devices allowing these media to be played. Because technology is constantly changing along with the prices of technology goods, the BLS often waits until a product matures and is used by a significant number of consumers before including it in the market basket. By not measuring the benefits of new products that consumers enjoy, this again will overstate the actual rate of inflation.

One final difficulty to note has to do with measuring the changing costs of health care. The CPI looks only at consumers' out-of-pocket spending on health care, and not the overall health care spending (including payments made by Medicare, Medicaid, and employer-provided insurance), which is 3 times larger. If price changes differ between out-of-pocket spending and total spending, the CPI will not reflect the true rise in costs.

One solution to these problems was the introduction of a new indicator by the BLS called C-CPI-U, or chained CPI for urban consumers. The C-CPI-U uses the same data as the CPI-U but applies a different formula to account for product substitutions made by consumers. Although the C-CPI-U does a better job at approximating a cost-of-living index, it takes longer to estimate because data must be collected over several years. The BLS reports the C-CPI-U, which has a base period of 1999, alongside CPI-U and CPI-W.

The difference in magnitudes between CPI-U and C-CPI-U vary from year to year; however, the trend has been for C-CPI-U to be lower than CPI-U by roughly 0.3% to 0.4% each year.

The Producer Price Index
The **producer price index (PPI)** measures the average changes in the prices received by domestic producers for their output. Before 1978 this index was known as the wholesale price index (WPI). The PPI is compiled by doing extensive sampling of nearly every industry in the mining and manufacturing sectors of our economy.

The PPI contains the following:

producer price index (PPI) A measure of the average changes in the prices received by domestic producers for their output.

- Price indexes for roughly 500 mining and manufacturing industries, including over 10,000 indexes for specific products and product categories.
- Over 3,200 commodity price indexes organized by type of product and end use.
- Nearly 1,000 indexes for specific outputs of industries in the service sector, and other sectors that do not produce physical products.
- Several major aggregate measures of price changes, organized by stage of processing, both commodity based and industry based.[3]

---

[2] National Research Council, *At What Price? Conceptualizing and Measuring Cost-of-Living and Price Indexes* (Washington, DC: National Academy Press), 2002, p. 28.

[3] This listing is excerpted from Chapter 14 of the *BLS Handbook of Methods*, 1997, found on the BLS Web site, www.bls.gov.

The PPI measures the net revenue accruing to a representative firm for specific products. Because the PPI measures net revenues received by the firm, excise taxes are excluded, but changes in sales promotion programs such as rebate offers or zero-interest loans are included. Because the products measured are the same from month to month, the PPI is plagued by the same problems discussed above for the CPI. These problems include quality changes, deleted products, and some manufacturers exiting the industry.

The GDP Deflator The **GDP deflator** shown in Figure 1 is our broadest measure of inflation. It is an index of the average prices for all goods and services in the economy, including consumer goods, investment goods, government goods and services, and exports. The prices of imports are excluded. Note that *deflation* occurred in the Great Depression. The spike in inflation occurred just after the end of World War II, when price controls were lifted. Since the mid-1980s, the economy has witnessed disinflation—inflation was present but generally at a decreasing rate.

GDP deflator An index of the average prices for all goods and services in the economy, including consumer goods, investment goods, government goods and services, and exports. It is the broadest measure of inflation in the national income and product accounts (NIPA).

FIGURE 1

Inflation from 1930 to 2013—GDP Deflator

The broadest measure of inflation, the GDP deflator, is used to graph inflation from 1930 to the present. Deflation occurred during the Great Depression. The spike in inflation occurred after World War II ended, when price controls were lifted. Since then, inflation has existed in a 1%–13% range. Since the mid-1980s, the U.S. economy has generally faced disinflation (inflation, but generally at a decreasing rate).

Adjusting for Inflation: Escalating and Deflating Series (Nominal Versus Real Values)

Price indexes are used for two primary purposes: escalation and deflation. An escalator agreement modifies future payments, usually increasing them, to take the effects of inflation into account. Deflating a series of data with an index involves adjusting some current value (often called the nominal value) for the impact of inflation, thereby creating what economists call a *real value*. Using the GDP deflator, for instance, to deflate annual GDP involves adjusting nominal GDP to account for inflation, thereby yielding real GDP, or GDP adjusted for inflation.

Escalator Clauses Many contracts, including commercial rental agreements, labor union contracts, and Social Security payments are subject to escalator clauses. An escalator clause is designed to adjust payments or wages for changes in the price level. Social

Security payments, for example, are adjusted upward almost every year to account for the rate of inflation.

Escalator clauses become important in times of rising or significant inflation. These clauses protect the real value of wages as well as payments such as Social Security. In fact, voting blocs and organizations such as AARP have been formed to protect those who depend on escalator clauses to maintain their standards of living.

Deflating Series: Nominal Versus Real Values   GDP grew by 24% from 2005 to 2013, but should we be celebrating? Not really, because inflation has eroded the purchasing power of that increase. The question is, by how much did GDP really increase?

First, remember that every index is grounded on a base year, and that the value for this base year is always 100. The base year used for the GDP deflator, for instance, is 2005. The formula for converting a nominal value, or *current dollar value,* to real value, or *constant dollar* value, is

$$\text{Real} = \text{Nominal} \times (\text{Base Year Index} \div \text{Current Year Index})$$

To illustrate, nominal GDP in 2013 was $16,633.4 billion. The GDP deflator, having been 100 in 2005, was 116.1 in 2013. Real GDP for 2013 (in 2005 dollars) was therefore:

$$\$14,326.8 \text{ billion} = \$16,633.4 \text{ billion} \times (100.0 \div 116.1).$$

Note that because the economy has faced some inflation—16.1% from 2005 to 2013—the nominal value of GDP has been reduced by this amount to arrive at the real value. In other words, of the 24% growth in nominal GDP, 16.1% was due to rising prices. If we subtract 16.1% from 24%, real growth of GDP from 2005 to 2013 was less than 8%, or about 1% per year. The recession of 2007–2009 played a large role in the very slow growth of real GDP over this time period.

The Effect of Overstating Inflation   Many federal benefits, including Social Security payments, food stamps, and veterans' benefits, are indexed to the CPI, which means that if inflation (as measured by the CPI) goes up by 3%, these benefits are increased by 3%. If the CPI overstates inflation, federal expenditures on benefits are higher. Although individuals initially benefit from the higher payments, overstating inflation in the long run makes real earnings appear smaller than what they actually are. This leads to a different set of issues for policymakers and our economy.

Because CPI had been estimated to overstate inflation, in 1999 the Department of Labor revised its measurement tools used for estimating inflation. As a result, today's CPI is a more accurate measure of inflation.

The Consequences of Inflation

Why do so many policymakers, businesspeople, and consumers dread inflation? Your attitude toward inflation will depend in large part on whether you live on a fixed income, whether you are a creditor or debtor, and whether you have properly anticipated inflation.

Many elderly people live on incomes that are fixed; often, only their Social Security payments are indexed to inflation. People on fixed incomes are harmed by inflation because the purchasing power of their income declines. If people live long enough on fixed incomes, inflation can reduce them from living comfortably to living in poverty.

Creditors, meanwhile, are harmed by inflation because both the principal on loans and interest payments are usually fixed. Inflation reduces the real value of the payments they receive, while the value of the principal declines in real terms. This means that debtors benefit from inflation; the real value of their payments declines as their wages rise with inflation. Many homeowners in the 1970s and 1980s saw the value of their real estate rise from inflation. At the same time, their wages rose, again partly due to inflation, but their mortgage payment remained fixed. The result was that a smaller part of the typical household's income was needed to pay the mortgage. Inflation thus redistributes income from creditors to debtors.

This result takes place only if the inflation is unanticipated. If lenders foresee inflation, they will adjust the interest rates they offer to offset the inflation expected over the period of the loan. Suppose, for instance, that the interest rate during zero inflation periods is roughly 3%. Now suppose that a lender expects inflation to run 5% a year over the next three years, the life of a proposed loan. The lender will demand an 8% interest rate to adjust for the expected losses caused by inflation. Only when lenders fail to anticipate inflation does it harm them, to the benefit of debtors.

But the effects of unexpected inflation do not stop there. When inflation is unexpected, the incentives individuals and firms face change. For example, suppose that inflation causes prices of everyday purchases along with wages to increase by 5%. If this inflationary effect was anticipated, then consumption decisions should not change, because *real* prices stay the same when prices and wages rise by the same amount. But if the price rise was unexpected, it might cause consumers to reduce their consumption, leading to lower spending in the economy. For firms, if an increase in money due to unexpected inflation causes demand for their products to rise at their original prices, firms might react by increasing production (and their costs) rather than adjusting their prices when actual demand has not changed. Therefore, unexpected inflation leads to faulty signals, which can reduce consumer and producer welfare.

Lastly, when inflation becomes rampant, individuals and firms expend resources to protect themselves from the harmful effects of rapidly rising prices, an effect that is especially prevalent in cases of hyperinflation.

Hyperinflation

hyperinflation An extremely high rate of inflation; above 100% per year.

Hyperinflation is an extremely high rate of inflation. Today, most economists refer to an inflation rate above 100% a year as hyperinflation. But in most episodes of hyperinflation, the inflation rates dwarf 100% a year. In 2008 in Zimbabwe, prices were more than doubling *every day*, for an annual inflation rate of 231,000,000%.

Hyperinflation is not new. It has been around since paper money and debt were invented. During the American Revolutionary War, the Continental Congress issued money until the phrase "not worth a continental" became part of the language. Germany experienced the first modern hyperinflation after World War I. Hungary experienced the highest rate of inflation on record during World War II. By the end of the war, it took over 800 octillion (8 followed by 29 zeros) Hungarian pengos to equal 1 prewar pengo.

Hyperinflation is usually caused by an excess of government spending over tax revenues (extremely high deficits) coupled with the printing of money to finance these deficits. Post–World War I Germany faced billions of dollars in war reparations that crippled the country. The German government found it difficult to collect enough taxes to pay the reparations, and instead it simply printed more money, causing the value of the currency to fall as prices rose. Over time, financial assets in banks and pension accounts became worthless and were essentially taxed away through hyperinflation.

Stopping hyperinflation requires restoring confidence in the government's ability to bring its budget under control. It usually requires a change in government and a new currency, and most important a commitment to reduce the growth of the money supply.

Millions, billions, and quadrillions are the types of numbers people have to deal with when using hyperinflated currencies.

ISSUE

The Consequences of Counterfeit Money on Inflation

Each day, hundreds of billions of U.S. dollars exchange hands in everyday transactions. A small fraction of these dollars are counterfeit, circulating throughout the economy as if they were genuine. When counterfeit money is created, who ends up paying for it?

Suppose you receive some money, and later realize one of the bills is fake (the ink runs, the paper is too thin, or the watermark is missing). What can you do? Many people assume they could go to a bank and exchange the fake bill for a real one. But most banks won't accept a fake bill because the bank would lose the money. Some people pass the fake to the next unsuspecting person, but this is a punishable offense. The law states that a counterfeit bill must be reported to the nearest U.S. Secret Service field office. By doing so, you still lose the money, as there is no compensation for turning in counterfeit money.

Thus, the responsibility lies with individuals and businesses to check the authenticity of the money received, and to refuse money that appears to be counterfeit. That is not always as easy as it sounds. A low-quality counterfeit might be detected by the naked eye or by touch, especially with the use of devices such as a counterfeit detector pen. But sophisticated counterfeiters produce high-quality counterfeits that are hard to detect. For example, one counterfeit-

ing method has been to remove the ink from a lower denomination bill and then reprint a higher denomination on the paper. The paper is real, making counterfeit detector pens ineffective, and the bill contains a watermark (however, the wrong one) and a security strip. These counterfeits are nearly indistinguishable from authentic bills, and can circulate for years without being noticed.

Who ultimately loses when counterfeit money is circulated? For low-quality bills, it is the last person to accept it. Restaurants and other businesses often receive counterfeits because cashiers are rushed. Consumers sometimes pass them to businesses thinking it won't hurt them. Because banks generally do not accept counterfeits, businesses end up losing.

When a business incurs a loss due to counterfeit money, this acts as a tax on the business. In other words, the supply curve shifts to the left, and prices rise. Therefore, even if individuals do not end

up with the counterfeit in their possession, they pay for them in the form of higher prices.

What happens when a high-quality counterfeit circulates for years in the economy; is it really fake? Literally, yes, but in terms of its economic impact, counterfeit money acts as real money if people accept it as real money. Ultimately, the government loses. Why? The government (the U.S. Treasury to be specific) is the only institution with the authority to print money. When another entity prints counterfeits, the amount of money in circulation rises, but the government never had the opportunity to use it first.

When more money chases a limited amount of goods and services in an economy, inflation arises. Because counterfeits produce the same effect as an increase in the money supply, inflation will occur. In sum, counterfeits hurt everyone, which is why governments invest in new technology to produce money with many security features.

Counterfeit detector pens are commonly used to monitor currency that comes into businesses. When counterfeit money doesn't get detected, businesses lose the money, which acts as a tax, shifting the supply curve to the left and causing prices to rise.

Scott Speakes/Corbis

Price — P_0, P_1; S_1, S_0, D; Quantity of Goods

Hyperinflation is an extreme case, yet it shows how inflation can have detrimental effects on an economy. This is why it is important to keep track of inflation, as it is an important measure of the health of an economy.

CHECKPOINT

INFLATION

- Inflation is a measure of the change in the cost of living.
- Inflation is a general rise in prices throughout the economy.
- Disinflation is a reduction in the rate of inflation, and deflation is a decline in overall prices in the economy.
- The CPI measures inflation for urban consumers and is based on a survey of a fixed market basket of goods and services each month.
- The PPI measures price changes for the output of domestic producers.
- The GDP deflator is the broadest measure of inflation and covers all goods and services in GDP.
- Escalator clauses adjust payments (wages, rents, and other payments such as Social Security) to account for inflation.
- Real (adjusted for inflation) values are found by multiplying the nominal (current dollar) values by the ratio of the base year index to the current year index.
- Hyperinflation is an extremely high rate of inflation.

QUESTIONS: Suppose you took out $20,000 in student loans at a fixed interest rate of 5%. Assume that after you graduate, inflation rises significantly as you are paying back your loans. Does this rise in inflation benefit you in paying back your student loans? Who is hurt more from unexpected higher inflation—a borrower or a lender?

Answers to the Checkpoint questions can be found at the end of this chapter.

◆ Unemployment

When people are unemployed, individual workers, their families, and the economy all suffer. Workers lose wages, and the economy loses what they could have produced. Consumer spending drops, and as we will see in later chapters, this drop in consumer spending can have a ripple effect, leading other workers to lose their jobs.

The Historical Record

The Census Bureau began collecting data on wages and earnings in the early 19th century, but it took the Great Depression to focus national attention on the need for consistent data on unemployment rather than specific instances of things such as factory closings. By the 1940s, the Department of Labor began collecting employment data using monthly surveys to get a more detailed picture of the labor force. As the Bureau of Labor Statistics has noted,

To know about unemployment—the extent and nature of the problem—requires information. How many people are unemployed? How did they become unemployed? How long have they been unemployed? Are their numbers growing or declining? Are they men or women? Are they young or old? Are they white or black or of Hispanic origin? Are they skilled or unskilled? Are they the sole support of their families, or do other family members have jobs? Are they more concentrated in one area of the country than another?[4]

Once the BLS has collected and processed the current employment statistics, policymakers use this information to craft economic policies. Before we discuss how these statistics are defined, collected, used, and made accurate, let's briefly look at the historical record of unemployment and its composition.

Figure 2 shows unemployment rates for the last century. Unemployment has varied from a high of 25% of the labor force in the middle of the Great Depression to a low of just over 1% during World War II. Unemployment during the past

Swim Ink 2, LLC/Corbis

A 1946 Census Bureau poster encouraging compliance with the initial unemployment survey.

[4] From the BLS Web site.

50 years has tended to hover around the 5% to 6% range, although it reached 10% during the 1981–1982 and 2007–2009 recessions.

Table 2 on the next page shows a breakdown of unemployment among various groups by gender, race, and education for 1980, 1990, 2000, and 2012. For blacks, unemployment has tended to be about double the rate of white unemployment, and the unemployment rate for Hispanics has usually exceeded that for whites by roughly 50%. Unemployment for college graduates is consistently low. Roughly half of all unemployment is normally from job losses, but this rose to two-thirds during the 2007–2009 downturn. The next largest group involves people who have not worked in some time and are looking to reenter the labor force. Finally, those people who quit their jobs or are new entrants into the labor force constitute a small percentage of the unemployed.

Now that we have some idea of the composition of the unemployed, let us consider just how these numbers are compiled. First, we need to examine how people get categorized as employed or unemployed.

Defining and Measuring Unemployment

The three major monthly numbers the BLS reports are the size of the labor force, number of people employed, and number unemployed. The unemployment rate is the number of people unemployed divided by the labor force.

Employed People are counted as *employed* if they have done any work at all for pay or profit during the survey week. Regular full-time work, part-time work, and temporary work are all included. People who have a job, but are on vacation, ill, having child care problems,

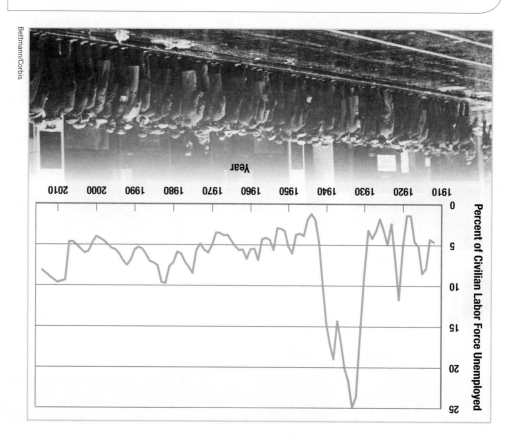

FIGURE 2

A Century of Unemployment (1912–2012)

Over the last century, unemployment has varied from a high of 25% of the labor force in the middle of the Great Depression to a low of just over 1% during World War II. Unemployment during the past 50 years has tended to hover around the 5%–6% range.

Bettmann/Corbis

TABLE 2 Unemployment Rates by Gender, Race, Education, Occupation, and Reason for Unemployment, 1980–2012

	1980	1990	2000	2012
Total unemployment	7.1	5.6	4.0	7.8
Gender				
Men	6.9	5.7	3.9	7.2
Women	7.4	5.5	4.1	7.3
Race or Ethnicity				
White	6.3	4.8	3.5	6.9
Black	14.3	11.4	7.6	14.0
Hispanic	10.1	8.2	5.7	9.6
Education				
Less than high school diploma	8.4	9.6	7.9	11.7
High school graduate	5.1	4.9	3.8	8.0
Less than bachelor's degree	4.3	3.7	3.0	6.9
College graduate and higher	1.9	1.9	1.5	3.9
Occupation				
Managerial and professional	2.5	2.1	1.7	3.9
Office and administrative support	3.6	4.3	3.6	8.4
Production occupations	6.5	8.7	6.3	10.4
Reason Why Unemployed				
Job loser	3.6	2.7	1.8	4.1
Job leaver	0.8	0.8	0.5	0.6
Reentrant	1.8	1.5	1.4	2.3
New entrant	0.8	0.5	0.3	0.8

Source: U.S. Department of Labor, Bureau of Labor Statistics.

on maternity or paternity leave, on strike, prevented from working because of bad weather, or engaged in some family or personal obligation are treated as employed. These people are considered to be employed because they have jobs to return to once their temporary situations have been resolved.

One other group, called unpaid family workers, is considered to be employed. These are people who work 15 or more hours a week in a family enterprise; they usually show up in agriculture and retail. Unpaid family workers who work fewer than 15 hours a week are not counted as employed.

Unemployed People are counted as unemployed if they do not have a job, but are available for work and have been actively seeking work for the previous four weeks. Actively looking for work includes efforts such as responding to online job ads, sending off résumés, scheduling job interviews, visiting school placement centers, and contacting private or public employment agencies.

Note the emphasis on being active in the job search. A *passive* job search that merely involves browsing online employment openings or talking to friends about jobs is not enough to characterize someone as unemployed. One exception involves workers who have been laid off but are expecting to be recalled; they do not need to seek other work to count as being unemployed. Aside from the only other exception—namely, people suffering a temporary illness—individuals must be engaged in a job search to be counted as unemployed.

Labor Force The **labor force** is the total number of those employed and unemployed. The unemployment rate is the number of unemployed divided by the labor force, expressed as a percent.

labor force The total number of those employed and unemployed.

The unemployment rate is the number of unemployed divided by the labor force, expressed as a percent.

The measurement of the labor force has important implications for the unemployment rate. To be counted in the labor force, one must either be employed or not employed but actively seeking work. As a result, a number of groups are not included in the labor force, including full-time students, retirees, children, and persons serving time in prison. If a person within these categories is not working, he or she is not counted in unemployment statistics because he or she is not in the labor force. A discussion of how changes in the labor force affect the unemployment rate appears later in this section.

Monthly Employment Surveys

The Census Bureau and the Department of Labor conduct different surveys to measure employment. The Census Bureau surveys households and the U.S. Department of Labor focuses on the payrolls of businesses and government agencies to produce their monthly reports.

The Household Survey Every month the Census Bureau, as part of the Current Population Survey, contacts roughly 60,000 households to determine the economic activity of people. The sample is drawn from over 700 geographical areas intended to represent the entire country, including urban and rural areas. The survey includes self-employed workers, unpaid family workers, agricultural workers, private household workers, and workers absent without pay.

The Census Bureau does not directly ask interviewees if they are employed. Rather, it asks a series of questions designed to elicit information that permits the Bureau to determine by its own standards whether people are employed or unemployed and whether they are in the labor force.

The Payroll Survey The payroll, or "establishment," survey focuses on roughly 400,000 companies and government agencies that are asked how many employees they currently have. If jobs are cut, this survey will immediately show a decrease in the number of employees.

According to the Bureau of Labor Statistics, "Both the payroll and household surveys are needed for a complete picture of the labor market. The payroll survey provides a highly reliable gauge of monthly change in nonfarm payroll employment. The household survey provides a broader picture of employment including agriculture and the self employed."[5]

The household survey provides a detailed demographic picture of the labor market and captures entrepreneurial activity missed by the payroll survey. In contrast, the payroll survey provides detailed information by industry and region of the country. Because the payroll survey has a larger sample, it is generally viewed as the most accurate gauge of employment and unemployment changes, but both surveys closely track each other.

[5] U.S. Department of Labor, Bureau of Labor Statistics. *Employment from the BLS Household and Payroll Surveys: Summary of Recent Trends*, 2013. Available at www.bls.gov.

Employment Trends

The surveys described in the previous section are important measures of employment and unemployment for the country as a whole as well as for individual states and cities included in the surveys. However, investors and economists are interested in trends in employment and how they affect the overall health of the economy. Although major companies are highlighted in the news for their decisions on hiring and layoff decisions, the majority of jobs in the country are generated by small and mid-sized companies. These employment decisions fluctuate often, and therefore investors are interested in statistics that might capture these short-term trends.

Weekly Jobs Report One report that has gained increasing attention is the Unemployment Insurance Weekly Claims Report, more commonly referred to as the Weekly Jobs Report, released by the U.S. Department of Labor each Thursday. The Weekly Jobs Report contains an estimate of the number of persons filing for unemployment benefits for the first time, and is used as a way to estimate trends in layoffs and in hiring. Economists are interested in seeing how the weekly data change from week to week. These data provide a more immediate estimate of unemployment than waiting for the monthly survey report.

Relationship Between Employment and the Unemployment Rate People often generalize the negative relationship between employment and the unemployment rate. Although these terms are negatively related, the relationship is not perfect. For example, it is possible for employment to grow and the unemployment rate to increase at the same time. Recall that the unemployment rate measures the number of people unemployed and seeking work divided by the labor force. The important point to highlight here is that the labor force is constantly changing.

The labor force changes for many reasons. For example, the labor force in the United States grows by around 1.5 million persons each year just from population growth (from natural births as well as from immigration). Therefore, even without considering any other factor influencing the labor force, the United States needs to generate numerous new jobs just to keep the unemployment rate steady. Further, people enter and leave the labor force for many reasons—college, retirement, family reasons, or just frustration with the job market. As a result of these factors, the unemployment rate is not perfectly correlated with employment numbers, as we will analyze in greater detail next.

Problems with Unemployment Statistics

Trying to measure personal situations as complex as employment, unemployment, and job seeking can be expected to generate its share of controversy and criticism. When the Department of Labor announces its results each month, commentators often note that these numbers understate unemployment, because they do not include chronically unemployed workers who have grown so frustrated and discouraged that they have dropped out of the labor force. Media pundits agonize over the plight of discouraged workers or the underemployed while discussing the impact of the latest numbers on the stock market.

How unemployment is measured depends on the intended use of the resulting measurements. Various uses for unemployment statistics include (1) gauging the state of the economy, (2) determining the divergence of supply and demand in labor markets, and (3) assessing the distribution of unemployment and the extent to which people are suffering from being out of work. In the United States, most unemployment statistics have been developed to gauge the state of the economy. The Bureau of Labor Statistics does, however, publish data about underemployment and discouraged workers.

Underemployment and Discouraged Workers It is not uncommon for people to take jobs that do not fully use their skills. In the early 1990s, many engineers and skilled workers who were employed in the defense industry saw their careers fall apart with the collapse of the Soviet Union. The "peace dividend" most people enjoyed generated excess supplies in defense-related labor markets. In the early 2000s, the collapse of many Internet start-ups and telecommunications firms eliminated the jobs of many highly skilled workers. More recently, the recession caused by the collapse of the housing market and the subsequent financial crisis put large numbers of construction, real estate, and Wall Street workers out of work.

As a result of these shake-ups, many people are unable to find jobs that enable them to duplicate their past standards of living. These individuals are *underemployed* in that they are forced to take jobs that do not fully—or in some cases even remotely—exploit their education, background, or skills.

Consider the following situation. After being laid off at the beginning of a recession, you spend several months looking for work, until finally you conclude that landing a job in the current downturn is impossible. You give up looking for work. Are you still unemployed? Not according to official statistics. Clearly, you would like to resume working; you have simply despaired of doing so anytime soon. Sufficiently discouraged to have quit *actively seeking work*, the BLS classifies you as being out of the labor force.

The deeper a recession, the more **discouraged workers** there will be. Today, the Census Bureau asks other questions of respondents to determine whether they fit into the discouraged worker category, listing these results separately.

Data from the Bureau of Labor Statistics in Figure 3 shows a breakdown of underemployment and discouraged workers. Discouraged workers who have given up looking for

discouraged workers To continue to be counted as unemployed, those without work must actively seek work (apply for jobs, interview, register with employment services, etc.). Discouraged workers are those who have given up actively looking for work and, as a result, are not counted as unemployed.

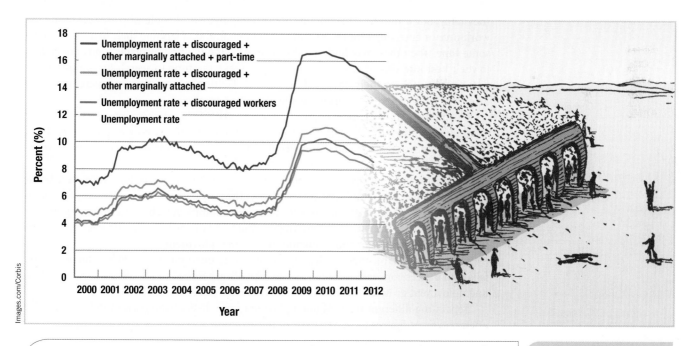

Unemployment Categories (2000–2012)

The Department of Labor categorizes unemployment into those unemployed and still actively seeking work, those who are discouraged (have quit looking), those who are marginally attached (those who looked for work in the past 12 months but not the last four weeks), and those working part time but who would prefer full-time work.

FIGURE 3

work due to poor employment prospects increase unemployment rates by a small amount. The same is true for other marginally attached workers—those who were available for work and actively looked for work during the last 12 months, but *not* in the last four weeks of the survey. The biggest group missing from the reported unemployment rate are those working part time for economic reasons. They would prefer a full-time job but have been unable to land one. Adding all of these categories nearly doubles the unemployment rate.

Other countries have different definitions of actively seeking work, classifying individuals engaged in passive job searches as unemployed. Notably, Canada and Europe have more relaxed search standards than the United States.

◉ CHECKPOINT

UNEMPLOYMENT

- People are counted as employed if they worked for pay or profit during the survey week.
- People are unemployed if they do not have a job but are available for work and have been actively seeking work for the previous four weeks.
- The labor force is the sum of the employed and unemployed. The unemployment rate is the number of unemployed divided by the labor force.
- Unemployment statistics do not account for underemployed and discouraged workers.

QUESTIONS: Does it seem reasonable to require that to be counted as unemployed, a person must be actively seeking work? Why not just count those who do not have a job but indicate they would like to work?

Answers to the Checkpoint questions can be found at the end of this chapter.

➲ Unemployment and the Economy

Inevitably, our economy will contain some unemployment. People who are reentering the workforce or entering it for the first time will often find that landing their first job can take some time. Then they may find, moreover, that taking the first available job is not always in their best interest—that it might be better to take the time to search for another position better matching their skills and personality. Getting information and searching more extensively can extend the period people remain unemployed.

Unemployment can occur because wages are artificially set above the market clearing or equilibrium wage. Both minimum wage laws and union bargaining can have this effect, helping those workers who are employed to earn more, but shutting some potential workers out of jobs.

Employers often keep wages above market equilibrium to reduce turnover, boost morale, and increase employee productivity. These *efficiency wages* give employees an incentive to work hard and remain with their present employers, because at other jobs they could get only market wages. These higher wages, however, can also prevent employers from hiring new workers, thus contributing to unemployment.

Changes in the business cycle will also generate unemployment. When the economy falls into a recession, sales decline, and employers are forced to lay off workers, therefore unemployment grows.

Separating different types of unemployment into distinct categories will help us apply unemployment figures to our analysis of the economy.

Types of Unemployment

There are three types of unemployment: frictional, structural, and cyclical. Each type has different policy ramifications.

Frictional Unemployment Do you recall how many different part-time jobs you held during high school? How about summer jobs while in college? If you have worked several types of jobs, you're not alone, as many reasons exist why one may leave a job. You may get bored; the business may close or reduce the staff it needs; you might move to a new city; or you could have been fired. If you're enrolled in school while working part-time jobs, generally you are not considered unemployed while between jobs, because being in school generally means you're not counted in the labor force. But the reasons for changing jobs are still relevant once you graduate and work full time.

As you pursue your career, chances are that you'll work for more than one company during your lifetime. **Frictional unemployment** describes the short-term duration of unemployment caused by workers switching jobs, often voluntarily, for a variety of reasons. Some workers quit their jobs to search for better positions. In some cases, these people may already have other jobs, but it may still take several days or weeks before they can report to their new employers. In these cases, people moving from one job to the next are said to be frictionally unemployed.

Frictional unemployment is natural for our economy and, indeed, necessary and beneficial. People need time to search for new jobs, and employers need time to interview and evaluate potential new employees.

Structural Unemployment **Structural unemployment** is roughly the opposite of frictional unemployment. Whereas frictional unemployment is assumed to be of rather short duration, structural unemployment is usually associated with extended periods of unemployment.

Structural unemployment is caused by changes in the structure of consumer demands or technology. Most industries and products inevitably decline and become obsolete, and when they do, the skills honed by workers in these industries often become obsolete as well.

Declining demand for cigarettes, for instance, has changed the labor market for tobacco workers. Farm work, textile finishing, and many aspects of manufacturing have all changed drastically in the last several decades. Farms have become more productive, and many sewing and manufacturing jobs have moved overseas because of lower wages there. People who are structurally unemployed are often unemployed for long periods and then become discouraged workers.

To find new work, those who are structurally unemployed must often go through extended periods of retraining. The more educated those displaced are, the more likely they will be able to retrain easily and adjust to a new occupation. One benefit of a growing economy is that retraining is more easily obtained when labor markets are tight.

Cyclical Unemployment **Cyclical unemployment** is the result of changes in the business cycle. If, for example, business investment or consumer spending declines, we would expect the rate of economic growth to slow, in which case the economy would probably enter a recession, as we will examine in later chapters. Cyclical unemployment is the difference between the current unemployment rate and what it would be at full employment, defined below.

Frictional and structural unemployment are difficult problems, and macroeconomic policies provide only limited relief. Cyclical unemployment, most economists agree, is where public policymakers can have their greatest impact. By keeping the economy on a steady, low-inflationary, solid growth path, policymakers can minimize the costs of cyclical unemployment. Admittedly, this is easier said than done given the various shocks that can affect the economy.

Defining Full Employment

Economists often describe the health of the economy by comparing its performance to *full employment*. We know full employment cannot be zero unemployment, because frictional and structural unemployment will always be present. Full employment today is generally taken to be equivalent to the natural rate of unemployment.

frictional unemployment
Unemployment for any economy that includes workers who voluntarily quit their jobs to search for better positions, or are moving to new jobs but may still take several days or weeks before they can report to their new employers.

structural unemployment
Unemployment caused by changes in the structure of consumer demands or technology. It means that demand for some products declines and the skills of this industry's workers often become obsolete as well. This results in an extended bout of unemployment while new skills are developed.

Music stores selling CDs are a dying breed as consumers buy most of their music online, causing structural unemployment in CD manufacturing and in the music retail industry.

cyclical unemployment
Unemployment that results from changes in the business cycle, and where public policymakers can have their greatest impact by keeping the economy on a steady, low-inflationary, solid growth path.

natural rate of unemployment
That level of unemployment at which price and wage decisions are consistent; a level at which the actual inflation rate is equal to people's inflationary expectations and where cyclical unemployment is zero.

The Natural Rate of Unemployment The **natural rate of unemployment** has come to represent several ideas to economists. First, it is often defined as that level of unemployment at which price and wage decisions are consistent—a level at which the actual inflation rate is equal to people's inflationary expectations. Natural unemployment is also considered to be the unemployment level at which unemployment is only frictional and structural, or cyclical unemployment is zero.

Economists often refer to the natural rate of unemployment as the *nonaccelerating inflation rate of unemployment* (NAIRU), defined as the unemployment rate most consistent with a low rate of inflation. It is the unemployment level at which inflationary pressures in the economy are at their minimum. We will discuss these issues in greater detail throughout the remainder of the book. For now, it is enough to remember that the NAIRU is the unemployment rate consistent with low inflation and low unemployment.

Full employment, or the natural rate of unemployment, is determined by such institutional factors as the presence or absence of employment agencies and their effectiveness. Many job seekers today, for example, search online postings on sites such as Indeed or LinkedIn, reducing the time it takes to match available employees with prospective employers. Other factors might include the demographic makeup of the labor force and the incentives associated with various unemployment benefit programs and income tax rates.

Changes in the Unemployment Rate Around the NAIRU In the previous chapter we studied how the business cycle leads to both periods of high economic growth and periods of recessions, fluctuating around a long-term trend. The unemployment rate follows a similar pattern, rising during recessions and falling during economic booms, but fluctuating around the NAIRU. In the United States, the NAIRU is very steady and has fallen slowly over the past 30 years from about 6% to roughly 5%, largely due to improvements in labor market efficiencies (such as the use of the Internet in job searches and the increase in part-time and temporary work) that has reduced the unemployment rate associated with low inflation.

Of particular importance is the length of time it takes the unemployment rate to return to the NAIRU when recessions push unemployment higher. To analyze this point, Figure 4 shows the unemployment rate over the past 50 years, along with the NAIRU. Periods of recession are shaded, most indicating cyclical unemployment as the unemployment rate line rises above the NAIRU. It is interesting to note that the time it takes the unemployment rate to return to the NAIRU varies. In most economic recoveries prior to 1990, the unemployment rate returned to the NAIRU fairly quickly. The

FIGURE 4

Unemployment Rate Versus the NAIRU

The average unemployment rate and NAIRU are shown from 1960 to 2013. Periods of recession are shaded. The rising unemployment line and flatter downward slopes following the last three recessions indicate a longer recovery period for jobs caused by the jobless recovery.

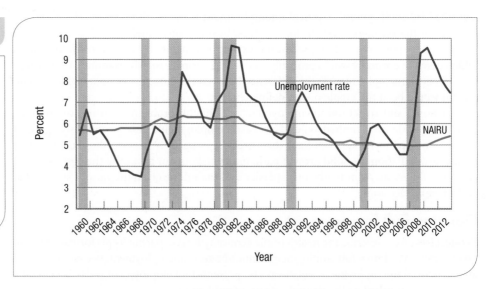

1990–1991 and 2001 recessions did not produce much cyclical unemployment; however, the unemployment rate initially rose during the recovery, leading to a "jobless recovery." But the longest jobless recovery occurred after the 2007–2009 recession, in which the unemployment rate stayed well above the NAIRU for several years.

Jobless Recoveries Prolong Unemployment Above NAIRU The previous chapter discussed some of the reasons why unemployment can stay high for so long after a recession is deemed over. It highlighted the four key markets—labor, financial, capital, and output—that influence one another and affect job growth. But the puzzle that economic growth does not coincide with job growth also deserves an explanation.

In the labor market, recessions tend to send people looking for other options—going back to college, seeking early retirement, or just taking time off until the economy improves. Some who are out of work during these periods take temporary or part-time jobs to support their loved ones until better work can be found. Although all of these people's jobs were affected, the government does not consider them as unemployed,

ISSUE

Why Do Unemployment Rates Differ So Much Within the United States?

In July 2013, the U.S. unemployment rate was 7.4%. However, in Nevada it was 9.5%. Meanwhile, in North Dakota, it was only 3.0%. Looking at metropolitan area unemployment rates reveals even starker differences: The unemployment rate in Yuma, Arizona, was 30.1%, while in Bismarck, North Dakota, it was 2.8%. Why do such large differences in unemployment exist between states and between cities?

In Europe, where citizens of the European Union are free to live and work in any other country within the union, differences in unemployment rates between member countries remain largely due to cultural reasons. People are hesitant to move to a country where people speak a different language or have a different culture. But in the United States, language and cultural issues between states are considerably less than between European countries—English is the primary language and Americans all basically watch the same types of movies and television shows.

Aside from the common language and culture, differences do arise in other areas, which helps to explain the differences in unemployment rate.

First, differences in taxes and regulations exist between states. Some states

Virtually no unemployment in North Dakota.

Fun and excitement abound for tourists in Las Vegas, but not for the large number of unemployed workers.

have lower taxes than others, and some states have environmental and work rules that are more business friendly than others.

Second, many industries tend to form a cluster in order to take advantage of economies of scale and scope. For example, industrial agglomeration in the computer industry centers in greater San Jose ("Silicon Valley"). Detroit has long been the automobile capital of the country, while Gary, Indiana, was once a major steel-producing town (in addition to being the birthplace of Michael Jackson). Economic trends tend to favor some industries over others. Biotechnology, eCommerce, and health care industries have experienced much growth over the past

decade, leading to employment growth in cities home to these industries. However, declines in manufacturing have increased unemployment in certain industrial clusters.

Finally, and perhaps most obvious, is that people prefer certain geographic areas to others. Significant population growth has occurred in the South and Mountain West, where warm weather and scenic beauty await, respectively. Many immigrants from Mexico prefer living in states bordering Mexico for cultural reasons. And throughout much of the past century, people have moved from rural areas to urban areas. How much would you sacrifice to live in a preferred area? People ask themselves this question often.

because they had either found temporary work or had left the labor force to pursue other options. Thus, the official unemployment rate reported during recessions tends to underestimate the actual number of people seeking work, a problem discussed in the previous section.

During an economic recovery, as jobs are being created, not only do the unemployed seek these jobs, but many of those who had left the labor force return to compete for these same jobs. When many would-be workers choose to leave the workforce during a prolonged economic downturn, competition for jobs can be more severe during an economic recovery when these workers return to the labor force.

The last few recessions saw many people temporarily leave the workforce to pursue nonwork options such as schooling, stay-at-home parenting, or volunteer work. These choices may explain why unemployment is slow to fall during economic recoveries, and one of the major reasons why jobless recoveries might remain a feature in future recessions.

Inflation, employment, unemployment, and gross domestic product (GDP) are the key macroeconomic indicators of our economic health. Our rising standards of living are closely tied to GDP growth. In the next chapter, we will investigate what causes our economy and living standards to grow over the long term.

 # CHECKPOINT

UNEMPLOYMENT AND THE ECONOMY

- Frictional unemployment is inevitable and natural for any economy as people change jobs and businesses open and close.

- Structural unemployment is typically caused by changes in consumer demands or technology. It is typically of long duration and often requires that the unemployed become retrained for new jobs.

- Cyclical unemployment is the result of changes in the business cycle. When a recession hits, unemployment rises, then falls when an expansion ensues.

- Macroeconomic policies have the most effect on cyclical unemployment.

- Full employment is typically defined as that level at which cyclical unemployment is zero or that level associated with a low nonaccelerating inflation rate.

QUESTION: The financial industry experienced a rapid expansion in the middle of the last decade as a result of the housing bubble, which created jobs for millions of workers in banks, mortgage companies, financial advising companies, and insurance companies. When the bubble burst, many of these workers became unemployed as the financial industry retrenched. For many, their skills were so specialized that they were unable to find new jobs at their old salaries. Were these people frictionally, structurally, or cyclically unemployed? Explain.

Answers to the Checkpoint question can be found at the end of this chapter.

chapter summary

Section 1: Inflation

Inflation is a measure of the general rise in prices throughout the economy. Prices for individual goods can fluctuate up or down, but the price level captures the overall trend in the movement of prices.

Market Basket

Price Level

How Inflation Is Measured

- **Consumer price index (CPI):** Measures the average change in prices of a market basket of consumer goods and services.

- **Producer price index (PPI):** Measures the average change in prices received by producers for their output.

- **GDP deflator:** The broadest measure of inflation, measuring the prices of all goods and services in the economy.

Calculating Inflation Using the CPI

CPI = (Cost in current period) ÷ (Cost in base period) × 100

Example: Suppose a market basket consists of pizza and soda

Base year prices: Pizza = $6 and Soda = $2
Current year prices: Pizza = $8 and Soda = $3

CPI = ($8 + $3) ÷ ($6 + $2) × 100 = 137.5 (average prices rose 37.5% since the base year)

Yekophotostudio/ Dreamstime.com

Melanie Blanding/Alamy

A severe drought in the summer of 2012 pushed corn prices higher, leading to higher prices on many goods.

The Main Causes of Inflation

- Strong consumer demand: Consumers spend more money, demand increases, and prices rise.

- Supply shocks on key inputs: Prices for inelastic goods such as food and inputs such as oil rise; higher prices are passed on to other industries and to consumers.

- Government printing money: The government prints money to finance its borrowing, more money is chasing a relatively fixed amount of goods and services, and therefore prices rise.

Disinflation Versus Deflation

Disinflation occurs when the rate of inflation falls, but is still positive.

Deflation occurs when the rate of inflation turns negative.

Hyperinflation is an extremely high rate of inflation. It typically is caused by excess government spending over tax revenues (high deficits) and the printing of money to finance deficits.

Eric Chiang

A price list of photocopying services in Zimbabwe in 2008 during hyperinflation.

Section 2: Unemployment

The **labor force** is the total number of people employed or unemployed. **Employed** persons are individuals age 16 and over who work for pay, whether full time, part time, or even temporary. **Unemployed** persons are those without jobs but are actively seeking work.

If you work part time at the local coffee shop after graduation while looking for a good job, you are not unemployed. Instead, you are underemployed, which still is considered employed.

What About Everyone Else?

Discouraged workers are those who have given up actively looking for work, and are not counted as unemployed.

Students who do not work are not counted in the labor force.

Retired persons and children under 16 are not counted in the labor force.

Institutionalized persons including persons in prison also are not counted in the labor force.

Section 3: Unemployment and the Economy

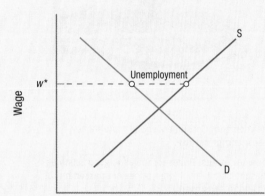

Unemployment is shown on a labor market diagram where the supply of labor (workers) exceeds the demand for labor (by firms).

The **natural rate of unemployment (NAIRU)** is the rate of unemployment that exists when prices and wages are equal to people's expectations. At the NAIRU, the economy is at "full employment."

NAIRU = frictional + structural unemployment

NAIRU is very stable in the United States at around 5% to 6%.

Types of Unemployment

- **Frictional unemployment:** Includes workers who voluntarily quit their jobs in search of better positions, or recent graduates seeking their first high-paying job.

- **Structural unemployment:** Longer term unemployment that is caused by changes in consumer demands or technology, and requires workers to be retrained for a career in another industry.

- **Cyclical unemployment:** Unemployment that results from the business cycle—when a recession hits, firms lay off workers until the economy recovers.

35mm film is hardly ever used anymore, and has led to structural unemployment as workers in the 35mm film industry find new employment.

KEY CONCEPTS

inflation, p. 442
price level, p. 443
disinflation, p. 443
deflation, p. 443
consumer price index (CPI), p. 444

producer price index (PPI), p. 445
GDP deflator, p. 446
hyperinflation, p. 448
labor force, p. 453
discouraged workers, p. 455

frictional unemployment, p. 457
structural unemployment, p. 457
cyclical unemployment, p. 457
natural rate of unemployment, p. 458

QUESTIONS AND PROBLEMS

Check Your Understanding

1. Describe the three measures of inflation in use today and the focus of each measure.

2. Who loses from unanticipated inflation? Who benefits?

3. Describe the possible losses to our society and the economy when people are unemployed.

4. Why do teenagers and young people have high unemployment rates?

5. Describe the three types of unemployment. What types of government programs would be most effective in combating each type of unemployment?

6. What is required for a person to be considered unemployed? How is the unemployment rate computed?

Apply the Concepts

7. You have several student loans that have interest rates that change every year. After graduation, you can consolidate these loans into a fixed rate single loan. You can consolidate now or one year from now. How do your expectations of the inflation rate during the next year affect your decision regarding when to consolidate?

8. Suppose you work hard at a job after graduation and after your first year, your effort is rewarded with a 3% raise when the average wage increase in your company is 2%. Then, the government releases its inflation report that states that inflation is running at 5%. Given this information, did your standard of living improve? Why or why not?

9. Since 1980, the U.S. population has grown 38%, while employment has increased by 45%. Further, the number of people unemployed has risen by only 15%. Are all of these indicators a sign of a strong or a weak labor market?

10. Assume you just lost your job and have decided to take a month-long break to travel to Europe before looking for a new position. Just as you return home from your trip, you are interviewed by the Department of Labor about your employment status. How would you be classified (employed, unemployed, or not in the labor force)?

11. The Bureau of Labor Statistics categorizes unemployed people into several groups, including job leavers, job losers, and discouraged workers. During a mild recession, which group would tend to increase the most? During a deep recession? During a boom?

12. In the beginning of a recovery after a recession, employment begins to rise and the news media report these data on job growth. Would such a report have an impact on the labor force? Would it affect the unemployment rate?

In the News

13. In early 2013, when the United States came close to experiencing a "fiscal cliff," one politician proposed introducing a trillion dollar coin to be minted by the government and sent to the U.S. Treasury to pay down the federal deficit ("Economics Is Platinum:

What the Trillion-Dollar Coin Teaches Us," Bloomberg.com, January 14, 2013). If such a coin were to be minted, what would be the likely effects on inflation? Is this a risk-free way of paying off a fiscal deficit? Why or why not?

14. Federal unemployment benefits were extended in 2013, allowing unemployed workers to receive up to 73 weeks of benefits depending on the unemployment rate in each state. This is an extension of a program that at its peak during the last recession offered up to a maximum of 99 weeks of unemployment benefits. How does extending the federal unemployment benefit program influence the unemployment rate?

Solving Problems

15. In January 1980, the CPI stood at 77.8, and by January 2006, it was 198.3. By what percent have consumer prices increased over this period? Assume college graduates entering the job market were being paid on average $1,200 a month in 1980, and in January 2006 the average was $3,000. Were these newer graduates paid more or less after adjusting for inflation?

16. Given the data for the United States between 1960 and 2010, complete the table below and answer the questions that follow.

Year	GDP (billions of dollars)	GDP Deflator (2000 = 100)	Real GDP (billions of 2000 dollars)	Population (millions)	Real GDP per Capita (in 2000 dollars)
1960	526.4	20.04	_____	180.7	14,537
1970	1,038.5	_____	3,772.3	205.1	_____
1980	_____	54.06	5,109.0	_____	22,437
1990	_____	81.61	_____	250.1	28,432
2000	9,817.0	_____	9,817.0	282.4	_____
2010	14,498.9	125.14	_____	308.7	_____

a. Between 1960 and 2010:
   i. GDP was how many times larger in 2010 than in 1960?
   ii. The price level was how many times larger in 2010 than in 1960?
   iii. Real GDP was how many times larger in 2010 than in 1960?
   iv. What is the relationship between these values?

b. What was the percentage change in real GDP per capita between 1960 and 2010? Were people in the United States better off in 2010 than in 1960?

c. What are some of the problems associated with using real GDP per capita as a measure of our well-being?

USING THE NUMBERS

17. According to By the Numbers, which of the previous four presidents (R. Reagan, G. H. W. Bush, B. Clinton, G. W. Bush) saw a fall in the Misery Index from the year he entered office to the year he left? Which presidents saw a rise in the Misery Index?

18. Using By the Numbers, compare the increase in the average prices of tuition at public and private colleges and universities with the increase in overall prices according to the consumer price index from 2001 to 2012.

ANSWERS TO QUESTIONS IN CHECKPOINTS

Checkpoint: Inflation

Inflation makes the value of a dollar fall in purchasing power. Therefore, if you borrow money when inflation is low and pay back the loan when inflation is higher, the money you are paying back is worth less than what you received. You benefit by being able to pay back your loans with money that is valued at less than before. Thus, unexpected inflation hurts lenders because the money they are being paid back is worth less in purchasing power than they had planned. Alternatively, had the inflation rate unexpectedly fallen, lenders would gain, as the money being paid back would be worth more in purchasing power than was expected.

Checkpoint: Unemployment

The reason for the requirement that a person actively seek work is to differentiate empirically those who profess to want a job (at possibly a higher wage than they can earn in the market) from those who are actively trying to obtain work.

Checkpoint: Unemployment and the Economy

Many workers became structurally unemployed because the skills they had acquired for the financial industry (and in many cases, specific to the housing industry) were not as useful in other industries. Therefore, as the financial industry became smaller after the housing bubble burst, many workers needed to find work in other industries, which required learning a new skill set.

Economic Growth

18

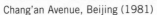

Chang'an Avenue, Beijing (1981)   Chang'an Avenue, Beijing (2007)

After studying this chapter you should be able to:

- Describe how economic growth is measured using real GDP and real GDP per capita.
- Discuss the relationship between a country's economic growth rate and its standard of living.
- Explain the power of compounding in making small differences much larger over time.
- Use the Rule of 70 to approximate the number of years it takes for an economy to double in size.
- Describe a production function and how it estimates economic output.
- Explain how the four factors of production contribute to economic growth.
- Describe the importance of innovation and technology in determining economic growth.
- Define infrastructure and explain its importance.
- Explain how the government promotes economic growth through the policies and laws it implements.
- Describe the relationship between economic freedom and economic growth.

economic growth Usually measured by the annual percentage change in real GDP, reflecting an improvement in the standard of living.

On a typical downtown street in Beijing in the 1980s, one would see thousands of bicycles and pedestrians among a trickling of cars owned by the privileged few. The skyline consisted of just a few large buildings.

How times have changed. Today, the bicycles in Beijing have largely been replaced with cars driven by millions of Chinese whose incomes have increased enough to afford one, the skyline is dominated by modern skyscrapers, and the pedestrians have largely moved underground, traveling on one of the world's most extensive and modern subway systems.

China's transformation from a poor, agricultural nation to an emerging world power with a growing middle and upper class has been remarkable. China's annual growth rate has averaged 9% over the past 20 years, compared to the average U.S. annual growth rate of 2% over the same period. Although a 7% difference might not seem significant, over 20 years the cumulative growth effect is staggering: China's real GDP grew 518% from 1992 to 2012, while in the United States real GDP grew 64%.

Economic growth plays a very powerful role in how people live and how standards of living change over time. Even small differences in growth rates turn into large differences over time.

Less than a generation ago, the United States, most of Europe, and the East Asian economies of Japan, Singapore, South Korea, Taiwan, and Hong Kong were the leaders of economic growth. These countries had consistent, strong growth while the rest of the world lagged behind.

Today, a much different picture emerges. Much of the developed world is still recovering from the devastating financial crisis and recession of 2007–2009, while a number of emerging countries now lead the world in terms of economic growth.

Most notable of high growth rates are the BRIC countries—*Brazil, Russia, India,* and *China.* In previous decades, each of these countries faced significant obstacles in achieving growth—Brazil with its high inflation, India with high poverty and population growth, and Russia and China with large populations and centralized governments. Today, as Table 1 on page 470 shows, these four countries have the highest growth rates among major industrialized nations. In fact, all four countries ranked in the top ten in total GDP in 2012, a feat almost inconceivable 30 years ago.

What changed in the BRIC countries that led to rapid growth? In Brazil, economic policies encouraged innovation, such as ethanol production, which allowed it to be energy self-reliant. In Russia, a new simplified tax code reduced corruption as market efficiency improved and its abundant natural resources were tapped. In India, dramatic growth in foreign direct investment by companies eager to seek a growing educated labor force at low wages led to new industries. And in China, huge government investment in infrastructure, export-led policies, and the opening of limited free markets allowed the economy to skyrocket. But these reasons alone do not tell the entire story. It is the combination of many efforts and policies that lead to long-run economic growth.

BY THE NUMBERS

Why Should We Care About Economic Growth?

Economic growth improves the standard of living of people through higher incomes and greater access to societal resources such as health care and clean water, which generally lead to a longer and healthier life.

Real GDP Per Capita (2012 dollars) — Year

World War II

Great Depression

Real GDP

2%
The average annual increase in real GDP over the period 1870 to 2012.

Real GDP per capita has grown 13 times since 1870 in the United States. After adjusting for inflation, growth has averaged 2% per year over this period and has led to a high U.S. standard of living. Economic growth results from increases in the labor force and its productivity, increases in capital, and improvements in technology.

The Benefits of Growth in the United States (1980–2012)

- Property crime per 100,000 population fell 46%.
- Percent of the population with a four-year college degree increased from 17% to 31%.
- Percent of the population with at least a high school diploma increased from 69% to 88%.

- Life expectancy increased from 73 to 78 years.
- 453% increase in federal government spending on science, space, and technology.
- 39% increase in the number of degree-granting colleges and universities.

42%
Reduction in global HIV/AIDS-related deaths per year from 2002 to 2012.

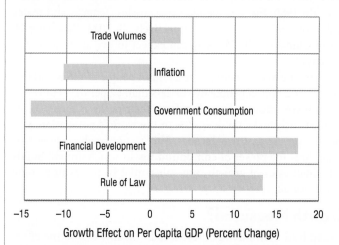

Growth Effect on Per Capita GDP (Percent Change)

Trade Volumes · Inflation · Government Consumption · Financial Development · Rule of Law

Good public policies promote growth. Implementing the rule of law, improving financial markets, and trading with other nations all promote growth. Higher government consumption and higher inflation harm growth.

Average Life Expectancy (2012) — Real GDP Per Capita (2012)

Japan · Switzerland · South Korea · Ireland · United States · Norway · Bolivia · India · Kenya · Nigeria · Chad · Zambia

Economic growth can lead to higher average life expectancies. Residents of rich countries generally live longer than residents of poor countries.

TABLE 1	Top 10 GDP in 2012 and Real GDP Growth Rate from 2002 to 2012	
Country	**GDP in 2012**	**Real GDP Growth (2002–2012)**
1. United States	$16.4 trillion	20% (1.83%/year)
2. China	$8.2 trillion	173% (10.58%/year)
3. Japan	$5.9 trillion	7% (0.67%/year)
4. Germany	$3.4 trillion	12% (1.16%/year)
5. France	$2.6 trillion	11% (1.11%/year)
6. Brazil	$2.5 trillion	45% (3.78%/year)
7. United Kingdom	$2.4 trillion	17% (1.58%/year)
8. Italy	$2.1 trillion	3% (0.25%/year)
9. India	$1.9 trillion	109% (7.65%/year)
10. Russia	$1.9 trillion	59% (4.84%/year)

Source: World Bank, *World Development Indicators.*

This chapter focuses on long-term economic growth and describes the conditions needed to sustain economic growth and improve standards of living. In the long run, all variables in the economy can adjust to changing conditions. The models in this chapter provide a framework for evaluating policies meant to encourage economic growth in the long run.

Why Is Economic Growth Important?

Economic growth is closely tied to how well people live. We already saw how a high growth rate in China changed the lives of much of its population—more people now can buy cars, computers, and other goods that previously were unaffordable. Economic growth improves the lives of people of all income levels, from the richest to the poorest citizens.

The benefits of economic growth extend beyond the goods people can buy. For example, economic growth leads to lower poverty rates and longer life expectancies as people can afford better medical care, more nutritious diets, and more leisure to reduce stress. The data speak for themselves: In 1980, the average life expectancies (females and males combined) in China and India were 67 and 54 years, respectively. In 2013, they were 75 and 66 years. Children born in China and India today can expect to live about a decade longer on average than their parents.

Still, according to estimates by the World Bank, over a billion people in the world live on less than $1.25 per day, and over 2 billion people live on less than $2 per day. However, the number of people living on these amounts has fallen from their peaks as many countries, such as the BRIC nations, which make up over 40% of the world's population, saw economic growth rates improve over the past two decades. This section analyzes how economic growth is measured and how the power of **compounding**, in which growth builds upon prior growth, can turn small rates of growth into substantial increases in income over time, leading to better lives for all.

compounding The ability of growth to build on previous growth. It allows a value such as GDP to increase significantly over time as income increases on top of previous increases in income.

How Is Economic Growth Measured?

Small differences in growth can lead to dramatic differences in income due to the effect of compounding. To show this, we first have to measure economic growth. Chapter 16 introduced the concepts of gross domestic product (GDP) and GDP per capita. As we saw, GDP is a measure of the total value of final goods and services produced in a country in one year, or simply a country's total annual output. GDP per capita is a country's GDP divided by its population, and provides a rough measure of a typical person's standard of living.

In this chapter, we revisit these concepts in a slightly different way by using the concept of real values introduced in Chapter 17. Specifically, we are concerned with **real GDP** and **real GDP per capita,** which are GDP and GDP per capita, respectively, measured in constant year dollars, such that the effects of inflation are removed, allowing for more accurate comparisons in output from year to year.

When a country's real GDP per capita increases, the average output per person is increasing (rather than just prices), and this generally translates into a higher standard of living for most of its residents. Therefore, this is a good indicator of how an economy grows over time.

In the United States, real GDP is measured by the Bureau of Economic Analysis (BEA). The BEA produces quarterly reports on the changes in U.S. GDP from the previous quarter, and is reported as an annualized rate (quarterly change multiplied by 4). For example, in January 2013, the BEA reported that the U.S. economy grew only 0.1% in the fourth quarter of 2012. This means that real GDP in the United States increased about 0.025% from the third quarter of 2012 to the fourth quarter of 2012, which equals a rise of 0.1% when annualized.

In addition, the BEA provides GDP growth data *year-over-year*. For example, the BEA reported that the U.S. economy grew 1.9% from the fourth quarter of 2011 to the fourth quarter of 2012. Why does the BEA report year-over-year growth? Year-over-year growth allows investors and policymakers to compare how the economy has grown over an entire 12-month period, without the seasonal ups and downs most economies experience. Table 2 shows the quarterly real GDP growth rates in 2012 using the annualized and year-over-year methods. The Annualized Rate column shows the seasonal fluctuations that influenced economic growth each quarter, while the Year-Over-Year column shows the growth rate for the preceding 12 months. Both measures are useful depending on whether one is analyzing trends in economic performance for a particular season or for the entire year.

real GDP The total value of final goods and services produced in a country in a year measured using prices in a base year.

real GDP per capita Real GDP divided by population. Provides a rough estimate of a country's standard of living.

Comparing Real GDP Growth Data in 2012   TABLE 2

	Annualized GDP Growth Rate	Year-Over-Year Growth Rate
1st quarter	+3.7%	+3.3%
2nd quarter	+1.2%	+2.8%
3rd quarter	+2.8%	+3.1%
4th quarter	+0.1%	+1.9%

Source: BEA Interactive Tables: GDP and the National Income and Product Accounts.

Small Differences in Growth Lead to Large Differences in Income Over Time

When we think of a stark contrast in living standards, we need look no further than the U.S.–Mexican border. Driving along the border, one can see tremendous differences in the quality of housing in Mexico versus that in the United States. Yet, how

The border between the U.S. and Mexico offers a glimpse at the sharp contrast between two nations with different growth paths.

did such a difference in standard of living occur? Did the U.S. economy grow that much faster? The surprising answer is that the U.S. growth rate over the past 100 years averaged just 1% higher than Mexico's growth rate. Perhaps more surprising is that Mexico's real GDP per capita is *above average* in the world. Even Mexico appears "rich" to countries such as Nicaragua and Honduras, whose real GDP per capita is only about one-fourth that of Mexico. If growth rates did not differ much between the United States and Mexico, or between Mexico and Nicaragua over the past century, why are the economies of these countries so different? The answer is the power of compounding growth.

Power of Compounding Growth Rates

Suppose you deposit $1,000 in a high-interest money market account that averages 10% in interest per year. If you simply let the interest accrue without adding any additional money to the account, that $1,000 would turn into $28,102 in 35 years. How is that possible? Money earns interest, in this case 10%. But interest also earns interest. In fact, jump ahead 34 years, when your $1,000 is worth $25,548. In year 35, earning 10% on $25,548 equals over $2,500 in interest, bringing your total to $28,102. In that year, you earned over 2.5 times in interest than the $1,000 you originally put in. That is the power of compounding growth.

Suppose instead that your money grew at 5% per year. What do you think the return will be? One-half of the 10% amount of $28,102? No . . . saving $1,000 at 5% would result in a total value of $5,516 in 35 years, significantly less than half of the $28,102 had the interest rate been 10%. This example shows that small differences in interest equal big changes over time. Suppose that your money grew at 9%, just 1% less than 10%. Your $1,000 would be worth $20,414 in 35 years, a drop of almost $8,000 over this period.

These numerical examples highlight the importance of small differences in growth between the United States and Mexico over time. By growing just 1% faster over a 100-year period, two countries can end up having real GDP per capita several times apart (about 4 times in the case of the United States and Mexico and about 4 times between Mexico and Nicaragua). Over the past 100 years, the United States grew 2% a year on average, Mexico grew 1.2% a year on average, and Nicaragua grew 0.3% a year on average.

At 5% = $5,516   At 10% = $28,102

Doubling the interest rate on a $1,000 deposit generates over 5 times more earnings over 35 years.

Rule of 70

Calculating compounding growth over a long period requires the use of a formula and calculator. Luckily, there is an easy way to *approximate* the number of years it takes for an amount to double in value by using the **Rule of 70**. The Rule of 70 states that the number of years required for a value (such as a nation's GDP) to double in size is equal to 70 divided by the growth rate:

Number of years to double value = 70 / growth rate

Rule of 70 Provides an estimate of the number of years for a value to double, and is calculated as 70 divided by the annual growth rate.

For example, if the growth rate is 10%, it would take about 70/10 = 7 years for an initial value to double (e.g., from $1,000 to $2,000), 14 years to double again (from $2,000 to $4,000), 21 years to double again (from $4,000 to $8,000), and so on.

Can Economic Growth Bring a Billion People Out of Poverty?

Poverty is a global concern. Although definitions of poverty vary from country to country, the World Bank defines *extreme poverty* as a person living on less than $1.25 per day (in real inflation-adjusted dollars). According to World Bank estimates, in 1990 over 2 billion people in the world lived in poverty. Twenty years later, that number had been cut nearly in half. This drop in extreme poverty is even more remarkable considering that the world's population grew from 5.3 billion to 6.8 billion over this period.

How did a billion people find themselves no longer in extreme poverty? Much of the drop can be attributed to economic growth in developing countries such as China and India, and more recently countries in Africa. In China alone, 20 years of solid growth pulled more than 500 million people above the extreme poverty threshold. Although average wages remain low compared to those in the United States or Europe, a typical factory worker making $250 per month can live a modest life in China, where the cost of living is significantly lower, and clearly a better life than in 1990 when average monthly wages were only $20 per month.

India is another country that has begun to see significant reductions in extreme poverty. Although poverty rates remain much higher in India than in Chi-na, India's growth rate of over 7% led to tens of millions exiting poverty each year. And since 2005, many countries in Africa have begun seeing their poverty rates fall, as greater investment in natural resource industries has led to strong economic growth on the mineral- and oil-rich continent.

Clearly, economic growth is a powerful factor, even during times of economic downturn. During the most recent global economic downturn, when average incomes around the world dropped and average food prices rose, one might conclude that the number of people living in poverty would increase. Although poverty based on higher thresholds such as those in the United States and Europe have increased, extreme poverty as defined by the $1.25 per day threshold continued to fall. In fact, Jim Yong Kim, the president of the World Bank, announced in 2013 that extreme poverty can be eliminated by 2030.

In sum, economic growth is arguably the most important contributor to reducing extreme poverty worldwide. Yet, not all problems with poverty have been resolved. First, while extreme poverty has fallen precipitously, poverty as defined by the higher $2 per day threshold has dropped less than 20% since 1990. In other words, while much progress has been made to

Strong economic growth in India over the past 20 years has brought hundreds of millions of people out of poverty, allowing a much more comfortable life for the next generation.

eliminate extreme poverty, nearly a third of the world's population remains very poor.

Hence, economic growth remains one of the most important, if not the most important, macroeconomic objective pursued by policymakers in order to continue the progress of reducing poverty worldwide.

Source: "Global Poverty: A Fall to Cheer," *The Economist*, March 12, 2012. "Is It Crazy to Think We Can Eradicate Poverty?" *The New York Times,* April 30, 2013.

The Rule of 70 is fairly accurate for small growth rates. For larger growth rates, especially above 10%, the Rule of 70 becomes slightly less accurate over time. Table 3 on the next page provides a comparison between actual values and estimated values using the Rule of 70 for 5% and 10% growth rates. The smaller growth rate keeps the Rule of 70 estimated values closer to the actual values than the larger growth rate.

Although the Rule of 70 does not provide an exact estimate of compounded values over time, its ease of use makes it a valuable tool in understanding the power of compounding growth rates over time.

In all examples so far, we have shown how compounding growth can lead to much improved lives over time. However, it is also important to note that the reverse can be true: The compounding effect also makes debts significantly larger over time.

Do you keep a balance on a credit card? If so, you're not alone. The average American household carries about $15,000 in credit card balances each month. Most credit cards

TABLE 3	Accuracy of the Rule of 70			
	5% Growth Rate		10% Growth Rate	
	Actual	**Using Rule of 70**	**Actual**	**Using Rule of 70**
Initial:	$1,000	$1,000	$1,000	$1,000
14 years:	$1,979	$2,000	$3,797	$4,000
28 years:	$3,920	$4,000	$14,421	$16,000

charge interest rates on unpaid balances between 12% and 18%, some even more. Suppose an individual has $15,000 in debt at a 17.5% interest rate. If no payments are made on this debt (let's assume a minimum monthly payment is not required), the Rule of 70 says that the debt will double about every 4 years (70/17.5). If no payments are made on this debt, that $15,000 will turn into $30,000 in 4 years, $60,000 in 8 years, $120,000 in 12 years, and $240,000 in 16 years. Paying off credit card balances can lead to significant savings over time.

In sum, the power of compounding means that policies aimed at increasing the annual rate of economic growth can have powerful long-run effects, resulting in some countries becoming rich while others that do not achieve such growth remain poor. The benefits of economic growth are highlighted through the remarkable rise in income over time that leads to a higher standard of living for all citizens. But what exactly spurs economic growth? That is a question we answer in the next section.

 CHECKPOINT

WHY IS ECONOMIC GROWTH IMPORTANT?

- Economic growth is measured by the increase in real GDP and real GDP per capita. In the United States, it is measured by the BEA on a quarterly basis as an annualized percentage change as well as a year-over-year change.

- Small differences in growth rates translate into large differences in income over time. Just a 1% difference in growth over time can make one country appear rich and another country appear poor.

- The Rule of 70 provides an easy way to approximate the number of years required for a value to double.

QUESTIONS: In 2012, the average Chinese manufacturing worker earned about $3,000 a year, while the average U.S. manufacturing worker earned $48,000 a year. Suppose that the U.S. growth rate is 3% per year (income doubles about every 24 years using the Rule of 70), while China's growth rate is 9% per year (income doubles about every 8 years using the Rule of 70). If these growth rates do not change, in what year would the typical Chinese worker earn $48,000 a year? In what year would the typical Chinese worker catch up to the American worker if U.S. wages continue to increase by 3% per year?

Answers to the Checkpoint questions can be found at the end of this chapter.

Thinking About Short-Run and Long-Run Economic Growth

Up to this point, we have discussed why economic growth is good and how it is measured. Next, we need to discuss the differences between short-run and long-run growth and the factors that determine economic growth.

Short-Run Versus Long-Run Growth

The first step to understanding how growth occurs is to understand the difference between short-run and long-run growth.

Short-Run Growth Involves a Fixed Capacity Short-run growth occurs when an economy makes use of existing but underutilized resources. For example, abandoned shopping centers or malls could easily be reopened with new stores. Idle construction equipment and unemployed workers could quickly be put into use on a new project. In these cases, the resources to produce goods and services are available but are not being used.

Short-run growth is common when countries are recovering from an economic downturn, or when obstacles preventing resources from being fully used (such as restrictions on land use or high mandatory benefits for workers) are loosened. But to sustain growth beyond the small fluctuations common in the business cycle, efforts to expand an economy's ability to produce are necessary. This leads to long-run growth.

Long-Run Growth Involves Expanding Capacity Long-run growth occurs when an economy finds new resources or finds ways to use existing resources better. In other words, the capacity to produce goods and services increases, leading to long-run growth. For example, suppose natural gas deposits that are estimated to be abundant in the United States are explored, leading to an expansion in production of natural gas powered vehicles (NGVs). This may lead to an expansion of production capacity in the United States through the reduction of its dependence on foreign oil and through the development of more environmentally friendly cars.

In Chapter 2, we introduced production possibility frontiers (PPF) to illustrate the maximum productive capacity of an economy if all resources are fully utilized. We can use PPF diagrams to show the difference between short-run and long-run economic growth.

In Figure 1 on the next page, the left panel shows an economy initially producing at point *a* inside of its PPF, indicating underutilized resources such as idle equipment or excess labor. By putting these resources to work, an economy can work its way toward production capacity on the PPF line at point *b,* representing short-run growth. Long-run growth, illustrated in the right panel, requires an economy to find new resources such as

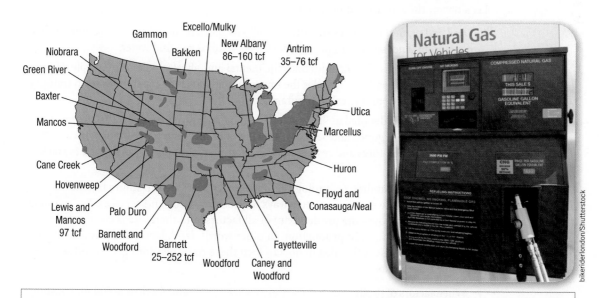

Natural gas deposits are so abundant in the United States that it has been dubbed the "Saudi Arabia of Natural Gas."

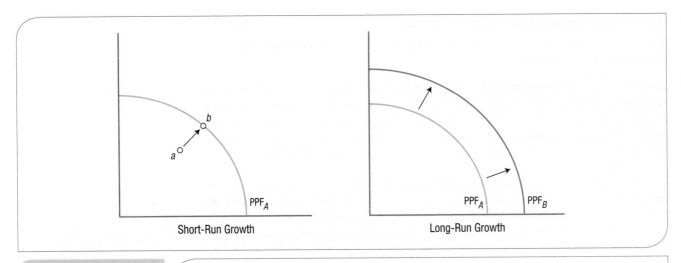

Short-Run Growth

Long-Run Growth

FIGURE 1

Short-Run Versus Long-Run Growth Illustrated on PPF Diagrams

Short-run economic growth occurs when underutilized resources are placed into production. In a PPF diagram, this is shown as a movement from a point inside the PPF to a point closer to or on the PPF (such as from *a* to *b*). Long-run economic growth occurs when new resources are found or existing resources are used more efficiently, thus expanding an economy's capacity to produce. In this case, PPF_A expands outward to PPF_B, allowing for more production possibilities.

new natural resources or improved human capital in its workforce, or new ideas to make better use of existing resources. Such improvements in production capacity will shift PPF_A outward to PPF_B, allowing for more production possibilities.

Factors of Production

Achieving long-run growth requires an economy to acquire new resources or to find better ways to use the resources it has to generate goods and services people desire either domestically or abroad through trade. In Chapter 2, we introduced these resources as the four factors of production, which are the building blocks for production and economic growth. Let's review these factors of production.

1. Land and natural resources (denoted as "N") includes land and any raw resources that come from land, such as mineral deposits, oil, natural gas, and water.

2. Labor (denoted as "L") includes both the mental and physical talents of people. Human capital (denoted as "H") includes the improvements to labor capabilities from training, education, and apprenticeship programs.

3. Physical capital (denoted as "K") includes all manufactured products that are used to produce other goods and services. This includes machinery used in factories, cash registers in stores and restaurants, and communications networks used to track shipments.

4. Entrepreneurial ability, technology, and ideas (A) describe the ability to take resources and use them in creative ways to produce goods and services. For example, technology improves the productivity of all factors, and therefore is considered a highly valuable input in production. In other words, land, labor, and physical capital are not useful unless the idea of how to turn these resources into goods and services people want exists.

When factors of production are used to produce goods and services useful for consumption, a measurement tool is needed to calculate the extent to which inputs (resources) are turned into outputs (goods and services). The relationship between the amount of inputs used in production and the amount of output produced is called a production function.

Production Function

A **production function** shows the output that is produced using different combinations of inputs combined with existing technology. Although many types of production functions exist, most are variations of the classical form: Output = f(L, K), which means that output is determined by some function of available labor or capital.

production function Measures the output that is produced using various combinations of inputs and a fixed level of technology.

Every country, industry, and even firm can have a different production function that measures how much output it can produce given the physical inputs and technology available. No two countries will produce exactly the same type or amount of products given the resources they have. Thus, a production function is a very important tool used to determine whether a country is using its limited resources efficiently and to what extent it can experience long-run growth.

Suppose f(L, K) = L + K for simplicity. This means that if an economy has 10 units of labor and 10 units of capital, total output would equal 10 + 10 = 20. Although most production functions are not this simple, the idea is that more inputs can produce more output by some function.

Because inputs are not limited to just labor and capital, a more realistic production function would look like the following:

$$\text{Output} = A \times f(L, K, H, N)$$

where total output equals technology (A) times a function of available labor (L), physical capital (K), human capital (H), and land and natural resources (N).

This equation helps to explain how an entire economy grows. For example, having a more educated labor force or having more capital will contribute to higher productive capacity of the economy (shifting the PPF outward).

But what we are truly interested in is how growth affects the lives of people living in those countries. For example, India's GDP has grown at a very fast pace, but so has its population. The important question is how economic growth affects the standard of living of the average person, or output per person. One way to achieve a close (but not exact) measure of output per person is to revise the above production function to one that measures output per worker.

To do so, assume that the production function exhibits constant returns to scale (a reasonable assumption). This means that any proportional change in the number of inputs results in the same proportional change in output. For example, if we divide all inputs by L, we would be able to calculate the output per worker as follows:

$$\text{Output per worker} = A \times f(L/L, K/L, H/L, N/L)$$

This equation shows that output per worker equals technology times a function of physical capital per worker, human capital per worker, and land and natural resources per worker.

JOSEPH SCHUMPETER (1883–1950)

Joseph Schumpeter drew attention to the critical role of the entrepreneur in the process of economic development. He famously coined the term "creative destruction" to describe the innovative dynamism of capitalism but came to the surprising conclusion that the system he exalted was ultimately doomed by the forces it helped create.

Born in Triesch, Moravia, in 1883, Schumpeter studied law and economics at the University of Vienna. In 1932, he emigrated to the United States, where he became an influential economics professor at Harvard University.

Schumpeter was a confirmed elitist who suffered from self-doubt and depression. Although he enjoyed telling audiences that he "aspired to become the greatest economist, horseman, and lover in the world," he would then throw in the punchline, "but things are not going well with the horses." Even though his career was in the shadow of the more famous John Maynard Keynes, he considered himself to be the greater economist.

In 1939, he published *Business Cycles,* which linked entrepreneurial activity to business cycles. He identified "waves of innovation," and paradoxically, connected innovation with the downturns or depressions in the business cycle, as new products competed with the old. Depressions, in his view, were part of the process of adapting to new innovations.

In 1942, Schumpeter published *Capitalism, Socialism and Democracy,* considered by many to be his masterpiece. He wrote about the future of capitalism, which he described as *creative destruction.* The influence of Schumpeter's work is still seen today in the study of modern growth theory.

Sources: Thomas McCraw, *Prophet of Innovation: Joseph Schumpeter and Creative Destruction* (Cambridge, MA: Harvard University Press), 2007; Paul Strathern, *A Brief History of Economic Genius* (New York: Texere), 2001.

Because we are concerned with output per worker, having more people will not automatically lead to a better standard of living (hence, L/L = 1). However, having more capital per person or more human capital (education) will increase the productivity of labor as each worker produces more output. Therefore, increases in capital will lead to improved standards of living.

To this point, we have discussed the importance of economic growth and defined the building blocks for economic growth using the factors of production that enter into the production function. The next section will use the production function to discuss ways in which an economy achieves growth by way of increasing productivity.

CHECKPOINT

THINKING ABOUT SHORT-RUN AND LONG-RUN ECONOMIC GROWTH

- Short-run growth occurs from using resources that have been sitting idle or underutilized, and is represented in a PPF diagram as a movement from a point within the PPF toward the PPF.

- Long-run growth occurs when the productive capacity of an economy is expanded through more resources or better uses of existing resources, and is shown in a PPF diagram as an outward shift of the PPF.

- The primary factors of production are land and natural resources, labor (and human capital), physical capital, and technology (entrepreneurial ability and ideas).

- A production function measures the amount of output that can be produced using different combinations of inputs. Production functions vary by firms, industries, and countries.

- Output per person adjusts the production function for changes in population growth in a country.

QUESTION: The Ivory Coast (Côte d'Ivoire) in West Africa is a country with abundant natural resources, a long coastline, and a stable currency that is tied to the euro and managed by the French Treasury. Despite these benefits, it remains an extremely poor country with an unstable government. What does this finding suggest about the Ivory Coast's overall factors of production and its production function compared to a country, say Iceland, with fewer physical resources but a significantly higher standard of living?

Answers to the Checkpoint question can be found at the end of this chapter.

Applying the Production Function: Achieving Economic Growth

The production function allows us to measure how inputs are converted into outputs. The extent to which inputs are converted into outputs is referred to as **productivity.** For example, when worker productivity grows, each worker is producing more output for each hour devoted to production.

productivity How effectively inputs are converted into outputs. Labor productivity is the ratio of the output of goods and services to the labor hours devoted to the production of that output. Higher productivity and higher living standards are closely related.

Productivity is a key driver of wages and incomes. The primary reason that the American standard of living is so high is that American workers produce more per hour than do workers in most other countries. Many people in the developing world eke out a living using tools that would remind us of an earlier century. This lower productivity is reflected in their lower standard of living.

The factors of production discussed in the previous section play an important role in increasing economic growth. As the quantity of each factor rises, output rises according to the production function for each industry. In addition, technology plays an important role in enhancing the productive output of all other resources.

A country's output is measured by the value of the goods and services it produces, which can increase based on their quantity or quality. In other words, highly productive countries are able to produce many goods that are high in value. One reason why Japan remains one of the world's richest countries is that its labor force is highly productive—using abundant capital, human capital, and technology, Japan's labor force produces many high-priced products such as cars, robots, and advanced electronics.

Let's look at each factor of production in turn to examine what increases productivity and economic growth.

Achieving More Land or Natural Resources

Natural resources are the building blocks of production; however, they are not a significant driver of economic growth. Countries that are abundant in land and natural resources have an advantage that can translate into economic growth only if such resources are used effectively. Countries that discovered new natural resources have experienced higher rates of growth. For example, new oil deposits have been discovered in Angola and Cameroon over the past decade. These discoveries led to significant investment by oil companies from China, India, and the United States in these countries, which contributed to a higher growth rate.

Growth of the Labor Force

Many countries have experienced significant population growth, leading to an increase in the labor supply. In the United States, population growth has been spurred by a relatively open immigration policy compared to other countries. In addition to population growth, labor force participation increased over the last few decades, as more women entered the workforce and as government policies were implemented to make work more attractive. An increase in the labor force generally leads to greater output, but not necessarily more output per person. In order for economic growth to improve the standard of living of its citizens, countries must not only expand the quantity of its labor force, but also the quality of labor to ensure that economic growth exceeds population growth.

Increasing the Quality of the Labor Force

One source of productivity growth comes from improvements to the labor force from **investment in human capital.** Human capital is a term economists use to describe skills, knowledge, and the quality of workers. On-the-job training and general education can improve the quality of labor. In many ways, increasing capital and a highly skilled labor force go together: Well-trained workers are needed to run the highly productive, often highly complex, machines. Unskilled workers are given the least important jobs and earn the lowest wages.

investment in human capital Improvements to the labor force from investments in skills, knowledge, and the overall quality of workers and their productivity.

By investing in human capital, nations can ultimately raise their growth rates by improving worker productivity. Government programs that raise the literacy rate, such as universal public education, also raise the rate of economic growth.

Increasing the Capital-to-Labor Ratio

When a farmer in the small Himalayan country of Bhutan plows his field with a crude plow hitched to a couple of yaks, the amount of land he can plant and harvest is miniscule. American farmers, in contrast, use equipment that allows them to plow, plant, fertilize, water, and harvest thousands of acres; they have a high **capital-to-labor ratio.** This raises U.S. farm productivity many orders of magnitude above that of poor Bhutanese farmers. The ultimate result of this productivity is that American farmers earn a far higher income than their counterparts in the developing world.

capital-to-labor ratio The capital employed per worker. A higher ratio means higher labor productivity and, as a result, higher wages.

Developing countries have large labor forces, but little capital. Developed nations like the United States, on the other hand, have limited labor supplies, and each worker works with a large array of capital equipment. As a rule, the more capital employed by workers, the greater their productivity and the higher their earnings.

Although a powerful contributor to productivity, capital is subject to **diminishing returns to capital.** For example, suppose that the farmer in Bhutan buys a tractor to replace his yaks. The increase in productivity would be dramatic. Now suppose that the farmer invests in an irrigation system. Surely the irrigation system will further increase productivity, but likely not as much as the tractor did. In other words, a farmer is likely to purchase the most essential equipment first. Each subsequent piece of equipment will

diminishing returns to capital Each additional unit of capital provides a smaller increase in output than the previous unit of capital.

Using expensive tractors and other capital equipment, U.S. farmers are more productive than Bhutanese farmers who rely on wooden plows pulled by yaks.

increase production but by a smaller amount than the previous one. For this reason, countries with abundant capital will not gain as much per additional piece of capital than countries with little capital with which to start. This is one reason why developing countries may initially grow faster than developed countries, a phenomenon called the catch-up effect.

The **catch-up effect** describes the idea that developing countries are able to achieve greater productivity for each unit of capital invested because they have the advantage of using technologies that have already been developed by other countries. This has allowed many developing countries to achieve a higher rate of growth compared to developed countries.

An example of the catch-up effect is China's expanding high-speed rail network. High-speed rail networks were largely invented and perfected by the Japanese, Germans, and French. However, large development costs required substantial government subsidies. China, on the other hand, had the advantage of building its rail network using existing technologies. As a result, China was able to expand its rail network at a lower price per mile, allowing it to catch up and to develop an even more advanced rail network than its predecessors. But because all factors face diminishing returns, the catch-up effect tends to slow over time unless new technologies are developed to keep the growth rate high.

Improvements in Technology and Ideas

Technological improvements can come from various sources and play *the* major role in improving productivity, raising the standard of living, and increasing economic growth. These include enterprising individuals who discover innovative products and production methods, from Henry Ford's auto assembly

THOMAS MALTHUS (1766–1834)

Thomas Malthus was raised in Surrey, England, the son of a wealthy eccentric country gentleman. Home-schooled by his father and a tutor, he had learned enough to be accepted to Cambridge University. After attending Cambridge, he spent several years as a clergyman before accepting a teaching post in political economy at the college of the East India Company, making him the first academic economist in history.

In 1793, the pamphleteer William Godwin published *Political Justice,* describing a utopian future with no war, poverty, crime, injustice, or disease. Malthus argued against the book's conclusions during a lengthy discussion with his father, who agreed with the book, but nevertheless suggested that Malthus set down his ideas in print.

The result was "An Essay on the Principle of Population as It Affects the Future Improvement of Society." Malthus argued that the origins of poverty were rooted in an unavoidable contradiction: Population, when allowed to grow without limits, increases geometrically, while the food supply could only increase arithmetically. He argued that English Poor Laws spread pauperism because any improvement in conditions of the poor would simply lead to population increases and to rising food prices and scarcities.

He even went so far as to suggest that "a proclamation should be read out at marriage ceremonies warning couples that they would have to bear the financial burden and consequences of their passion."

His dire predictions about world starvation led Thomas Carlyle a few decades later to describe the economics profession as the "Dismal Science." Although the predictions of inadequate food supply did not fully materialize due to the invention of agricultural technologies and fertilizer, the "Dismal Science" remains today as an alternative name for economics.

Sources: Paul Strathern, *A Brief History of Economic Genius* (New York: Texere), 2002; Howard Marshall, *The Great Economists: A History of Economic Thought* (New York: Pitman Publishing), 1967; Donald Winch, "Malthus," in *Three Great Economists* (Oxford: Oxford University Press), 1997, pp. 105–218.

line to Steve Jobs's role in developing the Apple home computer, iPod, iPhone, and iPad that have changed the way we live, work, and socialize. Technology has also improved as a result of advancements in telecommunications, the Internet, and biotechnology.

Technological progress is the primary explanation for the extraordinary economic growth the United States has enjoyed over the last century. In the production function, technology enhances the productive capacity of all other resources.

Technologies that kept our economy expanding have also helped many other countries to grow. In the developing world, growth most often comes from foreign companies building factories that employ locals at low wages. These companies often pay more than workers could have hoped to earn on their own. These higher earnings become the grubstake to ensure better education and earnings for their children.

Today, new technologies are helping many developing nations accelerate their growth. Wireless service has improved communications, inexpensive vaccinations and health education programs have reduced mortality rates, and the global movement of capital and production facilities has created new job opportunities.

catch-up effect Countries with smaller starting levels of capital experience larger benefits from increased capital, allowing these countries to grow faster than countries with abundant capital.

Including Everything Else: Total Factor Productivity

We have shown that productivity can be measured by how well a country uses its resources to produce goods and services. However, a country's productivity is not entirely dependent on the amount of inputs it has. True, a country with more inputs such as physical and

ISSUE

The Role of Social Media in Promoting Economic Growth

Social media have changed the way individuals communicate with friends, co-workers, and family members. They also have changed the way people buy goods and services and the way businesses market their products. Social media allow both individuals and firms to do more with fewer resources, contributing to greater productivity, a driver of economic growth.

It wasn't that long ago when the most common way to find deals and sales was to comb through the local newspaper and advertising inserts. However, print newspaper readership has declined precipitously as online news sources, including news alerts through social media sites such as Twitter, take their place. Because firms have longed relied on newspapers as a source of advertising, a change was needed to adapt to the growth of social media.

And the collection of information does not stop there. The power of consumer-to-consumer persuasion has made online product feedback an im-

portant source of advertising. Customers who rate products and services after their purchase (often following an email solicitation from sellers) provide influential information to potential customers who are likely to trust product reviews from previous users, especially if a large percentage of previous users are satisfied with their purchases.

Further, businesses have been formed to harness the powerful role of consumer-to-consumer commerce that social media facilitate. Beginning with eBay and Craigslist over a decade ago, today, companies such as Groupon and Angie's List allow individuals to promote products to other consumers. Com-

bined with global-positioning devices that help potential consumers locate nearby merchants, such changes in the way businesses interact with potential consumers have reduced the time it requires for new products to be introduced into the market.

Much like prior innovations that have changed the way we live, social media have made markets more efficient by allowing buyers and sellers to interact more seamlessly. In doing so, productivity rises and contributes to economic growth. But as we have seen before, inventions sometimes come and go; therefore, the next big invention might be right around the corner.

total factor productivity The portion of output produced that is not explained by the number of inputs used in production.

human capital will likely produce more output. However, external factors influence the ability of inputs to be used effectively. The measure of output that is not explained by the number of inputs used in production is called **total factor productivity.**

Total factor productivity captures the factors that influence the overall effectiveness of inputs. For example, suppose a major hurricane sweeps through a region, knocking out power and communications for a week. Factories would likely be less productive despite having all of its workers and equipment available. Some equipment might not be able to run without electricity, and the morale of workers after a hurricane might make them less motivated to work. Such effects on output would not be captured by the number of inputs available.

Another factor affecting total factor productivity is the value of new innovations, which increases the efficiency of inputs used in production. For example, social media were originally designed to allow individuals to communicate better with one another through sites such as Facebook and Twitter. However, an external effect occurred when firms began to use these sites to market their products, which led to a dramatic change in how people learn about various products and improved the efficiency of production and consumption. The Issue on the previous page discusses the role social media have had on economic growth.

Total factor productivity also is influenced by the institutions in place within a country. For example, a country can have a very educated labor force but policies in place that prevent its human capital from being used efficiently. The country could be engaged in frequent military conflicts, preventing its resources from being used to improve the lives of its citizens. Or, a country may have a weak legal system or property rights, or a lack of economic freedom that prevents its markets from producing what people want. These institutional factors are largely influenced by the government. In the next section, we discuss government's role in fostering economic growth.

 CHECKPOINT

APPLYING THE PRODUCTION FUNCTION: ACHIEVING ECONOMIC GROWTH

- Productivity is the key driver for economic growth, and rises when labor is able to produce greater quantities and higher values of output.

- Increased productivity of labor can come from increases in land and natural resources, the quality of the labor force, the capital-to-labor ratio, and improvements in technology.

- Physical capital is subjected to diminishing returns, which allows countries with less starting capital to experience a catch-up effect as they acquire more capital.

- Total factor productivity measures the portion of output that is not explained by the amount of inputs placed in use. It captures the external effects that influence the productivity of all inputs.

QUESTION: In June 2010, Warren Buffett, one of the world's richest individuals, pledged that "more than 99% of my wealth will go to philanthropy during my lifetime or at death" and noted that he would give this approximately $30 billion in installments to the Bill & Melinda Gates Foundation. The foundation focuses on grants to developing nations, helping the poorest of the poor. What suggestions would you give the foundation to help these developing nations grow?

Answers to the Checkpoint question can be found at the end of this chapter.

⊙ The Role of Government in Promoting Economic Growth

Government plays an important role in how well a country utilizes its resources in production. The policies and incentives put into place affect a country's total factor productivity. We will discuss some of the key ways in which government plays a role in influencing productivity.

Government as a Contributor to Physical Capital, Human Capital, and Technology

The government is the single largest consumer of goods and services in the United States. Each year, the U.S. government spends over $350 billion on purchases including highways, bridges, transportation systems, public education, military equipment, and more. By investing heavily in capital goods, the government is promoting a higher level of labor productivity in the country.

Physical Capital: Public Capital and Private Investment One of the reasons why some nations are rich and others are poor lies in the different levels of infrastructure development among various countries. The focus on infrastructure means that there is something important that lies behind our aggregate production: We do not just increase capital, increase labor, improve technology, and turn a crank to obtain economic growth.

Infrastructure is defined as a country's public capital. It includes dams, roads, and bridges; transportation networks, such as air and rail lines; power-generating plants and power transmission lines; telecommunications networks; and public education facilities. These items are tangible public goods that can easily be measured. All are crucial for economic growth.

The government also encourages private investment in physical capital through tax incentives and other subsidies to firms willing to invest in capital projects. Industries that receive the largest tax incentives include aerospace, defense, energy, and telecommunications.

> **infrastructure** The public capital of a nation, including transportation networks, power-generating plants and transmission facilities, public education institutions, and other intangible resources such as protection of property rights and a stable monetary environment.

Human Capital: Public Education and Financial Aid The government plays an important role in ensuring that every person has access to a minimum level of education. In the United States, state laws mandate that children stay in school until a minimum age, typically 16. Public schools and universities are highly subsidized by local and state governments to provide affordable access to educational opportunities.

Besides providing funding directly to schools and universities, the government offers various forms of need-based and merit-based financial assistance directly to students to use toward educational expenses. These include Pell Grants and the G.I. Bill, federal subsidized loans, and various types of tax incentives that allow qualified students (or their parents) to deduct a portion of their tuition and fees from their taxable income or from their taxes directly. The government also allows teachers to deduct certain expenses from their taxes, and provides tax-exempt status for organizations whose mission is to provide scholarships, such as the prestigious National Merit Scholarship Program. These grants, loans, and tax incentives contribute to the government's role in promoting human capital.

Technology: Government R&D Centers and Federal Grants Some of the largest research centers in the country are government funded. These include Los Alamos National Laboratory and Sandia National Laboratories (part of the Department of Energy), the National Institutes of Health, the National Aeronautics and Space Administration (NASA), and the National Oceanic and Atmospheric Administration (NOAA), just to name a few. These government research centers employ thousands of scientists, researchers, and doctors for the purpose of advancing knowledge and inventing products that enhance the lives of all citizens and promote economic growth.

In addition to running research centers, the government provides funds directly to public and private research centers as well as to individual researchers. Among the largest grantors of funds is the National Science Foundation (NSF), founded in 1950. In 2012,

Richard Robinson/Los Alamos National Laboratory

The Los Alamos National Laboratory in New Mexico is one of the largest government research centers in the country. During World War II, it was a secret lab that housed the "Manhattan Project," which ultimately produced the world's first atomic bomb.

the NSF provided nearly $7 billion in grants to nearly 12,000 projects, and has maintained its mission of promoting research essential for a nation's economic health and global competitiveness.

Government as a Facilitator of Economic Growth

A second major role of government in promoting economic growth is to ensure that an effective legal system is in place to enforce contracts and to protect property rights, and that the financial system is kept stable. These are the less tangible yet equally important components of a country's infrastructure.

Enforcement of Contracts The legal enforcement of contract rights is an important component of an infrastructure that promotes economic growth and well-being. Without contract enforcement, people are less likely to be willing to enter into contracts, for example, to produce and deliver goods for payment at some future date. Therefore, contract enforcement promotes economic growth by ensuring that production and purchasing commitments made by producers and consumers are honored.

Protection of Property Rights A stable legal system that protects property rights is essential for economic growth. Many developing countries do not systematically record the ownership of real property: land and buildings. Although ownership is often informally recognized, without express legal title, the capital locked up in these informal arrangements cannot be used to secure loans for entrepreneurial purposes. As a result, valuable capital sits idle; it cannot be leveraged for other productive purposes.[1]

In addition, a legal system that recognizes and protects ideas (or intellectual property) is critical to encouraging innovation. Common legal protections for ideas include patents (for inventions), copyrights (for written work), and trademarks (for names and symbols). Every country has its innovators; the question is whether these people are offered enough of an incentive to devote their efforts to coming up with the innovations that drive economic growth. The extent to which countries establish intellectual property rights varies, and even when such protections exist, enforcement of the protections varies.

Stable Financial System Another important component of a nation's infrastructure is a stable and secure financial system. Such a financial system keeps the purchasing power of the currency stable, facilitates transactions, and permits credit institutions to arise. The recent global financial turmoil is an example of the problems caused by financial instability. Further, bank runs, like those that caused major economic disruption in Uruguay and Argentina in 2001–2002, are less likely when a nation's financial environment is stable.

Unanticipated inflations or deflations are both detrimental to economic growth. Consumers and businesses rely on the monetary prices they pay for goods and services for information about the state of the market. If these price signals are constantly being distorted by inflation or deflation, the quality of business and consumer decisions suffers. Unanticipated price changes further lead to a redistribution of income between creditors and debtors. Financial instability is harmful to improving standards of living and generating economic growth.

Government as a Promoter of Free and Competitive Markets

A third role of government in promoting economic growth is maintaining competitive and efficient markets and the freedom for firms and individuals to pursue their interests.

Competitive Markets and Free Trade One of the challenges of government is choosing the right mix of policies to keep markets competitive and fair. Regulations are put into place to protect various interests, whether consumer welfare, worker rights and safety, or

---

[1] For an extensive discussion of this issue, see Hernando de Soto, *The Mystery of Capital: Why Capitalism Triumphs in the West and Fails Everywhere Else* (New York: Basic Books), 2000.

the environment. But government also must ensure such regulations not stand in the way of markets operating efficiently.

Competitive markets refer to the ability of firms to open and close businesses without unnecessary restrictions or other burdens. Free trade refers to the ability to buy and sell products with other countries without significant barriers such as tariffs or quotas. Allowing the market to function freely within the confines of sensible regulatory laws generally creates more potential for economic growth.

Economic Freedom   One of the measures used to gauge the ability of individuals and businesses to make investment and production decisions freely is the Index of Economic Freedom.

Unlike physical infrastructure such as roads and dams, which are easy to measure, attempting to measure the intangibles of doing business often requires subjective judgments. One reasonably objective measure is the 2013 Index of Economic Freedom.[2] This index incorporates information about freedoms in ten categories: business, trade, fiscal policy, government size, monetary policy, investment, finance, property rights, corruption, and labor.

Clearly, assigning some of these items a numeric value requires some subjective judgment. Even so, this index is one reasonable approach to measuring the overall infrastructure of a country.

Figure 2 portrays the relationship between economic freedom and per capita GDP measured by purchasing power parity (what income will buy in each country). Those nations with the most economic freedom have the highest per capita GDP and also the highest growth rates (not shown).

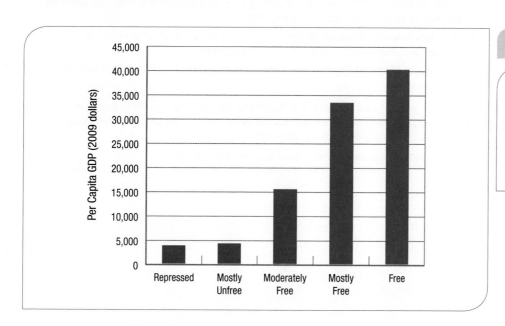

FIGURE 2

Economic Freedom and Per Capita GDP

The relationship between economic freedom and per capita GDP is shown here. Those nations with the most economic freedom also have the highest per capita GDP.

Economist Peter Bauer from the London School of Economics argued that "opportunities for private profit, not government plans, held the key to development. Governments had the limited though crucial role of protecting property rights, enforcing contracts, treating everybody equally before the law, minimizing inflation and keeping taxes low."[3] Today, his ideas are part of a new conventional

---

[2] Heritage Foundation, *2013 Index of Economic Freedom* (Washington, DC), 2013.
[3] "Economic Focus: A Voice for the Poor," *The Economist,* May 4, 2002, p. 76.

wisdom that government should act as a promoter rather than as a provider of economic growth.

In this chapter, we have seen that economic growth in the long run comes from improvements in labor productivity, increases in capital, or improvements in technology. Investments in human capital and greater economic freedom also lead to higher growth rates and higher standards of living.

In the long run, all of these factors generate growth and higher standards of living. Yet, what are we to do if the economy collapses in the short run? The Great Depression of the 1930s was to prove that for a reasonably long period (a decade), the economy could be mired in a slowdown with high unemployment rates and negative growth. A deep economy-wide downturn inflicts high costs on both today's citizens and future generations. In the next chapter we turn to the first of our discussions on managing the economy in the short run.

 # CHECKPOINT

THE ROLE OF GOVERNMENT IN PROMOTING ECONOMIC GROWTH

- Government has an important role in promoting economic growth by providing physical and human capital, ensuring a stable legal system and financial markets, and promoting free and competitive markets.

- Infrastructure is a country's public capital, including dams, roads, transportation networks, power-generating plants, and public schools.

- Governments provide capital and technology by purchasing public capital and providing incentives for private investment, supporting education through subsidies and financial aid, and supporting research and development.

- Other less tangible infrastructure elements include protection of property rights, enforcement of contracts, and a stable financial system.

- The Index of Economic Freedom measures a country's infrastructure, which supports economic growth.

QUESTION: Imagine a country with a "failed government" that can no longer enforce the law. Contracts are not upheld and lawlessness is the order of the day. How well could an economy operate and grow in this environment?

Answers to the Checkpoint question can be found at the end of this chapter.

chapter summary

Section 1: Why Is Economic Growth Important?

Economic growth is the most important factor influencing a country's standard of living. Economic growth is measured by a nation's ability to increase **real GDP** and **real GDP per capita.** Using *real* values instead of *nominal* values allows a country to compare growth from year to year without having to take into account the effects of inflation. Countries with high economic growth have seen rising incomes and better lives for their citizens.

The Rule of 70 is a simple tool used to estimate the number of years needed to double a value given a constant growth rate.

Number of years = 70 / growth rate

Examples: Number of years to double at growth rate of:

1% = 70/1% = 70 years

2% = 70/2% = 35 years

5% = 70/5% = 14 years

10% = 70/10% = 7 years

20% = 70/20% = 3.5 years

Small differences in growth can equal big differences over time due to the power of **compounding.**

Using the Rule of 70 to estimate 5% versus 10% growth:

Year	Value at 5%	Year	Value at 10%
2015	$1,000	2015	$1,000
		2022	$2,000
2029	$2,000	2029	$4,000
		2036	$8,000
2043	$4,000	2043	$16,000

In 28 years, the initial $1,000 is worth $16,000 at 10% growth versus $4,000 at 5% growth.

Section 2: Thinking About Short-Run and Long-Run Economic Growth

Short-Run Versus Long-Run Growth

Short-run growth occurs when an economy makes use of existing or underutilized resources, and is shown as a movement from inside a PPF toward the PPF (such as from point *a* to point *b*).

Long-run growth requires an expansion of production capacity through an increase in resources or technology, and is shown by a shift of the PPF (such as from PPF_A to PPF_B).

Factors of Production

- **Land (N):** includes land and natural resources
- **Labor (L):** within labor is human capital **(H),** labor improved by education or training
- **Capital (K):** manufactured goods used in the production process
- **Entrepreneurial ability (A):** ideas and technology

Short and Long-Run

A **production function** is the method by which firms turn factors of production into goods and services.

Section 3: Applying the Production Function: Achieving Economic Growth

Productivity is the ability to turn a fixed amount of inputs (factors of production) into more outputs (goods and services).

Ways to Increase Productivity

- Increasing access to natural resources
- Improving quality of labor (human capital)
- Increasing the capital-to-labor ratio
- Promoting innovation and technology

Rising productivity leads to growing incomes and a better standard of living.

Total factor productivity is a measurement of productivity taking into account all other factors other than the quantity and quality of inputs that could influence production. Examples include natural disasters, climate, or cultural norms that influence the effectiveness of productive inputs.

Section 4: The Role of Government in Promoting Economic Growth

The government can promote economic growth by investing in physical capital, human capital, and technology.

Government involvement in promoting economic growth occurs by way of:

- **Physical capital:** The building and maintenance of the country's public capital (infrastructure), which includes roads, bridges, airports, power plants, and telecommunications networks.

- **Human capital:** Providing subsidized public college education, financial aid grants and loans.

- **Technology:** Funding research and development, and the establishment of major government research labs.

West Point, the United States Military Academy, is an example of government promoting physical capital (the campus and buildings), human capital (education), and technology (research by its faculty).

Government As a Guarantor of Economic Growth

- **Enforcement of contracts:** A strong legal system.

- **Protection of property rights:** Ensuring that monetary rewards are provided to innovators.

- **Stable financial system:** A functioning and stable monetary system ensures investment is undertaken when the opportunity arises.

- **Promoting free and competitive markets:** International trade allows for specialization and gains from trade, and competitive markets ensure firms do not exploit market power, their ability to set prices for goods and services in a market.

The **Index of Economic Freedom** ranks 184 nations in terms of overall environment for promoting economic growth. In 2013, Hong Kong ranked first, and the United States came in tenth.

KEY CONCEPTS

economic growth, p. 468
compounding, p. 470
real GDP, p. 471
real GDP per capita, p. 471
Rule of 70, p. 472

production function, p. 477
productivity, p. 478
investment in human capital, p. 479
capital-to-labor ratio, p. 479
diminishing returns to capital, p. 479

catch-up effect, p. 480
total factor productivity, p. 482
infrastructure, p. 483

QUESTIONS AND PROBLEMS

Check Your Understanding

1. Although abundant natural resources can be a blessing to a country, are they necessary to ensure economic growth and a prosperous economy?

2. Why does a small difference in the economic growth rate lead to big differences over time?

3. What are some ways in which countries can improve labor productivity?

4. In what ways do governments help to build technology and ideas?

5. Why is investment in human capital good for both individuals and fostering economic growth for the economy as a whole?

6. Why is a stable financial system important to economic growth?

Apply the Concepts

7. The standard of living we enjoy today is largely due to the investments of earlier generations of Americans. Do you agree? Why or why not?

8. What role might foreign investment play in helping developing nations improve their growth rate and increase income levels?

9. Higher levels of savings and investment lead to greater rates of economic growth. What can government do to encourage more savings and investment?

10. Per capita income (or output) is the general measure used to compare the standards of living between countries. If a country's population growth is higher than its economic growth, what happens to per capita income? What are some of the limitations to using per capita income as a measure to compare the well-being of different countries?

11. In 1988, Nobel Prize–winner Robert Lucas suggested that differences in growth rates between Egypt and India raise the most fundamental economic question of what causes economic growth. What makes this issue of growth so important? Is a long-term growth rate of 1.4% so different from one of 3.4%?

12. One of the potential negative consequences of both economic and population growth is that we will eventually exhaust the Earth's natural resources, leading to our demise. What kind of activities might prevent this from happening?

In the News

13. Severe budget cuts at the federal and state level caused Education Secretary Arne Duncan to warn Congress about the long-term effects of education cuts on global competitiveness and economic growth ("Duncan Warns Congress on Impact of 'Sequestration' on Education Programs," *Washington Post*, February 14, 2013). In 2013, nearly two-thirds of states still spent less money on education per student than in 2008; meanwhile, countries in Europe and Asia have increased spending on education despite the economic downturn. If the reduction in education spending in the United States does in fact slow economic growth, explain why the effects of the slower growth will be felt much more by your grandchildren than by you today.

14. Energy independence has been a goal for each of the presidential administrations since Richard Nixon in the 1970s ("U.S. Inches Toward Goal of Energy Independence," *The New York Times*, March 22, 2012). But the increased focus on alternative energy sources, such as natural gas, wind, water, and solar, along with greater emphasis on fuel-saving technology (hybrid and plug-in cars) has only taken on greater significance in the last decade. How does achieving energy independence contribute to labor productivity and economic growth?

Solving Problems

15. Suppose you receive a stock tip that allows you to earn a 14% annual return. At this constant rate, about how long will it take to double your money using the Rule of 70?

16. Suppose a new colony is created on the moon with the following production function: output $= A \times (L + K + H + N)$. If L, K, H, and N each equal 5, and technology (A) equals 3, how much output would this new colony produce?

USING THE NUMBERS

17. According to By the Numbers, approximately how many years did it take for real GDP per capita in the United States to double from $5,000 to $10,000? How about from $25,000 to $50,000? During which period was economic growth stronger in terms of annual growth?

18. According to By the Numbers, what is the range of life expectancies for the countries whose GDP per capita was less than $5,000 in 2012? Compare these life expectancies with those with GDP per capita greater than $35,000. Is there a strong correlation between GDP per capita and life expectancy?

ANSWERS TO QUESTIONS IN CHECKPOINTS

Checkpoint: Why Is Economic Growth Important?

If incomes in China double every 8 years (as shown in the table), Chinese workers would earn $48,000 in year 2044, equaling what American workers earned in 2012. If growth continues at the same rate, Chinese workers would earn the same as American workers in the year 2060, less than 50 years from today.

Year	U.S. 3% growth rate	China's 9% growth rate
2012	$48,000	$3,000
2020		$6,000
2028		$12,000
2036	$96,000	$24,000
2044		$48,000
2052		$96,000
2060	$192,000	$192,000

Checkpoint: Thinking About Short-Run and Long-Run Economic Growth

Every factor of production contributes to economic growth. Although the Ivory Coast is abundant in natural resources and labor compared to Iceland, it lacks the human capital, physical capital, and technology that are important components in the production function. In addition, the lack of stability in the country from recent civil and military strife has left many of its resources underutilized for productive purposes, further inhibiting the Ivory Coast from achieving higher long-run growth.

Checkpoint: Applying the Production Function: Achieving Economic Growth

An organization such as the Bill & Melinda Gates Foundation can help people improve their health through vaccinations, clean water, and sanitation, thereby enabling them to improve their productivity and earning power. Then, focus can be put on schools and improving education. All of this focus on human capital broadly can be accomplished with grants to communities or parents (by subsidizing them to send their kids to school) in developing nations.

Checkpoint: The Role of Government in Promoting Economic Growth

Not very well. Large-scale businesses that we are accustomed to could not exist. What's left is small individual businesses that serve small local populations. Growth is stymied, and everyone ekes out a small living. Countries such as Somalia are in this no-win situation.

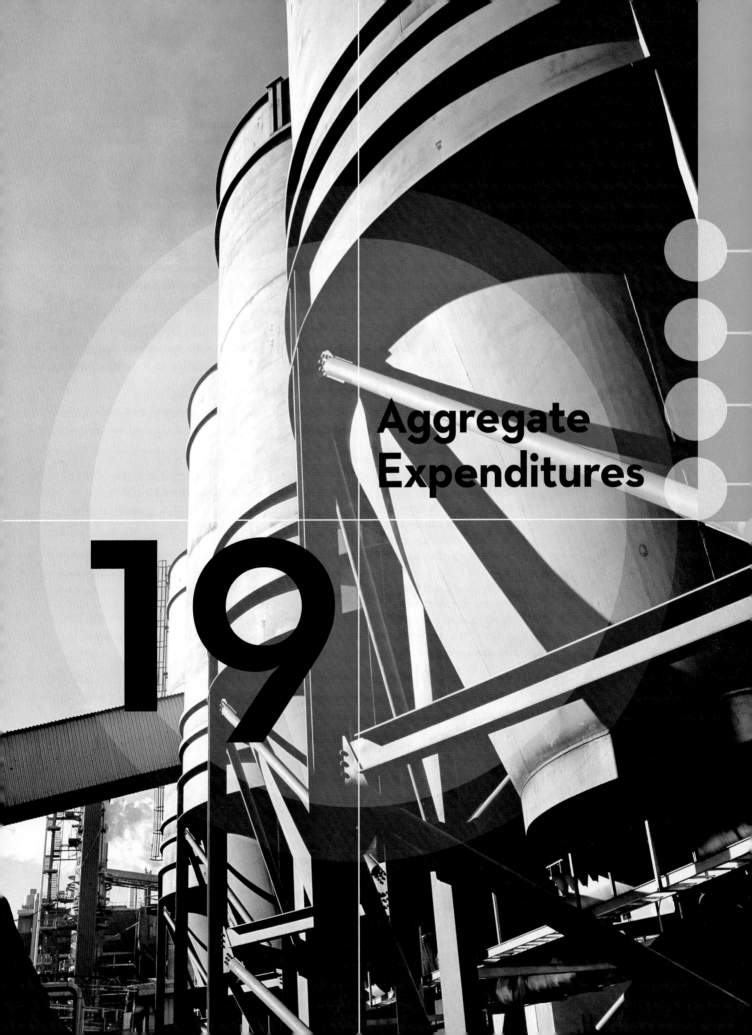

19

Aggregate Expenditures

Madawaska, Maine, near the northern end of U.S. 1 that extends all the way south to Key West, Florida, is like many other idyllic small towns in America—picturesque, friendly, and highly dependent on one industry to provide jobs for its residents. For Madawaska, it is the local paper mill, which provides jobs to 650 of its 4,500 residents. The salaries earned by its workers help to keep the rest of the town employed, including workers in restaurants and cafés, pharmacies, banks, and gas stations that serve the paper mill workers and their families.

During the depth of the 2007–2009 recession, when Madawaska's paper mill was on the brink of closure, not only did its workers face potential unemployment, but so did the rest of the community, which depends on people with jobs at the paper mill to support their businesses. Towns such as Madawaska highlight the interdependency of the economy in which the loss of one job results in a reduction in spending that affects other jobs. In February 2010, the workers at the paper mill took the unusual step of accepting an 8.5% wage cut in order to keep the company (and town) from closing down.

The real economic crisis of Madawaska has been seen in recent years throughout the U.S. economy, in cities big and small, as the recession and slow recovery led to high unemployment and low income growth, which subsequently led to less money being spent on clothing, electronics, travel, and cars, causing a chain reaction downward in consumption. This chain reaction is what John Maynard Keynes alluded to when he published *The General Theory of Employment, Interest and Money* in 1936, which discussed the importance of aggregate spending and the government's role in stabilizing the macroeconomy.

Today, the ideas of John Maynard Keynes are frequently in the news. The phrase "Government Must Act!" is echoed by people of all political views when facing economic hard times. But *how* should government act and to *what extent* should it act?

These are the more contentious questions that are debated today. Stimulus packages, tax cuts, farm subsidies, laws and regulations, and even financial aid for college students are all part of a huge arsenal of tools available to government policymakers.

The American Recovery and Reinvestment Act of 2009 was one such stimulus policy passed by Congress. Among its efforts to boost economic activity and to create jobs were money designated for construction projects, tax cuts for most workers, and an increase in unemployment benefits. The goal of the stimulus was to put money into the hands (through jobs, tax cuts, and cash benefits) of those most likely to spend it in their communities, thus carrying a positive ripple effect through to other businesses that depend on consumer spending.

But Keynesian policies have not been without their critics as the size of government grew. Spending by government (federal, state, and local) has increased from 10% of GDP in the 1930s to over 30% today as the size and scope of government programs expand. Although many people benefit from these programs, some believe government has overreached and they would prefer something smaller and simpler.

This sort of thinking is not new. In fact, over a century ago, government policies were rarely used to intervene in the workings of the economy, even when the economy entered a downturn. Classical economists, as they are called, viewed the role of the government as providing the necessary framework upon which the market could operate—maintaining competition, providing central banking services, providing for national defense, administering the legal system, and so forth. But government was not expected to play a role in promoting full employment, stabilizing prices, or stimulating economic growth—the economy was supposed to do this on its own. The belief at the time was that economic downturns were *self-correcting*, meaning that if the economy were left alone, the forces of supply and demand would naturally bring the economy back into equilibrium.

To classical economists, this is how the self-correcting mechanism worked. Suppose a lack of consumer confidence caused surpluses in the product markets. Businesses would lower prices to get the goods out the door, bringing product markets back into equilibrium. Lower prices pinch profit margins, therefore businesses would seek to lower costs,

BY THE NUMBERS

The Role of Spending in the Economy

Spending plays a vital role in spurring economic activity and creating growth and jobs. Spending occurs by consumers, investors, foreigners, and government. During economic downturns, government plays an increasingly important role in trying to influence the economy.

Government spending as a percentage of GDP rises during economic recessions (shaded).

Olivier Le Queinec/Dreamstime.com

Average government spending per person varies significantly across countries. The U.S. government spends less per person than governments of other developed countries.

Country	Government Spending Per Person (in U.S. Dollars)
India	233
China	1,512
Mexico	2,595
Russia	2,905
World	3,335
Brazil	4,248
United States	11,276
Germany	18,585
Japan	20,173
Canada	21,831
France	22,226
Australia	24,014
Sweden	31,791

Susan Law Cain/Dreamstime.com

$2,080,300,000,000
Total U.S. private domestic investment spending in 2012.

$2,210,600,000,000
Total U.S. spending by foreign consumers (exports) in 2012.

The top categories of personal consumption expenditures in the United States in 2012:

Goods

1. Food/Groceries — $832.6 billion
2. Gasoline/Energy — $447.1 billion
3. Motor Vehicles/Parts — $425.6 billion
4. Clothing/Footwear — $368.9 billion
5. Recreational Goods — $359.9 billion

Services

1. Housing/Utilities — $1,976.5 billion
2. Health Care — $1,841.9 billion
3. Financial Services/Insurance — $831.0 billion
4. Restaurants/Hotels — $730.9 billion
5. Recreational Services — $415.6 billion

Combined spending among state and local governments roughly equals federal spending. Total spending among all governments exceeded $6 trillion in 2012. (Values in billions.)

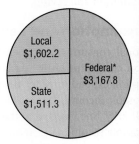

Local $1,602.2
Federal* $3,167.8
State $1,511.3

Ken Cole/Dreamstime.com

*Federal spending excludes intergovernmental transfers (money given to state and local governments).

the chief of which is labor. Just as the paper mill workers in Madawaska took a pay cut in order to keep their jobs, workers (in the classical view) would take pay cuts to deal with price adjustments in product markets. This is the self-correcting mechanism in product and labor markets.

What about capital markets? In the classical view, savings (and by extension, consumption) and investment are determined by interest rates. If investment is too low relative to saving, interest rates would fall, reducing saving and stimulating business investment. In this way, capital markets worked with product and labor markets to keep the economy chugging away at full employment.

That classical perspective was challenged during the Great Depression by Keynes, who turned away from the classical framework with its three separate and distinct competitive markets operating through prices, wages, and interest rates. He focused instead on the economy as a whole and on aggregate spending.

In this chapter, we develop the aggregate expenditures model, which is commonly referred to as the Keynesian model. It can be used to analyze short-run macroeconomic fluctuations. This model will give you the tools to understand why policymakers took such an aggressive approach to the 2007–2009 downturn. Keynes's focus was on aggregate spending, and how consumption spending is a key component to explaining how the economy reaches short-term equilibrium employment, output, and income. Using this model, we will see why an economy can get stuck in an undesirable place, and why policies are useful in smoothing out the business cycle.

⊙ Aggregate Expenditures

Recall that when we discussed measuring gross domestic product (GDP), we concluded that it could be computed by adding up either all spending or all income in the economy. We saw that the expenditures side consists of consumer spending, business investment spending, government spending, and net foreign spending (exports minus imports). Thus, **aggregate expenditures** are equal to:

$$GDP = AE = C + I + G + (X - M)$$

> **aggregate expenditures** Consist of consumer spending, business investment spending, government spending, and net foreign spending (exports minus imports): $GDP = C + I + G + (X - M)$.

Some Simplifying Assumptions

In this chapter, we first will focus on a simple model of the private economy that includes only consumers and businesses. Later in the chapter, we will incorporate government spending, taxes, and the foreign sector into our analysis. Second, we will assume that all saving is personal saving as opposed to national saving, which includes business saving and government saving. Third, because Keynes was modeling a depression economy, we follow him in assuming that there is considerable slack in the economy, much like the economy of the past several years. Unemployment is high and other resources are sitting idle, which means that if demand were to rise, businesses could quickly increase output without any upward pressure on costs. We will assume, therefore, that the aggregate price level (the CPI, PPI, or GDP deflator) is fixed. Taking into account these assumptions, which make the analysis easier but do not affect the key points, let us begin by looking at consumption and saving.

Consumption and Saving

> **consumption** Spending by individuals and households on both durable goods (e.g., autos, appliances, and electronic equipment) and nondurable goods (e.g., food, clothing, and entertainment).

Personal consumption expenditures (C) represent roughly 70% of GDP, and for this reason **consumption** is a major ingredient in our model. Figure 1 shows personal consumption expenditures for the years since 1980. Notice how closely consumption parallels disposable income.

The 45° line inserted in the figure represents all points where consumption is equal to disposable income (Y_d). If an economy spends its entire annual income, saving nothing, the 45° line would represent consumption. Consequently, annual **saving** (S) is equal to the vertical difference between the 45° reference line and annual consumption ($S = Y_d - C$). After all, what can you do with income except spend it or save it?

> **saving** The difference between income and consumption; the amount of disposable income not spent.

FIGURE 1

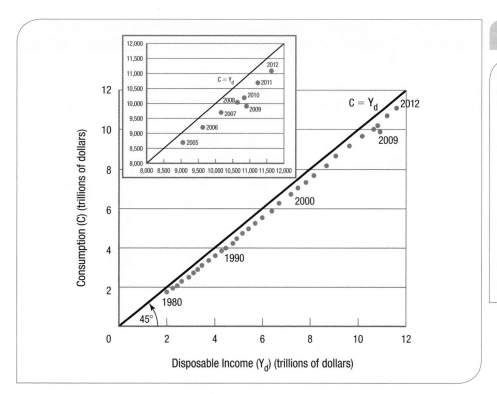

Consumption and Disposable Income

This graph shows personal consumption spending (C) for the years since 1980. The 45° line inserted in the figure represents the points at which consumption is equal to disposable income (Y_d). If an economy spends its entire annual income, saving nothing, the 45° line would represent consumption. Annual saving (S) is equal to the vertical difference between the 45° reference line and annual consumption ($S = Y_d - C$).

Notice that consumption spending increased every year since 1980 except in 2009, when disposable income rose but consumption dropped. This was an important contributor to the depth of the 2007–2009 recession. In fact, the last time annual consumption spending dropped occurred in 1933, during the depth of the Great Depression.

Keynes began his theoretical examination of consumption by noting the following:

The fundamental psychological law, upon which we are entitled to depend with great confidence both a priori from our knowledge of human nature and from the detailed facts of experience, is that men are disposed, as a rule and on the average, to increase their consumption as their income increases, but not by as much as the change in their income.[1]

Consumption spending grows, in other words, as income grows, but not as fast. Therefore, as income grows, saving will grow as a percentage of income. Notice that this approach to analyzing saving differs from the classical approach. Classical economists assumed that the *interest rate* is the principal determinant of saving and, by extension, one of the principal determinants of consumption. Keynes, in contrast, emphasized *income* as the main determinant of consumption and saving.

Table 1 on the next page portrays a hypothetical consumption function of the sort Keynes envisioned. As income grows from $4,000 to $4,200, consumption increases by $150 ($4,150 − $4,000) and saving grows from $0 to $50. Thus, the *change* in income of $200 is divided between consumption ($150) and saving ($50). Note that at income levels below $4,000, saving is negative; people are spending more than their current income either by using credit or drawing on existing savings to support consumption.

Average Propensities to Consume and Save The percentage of income that is consumed is known as the **average propensity to consume** (APC); it is listed in column (4) of Table 1. It is calculated by dividing consumption spending by income (C/Y). For example, when income is $5,000 and consumption is $4,750, APC is 0.95, meaning that 95% of the income is spent.

average propensity to consume
The percentage of income that is consumed (C/Y).

---

[1] John Maynard Keynes, *The General Theory of Employment, Interest and Money* (New York: Harcourt Brace Jovanovich) 1936, p. 96.

TABLE 1	Hypothetical Consumption and Saving and Propensities to Consume and Save

(1) Income or Output Y (in $)	(2) Consumption C (in $)	(3) Saving S (in $)	(4) APC C ÷ Y	(5) APS S ÷ Y	(6) MPC ΔC ÷ ΔY	(7) MPS ΔS ÷ ΔY
3,000	3,250	−250	1.08	−0.08	0.75	0.25
3,200	3,400	−200	1.06	−0.06	0.75	0.25
3,400	3,550	−150	1.04	−0.04	0.75	0.25
3,600	3,700	−100	1.03	−0.03	0.75	0.25
3,800	3,850	−50	1.01	−0.01	0.75	0.25
4,000	4,000	0	1.00	0.00	0.75	0.25
4,200	4,150	50	0.99	0.01	0.75	0.25
4,400	4,300	100	0.98	0.02	0.75	0.25
4,600	4,450	150	0.97	0.03	0.75	0.25
4,800	4,600	200	0.96	0.04	0.75	0.25
5,000	4,750	250	0.95	0.05	0.75	0.25
5,200	4,900	300	0.94	0.06	0.75	0.25
5,400	5,050	350	0.94	0.06	0.75	0.25
5,600	5,200	400	0.93	0.07	0.75	0.25

average propensity to save The percentage of income that is saved (S/Y).

The **average propensity to save** (APS) is equal to saving divided by income (S/Y); it is the percentage of income saved. Again, if income is $5,000 and saving is $250, APS is 0.05, or 5% is saved. The APS is shown in column (5) of Table 1.

Notice that if you add columns (4) and (5) in Table 1, the answer is always 1. That is because Y = C + S, therefore all income is either spent or saved. Similar logic dictates that the two percentages spent and saved must total 100%, or that APC + APS = 1.

Marginal Propensities to Consume and Save *Average* propensities to consume and save represent the proportion of income that is consumed or saved. *Marginal* propensities measure what part of *additional* income will be either consumed or saved. This distinction is important because changing policies by government policymakers means that income changes and consumers' reactions to their *changing* incomes is what we will see later drives changes in the economy.

marginal propensity to consume The change in consumption associated with a given change in income (ΔC/ΔY).

The **marginal propensity to consume** (MPC) is equal to the change in consumption associated with a given change in income. Denoting change by the delta symbol (Δ), MPC = ΔC/ΔY. Thus, for example, when income grows from $5,000 to $5,200 (a $200 change), and consumption rises from $4,750 to $4,900 (a $150 change), MPC is equal to 0.75 ($150/$200).

Notice that this result is consistent with Keynes's fundamental psychological law quoted earlier, holding that people "are disposed, as a rule and on the average, to increase their consumption as their income increases, but not by as much as the change in their income." In Table 1, the MPC for all changes in income is 0.75, as shown in column (6).

marginal propensity to save The change in saving associated with a given change in income (ΔS/ΔY).

The **marginal propensity to save** (MPS) is equal to the change in saving associated with a given change in income; MPS = ΔS/ΔY. Therefore, when income grows from $5,000 to $5,200, and saving grows from $250 to $300, MPS is equal to 0.25 ($50/$200). Column (7) lists MPS.

Note once again that the sum of the MPC and the MPS will always equal 1, because the only things that can be done with a change in income is to spend or save it. A small word of warning, however: Though APC + APS = 1 and MPC + MPS = 1, most of the time APC + MPS ≠ 1 and APS + MPC ≠ 1. Try adding a few different columns from Table 1 and you will see that this is true.

Figure 2 graphs the consumption and saving schedules from Table 1. The graph in Panel A extends the consumption schedule back to zero income, where consumption is equal to $1,000 and saving is equal to −$1,000. (Remember that Y = C + S, therefore if Y = 0 and C = $1,000, then S must equal −$1,000. With no income, people in this economy would continue to spend, either borrowing money or drawing down their accumulated savings to survive.) The 45° line in panel A is a reference line where Y = C + S. At the point at which the consumption schedule crosses the reference line (point *a*, Y = $4,000), saving is zero because consumption and income are equal.

The saving schedule in panel B plots the difference between the 45° reference line (Y = C + S) and the consumption schedule in panel A. For example, if income is $4,000, saving is zero (point *f* in panel B), and when income equals $5,000, saving equals $250 [line (*b* − *c*) in panel A, point *g* in panel B]. Saving is positively sloped, again reflecting Keynes's fundamental law; the more people earn, the greater percentage of income they will save (the average propensity to save rises as income rises). Make a mental note that the saving schedule shows how much people *desire* to save at various income levels.

How much people will *actually* save depends on equilibrium income, or how much income the economy is generating. We are getting a bit ahead of the story here, but planting this seed will help you when we get to the section where we determine equilibrium income in the economy.

Note finally that the consumption and saving schedules in our example are straight-line functions. This need not be the case, but it simplifies some of the relationships to graph them like this at this point. When the consumption and saving schedules are linear,

Suppose you receive some birthday money from your aunt. What portion of this money would you spend and what portion would you save? These portions are your marginal propensity to consume and marginal propensity to save, respectively.

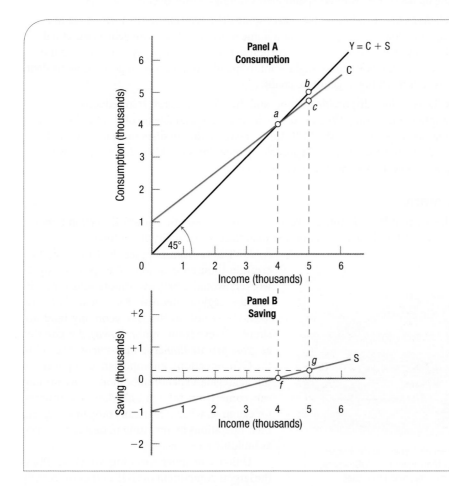

FIGURE 2

Consumption and Saving

The consumption and saving schedules from Table 1 are graphed here. Panel A extends the consumption schedule back to zero income, where consumption is equal to $1,000 and saving is equal to −$1,000. At the point where the consumption schedule crosses the reference line (point *a*, Y = $4,000), saving is zero. The saving schedule in panel B simply plots the difference between the 45° reference line and the consumption schedule in panel A. Thus, when income = $5,000, saving = $250 [line (*b* − *c*) in panel A, point *g* in panel B].

the MPC is the slope of the consumption function, and the MPS is the slope of the saving schedule. In this case, MPC = 0.75 and MPS = 0.25, which tells us that every time income changes by $1,000, consumption will change by $750 and saving will change by $250.

Other Determinants of Consumption and Saving   Income is the principal determinant of consumption and saving, but other factors can shift the saving and consumption schedules. These factors include the wealth of a family, their expectations about the future of prices and income, family debt, and taxation.

- *Wealth*   The more wealth a family has, the higher its consumption at all levels of income. Wealth affects the consumption schedule by shifting it up or down, depending on whether wealth rises or falls. When the stock market was soaring in the late 1990s, policymakers worried about the wealth effect, that as many households saw their wealth dramatically expand, rising consumption might cause the economy's inflation rate to rise. As it turned out, the stock market collapsed in 2000, and again in 2008, and the economy moved into recession. Then, economists began worrying about the negative impact of this wealth effect as trillions of dollars of wealth evaporated from the stock market before it eventually recovered.

- *Expectations*   Expectations about future prices and incomes help determine how much a person will spend today. If you anticipate that prices will rise next week, you will be more likely to purchase more products today. What are sales, after all, but temporary reductions in price designed to entice customers into the store today? Similarly, if you anticipate that your income will soon rise—perhaps you are about to graduate from medical school— you will be more inclined to incur debt today to purchase something you want, as was the case with high school student LeBron James, driving around in a Hummer, knowing that when he was drafted into the NBA, he would be making a fortune. Lotto winners who receive their winnings over a 20-year span often spend much of the money early on, running up debts. Few winners spend their winnings evenly over the 20 years.

- *Household Debt*   Most households carry some debt, typically in the form of credit card balances, auto loans, student loans, or a home mortgage. The more debt a household has, the less able it is to spend in the current period as it makes payments toward the debt. Although the household might want to spend more money on goods now, its debt level restricts its ability to get more credit.

- *Taxes*   Taxes reduce disposable income, and therefore taxes result in reduced consumption and saving. When taxes are increased, spendable income falls, therefore consumption is reduced by the MPC times the reduction in disposable income, and saving falls by the reduction in disposable income times the MPS. Tax reductions have the opposite effect, as we will see later in this chapter.

investment   Spending by businesses that adds to the productive capacity of the economy. Investment depends on factors such as its rate of return, the level of technology, and business expectations about the economy.

Investment

When the town of West Point, Georgia, received the news that South Korean automaker Kia Motors was building a $1 billion car manufacturing facility in its town, its residents couldn't have been happier. Not only was Kia creating thousands of jobs, the spending by its workers would create even more jobs throughout the region. Because Kia's manufacturing facility was new to the U.S. economy (and not simply a move from another town), it is counted as *gross private domestic investment* (the "I" in the GDP equation), an important component of the aggregate expenditures model. **Investment** can come from foreign and domestic sources, for example, when American companies expand their operations by investing in new capital such as building a new factory.

Unlike consumer spending, which at 70% is the largest component of GDP and until recently held fairly steady from year to year, gross private

Many residents in West Point, Georgia, were excited when South Korean auto manufacturer Kia built a large factory in their town in 2008, saving the town's economy after decades of factory closings and job losses.

ZUMA Press, Inc./Alamy

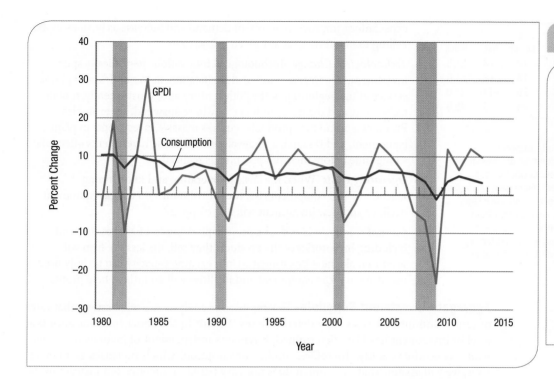

FIGURE 3

Changes in Consumption and Gross Private Domestic Investment
The annual percentage changes in consumption and gross private domestic investment (GPDI) are shown here. Consumption is relatively stable, but investment spending is highly volatile, with annual fluctuations ranging from −23% to +30%. The shaded bars represent recessions.

domestic investment is volatile. Sure, large investment deals like Kia's new plant in West Point, Georgia, are a huge boost to the economy, but such investments tend to be sporadic. The annual percentage changes in consumption and investment spending from 1980 to 2012 are shown in Figure 3.

Notice that although consumption until 2008 plodded along with annual increases between 3% and 10%, investment spending has undergone annual fluctuations ranging from −23% to +30%. Investment constitutes roughly 15% of GDP, therefore its volatility often accounts for our recessions and booms.

The economic boom of the 1990s, for instance, was fueled by investments in information technology infrastructure, including massive investments in telecommunications. In the 1990s, people believed that Internet traffic would grow by 1,000% a year, doubling every three months or so. This belief led many companies to lay millions of miles of fiber optic cable. When the massive investments made in computer hardware and software over that same decade are taken into account, it is no wonder that the economy grew at a breakneck pace.

But this increase came to a halt in the early 2000s, when businesses—especially the telecoms—discovered that they had built up a massive excess capacity, and thus bandwidth prices plummeted. The resulting plunge in investment between 2000 and 2001 can be seen in Figure 3. Investment recovered by 2003, then collapsed from 2007 to 2009 as the housing and financial crises took their toll.

Investment Demand Investment levels depend mainly on the rate of return on capital. Investments earning a high rate of return are the investments undertaken first (assuming comparable risk), with those projects offering lower returns finding their way into the investment stream later. Interest rate levels also are important in determining how much investment occurs, because much of business investment is financed through debt. As interest rates fall, investment rises, and vice versa.

Although the rate of return on investments is the main determinant of investment spending, other factors influence investment demand, including expectations, technological change, capital goods on hand, and operating costs.

- *Expectations* Projecting the rate of return on investment is not an easy task. Returns are forecasted over the life of a new piece of equipment or factory, yet many changes in the economic environment can alter the actual return on these investments. As business

Inventories	% Higher	% Same	% Lower	Net	Index
Feb 2013	22	59	19	+3	51.5
Jan 2013	20	62	18	+2	51.0
Dec 2012	14	58	28	−14	43.0
Nov 2012	18	54	28	−10	45.0

Each month, the Institute of Supply Management provides a forecast of investment demand by asking businesses whether their inventories have increased, decreased, or stayed the same since the previous month. Investors cheer falling inventories, such as that from November 2012 to December 2012, because it is a sign that businesses will boost factory production and investment in new facilities.

expectations improve, investment demand will increase as businesses are willing to invest more at any given interest rate.

- *Technological Change* Technological innovations periodically spur investment. The introduction of electrification, automobiles, and phone service at the beginning of the 20th century and, most recently, mobile technology and the new products they have spawned, are examples. Producing brand new products requires massive investments in plants, equipment, and research and development. These investments often take a long time before their full potential is realized.

- *Operating Costs* When the costs of operating and maintaining machinery and equipment rise, the rate of return on capital equipment declines and new investment will be postponed.

- *Capital Goods on Hand* The more capital goods a firm has on hand, including inventories of the products they sell, the less the firm will want to make new investments. Until existing capacity can be fully used, investing in more equipment and facilities will do little to help profits.

Aggregate Investment Schedule To simplify our analysis, we will assume that rates of return and interest rates fully determine investment in the short run. But once that level of investment has been determined, it remains independent of income, or *autonomous,* as economists say. Therefore, unlike consumption, which increases as incomes rises, we will assume that investment does not vary based on income, but instead on the rates of return that determine how potentially profitable investment will be. Figure 4 shows the resulting aggregate investment schedule that plots investment spending with respect to income.

FIGURE 4

The Investment Schedule

The aggregate investment schedule, relating investment spending to income, is shown here. Because aggregate investment is I_0 at all income levels, the curve is a horizontal straight line. This assumption simplifies the aggregate expenditures model.

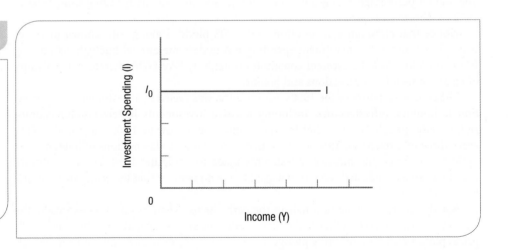

Because we have assumed that aggregate investment is I_0 at all income levels, the curve is a horizontal straight line. Investment is unaffected by different levels of income. This is a simplifying assumption that we will change in later chapters when we look at its implications.

Our emphasis in this section has been on two important components of aggregate spending: consumption and investment. Consumption is about 70% and investment is about 15% of aggregate spending. Consumption is relatively stable, but investment is volatile and especially sensitive to expectations about conditions in the economy. We have seen that, on average, some income is spent (APC) and some is saved (APS). But, it is that portion of *additional* income that is spent (MPC) and saved (MPS) that is most important for where the economy settles or where it reaches equilibrium, as we will see in the next section.

CHECKPOINT

AGGREGATE EXPENDITURES

- Before the Great Depression, classical economists (as they are now referred to) looked at three primary markets and thought these markets would keep the economy operating around full employment.

- Keynes argued that the economy is largely influenced by the amount of spending that occurs, and therefore analyzed the economy by looking at aggregate expenditures.

- Aggregate expenditures are equal to C + I + G + (X − M), with consumption being roughly 70% of aggregate spending.

- Keynes argued that saving and consumption spending are related to income. As income grows, consumption will grow but not as fast.

- The marginal propensities to consume (MPC) and save (MPS) are equal to $\Delta C/\Delta Y$ and $\Delta S/\Delta Y$, respectively. They represent the change in consumption and saving associated with a change in income.

- Other factors affecting consumption and saving include wealth, expectations about future income and prices, the level of household debt, and taxes.

- Investment levels depend primarily on the rate of return on capital.

- Other determinants of investment demand include business expectations, technology change, operating costs, and the amount of capital goods on hand.

- Consumption is relatively stable. In contrast, investment is volatile.

QUESTION: Why is investment spending generally much more volatile than consumption spending?

Answers to the Checkpoint question can be found at the end of this chapter.

The Simple Aggregate Expenditures Model

Now that we have stripped the government and foreign sectors from our analysis at this point, aggregate expenditures (AE) will consist of the sum of consumer and business investment spending (AE = C + I). Figure 5 on the next page shows a simple aggregate expenditures model based on consumption and investment. Aggregate expenditures based on the data in Table 1 are shown in panel A of Figure 5; panel B shows the corresponding saving and investment schedules.

Let us take a moment to remind ourselves what these graphs represent. The 45° line in Panel A represents the situation when income exactly equals spending, or Y = AE. In other words, no savings occur at any level of income. All other lines represent situations in which income does not exactly equal spending at all levels of income. Point *a* in both panels is that level of income ($4,000) at which saving is zero and all income is spent. Saving is, therefore, positive for income levels above $4,000 and negative at incomes below. The vertical distance *ef* in panel A represents investment (I_0) of $100; it is equal to I_0 in panel B. Note that the vertical axis of panel B has a different scale from that of panel A.

Macroeconomic Equilibrium in the Simple Model

The important question to ask is where this economy will come to rest. Or, in the language of economists, at what income will this economy reach **Keynesian macroeconomic equilibrium?** By equilibrium, economists mean that income at which there are no net pressures pushing the economy to move to a higher or lower level of income and output.

To find this equilibrium point, let's begin with the economy at an income level of $4,000. Are there pressures driving the economy to grow or decline? Looking at point *a* in panel A of Figure 5, we see that the economy is producing $4,000 worth of goods and services and $4,000 in income. At this income level, however, consumers and businesses want to spend $4,100 ($4,000 in consumption and $100 in investment). Because aggregate expenditures (AE) exceed current income and output, there are more goods being

Keynesian macroeconomic equilibrium In the simple model, the economy is at rest; spending injections (investment) are equal to withdrawals (saving), or I = S, and there are no net inducements for the economy to change the level of output or income. In the full model, all injections of spending must equal all withdrawals at equilibrium: I + G + X = S + T + M.

FIGURE 5

Equilibrium in the Aggregate Expenditures Model

Ignoring government spending and net exports, aggregate expenditures (AE) consist of consumer spending and business investment (AE = C + I). Panel A shows AE and its relationship with income (Y); when spending equals income, the economy is on the Y = AE line. Panel B shows the corresponding saving and investment schedules. Point *a* in both panels shows where income equals consumption and saving is zero. Therefore, saving is positive for income levels above $4,000 and negative at incomes below $4,000. The vertical distance *ef* in panel A represents investment ($100); it is equal to I_0 in panel B. Equilibrium income and output is $4,400 (point *e*), because this is the level at which businesses are producing just what other businesses and consumers want to buy.

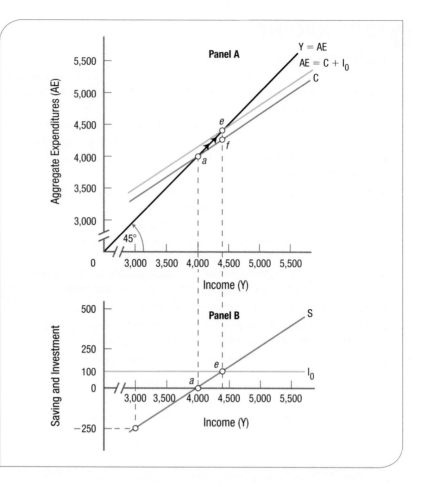

demanded ($4,100) than are being supplied at $4,000. As a result, businesses will find it in their best interests to produce more, raising employment and income and moving the economy toward income and output level $4,400 (point *e*).

Once the economy has moved to $4,400, what consumers and businesses want to buy is exactly equal to the income and output being produced. Businesses are producing $4,400, aggregate expenditures are equal to $4,400, and there are no pressures on the economy to move away from point *e*. Income of $4,400, or point *e*, is an equilibrium point for the economy.

Panel B shows this same equilibrium, again as point *e*. Is it a coincidence that saving and investment are equal at this point where income and output are at equilibrium? The answer is no. In this simple private sector model, saving and investment will always be equal when the economy is in equilibrium.

Remember that aggregate expenditures are equal to consumption plus business investment (AE = C + I). Recall also that *at equilibrium*, aggregate expenditures, income, and output are all equal; what is demanded is supplied (AE = Y). Finally, keep in mind that income can either be spent or saved (Y = C + S). By substitution, we know that, at equilibrium,

$$AE = Y = C + I$$

We also know that

$$Y = C + S$$

Substituting C + I for Y yields

$$C + I = C + S$$

Canceling the C's, we find that, *at equilibrium,*

$$I = S$$

Thus, the location of point *e* in panel B is not just coincidental; at equilibrium, actual saving and investment are always equal. Note that at point *a,* saving is zero, yet investment spending is $100 at I_0. This difference means businesses desire to invest more than people desire to save. With *desired* investment exceeding *desired* saving, this cannot be an equilibrium point, because saving and investment must be equal in order for the economy to be at equilibrium. Indeed, income will rise until these two values are equal at point *e.*

What is important to take from this discussion? First, when intended (or desired) saving and investment differ, the economy will have to grow or shrink to achieve equilibrium. When desired saving exceeds desired investment—at income levels above $4,400 in panel B—income will decline. When intended saving is below intended investment—at income levels below $4,400—income will rise. Notice that we are using the words "intended" and "desired" interchangeably.

Second, at equilibrium all **injections** of spending (investment in this case) into the economy must equal all **withdrawals** (saving in this simple model). Spending injections increase aggregate income, while spending withdrawals reduce it. This fact will become important as we add government and the foreign sector to the model.

The Multiplier Effect Given an initial investment of $100 ($I_0$), equilibrium is at an output of $4,400 (point *e*). Remember that at equilibrium, what people *withdraw* from the economy (saving) is equal to what others are willing to *inject* into the spending system (investment). In this case both values equal $100. Point *e* is an equilibrium point because there are no pressures in the system to increase or decrease output; the spending desires of consumers and businesses are satisfied.

The Multiplier Let us assume *full employment* occurs at output $4,800. How much would investment have to increase to move the economy out to full employment? As Figure 6 on the next page shows, investment must rise to $200 ($I_1$), an increase of $100. With this new investment, equilibrium output moves from point *e* to point *b,* and income rises from $4,400 to $4,800.

What is remarkable here is that a mere $100 of added spending (investment in this case) caused income to grow by $400. This phenomenon is known as the **multiplier** effect. Recognizing it was one of Keynes's major insights. How does it work?

In this example, we have assumed the marginal propensity to consume is 0.75. Therefore, for each added dollar received by consumers, $0.75 is spent and $0.25 is saved. Thus, when businesses invest an additional $100, the firms providing the machinery will spend $75 of this new

injections Increments of spending, including investment, government spending, and exports.

withdrawals Activities that remove spending from the economy, including saving, taxes, and imports.

multiplier Spending changes alter equilibrium income by the spending change times the multiplier. One person's spending becomes another's income, and that second person spends some (the MPC), which becomes income for another person, and so on, until income has changed by $1/(1 - MPC) = 1/MPS$. The multiplier operates in both directions.

JOHN MAYNARD KEYNES (1883–1946)

In 1935, John Maynard Keynes boasted in a letter to playwright George Bernard Shaw of a book he was writing that would revolutionize "the way the world thinks about economic problems." This was a brash prediction to make, even to a friend, but it was not an idle boast. His *General Theory of Employment, Interest and Money* did change the way the world looked at economics.

Keynes belongs to a small class of economic earth-shakers which includes Karl Marx and Adam Smith. His one-man war on classical theory launched a new field of study known as macroeconomics. His ideas would have a profound influence on theorists and government policies for decades to come.

Keynes was once asked if there was any era comparable to the Great Depression. He replied, "It was called the Dark Ages and it lasted 400 years." His prescription to President Franklin D. Roosevelt was to increase government spending to stimulate the economy. Sundeep Reddy reports that "during a 1934 dinner . . . after one economist carefully removed a towel from a stack to dry his hands, Mr. Keynes swept the whole pile of towels on the floor and crumpled them up, explaining that his way of using towels did more to stimulate employment among restaurant workers" (*The Wall Street Journal,* January 8, 2009, p. A10).

During the world economic depression in the early 1930s, Keynes became alarmed when unemployment in England continued to rise after the first few years of the crisis. Keynes argued that *aggregate expenditures,* the sum of consumption, investment, government spending, and net exports, determined the levels of economic output and employment. When aggregate expenditures were high, the economy would foster business expansion, higher incomes, and high levels of employment. With low aggregate spending, businesses would be unable to sell their inventories and would cut back on investment and production.

The ideas formulated by Keynes dramatically changed the way government policy is used throughout the world. Today, as many countries face a slow economic recovery, governments have taken a more proactive role in their economies in hopes of avoiding another downturn of the magnitude seen in the 1930s.

FIGURE 6

Saving and Investment

When investment is $100, equilibrium employment occurs at an output of $4,400 (point *e*). When investment rises to $200 (I₁), equilibrium output climbs to $4,800 (point *b*). Thus, $100 of added investment spending causes income to grow by $400. This is the multiplier at work.

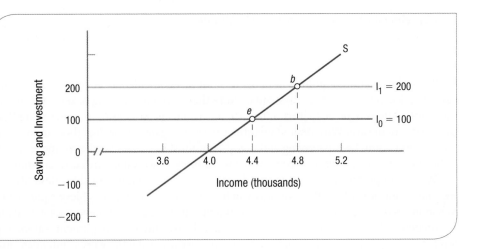

income on more raw materials, while saving the remaining $25. The firms supplying the new raw materials have $75 of new income. These firms will spend $56.25 of this (0.75 × $75.00), while saving $18.75 ($56.25 + $18.75 = $75.00). This effect continues on until the added spending has been exhausted. As a result, income will increase by $100 + $75 + $56.25 .... In the end, income rises by $400. Figure 7 outlines this multiplier process.

The general formula for the spending multiplier (k) is

$$k = 1/(1 - MPC)$$

Alternatively, because MPC + MPS = 1, the MPS = 1 − MPC, therefore

$$k = 1/MPS$$

Thus, in our simple model, the multiplier is

$$1/(1 - 0.75) = 1/0.25 = 4$$

As a result of the multiplier effect, new spending will raise equilibrium by 4 times the amount of new spending. Note that any change in spending (consumption,

FIGURE 7

The Multiplier Process

An initial $100 of spending generates more spending because of the multiplier process shown in this figure. With an MPC = 0.75 in the second round, $75 is spent and $25 is saved. In the third round, $56.25 of the previous $75 is spent and $18.75 is saved, and so on. Total spending is $400, and total saving is $100 when all rounds are completed.

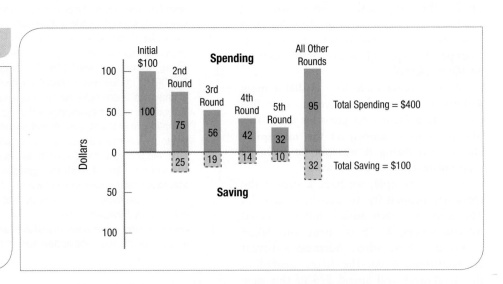

investment—and as we will see in the next section—government spending or changes in net exports) will also have this effect. Spending is spending. Note also—and this is important—the multiplier works in both directions.

The Multiplier Works in Both Directions

If spending increases raise equilibrium income by the increase times the multiplier, a spending decrease will reduce income in corresponding fashion. In our simple economy, for instance, a $100 decline in investment or consumer spending will reduce income by $400.

This is one reason why recession watchers are always concerned about consumer confidence. During a recession, income declines, or at least the rate of income growth falls. If consumers decide to increase their saving to guard against the possibility of job loss, they may inadvertently make the recession worse. As they pull more of their money out of the spending stream, *withdrawals* increase, and income is reduced by a multiplied amount as other agents in the economy feel the effects of this reduced spending. The result can be a more severe or longer lasting recession.

This was the case when consumer spending peaked in the summer of 2008. After that, auto sales plummeted and housing prices and sales fell. As the recession that started in December 2007 progressed and jobs were lost, consumers reduced their spending. As their confidence in the economy evaporated, households began to save more, consumer spending declined further, and the economy sunk into a deeper recession. Figure 8 shows how consumer spending (downward arrow) fell and saving rose (upward arrow) after September 2008. Leading up to the recession, saving was less than 1% of personal income, but by mid-2009 it had grown to 7%. Before the recession, aggregate household debt had soared, and part of what we are seeing in Figure 8 may reflect households spending less in order to pay off debt and return to more sustainable levels of debt.

paradox of thrift When investment is positively related to income and households *intend* to save more, they reduce consumption, income, and output, reducing investment so that the result is that consumers *actually* end up saving less.

Paradox of Thrift The implication of Keynesian analysis for actual aggregate household saving and household intentions regarding saving is called the **paradox of thrift.** As we saw in Figure 8, if households *intend* (or desire) to save more, they will reduce

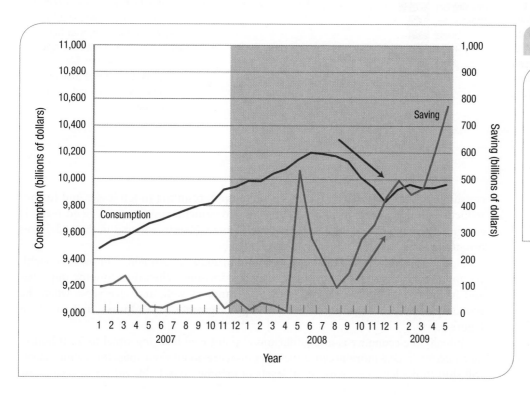

FIGURE 8

Consumption and Saving, 2007–2009

Consumption declined as the recession developed, and consumer worries about job losses and the decline in housing prices resulted in households saving more. The shaded area on the right represents the recession.

ISSUE

Do High Savings Rates Increase the Risk of a Long Recession?

Everyone has a frugal friend or relative who saves every penny possible, or a shopaholic friend who can't seem to save any money at all. These differences in savings rates often are influenced by economic and demographic factors.

People with higher incomes tend to save a larger portion of their incomes than those with lower incomes. Older people tend to save more than younger people. And those living in rural areas tend to save more than those in urban areas. Yet, although these factors explain savings rates *within* a country, they do not fully explain the savings rate across countries. In other words, cultural differences play an important role as well.

The following table shows the average household saving rate in a sample of twelve countries in 2012. China and India rank at the top of this list, despite having a lower income per capita than any other country on the list. The United States, which has the highest income per capita among the countries shown, has a savings rate toward the bottom. And some countries have seen dramatic changes in their savings rate, such as Japan, which had one of the high-est savings rates 30 years ago but today has the lowest savings rate among the countries shown.

The savings rate plays an important role in an economy. A high savings rate, such as that in China, India, and France, gives a country's banking system a vote of confidence; people trust putting their money into financial institutions and expect the money will be available when desired. Also, savings provide opportunities for others to borrow, providing inexpensive access to loans for investment.

However, a high savings rate can also make a country vulnerable in times of recession. The adverse effects of a high savings rate occurred in Japan in the 1990s. Facing a difficult recession, a

Xiye/Dreamstime.com

high savings rate prevented government incentives to jumpstart consumption and investment from being effective. In other words, the multiplier was too low to pull the economy out of recession, resulting in a decadelong recession referred to as the *Lost Decade*.

Today, Japan's savings rate is among the lowest in the world, as income growth stalled and consumerism rose. Yet, a greater willingness to spend portends well in terms of its ability to recover from the next recession. On the other hand, China and India, which have enjoyed high growth rates and high savings rates, may one day face an enduring recession if their dynamic growth machines eventually sputter.

Average Household Savings Rate (2012)

(bar chart showing savings rates for China, India, France, Switzerland, Sweden, Germany, Australia, United Kingdom, United States, Canada, Korea, Japan; x-axis from 0 to 40% in increments of 5)

consumption, thereby reducing income and output, resulting in job losses and further reductions in income, consumption, business investment, and so on. The end result is an aggregate equilibrium with lower output, income, investment, and in the end, lower *actual* aggregate saving.

Notice that we have modified our assumption about investment—it now varies with economic conditions and is positively related to income. When the economy improves and income (or output) rises, investment expands as well, and vice versa when the economy sours. This is shown in our simple aggregate expenditures framework in Figure 9.

Initially the economy is in equilibrium at point e with saving equal to S_0. If households *desire* to save more because they feel insecure about their jobs, the savings curve will shift to the left to S_1. Now at all levels of income households *intend* to save more.

FIGURE 9

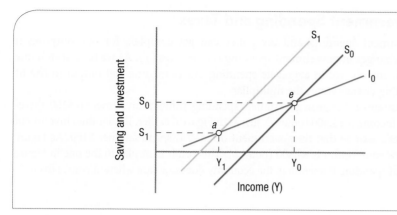

Income (Y)

Paradox of Thrift
When consumers intend to save
more and consume less (the
saving schedule shifts from S_0
to S_1), and if investment is a
rising function of income, the
end result is that at equilibrium,
households actually end up
saving less (point *a*).

This sets up the chain reaction described above, leading to a new equilibrium at point *a*, where equilibrium income has fallen to Y_1 and *actual* saving has declined to S_1. The paradox is that if everyone tries to save more (even for good reasons), in the aggregate they may just save less.

 CHECKPOINT

THE SIMPLE AGGREGATE EXPENDITURES MODEL

- Ignoring both government and the foreign sector in a simple aggregate expenditures model, macroeconomic equilibrium occurs when aggregate expenditures are just equal to what is being produced.

- At equilibrium, aggregate saving equals aggregate investment.

- The multiplier process amplifies new spending because some of the new spending is saved and some becomes additional spending. And some of that spending is saved and some is spent, and so on.

- The multiplier is equal to $1/(1 - MPC) = 1/MPS$.

- The multiplier works in both directions. Changes in spending are amplified, changing income by more than the initial change in spending.

- The paradox of thrift results when households *intend* to save more, but at equilibrium they end up saving less.

QUESTION: Business journalists, pundits, economists, and policymakers all pay attention to the results of the Conference Board's monthly survey of 5,000 households, called the Consumer Confidence Index. When the index is rising, this is good news for the economy, and when it is falling, concerns are often heard that it portends a recession. Why is this survey important as a tool in forecasting where the economy is headed in the near future?

Answers to the Checkpoint question can be found at the end of this chapter.

The Full Aggregate Expenditures Model

With the simple aggregate expenditures model of the domestic private sector (individual consumption and private business investment), we concluded that at equilibrium, saving would equal investment, and that changes in spending lead to a larger change in income. This multiplier effect was an important insight by Keynes. To build the full aggregate expenditures model, we now turn our attention to adding government spending and taxes and the impact of the foreign sector.

Adding Government Spending and Taxes

Although government spending and tax policy can get complex, for our purposes it involves simple changes in government spending (G) or taxes (T). As we have seen in the previous section, any change in aggregate spending causes income and output to rise or fall by the spending change times the multiplier.

Figure 10 illustrates a change in government spending. Initially, investment is $100, therefore equilibrium income is $4,400 (point *e*), just as in Figure 6 earlier. Rather than investment rising by $100, let's assume that the government decides to spend another $100. As Figure 10 shows, the new equilibrium is $4,800 (point *b*). This result is similar to the one in Figure 6, confirming that spending is spending; the economy does not care where it comes from.

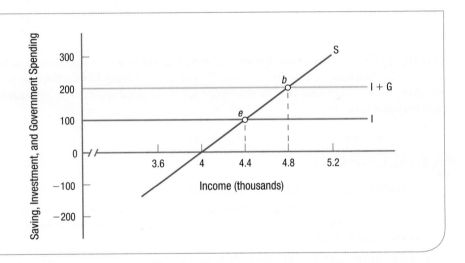

A quick summary is now in order. Equilibrium income is reached when *injections* (here I + G = $200) equal *withdrawals* (in this case S = $200). It did not matter whether these injections came from investment alone or from investment and government spending together. The key is spending.

Changes in spending modify income by an amount equal to the change in spending times the multiplier. How, then, do changes in taxes affect the economy? The answers are not as simple in that case.

Tax Changes and Equilibrium   When taxes are increased, money is withdrawn from the economy's spending stream. When taxes are reduced, money is injected into the economy's spending stream because consumers and businesses have more to spend. Thus, taxes form a wedge between income and that part of income that can be spent, or disposable income. Disposable income (Y_d) is equal to income minus taxes ($Y_d = Y - T$). For simplicity, we will assume that all taxes are paid in a lump sum, thereby removing a certain fixed sum of money from the economy. This assumption does away with the need to worry now about the incentive effects of higher or lower tax rates.

Returning to the model of the economy we have been developing, consumer spending now relates to disposable income (Y − T) rather than just to income. Table 2 reflects this change, using disposable income to determine consumption. With government spending and taxes (fiscal policy) in the model, spending *injections* into the economy include government spending plus business investment (G + I). *Withdrawals* from the system include saving and taxes (S + T).

Again, equilibrium requires that *injections* equal *withdrawals*, or in this case,

$$G + I = S + T$$

In our example, Table 2 shows that G + I = S + T at income level $4,500 (the shaded row in the table). If no tax had been imposed, equilibrium would have been at the point

Keynesian Equilibrium Analysis with Taxes

TABLE 2

Income or Output (Y), in $	Taxes (T), in $	Disposable Income (Y_d), in $	Consumption (C)	Saving (S)	Investment (I)	Government Spending (G)
4,000	100	3,900	3,925	−25	100	100
4,100	100	4,000	4,000	0	100	100
4,200	100	4,100	4,075	25	100	100
4,300	100	4,200	4,150	50	100	100
4,400	100	4,300	4,225	75	100	100
4,500	100	4,400	4,300	100	100	100
4,600	100	4,500	4,375	125	100	100
4,700	100	4,600	4,450	150	100	100
4,800	100	4,700	4,525	175	100	100
4,900	100	4,800	4,600	200	100	100
5,000	100	4,900	4,675	225	100	100

at which $S = G + I$, and thus at an income of $4,800 (point *b* in Figure 10, not shown in Table 2). Therefore, imposing the tax reduces equilibrium income by $300. Because taxes represent a withdrawal of spending from the economy, we would expect equilibrium income to fall when a tax is imposed. Yet, why does equilibrium income fall by only $300, and not by the tax multiplied by the multiplier, which would be $400?

The answer is that consumers pay for this tax, in part, by *reducing* their saving. Specifically, with the MPC at 0.75, the $100 tax payment is split between consumption, reduced by $75, and saving, reduced by $25. When this $75 decrease in consumption is multiplied by the multiplier, this yields a decline in income of $300 ($75 × 4). The *reduction* in saving of $25 *dampens* the impact of the tax on equilibrium income because those funds were previously withdrawn from the spending stream. Changing the withdrawal category from saving to taxes does not affect income: Both are withdrawals.

Equilibrium is shown at point *g* in Figure 11. At point *g*, $I + G = S + T$, with equilibrium income equal to $4,500 and taxes and saving equal to $100 each.

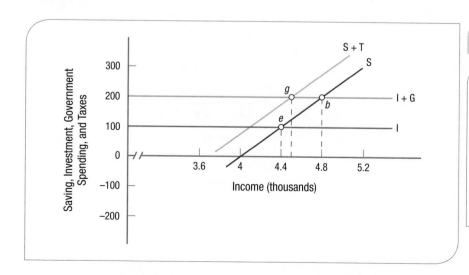

FIGURE 11

Saving, Investment, Government Spending, and Taxes

Tax increases or decreases have less of a direct impact on income, employment, and output than an equivalent change in government spending. Some of a tax increase will come from saving and some of a tax decrease will go into saving, thereby reducing the effect of these tax changes.

The result is that a tax increase (or decrease, for that matter) will have less of a direct impact on income, employment, and output than will an equivalent change in government spending. For this reason, economists typically describe the "tax" multiplier as being smaller than the "spending" multiplier.

The Balanced Budget Multiplier

By now you have probably noticed a curious thing. Our original equilibrium income was $4,400, with investment and saving equal at $100. When the government was introduced with a balanced budget (G = T = $100), income rose by $100 to $4,500, while equilibrium saving and investment remained constant at $100.

This has led to what economists call the **balanced budget multiplier.** Equal changes in government spending and taxation (a balanced budget) lead to an equal change in income. Equivalently, the balanced budget multiplier is equal to 1. If spending and taxes are increased by the same amount, income grows by this amount, hence a balanced budget multiplier equal to 1. Note that the balanced budget multiplier is 1 no matter what the values of MPC and MPS.

balanced budget multiplier
Equal changes in government spending and taxation (a balanced budget) lead to an equal change in income (the balanced budget multiplier is equal to 1).

Adding Net Exports

Thus far we have essentially assumed a closed economy by avoiding adding foreign transactions: exports and imports. We now add the foreign sector to complete the aggregate expenditures model.

The impact of the foreign sector in the aggregate expenditures model is through net exports: exports minus imports (X − M). Exports are *injections* of spending into the domestic economy, and imports are *withdrawals.* When Africans purchase grain from American farmers, they are injecting new spending on grain into our economy. Conversely, when we purchase French wine, we are withdrawing spending (as saving does) and injecting these funds into the French economy.

Figure 12 adds net exports to Figure 10 with investment and government spending. By adding $100 of net exports to the previous equilibrium at point *b,* equilibrium moves to $5,200 (point *c*). Again, we see the multiplier at work as the $100 in net exports leads to a $400 increase in income.

With the foreign sector included, all injections into the economy must equal all withdrawals; therefore at equilibrium,

$$I + G + X = S + T + M$$

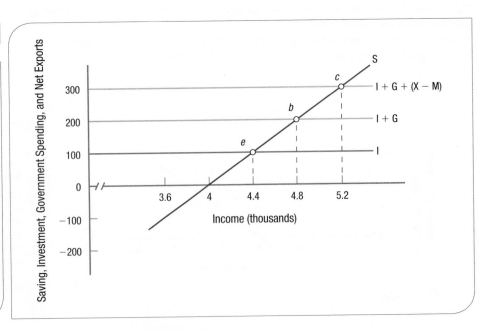

FIGURE 12

Saving, Investment, Government Spending, and Net Exports

Adding investment (I), government spending (G), and net exports (X − M) causes income and output to rise or fall by the spending change times the multiplier. In this figure, we have added net exports (X − M) of $100 to the investment and government spending in Figure 10 to get I + G + (X − M). Thus, an increase in investment spending, government spending, and net exports has the same effect on income and output.

Thus, if we import more and all other spending remains the same, equilibrium income will fall. This is one reason why so many people focus on the trade deficit or net exports (X − M) figures each month.

The aggregate expenditures model illustrates the importance of spending in an economy. Investment, government spending, and exports all increase income, whereas saving, taxes, and imports reduce it. Further, the fact that consumers spend and save some of the *changes* in income (MPC and MPS) gives rise to a spending multiplier that magnifies the impact of changes in spending on the economy.

Recessionary and Inflationary Gaps

Keynesian analysis illustrated what was needed to get the economy out of the Great Depression: an increase in aggregate spending. Without an increase in spending, an economy can be stuck at a point below full employment for an extended period of time. Therefore, Keynes argued that if consumers, businesses, and foreigners were unwilling to spend (their economic expectations were clearly dismal), government should. This was also the basic rationale for the 2009 stimulus package passed by Congress and signed by President Obama. Finally, this leads to the question of just how much additional spending is needed to return the economy to full employment.

ISSUE

Was Keynes Right About the Great Depression?

There is little disagreement that the Great Depression was one of the most important events in the United States in modern history. Good aggregate data were not yet available, but President Roosevelt and congressional leaders knew something was very wrong.

Within a couple of years, 10,000 banks collapsed, farms and businesses were lost, the stock market lost 85% of its value from the beginning of the decade, and soup kitchens fed a growing horde as unemployment soared to nearly 25%, up from 3.2% in 1929. Worse, the Great Depression persisted: It did not look to be temporary; there was no end in sight.

The aggregate expenditures model we have just studied provides some insight into the Great Depression. The figure plots hypothetical saving and investment curves over the actual data for 1929 and 1933. Both government and the foreign sector were tiny at this time, therefore the simple aggregate expenditures model effectively illustrates why the Great Depression did not show signs of much improvement; by 1939, the unemployment rate was still over 17%.

Saving and investment were over $16 billion in 1929, or roughly a healthy 15% of GDP (point *a*). By 1933, investment collapsed to just over $1 billion (a 91% decline), and the economy was in equilibrium at an income of roughly half of that in 1929 (point *b*). Government spending remained at roughly the same levels while net exports, a small fraction of aggregate

expenditures, fell by more than half of their previous levels.

Keynes had it right: Unless something happened to increase investment or exports (not likely given that the rest of the world was suffering economically as well), the economy would remain mired in the Great Depression (point *b*). He suggested that government spending was needed. Ten years later (1943), the United States was in the middle of World War II, and aggregate expenditures swelled as government spending rose by a factor of 10. The Great Depression was history.

recessionary gap The increase in aggregate spending needed to bring a depressed economy back to full employment; equal to the GDP gap divided by the multiplier.

Recessionary Gap The **recessionary gap** is the increase in aggregate spending needed to bring a depressed economy back to full employment. Note that it is not the difference between real GDP at full employment and current real GDP, which is called the GDP gap. If full employment income is $4,400 and our current equilibrium income is $4,000, the recessionary gap is the added spending ($100) that when boosted by the multiplier (4 in this case) will close a GDP gap ($400).

inflationary gap The spending reduction necessary (when expanded by the multiplier) to bring an overheated economy back to full employment.

Inflationary Gap If aggregate spending generates income above full employment levels, the economy will eventually heat up, creating inflationary pressures. Essentially, the economy is trying to produce more output and income than it can sustain for very long. Thus, the excess aggregate spending exceeding that necessary to result in full employment is the **inflationary gap.** Using our previous example, if full employment is an income of $4,400 and our current equilibrium is $4,800, a reduction in spending is needed to close the $400 GDP gap and to prevent inflation from building. In this case, a reduction in aggregate expenditures of $100 with a multiplier of 4 would bring the economy back to full employment at $4,400. In sum, changes in aggregate expenditures expanded by the multiplier can help bring an economy facing either recessionary or inflation pressures back into equilibrium sooner.

This Keynesian approach to analyzing aggregate spending revolutionized the way economists looked at the economy and led to the development of modern macroeconomics. In the next chapter, we extend our analysis to the aggregate demand and supply model, a modern extension of this aggregate expenditures model to account for varying price levels and the supply side of the macroeconomy.

 CHECKPOINT

THE FULL AGGREGATE EXPENDITURES MODEL

- Government spending affects the economy in the same way as other spending.
- Tax increases withdraw money from the spending stream but do not affect the economy as much as spending reductions, because these tax increases are partly offset by decreases in saving.
- Tax decreases inject money into the economy but do not affect the economy as much as spending increases, because tax reductions are partly offset by increases in saving.
- Equal changes in government spending and taxes (a balanced budget) result in an equal change in income (a balanced budget multiplier of 1).
- A recessionary gap is the new spending required that, when expanded by the multiplier, moves the economy to full employment.
- An inflationary gap is the spending reduction necessary (again when expanded by the multiplier) to bring the economy back to full employment.

QUESTION: If the government is considering reducing taxes to stimulate the economy, does it matter if the MPS is 0.25 or 0.33?

Answers to the Checkpoint question can be found at the end of this chapter.

chapter summary

Section 1: **Aggregate Expenditures**

Gross domestic product (GDP) is measured by spending or income. Using the spending approach, GDP is equal to aggregate expenditures (AE). Therefore:

$$GDP = AE = C + I + G + (X - M)$$

45 Degree and Consumption Line

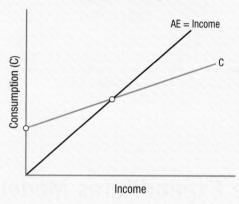

The 45° line shows where total spending (AE) equals income. No borrowing or saving exists.

The consumption line (C) starts above the origin on the vertical axis (even with no income, one still consumes by borrowing). As income increases, consumption rises, but not as fast as income (the slope of C depends on the MPC).

When C crosses AE, spending equals income (on the 45° line). When C is below the AE line, saving is positive.

Investment spending fluctuates much more than consumption year to year.

Disposable income, Y_D, is income after all taxes have been paid. Disposable income can either be spent (C) or saved (S). Thus, $Y_D = C + S$.

The portion that is consumed or saved is an important concept in the aggregate expenditures model:

Marginal propensity to consume (MPC) = $\Delta C / \Delta Y_D$

Marginal propensity to save (MPS) = $\Delta S / \Delta Y_D$

MPC + MPS = 1 (all money is either spent or saved)

Even with little to no income, college students still consume goods and services, often by borrowing against future income.

Determinants of Consumption and Saving

The aggregate expenditures model states that income is the main determinant of consumption and saving. But other factors also can shift the consumption schedule, such as:

- Wealth
- Expectations
- Household debt
- Taxes

Determinants of Investment Demand

Investment demand is assumed to be independent of income, but certain factors can shift investment demand, such as:

- Expectations
- Technological change
- Operating costs
- Capital goods on hand

Section 2: Simple Aggregate Expenditures Model

Ignoring government spending and net exports, aggregate expenditures (AE) are the sum of consumer and business investment: AE = C + I. Because AE also equals C + S at equilibrium, this means that savings = investment.

The **multiplier effect** occurs when a dollar of spending generates many more dollars of spending in the economy.

The **multiplier** is equal to:

1/(1 − MPC) or 1/MPS.

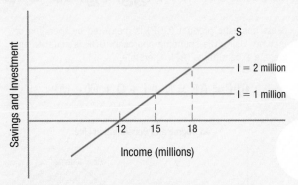

With no investment, income = $12 million. With $1 million in investment, income rises to $15 million, an increase of $3 million. The multiplier in this example is 3.

Section 3: The Full Aggregate Expenditures Model

Government spending affects the economy just like any other spending, and so does spending by foreign consumers (exports). In the full aggregate expenditures model, all forms of spending are analyzed, including C, I, G, and (X − M).

If the multiplier for an economy is 5, a $1 million increase in investment increases income by $5 million. The same effect occurs with a $1 million increase in government spending or $1 million increase in net exports. Essentially, spending is spending, no matter where it comes from.

A general way to analyze policies that increase or decrease aggregate output is to categorize activities as either an **injection** or a **withdrawal:**

Injections increase spending in an economy, and include investment (I), government spending (G), and exports (X).

Withdrawals decrease spending in an economy, and include savings (S), taxes (T), and imports (M).

In equilibrium, all injections must equal all withdrawals:

$$I + G + X = S + T + M$$

Whenever the economy moves away from its full employment equilibrium, one of two gaps is created:

Recessionary gap: The increase in aggregate spending (that is then multiplied) to bring a depressed economy to full employment.

Inflationary gap: The reduction in aggregate spending (again expanded by the multiplier) needed to reduce income to full employment levels.

Purchasing an American-made car injects spending into the economy, and the economic benefits are enhanced by the multiplier.

Purchasing a foreign-made car, however, results in a withdrawal because money leaves the country, and this effect is compounded by the multiplier.

KEY CONCEPTS

QUESTIONS AND PROBLEMS

Check Your Understanding

1. Describe the important difference between the average propensity to consume (APC) and the marginal propensity to consume (MPC).

2. List the factors that influence an individual's marginal propensity to consume.

3. Explain why we wouldn't expect investment to grow sufficiently to pull the economy out of a depression.

4. Define the simple Keynesian multiplier. Describe why a multiplier exists.

5. Explain why a $100 reduction in taxes does not have the same impact on output and employment as a $100 increase in government spending.

6. How do injections and withdrawals into an economy affect its income and output?

Apply the Concepts

7. Assume a simple Keynesian depression economy with a multiplier of 4 and an initial equilibrium income of $3,000. Saving and investment equal $400, and assume full employment income is $4,000.

   a. What is the MPC equal to? The MPS?

   b. How much would government spending have to rise to move the economy to full employment?

   c. Assume that the government plans to finance any spending by raising taxes to cover the increase in spending (it intends to run a balanced budget). How much will government spending and taxes have to rise to move the economy to full employment?

   d. From the initial equilibrium, if investment grows by $100, what will be the new equilibrium level of income and savings?

8. Other than reductions in interest rates that increase the level of investment by businesses, what factors would result in higher investment at existing interest rates?

9. The simple aggregate expenditures model discussed in this chapter concluded that one form of spending was just as good as any other; increases in all types of spending lead to equal increases in income. Is there any reason to suspect that private investment might be better for the economy than government spending?

10. Assume that the economy is in equilibrium at $5,700, and full employment is $4,800. If the MPC is 0.67, how big is the inflationary gap?

11. How does the economy today differ from that of the Great Depression, the economy Keynes used as the basis for the macroeconomic model discussed in this chapter?

12. In modern politics, the word Keynesian often is synonymous with "big government" spending. Does this characterization accurately reflect the role of government in spurring economic activity? How would a tax cut be characterized today versus in Keynes's time?

In the News

13. In recent years banks have encouraged their customers to save by giving incentives to join programs that automatically transfer money from checking accounts to savings accounts. For example, a bank might offer to round debit transactions to the nearest dollar, transferring the change to one's savings account, and then boost this amount with a match up to a certain amount ("Just Save Already: Bank Gimmicks for Saving Only Sound Good," *Daily Finance*, September 11, 2009). Although these programs were intended to encourage customers to save, some economists are not very enthusiastic about these programs. What reasons, both practical and theoretical, might cause some to be concerned?

14. The $787 billion stimulus package passed in 2009 was designed to jumpstart the economy reeling from the worst economic recession since the Great Depression by injecting the economy with large amounts of government spending ("Much Ado About Multipliers," *The Economist*, September 24, 2009). Explain how this spending, as designed, was meant to create a much greater economic effect than the $787 billion spent. What factors might explain why the full economic effect of the stimulus may have fallen short of expectations?

Solving Problems

15. Using the aggregate expenditures table below, answer the questions that follow.

Income (Y), in $	Consumption (C), in $	Saving (S), in $
2,200	2,320	−120
2,300	2,380	−80
2,400	2,440	−40
2,500	2,500	0
2,600	2,560	40
2,700	2,620	80
2,800	2,680	120
2,900	2,740	160
3,000	2,800	200

a. Compute the APC when income equals $2,300 and the APS when income equals $2,800.

b. Compute the MPC and MPS.

c. What does the simple Keynesian multiplier equal?

d. If investment spending is equal to $120, what will be equilibrium income?

e. Using the following graph, show saving, investment, and equilibrium income.

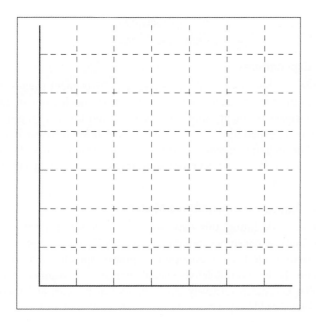

16. Use the figure below to answer the following questions.

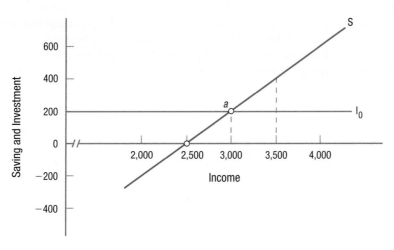

a. What are the MPC, the MPS, and the multiplier?

b. If the economy is currently in equilibrium at point *a,* and full employment income is $4,000, how much in *additional* expenditures is needed to move this economy to full employment? What is this level of spending called?

c. Assume that the economy is currently in equilibrium at point *a* and full employment income is $4,000. How much of a tax decrease would be required to move the economy to full employment?

⊕ USING THE NUMBERS

17. According to By the Numbers, in what year (since 1973) did the U.S. government spend the most as a percentage of GDP? In what year did it spend the least? How do your answers correspond to the business cycle?

18. According to By the Numbers, the U.S. government spends less per person than any other developed country on the list. Does this mean that the overall size of the U.S. government is smaller than that of the other developed countries? Why or why not?

Checkpoint: Aggregate Expenditures

Consumer spending, while 5 times larger in absolute size than investment spending, involves many small expenditures by households that do not vary much from month to month, such as rent (or mortgage payment), food, and utilities. Consumers change habits, but slowly. Business investment expenditures are typically on big-ticket items such as new factories and equipment, but such investments occur only when businesses have favorable expectations about the economy. When expectations sour, investment typically falls by all firms in an industry.

Checkpoint: The Simple Aggregate Expenditures Model

When consumer confidence is declining, this may suggest that consumers are going to spend less and save more. Because consumer spending is roughly 70% of aggregate spending, a small decline represents a significant reduction in aggregate spending and may well mean that a recession is on the horizon. Relatively small changes in consumer spending coupled with the multiplier can mean relatively large changes in income, and therefore forecasters and policymakers should keep a close eye on consumer confidence.

Checkpoint: The Full Aggregate Expenditures Model

Yes, it does matter. If the tax reduction is going to be $100, for example, and the MPS is 0.25, the multiplier is 4, and the income increase will be $75 \times 4 = $300. Keep in mind that in this case, one-fourth of the tax reduction will go into saving and will not be amplified by the multiplier. However, with a MPS of 0.33, the multiplier will be 3, and one-third will not be multiplied (will go into saving), therefore the increase in income will be $66.6 \times 3 = $200.

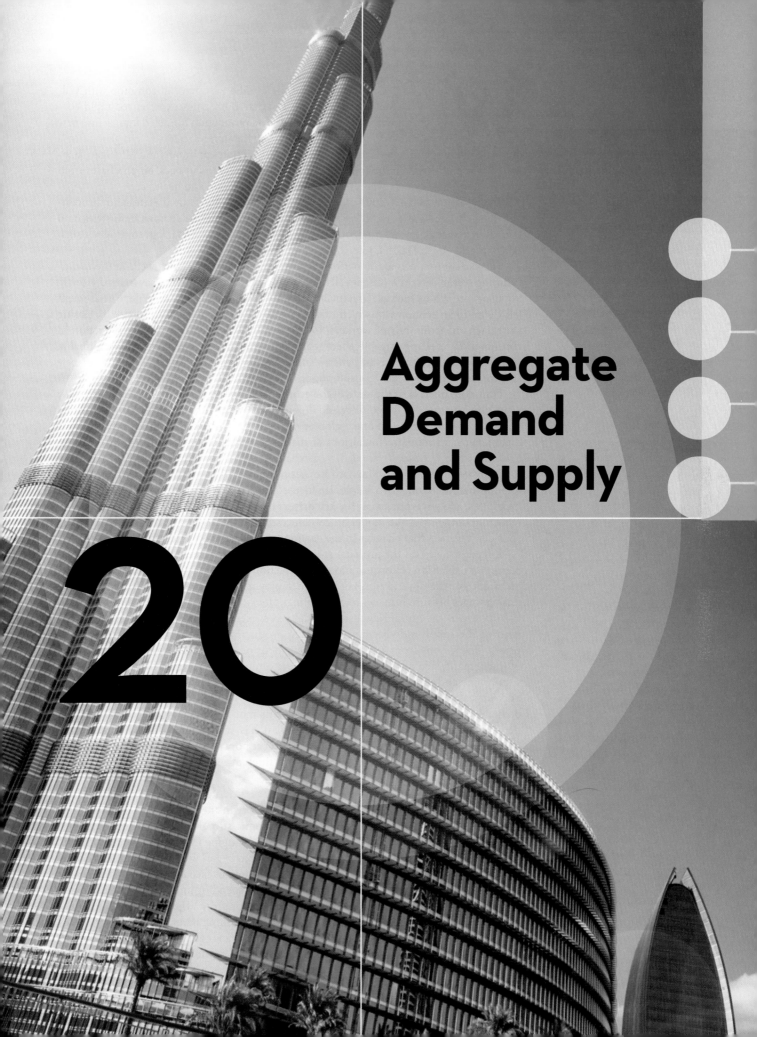

Aggregate Demand and Supply

20

What does Dubai, a large city in the Middle East, have in common with Williston, a small town in North Dakota? Both cities experienced rapid economic growth in the past decade as oil production funneled money into new construction and infrastructure, drawing in new residents and generating a dramatic rise in spending. Meanwhile, in the industrial states of Illinois and Michigan, stagnant wages and persistent unemployment forced residents to cut back on purchases from vacations and new cars to even some necessities, such as food and health care.

The recession of 2007–2009 created much hardship in the United States and throughout the global economy. However, the extent to which different regions, industries, and households were affected varied, from the extreme to not at all. In fact, in some areas, such as in western North Dakota, jobs were plentiful and lives improved.

The variation in economic performance extended to industries as well. In the manufacturing sector, certain industries all but closed, while other industries saw record growth. Popular store chains such as Circuit City, Borders, Linens 'n Things, and Filene's Basement fell victim to an economy in which many consumers were not eager to spend. By closing stores, tens of thousands of workers lost their jobs, which led to a greater reduction in consumption, creating a ripple effect that made economic recovery even more difficult. Meanwhile, the health care and energy industries flourished, creating thousands of new jobs that will lead to greater consumption.

How does one assess the state of the economy and evaluate the effectiveness of policy when different areas of the country and different industries vary in performance? It would be dangerous to look at just one region or one industry (or even one time of the year, for that matter) and come to conclusions or make policy recommendations for the nation as a whole.

British economist John Maynard Keynes recognized the need to develop tools to analyze the macroeconomy as a whole. He focused on aggregate expenditures by consumers, businesses, and governments as the key drivers for the economy that determined employment and output. But the model he developed during the Great Depression did not fully consider the effect that changes in the economy would have on prices. Why?

Keynes focused on the problem at hand, when resources were underutilized. For this reason, an expansion of consumption or production did not create much upward pressure on prices. For example, in times of high unemployment, more labor can be hired without raising wages because firms with job openings often are inundated with applicants.

Therefore, the initial Keynesian model was a fixed price model, one that essentially ignored the supply side because increasing production would occur without a rise in prices. The lessons from Keynes, with their focus on spending, formed the foundation of the demand side of the modern macroeconomic model. In this chapter, we add the supply side and move from a fixed price model to a flexible price model, where prices and wages adjust to macroeconomic conditions. We call this model the aggregate demand–aggregate supply (AD/AS) model. This model looks a lot like the supply and demand model developed in Chapter 3, but it has several important differences: It measures real output of the aggregate (overall) economy, it uses the average price level for an economy, and it focuses on short-run fluctuations around a long-run equilibrium output.

The response of prices and wages does not always change in a consistent manner. As we will see, sometimes prices and wages can be *sticky* in the short run, a condition that allows an economy to respond positively to economic stimulus policies. But in the long run, prices and wages tend to be very responsive to changing macroeconomic conditions.

This flexible price model expands the analysis that began with Keynes to many more modern problems facing economies. And when economies face a deep recession like that in 2007–2009, with high unemployment and reduced spending and investment, the policy prescriptions from Keynesian analysis return to the forefront. The beauty of this AD/AS approach is that it builds on skills you already have: defining demand and supply curves, assessing changes in economic facts, and determining a new equilibrium. These techniques provide policymakers with a way of looking at the overall economy when many factors and differences in economic performance prevail across regions and industries.

:: BY THE NUMBERS

The Sheer Size of Aggregate Demand and Aggregate Supply

Aggregate demand and aggregate supply are made up of many components in the economy. Factors that influence the extent to which consumers, businesses, and governments spend make up aggregate demand, while various short-run and long-run factors influence producers and aggregate supply.

A snapshot of industries that contributed to a country's aggregate demand or aggregate supply in 2012:

Aggregate Demand

China: Consumers purchased 19.3 million cars worth over $300 billion.

Japan: Consumers purchased 16 billion pounds of fish worth $14 billion.

United Arab Emirates: Businesses spent $1.5 billion building new hotels.

Israel: Government spent $15.2 billion for military preparedness.

Aggregate Supply

United States: Produced movies that earned $11 billion domestically.

France: Produced 1.2 billion gallons of wine worth $23.4 billion.

Saudi Arabia: Produced 4.1 billion barrels of oil worth $400 billion.

Brazil: Produced 6.5 billion pounds of coffee worth $5.8 billion.

Botswana: Mined 22.9 million carats of diamonds worth $4 billion.

Energy consumption contributes to aggregate demand and also influences aggregate supply through its effect on input prices. Oil consumption (in billions of barrels) in 1982 and 2012 in the United States and China:

5.6	6.8		3.6
		0.6	
1982	2012	1982	2012
United States		China	

$78,900,000,000,000

Total World Aggregate
Demand in 2012

525%

Increase in NASDAQ stock index value from 1995 to 2000, creating immense wealth that increased aggregate demand.

Home ownership provides a wealth effect that influences aggregate demand. States with the highest and lowest rates of home ownership in 2012.

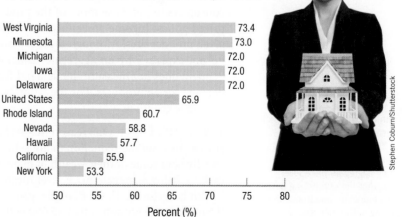

State	Percent (%)
West Virginia	73.4
Minnesota	73.0
Michigan	72.0
Iowa	72.0
Delaware	72.0
United States	65.9
Rhode Island	60.7
Nevada	58.8
Hawaii	57.7
California	55.9
New York	53.3

Percent (%)

98% of all apparel and 99% of all footwear sold in the United States is imported. Imports reduce aggregate demand because money is flowing out of the country to pay for these goods.

This chapter begins with an analysis of aggregate demand and its determinants. We then turn to aggregate supply, studying the differences between a long-run aggregate supply curve and a short-run aggregate supply curve, and the determinants of each. Finally, we put the aggregate demand and aggregate supply curves together to analyze macroeconomic equilibrium. The AD/AS model gives you the tools to analyze tradeoffs between economic output and inflation. It will allow you to understand the causes of recessions and inflation, and how government policy is sometimes used to correct these problems.

⊜ Aggregate Demand

aggregate demand The output of goods and services (real GDP) demanded at different price levels.

The **aggregate demand** (AD) curve (or schedule) shows the output of goods and services (real GDP) demanded at different price levels. The aggregate demand curve in Figure 1 looks like the product demand curves we studied earlier. They both slope downward, showing how output rises as prices fall, and vice versa. However, it's important to remember that these two curves and the reasons they slope downward are different.

The Aggregate Demand Curve

The aggregate demand curve shows the amount of real goods and services (output = real GDP) that will be purchased at various price levels.

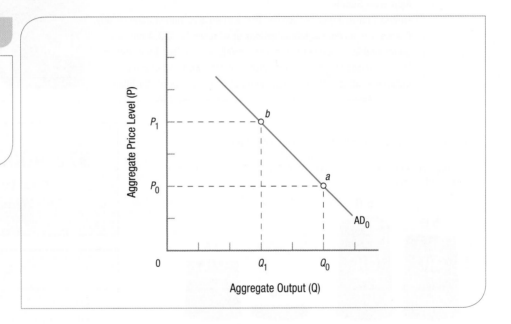

Why Is the Aggregate Demand Curve Negatively Sloped?

In Chapter 3, we studied why product demand curves slope downward due to *income* and *substitution* effects. To review, an income effect occurs when the price of a given product falls, causing consumers' spendable income to rise, allowing them to afford more of all goods. A substitution effect occurs when the price of a product falls, causing consumers to purchase more of the product because they substitute it for other higher priced goods. Income and substitution effects work the other way when the price of a given product rises. Although these explanations work for a product demand curve, they do not explain why an aggregate demand curve slopes downward, because aggregate demand does not measure the demand for just one product, but rather it measures the demand for all products. For the latter, we need to look at other factors influencing the aggregate economy.

wealth effect Households usually hold some of their wealth in financial assets such as savings accounts, bonds, and cash, and a rising aggregate price level means that the purchasing power of this monetary wealth declines, reducing output demanded.

The Wealth Effect One reason that real output declines when the aggregate price level rises is the resulting reduction in household wealth, called the **wealth effect.** Households usually hold some of their wealth in financial assets such as savings accounts, bonds, and cash. A rising aggregate price level means that the purchasing power of this monetary wealth is declining. If, for example, you have $5,000 in a savings account and prices rise throughout the economy, that $5,000 will now purchase less than before. This reduction in household purchasing power means that some purchases are put on hold, thereby reducing output demanded. This is represented by a movement from point *a* to point *b* in Figure 1.

Impact on Exports When the U.S. aggregate price level rises, American goods become more expensive in the global marketplace. Higher prices mean that our goods are less competitive with the goods made in other countries. The result is that foreigners purchase fewer American products, and our exports decline. A decrease in exports means that the demand for domestically produced goods and services (the quantity purchased by foreign consumers, a component of real GDP) also declines. Therefore, higher prices result in lower real output.

Interest Rate Effects Interest rates are the prices paid for the use of money. If we assume for a moment that the quantity of money is fixed, then as aggregate prices rise, people will need more money to carry out their economic transactions. As people demand more money, the cost of borrowing money—interest rates—will go up. Rising interest rates mean reduced business investment, which results in a drop in quantity demanded for real GDP, shown in Figure 1 as a movement from point *a* to *b* and falling real output.

In summary, the aggregate demand curve is negatively sloped because of three factors. When the aggregate price level rises, this lowers household purchasing power because of the wealth effect. A rising aggregate price level also lowers the amount of exports because our goods are now more expensive. Furthermore, a rising aggregate price level increases the demand for money and therefore drives up interest rates. Rising interest rates reduce business investment and reduce the quantity demanded of real GDP. In each case, as aggregate prices rise from P_0 to P_1, quantity demanded of real GDP falls from Q_0 to Q_1.

Determinants of Aggregate Demand

We have seen that the aggregate demand curve is negatively sloped. Everything else held constant, a change in the aggregate price level will change the quantity of real GDP demanded along the aggregate demand curve. The *determinants* of aggregate demand are those factors that shift the *entire* aggregate demand curve when they change. They are the "everything else held constant." These include the components of GDP: consumption, investment, government spending, and net exports.

If one of these components of aggregate spending changes, the aggregate demand curve will shift, as shown in Figure 2. At first, aggregate demand is AD$_0$, therefore a shift

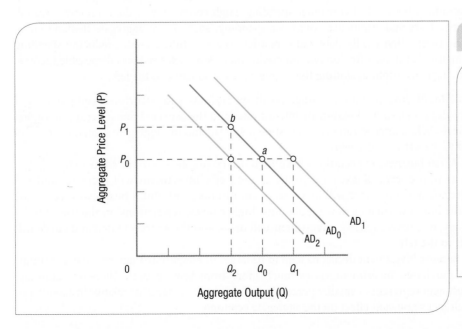

FIGURE 2

Shifts in the Aggregate Demand Curve

The determinants of aggregate demand include the components of GDP and aggregate spending: consumption, investment, government spending, and net exports. A change in one will shift the aggregate demand curve, as shown here. At first, aggregate demand is AD$_0$, therefore a shift to AD$_1$ represents an increase in aggregate demand; more real output is demanded at all price levels. A decline in aggregate demand to AD$_2$ means that less real output is being demanded at all price levels.

to AD_1 represents an increase in aggregate demand; more real output is demanded at the same price level, P_0. If, for example, businesses decide to invest more in new technology, more real output is now demanded at the current price level, P_0, and at all other price levels. For similar reasons, a decrease in aggregate demand to AD_2 means that less real output is being demanded. If consumers fear the onset of a recession and decide to reduce spending to increase their savings, then less output will be demanded at all price levels.

Let's look at these determinants of aggregate demand more closely. What might cause the various components of aggregate expenditures to change, shifting the AD curve?

Consumer Spending Consumer spending is the largest component of aggregate demand, representing about 70% of total spending in an economy. The level of spending as a percentage of overall output is relatively stable over time. Still, consumer spending is affected by four major factors: wealth, consumer confidence, household debt, and taxes. Because consumer spending represents such a large part of the economy, even small changes in these factors can have a significant impact on the economy. And in times when consumption changes a lot, the effect on the economy can be dramatic.

For example, when the technology-heavy NASDAQ Stock Market surged in the late 1990s, Federal Reserve Chairman Alan Greenspan became concerned that a consequent surge in consumer spending from the newly added wealth would increase aggregate demand to AD_1 in Figure 2, resulting in higher inflation. (We'll see why spending can lead to inflation a little later in this chapter.) When the NASDAQ collapsed in the early 2000s, the Federal Reserve then became worried that sinking consumer confidence (caused by falling wealth) would reduce consumption spending, thereby making the recession worse. In late 2008 and early 2009, falling housing prices and a stock market slump, coupled with reduced consumer confidence, caused an unusually large drop in consumer spending that was an important factor in the depth of the recession.

Note that changes in wealth have two similar but distinct impacts on aggregate demand. First, as described earlier, when aggregate prices rise, the purchasing power of financial assets falls, reducing the *amount* of goods and services that can now be purchased with this money. This is a movement along an existing aggregate demand curve to a higher price level (point *a* to *b* in Figure 2).

Second, described here, is a decrease in wealth (for example, caused by a stock market crash) that reduces consumption *at all price levels.* In this case, the entire aggregate demand curve shifts from AD_0 to AD_2 in Figure 2. This is the impact of changing wealth on consumer spending that is usually the focus of attention by the media and policymakers.

Consumer expectations and confidence about the economy play a significant role in determining the level of consumer spending. High confidence in the economy eases job security fears and stimulates consumer spending, shifting the aggregate demand curve to the right. High family debt ratios restrict access to future credit, reducing spending on high-ticket items often bought on credit. Increasing taxes reduces disposable income, reducing consumption, shifting the aggregate demand curve to the left.

Investment Investment (spending, mostly by businesses for structures, equipment, and software) is determined mainly by interest rates and the expected rate of return on capital projects. When interest rates rise, investment will fall and the aggregate demand curve will shift to the left, and vice versa.

When business expectations become more favorable—perhaps some new technology is introduced, or excess capacity is reduced—investment will increase, and the aggregate demand curve will increase, or shift to the right. But if businesses see clouds on the horizon, such as new regulations, higher taxes, restrictions on the use of technology, or excess capacity, investment will drop, and the aggregate demand curve will shift to the left.

Because investment decisions tend to be larger in magnitude than everyday consumption purchases, investment varies much more from year to year. Therefore, although investment represents a smaller percentage of aggregate demand, its relative instability can result in a significant effect on the aggregate economy.

Government Spending and Net Exports Government spending and net exports have essentially the same effect on the aggregate economy as consumer and investment spending. When government spending or net exports rise, aggregate demand increases, and vice versa.

When the national income of a foreign country rises, some of this money is used to buy more American goods and services. The increase in demand for U.S. goods and services in other countries results in more exports, which increases U.S. aggregate demand. A change in foreign exchange rates will also affect aggregate demand. An appreciation, or rise, in the value of the euro, for instance, will result in Europeans buying more American goods because a euro will buy more. Again, this change increases U.S. exports and U.S. aggregate demand. These effects on aggregate demand are offset by increases in imports of foreign goods, because goods are being demanded from outside of the United States.

A quick summary is now in order. The aggregate demand curve shows the quantities of real GDP demanded at different price levels. (The derivation of the AD curve using the Keynesian fixed price model is shown in the Appendix to this chapter.) The aggregate demand curve slopes downward because of the wealth effect (the value of monetary assets falls when the price level rises), because exports fall as domestic prices rise, and because rising prices raise interest rates, which reduce investment. On the other hand, changes in one of the determinants of aggregate demand shift the aggregate demand curve. Table 1 summarizes the determinants of aggregate demand.

Again, the determinants of aggregate demand are those "other factors held constant": consumption, investment, government spending, and net exports. If one of those determinants changes, the entire aggregate demand curve will shift. Keep in mind that changes

A favorable exchange rate for the euro makes shopping trips to New York for Europeans less expensive, providing a boost to U.S. aggregate demand.

The Determinants of Aggregate Demand (the aggregate demand curve shifts when these change)		**TABLE 1**
Determinant	**AD Increases**	**AD Decreases**
Consumer Spending		
• Wealth	Wealth increases	Wealth decreases
• Consumer expectations	Expectations improve	Expectations worsen
• Household debt	Debt falls	Debt rises
• Taxes	Taxes are cut	Taxes increase
Investment		
• Interest rates	Fall	Rise
• Expected rate of return on investment	Higher	Lower
Government Spending	Increases	Decreases
Net Exports	Increases	Decreases
• Income in other countries	Rising	Falling
• Exchange rate changes	Depreciating dollar	Appreciating dollar

ISSUE

Did the Collapse of the Housing Market Affect Aggregate Demand?

From 2006 to 2011, the U.S. housing market took a tremendous dive, with home values falling an average of 32% over this period. Some of the hardest hit cities, such as Phoenix, Las Vegas, and Miami, saw average home values drop by up to 60%.

We know how the housing market affected the economy by creating a near collapse of the financial system and the stock markets, along with causing a severe recession and high unemployment. But the drop in housing values also had an important direct impact on aggregate demand as homeowners altered their consumption patterns.

While much attention has been focused on households that borrowed to finance their houses or had used their homes to borrow additional money during the housing boom, in 2013 about 30% of homes in the United States did not have mortgages. These are homes that had mortgages that

had already been paid off, or were originally paid for in cash. Many of these homes without mortgages are owned by older individuals who spent much of their lives paying off their 15-year or 30-year mortgages.

When households own their homes outright, the value of these homes often represents a large proportion of their assets. For these homeowners, a drastic drop in the value of their homes creates a great deal of uncertainty. For example, it becomes more difficult to rely on the value of their homes to provide a comfortable retirement. Some, for example, sell their homes for something smaller and cheaper (especially once the kids move out), using the excess money for daily expenses. When the price of homes fell, those who planned to sell their homes found that they could not get enough money to live comfortably. Some even chose to return to work.

Blend Images/Alamy

As a result, the drop in housing values created a large wealth effect among homeowners. Homeowners felt poorer, and as a result, changed their consumption habits accordingly. Instead of relying on home values for future income, homeowners saved more to ensure a comfortable future. By increasing savings, there was a corresponding drop in consumption, decreasing aggregate demand. Indeed, the collapse of the housing market did more than just affect financial markets and labor markets—it had a direct impact on aggregate demand.

in the determinants are most important for policymaking. When a policy is enacted (say, lower tax rates), policymakers expect to stimulate consumer and investment spending, increasing aggregate demand, output, and employment.

As important as aggregate demand is in determining an economy's output, aggregate demand tells only one part of the story. The other part, aggregate supply, describes the impetus for businesses to create and produce goods and services, which we turn to next.

 # CHECKPOINT

AGGREGATE DEMAND

- The aggregate demand curve shows the relationship between real GDP and the price level.
- The aggregate demand curve has a negative slope because of the impact of the price level on financial wealth, exports, and interest rates.
- The determinants of aggregate demand are consumer spending, investment spending, government expenditures, and net exports. Changes in any of these determinants will shift the aggregate demand curve.

QUESTION: Consumer spending is related to disposable personal income (income minus taxes). In 2011 and 2012, the federal government reduced the payroll taxes paid by American workers from 6.2% to 4.2%. Describe how this change in taxes would affect consumption and aggregate demand.

Answers to the Checkpoint question can be found at the end of this chapter.

Aggregate Supply

The **aggregate supply** curve shows the real GDP that firms will produce at varying price levels. Even though the definition seems similar to that for aggregate demand, note that we have now moved from the spending side of the economy to the production side. We will consider two different possibilities for aggregate supply: the short run and the long run. In the short run, aggregate supply is positively sloped and prices rise when GDP grows. In contrast, long-run aggregate supply reflects the long-run state of the economy and is represented by a vertical curve. Growth occurs in the economy by shifting this vertical aggregate supply curve to the right. Let's begin by looking at the economy from the long-run perspective.

Long Run

The *vertical* **long-run aggregate supply (LRAS) curve** incorporates the assumptions of classical (pre-1930s) economic analysis. Classical analysis assumes that all variables are adjustable in the long run, where product prices, wages, and interest rates are flexible. As a result, the economy will gravitate to the position of full employment shown as Q_0 in Figure 3.

> **aggregate supply** The real GDP that firms will produce at varying price levels. In the short run, aggregate supply is positively sloped because many input costs are slow to change (they are *sticky*), but in the long run, the aggregate supply curve is vertical at full employment because the economy has reached its capacity to produce.

> **long-run aggregate supply (LRAS) curve** The long-run aggregate supply curve is vertical at full employment because the economy has reached its capacity to produce.

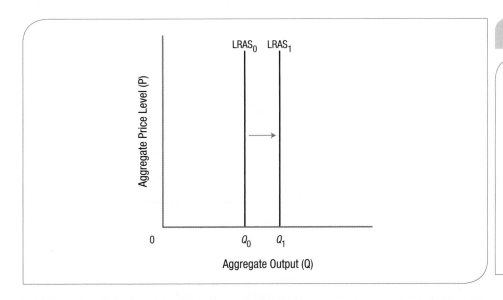

FIGURE 3

Long-Run Aggregate Supply

The long-run aggregate supply (LRAS) curve is vertical, reflecting the assumptions of classical economic analysis. In the long run, all variables in the economy can adjust, and the economy will settle at full employment at output Q_0. Changes in the amount of resources available, the quality of the labor force, and technology can shift the LRAS curve to the right to LRAS$_1$, at a new full employment output at Q_1.

Full employment is often referred to as the *natural rate of output* or *the natural rate of unemployment* by economists. This long-run output is an equilibrium level at which inflationary pressures are minimal. Once the economy has reached this level, further increases in output are extremely difficult to achieve; there is no one else to operate more machines, and no more machines to operate. As we will see later, attempts to expand beyond this output level only lead to higher prices and rising inflation.

In general terms, the vertical LRAS curve represents the full employment capacity of the economy and depends on the amount of resources available for production and the available technology. Full employment is determined by the capital available, the size and quality of the labor force, and the technology employed; in effect, the productive capacity of the economy. Remember from earlier chapters that these are also the big three factors driving economic growth (shifting the LRAS$_0$ curve to the right to LRAS$_1$) once a suitable infrastructure has been put in place.

The Shifting Long-Run Aggregate Supply Curve

Improving technology such as automation and digitalization are clear examples of an increase in productive capacity. But so is the enhancement of labor quality. As a greater percentage of people pursue college and postgraduate degrees, productivity increases and leads to economic growth. Finally, increased trade and globalization have allowed resources to flow more freely, allowing the United States to gain access to better or cheaper inputs and more specialized labor.

Each of the shifts in the LRAS curve takes time. It's not easy to improve the human capital of an entire nation or to develop new production technologies. Therefore, although the LRAS is of concern to the long-term welfare of the country, policymakers are often more concerned about short-run outcomes. We now turn to the short-run aggregate supply (SRAS) curve.

Short Run

short-run aggregate supply (SRAS) curve The short-run aggregate supply curve is positively sloped because many input costs are slow to change (*sticky*) in the short run.

Figure 4 shows the **short-run aggregate supply (SRAS) curve,** which is positively sloped because some input costs are slow to change in the short run. When prices rise, firms do not immediately see an increase in wages or rents because these are often fixed for a specified term; in other words, input prices are *sticky*. Thus, profits will rise with the rising prices and firms will supply more output as their profits increase.

FIGURE 4

Short-Run Aggregate Supply

The short-run aggregate supply (SRAS) curve is positively sloped because many input costs are slow to change in the short run (they are *sticky*).

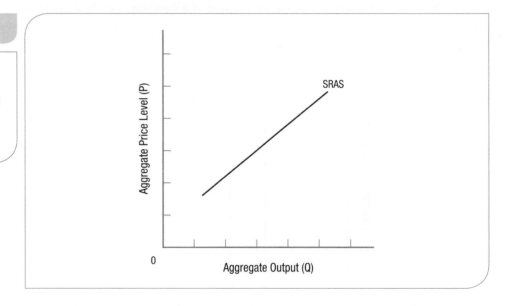

This situation, however, cannot last for long. As an entire industry or the economy as a whole increases its production, firms must start hiring more labor or paying overtime. As each firm seeks more employees, wages are driven up, increasing costs and forcing higher prices.

For the economy as a whole, a rise in real GDP results in higher employment and reduced unemployment. Lower unemployment rates mean a tightening of labor markets. This often leads to fierce collective bargaining by labor, followed by increases in wages, costs, and prices. The result is that a short-run increase in GDP is usually accompanied by a rise in the price level.

Determinants of Short-Run Aggregate Supply

We have seen that, because the aggregate supply curve is positively sloped in the short run, a change in aggregate output, other things held constant, will result in a change in the aggregate price level. The determinants of short-run aggregate supply—those other things held constant—include changes in input prices, productivity, taxes, regulation, the market power of firms, or business and inflationary expectations. When any of these determinants change, the entire SRAS curve shifts, as Figure 5 illustrates.

Input Prices Changes in the cost of land, labor, capital, or entrepreneurship will change the output that firms are willing to provide to the market. As we have seen, when world crude oil prices rise, it is never long before prices rise at the gasoline pump. Rising input

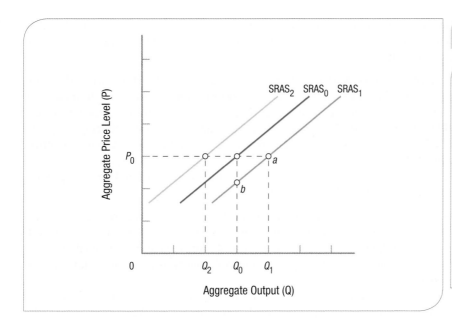

FIGURE 5

Shifts in Short-Run Aggregate Supply
The determinants of short-run aggregate supply include changes in input prices, productivity, taxes, regulation, the market power of firms, and business and inflationary expectations. If one of these determinants changes, the entire short-run aggregate supply curve shifts. Increasing productivity, for instance, will shift the short-run aggregate supply curve to the right, from $SRAS_0$ to $SRAS_1$. Conversely, raising taxes or adding inefficient regulations can shift the short-run aggregate supply curve to the left, from $SRAS_0$ to $SRAS_2$.

prices are quickly passed along to consumers, and the opposite is true as well. New discoveries of raw materials result in falling input prices, causing the prices for products incorporating these inputs to drop. This means that more of these products can be produced at a price of P_0 in Figure 5 as short-run aggregate supply shifts to $SRAS_1$ (point a), or now output Q_0 can be produced at a lower price on $SRAS_1$ (point b).

Productivity Changes in productivity are another major determinant of short-run aggregate supply. Rising productivity will shift the short-run aggregate supply curve to the right—from $SRAS_0$ to $SRAS_1$ in Figure 5—and vice versa. This is why changes in technology that increase productivity are so important to the economy. Technological advances, moreover, often lead to new products that expand short-run aggregate supply. They also increase the productive capability of the economy, which shifts LRAS to the right.

An example of a technological advance is the improvement in traffic-enhanced GPS navigational devices, which allows one to select the quickest route to a destination taking into account traffic and roadblocks (such as those caused by construction projects and car crashes) in real time. Such technological enhancements let commercial vehicles reduce their time on the road, reducing transportation costs to the company. These cost reductions lead to an increase in short-run aggregate supply. If these technologies expand the overall productive capacity of the economy, they can also increase long-run aggregate supply.

Taxes and Regulation Rising taxes or increased regulation can shift the short-run aggregate supply curve to the left, from $SRAS_0$ to $SRAS_2$ in Figure 5. Excessively burdensome regulation, though it may provide some benefits, raises costs so much that the new costs exceed the benefits. This results in a decrease in short-run aggregate supply. Often, no one knows how much regulation has increased costs until some sort of deregulation is instituted.

Alternatively, tax reductions such as investment tax credits reduce the costs of production, resulting in an increase in short-run aggregate supply. Similarly,

The dramatic rise in copper prices from 2006 to 2012 increased the cost of producing copper products, and contributed to a decrease in aggregate supply.

improving the process of satisfying regulations, such as reducing required paperwork, also can increase short-run aggregate supply even when the regulations themselves do not change.

Market Power of Firms   Monopoly firms charge more than competitive firms. Therefore, a change in the market power of firms can increase prices for specific products, thereby reducing short-run aggregate supply. When the Organization of Petroleum Exporting Countries (OPEC) formed in 1973, it raised oil prices roughly 10-fold by reducing the global supply of oil. Because at that time there were very few substitutes for oil, higher oil prices shifted the SRAS curve to the left.

Today, with many non-OPEC nations (such as Russia, Norway, and Canada) producing large quantities of oil, OPEC's power to raise prices has fallen.

Expectations   A change in business expectations also can change short-run aggregate supply. If firms perceive that the business climate is worsening, they may reduce their investments in capital equipment. This reduced investment results in reduced productivity, fewer new hires, or even the closing of marginally profitable plants, any of which can reduce aggregate supply in the short run.

A change in inflationary expectations by businesses, workers, or consumers can shift the short-run aggregate supply curve. If, for example, workers believe that inflation is going to increase, they will bargain for higher wages to offset the expected losses to real wages. The intensified bargaining and resulting higher wages will reduce aggregate supply.

To summarize, the short-run aggregate supply curve slopes upward because many input costs are slow to change (i.e., are *sticky*) in the short run. This SRAS curve can shift because of changes in input prices, productivity, taxes, regulation, the market power of firms, or business and inflationary expectations. Table 2 summarizes the determinants of short-run aggregate supply.

TABLE 2	Determinants of Short-Run Aggregate Supply (the short-run aggregate supply curve shifts when these change)		
Determinant		**SRAS Increases**	**SRAS Decreases**
Changes in Input Prices		Prices decline	Prices rise
Changes in Productivity			
• Technology		Improvements	Declines
• Changes in human capital		Improvements	Declines
Changes in Taxes and Regulations			
• Tax rates		Lower	Higher
• Subsidies		Higher	Lower
• Change in burdensome regulations		Reductions	Additions
Change in Market Power		Reductions	Increases
Changes in Business or Inflation Expectations			
• Business expectations		More positive	More negative
• Inflation expectations		Lower	Higher

CHECKPOINT

AGGREGATE SUPPLY

- The aggregate supply curve shows the real GDP that firms will produce at varying price levels.

- The vertical long-run aggregate supply (LRAS) curve represents the long-run full-employment capacity of the economy.

- Increasing resources or improved technology shift the LRAS curve, which represents economic growth.

- The short-run aggregate supply (SRAS) curve is upward sloping, reflecting rigidities in the economy because input and output prices are slow to change (sticky).

- The determinants of short-run aggregate supply include changes in input prices, productivity, taxes, regulations, the market power of firms, and business and inflationary expectations.

QUESTION: One of the consequences of the housing and financial crises of the last decade was the implementation of new regulations on the banking industry to prevent individuals and businesses from engaging in unscrupulous activities that might lead to another crisis. By implementing these new laws, business expectations are likely to change. Explain how new banking laws could affect business expectations and the SRAS curve.

Answers to the Checkpoint question can be found at the end of this chapter.

➔ Macroeconomic Equilibrium

Let us now put together our aggregate demand and aggregate supply model. A *short-run* **macroeconomic equilibrium** occurs at the intersection of the short-run aggregate supply and aggregate demand curves; see point *e* in Figure 6. In this case, point *e* also represents *long-run macroeconomic equilibrium* because the economy is operating at full employment, producing output Q_f.

Output level Q_f represents full employment. The SRAS curve assumes price level expectations equal to P_e, and thus Q_f is the natural rate of unemployment or output. Remember that the natural rate of unemployment is that unemployment level at which inflation is low and consistent with inflationary expectations in the economy.

macroeconomic equilibrium
Occurs at the intersection of the short-run aggregate supply and aggregate demand curves. At this output level, there are no net pressures for the economy to expand or contract.

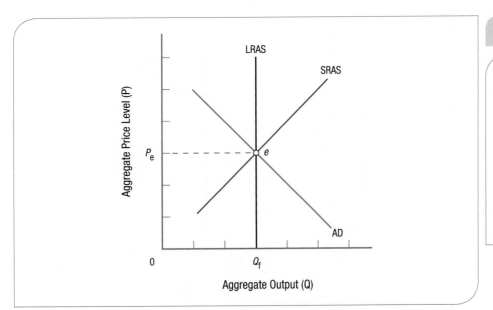

FIGURE 6

Macroeconomic Equilibrium

Point *e* represents a short-run macroeconomic equilibrium, the point at which the short-run aggregate supply curve and aggregate demand curve intersect. In this case, point *e* also represents a long-run macroeconomic equilibrium, because the economy is operating at full employment, producing output Q_f.

The Spending Multiplier

The spending **multiplier** is an important concept introduced into macroeconomics by John Maynard Keynes in 1936. The central idea is that new spending creates more spending, income, and output than just an amount equal to the new spending itself.

Let's assume, for example, that consumers tend to spend three-quarters and save one-quarter of any new income they receive. Now, assume that good weather encourages a family to spend the day at the annual county fair, spending $100 on food and rides. In other words, $100 of new spending is introduced into the economy. That $100 spent on food and rides adds $100 in income to the operator of the fair, because all spending equals income to someone else (whether that be the owner or the workers she hires). Of this additional income, suppose that $25 is saved and $75 is spent by the fair operator to fix a plumbing leak in her home. That $75 in spending becomes $75 in income to the plumber. Now that the plumber has $75 more income, suppose he saves $18.75 (25% of $75) and uses the rest ($56.25) to change the oil in his car, generating $56.25 in income to the mechanic, and so on, round-by-round.

Adding up all of the new spending (equal to the sum of $100 + $75 + $56.25 + . . .) from the initial $100 results in total spending increasing by $400. This represents an increase in output or GDP of $400. Adding up total new saving ($25 + 18.75 + . . .) equals $100, which means that the initial $100 in new spending has increased savings by the same amount through the multiplier process.

The proportion of *additional* income that consumers spend and save is known as the **marginal propensity to consume** and the **marginal propensity to save** (MPC and MPS). In our example, MPC = 0.75 and MPS = 0.25. The multiplier is equal to 4, given that $400 of new income was created with the introduction of $100 of new spending. The formula for the spending multiplier is equal to $1/(1 - MPC) = 1/MPS$, and in this case, is $1/(1 - 0.75) = 1/0.25 = 4$. This formula works as long as the aggregate price level is stable.

When the economy has many unemployed resources and excess capacity, the price level will remain constant and output will increase by the full magnitude of the multiplier. However, when the economy moves up the SRAS curve in the short run, its response to the same increase in aggregate spending is not as great. In Figure 7, aggregate demand increases the same amount as before. The new equilibrium is at point *a* with output of Q_f. But, output grows less because price increases or inflation eat up some of each spending

multiplier Spending changes alter equilibrium income by the spending change times the multiplier. One person's spending becomes another's income, and that second person spends some (the MPC), which becomes income for another person, and so on, until income has changed by $1/(1 - MPC) = 1/MPS$. The multiplier operates in both directions.

marginal propensity to consume The change in consumption associated with a given change in income.

marginal propensity to save The change in saving associated with a given change in income.

FIGURE 7

The Multiplier and Aggregate Demand and Supply

The spending multiplier magnifies new spending into greater levels of income and output because of round-by-round spending. Your spending becomes my income, and I spend some of that income, creating further income and consumption, and so on.

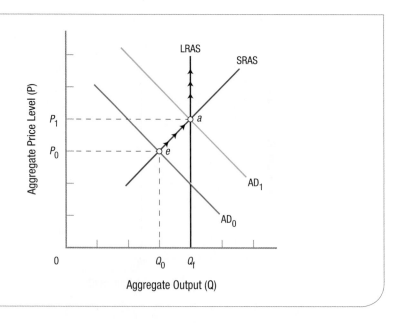

round, resulting in less real output. The multiplier is therefore less than the pure spending multiplier of 4 just discussed. Note that once aggregate demand is increased beyond AD_1, price increases soak up the entire increase in aggregate demand (along the LRAS curve) because real output does not change.

Let's take a moment to summarize where we are before we begin to use this model to understand some important macroeconomic events. Short-run macroeconomic equilibrium occurs at the intersection of AD and SRAS. It can also happen that this equilibrium represents long-run equilibrium, but not necessarily; equilibrium can occur at less than full employment. As we will see shortly, the Great Depression is one example of this. Increases in spending are multiplied and lead to greater changes in output than the original change in spending. For policymakers, this means that the difference between equilibrium real GDP and full-employment GDP (the GDP gap) can be closed with a smaller change in spending.

This leads us to the point where we can use the AD/AS model to analyze past macroeconomic events. By looking at these events through the AD/AS lens, we begin to see the options open to policymakers. In the next section, we look at what happened during the Great Depression, then examine both demand-pull and cost-push inflation. Each type of inflation presents unique challenges for policymakers.

The Great Depression

Figure 6 conveniently showed the economy in long-run equilibrium and short-run equilibrium at the same point. The Great Depression demonstrated, however, that an economy can reach short-run equilibrium at output levels substantially below full employment.

The 1930s Depression was a graphic example of just such a situation. Real GDP dropped by nearly 40% between 1929 and 1933. Unemployment peaked at 25% in 1932 and never fell below 15% throughout the 1930s.

Figure 8 shows the actual data for the Great Depression with superimposed aggregate demand and SRAS curves for 1929 and 1933. Investment is the most volatile of the GDP components, and it fell nearly 80% from 1929 to 1933. This drop in investment reduced spending, and therefore income and consumption, resulting in a deep depression. The increase in aggregate demand necessary to restore the economy back to 1929 levels was huge, and it was no wonder that a 6% increase in government spending had virtually no impact on the Depression. It wasn't until spending ramped up for World War II that the country popped out of the Depression.

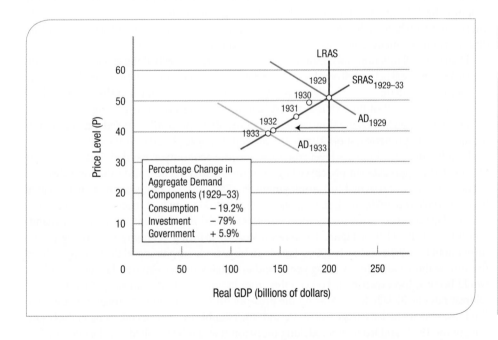

FIGURE 8

Aggregate Demand, Short-Run Aggregate Supply, and the Investment Decline During the Depression

Aggregate demand and short-run aggregate supply are superimposed on the real GDP and price level data for the Great Depression. Investment dropped nearly 80% and consumption declined nearly 20%. Together, these reductions in spending created a depression that was so deep that it took the massive spending for World War II to bring the economy back to full employment.

Demand-Pull Inflation

Demand-pull inflation occurs when aggregate demand expands so much that equilibrium output exceeds full employment output. Turning to Figure 9, assume that the economy is initially in long-run equilibrium at point *e*. If businesses become irrationally exuberant and expand investments in some area (such as telecommunications in the late 1990s), this expansion will push aggregate demand out to AD_1. The economy moves to a short-run equilibrium beyond full employment (point *a*), and the price level rises to P_1.

Demand-Pull Inflation

Demand-pull inflation occurs when aggregate demand expands and equilibrium output (point *a*) exceeds full employment output (Q_f). Because the LRAS curve has not shifted, the economy will in the end move into long-run equilibrium at point *c*. With the new aggregate demand at AD_1, prices have unexpectedly risen, therefore short-run aggregate supply shifts to $SRAS_2$ as workers, for example, adjust their wage demands upward, leaving prices permanently higher at P_2.

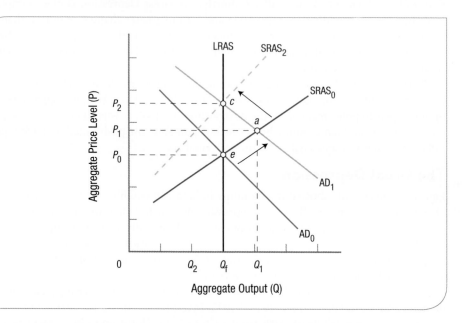

On a temporary basis, the economy can expand beyond full employment as workers incur overtime, temporary workers are added, and more shifts are employed. Yet, these activities increase costs and prices. And because long-run aggregate supply (LRAS) has not shifted, the economy will ultimately move to point *c* (if AD stays at AD_1), shifting short-run aggregate supply to $SRAS_2$ and leaving prices permanently higher (at P_2). In the long run, the economy will gravitate to points such as *e* and *c*. Policymakers could return the economy back to the original point *e* by instituting policies that reduce AD back to AD_0. These might include reduced government spending, higher taxes, or other policies that discourage investment, consumer spending, or exports.

Demand-pull inflation can continue for quite a while, especially if the economy begins on the SRAS curve well below full employment. Inflation often starts out slow and builds up steam.

Decadelong demand-pull inflation scenarios for the United States in the 1960s and for Japan in the last half of the 1980s and first half of the 1990s are shown in Figure 10.

For the United States, the slow escalation of the Vietnam conflict fueled a rising economy along the hypothetical short-run aggregate supply curve placed over the data in panel A. Early in the decade, the price level rose slowly as the economy expanded. But notice how the short-run aggregate supply curve began to turn nearly vertical and inflation rates rose as the economy approached full employment in 1969. Real output growth virtually halted between 1969 and 1970, but inflation was 5.3%. The economy had reached its potential.

The Japanese economy during the 1985–1995 period is a different example of demand-pull inflation. Panel B of Figure 10 shows a steadily growing economy with rising prices, throughout the 1980s and early 1990s. Japan ran huge trade surpluses and the yen appreciated (becoming more valuable). A rising yen would eventually reduce exports (Japanese products would become too expensive). To keep this from happening, the Japanese government kept interest rates artificially low, reducing the pressure on the yen and encouraging investment. But these policies fueled a huge real estate and stock bubble that began collapsing in the beginning of the 1990s and led to a decadelong recession that has been called "the lost decade."

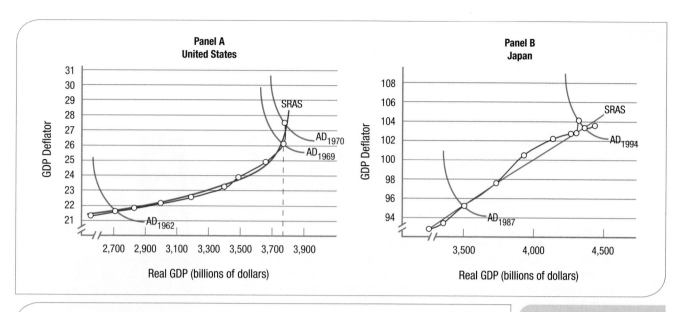

Demand-Pull Inflation, United States (1960s) and Japan (1985–1995)

This figure shows two examples of demand-pull inflation for the United States and Japan. Hypothetical aggregate demand and short-run aggregate supply curves are superimposed over the data for the two time periods. The Vietnam conflict expanded aggregate demand in the 1960s, and the U.S. economy experienced inflation over the entire decade and faced rising inflation rates as the economy approached full employment in 1969. Japan experienced demand-pull inflation as it enjoyed a huge trade surplus, which expanded the economy. Japanese policymakers kept interest rates artificially low, fueling a real estate and stock bubble that collapsed in the 1990s, resulting in a decadelong recession.

FIGURE 10

Demand-pull inflation can often take a while to become a problem. But once the inflation spiral gains momentum, it can pose a serious problem for policymakers.

Cost-Push Inflation

Cost-push inflation occurs when a supply shock hits the economy, shifting the short-run aggregate supply curve leftward, as from $SRAS_0$ to $SRAS_2$ in Figure 11. The 1973 oil shock is a classic example. Because oil is a basic input in so many goods and services we purchase,

cost-push inflation Results when a supply shock hits the economy, reducing short-run aggregate supply, and thus reducing output and increasing the price level.

FIGURE 11

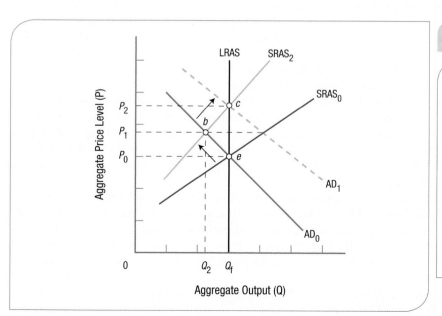

Cost-Push Inflation

Cost-push inflation is represented by an initial decline in short-run aggregate supply from $SRAS_0$ to $SRAS_2$. Rising resource costs or inflationary expectations will reduce short-run aggregate supply, resulting in a short-run movement from point *e* to point *b*. If policymakers wish to return the economy to full employment, they can increase aggregate demand to AD_1, but must accept higher prices as the economy moves to point *c*. Alternatively, they could reduce aggregate demand, but that would lead to lower output and lower employment.

ISSUE

Why Didn't Recent Stimulus Measures Lead to Inflation?

The 2007–2009 recession and the high unemployment that persisted for years after led policymakers to implement many policies to jumpstart the economy. These included government spending (stimulus) programs, tax rebates in 2009, a reduction in payroll taxes in 2011 and 2012, extension of unemployment benefits, loan modification programs, and more. Each of these policies was designed to encourage spending by consumers and thereby increase aggregate demand. By doing so, the AD/AS model presented in this chapter predicts that rightward shifts of the AD curve would lead to a higher aggregate price level, or inflation. Yet, inflation rates in the United States have remained low. How is that possible?

First, the AD curve might not have moved at all. Much of the government spending to increase aggregate demand was offsetting corresponding decreases in aggregate demand due to high unemployment, low consumer and business confidence, and low foreign demand for American goods. Thus, the role of such policies may have prevented a worsening of the economy by keeping aggregate demand in the same place as before. Using this explanation, the price level would not be affected at all.

Second, the recession created a large amount of underutilized resources. Keynes argued that during times of poor economic performance, many resources (such as labor and capital) remain underutilized. In such cases, an increase in aggregate demand, which subsequently increases demand for labor and capital, would merely be using resources that had been sitting idle. There would be little pressure on wages and prices to rise.

These reasons and others help to explain why the government was able to engage in various policies to increase the speed of economic recovery without the immediate threat of inflation. But once the economy recovers and idle resources are used up, any further government spending would likely lead to a higher aggregate price level. Indeed, inflation could arise in the future, leading to potential stagflation if economic growth remains low and unemployment remains high.

Inflation remained low despite an increase in government spending on infrastructure and tax cuts to encourage more spending by consumers.

Christopher Russell/Dreamstime.com

---

skyrocketing oil prices affected all parts of the economy. After a bout of cost-push inflation, rising resource costs push the economy from point *e* to point *b* in Figure 11. Note that at point *b*, real output has fallen (the economy is in a recession) and the price level has risen. Policymakers can increase demand to AD_1 and move the economy back to full employment at point *c*. For example, they might increase government spending, reduce taxes, or introduce policies that encourage consumption, investment, or net exports. But notice that this means an even higher price level. Alternatively, policymakers could reduce inflationary pressures by reducing aggregate demand, but this leads to an even deeper recession as output and employment fall further.

Figure 12 shows the striking leftward shift in equilibrium points for 1973–1975. Output stood still, while prices rose as the economy adjusted to the new energy prices. Superimposed over the annual data are two hypothetical short-run aggregate supply curves. Notice that it took the economy roughly three years to absorb the oil shock. Only after the economy had adjusted to the new prices did it continue on a path roughly equivalent to the pre-1973 SRAS curve.

Before the Great Depression, economic analysis focused on the behavior of individuals, households, and businesses. Little attention was paid to the macroeconomic stabilization potential of government policies. The federal government had its responsibilities under the Constitution in many areas—such as national defense, the enforcement of contracts, and tax collection—but managing the economy was not among them.

The Great Depression of the 1930s and John Maynard Keynes's *The General Theory* drastically changed how economists viewed the role of the federal government. During the

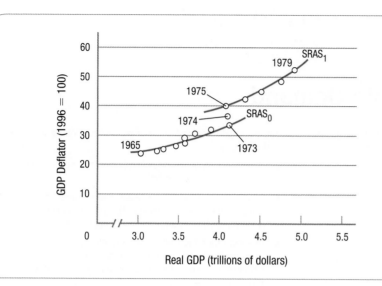

FIGURE 12

Cost-Push Inflation in the 1970s
The rise in equilibrium prices following the 1973 oil shocks was striking. From 1973 to 1975, prices rose, yet output stood still as the economy adjusted to the new energy prices. Superimposed over the actual annual data are two hypothetical short-run aggregate supply curves. Notice that it took the economy roughly three years to absorb the oil shock.

Depression, when unemployment reached 25% and bank failures wiped out personal savings, federal intervention in the economy became imperative. After the 1930s, the federal government's role grew to encompass (1) expanded spending and taxation and the resulting exercise of fiscal policy, (2) extensive new regulation of business, and (3) expanded regulation of the banking sector, along with greater exercise of monetary policy.

The next chapter focuses on how government spending and taxation combine to expand or contract the macroeconomy. When the economy enters a recession, fiscal policy can be used to moderate the impact and prevent another depression. Later chapters will explore the monetary system and the use of monetary policy to stabilize the economy and the price level. The AD/AS model will serve as a tool to analyze both fiscal and monetary policies. As you read these chapters, keep in mind that the long-run goals of fiscal and monetary policy are economic growth, low unemployment, and modest inflationary pressures.

 # CHECKPOINT

MACROECONOMIC EQUILIBRIUM

- Macroeconomic equilibrium occurs where short-run aggregate supply and aggregate demand cross.
- The spending multiplier exists because new spending generates new round-by-round spending (based on the marginal propensities to consume and save) that creates additional income.
- The formula for the spending multiplier is $1/(1 - MPC) = 1/MPS$.
- The multiplier is larger when the economy is in a deep recession or a depression.
- Policymakers can increase output by enacting policies that expand government spending, consumption, investment, or net exports, or reduce taxes.
- Demand-pull inflation occurs when aggregate demand expands beyond that necessary for full employment.
- Cost-push inflation occurs when short-run aggregate supply shifts to the left, causing the price level to rise along with rising unemployment.

QUESTIONS: Over the past decade, the price of petroleum products in the United States more than doubled, and gasoline and diesel fuel peaked at over $4.00 a gallon. Describe the impact of this price increase on short-run aggregate supply. How might it affect employment, unemployment, and the price level? Would the impact depend on whether consumers and businesses thought the price increase was permanent?

Answers to the Checkpoint questions can be found at the end of this chapter.

chapter summary

Section 1: **Aggregate Demand**

The **aggregate demand** curve shows the quantity of goods and services (real GDP) demanded at different price levels.

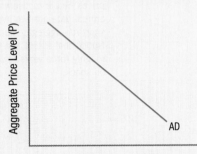

The determinants of aggregate demand include the components of aggregate spending:

1. Consumption spending
2. Investment spending
3. Government spending
4. Net exports

Changing any one of these aggregates will shift the aggregate demand curve.

The aggregate demand curve is downward sloping for three main reasons:

- Wealth effect: When price levels rise, the purchasing power of money saved falls.

- Export effect: Rising price levels cause domestic goods to be more expensive in the global marketplace, resulting in fewer purchases by foreign consumers.

- Interest rate effect: When price levels rise, people need more money to carry out transactions. The added demand for money drives up interest rates, causing investment spending to fall.

The housing market recovery has resulted in a boost to aggregate demand.

Section 2: **Aggregate Supply**

The **aggregate supply** curve shows the real GDP firms will produce at varying price levels.

In the short run, aggregate supply is upward-sloping (SRAS).

In the long run, aggregate supply is vertical (LRAS).

In the short run, prices and wages are sticky (think of menu prices staying the same for a period of time). Therefore firms respond by increasing output when prices rise.

In the long run, prices and wages adjust, therefore output is not affected by the price level.

Factors that shift the SRAS curve:

- Input prices
- Productivity
- Taxes and regulation
- Market power of firms
- Expectations

Factors that shift the LRAS curve:

- Increase in technology
- Greater human capital
- Trade
- Innovation and R&D

Electronic toll collection booths save time and reduce transportation costs to firms, leading to an increase in short-run aggregate supply and potentially long-run aggregate supply.

Section 3: Macroeconomic Equilibrium

A long-run macroeconomic equilibrium occurs at the intersection of the LRAS and AD curves, at full employment.

A short-run macroeconomic equilibrium occurs at the intersection of the SRAS and AD curves. Short-run equilibrium can occur below full employment (recession) or above full employment (inflationary pressure).

Long-Run Macro Equilibrium

Short-Run Equilibrium (recession)

Short-Run Equilibrium (inflation)

The spending **multiplier** exists because new spending generates income that results in more spending and income, based on the marginal propensities to consume and save.

Multiplier Example: MPC = 0.80 and MPS = 0.20

Round 1: $100 in new spending = $100 in new income

Round 2: $80 is spent and $20 is saved ($80 in new income)

Round 3: $64 is spent and $16 is saved

Round 4: $51.20 is spent and $12.80 is saved

Round 5: $40.96 is spent and $10.24 is saved

Round 6: $32.76 is spent and $8.20 is saved

...

Round n: $0.01 is spent and $0.00 is saved

Total effect of $100 in spending =

$500 in spending and $100 in savings

Multiplier = $1/(1 - MPC) = 1/(1 - 0.80) = 5$

Demand-pull inflation occurs when aggregate demand expands so much that equilibrium output exceeds full employment output. Temporarily, the economy can expand beyond full employment as workers incur overtime and more workers are added. But as wages rise, the economy will move to a new equilibrium, where prices are permanently higher.

Cost-push inflation occurs when a supply shock hits the economy, shifting the SRAS curve to the left. Cost-push inflation makes using policies to expand aggregate demand to restore full employment difficult because of the additional inflationary pressures added to the economy.

QUESTIONS AND PROBLEMS

Check Your Understanding

1. Describe the impact of rising interest rates on consumer spending.

2. When the economy is operating at full employment, why is an increase in aggregate demand not helpful to the economy?

3. When the economy is hit with a supply shock, such as oil prices rising from $25 a barrel to $75 a barrel, why is this doubly disruptive and harmful to the economy?

4. Explain why the aggregate supply curve is positively sloped during the short run and vertical in the long run.

5. List some examples of factors that will shift the aggregate demand curve.

6. List some examples of factors that will shift the long-run aggregate supply curve.

Apply the Concepts

7. There is little doubt that computers and the Internet have changed our economy. Information technology (IT) can boost efficiency in nearly everything: Markets are more efficient, IT is global, and IT improves the design, manufacture, and supply chain of products we produce. Use the aggregate demand and supply framework discussed in this chapter to show the impact of IT on the U.S. economy.

8. Unemployment can be caused by a reduction in aggregate demand or short-run aggregate supply. Both changes are represented by a leftward shift in the curves. Does it matter whether the shift occurs in aggregate demand or short-run aggregate supply? Use the AD/AS framework to show why or why not.

9. Why is cost-push inflation a more difficult problem for policymakers than demand-pull inflation?

10. Why is consumer confidence so important in determining the equilibrium level of output and employment?

11. As the Japanese yen appreciated in value during the 1980s and 1990s, more Japanese auto companies built manufacturing plants in other parts of Asia and in the United States. What impact did this have on net exports for the United States? Why did Japanese automakers build plants in the United States? Were the reasons similar to the reasons that American firms build plants (or establish offshore production) in China and other parts of Asia?

12. Some advocates have suggested that the United States should move to a universal health care plan paid for at the federal level, like Medicare, which would be funded out of general tax revenues. Such a plan, it is argued, would guarantee quality health care

to all. Ignoring all the controversy surrounding such a plan, would the introduction of universal health care paid for from general revenues have an impact on short-run aggregate supply? On long-run aggregate supply? Why or why not?

In the News

13. Oil production in the United States has increased significantly over the past decade as a result of improved oil extraction technologies, with some analysts predicting that the United States will surpass Saudi Arabia in overall energy production by the end of the decade ("U.S. Oil Output to Overtake Saudi Arabia's by 2020," Bloomberg.com, November 12, 2012). How do the increase in U.S. energy production and the subsequent reduction in the reliance on imported oil affect the U.S. aggregate demand and/or aggregate supply curves?

14. In early 2013, significant political gridlock in Congress involved automatic spending cuts by the government termed the *Sequester*. Many economists warned that allowing the drastic cuts to persist increased the risk of another recession ("The Sequester and Fiscal Policy," *The New York Times*, March 8, 2013). Using the AD/AS model and what you know about the multiplier, explain why economists would come to this conclusion.

Solving Problems

15. In the figure below, the economy is initially in equilibrium at full employment at point *e*. Assume that consumption falls by 100, leading to a shift in aggregate demand from AD_0 to AD_1.

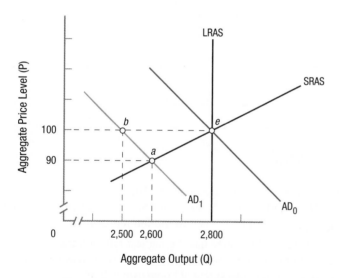

a. What is the new short-run equilibrium?

b. How large is the simple Keynesian multiplier in this case?

16. Use the table and grid below to answer the following questions:

a. In the grid, graph the aggregate demand and short-run aggregate supply curves (label them AD_0 and $SRAS_0$). What are equilibrium output and the price level?

b. Assume aggregate demand grows by 100% (output doubles at each price level). Graph the new aggregate demand curve and label it AD_1. What is the new equilibrium output and price level?

c. If full employment output is 600, what will be the long-run output and price level given the new aggregate demand curve?

Price Level	Output (short-run aggregate supply)	Output (aggregate demand)
150	1,000	200
125	800	400
100	600	600
75	400	800
50	200	1,000

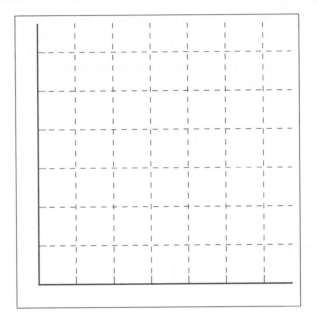

⊕ USING THE NUMBERS

17. According to By the Numbers, if the average price of a barrel of oil is $100, and total aggregate demand in 2012 was $15 trillion in the United States and $9 trillion in China, what percentage of aggregate demand did oil consumption represent in each country?

18. According to By the Numbers, which state has the highest rate of home ownership? Which state has the lowest rate of home ownership? What are some reasons why these states represent the highest rate and lowest rate of home ownership?

ANSWERS TO QUESTIONS IN CHECKPOINTS

Checkpoint: Aggregate Demand

A reduction in the payroll tax from 6.2% to 4.2% would increase disposable income and consumption, shifting aggregate demand to the right. However, because government spending is an element of aggregate demand, the loss in government revenue from the tax reduction may offset some of the increase in aggregate demand if government is forced to cut back on its spending.

Checkpoint: Aggregate Supply

Regulations typically add compliance costs to businesses, which would shift the SRAS curve leftward. However, if regulations are effective in preventing another financial crisis, then expectations may improve as businesses feel more confident in the economy. Such positive expectations would shift SRAS to the right. Yet, regulations also could add uncertainty to businesses, which could reduce expectations and shift SRAS back to the left. The overall effect is likely to depend on the type of regulations used and whether they actually generate more benefits than costs.

Checkpoint: Macroeconomic Equilibrium

Petroleum products are an important input in our economy. Higher oil prices will increase costs of transportation, and where oil is an important input (e.g., in the production of plastics), it will increase costs and reduce short-run aggregate supply. Over time, these cost increases will show up as a higher price level, reduced employment, and higher unemployment. If the economy continues to grow, these impacts will be masked, but will reduce the growth numbers. After the oil price shocks in the 1970s, the United States became much more energy efficient, which means today's price increases may not have quite the shock effect on the economy as was experienced in the 1970s. If the change is seen as permanent, consumers and businesses will begin making long-run adjustments to higher prices. For example, consumers will begin switching to more fuel-efficient cars (hybrids and smaller cars), and businesses will look at investing in energy-saving methods of distribution and production. If the price increases are just viewed as temporary, both groups might not adjust much at all.

Appendix
Deriving the Aggregate Demand Curve

The aggregate demand curve shows the quantities of goods and services (real GDP) demanded at different price levels. It can be derived using the aggregate expenditures model described in the previous chapter. To illustrate, panel A of Figure APX-1 shows aggregate expenditures (AE) curves at two different price levels. Remember that AE curves are drawn assuming fixed prices.

First, consider equilibrium point a on aggregate expenditures curve $AE(P_0)$. This point shows an equilibrium income of Y_0, which is equivalent to a real output of Q_0. Point a in panel B, therefore, represents a real output of Q_0 and a price level of P_0. However, if the aggregate price level rises to P_1, aggregate expenditures will decline to $AE(P_1)$ because at these higher prices, the same level of expenditures will not buy as much real output as before. The result is a new equilibrium at point b in both panels. Connecting points a and b in panel B, we have constructed aggregate demand curve AD, which represents the relationship between the price level and aggregate output.

FIGURE APX-1

Deriving the Aggregate Demand Curve

The aggregate demand curve, which shows the quantities of goods and services demanded at different price levels for the entire economy, can be derived using the aggregate spending model. Panel A shows aggregate expenditures curves at two different price levels. Point a on aggregate expenditures curve $AE(P_0)$ represents equilibrium income Y_0, equivalent to a real output of Q_0. Point a in panel B shows real output of Q_0 that is associated with equilibrium point a and its price level P_0. If the aggregate price level rises to P_1, aggregate spending will decline to $AE(P_1)$ in panel A. The result is a new equilibrium at point b in both panels. Connecting points a and b in panel B results in aggregate demand curve AD.

Fiscal Policy and Debt

21

When you apply for a loan to buy a car, you undoubtedly will go through a credit check and get a credit rating, which is a number that estimates the probability of you paying back the loan. The government also gets a credit rating for the loans it takes out. This rating, like yours, estimates the probability of the government paying back its loans.

On August 5, 2011, Standard and Poor's (S&P), a credit rating agency, did something it had never done in its history: lower the debt rating of the United States government from a perfect AAA rating to a slightly less than perfect AA+ rating. Although an AA+ rating is still excellent, this change was significant, because it suggested for the first time that the United States government is not immune from all and any hardships in paying its debts.

Why did the United States government lose its perfect debt rating? One reason was its extensive use of fiscal policy over the last several years. Fiscal policy is the use of government revenue collection (mainly taxation) and spending to influence the economy. In terms of taxation, when the government taxes something, individuals and businesses have less money to spend. Therefore, taxes put the brakes on various economic activities. However, in terms of spending, think of what it means to local employment if the government decides to improve the roads and bridges in a city. By their very nature, taxation and spending affect the economy.

In extraordinary times, governments use fiscal policy to influence the macroeconomy with the express purpose of smoothing fluctuations in the business cycle. During the last recession, in 2007–2009, the Obama Administration added almost $800 billion in additional government spending in an attempt to pull the economy out of its doldrums. If people would not spend, government would spend in their place: Spending was used to spur the economy when citizens were too scared to spend themselves. In inflationary times, government uses fiscal policy to pull money out of people's hands in an attempt to cool down spending and inflation.

Fiscal policy influences aggregate demand and aggregate supply, the model studied in the previous chapter, in many ways. However, fiscal policy that is used to stimulate the economy is often accompanied by persistent budget deficits and debt. Why and to what end? This chapter will examine these issues and focus on the problem of financing deficits by accruing debt.

Most Americans are accustomed to dealing with debt. Individuals might have a home mortgage, car loan, student loan, or credit card balances, while businesses often take out loans for capital purchases and other expenses to run their operations. Most debt is managed by making periodic payments toward the balance and interest. However, when debt becomes too high to be controlled, individuals and companies face financial distress and are sometimes forced to declare bankruptcy. In 2012, over 1.3 million individuals and over 42,000 businesses filed for bankruptcy.

As we will see, it is no surprise that governments also deal with debt. In recent years, deficits and the national debt have dominated economic headlines. The national debt grows when the government consistently spends more than the tax revenues it collects each year. In 2012, the U.S. government collected about $2.5 trillion in taxes, but spent more than $3.5 trillion. The difference of over $1 trillion represented the federal deficit that was added to the national debt.

Unlike debt for individuals and small companies, a government has a much larger arsenal of tools to prevent it from going bankrupt, including the power to tax and the ever-powerful ability to "print" money. But even those tools can sometimes be rendered useless, causing a government to rack up sizeable debt and increasing the burden of managing the debt. Further, when a government does default on its debt, it can create havoc in markets throughout the world.

In this chapter, we analyze the tools government uses to implement fiscal policy and study their effects on aggregate demand and aggregate supply, which affects income and output. We analyze the bias toward accruing public debt rather than raising taxes or reducing spending. Is the amount of the federal debt a problem, both now and in the future? If so, what can the government do about it? By the time you have finished studying this chapter, you should have a good sense of the scope of fiscal policy and the consequences on the economy of relying on public debt rather than balancing taxes and spending.

BY THE NUMBERS

Your Government and Its Financial Operation

The U.S. government is one of the largest institutions in the world, taking in revenues of nearly $2.5 trillion each year. Still, the government in recent years has spent much more, accruing deficits of over $1 trillion every year from 2009 to 2012 and adding to its public debt.

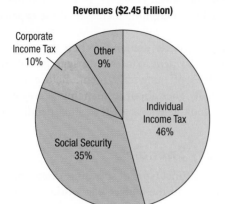

Revenues ($2.45 trillion)

- Corporate Income Tax 10%
- Other 9%
- Individual Income Tax 46%
- Social Security 35%

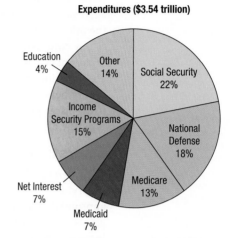

Expenditures ($3.54 trillion)

- Education 4%
- Other 14%
- Social Security 22%
- Income Security Programs 15%
- National Defense 18%
- Net Interest 7%
- Medicare 13%
- Medicaid 7%

The government collected $2.45 trillion in 2012 primarily from individual income taxes and Social Security (payroll) taxes. It spent $3.54 trillion, over half on national defense, Social Security, and Medicare.

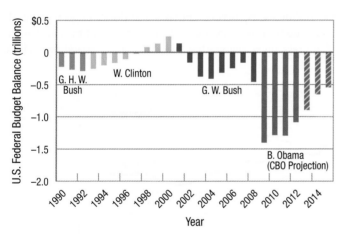

U.S. federal government expenditures exceeded revenues in every year since 1990 except from 1998 to 2001. The gap between spending and revenues expanded in 2008 as a result of the recession.

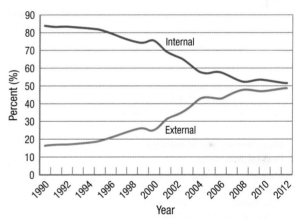

External (foreign held) debt has risen since 1990. Today, nearly 50% of total public debt is held externally.

Top Ten Creditors of U.S. Treasury Debt as of July 2013 (in billions)

China, Japan, Caribbean Nations, OPEC Nations, Brazil, Taiwan, Switzerland, Belgium, United Kingdom, Luxembourg

Hunter Breedlove/age fotostock

$16,738,598,000,000

Total U.S. national debt in July 2013.

$235,518,000,000

Total interest paid on the national debt in 2012.

→ Fiscal Policy and Aggregate Demand

When an economy faces underutilization of resources because it is stuck in equilibrium well below full employment, we saw that increases in aggregate demand can move the economy toward full employment without generating excessive inflation pressures. The recent recession provided evidence of this effect. However, in normal times, influencing aggregate demand brings with it a tradeoff: Output is increased at the expense of raising the price level.

In contrast, consider decreasing aggregate demand. When the economy is in an inflationary equilibrium *above full employment,* contracting aggregate demand dampens inflation but leads to another tradeoff: unemployment. Before we examine the theory behind how government actually goes about influencing aggregate demand by using fiscal policy, let's take a brief look at what categories of spending fiscal policy typically alters.

Discretionary and Mandatory Spending

The federal budget can be split into two distinct types of spending: discretionary and mandatory. Discretionary spending is the part of the budget that works its way through the appropriations process of Congress each year. **Discretionary spending** includes such programs as national defense (primarily the military), transportation, science, environment, income security (some welfare programs and a large portion of Medicaid), education, and veterans benefits and services. As Figure 1 shows, discretionary spending is now under 40% and has steadily declined as a percent of the budget since the 1960s, when it was over 60% of the budget.

Mandatory spending is authorized by permanent laws and does not go through the same appropriations process as discretionary spending. To change one of the entitlements of mandatory spending, Congress must change the law. Mandatory spending includes

discretionary spending The part of the budget that works its way through the appropriations process of Congress each year and includes such programs as national defense, transportation, science, environment, and income security.

mandatory spending Spending authorized by permanent laws that does not go through the same appropriations process as discretionary spending. Mandatory spending includes such programs as Social Security, Medicare, and interest on the national debt.

FIGURE 1

Discretionary and Mandatory Federal Spending

Mandatory spending includes programs authorized by law (also called entitlements) such as Social Security, Medicare, and the Supplemental Nutrition Assistance Program. Mandatory programs do not go through the normal Congressional appropriations process and have been growing. Discretionary programs are authorized each year by the appropriations process of Congress and include national defense, transportation, environment, and education spending. Discretionary spending has been steadily declining as a percent of the budget.

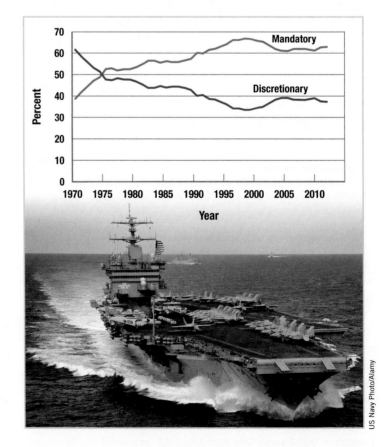

such programs as Social Security, Medicare, part of Medicaid, interest on the national debt, and some means-tested income-security programs, including SNAP (Supplementary Nutrition Assistance Program; formerly known as the Food Stamp Program) and TANF (Temporary Assistance to Needy Families). This part of the budget has been growing, as Figure 1 illustrates, and now accounts for over 60% of the budget.

Even though discretionary spending is only 37% of the budget, this is still roughly $1.3 trillion, and the capacity to alter this spending is a powerful force in the economy. Therefore, we are mainly concerned with discretionary spending when we consider fiscal policy.

Discretionary Fiscal Policy

The exercise of **discretionary fiscal policy** is done with the express goal of influencing aggregate demand. It involves adjusting government spending and tax policies to move the economy toward full employment, encouraging economic growth, or controlling inflation.

Some examples of the use of discretionary fiscal policy include tax cuts enacted during the Kennedy, Reagan, and George W. Bush administrations. These tax cuts were designed to expand the economy under the belief that people would spend their tax savings, both in the near term and the long run—they were meant to influence both aggregate demand and aggregate supply. Tax increases were enacted under the George H. Bush and Clinton administrations in the interest of reducing the government deficit and interest rates. The Roosevelt administration used increased government spending, although small amounts by today's standards, to mitigate the impact of the Great Depression.

Government Spending   Although discretionary fiscal policy can get complex, the impact of changes in government spending is relatively simple. As we know, a change in government spending or other components of GDP will cause income and output to rise or fall by the spending change *times* the multiplier.

This is illustrated in Figure 2 with the economy initially in equilibrium at point e, with real output equaling Q_0. If government spending increases, shifting aggregate demand from AD_0 to AD_1, aggregate output will increase from Q_0 to Q_f. Because the short run aggregate supply curve is upward sloping, some of the increase in output is absorbed by rising prices, reducing the pure spending multiplier discussed in earlier chapters.

discretionary fiscal policy
Involves adjusting government spending and tax policies with the express short-run goal of moving the economy toward full employment, expanding economic growth, or controlling inflation.

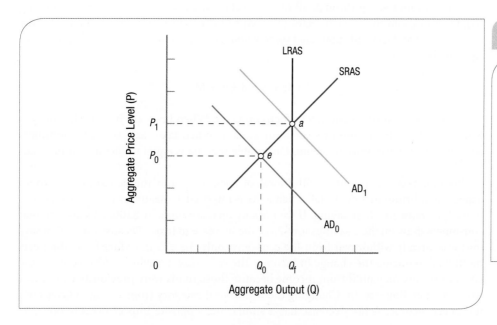

FIGURE 2

The Multiplier and Government Spending

The economy is initially in equilibrium at point *e*. As new government spending works its way through the economy round-by-round, both income and output are multiplied, but price increases absorb some of the increase in AD. Once the economy reaches full employment (point *a*), price increases absorb all of the increase in AD.

Once the economy reaches full employment (point *a*), further spending is not multiplied as the economy moves along the LRAS curve, and price increases absorb it all. Finally, keep in mind that the multiplier works in both directions.

Taxes   Changes in government spending modify income by an amount equal to the change in spending *times* the multiplier. How, then, do changes in taxes affect the economy? The answer is not quite as simple. Let's begin with a reminder of what constitutes spending equilibrium.

When the economy is in equilibrium,

$$GDP = C + I + G + (X - M)$$

At equilibrium, all spending *injections* into the economy equal all *withdrawals* of spending. To see why, let's simplify the above equation and begin with only a private economy, eliminating government (G) and the foreign sector, or net exports (X – M). Thus,

$$GDP = C + I$$

Gross domestic product (GDP) is equal to consumer plus business investment spending. Without government and taxes, GDP is just income (Y), therefore

$$Y = C + I$$

or, subtracting C from each side of the equation,

$$Y - C = I$$

Now, income minus consumption (Y – C) is just saving (S), therefore at equilibrium,

$$S = I$$

This simple equation represents a very important point: At equilibrium, *injections* (in this case, I) are just equal to *withdrawals* (S in this instance). Investment represents spending where saving is the removal of income from the spending and income stream.

Now, without going through all of the algebra, when we add government spending (G), taxes (T), and the foreign sector (X – M) to the equation, we have just added some *injections* (G) and (X) and subtracted some *withdrawals* (T) and (M), thus the equilibrium equation becomes

$$I + G + X = S + T + M$$

With this equation in hand, let's focus on taxes. When taxes are increased, money is withdrawn from the economy's spending stream. When taxes are reduced, consumers and businesses have more to spend. Disposable income is equal to income minus taxes (Y – T).

Because taxes represent a withdrawal of spending from the economy, we would expect equilibrium income to fall when a tax is imposed. Consumers pay a tax increase, in part, by *reducing* their saving. If we initially increase taxes by $100, let's assume that consumers draw on their savings for $25 of the increase in taxes. Because this $25 in savings was already withdrawn from the economy, only the $75 in reduced spending gets multiplied, reducing the change in income. The *reduction* in saving of $25 dampens the effect of the tax on equilibrium income because those funds were previously withdrawn from the spending stream. Changing the withdrawal category from saving to taxes does not affect income. A tax decrease has a similar but opposite impact because only the

ISSUE

How Big Was the Stimulus Multiplier, Really?

President Obama's $787 billion 2009 stimulus package set off a flurry of discussion among economists about the actual size of spending and tax multipliers. It is one thing in our simple models to show that these multipliers exist and assert the value based on the MPC (a multiplier of 4 in our model with an MPC of 0.75). But the economy is a complex machine and there are various leakages that keep the multiplier from reaching its theoretical Keynesian "depression" potential. Leakages are funds that do not find their way into the domestic consumption-income multiplication stream.

One important leakage is taxes. Income generated from one person's consumption is taxed, reducing the amount available for further consumption and income generation. Another important leakage is purchases of imports; when consumers buy imported goods, that money flows overseas and is not multiplied here. Both taxes and imports withdraw money from the spending stream, reducing the actual value of the multiplier. This explains why Congress and the president included a number of "Buy American" provisions in the 2009 stimulus plan.

What empirical value best represents the short-term stimulus multi-

plier? That is not an easy question to answer because many factors influence an economy's output, such as the trend in the business cycle. Therefore, it is difficult to narrow the effects of a specific government injection, such as the 2009 stimulus, from other factors that play a role.

Still, a number of empirical studies have attempted to estimate the multiplier and its effect on the economy. Conclusions from these studies ranged from the stimulus having a substantial effect on the economy's recovery to having virtually no effect at all. Looking more closely at the results, however, revealed more areas of consensus. For example, most studies showed the stimulus having a positive effect on employment, and that multipliers varied depending on the type of spending used. Spending on infrastructure and low-income assistance, for example, generally showed a higher multiplier than money given to states for education and law enforcement. The latter is likely because states may have substituted stimulus funds in place of other sources to balance their budgets.

Most studies estimate the overall multiplier of the 2009 stimulus to be between 1.5 and 2, which means that the increase in GDP is just modestly

James Nazz/Corbis

higher than the increase in government spending. The implications of these multiplier estimates on fiscal policy are significant. If actual multipliers are far below their intended targets, the ability of fiscal policy to influence economic outcomes decreases significantly.

Some economists claimed that the 2009 stimulus did not give the bang for the buck that policymakers promised. Still, we will never know how the economy would have fared without the stimulus. Therefore, the role of fiscal policy remains an important debate among economists and policymakers.

Source: Dylan Matthews, "Did the Stimulus Work? A Review of the Nine Best Studies on the Subject," *The Washington Post,* August 24, 2011.

MPC part is spent and multiplied, and the rest is saved and thus withdrawn from the spending stream.

The result is that a tax increase (or decrease, for that matter) has less of a direct impact on income, employment, and output than an equivalent change in government spending. Another way of saying this is that the government tax multiplier is *less* than the government spending multiplier. Therefore, added spending leads to a larger increase in GDP when compared to the same reduction in taxes. The 2009 $787 billion stimulus package was more heavily structured toward spending partly for this reason.

Transfers Transfer payments are money payments directly paid to individuals. These include payments for such items as Social Security, unemployment compensation, and welfare. In large measure, they represent our social safety net. We will ignore them as part of the discretionary fiscal policy, because most are paid as a matter of law, but we will see later in the chapter that they are very important as a way of stabilizing the economy.

Expansionary and Contractionary Fiscal Policy

Expansionary fiscal policy involves increasing government spending, including the improvement of infrastructure such as roads and bridges and investment in human capital via education and research; increasing transfer payments such as unemployment compensation or welfare payments; or decreasing taxes—all to increase aggregate demand. These policies put more money into the hands of consumers and businesses. In theory, these additional funds should lead to higher spending. The precise effect expansionary fiscal policies have, however, depends on whether the economy is at or below full employment.

When the economy is below full employment, an expansionary policy will move the economy to full employment, as Figure 3 shows. The economy begins at equilibrium at point e, below full employment. Expansionary fiscal policy increases aggregate demand from AD_0 to AD_1, and equilibrium output rises to Q_f (point f) as the price level rises to P_1. In this case, one good outcome results—output rises to Q_f—though it is accompanied by one less desirable result, the price level rising to P_1.

FIGURE 3

Expansionary Fiscal Policy Below Full Employment

When the economy is below full employment, expansionary policies move it to full employment. Here, the economy begins at equilibrium at point e, below full employment. Expansionary fiscal policy increases aggregate demand from AD_0 to AD_1, raising equilibrium output to Q_f and the price level to P_1 (point f).

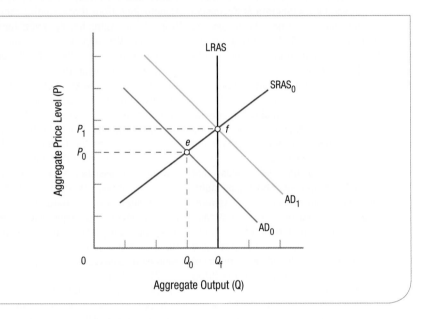

Figure 4 shows what happens when the economy is at full employment: An expansionary policy raises prices without producing any long-run improvement in real GDP. In this figure, the initial equilibrium is already at full employment (point e), therefore increasing aggregate demand moves the economy to a new output level above full employment (point a), thereby raising prices to P_1. This higher output is only temporary, however, as workers and suppliers adjust their expectations to the higher price level, thus shifting short-run aggregate supply upward to $SRAS_2$. Short-run aggregate supply declines because workers and other resource suppliers realize that the prices they are paying for products have risen; hence, they demand higher wages or prices for their services. This higher demand just pushes prices up further, until finally workers adjust their inflationary expectations and the economy settles into equilibrium at point b. At this point, the economy is again at full employment, but at a higher price level (P_2) than before.

When an economy moves to a point beyond full employment, as just described, economists say an *inflationary spiral* has set in. The explanation for this phenomenon was suggested earlier. Still, we can already see that one way to reduce such inflationary pressures is by a **contractionary fiscal policy**: reducing government spending, transfer payments, or raising taxes (increasing withdrawals from the economy). Figure 5 shows the result of

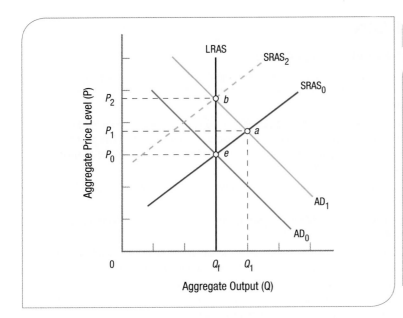

FIGURE 4

Expansionary Fiscal Policy at Full Employment

When an economy is already at full employment, expansionary policies lead to no long-run improvement in real GDP. Beginning at full employment (point e), increasing aggregate demand moves the economy to an output level above full employment (point a). This higher output is only temporary, however, as workers and suppliers adjust their expectations to the higher price level (P_1), thus shifting short-run aggregate supply left toward $SRAS_2$. But this just pushes prices up further, until finally workers adjust their inflationary expectations, and the economy settles into a new long-run equilibrium at point b, where the economy is once again at full employment, but at a higher price level (P_2).

contractionary policy. The economy is initially overheating at point e, with output above full employment. Contractionary policy reduces aggregate demand to AD_1, bringing the economy back to full employment at price level P_1 and output Q_f.

Exercising demand-side policy requires tradeoffs between increasing output at the expense of raising the price levels, or else lowering price levels by accepting a lower output. When recession threatens, the public is often happy to trade higher prices for greater employment and output. One would think the opposite would be true when an inflationary spiral loomed on the horizon. Politicians, however, are loath to support contractionary policies that control inflation by reducing aggregate demand, because high unemployment can cost politicians their jobs. As a result, the demand-side fiscal policy tools—government spending, transfer payments, and taxes—may remain unused. In these instances, politicians often look to the Federal Reserve to use its tools and influence to keep inflation in check. We will examine the Federal Reserve in later chapters.

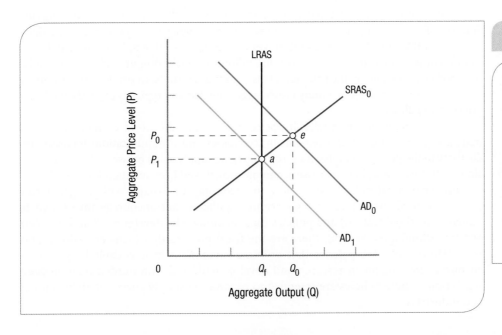

FIGURE 5

Contractionary Fiscal Policy to Reduce Inflation

In this figure, the economy is overheating at point e, with output above full employment. Contractionary policies reduce aggregate demand to AD_1, bringing the economy back to full employment at price level P_1. These policies prevent an inflationary spiral, but the fall in aggregate output leads to an increase in unemployment.

CHECKPOINT

FISCAL POLICY AND AGGREGATE DEMAND

- Demand-side fiscal policy involves using government spending, transfer payments, and taxes to change aggregate demand and equilibrium income, output, and the price level in the economy.

- In the short run, government spending raises income and output by the amount of spending times the multiplier. Tax reductions have a smaller impact on the economy than government spending because some of the reduction in taxes is added to saving and is therefore withdrawn from the economy.

- Expansionary fiscal policy involves increasing government spending, increasing transfer payments, or decreasing taxes.

- Contractionary fiscal policy involves decreasing government spending, decreasing transfer payments, or increasing taxes.

- When an economy is at full employment, expansionary fiscal policy may lead to greater output in the short term, but will ultimately just lead to higher prices in the longer term.

- Politicians tend to favor expansionary fiscal policy because it can bring with it increases in employment although with increasing inflation. Politicians tend to shun contractionary fiscal policy because it brings unemployment.

QUESTION: The 2009 $787 billion stimulus package cost roughly $2,500 per person or $10,000 for a family of four. The time required for the government to spend that sum on infrastructure projects (funding approvals, environmental clearances, and so on) means that the spending stretched over two to four years. Why didn't Congress just send a $2,500 check to each woman, man, and child in America to speed up the impact on the economy?

Answers to the Checkpoint question can be found at the end of this chapter.

Fiscal Policy and Aggregate Supply

supply-side fiscal policies
Policies that focus on shifting the long-run aggregate supply curve to the right, expanding the economy without increasing inflationary pressures. Unlike policies to increase aggregate demand, supply-side policies take longer to have an impact on the economy.

Fiscal policies that influence aggregate supply are different from policies that influence aggregate demand, as they do not always require tradeoffs between price levels and output. That is the good news. The bad news is that **supply-side fiscal policies** require more time to work than do demand-side fiscal policies. The focus of fiscal policy and aggregate supply is on long-run economic growth.

Figure 6 shows the impact that fiscal policy can have on the economy over the long run. The goal of these fiscal policies is to shift the long-run aggregate supply curve to the right, here from $LRAS_0$ to $LRAS_1$. This shift moves the economy's full employment equilibrium from point *a* to point *b*, thereby expanding full-employment output while keeping inflation in check. In Figure 6, the price level falls as output expands. In practice, this would be unusual because when the economy grows, aggregate demand typically expands and keeps prices from falling.

Figure 6 may well reflect what happens in general as the world economy embraces trade and globalization. Improvements in technology and communications increase productivity to the point that global long-run aggregate supply shifts outward. These changes, along with freer trade, help increase economic growth and keep inflation low.

Just what fiscal policies will allow the economy to expand without generating price pressures? First, there are government policies that encourage investment in human capital (education) and policies that encourage the development and transfers of new technologies. Second, there are the fiscal policies that focus on reducing tax rates. Third, there are policies that promote investment in new capital equipment, encourage investment in research and development, and trim burdensome business regulations. These policies are intended to expand the supply curves of all businesses and industries.

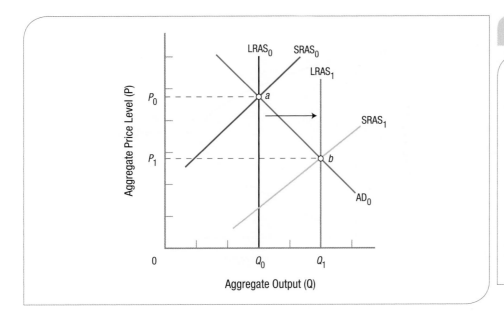

FIGURE 6

Fiscal Policy and Aggregate Supply
The ultimate goal of fiscal policy directed at aggregate supply is to shift the long-run aggregate supply curve from $LRAS_0$ to $LRAS_1$. This moves the economy's full employment equilibrium from point a to point b, expanding output while keeping inflation in check. With these fiscal policies, the inflationary pressures are reduced as output expands, but these policies take a longer time to have an impact.

Infrastructure Spending

Governments can do a great deal to create the right environment to encourage economic growth. We already have seen the benefits of building and maintaining a nation's infrastructure, including roads, bridges, dams, and communications networks, or setting up a fair and efficient legal system and stable financial system. Further, the higher the levels of human capital and the more easily technology is transferred to other firms and industries (the public good aspect of technology), the more robust economic growth. Therefore, long-run growth is enhanced through investments in higher education and research and development.

Reducing Tax Rates

Reducing tax rates has an impact on both aggregate demand and aggregate supply. Lower tax rates increase aggregate demand because households now have more money to spend. At the same time, lower tax rates mean that take-home wages rise and this may encourage more work effort. Also, entrepreneurial profits are taxed at lower rates, encouraging more people to take risks and start businesses. At different times, policymakers have lowered taxes to stimulate consumption: John F. Kennedy reduced tax rates in the early 1960s and George W. Bush in 2001 and 2008 provided tax rebates to taxpayers as part of economic stimulus packages. President Obama's 2009 stimulus program included tax credits along with increases in government spending.

At other times, administrations have reduced marginal tax rates, the rate paid on the next dollar earned, with the express purpose of stimulating incentives to work and for businesses to take risks. President Kennedy reduced the top marginal rate from 70% to 50%, and President Reagan reduced the top marginal rate from 50% to 28%.

Clearly, high marginal income tax rates can have adverse effects on the economy. Still, there is considerable controversy regarding the benefits of the supply-side approach to macroeconomic fiscal policy. The supply-side movement that resulted in the marginal tax rate reductions in the 1980s by the Reagan administration was partially driven by reference to a simple tax revenue curve drawn by economist Arthur Laffer showing how reducing tax *rates* could increase tax *revenues*.

The **Laffer curve** in Figure 7 on the next page shows that if tax rates are 0% or 100%, tax revenues will be zero (the latter because there would be no incentive to earn income). In between these two extreme tax rates, tax revenues will be positive. Laffer argued that high tax rates (such as the one that generates revenues at point *a* on the Laffer curve)

Laffer curve Shows a hypothetical relationship between income tax rates and tax revenues. As tax rates rise from zero, revenues rise, reach a maximum, then decline until revenues reach zero again at a 100% tax rate.

FIGURE 7

The Laffer Curve

The Laffer curve shows the relationship between average tax rates and total tax revenues. As the tax rate rises from 0%, tax revenues increase. At point *c*, tax revenues are maximized. If tax rates continue to rise, Laffer's argument was that the government could obtain revenues at point *a* based on a high tax rate, and equal revenues at point *b* based on a lower tax rate. The tax rates that correspond to points b and c are often debated by economists.

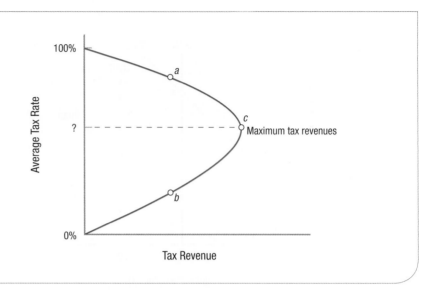

create disincentives to work and invest. He claimed that a lower tax rate would generate the same amount of revenue, seen as point *b* on the curve. Economists debate about what the tax rate corresponding to point *b* would be. Further, it raises a bigger debate about the tax rate at which the disincentive to work begins to reduce tax revenues. In other words, what tax rate corresponds to point *c* on the Laffer curve?

Expanding Investment and Reducing Regulations

We have already seen how closely standards of living are tied to productivity. Investment increases the capital with which labor works, thereby increasing productivity. Rising productivity drives increased economic growth and raises the average standard of living, shifting the long-run aggregate supply curve to the right.

Investment can be encouraged by such policies as investment tax credits (direct reductions in taxes for new investment) and more rapid depreciation schedules for plant and equipment. When a firm can expense (depreciate) its capital equipment over a shorter period of time, it cuts its taxes now rather than later, and therefore earns a higher return on the capital now. Similarly, government grants for basic research help firms increase their budgets for research and development, which results in new products and technologies brought to market.

Nowhere is this impact more evident than in the health care field. The National Institutes of Health, part of the U.S. Department of Health and Human Services, invests over $30 billion in health care research each year, mostly in grants to medical schools, universities, and research institutions. These investments have enabled new medicines to be developed at a much faster rate than previously. And beyond the obvious benefits this has for the people who require such medicines, investments of this sort pay dividends for the entire economy. As health care improves, workers' absentee rates are lower and productivity rises.

Another way of increasing long-run aggregate supply involves repealing unnecessarily onerous regulations that hamper business and add to costs. Clearly, some regulation of business activities is needed, as the recent financial industry meltdown has shown. Still, these regulations should be subjected to rigorous cost-benefit analyses. Otherwise, excessive regulations end up adding to the costs of the products we buy, without yielding significant benefits. Examples of excessively regulated industries have included trucking and the airlines. When these industries were deregulated in the 1980s, prices fell and both industries expanded rapidly. Today, some economists argue that the

Chromosome genetics research has led to significant advances in medical cures, and is an example of how fiscal policy can expand aggregate supply.

Pgiam/Getty Images

Federal Drug Administration's drug approval process is too long and costly; bringing a new drug to market can cost over $1 billion.

Fiscal policies to increase aggregate supply are promoted mainly through the government's encouragement of human capital development and technology improvements, its power to tax, its ability to promote investment in infrastructure and research, and the degree and efficiency of regulation. Cutting marginal tax rates, offering investment tax credits, and offering grants for research are the favored policies. The political fervor of the 1980s supply-side movement has largely dissipated as marginal income tax rates have declined. But fiscal policies to encourage growth in long-run aggregate supply are still an important part of the government's long-term fiscal policy arsenal.

 ## CHECKPOINT

FISCAL POLICY AND AGGREGATE SUPPLY

- The goal of fiscal policies that influence aggregate supply is to shift the long-run aggregate supply curve to the right.

- Expanding long-run aggregate supply can occur through higher investments in human capital and a focus on technological infrastructure with "public good" benefits.

- The Laffer curve suggested that reducing tax rates could lead to *higher* revenues in some cases.

- Other fiscal policies to increase long-run aggregate supply include providing incentives for business investment and reducing burdensome regulation.

- The major limitation of fiscal policies to influence long-run aggregate supply is that they take a longer time to have an impact compared to polices aimed at influencing aggregate demand.

QUESTIONS: Some economists have suggested that an improved tax structure would entail a reduction in income taxes for individuals, corporations (corporate income tax), and investors (capital gains taxes), that are offset by an increase in consumption taxes (such as sales and excise taxes). Which part(s) of this type of proposal would be consistent with supply-side economics? Why?

Answers to the Checkpoint questions can be found at the end of this chapter.

Implementing Fiscal Policy

Implementing fiscal policy is often easier said than done. It is often a complex and time-consuming process. Three disparate entities—the Senate, House, and the president—must collectively agree on specific spending and tax policies. Ideally, these decisions are made in the open with the public fully informed. The complexities of the budgeting process and its openness (not a bad thing in itself) give rise to several inherent difficulties. We will briefly consider some problems having to do with the timing of fiscal decisions and the political pressures inherent in the process, after first looking at the automatic stabilization mechanisms contained in the federal budgeting process.

Automatic Stabilizers

There is a certain degree of stability built into the U.S. macroeconomic system. Tax revenues and transfer payments are the two principal **automatic stabilizers;** without any overt action by Congress or other policymakers, these two components of the federal budget expand or contract in ways that help counter movements of the business cycle.

When the economy is growing at a solid rate, tax receipts rise because individuals and firms are increasing their taxable incomes. At the same time, transfer payments decline, because fewer people require welfare or unemployment assistance. Rising tax

automatic stabilizers Tax revenues and transfer payments automatically expand or contract in ways that reduce the intensity of business fluctuations without any overt action by Congress or other policymakers.

revenues and declining transfer payments have contractionary effects, and act as a brake to slow the growth of GDP, helping to keep the economy from overheating, or keeping it from generating inflationary pressures. When the economic boom ends, and the economy goes into a downturn, the opposite happens: Tax revenues decline and transfer payments rise. These added funds getting pumped into the economy help cushion the impact of the downturn, not just for the recipients of transfer payments, but for the economy as a whole.

The income tax is a powerful stabilizer because of its progressivity. When incomes fall, tax revenues fall faster because people do not just pay taxes on smaller incomes, but they pay taxes at lower rates as their incomes fall. Disposable income, in other words, falls more slowly than aggregate income. But when the economy is booming, tax revenues rise faster than income, thereby withdrawing spending from the economy. This helps to slow the growth in income, thus reducing the threat of an inflationary spiral.

The key point to remember here is that automatic stabilizers reduce the intensity of business fluctuations. Automatic stabilizers do not eliminate fluctuations in the business cycle, but they render business cycles smoother and less chaotic. Automatic stabilizers act on their own, whereas discretionary fiscal policy requires overt action by policymakers, and this fact alone creates difficulties.

Fiscal Policy Timing Lags

Using discretionary fiscal policy to smooth the short-term business cycle is a challenge because of several lags associated with its implementation. First, most of the macroeconomic data that policymakers need to enact the proper fiscal policies are not available until at least one quarter (three months) after the fact. Even then, key figures often get revised for the next quarter or two. The **information lag,** therefore, creates a one- to six-month period before informed policymaking can even begin.

Even if the most recent data suggest that the economy is trending into a recession, it may take several quarters to confirm this fact. Short-term (month-to-month or quarter-to-quarter) variations in key indicators are common and sometimes represent nothing more than randomness in the data. This **recognition lag** is one reason why recessions and recoveries are often well under way before policymakers fully acknowledge a need for action.

Third, once policymakers recognize that the economy has trended in a certain direction, fiscal policy requires a long and often contentious legislative process, referred to as a **decision lag.** Not all legislators have the same goals for the economy; therefore, any new government spending must first survive an arduous trip through the political sausage machine. Once some new policy has become law, it often requires months of planning, budgeting, and implementation to set up a new program. This process, the **implementation lag,** rarely consumes *less* than 18 to 24 months.

The problem these lags pose is clear: By the time the fiscal stimulus meant to jumpstart a sputtering economy kicks in, the economy may already be on the mend. And if so, the exercise of fiscal policy can compound the effects of the business cycle by overstimulating a patient that is already recovering.

Some of these lags can be reduced by expediting spending already approved for existing programs rather than implementing new programs. This was the approach Congress and the administration wanted to take with the 2009 stimulus package. Congress allocated part of the increased spending to "shovel-ready" projects to reduce the time for this spending to have an impact on the economy. Also, the lags associated with tax changes are much shorter, given that new rates can go into withholding tables and take effect within weeks of enactment. Therefore, policymakers often include tax changes because of their shorter implementation lags.

information lag The time policymakers must wait for economic data to be collected, processed, and reported. Most macroeconomic data are not available until at least one quarter (three months) after the fact.

recognition lag The time it takes for policymakers to confirm that the economy is in a recession or a recovery. Short-term variations in key economic indicators are typical and sometimes represent nothing more than randomness in the data.

decision lag The time it takes Congress and the administration to decide on a policy once a problem is recognized.

implementation lag The time required to turn fiscal policy into law and eventually have an impact on the economy.

Political gridlock can delay fiscal policy legislation for months or years.

Olivier Douliery-Pool/Getty Images

The Government's Bias Toward Borrowing and Away from Taxation

Because of the uncertainties surrounding the economy, politicians often take their own interests into account when considering fiscal policy, if not for economic reasons then very likely for political ones. In times of recessions or slow economic recovery, those on the left tend to favor more government spending and transfer payments, while those on the right tend to favor reductions in taxes. Both policies are expansionary and lead to greater deficits, especially as tax receipts fall due to lower incomes and fewer jobs.

But in order to balance the budget over the long run, such policies generally need to be reversed in good times so that government spending is reduced and taxes raised, along with the generation of more tax receipts from higher incomes and more jobs. But politicians often are reluctant to do so. Even in good economic times, tax hikes are politically dangerous, and so are major cuts to government spending programs and transfer programs. The result is that fiscal policy is financed by deficits. Deficits persist in our system of government.

Public choice theory involves the economic analysis of public and political decision making. James Buchanan, considered the father of public choice theory, essentially fused the disciplines of economics and political science. Buchanan contrasted Adam Smith's description of social benefits that arise from private individuals acting in their own self-interest with the harm that frequently results from politicians doing the same thing. Competition among individuals and firms for jobs, customers, and profits creates wealth, and thus it benefits the entire society. Self-interested politicians, however, often instigate government interventions that are harmful to the larger economy.

Public choice economists such as Buchanan argue that deficit spending reduces the perceived cost of current government operations. The result is that taxpayers permit some programs to exist that they would oppose if required to pay the full cost today. But this situation, public choice economists charge, amounts to shifting the cost of government to the next generation, and has led to the steady expansion of the federal government.

Public choice analysis helps us to understand why deficits seem inevitable: We do not pay the full costs of today's programs. In the past 50 years, the federal government has run a deficit in 45 of these years, despite significant growth of the economy over this time. The next section focuses on the role of deficits and public debt on the economy.

public choice theory The economic analysis of public and political decision making, looking at issues such as voting, the impact of election incentives on politicians, the influence of special interest groups, and rent-seeking behaviors.

 CHECKPOINT

IMPLEMENTING FISCAL POLICY

- Automatic stabilizers reduce the intensity of business fluctuations. When the economy is booming, tax revenues are rising and unemployment compensation and welfare payments are falling, dampening the boom. When the economy enters a recession, tax revenues fall and transfer payments rise, cushioning the decline. This happens automatically.

- Fiscal policymakers face information lags (the time it takes to collect, process, and provide data on the economy), recognition lags (the time required to recognize trends in the data), decision lags (the time it takes for Congress and the administration to decide on a policy), and implementation lags (the time required by Congress to pass a law and see it put in place).

- These lags can often result in government policy being mistimed. For example, expansionary policy taking effect when the economy is well into a recovery or failing to take effect when a recession is underway can make stabilization worse.

- Public choice economists argue that deficit spending reduces the perceived cost of the current government operations, and therefore politicians are more willing to enact expansionary policies that lead to deficits and a higher public debt.

QUESTION: Suppose that the president wishes to enact fiscal policies that would generate the most immediate effect on the economy, and thus improve his chances of re-election. What type of policies would he tend to favor and why?

Answers to the Checkpoint question can be found at the end of this chapter.

Financing the Federal Government

In the late 1990s, some economists argued that spending should be reduced, taxes increased, or a contractionary monetary policy implemented to cool down an economy and stock market that were overheating. Their advice was partly heeded, in that tax rates were increased as the economy entered a boom, and the federal budget ended the 1990s in surplus. The recession of 2001, caused in part by the fall in the stock market and a reduction in investment, moved the budget back into deficit. Let's first define deficits, surpluses, and public debt before studying their impact on the economy.

Defining Deficits and the National Debt

deficit The amount by which annual government spending exceeds tax revenues.

surplus The amount by which annual tax revenues exceed government expenditures.

A **deficit** is the amount by which annual government spending exceeds tax revenues. A **surplus** is the amount by which annual tax revenues exceed government expenditures. In 2000, the budget surplus was $236.2 billion. By 2002, tax cuts, a recession, and new commitments for national defense and homeland security had turned the budget surpluses of 1998–2001 into deficits—a deficit of $157.8 billion for fiscal year 2002. The effects of the deep recession in 2007–2009, and the extent of fiscal policies used, changed the magnitude of the deficit picture again. Government intervention and support for the financial and automobile industries and a nearly $800 billion stimulus package to soften the recession resulted in a 2009 deficit of over $1.4 trillion. However, the economic recovery since 2009 has reduced the deficit from its peak.

public debt The total accumulation of past deficits and surpluses; it includes Treasury bills, notes, and bonds, and U.S. Savings Bonds.

The **public debt,** or *national debt*, is the total accumulation of past deficits less surpluses. Gross public debt in 2013 was over $16 trillion, but public debt held by the public was only three-quarters of that amount (about $12 trillion). Some agencies of government, such as the Social Security Administration, the Treasury Department, and the Federal Reserve, hold some debt; one agency of government owes money to another. Debt held by the public (including foreign governments) is debt that represents a claim on government assets, not simply intergovernmental transfers.

Figure 8 shows the public debt held by the public as a percentage of gross domestic product (GDP) since 1940. During World War II, public debt exceeded GDP. It then

FIGURE 8

Public Debt Held by the Public as a Percent of GDP

The public debt as a percentage of GDP has varied considerably since 1940. During World War II, public debt exceeded GDP. It then trended downward until the early 1980s, when public debt began to climb again. In 2012, public debt held by the public (as opposed to government institutions) exceeded 70% of GDP.

Eric Chiang

trended downward until the early 1980s, when public debt began to climb again. Public debt held by the public as a percentage of GDP fell from the mid-1990s until 2000, first because of growing budget surpluses in the late 1990s, then because of falling interest rates (what the government has to pay on the debt), but it has risen since then. Public debt held by the public (as opposed to government institutions) has surpassed 70% of GDP.

ISSUE

How Big Is the Economic Burden of Interest Rates on the National Debt?

The federal government paid almost $250 billion in interest payments on the national debt in 2012. This is money that could have been used for other public programs. In fact, interest payments on the debt were greater than the amount the government paid for education, transportation infrastructure, low-income housing, and Homeland Security combined.

Although interest payments on the debt are large, they represent a small portion of the federal budget and an even smaller portion of GDP. Interest on the debt as a percentage of GDP, as shown in the figure, was steady from 1950 to 1980, hovering around 1.5%. This percentage more than doubled during the 1980s because of high inflation and interest rates, and rising deficits. In the mid-1990s, interest rates dropped and deficits fell, even becoming surpluses for a short time. Consequently, interest as a percentage of GDP dropped toward the level it was in the 1950s. To-

day, budget deficits are again rising, but with interest rates at record lows, interest payments remain a small percentage of GDP.

The fact that rising debt has not led to dramatic borrowing costs highlights the important role that interest rates have on the economy. Many individuals, firms, and foreign governments hold long-term (up to 30-year) Treasury bonds, During the economic crisis in the early 1980s, interest rates on 30-year Treasury bonds reached 15%, guaranteeing a bondholder a 15% annual return for 30 years.

Today, those 15% bonds from the 1980s are maturing, and new 30-year bonds are paying less than 4%, resulting in tremendous savings to the government in financing the national debt. For example, an average interest rate of 2% saves the U.S. federal government $500 billion per year compared to a 5% interest rate, and saves over $1 trillion per year compared to an 8% interest rate.

Why have long-term interest rates remained low despite the high debt and a debt downgrade in U.S. bonds? One reason is that volatility in stock markets makes U.S. debt still one of the safest investments in the world. Second, foreign governments perceive the U.S. dollar as a valuable hard currency, and thus buy our bonds as a way to build up their national reserves. For these reasons and more, the U.S. government has little trouble selling bonds at low interest rates.

Despite the current favorable conditions under which the U.S. government finances its debt, it must still focus on keeping debt in check for a number of reasons. First, interest payments on external (foreign) holdings of U.S. debt are a leakage from our economy. Second, bond prices can change quickly, increasing the burden of the debt. Third, as interest rates rise in the future, low interest rate bonds issued today will mature and may be replaced by higher interest rate bonds.

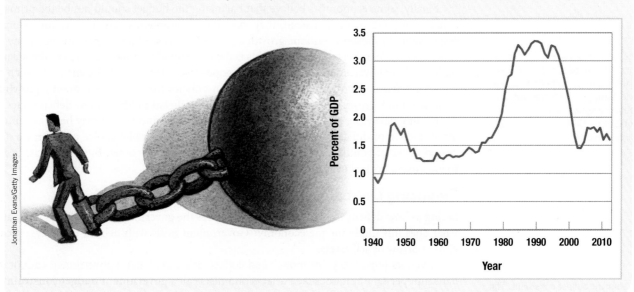

Public debt is held as U.S. Treasury securities, including Treasury bills, notes, bonds, and U.S. Savings Bonds. Treasury bills, or T-bills, as they are known, are short-term instruments with a maturity period of a year or less that pay a specific sum at maturity. T-bills do not pay interest. Rather, they are initially sold at a discount, and their yields are then determined by the time to maturity and the discount. T-bills are the most actively traded securities in the U.S. economy, and they are highly liquid, providing the closest thing there is to risk-free returns.

Treasury notes are financial instruments issued for periods ranging from 1 to 10 years, whereas Treasury bonds have maturity periods exceeding 10 years. Both of these instruments have stated interest rates and are traded sometimes at discounts and sometimes at premiums.

Today, interest rates on the public debt are between 1% and 4%. This relatively low rate has not always been the case. In the early 1980s, interest rates varied from 11% to nearly 15%. Inflation was high and investors required high interest rates as compensation. When rates are high, government interest costs on the debt soar.

Balanced Budget Amendments

Although federal budget deficits have been the norm for the past 50 years, the recent severe recession led to record deficits, leading many politicians to propose federal balanced budget amendments requiring the federal government to balance its budget every year. Balanced budget amendments are not new. They exist for most state governments. At the federal level, however, such rules have not existed since the 1930s.

Most balanced budget amendments require an **annually balanced budget,** which means government would have to equate its revenues and expenditures every year. Most economists, however, believe such rules are counterproductive. For example, during times of recession, tax revenues tend to fall due to lower incomes and higher unemployment. To offset these lost revenues, an annually balanced budget would require deep spending cuts or tax hikes (in other words, contractionary policy) during a time when expansionary policies are needed. Many economists believe that balanced budget rules of the early 1930s turned what probably would have been a modest recession into the global Depression.

An alternative to balancing the budget annually would be to require a **cyclically balanced budget,** in which the budget is balanced over the course of the business cycle. The basic idea is to restrict spending or raise taxes when the economy is booming, allowing for a budget surplus. These surpluses would then be used to offset deficits accrued during recessions, when increased spending or lower taxes are appropriate. To some extent, balancing the budget over the business cycle happens automatically as long as fiscal policy is held constant due to the automatic stabilizers discussed earlier. However, the business cycle takes time to define (due to lags), making it difficult to enforce such a rule in practice.

Finally, some economists believe that balancing the budget should not be the primary concern of policymakers; instead, they view the government's primary macroeconomic responsibility to foster economic growth and stable prices, while keeping the economy as close as possible to full employment. This is the **functional finance** approach to the federal budget, where governments provide public goods and services that citizens want (such as national defense, education, etc.) and focus on policies that keep the economy growing, because rapidly growing economies do not have significant public debt or deficit issues.

In sum, balancing the budget annually or over the business cycle may be either counterproductive or difficult to do. It is not a solution to the public choice problem we discussed above of politicians' incentives to spend and not raise taxes. Budget deficits begin to look like a normal occurrence in our political system.

Financing Debt and Deficits

Seeing as how deficits may be persistent, how does the government deal with its debt, and what does this imply for the economy? Government deals with debt in two ways. It can either borrow or sell assets.

Given its power to print money and collect taxes, the federal government cannot go bankrupt per se. But it does face what economists call a **government budget constraint:**

$$G - T = \Delta M + \Delta B + \Delta A$$

annually balanced budget Federal expenditures and taxes would have to be equal each year.

cyclically balanced budget Balancing the budget over the course of the business cycle by restricting spending or raising taxes when the economy is booming and using these surpluses to offset the deficits that occur during recessions.

functional finance Essentially ignores the impact of the budget on the business cycle and focuses on fostering economic growth and stable prices, while keeping the economy as close as possible to full employment.

government budget constraint The government budget is limited by the fact that $G - T = \Delta M + \Delta B + \Delta A$.

where

> G = government spending
> T = tax revenues, thus $(G - T)$ is the federal budget deficit
> ΔM = the change in the money supply (selling bonds to the Federal Reserve)
> ΔB = the change in bonds held by public entities, domestic and foreign
> ΔA = the sales of government assets

The left side of the equation, $G - T$, represents government spending minus tax revenues. A positive $(G - T)$ value is a budget deficit, and a negative $(G - T)$ value represents a budget surplus. The right side of the equation shows how government finances its deficit. It can sell bonds to the Federal Reserve, sell bonds to the public, or sell assets. Let's look at each of these options.

- **$\Delta M > 0$:** First, the government can sell bonds to government agencies, especially the Federal Reserve, which we will study in depth in a later chapter. When the Federal Reserve buys bonds, it uses money that is created out of thin air by its power to "print" money. When the Federal Reserve pumps new money into the money supply to finance the government's debt, it is called monetizing the debt.

- **$\Delta B > 0$:** If the Federal Reserve does not purchase the bonds, they may be sold to the public, including corporations, banks, mutual funds, individuals, and foreign entities. This also has the effect of financing the government's deficit.

- **$\Delta A > 0$:** Asset sales represent only a small fraction of government finance in the United States. These sales include auctions of telecommunications spectra and offshore oil leases. Developing nations have used asset sales, or privatization, in recent years to bolster sagging government revenues and to encourage efficiency and development in the case where a government-owned industry is sold.

Thus, when the government runs a deficit, it must borrow funds from somewhere, assuming it does not sell assets. If the government borrows from the public, the quantity of publicly held bonds will rise; if it borrows from the Federal Reserve, the quantity of money in circulation will rise.

The main idea from this section is that deficits must be financed in some form, whether by the government borrowing or selling assets, or paid for by a combination of rising private savings and falling investment. As we'll see in the next section, rising levels of deficits and the corresponding interest rates raise some important issues about the ability of a country to manage its debt burden.

 ## CHECKPOINT

FINANCING THE FEDERAL GOVERNMENT

- A deficit is the amount that government spending exceeds tax revenue in a particular year.
- The public (national) debt is the total accumulation of past deficits less surpluses.
- Approaches to financing the federal government include annually balancing the budget, balancing the budget over the business cycle, and ignoring the budget deficit and focusing on promoting full employment and stable prices.
- The federal government's debt must be financed by selling bonds to the Federal Reserve ("printing money" or "monetizing the debt"), by selling bonds to the public, or by selling government assets. This is known as the government budget constraint.

QUESTION: One reason why state governments have been more willing to pass balanced budget amendments than the federal government is the difference between mandatory and discretionary spending. What are some expenses of the federal government that are less predictable or harder to cut that make balanced budget amendments more difficult to pursue?

Answers to the Checkpoint question can be found at the end of this chapter.

➔ Why Is the Public Debt So Important?

We have seen that politicians have a bias toward using expansionary fiscal policy and not contractionary fiscal policy, and also have a bias toward using debt rather than taxes to finance the ensuing deficits. This explains the persistence of federal debt. We have seen that balancing the federal budget by passing an amendment is not an ideal solution. The question then becomes, How big a problem is persistent deficits? Should we be worrying about this now?

Figure 9 shows the debt of mostly developed nations in 2012. Japan, Greece, and Italy had a large debt relative to their GDP. Although many countries had debt below 100% of GDP and deficits below 6% of GDP, Greece, Japan, Italy, the United Kingdom, and the United States are exceptions. China, Russia, and Chile had low debt ratios (debt/GDP) and Chile had a budget surplus in 2012. As an economy moves toward the upper left portion of the figure, problems begin to rise.

FIGURE 9

Public Debt and Deficits as a Percent of GDP

This figure shows the relationship between public debt and deficits for several nations. Those countries with high deficits tend to have high debt-to-GDP ratios.

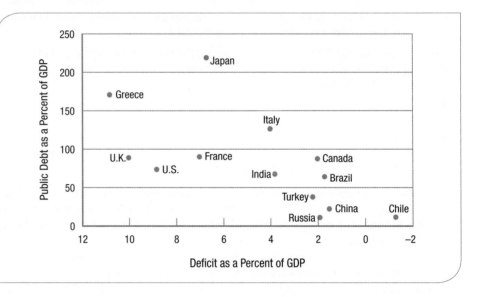

Politicians frequently warn that the federal government is going bankrupt, or that we are burdening future generations with our own enormous public debt. After all, total (gross) public debt exceeds $16 trillion and private debt held by the public totals about $12 trillion, meaning that every baby born in the United States begins life saddled with over $38,000 in public debt. Before you start panicking, let's examine the burden of the public debt.

Is the Size of the Public Debt a Problem?

The national debt held by the public represents over 70% of U.S. GDP. Is this amount of debt a cause for immediate concern? It really depends on the costs of financing the debt. What is the burden of the interest rate payments on the debt?

Think about it another way. Suppose that you earn $50,000 a year and have $35,000 in student loan debt, equal to 70% of your annual income. Is this a problem? It would be if the interest rate on the student loans were 20% a year, because interest payments of $7,000 per year would take up a significant chunk (14%) of your gross salary. But if the interest rate is 3%, the debt burden from the interest ($1,050 per year) would not be as substantial, representing only about 2% of your gross salary.

For the U.S. national debt, current interest rates are relatively low due in large part to aggressive action by the Federal Reserve. Interest costs on the national debt were about $250 billion in 2012, representing about 7% of the federal budget. That is not an overwhelming amount.

Wouldn't it be wise to pay the debt down or pay it off? Not necessarily. Many people today "own" some small part of the public debt in their pension plans, but many others do not. If taxes were raised across the board to pay down the debt, those who did not own any public debt would be in a worse position than those who did.

Servicing the debt requires taxing the general public to pay interest to bondholders. Most people who own part of the national debt (or who indirectly own parts of entities that hold the debt) tend to be richer than those who do not. This means that money is taken from those across the income or wealth distribution and given to those near the top. Still, the fact that taxes are mildly progressive mitigates some, and perhaps even all, of this reverse redistribution problem.

Thus, the public debt is not out of control, at least based on the economy's ability to pay the interest costs. However, rising interest rates will raise the burden of this debt. Even so, at its current size, the public debt is manageable as long as it does not experience another spike in the near term.

When a country's debt as a percentage of GDP becomes too high, it can no longer service the debt, leading to a potential default.

Another consideration is whether the debt is mostly held externally (i.e., financed by foreign governments, banks, and investors) as is the case of many developing countries. These countries have discovered that relying on foreign sources of financing has its limits.

Does It Matter If Foreigners Hold a Significant Portion of the Public Debt?

The great advantage of citizens being creditors as well as debtors with relation to the public debt is obvious. Men readily perceive that they can not be much oppressed by a debt which they owe to themselves.

—ABRAHAM LINCOLN (1864)

Consider first, as Abraham Lincoln noted in 1864, that much of the national debt held by the public is owned by American banks, corporations, mutual funds, pension plans, and individuals. As a people, we essentially own this debt—this is **internally held debt.** Hence, the taxes collected from a wide swath of the American public to pay the interest on the debt are paid back out to yet another group of Americans. As Table 1 shows, however, foreigners own nearly half of the public debt held by the public. This is **externally held debt.**

Of the interest paid on the $16 trillion gross public debt, about 29% goes to federal agencies holding this debt—the Social Security Administration, the Federal Reserve, and other federal agencies—38% goes to the American private sector, and 34% goes to foreigners.

The interest paid on externally held debt represents a real claim on our goods and services, and thus can be a real burden on our economy. Debt held by the public has grown, and the portion of the debt held by foreigners has expanded. Until the mid-1990s, foreigners held roughly 20% of publicly held debt.

internally held debt Public debt owned by U.S. banks, corporations, mutual funds, pension plans, and individuals.

externally held debt Public debt held by foreigners, which is roughly equal to half of the outstanding U.S. debt held by the public.

Distribution of National Debt, as of January 2013 (trillions)	Amount	Percent	TABLE 1
Held by the Federal Reserve and government agencies	$4.821	28.8%	
Held by the public	11.917	71.2	
Held by foreigners	5.601	33.5	
Held domestically	6.316	37.7	
Total national debt	16.738	100.0	

Traditionally much of the U.S. debt is held internally, but this is changing. In just a decade, foreign holdings have doubled to nearly 50% of debt held by the public, and nearly half of this is held by China and Japan. Why such a rapid expansion of foreign holdings since the 1990s? One reason is that these countries are buying our debt to keep their currencies from rising relative to the dollar. When their currencies rise, their exports to America are more costly, and as a result sales fall, hurting their economies. Better to accumulate U.S. debt than see their export sectors suffer.

However, the increased reliance on external financing of our debt raises some concerns. For example, the significant amount of our debt held by China makes our economy more vulnerable to policy changes by the Chinese government and/or businesses that hold our debt. On the positive side, however, creditors such as China are likely to maintain strong economic and political ties with the United States; besides, China eventually will want its money back.

Does Government Debt Crowd Out Consumption and Investment?

As we saw in the budget constraint section earlier, when the government runs a deficit, it must sell bonds to either the public or the Federal Reserve. If it sells bonds to the Federal Reserve (prints money) when the economy is near full employment, the money supply will grow and inflation will result.

Alternatively, when the federal government spends more than tax revenues permit, it can sell bonds to the public. But doing so drives up interest rates as the demand for loanable funds (this time by the government rather than the public sector) increases. As interest rates rise, consumer spending on durable goods such as cars and appliances, often bought on credit, falls. It also reduces private business investment. Therefore, while deficit spending is usually expansionary, the consequence is that future generations will be bequeathed a smaller and potentially less productive economy, resulting in a lower standard of living. This is the **crowding-out effect** of deficit spending. However, in a severe recession when consumers and businesses are not eager to buy or invest, the crowding-out effect is less pronounced, making fiscal policy more powerful.

crowding-out effect Arises from deficit spending requiring the government to borrow, thus driving up interest rates and reducing consumer spending and business investment.

The crowding-out effect also can be mitigated if the funds from deficit spending are used for public investment. Improvements in the nation's transportation infrastructure, education establishment, and research facilities, for instance, are all aimed at improving the economy's future productive capacity. If the investments expand the nation's productive capacity enough, growth will be such that the debt-to-GDP ratio may fall. But if all or most of the deficit is spent on current consumption, growth in GDP may be weak and the debt-to-GDP ratio will most likely rise.

How Will the National Debt Affect Our Future? Are We Doomed?

If the federal debt is not an enormous burden now, what about in the future? Here there is a large cause for concern. Economists have argued that economic growth depends on the **fiscal sustainability** of the federal budget. For a fiscal policy to be fiscally sustainable, the present value (current dollar value) of all projected future revenues must be equal to the present value of projected future spending. If the budget is not fiscally sustainable, an intergenerational tax burden may be created, with future generations paying for the spending of the current generation.

fiscal sustainability A measure of the present value of all projected future revenues compared to the present value of projected future spending.

Clearly, some tax burden shifting is sensible. When current fiscal policy truly invests in the economy, future generations benefit, and therefore, some of the present costs may justifiably be shifted to them. Investments in infrastructure, education, research, national defense, and homeland security are good examples.

However, the federal government has immense obligations that extend over long periods that are unrelated to economic investment. Its two largest programs, Social Security and Medicare, account for over 35% of all federal spending. People who are just beginning to enter retirement can expect to live for two or three more decades. Add to this the fact that medical costs are growing at rates significantly higher than economic growth as new and more sophisticated treatments are developed and demanded.

The intergenerational impact results from the fact that Social Security and Medicare are pay-as-you-go programs. The current working generation, in other words, funds the older generation's benefits; there are no pooled funds waiting to be tapped as needed. Thus, these two programs represent huge unfunded liabilities to younger (and yet to be born) generations.

With the current national debt held by the public at $12 trillion, and total future liabilities (the money that has been promised, such as for Social Security and Medicare, but have not been paid) over next 75 years estimated to be about $87 trillion, the implications for future budgeting are significant. In other words, without some significant change in economic or demographic growth, taxes will have to be increased on a massive scale at some point, or else the benefits for Social Security and Medicare will have to be drastically cut.

If these estimates of fiscal imbalance are on track, fiscal policy is headed for a train wreck as the baby boomers keep retiring. The public choice analysis discussed earlier suggests that politicians will try to keep this issue off the agenda for as long as possible, one side fighting tax increases while the other resists benefit reductions. Clearly, given the magnitudes discussed here, this problem will be difficult to solve once it reaches crisis proportions.

We started this chapter by talking about the government's ability to address fluctuations in the business cycle by using fiscal policy to affect aggregate demand and aggregate supply. But given the government's penchant for expansionary policy, persistent budget deficits tend to result. Unlike for individuals, the federal government has the ability to incur debt for some time because of its ability to print money and borrow from the public. And while the federal government is currently able to safely manage its debt, this picture may change down the road as Social Security and Medicare liabilities continue to grow. The implication is that we are better off dealing with this future problem now rather than later.

 # CHECKPOINT

WHY IS THE PUBLIC DEBT SO IMPORTANT?

- Interest payments on the debt exceed 7% of the federal budget. These funds could have been spent on other programs.

- About half of the public debt held by the public is held by domestic individuals and institutions, and half is held by foreigners. The domestic half is internally held and represents transfers among individuals, but that part held by foreigners is a real claim on our resources.

- When the government pays for the deficit by selling bonds, interest rates rise, crowding out some consumption and private investment and reducing economic growth. To the extent that these funds are used for public investment and not current consumption, this effect is mitigated.

- The rising costs of Social Security and Medicare represent the biggest threat to the long-run federal budget. Either the costs of such programs eventually need to be reduced, or additional taxes will be required to cover these rising expenses.

QUESTIONS: Suppose China and Japan, the two largest external creditors of U.S. public debt, choose to diversify their asset holdings by selling some of their U.S. Treasury bonds. How will this affect the government's ability to finance its debt? What might happen to consumption and investment in the United States?

Answers to the Checkpoint questions can be found at the end of this chapter.

chapter summary

Section 1: **Fiscal Policy and Aggregate Demand**

Fiscal policy describes the use of government taxation and spending to influence the economy. Specifically, it involves three main tools: taxation, government spending on goods and services, and transfer payments.

Contractionary fiscal policy includes reducing government spending or transfer payments, or raising taxes. The effect is a shift of the AD curve to the left, decreasing prices and aggregate output.

Expansionary fiscal policy includes increases in government spending or transfer payments, or reducing taxes. The effect is a shift of the AD curve to the right.

The **multiplier effect** allows each dollar of government spending to expand aggregate output by a multiple of the amount spent. Changes in government spending have a larger multiplier than changes in taxes.

Kirby Hamilton/Getty Images

Unemployment benefits generally produce a high multiplier effect because recipients are likely to spend all of the money quickly.

Using expansionary fiscal policy to shift AD during a recession can reduce the time required to achieve full employment, Q_f. The tradeoff of such policies is potential inflation, although the effect is small when used in a deep recession.

Section 2: **Fiscal Policy and Aggregate Supply**

The goal of **supply-side fiscal policy** is to shift the LRAS curve to the right. Such policies do not require a tradeoff between output and prices; however, these policies require more time to work.

Danny Lehman/Corbis

Maintaining highways such as the treacherous Trans-Alaskan Highway can increase aggregate supply if better roads increase productivity.

Common Supply-Side Policies

- **Infrastructure Spending:** Improving roads and communications networks, stabilizing legal and financial systems, and improving human capital and technologies (R&D).

- **Cuts in Tax Rates:** Increases aggregate supply by providing firms incentives to expand or for individuals to work more.

- **Elimination of Burdensome Regulations:** Leads to greater efficiency if the costs of regulation outweigh its benefits.

Section 3: Implementing Fiscal Policy

The economy contains **automatic stabilizers:**

When the economy is strong:

Tax receipts rise   Transfer payments fall

(both have contractionary effects to fight inflation)

When the economy is weak:

Tax receipts fall   Transfer payments rise

(both have expansionary effects to offset the recession)

Using fiscal policy involves **timing lags:**

- **Information lag:** Time required to acquire macroeconomic data.
- **Recognition lag:** Time required to recognize trends in the data.
- **Decision lag:** Legislative process to enact policies.
- **Implementation lag:** Time required after laws are passed to set up programs.

Passing new fiscal policy can take a lot of time, especially in a divided Congress.

Section 4: Financing the Federal Government

The **federal deficit** is the annual amount that the government spends that is above the amount it receives in tax revenues. The public (or national) debt is the accumulation of all past deficits and surpluses.

How Does the Government Finance Its Deficit $(G - T)$?

- The Federal Reserve prints money to buy bonds: ΔM
- Treasury bonds held domestically and externally: ΔB
- Sales of government assets: ΔA

U.S. Savings Bonds are one form of financing government debt.

Section 5: Why Is the Public Debt So Important?

The U.S. government pays about $250 billion per year in interest payments on the public debt. Although this is a manageable expense, rises in interest rates and rising future liabilities can make debt a more significant problem in the future.

Social Security and Medicare liabilities rise each year as Americans live longer and health care costs rise. These two components pose a big concern for future debt.

About half of U.S. public debt is held externally, by foreign governments and investors. Of this amount, nearly half, or about $2.4 trillion, is held by China and Japan.

Borrowing money to finance the debt raises interest rates, making it more expensive for individuals and businesses to borrow money. This is the **crowding-out effect.**

KEY CONCEPTS

QUESTIONS AND PROBLEMS

Check Your Understanding

1. Explain why government spending theoretically gives a bigger boost to the economy than tax cuts.

2. Explain why increasing government purchases of goods and services is expansionary fiscal policy. Would increasing taxes or reducing transfer payments be contractionary or expansionary? Why?

3. Changes in tax rates affect both aggregate demand and aggregate supply. Explain why this is true.

4. What is one benefit to businesses when the government budget is in surplus?

5. How might interest paid on the national debt lead to greater income inequality?

6. Is the absolute size of the national debt or the national debt as a percent of GDP the best measure of its importance to our economy? Explain.

Apply the Concepts

7. One argument often heard against using fiscal policy to tame the business cycle is that the lags associated with getting a fiscal policy implemented are so long that when the program is finally passed and implemented, the business cycle has moved on to the next phase and the new program may not be necessary and may even be potentially destabilizing at that point. Does this argument seem reasonable? What counterarguments can you make in support of using fiscal policy?

8. As mandatory federal spending becomes increasingly a larger share of the budget, should we worry that the economic stabilization aspects of fiscal policy are becoming so limited as to be ineffective?

9. Our current personal income tax system is progressive: Income tax rates rise with rising incomes and are lower for low-income individuals. Some policymakers have favored a "flat tax" as a replacement for our modestly progressive income tax system. Most exemptions and deductions would be eliminated, and a single low tax rate would be applied to personal income. Would such a change in the tax laws alter the automatic stabilization characteristics of the personal income tax?

10. In 1962 in a speech before the Economic Club of New York, President Kennedy argued that " . . . it is a paradoxical truth that taxes are too high today and tax revenues are too low—and the soundest way to raise revenues in the long run is to cut rates now." Is President Kennedy's argument consistent with supply-side economics? Why or why not?

11. A balanced budget amendment to the Constitution requiring Congress to balance the budget every year is introduced in Congress every so often. What sort of problems would the passage of such an amendment introduce for policymakers and the economy? What would be the benefit of the passage of such an amendment?

12. If the economy (gross domestic product) is growing faster than the growth of the national debt held by the public (both domestic and foreign), how does that affect the ability of the government to manage the national debt? What arguments can you make to rebut the common assertion that the national debt is bankrupting the country?

In the News

13. The last two of elections have seen more states and municipalities passing ballot measures legalizing some forms of soft drugs such as marijuana for medicinal or recreational purposes ("Marijuana Legalization Wins Majority Support in Poll," *The Los Angeles Times*, April 4, 2013). Previously, sales of such drugs took place in the informal or underground economy, where taxes are avoided and crime runs high. What would be some fiscal policy justifications for legalizing soft drugs?

14. In June of 2009, *The Economist* discussed the ability to manage a country's debt:

    Arithmetically, a government's debt burden is sustainable if it can pay the interest without borrowing more. Otherwise the government will eventually fall into a debt trap, borrowing ever more just to service earlier debt.

    What kind of problems might cause a country to fall into a debt trap as described above? What policies enacted today could reduce the probability of falling into a debt trap?

Solving Problems

15. Suppose a small economy has two income tax rates: 15% for all income up to $50,000 and 30% for any income earned above $50,000. Suppose that prior to the recession, the economy had five workers earning the following salaries:

Amy	$20,000
Betty	$40,000
Charlie	$60,000
Dimitry	$80,000
Evelyn	$100,000

    a. Calculate the total tax revenues paid by the five workers. What percent of total income does this represent?

    b. Now assume that a recession causes each of the five salaries to fall by 25%. Given the lower salaries, what would be the total tax revenues paid by the five workers? What percent of total income does this represent?

    c. Explain how this progressive tax structure acts as an automatic stabilizer.

16. Suppose an economy has a national debt of $10 billion, and the average interest rate on this debt is currently 3%. Its GDP is $20 billion. What percentage of this economy's GDP is spent on interest payments on its debt? Suppose that next year one of two events occurs: (1) GDP and interest rates stay the same, but the economy adds $2 billion to its national debt, (2) GDP and the national debt stays the same, but interest rates increase to 4%. Which of these two events would increase the interest rate burden of the national debt more? Show your calculations.

USING THE NUMBERS

17. According to By the Numbers, what percent of total national debt and foreign held debt is held by China? How about OPEC nations? What does this suggest about the relative importance of U.S. relations with China and OPEC nations?

18. According to By the Numbers, in which year between 1990 and 2012 did the United States have the biggest budget surplus and what was that value? In which year did it have the biggest budget deficit and what was that value?

Checkpoint: Fiscal Policy and Aggregate Demand

Although the money would have hit the economy sooner, a significant portion of the proceeds would have been saved or used to pay existing bills, potentially limiting the stimulative impact of *added* spending. The other benefit of the infrastructure package is that by being spread out over several years, it won't just be a big jolt to the economy that ends as fast as it began. Thus, the impact on employment and business planning was smoother.

Checkpoint: Fiscal Policy and Aggregate Supply

Supply-side economics focuses on providing incentives for individuals to work and for businesses to invest, and therefore advocate lower tax rates. The reduction in the individual, corporate, and capital gains taxes would each be consistent with supply-side economics. However, if a portion of these tax savings is offset through higher consumption taxes, this would not be consistent with supply-side economics because such a tax would discourage consumption and negatively affect business and investment outlook.

Checkpoint: Implementing Fiscal Policy

The president would favor policies that could be implemented quickly, such as "shovel ready" infrastructure projects that have already been approved, the expansion of unemployment benefits which can take effect immediately, or tax cuts that can be applied in the current tax year. The president would not favor policies that require a new law to be passed, as such policies may take years before being implemented.

Checkpoint: Financing the Federal Government

The federal government must satisfy its mandatory spending requirements, including Social Security, unless it passes a law to reform such spending. Also, the federal government must pay for national defense, including wars, which are unpredictable. Also unpredictable are expenses related to natural disasters, which require action by various federal agencies. Because of the combination of various mandatory spending programs and unpredictable discretionary spending requirements, the federal government would find it difficult in practice to enforce a balanced budget amendment.

Checkpoint: Why Is the Public Debt So Important?

If China and Japan reduce their holdings of U.S. debt, interest rates would need to rise in order to attract other investors to purchase these bonds. Rising interest rates would adversely affect consumption and investment in the United States, potentially slowing economic growth.

Saving, Investment, and the Financial System

22

After studying this chapter you should be able to:

- Describe the functions of money.

- Define the money supply according to M1 and M2.

- Use the loanable funds model to show how savers and borrowers are brought together.

- Explain how the financial system makes it easier for savers and borrowers.

- Describe the relationship between the price of bonds and interest rates.

- Describe the tradeoff between risk and return and how that influences the return on investment for bonds and stocks.

- Explain how the compounding effect makes debt and savings much larger over time.

- Understand how retirement savings programs function and the benefits they provide.

On August 13, 2004, the city of Athens, Greece, celebrated as the Summer Olympic Games returned to its historic homeland, the place where Olympic athletes nearly 3,000 years ago competed on the same land as athletes in the current games were about to compete.

Indeed, it was a proud moment for Greeks, and for their government, which had borrowed billions of dollars to build new stadiums, a modern transportation network, and a new airport, and to give the city a significant facelift to showcase its growing economic prosperity to a worldwide audience. Where did the government get this money? It borrowed money from banks and from the public by issuing bonds, and there was plenty of money to be borrowed. The Olympics were the ultimate showpiece of a nation on the rise.

No one could have predicted on that proud day that in less than a decade, that same city would be engulfed in financial turmoil, with large government debt, protests and riots, and a country in complete despair. What happened in Greece that led to such a dramatic reversal in fortune?

In short, it was a breakdown of financial institutions caused by a global recession along with uncontrolled government debt that caused long-term interest rates to skyrocket from 4% in 2009 to 27% in 2012. With interest rates so high, the ability to borrow, whether by the government, by businesses, or by consumers, became prohibitive, leading to a drastic decline in consumption and investment and subsequently a rise in unemployment. Clearly, Greece headed into a vicious cycle that threatened not only the country but the stability of the euro, the currency it shares with much of Europe.

Although Greece was not the only country to have undergone a financial crisis, it was one of the most difficult cases because of the challenges that affected the banks, bond market, and stock market—which form what we refer to as a country's financial system. The financial system plays an important role in the health of the macroeconomy, and when the system breaks down, as it did in Greece, the economy often goes down with it.

Up to now, we have looked at how the federal government tries to manage the macroeconomy through fiscal policy, by using government taxation and spending. We now want to look at the government's other policy approach—monetary policy. To analyze how government uses monetary policy to influence the macroeconomy, we must first lay the foundation by examining the financial system and the role of money, which is the subject of this chapter. Building on this foundation, in the following chapters we will see how financial institutions create money and how the government enacts policies that encourage the financial system to do things that mitigate fluctuations in the macroeconomy.

We begin by looking at money: what it is and what it does. We then examine why people save and why firms borrow. We next show how the market for loanable funds brings these two groups together, and how the financial system makes this process easier and better for all. The chapter concludes with an overview of financial tools that illustrates the importance of financial literacy in our everyday lives.

After completing this chapter, you will have gained an appreciation of how the financial system allows us to buy and sell items in an efficient manner, using forms of payment that have become increasingly electronic in the digital age. But more than that, the financial system allows all economic transactions to function efficiently by channeling funds from savers to borrowers. Without it, countries would essentially break down, as did Greece, affecting millions of lives.

BY THE NUMBERS

The Financial System and Its Sheer Size and Scope

The U.S. financial system consists of commercial banks, money markets, and government institutions that issue and manage money. It is connected with the global financial system, consisting of banks and financial institutions around the world that influence one another.

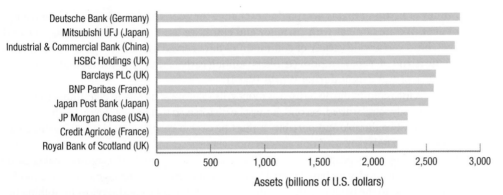

Bank assets (billions of U.S. dollars):
- Deutsche Bank (Germany)
- Mitsubishi UFJ (Japan)
- Industrial & Commercial Bank (China)
- HSBC Holdings (UK)
- Barclays PLC (UK)
- BNP Paribas (France)
- Japan Post Bank (Japan)
- JP Morgan Chase (USA)
- Credit Agricole (France)
- Royal Bank of Scotland (UK)

Assets (billions of U.S. dollars): 0, 500, 1,000, 1,500, 2,000, 2,500, 3,000

The largest banks in the world measured in billions of U.S. dollars in assets as of December 2012. Twenty years ago, Japanese and American banks dominated the top ten. In 2012, just two Japanese banks and one American bank remained in the top ten.

The world's most circulated currencies:

Glyn Thomas/Alamy

ANDREW WALTERS/Alamy

Hans-Joachim Schneider/Alamy

Glyn Thomas/Alamy

Glyn Thomas/Alamy

Glyn Thomas/Alamy

imagebroker/Alamy

INTERFOTO/Alamy

The eight most circulated currencies in the world. Although more printed euro bills exist in circulation than U.S. dollars, the U.S. dollar remains by far the largest reserve "hard" currency held around the world (mostly in electronic form).

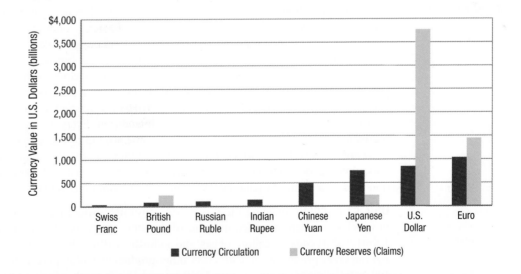

Currency Value in U.S. Dollars (billions): $4,000, 3,500, 3,000, 2,500, 2,000, 1,500, 1,000, 500, 0

Currencies: Swiss Franc, British Pound, Russian Ruble, Indian Rupee, Chinese Yuan, Japanese Yen, U.S. Dollar, Euro

■ Currency Circulation   ■ Currency Reserves (Claims)

$20,800,000,000,000

Total Value of U.S. Retirement Accounts as of April 2013.

$807,600,000,000

Total Credit Card Debt in the United States as of April 2013.

→ What Is Money?

Anything can serve as money, from the cowrie shells of the Maldives to the huge stone disks used on the Pacific islands of Yap. And now, it seems, in this electronic age nothing can serve as money too.

NIALL FERGUSON, *THE ASCENT OF MONEY*

money Anything that is accepted in exchange for goods and services or for the payment of debt.

Money is anything that is accepted in exchange for goods and services or for the payment of debt. We are familiar with currency and coins; we use them nearly every day. Over the ages, however, a wide variety of commodities have served as money—giant circular stones on the island of Yap, wampum (trinkets) among early Native Americans, and cigarettes in prisoner-of-war camps during World War II.

First, for a commodity to be used as money, its value must be easy to determine. Therefore, it must be easily standardized. Second, it must be divisible, so that people can make change. Third, money must be durable and portable. It must be easy to carry (so much for the giant circular stones, which today are used only for ceremonial purposes in Yap.) Fourth, a commodity must be accepted by many people as money if it is to act as money. As Niall Ferguson makes clear in the quote above, today we have "virtual" money, in the sense that digital money is moved from our employer to the bank and then to the retailer for our goods and services in nothing but a series of electronic transactions. This is really the ultimate in **fiat money:** money without any intrinsic value but accepted as money because the government has made it legal tender.

fiat money Money without intrinsic value but nonetheless accepted as money because the government has decreed it to be money.

Money is so important that nearly every society has invented some form of money for its use. We begin our examination of money by looking at its functions.

The Functions of Money

Money has three primary functions in our economic system: as a medium of exchange, as a measure of value (unit of account), and as a store of value. These uses make money unique among commodities.

barter The direct exchange of goods and services for other goods and services.

Medium of Exchange Let us start with a primitive economy. There is no money. To survive, you have to produce everything yourself: food, clothing, housing. It is a fact that few of us can do all of these tasks equally well. Each one of us is better off specializing, providing those goods and services we are more efficient at supplying. Say I specialize in dairy products and you specialize in blacksmithing. We can engage in **barter,** which is the direct exchange of goods and services. I can give you gallons of milk if you make me a pot for cooking. A *double coincidence of wants* occurs if, in a barter economy, I find someone who not only has something I want, but who also wants something I have. What happens if you, the blacksmith, are willing to make the cooking pot for me but want clothing in return? Then I have to search out someone who is willing to give me clothing in exchange for milk; I will then give you the clothing in exchange for the cooking pot. You can see that this system quickly becomes complicated. This is why barter is restricted to primitive economies.

Consider what happens when money is introduced. Everyone can spend their time producing goods and services, rather than running around trying to match up exchanges. Everyone can sell their products for money, and then can use this money to buy cooking pots, clothing, or whatever else they want. Thus, money's first and most important function is as a **medium of exchange.** Without money, economies remain primitive.

medium of exchange Money is a medium of exchange because goods and services are sold for money, then the money is used to purchase other goods and services.

Unit of Account Imagine the difficulties consumers would have in a barter economy in which every item is valued in terms of the other products offered—12 eggs are worth 1 shirt, 1 shirt equals 3 gallons of gas, and so forth. A 10-product economy of this sort, assigning every product a value for every other product, would require 45 different prices. A 100-good economy would require 4,950 prices.[1] This is another reason why only the most primitive economies use barter.

---

[1] The formula for determining the number of prices needed when N goods are in an economy is $[N(N-1)]/2$. Thus, for 10 goods, the result is $[10(10-1)]/2 = 90/2 = 45$.

Once again, money is able to solve a problem inherent to the barter economy. It reduces the number of prices consumers need to know to the number of products on the market; a 100-good economy will have 100 prices. Thus, money is a **unit of account,** or a measure of value. Dollar prices give us a yardstick for measuring and comparing the values of a wide variety of goods and services.

Admittedly, ascribing a dollar value to some things, such as human life, love, and clean air, can be difficult. Still, courts, businesses, and government agencies manage to do so every day. For example, if someone dies and the court determines this death was due to negligence, the court tries to determine the value of the life to the person's survivors—not a pleasant task, but one that has to be undertaken. Without a monetary standard, such valuations would be not just difficult, but impossible.

Store of Value Using cherry tomatoes as a medium of exchange and unit of account might be handy, except that they have the bad habit of rotting. Money lasts, enabling people to save the money they earn today and use it to buy the goods and services they want tomorrow. Thus, money is a **store of value.** It is true that money is not unique in preserving its value. Many other commodities, including stocks, bonds, real estate, art, and jewelry are used to store wealth for future purchases. Indeed, some of these assets may rise in value, and therefore might be preferred to money as a store of value. Why, then, use money as a store of wealth at all?

The answer is that every other type of asset must be converted into money if it is to be spent or used to pay debts. Converting other assets into cash involves transaction costs, and for some assets, these costs are significant. An asset's **liquidity** is determined by how fast, easily, and reliably it can be converted into cash.

Money is the most liquid asset because, as the medium of exchange, it requires no conversion. Stocks and bonds are also liquid, but they do require some time and often a commission fee to convert into cash. Prices in stock and bond markets fluctuate, causing the real value of these assets to be uncertain. Real estate requires considerable time to liquidate, with transaction costs that often approach 10% of a property's value.

Money differs from many other commodities in that its value does not deteriorate in the absence of inflation. When price levels do rise, however, the value of money falls: If prices double, the value of money is cut in half. In times of inflation, most people are unwilling to hold much of their wealth in money. If hyperinflation hits, money will quickly become worthless as the economy reverts to barter.

Money, then, is crucial for a well-functioning modern economy. All of its three primary functions are important: medium of exchange, unit of account, and store of value.

unit of account Money provides a yardstick for measuring and comparing the values of a wide variety of goods and services. It eliminates the problem of double coincidence of wants associated with barter.

store of value The function that enables people to save the money they earn today and use it to buy the goods and services they want tomorrow.

liquidity How quickly, easily, and reliably an asset can be converted into cash.

In Australia, when people use "plastic money," they aren't referring to just credit and debit cards, but also to polymer-based banknotes that are much more durable than paper currency (no tears or handwritten scribbles on these notes). Today, over thirty countries use at least one denomination of currency literally "made of plastic."

Defining the Money Supply

How much money is there in the U.S. economy? One of the tasks assigned to the Federal Reserve System (the Fed), the central bank of the United States, is that of measuring our money supply. The Fed has developed several different measures of monetary aggregates, which it continually updates to reflect the innovative new financial instruments our financial system is constantly developing. The monetary aggregates the Fed uses most frequently are M1, the narrowest measure of money, and M2, a broader measure. An even broader measure called M3 was published until 2006 when the Fed decided the additional benefit of this measure was not worth the costs of collecting the data.

ISSUE

Where Did All the Dollar Coins Go?

When is the last time you received a presidential, Sacagawea, or Susan B. Anthony dollar as change for some purchase you made? For most of us, the answer approaches never. Why don't dollar coins circulate in the United States?

The benefits of a dollar coin are clear: Coins last much longer than dollar bills, which tend to deteriorate within 18 months. Annual savings from minting coins over printing dollar bills runs to $500 million a year, because although production costs are higher, coins circulate longer than bills, making total costs lower for coins. This is why the U.S. Treasury has tried twice recently to introduce dollar coins.

Introducing dollar coins faces several serious hurdles. First, several industries will incur added costs. For example, banks will have additional costs to sort, store, and wrap the coins, and vending machines must be altered to accept the coins. The coins cannot be too big, or the public will reject them as being too heavy; this was the problem with the Kennedy half-dollar and the silver dollars of the past. But a small dollar, roughly the size of a quarter, generates confusion—Is it a dollar or a quarter?—and again has been rejected by the public.

Other countries have successfully introduced dollar coins: Canada has $1 and $2 coins and Britain has £1 and £2 coins. All are circulated widely. What do we need to do to launch a successful dollar coin in the United States?

After reviewing the experiences of other countries, the General Accounting Office (GAO) concluded that a successful introduction of a dollar coin would require that the government develop a substantial awareness campaign (a heavy, extended advertising campaign) to overcome initial public resistance. Second, the Treasury must mint sufficient coins for acceptance by the public. Third, and probably most important, the dollar bill would have to be eliminated. A key element in the general acceptance of the dollar coins in Canada was that the populace had no choice: The dollar bill was removed from circulation at the same time the dollar coin was introduced.

This being the case, why did the U.S. Treasury try once again in 2007 to launch a dollar coin without removing the paper dollar from circulation? These new coins were based on the popularity of the state quarters program, through which each year five state quarters were released into general circulation. The new dollar coins

United States Mint image

released in 2007 were engraved with an image of George Washington, and eventually over the years all of the presidents would be represented. But despite the government's efforts to market the new coins, the public again shunned their use, forcing the government to store millions of uncirculated dollar coins in vaults. In December 2011, the government suspended their production, announcing that only a limited number of each presidential dollar coin would be produced to satisfy the demand from coin collectors.

Given the potential annual savings, we will undoubtedly see further attempts at introducing a dollar coin in the United States. But until the idea of using dollar coins is accepted by most Americans, the U.S. paper dollar will continue to reign supreme.

More specifically, the Fed defines M1 and M2 as follows:

M1 The narrowest definition of money; includes currency (coins and paper money), traveler's checks, demand deposits (checks), and other accounts that have check-writing or debit capabilities. The most liquid instruments that might serve as money.

M2 A broader definition of money that includes "near monies" that are not as liquid as cash, including deposits in savings accounts, money market accounts, and money market mutual fund accounts.

M1 equals:
- Currency (banknotes and coins)
+ Traveler's checks
+ Demand deposits
+ Other checkable deposits

M2 equals:
- M1
+ Savings deposits
+ Money market deposit accounts
+ Small-denomination (less than $100,000) time deposits
+ Shares in retail money market mutual funds

Narrowly Defined Money: M1 Because money is used mainly as a medium of exchange, when defined most narrowly it includes currency (banknotes and coins), demand deposits (checking accounts), and other accounts that have check-writing capabilities. Currency represents slightly less than half of M1, with banknotes constituting more than 90% of currency;

coins form only a small part of M1. Checking accounts represent the other half of the money supply, narrowly defined. Currently, M1 is equal to roughly $2.5 trillion. It is the most liquid part of the money supply.

Checking accounts can be opened at commercial banks and at a variety of other financial institutions, including credit unions, mutual savings banks, and savings and loan associations. Also, many stock brokerage firms offer checking services on brokerage accounts.

A Broader Definition: M2 A broader definition of money, M2, includes the "near monies": money that cannot be drawn on instantaneously but that is nonetheless accessible. This includes deposits in savings accounts, money market deposit accounts, and money market mutual fund accounts. Many of these accounts have check-writing features similar to demand deposits.

Certificates of deposit (CDs) and other small-denomination time deposits can usually be cashed in at any time, although they often carry penalties for early liquidation. Thus, M2 includes the highly liquid assets in M1 and a variety of accounts that are less liquid, but still easy and inexpensive to access. This broader definition of money brings the current money supply up to over $10 trillion.

When economists speak of "the money supply," they are usually referring to M1, the narrowest definition. Even so, the other measures are sometimes used. The index of leading economic indicators, for instance, uses M2, adjusted for inflation, to gauge the state of the economy. Economists sometimes disagree on which is the better measure of the money supply; although M1 and M2 tend to have similar trends, they have deviated significantly in certain periods. For the remainder of this book, the money supply will be considered to be M1 unless otherwise specified.

The monetary components that make up the money supply serve many purposes. But at its essence, it channels funds from savers to borrowers, an important function of the financial system that barter societies are unable to do. In the next section, we look at a simple model of loanable funds to show how savers and borrowers come together to make moneylending possible and contribute to economic growth.

 CHECKPOINT

WHAT IS MONEY?

- Money is anything accepted in exchange for goods and services and for the payment of debts.

- The functions of money include: a medium of exchange, a unit of account, and a store of value.

- *Liquidity* refers to how fast, easily, and reliably an asset can be converted into cash.

- M1 is currency plus demand deposits plus other checkable deposits.

- M2 is equal to M1 plus savings deposits plus other savings-like deposits.

QUESTION: The U.S. penny, with Abraham Lincoln's image on the front, has been in circulation since 1909. Back then, pennies were inexpensive to produce and could be used to purchase real items. Today, a U.S. penny actually costs the government more than one cent to produce, and it is virtually unusable in any coin-operated machine and impractical to use in stores. How has the role of the penny changed over the past century in terms of its monetary functions (medium of exchange, unit of account, and store of value)?

Answers to the Checkpoint question can be found at the end of this chapter.

The Market for Loanable Funds

The market for loanable funds is a model that describes the financial market for saving and investment. Initially, we will assume that savers deal directly with investors. This simplifies our analysis. We then will bring in financial intermediaries (banks, mutual funds, and other financial institutions) to describe the benefits of a well-functioning financial system.

Supply and Demand for Loanable Funds

Why do people save? Why do they borrow? The first thought might be that people save because they *can* save. Unlike barter economies, money makes saving possible.

People supply funds to the loanable funds market because they do not spend all of their income; they save. There are many reasons why individuals save. People save "for a rainy day": They put away some of their income when times are good to take care of them when times turn bad. Saving behavior is also a cultural phenomenon: Many countries have savings rates far higher than that in the United States.

The reward for not spending today is the *interest* received on savings, enabling people to spend more in the future. Therefore, in the market for loanable funds shown in Figure 1, the quantity of loanable funds is measured on the horizontal axis, and the price of the funds (interest rate) is measured on the vertical axis. In this market, the supply curve represents savers, while the demand curve represents borrowers.

FIGURE 1

The Market for Loanable Funds

This market represents supply and demand for funds. Savers spend less than they earn and supply the excess funds to the market. Borrowers (primarily businesses) have potential profit-making investment opportunities, and this leads to their demand for funds. Equilibrium is at point *e*.

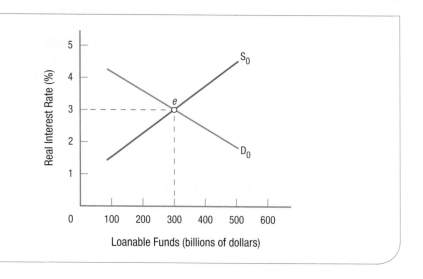

The supply of funds to the loanable funds market, shown as S_0, is positively related to the interest rate. Because interest rates are the price (reward) that savers receive, higher interest rates result in more saving (funds) supplied to the market. This results in an upward sloping supply curve much like other supply curves we studied earlier, and is just another example of people reacting to incentives.

The demand for loanable funds comes from people who want to purchase goods and services, such as taking out a loan to go to college, taking out a mortgage on a house, or who, as entrepreneurs, want to start or expand a business. Firms are borrowers, too. Firms may want to invest in new plants, additional equipment, expanded warehouse facilities, or engage in additional research and development on new products. The specific investment depends on the industry. For firms in the oil industry, it might be for an offshore oil platform or refinery. For a start-up network firm such as ZocDoc, which has a growing number of subscribers but limited financial capital, the loanable funds might be used for another server farm.

Building a new server farm requires a substantial amount of cash, often obtained by borrowing in the loanable funds market.

The demand for loanable funds, shown as D_0 in Figure 1, slopes downward because when the interest rate is high, fewer projects will have a rate of return high enough to justify the investment. A project will be undertaken only if its expected return (its benefit) is higher than the cost of funding the project. When oil prices are high, for example, an oil platform might have a high enough return to justify paying a high interest rate, but the expected returns on a new plane for a small airline may not be. As interest rates fall, more projects become profitable and the amount of funds demanded rises.

Keep in mind that when we refer to interest rates we are referring to *real* interest rates (adjusted for inflation) that reflect the real cost of borrowing and the real return to savers.

The loanable funds market reaches equilibrium in Figure 1 at a 3% real interest rate and $300 billion in funds traded in the market. If for some reason the real interest rate *exceeded* 3%, savers would provide more funds to the market than investors want and interest rates would fall until the market reached point *e*. In a similar way, if interest rates were somehow *below* 3%, investors would want more funds than savers would be willing to provide and, again, the market would push interest rates up to 3% at point *e*. Not surprisingly, this market is similar to the competitive markets for other goods and services we have discussed earlier. When compared to most markets, financial markets are typically more competitive and often reach equilibrium more quickly if something changes in the market. Let's now use this model to analyze various impacts (private and public) on the market for loanable funds.

Just as in other markets, the market for loanable funds is subject to factors that shift the supply or demand for loanable funds. When this occurs, interest rates and the level of saving and investment also change.

Shifts in the Supply of Loanable Funds

A shift in the supply curve of loanable funds occurs when a factor increases or decreases the country's willingness to save (either by private individuals or the public government) at any given interest rate. Changes in economic outlook, incentives to save, income or asset prices, and government deficits can influence savings patterns.

Economic Outlook Suppose households decide to save a larger proportion of their income because they fear job loss in a recession. If households decide to save more, the amount of funds provided to the market at all interest rates will increase, shifting the supply of loanable funds from S_0 to S_1 in Figure 2. Equilibrium will move from point *e* to point *a*, real interest rates will fall, and both saving and investment will rise from $300 billion to $400 billion. Similarly, if a recession ends and people go on a buying spree, savings will fall. In Figure 2, this would be a shift in the supply curve from S_1 to S_0.

Incentives to Save Governments and companies offer various incentives to individuals to save, such as retirement contribution plans and other tax incentives. Adjusting such incentives will change the level of savings accordingly.

Income or Asset Prices As incomes rise, people generally save a larger proportion of their income, all else equal. Asset prices, however, tend to work the other way. As home prices and stock values increase, people *feel* wealthier (without necessarily having more income) and will spend more and save less. The opposite effects occur when incomes fall or asset prices fall.

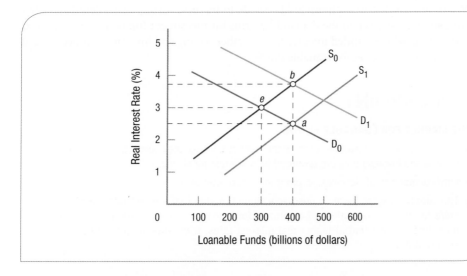

FIGURE 2

Changes in Supply, Demand, and Interest Rates

If savers decide to save more, the supply of funds will grow to S_1. At the new equilibrium, point *a*, interest rates fall and the amount of funds traded rises. Anything that increases the rate of return on investment (investment tax credits or increased demand for the firm's product) will result in the demand for funds increasing and a new equilibrium at point *b*.

Government Deficits The supply of loanable funds includes both private and public saving. When a government runs a budget surplus, additional loanable funds are provided to the market. But when a government incurs a budget deficit, this reduces the supply of loanable funds available to investors and borrowers.

Shifts in the Demand for Loanable Funds

We have seen how changes in savings can shift the supply of loanable funds. Now let's turn our attention to the demand side. Anything that changes the rate of return on potential investment will cause the demand for loanable funds to change. Let's keep saving on the initial supply curve, S_0, in Figure 2.

Investment Tax Incentives Investment tax credits effectively reduce tax payments for firms building new factories or buying new equipment. These laws give firms incentives to invest by increasing their *after-tax* rate of return, and often are created in bad economic times with the expectation of a quick jolt to investment demand.

An increase in investment demand would shift the demand for loanable funds from D_0 to D_1 in Figure 2 and results in both higher real interest rates (3.75%) and higher investment ($400 billion). An increase in business taxes would have the opposite effect on demand.

Technological Advances New technologies that increase productivity or create new products give businesses an incentive to increase production, which often results in plant expansion or the need to build an additional facility, increasing the demand for loanable funds.

Regulations Government regulations tend to influence the level of business investment. When regulations reduce corruption and instill confidence in firms and entrepreneurs, demand for investment will rise. But when regulations impose higher costs or make plant expansion difficult, the demand for investment will fall because the return on investment is reduced.

Product Demand When demand for a firm's product or service increases, the return on investment rises. This increases the demand for loanable funds. The opposite is true when product demand falls.

Business Expectations When business sentiment about the economy rises, firms will tend to increase their investment demand which increases the demand for loanable funds. When business sentiment falls, investment demand decreases and so does demand for loanable funds.

In summary, the market for loanable funds works just like any other market where one can use the familiar tools of supply and demand analysis. The only slight difference is that the price is represented by the real interest rate on loanable funds.

We have seen that when households decide to increase saving, real interest rates fall and investment rises. When the demand by firms for investment funds rises, real interest rates rise along with expanded investment. Together, saving and investment move toward equilibrium in the market for loanable funds.

CHECKPOINT

THE MARKET FOR LOANABLE FUNDS

- Households supply loanable funds to the market because they spend less than their income and because they are rewarded with interest for saving.

- Firms demand funds to invest in profitable opportunities.

- The supply curve of funds is positively sloped; higher real interest rates bring more funds into the market. The demand for loanable funds is negatively sloped, reflecting the fact that at higher real interest rates, fewer investment projects are profitable.

- Any policy that provides additional incentives for households to save will increase the supply of loanable funds, resulting in lower interest rates and greater investment.

- Anything that increases the potential profitability (rate of return) of business investments will increase the demand for loanable funds, resulting in higher interest rates and investment.

QUESTIONS: The economic recession of 2007–2009 brought about many consequences, most notably a fall in business confidence in which firms became reluctant to invest and expand their operations, and an increased fear of job loss among workers. How do these two events affect the supply of savings and the demand for borrowing? What happens to the supply and demand curves found in Figure 2? Once the economy recovers, what is supposed to happen to these curves?

Answers to the Checkpoint questions can be found at the end of this chapter.

→ The Financial System

The previous section discussed how savers and borrowers interact in a market such that those who demand money for various reasons are able to turn to those who have extra money to save. The interest rate is what keeps this market in equilibrium between savers and borrowers. But how does one actually go about saving or borrowing money?

Suppose you have an extra $1,000 that you want to save for the future, and a buddy from your old high school asks you to invest in a new skateboard shop he plans to open on campus. Do you lend your money to him?

That should depend on a number of factors. First, will your friend be paying you interest or a share of his profits? Second, how risky would such an investment be? Is your friend borrowing from you because he can't qualify for a small business loan elsewhere? Third, when will you expect to get your money back? Next year, or just whenever the business makes enough profit to pay you back? Or perhaps never if the shop goes bust.

These are important questions to evaluate before making financial decisions about your money. Often, the time it takes to evaluate proposals such as lending money to your buddy and to everyone else you know looking to borrow money can be significant and costly. For this reason, many individuals instead choose to save by putting money into banks, bonds, and stocks, which together represent the financial system.

Should you invest your money here?

The Bridge Between Savers and Borrowers

The **financial system** is a complex set of institutions that, in the broadest sense, allocates scarce resources (financial capital) from savers, those who are spending less than they earn, to borrowers, those who want to use these resources to invest in potentially profitable projects. Both savers and borrowers can include households, firms, and governments, but our focus is on households as savers and firms as borrowers. As we have seen, savers expect to earn interest on their savings and borrowers expect to pay interest on what they borrow. Households may save for a down payment on a house or a new car, and firms borrow to invest in new plants, equipment, or research and development.

Financial institutions or **financial intermediaries** are the bridge between savers and borrowers. They include, among others, commercial banks, savings and loan associations, credit unions, insurance companies, securities firms (brokerages), and pension funds. The complexity of a country's financial institutions often is a sign of economic efficiency and growth, as these financial firms take savings from savers and loan them to borrowers.

financial system A complex set of institutions, including banks, bond markets, and stock markets, that allocate scarce resources (financial capital) from savers to borrowers.

financial intermediaries Financial firms (banks, mutual funds, insurance companies, etc.) that acquire funds from savers and then lend these funds to borrowers (consumers, firms, and government).

The Roles of Financial Institutions

Financial institutions fulfill three important roles that facilitate the flow of funds to the economy. They (1) reduce information costs, (2) reduce transaction costs, and (3) spread risk by diversifying assets.

Reducing Information Costs Information costs are the expenses associated with gathering information on individual borrowers and evaluating their creditworthiness. Savers (in this case, lenders) would have a difficult time without financial institutions. For example, when deciding whether to lend your buddy money to open his skateboard shop, you might know plenty about your friend's personality and habits, but have few ways to determine if his shop was safe to lend to or was unsound, or even just a fraud. Financial institutions reduce information costs by screening, evaluating, and monitoring firms to see that they are creditworthy and use the borrowed funds loaned in a prudent manner.

Reducing Transaction Costs Transaction costs are those associated with finding, selecting, and negotiating contracts between individual savers and borrowers. Suppose your buddy needs much more than $1,000, and asks all of his friends to lend him money. Trying to set up contracts individually between many lenders and a borrower can be time-consuming and costly, especially if every lender wants to make sure the business is a sound investment. Financial institutions reduce transaction costs by providing standardized financial products, including savings accounts, stocks, bonds, annuities, mortgages, futures, and options. In your case, you and your friends might put your money into a savings account, while your buddy applies for a loan at that bank.

Diversifying Assets to Reduce Risk Firms need funds for long-term investments, but savers want access to their money at a moment's notice and would want their funds invested in a number of diversified projects to reduce risk. In other words, you might not want to put your entire savings into one risky loan. Financial institutions accept funds from savers and pool this money into a portfolio of diversified financial instruments (stocks, bonds, etc.), reducing overall risk and at the same time permitting savers access to their funds when needed. In addition, they can also offer securities with different risk profiles to savers, from relatively safe CDs and savings accounts to more risky domestic and foreign stocks. In so doing, these institutions allow a greater flow of funds between savers and borrowers, greatly increasing the efficiency of investment in the economy.

The role of financial institutions in funneling funds from savers to investors is essential, because the people who save are often not the same people with profitable investment opportunities. Without financial institutions, investment would be a pale version of what we see today, and the economy would be a fraction of its size.

Types of Financial Assets

return on investment The earnings, such as interest or capital gains, that a saver receives for making funds available to others. It is calculated as earnings divided by the amount invested.

Savers have many options when it comes to where to put their money. The primary difference among the many types of financial assets available is the **return on investment (ROI)** one can achieve. A return on investment can be determined by the interest rate earned on savings accounts or CDs, or the capital gains, dividends, and other interest earned from investing in stocks or bonds. The ROI of an asset largely depends on the risk of the asset, with lower risk assets generally earning a lower ROI and higher risk assets earning a higher ROI.

The simplest way to save is to deposit money into a checking or savings account at your local bank. This is also the lowest risk approach to saving, because all savings up to $250,000 per account are insured by the Federal Deposit Insurance Corporation (FDIC) as long as the bank is a member. In its 80-year history, no saver's deposit insured with the FDIC has ever been lost, even when a bank has gone bankrupt.

The advantages of placing savings in banks are clear—savers have easy access to their money (high liquidity) in addition to virtually no risk. The disadvantage is that savings and checking accounts pay very low interest, and in some cases no interest at all.

Thus, in order to increase earnings on savings, savers must either (1) choose financial assets with lower liquidity, or (2) choose assets that carry a higher level of risk. One way to achieve this is to invest in bonds and stocks, to which we now turn our attention.

Savers can invest their funds *directly* in businesses by purchasing a bond or shares of stock from a firm using one of many brokerage firms easily accessible by ordinary individuals. Savers can also invest *indirectly* by providing funds to a financial institution (bank or mutual fund, for example) that channels those funds to borrowers. A share of stock represents partial ownership of a corporation, and its value is determined by the earning capacity of the firm. A bond, on the other hand, represents debt of the corporation. Bonds are typically sold in $1,000 denominations and pay a fixed amount of interest. If you own a bond, you are a creditor of the firm.

Bond Prices and Interest Rates

We examined real interest rates when we described the loanable funds market, and we described several direct and indirect financial instruments such as stocks, savings accounts, and bonds. But most of the loanable funds are in the form of corporate or government *bonds*. As of April 2013, the total value of loans made by U.S. commercial banks was about $7.3 trillion, the total value of the U.S. bond market was about $38 trillion, and the total value of stocks traded in U.S. stock exchanges was about $17 trillion.

Because of the sheer size of the U.S. bond market, economists often look at financial markets from the viewpoint of the supply and demand for bonds. They often consider policy implications by their impact on the price of bonds and the quantity traded. It can be a little confusing because bond prices and interest rates are inversely related—when interest rates go up, bond prices go down, and vice versa. Let's take a quick look at the characteristics of bonds to help you see why interest rates and bond prices move in opposite directions. Understanding this will give you a better understanding of how monetary policy actually works.

To see why bond prices and interest rates are inversely related, we need to analyze bond contracts more closely. A bond is a contract between a seller (the company or government issuing the bond) and a buyer that determines the following:

- Coupon rate of the bond
- Maturity date of the bond
- Face value of the bond

The seller agrees to pay the buyer a fixed rate of interest (the coupon rate) on the face value of the bond (usually $1,000 for a corporate bond, but much larger values for government bonds) until a future fixed date (the maturity date of the bond). For example, if XYZ Company issues a bond with a face value of $1,000 at a coupon rate of 5%, it agrees to pay the bondholder $50 per year until the maturity date of the bond. Note that this $50 payment per year is *fixed* for the life of the bond.

Once a bond is issued, it is subject to the forces of the marketplace. As economic circumstances change, people may be willing to pay more or less for a bond that originally sold for $1,000. The *yield* on a bond is the percentage return earned over the life of the bond. Yields change when bond prices change.

Assume, for instance, that when a $1,000 bond is issued, general interest rates are 5%, so that the bond yields an annual interest payment of $50. For simplicity, let's assume that the bond is a perpetuity bond—that is, the bond has no maturity date. The issuer of the bond has agreed to pay $50 a year *forever* for the use of this money.

Assume that market interest rates rise to 8%. Just how much would the typical investor now be willing to pay for this bond that returns $50 a year? We can approach this intuitively. If we can buy a $1,000 bond now that pays $80 per year, why would we pay $1,000 for a similar bond that pays only $50? Would we pay more or less for the bond that pays $50? If we can get a bond that pays $80 for $1,000, we would pay *less* for a bond paying $50.

There is a simple formula we can use for perpetuity bonds:

$$\text{Yield} = \frac{\text{Interest Payment}}{\text{Price of Bond}}$$

Or rearranging terms:

$$\text{Price of Bond} = \frac{\text{Interest Payment}}{\text{Yield}}$$

The new price of the bond will be $625 ($50 ÷ 0.08 = $625). Clearly, as market interest rates went up, the price of this bond fell. Conversely, if market interest rates were to fall, say, from 5% to 3%, the price of the bond would rise to $1,666.67 ($50 ÷ 0.03 = $1,666.67).

Keep this relationship between interest rates and bond prices in mind when we focus on the tools of monetary policy in the next couple of chapters, for this approach to bond pricing is important to understanding how the government manages the money supply through the purchase and sale of bonds.

Stocks and Investment Returns

An alternative to placing savings into banks or bonds is to purchase shares of stock (also known as equity) in a company. When one buys a share of stock, this share represents one fraction (of the total shares issued) of ownership in the company, and subsequently one vote at shareholder meetings and one share of any dividends (periodic payments to shareholders).

The buying and selling of stock shares occurs in stock exchanges (such as the New York Stock Exchange or NASDAQ). The price of a share of stock is determined by supply and demand just as in any other market, and for every buyer of a share of stock there must be a seller.

Compared to bonds, stocks tend to be riskier investments, because shares, representing partial ownership as opposed to a creditor of a company, become worthless when a company goes bankrupt. Bonds are generally considered safer investments because bondholders are the first to be repaid when businesses face financial trouble. However, stockholders get to share in the company's profits through dividend payments and the increase in share values, which can be substantial when a company succeeds. Both bonds and stocks are less liquid than savings and checking accounts, as both require the asset to be sold and a small commission paid in order to convert the asset into cash.

tradeoff between risk and return The pattern of higher risk assets offering higher average annual returns on investment than lower risk assets.

Which pays more over the long run, bonds or stocks? Given their higher risk, stocks tend to reward investors with a higher average return on investment over the long run, which follows the general rule of the **tradeoff between risk and return.** Riskier assets typically offer a greater return, otherwise investors would not choose to take such risks. With the exception of a few periods during which the stock market dropped considerably (such as the crash in technology stocks from 2000 to 2001 and the stock market crash from late 2007 to early 2009 when many companies went bankrupt or nearly bankrupt), stocks generally trend upward, providing an average return on investment higher than what can be earned through less risky bonds and the least risky savings accounts and CDs, which are FDIC insured.

The complexity of the financial system offers savers and borrowers many opportunities to conduct economic transactions quickly and efficiently. But because the financial system also can be subject to corruption, financial institutions are heavily regulated to ensure the soundness and safety of the financial system and to increase the transparency and information to investors. The agencies regulating financial markets include the Securities and Exchange Commission (SEC), the Federal Reserve System, the FDIC, and another half-dozen or so federal agencies, along with all the state agencies regulating firms in this market.

Although heavily regulated, financial markets are complex environments that are occasionally subjected to meltdowns that can lead the economy into a recession and result in huge losses for the affected firms. When meltdowns occur, the bridge that financial intermediaries bring between savers and lenders can collapse.

CHECKPOINT

THE FINANCIAL SYSTEM

- Financial institutions are financial intermediaries that build a bridge between savers and borrowers.
- Financial institutions reduce transaction costs, information costs, and risk, making financial markets more efficient.
- Efficient financial markets foster growth because they maximize the amount of funds channeled from savers to borrowers.
- Financial assets include savings and checking accounts, certificates of deposit (CDs), bonds, stocks, and mutual funds.
- Bond prices and interest rates are inversely related.

QUESTION: In 2008, voters in California approved the construction of a high-speed rail system connecting Anaheim (near Los Angeles) and San Francisco by 2030, at a cost of over $65 billion. A portion of this cost will be financed by institutions such as Goldman Sachs, an investment banking and securities firm, while a larger portion will be financed by the issuance of bonds to investors and local governments, with the rest financed by private investors who will own shares in the rail system. Explain how financial intermediation is necessary in order to make this project a reality. Why couldn't the state government just pay for it by using tax revenues it collects this year?

Answers to the Checkpoint question can be found at the end of this chapter.

Financial Tools for a Better Future

Now that we have discussed the role of money, the market for loanable funds, and financial intermediaries, we should step back and ask ourselves how we can apply what we have learned to our everyday finances and our future. As a caveat, it is always best to seek financial advice from a trusted professional who has your best interests in mind. This section is meant to introduce you to the basic financial concepts encountered when borrowing and saving money.

Short-Term Borrowing

As a college student, your income is low to nonexistent as you invest (very wisely) in human capital by pursuing a college degree that will increase your earning potential during your working years. That means that in the near term, you will likely accumulate debt in the form of student loans, credit card balances, and car loans. Eventually, a home mortgage might also necessitate more borrowing.

Interest rates on personal debt vary considerably, with small differences leading to substantial payments over the long run, as we will see shortly. Student loans funded by the government typically offer low interest rates in addition to allowing you to defer payments until after you graduate. These loans often provide the lowest cost of borrowing to get you through until your income rises.

The most common short-term loan, however, comes in the form of credit card debt. Credit card companies typically charge a higher interest rate, although on occasion may provide **teaser rates**—offers of low or even zero interest for a limited time on purchases and/or balance transfers. They are called *teasers* because credit card companies hope that you actually *don't* pay off your balance at the end of the offer period. Interest rates after the offer period increase considerably, and often are higher than other borrowing rates. In addition, many credit cards charge balance transfer fees of 3% to 5% of the transferred amount, which means the 0% offer that you enjoy for a limited time is not truly 0%.

Because of the high costs of holding credit card debt, it is generally advisable to:

1. Keep credit card balances to a minimum.
2. Find lower cost borrowing opportunities (such as student loans or bank loans) to keep higher interest credit card balances lower.

teaser rates Promotional low interest rates offered by lenders for a short period of time to attract new customers and to encourage spending.

3. Avoid applying for too many credit cards, because fees can rack up and credit scores can be negatively affected by excessive credit applications.

4. Never miss a minimum payment, for *any amount*, even for a month. Every missed payment remains on credit reports for years, potentially raising costs for future car loans and home mortgages, and even making insurance and certain jobs harder to find.

The Power (or Danger) of Compounding Interest

Interest rates are an important factor in deciding how to go about borrowing, or saving, money. For the most part, we see interest rates as being quite low, typically less than 10%. The exceptions typically are for credit card debt or high-risk lending when the borrower has a greater likelihood of defaulting on the loan.

But even for low interest rates, the effect on long-run payments can be substantial due to the **compounding effect.** Compounding occurs when interest is calculated and added on a periodic (often daily) basis to money borrowed or saved in addition to the interest already charged or earned. Let's use annual terms for simplicity. Suppose you borrow $1,000 at a 10% interest rate. Table 1 shows how compounding interest can add up quickly. After a year, you pay 10% × $1,000 = $100 in interest. Suppose you do not make any payments on the debt. The next year, you pay 10% × $1,100 (the original debt + interest already charged) = $110 in interest.

Plastic surgery for your debt.

Roderick Chen/First Light/Corbis

compounding effect The effect of interest added to existing debt or savings leading to substantial growth in debt or savings over the long run.

TABLE 1	Compounding Interest and Debt		
Year	Starting Value	10% Interest	Ending Value
1	$1,000.00	$100.00	$1,100.00
2	$1,100.00	$110.00	$1,210.00
3	$1,210.00	$121.00	$1,331.00
4	$1,331.00	$133.10	$1,464.10
5	$1,464.10	$146.41	$1,610.51
...	...	...	...
28	$13,109.99	$1,311.00	$14,420.99
29	$14,420.99	$1,442.10	$15,863.09
30	$15,863.09	$1,586.31	$17,449.40

This may not seem like much. But suppose you do not make any payments on the debt for 30 years. Your original $1,000 debt will become $17,449! In fact, in year 30 alone, nearly $1,600 in interest would be added to the debt, more than the original borrowed amount. That is the danger of compounding interest on borrowed debt, and an important reason to seek low interest rates and make adequate payments. The good news, however, is that while compounding works against those with debt, it helps those who save, leading to higher future wealth.

Risk Assessment and Asset Allocation

As you work and accumulate savings, an important question is how to go about putting unspent money into assets that will grow over the years until you eventually need it.

The simplest and most liquid means of saving might be to keep money in cash stashed in a safe place or just letting money sit in a checking or savings account at your local bank.

Although these methods give you the quickest access to your money, they are unlikely to provide much gain in value. Most checking accounts and even savings accounts pay no interest (if they do it's often less than 1% these days). With inflation, when you eventually want to use the money, the purchasing power of that money has decreased. How does one go about choosing an asset that pays higher returns?

An important consideration when choosing the type of investment is assessing your tolerance for risk. Would you be frantic if you see your savings fluctuate up and down each day? Would you instead prefer to see steady growth of your savings? Or would you be willing to accept some volatility, the fact that some investments may fall in value, in exchange for a chance of higher growth over the long term?

Risk tolerance should reflect the type of investment instruments purchased. A less risky portfolio would contain a large portion of savings in assets such as CDs and high-rated bonds, and "blue chip" stocks. A more risky portfolio would contain a greater portion of savings in growth stocks and high-return bonds.

As described in the previous section, a tradeoff between risk and return exists, where riskier assets typically offer a greater average return. This choice between risk and return not only affects one's personal investments, but also affects how one goes about saving for the future and for retirement, which we discuss next.

Saving for the Future: Employer-Based Programs

Upon graduating from college, among the exciting challenges facing the new graduate is seeking a good job and earning a salary that, hopefully, allows for a more comfortable life. But besides earning more money, decisions must be made about how to *save* for the future.

Suppose you find your dream job and begin work. Besides the Social Security (FICA) tax that is taken out of each paycheck to fund retirement benefits, you are asked whether you want to contribute to your employer's retirement program. Do you contribute, and if so, how much? 3%? 6%? More? And once you contribute to an account, in what type of assets do you invest that money? Safe or risky assets, or some combination? The tradeoff between risk and return becomes a very important factor in these decisions.

Let's begin by looking at employer-based savings programs, the most common being the 401(k) (offered by most private and public companies), though similar programs exist for government employees and tax-exempt organizations [such as 403(b)], and for teachers (such as TIAA-CREF).

To Contribute or Not to Contribute? Most retirement savings programs allow (or in some cases, require) employees to contribute a certain percentage of their wage earnings into a retirement account. Many companies will then offer a full or partial match of the contribution up to 3% to 4% of one's salary.

If your employer offers to match savings contributions, this is essentially "free money" that gets added to your savings, dramatically increasing your return as long as you satisfy the **vesting period,** the minimum years of employment required for the employer-paid portion to become permanent in the account, even if you leave the company.

Suppose you contribute $1,000 into the savings program, and your employer matches it with another $1,000. You will have instantly earned a 100% return on your investment as long as the vesting period has been satisfied. Try finding another financial asset that offers this high a return!

Another benefit of 401(k) (or similar) programs is that contributions are tax-deferred, meaning that an employee does not pay income tax on the contributed amount until the money is eventually withdrawn. Why does this matter?

Suppose you earn $75,000 in taxable income. This means you are in the 25% tax bracket for most income earned. Suppose you increase your 401(k) contribution by $1,000. How much does your take-home pay fall? Because you normally would pay 25% in income tax on the $1,000, your take-home pay would fall by only $1,000(1 − 0.25) = $750. Essentially, you give up $750 now to add an additional $1,000 into your retirement account. That is $250 (33%) in extra savings right from the start, on top of the investment earnings on that additional amount over your working life.

vesting period The minimum number of years a worker must be employed before the company's contribution to a retirement account becomes permanent.

A downside of most retirement plans is the restriction on when you can use the savings. The minimum age for withdrawing money from most 401(k) accounts is 59.5 years. Withdrawing money before this age incurs (with few exceptions) a 10% early withdrawal penalty.

In What Assets Should One Invest? Suppose you have decided to contribute to your employer's retirement plan and to take advantage of the employer match and tax benefits. Now you are given online access to your account, where you see myriad options on where to invest your money.

As with all investments, risk assessment is an important consideration when it comes to managing retirement accounts. Most accounts allow you to choose a portfolio of investments ranging from safe assets (such as Treasury bills) to risky assets (such as high-growth stocks). Many financial advisors suggest that you choose a higher risk portfolio in your younger years, then gradually reduce your risk as you approach retirement. Why? Let's use the 2007–2009 stock market crash as an example.

Between October 2007 and March 2009, major stock market indexes fell by nearly 50%. Retirement accounts that were invested fully in stocks fell drastically in value. Suppose you are 60 years old and near retirement. You spent your entire life saving and suddenly see your savings drop by 50%. This could drastically affect your quality of life during retirement. Had you transitioned to safer assets as you aged, your savings would not have dropped as much. But this would not be the case for younger workers, because stock market drops tend to have a smaller impact over the long run; in fact, temporary stock market drops can even *improve* outcomes in the long run, as described in the Issue on the next page.

Other Retirement Savings Tools: Social Security, Pensions, and IRAs

Besides employer-sponsored retirement contribution funds, other programs exist that allow individuals to save for their future. These include Social Security, employer-based pension programs, and individual retirement arrangement (IRA, also known as individual retirement account) programs.

Social Security Social Security is another form of retirement savings that nearly every American participates in from the time they start working as a teenager. The payroll tax (FICA) is 12.4% (of which 6.2% is paid by employees and 6.2% is paid by employers) of wage earnings up to a maximum of $113,700 in 2013. Unlike 401(k) contributions, the money you contribute to FICA is not yours, but rather is used to pay the benefits of those currently collecting Social Security benefits. Benefits are determined by a formula based on one's lifetime contributions.

The minimum age to begin collecting Social Security is 62, though if you wait until age 67, monthly benefits will be greater, and potentially will pay more overall if you live longer. Of course, if you have a family history of shorter lifespans, it might be a good idea to start collecting sooner.

Some have argued that Social Security is unfair to the poor, who generally have lower life expectancies than the rich. If the minimum age for collecting Social Security rises due to a shortfall of funds, those with lower life expectancies might not collect anything (except for a portion that can be bequeathed to a spouse or heir).

pensions A retirement program into which an employer pays a monthly amount to retired employees until they die.

Pension Plans **Pensions** are an alternative to 401(k)-type accounts. Pensions are monthly payments made by your employer from the day you retire until you die, based on the number of years you worked at the company. For example, a person who worked at a company 30 years might receive a pension of $3,000 per month upon retirement for the rest of his or her life, while someone who worked only 10 years might receive $1,000 per month.

Because pension benefits are difficult for companies to predict as people live longer, employers are increasingly switching to fixed-contribution plans such as a 401(k), where employer contributions are made up front. But a few notable jobs retain comfortable

ISSUE

Did the 2007–2009 Stock Market Crash Affect Long-Term Savings?

From October 2007 to March 2009, major U.S. stock market indices (Dow, NASDAQ, and S&P 500) fell by more than 50% from their peaks. Investment savings accounts that took decades to accumulate saw their values drop in half in less than 17 months. The same was true for many retirement accounts, such as 401(k) and IRA accounts, which often are heavily invested in stocks. Indeed, this was a bleak period to follow one's retirement savings, not to mention the equally devastating loss in housing values during this period. Would the drop in stock values create long-term consequences for retirement? The answer may be surprising.

In 2012, many American workers were pleased to find that their retirement accounts had recovered, and in many cases, well surpassed the amounts they had at their previous peaks. How was this possible, given that the stock market had not yet fully recovered?

The answer is that although money invested up to October 2007 suffered a severe decline in value, workers continued to contribute to their retirement plans, and employer-matching added to the new funds. As new money entered retirement plans during the stock market decline, these funds were invested in assets at their new *lower* prices. When stock values recovered, old funds regained their values, while new funds saw healthy gains in value. The following example illustrates two scenarios using hypothetical numbers.

Scenario 1: Stocks fall 50% over the next year, then fully recover three years later

Scenario 2: Stock market stays at the same exact level for the entire four-year period

Description	Scenario 1	Scenario 2
Initial Account Balance:	$100,000	$100,000

Change in Value after Event:
   Scenario 1: 50% fall in stock prices
   Scenario 2: No change in stock prices
	–$50,000	–$0

Account Balance After Event:	$50,000	$100,000
New Contributions Over Four Years:	+$30,000	+$30,000

Earnings on New Contributions:
   Scenario 1: Purchased at an average of 40% below peak prices, resulting in a 67% gain
   Scenario 2: Purchased at original stock prices, with no increase in value
	+$20,000	+$0

Change in Value of Original Contributions:
   Scenario 1: Full recovery in stock prices
   Scenario 2: No change in stock prices
	+$50,000	+$0

Total Value of Account	**$150,000**	**$130,000**

This hypothetical scenario shows that a drop in the stock market may not cause a major problem for retirement savings over the long run *as long as* one continues to work and contribute toward retirement. And the younger the worker, the less of an impact short-term stock market corrections will have, because a smaller balance would be affected by the market drop, while new funds invested at lower prices can earn substantial gains (assuming no withdrawals or loans are made from the account). Unfortunately, some people dumped stocks after they fell, and got conservative with new money. The moral of the story: Don't panic. Slow and steady wins the race.

Sanford/Agliolo/Corbis

pensions: The president of the United States receives a pension of about $200,000 every year after leaving office.

Finally, in addition to personal savings, investments, 401(k) and pensions plans, many individuals choose to save using individual retirement arrangements (IRAs).

Individual Retirement Arrangements (IRAs) Similar to 401(k) programs, traditional IRA programs allow one to save pretax (tax-deferred) dollars up to a certain limit, which, as discussed above, gives an immediate boost to savings compared to posttax dollars. Traditional IRA accounts allow one to invest in a broad range of stocks, bonds, and other assets. The minimum age to withdraw funds without penalty is 59.5 years, and taxes are paid on money withdrawn. (Note that most retirees are in lower tax brackets compared to their tax bracket during their working years.)

An alternative to a traditional IRA is a Roth IRA, which allows posttax dollars to be contributed up to a certain limit each year. Why would one contribute posttax dollars as opposed to pretax dollars? First, with a Roth IRA, money that you contribute (but not the earnings on contributions except in certain circumstances) can be withdrawn anytime without penalty. Second, Roth IRAs do not incur any taxes upon withdrawal after age 59.5, including the interest and capital gains the account accumulates over its life. Thus, while one pays taxes upfront on initial contributions, no taxes are paid on earnings, which can be very substantial with compounding.

Saving for the future is an important financial decision. Fortunately, many programs such as 401(k), Social Security, and IRAs make the process easier.

 CHECKPOINT

FINANCIAL TOOLS FOR A BETTER FUTURE

- Credit cards typically are an expensive way to finance borrowing, even with teaser rates.
- Debt and savings rise rapidly over the long run due to the compounding effect.
- A tradeoff exists between risk and return: The greater the risk, the higher the average return on investment.
- Company-sponsored retirement accounts such as a 401(k) allow employees to contribute pretax dollars and receive matching company contributions.
- Social Security is a program into which current contributors (workers) pay for benefits of the recipients (retirees) by way of a payroll tax on wages.
- Individual retirement arrangements (IRA) are similar to 401(k) programs except that they are not company sponsored and they provide greater investment choices.

QUESTIONS: Suppose Amy is very risk averse with her money, while Jose likes to invest in riskier assets in hopes of a higher return. What type of assets would be best suited for each person? Supposing the tradeoff between risk and return holds true over the next 30 years, how would Amy's savings compare to Jose's given the compounding effect (assuming each saves the same amount)?

Answers to the Checkpoint questions can be found at the end of this chapter.

chapter summary

Section 1: **What Is Money?**

Money is anything that is accepted in exchange for goods and services or for the payments of debts.

Three Primary Functions of Money

1. **Medium of exchange:** Eliminates the double coincidence of wants common to barter.
2. **Unit of account:** Reduces the number of prices needed to just one per good.
3. **Store of value:** Allows people to save now and spend later.

Two Primary Money Supply Measures

M1 = currency (banknotes and coins), traveler's checks, and demand deposits (checking accounts).

M2 = M1 + "near monies" (savings accounts, money market deposit accounts, small-denomination time deposits, and money market mutual fund accounts).

An asset's **liquidity** is determined by how fast, easily, and reliably it can be converted into cash.

Most Liquid

Least Liquid

Section 2: **The Market for Loanable Funds**

The **market for loanable funds** describes the financial market for saving and investment.

Savers provide more funds to the loanable funds market as interest rates increase.

Firms demand more funds for investment opportunities as interest rates fall.

Factors affecting the willingness to save or borrow lead to a change in the market for loanable funds. For example, growing business confidence increases firms' willingness to invest, thus shifting the demand for loanable funds to the right, causing interest rates to rise.

Section 3: **The Financial System**

James Leynse/Corbis

Banks, savings and loans associations, credit unions, insurance companies, securities firms (brokerages), and pension funds are all types of financial intermediaries that take savings from savers and loan the funds to borrowers.

Financial intermediaries accept funds from savers and efficiently channel these to borrowers, reducing transaction and information costs, as well as lowering risk.

A bond is a contract between a seller (government or company) and a buyer. As a general rule, as market interest rates rise, the value of bonds (paying fixed dollars of interest) fall, and vice versa.

How to Calculate the Price of a Perpetuity Bond

Price of Bond = Annual Interest Payment ÷ Yield (%)

Example: If a bond pays $100 per year, and the yield is 6%, the price of the bond is $100 ÷ 0.06 = $1,667.

Section 4: **Financial Tools for a Better Future**

The **compounding effect** is powerful because it causes debt (if no payments are made) and savings to increase dramatically over time.

$10,000 in savings today invested at:

5%: equals $43,219 in 30 years

10%: equals $174,495 in 30 years

$10,000/year saved ($300,000 total over 30 years) invested at:

5%: equals $707,608 in 30 years

10%: equals $1,819,435 in 30 years

Tradeoff Between Risk and Return: The greater the risk involved, the higher the average annual return on investment.

Richard Cano/Getty Images

U.S. Savings Bonds and Treasury securities are among the safest assets in the world. Because of their low risk, the interest rates paid also are very low.

Programs for Retirement Savings

- Employer-sponsored programs
  - Fixed contribution plans, such as 401(k), 403(b), and TIAA-CREF, allow workers to contribute pretax dollars and employers to partially match contributions.
  - **Pensions** are monthly payments made by employers to their retired employees based on length of employment with the company.
- Government-sponsored programs
  - Social Security: Current workers pay benefits of retirees through the payroll tax on wages.
- Other retirement programs
  - IRAs use pretax dollars to fund investments; taxes are paid upon withdrawal after age 59.5.
  - Roth IRAs use after-tax dollars to fund investments. Contributed funds (but not earnings on those contributions) can be withdrawn anytime without penalty, and no taxes are paid on withdrawals (including earnings on investment) after one reaches the age of 59.5.

KEY CONCEPTS

money, p. 578
fiat money, p. 578
barter, p. 578
medium of exchange, p. 578
unit of account, p. 579
store of value, p. 579

liquidity, p. 579
M1, p. 580
M2, p. 580
financial system, p. 585
financial intermediaries, p. 585
return on investment, p. 586

tradeoff between risk and return,
  p. 588
teaser rates, p. 589
compounding effect, p. 590
vesting period, p. 591
pensions, p. 592

QUESTIONS AND PROBLEMS

Check Your Understanding

1. Describe the three functions of money.

2. What is a barter economy? Describe why such an approach is a difficult way for a modern economy to exist.

3. Explain the important difference between M1 and M2.

4. What gives our money its value if there is no gold or silver backing the currency?

5. What happens to savings if the real interest rate goes up? What happens to the demand for borrowing?

6. Explain why bond prices and interest rates are inversely related.

Apply the Concepts

7. List the following assets from most liquid to least liquid: a house (real estate); cash; a one-carat diamond; a savings account; 100 shares of Google stock; a Harley-Davidson motorcycle; a checking account; your old leather jacket.

8. At many game centers (such as Chuck E. Cheese's), it is common for kids to play carnival-type games to win prize tickets, which are then redeemed for a variety of prizes based on the number of tickets earned. In what ways do these prize tickets illustrate the three functions of money?

9. How do recessions affect the market for loanable funds? What happens to the supply of savings? What happens to the demand for borrowing? What is the effect on real interest rates?

10. Most individuals with average wealth choose to save their money using a financial intermediary such as a bank or a mutual fund. However, individuals with greater wealth are more likely to invest in individual stocks or directly in new or existing businesses. Explain why persons of different wealth are likely to show differences in how they save, and how financial intermediaries play a role.

11. Why would it be better to put $1,000 each year into a retirement account than to wait ten years and put in $10,000 all at once? Would it make much of a difference in the long run?

12. Why have pensions become a less common form of retirement benefit offered by companies?

In the News

13. A proposal in the government budget set forth in 2013 placed a limit on the total amount of savings that can be accumulated in tax-preferred retirement accounts to about $3 million (*U.S. News and World Report,* April 10, 2013). The White House has argued that wealthy individuals have accumulated "substantially more than is needed to fund reasonable levels of retirement saving," and that the tax deductions from these excess savings cost the government billions each year. How do these sorts of proposals affect the market for loanable funds?

14. At the trough of the last recession in 2009, major stock market indexes had dropped in half from their peak in 2007. This led many stock analysts to argue that bonds had outperformed stocks and also were safer investments. However, a report published by Morningstar Investment Management titled "Are Bonds Going to Outperform Stocks Over the Long Run? Not Likely" contradicted these analysts by comparing returns on stocks and bonds over periods of more than 40 years, and showing that stock returns easily beat those of bonds. Why would the argument that bonds perform better than stocks lead to a self-fulfilling prophecy if investors sell stocks and buy bonds? Which argument better reflects the theory of the tradeoff between risk and return?

Solving Problems

15. Suppose a small country has the following monies in circulation:

    Cash/currency: $1 million

    Demand deposits: $2 million

    Other checkable deposits: $2 million

    Small-denomination time deposits: $4 million

    Savings deposits: $5 million

    Money market deposit accounts: $5 million

    Calculate the value of M1 and M2 for this country.

16. Suppose you paid $1,000 for a perpetuity bond that pays $40 a year forever to the bondholder. Now suppose that due to aggressive policy by the Fed, general interest rates fall from 4% to 1%. What would be the price of the bond if it continues to pay $40 per year?

⊕ USING THE NUMBERS

17. According to By the Numbers, which bank had the largest amount of assets in 2012, and what was this value? How much in assets did a bank need to reach the top ten largest banks in the world in 2012?

18. According to By the Numbers, how much in U.S. dollars is currently in circulation in the world? How much in U.S. dollars is held in reserves in the world? Describe how these numbers compare to the euro and the Japanese yen.

ANSWERS TO QUESTIONS IN CHECKPOINTS

Checkpoint: What Is Money?

Because the purchasing power of the penny has fallen significantly since its first introduction, its monetary role also has diminished. It still serves as a medium of exchange, though the ease of its use has become so difficult that pennies often are left in coin jars, tip jars, and charity bins as opposed to kept for everyday use. Its function as a unit of account remains, since most prices are still quoted to the nearest penny. And its function as a store of value remains, though it requires a substantial jar of pennies before it is worth the time taking it to a coin exchange machine or to the bank.

Checkpoint: The Market for Loanable Funds

A fall in business confidence would reduce the demand for loanable funds, shifting the demand curve to the left in Figure 2. Meanwhile, increased insecurity about jobs will encourage people to save more, shifting the supply of savings to the right. These shifts create a huge surplus of funds at the original interest rate, and therefore interest rates would fall until a new equilibrium is reached. As the economy recovers, businesses resume their investments and consumers begin spending again, and the demand curve will shift back to the right and the supply curve would shift to the left. Interest rates would trend upwards.

Checkpoint: The Financial System

The high-speed rail system is a multi-year, costly project that is too large to be paid for using taxes from any one year. Even if the state government pays for it using taxes over many years, it still must borrow the money first before paying it back using taxes collected in the future. Therefore, financial intermediation by banks is required. But the rail project will use more than just banks. It also relies heavily on the bond market, relying on investors willing to lend money for a relatively long period of time before being paid back with interest. Lastly, it relies on the equity markets, by selling partial ownership of the new rail system to investors willing to put up billions in hopes of a profitable return in the future once the rail line goes into service.

Checkpoint: Financial Tools for a Better Future

Because Amy is more risk averse with her money, she would choose a low risk portfolio containing safer bonds and stocks, while Jose, being more risk preferring, would invest in growth stocks and high yield bonds. If the tradeoff between risk and return holds, Jose's savings would grow at a higher average annual rate than Amy's. With compounding, Jose's savings over the long run will likely be substantially larger than Amy's. One exception might be if a stock market crash occurs at the end, in which Jose's savings would fall if he didn't reduce the riskiness of his portfolio in the later years. Even so, with the power of compounding, Jose's portfolio would likely be much higher than Amy's even if a stock market crash did occur.

23

Money Creation and the Federal Reserve

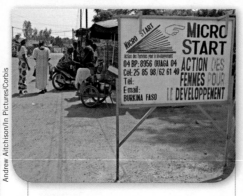

A microloan bank in Burkina Faso.

Afghan women attend a village meeting to make payments on their microloans.

In small towns and villages throughout Central and South Asia, Africa, and Latin America, entrepreneurship is flourishing. These are not your typical high-tech start-ups or research and development centers, but rather primitive small shops selling basic goods and services. Many got their start using a microloan—a small loan (as little as $50) offered by organizations aiming to promote business enterprise among individuals who would not qualify for traditional bank loans.

These small loans and the new businesses they help create (largely by women in the poorest parts of the world) have been credited with bringing more people out of poverty in recent years than direct foreign aid has. How can a tiny loan of $50 have such a positive effect on the economy?

Quite easily, in fact. In Bangladesh, Fatima takes her $50 loan and buys cotton to make a dozen sharis. She sells the sharis at the local outdoor market for a total of $120, of which she uses $50 to pay back her microloan and $70 to buy more cotton to make even more sharis. Only this time, she is debt-free, allowing her to use all her proceeds to expand her business and provide income for her family. Meanwhile, the $50 she paid back will be loaned to another entrepreneur, allowing another small business to get its start.

When a small loan is used to create a new business, jobs are created, which allows people to spend money at other businesses (also likely started from a microloan). The collective power of new businesses, jobs, and increased spending leads to healthy economic growth in the village, and it all started from a single microloan. Now, multiply this one case by the thousands of microloans being made available throughout the developing world, and the effect on reducing poverty is staggering. This example represents a microcosm of the global economy and the money creation process in which financial intermediaries play an important role.

During the recent 2007–2009 recession and ensuing economic recovery, the opposite effect was happening in the United States. The downturn caused a steep decline in consumer and business confidence. Individuals and firms were not in a spending mood as jobs were lost and wages cut, on top of falling home and stock prices.

When consumers are not eager to spend, businesses suffer. Business owners develop a much bleaker view of the economy and reduce investment. Businesses may even cut jobs, jobs that are important for economic recovery.

But this wasn't the entire story. Financial institutions during this time also lacked a willingness to lend to individuals and businesses that actually wanted to spend and invest. Why weren't the banks eager to lend? And why did the lack of lending slow the economic recovery?

The answer is surprisingly similar to the situation of the villager seeking a small loan. When the financial industry was jolted by massive losses in the aftermath of the housing

BY THE NUMBERS

Banks and the Federal Reserve

Banks create money by accepting deposits and making loans. This process is aided by the Federal Reserve, which influences interest rates and sets reserve requirements for member banks.

The monetary base is the sum of all currency in circulation and reserves held by banks. It grew steadily until the recent financial crisis, when aggressive action by the Federal Reserve caused the monetary base to skyrocket.

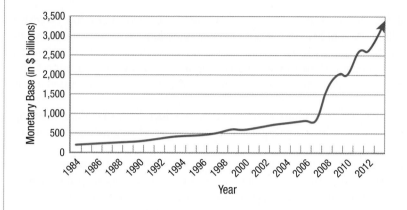

$3,398,930,000,000

Size of the U.S. monetary base in August 2013.

$1,672,936,000,000

Size of the euro monetary base in August 2013.

Bank failures were a major problem during the Great Depression in the 1930s, during the savings and loan crisis of the 1980s, and again during the most recent financial crisis. In fact, more banks failed in 2010 and 2011 than during the 40-year period from 1940 to 1979.

*bar represents a partial decade

In 2008, Washington Mutual became the largest bank to fail in U.S. history.

Individual bank accounts are protected against bank failure by the Federal Deposit Insurance Corporation (FDIC). No FDIC insured deposit has ever been lost in its history.

Year	FDIC Insured Limit
1934	$2,500
1935	$5,000
1950	$10,000
1966	$15,000
1969	$20,000
1974	$40,000
1980	$100,000
2008	$250,000

The Federal Reserve intervened heavily during the 2007–2009 financial crisis by increasing its purchases of underperforming assets from struggling banks. By doing so, the Fed altered its balance sheet in both its overall size and composition of assets.

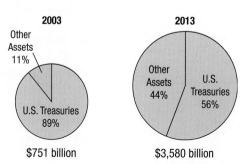

and construction collapse, many banks failed while others barely survived or required government bailouts. The scare faced by banks led to a severe tightening in lending practices (which, ironically, is the type of prudent lending that might have prevented the financial crisis to begin with). The unwillingness of banks to lend money prolonged the period of time necessary for economic recovery.

In times when individuals and businesses are unwilling to spend and banks unwilling to lend, people begin to look elsewhere for help. For the small village, it was the emergence of the microloan organizations. For the U.S. economy, people turned to the government to take action.

The Federal Reserve (or Fed), the central bank of the United States, has extensive power in controlling the supply of money and interest rates, key elements in its arsenal of tools to jumpstart the economy when markets fail to do so on their own. In recent years, the Fed has taken dramatic steps to make borrowing less expensive for consumers and homeowners, and to provide banks with more capital and the confidence to lend to qualified borrowers.

This chapter takes a detailed look at the process by which banks go about creating money, as if out of thin air, by accepting deposits by savers and channeling these funds to borrowers.

We then study in more detail the role of the Federal Reserve, the guarantor of our money and our financial system. We will look at the history of the Fed, what it does with our money, and why it is called "the lender of last resort." Lastly, we analyze the policies and tools the Fed can use to influence the money supply and interest rates.

How Banks Create Money

When most people think of money being created, the typical images conjured up are of large machines at government institutions printing sheets of crisp new banknotes or a large mint hammering out shiny new coins. Although this is indeed money creation in the literal sense, in reality currency represents less than half of the money supply, as we saw in the previous chapter.

Most money that we use every day does not involve cash and coins, but rather a sophisticated system of electronic debits and credits to our bank accounts. For example, unless one works primarily for cash tips or runs a small business where most purchases are paid for in cash, most of us will receive either a physical paycheck or a direct deposit of our wages into our bank accounts. Similarly, when we make purchases, most of us might use a debit or a credit card.

Given that most transactions today do not involve cash, the idea of *creating money* takes on an additional meaning, one in which banks play a very important role in its process.

Creating Money as if Out of Thin Air

Suppose that you run a small tutoring service helping students at your school succeed in (or at least pass) their economics courses. Some of your clients pay you with a personal check at the end of their session, while others give you cash. Let's assume that this month, you received a total of $500 in checks, which you deposit into your checking account, and $500 in cash, which you keep in your safe at home. Your goal is to save as much of your tutoring earnings as possible in order to buy a new car. Aside from the potential forgone interest earnings and the temptation to spend the cash, does it really matter whether you put the cash in the bank or not?

To you, it doesn't. If you need the money, you could just as easily go to an ATM to withdraw the cash as it is to take the cash out of your safe. But for the economy, there is in fact an important difference. The $500 you hold in cash is available to you—and only you—to use. However, the $500 in checks you had deposited in your bank account is money that *others* can use until you eventually need it. How is it that other people can use your money and yet this money is still available for you to take out when you need it?

Banks hold deposits from many customers at one time, and only a small portion is withdrawn on any given day, which the banks service using the reserves they keep on hand. The rest is lent out to borrowers who pay interest to the bank, part of which is then used to pay interest on the deposits the bank holds. The deposits and lending that occur in a bank starts the money creation process.

To illustrate the power of the money creation process, suppose you decide to take your $500 in cash and deposit it into your checking account. Let's analyze how the bank uses this money using a simplified balance sheet comparing a bank's assets (money the bank claims) and liabilities (money the bank owes) called a T-account. Liabilities are shown on the right side of the T-account. When you deposit money into the bank, it becomes a liability for the bank—the bank owes you this money. To balance out this liability, however, the bank now has an asset consisting of the cash from your deposit. Assets are shown on the left side of the T-account.

The following T-account shows an increase in the bank's assets by $500 (the cash that you deposit that the bank now holds). On the right side, the bank's liabilities increase by $500 because it must give back the $500 when you ask for it.

T-Account After Initial Cash Deposit	
Assets	**Liabilities**
+$500 (cash)	+$500 (increase in your checking account balance)

It is important to note that based on this initial transaction, no new money has been created in the economy. Why? Cash and demand deposits (checking accounts) are both components of the money supply measured as M1. By taking cash and converting it into a checkable deposit, there is now $500 less cash in circulation, but $500 more in checkable deposits, for a net change in M1 of 0.

But the process is just beginning. Now that the bank has additional cash reserves, it can lend some of this money to someone else. Suppose another customer at the same bank, Jenna, is running low on cash and needs to take out a small loan of $300 to cover bills that are coming up at the end of the month. How would the bank handle this?

The bank would create a $300 loan for Jenna (which becomes an asset to the bank), and add $300 to Jenna's checking account for her to use when needed. The following shows the new T-account for the bank.

T-Account After Loan to Jenna	
Assets	**Liabilities**
+$500 (cash)	+$500 (increase in your checking account)
+$300 (loan to Jenna)	+$300 (increase in Jenna's checking account)

After the loan to Jenna is made, the total amount of checkable deposits has now increased by $800 based on the initial $500 cash deposit. In other words, the bank has *created* $300 in money, as if out of thin air, simply by making a loan to Jenna.

The obvious question would now be—Couldn't the bank just keep making infinite amounts of loans? The answer is that the bank needs to have enough funds in place should you or Jenna decide to make a withdrawal from your account to pay bills or make purchases. Thus, a bank's ability to make loans is limited to a certain percentage of its total

reserve ratio The percentage of a bank's total deposits that are held in reserves, either as cash in the vault or as deposits at the regional Federal Reserve Bank.

reserve requirement The required ratio of funds that commercial banks and other depository institutions must hold in reserve against deposits.

customer deposits. In other words, a bank must keep some reserves (such as cash) on hand to cover day-to-day withdrawals. The level of reserves a bank holds as a percentage of total deposits is called its **reserve ratio.** Further, the government requires that banks maintain a minimum level of reserves called the **reserve requirement.**

In our example, the reserve ratio is calculated by: reserves/total deposits, which in this case is $500/($500 + $300) = 62.5%. Because most reserve requirements are much lower than this percentage, this bank is considered highly liquid, and may continue to make more loans using your initial cash deposit until the reserve ratio drops down toward its reserve requirement.

Up until now, we have assumed that all loans and deposits occurred at the same bank, but this need not be true. In fact, most money transactions in our economy take place between banks. But the way in which we analyzed loans and deposits and how that leads to money being created does not change. Our example above describes the process of a fractional reserve banking system.

Fractional Reserve Banking System

Banks loan money for consumer purchases and business investments. Assume that you deposit $1,000 into your checking account and the bank then loans this $1,000 to a local business to purchase some machinery. If you were to go to the bank the next day and ask to withdraw your funds, how would the bank pay you? The bank could not pay you if you were its only customer. Banks, however, have many customers, and the chance that all these customers would want to withdraw their money on the same day is small.

Such "runs on the bank" are rare, normally occurring only when banks or a country's currency are in trouble. In the United States, the Federal Deposit Insurance Corporation (FDIC) protects bank deposits (up to $250,000 per account) from bank failure. When a bank gets into financial trouble, the FDIC typically arranges for another (healthy) bank to take over the failing bank, resulting in virtually no interruption of services to the bank's customers. The bank takeover usually occurs late on a Friday and the bank reopens on Monday morning under a new name. Because most accounts are insured, it is business as usual on Monday.

It was the possibility of bank runs that led to the **fractional reserve banking system.** When someone deposits money into a bank account, the bank is required to hold part of this deposit in its vault as cash, or else in an account with the regional Federal Reserve Bank. We will learn more about the Federal Reserve System later in this chapter, but for the moment, let us continue to concentrate on how fractional reserve banking permits banks to create money.

A bit of unusual economic graffiti found on a Venice, California, ATM.

fractional reserve banking system Describes a banking system in which a portion of bank deposits are held as vault cash or in an account with the regional Federal Reserve Bank, while the rest of the deposits are loaned out to generate the money creation process.

excess reserves Reserves held by banks above the legally required amount.

The Money Creation Process Banks create money by lending their **excess reserves,** or reserves above the reserve requirement. When money is loaned out, it eventually is deposited back into the original bank or some other bank. The bank will again hold some of these new deposits as reserves, loaning out the rest. The whole process continues until the entire initial deposit is held as reserves somewhere in the banking system.

Assume that the Federal Reserve sets the reserve requirement at 20%. This means that banks must hold 20% of each deposit as reserves, whether in their vaults or in accounts with the regional Federal Reserve Bank. Now assume that you take $1,000 out of your personal safe at home and take it to Bank A. Bank A puts 20% of your $1,000 into its vault as reserves and loans out the rest. Its T-account balance sheet now reads:

Bank A	
Assets	**Liabilities**
Reserves +$200	Deposits +$1,000
Loans +$800	

As the balance sheet indicates, your $1,000 deposit is now a liability for Bank A. But the bank also has new assets, split between reserves and loans. In each of the transactions that follow, we assume banks become fully *loaned-up,* loaning out all they can and keeping in reserves only the amount required by law.

Assume that Bank A loans out the $800 it has in excess funds to a local gas station, and assume that this money is deposited into Bank B. Bank B's balance sheet now reads:

Bank B	
Assets	**Liabilities**
Reserves +$160	Deposits +$800
Loans +$640	

Bank B, in other words, has new deposits totaling $800. Of this, the bank must put $160 into reserves; the remaining $640 it loans out to a local winery. The winery deposits these funds into its bank, Bank C. This bank's balance sheet shows:

Bank C	
Assets	**Liabilities**
Reserves +$128	Deposits +$640
Loans +$512	

Summing up the balance sheets of the three banks shows that total reserves have grown to $488 ($200 + $160 + $128), loans have reached $1,952 ($800 + $640 + $512), and total deposits are $2,440 ($1,000 + $800 + $640). Your original $1,000 new deposit has caused the money supply to grow.

Banks A, B, C	
Assets	**Liabilities**
Reserves +$488	Deposits +$2,440
Loans +$1,952	

This process continues until the entire $1,000 of the original deposit has been placed in reserves, thus raising total reserves by $1,000. By this point, all the banks together will have loaned out a total of $4,000. A summary balance sheet for all banks reads:

All Banks	
Assets	**Liabilities**
Reserves +$1,000	Deposits +$5,000
Loans +$4,000	

Notice what has happened. Keeping in mind that demand deposits form part of the money supply, your original deposit of $1,000—cash that was injected into the banking system—has turned into $5,000 in deposits, a $4,000 increase in the money supply. Bank reserves, in other words, have gone up by your initial deposit, but beyond this, an added $4,000 has been created. And this was made possible because banks were allowed to loan part of your deposit to consumers and businesses.

The ability of banks to take an initial deposit of cash and turn it into loans and deposits many times over (5 times the initial deposit in our example) demonstrates the power of the banking system to create money. Moreover, the initial deposit of cash need not come from an individual; in fact, much of the money creation that occurs in the economy begins with deposits made by the government, as we will see later in this chapter.

CHECKPOINT

HOW BANKS CREATE MONEY

- Money is created when banks make loans to customers, because these funds are eventually deposited into other banks as checkable deposits.
- The fractional reserve system permits banks to create money through their ability to accept deposits and make loans.
- The reserve ratio is the fraction of total customer deposits held in reserves.
- The reserve requirement is the minimum reserve ratio banks must follow.
- A T-account is a simplified bank balance sheet showing assets (money banks lay claim to) and liabilities (money banks owe).

QUESTIONS: Suppose that you go to your bank and withdraw $1,000 from your checking account to spend on your Spring Break vacation to the Caribbean. If the bank has plenty of cash to pay you without falling below its reserve requirement or changing the amount of loans it has, would the money supply M1 change? Would the money supply change if the bank had planned to loan out its excess reserves?

Answers to the Checkpoint questions can be found at the end of this chapter.

The Money Multiplier and Its Leakages

We have just seen how banks create new money when they make loans using the deposits of their customers. As money gets deposited and loaned out from banks over and over, an initial amount of money can generate new deposits and loans many times over. Just how much money can an initial deposit actually create? We can use the money multiplier to find out.

Bank Reserves and the Money Multiplier

In theory, money creation can be infinite if banks loaned out 100% of all money deposited, and all loaned money found its way back into another bank following their business transactions. But this is highly unlikely due to several factors, the most important being reserves held by the bank.

Because all banks are required to hold a certain percentage of their deposits as reserves in their vault or at their regional Fed bank, the maximum amount of money that can be created is limited by the reserve requirement.

Given a bank's reserve requirement, the *potential* or *maximum* amount the money supply can increase (or decrease) when a dollar of new deposits enter (exit) the system is called the **money multiplier.** The money multiplier is defined as:

$$\text{Money Multiplier} = \frac{1}{\text{Reserve Requirement}}$$

money multiplier Measures the *potential* or *maximum* amount the money supply can increase (or decrease) when a dollar of new deposits enter (exit) the system and is defined as 1 divided by the reserve requirement. The actual money multiplier will be less, because some banks hold excess reserves.

Thus, if the reserve requirement is 20%, as in our example in the previous section, the money multiplier is 1/0.20 = 5. Therefore, an initial deposit of $1,000 will create an additional $4,000 in money for a total of $5,000, a five-fold increase.

The money multiplier is important to economic policy because money can be initially deposited into the banking system in two ways. The first approach, described earlier, is a cash deposit made by a bank customer. The second approach occurs when the government injects new money into the banking system through the power it has to print money.

When the government "prints money," it does not mean it is printing banknotes and spending it at the mall. Instead, the government typically adds reserves electronically to banks in exchange for bonds and other assets. This money did not exist before the Fed created it by just a stroke of a computer key. When these funds are added to bank reserves, that in itself increases the money supply (unlike a customer's cash which is already counted in the money supply). Further, the effect is compounded by the money multiplier. The government therefore possesses tremendous power in influencing the money supply through its ability to print money and via the money multiplier.

But the ability of the government to expand the money supply is subjected to various factors preventing the full money multiplier from taking place. In other words, the money multiplier formula gives us the *potential* money multiplier. The actual money multiplier will be smaller because of leakages from the banking system. How much smaller?

Money Leakages

The potential money multiplier and the actual money multiplier are rarely the same because of money **leakages.** A leakage is money that leaves the money creation process of deposits and loans due to an action taken by a bank, an individual, a business, or a foreign government.

leakages A reduction in the amount of money that is used for lending that reduces the money multiplier. It is caused by banks choosing to hold excess reserves and from individuals, businesses, and foreigners choosing to hold more cash.

Bank Leakages Banks are in the business of making loans. If they don't, they likely will not stay in business for long, especially if all they do is accept deposits and pay interest on those deposits. For any bank, profits come from the interest charged on loans made to borrowers. For this reason, it is generally presumed that banks will be *loaned-up*, or maximize the amount of loans they can make given the reserve requirement.

However, in recent years, many banks chose not to be loaned-up. Instead, banks chose to keep excess reserves, or reserves above the legally required amount. Why would a bank choose not to loan out the maximum amount of money allowed?

The lessons from the last financial crisis point to the answer. The recession caused many loan defaults and foreclosures as workers were laid off or faced wage cuts. Whenever a borrower defaults on a loan, the amount of that loan is removed (written off) from the bank's assets; however, the bank still owes the people whose deposits made those funds available. Banks absorb these losses through the profits they earn from charging interest to those who pay back their loans. If a large number of borrowers default on their loans, the bank risks a **solvency crisis,** when its liabilities exceed its assets. This means that the bank owes more than what is owed to it, increasing the likelihood of bankruptcy.

solvency crisis A situation when a bank's liabilities exceed its assets.

Returning to our earlier example, suppose that Jenna used her $300 loan to pay off her bills (transferring money from her account to her creditor's account) but then defaults on her loan. The bank's balance sheet would now read:

Assets	Liabilities
+$500 (cash)	+$500 (increase in your checking account)
+$300 (loan to Jenna)	+$300 (increase in Jenna's creditor's account)
−$300 (Jenna's default)	−$300 (bank equity)

The difference between assets and liabilities is a bank's equity, or value that is shared by the bank's stockholders. Although equity is not a liability, it appears in the liabilities column because ultimately any gains are distributed to shareholders like a liability. When liabilities exceed assets, as in the case above, the bank has negative equity (shown as −$300 on the right-hand side of the T-account). When this occurs, the bank is insolvent; in other words, it's broke.

To reduce the risk of a solvency problem leading to bankruptcy, banks often hold excess reserves during tough economic times to ensure that they have the ability to absorb a higher rate of defaults. Further, banks also choose to be more cautious about to whom they lend money. The following Issue highlights the striking difference in lending practices before and after the financial crisis, and how it has affected the money multiplier.

When banks choose not to loan all of their excess reserves, the actual money multiplier is reduced because the reduction in loans recirculates less money back through the banking system.

As we saw in the chapter opener, the willingness of banks to lend generates a powerful effect on the economy. We now know that this is due to the money multiplier. However, the lack of lending creates the opposite effect, which makes bank leakages an extremely important obstacle to economic growth.

Leakages by Individuals and Businesses Earlier in the chapter, we saw how holding cash reduces the ability of banks to create money. Why would people choose to hold more cash?

One factor might be the interest rate the bank pays on deposits. If interest rates paid on savings and checking accounts at the bank are near 0, as they has been for much of the past few years, one might choose to hold more savings in cash out of convenience, or make fewer trips to the bank by making larger withdrawals from an ATM. Another factor

ISSUE

Did Tighter Lending Practices Reduce the Money Multiplier?

In 2005, virtually anyone could go into a bank, apply for a home mortgage using a "no-doc" application process that allowed borrowers to state their income without verification (hence their nickname "liar loans"), and obtain a substantially larger loan than what one would normally qualify for. In addition, new mortgage tools such as teaser loans and interest-only loans allowed borrowers to lower their monthly payments (for a few years), allowing one to borrow even more.

During this heyday of easy lending, how did banks fare? Here's a hint: Between mid-2004 and mid-2007, not a single bank in the United States went bankrupt. Life seemed to be good for the banking industry and for borrowers aspiring to buy their dream home. Or was it too good to be true?

In late 2007, the housing industry came crashing down. Borrowers whose teaser rates expired saw their monthly payments double or triple, and many who could no longer afford the pay-

ments could not sell their homes, which had fallen in value. In the end, massive defaults and foreclosures that occurred between 2008 and 2011 led to hundreds of bank failures.

The consequences of the housing crisis led banks to tighten their lending practices severely. Instead of loans that were too easy to get, loans suddenly became too hard to qualify for. Banks now require substantial proof of income and assets, and sometimes even that isn't enough. Some banks now require proof (such as a résumé) that a borrower could easily find another job if she or he lost her or his current one.

The reaction of banks and the tightening of credit created another problem: a large drop in the U.S. money multiplier. The Federal Reserve Bank of St. Louis estimated the money multiplier for the U.S. since 1984, shown in the figure below. The estimates show that the money multiplier has gradually fallen since the 1990s, but fell dramatically between 2008 and 2009, when the money multiplier dropped from 1.7 to less than 1.0.

With a sharp drop in lending, this had the troubling effect of diminished economic activity as banks tightened their lending practices. When the money multiplier drops this much, the ability of the Fed to use its tools effectively decreases. But this doesn't mean that the Fed stops working; instead, the Fed compensated for the low money multiplier by injecting even more money into the banking system, dramatically increasing the monetary base (currency in circulation + reserves).

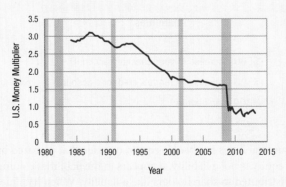

might be a general rise in fear about the financial system. Despite the existence of the FDIC, when banks are in trouble, people begin to believe that their money is less safe in banks and start to hold more cash.

When individuals choose to keep money in cash rather than deposit it in a bank, a leakage in the money supply occurs because that money is not available to be loaned to someone else. The cycle of lending and saving that would be generated from that money comes to a halt, and the actual money multiplier is reduced.

Individuals are not the only ones to hold cash. Most businesses conduct a portion of their transactions using cash. Therefore, at any one time, a business will be holding a certain fraction of its money in cash rather than in a bank. The percentage of cash holdings varies by business, but regardless represents a leakage in the money supply. As businesses hold more cash, as do individuals, this diminishes their deposits, thus reducing the actual money multiplier.

The Effect of Foreign Currency Holdings Most Americans are accustomed to using debit and credit cards for daily transactions, reducing the need to hold cash. Yet, surprisingly, the U.S. government continues to print billions of new U.S. dollars each year. If Americans generally are holding smaller amounts of cash, who then is holding all of these dollars?

The answer is foreign consumers, businesses, and governments. Because of the relative stability of the U.S. dollar, many countries hold U.S. dollars in reserves in order to provide support to their own currencies. Some countries, such as El Salvador and Ecuador, have abandoned their own currency altogether, choosing to use the U.S. dollar as their only legal form of currency. The prominent role that the U.S. dollar plays as the world's most popular reserve currency causes the majority of U.S. dollars (about two-thirds, in fact) to be held outside of the United States. Because of the sheer volume of U.S. currency being held as cash throughout the world, this has the effect of reducing the actual money multiplier relative to its potential. But keep in mind that this is not necessarily a bad thing. A popular currency allows the U.S. government to print more without worrying about a significant decrease in its value relative to other currencies.

What Is the Actual Money Multiplier in the Economy?

Given the leakages described earlier, economists have studied and estimated the actual value of the money multiplier that ultimately influences economic growth. What they have found is that leakages in the U.S. economy tend to be large, due to significant cash holdings by foreigners and banks' unwillingness to lend when the perceived risks of default are high.

To study the effect of leakages on the actual money multiplier, it is useful to modify our original money multiplier formula (1/Reserve Requirement) by adding the bank and cash leakages to the formula to create a *leakage-adjusted money multiplier.*

A leakage-adjusted money multiplier takes into account the required reserve requirement along with excess reserves held by banks and cash held by individuals, businesses, and foreigners. Higher values of these components translate to greater leakages and therefore a lower actual money multiplier.

For example, suppose that the reserve requirement is 20% but the existence of leakages doubles the percentage held in reserves and cash to 40%. These money leakages cause the money multiplier to drop from 5 (1/0.20) to 2.5 (1/0.40), a significant reduction in money creation in the economy.

Empirical data has shown that money leakages tend to increase during economic recessions, when banks are more reluctant to lend and people are more likely to hold cash. We will see in the next chapter that the resulting decrease in the money multiplier adds to the challenges of using monetary policy to pull the economy out of a recession.

During the 2007–2009 recession, the money multiplier fell precipitously from 1.7 to less than 1. A money multiplier of less than 1 means that fewer loans were being made than the new money introduced into the economy. This is very important because actions by the government to increase the money supply result in less bang for the buck when the money multiplier is smaller. Such an effect renders monetary policy much more challenging.

Eric Chiang

Got jars of coins? Coins represent a cash leakage. Businesses such as Coinstar convert coins into banknotes or gift cards that are more likely to be spent, helping to bring money back into the banking system.

The fact that banks can create money by making loans represents a great deal of power. This power is mitigated by leakages and their effect on the actual money multiplier. Government can encourage this money creation process by injecting banks with new money. The question then becomes, How do they go about doing this? Once we understand how the government, meaning the Fed, creates money, we can then go on in the next chapter to discuss the short- and long-run results of this monetary policy.

The institution charged with overseeing the money supply and creating money out of thin air is the Federal Reserve System. Let us turn to a brief survey of the Federal Reserve System. Here we consider how it is organized, what purposes it serves, and what functions it has. The next chapter takes a closer look at the Fed in action.

CHECKPOINT

THE MONEY MULTIPLIER AND ITS LEAKAGES

- The potential money multiplier is equal to 1 divided by the reserve requirement. This is the maximum value for the multiplier.

- Money leakages are caused by banks choosing to hold excess reserves and by individuals, businesses, and foreigners holding a portion of their funds in cash rather than depositing it in a bank. Leakages reduce the money multiplier.

- The leakage-adjusted money multiplier takes leakages into account and provides a more realistic estimate of the money multiplier in the economy.

QUESTIONS: In the following table, calculate the potential money multiplier for each of the following reserve requirements if banks fully loan out all of their excess reserves. If banks were not required to hold any reserves, how big could the money multiplier potentially be? Is this a realistic money multiplier? Why or why not?

Reserve Requirement	Potential Money Multiplier
50%	
33.3%	
25%	
20%	
10%	

Answers to the Checkpoint questions can be found at the end of this chapter.

The Federal Reserve System

Federal Reserve System The central bank of the United States.

The **Federal Reserve System** is the central bank of the United States. It controls an immense power to create money in the economy.

Early in U.S. history, banks were private and chartered by the states. In the 1800s and early 1900s, bank panics were common. After an unusually severe banking crisis in 1907, Congress established the National Monetary Commission. This commission proposed one central bank with sweeping powers. But a powerful national bank became a political issue in the elections of 1912, and the commission's proposals gave way to a compromise that is today's Federal Reserve System.

The Federal Reserve Act of 1913 was a compromise between competing proposals for a huge central bank and for no central bank at all. The act declared that the Fed is "to provide for the establishment of Federal Reserve Banks, to furnish an elastic currency, to afford means of rediscounting commercial paper, to establish a more effective supervision of banking in the United States, and for other purposes."

Since 1913, other acts have further clarified and supplemented the original act, expanding the Fed's mission. These acts include the Employment Act of 1946, the International Banking Act of 1978, the Full Employment and Balanced Growth Act of 1978, the Depository Institutions Deregulation and Monetary Control Act of 1980, and the Federal Deposit Insurance Corporation Improvement Act of 1991.

The original Federal Reserve Act, the Employment Act of 1946, and the Full Employment and Balanced Growth Act of 1978 all mandate national economic objectives. These acts require the Fed to promote economic growth accompanied by full employment, stable prices, and moderate long-term interest rates. As we will see in the next chapter, meeting all of these objectives at once has often proved difficult.

The Federal Reserve is considered to be an independent central bank, in that its actions are not subject to executive branch control. The entire Federal Reserve System is, however, subject to oversight from Congress. The Constitution invests Congress with the power to coin money and set its value, and the Federal Reserve Act delegated this power to the Fed, subject to Congressional oversight. Though several presidents have disagreed with Fed policy over the years, the Fed has always managed to maintain its independence from the executive branch.

Experience in this country and abroad suggests that independent central banks are better at fighting inflation than are politically controlled banks. The main reason is that an independent central bank is less likely to be influenced by short-term political pressures to engage in excessive expansionary monetary policy to hasten a recovery.

The Structure of the Federal Reserve

The Federal Reserve Act of 1913 passed by Congress led to the establishment of *regional* banks governed by a central authority. The intent was to provide the Fed with a broad perspective on the economy, with the regional Federal Reserve Banks contributing economic analysis from all parts of the nation, while still investing a central authority with the power to carry out a national monetary policy.

The Fed is composed of a central governing agency, the Board of Governors, located in Washington, D.C., and twelve regional Federal Reserve Banks in major cities around the nation. Figure 1 shows the twelve Fed districts and their bank locations.

The Board of Governors The Fed's Board of Governors consists of seven members who are appointed by the president and confirmed by the Senate. Board members serve terms of 14 years, after which they cannot be reappointed. Appointments to the Board are staggered such that one term expires on January 31 of every even-numbered year. The chairman and the vice chairman of the Board must already be Board members;

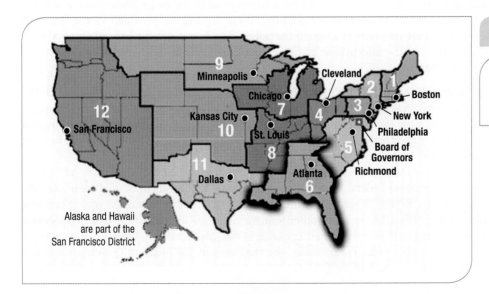

FIGURE 1

Regional Federal Reserve Districts
The twelve regional Federal Reserve districts and their bank locations.

they are appointed to their leadership positions by the president, subject to Senate confirmation, for terms of four years. The Board of Governors' staff of nearly 2,000 helps the Fed carry out its responsibilities for monetary policy, and banking and consumer credit regulation.

Federal Reserve Banks Twelve Federal Reserve Banks and their branches perform a variety of functions, including providing a nationwide payments system, distributing coins and currency, regulating and supervising member banks, and serving as the banker for the U.S. Treasury. Table 1 lists all regional banks and their main locations. Each regional bank has a number and letter associated with it. If you look at your money, you will see that all U.S. currency bears the designation of the regional bank where it was first issued, as shown in Table 1.

TABLE 1	Federal Reserve Regional Banks	
Number	**Bank**	**Letter**
1	Boston	A
2	New York	B
3	Philadelphia	C
4	Cleveland	D
5	Richmond	E
6	Atlanta	F
7	Chicago	G
8	St. Louis	H
9	Minneapolis	I
10	Kansas City	J
11	Dallas	K
12	San Francisco	L

Each regional bank also provides the Federal Reserve System and the Board of Governors with information on economic conditions in its home region. Eight times a year this information is compiled into a report—called the Beige Book—that details the economic conditions around the country. These reports are provided to the Board of Governors first, and later released to the public. The Board and the Federal Open Market Committee use the information the Beige Book contains to determine the course of the nation's monetary policy.

Federal Open Market Committee The **Federal Open Market Committee (FOMC)** oversees open market operations, the main tool of monetary policy. Open market operations involve the buying and selling of government securities. How these open market operations influence reserves available to banks and other thrift institutions will become clear shortly.

The FOMC is composed of the seven members of the Board of Governors and five of the twelve regional Federal Reserve Bank presidents. The president of the Federal Reserve Bank of New York is a permanent member because actual open market operations take place at the New York Fed. The other four members are appointed for rotating one-year terms. All regional presidents participate in FOMC deliberations, but only those serving on the committee vote. Traditionally, the chairman of the Board of Governors has also served as the chairman of the FOMC.

Federal Open Market Committee (FOMC) A twelve-member committee that is composed of members of the Board of Governors of the Fed and selected presidents of the regional Federal Reserve Banks. It oversees open market operations (the buying and selling of government securities), the main tool of monetary policy.

The Fed as Lender of Last Resort The essence of banking, as we have seen, is that banks take in short-term deposits (liabilities) and make long-term, often illiquid, loans (assets). This puts banks in the unique position of facing extraordinary withdrawals when people panic and all want their money at the same time. Banks typically do not have sufficient reserves to stem a full-fledged financial panic. They cannot turn these long-term loans into cash. During a panic, banks would be forced to dump the securities or loans onto the market at a deep discount (or "take a haircut" in modern parlance), potentially forcing them into insolvency. Lending to banks during financial panics—being a lender of last resort—is a principal reason for the existence of central banks.

The value of the Fed's ability to provide loans during a financial crisis stood out during the financial panic in late 2008. The Fed extended credit where none was available. As markets collapse during financial panics, banks become reluctant to lend out money to businesses and to other banks that need cash in an emergency. This is when the Fed steps in.

In just a few months, the Fed extended more than $2 trillion in loans to banks and other financial institutions, and by doing so changed the allocation of assets in its balance sheet in ways not seen since it was created in 1913. Specifically, instead of holding primarily government treasury securities, in late 2008 the Fed was holding more bank assets (such as mortgage-backed securities) than treasury securities.

Had the Fed and its lender of last resort capability not been available, the 2007–2009 recession would have been much deeper and could possibly have resulted in another depression. The ability of the Fed to make loans and inject the banking system with new money allows the fractional banking process to work and prevents the economy from facing a much worse financial crisis.

 CHECKPOINT

THE FEDERAL RESERVE SYSTEM

- The Federal Reserve System is the central bank of the United States.
- The Federal Reserve is structured around twelve regional banks and a central governing agency, the Board of Governors.
- The Federal Open Market Committee (FOMC) oversees open market operations for the Federal Reserve.
- The Federal Reserve serves as the lender of last resort, stepping in to loan money to banks that are facing cash emergency shortages.

QUESTION: If a large portion of a bank's customers want their money back at the same time and other banks won't lend to it, what can the Federal Reserve do to prevent a run on the bank?

Answers to the Checkpoint question can be found at the end of this chapter.

The Federal Reserve at Work: Tools, Targets, and Policy Lags

With an ability to alter the money supply, both directly and indirectly through the money multiplier, the Federal Reserve has remarkable powers to conduct monetary policy, its primary role. And because it acts independently of political parties, the Fed is able to set monetary policy with remarkable efficiency, especially compared to fiscal policy, which involves the ever common wrangling between political parties in Congress and the president. For this reason, monetary policy is often looked at as a way to provide quicker remedies to economic conditions facing the country.

But how is monetary policy actually carried out? Quite remarkably, the Federal Reserve uses just three primary tools for conducting monetary policy:

- **Reserve requirements**—The required ratio of funds that commercial banks and other depository institutions must hold in reserve against deposits.
- **The discount rate**—The interest rate the Federal Reserve charges commercial banks and other depository institutions to borrow reserves from a regional Federal Reserve Bank.
- **Open market operations**—The buying and selling on the open market of U.S. government securities, such as Treasury bills and bonds, to adjust reserves in the banking system.

Reserve Requirements

The Federal Reserve Act specifies that the Fed must establish reserve requirements for all banks and other depository institutions. As we have seen, this law gives rise to a fractional reserve system that enables banks to create new money, expanding demand deposits through loans. The potential expansion depends on the money multiplier, which in turn depends on the reserve requirement. By altering the reserve ratio, the Fed can alter reserves in the system and alter the supply of money in the economy.

Banks hold two types of reserves: required reserves and excess reserves above what they are required to hold. Roughly 15,000 depository institutions, ranging from banks to thrift institutions, are bound by the Fed's reserve requirements. Reserves are kept as vault cash or in accounts with the regional Federal Reserve Bank. These accounts not only help satisfy reserve requirements, but are also used to clear many financial transactions.

Banks are assessed a penalty if their accounts with the Fed are overdrawn at the end of the day. Given the unpredictability of the volume of transactions that may clear a bank's account on a given day, most banks choose to maintain excess reserves.

At the end of the day, banks and other depository institutions can loan one another reserves or trade reserves in the federal funds market. One bank's surplus of reserves can become loans to another institution, earning interest (the **federal funds rate**). A change in the federal funds rate reflects changes in the market demand and supply of excess reserves.

federal funds rate The interest rate financial institutions charge each other for overnight loans used as reserves.

In 2008, the Fed changed its long-standing law of not paying interest on reserves. The new law allowed banks to earn interest on the reserves it deposits at the Fed. This law changed the incentives faced by banks by reducing the opportunity cost of choosing not to lend. In other words, in tough economic times, banks may choose to forgo making loans (especially risky ones) in favor of earning interest on their excess reserves deposited at the Fed. As we saw in the previous section, when banks hold more excess reserves, the money multiplier falls.

By raising or lowering the reserve requirement, the Fed can add reserves to the system or squeeze reserves from it, thereby altering the supply of money. Yet, changing the reserve requirement is almost like doing surgery with a bread knife; the impact is so massive and imprecise that the Fed rarely uses this tool.

Discount Rate

discount rate The interest rate the Federal Reserve charges commercial banks and other depository institutions to borrow reserves from a regional Federal Reserve Bank.

The **discount rate** is the rate regional Federal Reserve Banks charge depository institutions for short-term loans to shore up their reserves. The discount window also serves as a backup source of liquidity for individual depository institutions.

The Fed extends discount rate credit to banks and other depository institutions typically for overnight balancing of reserves. The rate charged is roughly 1 percentage point higher than the FOMC's target federal funds rate. However, most banks avoid using the discount window out of fear that it might arouse suspicion by both their customers and by the Fed that they are facing financial trouble.

But during the banking crisis that started in 2007, the government was more interested in banks making prudent decisions than avoiding the stigma of borrowing from the Fed. To encourage banks to use the discount window when needed, in August 2007 the rate was lowered to 0.5 percentage point above the federal funds rate. As noted earlier, the federal funds rate is the interest rate that banks and other financial institutions with excess reserves charge other banks for overnight loans to help them shore up their reserves. As we will see in the following, this is an important target for Federal Reserve policy.

Neither the discount rate nor the reserve requirement, however, gives the Fed as much power to implement monetary policy as open market operations. Open market operations allow the Fed to alter the supply of money and system reserves by buying and selling government securities.

Open Market Operations

When one private financial institution buys a government security from another, funds are redistributed in the economy; the transaction does not change the amount of reserves in the economy. When the Fed buys a government security, however, it pays some private financial institution for this bond; therefore, it adds to aggregate reserves by putting new money into the financial system.

Open market operations are powerful because of the dollar-for-dollar change in reserves that comes from buying or selling government securities. When the FOMC buys a $100,000 bond, $100,000 of new reserves is instantly put into the banking system. These new reserves have the potential to expand the money supply as banks make loans.

Open market operations are the most important of the Fed's tools. When the Fed decides on a policy objective, the volume of bonds being traded in open market operations to achieve that objective can be staggering. With the bond market valued in the trillions, it requires billions of dollars in bond transactions in order for the FOMC to push the federal funds rate toward its target.

open market operations The buying and selling of U.S. government securities, such as Treasury bills and bonds, to adjust reserves in the banking system.

The Federal Funds Target The target federal funds rate is the Fed's primary approach to monetary policy. As we will see in the next chapter, targeting the federal funds rate through open market operations gives the Fed an ability to influence the price level and output in the economy, a very powerful effect. The FOMC meetings result in a decision on the target federal funds rate, which is announced at the end of the meeting. Keep in mind that the federal funds rate is not something that the Fed directly controls. Banks lend overnight reserves to each other in this market, and the forces of supply and demand set the interest rate.

The Fed uses open market operations to adjust reserves and thus change nominal interest rates with the goal of nudging the federal funds rate toward the Fed's target. When the Fed buys bonds, its demand raises the price of bonds, lowering nominal interest rates in the market. The opposite occurs when the Fed sells bonds and adds to the market supply of bonds for sale, lowering prices and raising the nominal interest rate. The Fed has actually been pretty good at keeping the federal funds rate near the target, as Figure 2 illustrates.

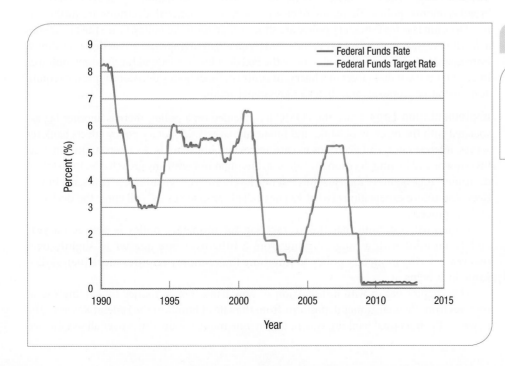

FIGURE 2

The Federal Funds Rate and Target Federal Funds Rate

In the last two decades, the Fed has been very successful at hitting its federal funds target rate.

In summary, typically the Fed sets a target for the federal funds rate and then uses open market operations to manipulate reserves to alter the money supply. Changing the money supply alters market interest rates to bring the federal funds rate in line with the Fed's target. Open market purchases increase reserves, reducing the need for banks to borrow, lowering the federal funds rate, and vice versa for open market sales. The key thing to note here is that the Fed does not directly control the money supply: It proceeds indirectly, though it has been very successful in meeting its goals.

Monetary Policy Lags

Although the Fed has a remarkable ability to use tools that have important impacts on interest rates, bank reserves, and the money supply, they can still take time to have an effect on the economy. Like fiscal policy, monetary policy is subject to four major lags: information, recognition, decision, and implementation. The combination of these lags can make monetary policy difficult for the Fed. Not only does the Fed face a moving bull's-eye in terms of its economic targets, but often it can be difficult for the Fed to know when its own policies will take effect and what their effect will be.

Information Lags We discussed information lags when we discussed fiscal policy lags: Economic data are available only after a lag of one to three months. Therefore, when an economic event takes place, changes may ripple throughout the economy for up to three months before monetary authorities begin to see changes in their data. Many economic measures published by the government, moreover, are subject to future revision. It is not uncommon for these revisions to be so significant as to render the original number meaningless. Thus, it might take the Fed several quarters to identify a changing trend in prices or output clearly.

Recognition Lags Simply seeing a decline in a variable in one month or quarter does not necessarily mean that a change in policy is warranted. Data revisions upward and downward are common. In the normal course of events, for instance, unemployment rates can fluctuate by small amounts, as can GDP. A quarter-percent decline in the rate of growth of GDP does not necessarily signal the beginning of a recession, although it could. Nor does a quarter-percent increase in GDP mean that the economy has reached the bottom of a recession; double-dip recessions are always a possibility. Because of this recognition lag, policymakers are often unable to recognize problems when they first develop.

Decision Lags The Federal Reserve Board meets roughly on a monthly basis to determine broad economic policy. Therefore, once a problem is recognized, decisions are forthcoming. Decision lags for monetary policy are shorter than for fiscal policy. Once the Fed makes a decision to, say, avert a recession, the FOMC can begin to implement that decision almost immediately. As Figure 2 illustrates, once the Fed decides on a federal funds target, nominal interest rates track that target in a hurry. In contrast, fiscal policy decisions typically require administrative proposals and then Congressional action.

Implementation Lags Once the FOMC has decided on a policy, there is another lag associated with the reaction of banks and financial markets. Monetary policy affects bank reserves, interest rates, and decisions by businesses and households. As interest rates change, investment and buying decisions are altered, but often not with any great haste. Investment decisions hinge on more than just interest rate levels. Rules, regulations, permits, tax incentives, and future expectations (what Keynes called "animal spirits") all enter the decision-making process.

Economists estimate that the average lag for monetary policy is between a year and 18 months, with a range varying from a little over one quarter to slightly over two years. Using monetary policy to fine-tune the economy requires more than skill—some luck helps.

This chapter began with a discussion of how banks create money by lending excess reserves from their customer deposits or from the sale of bonds to the Federal Reserve. The power of the fractional banking system to generate money many times over allows the Fed

ISSUE

What Can the Fed Do When Interest Rates Reach 0%?

At the height of the 2007–2009 recession, the Federal Reserve used aggressive expansionary policy to prevent a much more severe recession or even a depression. The Fed did so by reducing the federal funds rate target, the interest rate that influences almost all other interest rates in the economy. By December 2008, the Federal Reserve had lowered the federal funds rate target to essentially 0%. Yet, the economy was still struggling and needed additional help to prevent a deeper recession. But with interest rates already at 0%, what else could the Fed do?

The Fed developed new ways to expand the money supply without using its regular open market operations. First, it purchased poorly performing assets from banks, such as mortgage-backed securities, in an effort to remove these bad assets from bank balance sheets.

Second, in August 2007 the Fed reduced the difference between the federal funds target rate and the discount rate and used *term auction facilities* to encourage borrowing by banks that typically would not borrow from the Fed out of fear it would signal that the bank was

in trouble. In an effort to reduce this stigma, the Fed essentially auctioned money for banks to borrow, taking interest rate bids from banks. This tool allowed many banks to borrow money at rates lower than the discount rate without facing the consequences from doing so. It also improved bank liquidity, making it easier for banks to lend to individuals and businesses.

Then came the tool often considered to be the last resort to stimulating the economy, *quantitative easing*, or QE. With quantitative easing, the Fed purchased huge amounts of bank debt, mortgage-backed securities, and long-term treasury notes, all with money it created electronically. Between 2008 and 2013, four rounds of quantitative easing (called QE1, QE2, QE3, and QE4, respectively) dramatically increased the Fed's balance sheet and more than doubled the monetary base (currency in circulation plus bank reserves).

It is difficult to quantify the success of the Fed's efforts. Critics of the Fed's actions point to the fact that unemployment remained high and economic growth barely improved years after the

recession ended. But supporters of the Fed argue that had the Fed not taken these actions, the economy might have entered a depression.

In situations such as these, economists often wonder about the *counterfactual*, or what would have happened if the Fed hadn't engaged in these policies. The reality is that we may never know, because once a decision is made, it is not possible to determine what would have happened using another approach. Regardless, the positive signs of an improving economy suggest that whether or not the Fed's actions played a pivotal role, there is no question that the Fed's power in controlling the money supply remains a very powerful tool that influences our lives in many ways.

to wield this power in several ways, mainly by targeting the federal funds rate using open market operations. The next chapter looks more deeply into how the Fed uses its monetary tools to balance its goals of keeping income growing and prices stable.

 CHECKPOINT

THE FEDERAL RESERVE AT WORK: TOOLS, TARGETS, AND POLICY LAGS

- The Fed's tools include altering reserve requirements, changing the discount rate, and open market operations (the buying and selling of government securities).
- The Fed uses open market operations to keep the federal funds rate at target levels.
- The Fed's policies, as with fiscal policy, are subject to information, recognition, decision, and implementation lags. Unlike fiscal policy, the Fed's decision lags tend to be shorter because Fed policies are not subjected to lengthy legislative processes.

QUESTIONS: Of the three tools used by the Fed, open market operations are the most common. Why is the Fed more hesitant about adjusting the reserve requirement and the discount rate? What can go wrong?

Answers to the Checkpoint questions can be found at the end of this chapter.

chapter summary

Section 1: **How Banks Create Money**

Money is created when banks make loans that eventually get deposited back into the system, generating checkable deposits. Part of these deposits are held as new reserves while the rest is again loaned out, creating even more money as it gets deposited back into the system.

$100
$100 deposit

$90
90% loaned out

$10
10% reserve

$81
90% loaned out

$9
10% reserve

In a **fractional reserve banking system,** banks accept deposits and hold only a certain portion in reserves, loaning out the rest.

T-Accounts and Reserve Ratios

A T-account is a simple balance sheet showing a bank's assets (money the bank claims) on the left side and liabilities (money the bank owes) on the right side.

Assets	Liabilities
Cash reserves	Deposits by customers
Loans made	

A bank can continue to make loans as long as its **reserve ratio,** calculated as its reserves as a percentage of its total customer deposits, is equal to or higher than the **reserve requirement.**

Reserve ratio = Reserves/Customer Deposits

Section 2: **The Money Multiplier and Its Leakages**

The **money multiplier** is the maximum amount the money supply can increase (or decrease) when a dollar of new deposits enter (or exit) the system.

Money Multiplier = 1/Reserve Requirement

Examples:

If the reserve requirement is 25%, the money multiplier = 1/0.25 = 4

If the reserve requirement is 15%, the money multiplier = 1/0.15 = 6.67

A **leakage-adjusted money multiplier** takes into account the excess reserves and cash holdings that reduce the loans made and therefore reduces the actual money multiplier.

The actual money multiplier found in the economy is often lower than the potential money multiplier due to **leakages** caused by:

1. Banks choosing to hold excess reserves by not lending out the maximum amount allowed.
2. Individuals and businesses holding money in cash rather than in a bank.

Ocean/Corbis

Stashing cash under the mattress creates a leakage in the money supply because this money cannot be loaned out to another borrower.

Section 3: The Federal Reserve System

Hisham Ibrahim/Corbis

The Fed is composed of a seven-member Board of Governors and twelve regional Federal Reserve Banks. The regional banks and their branches conduct the following services:

1. Provide a nationwide payments system.
2. Distribute coins and currency.
3. Regulate and supervise member banks.
4. Serve as the banker for the U.S. Treasury.

The **Federal Reserve System** is the central bank of the United States. It was established by the Federal Reserve Act of 1913 and is required by law to promote economic growth accompanied by full employment, stable prices, and moderate long-term interest rates.

The Federal Reserve is the Guarantor of the Financial System

Its actions are not subject to executive branch oversight, although the entire Federal Reserve System is subject to oversight by Congress.

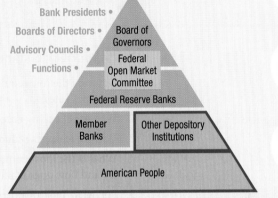

Source: www.doctorhousingbubble.com—taken from the Federal Reserve's website on 'Fed 101'

Section 4: The Federal Reserve at Work: Tools, Targets, and Policy Lags

The Fed uses three major tools to conduct monetary policy:

1. **Reserve requirements:** Establishing the minimum level of reserves banks must hold.
2. **Discount rate:** Setting the interest rate at which banks can borrow from the Fed.
3. **Open market operations:** Buying and selling government securities to target the federal funds rate.

The Fed targets the **federal funds rate,** an interest rate that influences nearly all other interest rates. The federal funds rate has been near 0% for the past few years.

Monetary policy is subject to lags:

- Information lag: The time it takes for economic data to become available.
- Recognition lag: The time before a trend in the data is certain enough to warrant a change in policy.
- Decision lag: The time it takes for the Federal Reserve Board to meet and make policy decisions.
- Implementation lag: The time it takes for banks and financial markets to react to the policy change.

Compared to fiscal policy lags, monetary policy lags, especially decision lags, are often shorter because decisions do not require the cooperation of Congress and the president.

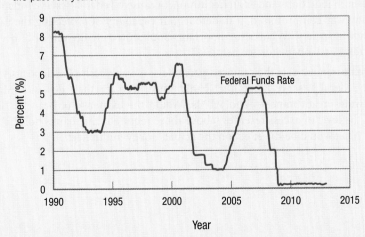

reserve ratio, p. 606
reserve requirement, p. 606
fractional reserve banking system,
  p. 606
excess reserves, p. 606
money multiplier, p. 608

leakages, p. 609
solvency crisis, p. 609
Federal Reserve System, p. 612
Federal Open Market Committee
  (FOMC), p. 614

federal funds rate, p. 616
discount rate, p. 616
open market operations, p. 617

QUESTIONS AND PROBLEMS

Check Your Understanding

1. Describe the role required reserves play in determining how much money the banking system creates.

2. Why are checking accounts (demand deposits) considered a liability to the bank?

3. Why do leakages reduce the money multiplier from its potential?

4. What is the most common tool used by the Federal Reserve to conduct monetary policy and how does it affect interest rates?

5. For what type of borrowing do the federal funds rate and the discount rate apply? Which rate is used in more transactions in the United States?

6. Why are monetary policy lags generally shorter than fiscal policy lags?

Apply the Concepts

7. The U.S. government produces billions of dollars in banknotes and coins for use in everyday transactions. Explain why currency alone does not represent money creation.

8. During an economic boom, banks tend to increase their willingness to lend. How does this trend influence the actual money multiplier?

9. The Federal Deposit Insurance Corporation (FDIC) insures individual bank accounts up to $250,000 per account. Does the existence of this insurance eliminate the need for reserve requirements? Does it essentially prevent "runs" on banks?

10. Many central banks in the world are independent in the sense that they are partially isolated from short-run political considerations and pressures. How is this independence attained? How important is this independence to policymaking at the Federal Reserve?

11. Alan Greenspan, a former chairman of the Fed, noted that "the Federal Reserve has to be independent in its actions and as an institution, because if Federal Reserve independence is in any way compromised, it undercuts our capability of protecting the value of the currency in society." What is so important about protecting the value of the currency? How does Fed independence help?

12. The reserve requirement sets the required percentage of vault cash plus deposits with the regional Federal Reserve Banks that banks must keep for their deposits. Many banks have widespread branches and ATMs. Would the existence of branches and ATMs affect the level of excess reserves (above those required) that banks hold? Why or why not? What would be the effect on the actual money multiplier?

In the News

13. Eric Keetch offered an interesting anecdote in the *Financial Times* (August 12, 2009):

    In a sleepy European holiday resort town in a depressed economy and therefore no visitors, there is great excitement when a wealthy Russian guest appears in the local hotel reception, announces that he intends to stay for an extended period and places a €100 note on the counter as surety while he demands to be shown the available rooms.

    While he is being shown the room, the hotelier takes the €100 note round to his butcher, who is pressing for payment.

    The butcher in turn pays his wholesaler who, in turn, pays his farmer supplier.

    The farmer takes the note round to his favorite "good time girl" to whom he owes €100 for services rendered. She, in turn, rushes round to the hotel to settle her bill for rooms provided on credit.

    In the meantime, the Russian returns to the lobby, announces that no rooms are satisfactory, takes back his €100 note and leaves, never to be seen again.

    No new money has been introduced into the local economy, but everyone's debts have been settled.

    What's going on here? In the end, no new money was introduced into the town, but all debts were paid. Is the money multiplier infinite? How do you explain what has happened? Did local GDP increase as a result of all debts being paid?

14. In the December 12, 2012, FOMC meeting, Chairman Ben Bernanke announced the start of QE4, a new round of quantitative easing in which the Fed committed to purchasing $85 billion in assets per month in order to keep the federal funds rate near 0% until the unemployment rate fell below 6.5%. The effect of this announcement resulted in the expectation that interest rates will remain extremely low until at least mid-2015. How might this announcement affect the lives of ordinary individuals, and what impact might this have on the economy?

Solving Problems

15. Assume that First Purity Bank begins with the balance sheet below and is fully loaned-up. Answer the questions that follow.

First Purity Bank	
Assets	**Liabilities**
Reserves +$700,000	Deposits +$2,000,000
Loans +$1,300,000	

    a. What is the reserve requirement equal to?
    b. If the bank receives a new deposit of $1 million and the bank wants to remain fully loaned-up, how much of this new deposit will the bank loan out?
    c. When the new deposit to First Purity Bank works itself through the entire banking system (assume all banks keep fully loaned-up), by how much will total deposits, total loans, and total reserves increase?
    d. What is the potential money multiplier equal to in this case?

16. Suppose that the leakage-adjusted money multiplier can be calculated using a modification of our money multiplier formula:

    1/(Reserve Requirement + Excess Reserves + Cash Holdings)

    where each component in the denominator is expressed as a percentage.

Suppose that the reserve requirement is 25%, but banks on average hold an additional 10% of their deposits as excess reserves. Further, assume that individuals and businesses choose to hold 15% of their borrowed funds in cash. Compare the potential money multiplier with the leakage-adjusted money multiplier. Does the existence of leakages make a significant impact on the ability to conduct monetary policy? Explain why or why not.

USING THE NUMBERS

17. According to By the Numbers, by what percentage did the U.S. monetary base increase from 2000 to 2005? How about from 2005 to 2010? Why are the percentage changes in these periods so different?

18. According to By the Numbers, during which decade did the greatest number of U.S. banks fail? During which decade did the second most number of U.S. banks fail?

ANSWERS TO QUESTIONS IN CHECKPOINTS

Checkpoint: How Banks Create Money

The basic transaction reduces your checking account by $1,000 and adds $1,000 in cash for your trip. Therefore, M1 would stay the same because cash and checkable deposits are both part of M1. However, by withdrawing $1,000 from the bank, this is $1,000 that could be loaned out by the bank and lead to money creation. Therefore, by making the withdrawal, the money supply would drop if the bank had planned to loan out its excess reserves.

Checkpoint: The Money Multiplier and Its Leakages

The potential money multipliers are 2, 3, 4, 5, and 10. If banks were not required to hold any reserves, the money multiplier could theoretically be infinite if every bank loans out 100% of its deposits. This is not likely, however, due to the many leakages that occur in the banking system. Banks would still hold some reserves, just as banks currently hold excess reserves over the required limit. No bank would want to be at the mercy of a small bank run that would lead to its ruin, therefore it would keep some currency reserves on hand. Also, individuals, businesses, and foreign governments may choose to hold a portion of their assets in cash, preventing this money from working its way through the money creation process.

Checkpoint: The Federal Reserve System

The Federal Reserve has the power to loan the struggling bank the money to satisfy the withdrawals. However, such withdrawals are often a sign of deeper underlying troubles at the bank. The question then becomes whether to let the bank fail and be taken over by a solvent bank, or to help it survive by purchasing bad debts and recapitalizing the bank.

Checkpoint: The Federal Reserve at Work: Tools, Targets, and Policy Lags

Open market operations are very effective because they influence virtually all interest rates. Reducing the reserve requirement can certainly boost lending; however, reducing it too much can put banks at risk should defaults rise. Adjusting the discount rate is generally less effective, because bank customers and investors often view borrowing from the discount window as a warning sign of the bank's deteriorating financial health. As a result, the Fed typically keeps the discount rate at a fixed level slightly above the federal funds rate.

24

Monetary Policy

An investor awaiting the Fed statement.

After studying this chapter you should be able to:

- Explain the goals of monetary policy and how the Fed uses expansionary and contractionary policies to achieve them.

- Describe how monetary policy affects interest rates and aggregate demand, and subsequently prices and output.

- Describe the equation of exchange and its implications for monetary policy in the long run.

- Contrast classical long-run monetary theory concerning the effectiveness of monetary policy in the short run with the explanations of the Keynesians and monetarists.

- Describe why the Fed targets price stability in the long run and inflation rates and output in the short run.

- Determine the effectiveness of monetary policy when demand or supply shocks occur.

- Describe the controversy over whether the Fed should have discretion or be governed by simple monetary rules.

- Describe the federal funds target, the Taylor rule, and how they are used in modern monetary policymaking.

- Explain why some policymakers have questioned the role of the Fed after it used extraordinary powers in response to the financial crisis of 2008.

- Discuss the monetary policy challenges faced by the Fed and the European Central Bank following the last recession and the Eurozone crisis.

Information received since the Federal Open Market Committee met in January suggests a return to moderate economic growth following a pause late last year. Labor market conditions have shown signs of improvement in recent months but the unemployment rate remains elevated . . . . To support continued progress towards maximum employment and price stability, the Committee expects that a highly accommodative stance of monetary policy will remain appropriate for a considerable time . . . .

—EXCERPT FROM THE FOMC STATEMENT OF MARCH 20, 2013

A t 2:00 P.M. on an ordinary weekday afternoon, the Federal Reserve (Fed) concludes its meeting of the Federal Open Market Committee, and just 15 minutes later, at 2:15 P.M. a meeting statement is released. To the twelve voting members of this committee, which meets about every six weeks, it's just another day on the job. But this is not your ordinary everyday job.

On Wall Street, millions of investors, physically present at a stock exchange or virtually present via their online brokerage accounts, anxiously await this Fed statement. Corporate executives, just coming back from lunch, immediately search their news app for the latest statement release.

Government policymakers in Ecuador and El Salvador tune in to the news to hear the Fed statement because it affects their countries' interest rates and their currency, which in fact is *the U.S. dollar*. And markets in the rest of the world await the Fed statement to determine how their own economies will be affected.

Indeed, in a matter of minutes after the release of the Fed statement, the twelve members of the Federal Open Market Committee will have affected the lives of hundreds of millions of people. How do such ordinary people carry such tremendous power?

The Federal Open Market Committee is the body within the Federal Reserve that controls U.S. monetary policy. Their economic policy decisions affect not only the U.S. economy but the entire world economy.

Although not every Fed meeting statement produces a dramatic flurry of reactions, the ability of the Fed to exert powerful policy action in times of economic fluctuation makes its meeting statement the most dissected piece of economic news in the world. Even the most slightly nuanced wording of the statement can generate mass market activity as people attempt to predict how the Fed will act not only today, but in months and years ahead.

This chapter studies the remarkable influence the Fed has to alter the macroeconomy using the tools that form the basis of monetary policy. The Federal Reserve Act mandates that the Fed implement monetary policies that will promote economic growth accompanied by high employment, stable prices, and moderate long-term interest rates. In the previous chapter, we saw how the Federal Reserve System is organized and described the three monetary policy tools the Fed uses, which are setting reserve requirements, setting the discount rate, and conducting open market operations. In this chapter, we look at what monetary policy aims to achieve and how the Fed undertakes monetary policy to deal with economic fluctuations.

BY THE NUMBERS

Monetary Policy In Action

Among the tools used by the Federal Reserve to conduct monetary policy are setting the discount rate and conducting open market operations targeting the federal funds rate. The interest rates targeted by the Fed have a profound impact on the entire economy.

The Fed's decisions on the discount and federal funds rate influence other interest rates of concern to consumers and firms. Notice how the average 30-year mortgage rate and the prime rate track the Fed's discount and federal funds rate.

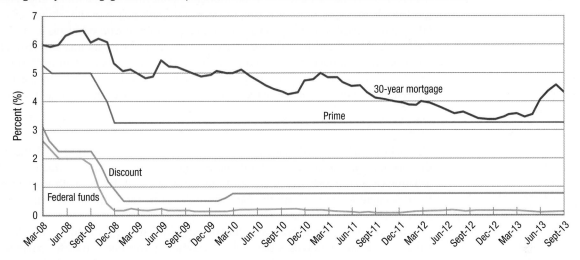

With the federal funds rate near 0%, the Fed used other mechanisms to provide relief to the economy, especially the purchase of mortgage-backed assets from banks and other financial institutions. As of April 2013, the Fed held over $1.2 trillion in non-treasury assets, of which mortgage-backed securities represented almost 90% of this amount.

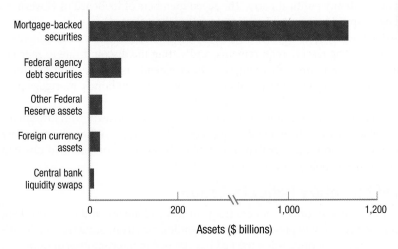

Assets ($ billions)

8,630,731,033
Total number of $100 bills in circulation in April 2013.

As the Fed increased the money supply, other countries have increased their holdings of U.S. dollars, mainly as reserves. Part of this is held in actual banknotes, mostly $100 bills. Where are all these $100 bills?

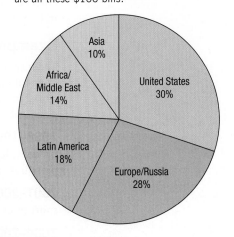

$1,169,129,096,488
Total amount of U.S. dollars and coins in circulation in April 2013.

The first part of this chapter describes the monetary policy process. We show how expansionary monetary policy is utilized during economic downturns and contractionary monetary policy during economic booms. We then consider the question: How do changes in the money supply affect the economy? We will see that money has no effect on the economy's real growth in the long run but can have sizeable effects in the short run. We examine the impact of monetary policy on controlling demand and supply shocks and how the Fed actually tries to manage the economy. We will see that the Fed's control over the economy is indirect and that good monetary policymaking is both art and science.

This chapter goes on to examine modern monetary policy in the context of financial crises and political wrangling. What can the Fed do to deal with problems in the financial system? And how have the Fed's aggressive actions during the recent financial crisis changed the perceptions of policymakers and the public about the role of government? The chapter concludes by looking at monetary policy challenges faced by the Fed and the European Central Bank, both of which have recently dealt with financial crises not seen in generations.

What Is Monetary Policy?

Throughout the study of macroeconomic principles, we have emphasized the effect of the business cycle in creating natural ups and downs in the economy, which often lead to inflation or unemployment. The rest of our study has dealt largely with ways to manage these fluctuations and to limit the harm from deviating too far from the long-run growth path of the economy.

One way of managing economic fluctuations is the use of fiscal policy, which we studied earlier. Fiscal policy uses the tools of taxation, government transfer payments, and government spending. The other way of managing economic fluctuations is the use of monetary policy, which deals with how the money supply is controlled to target interest rates in an economy.

The Twin Goals of Monetary Policy

The authority to control a nation's monetary policy is typically held by a country's central bank. In the United States, the central bank is the Federal Reserve, an independent organization unaffiliated with any political party. The seven members of its Board of Governors are appointed by the president for a 14-year term rather than elected.

As discussed in the previous chapter, the Fed uses its primary tools of conducting open market operations, setting reserve requirements, and setting the discount rate to manage the money supply in the economy. By doing so, it has tremendous influence on the interest rates on savings accounts, money market accounts, government bonds, mortgage payments, student loans, car loans, and credit card balances.

The Fed uses these tools to promote its twin goals of economic growth with low unemployment, and stable prices with moderate long-term interest rates. When the economy enters a boom or a recession that threatens the stability of these factors, the Fed can step in to enact an appropriate policy to counteract the effect.

Examples of Monetary Policy in Action

The business cycle of the economy produces frequent ups and downs, and the Fed is kept busy anticipating and reacting to prevent major economic crises from occurring. Let's take a brief look at a few recent periods when the Fed has stepped in to promote economic and price stability.

1998–1999: The peak of the Internet growth, when new "dot.com" companies sprouted up daily, led to tremendous economic growth. But along with growth came inflationary pressures, and the Fed responded by raising interest rates.

2001–2003: With the dramatic collapse in the price of technology stocks along with the short recession in 2001, the Fed lowered interest rates to stimulate employment.

2004–2006: The housing bubble led to strong growth throughout the economy and inflationary pressures crept up (especially in industries related to housing), leading the Fed to raise interest rates again.

2007–2009: When the housing bubble collapsed, unemployment rose significantly and the Fed dramatically reduced interest rates to record lows.

2010–2013: A slow economic recovery with persistent unemployment resulted in the Fed committing to holding interest rates at record lows.

Why Is the Interest Rate So Important to the Economy?

Examine the economic decisions you make every day, and you might find the influence interest rates have quite remarkable. Interest rates affect the manner in which we borrow and consume, and the way in which we save and invest.

Suppose you are looking to buy a new car, and have budgeted $2,000 for a down payment and $400 a month toward the monthly payment and interest on a five-year loan. How much of a car can you afford with this budget?

It depends a great deal on the interest rate. Suppose the current interest rate on a car loan is 8.99%. Using the money you have, you would be able to afford a car costing up to $21,275. But now suppose that the interest rate on a car loan is 2.99%. At the lower interest rate, you would be able to afford a car costing up to $24,265, or almost $3,000 in extra spending without changing your monthly payment.

This extra $3,000 in potential spending resulting from the lower interest rate adds to the amount of consumption in the economy. Recall from Chapter 20 that aggregate demand is the sum of consumption, investment, government spending, and net exports. Just as lower interest rates make cars more affordable, they also make homes more affordable, along with equipment purchases by businesses. Therefore, a reduction in interest rates promotes greater consumption and investment, which leads to an increase in aggregate demand, shifting the aggregate demand curve to the right.

When Is It Optimal to Loosen or Tighten Monetary Policy?

By influencing interest rates, the Fed influences aggregate demand. Specifically, the Fed loosens monetary policy in times of recessionary concerns and tightens monetary policy in times of inflationary concerns.

- **Loosening monetary policy:** Reducing interest rates → increases consumption and investment → increases aggregate demand.

- **Tightening monetary policy:** Raising interest rates → decreases consumption and investment → decreases aggregate demand.

Let's explore "loosening" and "tightening" a bit more.

Expansionary Monetary Policy During times of economic downturn, the Fed will engage in **expansionary monetary policy** by conducting open market operations. By buying government bonds from banks using money it creates, the Fed puts more money into the economy, thus expanding the money supply and reducing interest rates. Lower interest rates tend to reduce the proportion of income people save and increase the amount they consume or invest, all else equal. When the amount of consumption or investment increases, it leads to an increase in aggregate demand (AD).

As interest rates are lowered, consumers and businesses find the cost of borrowing decreasing as well. For a business, this may mean that it would be easier to finance an expansion of a factory or the building of a new restaurant or store. To a consumer, a lower interest rate on a home or car purchase can significantly reduce monthly payments, freeing up some money for other purchases. As borrowing increases to finance consumption or investment, AD again increases.

Further, a reduction in interest rates, in particular on treasury securities, means that the government is spending less on financing the national debt. By spending less on financing the debt, the government is then able to spend more on other purchases, which contributes to an increase in AD.

Finally, as the interest rate falls, American bonds become less attractive to foreign investors, and this often leads to a decline in the value of the U.S. dollar in foreign exchange markets. A falling dollar makes American products cheaper relative to foreign products, which stimulates exports and reduces imports, increasing AD.

A lower interest rate allows one to afford a better car (or at least fancier rims) with the same monthly payment.

Chris Wallbank/Fast Ford Magazine via Getty Images

expansionary monetary policy Fed actions designed to increase excess reserves and the money supply to stimulate the economy (expand income and employment).

In sum, expansionary monetary policy is used when the economy is facing a recessionary gap, in which output falls below the level needed to reach full employment. By engaging in expansionary policy, the aggregate demand curve shifts to the right as shown in Figure 1, expanding output at every price level.

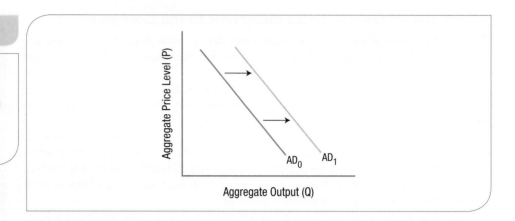

contractionary monetary policy
Fed actions designed to decrease excess reserves and the money supply to shrink income and employment, usually to fight inflation.

Contractionary Monetary Policy The opposite of expansionary monetary policy is **contractionary monetary policy,** according to which the Fed sells bonds, taking money out of the economy to reduce the money supply and raise interest rates. The Fed uses contractionary monetary policy when inflationary pressures build up. When do inflationary periods typically occur?

Inflationary pressures typically occur following a period of strong economic growth, such as during the housing bubble a decade ago. As eager consumers and investors bid up prices for homes, demand for related items such as furniture, appliances, and even plane tickets for those who bought second homes far away increased. As demand for goods and services rise, prices tend to rise as well. If prices rise too much, this would have consequences on the economy as the purchasing power of savings erodes.

To stem the growth of inflation, the Fed would reduce the money supply, thereby increasing the interest rate to slow the growth of demand. In this case, rising interest rates would lead to a fall in consumption and investment. Government would spend more financing the national debt, reducing what it can spend on other goods and services. And a rise in the value of the dollar from increased demand for higher interest bonds makes American goods more expensive, reducing net exports. Each of these effects causes the aggregate demand curve to shift to the left as shown in Figure 2, reducing output at every price level and putting downward pressure on prices.

Up until now, we have assumed that monetary policy affects the interest rate, which subsequently influences the aggregate demand curve. But how does a simple change in the money supply influence goods and services in the real economy? The next section explores this question by analyzing how prices and output change in the short run and long run.

CHECKPOINT

WHAT IS MONETARY POLICY?

- Monetary policy involves the control of the money supply to target interest rates in order to stabilize fluctuations in the business cycle.

- The Federal Reserve implements monetary policy; its goals are to promote economic growth by maintaining full employment, stable prices, and moderate long-term interest rates.

- Interest rates are crucial because they directly influence the components of aggregate demand, including consumption and investment.

- Expansionary monetary policy is used during times of recessions, and involves expanding the money supply to reduce interest rates.

- Contractionary monetary policy is used during times of rising inflation, and involves reducing the money supply to raise interest rates.

- By increasing or decreasing aggregate demand, the Fed can move the economy back toward the long-run economic output level.

QUESTION: Suppose the government passes legislation limiting the maximum interest rate that can be charged on student loans, reducing the monthly payment on your loans. How is this legislation similar to an expansionary monetary policy?

Answers to the Checkpoint question can be found at the end of this chapter.

 ## Monetary Theories

In discussing the theories that justify the use of monetary policy, it is best to differentiate the long run from the short run. We will see that money has no effect on the real economy (such as employment and output) in the long run but can have an effect in the short run.

The Short Run Versus the Long Run: What's the Difference?

One of the important concepts covered in Chapter 20 is the comparison between the short-run aggregate supply curve (SRAS) and the vertical long-run aggregate supply curve (LRAS). Recall that the LRAS curve is vertical because economic output is always fixed in the long run at the full employment output when wages and prices are flexible. Only factors that increase the productivity of inputs can shift the LRAS curve. The SRAS curve, however, is upward sloping because higher prices can cause temporary increases in output. This is due to sticky wages and prices.

We now build on the AD/AS model by explaining how changes in the money supply, which directly affect the aggregate demand curve, might change prices and output in the economy. The main determinant—you guessed it—depends on whether the aggregate supply curve is vertical (i.e., in the long run) or upward sloping (i.e., in the short run).

Let's begin by looking at the long run, which is the analysis most commonly associated with the classical theory.

The Long Run: The Classical Theory

Classical economists focused on long-run adjustments in economic activity. In the long run, wages, prices, and interest rates are flexible, allowing the labor, product, and capital markets to adjust to keep the economy at full employment.

A product of the classical theory is the *quantity theory of money*, which is defined by the **equation of exchange:**

$$M \times V = P \times Q$$

where M is the supply of money, V is the velocity of money (the average number of times per year a dollar is spent on goods and services), P is the price level, and Q is the economy's

equation of exchange The heart of classical monetary theory uses the equation $M \times V = P \times Q$, where M is the supply of money, V is the velocity of money (the average number of times per year a dollar is spent on goods and services, or the number of times it turns over in a year), P is the price level, and Q is the economy's output level.

real output level. Note that the right side of the equation—the aggregate price level times the level of output—is equal to nominal GDP.

In the long run, when the economy is at full employment, the implications for monetary policy are straightforward. Because velocity (V) is assumed to be fixed by existing monetary institutions (for example, the amount of cash you use on a monthly basis is generally consistent), and aggregate output (Q) is assumed to be fixed at full employment, any change in the money supply (M) will translate directly to a change in prices (P), or in other words, inflation.

Suppose you sell your grandma's old LP records on eBay. Last month you listed five records for sale and sold them at an average winning bid of $20 each. Now suppose that this month a 10% increase in the money supply causes more people to want to buy records. If you again list only five records for sale, what will likely happen? There is more money to spend on the same amount of goods. Buyers might bid up the price to say, $22. In the end, prices rise in the exact proportion to the rise in the money supply. This is the essence of the classical theory—that increases in the money supply translate into an immediate and proportional rise in the aggregate price level with no change in real output (Q). As a result, monetary policy is ineffective.

Panel A of Figure 3 illustrates how the quantity theory works within an aggregate demand and supply model. The economy is initially in long-run equilibrium at point e with full employment output of $15 trillion and an initial money level of $2.0 trillion. Increasing the money supply to $2.2 trillion (a 10% increase) shifts aggregate demand upward to $AD_{(\$2.2T)}$, resulting in a new equilibrium at point b where the aggregate price level increases to 110 (a 10% increase), yet real output remains constant at $15 trillion. This positive relationship between changes in the supply of money and inflation is evident in the plot shown in panel B, which shows the strong correlation between average monetary growth and inflation for 30 countries from 1972 to 2012. This suggests that any central bank that wants to avoid high inflation must avoid rapid growth of its money supply.

Quantity theory provides a good explanation of the long-run impact of monetary growth in the larger economy. But do people really catch on so quickly to money growth? Typically not. The realization that wages and prices can be "sticky" led economists to develop theories of how prices and output can change in the short run, leading to a SRAS curve that differs from a LRAS curve. The most notable theories include the Keynesian and monetarist models.

Short-Run Effects of Monetary Policy

If the short-run effects of money were the same as in the long run, that would be the end of the story. In contrast to the long run, changes in the money supply can have an effect on the real economy in the short run, not just on the price level. To explain this, let's start by returning to our earlier example to show how money supply growth can affect economic output.

IRVING FISHER (1867–1947)

Irving Fisher was one of the ablest mathematical economists of the early 20th century. A staunch advocate of monetary reform, his theories influenced economists as different as John Maynard Keynes and Milton Friedman.

Born in upstate New York in 1867, Fisher studied mathematics, science, and philosophy at Yale University. In 1905, Fisher was in a phone booth in Grand Central Terminal in New York City when someone stole his briefcase, which contained his manuscript of *The Nature of Capital and Income*, one of the first economics books about the stock market. He rewrote the book in the next year, making copies of each chapter as it was finished and always closing the doors to phone booths after that.

Monetarists owe a great debt to Fisher's next great book, *The Purchasing Power of Money*, in which he offered an "equation of exchange": $MV = PT$ (where T is the number of transactions taking place, or output). Classical economists have used variations of the formula to suggest that inflation is caused by increases in the money supply.

Fisher was prim and straight-laced, disciplined, and did not drink alcohol or coffee or tea, smoke, eat chocolate, or use pepper. His lack of humor and sometimes controversial economic beliefs (such as 100% bank reserves) led some to regard him as quite odd.

But among his many skills and interests, Fisher was a successful inventor and businessman. In 1925, he patented the "visible card index" system, an early version of the Rolodex, and earned a fortune. Unfortunately, within a few years he would lose everything in the stock market crash of 1929, an event that he famously failed to predict. His insistence of an imminent recovery during the early Depression years caused irreparable damage to a well-earned reputation as one of America's greatest economists.

Sources: Justin Fox, The Myth of the Rational Market (New York: HarperCollins), 2009, p. 3; Robert Allen, *Irving Fisher: A Biography* (Cambridge, MA: Blackwell), 1993, p. 9.

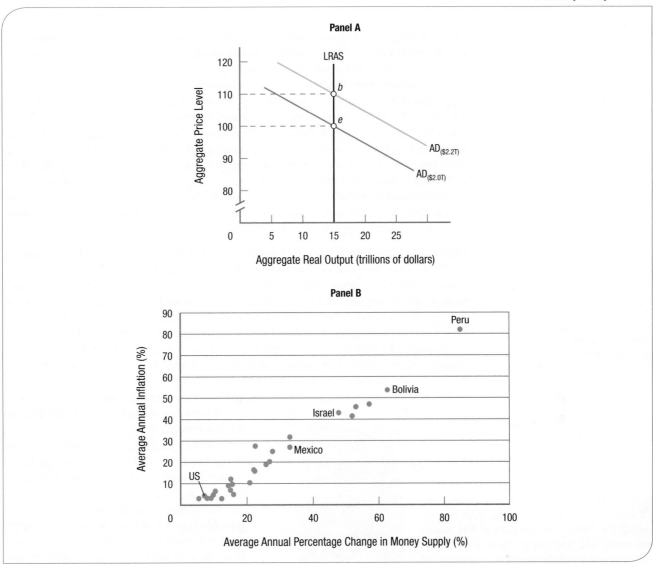

The Impact of a Change in the Money Supply in the Long Run: Theory and Evidence

The quantity theory of money is shown using aggregate demand and aggregate supply. The economy is initially in equilibrium at point *e*. The long-run aggregate supply curve is vertical (long-run full employment at $15 trillion), while the aggregate demand curve reflects a money supply of $2.0 trillion. Increasing the money supply to $2.2 trillion (a 10% increase) shifts aggregate demand upward to AD$_{($2.2T)}$, resulting in a new equilibrium at point *b*, where the aggregate price level rises by 10%, yet real output remains constant. The price level rise is equal to the percentage increase in the money supply. Monetary growth and inflation for thirty countries from 1972 to 2012 supports this theory.

FIGURE 3

Money Illusion and Sticky Wages and Prices Suppose you continue to sell your grandma's records on eBay, listing five for sale each month. And every month, you notice that the average winning bids keep rising, first to $22, then to $25, then to $30, or even higher. This increase in the sales price makes you happy because you feel richer each month compared to the previous month. You think you are benefitting from the growing popularity of your grandma's good taste in music.

How would you use your additional income? Most people would spend it by going out to eat more or buying more clothes. This extra spending (by you and everyone who *feels* richer) results in a temporary increase in economic output. But then you notice that the items you typically buy each month start increasing in price, so much so that despite earning more money, you end up buying about the same amount of goods as you did before. In other words, after prices caught up, you're no better off than when you made only $20 per record. What you have discovered is that grandma's records are not growing in popularity. Rather, growth in the money supply is causing an increase in all prices. You misperceived that you were wealthier when you really were not.

The example above illustrates the misperceptions in wealth that occur when the money supply grows, and is known as *money illusion*. But money illusion is not the only distinguishing factor between the short run and the long run. Another short-run effect is that wages and prices tend to react slowly to changes in the economy. Most workers' wages do not change with every paycheck; similarly, the prices of many goods and services we buy do not change every day. This delayed reaction in wages and prices to economic conditions makes them *sticky*. This is not the first time we have studied the effects of sticky wages and sticky prices—we studied them previously when explaining why the SRAS curve slopes upward. But now we look at how an upward sloping SRAS curve can make monetary policy effective in the short run by looking at two opposing views on the effectiveness of monetary policy in the short run.

Keynesian Model Developed by John Maynard Keynes during the Great Depression of the 1930s, Keynesian analysis has had a profound effect on policymakers and economists that continues today. According to Keynesian theory, an increase in the money supply leads more people to buy interest-earning assets (bonds), causing the price of bonds to rise and the interest rate to fall. Lower interest rates should normally lead to an increase in investment that increases aggregate demand, which increases income, output, and employment.

liquidity trap When interest rates are so low that people believe rates can only rise, they hold on to money rather than investing in bonds and suffering the expected capital loss.

However, Keynesians believed that this outcome occurs only when the economy is healthy. During times of recession, people become fearful and don't buy as much, leading to massive excess capacity for businesses. Reducing interest rates might not lead to greater investment, because firms are unable to sell what they were currently producing, and therefore would be reluctant to invest more.

Further, when interest rates fall to very low levels, Keynes argued that people simply hoard money because it's not worth holding bonds that pay so little interest. Keynes referred to this phenomenon as the **liquidity trap.** In a liquidity trap, an increase in the money supply does not result in a decrease in interest rates; thus there is no change in investment, and consequently no change in income or output. Monetary policy is totally ineffective. This was one reason Keynes argued that fiscal policy, especially government spending, was needed to get the economy out of the Depression.

Monetarist Model Milton Friedman challenged the Keynesian view by arguing that government spending inherent to fiscal policy must be financed either by increased taxation and/or increased borrowing. His monetarist theory states that higher taxation means consumers and firms have less money to consume and invest, while increased borrowing leads to higher interest rates, which also reduces consumption and investment. Thus, monetarists believe that the crowding out effect makes fiscal policy ineffective.

Friedman pioneered the notion that consumption is not only based on income, but also on wealth, an idea he referred to as the *permanent income hypothesis.*

With Friedman's approach, when the money supply increases, interest rates fall,

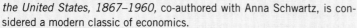

NOBEL PRIZE
MILTON FRIEDMAN (1912-2006)

Milton Friedman may be the best-known economist of the latter half of the 20th century. During the 1980s, his advocacy of free market economics and "monetarist" theories had a dramatic impact on policymakers, notably President Ronald Reagan and British Prime Minister Margaret Thatcher. His book, *A Monetary History of the United States, 1867–1960,* co-authored with Anna Schwartz, is considered a modern classic of economics.

Born in 1912 in Brooklyn, New York, to poor immigrant parents, Friedman was awarded a scholarship to Rutgers University but paid for his additional expenses by waiting on tables and clerking in a store. He eventually went on to graduate school at the University of Chicago to study economics, and then to Columbia University.

In 1946, he accepted a professorship at the University of Chicago where he delved into the role of money in business cycles. In 1950, Friedman worked in Paris for the Marshall Plan, studying a precursor to the Common Market. He came to believe in the importance of flexible exchange rates between members of the European community.

Friedman's views were explicitly counter to the Keynesian belief in a range of activist government policies to stabilize the economy. Friedman emphasized the importance of monetary policy in determining the level of economic activity, and advocated a consistent policy of steady growth in the money supply to encourage stability and economic growth.

Friedman was awarded the Nobel Prize in Economics in 1976 for his work on monetary theories and also for his concept of "permanent income," the idea that people based their savings habits on the typical amount they earn instead of on increases or decreases they may view as temporary.

and individuals rebalance their asset portfolios by exchanging money for other assets, not only bonds—for example, real estate and consumer durables such as cars and recreational equipment. Therefore, falling interest rates will lead to higher investment and/or consumption. This leads to an increase in aggregate demand and ultimately an increase in income, output, and/or the price level.

Therefore, monetarists believe that monetary policy can be effective in the short run. But, like classical economists, monetarists believe that an increase in money will ultimately increase prices in the long run. As Milton Friedman famously remarked: "Inflation is always and everywhere a monetary phenomenon."

Figure 4 illustrates the monetarist approach that a change in output will occur only in the short run. The economy is initially in long-run equilibrium at point e, with output at $15 trillion and a price level of 100. A 10% increase in the money supply from $2.0 trillion to $2.2 trillion shifts the aggregate demand curve from AD_0 to AD_1, initially raising output to $16 trillion and the aggregate price level to 104 (point b). Over time, as prices adjust, the SRAS curve will shift left and the economy will move back to its full employment output ($15 trillion), raising prices in the long run by 10% to 110 (point c).

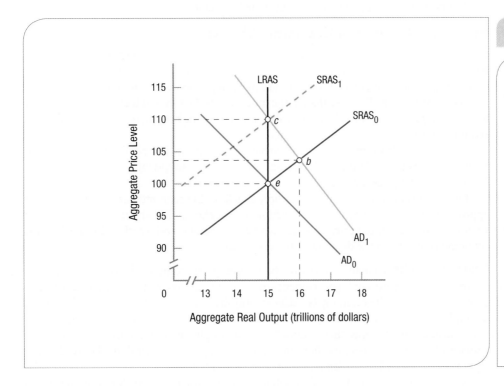

FIGURE 4

Monetarist Theory on Money Supply

Monetarists argue that a change in output will last only for the short run; in the long run, the economy will move back to full employment. The economy begins in equilibrium at point e. An increase in the money supply of 10% shifts the aggregate demand curve from AD_0 to AD_1, resulting in higher short-run output, $16 trillion, and a higher price level (point b). Over time, the economy will move back to full employment ($15 trillion), increasing the price level in the long run to 110 (a 10% increase). The long-run aggregate supply curve is therefore vertical at full employment output ($15 trillion).

Summary of the Effectiveness of Monetary Policy

Let's summarize the theories of the effectiveness of monetary policy.

Long Run: Changes in the money supply show up directly as increases in the price level because both velocity and output are considered fixed in the equation of exchange ($M \times V = P \times Q$). Because classical economists focused on the long run, they saw no use for monetary policy.

Short Run: Keynes believed that when the economy is well below full employment, monetary policy is ineffective because investment is more influenced by business expectations about the economy than interest rates. Further, Keynes suggested that once interest rates get very low, monetary policy might confront a "liquidity trap," where money is just hoarded. Thus, Keynesians favor fiscal policy to move the economy toward full employment.

Monetarists, on the other hand, do see a role for monetary policy. In the short run, changes in the money supply reduce interest rates, which in turn stimulate both investment and consumption. Consumer spending is related to wealth (not just income), and

TABLE 1	Summary of Monetary Theories	
	Short Run	**Long Run**
Classical Theory	Does not exist; economy always self-adjusts	Economy self-adjusts due to flexible prices. Money leads only to price changes.
Keynesian Theory	Fiscal policy is effective, while monetary policy is ineffective in times of deep recession.	Economy adjusts to long-run equilibrium; increased money supply leads to higher prices.
Monetarist Theory	Fiscal policy is ineffective because government spending crowds out consumption and investment, while monetary policy is effective.	Economy adjusts to long-run equilibrium; increased money supply leads to higher prices.

changes in interest rates induce portfolio adjustments that alter consumer spending for durable goods.

A summary of the three theories is provided in Table 1.

Monetary Policy and Economic Shocks

Our discussion thus far suggests that the Fed's approach to monetary policy should be based on both short- and long-run considerations. Low inflation represents a reasonable long-run goal, while income and output are more appropriate for the shorter term.

Economists generally agree that, in the long run, the Fed should focus on price stability because low rates of inflation have been shown to create the best environment for long-run economic growth.

We have seen from the equation of exchange that, in the long run, aggregate supply is vertical and fixed at full employment, and changes in the supply of money result directly in changes in the price level.

But in the short run, demand and supply shocks to the economy may require differing approaches to monetary policy. The direction of monetary policy and its extent depend on whether it focuses on the price level or income and output, and whether the shock to the economy comes from the demand or the supply side.

Demand Shocks Demand shocks to the economy can come from reductions in consumer demand, investment, government spending, or exports, or from an increase in imports. For example, the economy faced a demand shock in 2008 when households, fearing unemployment after the housing bubble burst, increased saving and reduced spending. Let's consider an economy that is initially in full employment equilibrium at point e in panel A of Figure 5. A *demand shock* then reduces aggregate demand to AD_1. At the new equilibrium (point a), the price level and output both fall.

An expansionary monetary policy will increase the money supply, lower interest rates, and thereby shift aggregate demand back to AD_0, restoring employment and output to full employment. In this case, targeting either a stable price level (100) or the original income and output level ($15 trillion) will bring the economy back to the same point of equilibrium, point e, where *both* targets are reached.

A positive demand shock produces a corresponding, though opposite, result. The positive demand shock will jolt output and the price level upward. Contractionary monetary policy will reduce both of them, restoring the economy to its original equilibrium.

For demand shocks, therefore, no conflict arises between the twin goals of monetary policy. Not only is the objective of full employment compatible with the objective of stable prices, but by targeting either one of these objectives, the Fed takes steps that work to bring about the other.

Supply Shocks Supply shocks can hit the economy for many reasons, including changes in resource costs such as a rise in oil prices, changes in inflationary expectations, or changes in technology. Looking at panel B of Figure 5, let us again consider an economy

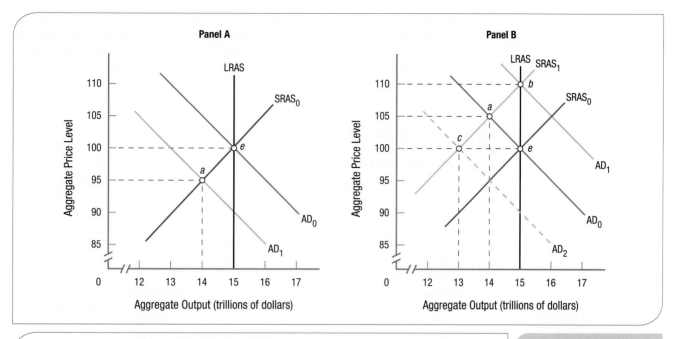

Demand Shocks, Supply Shocks, and Monetary Policy

Monetary policy can be effective in counteracting a demand shock. In panel A, the economy begins in full employment equilibrium at point *e* and then a demand shock reduces aggregate demand to AD_1, resulting in a new equilibrium (point *a*). Expansionary monetary policy will shift aggregate demand back to AD_0. This policy restores output back to full employment ($15 trillion), while restoring prices to their original level (100). Monetary policy is less effective in counteracting a supply shock. In panel B, a negative supply shock shifts short-run aggregate supply from $SRAS_0$ to $SRAS_1$. The new equilibrium (point *a*) is at a *higher* price level, 105, and *lower* output, $14 trillion, a doubly negative result. The Fed could use expansionary monetary policy to shift AD_0 to AD_1; this would restore the economy to full employment output of $15 trillion (point *b*), but at an even higher price level (110). Alternatively, the Fed could focus on price level stability, using contractionary monetary policy to shift aggregate demand to AD_2, but this would further deepen the recession by pushing output down to $13 trillion (point *c*).

FIGURE 5

initially in full employment equilibrium at point *e*. Assume that a negative shock to the economy, say, an oil price spike, shifts short-run aggregate supply from $SRAS_0$ to $SRAS_1$. The new equilibrium (point *a*) occurs at a *higher* price level (105) and a *lower* output of $14 trillion.

This doubly negative result means that a supply shock is very difficult to counter. The Fed could use expansionary monetary policy to shift AD_0 to AD_1; this would restore the economy to full employment output of $15 trillion (point *b*), but at an even higher price level (110). Alternatively, the Fed could focus on price level stability, using contractionary monetary policy to shift aggregate demand to AD_2, but this would further deepen the recession by pushing output down to $13 trillion (point *c*).

For a negative supply shock, not only has price level stability worsened, but so has output and income. Contrast this with the situation earlier, when a demand shock worsened the economy for one of its targets, but improved it for the other. Supply shocks are difficult to counteract because of their doubly negative results.

Implications for Short-Run Monetary Policy There is general agreement among economists that monetary policy should focus on price stability in the long run, while focusing on output or income in the short run. When a demand shock strikes, following this short-run policy course has the same effect as using price stability as the goal. When a supply shock occurs, however, targeting nominal income or output is preferable, because it permits the Fed to spread the shock's impact between income and output losses and price level increases. By increasing aggregate demand, the economy will suffer some added increase in the price level, but output will rise, reducing the severity of any recession. The Fed will probably not try to push the economy back to full employment (from point *a* to point *b* in the right panel in Figure 5) immediately, because this action would result in much higher inflation. Moving the economy back to full employment is typically spread over several periods.

 CHECKPOINT

MONETARY THEORIES

- The classical equation of exchange is: $M \times V = P \times Q$. In the long run, velocity (*V*) and output (*Q*) were assumed to be fixed. Therefore, changes in the money supply translated directly into changes in the price level: $\Delta M = \Delta P$.

- In the short run, Keynesian monetary analysis suggests that changes in the money supply change interest rates, leading to changes in investment and aggregate demand when the economy is healthy. However, in a deep recession, changes in the money supply have no effect on the real economy.

- Monetarists suggest that in the long run, the economy functions in the way that classical economists described, but they see monetary policy affecting interest rates in the short run, which in turn changes investment *and/or* consumption, changing aggregate demand and thus affecting output *and/or* the price level.

- In the long run, the Fed targets price stability. Low rates of inflation are most conducive to long-run economic health.

- Monetary policy can focus on either a stable price level or output when a shock to the economy comes from the demand side. The objective of full employment is compatible with the objective of stable prices.

- Supply shocks present a more serious problem for monetary policy. A negative supply shock reduces output but increases the price level. Expansionary monetary policy to increase output further increases the price level, and contractionary policy to reduce the price level worsens the recession.

QUESTION: Much of the recent political debate has focused on the approach needed to speed the recovery of the economy and on dealing with the national debt. The common debate typically involves those who prefer a smaller government (reduced taxation with a dramatic reduction in government spending) versus those who prefer increased government spending funded by higher taxes. Which general theories described in this section best resemble the two sides of the debate?

Answers to the Checkpoint question can be found at the end of this chapter.

Modern Monetary Policy

When the Fed engages in expansionary monetary policy, it is buying bonds using money it creates by adding to the existing bank reserves deposited at the Fed. Other terms used to describe this process include **easy money, quantitative easing,** and **accommodative monetary policy.** It is designed to increase excess reserves and the money supply, and ultimately reduce interest rates to stimulate the economy and expand income and employment. The opposite of an expansionary policy is contractionary monetary policy, also referred to as **tight money** or **restrictive monetary policy.** Tight money policies are designed to shrink income and employment, usually in the interest of fighting inflation. The Fed brings about tight monetary policy by selling bonds, thereby pulling reserves from the financial system.

The Federal Reserve Act gives the Board of Governors significant discretion over conducting monetary policy. It sets out goals but leaves it up to the discretion of the Board of Governors how best to reach these objectives. As we have seen, the Fed attempts to frame monetary policy to keep inflation low over the long run, but also to maintain enough flexibility to respond in the short run to demand and supply shocks.

easy money, quantitative easing, or accommodative monetary policy Fed actions designed to increase excess reserves and the money supply to stimulate the economy (expand income and employment). *See also* expansionary monetary policy.

tight money or **restrictive monetary policy** Fed actions designed to decrease excess reserves and the money supply to shrink income and employment, usually to fight inflation. *See also* contractionary monetary policy.

Rules Versus Discretion

The complexities of monetary policy, especially in dealing with a supply shock, have led some economists, most notably Milton Friedman, to call for a **monetary rule** to guide monetary policymakers. Other economists argue that modern economies are too complex to be managed by a few simple rules. Constantly changing institutions, economic behaviors, and technologies mean that some discretion, and perhaps even complete discretion, is essential for policymakers. Also, if policymakers could use a simple and efficient rule on which to base successful monetary policy, they would have enough incentive to adopt it voluntarily, because it would guarantee success and their job would be much easier.

Milton Friedman argued that variations in monetary growth were a major source of instability in the economy. To counter this problem, which is compounded by the long and variable lags in discretionary monetary policy, Friedman advocated the adoption of monetary growth rules. Specifically, he proposed increasing the money supply by a set percentage every year, at a level consistent with long-term price stability and economic growth.

Friedman and other monetarists, like the classical economists before them, believed the economy to be inherently stable. If they are correct, then generating a steady increase in the money supply should reduce the potentially destabilizing effects monetary policy can have on the economy.

If the change in aggregate demand is small or temporary, a monetary growth rule will probably function well enough. But if the shock is large, persistent, or continual, as was the case during the Great Depression and the recent financial crisis, a discretionary monetary policy aimed at bringing the economy back to full employment more quickly would probably be preferred.

In some cases, a monetary rule keeps policymakers from making things worse by keeping them from doing anything. Yet, the monetary rule also prevents policymakers from aiding the economy when a policy change is needed. Policymakers argue that they need to be able to balance one goal against another, rather than being tied down by strict rules that in the end do nothing.

Monetary targeting, the practice of setting a fixed rate for money supply growth, suggested by Milton Friedman, was the focus of the Fed from 1970 to 1980 but wasn't considered successful.

The alternative to setting money growth rules that modern monetary authorities around the world have tried is the simple rule of **inflation targeting,** which is setting targets on the inflation rate, usually around 2% per year. If inflation (or the forecasted rate of inflation) exceeds the target, contractionary policy is employed; if inflation falls below the target, expansionary policy is used. Inflation targeting has the virtue of explicitly iterating that the long-run goal of monetary policy is price stability.

Assume once more that a negative demand shock hits the economy. Inflation targeting means that discretionary expansionary monetary policy will be used to bring the economy back to full employment. But now consider a negative supply shock from an increase in the price of energy or some other raw material. Inflation targeting means that contractionary monetary policy should be used to reduce the inflation spiral. As we saw, however, contractionary policy would deepen the recession, and in reality, few monetary authorities would stick to an inflation-targeting approach in this situation. They would be more likely to stimulate the economy slightly, hoping to move it back to full employment with only a small increase in inflation. The result is that inflation targeting could soon lose its credibility and effectiveness.

The Federal Funds Target and the Taylor Rule

If not monetary targeting or inflation targeting, what other rule can the Fed use? We know that the Fed alters the federal funds rate as its primary monetary policy instrument. Under what circumstances will the Fed change its federal funds target? The Fed is concerned with two major factors: preventing inflation and preventing and moderating recessions. Professor John Taylor of Stanford University studied the Fed and how it makes decisions and he empirically found that the Fed tended to follow a general rule that has become known as the **Taylor rule** for federal funds targeting:

monetary rule Keeps the growth of money stocks such as M1 or M2 on a steady path, following the equation of exchange (or quantity theory), to set a long-run path for the economy that keeps inflation in check.

inflation targeting The central bank sets a target on the inflation rate (usually around 2% per year) and adjusts monetary policy to keep inflation in that range.

Taylor rule A rule for the federal funds target that suggests that the target is equal to 2% + Current Inflation Rate + 1/2(Inflation Gap) + 1/2(Output Gap). Alternatively, it is equal to 2% plus the current inflation rate plus 1/2 times the difference between the current inflation rate and the Fed's inflation target rate plus 1/2 times the output gap (current GDP minus potential GDP).

$$\text{Federal Funds Target Rate} = 2 + \text{Current Inflation Rate} + 1/2(\text{Inflation Gap}) + 1/2(\text{Output Gap})$$

The Fed's inflation target is typically 2%, the inflation gap is the current inflation rate minus the Fed's inflation target, and the output gap is current GDP minus potential GDP. If the Fed tries to target inflation around 2%, the current inflation rate is 4%, and output is 3% below potential GDP, then the target federal funds rate according to the Taylor rule is:

$$
\begin{aligned}
\text{FF}_{\text{Target}} &= 2 + 4 + 1/2(4 - 2) + 1/2(-3) \\
&= 2 + 4 + 1/2(2) + 1/2(-3) \\
&= 2 + 4 + 1 - 1.5 \\
&= 5.5\%.
\end{aligned}
$$

Notice that the high rate of inflation (4%) drives the federal funds target rate upward while the fact that the economy is below its potential reduces the rate. If the economy were operating at its potential, the federal funds target would be 7%, because the Fed would not be worried about a recession and would be focused on controlling inflation.

Figure 6 shows how closely the Taylor rule tracks the actual federal funds rate. Some economists have blamed the large spread between the two rates during the period between 2003 and 2007 for the housing boom that precipitated the financial crisis in 2008. They argue that the extremely low interest rates fueled the housing boom.

More important, what the Taylor rule tells us is that when the Fed meets to change the federal funds target rate, the two most important factors are whether inflation is different from the Fed's target (typically 2%) and whether output varies from potential GDP. If output is below its potential, a recession threatens and the Fed will lower its target, and vice versa when output exceeds potential and inflation threatens to exceed the Fed's target.

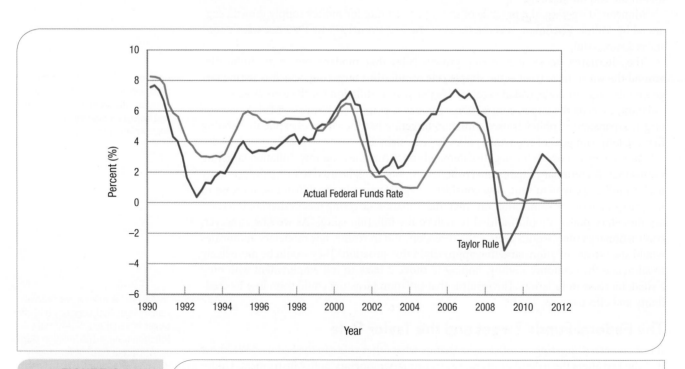

FIGURE 6

Actual Federal Funds Rate and the Taylor Rule

The Taylor rule tracks the actual federal funds rate quite closely. Some economists have argued that the low federal funds rate during the period from 2003 to 2007 was the cause of the housing boom that precipitated the financial crisis in 2008 and the ensuing recession.

A Recap of the Fed's Policy Tools

Now is a good time to summarize the monetary policy actions that the Fed can take to achieve its twin goals of price stability and full employment, Q_f.

When output exceeds potential output ($Q > Q_f$), firms are operating above their capacities and costs will rise, adding an inflationary threat that the Fed wants to avoid. Therefore, the Fed would increase the real interest rate to cool the economy. When output is below potential ($Q < Q_f$), the Fed's goal is to drive the economy back to its potential and avoid a recession and the losses associated with an economy below full employment. The Fed does this by lowering the real interest rate. This reflects the Fed's desire to fight recession when output is below full employment and fight inflation when output exceeds its potential.

Today, monetary authorities set a target interest rate and then use open market operations to adjust reserves and keep the federal funds rate near this level. The Fed's interest target is the level that will keep the economy near potential GDP and/or keep inflationary pressures in check. When GDP is below its potential and a recession threatens the economy, the Fed uses expansionary policy to lower interest rates, expanding investment, consumption, and exports. When output is above potential GDP and inflation threatens, the Fed uses a higher interest rate target to slow the economy and reduce inflationary pressure.

When inflation becomes a problem in the short run (assuming initially no change in output), the Fed will act in a similar manner. It will increase interest rates to slow the economy and reduce inflationary pressures. Raising interest rates is never a politically popular act, but the Fed will be forced to balance future economic growth against rising inflationary expectations. As former Fed Chairman William McChesney Martin said, "The job of a good central banker is to take away the punchbowl just as the party gets going."

Transparency and the Federal Reserve

How does the Fed convey information about its actions, and why is this important? For many years, decisions were made in secrecy, and often they were executed in secrecy: The public did not know that monetary policy was being changed. Because monetary policy affects the economy, the Fed's secrecy stimulated much speculation in financial markets about current and future Fed actions. Uncertainty often led to various counterproductive actions by people guessing incorrectly. These activities were highly inefficient.

When Alan Greenspan became head of the Fed in 1987, this policy of secrecy started to change. By 1994, the Fed released a policy statement each time it changed interest rates, and by 1998 it included a "tilt" statement forecasting what would probably happen in the next month or two. By 2000, the FOMC released a statement after each of its eight yearly meetings even if policy remained the same. As the chapter opener describes, the FOMC statement is now one of the most anticipated pieces of economic news.

This new openness has come about because the Fed recognized that monetary policy is mitigated when financial actors take counterproductive actions when they are uncertain about what the Fed will do. In the words of William Poole, former president of the Federal Reserve Bank of St. Louis,

> *Explaining a policy action—elucidating the considerations that led the FOMC to decide to adjust the intended funds rate, or to leave it unchanged—is worthwhile. Over time, the accumulation of such explanations helps the market, and perhaps the FOMC itself, to understand what the policy regularities are. It is also important to understand that many—perhaps most—policy actions have precedent value. . . . One of the advantages of public disclosure of the reasons for policy actions is that the required explanation forces the FOMC to think through what it is doing and why.*[1]

---

[1] William Poole, "Fed Transparency: How, Not Whether," The Federal Reserve Bank of St. Louis, *Review*, November/December 2003, p. 5.

ISSUE

The Record of the Fed's Performance

Determining how to measure the impact of Federal Reserve policy on our huge, complex economy is not easy. The figure shows how three variables—unemployment, inflation, and interest rates—have fared during the tenure of the four Fed chairmen over the last four decades.

Before 1980, when Arthur Burns headed the Fed, inflation was rising. An oil supply shock in 1973 was met with accommodative monetary policy and aggregate demand expanded.

The economy was hit with a second oil price shock in the late 1970s. By the early 1980s, inflation rose to double digits, peaking at over 14% in 1980. Paul Volcker, the head of the Fed at that time, tightened monetary policy to induce a recession (1981–1982) to reduce inflation. By the end of his term, inflation had been reduced to little more than 4%, a remarkable feat.

During the 1990s, the Greenspan Fed alternated between encouraging output growth (mid-1990s) and fighting inflation (early and late 1990s). The Fed under Greenspan did a good job of keeping the economy near full employment. Interest rates trended down and inflation was moderate during the 1990s and early 2000s. But a housing bubble, partly the result of the extremely low interest rates from 2003 to 2007, followed by its collapse in 2008, brought on a financial panic and a deep recession.

The problems stemming from the housing collapse and financial crisis became a challenge for Fed chairman Ben Bernanke. In 2008, the Fed under Bernanke lowered the fed funds rate to almost 0%. In addition, the Bernanke Fed continued to expand the monetary base by purchasing long-term assets from banks when interest rates had already hit the floor. As the chart shows, unemployment trended down and the short period of deflation in 2009 was corrected.

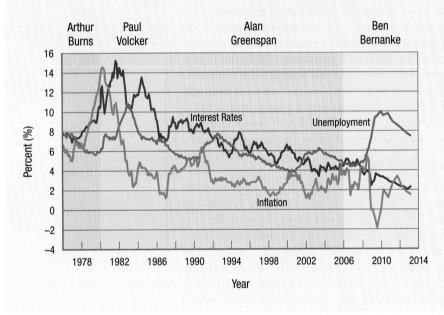

Fed transparency helps the public understand why it is taking certain actions. This helps the market understand what the Fed does in certain circumstances, and what the Fed is likely to do in similar situations in the future. The Fed also includes a "looking forward" or "tilt" comment after each meeting, which provides a summary of the Fed's outlook on the economy and information on the target federal funds rate. Transparency helps the Fed implement its monetary policy.

Until very recently, the performance of monetary authorities over the previous several decades illustrated how effective discretionary monetary policy could be. Price stability was remarkable, unemployment and output levels were near full employment levels, interest rates were kept low, and economic growth was solid.

The recent global financial crisis has tested the limits of central banks in preventing economic catastrophe. On the one hand, some economists such as Janet Yellen (often referred to as "doves") argue that greater Fed action is needed in times of economic hardship, while others ("hawks") warn against the inflationary effects of too much monetary policy action. The concluding section of this chapter looks at the actions of the Fed and the European Central Bank in stemming the economic effects from a crisis, and how economic "doves" have gained significant influence in the way monetary policy has been implemented.

CHECKPOINT

MODERN MONETARY POLICY

- In the long run, the Fed targets price stability. Low rates of inflation are most conducive to long-run economic growth.

- In the past, monetary targeting was used to control the rate of growth of the money supply. Later, an alternative approach of inflation targeting, targeting the inflation rate to around 2%, became more prevalent.

- The Fed sets a target federal funds rate and then uses open market operations to adjust reserves and keep the federal funds rate near this level.

- The Taylor rule is a general rule that ties the federal funds rate target to the inflation gap and the output gap for the economy, and has done a good job in estimating the actual federal funds rate target set by the Fed.

- When inflation rises, the Fed uses contractionary monetary policy to increase the federal funds rate to slow the economy. When the economy drifts into a recession and inflationary pressures fall, the Fed does the opposite and reduces the federal funds rate, giving the economy a boost.

- Fed transparency helps us to understand why the Fed makes particular decisions and also what the Fed will probably do in similar circumstances in the future.

QUESTION: "When central bankers aggressively bang the drum on inflation, bond investors quickly head for the exits. So it is not surprising that waves of selling have engulfed global government debt markets" (Michael Mackenzie, *Financial Times*, May 11, 2008, p. 23). Why should bond investors sell when the Fed or other central bankers decide that inflation is a growing problem?

Answers to the Checkpoint question can be found at the end of this chapter.

New Monetary Policy Challenges

For much of the past century, since the Federal Reserve Act created the Federal Reserve and with it monetary policy, policies were quite predictable and the role of the Fed was seen as an ever present but never overreaching government body. A similar sentiment was felt toward the European Central Bank (ECB), formed in 1998 in the seventeen-member (as of 2013) Eurozone.

These perceptions have changed in recent years after both the United States and Europe experienced the worst financial crisis in nearly a century. Extraordinary times called for extraordinary efforts by the Fed and the ECB, using monetary policy beyond what is used in normal times. In the United States, the recession of 2007–2009 and the subsequent slow recovery led the Fed to take drastic actions never seen in its past. More recently, the ECB made large rescue packages for member nations that neared default on their debt, taking new drastic measures to save the euro from collapse. This section presents a brief summary of the challenges faced by the Fed and the ECB, and how both have used extraordinary powers to limit the economic impact of the crises.

The Fed: Dealing with an Economic Crisis Not Seen in 80 Years

The financial meltdown that plagued the global economy in the latter part of the last decade was caused by a perfect storm of conditions. First, a world savings glut and unusually low interest rates from 2002 to 2005 led to a housing bubble. Second, financial risk was not properly accounted for, as consumers were eager to buy homes (sometimes second homes) and banks were so eager to lend that they ignored previous lending standards. Third, investors and financial institutions (including pension funds) bought trillions of dollars of assets that depended on housing values increasing consistently over the years.

When the housing bubble collapsed, the house of cards collapsed as well. Falling home values and rising mortgage payments caused homeowners to default, leading to many foreclosures. The foreclosures caused assets dependent on housing values to plummet, resulting in trillions of dollars in losses by financial firms and investors. Banks found themselves in trouble, and the government bailed out the banks by buying up bad loans to provide capital and liquidity in order to prevent bank runs and a sharp fall in lending.

In response to the financial crisis, the Fed used its normal monetary policy tools and some that it hadn't used since the 1930s. By December 2008, the Fed had lowered its federal funds target rate, using its normal monetary policy tool, to essentially 0%. By this time, the Fed turned to extraordinary measures when it began making massive loans to banks and buying large amounts of risky mortgage-backed securities. The Fed's balance sheet ballooned in size from less than $1 trillion in 2008 to over $3 trillion in 2012, a level that well exceeds that in normal times. Further, its balance sheet allocation changed dramatically from one consisting of about 90% in safe treasury securities to one comprising nearly half in more risky assets such as mortgage-backed securities.

The Fed was the prime mover in dealing with the financial crisis, once it recognized it. One can argue that it took too long for the Fed to recognize the problem, and the Fed may have encouraged the housing bubble by keeping interest rates very low for too long. Further, the government's response in bailing out financial institutions and other industries, along with a dramatic increase in the monetary base, led some to believe that the Fed overstepped its authority by exercising powers it did not have (such as its role in buying up troubled assets from banks) and expanding the monetary base too far, risking widespread inflation in the future.

But as Fed Chairman Ben Bernanke said, if your neighbor's house is on fire because he was smoking in bed, you deal with the fire first because if you don't, your own house can burn down. You deal with your neighbor's smoking problem later.

Recessions that follow a banking crisis are typically twice as long and result in nearly 4 times the loss in GDP.[2] New rules imposed on financial firms since the crisis have included higher capital requirements, restrictions on leverage, and tighter regulations. The Fed was not alone in taking drastic action. The Fed's counterpart in Europe, the ECB, took extraordinary action as well.

The Eurozone Crisis and the Role of the European Central Bank

The Eurozone was created during a 1992 meeting in the Netherlands by twelve European nations that envisioned a single currency that would reduce transaction costs and facilitate and expand trade. The meeting resulted in the signing of the Maastricht Treaty, which set the monetary criteria that each member nation had to satisfy before joining the Eurozone. These criteria included, among others:

1. Maintaining an inflation rate no higher than 1.5% above the average of the three member countries with the lowest inflation.

2. Maintaining long-term interest rates (on 10-year bonds) no higher than 2% above the average of the three member countries with the lowest interest rates.

3. Maintaining annual deficits of less than 3% of GDP.

4. Maintaining total debt of less than 60% of GDP.

5. Having no major currency devaluation in the preceding two years.

When the euro was introduced in 1999, eleven of the twelve treaty members met the monetary criteria. Greece took two extra years to satisfy the criteria and was admitted into the Eurozone in 2001.

Why were such stringent criteria needed? When a common currency is adopted, monetary policy becomes shared by all members. Therefore, a monetary crisis in one country can quickly spread to all countries. Germany, the largest and wealthiest member of the Eurozone, traditionally had maintained low inflation and a very stable economy. Although Germany had much to gain from the Eurozone, it also faced risks by integrating its monetary policy with countries whose economies were less stable. Because of Germany's fear of inflation, the Eurozone was set up in a way that prescribed austerity measures as opposed

---

[2] Financial Services Authority, *The Turner Review: A Regulatory Response to the Global Banking Crisis* (London: FSA), 2009.

to monetary expansion as a cure for debt. However, the severity of the Eurozone crisis that would ensue a decade later changed this focus, as even Germany had to accept that extraordinary actions were needed.

Still, for much of the first decade, the euro was a success, with member nations keeping their debt under control while the ECB implemented monetary policy for the entire Eurozone. However, that changed in the mid-2000s, when several member nations saw their debts rise, requiring some to sell securities (sovereign debt) on future cash revenues to keep their debt-to-GDP ratio from exceeding the Eurozone limit. However, these quick fixes worked only for a short period. A bigger crisis was brewing that would test the ability of the ECB to save the euro from collapse.

From 2008 to 2013, nearly half of the Eurozone nations faced some sort of financial crisis. In each situation, the ECB used its normal monetary policy tools in addition to extraordinary measures to lessen the economic impact of the crisis.

- **Ireland:** Ireland was one of the first member nations to face difficulties when its property bubble burst, causing all of its major banks to face insolvency in 2008. This led the Irish government to pass a law guaranteeing all bank deposits and the ECB to step in and lend billions of euros to Irish banks, an action that up to that point had never been taken on this scale.

- **Greece:** The global recession devastated Greece's shipping industry, which led to deficits and then a debt crisis in 2010. By 2012, interest rates had risen to over 25%. Further, public riots threatened Greece's ability to maintain public support for the euro and the conditions required to remain in the Eurozone. An agreement in 2012 resulted in the ECB loaning funds at favorable terms and returning billions in profits it had earned on previously held Greek bonds. In exchange, Greece agreed to debt-cutting measures, structural reforms, and greater scrutiny of its budget.

- **Portugal:** Portugal became the third country to receive a bailout package from the ECB in 2011 in exchange for promises of budget cuts and structural reforms. However, attempts at cutting the budget mostly failed, and several new laws to restrict spending were struck down by Portuguese courts in 2013. The crisis increased unemployment, which had reached 18% by mid-2013.

- **Cypress:** In 2013, Cypress became the fourth nation to receive a bailout package when heavy investments by investors and banks in private Greek industries went sour. It also became the first nation to borrow funds from the European Stability Mechanism (ESM), created by the ECB in September 2012 to provide loans to Eurozone members facing financial difficulties. Unlike Ireland's guarantee of all deposits, leadership in Cypress bent to popular demands that investors and banks not be bailed out, which further threatened the stability of its economy.

- **Spain:** Spain has faced an unrelenting economic crisis since 2008, as uncontrolled debt and unemployment led to many leadership changes in its government. In 2013, the unemployment rate reached 25%, and over 50% for those under the age of 30. Throughout this period, the ECB had stepped in by buying Spanish government bonds and making extraordinary amounts of loans (around 350 billion euros) to Spanish banks, including new loans from the ESM.

- **Italy:** Italy has long had a high debt-to-GDP ratio, even before the crisis in other countries began. It has taken many steps to reduce its debt, which has stood over 100% of its GDP for much of the past decade, though much work remains. A key obstacle facing Italy has been the lack of economic growth. While other Eurozone nations experienced economic growth following the global economic crisis, Italy's economy remained in a recession dating from 2011.

Ireland went from being the second wealthiest member of the Eurozone (after Luxembourg) to one facing the biggest financial crisis in 2008.

- **Slovenia:** In 2007, Slovenia became the 13th member of the Eurozone and the first new member since the original twelve treaty members. However, Slovenia's economy is considerably smaller than the rest of the Eurozone, and banks were never fully privatized, resulting in political influences in banking decisions. These factors made Slovenia more prone to economic downturns, and led to its financial crisis in 2013.

In sum, the ECB took extraordinary actions that it had never taken in its history to prevent financial crises in individual countries from causing the collapse of the Eurozone. First, the ECB provided loans to banks and bought government debt, and created the ESM in 2012 to manage funds being disbursed. Second, the ECB negotiated deals with private

ISSUE

The Challenges of Monetary Policy with Regional Differences in Economic Performance

In late 2011, the Eurozone reached a crisis when several of its members, notably Greece and Portugal, neared default on their national debts. Others soon followed. The worry among leaders, particularly in Germany, was that the poorer members of the Eurozone might cause the euro to collapse, bringing the European economy down with it.

Many have pointed to Europe as an experiment with monetary policy integration gone wrong: Members of the Eurozone were too different, not only culturally, but also economically. Prior to its formation in 1999, the richest member of the Eurozone, Luxembourg, had a GDP per capita that was more than twice the level of that of Portugal, which at the time was the poorest member of the original eleven countries, until Greece joined in 2001. In 2007, countries in Eastern Europe began joining, further spreading the difference between the richest and poorest members, which would all share the same currency and monetary policy determined by the European Central Bank (ECB).

Although each member nation would have representation in the ECB based on population, decisions are dominated by Germany and France, the two largest members. The challenge faced by the ECB is formulating a common monetary policy

that best fits the economic conditions faced by its members. This is not easy.

When one part of the Eurozone is booming (say Belgium) and would benefit from contractionary monetary policy, while another is struggling with debt (Greece) and requires expansionary monetary policy, choosing a common monetary policy involves placing the priority of one country's economic concerns over another.

But is the situation in Europe the only one in which a common monetary policy needs to address wide variations in economic performance? The answer is no, and the best example of another monetary zone facing similar problems may surprise you . . . the United States.

The United States shares many similarities with the Eurozone when it comes to monetary policy. Although the United States is one country, wide variations in economic performance still exist. In 2010, Maryland's per capita income of $70,000 was almost twice that of Mississippi's $36,000. Unemployment in North Dakota was less than 3% while in Nevada it was over 13%. Regions with rapid economic growth faced inflationary concerns, while struggling regions grappled with high unemployment.

Further, U.S. monetary policy also must take into account territories that

European Central Bank in Frankfurt, Germany.

Walter Bibikow/JAI/Corbis

use the U.S. dollar, such as Puerto Rico, whose per capita income is even lower than Mississippi's. And finally, some countries—such as Ecuador, El Salvador, and Panama—have unilaterally adopted the U.S. dollar as their official currency, and hence U.S. monetary policy. The Fed's decisions have a direct impact on all economies that use the U.S. dollar.

In sum, large monetary unions such as the Eurozone and the United States must weigh the priorities of one region against another when considering the policies they implement. Such a task makes the statement that *monetary policy is as much art as science* a realistic description facing central banks today.

banks and other investors to write off portions of debt and to restructure existing loans to governments. Third, it demanded that governments pass austerity measures, enact structural reforms, and be subjected to greater scrutiny. Like the Fed, the ECB's balance sheet ballooned during the crisis, from about 1 trillion euros in 2007 to over 3 trillion euros in 2012. Why was the ECB so eager to take extraordinary actions to prevent countries from defaulting on their debt?

Clearly, the number of Eurozone nations facing a financial crisis had reached a critical point. If any nation defaults and pulls out of the Eurozone, it could trigger a global loss of confidence in the euro. For example, investors might be less willing to invest in euro-denominated bonds and assets if the long-term stability of the currency came into question. Such a loss of confidence would itself reduce the stability of the euro, leading to a self-fulfilling prophecy. Imagine what would happen if a U.S. state became so much in debt that it chose to give up the U.S. dollar and create its own, much devalued, state currency. The impact could be significant. In Europe, it almost became reality in 2013.

However, the ECB used aggressive monetary policies to reduce the likelihood of a nation's exit from the Eurozone. Just as the Fed stepped in to prevent regional crises in the United States by injecting financial capital and reducing interest rates, the ECB used expansionary monetary policies to help member nations facing economic crises. This is much easier said than done, as the Issue described, when different areas of a currency zone face varying levels of economic performance.

Today, many of the financial crises have stabilized for the time being, though by no means have they been resolved. Although Ireland's banks were recapitalized and interest rates in Greece returned to normal levels, the economies of the Eurozone nations remain tenuous, which means that the ECB will likely continue to exert its influence for years to come.

In the United States, the housing market has started to recover, stock markets have set new highs, and banks have strengthened their balance sheets. Still, as in Europe, problems such as persistent unemployment and deficits remain in the United States, which means that the Fed will continue to rely on monetary tools to prevent problems from home and abroad from engulfing the economy.

The next chapter is devoted to analyzing the major macroeconomic policy challenges involving both fiscal policy and monetary policy, allowing you to use the macroeconomic tools learned thus far to sketch out solutions.

 CHECKPOINT

NEW MONETARY POLICY CHALLENGES

- To control the financial panic of 2008, the Fed used its normal monetary policy tools and some that it hadn't used since the 1930s.

- The European Central Bank is the Fed's counterpart in Europe, setting the monetary policy for the seventeen-member Eurozone.

- A long and severe debt crisis occurred when several European nations neared default on their loans and came close to exiting the Eurozone, requiring extraordinary actions, including bailout loans, by the ECB to keep the effects of the crisis from spreading to the entire Eurozone.

QUESTION: The collapse of the financial markets in late 2008 resulted in the Fed reducing interest rates to near 0%. Was it likely that the U.S. economy in 2009 sank into a Keynesian liquidity trap?

Answers to the Checkpoint question can be found at the end of this chapter.

chapter summary

Section 1: **What Is Monetary Policy?**

Monetary policy is the process by which a country's money supply is controlled to target interest rates that subsequently influences economic output and prices.

Importance of Interest Rates on the Economy

Higher interest rates affect aggregate demand by:

1. Making borrowing more expensive, forcing consumers and firms to cut spending and investing.

2. Giving people more incentive to save than spend.

3. Forcing the government to spend more on financing the national debt.

4. Increasing the value of the U.S. dollar, making U.S. exports more expensive.

Twin Goals of Monetary Policy

1. Economic growth and full employment

2. Stable prices and moderate long-term interest rates

Bills, bills, bills. Higher interest rates cause debt payments to take a bigger portion of each paycheck, leaving less to spend on other goods.

Image Source/Corbis

Expansionary monetary policy: More money → lower interest rates → higher C, I, G, and (X – M) = increase in aggregate demand and output.

Contractionary monetary policy: Less money → higher interest rates → lower C, I, G, and (X – M) = decrease in aggregate demand and output.

Section 2: **Monetary Theories**

The **quantity theory of money** is a product of the classical school of thought, which concludes that the economy will tend toward equilibrium at full employment in the long run.

Classical theorists do not believe that monetary policies are effective at all.

Keynesians and monetarists believe that monetary policy can be effective in the short run, but not in the long run.

Equation of Exchange (Classical Theory)

$$M \times V = P \times Q$$

$$\uparrow \qquad \uparrow$$

Fixed   **Fixed**

$$\Delta M = \Delta P$$

Because velocity (V) and output (Q) are believed to be fixed in the long run, any change in the money supply (M) results in a change in prices (P).

Keynesian Money Theory

Increasing the money supply leads to greater investment when the economy is healthy. In times of severe recession, however, monetary policy is ineffective.

Fiscal policy is the preferred approach to restore the economy.

Tim Gidal/Picture Post/Getty Images

John Maynard Keynes

Monetarist Theory

Increasing the money supply reduces interest rates, which leads to greater consumption and investment. Monetary policy is therefore effective in the short run.

Believes fiscal policy crowds out consumption and investment, thus is ineffective.

Bettmann/Corbis

Milton Friedman

Demand Shocks Versus Supply Shocks

Demand shocks affect the AD curve.

- Caused by factors such as consumer confidence, business sentiment, or export demand.
- Monetary policy is easier because targeting one goal automatically targets the other.

Supply shocks affect the SRAS curve.

- Caused by factors such as changing input prices or technological innovation.
- Monetary policy is difficult because targeting one goal makes the other target worse.

Volker Moehrke/Corbis

Rising oil and fuel prices cause a negative supply shock that is difficult to counteract with monetary policy.

Section 3: **Modern Monetary Policy**

Rules: Money grows by a fixed amount each year, preventing monetary policy from causing too drastic an effect because the economy is inherently stable in the long run.

versus

Discretion: Flexible money approach based on current economic conditions; useful in severe recessions when constant money growth might not be enough.

Magictorch/Ikon Images/Corbis

Alternative to money targeting is **inflation targeting:** implementing policy to keep inflation at about 2% to faciliate long-term economic growth.

Taylor rule: Used to approximate the Fed's actions on interest rates based on economic conditions:

Fed Funds Rate Target = 2 + Inflation Rate + 1/2 (Inflation Gap) + 1/2(Output Gap)

Section 4: **New Monetary Policy Challenges**

The U.S. financial crisis in 2008 created a major challenge to the Fed, which had lowered the federal funds rate to near 0% and still faced an economy in deep recession.

The seventeen member nations that form the Eurozone share a monetary policy set by the European Central Bank (ECB). In recent years, ECB has used aggressive monetary policy actions to prevent the effects of financial crises in individual nations from engulfing the entire region.

To continue expansionary monetary policy with interest rates at 0%, the Fed engaged in various **quantitative easing** strategies, including purchasing long-term assets from banks to expand the monetary base.

Andy Rain/epa/Corbis

Protests on quantitative easing arose because people feared high potential inflation, which will reduce the value of money and savings.

KEY CONCEPTS

expansionary monetary policy, p. 629
contractionary monetary policy,
  p. 630
equation of exchange, p. 631
liquidity trap, p. 634

easy money, quantitative easing, or
  accommodative monetary policy,
  p. 638
tight money or restrictive monetary
  policy, p. 638

monetary rule, p. 639
inflation targeting, p. 639
Taylor rule, p. 639

QUESTIONS AND PROBLEMS

Check Your Understanding

1. Why is it important for the Federal Reserve Board to be independent of the executive branch of the federal government?

2. When the interest rate falls, why do people desire higher money balances?

3. Describe how open market operations alter the supply of money.

4. What does the equation of exchange, $M \times V = P \times Q$, help to explain?

5. How is the impact of expansionary monetary policy different when the economy is considerably below full employment than when it is at full employment?

6. How do sticky wages and prices make monetary policy effective in the short run?

Apply the Concepts

7. Suppose a rise in consumer confidence causes aggregate demand to increase, resulting in a short-run equilibrium that is above full employment output. What type of monetary policy might the Fed use to reduce inflationary pressures and to bring the economy back to full employment?

8. It seems that each time the Fed raises interest rates, the stock market has an awful few days. Why do higher interest rates have such an impact on the stock market?

9. If the Fed persistently pursues an easy money policy, what is the likely outcome?

10. When NASA scientists were operating the Mars rovers to get them to drive across the Martian landscape and collect and analyze rocks and crevices, the scientists complained that the 20-minute delay between when they issued a command and when the rovers responded made their job more challenging. Isn't this somewhat similar to what monetary policymakers face? How is it different?

11. Suppose another spike in energy prices causes a negative supply shock to occur. What type of monetary policy should the Fed use if the goal is to maintain price stability in the economy? What are the consequences of doing so?

12. Explain how the housing bubble at the beginning of the 21st century led to the Taylor rule target exceeding the actual federal funds rate. Could increasing the federal funds rate during this time have helped to reduce the severity of the last recession?

In the News

13. *There are two forces that cause the economy to grow. One is real, the other is an illusion. The real force—entrepreneurial innovation and creativity—comes naturally as long as government policies do not drive it away. The artificial force is easy money. An increased supply of money, by creating an illusion of wealth, can increase spending in the short run, but this eventually turns into inflation. Printing money cannot possibly create wealth; if it could, counterfeiting would be legal.*[3]

---

[3] Brian Wesbury, "Economic Rehab," *The Wall Street Journal*, June 7, 2006, p. A14.

Does this quote illustrate the short-run versus the long-run aspects of monetary policy? Why or why not?

14. *The Economist* commented on the Greek debt crisis in an aptly titled article on February 11, 2012, "Brinkmanship in Athens," as Greece led the European economy to the edge as a battle brewed between Greek political leaders attempting to satisfy its citizens' demands and the European Central Bank, which held the much needed rescue funds but demanded major fiscal reforms in return. Using an AD/AS model, explain how a major monetary stimulus from the European Central Bank would affect Greece's economy. Next, explain what the required austerity measures (i.e., budget cuts) might do to the economy. Do these measures conflict with each other? Explain.

Solving Problems

15. Why are supply shocks so much harder than demand shocks for monetary policy to adjust to? Use the grid below to show your answer to this question.

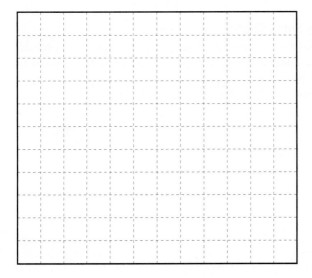

16. In 2012, the U.S. inflation rate was 2.1% and output was 4.8% below its long-run potential output due to the slow recovery of the economy. Assuming that the inflation target is 2%, what would be the federal funds target rate if the FOMC used the Taylor rule? How does this compare to the actual federal funds rate of 0.1%?

⊞ USING THE NUMBERS

17. According to By the Numbers, what were the approximate interest rates for the following types of loans in September 2013: federal funds rate, discount rate, prime rate, 30-year mortgage rate? Why aren't these interest rates all the same?

18. According to By the Numbers, in what region outside of the United States is the largest percentage of U.S. $100 bills in circulation held? Why is the answer not China, which holds the most U.S. debt?

ANSWERS TO QUESTIONS IN CHECKPOINTS

Checkpoint: What Is Monetary Policy?

Expansionary monetary policy reduces interest rates in order to spur consumption and investment, leading to an increase in aggregate demand. A reduction in interest rates placed on student loans by the government, although technically not monetary policy, produces a similar effect. When your monthly payments are reduced due to the interest rate reduction, you now have extra money to spend on other items. This extra consumption contributes to an increase in aggregate demand, much like an expansionary monetary policy would do.

Checkpoint: Monetary Theories

Those who prefer a large government role in the economy would best resemble Keynesians who believe in fiscal policy to increase aggregate demand. Those who advocate for a smaller government might be considered monetarists, who believe that fiscal policy tends to crowd out consumption and investment. Those who do not believe in either fiscal or monetary policy interventions might resemble classical theorists who believe that the economy should be left to market forces.

Checkpoint: Modern Monetary Policy

When the Fed begins to view inflation as a growing problem, it usually means that some form of contractionary monetary policy is to follow. This typically means that interest rates will rise and, most important for bond investors, bond prices will *fall* and bondholders will incur capital losses.

Checkpoint: New Monetary Policy Challenges

Reducing interest rates to low levels to stimulate credit and the economy was probably not sufficient by itself. But as consumer spending dropped off, business avoided new investments as markets declined or disappeared, suggesting that the economy may have been in a liquidity trap. Keynesian analysis got the nod from policymakers with the $787 billion fiscal stimulus package.

25

Macroeconomic Policy: Challenges in a Global Economy

Between 2003 and 2007, the U.S. housing market achieved gains at a rate never before seen in its history. As soon as a house or condo was put on the market, buyers were eager to snatch it up. Banks were eager to lend to these buyers and bent over backward to accommodate them, even lowering standards if need be. If they did not, other banks were ready to jump in. The upshot: new types of loans targeted to borrowers who otherwise would not have qualified for conventional loans. And the government facilitated the process by keeping interest rates low.

These factors provided incentives for individuals and firms to consume and produce. Luxury condominiums were built throughout the country, especially in popular vacation destinations such as Miami, Phoenix, and Las Vegas. New housing developments formed, each adding hundreds or thousands of homes with the expectation that buyers would come. And they did, helped by banks that became even more aggressive in their lending, advertising attractive mortgages that required no down payment, interest-only payments, and little to no credit.

Over this period, average home prices in the United States increased by 41%. In Nevada and Arizona, home prices rose by almost 80%. The growth in the housing market spurred other industries, such as home furnishings, insurance, and even automobiles. Individuals were eager to buy, developers were eager to build, banks were eager to lend, and investors were eager to put money in securities backed by the value of housing.

Unfortunately, the house of cards eventually collapsed in late 2007, with the effects still felt five years later. The worst financial crisis in generations led to a restricted lending market, a severe recession, and a long jobless recovery.

What does macroeconomics have to say about the effects of a deep economic recession and a slow economic recovery? Quite a bit, actually. We have seen in previous chapters how the Fed and the federal government intervene in markets to promote long-term economic growth and stability in employment and prices. But this is much harder than it might appear to be: There is no magic formula easily discernible to all that will correct each problem.

Before the 1930s, common wisdom was that the economy was best left alone. The Great Depression changed that, and ever since then the government's role in economic stabilization—smoothing the business cycle—expanded substantially.

This chapter studies the economic policies that address the macroeconomic issues facing the world today: persistent unemployment, long-run inflation, debt, and economic growth. One challenge is the existence of a potential tradeoff between inflation and unemployment. Another is the potential tradeoff between debt reduction and economic growth. These potential tradeoffs influence the macroeconomic policies chosen to guide the economy.

The chapter begins with a broad overview of the factors leading to the 2007–2009 Great Recession (as it is now known) and the slow recovery, and includes a short discussion of policy options. The chapter then studies several theories regarding the effectiveness of macroeconomic policy, including the Phillips curve on the potential tradeoff between unemployment and inflation, the rational expectations argument about the ultimate ineffectiveness of policy, and the new Keynesian response.

Finally, we discuss the economic issues that influence the future of our economy. We focus on the effects of deficits and growing debt, persistent unemployment, and globalization. We use the macroeconomic tools discussed throughout the book to analyze how economic policies affect our economy and our standard of living.

The Great Recession and Macroeconomic Policy

The 18-month recession that lasted from December 2007 to July 2009 was dubbed the Great Recession, not because of its length, which was not much longer than the typical recession, but rather for its severity and the impact it had on so many industries and countries. Further, the economic recovery that took place after the recession was slow, requiring many years for economic indicators to return to their prerecession levels. The unemployment rate, for example, remained above 7% even four years after the recession ended. This section presents the factors that led to the Great Recession and the macroeconomic policies used to mitigate its effects.

BY THE NUMBERS

The Long Road Back: The Great Recession and the Jobless Recovery

The Great Recession was caused by the collapse of the housing market, which led to reduced consumer sentiment and lower retail sales. Persistent unemployment ensued and the Fed used unprecedented monetary policy actions to speed up the economic recovery.

Median existing home prices rose significantly in the early years of the 21st century but fell quickly in the latter part of the decade. Housing prices have since risen again.

Consumer sentiment fell from 2007 to 2009. It has since risen with the economic recovery; however, as of 2013 consumer sentiment had not returned to its prerecession peak.

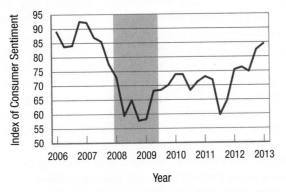

Monthly real retail sales fell over 10% from 2007 to 2009. It took four years for real retail sales to recover and to surpass the level reached in 2007.

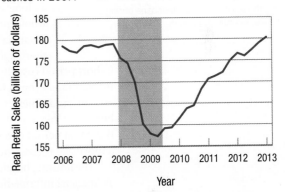

7,163,000
Total jobs lost during the Great Recession (December 2007–June 2009).

5,485,000
Total jobs created over four years of recovery (July 2009–June 2013).

The Federal Reserve undertook four rounds of quantitative easing (QE) after short-term interest rates were effectively lowered to 0%. The value of assets purchased in each round:

QE1 (December 2008–March 2010): $1,425 billion

QE2 (November 2010–June 2011): $600 billion

QE3 (September 2012– ?): $40 billion/month ($520 billion through October 2013)

QE4 (December 2012– ?): $45 billion/month ($450 billion through October 2013)

Credit Application

The Fed's actions kept long-term interest rates low, encouraging consumers and businesses to borrow in order to consume and invest. But would lenders lend?

From the Housing Bubble to the Financial Crisis

Owning a home is a dream shared by most people. During the first few years of the 21st century, a glut in worldwide savings and the Fed's aggressive expansionary monetary policies following the 2001 recession led to low mortgage rates, helping many to achieve that dream of home ownership. Renters bought their first homes. Existing homeowners moved into larger homes or bought second homes. The resulting higher than normal demand drove up the price of housing. After a few years of rising prices, people started to think prices could only go up. This led some people to become speculators, which led to house "flipping"—purchasing a home with the intention of selling it as soon as possible for a tidy profit.

Builders provide homes, but usually a third party brings the transaction to a close: A financial intermediary provides the financing for home buyers in the form of a mortgage. For many years, the standard mortgage was a 30-year mortgage with a fixed interest rate. The person taking out the mortgage to purchase the home made monthly payments, which consisted of interest on the loan and some payment toward the loan amount (the principal). Financial intermediaries, such as banks, usually had high standards that would-be home buyers had to meet. Further, a home buyer's income and credit quality were rigorously checked by the financial intermediaries.

First homes, bigger homes, and second homes were the goals of many Americans during the housing bubble of the early 21st century.

This changed at the beginning of the new century, as banks eager to cash in on the lucrative housing market made loans easier to obtain. And, as long as housing prices kept rising, the borrower's collateral (the house) would protect the bank from losing money if the loan could not be repaid. Financial intermediaries encouraged home buying by offering adjustable-rate mortgages (ARMs). These mortgages offered a below-market interest rate for a short period (usually three or five years); the rate would then adjust based on the market interest rate. From a buyer's point of view, a below-market rate, at least in the short term, was an inducement to buy. From a bank's point of view, below-market rates generated business: They could expect ARM holders to seek out fixed interest rate mortgages after the initial period ended, which meant a second round of origination fees (paid whenever a mortgage is taken out).

The housing boom of 2003 to 2007 saw even more innovations in the mortgage market, as financial intermediaries felt competitive pressure from new mortgage brokers and Wall Street firms that were only too happy to meet the growing demand. Two key things happened: Mortgage credit standards fell, and the market for collateralized debt obligations (CDOs) developed.

Subprime Mortgages and Collateralized Debt Obligations

subprime mortgage Mortgages that are given to borrowers who are a poor credit risk. These higher-risk loans charge a higher interest rate, which can be profitable to lenders if borrowers make their payments on time.

Subprime mortgages are loans made to borrowers with poor credit. These loans carried high interest rates that were profitable for the banks as long as borrowers made payments on time. Because the economy was strong, defaults were minimal. Further, many financial institutions reduced their risk by selling off these loans to other investors in the form of CDOs, also known as mortgage-backed securities (which make up most CDOs).

CDOs are essentially bonds backed by a collection of mortgages: prime, subprime, home equity, and other ARMs. Banks holding mortgages found they could offset the risk of default by selling them to consolidators who put together enormous packages of CDOs, with the mortgaged homes standing as the collateral behind the security offered. Wall Street then sold off slices of these mortgage pools to investors interested in the steady income from mortgage payments. Mortgages to subprime borrowers—people with a lower ability to pay or who were poor credit risks for other reasons—could be combined with solid mortgages, a little like diluting poison in a large lake to dissipate its effects.

Banks and mortgage companies now were evaluating mortgage clients for loans that they did not intend to keep. They were simply collecting an origination fee and then immediately selling the mortgage to Wall Street. What in the past had been a long-term investment for banks and mortgage companies became nothing more than a business of advertising and selling loans quickly. Because Wall Street could package and sell as many loans as mortgage brokers could provide, banks had less incentive to keep high lending standards based on credit history and large down payments. Risk was being transferred elsewhere. People, no matter how bad their credit history, could get a loan for a piece of real estate without putting any money down. In one extreme and famous case, a farm laborer with an annual income of $14,000 was given a $720,000 loan on a Bakersfield, California, home.

Trouble started in 2007 when some of the people who took on subprime mortgages started to default. These people were stretched too thin. When their ARMs reset, they faced higher payments, sometimes double or triple the original monthly payments. Worse, the spike in foreclosures as well as homeowners trying to sell their homes to escape rising mortgage payments caused the value of houses to fall, which meant that borrowers wishing to refinance their homes (to make mortgage payments affordable again) were being turned away because the amount they were seeking to borrow exceeded the value of their now lower-value home.

Compounding this, another problem arose. Risk ratings by bond rating agencies whose job it is to rate packages of mortgages turned out to be faulty. Wall Street knew the minimum requirements needed for a rating agency to assign a AAA rating to a CDO, and they manipulated the components to get that all-important rating. Also, rating firms were paid 6 times their normal fee to give the AAA rating to the mortgage packages, and were only paid *if the CDO got the AAA rating*, giving ratings agencies an incentive to lower standards. Investors wanted bonds with the security of a AAA rating, which gave the appearance of high-yield, low-risk investments. The bond packages sold well all over the world. The risk of each CDO was underestimated because of the overly rosy ratings.

Two more problems would make this a growing house of cards. Because the mortgage packages were seen as low-risk investments, many investors borrowed money at the low prevailing interest rates to purchase greater quantities. They **leveraged** their capital to earn greater returns. But with leverage comes additional risk: A small drop in prices can easily wipe out a highly leveraged account. Table 1 shows how a leveraged investment magnifies the risk of losing money. In this case, a 10% drop in value of the security wipes out the leveraged account, while the nonleveraged account sees its value drop by just 10%. A leveraged account magnifies both gains and losses.

To protect against this risk, investors purchased **credit default swaps,** an instrument developed by the financial industry to act as an insurance policy against defaults. The biggest issuer of credit default swaps, the American Insurance Group (AIG), sold several *trillion* dollars of these swaps with only a few *billion* dollars in capital to back them up. Here again we see risk underestimated, and therefore mispriced.

leverage Occurs when investors borrow money at low interest rates to purchase investments that may provide higher rates of return. The risk of highly leveraged investments is that a small decrease in price can wipe out one's account.

credit default swap A financial instrument that insures against the potential default on an asset. Because of the extent of defaults in the last financial crisis, issuers of credit default swaps could not repay all of the claims, bankrupting these financial institutions.

The Magnified Risk of Leveraged Investments	TABLE 1

Nonleveraged Investment	Leveraged Investment
Initial account value: $10,000	Initial account value: $10,000
Leverage ratio: 1:1	Leverage ratio: 10:1
Value of invested assets: $10,000 ($10,000 × 1)	Value of invested assets: $100,000 ($10,000 × 10)
Event: 10% drop in invested assets	Event: 10% drop in invested assets
Drop in value of investment: $1,000 ($10,000 × 10%)	Drop in value of investment: $10,000 ($100,000 × 10%)
New account value: $9,000	New account value: $0

Collapsing Financial Markets This brings us to the central event that brought down the financial system. By 2007, $25 *trillion* of American CDOs were in investment portfolios of banks, pension funds, mutual funds, hedge funds, and other financial institutions worldwide. The rate of subprime mortgage defaults was on the rise: Up to a quarter of the mortgages in CDOs might default, representing a default rate 10 times greater than that anticipated by the AAA rating models. Because investors did not know what exactly was in their CDOs (the prospectuses were impenetrable), they panicked and tried to sell these investments.

The collapse of the housing market forced many homeowners out of their homes and contributed to the severity of the 2007–2009 recession.

Because the CDOs were too complex to evaluate, the market collapsed. Buyers evaporated, and prices fell as people began dumping CDOs at fire-sale prices. AIG could not cover the losses it had insured and went bankrupt. For banks, this was a catastrophe. Their CDOs were virtually worthless, and an important part of the banks' capital was wiped out. To raise capital, banks called in loans and reduced lines of credit to businesses, which reduced the money supply, contracted the economy, caused job losses, and deepened the recession.

In sum, the financial crisis was caused by a savings glut that led to low interest rates, which fueled a housing boom that led to new financial instruments and investment securities that depended on the value of housing staying high. A financial house of cards was created, and when one card at the bottom (subprime loans) lost strength, the entire edifice fell. Because all types of financial institutions worldwide were investors in CDOs, credit dried up, creating a credit crisis that precipitated a worldwide recession.

The Government's Policy Response

As long as the financial system takes on risks that it misperceives, we will have financial crises. Let's look at the government's policy response to the financial crisis:

- Bear Stearns: In July 2007, Bear Stearns, a large Wall Street investment bank, liquidated two hedge funds that invested in mortgage-backed securities as they started to collapse. By March 2008, with Bear Stearns on the verge of bankruptcy due to its holdings of mortgage-backed securities, the Fed engineered a takeover of Bear Stearns by Chase Bank. In essence, the Fed was bailing out a rogue bank. This kept a lid on things for a while, but not for long.

- Lehman Brothers: Stung by criticism of its Bear Stearns bailout, the Fed let Lehman Brothers, the fourth largest commercial bank, fail on September 15, 2007. The Fed and the Treasury thought they were sending a message to the financial markets that imprudent behavior such as that displayed by Lehman Brothers would result in tremendous costs to stockholders and executives. Unfortunately, this decision sent the financial markets into a tailspin, as banks lost faith in other banks, and insolvencies rose throughout the financial sector.

- AIG: The market received another shock in September when AIG announced it was bankrupt. The news of its bankruptcy turned AAA-rated CDO bonds into highly discounted junk bonds. To stem the panic, the Fed lent AIG over $100 billion.

- TARP: In October 2008, Congress responded to the crisis by passing the $700 billion Troubled Asset Relief Program (TARP), authorizing the U.S. Treasury to purchase CDOs from banks to shore up their capital. The U.S. Treasury ended up investing in banks by injecting government money for preferred equity (stock), thereby increasing bank capital and eliminating insolvency.

- Public Concerns: Policymakers were concerned about public confidence in banks and worried that depositors might begin withdrawing funds, putting banks at further risk of failure. The Federal Deposit Insurance Corporation (FDIC) increased its guarantee on deposits from $100,000 to $250,000 per account.

- The 2009 Stimulus Package: One of President Obama's first pieces of legislation in his first term was passing the $787 billion American Recovery and Reinvestment Act, a fiscal policy aimed to boost aggregate demand following the financial crisis and recession.

- Industry Bailouts: The financial crisis had also depressed consumer demand, which led many industries to face collapse. In 2009, the government loaned significant sums of money to General Motors, Chrysler, and Ford to save the U.S. automobile industry. Today, the U.S. automobile industry is profitable and strong: In 2012, each of the three major automobile companies made substantial profits and combined earned a profit of $13.2 billion.

- Fed's Quantitative Easing Programs: Over the next several years, the Fed would continue to buy mortgage-backed securities in order to remove these risky assets from bank balance sheets. The effort was unprecedented, with the Fed accumulating over $1 trillion in mortgage-backed securities by 2012.

These extraordinary efforts prevented the widespread bank failures that had plagued the economy during the Great Depression and during the Savings and Loan Crisis in the 1980s. For the Fed, it was crucial to maintain public confidence and keep the recession from becoming a full-blown depression. The Fed stepped far outside of its usual role of managing the money supply, interest rates, inflation, and unemployment, and took extraordinary, lender-of-last-resort measures to prevent a financial sector meltdown.

This brief summary of the government's response during the financial crisis outlines the breadth and depth of fiscal and monetary policies designed to avert a catastrophe. They have succeeded, but the cost may not be known for a decade.

The Financial Crisis and Its Effects

The economy grew nicely between 2005 and the end of 2007. Inflation was low and the economy grew at about 2.5% a year. When we discussed lags in a previous chapter, we saw how it takes time to ascertain when an economy enters a recession. In hindsight, it is easy to see when this recession started. Figure 1 shows hypothetical aggregate demand and short-run

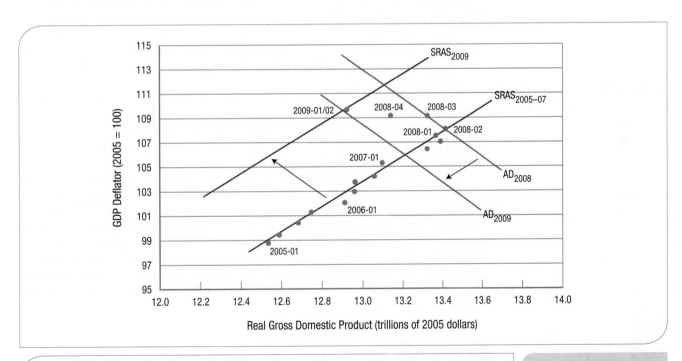

The 2007–2009 Recession

This figure illustrates the 2007–2009 downturn by using real GDP and the GDP deflator data for 2005 through 2009 and superimposing hypothetical aggregate demand and short-run aggregate supply curves on the data. Because of the financial crisis, consumer spending declined, reducing aggregate demand in 2008 and 2009. Layoffs ensued and short-run aggregate supply declined as well. During this period, real output declined by over 4%.

FIGURE 1

aggregate supply curves superimposed over the actual data for the years 2005 to 2009. Follow the dots and you can see progressive growth in real GDP until the end of 2007. This recession began at the end of 2007 and accelerated in 2008 until the middle of 2009. Real GDP declined by over 4% and unemployment reached 10% of the labor force.

How can we explain this shift in aggregate demand and short-run aggregate supply? The recession was brought on by the financial crisis, which in turn was brought on by the mispricing of the risk of subprime mortgages and by excessive consumer debt. At the onset of the financial crisis, jobs were cut as consumers reduced their spending: They tightened their belts in an effort to reduce household debt levels and hunkered down for what they perceived as a severe recession on the way. As a result, 7 million people lost their jobs during this two-year period. Job losses reduced consumer confidence, further reducing consumer spending, which shifted aggregate demand from AD_{2008} toward AD_{2009}. As demand dropped, businesses reduced their production capacity through layoffs and plant closings, shifting short-run aggregate supply leftward from its original trajectory at $SRAS_{2005-2007}$ to that shown as $SRAS_{2009}$.

Toward the end of the recession, prices began to fall as *deflation* set in for most of 2009. We have spent a considerable time in this book studying the harmful effects of inflation, yet now the economy faced deflation. Deflation can be a problem because it increases the *real* value of existing debt, making the debt more burdensome and requiring more purchasing power to make interest payments or pay off the debt. Policymakers faced the problem of preventing debt from becoming a more serious burden on households, which would further reduce aggregate demand and deepen the recession.

Financial Crises and Macroeconomic Policy

For most college students, the 2007–2009 financial crisis and the accompanying recession represents their first experience with a *serious* downturn in the economy. The previous two slumps (1990–1991 and 2001) were shallow and lasted only eight months, but were followed by a period of slow job growth.

The savings and loan collapse (our last banking crisis) happened nearly 30 years ago, therefore most people under 45 cannot recollect its impact. Over the last 40 years, Europe, the United States, Australia, and New Zealand have endured a total of 18 bank-centered financial crises.

One of the themes of financial crises is excessive debt accumulation by consumers, firms, banks, and government, which creates a greater risk to the economy during downturns. Bailouts resulting from financial crises are expensive and recessions are costly both for the government and for the people unemployed. More distressing is that recessions associated with bank-centered financial crises tend to last much longer.

The tools we learned about in previous chapters helped us to understand how the government managed the most recent financial crisis. Let's take a further step, adding in some challenges to the effective use of policy to smooth the business cycle. The next section focuses on the effectiveness of macroeconomic policy by considering the Phillips curve, which proposes a tradeoff between unemployment and inflation. If this tradeoff exists, policymaking becomes simple: Pick some rate of unemployment and face a corresponding rate of inflation. We also look at how the rational expectations model questions whether using macroeconomic policy to correct fluctuations in the business cycle can ever be effective at all.

 CHECKPOINT

THE GREAT RECESSION AND MACROECONOMIC POLICY

- A world savings glut and low interest rates from 2003–2007 led to a housing price bubble. Consumers were eager to buy homes, developers were eager to build them, banks were eager to lend money to purchasers, and investors were eager to invest in CDOs.

- Financial risk was not properly accounted for in the period leading up to the financial crisis, and ratings agencies gave too many CDOs a AAA rating that wasn't deserved.

- When the housing bubble collapsed, foreclosures on subprime mortgages sent the economy into a recession.
- To control the panic, the Fed used its normal monetary policy tools and some that it hadn't used since the 1930s in its role as lender of last resort.
- Congress used fiscal policy in an attempt to nullify the drop in aggregate demand caused by the financial crisis.

QUESTION: The U.S. housing bubble in the early 21st century was caused by a number of factors that provided incentives to individuals to buy houses, to businesses to build and sell houses, and to financial institutions to loan money. In hindsight, what are some policies that the government could have implemented to mitigate this housing bubble?

Answers to the Checkpoint question can be found at the end of this chapter.

Effectiveness of Macroeconomic Policy: Phillips Curves and Rational Expectations

The persistent unemployment that occurred after the 2007–2009 recession in what is known as a jobless recovery had economists debating the right policy to use. Fiscal policy was undertaken to boost market activity, at the cost of rising debt. And significant monetary policy actions were taken to inject the economy with more money, at the cost of potential inflation. Questions that arise from these policies include whether the effort to reduce unemployment could result in higher inflation, or whether macroeconomic policy has any short-term effects at all. We address these issues in this section by studying two theories developed in the 1950s and 1960s: the Phillips curve and rational expectations.

With Phillips curve analysis, it first seemed that fiscal policy was easy: Pick an unemployment rate from column A and get a corresponding inflation rate from column B. Unfortunately, reality turned out to be much more complex. With rational expectations, the question was whether policy could ever be effective at all.

Unemployment and Inflation: Phillips Curves

Does a relationship exist between unemployment and inflation? In his early work, A. W. Phillips compared the rate of change in money wages to unemployment rates in Britain over the years 1861 to 1957. The negatively sloped curve shown in Figure 2 reflects his estimate of how these variables were related and has been called a **Phillips curve** in his honor. As you can see, when unemployment rises, wage rates fall.

Phillips curve The original curve posited a negative relationship between wages and unemployment, but later versions related unemployment to inflation rates.

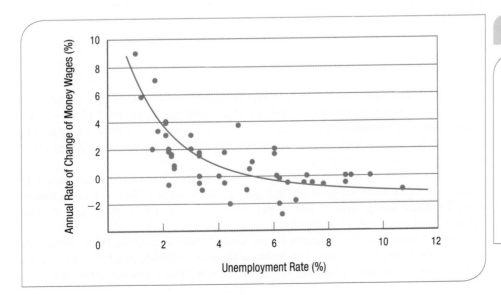

FIGURE 2

The Original Phillips Curve for Britain (1861–1957)

A. W. Phillips compared the rate of change in money wages to unemployment rates in Britain from 1861 to 1957. The resulting nonlinear, negatively sloped curve is the first example of a Phillips curve. When unemployment rises, wage rates fall, and vice versa. Note that some dots represent multiple years.

What explains this negative relationship between wages and unemployment? Labor costs or wages are typically a firm's largest cost component. As the demand for labor rises, labor markets will tighten, making it difficult for employers to fill vacant positions. Hence, wages rise as firms bid up the price of labor to attract more workers. The opposite happens when labor demand falls: Unemployment rises and wages decline.

This relationship can be seen in specific industries that have seen spikes or downturns in employment. For example, demand for health care professionals increased in the past decade, reducing unemployment in the industry. Those who pursue a career in nursing, medicine, or other health-related fields saw their salaries increase relative to those in other careers. On the other hand, the collapse of the financial and housing sectors forced many realtors, loan specialists, and construction workers out of work. Those lucky enough to find work often made less than they did during the housing boom.

The market relationship between wages and unemployment will clearly affect prices. But worker productivity also plays an important role in determining prices.

Productivity, Prices, and Wages We might think that whenever wages rise, prices must also rise. Higher wages mean higher labor costs for employers—costs that businesses then pass along as higher prices. But this is not always the case. If worker productivity increases enough to offset the wage increase, then product prices can remain stable. The basic relationship among wages, prices, and productivity is

Inflation = Increase in Nominal Wages − Rate of Increase in Labor Productivity

For example, when wages increase by 5% and productivity increases by 3%, inflation is 2%. Given this relationship, the Phillips curve can be adapted to relate productivity to inflation and unemployment, as shown in Figure 3.

FIGURE 3

The Phillips Curve

A rise in wages may cause a rise in prices, but if worker productivity increases sufficiently to offset the wage increase, product prices can remain stable. When the rates of change in productivity and wages are equal, inflation is zero (point a). This is the natural rate of unemployment. If policymakers want to use expansionary policy to reduce unemployment from u_n to u_1, they must be willing to accept inflation of p_1. Reducing unemployment further to u_2 would raise inflation to p_2 as labor markets tighten and wages rise more rapidly than productivity.

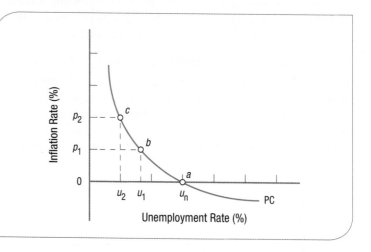

Notice that when the rates of change in productivity and wages are equal, inflation is zero (point a). This occurs at the natural rate of unemployment, the unemployment rate when inflationary pressures are nonexistent. Therefore, higher rates of productivity growth mean that for a given level of unemployment, inflation will be less (the Phillips curve would shift in toward the origin).

If policymakers want to use expansionary policy to reduce unemployment from u_n to u_1, then according to the curve shown in Figure 3, they must be willing to accept inflation of p_1. To reduce unemployment further to u_2 would raise inflation to p_2 as labor markets tightened and wages rose more rapidly.

Figure 4 shows the Phillips curve for the United States during the 1960s. Notice the nearly smooth negative relationship between the two variables, much like that in the last two figures. As unemployment fell, inflation rose. This empirical relationship led

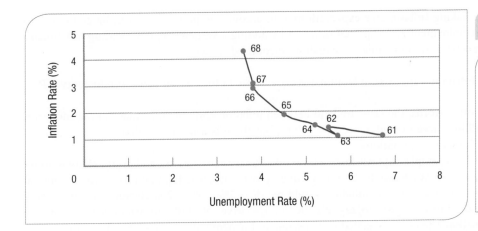

FIGURE 4

The Phillips Curve—1960s

The Phillips curve for the United States during the 1960s gives a smooth negative relationship between inflation and unemployment, much like that found in the last two figures. Using this relationship, policymakers concluded that an inflation rate of 3% to 4% was required to keep unemployment below 4%.

policymakers to believe that the economy presents them with a menu of choices. By accepting a minor rise in inflation, they could keep unemployment low. Alternatively, by accepting a rise in unemployment, they could keep inflation near zero.

But just as policymakers were getting used to the ease of making policy by accepting moderate inflation in exchange for lower unemployment rates, the economy played a big trick on them. As Figure 5 shows, the entire Phillips curve began shifting outward during the early 1970s.

What looked to be an easy tradeoff between inflation and unemployment turned ugly. Unemployment rates that, in the 1960s, had been associated with modest inflation of 2% to 3% quickly began requiring twice that rate in the early 1970s. By the late 1970s, these same unemployment rates were generating annual inflation rates approaching double digits. The reason for these shifts turned out to be the oil supply shocks of the mid-1970s and the rising inflationary expectations that followed.

The Importance of Inflationary Expectations Workers do not work for the sake of earning a specific dollar amount, or a specific nominal wage. Rather, they work for the sake of earning what those wages will buy—for real wages. Consequently, when they bargain for wage increases, workers will take their past experiences with inflation into account.

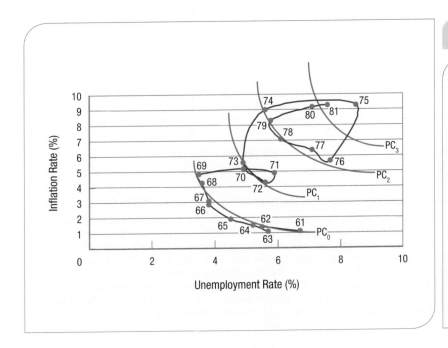

FIGURE 5

The Phillips Curve from 1961–1981: Instability and Supply Shocks

Just as policymakers were getting used to accepting moderate inflation in exchange for lower unemployment rates, the economy surprised them. The entire Phillips curve began shifting outward during the early 1970s. Unemployment rates that, in the 1960s, had been associated with modest inflation of 2% to 3% quickly began requiring twice that rate. The inflation-unemployment tradeoff worsened throughout the 1970s and into the early 1980s, largely due to oil price shocks and rising inflationary expectations. Inflation and unemployment continued to rise, creating stagflation. By 1980, annual inflation was over 9%, and unemployment was over 7%.

inflationary expectations The rate of inflation expected by workers for any given period. Workers do not work for a specific nominal wage but for what those wages will buy (real wages), therefore their inflationary expectations are an important determinant of what nominal wage they are willing to work for.

Taking **inflationary expectations** into account, wage increases can be connected to unemployment and expected inflation by adding a variable, p^e, representing inflationary expectations, to the inflation equation introduced earlier:

$$\text{Inflation} = \text{Increase in Nominal Wages} - \text{Rate of Increase in Labor Productivity} + P^e$$

In other words, the same tradeoff between inflation and unemployment in the short-run Phillips curve existed as we saw before, but there is a unique tradeoff for each level of inflationary expectations.

For example, suppose there are no inflationary expectations, and productivity is growing at a 3% rate when the economy's unemployment rate is 4%. In this scenario, if nominal wages increase by 5%, inflation would be 5% − 3% + 0% = 2%. However, if inflationary expectations (p^e) grow to, say, 4%, the Phillips curve will shift outward in Figure 5, and the inflation rate now associated with 4% unemployment will be 5% − 3% + 4% = 6%.

Inflationary Expectations and the Phillips Curve
Panel B of Figure 6 shows a Phillips curve augmented by inflationary expectations. The economy begins in equilibrium at full employment with zero inflation (point a in panel B). Panel A shows the aggregate demand and supply curves for this economy in equilibrium at point a. Note that the economy is producing at full employment output of Q_f, and this translates to the natural rate of unemployment, u_n, in panel B.

The Phillips curve in panel B is initially PC_0 ($p^e = 0\%$). Thus, inflation is equal to zero and so are inflationary expectations (p^e).

Now assume, however, that policymakers are unhappy with the economy's performance and want to reduce unemployment below u_n. Using expansionary policies, they

FIGURE 6

Aggregate Demand, Aggregate Supply, and the Expectations-Augmented Phillips Curve

Panel A shows the economy's aggregate demand and supply curves, and panel B shows the economy's Phillips curve, augmented by inflationary expectations. Using expansionary policies to reduce unemployment below u_n, policymakers shift aggregate demand in panel A from AD_0 to AD_1. This moves the economy to point b, with real output and the price level rising to Q_1 and P_1. Unemployment declines to u_1 (point b in panel B), but inflation rises to something approaching 5%. If policymakers attempt to hold unemployment below the natural rate, the economy will endure accelerating inflation. The long-run Phillips curve (LRPC) in panel B shows the relationship between inflation and unemployment when the inflation rate is just equal to inflationary expectations.

shift aggregate demand in panel A from AD_0 to AD_1. This moves the economy to point b; real output and the price level rise, to Q_1 and P_1.

In panel B, meanwhile, the unemployment rate has declined to u_1 (point b), but inflation has risen to 5%. Workers had anticipated zero inflation; this *unanticipated inflation* means that real wages have fallen. Therefore, workers will begin asking for raises, and employers wanting to keep turnover at a minimum may well begin offering higher wages.

The Long-Run Phillips Curve The long-run Phillips curve (LRPC), shown in panel B of Figure 6 as the vertical line at full employment (unemployment $= u_n$), shows the long-term relationship between inflation and unemployment when the inflation rate and the expected inflation rate are equal. The LRPC is the Phillips curve counterpart to the vertical long-run aggregate supply curve (LRAS) in panel A.

Accelerating Inflation As nominal wages rise, the result in panel A is that, over time, the short-run aggregate supply curve shifts leftward to $SRAS_1$, thus moving the economy back to full employment at point c. In panel B, with inflation now running at 5%, the Phillips curve shifts outward to PC_1 ($p^e = 5\%$). Workers, however, now expect 5% inflation, and the economy moves back to point c. Unemployment has moved back to its natural rate, but inflationary expectations have risen to 5%. The aggregate price level, meanwhile, has risen from P_0 to P_2, or 5%.

At this point, in order for policymakers to move the economy back to u_1 (or Q_1), they must repeat the process of expanding aggregate demand, only this time, the economy is starting from a higher Phillips curve because inflationary expectations are already elevated.

The implications of this analysis for fiscal and monetary policymakers who want to fine-tune the economy and keep unemployment below the natural rate are not pleasant. If policymakers want to keep unemployment below the natural rate, they must continually increase aggregate demand so that inflation will always exceed what is expected. Thus, policymakers must be willing to incur a permanently *accelerating* rate of inflation—hardly a popular idea.

In the late 1970s and early 1980s, oil price shocks and rising inflationary expectations caused both inflation and unemployment to rise, creating what economists call **stagflation.** Where under the original Phillips curve the conclusion was that rising unemployment would be met by *falling* inflation, the 1970s witnessed rising unemployment and *rising* inflation as the Phillips curve shifted outward. By 1980, inflation was over 9% and unemployment was over 7%.

An oil crisis in the late 1970s caused inflation to spike and unemployment to rise, creating what economists call stagflation.

Returning Inflation to Normal Levels To eliminate inflationary pressures when they arise, policymakers must be willing to curtail growth in aggregate demand and accept the resulting higher rates of unemployment for a certain transition period. How long it takes to reduce inflation and return to the natural rate of unemployment will depend on how rapidly the economy adjusts its inflationary expectations. Policymakers can speed this process along by ensuring their policies are credible, for instance, by issuing public announcements that are consistent with contractionary policies in both the monetary and fiscal realms.

Figure 7 on the next page illustrates how inflationary expectations are reduced to bring about a more favorable tradeoff. Initially, the economy is in equilibrium at point a, with the economy at the natural rate of unemployment of 6% and inflation at 10%.

To reduce inflationary expectations, policymakers must be willing to reduce aggregate demand and push the economy into a recession, increasing unemployment to 8%. As aggregate demand slumps, wage and price pressures will soften, reducing inflationary expectations. As these expectations decline, the Phillips curve shifts inward, from PC_2 to

stagflation Simultaneous occurrence of rising inflation and rising unemployment.

FIGURE 7

Phillips Curves and Disinflation

In the disinflation process, the economy initially is in equilibrium at point *a*. To reduce inflationary expectations, policymakers must reduce aggregate demand and push the economy into a recession, increasing unemployment to 8%. As aggregate demand slumps, wage and price pressures soften, reducing inflationary expectations. As these expectations decline, the entire Phillips curve shifts inward, from PC$_2$ to PC$_1$. If the process goes on long enough, the Phillips curve will shift back to PC$_0$. The arrows here show the path the economy must take back to roughly stable prices at the natural unemployment rate.

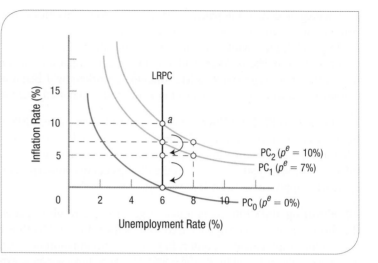

PC$_1$, and if the process goes on long enough, the Phillips curve will eventually shift back to PC$_0$. The arrows in Figure 7 show the path the economy must take to lower inflation rates. How fast this occurs depends on the severity of the recession and the confidence the public has that policymakers are willing to stay the course.

In 1981, the Reagan administration launched a long-term program designed to increase economic growth and reduce inflation. The Reagan administration took the view that stagflation had arisen from a substantial increase in the government's role in the economy, and responded with policies that reduced government spending, taxes, and regulations. This

 ISSUE

The Bernanke Inflation Jump—When?

After the federal funds target rate was lowered to an effective rate of 0% in December of 2008, the Federal Reserve embarked on a series of alternative bond buying activities (such as the purchase of risky mortgage-backed securities) in order to continue its use of expansionary monetary policy to speed the economic recovery. These quantitative easing policies became known by their sequence, from QE1 to QE4.

During this time, the Fed altered its balance sheet from one containing mostly safe U.S. Treasury bonds to one that at one point consisted of over $1 trillion worth of risky mortgage-backed securities. These efforts at easing credit markets through bond purchases cannot be sustained long-term, because inflation would result. In fact, the vast amount of bond purchases has already set the stage for a rise in inflation as consumer and business confidence continues to rise. There's simply too much money chasing a limited amount of output.

Economists predict that as the economy recovers, the Fed will eventually halt its QE programs, causing interest rates to rise. But before it does, the Fed continues to walk a fine line between easing credit markets and keeping inflation in check. When the Fed announced QE3 and QE4 in 2012, it did not provide a specific end date; instead, it committed to keeping interest rates low until the unemployment rate falls toward the natural rate.

However, this uncertainty added to the nervousness that businesses and investors experienced as different people held different expectations about the Fed's actions. In fact, markets in 2013 battled between optimism as the economy continued to recover and fear that it would come to a screeching halt once the Fed inevitably ends its expansionary monetary policies to prevent a rise in inflation. Alternatively, the Fed could have announced the end date right away.

Two questions remain. First, did the Fed's failure to set an end date produce enough uncertainty that it harmed the economy more than its policies helped? After all, when consumers and businesses face too much uncertainty, they hold off on spending and investing until the uncertainty clears up. Second, does the economy have enough momentum to sustain economic growth without expansionary monetary policy? Time will tell.

aggressive plan of wringing stagflation out of the U.S. economy took the better part of the 1980s. Inflation that took over a decade to develop required nearly another decade to be resolved. Fed Chairman Paul Volcker, who insisted on keeping interest rates high in the face of fierce public opposition, deserves much of the credit for this triumph over inflation.

This lesson about the importance of restraining monetary growth and focusing on stable prices was not lost on the next Fed chairman, Alan Greenspan. Throughout the 1990s, the Fed maintained a tight watch on inflation, which fell from around 4% to near 1%.

The importance of keeping inflation low has continued to influence policymaking today. As long as the threat of inflation remains low, policymakers have been willing to use expansionary policy to promote economic growth and reduce unemployment, exactly what the Phillips curve suggests would be effective. These policies assume that inflation expectations adjust with a noticeable lag, allowing some tradeoff between inflation and unemployment to exist. Some economists, however, argue that consumers and businesses adapt their expectations so rapidly that their behavior tends to nullify much of policymakers' actions, which we will discuss next.

Rational Expectations and Policy Formation The use of expectations in economic analysis is nothing new. Keynes believed that expectations are driven by emotions. He suggested that investors in the stock market will jump on board trends without attempting to understand the underlying market dynamics. Milton Friedman developed his model of expectations using what are known as **adaptive expectations,** whereby people are assumed to perform a simple extrapolation from past events. Workers, for example, are assumed to expect that past rates of inflation, averaged over some time period, will continue into the future. Adaptive expectations are represented by a *backward-looking* model of expectations, which contrasts with the rational expectations model.

In the **rational expectations** model developed by Robert Lucas, rational economic agents are assumed to make the best possible use of all publicly available information about what the future holds before making decisions. This does not mean that every individual's predictions about the future will be correct. Those errors that do occur will be randomly distributed, such that the expectations of large numbers of people will average out to be correct.

Assume that the economy has been in an equilibrium state for several years with low inflation (2%) and unemployment (6%). In such a stable environment, the average person would expect the inflation rate to stay right about where it is indefinitely. But now assume that the Fed announces it is going to increase the rate of growth of the money supply significantly. Basic economic theory tells us that this action will translate into higher prices, bringing about higher future inflation rates. Knowing this, households and businesses will revise their inflationary expectations upward.

As this example shows, people do not rely only on past experiences to formulate their

adaptive expectations Inflationary expectations are formed from a simple extrapolation from past events.

rational expectations Rational economic agents are assumed to make the best possible use of all publicly available information, then make informed, rational judgments on what the future holds. Any errors in their forecasts will be randomly distributed.

NOBEL PRIZE ROBERT LUCAS

In the 1970s, a series of articles by Robert E. Lucas changed the course of contemporary macroeconomic theory and profoundly influenced the economic policies of governments throughout the world. His development of the rational expectations theory challenged decades of assumptions about how individuals respond to changes in fiscal and monetary policies.

Lucas was born in 1937 in Yakima, Washington. His father was a welder, who advanced through the ranks to become president of a refrigeration company. Lucas was awarded a scholarship to the University of Chicago. He had wanted to be an engineer, but the University of Chicago did not have an engineering school, so he studied history instead. After briefly attending the University of California, Berkeley, where he developed an interest in economics, he returned to the University of Chicago, earning his Ph.D. in 1964. One of his professors was Milton Friedman, whose skepticism about interventionist government policies influenced a generation of economists. Lucas began his teaching career at Carnegie-Mellon University and later became a professor at the University of Chicago.

Before Lucas, economists accepted the Keynesian idea that expansionary policies could lower the unemployment rate. Lucas, however, argued that the rational expectations of individual workers and employers would adjust to the changing inflationary conditions, and unemployment rates would rise again. Lucas developed mathematical models to show that temporarily cutting taxes to increase spending was not a sound policy because individuals would base their decisions on expectations about the future, and these temporary tax cuts would find their way into savings and not added spending. In other words, individuals were rational, forward thinking, and perfectly able to adapt to changing economic information.

When the Royal Swedish Academy of Sciences awarded Lucas the Nobel Prize in 1995, it credited Lucas with "the greatest influence on macroeconomic research since 1970."

expectations of the future, but instead use all information available to them, including current policy announcements and other information that gives them reason to believe the future might hold certain changes. If adaptive expectations are backward looking, rational expectations are *forward looking*.

Policy Implications of Rational Expectations Do individuals and firms really form their future expectations as the rational expectations hypothesis suggests? If so, the implications for macroeconomic policy would be enormous; indeed, it could leave macroeconomic policy ineffective.

To illustrate, let us assume that the economy depicted in Figure 8 is operating at full employment at point *a*. Short-run aggregate supply curve SRAS$_0$ ($P = 100$) reflects current inflationary expectations. Suppose the Fed announces that it intends to increase the money supply.

FIGURE 8

Rational Expectations: The Policy Ineffectiveness Hypothesis

Rational expectations theory suggests that macroeconomic policy will be ineffective, even in the short term. Assume that the economy is operating at full employment (point *a*) and short-run aggregate supply curve SRAS$_0$ ($P = 100$). Now suppose that the Fed announces that it intends to increase the money supply. Expanding the money supply will shift aggregate demand from AD$_0$ to AD$_1$, and this will increase the demand for labor and raise nominal wages. Yet, as soon as the Fed announces it is going to increase the money supply, rational economic agents will use this information immediately to raise their inflationary expectations. Thus, output will remain unchanged, though the price level rises immediately to 110.

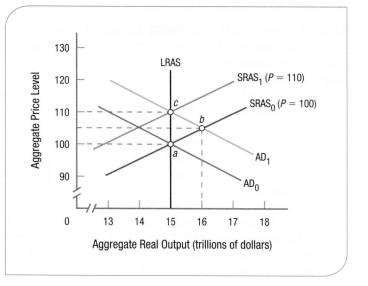

Expanding the money supply will shift aggregate demand from AD$_0$ to AD$_1$. This will increase the demand for labor and raise nominal wages. But what happens next?

Natural rate theorists, using adaptive expectations, would argue that workers will be fooled into thinking that the increase in money wages represents a real raise, thus driving output and employment up to $16 trillion (point *b*). After a time, however, workers will realize that real wages have not risen because prices have risen by at least as much as wages. Aggregate supply will then fall to SRAS$_1$ ($P = 110$) as price expectations climb and the economy gradually moves back to full employment at a higher price level (point *c*). In this scenario, the Fed's policy succeeds in raising output and employment in the short term, but at the expense of a long-term rise in the cost of living.

Contrast this with the rational expectations model. When the Fed announces that it is going to increase the money supply, perfectly rational individuals and firms will listen to this information and immediately raise their inflationary expectations. In Figure 8, output will remain unchanged because the price level will rise immediately to 110. No one gets fooled into temporarily increasing output or employment, even though the increase in the money supply still drives up prices. Therefore, any announcement of a policy change will result in an immediate move to a new long-run equilibrium, leaving the short-term aspects of the policy change ineffective.

This suggests that if the Fed wants to use an increase in the money supply to raise output and employment in the short term, the only way it can do so is by *not* announcing its plans; it must essentially force individuals and firms to make decisions with substantially incomplete information.

A Critique of Rational Expectations To date, empirical assessments of the ineffectiveness of macroeconomic policy based on rational expectations have yielded mixed results. In general, these studies do not support the policy ineffectiveness proposition. That is, macroeconomic policies do have a real impact on the economy, and monetary policies are credited with keeping inflation low over the past three decades.

New Keynesian economists have taken a different approach to critiquing rational expectations theory. Both the adaptive and the rational expectations models assume that labor and product markets are highly competitive, with wages and prices adjusting quickly to expansionary or contractionary policies. The new Keynesians point out, however, that labor markets are often beset with imperfect information, and that efficiency wages often bring about short-term wage stickiness.

Imperfect information occurs when firms and workers do not have up-to-the-minute information on economic fluctuations due to timing lags, causing wages and prices to not react quickly. **Efficiency wage theory** disputes the notion that labor markets are like competitive commodity markets with equal prices. For all labor is not equal. People need incentives to work hard, and paying workers an efficiency wage, or a wage above the market-clearing level, is one form of motivation to improve morale and productivity.

Imperfect information and efficiency wages suggest that wages and prices may be sticky because workers and firms are either unable or unwilling to make adjustments quickly to changes in the economy. This means that neither workers nor firms can react quickly to changes in monetary or fiscal policy. And this would give such policies a chance of a short-term impact.

Although the policy ineffectiveness proposition has not found significant empirical support, rational expectations as a concept has profoundly affected how economists approach macroeconomic problems. Nearly all economists agree that policy changes affect expectations, and that this affects the behavior of individuals and firms that potentially reduce the effectiveness of monetary and fiscal policy.

This section has considered two challenges to the effectiveness of macroeconomic policy. First, we looked at the Phillips curve, and showed that policies attempting to address unemployment could lead to inflation and a build-up in inflationary expectations. In other words, policymakers do not face an easy choice between rates of unemployment and rates of inflation. Second, we looked at rational expectations and showed how expectations could mitigate the effectiveness of policy.

In the next section, we now want to apply these concepts to macroeconomic issues that are important in our future: jobless recoveries, debt and long-run inflation, and the role of globalization in influencing economic growth.

efficiency wage theory Employers often pay their workers wages above the market-clearing level to improve morale and productivity, reduce turnover, and create a disincentive for employees to shirk their duties.

CHECKPOINT

EFFECTIVENESS OF MACROECONOMIC POLICY: PHILLIPS CURVES AND RATIONAL EXPECTATIONS

- The Phillips curve represents the negative relationship between the unemployment rate and the inflation rate. When the unemployment rate goes up, inflation goes down, and vice versa.

- Phillips curves are affected by inflationary expectations. Rising inflationary expectations by the public would be reflected in a shift in the Phillips curve to the right, worsening the tradeoff between inflation and unemployment.

- If policymakers use monetary and fiscal policy to attempt to keep unemployment continually below the natural rate, they will face accelerating inflation. Reducing inflation requires that policymakers curtail aggregate demand and accept higher rates of unemployment during the transition period back to low inflation.

- Adaptive expectations assume that individuals and firms extrapolate from past events; it is a *backward-looking* model. Rational expectations assume that individuals and firms make the best possible use of all publicly available information; it is a *forward-looking* model of expectations.

- Rational expectations analysis leads to the conclusion that policy changes will be ineffective in the short run because individuals will immediately adjust to the long-run consequences of the policy.

- Market imperfections and information problems are two reasons why the policy ineffectiveness conclusions of rational expectations analysis have met with mixed results empirically.

QUESTIONS: If an economy has high unemployment but low inflation, what would the Phillips curve suggest to be an appropriate macroeconomic policy? Would your answer change if inflationary expectations rise? If we assume that all individuals and firms have excellent foreknowledge as described by the rational expectations model, would that change your answer?

Answers to the Checkpoint questions can be found at the end of this chapter.

Macroeconomic Issues That Confront Our Future

Macroeconomic theory developed over the last 200 years, especially during the 80 years after Keynes. Until recently, economists thought they had the understanding and the tools to make depressions or deep recessions a thing of the past. For the last 30 years, a general consensus grew among economists that monetary policy should handle most of the task of keeping the economy on a steady low-inflation growth path. The recent financial crisis and subsequent recession has made the profession question that conclusion. This downturn has reinvigorated those who felt that fiscal policy should have more of a role, as well as those who felt that government should have a smaller role overall.

This section uses the theories and tools we have learned to understand the important issues that confront our economy today and will do so in the future. Specifically, what are the pressing macroeconomic issues that will have the greatest effect on the next generation? What do macroeconomic theories tell us that policymakers can do?

If you take one idea away from this course it should be that there is *not* one economic model or one economic policy that fits all occasions or circumstances. It often seems that one set of policymakers see "cutting taxes" as the universal cure-all while others see "more government spending" as the only solution. Both are wrong. Different circumstances call for different approaches.

In the following, we set out the key points surrounding three important issues facing our economy today and likely in the future: (1) the existence of jobless recoveries and persistent unemployment, (2) growing debt and the threat of long-run inflation, and (3) the importance of achieving economic growth in a globalized economy. Throughout this book, we have presented different models and the circumstances in which macroeconomic policy can be effective in these situations.

Are Recoveries Becoming "Jobless Recoveries"?

Globalization, new technologies, and improved business methods are making the jobs of policymakers much more difficult and may even be changing the nature of the business cycle. The 1990–1991, 2001, and 2007–2009 recessions all deviated significantly from what has happened in past business cycles in that they were followed by jobless recoveries.

Taming the business cycle has proven to be just as much of an art as a science. Whenever economists believe they have finally gotten a handle on controlling the economy, some new event or transformation of the economy has taken place, humbling the profession. There is no doubt that between 1983 and 2007, the federal government and the Fed did a remarkable job of keeping the economy on a steady upward growth path, with only two minor recessions. The 1990–1991 and 2001 recessions were mild, but the recoveries coming out of these recessions were weak, especially for those out of work and looking for a job.

Recall what we described as a jobless recovery in an early chapter of this book. When output begins to grow after a trough, employment usually starts to grow. But when output begins to rise yet employment growth does not resume, the recovery is called a **jobless recovery.**

We have already seen that business cycles vary dramatically in their depth and duration. The Great Depression was the worst downturn in American history, while the 2001 recession was one of the mildest. During that recession, the unemployment rate never rose above 6% and real output (GDP) fell only one-quarter of 1% throughout the downturn. But if the recession was mild, the recovery was not as strong as in typical business cycles.

Figure 9 shows how the 2007–2009 recession compares to the two previous downturns and their recoveries. It indexes real output for all three downturns so that the most recent recession and recovery can be compared to those previous business cycles. Specifically, real GDP for each business cycle is indexed to the peak of the cycle. This involves dividing each quarter's output by output at the peak and multiplying by 100 to index the values to 100. Thus, if one quarter after the peak, output has fallen by 1%, the index would be 99 at that point. In this way we can get a graphical picture of how output is doing throughout the course of each cycle.

jobless recovery A phenomenon that takes place after a recession, when output begins to rise, but employment growth does not.

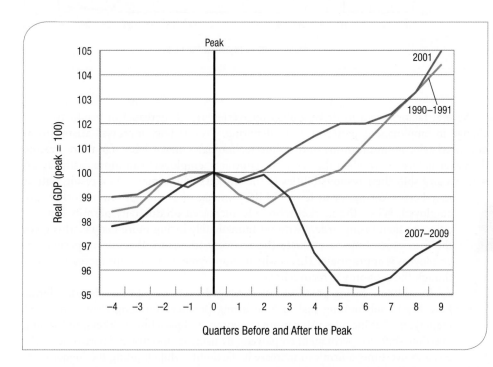

FIGURE 9

Real GDP Growth Relative to the Peak of the Business Cycle

The 2007–2009 recession is compared to the previous two recessions in 1990–1991 and 2001 by indexing real output to the peak of the business cycle. The 2007–2009 downturn was deeper; in both of the previous recessions, GDP was back to the previous peak at this point in the cycle.

Notice in this figure that both the 1990–1991 and 2001 recessions lasted just under three quarters (eight months each). For the 1990–1991 recession, this is shown by the two-quarter drop in real GDP to a little below 99, then the economy resumed an upward path. The 2001 downturn shows a slight dip in the first quarter, but then quickly rises back above 100. Clearly, both of these recessions were mild indeed.

In contrast, the 2007–2009 recession was considerably more severe than both of the previous downturns. A year and a half into this recession, real output fell by over 4% and the decline in the economy was just leveling off.

Figure 10 on the next page presents the same type of indexed graph for employment, though indexing the values monthly. Notice that for the 1990–1991 and 2001 recessions, employment had not reached its prior peak even after two years. In fact, employment took nearly three years to return to peak levels after the 1990–1991 recession, and nearly four years after the 2001 recession. In the past, the turnaround in employment to the previous peak was typically reached in two years. Likewise, after the 2007–2009 recession ended in June 2009, unemployment still remained above 7% four years later in mid-2013.

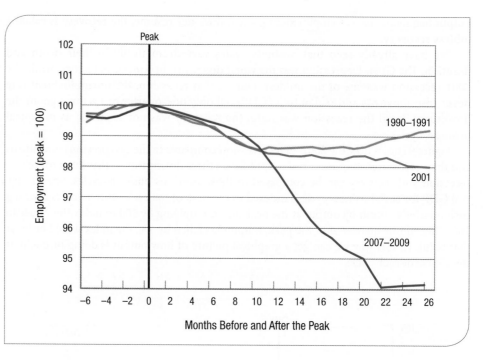

FIGURE 10

Employment Growth Relative to the Peak of the Business Cycle

Employment in the 2007–2009 recession is compared to the previous two recessions in 1990–1991 and 2001 by indexing employment to the peak of the business cycle. This downturn was deeper than the previous recessions, when it took three to four years to get back to peak employment levels.

seewhatmitchsee/Alamy

Increased technology and productivity has enabled companies to use fewer workers to run their operations. In 2012, Pinterest had only 100 employees for its 40 million subscribers, a ratio of one employee per 400,000 users.

Several factors seem to drive jobless recoveries: rapid increases in productivity, a change in employment patterns, and offshoring. Productivity increases arising from improved telecommunications and online technologies make labor far more flexible than ever before. Now when the economy contracts, employers can more easily lay off workers and shift their responsibilities to the workers who remain. As a result, output may keep growing, or at least not drop much, even though fewer workers are employed. When the market rebounds, increased productivity permits firms to adjust to their rising orders without immediately hiring more people. This gives the firm more time to evaluate the recovery to ensure that hiring permanent employees is appropriate. This is why unemployment often keeps increasing even though the economy is recovering.

In addition, hiring practices have changed over the past few decades. Firms have begun substituting just-in-time hiring practices for long-term permanent employees. This includes using more temporary and part-time workers, and adding overtime shifts for permanent employees. By using temporary and part-time workers, and overtime, a firm can increase its flexibility while limiting the higher costs associated with hiring permanent employees until it has had time to evaluate the recovery and the demand for its products.

Because the current and past two recoveries have been slow to add jobs, economists and policymakers are concerned that jobless recoveries have become the norm following recessions. The consequence of jobless recoveries is that reducing unemployment requires much more government action than before, especially expansionary fiscal and monetary policies. What type of fiscal and monetary policies can be used to address jobless recoveries?

Expansionary fiscal policy is most effective when government spending or tax cuts generate economic activity through the spending multiplier, which translates into jobs being created. Alternatively, fiscal policy can be used to provide incentives for employers to hire workers (such as tax incentives for hiring veterans) or employee incentives (such as increased tax deductions for low-income workers).

Alternatively, expansionary monetary policy can be used to promote employment. For example, increasing the money supply and lowering interest rates reduce the cost of financing major projects, creating jobs. The Fed's recent quantitative easing programs that bought up risky mortgage-backed assets reduced long-term interest rates, creating another boost to consumption and investment.

Although plenty of policy options exist to address jobless recoveries, they do not come without costs. For example, a reduction in consumer or business confidence can reduce the willingness of consumers and firms to spend, diminishing the multiplier. Increased government spending can lead to greater debt and higher interest rates, which can crowd out private consumption and investment. Therefore, the intended effects of fiscal policy are mitigated. Further, increased money supply and quantitative easing programs can lead to inflation in the long run, as more money chases an economy's output. Such effects can mitigate the long-term benefits of monetary policy.

In sum, the potential consequences of using expansionary fiscal and monetary policies to reduce the unemployment rate are higher debt and potential inflation, important issues to which we turn next.

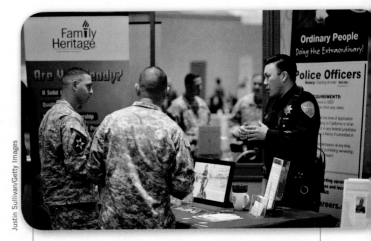

The *VOW to Hire Heroes Act* is an example of fiscal policy used to encourage employers to hire veterans returning from active duty.

Will Rising Debt and Future Debt Obligations Lead to Inflation?

Much of the debate among policymakers in recent years has centered on rising deficits and national debt. Indeed, fiscal deficits and national debt (at least in nominal terms) have risen to levels not seen in our history. The concern over debt has changed the politics in Washington, as a bitter debate ensued regarding the use of expansionary policies (such as stimulus spending and quantitative easing) to promote economic growth versus austerity measures (cost cutting) to reduce the deficit and the burden of the debt on future generations.

Rising Future Debt Obligations: Health Care and Social Security
Even if the current deficits are brought under control using a combination of government spending cuts and tax increases, the long-term debt obligations relating to Social Security payments and rising health care costs pose a bigger question about the ability to keep deficits and debt under control over the long term.

As greater numbers of baby boomers (those born soon after the end of World War II) retire, more will begin receiving Social Security and Medicare benefits. In addition to greater numbers of beneficiaries, the cost of the benefits also rises. Social Security benefits increase based on the rate of inflation, while Medicare payments rise as the cost of health care increases.

Although recent legislation has slowed the rise in health care costs, the overall cost remains unsustainable in the long term. In addition, the long-term debt obligations stemming from health care and Social Security do not fully appear in current deficit statistics, because these expenses are budgeted and paid out during the year in which the costs are incurred. Therefore, if costs rise faster than revenues, deficits will persist, adding to the national debt.

The Cost of Financing Debt
The cost of financing debt depends on the interest rate. Fortunately, the United States has enjoyed very low interest rates for much of the past decade. This not only helps individuals and firms looking to borrow, but also the government in financing its debt. A new 30-year Treasury bond issued in 2013 paid only about 3% per year. In 1984, a new 30-year Treasury bond paid over 13% per year. A difference of 10% in the interest rate represents a tremendous savings to the government.

Another factor in the cost of financing debt is the willingness of countries to hold U.S. debt. Part of this depends on the demand for the U.S. dollar. The U.S. dollar remains the most widely held currency in the world. When U.S. dollars are held by foreigners, this amounts to an interest-free loan to the U.S. government, because no interest is paid on currency. The willingness of people around the world to use and hold dollars allows the government to print these dollars without the immediate worry of inflation.

The Effects of Debt on Inflation Addressing debt can be undertaken with fiscal policy as well as monetary policy. Fiscal policy to curb debt includes raising taxes or reducing government spending. However, neither of these policies is popular, especially the reduction of Social Security or health care benefits that make up over 40% of government spending. Further, contractionary fiscal policy can curtail economic growth, which is especially dangerous when recovering from a severe recession like the one from 2007–2009. For this reason, policymakers have turned to monetary policy.

One of the dangers of using monetary policy to help address deficit and debt issues occurs with **monetized debt,** which is debt that is paid for by an increase in the money supply. In other words, debt is reduced by way of a lower real value of the dollar. Because U.S. Treasury securities have long been sought after as a safe investment by individuals, firms, as well as governments around the world, the U.S. government has not had to worry about the inflationary effects of its monetary policy in recent years.

However, should world demand for U.S. Treasury securities fall as countries diversify their holdings to other assets (such as euro-denominated assets or gold-backed assets), the value of the U.S. dollar may fall. Because we purchase many goods and services from other countries, a weaker dollar increases the prices of many goods and services, leading

monetized debt Occurs when debt is reduced by increasing the money supply, thereby making each dollar less valuable through inflation.

 ISSUE

Inflating Our Way Out of Debt: Is This an Effective Approach?

In late 2012, the news media posted headlines about the possibility of the Fed authorizing the minting of a *trillion dollar coin* that would be used to pay for most of the year's fiscal deficit. By doing so, the minted coin would be sent to the U.S. Treasury to pay down the debt. Would such a strategy really work? Would there be any effects on the economy or on ordinary Americans?

Although this type of policy is highly unlikely to occur (though more than one prominent economist has endorsed the plan), what may surprise you is that the Fed has used similar types of policies for years to address our rising national debt.

When the money supply is increased, the Fed is using money that is created out of thin air to purchase treasury bonds (debt) from banks and other institutions. In other words, part of the government's debt is held by other parts of the government using money it creates through its power to print money. Does this sound like an easy solution?

Certainly, it's easier than implementing fiscal policies to combat debt, which would require the raising of taxes or the reduction of government spending, neither of which is popular, especially when much of government spending is used for our national defense or to take care of our senior citizens. Therefore, the government has relied more on monetary policy. When money is created to purchase debt instruments, this is referred to as monetizing debt.

As we studied in an earlier chapter, money is neutral. When more money chases a fixed output, prices must rise. Because aggregate demand was depressed after the last recession, inflation did not immediately rise. However, as consumer and business confidence improve, all of the money sitting on the sidelines will eventually enter into the economy and drive prices higher, leading to inflation. As inflation rises, the real value of the national debt falls.

Who, then, ends up paying for this reduction in debt caused by inflation?

American Mint, LLC

The answer is everyone who holds dollar-denominated assets, such as those with a savings or retirement account, or holders of bonds including foreign investors and governments. When prices rise, the real value of savings falls. In addition, a rise in inflationary expectations causes banks to raise interest rates, and can lead to an inflation spiral described in the chapter, resulting in even higher prices. In sum, the costs of financing debt by way of inflation are spread among everyone. Regardless of whether fiscal or monetary policy is used, we will all feel the effect of the debt in one way or another.

to inflation. Therefore, although a weaker dollar and inflation both reduce the burden on the existing debt, a higher rate of inflation reduces the purchasing power of one's income and savings, thereby reducing the standard of living.

In order to stem the effects of higher inflation, contractionary monetary policy is needed once the economy has recovered enough to withstand an increase in interest rates. Such policies are not popular. In 2013, the fear of the Fed ending its quantitative easing polices scared many investors who worried about the start of another recession. Still, controlling inflation is the key to preventing more serious problems for the economy. Ultimately, a higher inflation rate may hinder productivity and economic growth, which is increasingly important in a globalized economy.

Will Globalization Lead to Increased Obstacles to Economic Growth?

Economic growth has been the driving force in improving our standard of living. However, the world is changing, and countries that historically have not experienced high rates of economic growth have begun to flourish. Countries such as China, India, Russia, and Brazil have surpassed the growth rates of the United States, Japan, and the countries of Europe over the last decade. Further, smaller developing countries, such as Gabon, Ethiopia, and Vietnam, have seen stellar growth rates that have pulled millions out of poverty.

Why has economic growth spread throughout the world in this way, and what does this entail for developed nations such as the United States?

One of the most important changes to the world economy over the past generation has been the dramatic increase in international trade, international factor movements (foreign investment and immigration), offshoring (the movement of factories overseas), and international banking. The integration of the world's economies has allowed more countries to specialize and reap the gains from trade that result.

For developed countries such as the United States, Japan, and countries in Europe, increased globalization means increased competition for resources, especially talented labor, which now has many more opportunities than it did in the past. Therefore, pressures to innovate and to increase productivity have increased with globalization.

What does this mean for macroeconomic policy? Not only does fiscal and monetary policy need to be tailored to fit the problems inherent in our own country, but how these policies affect other countries becomes important as well.

Fiscal policies such as implementing trade restrictions or providing support for domestic industries tend to help one country at the expense of its trading partners. Taking these policies too far may encourage other countries to take similar actions, which would lead to fewer exports and a reduction in trade and economic growth.

Ethiopia, which experienced one of the worst famines in world history in 1985, today has an emerging economy with a high growth rate as it focuses on infrastructure, manufacturing, and trade.

Monetary policies also affect other nations through trade and the exchange rate. Expansionary monetary policy, such as reducing the interest rate, has the effect of lowering the value of one currency against others. When this occurs, the price of imports rises and the price of exports falls, helping to improve the trade balance as consumers react by purchasing more domestically produced goods than foreign-made goods. But again, such policies can lead to retaliatory actions if taken too far.

We turn our attention in the next two chapters to international trade and open economy macroeconomics. Both chapters deal with how countries interact with other countries, either through the trade of goods and services or through the exchange of currencies. Both have important implications for the ability of countries to grow and to improve their standards of living.

 CHECKPOINT

MACROECONOMIC ISSUES THAT CONFRONT OUR FUTURE

- No single macroeconomic model can solve all economic problems.

- Jobless recoveries are spurred by increases in labor productivity, changes in employment patterns, and increased use of offshoring. Fiscal and monetary policies provide incentives to consume and invest, leading to job growth.

- Rising deficits were caused by expansionary fiscal policies used to stem the effects of the financial crisis. Future concerns of deficits and debt center on the rising costs of Social Security payments and Medicare costs, making the use of fiscal policy to mitigate rising debt difficult.

- Rising interest rates in the future will increase borrowing costs, making it more difficult to finance debt. Increased use of expansionary monetary policy can lead to long-run inflation, reducing the debt burden but also reducing the purchasing power of savings.

- Globalization has increased the growth rates of many developing countries. Increased competition from abroad has made it more challenging for developed nations to maintain high growth rates over time.

- Fiscal policies related to trade openness and protectionism along with monetary policies related to exchange rates can affect an economy's growth rate. However, taking these policies too far can lead to retaliation by trading partners that are adversely affected.

QUESTIONS: In 2009 inflation was negative; average prices *fell*. The 2007–2009 recession was partly the result of American households carrying too much debt (both in mortgages and on credit cards). Households set out to reduce their debt levels by reducing spending, causing a deeper recession in 2009. Is deflation a help or hindrance to using monetary and fiscal policy to stimulate the economy? Why?

Answers to the Checkpoint questions can be found at the end of this chapter.

chapter summary

Section 1: The Great Recession and Macroeconomic Policy

Events Leading to the Great Recession

- A glut in worldwide savings in the early years of the 21st century reduced interest rates.

- Low interest rates and easy bank loans fueled a housing bubble.

- Risky subprime mortgages were packaged into securities that were inadequately investigated and given perfect AAA ratings.

- Loan defaults led to a reduction in home prices and the collapse of mortgage-backed securities.

- Banks lost money from poor investments, insurance companies could not cover losses, and the contagion spread to other industries and eventually to the entire economy.

Philip Gangler/Shutterstock

The Government's Policy Response

- Passed the $700 billion Troubled Asset Relief Program (TARP) to bail out banks nearing bankruptcy.

- Loaned over $100 billion to AIG to prevent its insolvency in insuring risky assets by financial institutions.

- Passed the $787 billion American Recovery and Reinvestment Act (Stimulus Package).

- Bailed out the U.S. automobile industry.

- Reduced the federal funds rate target to 0% and began a series of quantitative easing (QE) programs to purchase risky assets from banks.

Section 2: Effectiveness of Macroeconomic Policy: Phillips Curves and Rational Expectations

The **Phillips curve** shows a negative relationship between unemployment rates and inflation. As unemployment falls, firms bid up the price of labor. Greater employment increases aggregate demand, pushing prices higher.

The Phillips curve presented policymakers with a menu of choices. By accepting modest inflation, they can keep unemployment low.

Fanatic Studio/Alamy

Phillips curves are affected by **inflationary expectations.** Rising inflationary expectations by the public would be reflected in a shift in the Phillips curve to the right, worsening the tradeoff between inflation and unemployment.

If policymakers use monetary and fiscal policy to attempt to keep unemployment continually below the natural rate, they will face accelerating inflation.

Once inflation reaches a high level, the risk of **stagflation** occurs, in which high inflation is coupled with high unemployment. Reducing stagflation requires tough contractionary monetary policies to bring down inflation.

The adaptive expectations model assumes that people form their future expectations based on their past experiences. Therefore, it is a backward-looking model of expectations.

The rational expectations hypothesis suggests that policymakers cannot stimulate output in the short run by raising inflation unless they keep their actions secret.

Market imperfections and information problems are two reasons why the policy ineffectiveness conclusions of rational expectations analysis have met with mixed results empirically.

The rational expectations model assumes that rational economic agents use all publicly available information in forming their expectations, and is a forward-looking model of expectations.

Lucian Milasan/Alamy

Efficiency wages are paid in many professions as a way to keep employees from shirking or leaving the company. The existence of efficiency wages brings about wage stickiness, which makes rational expectations less likely.

Section 3: Macroeconomic Issues That Confront Our Future

The use of fiscal policy or monetary policy, or both, depends on the type of issues confronting our economy. Important issues facing our country today and in the future include:

- Jobless recoveries, which are common after severe financial crises.

- Rising deficits and debt.

- Higher long-term inflation.

- Globalization and its effect on economic growth.

Ilya Terentyev/iStockphoto

The growing population of seniors and the rising costs of Social Security and health care benefits are major factors affecting potential debt in the long run.

Using fiscal or monetary policy creates both benefits and costs that need to be weighed against each other to determine their effectiveness in solving the problems facing our economy.

KEY CONCEPTS

subprime mortgage, p. 656
leverage, p. 657
credit default swap, p. 657
Phillips curve, p. 661

inflationary expectations, p. 664
stagflation, p. 665
adaptive expectations, p. 667
rational expectations, p. 667

efficiency wage theory, p. 669
jobless recovery, p. 671
monetized debt, p. 674

QUESTIONS AND PROBLEMS

Check Your Understanding

1. The Phillips curve for the United States in the 1960s shown in Figure 4 becomes very steep after unemployment drops below 4%, and rather shallow as unemployment exceeds 6%. Why is a typical Phillips curve shaped this way?

2. Does the long-run Phillips curve make it difficult (if not impossible) for policymakers to increase output and employment beyond full employment in the long run?

3. Explain why inflation accelerates if policymakers use monetary and fiscal policy to keep unemployment below the natural rate.

4. Does having rational expectations mean that all economic actors act rationally and are always correct?

5. Would policymakers prefer a Phillips curve with a steep or a shallow slope? Why?

6. A negative supply shock (a huge natural disaster or significant energy price spike) would do what to the short-run Phillips curve? To the long-run Phillips curve?

Apply the Concepts

7. Why would policymakers want to drive unemployment below the natural rate, given that inflation will result?

8. Why are inflationary expectations so important for policymakers to keep under control? When a supply shock such as an oil price spike hits the economy, does it matter how fast policymakers attempt to bring the economy back to full employment?

9. How are the long-run Phillips curve (LRPC) and the long-run aggregate supply (LRAS) curve related?

10. Would the credibility of policymakers' (Congress and the Fed) commitment to keeping inflation low have an effect on inflationary expectations when the economy is beset by a supply shock?

11. Explain why those who favor the rational expectations approach to modeling the economy do not favor discretionary policymaking.

12. If efficiency wages are widespread throughout the economy but most workers feel they are significantly underpaid, will paying workers more prevent them from shirking?

In the News

13. Fed Chairman Ben Bernanke noted that "in the 1970s the public had little confidence that the Fed would keep inflation low and stable." As a result, when oil prices rose, wages and prices quickly followed. This caused the Fed to have to increase interest rates sharply to curtail inflation. Do people have a different perspective on the Fed today than they did in the past?

14. About every year, Congress is tasked with increasing the debt ceiling that allows the government to continue borrowing. In past decades, such legislation would pass easily because it was authorizing the payment of expenses already incurred. However, in recent years, congressional leaders took the drastic approach to oppose raising the debt

ceiling as a way to reign in government spending. If these leaders were successful in preventing the debt ceiling from being raised, what would be some benefits and costs of this action?

Solving Problems

15. In Canada, the consensus estimate of the natural rate of unemployment was 4.5% in 1970 and 7% in 2005. A minority view has claimed that the change to 7% is beyond explanation and must be too high. A similar change has taken place in the United States over this period, but the consensus estimate of the natural rate of unemployment is closer to 5.5% today. What would be the result if the Bank of Canada (the central bank of Canada) and the Federal Reserve in the United States assumed that the natural rate was 7% when it really was closer to 5.5%?

16. When the recessions of 1990–1991 and 2001 ended, unemployment kept rising and it took roughly two-and-a-half years before unemployment returned to where it was at the *trough* of the recession. The figure below shows the path of unemployment (indexed to 100 = trough level) after the recession had officially ended.

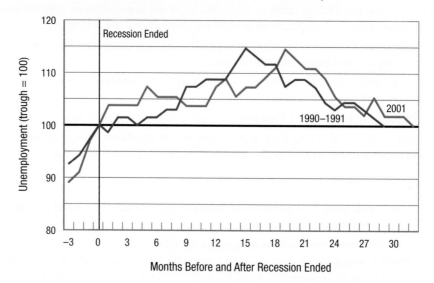

Following the 1990–1991 recession, unemployment only returned to its lowest level (at the peak before the recession) after four-and-a-half years, and with the recession of 2001, unemployment never returned to its lowest level. Does this phenomenon of unemployment continuing to rise after a recession has ended help foster the conclusion that these two recoveries were jobless recoveries?

USING THE NUMBERS

17. According to By the Numbers, in which year did the median value of existing homes peak? By what percentage did the median existing home price increase from the year 2000 until its peak? By what percentage did the median existing home price fall from its peak to the year 2012?

18. According to By the Numbers, what was the value of monthly real retail sales when it reached its lowest point in 2009? By what percentage did monthly real retail sales increase from 2009 to 2013?

ANSWERS TO QUESTIONS IN CHECKPOINTS

Checkpoint: The Great Recession and Macroeconomic Policy

Had it been known that the collapse of the housing market bubble would have caused a severe financial crisis, the government could have implemented macroeconomic policies to slow the rise in housing prices. For example, the government could (1) use contractionary monetary policy to push interest rates higher, making it more expensive to borrow money; (2) pass regulations on financial institutions requiring greater scrutiny of potential borrowers; (3) limit the types of risky loans that could be created; and (4) eliminate tax incentives on housing market profits to limit house flipping.

Checkpoint: Effectiveness of Macroeconomic Policy: Phillips Curves and Rational Expectations

The Phillips curve would suggest that unemployment can be reduced by accepting a higher rate of inflation. As long as inflation is very low, a small rise in inflation would be a small cost to pay for pushing the unemployment rate down. However, if inflationary expectations rise, it would require a greater inflation rate to achieve a lower unemployment rate. Here, policymakers must be careful not to let inflation exceed a level that might cause larger problems for the economy. Finally, if individuals and firms acted according to the rational expectations model, any increase in inflation would never lead to a reduction in unemployment. In this case, macroeconomic policy is ineffective in the short run, and the best prescription would be to leave the market alone to correct itself over time.

Checkpoint: Macroeconomic Issues That Confront Our Future

On balance, it is a hindrance when households and businesses attempt to reduce debt levels. Falling prices increase the real value of debt, while declining real income makes it harder to pay off. Declining demand and prices for output provides little incentive for business to invest and expand. Deflation is a symptom of a declining economy and was a concern of monetary policymakers at the onset of the financial crisis in 2008. It is a factor that policy stimulus must overcome.

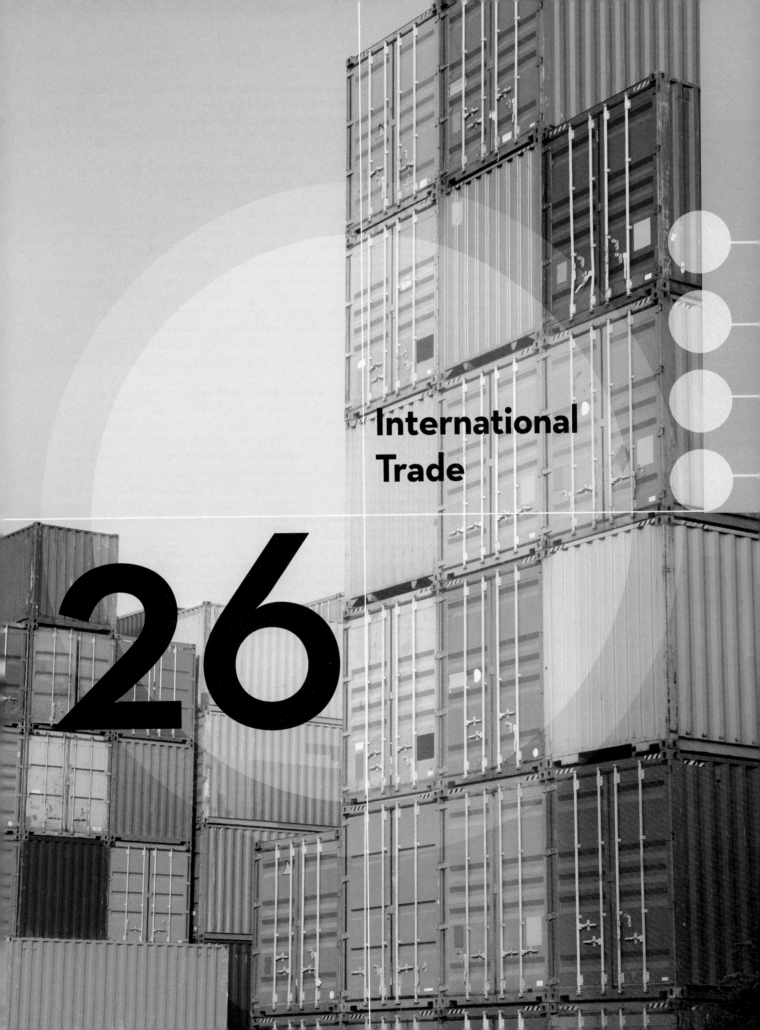

International Trade

26

Every day at the Port of Los Angeles, up to ten mega container ships arrive, each containing 10,000 to 16,000 TEU (*20-foot equivalent units,* or 20 feet × 8 feet × 8.5 feet standard containers) of goods from around the world. A standard tractor trailer can transport two TEUs, which means that up to 80,000 tractor trailers full of goods are brought into the United States each day, *at just one port.*

These cargo ships and trucks transport the goods we enjoy every day that are made in China, France, Brazil, Kenya, Australia, and the 180 other countries with which the United States has trading relations.

Take a quick look in your closet, and count how many countries contributed to your wardrobe—shirts tailored in Hong Kong, shoes made in Italy, sweaters made in Norway, jackets made in China, and the list goes on. On occasion, you might come across something made in the United States, although it is a rarity in the apparel industry. Most Americans wear foreign-made clothing, over half of us drive foreign cars, and even American cars contain many foreign components. Australian wines, Swiss watches, Chilean sea bass, and Brazilian coffee have become common in the United States. We also buy services from other countries, for example, when we travel to Europe and stay in hotels and use its high-speed trains. The opportunity to buy goods and services from other countries gives consumers more variety to choose from, and also provides an opportunity to buy products at lower prices.

Although the United States buys many goods from other countries, it also sells many goods to other countries—just not clothing. The "Made in USA" label is highly respected throughout the world, and the United States sells commercial airplanes, cars and trucks, tractors, high-tech machinery, and pharmaceuticals to individual consumers and businesses in other countries. It also sells agricultural goods and raw materials, such as soybeans, copper, and wood pulp. And it sells services too, such as medical care, tourist services when foreigners visit the United States, higher education (foreign students studying at American colleges), and entertainment, including movies, software, and music.

Trade is now part of the global landscape. Worldwide foreign trade has quadrupled over the past 25 years. In the United States today, the combined value of exports and imports approaches $5 trillion a year. Twenty-five years ago, trade represented under 20% of gross domestic product (GDP); today it accounts for over 30% of GDP. Nearly a tenth of American workers owe their jobs to foreign consumers. Figure 1 shows the current composition of U.S. exports and imports. Note that the United States imports and exports a lot of capital goods—that is, the equipment and machinery used to produce other goods. Also, we export about 50% more services than we import, services such as education and health care. Third, petroleum products represent approximately 13% of imports, totaling $350 billion a year.

FIGURE 1

U.S. Trade by Sector (2012)

This figure shows trade by sector. The United States imports and exports large amounts of capital goods, the equipment and machinery used to produce other goods. Also, nearly one-third of United States exports are services such as education and health care.

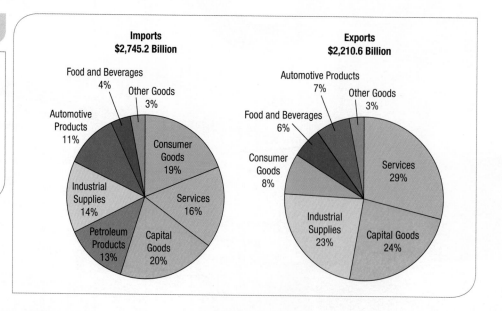

Imports
$2,745.2 Billion

Food and Beverages 4%
Other Goods 3%
Automotive Products 11%
Consumer Goods 19%
Industrial Supplies 14%
Services 16%
Petroleum Products 13%
Capital Goods 20%

Exports
$2,210.6 Billion

Automotive Products 7%
Other Goods 3%
Food and Beverages 6%
Consumer Goods 8%
Services 29%
Industrial Supplies 23%
Capital Goods 24%

BY THE NUMBERS

International Trade

Most economists would agree that trade has been a net benefit to the world. The 1947 General Agreement on Tariffs and Trade (GATT) lowered tariffs and led to expanded trade and higher standards of living around the world.

Trade deficits (negative trade balances) were not a problem until the mid-1970s, when the United States began importing more than it exported. The recent recession resulted in exports rising while imports fell.

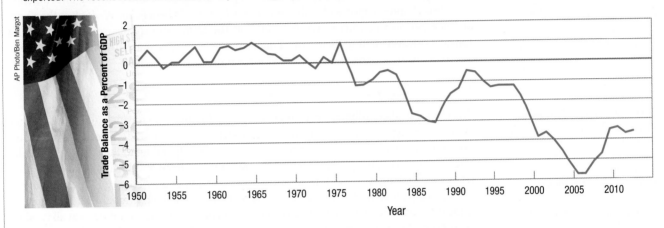

Trade Balance as a Percent of GDP vs. Year (1950–2010)

Tariff barriers (a tax on imports) are relatively low in most countries.

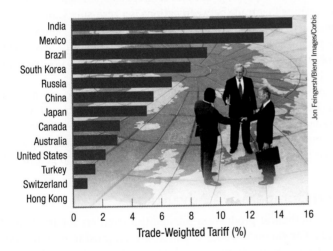

India
Mexico
Brazil
South Korea
Russia
China
Japan
Canada
Australia
United States
Turkey
Switzerland
Hong Kong

Trade-Weighted Tariff (%)
0 2 4 6 8 10 12 14 16

Medical tourism is growing because health costs are lower overseas, even including the costs of travel.

Cost of Various Medical Procedures

Procedure	United States	Thailand	Costa Rica
Heart Bypass	$144,317	$22,500	$35,000
Heart Valve	177,665	18,500	31,000
Hip Replacement	100,047	12,000	14,500
Knee Replacement	65,918	10,500	11,700
Hysterectomy	31,474	4,500	7,000
Spinal Fusion	103,761	9,700	22,000

3,150,000
Number of American cars sold in China in 2012.

U.S. public sentiment about lowering trade barriers is mixed, and some even oppose helping displaced workers.

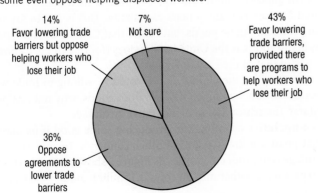

14%
Favor lowering trade barriers but oppose helping workers who lose their job

7%
Not sure

43%
Favor lowering trade barriers, provided there are programs to help workers who lose their job

36%
Oppose agreements to lower trade barriers

China, once a world powerhouse, slipped in the 20th century but is coming back.

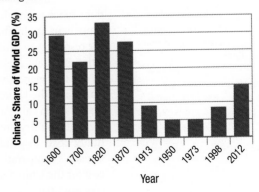

China's Share of World GDP (%)
0 5 10 15 20 25 30 35

1600 1700 1820 1870 1913 1950 1973 1998 2012
Year

Does all of this world trade make consumers and producers better off? This chapter examines the effects of trade on both the importing (buying) and exporting (selling) countries, and how trade affects the prices and availability of goods and services in each country.

Improved communication and transportation technologies have worked together to promote global economic integration. In addition, most governments around the world have reduced their trade barriers in recent years.

Trade must yield significant benefits or it would not exist. After all, there are no laws requiring countries to trade, just agreements permitting trade and reducing impediments to it. This chapter begins with a discussion of why trade is beneficial. We look at the terms of trade between countries. We then look at the tariffs and quotas sometimes used to restrict trade, calculating their costs. Finally, we will consider some arguments critics have advanced against increased trade and globalization.

The Gains from Trade

autarky A country that does not engage in international trade, also known as a closed economy.

imports Goods and services that are purchased from abroad.

exports Goods and services that are sold abroad.

Economics studies voluntary exchange. People and nations do business with one another because they expect to gain through these transactions. Foreign trade is nearly as old as civilization. Centuries ago, European merchants were already sailing to the Far East to ply the spice trade. Today, people in the United States buy cars from South Korea and electronics from China, along with millions of other products from countries around the world.

Virtually all countries today engage in some form of international trade. Those that trade the least are considered *closed economies*. A country that does not trade at all is called an **autarky.** Most countries, however, are *open economies* that willingly and actively engage in trade with other countries. Trade consists of **imports,** goods and services purchased from other countries, and **exports,** goods and services sold abroad.

Many people assume that trade between nations is a zero-sum game: a game in which, for one party to gain, the other party must lose. Poker games fit this description; one person's winnings must come from another player's losses. This is not true of voluntary trade. Voluntary exchange and trade is a positive-sum game, meaning that both parties to a transaction can gain.

To understand how this works, and thus why nations trade, we need to consider the concepts of absolute and comparative advantage. Note that nations per se do not trade; individuals in specific countries do. We will refer to trade between nations but recognize that individuals, not nations, actually engage in trade. We covered this earlier, in Chapter 2, but it is worthwhile to go through it again.

International trade allows consumers to buy goods (such as televisions) produced in many countries. Competition from trade allows for greater variety and lower prices.

Absolute and Comparative Advantage

absolute advantage One country can produce more of a good than another country.

comparative advantage One country has a lower opportunity cost of producing a good than another country.

Figure 2 shows hypothetical production possibilities frontiers for the United States and Canada. For simplicity, both countries are assumed to produce only beef and guitars. Given the production possibility frontiers (PPFs) in Figure 2, the United States has an absolute advantage over Canada in the production of both products. An **absolute advantage** exists when one country can produce more of a good than another country. In this case, the United States can produce twice as much beef and 5 times as many guitars as Canada. This is not to say that Canadians are inefficient in producing these goods, but rather that Canada does not have the resources to produce as many goods as the United States does (for one thing, its population is barely a tenth the size of that of the United States).

At first glance, we may wonder why the United States would be willing to trade with Canada. If the United States can produce so much more of both goods, why not just produce its own cattle and guitars? The reason lies in comparative advantage.

One country enjoys a **comparative advantage** in producing some good if its opportunity costs to produce that good are lower than the other country's. In this example, Canada's comparative advantage is in producing cattle. As Figure 2 shows, the opportunity cost for the United States to produce another million cows is 1 million guitars; each added cow essentially costs 1 guitar.

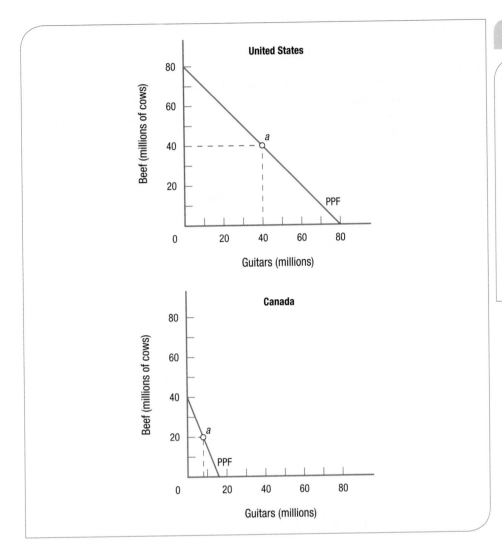

FIGURE 2

Production Possibilities for the United States and Canada

The production possibilities frontiers (PPF) shown here assume that the United States and Canada produce only beef and guitars. In this example, the United States has an absolute advantage over Canada in producing both products; the United States can produce twice as many cattle and 5 times as many guitars as Canada. Canada nonetheless has a comparative advantage over the United States in producing beef.

Contrast this with the situation in Canada. For every guitar Canadian manufacturers forgo making, they can produce 2.5 more cows. This means cows cost only 0.4 guitar in Canada (1/2.5 = 0.4). Canada's comparative advantage is in producing cattle, because a cow costs 0.4 guitar in Canada, while the same cow costs an entire guitar in the United States. By the same token, the United States has a comparative advantage in producing guitars: 1 guitar in the United States costs 1 cow, but the same guitar in Canada costs 2.5 cows.

Table 1 summarizes the opportunity costs of each good in each country and shows which country has the comparative advantage for each good. These relative costs suggest that the United States should focus its resources on guitar production and that Canada should specialize in beef.

Comparing Opportunity Costs for Beef and Guitar Production			TABLE 1
	U.S. Opportunity Cost	**Canada Opportunity Cost**	**Comparative Advantage**
Beef production	1 guitar	0.4 guitar	Canada
Guitar production	1 cow	2.5 cows	United States

Gains from Trade

To see how specialization and trade can benefit both countries even when one has an advantage in producing more of both goods, assume that the United States and Canada at first operate at point *a* in Figure 2, producing and consuming their own beef and guitars. As we can see, the United States produces and consumes 40 million cattle and 40 million guitars. Canada produces and consumes 20 million cattle and 8 million guitars. This initial position is similarly shown as points *a* in Figure 3.

FIGURE 3

The Gains from Specialization and Trade to the United States and Canada

Assume Canada specializes in cattle. If the two countries want to continue consuming 60 million cows between them, the United States needs to produce only 20 million. This frees up resources for the United States to begin producing more guitars. Because each cow in the United States costs 1 guitar to produce, reducing beef output by 20 million cattle means that 20 million more guitars can be produced. When the two countries trade their surplus products, both are better off than before.

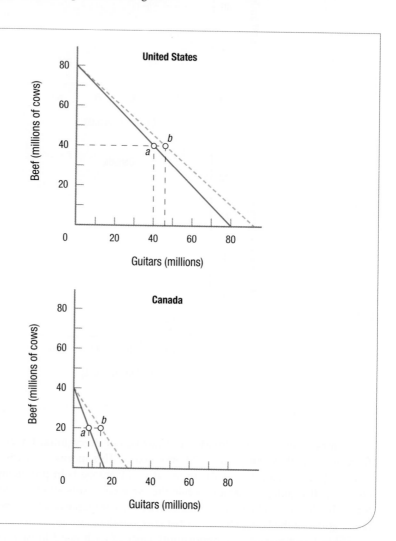

Assume now that Canada specializes in producing cattle, producing all that it can—40 million cows. We will assume that the two countries want to continue consuming 60 million cows between them. This means that the United States needs to produce only 20 million cattle, because Canada is now producing 40 million. This frees up some American resources to produce guitars. Because each cow in the United States costs a guitar, reducing beef output by 20 million cattle means that 20 million more guitars can now be produced.

Thus, the United States is producing 20 million cattle and 60 million guitars. Canada is producing 40 million cattle and no guitars. The combined production of cattle remains the same, 60 million, but guitar production has increased by 12 million (from 48 to 60 million).

The two countries can trade their surplus products and will be better off. This is shown in Table 2. Assuming that they agree to share the added 12 million guitars between them equally, Canada will trade 20 million cattle in exchange for 14 million guitars. Points *b* in Figure 3 show the resulting consumption patterns for each country. Each consumes the same quantity of beef as before trading, but each country now has 6 million more guitars: 46 million for the United States and 14 million for Canada. This is shown in the last column of the table.

The Gains from Trade			TABLE 2
Country and Product	Before Specialization	After Specialization	After Trade
United States			
Cows	40 million	20 million	40 million
Guitars	40 million	60 million	46 million
Canada			
Cows	20 million	40 million	20 million
Guitars	8 million	0	14 million

One important point to remember is that even when one country has an absolute advantage over another, countries still benefit from trade. The gains are small in our example, but they will grow as the two countries approach one another in size and their comparative advantages become more pronounced.

Practical Constraints on Trade   At this point, we should take a moment to note some practical constraints on trade. First, every transaction involves costs. These include transportation, communications, and the general costs of doing business. Over the last several

ISSUE

The Challenge of Measuring Imports and Exports in a Global Economy

Before the growth of globalization of manufacturing, the brand names of products would indicate their origin. For example, Sony televisions were made in Japan, Nokia telephones were made in Finland, and a Ford car would be made in the United States using American steel, engines, cloth, and, of course, American labor.

Today, a product's brand name does not tell the entire story. Production has become very complex, with parts sourced from around the world. With such complexities in trade, how then are imports and exports measured?

Do sales of Levi's jeans count as American exports? Although Levi's are an American brand that has for much of its history been produced in the United States, today nearly all Levi's jeans are made in Asia. Therefore, the American-brand jeans we buy count as an *import*. On the other hand, we also consume many products that may seem foreign, but are made in America. The majority of Toyota and Honda cars, for example, are assembled in American

factories using American steel, glass, and other materials. The same is true to a lesser extent for luxury brands such as BMW, which produces many compact cars in South Carolina. For all but a few parts (such as the engine and transmission) that are made in Japan or Germany, these cars are as American as apple pie, and are not counted as imports.

In order to measure imports and exports accurately, the United States Bureau of Economic Analysis tabulates data from documents collected by U.S. Customs and Border Protection, which details the appraised value (price paid) for all shipments of goods into and out of the ports of entry (whether by land, air, or sea). The value of imported and exported services is more difficult to measure, and is based on a survey of monthly government and industry reports to determine the value of all services bought from and sold to foreigners.

> PARTS CONTENT INFORMATION
> FOR VEHICLES IN THIS CARLINE:
> U.S./CANADA PARTS CONTENT: 75.0%
> MAJOR SOURCES OF FOREIGN PARTS CONTENT:
> JAPAN : 15.0%
>
> FOR THIS VEHICLE:
> FINAL ASSEMBLY POINT:
> SAN ANTONIO, TEXAS,   U.S.A.
> COUNTRY OF ORIGIN:
> ENGINE PARTS: U.S.A.
> TRANSMISSION PARTS: U.S.A.
> NOTE: Parts content does not include final assembly, distribution, or other non—parts costs.
>
> This Toyota Tundra was assembled in the U.S.A. by Toyota Motor Manufacturing, Texas, Inc., which employs thousands of American workers at its plant in San Antonio, Texas and uses hundreds of U.S. suppliers.
>
> WARNING: NOT TO BE REMOVED EXCEPT AFTER SALE OR LEASE TO A CONSUMER.
> TUNDRA   13

A domestic content label of an "imported" Toyota truck.

The globalized economy has been spurred in large part due to falling transportation and communication costs in the past few decades. Companies face ever greater competition, applying more pressure to reduce production costs. The expansion of the production process to a worldwide factory is just one way our economy has changed, and this trend is likely to continue into the future.

decades, however, transportation and communication costs have declined all over the world, resulting in growing world trade.

Second, the production possibilities frontiers for nations are not linear; rather, they are governed by increasing costs and diminishing returns. Countries find it difficult to specialize only in one product. Indeed, specializing in one product is risky because the market for the product can always decline, new technology might replace it, or its production can be disrupted by changing weather patterns. This is a perennial problem for developing countries that often build their exports and trade around one agricultural commodity.

Although it is true that trading partners benefit from trade, some individuals and groups within each country may lose. Individual workers in those industries at a comparative disadvantage are likely to lose their jobs, and thus may require retraining, relocation, or other help if they are to move smoothly into new occupations.

When the United States signed the North American Free Trade Agreement (NAFTA) with Canada and Mexico, many U.S. workers experienced this sort of dislocation. Some U.S. jobs went south to Mexico because of lower wages. States such as Texas and Arizona experienced greater levels of job dislocation due to their proximity to Mexico. Still, by opening up more markets for U.S. products, NAFTA has stimulated the U.S. economy. The goal is that displaced workers, newly retrained, will end up with new and better jobs, although there is no guarantee this will happen.

 CHECKPOINT

THE GAINS FROM TRADE

- An absolute advantage exists when one country can produce more of a good than another country.

- A comparative advantage exists when one country can produce a good at a lower opportunity cost than another country.

- Both countries gain from trade when each specializes in producing goods in which they have a comparative advantage.

- Transaction costs, diminishing returns, and the risk associated with specialization all place some practical constraints on trade.

QUESTIONS: When two individuals voluntarily engage in trade, they both benefit or the trade wouldn't occur—one party wouldn't choose to be worse off after the trade. Is the same true for nations? Is everyone in both nations better off?

Answers to the Checkpoint questions can be found at the end of this chapter.

➲ The Terms of Trade

How much can a country charge when it sells its goods to another country? How much must it pay for imported goods? The terms of trade determine the prices of imports and exports.

To keep things simple, assume that each country has only one export and one import, priced at P_x and P_m. The ratio of the price of the exported goods to the price of the imported goods, P_x/P_m, is the terms of trade. Thus, if a country exports computers and imports coffee, with two computers trading for one ton of coffee, the price of a computer must be one-half the price of a ton of coffee.

terms of trade The ratio of the price of exported goods to the price of imported goods (P_x/P_m).

When countries trade many commodities, the **terms of trade** are defined as the average price of exports divided by the average price of imports. This can get a bit complicated, given that the price of each import and export is quoted in its own national currency, while the exchange rate between the two currencies may be constantly changing. We will ignore these complications by translating currencies into dollars, focusing our attention on how the terms of trade are determined and the impact of trade.

Determining the Terms of Trade

To get a feel for how the terms of trade are determined, let us consider the trade in golf clubs between the United States and South Korea. We will assume the United States has a comparative advantage in producing golf clubs; all prices are given in dollars.

Panel A of Figure 4 shows the demand and supply of sets of golf clubs in the United States. The upward sloping supply curve reflects increasing opportunity costs in golf club production. As the United States continues to specialize in golf club production, resources less suited to this purpose must be employed, resulting in rising costs for golf club production. Because of this rise in costs as ever more resources are shifted to golf clubs, the United States will eventually lose its comparative advantage in golf club production. This represents one limit on specialization and trade.

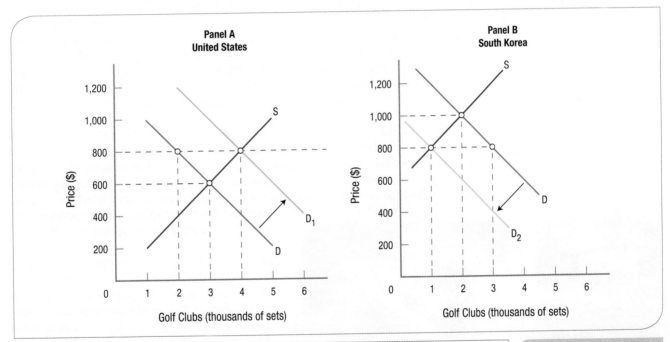

FIGURE 4

Determining the Terms of Trade

Panel A shows the demand and supply of golf clubs in the United States; the upward slope of the supply curve reflects increasing opportunity costs to produce more golf clubs. The United States begins in pretrade equilibrium at $600 and South Korea's initial equilibrium is at $1,000. With trade, Korean consumers will begin buying American golf clubs because of their lower price. American golf club makers will increase production to meet this new demand. Korean golf club firms will see sales of their golf clubs decline as prices begin to fall. Ignoring transport costs, trade will continue until prices reach $800. At this point, American exports (2,000) are just equal to Korean imports (2,000).

Let us assume that the United States begins in pretrade equilibrium, with the price of sets of golf clubs at $600 each. Panel B shows South Korea initially in equilibrium with a higher price of $1,000. Because prices for golf clubs from the United States are lower, when trade begins, Korean consumers will begin buying U.S. golf clubs.

American golf club makers will increase production to meet this new demand. Korean golf club firms, conversely, will see the sales of their golf clubs decline. For now, let us ignore transport costs, such that trade continues until prices reach $800. At this point, U.S. exports (2,000 sets of golf clubs) are just equal to Korean imports. Both countries are now in equilibrium, with the price of golf clubs somewhere between the two pretrade equilibrium prices ($800 in this case).

Imagine this same process simultaneously working itself out with many other goods, including some at which the Koreans have a comparative advantage, such as interactive televisions. As each product settles into an equilibrium price, the terms of trade between these two countries is determined.

The Impact of Trade

Our examination of absolute and comparative advantage has thus far highlighted the benefits of trade. A closer look at Figure 4, however, shows that trade produces winners and losers.

Picking up on the previous example, golf club producers in the United States are happy, having watched their sales rise from 3,000 to 4,000 units. Predictably, management and workers in this industry will favor even more trade with South Korea and the rest of the world. Yet, domestic consumers of golf clubs are worse off, because after trade they purchase only 2,000 sets at the higher equilibrium price of $800.

Contrast this situation in the net exporting country, the United States, with that of the net importer, South Korea. Korean golf club producers are worse off than before because the price of golf clubs fell from $1,000 to $800, and their output was reduced to 1,000 units. Consequently, they must cut jobs, leaving workers and managers in the Korean golf club industry unhappy with its country's trade policies. Korean consumers, however, are beneficiaries of this expanded trade, because they can purchase 3,000 sets of golf clubs at a lower price of $800 each.

These results are not merely hypothetical. This is the story of free trade, which has been played out time and time again: Some sectors of the economy win, and some lose. American consumers have been happy to purchase Korean televisions such as Samsung and LG, given their high quality and low prices. American television producers (such as RCA and Zenith) have not been so pleased, nor have their employees, having watched television factories close and workers displaced as competition from abroad forced these companies out of business.

Trade allows American golf club producers to expand sales globally, while Korean golfers benefit from their availability.

Similarly, the ranks of American textile workers have been decimated over the past three decades as domestic clothing producers have increasingly become nothing but designers and marketers of clothes, shifting their production overseas to countries in which wages are lower. American-made clothing is now essentially a thing of the past.

To be sure, American consumers have enjoyed a substantial drop in the price of clothing, because labor forms a significant part of the cost of clothing production. Still, being able to purchase inexpensive T-shirts made in China is small consolation for the unemployed textile worker in North Carolina.

The undoubted pain suffered by the losers from trade often is translated into pressure put on politicians to restrict trade in one way or another. The pain is often felt more strongly than the "happiness" felt by those who benefit from trade.

How Trade Is Restricted

Trade restrictions can range from subsidies provided to domestic firms to protect them against lower priced imports to embargoes by which the government bans any trade with a country. Between these two extremes are more intermediate policies, such as exchange controls that limit the amount of foreign currency available to importers or citizens who travel abroad. Regulation, licensing, and government purchasing policies are all frequently used to promote or ensure the purchase of domestic products. The main reason for these trade restrictions is simple: The industry and its employees actually feel the pain and lobby extensively for protection, while the huge benefits of lower prices are diffused among millions of consumers whose benefits are each so small that fighting against a trade barrier isn't worth their time.

The most common forms of trade restrictions are tariffs and quotas. Panel A of Figure 5 shows the average U.S. tariff rates since 1900. Some economists have suggested that the

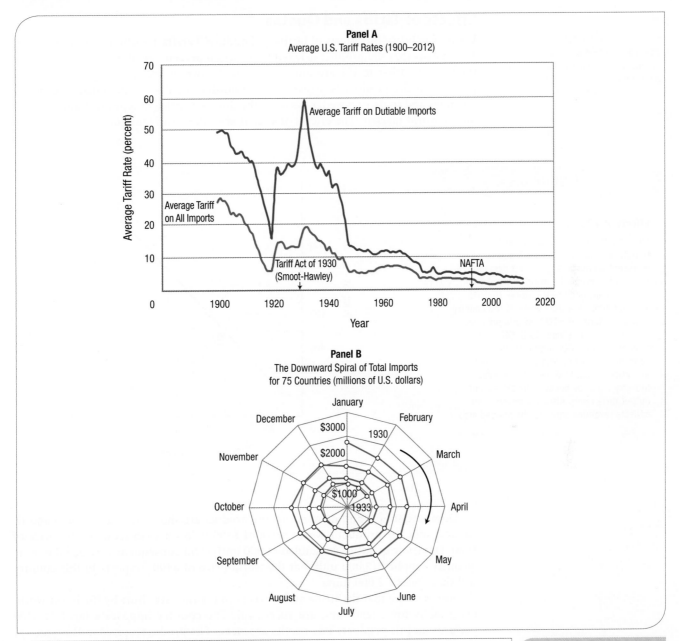

Panel A
Average U.S. Tariff Rates (1900–2012)

Panel B
The Downward Spiral of Total Imports
for 75 Countries (millions of U.S. dollars)

Average U.S. Tariff Rates, 1900–2012, and the Downward Spiral of World Imports, 1930–1933

Tariffs and quotas are the most common forms of trade restrictions. Panel A shows that tariff rates in the United States peaked during the Great Depression. Over the last several decades, tariffs have steadily declined to an average of about 2% today. When tariffs jumped with the passage of the Smoot-Hawley Act in 1930, world imports spiraled downward as shown in panel B. As trade between nations declined, incomes, output, and employment also fell worldwide. In panel B, total monthly imports in millions of U.S. dollars for 75 countries is shown spiraling downward from $2,738 million in January 1930 to $1,057 million in March 1933.

Source: Charles Kindleberger, *The World Depression 1929–1939* (Berkeley: University of California Press), 1986, p. 170.

FIGURE 5

tariff wars that erupted in the 1920s and culminated in the passage of the Smoot-Hawley Act in 1930 were an important factor underlying the severity of the Great Depression. Panel B shows the impact of higher tariffs on worldwide imports from 1930 to 1933. The higher tariffs reduced trade, leading to a reduction in income, output, and employment, and added fuel to the worldwide depression. Since the 1930s, the United States has played a leading role in trade liberalization, with average tariff rates declining to a current rate of roughly 2%.

Effects of Tariffs and Quotas

tariff A tax on imported products. When a country taxes imported products, it drives a wedge between the product's domestic price and its price on the world market.

What exactly are the effects of tariffs and quotas? **Tariffs** are often *ad valorem* taxes. This means that the product is taxed by a certain percentage of its price as it crosses the border. Other tariffs are unit taxes (also known as *specific tariffs*): A fixed tax per unit of the product is assessed at the border. Tariffs are designed to generate revenues and to drive a wedge between the domestic price of a product and its price on the world market. The effects of a tariff are shown in Figure 6.

FIGURE 6

Effects of a Tariff

What are the effects of a typical tariff? Supply and demand curves S and D represent domestic supply and demand. Assume the product's world price of $400 is lower than its domestic price. Imports will therefore be 2,000 units. If the country imposes a tariff of $100 on this product, the domestic price rises to $500, and imports fall to 1,000 units. Domestic consumers now buy less of the product at higher prices. However, the domestic industry is happy because its prices and output have risen. Also, the government collects revenues equal to the shaded area.

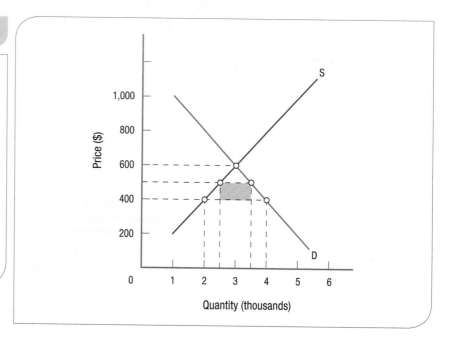

Domestic supply and demand for the product are shown in Figure 6 as S and D. Assume that the product's world price of $400 is lower than its domestic price of $600. Domestic quantity demanded (4,000 units) will consequently exceed domestic quantity supplied (2,000 units) at the world price of $400. Imports to this country will therefore be 2,000 units.

Now assume that the firms and workers in the industry hurt by the lower world price lobby for a tariff and are successful. The country imposes a tariff of $100 per unit on this product. The results are clear. The product's price in this country rises to $500 and imports fall to 1,000 units (3,500 − 2,500). Domestic consumers buy less of the product at higher prices. Even so, the domestic industry is happy, because its prices and output have risen. The government, meanwhile, collects revenues equal to $100,000 ($100 × 1,000), the shaded area in Figure 6. These revenues can be significant: In the 1800s, tariffs were the federal government's dominant form of revenue. It is only in the last century that the federal government has come to rely more on other sources of revenue, including taxes on income, sales, and property.

Figure 7 shows the effects of a **quota.** They are similar to what we saw in Figure 6, except that the government restricts the quantity of imports into the country to 1,000 units. Imports fall to the quota level, and consumers again lose, because they must pay higher prices for less output. Producers and their employees gain as prices and employment in the domestic industry rise. For a quota, however, the government does not collect revenue. Then who gets this revenue? The foreign exporting company gets it in the form of higher prices for its products. This explains why governments prefer tariffs over quotas.

quota A government set limit on the quantity of imports into a country.

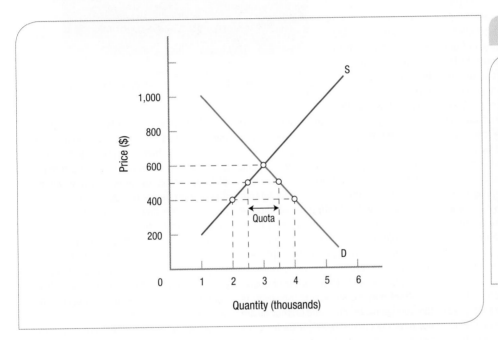

FIGURE 7

Effects of a Quota

What are the effects of a quota? They are similar to the effects of a tariff, except that the government restricts the quantity of imports into the country to 1,000 units. Imports fall to the quota level, and again consumers lose as they must pay higher prices for less output. Producers and their employees gain as prices and employment in the domestic industry rise. With a quota, however, the government does not collect revenues.

The United States imposed quotas on Japanese automobiles in the 1980s. The primary effect of these quotas was initially to raise the minimum standard equipment and price dramatically for some Japanese cars and ultimately to increase the number of Japanese cars made in American factories. If a firm is limited in the number of vehicles it can sell, why not sell higher priced ones where the profit margins are higher? The Toyota Land Cruiser, for instance, was originally a bare-bones SUV selling for under $15,000. With quotas, this vehicle was transformed into a luxury behemoth with all the bells and whistles standard. Although quotas on Japanese automobiles have long expired, Japanese automakers continue to produce a wide array of luxury automobiles today.

One problem with tariffs and quotas is that when they are imposed, large numbers of consumers pay just a small amount more for the targeted products. Few consumers are willing to spend time and effort lobbying Congress to end or forestall these trade barriers from being introduced. Producers, however, are often few in number, and they stand to gain tremendously from such trade barriers. It is no wonder that such firms have large lobbying budgets and provide campaign contributions to political candidates.

ISSUE

Do Foreign Trade Zones Help or Hurt American Consumers and Workers?

Driving through the gates of the Cartago *Zona Franca* in Costa Rica, one encounters a remarkable sight in a historic Central American town: large factories adorned with the names of large American companies in industries including pharmaceuticals, semiconductors, medical supplies, and household products. What are these companies doing in Costa Rica, and why did they choose to locate within this small gated compound?

In Cartago, as well as in other cities throughout the world, clusters of multinational companies engage in manufacturing activities. These companies are taking advantage of the benefits offered by foreign trade zones, also commonly known as free trade zones or export processing zones.

A foreign trade zone is a designated area in a country where foreign companies can import inputs, without tariffs, to be used for product assembly by local workers who are often paid a fraction of what equivalent workers would be paid in the company's home country. By operating in a foreign trade zone, all inputs coming into a country are exempted from tariffs as long as the finished products (with some exceptions) are then exported from the country. Further, companies are often exempted from other taxes levied by the government.

Countries such as China, the Philippines, and Costa Rica establish foreign trade zones to attract foreign investment, which creates well-paying jobs relative to wages paid by domestic companies. Countries with high literacy rates, like Costa Rica, are especially attractive because their workers can perform semiskilled tasks such as assembling electronic and computer products or handling customer service calls. Foreign trade zones also are prevalent along border towns, such as those in Mexico, where easy transportation to and from the United States allows inputs and products to flow rapidly.

Although companies operating in foreign trade zones benefit from lower production costs and the host country benefits from jobs created, not everyone is in favor of foreign trade zones. Various unions in the United States view foreign trade zones as facilitating the offshoring of American jobs. Offshoring (also commonly referred to as outsourcing) occurs when part of the production process (typically the labor-intensive portions) is sent to countries with lower input costs.

What may be surprising, however, is that foreign trade zones and offshoring are not one-way streets. Foreign trade zones are not limited to developing countries with low labor costs. The United States has many foreign trade zones established for the same purpose: to attract foreign companies to invest in manufacturing plants. Although American labor costs are high, they often are lower than wages in European countries or in Japan. By moving production to the United States, European and Japanese companies produce goods such as cars while enjoying the same tax benefits described earlier by American companies operating abroad.

Foreign trade zones have long been a part of the U.S. economy. Today, foreign trade zones exist throughout the country.

Most of the arguments against offshoring are based on anecdotal evidence—a plant closing here, a closing there, and so on. But in the mid-2000s, the Bureau of Labor Statistics developed a survey to quantify the levels of both offshoring and inshoring (the flow of jobs to the United States by firms from other countries). In the year 2012, statistics showed that the *net* effect was roughly equal, that almost as many jobs were created by foreign companies in the United States as jobs lost from American companies moving production facilities overseas.

As we have seen, there are both winners and losers in trade. But in general, economists found that there is a net increase in income to U.S. residents from offshoring. When all impacts are considered, including savings to consumers from lower product costs, imports of U.S. goods by foreigners, profits to U.S. affiliates, and the value of labor reemployed, the benefits tend to outweigh the costs. Clearly, those who lose their jobs suffer. But with a policy to provide training to displaced workers, the savings from offshoring can lead to greater investment and growth in the long run.

CHECKPOINT

THE TERMS OF TRADE

- The terms of trade are determined by the ratio of the price of exported goods to the price of imported goods.

- The terms of trade are set by the markets in each country and by exports and imports that eventually equalize the prices.

- Trade leads to winners and losers in each country and in each market.
- Trade restrictions vary from subsidies to domestic firms to government bans on the import of foreign products.
- Tariffs are taxes on imports that protect domestic producers and generate revenue for the government.
- Quotas represent restrictions on the volume of particular imports that can come into a country. Quotas do not generate revenue for governments and are infrequently used.

QUESTION: When the government imposes a quota on foreign trucks, who benefits and who loses?

Answers to the Checkpoint question can be found at the end of this chapter.

Arguments Against Free Trade

We have seen the benefits of trade, and have looked at how trade undoubtedly benefits some and harms others. Those who are harmed by trade often seek to restrict trade, primarily in the form of tariffs and quotas. Because trade leads to some loss, those who are harmed by trade have made arguments against free trade.

The arguments against free trade fall into two camps. Traditional economic arguments include protection for infant industries, protection against dumping, low foreign wages, and support for industries judged vital for national defense. More recent arguments focus on globalization (social and economic) concerns that embody political-economy characteristics. These include domestic employment concerns, environmental concerns, and the impact of globalization on working conditions in developing nations. In what follows, we take a critical look at each of these arguments, showing that most of these arguments do not have a solid empirical basis.

Traditional Economic Arguments

Arguments against trade are not new. Despite the huge gains from trade, distortions (subsidies and trade barriers) continue because changing current policies will hurt those dependent on subsidies and trade restrictions, and these firms and workers will show their displeasure in the voting booth. All of these traditional economic arguments against free trade seem reasonable on their face, but on closer examination, they look less attractive.

Infant Industry Argument An **infant industry,** it is argued, is one that is too underdeveloped to achieve comparative advantage or perhaps even to survive in the global market. Such an industry may be too small or undercapitalized, or its management and workers may be too inexperienced, to compete. Unless the industry's government provides it with some protection through tariffs, quotas, or subsidies, it might not survive in the face of foreign competition.

In theory, once the infant industry has been given this protection, it should be able to grow, acquiring the necessary capital and expertise needed to compete internationally. Germany and the United States used high tariffs to protect their infant manufacturing sectors in the 1800s, and Japan continued to maintain import restrictions up until the 1970s.

Although the infant industry argument sounds reasonable, it has several limitations. First, protecting an industry must be done in a way that makes the industry internationally competitive. Many countries coddle their firms, and these producers never seem to develop into "mature," internationally viable firms. Once protection is provided (typically a protective tariff), it is difficult to remove after an industry has matured. The industry and its workers continue to convince policymakers of the need for continued protection.

Second, infant industry protection often tends to focus on capital manufacturing. Countries with huge labor supplies would do better to develop their labor-intensive industries first, letting more capital-intensive industries develop over time. Every country, after

infant industry An industry so underdeveloped that protection is needed for it to become competitive on the world stage or to ensure its survival.

all, should seek to exploit its comparative advantages, but it is difficult to determine which industries have a chance of developing a comparative advantage in the future and should be temporarily protected.

Third, many industries seem to be able to develop without protections, therefore countries may be wasting their resources and reducing their incomes by imposing protection measures.

Clearly, the infant industry argument is not valid for advanced economies such as those of the United States, much of Europe, and Japan. The evidence for developing nations shows some benefits but is mixed for the reasons noted above.

Antidumping **Dumping** means that goods are sold at lower prices (often *below cost*) abroad than in their home market. This is typically a result of government subsidies.

In the same way that price discrimination improves profits, firms can price discriminate between their home markets and foreign markets. Let's assume that costs of production are $100 per unit for all firms (domestic and foreign). A state subsidy of $30 a unit, for example, reduces domestic costs to $70 per unit and permits the firm to sell its product in world markets at these lower prices. These state subsidies give these firms a cost advantage in foreign markets.

Firms can use dumping as a form of predatory pricing, using higher prices in their domestic markets to support unrealistically low prices in foreign markets. The goal of predatory pricing is to drive foreign competitors out of business. When this occurs, the firm doing the dumping then comes back and imposes higher prices. In the long run, these higher prices thereby offset the company's short-term losses.

Dumping violates American trade laws. If the federal government determines that a foreign firm is dumping products onto the American market, it can impose antidumping tariffs on the offending products. The government, however, must distinguish among dumping, legitimate price discrimination, and legitimate instances of lower cost production arising from comparative advantage.

Low Foreign Wages Some advocates of trade barriers maintain that domestic firms and their workers need to be protected from displacement by cheap foreign labor. Without this protection, it is argued, foreign manufacturers that pay their workers pennies an hour will flood the market with low-cost products. As we have already seen, this argument has something to it: Workers in advanced economies can be displaced by low-wage foreign workers. This is what has happened in the American textile industry.

Once a handful of American clothing manufacturers began moving their production facilities overseas, thereby undercutting domestic producers, other manufacturers were forced to follow them. American consumers have benefited from lower clothing prices, but many displaced textile workers are still trying to get retrained and adapt to work in other industries. More recently, many manufacturing jobs have drifted overseas, and high-technology firms today are shifting some help desk facilities and computer programming to foreign shores.

On balance, however, the benefits of lower priced goods considerably exceed the costs of lost employment. The federal government has resisted imposing protection measures for the sake of protecting jobs, instead funding programs that help displaced workers transition to new lines of work.

National Defense Argument In times of national crisis or war, the United States must be able to rely on key domestic industries, such as oil, steel, and defense. Some have argued that these industries may require some protection even during peacetime to ensure that they are already well established when a crisis strikes and importing key products may be impossible. Within limits, this argument is sound. Still, the United States has the capacity to produce such a wide variety of products that protections for specific industries would seem to be unjustified and unnecessary.

So what are we to make of these traditional arguments? Although they all seem reasonable, they all have deficiencies. Infant industries may be helped in the short run, but protections are often extended well beyond what is necessary, resulting in inefficient firms that are vulnerable on world markets. Dumping is clearly a potential problem, but distinguishing real cases of dumping and comparative advantage has often proven difficult in practice. Low foreign wages are often the only comparative advantage a developing nation has to offer the world economy, and typically, the benefits to consumers vastly outweigh the loss to a particular industry. Maintaining (protecting) industries for national defense has merit and may be appropriate for some countries, but for a country as huge and diversified as the United States, it is probably unnecessary.

Recent Globalization Concerns

Expanded trade and globalization have provided the world's producers and consumers with many benefits. Some observers, however, have voiced concerns about globalization and its effects on domestic employment, the global environment, and working conditions in developing nations. Let's look at each one of these globalization concerns.

The steel industry is one of several that are considered key domestic industries vital in times of national crisis. Therefore, industry executives frequently argue for protection against foreign competition.

Trade and Domestic Employment Some critics argue that increased trade and globalization spell job losses for domestic workers. We have seen that this can be true. Some firms, unable to compete with imports, will be forced to lay off workers or even close their doors. Even so, increased trade usually allows firms that are exporters to expand their operations and hire new workers. These will be firms in industries with comparative advantages. For the United States, these industries tend to be those that require a highly skilled workforce, resulting in higher wages for American workers.

Clearly, those industries that are adding workers and those that are losing jobs are different industries. For workers who lose their jobs, switching industries can be difficult and time-consuming, and often it requires new investments in human capital. American trade policy recognizes this problem, and the Trade Adjustment Assistance (TAA) program provides workers with job search assistance, job training, and some relocation allowances. In some industries sensitive to trade liberalization, including textiles and agriculture, trade policies are designed to proceed gradually, thus giving these industries and their workers some extra time to adjust.

Possible employment losses in some noncompetitive industries do not seem to provide enough justification for restricting trade. By imposing trade restrictions such as tariffs or quotas in one industry, employment opportunities in many other industries may be reduced. Open, competitive trade encourages producers to focus their production on those areas in which the country stands at a comparative advantage. Free trade puts competitive pressure on domestic firms, forcing them to be more productive and competitive, boosting the flow of information and technology across borders, and widening the availability of inputs for producers. At the end of the day, consumers benefit from these efficiencies, having more goods to choose from and enjoying a higher standard of living.

Trade and the Environment Concerns about globalization, trade, and the environment usually take one of two forms. Some people are concerned that expanded trade and globalization will lead to increased environmental degradation as companies take advantage of lax environmental laws abroad, particularly in the developing world. Others worry that attempts by the government to strengthen environmental laws will be challenged by trading partners as disguised protectionism.

Domestic environmental regulations usually target a product or process that creates pollution or other environmental problems. One concern in establishing environmental regulations, however, is that they not unfairly discriminate against the products of another country. This is usually not a serious problem. Nearly all trade agreements, including the World Trade Organization Agreements and NAFTA, have provisions permitting countries to enforce measures "necessary to protect human, animal or plant life or health" or to conserve exhaustible natural resources. Nothing in our trade agreements prevents the United States from implementing environmental regulations as long as they do not unreasonably discriminate against our trading partners.

Will free trade come at the expense of the environment? Every action involves a tradeoff. Clearly, there can be cases in which the benefits of trade accruing to large numbers of people result in harm to a more concentrated group. However, trade policies can also be complementary to good environmental policies. For example, increased free trade in agriculture encourages countries with fertile lands to specialize in growing crops while discouraging countries from farming marginal lands that require the use of environmentally damaging pesticides and chemicals.

We have seen that trade raises incomes in developed and developing countries. And environmental protection is an income elastic good: As incomes rise, the demand for environmental protections rises and its environmental protection efforts begin to improve.

In poor, developing nations, environmental protection will not at first be a priority. Critics of globalization are concerned that because environmental and labor standards in many developing nations are well below those of the developed countries, there will be pressure to adopt these lower standards in rich nations due to trade and foreign direct investment. But as Bhagwati and Hudec argue, there has been no systematic "race to the bottom" and many corporations often have the highest environmental and labor standards in the developing world.[1] Also, it is worth noting that over time, as incomes rise, environmental protection takes on added importance even in poorer nations. On balance, trade probably benefits the environment over the longer term, as incomes grow in developing nations and environmental protections take on greater importance.

Trade and Its Effect on Working Conditions in Developing Nations Some antiglobalization activists argue that trade between the United States and developing countries, where wages are low and working conditions are deplorable, exploits workers in these developing countries. Clearly, such trade does hurt American workers in low-wage, low-skilled occupations who cannot compete with the even lower wage workers overseas. But it is not clear that workers in developing countries would be helped if the United States were to cut off its trade with those countries that refuse to improve wages or working conditions.

Restricting trade with countries that do not raise wages to levels we think acceptable or bring working conditions up to our standards would probably do more harm than good. Low wages reflect, among other factors, small investments in human capital, low productivity, and meager living standards characteristic of developing nations. Blocking trade with these nations may deprive them of their key chance to grow and to improve in those areas in which we would like to see change.

Liberalized trade policies, economic freedom, and a legal system that respects property rights and foreign capital investment probably provide the best recipe for

---

[1] Jagdish Bhagwati and Robert Hudec (eds.), *Fair Trade and Harmonization, Vol. 1: Economic Analysis* (Cambridge, MA: MIT Press), 1996.

rapid development, economic growth, environmental protection, and improved wages and working conditions.

In summary, trade does result in job losses in some industries, but the gain for consumers and the competitive pressures that trade puts on domestic companies is beneficial to the economy as a whole. Trade raises incomes in developing nations, resulting in a growing demand for more environmentally friendly production processes. Trade is not the reason for low environmental standards in developing countries; they result from low incomes, low standards of living, and poor governmental policies. Trade brings about higher levels of income and ultimately better working conditions.

CHECKPOINT

ARGUMENTS AGAINST FREE TRADE

- The infant industry argument claims that some industries are so underdeveloped that they need protection to survive in a global competitive environment.

- Dumping involves selling products at different prices in domestic and foreign markets, often with the help of subsidies from the government. This is a form of predatory pricing to gain market share in the foreign market.

- Some suggest that domestic workers need to be protected from the low wages in foreign countries. This puts the smaller aggregate loss to small groups ahead of the greater general gains from trade. Also, for many countries, a low wage is their primary comparative advantage.

- Some argue that select industries need protection to ensure that they will exist for national defense reasons.

- Clearly, globalization has meant that some U.S. workers have lost jobs to foreign competition, and some advocates would restrict trade on these grounds alone. But on net, trade has led to higher overall employment. The U.S. government recognizes these issues and has instituted a Trade Adjustment Assistance (TAA) program to help workers who lose their jobs transition to new employment.

- Concern about the environment is often a factor in trade negotiations. Those concerned about globalization want to ensure that firms do not move production to countries with lax environmental laws, while others are concerned that environmental regulation not be used to justify protectionism. Trade ultimately raises income and environmental awareness in developing nations.

- Some antiglobalization activists consider shifting production to countries with low wages as exploitation and demand that wages be increased in other countries. Globalization has typically resulted in higher wages in developing nations, but not up to the standards of developed nations.

QUESTION: Trade between the United States and China increased significantly over the last two decades. China is now the United States' second largest trading partner after Canada. Expanding trade has led to significant reductions in the price of many goods, including technology goods such as computers and tablets. However, some people have been vocal against policies that promote freer trade with China. What are some reasons why people would be against greater trade with China?

Answers to the Checkpoint question can be found at the end of this chapter.

chapter summary

Section 1: **The Gains from Trade**

Absolute advantage: occurs when one country can produce more of a good than another country.

Comparative advantage: occurs when a country can produce a good at a lower opportunity cost than another country.

The United States has a comparative advantage in both soybean production (due to an abundance of fertile land) and commercial aircraft production (due to an abundance of technology and human capital).

Trade is a **positive-sum game,** which means that both countries in a trading relationship can gain compared to not trading.

Section 2: **The Terms of Trade**

The **terms of trade** determine the prices of imports and exports. When countries trade many commodities, the terms of trade are defined as the average price of exports divided by the price of imports.

The Effect of Trade on Prices

Before trade, the prices charged for one good may be different in the two countries. The country with the lower price is likely to export the good; greater demand for that country's good pushes prices higher. The country with the higher price is likely to import the good; lesser demand for that country's good pushes prices lower. Market forces therefore push prices toward an equilibrium under free trade.

Price in Country A

Imports push prices down

Equilibrium price with trade

Exports push prices up

Price in Country B

Tariffs are a tax on imports. They raise the domestic price of the good to the *world price + tariff.*

Winners: Domestic producers gain area A. Government gains area C in tariff revenues.

Losers: Domestic consumers lose areas A + B + C + D due to higher prices.

Net Loss: Areas B + D (deadweight loss from the tariff)

Historically, trade barriers have been high. In the 1930s, the Smoot-Hawley Act placed an average tax of 60% on most imported goods, arguably prolonging the Great Depression. Trade barriers have fallen since, and in the past three decades have fallen dramatically to nearly free trade with all countries.

Section 3: **Arguments Against Free Trade**

Many strong arguments against free trade exist. In each case, trade protection in the form of a tariff or quota is sought to protect the domestic industry.

Infant Industry Argument: States that a new industry requires protection to survive against established foreign competition. The problem is determining when these industries mature.

Antidumping Argument: Occurs when a foreign firm sells its goods below cost or at a price below what it charges in its domestic market.

Key Industries Argument: States that a country must be able to rely on its domestic industries for critical goods such as food, oil, steel, and defense equipment in times of conflict when trade might not be possible.

Environmental Degradation Argument: States that countries producing mass goods allow their environments to deteriorate. However, studies show that as countries develop and incomes grow, demand for environmental protection rises.

In the early 1980s, Harley-Davidson sought infant industry protection against competition from established lower cost Japanese motorcycles, giving it time to retool its factories to be more competitive.

Protection Against Cheap Labor Argument: Argues that domestic workers need to be protected from cheap foreign labor. Most economists estimate that the benefits from lower priced imports from free trade exceed the costs of lost employment. Further, increased trade generates jobs in export industries.

Exploitation of Foreign Workers Argument: Argues that trading with developing countries where wages are low and working conditions are deplorable exploits workers in these countries. But restricting trade would probably do more harm than good. Trade may be their only chance to grow and improve their standard of living.

Although working conditions in factories in developing countries look miserable, they often are better than working conditions before trade. In addition, trade increases demand for workers, which leads to higher wages.

South Korea sustained environmental degradation during its economic development in the 1980s and 1990s. Today, it invests heavily in environmental protection and sustainable cities like Songdo outside the capital of Seoul.

autarky, p. 686
imports, p. 686
exports, p. 686
absolute advantage, p. 686

comparative advantage, p. 686
terms of trade, p. 690
tariff, p. 694
quota, p. 695

infant industry, p. 697
dumping, p. 698

QUESTIONS AND PROBLEMS

Check Your Understanding

1. What is the difference between absolute and comparative advantage? Why would Michelle Wie, who is better than you at both golf and laundry, still hire you to do her wash?

2. If the United States has a comparative advantage in the production of strawberries compared to Iceland, how might trade affect the prices of strawberries in the two countries?

3. Who are the beneficiaries from a large U.S. tariff on French and German wines? Who are the losers?

4. Why does a quota generate a larger loss to the importing country than a tariff that restricts imports to the same quantity?

5. What is the difference between an infant industry and a key industry? Why do producers in both industries desire protection against foreign imports?

6. How could free trade between the United States and China potentially lead to *more* jobs in the United States?

Apply the Concepts

7. South Korean film production companies have been protected for half a century by policies enacted to protect an infant industry. But beginning in July 2006, the days that local films *must* be shown by any movie house was reduced to 73 from 146. South Korean film celebrities and the industry fought the changes even though local films commanded half the box office. Why would a country enact special protection for the local film industry? Who would be the major competitor threatening the South Korean film industry? If films made by the local industry must be shown at least 146 days a year, does the local industry have much incentive to develop good films and be competitive with the rest of the world?

8. Expanding trade in general benefits both countries, or they would not willingly engage in trade. But we also know that consumers and society often gain while particular industries or workers lose. Because society and consumers gain, why don't the many gainers compensate the few losers for their loss?

9. Some activist groups are calling for "fair trade laws" by which other countries would be required to meet or approach our environmental standards and provide wage and working conditions approaching those of developed nations in order to be able to trade with us. Is this just another form of rent seeking by industries and unions for protection from overseas competition?

10. Why is there free trade between states in the United States but not necessarily between countries?

11. Remittances from developed countries amount to over $325 billion each year. These funds are sent to their home countries by migrants in developed nations. Is this similar to the gains from trade discussed in this chapter, or are these workers just taking jobs that workers in developed countries would be paid more to do in the absence of the migrants?

12. Suppose Brazil developed a secret process that effectively quadrupled its output of coffee from its coffee plantations. This secret process enabled it to significantly undercut the prices of U.S. domestic producers. Would domestic producers receive a sympathetic ear to calls for protection from Brazil's lower cost coffee? How is this case different from that of protection against cheap foreign labor?

In the News

13. Economist Steven Landsburg (*New York Times,* January 16, 2008, p. A23) made the point that "bullying and protectionism have a lot in common. They both use force (either directly or through the power of the law) to enrich someone else at your involuntary expense. If you're forced to pay $20 an hour to an American for goods you could have bought from a Mexican for $5 an hour, you're being extorted." He also argued, "Surely we have fellow citizens who are hurt by those [trade] agreements, at least in the limited sense that they'd be better off in a world where trade flourishes, except in this one instance. What do we owe those fellow citizens?" The United States has programs to educate and retrain workers displaced by free trade agreements. Do we even owe them that? Why?

14. *The Economist* (November 21, 2009) suggested that in a highly globalized world where production is easily moved to other countries, there is an inherent tension between our desire to reduce carbon emissions to stem global climate change and our commitment to free trade. Do you agree? Why or why not?

Solving Problems

15. The figure below shows the production possibilities frontiers (PPFs) for Italy and India for their domestic production of olives and tea. Without trade, assume that each is consuming olives and tea at point *a*.

a. If Italy and India were to consider specialization and trade, what commodity would each specialize in? What is India's opportunity cost for tea and olives? What is Italy's opportunity cost for tea and olives?

b. Assume that the two countries agree to specialize entirely in one product (the one for which each country has a comparative advantage), and agree to split the total output between them. Complete the table below. Are both countries better off after trade?

Country and Product	Before Specialization	After Specialization	After Trade
Italy			
Olives	6 million tons	_____	_____
Tea	10 million tons	_____	_____
India			
Olives	2 million tons	_____	_____
Tea	30 million tons	_____	_____

16. The following figure shows the annual domestic demand and supply for 10 GB compact flash cards for digital cameras.

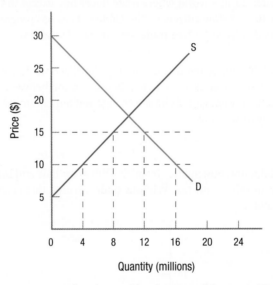

a. Assume that the worldwide price of these 10 GB cards is $10. What percent of United States sales would be imported?

b. Assume the U.S. government puts a $5 tariff per card on imports. How many 10 GB flash cards would be imported into the United States?

c. Given the tariff in question (b), how much revenue would the government collect from this tariff?

d. Given the tariff in question (b), how much more sales revenue would domestic companies enjoy as a result of the tariff?

❖ USING THE NUMBERS

17. According to By the Numbers, approximately when was the last time the United States had a trade surplus? As a percentage of GDP, what was the highest trade surplus the United States has achieved? What was the highest trade deficit the United States has achieved?

18. According to By the Numbers, most of the developed countries (Canada, Australia, the United States, Switzerland, and Hong Kong) have relatively low tariff barriers while much of the developing world still has high tariffs on imports. What reasons might account for why these countries continue to have high tariffs?

ANSWERS TO QUESTIONS IN CHECKPOINTS

Checkpoint: The Gains from Trade

Yes, in general, nations would not trade unless they benefit. However, as we have seen, even though nations as a whole gain, specific groups—industries and their workers who do not have a comparative advantage relative to other countries—lose.

Checkpoint: The Terms of Trade

When a quota is imposed, the first beneficiary is the domestic industry. Competition from foreign competition is limited. If the market is important enough (automobiles), the foreign companies build new plants in the United States and compete as if they are domestic firms. A second beneficiary is foreign competitors, in that they can increase the price or complexity of their products and increase their margins. Losers are consumers and, to some extent, the government, because a tariff could have accomplished the same reduction in imports and the government would have collected some revenue.

Checkpoint: Arguments Against Free Trade

Growth in the volume of trade with China has led to lower prices on many goods Americans enjoy. However, although trade with China has led to significant benefits to Americans, the sentiment is not always positive for a number of reasons. First, many believe that China's low prices (through its low wages as well as government efforts to keep the value of the U.S. dollar strong) forced many American factories to close or move overseas, causing job losses. Second, some believe China holds an unfair advantage due to poor working conditions and low environmental standards. Third, some believe that quality standards for Chinese products are low, leading to safety issues. These and other reasons have created a backlash against efforts to further reduce trade barriers between the two nations. However, these concerns have not diminished the benefits of low prices and the many American jobs generated through increased exports of American-made products to a growing consumer market in China.

27

Open Economy
Macroeconomics

After studying this chapter you should be able to:

- Define the current account and the capital account in the balance of payments between countries.

- Explain the difference between nominal and real exchange rates.

- Describe the effects of currency appreciation or depreciation on imports and exports.

- Describe the effects of changes in inflation rates, disposable income, and interest rates on exchange rates.

- Explain the differences between fixed and flexible exchange rate systems.

- Describe the implications for fiscal and monetary policies of fixed and flexible exchange rate systems.

Y ou probably are aware of international finance if you have traveled abroad. To purchase goods and services in another country, you need to have an amount of that country's currency. True, you can use credit cards for major purchases, but you still need some currency for daily transactions. In Britain, you need to pay in British pounds; in France, you need euros. British and French shopkeepers and public transportation officials will not accept U.S. dollars. This means that at the beginning of your trip, whether at the airport or at a bank, you have to exchange your dollars for the currency of the country you are visiting.

This process of exchanging money applies to international trade as well. You may pay dollars for your Burberry scarf or Louis Vuitton handbag in a store in the United States, but eventually your dollars have to be converted to pounds or euros when your payments make their way back to Britain or France, respectively. And if U.S. companies export goods abroad, they will want to bring dollars back to the United States, whether the goods are paid for originally in dollars or not.

Furthermore, in today's open economies, individuals can hold domestic and foreign financial assets. Your own financial portfolio might include foreign stocks, bonds, and currency, as well as domestic stocks and bonds. Buying and selling foreign securities and goods involves the buying and selling of foreign currency, also known as foreign exchange.

We can see that foreign exchange transactions for tourism, trade, and investment would seem to be large in number and amount. In fact, foreign exchange transactions dwarf the volume of exports and imports, often by as much as 30 to 40 times, in the same way that the annual value of all stock transactions far surpasses the market value of all companies on the New York Stock Exchange. Most foreign exchange transactions are conducted not for trade but for financial or speculative purposes. The social benefit to emerge from this speculation is a highly liquid foreign exchange market that ensures the possibility of trade. The large volume of speculative trade in currencies means that there will always be a market for international trade.

In this chapter, we want to look at foreign exchange markets to get a sense of how policymaking in the United States is affected by an open worldwide economy. We start with balance of payments accounts, which are to open economy macroeconomics what national income accounts are to an individual country's macroeconomic accounts. This accounting structure is the basis for open economy analysis. We then examine the foreign exchange market in detail, looking at both the trade and financial aspects of those common foreign currency events: currency appreciation and depreciation. Finally, we put this all together when we view fixed and flexible exchange rate systems and discuss how an open economy affects monetary and fiscal policymaking.

The Balance of Payments

All open economies have balance of payments accounts. Open financial markets permit economies to run trade surpluses and deficits.

A simplified version of the U.S. balance of payments accounts for 2012 is shown in Table 1 on page 712. These accounts were compiled by the Bureau of Economic Analysis of the U.S. Department of Commerce. The balance of payments represents all payments received from foreign countries and all payments made to them. Notice that the accounts are split into two broad divisions, the current account and the capital account.

The Current Account

The **current account** includes payments for imports and exports of goods and services, incomes flowing into and out of the country, and net transfers of money.

Imports and Exports   In 2012, U.S. exports of goods and services totaled $2,213.7 billion, with imports totaling $2,729.5 billion. This exchange produced a trade deficit of $515.8 billion because we imported more than we exported. Some balance of payments

current account Includes payments for imports and exports of goods and services, incomes flowing into and out of the country, and net transfers of money.

BY THE NUMBERS

The Foreign Exchange Market

The foreign exchange market is the world's largest trading exchange, far surpassing the total value of all bond and stock transactions throughout the world. Currencies are traded 24 hours a day from Sunday 5 P.M. EST to Friday 5 P.M. EST in major foreign exchanges in London, Tokyo, New York, and Sydney.

The most traded currencies in the world are shown. Because each transaction involves two currencies, the percentages add up to 200%. The U.S. dollar is involved in 84.9% of all foreign exchange transactions.

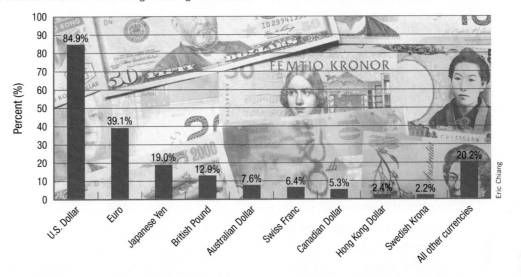

Eric Chiang

$3.98 trillion

Total value of currency traded *each day* in foreign exchange markets.

90%

Percent of foreign exchange trades that are speculative (investors attempting to earn profits).

Approximately twenty nations peg their currencies (maintain a fixed exchange rate) to the U.S. dollar. Three nations (as of 2013)—Panama, Ecuador, and El Salvador—have gone even further, adopting the U.S. dollar as their official currency.

Mark Wilson/Getty Images

Foreign exchange swaps, or contracts to buy and sell a fixed amount of foreign currency on two different dates, are the most common type of foreign exchange transaction, followed by spot transactions, which are foreign currency trades at the current exchange rate. Together, these transactions comprise nearly 82% of all foreign exchange transactions. The remaining 18% includes other foreign exchange trades such as options and futures.

Selected Currencies Pegged to the U.S. Dollar

Country/Region	Exchange Rate per $ (October 1, 2013)
Bahamas	1 Bahamian dollar
Djibouti	179 francs
East Caribbean	2.7 East Caribbean dollars
Hong Kong	7.8 Hong Kong dollars
Jordan	0.71 dinar
Lebanon	1,500 pounds
Qatar	3.64 riyal
Saudi Arabia	3.75 riyal
United Arab Emirates	3.67 dirham
Venezuela	6.3 bolivar

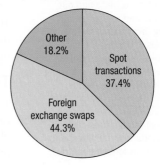

TABLE 1	The Balance of Payments 2012 (billions of U.S. dollars)	
Current Account		
Exports	2,213.7	
Imports	2,729.5	
Balance of trade (exports – imports)		–515.8
Income received (inflow)	742.1	
Income payments (outflow)	543.5	
Balance on income (inflow – outflow)		198.6
Net transfers		–134.1
Current account balance		–451.3
Capital Account		
Change in foreign-owned assets in the United States	388.3	
Change in U.S.-owned assets abroad	–17.9	
Net increase in foreign-owned holdings		406.2
Statistical discrepancy		45.1
Capital account		451.3

accounts break exports and imports into separate categories of goods and services; here they are combined. This component of the current account is known as the balance of trade.

Income Another source of foreign payments to the United States comprises income flows, which include wages, rents, interest, and profits that Americans earn abroad ($742.1 billion in 2012) minus the corresponding income foreigners earn in the United States ($543.5 billion). On balance, foreigners earned $198.6 billion less in the United States than U.S. citizens and corporations earned abroad in 2012.

Transfers Direct transfers of money also take place between the United States and other countries. These transfers include foreign aid, funds sent to such international organizations as the United Nations, and stipends paid directly to foreign students studying in the United States or U.S. students studying abroad. These transfers also include the money that people working in the United States send back to their families in foreign countries. Net transfers for 2012 totaled –$134.1 billion.

Adding all current account categories for 2012 yields a current account deficit of $451.3 billion. In 2012, the United States paid out $451.3 billion more than it received. Therefore, the United States had to borrow $451.3 billion from the rest of the world, or the net holdings of U.S. assets by foreigners must have increased by that same amount, or some combination of the two.

The Capital Account

The **capital account** summarizes the flow of money into and out of domestic and foreign assets. This account includes investments by foreign companies in domestic plants or subsidiaries—a Toyota truck plant in Tennessee, for example. Note that the profits from such investments flow abroad, and thus they are in the income payments

capital account Summarizes the flow of money into and out of domestic and foreign assets, including investments by foreign companies in domestic plants or subsidiaries, and other foreign holdings of U.S. assets, including mutual funds, stocks, bonds, and deposits in U.S. banks. Also included are U.S. investors' holdings of foreign financial assets, production facilities, and other assets in foreign countries.

(outflow) category of the current account. Other foreign holdings of U.S. assets include portfolio investments such as mutual funds, stocks, bonds, and deposits in U.S. banks. American investors hold foreign financial assets in their portfolios, including foreign stocks and bonds. And American companies own plants and other assets in foreign countries.

Because the United States ran a current account deficit in 2012, it must run a capital account surplus. Net capital inflows into the United States must equal $451.3 billion to offset the current account deficit. Indeed, foreign-owned assets in the United States rose by $388.3 billion, while U.S. ownership of foreign assets actually fell by $17.9 billion (meaning that foreign investors bought back assets previously acquired by U.S. investors abroad), resulting in a net inflow of capital of $406.2 billion. Because many accounts are subjected to estimation errors, a statistical discrepancy value of $45.1 billion is added to the net inflow of capital to bring the total capital account surplus to $451.3 billion.

The key point to remember is that balance of payments accounts have to show a balance: A deficit in the current account must be offset by a corresponding surplus in the capital account, and vice versa. Keep this point in mind as we go on to look at foreign exchange and policy implications of an open economy.

The iconic Plaza Hotel in New York City, which has appeared in several dozen movies, was purchased by foreign investors in 2004. The inflow of funds to the United States used to purchase the hotel appeared in the U.S. capital account that year.

⬤ CHECKPOINT

THE BALANCE OF PAYMENTS

- The balance of payments represents all payments received from foreign countries and all payments made to them.
- The balance of payments is split into two categories: current and capital accounts.
- The current account includes payment for exports and imports, income flows, and net transfers of money.
- The capital account summarizes flows of money into and out of domestic and foreign assets.
- The sum of the current and capital account balances must equal zero.

QUESTION: China and Russia both have a high savings rate as a percent of GDP. The lack of consumption relative to domestic investment leads to substantial net exports. Would this situation lead to a current account surplus or a current account deficit? Why?

Answers to the Checkpoint question can be found at the end of this chapter.

⮕ Exchange Rates

As we saw in the chapter opening, if you wish to go abroad or to buy a product directly from a foreign firm, you need to exchange dollars for foreign currency. Today, credit cards automatically convert currencies for you, making the transaction more convenient. This conversion does not, however, alter the transaction's underlying structure.

When you decide to travel abroad, the value of the dollar compared to the currency where you are going determines how expensive your trip will be. Figure 1 on the next page shows the trade-weighted exchange index value of the dollar compared to a wide range of currencies. The value of the dollar has generally been slowly rising until the early part of this century. This section looks at the issues of exchange rates and their determination.

Defining Exchange Rates

The **exchange rate** is defined as the rate at which one currency, such as U.S. dollars, can be exchanged for another, such as British pounds. The exchange rate is nothing more than the price of one currency for another. Table 2 on the next page shows exchange rates for

exchange rate The rate at which one currency can be exchanged for another, or just the price of one currency for another.

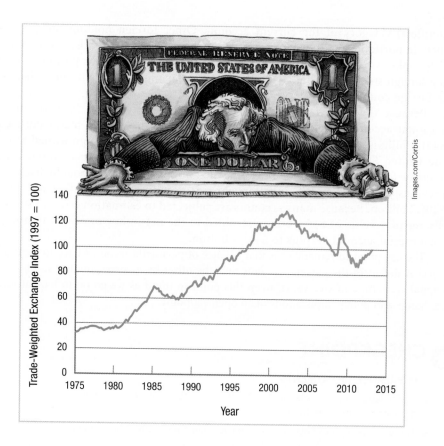

Images.com/Corbis

FIGURE 1

The Value of the Dollar

The trade-weighted exchange index, a weighted average of the foreign exchange value of the dollar against a broad group of U.S. trading partners, is shown. Generally, the value of the dollar rose between 1975 and the early 2000s. After that, rising deficits and low interest rates put downward pressure on the dollar, although it has risen again in recent years.

selected countries for a specific date (October 1, 2013), as found on the Web site xe.com. Exchange rates can be quoted in one of two ways: (1) the price (in domestic currency) of one unit of foreign currency, or (2) the number of units of a foreign currency required to purchase one unit of domestic currency. As Table 2 illustrates, exchange rates are often listed from both perspectives.

TABLE 2	Exchange Rates (October 1, 2013)	
	Exchange Rates	
	U.S. Dollars	**Currency per U.S. Dollar**
Australia (dollar)	0.931	1.074
Brazil (real)	0.443	2.255
Britain (pound)	1.605	0.623
Canada (dollar)	0.970	1.031
China (yuan)	0.163	6.123
India (rupee)	0.016	62.648
Japan (yen)	0.010	97.809
Mexico (peso)	0.076	13.206
Russia (ruble)	0.031	32.369
Switzerland (franc)	1.105	0.905

Source: xe.com

Nominal Exchange Rates According to Table 2, 1 British pound will buy 1.60 dollars. Equivalently, 1 dollar will purchase 0.62 pound. These numbers are reciprocal measures of each other ($1 \div 1.60 = 0.62$).

Real Exchange Rates A **nominal exchange rate** is the price of one country's currency for another. The **real exchange rate** takes the price levels of both countries into account. Real exchange rates become important when inflation is an issue in one country. The real exchange rate between two countries is defined as

$$e_r = e_n \times (P_d/P_f),$$

where e_r is the real exchange rate, e_n is the nominal exchange rate, P_d is the domestic price level, and P_f is the foreign price level.

The real exchange rate is the nominal exchange rate multiplied by the ratio of the price levels of the two countries. In plain words, the real exchange rate tells us how many units of the foreign good can be obtained for the price of one unit of that good domestically. The higher this number, the cheaper the good abroad becomes. If the real exchange rate is greater than 1, prices abroad are lower than at home. In a broad sense, the real exchange rate may be viewed as a measure of the price competitiveness between the two countries. When prices rise in one country, its products are not as competitive in world markets.

Let us take British and American cars as an example. Assume that Britain suffers significant inflation, which pushes the price of Land Rovers up by 15% in Britain. The United States, meanwhile, suffers no such inflation of its price level. If the dollar-to-pound exchange rate remains constant for the moment, the price of Land Rovers in the U.S. market will climb, while domestic auto prices remain constant.

Now Land Rovers are not as competitive as before, resulting in fewer sales. Note, however, that the resulting reduction in U.S. purchases of British cars and other items will reduce the demand for British pounds. This puts downward pressure on the pound, reducing its exchange value and restoring some competitiveness. Markets do adjust! We will look at this issue in more detail later in the chapter.

Purchasing Power Parity **Purchasing power parity** (PPP) is the rate of exchange that allows a specific amount of currency in one country to purchase the same quantity of goods in another country. Absolute PPP would mean that nominal exchange rates equaled the same purchasing power in each country. As a result, the real exchange rate would be equal to 1. For example, PPP would exist if $4 bought a meal in the United States, and the same $4 converted to British pounds (about £2.5) bought the same meal in London.

If you have traveled abroad, you know that PPP is not absolute. Some countries, such as India and Thailand, are known as inexpensive countries, while others, such as Norway and Switzerland, can be expensive. *The Economist* annually publishes a "Big Mac Index," a lighthearted attempt to capture the notion of PPP.

nominal exchange rate The rate at which one currency can be exchanged for another.

real exchange rate The price of one country's currency for another when the price levels of both countries are taken into account; important when inflation is an issue in one country; it is equal to the nominal exchange rate multiplied by the ratio of the price levels of the two countries.

purchasing power parity The rate of exchange that allows a specific amount of currency in one country to purchase the same quantity of goods in another country.

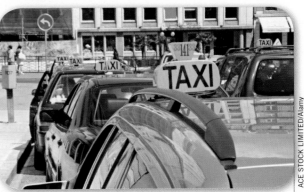

An hour-long massage in Bangkok, Thailand, can cost as little as $8, while a quick ten-minute cab ride in Geneva, Switzerland, can run $30. Exchange rates often do not result in purchasing power parity between nations.

TABLE 3	Measures of Purchasing Power Parity				

	Big Mac Prices				
	In Local Currency	In Dollars	Implied PPP of the Dollar	Actual Dollar Exchange Rate (October 2013)	Under (–)/Over (+) against the Dollar (%)
United States	US$ 4.37	4.37	1.00	—	—
Argentina	Peso 19.0	3.82	4.35	5.79	–25
Britain	Pound 2.69	4.25	0.62	0.62	0
Canada	CAD$ 5.41	5.39	1.24	1.03	+20
China	Yuan 16.0	2.57	3.66	6.12	–40
India	Rupee 89.0	1.67	20.38	62.65	–67
Japan	Yen 320.0	3.51	73.27	97.81	–25
Mexico	Peso 37.0	2.90	8.47	13.21	–36
Norway	Krona 43.0	7.84	9.85	5.99	+64
Switzerland	CHF 6.5	7.12	1.49	0.91	+63
Taiwan	NT$ 75.0	2.54	17.17	29.57	–42
Thailand	Bhat 87.0	2.92	19.92	31.38	–37
Venezuela	Bolivar 39.0	9.08	8.93	6.29	+42

Prices of fast food in different nations often do not result in purchasing power parity.

Source: "The Big Mac Index," © The Economist Newspaper Limited, London (July 28, 2011 and July 13, 2013).

Table 3 presents some recent estimates of PPP and the Big Mac Index. It also shows the PPP implied by the relative cost of Big Macs, along with the actual exchange rate. When comparing these two, we get an approximate over- or understating of the exchange rate. Keep in mind that the cost of a McDonald's Big Mac may be influenced by many unique local factors (trade barriers on beef, customs duties, taxes, competition), and therefore it may not reflect real PPP. Also, in some countries where beef is not consumed, chicken patties are substituted; and in still other countries, vegetarian patties are used.

Although not perfect, changes in the Big Mac Index often are reflective of movements in true PPP, given that simultaneous changes in several of the factors that distort the index often reflect real changes in the economy.

Exchange Rate Determination

We have seen that people and institutions have two primary reasons for wanting foreign currency. The first is to purchase goods and services and conduct other transactions under the current account. The second is to purchase foreign investments under the capital account. These transactions create a demand for foreign currency and give rise to a supply of domestic currency available for foreign exchange.

A Market for Foreign Exchange Figure 2 shows a representative market for foreign exchange. The horizontal axis measures the quantity of dollars available for foreign exchange, and the vertical axis measures the exchange rate in British pounds per U.S. dollar. The demand for dollars as foreign exchange is downward sloping; as the exchange rate falls, U.S. products become more attractive, and more dollars are desired.

Suppose, for example, that the exchange rate at first is $1 = £1 and that the U.S. game company Electronic Arts manufactures and sells its games at home and in Britain for $50 (£50). Then suppose that the dollar *depreciates* by 50%, such that $1.00 = £0.50. If

FIGURE 2

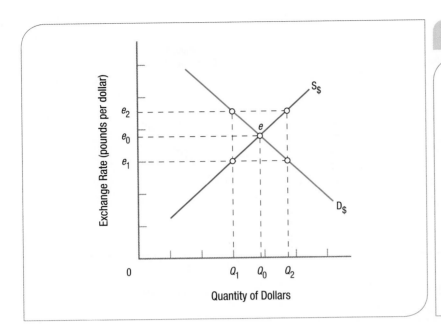

The Foreign Exchange Market for Dollars

A market for foreign exchange is shown here. The horizontal axis measures the quantity of dollars available for foreign exchange, and the vertical axis measures the exchange rate in pounds per dollar. If exchange rates are fully flexible and the exchange rate is initially e_1, there is excess demand for dollars: Q_2 minus Q_1. The dollar will appreciate and the exchange rate will move to e_0. Alternatively, if the exchange rate is initially e_2, there is an excess supply of dollars. Because there are more dollars being offered than demanded, the dollar will depreciate. Eventually, the market will settle into an exchange rate of e_0, where precisely the quantity of dollars supplied is the quantity demanded.

the dollar price of a game remains at $50 in the United States, the pound price of games in Britain will fall to £25 because of the reduction in the exchange rate. This reduction will increase the sales of games in Britain and increase the quantity of dollars British consumers need for foreign exchange.

The supply of dollars available for foreign exchange reflects the demand for pounds, because to purchase pounds, U.S. firms or individuals must supply dollars. Not surprisingly, the supply curve for dollars is positively sloped. If the dollar were to *appreciate*, say, moving to $1 = £2, British goods bought in the United States would look attractive because their dollar price would be cut in half. As Americans purchased more British goods, the demand for pounds would grow, and the quantity of dollars supplied to the foreign exchange market would increase.

Flexible Exchange Rates Assume that exchange rates are fully flexible, such that the market determines the prevailing exchange rate, and that the exchange rate in Figure 2 is initially e_1. At this exchange rate, there is an excess demand for dollars because quantity Q_2 is demanded but only Q_1 is supplied. The dollar will **appreciate,** or rise in value relative to other currencies, and the exchange rate will move in the direction of e_0 (more pounds are required to purchase a dollar). As the dollar appreciates, it becomes more expensive for British consumers, thus reducing the demand for U.S. exports. Because of the appreciating dollar, British imports are more attractive for U.S. consumers, increasing U.S. imports. These forces work to move the exchange rate to e_0, closing the gap between Q_2 and Q_1.

Alternatively, if the exchange rate begins at e_2, there will be an excess supply of dollars. Because more dollars are being offered than demanded, the value of dollars relative to British pounds will decline, or **depreciate.** American goods are now more attractive in Britain, increasing American exports and the demand for dollars, while British goods become more expensive for American consumers. Eventually, the market will settle into an exchange rate of e_0, at which precisely the quantity of dollars supplied is the quantity demanded.

Currency Appreciation and Depreciation A currency appreciates when its value rises relative to other currencies and depreciates when its value falls. This concept is clear enough in theory, but it can get confusing when we start looking at charts or tables that show exchange rates. The key is to be certain of which currency is being used to measure the value of other currencies. Does the table you are looking at show the pound price of the dollar or the dollar price of the pound?

Figure 3 on the next page shows the exchange markets for dollars and pounds. Panel A shows the market for dollars, where the price of dollars is denominated in pounds (£/$),

appreciation (currency) When the value of a currency rises relative to other currencies.

depreciation (currency) When the value of a currency falls relative to other currencies.

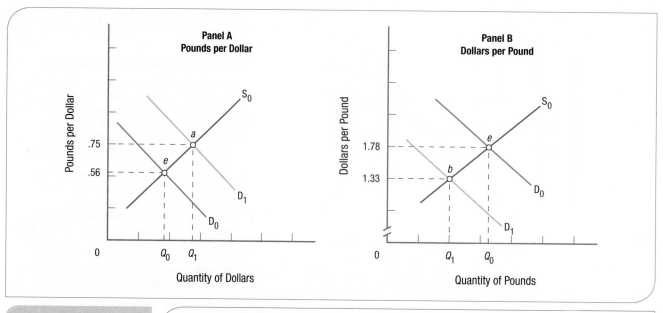

FIGURE 3

The Foreign Exchange Market

Data for dollars and pounds are graphically represented here. Panel A shows a market for dollars in which the price of dollars is denominated in pounds (£/$). In panel A, the market is in equilibrium at £0.56 per dollar (point *e*). Panel B shows the equivalent market for pounds in equilibrium at $1.78 per pound (again at point *e*). A rise in the demand for dollars means that the dollar appreciates to £0.75 per dollar (point *a* in panel A). Panel B shows that the corresponding decline in demand for pounds (from D_0 to D_1) leads to a depreciation of the pound as the exchange rate falls from $1.78 to $1.33 per pound (point *b*).

Note that a depreciating pound in panel B indicates a decline in the exchange rate, but this simultaneously represents an appreciating dollar. Thus, graphs can be viewed as reflecting either appreciation or depreciation, depending on which currency is being used to establish the point of view.

just as in Figure 2. This market is in equilibrium at £0.56 per dollar (point *e*). Panel B shows the equivalent market for pounds; it is in equilibrium at $1.78 per pound (again at point *e*). Note that $1 \div 0.56 = 1.78$, therefore panels A and B represent the same information, just from different viewpoints.

Assume that there is a rise in the demand for dollars. In panel A, the dollar appreciates to £0.75 per dollar (point *a*), thus leading to a rise in the exchange rate. In panel B, the corresponding decline in demand for pounds (from D_0 to D_1) leads to a depreciation of the pound and a fall in the exchange rate from $1.78 to $1.33 per pound (point *b*). Notice that the pound's depreciation in panel B produces a decline in the exchange rate, but this decline simultaneously results in appreciation of the dollar. These graphs could be viewed as showing either an appreciation or a depreciation, depending on which currency represents your point of view.

For our purposes, we will try to use figures that show the exchange rate rising when the focus currency appreciates. Still, you need to be aware that exchange rates can be represented in two different ways. Exchange rate graphs are difficult and sometimes confusing, therefore you will need to think through each graph you encounter.

Determinants of Exchange Rates What sort of conditions will cause currencies to appreciate or depreciate? First, a change in our tastes and preferences as consumers for foreign goods will result in currency appreciation or depreciation. For example, if we desire to purchase more foreign goods, this will lead to an increase in the demand for foreign currency and result in the depreciation of the dollar.

Second, if our income growth exceeds that of other countries, our demand for imports will grow faster relative to the growth of other nations. This will lead again to an increase in demand for foreign currency, resulting in the depreciation of the dollar.

Third, rising inflation in the United States relative to foreign nations makes our goods and services relatively more expensive overseas and foreign goods more attractive here at home. This results in growing imports, reduced exports, and again leads to a depreciation of the dollar.

Fourth, falling interest rates in the United States relative to foreign countries makes financial investment in the United States less attractive. This reduces the demand for dollars, leading once again to a depreciation of the dollar.

Note that if we reverse these stories in each case, the dollar will appreciate.

Exchange Rates and the Current Account

As we have already seen, the current account includes payments for imports and exports. Also included are changes in income flowing into and out of the country. In this section, we focus on the effect that changes in real exchange rates have on both of these components of the current account. We will assume that import and export demands are highly elastic as prices change due to changes in the exchange rate.

Changes in Inflation Rates Let's assume that inflation heats up in Britain, such that the British price level rises relative to U.S. prices, or the dollar appreciates relative to the pound. Production costs rise in Britain, therefore British goods are more expensive. American goods appear more attractive to British consumers, therefore exports of American goods rise, improving the U.S. current account. American consumers purchase more domestic goods and fewer British imports because of rising British prices, further improving the American current account. The opposite is true for Britain: British imports rise and exports fall, hurting the British current account.

These results are dependent on our assumption that import and export demands are highly elastic with real exchange rates. Thus, when exchange rates change, exports and imports will change proportionally more than the change in exchange rates.

Changes in Domestic Disposable Income If domestic disposable income rises, U.S. consumers will have more money to spend, and given existing exchange rates, imports will rise because some of this increased consumption will go to foreign products. As a result, the current account will worsen as imports rise. The opposite occurs when domestic income falls.

Exchange Rates and the Capital Account

The capital account summarizes flows of money or capital into and out of U.S. assets. Each day, foreign individuals, companies, and governments put billions of dollars into Treasury bonds, U.S. stocks, companies, and real estate. Today, foreign and domestic assets are available to investors. Foreign investment possibilities include direct investment in projects undertaken by multinational firms, the sale and purchase of foreign stocks and bonds, and the short-term movement of assets in foreign bank accounts.

Because these transactions all involve capital, investors must balance their risks and returns. Two factors essentially incorporate both risk and return for international assets: interest rates and expected changes in exchange rates.

Interest Rate Changes If the exchange rate is assumed to be constant, and the assets of two countries are *perfectly substitutable*, then an interest rate rise in one country will cause capital to flow into it from the other country. For example, a rise in interest rates in the United States will cause capital to flow from Britain, where interest rates have not changed, into the United States, where investors can earn a higher rate of return on their investments. Because the assets of both countries are assumed to be perfectly substitutable, this flow will continue until the interest rates (r) in Britain and the United States are equal, or

$$r_{US} = r_{UK}$$

Everything else being equal, we can expect capital to flow in the direction of the country that offers the highest interest rate, and thus, the highest return on capital. But "everything else" is rarely equal.

Expected Exchange Rate Changes Suppose that the exchange rate for U.S. currency is *expected to appreciate* ($\Delta\varepsilon > 0$). The relationship between the interest rates in the United States and Britain becomes

$$r_{US} = r_{UK} - \Delta\varepsilon$$

Investors demand a higher return in Britain to offset the expected depreciation of the British pound relative to the U.S. dollar. Unless interest rates rise in Britain, capital will flow out of Britain and into the United States until U.S. interest rates fall enough to offset the expected appreciation of the dollar.

If capital is not perfectly mobile and substitutable between two countries, a *risk premium* can be added to the relationship just described; thus,

$$r_{US} = r_{UK} - \Delta\varepsilon + x$$

where x is the risk premium. Expected exchange rate changes and risk premium changes can produce enduring interest rate differentials between two countries.

If the dollar falls relative to the yen, the euro, and the British pound, this is a sign that foreign investors were not as enthusiastic about U.S. investments. Low interest rates and high deficits may have convinced foreign investors that it was not a good time to invest in the United States. The United States is more dependent on foreign capital than ever before. Today, about half of U.S. Treasury debt held by the public is held by foreigners. Changes in inflation, interest rates, and expectations about exchange rates are important.

Exchange Rates and Aggregate Supply and Demand

How do changes in nominal exchange rates affect aggregate demand and aggregate supply? A change in nominal exchange rates will affect imports and exports. Consider what happens, for example, when the exchange rate for the dollar depreciates. The dollar is weaker, and thus the pound (or any other currency) will buy more dollars. American products become more attractive in foreign markets, therefore American exports increase and aggregate demand expands. Yet, because some inputs into the production process may be imported (raw materials, computer programming services, or call answering services), input costs will rise, causing aggregate supply to contract.

Let us take a more detailed look at this process by considering Figure 4. Assume that the economy begins in equilibrium at point *e*, with full employment output Q_f and the

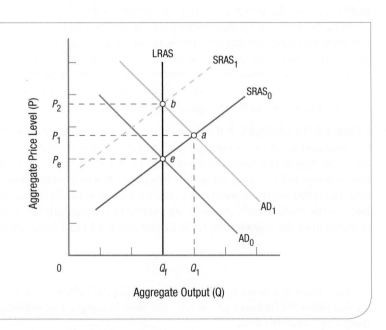

FIGURE 4

Exchange Rates and Aggregate Demand and Supply

Assume that the economy initially begins in equilibrium at point *e*, with full employment output Q_f and the price level at P_e. Assume that the dollar depreciates. This will increase exports, shifting aggregate demand from AD_0 to AD_1 and raising prices to P_1 and output to Q_1 in the short run. In the long run, short-run aggregate supply will shift from $SRAS_0$ to $SRAS_1$, as workers readjust their wage demands in the long run, thus moving the economy to point *b*. As the economy adjusts to a higher price level, the benefits from currency depreciation are greatly reduced.

price level at P_e. As the dollar depreciates, this will spur an increase in exports, thus shifting aggregate demand from AD_0 to AD_1 and raising prices to P_1 in the short run. Initially, output climbs to Q_1, but because some of the economy's inputs are imported, short-run aggregate supply will decline, mitigating this rise in output. In the short run, the economy will expand beyond Q_f, and prices will rise.

In the longer term, as domestic prices rise, workers will realize that their real wages do not purchase as much as they did before, because import prices are higher. As a result, workers will start demanding higher wages just to bring them back to where they were originally. This shifts short-run aggregate supply from $SRAS_0$ to $SRAS_1$, thereby moving the economy from point *a* in the short run to point *b* in the long run. As the economy adjusts to a higher price level, the original benefits accruing from currency depreciation will be greatly reduced.

Currency depreciation works because imports become more expensive and exports less so. When this happens, consumer income no longer goes as far, because the price of domestic goods does not change, but the cost of imports rises. In countries where imports form a substantial part of household spending, major depreciations in the national currency can produce significant declines in standards of living. Such depreciations (or devaluations) have occasioned strikes and, in some cases, even street riots; examples in recent decades include such actions in Argentina, Brazil, Mexico, and Indonesia.

What are the implications of all this for policymakers? First, a currency depreciation or devaluation can, after a period, lead to inflation. In most cases, however, the

ISSUE

Would a Stronger Chinese Yuan Be Good for Americans?

Much discussion in recent years has focused on the accusation that the Chinese government manipulated the value of its currency, the yuan. What exactly did China do?

When Americans purchase goods from China (and we purchase a whole lot of goods), normally dollars must be exchanged for yuan to pay for these goods. Factories in China need to pay their workers in yuan so that their workers can pay their rent and buy groceries. When dollars are exchanged for yuan, demand for yuan increases, which raises its value. Therefore, the yuan should appreciate against the dollar.

When the yuan appreciates, it takes more dollars to obtain the same amount of yuan as before. Therefore, goods made in China, from toys you buy for your nephews and nieces to shoes, clothes, and electronics you buy for yourself, become more expensive.

To prevent the prices of China's exports from rising too much in the United States, the Chinese government bought up many of these dollars flowing into China, preventing them from being sold on the foreign exchange market. By holding U.S. dollars, the dollar value is kept from falling. In 2013, China held over 1 trillion in U.S. dollars.

Who benefited from this policy and who lost out? The actions by the Chinese government to prevent the yuan from appreciating keeps prices of Chinese-made goods low for ordinary American consumers, especially benefiting those with limited budgets. Thanks, China, for helping the U.S. consumer.

Who lost out? China's policy made it harder for American (and other non-Chinese) companies to compete against Chinese imports.

If the winners from this policy are American consumers and the losers are American businesses and their workers, policymakers are faced with quite a dilemma. Pressuring the Chinese to let its currency appreciate might be good for American companies, though it will lead to higher prices for many

Are you ready to pay more for everyday purchases? If the Chinese yuan appreciates, you may.

goods that we buy. Are we ready to see the cost of this policy come out of our pockets? Many Americans would be reluctant to support such an outcome, because it would have a similar effect as an increase in taxes or inflation. Both reduce the purchasing power of our income and savings.

Indeed, you can see that the debate about currency manipulation goes beyond whether one side is playing by the rules. Sometimes, fairness can be a costly proposition.

causation probably goes the other way: Macroeconomic policies or economic events force currency depreciations.

Trade balances usually improve with an exchange rate depreciation. Policymakers can get improved current account balances without inflation by pursuing devaluation first, then pursuing fiscal contraction (reducing government spending or increasing taxes), and finally moving the economy back to point *e* in Figure 4. But here again, the real long-run benefit is more stable monetary and fiscal policies.

CHECKPOINT

EXCHANGE RATES

- Nominal exchange rates define the rate at which one currency can be exchanged for another.
- Real exchange rates are the nominal exchange rates multiplied by the ratio of the price levels of the two countries.
- Purchasing power parity (PPP) is a rate of exchange that permits a given level of currency to purchase the same amount of goods and services in another country.
- A currency appreciates when its value rises relative to other currencies. Currency depreciation causes a currency to lose value relative to others.
- Inflation causes depreciation of a country's currency, worsening its current account. Rising domestic income typically results in rising imports and a deteriorating current account.
- Rising interest rates cause capital to flow into the country with the higher interest rate, and expectations about a future currency appreciation or depreciation affect the capital account.
- Currency appreciation and depreciation have an effect on aggregate supply and demand. For example, currency depreciation expands aggregate demand as exports increase, but some (now higher-priced) imported inputs are inputs into production, reducing aggregate supply.

QUESTION: Cities along the U.S.–Canadian border, such as Vancouver, Niagara Falls, Detroit, and Buffalo, receive a substantial number of day visitors. For example, Americans might cross the border into Niagara Falls for a day of sightseeing, while Canadians might cross the border into Detroit to shop. Suppose that the value of the Canadian dollar appreciates against the U.S. dollar. How does this change affect tourism, businesses that depend on day-trippers, and the current account of the United States and Canada?

Answers to the Checkpoint question can be found at the end of this chapter.

→ Monetary and Fiscal Policy in an Open Economy

How monetary and fiscal policy is affected by international trade and finance depends on the type of exchange rate system in existence. There are several ways that exchange rate systems can be organized. We will discuss the two major categories: fixed and flexible rates.

Fixed and Flexible Exchange Rate Systems

A **fixed exchange rate** system is one in which governments determine their exchange rates, then adjust macroeconomic policies to maintain these rates. A **flexible** or **floating exchange rate** system, in contrast, relies on currency markets to determine the exchange rates consistent with macroeconomic conditions.

Before the Great Depression, most of the world economies were on the gold standard. According to Peter Temin, the gold standard was characterized by "(1) the free flow of gold between individuals and countries, (2) the maintenance of fixed values of

fixed exchange rate Each government determines its exchange rate, then uses macroeconomic policy to maintain the rate.

flexible or floating exchange rate A country's currency exchange rate is determined in international currency exchange markets, given the country's macroeconomic policies.

national currencies in terms of gold and therefore each other, and (3) the absence of an international coordinating organization."[1]

Under the gold standard, each country had to maintain enough gold stocks to keep the value of its currency fixed to that of others. If a country's imports exceeded its exports, this balance of payments deficit had to come from its gold stocks. Because gold backed the national currency, the country would have to reduce the amount of money circulating in its economy, thereby reducing expenditures, output, and income. This reduction would lead to a decline in prices and wages, a rise in exports (which were getting cheaper), and a corresponding drop in imports (which were becoming more expensive). This process would continue until imports and exports were again equalized and the flow of gold ended.

In the early 1930s, the U.S. Federal Reserve pursued a contractionary monetary policy intended to cool off the overheated economy of the 1920s. This policy reduced imports and increased the flow of gold into the United States. With France pursuing a similar deflationary policy, by 1932 these two countries held more than 70% of the world's monetary gold. Other countries attempted to conserve their gold stocks by selling off assets, thereby spurring a worldwide monetary contraction. As other monetary authorities attempted to conserve their gold reserves, moreover, they reduced the liquidity available to their banks, thereby inadvertently causing bank failures. In this way, the Depression in the United States spread worldwide.

As World War II came to an end, the Allies met in Bretton Woods, New Hampshire, to design a new and less troublesome international monetary system. Exchange rates were set, and each country agreed to use its monetary authorities to buy and sell its own currency to maintain its exchange rate at fixed levels.

The Bretton Woods agreements created the International Monetary Fund to aid countries having trouble maintaining their exchange rates. In addition, the World Bank was established to loan money to countries for economic development. In the end, most countries were unwilling to make the tough adjustments required by a fixed rate system, and it collapsed in the early 1970s. Today, we operate on a flexible exchange rate system in which each currency floats in the market.

Pegging Exchange Rates Under a Flexible Exchange Rate System

Although most currencies fluctuate in value based on their relative demand and supply on the foreign exchange market, a number of countries use macroeconomic policies to peg their currency (maintain a fixed exchange rate) to another currency, most commonly the U.S. dollar or the euro.

A common reason for a country to peg its currency to another is to maintain a close trade relationship, because fixed exchange rates prevent fluctuations in prices due to changes in the exchange rate. For example, most OPEC nations peg their currencies to the U.S. dollar as a result of their dependency on oil exports, a significant portion of which goes to the United States. Many Caribbean nations that depend on tourism and trade with the United States also peg their currencies to the U.S. dollar.

Some countries do not maintain a strict fixed exchange rate with the U.S. dollar, but will intervene to control the exchange rate. For example, China has intervened in foreign exchange markets for strategic purposes, propping up the value of the U.S. dollar by holding dollars instead of exchanging them on the foreign exchange market. By keeping the U.S. dollar strong, the price of Chinese exports is kept low for American consumers, allowing China to continue expanding their export volume.

Another reason for maintaining a fixed exchange rate is to improve monetary stability and to attract foreign investment. For example, several countries in western Africa

---

[1] Peter Temin, *Lessons from the Great Depression: The Lionel Robbins Lectures for 1989* (Cambridge, MA: MIT Press), 1989, p. 8.

When traveling to Panama, it is not necessary to exchange money. Panama's official currency is the U.S. dollar.

peg their unified currency, the CFA franc, to the euro. By maintaining a fixed exchange rate, a country is essentially giving up its ability to conduct independent monetary policy. However, some countries such as Mexico and Argentina, both of which had pegged their currencies to the U.S. dollar in the past, were forced to abandon their efforts due to high inflation, which made their products too expensive in world markets.

Finally, some countries chose to abandon their currency altogether by adopting another country's currency as their own. Panama, Ecuador, and El Salvador all chose to adopt the U.S. dollar as their official currency, a process known as **dollarization.** Not only did they give up their ability to use monetary policy, they also eliminated the risk of being unable to maintain fixed exchange rates with their original currencies.

There clearly are many approaches to foreign exchange used. But how does a fixed versus a flexible exchange rate system affect each country's ability to use fiscal and monetary policy? We answer this question next.

Policies Under Fixed Exchange Rates

dollarization Describes the decision of a country to adopt another country's currency (most often the U.S. dollar) as its own official currency.

When the government engages in expansionary policy, aggregate demand rises, resulting in output and price increases. Figure 5 shows the result of such a policy as an increase in aggregate demand from AD_0 to AD_1, with the economy moving from equilibrium at point a to point b in the short run and the price level rising from P_0 to P_1. A rising domestic price level means that U.S. exports will decline as they become more expensive. As incomes rise, imports will rise. Combined, these forces will worsen the current account, moving it into deficit or reducing a surplus, as net exports decline.

An expansionary monetary policy, combined with a fiscal policy that is neither expansionary nor contractionary, will result in a rising money supply and falling interest rates. This causes aggregate demand to rise to AD_1 as shown in Figure 5. Lower interest rates result in capital flowing from the United States to other countries. This reduces the U.S. money supply.

The greater the capital mobility, the more the money supply is reduced, and the more aggregate demand moves back in the direction of AD_0. With perfect capital mobility, monetary policy would be ineffective. The amount of capital leaving the United States would be just equal to the increase in the money supply to begin with, and interest rates would be returned to their original international equilibrium.

Keeping exchange rates fixed and holding the money supply constant, an expansionary fiscal policy will produce an increase in interest rates. As income rises, there will be

---

FIGURE 5

Monetary and Fiscal Policy in an Open Economy

When the government engages in expansionary policy, aggregate demand rises, resulting in output and price increases. A rising domestic price level reduces exports while rising incomes increases imports, worsening the current account.

An expansionary monetary policy (holding fiscal policy constant), increases the money supply and reduces interest rates. Lower interest rates result in capital outflow, pushing the money supply back down and moving aggregate demand back toward AD_0.

An expansionary fiscal policy (holding monetary policy constant), increases interest rates, leading to capital inflow, pushing aggregate demand further to the right to AD_2.

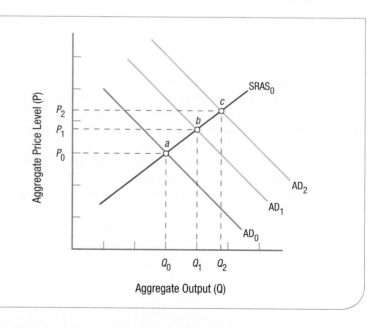

a greater transactions demand for money, resulting in higher interest rates. Higher interest rates mean that capital will flow into the United States.

As more capital flows into U.S. capital markets, interest rates will be reduced, adding to the expansionary impact of the original fiscal policy. Expansionary fiscal policy is reinforced by an open economy with fixed exchange rates as aggregate demand increases to AD_2.

Policies Under Flexible Exchange Rates

Expansionary monetary policy under a system of flexible exchange rates, again holding fiscal policy constant, results in a growing money supply and falling interest rates. Lower interest rates lead to a capital outflow and a balance of payments deficit, or a declining surplus. With flexible exchange rates, consumers and investors will want more foreign currency; thus, the exchange rate will depreciate. As the dollar depreciates, exports increase; U.S. exports are more attractive to foreigners as their currency buys them more. The net result is that the international market works to reinforce an expansionary policy undertaken at home.

Permitting exchange rates to vary and holding the money supply constant, an expansionary fiscal policy produces a rise in interest rates as rising incomes increase the transactions demand for money. Higher interest rates mean that capital will flow into the United States, generating a balance

NOBEL PRIZE ROBERT MUNDELL

Awarded the Nobel Prize in 1999, Robert Mundell is best known for his groundbreaking work in international economics and for his contribution to the development of supply-side economic theory. Born in Canada in 1932, he attended the University of British Columbia as an undergraduate and earned his Ph.D. from the Massachusetts Institute of Technology in 1956. For a year, he served as a postdoctoral fellow at the University of Chicago, where he met the economist Arthur Laffer, his collaborator in the development of supply-side theory.

Supply-side economists advocated reductions in marginal tax rates and stabilization of the international monetary system. This approach was distinct from the two dominant schools of economic thought, Keynesianism and monetarism, although it shared some ideas with both. Mundell's work had a major influence on the economic policies of President Ronald Reagan and Federal Reserve Chairman Paul Volcker, whose tight money policies helped curb inflation.

Mundell's early research focused on exchange rates and the movement of international capital. In a series of papers in the 1960s that proved to be prophetic, he speculated about the impacts of monetary and fiscal policy if exchange rates were allowed to float, emphasizing the importance of central banks acting independently of governments to promote price stability. At the time, his work may have seemed purely academic. Within ten years, however, the Bretton Woods system of fixed exchange rates tied to the dollar broke down, exchange rates became more flexible, capital markets opened up, and Mundell's ideas were borne out.

In another feat of near prophecy, Mundell wrote about the potential benefits and disadvantages of a group of countries adopting a single currency, anticipating the development of the European currency, the euro, by many years. Since 1974, Mundell has taught at Columbia University.

of payments surplus or a smaller deficit, causing the exchange rate to appreciate as foreigners value dollars more. As the dollar becomes more valuable, exports decline, moving aggregate demand back toward AD_0 in Figure 5. With flexible exchange rates, therefore, an open economy can hamper fiscal policy.

These movements are complex and go through several steps. Table 4 summarizes them for you. The key point to note is that under our flexible exchange rate system now, an open

Summary of the Effects of an Open Economy on Monetary and Fiscal Policy in a Fixed and Flexible Exchange Rate System		**TABLE 4**
	Flexible Exchange Rate	**Fixed Exchange Rate**
Monetary policy (fiscal policy constant)	Reinforced	Hampered
Fiscal policy (monetary policy constant)	Hampered	Reinforced

economy reinforces monetary policy and hampers fiscal policy. No wonder the Fed has become more important.

Several decades ago, presidents and Congress could adopt monetary and fiscal policies without much consideration of the rest of the world. Today, economies of the world are vastly more intertwined, and the macroeconomic policies of one country often have serious impacts on others. Today, open economy macroeconomics is more important, and good macroeconomic policymaking must account for changes in exchange rates and capital flows.

During the financial crisis and recession of 2007–2009, the implications of monetary policy on exchange rates became important, as countries throughout the world were eager to use expansionary monetary policy to curtail the severity of the crisis. However, taking

ISSUE

Would Flexible Exchange Rates in OPEC Nations Affect Oil Markets?

For several decades, many OPEC nations have pegged their currencies to the U.S. dollar as a way to facilitate trade of crude oil, their largest export, to the world market and especially the United States, one of their largest customers.

However, in the past decade, several OPEC nations, such as Kuwait, have moved off of the peg, choosing to let their currencies fluctuate and also to trade oil in other currencies including the euro. How would a move to flexible exchange rates affect international trade of goods and services, particularly oil?

The price of a barrel of crude oil is determined on world markets, typically in U.S. dollars. When the value of the dollar changes, the value of OPEC currencies pegged to the dollar remains the same, thereby preventing dramatic changes in oil prices resulting from exchange rate changes in the supplying country.

However, in recent years many countries, such as India and China, have increased their demand for oil. If the U.S. dollar depreciates against the Chinese yuan or Indian rupee, oil becomes cheaper for Indians and Chinese, all else equal. Therefore, a depreciation of the dollar would increase the demand for oil on world markets, pushing up prices that all consumers must pay. In sum, fluctuations in the value of the dollar affect oil prices from the demand side.

What would happen if more OPEC nations removed their currency peg? Initially, oil prices would likely not change too much as long as the value of the U.S. dollar does not deviate much. However, if the U.S. dollar faces a significant depreciation, the price of oil will rise because of its reduced purchasing power. This is what Kuwait wants.

In sum, the existence of fixed and flexible exchange rates carries important implications for the prices of imported and exported goods, which constitute a large percentage of economic activity in nearly all countries. Fixed exchange rates tend to stabilize the prices of

Gas prices in Gibraltar quoted in both British pounds and euros per liter.

traded goods as long as economies face similar levels of economic and monetary growth. Flexible exchange rates allow countries to adjust their policies to correct deficits or surpluses in their current accounts; however, the effect on the prices of traded goods, such as oil, can be more unpredictable.

such action unilaterally can lead to adverse effects in other countries due to its effect on exchange rates, which affect trade and current accounts.

Therefore, in October of 2008, six central banks including the Fed and the European Central Bank took a rare action of coordinated monetary policy, in which the central banks jointly announced a reduction in their target interest rates. As a result, countries engaging in a similar level of expansionary policy would prevent instability in exchange rates. As Fed Chairman Ben Bernanke put it, "the coordinated rate cut was intended to send a strong signal to the public and to markets of our resolve to act together to address global economic challenges."[2] The coordinated efforts of central banks continued over several years, especially when the Eurozone crisis intensified in 2011.

The global economy is connected not only through trade and currency exchanges. Nearly all economic decisions have effects that extend beyond our country's borders, from the types of goods that consumers purchase, to the goods firms produce and where they produce them, to how governments set policies that affect their citizens and those in other countries. As you complete your degree and prepare for your career, keep in mind the statement from Chapter 1 that has been illustrated throughout this book: *Economics is all around us.*

 ## CHECKPOINT

MONETARY AND FISCAL POLICY IN AN OPEN ECONOMY

- A fixed exchange rate is one in which governments determine their exchange rates and then use macroeconomic policy to maintain these rates.

- Flexible exchange rates rely on markets to set the exchange rate given the country's macroeconomic policies.

- Some countries peg their currency to another to facilitate trade, to promote foreign investment, or to maintain monetary stability.

- Fixed exchange rate systems hinder monetary policy, but reinforce fiscal policy.

- Flexible exchange rates hamper fiscal policy, but reinforce monetary policy.

QUESTION: The United States seems to rely more on monetary policy to maintain stable prices, low interest rates, low unemployment, and healthy economic growth. Does the fact that the United States has really embraced global trade (imports and exports combined are over 30% of GDP) and has a flexible (floating) exchange rate help explain why monetary policy seems more important than fiscal policy?

Answers to the Checkpoint question can be found at the end of this chapter.

---

[2] Ben Bernanke, *Policy Coordination Among Central Banks,* Speech at the Fifth European Central Banking Conference, The Euro at Ten: Lessons and Challenges, Frankfurt, Germany, November 14, 2008. [URL]http://www.federalreserve.gov/newsevents/speech/bernanke20081214a.htm

chapter summary

Section 1: **The Balance of Payments**

The **current account** includes payments for imports and exports of goods and services, incomes flowing into and out of the country, and net transfers of money.

The **capital account** includes flows of money into and out of domestic and foreign assets.

The sum of the current account and capital account balances must equal zero.

When foreign tourists visit Miami Beach, the money that is spent adds to the U.S. current account. When a foreign tourist purchases a vacation condo, the purchase of this asset increases the U.S. capital account.

Foreign investment in the United States includes foreign ownership of domestic plants or subsidiaries; investments in mutual funds, stocks, and bonds; and deposits in U.S. banks. Similarly, U.S. investors hold foreign financial assets in their portfolios and own interests in foreign facilities and companies.

Section 2: **Exchange Rates**

The **exchange rate** defines the rate at which one currency can be exchanged for another.

A **nominal exchange rate** is the price of one country's currency for another.

The **real exchange rate** takes price levels into account. The real exchange rate (e_r) is the nominal exchange rate (e_n) multiplied by the ratio of the price levels of the two countries:

$$e_r = e_n \times (P_d / P_f)$$

If exchange rates are fully flexible, markets determine the prevailing exchange rate. If there is an excess demand for dollars, the dollar will appreciate, or rise in value. If there is an excess supply of dollars, the value of dollars will decline, or depreciate.

The **purchasing power parity** of a currency is the rate of exchange at which some currency in one country can purchase the same goods in another country.

Many services, such as playing a video game at a gaming center, are not easily traded. Therefore, price differences will exist based on the country's standard of living, and often will not reflect purchasing power parity with other countries.

It is important to keep in mind which currency is being used to measure the price of others. Graphs can be viewed as showing either an appreciation or a depreciation, depending on which currency is being considered.

In the figure, an increase in demand for U.S. dollars leads to its appreciation from 0.60 pounds per dollar to 0.75 pounds per dollar.

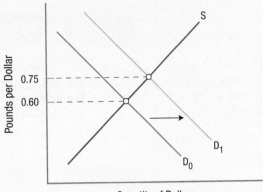

Real exchange rates affect the payments for imports and exports, and also affect the current account. Inflation causes depreciation of a country's currency, worsening its current account.

Interest rates can differ between countries due to expected exchange rate changes ($\Delta \varepsilon$) and a risk premium (x) when capital is not perfectly substitutable between countries.

$$r_{US} = r_{UK} - \Delta \varepsilon + x$$

A shopping trip to the United States by British tourists increases demand for the dollar.

Interest rates and exchange rate expectations affect the capital account. An interest rate rise in one country will cause capital to flow into it from the other country.

Section 3: Monetary and Fiscal Policy in an Open Economy

A **fixed exchange rate system** is one in which governments determine their exchange rates, then use macroeconomic adjustments to maintain these rates.

A **flexible** or **floating exchange rate system** relies on currency markets to determine the exchange rates, given macroeconomic conditions.

Some countries choose to peg their currency to another in order to facilitate trade, attract foreign investment, or promote monetary stability.

Ecuador took an extreme form of fixed exchange rate by adopting the U.S. dollar as its official currency (a process known as **dollarization**).

Fixed exchange rate systems hinder monetary policy, but reinforce fiscal policy.

Flexible exchange rates hamper fiscal policy, but reinforce monetary policy.

current account, p. 710   real exchange rate, p. 715   fixed exchange rate, p. 722

capital account, p. 712   purchasing power parity, p. 715   flexible or floating exchange rate,

exchange rate, p. 713   appreciation (currency), p. 717   p. 722

nominal exchange rate, p. 715   depreciation (currency), p. 717   dollarization, p. 724

QUESTIONS AND PROBLEMS

Check Your Understanding

1. Describe the balance of trade. What factors contribute to our trade deficit?

2. Mexican immigrants working in the United States often send money back home (known as remittances) to help their families or to add to their savings account for the future. In 2012, these remittances surpassed $22 billion. How are these transfers recorded in the balance of payments accounts?

3. What is the important difference between the current account and the capital account, given that the sum of the two values must equal 0?

4. If the euro appreciates by 30%, what will happen to imports of Mercedes-Benz automobiles in the United States?

5. Describe the difference between fixed and flexible exchange rates.

6. Describe the difference between the nominal and real exchange rates. What does rising inflation do to a country's real exchange rate?

Apply the Concepts

7. Assume that global warming and especially high temperatures in Northern California have rendered it impossible for wine grapes in the Napa Valley (and all over California) to grow properly. Unable to get California wines, demand jumps dramatically for Australian wines. How would this affect the Australian dollar? Is this good for other Australian exports?

8. If the European economies begin having a serious bout of stagflation—high rates of both unemployment and inflation—will this affect the value of the dollar? Explain.

9. Trace through the reasoning why monetary policy is enhanced by a flexible exchange rate system.

10. Zimbabwe devalued its currency in mid-2006, essentially turning a $20,000 Zimbabwe bill into a $20 bill. People were permitted only three weeks during which to turn in their old currency for new notes; individuals were limited to $150 a day and companies were restricted to $7,000 a day. Who do you think were the losers from this devaluation, especially considering the limited turn-in period for the old currency?

11. Exchange rates and purchasing power parity should be the same between countries. If it costs 300 U.S. dollars to purchase an iPad in the United States and 400 Australian dollars to purchase one in Sydney, then the exchange rate between the Australian dollar and the U.S. dollar should be 4:3. Why might purchasing power parity be different from the exchange rate?

12. When the dollar gets stronger against the major foreign currencies, does the price of French wine rise or fall in the United States? Would this be a good time to travel to Australia? What happens to U.S. exports?

In the News

13. In the latter half of 2012, the worldwide musical hit *Gangnam Style* by South Korean K-pop singer Psy, contributed to a boost in tourism to South Korea ("Gangnam Brings Fans—and Tourism Revenue—to Korea," CNBC.com, January 23, 2013). Record numbers of tourists from China, Japan, and even the United States wanting to see the Gangnam district in person helped South Korea's economy in 2012. How does an increase in South Korean tourism affect the foreign exchange market for the South Korean won (its currency)?

14. The Eurozone crisis has led more than one nation to consider abandoning the euro and returning to its previous currency ("Pondering a Dire Day: Leaving the Euro," *New York Times*, December 12, 2011). If a nation were to exit the Eurozone and significantly devalue its currency against the euro and other major currencies, what are some implications for trade, the current account, and the standard of living for its citizens?

Solving Problems

15. Assume that the following exchange rates prevail:

	(U.S. $ Equivalent)
Argentina	0.1904 (peso)
Canada	0.9648 (dollar)
Mexico	0.0812 (peso)
Bahrain	2.6525 (dinar)

How many Mexican pesos does it take to get 1 Bahraini dinar? If you had 20 U.S. dollars, could you take a ferry ride in Canada if it cost 25 Canadian dollars? If someone gave you 50 Argentinean pesos to settle a 150 Mexican peso bet, would it be enough?

16. Suppose that you are given an opportunity to work in Tokyo over the summer as an English tutor, and you are provided with all living expenses and a 500,000-yen cash stipend which you plan to save and bring home. If the exchange rate is 103 yen per U.S. dollar, how much is your stipend worth in dollars if you traded your money right away? Suppose you predict that the exchange rate will change in the next few months to 92 yen per dollar. Would you receive more dollars if you wait until after the exchange rate changes?

USING THE NUMBERS

17. According to By the Numbers, if approximately $4 trillion of currency is traded each day in foreign exchange markets, about how much of this is traded in U.S. dollars? Euros? Japanese yen?

18. According to By the Numbers, if you travel to Jordan to visit the archaeological site of Petra and exchange 200 U.S. dollars, about how many Jordanian dinars would you receive? If you had traveled to Petra last year, would the amount of money received for your $200 have been different?

ANSWERS TO QUESTIONS IN CHECKPOINTS

Checkpoint: The Balance of Payments

When a country has a high savings rate (relative to domestic investment), it is likely that its exports will exceed imports, resulting in a trade surplus. Both China and Russia are net exporters, which shows up as a current account surplus in their balance of payments accounts.

Checkpoint: Exchange Rates

When the Canadian dollar appreciates against the U.S. dollar, Canadian tourists visiting the United States receive more U.S. dollars for each Canadian dollar. Therefore, purchases by

Canadian tourists in the United States become cheaper. As a result, demand rises, helping American businesses that depend on Canadian tourists. Also, the increased flow of money into the United States helps improve the U.S. current account. Meanwhile, the opposite occurs for American tourists to Canada, who find it more expensive to visit Canada. Because the higher cost of travel will discourage some Americans from visiting Canada, Canadian businesses, such as those in Niagara Falls, will suffer. Also, the reduction in money being spent by Americans in Canada will hurt Canada's current account.

Checkpoint: Monetary and Fiscal Policy in an Open Economy

As noted in this section, monetary policy is reinforced when exchange rates are flexible, while fiscal policy is hindered. This is probably only a partial explanation, because fiscal policy today seems driven more by "events" and other priorities, and less by stabilization issues.

The recent deep recession required heavy doses of both monetary and fiscal policy to keep the economy from a devastating downturn. Additional government spending, while huge, didn't seem to pack the punch many thought it would. Maybe flexible exchange rates kept it from being as effective as anticipated.

Sources for By the Numbers

Chapter 1

Total number of bachelor's degrees granted by major: *Digest of Education Statistics,* National Center for Education Statistics, U.S. Department of Education.

Technology company CEO majors: "Study Finds Most Likely Tech Sector CEO Is Dave the Ivy League Ex-Yahoo Econ Major," *Forbes,* September 28, 2012.

Fortune 100 company CEO majors: "The Education of Fortune 100 CEOs," Curran Career Consulting, January 2011.

Percent of Fortune 500 companies founded by immigrants or their children: "The 'New American' Fortune 500," Partnership For a New American Economy, June 2011.

Average percentage of income spent on various categories: Bureau of Labor Statistics, U.S. Department of Labor.

Median salaries for economics jobs: Payscale.com

Chapter 2

Farm productivity yields: Crop Quick Stats, National Agricultural Statistics Service, U.S. Department of Agriculture.

Cost of firing workers: "You're Fired: What It Costs to Sack a Worker," *The Economist,* September 16, 2008.

U.S. Trade balance: U.S. Department of Commerce.

American attitudes on environment and economic growth: "Who Cares? Don't Count on Public Opinion to Support Mitigation," *The Economist,* December 3, 2009.

Chapter 3

Gaming revenues by state: State of the States: The AGA Survey of Casino Entertainment, American Gaming Association.

Prices of precious metals: cnbc.com

Total value of the worldwide virtual goods market: "Virtual goods revenue to hit $7.3 billion this year," Bloomberg Business Week, November 15, 2010.

Total number of water bottles consumed: Beverage Marketing Corporation, www.beveragemarketing.com

Total sales of bottled water: Beverage Marketing Corporation, www.beveragemarketing.com

College and university enrollment: National Postsecondary Student Aid Study, U.S. Department of Education.

Chapter 4

Rent control price differences: Author estimates using available market data.

Federal telephone support by state: Universal Service Monitoring Report, CC Docket 98-202, Table 1.13, www.FCC.gov

Total U.S. farm support: Farm Subsidy Database, The Environmental Working Group, farm.ewg.org

Minimum wage by state: U.S. Department of Labor.

U.S. farm subsidies: Farm Subsidy Database, The Environmental Working Group, farm.ewg.org

Chapter 5

Elasticity of various goods: Compiled from numerous studies reporting estimates for price elasticity of demand.

Elasticity of food by country: Cross-price elasticities of demand across 114 countries, U.S. Department of Agriculture, March 2010.

Alternative fuels: AutoblogGreen, green.autoblog.com/2010/03/06/u-s-annual-energy-outlook-predicts-alternative-vehicles-wont

Parking alternatives: David A. Hensher and Jenny King (2001), "Parking Demand and Responsiveness to Supply, Price and Location in Sydney Central Business District," *Transportation Research* Part A, Vol. 35, No. 3, March 2001, pp. 177–196.

Average rise in public university tuition: National Center for Education Statistics, U.S. Department of Education.

Average fall in international calling rates: Author calculation using data from the Federal Communications Commission.

Chapter 6

U.S. distribution of household budgets: Bureau of Labor Statistics, U.S. Department of Labor.

Consumer expenditures in various categories: Bureau of Labor Statistics, U.S. Department of Labor.

Total number of passenger cars: U.S. Bureau of Transportation Statistics, U.S. Department of Transportation.

Charitable donations: www.givingUSA.com

Organic foods sales: 2012 Organic Industry Survey, Organic Trade Association.

NBA Jerseys: "Top-Selling NBA Jerseys in the United States and Internationally," *Forbes,* June 21, 2012.

Chapter 7

The cost of industrial robots: Bureau of Labor Statistics, U.S. Department of Labor.

Productivity rates: Bureau of Labor Statistics, U.S. Department of Labor.

Revenue needed to support new semiconductor plant: Author estimate based on various sources.

Time spent on government paperwork: U.S. Government Printing Office, www.gpo.gov

Apple iPad cost breakdown: Digital Manufacturing: How It's Made, www.manufacturingdigital.com/news_archive/tags/apple/apple-ipa

Online flight bookings: U.S. Department of Transportation.

Online flight check-ins: Airline IT Trends Survey, SITA www.sita.aero/surveys-reports/industry-surveys-reports/airline-it-trends-survey-2012

Chapter 8

Farm and farm-related employment by region: U.S. Department of Agriculture, maps.ers.usda.gov/mapimages/ers_reg_color.jpg

Top tea producers: Tip Top Tens, www.tiptoptens.com/2011/05/07/top-10-tea-producing-countries

World tea production: Food and Agricultural Organization of the United Nations.

World coffee production: Food and Agricultural Organization of the United Nations.

Average price of soybeans, wheat, and corn: Economic Research Service, U.S. Department of Agriculture.

Chapter 9

Television viewership by championship: Compiled using various media reports.

Most expensive drugs: www.forbes.com/2010/02/19/expensive-drugs-cost-business-healthcare-rare-diseases.html

Cost of a ride on Virgin Galactic: www.virgingalactic.com

Windows market share: www.netmarketshare.com/operating-system-market-share.aspx?qprid=10&qpcustomd=0

Electricity demand: U.S. Energy Information Administration, U.S. Department of Energy, www.eia.gov/forecasts/aeo/MT_electric.cfm

Chapter 10

Largest fast-food chains: "The Most Popular Fast Food Restaurants in America," Business Insider, July 12, 2012.

Wireless market share: US Wireless Data Market Q1 2011 Update, Chetan Sharma Consulting, www.chetansharma.com

Total number of marathons in the United States: www.MarathonGuide.com

Total number of Nike shoe models produced: www.Solepedia.com

Largest and smallest universities and colleges in the United States: Individual university websites and TopTenz.net

Chapter 11

Pay for undergraduate majors: 2010–11 College Salary Report, Payscale.com

Average salary for women compared to men: "Female Grads Earn $8,000 Less Than Men," CNNMoney, October 23, 2012.

Average cost of benefits as a percent of salary for full-time workers: Bureau of Labor Statistics, U.S. Department of Labor.

Average starting salaries for various professions: NACE 2011 Survey, National Association of Colleges and Employers.

Percent of workers with flexible work hours: Bureau of Labor Statistics, U.S. Department of Labor.

Projected job growth by state: "Which States Are Poised for Job Growth?" The Wall Street Journal, October 20, 2011.

Chapter 12

Percentage of high school graduates enrolling in college and percentage of college graduates pursuing postgraduate degrees: Digest of Education Statistics, National Center for Education Statistics, U.S. Department of Education.

Total number of patents granted in 1980 and 2012: U.S. Patent Statistics Report, U.S. Patent and Trademark Office.

U.S. venture capital funds by year: Dow Jones Financial Information Services; Thomson Reuters; National Venture Capital Association.

Length of high-speed rail track by country: International Union of Railways.

Chapter 13

Hybrid car sales by year: Alternative Fuels and Advanced Vehicle Data Center; U.S. Department of Energy.

Number of electric bicycles in China: "An Electric Boost for Bicyclists," The New York Times, January 31, 2010.

Increase in wind energy generated in the United States: U.S. Energy Information Administration, U.S. Department of Energy.

Annual savings from the use of compact fluorescent bulbs: Energy Star, U.S. Environmental Protection Agency.

Acres of arable land per person in the United States and China: World Development Indicators, The World Bank.

Amount of solid waste by product (recovered and not recovered): Municipal Solid Waste Generation, Recycling, and Disposal in the United States: Facts and Figures for 2011, U.S. Environmental Protection Agency.

Average gasoline tax in the United States: American Petroleum Institute.

Average gasoline tax in Britain: Fuel Duty Rates, HM Revenue & Customs.

European Union Atlantic cod catch by year: European Commission, EU Market Observatory for Fisheries and Aquaculture Products.

Wind generation capacity by state: AWEA 4th Quarter 2012 Public Market Report, American Wind Energy Association.

Chapter 14

Which device can you not live without?: The New York Times and Forrester Research.

Internet penetration rates: Internet World Stats, www.internetworldstats.com.

Number of Google Plus users: Google Blog, googleblog.blogspot.com

Number of Facebook users: Facebook, Inc.

Word processing market share: Author estimate based on available market data.

Number of online movie downloads and streaming views: "Internet To Surpass DVD in Movie Consumption, Not Revenue," The Los Angeles Times, March 23, 2012.

Chapter 15

U.S. poverty threshold: U.S. Census Bureau, U.S. Department of Commerce.

U.S. minimum wage: Wage and Hour Division, U.S. Department of Labor.

Poverty rates across the world: The World Factbook, Central Intelligence Agency.

Number of Medicaid recipients: Medicaid Spending and Enrollment Detail for CBO's May 2013 Baseline, Congressional Budget Office.

Average monthly U.S. housing subsidy: Author calculation using budget and recipient data from the U.S. Department of Housing and Urban Development.

Percentage of Americans receiving food stamps: Supplemental Nutrition Assistance Program (SNAP) Data System, Economic Research Service, U.S. Department of Agriculture.

Chapter 16

U.S. unemployment rate and real GDP growth by year: Bureau of Economic Analysis, U.S. Department of Commerce; Bureau of Labor Statistics, U.S. Department of Labor.

U.S. savings rate by year: Bureau of Economic Analysis, U.S. Department of Commerce.

U.S. gross domestic product: Bureau of Economic Analysis, U.S. Department of Commerce.

Gross world product: World Development Indicators, The World Bank.

State unemployment rates: Bureau of Labor Statistics, U.S. Department of Labor.

U.S. Index of Housing Prices: Standard and Poor's Case-Shiller Home Price Indices.

Chapter 17

The Misery Index by year: miseryindex.us

State and federal unemployment benefits: Pew Analysis of Congressional Budget Office data.

Average cost of tuition at public and private universities by year and consumer price index:

National Center for Education Statistics, U.S. Department of Education; U.S. Bureau of Labor Statistics, U.S. Department of Labor.

The social costs of unemployment: Author calculations based on available data.

Chapter 18

U.S. real GDP per capita by year: Bolt, J. and J. L. van Zanden (2013), "The First Update of the Maddison Project, Re-Estimating Growth Before 1820," Maddison Project Working Paper 4; Federal Reserve Economic Data (FRED), Economic Research Division, Federal Reserve Bank of St. Louis.

The benefits of growth in the United States: National Center for Education Statistics, U.S. Department of Education; Uniform Crime Reporting Statistics, U.S. Department of Justice; U.S. Centers for Disease Control and Prevention; U.S. Congressional Budget Office.

Reduction in global HIV/AIDS-related deaths per year: UNAIDS.org

Growth effect on per capita GDP: Dollar, David; Kraay, Aart (2002), "Growth Is Good for the Poor," *Journal of Economic Growth*, 7, 195–225.

Real GDP per capita and average life expectancy by country: World Development Indicators, The World Bank.

Chapter 19

Government spending as a percentage of GDP by year: U.S. Congressional Budget Office; usgovernmentspending.com

Average government spending per person by country: The World Factbook, Central Intelligence Agency.

Total U.S. private domestic investment spending: Bureau of Economic Analysis, U.S. Department of Commerce.

Total U.S. spending by foreign consumers (exports): Bureau of Economic Analysis, U.S. Department of Commerce.

Top categories of personal consumption expenditures: Bureau of Economic Analysis, U.S. Department of Commerce.

Spending by local, state, and federal governments: usgovernmentspending.com

Chapter 20

Aggregate demand and aggregate supply statistics: China Association of Automobile Manufacturers; Ministry of Agriculture of France; The Numbers, Nash Information Services; diamonds.net; and author estimates based on available sources.

Oil consumption in the United States and China in 1982 and 2012: U.S. Energy Information Administration, U.S. Department of Energy.

Total world aggregate demand: The World Factbook, Central Intelligence Agency.

Increase in NASDAQ stock index value: cnbc.com

Rates of home ownership by state: U.S. Census Bureau, U.S. Department of Commerce.

Chapter 21

U.S. federal government revenues: U.S. Congressional Budget Office.

U.S. federal government expenditures: U.S. Congressional Budget Office.

U.S. net government expenditures by year: Historical Tables, Office of Management and Budget, The White House.

U.S. external (foreign held) debt by year: U.S. Department of the Treasury.

Top ten creditors of U.S. Treasury Debt: U.S. Department of the Treasury.

Total U.S. national debt: brillig.com/debt_clock

Total interest paid on the U.S. national debt: Bureau of Economic Analysis, U.S. Department of Commerce.

Chapter 22

The largest banks in the world: www.relbanks.com/worlds-top-banks/assets

The eight most circulated currencies and currency reserves in the world: International Monetary Fund.

Total value of U.S. retirement accounts: ICI Retirement Industry Report, Investment Company Institute.

Total credit card debt in the United States: U.S. Federal Reserve.

Chapter 23

U.S. monetary base by year: Federal Reserve Economic Data (FRED), Economic Research Division, Federal Reserve Bank of St. Louis.

Euro monetary base: European Central Bank.

Number of U.S. bank failures by year: Historical Statistics on Banking, Federal Deposit Insurance Corporation.

Federal Deposit Insurance Corporation insured limits: Federal Deposit Insurance Corporation.

Federal Reserve balance sheet in 2003 and 2013: U.S. Federal Reserve.

Chapter 24

U.S. 30-year mortgage, prime, discount, and federal funds rate by quarter: Federal Reserve Economic Data (FRED), Economic Research Division, Federal Reserve Bank of St. Louis; U.S. Federal Reserve.

Composition of non-treasury assets held by the Federal Reserve: U.S. Federal Reserve.

Total number of $100 bills in circulation: *Treasury Bulletin*, Financial Management Service, U.S. Department of the Treasury.

Total amount of U.S. dollars and coins in circulation: *Treasury Bulletin*, Financial Management Service, U.S. Department of the Treasury.

Holdings of U.S. $100 bills by region: U.S. Federal Reserve.

Chapter 25

U.S. median existing home prices by year: Standard and Poor's Case-Shiller Home Price Indices.

U.S. Index of Consumer Sentiment: University of Michigan: Consumer Sentiment Index.

U.S. monthly real retail sales: Federal Reserve Economic Data (FRED), Economic Research Division, Federal Reserve Bank of St. Louis.

Total U.S. jobs lost during the Great Recession: Bureau of Labor Statistics, U.S. Department of Labor.

Total U.S. jobs created during the economic recovery: Bureau of Labor Statistics, U.S. Department of Labor.

Value of assets purchased by the Federal Reserve quantitative easing programs: U.S. Federal Reserve.

Chapter 26

Trade deficit as a percent of GDP: Foreign Trade Division, U.S. Census Bureau, U.S. Department of Commerce.

Trade-weighted tariff barriers: World Development Indicators, The World Bank.

Medical tourism services: Companion Global Healthcare, Inc.

Number of American cars sold in China: Author estimate based on sales reports from Ford, Chrysler, and General Motors.

U.S. public sentiment on lower trade barriers: Constrained Internationalism: Adapting to New Realities: Results of a 2010 National Survey of American Public Opinion, Chicago Council on Global Affairs.

China's share of world GDP: Historical Statistics of the World Economy: 1–2008 AD, Angus Maddison; World Economic Outlook Database, International Monetary Fund.

Chapter 27
The most traded currencies in the world: 2013 Triennial Central Bank Survey, Bank of International Settlements.

Total value of currency traded each day in foreign exchange markets: 2013 Triennial Central Bank Survey, Bank of International Settlements.

Percent of foreign exchange trades that are speculative: various sources.

Value of currencies pegged to the U.S. dollar: xe.com

Composition of foreign exchange transactions: 2013 Triennial Central Bank Survey, Bank of International Settlements.

Glossary

absolute advantage One country can produce more of a good than another country.

accounting profit The difference between total revenue and explicit costs. These are the profits that are taxed by the government.

adaptive expectations Inflationary expectations are formed from a simple extrapolation from past events.

agency shop Employees are not required to join the union, but must pay dues to compensate the union for its services.

aggregate demand The output of goods and services (real GDP) demanded at different price levels.

aggregate expenditures Consist of consumer spending, business investment spending, government spending, and net foreign spending (exports minus imports): $GDP = C + I + G + (X - M)$.

aggregate supply The real GDP that firms will produce at varying price levels. In the short run, aggregate supply is positively sloped because many input costs are slow to change (they are *sticky*), but in the long run, the aggregate supply curve is vertical at full employment because the economy has reached its capacity to produce.

allocative efficiency The mix of goods and services produced is just what the society desires.

altruism Actions undertaken merely out of goodwill or generosity.

annually balanced budget Federal expenditures and taxes would have to be equal each year.

antitrust law Laws designed to maintain competition and prevent monopolies from developing.

appreciation (currency) When the value of a currency rises relative to other currencies.

asymmetric information Occurs when one party to a transaction has significantly better information than another party.

autarky A country that does not engage in international trade, also known as a closed economy.

automatic stabilizers Tax revenues and transfer payments automatically expand or contract in ways that reduce the intensity of business fluctuations without any overt action by Congress or other policymakers.

average cost pricing rule Requires a regulated monopolist to produce and sell output where price equals average total cost. This permits the regulated monopolist to earn a normal return on investment over the long term and therefore remain in business.

average fixed cost Equal to total fixed cost divided by output (FC/Q).

average product Output per worker, found by dividing total output by the number of workers employed to produce that output (Q/L).

average propensity to consume The percentage of income that is consumed (C/Y).

average propensity to save The percentage of income that is saved (S/Y).

average total cost Equal to total cost divided by output (TC/Q). Average total cost is also equal to AFC + AVC.

average variable cost Equal to total variable cost divided by output (VC/Q).

balanced budget multiplier Equal changes in government spending and taxation (a balanced budget) lead to an equal change in income (the balanced budget multiplier is equal to 1).

barriers to entry Any obstacle that makes it more difficult for a firm to enter an industry, and includes control of a key resource, prohibitive fixed costs, and government protection.

barter The direct exchange of goods and services for other goods and services.

behavioral economics The study of how human psychology enters into economic behavior as a way to explain why individuals sometimes act in predictable ways counter to economic models.

budget line Graphically illustrates the possible combinations of two goods that can be purchased with a given income, given the prices of both goods.

bundling A strategy of packaging several products into a single product with a single price. Bundling allows firms to capture customers of related products by making it more attractive to use the same firm's products.

business cycles Alternating increases and decreases in economic activity that are typically punctuated by periods of recession and recovery.

capital Includes manufactured products such as tractors, welding equipment, and computers that are used to produce other goods and services. The payment to capital is referred to as interest.

capital account Summarizes the flow of money into and out of domestic and foreign assets, including investments by foreign companies in domestic plants or subsidiaries, and other foreign holdings of U.S. assets, including mutual funds, stocks, bonds, and deposits in U.S. banks. Also included are U.S. investors' holdings of foreign financial assets, production facilities, and other assets in foreign countries.

capital-to-labor ratio The capital employed per worker. A higher ratio means higher labor productivity and, as a result, higher wages.

cartel An agreement between firms (or countries) in an industry to formally collude on price and output, then agree on the distribution of production.

casual user A consumer who purchases a good only after the good has matured in the market and is more sensitive to price.

catch-up effect Countries with smaller starting levels of capital experience larger benefits from increased capital, allowing these countries to grow faster than countries with abundant capital.

ceteris paribus Assumption used in economics (and other disciplines as well), where other relevant factors or variables are held constant.

change in demand Occurs when one or more of the determinants of demand changes, shown as a shift in the entire demand curve.

change in quantity demanded Occurs when the price of the product changes, shown as a movement along an existing demand curve.

change in quantity supplied Occurs when the price of the product changes, shown as a movement along an existing supply curve.

change in supply Occurs when one or more of the determinants of supply change, shown as a shift in the entire supply curve.

circular flow diagram Illustrates how households and firms interact through product and resource markets and shows that economic aggregates can be determined by either examining spending flows or income flows to households.

closed shop Workers must belong to the union before they can be hired.

Coase theorem If transaction costs are minimal (near zero), a bargain struck between beneficiaries and victims of externalities will be efficient from a resource allocation perspective. As a result, the socially optimal level of production will be reached.

collateral An asset used to secure a loan that can be sold if the borrower fails to repay a loan.

command and control policies Environmental policies that set standards and issue regulations, which are then enforced by the legal and regulatory system.

comparative advantage One country has a lower opportunity cost of producing a good than another country.

complementary goods Goods that are typically consumed together. When the *price* of a complementary good rises, the *demand* for the other good declines, and vice versa. Complements have a negative cross elasticity of demand.

compounding The ability of growth to build on previous growth. It allows a value such as GDP to increase significantly over time as income increases on top of previous increases in income.

compounding effect The effect of interest added to existing debt or savings leading to substantial growth in debt or savings over the long run.

concentration ratio The share of industry shipments or sales accounted for by the top four or eight firms.

constant cost industry An industry that, in the long run, faces roughly the same prices and costs as industry output expands. Some industries can virtually clone their operations in other areas without putting undue pressure on resource prices, resulting in constant operating costs as they expand in the long run.

constant returns to scale A range of output where average total costs are relatively constant. The expansion of fast-food restaurant franchises and movie theaters, which are essentially replications of existing franchises and theaters, reflect this.

consumer price index (CPI) A measure of the average change in prices paid by urban consumers for a typical market basket of consumer goods and services.

consumer surplus The difference between market price and what consumers (as individuals or the market) would be willing to pay. It is equal to the area above market price and below the demand curve.

consumption Spending by individuals and households on both durable goods (e.g., autos, appliances, and electronic equipment) and nondurable goods (e.g., food, clothing, and entertainment).

contestable markets Markets that look monopolistic but where entry costs are so low that the sheer threat of entry keeps prices low.

contractionary fiscal policy Involves increasing withdrawals from the economy by reducing government spending, transfer payments, or raising taxes to decrease aggregate demand to contract output and the economy.

contractionary monetary policy Fed actions designed to decrease excess reserves and the money supply to shrink income and employment, usually to fight inflation.

core user A consumer who has a very high willingness to pay for a new product or service and is among the first to purchase it.

corporation A business structure that has most of the legal rights of individuals, and in addition, can issue stock to raise capital. Stockholders' liability is limited to the value of their stock.

cost-benefit analysis A methodology for decision making that looks at the discounted value of the costs and benefits of a given project.

cost-push inflation Results when a supply shock hits the economy, reducing short-run aggregate supply, and thus reducing output and increasing the price level.

coupon rate A periodic fixed payment to the bond holder measured as an annual percent of the bond's face value.

credit default swap A financial instrument that insures against the potential default on an asset. Because of the extent of defaults in the last financial crisis, issuers of credit default swaps could not repay all of the claims, bankrupting these financial institutions.

cross elasticity of demand Measures how responsive the quantity demanded of one good is to changes in the price of another good. Substitute goods have positive cross elasticities: An increase in the price of one good leads consumers to substitute (buy more of) the other good whose price has not changed. Complementary goods have negative cross elasticities: An increase in the price of a complement leads to a reduction in sales of the other good whose price has not changed.

crowding-out effect Arises from deficit spending requiring the government to borrow, thus driving up interest rates and reducing consumer spending and business investment.

current account Includes payments for imports and exports of goods and services, incomes flowing into and out of the country, and net transfers of money.

cyclical unemployment Unemployment that results from changes in the business cycle, and where public policymakers can have their greatest impact by keeping the economy on a steady, low-inflationary, solid growth path.

cyclically balanced budget Balancing the budget over the course of the business cycle by restricting spending or raising taxes when the economy is booming and using these surpluses to offset the deficits that occur during recessions.

deadweight loss The reduction in total surplus that results from the inefficiency of a market not in equilibrium.

decision lag The time it takes Congress and the administration to decide on a policy once a problem is recognized.

decreasing cost industry An industry that, in the long run, faces lower prices and costs as industry output expands. Some industries enjoy economies of scale as they expand in the long run, typically the result of technological advances.

deficit The amount by which annual government spending exceeds tax revenues.

deflation A decline in overall prices throughout the economy. This is the opposite of inflation.

demand The maximum amount of a product that buyers are willing and able to purchase over some time period at various prices, holding all other relevant factors constant (the *ceteris paribus* condition).

demand curve A graphical illustration of the law of demand, which shows the relationship between the price of a good and the quantity demanded.

demand for labor Demand for labor is derived from the demand for the firm's product and the productivity of labor.

demand schedule A table that shows the quantity of a good a consumer purchases at each price.

demand-pull inflation Results when aggregate demand expands so

much that equilibrium output exceeds full employment output and the price level rises.

depreciation (currency) When the value of a currency falls relative to other currencies.

determinants of demand Nonprice factors that affect demand, including tastes and preferences, income, prices of related goods, number of buyers, and expectations.

determinants of supply Nonprice factors that affect supply, including production technology, costs of resources, prices of other commodities, expectations, number of sellers, and taxes and subsidies.

diminishing marginal returns An additional worker adds to total output, but at a diminishing rate.

diminishing returns to capital Each additional unit of capital provides a smaller increase in output than the previous unit of capital.

discount rate The interest rate the Federal Reserve charges commercial banks and other depository institutions to borrow reserves from a regional Federal Reserve Bank.

discouraged workers To continue to be counted as unemployed, those without work must actively seek work (apply for jobs, interview, register with employment services, etc.). Discouraged workers are those who have given up actively looking for work and, as a result, are not counted as unemployed.

discretionary fiscal policy Involves adjusting government spending and tax policies with the express short-run goal of moving the economy toward full employment, expanding economic growth, or controlling inflation.

discretionary spending The part of the budget that works its way through the appropriations process of Congress each year and includes such programs as national defense, transportation, science, environment, and income security.

diseconomies of scale A range of output where average total costs tend to increase. Firms often become so big that management becomes bureaucratic and

unable to control its operations efficiently.

disinflation A reduction in the rate of inflation. An economy going through disinflation is still facing inflation, but at a declining rate.

disposable personal income Personal income minus taxes.

dollarization Describes the decision of a country to adopt another country's currency (most often the U.S. dollar) as its own official currency.

dominant strategy Occurs when a player chooses the same strategy regardless of what his or her opponent chooses.

double-dip recession A recession that begins after only a short period of economic recovery from the previous recession.

dumping Selling goods abroad at lower prices than in home markets, and often below cost.

easy money, quantitative easing, or accommodative monetary policy Fed actions designed to increase excess reserves and the money supply to stimulate the economy (expand income and employment). *See also* expansionary monetary policy.

economic costs The sum of explicit (out-of-pocket) and implicit (opportunity) costs.

economic discrimination When workers of equal ability are paid different wages or in any other way discriminated against because of race, color, religion, gender, age, national origin, or disability.

economic growth Usually measured by the annual percentage change in real GDP, reflecting an improvement in the standard of living.

economic profit Profit in excess of normal profits. These are profits in excess of both explicit and implicit costs.

economics The study of how individuals, firms, and society make decisions to allocate limited resources to many competing wants.

economies of scale As a firm's output increases, its LRATC tends to decline. This results from specialization of labor and management, and potentially a better use of capital and complementary production techniques.

economies of scope By producing a number of products that are interdependent, firms are able to produce and market these goods at lower costs.

efficiency How well resources are used and allocated. Do people get the goods and services they want at the lowest possible resource cost? This is the chief focus of efficiency.

efficiency wage theory Employers often pay their workers wages above the market-clearing level to improve morale and productivity, reduce turnover, and create a disincentive for employees to shirk their duties.

elastic demand The absolute value of the price elasticity of demand is greater than 1. Elastic demands are very responsive to changes in price. The percentage change in quantity demanded is greater than the percentage change in price.

elastic supply Price elasticity of supply is greater than 1. The percentage change in quantity supplied is greater than the percentage change in price.

elasticity of demand for labor The percentage change in the quantity of labor demanded divided by the percentage change in the wage rate.

entrepreneurs Entrepreneurs combine land, labor, and capital to produce goods and services. They absorb the risk of being in business, including the risk of bankruptcy and other liabilities associated with doing business. Entrepreneurs receive profits for this effort.

equation of exchange The heart of classical monetary theory uses the equation $M \times V = P \times Q$, where M is the supply of money, V is the velocity of money (the average number of times per year a dollar is spent on goods and services, or the number of times it turns over in a year), P is the price level, and Q is the economy's output level.

equilibrium Market forces are in balance when the quantities demanded by consumers just equal the quantities supplied by producers.

equilibrium price Market equilibrium price is the price that results when quantity demanded is just equal to quantity supplied.

equilibrium quantity Market equilibrium quantity is the output that results when quantity demanded is just equal to quantity supplied.

equity The fairness of various issues and policies.

essential facility An input that is needed to produce a product or to allow a person to consume a product.

excess reserves Reserves held by banks above the legally required amount.

exchange rate The rate at which one currency can be exchanged for another, or just the price of one currency for another.

expansionary fiscal policy Involves increasing government spending, increasing transfer payments, or decreasing taxes to increase aggregate demand to expand output and the economy.

expansionary monetary policy Fed actions designed to increase excess reserves and the money supply to stimulate the economy (expand income and employment).

explicit costs Those expenses paid directly to another economic entity, including wages, lease payments, taxes, and utilities.

exports Goods and services that are sold abroad.

externalities The impact on third parties of some transaction between others in which the third parties are not involved. An external cost (or negative externality) harms the third parties, whereas external benefits (positive externalities) result in gains to them.

externally held debt Public debt held by foreigners, which is roughly equal to half of the outstanding U.S. debt held by the public.

face value The value of a bond that is paid upon maturity. This value is fixed, and therefore not the same as the market value of a bond, which is influenced by changes in interest rates and risk.

federal funds rate The interest rate financial institutions charge each other for overnight loans used as reserves.

Federal Open Market Committee (FOMC) A twelve-member committee that is composed of members of the Board of Governors of the Fed and selected presidents of the regional Federal Reserve Banks. It oversees open market operations (the buying and selling of government securities), the main tool of monetary policy.

Federal Reserve System The central bank of the United States.

fiat money Money without intrinsic value but nonetheless accepted as money because the government has decreed it to be money.

financial capital The money required by businesses to purchase inputs for production and to run their operations.

financial intermediaries Financial firms (banks, mutual funds, insurance companies, etc.) that acquire funds from savers and then lend these funds to borrowers (consumers, firms, and government).

financial system A complex set of institutions, including banks, bond markets, and stock markets, that allocate scarce resources (financial capital) from savers to borrowers.

firm An economic institution that transforms resources (factors of production) into outputs.

fiscal sustainability A measure of the present value of all projected future revenues compared to the present value of projected future spending.

fixed costs Costs that do not change as a firm's output expands or contracts, often called overhead. These include items such as lease payments, administrative expenses, property taxes, and insurance premiums.

fixed exchange rate Each government determines its exchange rate, then uses macroeconomic policy to maintain the rate.

flat tax A tax that is a constant proportion of one's income.

flexible or **floating exchange rate** A country's currency exchange rate is determined in international currency exchange markets, given the country's macroeconomic policies.

fractional reserve banking system Describes a banking system in which a portion of bank deposits are held as vault cash or in an account with the regional Federal Reserve Bank, while the rest of the deposits are loaned out to generate the money creation process.

framing bias Describes when individuals are steered into making one decision over another or are convinced they are receiving a higher value for a product than what was paid for it.

free rider The ability of an individual to avoid paying for a public good because he or she cannot be excluded from enjoying the good once provided.

frictional unemployment Unemployment for any economy that includes workers who voluntarily quit their jobs to search for better positions, or are moving to new jobs but may still take several days or weeks before they can report to their new employers.

functional distribution of income The distribution of income for resources or factors of production (land, labor, capital, and entrepreneurial ability).

functional finance Essentially ignores the impact of the budget on the business cycle and focuses on fostering economic growth and stable prices, while keeping the economy as close as possible to full employment.

game theory The study of how individuals and firms make strategic decisions to achieve their goals when other parties or factors can influence that outcome.

GDP deflator An index of the average prices for all goods and services in the economy, including consumer goods, investment goods, government goods and services, and exports. It is the broadest measure of inflation in the national income and product accounts (NIPA).

GDP per capita A country's GDP divided by its population. GDP per capita provides a useful measure of a country's relative standard of living.

Gini coefficient A precise method of measuring the position of the Lorenz curve, defined as the area between the Lorenz curve and the equal distribution line divided by the total area below the equal distribution line.

government budget constraint The government budget is limited by the fact that $G - T = \Delta M + \Delta B + \Delta A$.

government failure The result when the incentives of politicians and government bureaucrats do not align with the public interest.

government spending Includes the wages and salaries of government employees (federal, state, and local); the purchase of products and services from private businesses and the rest of the world; and government purchases of new structures and equipment.

gross domestic product (GDP) A measure of the economy's total output; it is the most widely reported value in the national income and product accounts (NIPA) and is equal to the total market value of all final goods and services produced by resources in a given year.

gross private domestic investment (GPDI) Investments in such things as structures (residential and nonresidential), equipment, and software, and changes in private business inventories.

Herfindahl-Hirschman index (HHI) A way of measuring industry concentration, equal to the sum of the squares of market shares for all firms in the industry.

horizontal summation Market demand and supply curves are found by adding together how many units of the product will be purchased or supplied at each price.

hyperinflation An extremely high rate of inflation; above 100% per year.

implementation lag The time required to turn fiscal policy into law and eventually have an impact on the economy.

implicit costs The opportunity costs of using resources that belong to the firm, including depreciation, depletion of business assets, and the opportunity cost of the firm's capital employed in the business.

imports Goods and services that are purchased from abroad.

incentives The factors that motivate individuals and firms to make decisions in their best interest.

incidence of taxation Refers to who bears the economic burden of a tax. The economic entity bearing the burden of a particular tax will depend on the price elasticities of demand and supply.

income A flow measure reflecting the funds received by individuals or households over a period of time, usually a week, month, or year.

income deficit The difference between the poverty threshold and a family's income.

income effect (labor) Higher wages mean that you can maintain the same standard of living by working fewer hours. The impact on labor supply is generally negative.

income effect When higher prices essentially reduce consumer income, the quantity demanded for normal goods falls.

income elasticity of demand Measures how responsive quantity demanded is to changes in consumer income.

increasing cost industry An industry that, in the long run, faces higher prices and costs as industry output expands. Industry expansion puts upward pressure on resources (inputs), causing higher costs in the long run.

increasing marginal returns A new worker hired adds more to total output than the previous worker hired, so that both average and marginal products are rising.

indifference curve Shows all the combinations of two goods where the consumer is indifferent (gets the same level of satisfaction).

indifference map An infinite set of indifference curves in which each curve represents a different level of utility or satisfaction.

industry standard A common format that is used, for example, in televisions, in digital recorders, or in software programs.

inelastic demand The absolute value of the price elasticity of demand is less than 1. Inelastic demands are not very responsive to changes in price. The percentage change in quantity demanded is less than the percentage change in price.

inelastic supply Price elasticity of supply is less than 1. The percentage change in quantity supplied is less than the percentage change in price.

infant industry An industry so underdeveloped that protection is needed for it to become competitive on the world stage or to ensure its survival.

inferior goods Goods that have income elasticities that are negative. When consumer income grows, quantity demanded falls for inferior goods.

inflation A measure of changes in the cost of living. A general rise in prices throughout the economy.

inflation targeting The central bank sets a target on the inflation rate (usually around 2% per year) and adjusts monetary policy to keep inflation in that range.

inflationary expectations The rate of inflation expected by workers for any given period. Workers do not work for a specific nominal wage but for what those wages will buy (real wages), therefore their inflationary expectations are an important determinant of what nominal wage they are willing to work for.

inflationary gap The spending reduction necessary (when expanded by the multiplier) to bring an overheated economy back to full employment.

informal economy Includes all transactions that are conducted but are not licensed and/or generate income that is not reported to the government (for tax collection).

information lag The time policymakers must wait for economic data to be collected, processed, and reported. Most macroeconomic data are not available until at least one quarter (three months) after the fact.

infrastructure The public capital of a nation, including transportation networks, power-generating plants and transmission facilities, public education institutions, and other intangible resources such as protection of property rights and a stable monetary environment.

injections Increments of spending, including investment, government spending, and exports.

intellectual property rights A set of exclusive rights granted to a creator of an invention or creative work, allowing the owner to earn profits over a fixed period of time. The types of protection include patents, copyrights, trademarks, and industrial designs.

interconnection The physical linking of a network to another network's essential facilities. Interconnection promotes competition by ensuring that no firm has exclusive access to a set of customers.

internally held debt Public debt owned by U.S. banks, corpora-tions, mutual funds, pension plans, and individuals.

intertemporal pricing A type of versioning in which goods are differentiated by the level of patience of consumers. Less patient consumers pay a higher price than more patient consumers.

investment Spending by businesses that adds to the productive capacity of the economy. Investment depends on factors such as its rate of return, the level of technology, and business expectations about the economy.

investment in human capital Improvements to the labor force from investments in skills, knowledge, and the overall quality of workers and their productivity.

jobless recovery A phenomenon that takes place after a recession, when output begins to rise, but employment growth does not.

Keynesian macroeconomic equilibrium In the simple model, the economy is at rest; spending injections (investment) are equal to withdrawals (saving), or I = S, and there are no net inducements for the economy to change the level of output or income. In the full model, all injections of spending must equal all withdrawals at equilibrium: I + G + X = S + T + M.

kinked demand curve An oligopoly model that assumes that if a firm raises its price, competitors will not raise theirs; but if the firm lowers its price, all of its competitors will lower their price to match the reduction. This leads to a kink in the demand curve and relatively stable market prices.

labor Includes the mental and physical talents of individuals who produce products and services. The payment to labor is called wages.

labor force The total number of those employed and unemployed. The unemployment rate is the number of unemployed divided by the labor force, expressed as a percent.

Laffer curve Shows a hypothetical relationship between income tax rates and tax revenues. As tax rates rise from zero, revenues rise, reach a maximum, then decline until revenues reach zero again at a 100% tax rate.

laissez-faire A market that is allowed to function without any government intervention.

land Includes natural resources such as mineral deposits, oil, natural gas, water, and land in the usual sense of the word. The payment to land as a resource is called rent.

law of demand Holding all other relevant factors constant, as price increases, quantity demanded falls, and as price decreases, quantity demanded rises.

law of diminishing marginal utility As we consume more of a given product, the added satisfaction we get from consuming an additional unit declines.

law of supply Holding all other relevant factors constant, as price increases, quantity supplied will rise, and as price declines, quantity supplied will fall.

leakages A reduction in the amount of money that is used for lending that reduces the money multiplier. It is caused by banks choosing to hold excess reserves and from individuals, businesses, and foreigners choosing to hold more cash.

leverage Occurs when investors borrow money at low interest rates to purchase investments that may provide higher rates of return. The risk of highly leveraged investments is that a small decrease in price can wipe out one's account.

liquidity How quickly, easily, and reliably an asset can be converted into cash.

liquidity trap When interest rates are so low that people believe rates can only rise, they hold on to money rather than investing in bonds and suffering the expected capital loss.

lock-in strategies Techniques used by firms to raise the switching costs for its customers, making it less attractive to leave the network.

long run A period of time sufficient for firms to adjust all factors of production, including plant capacity. Existing firms can expand or build new plants, or firms can enter or exit the industry.

long-run aggregate supply (LRAS) curve The long-run aggregate supply curve is vertical at full employment because the economy has reached its capacity to produce.

long-run average total cost In the long run, firms can adjust their plant sizes so that LRATC is the lowest unit cost at which any particular output can be produced in the long run.

Lorenz curves A graphical method of showing the income distribution by cumulating families of various income levels on the horizontal axis and relating this to their cumulative share of total income on the vertical axis.

lump-sum tax A fixed amount of tax regardless of income, and is a type of regressive tax.

luxury goods Goods that have income elasticities greater than 1. When consumer income grows, quantity demanded of luxury goods rises more than the rise in income.

M1 The narrowest definition of money; includes currency (coins and paper money), traveler's checks, demand deposits (checks), and other accounts that have check-writing or debit capabilities. The most liquid instruments that might serve as money.

M2 A broader definition of money that includes "near monies" that are not as liquid as cash, including deposits in savings accounts, money market accounts, and money market mutual fund accounts.

macroeconomic equilibrium Occurs at the intersection of the short-run aggregate supply and aggregate demand curves. At this output level, there are no net pressures for the economy to expand or contract.

macroeconomics The broader issues in the economy such as inflation, unemployment, and national output of goods and services.

mandatory spending Spending authorized by permanent laws that does not go through the same appropriations process as discretionary spending. Mandatory spending includes such programs as Social Security, Medicare, and interest on the national debt.

marginal cost The change in total costs arising from the production of additional units of output

($\Delta TC/\Delta Q$). Because fixed costs do not change with output, marginal costs are the change in variable costs associated with additional production ($\Delta VC/\Delta Q$).

marginal cost pricing rule Regulators would prefer to have natural monopolists price where P = MC, but this would result in losses (long term) because ATC > MC. Thus, regulators often must use an average cost pricing rule.

marginal factor cost (MFC) The added cost associated with hiring one more unit of labor. For competitive firms, it is equal to the wage; but for monopsonists, it is higher than the new wage (W) because all existing workers must be paid this higher new wage, making MFC > W.

marginal physical product of labor The additional output a firm receives from employing an added unit of labor (MPP$_L$ = $\Delta Q \div \Delta L$).

marginal product The change in output that results from a change in labor ($\Delta Q/\Delta L$).

marginal propensity to consume The change in consumption associated with a given change in income.

marginal propensity to save The change in saving associated with a given change in income.

marginal revenue The change in total revenue from selling an additional unit of output. Because competitive firms are price takers, P = MR for competitive firms.

marginal revenue product The value of another worker to the firm is equal to the marginal physical product of labor (MPP$_L$) times marginal revenue (MR).

marginal utility The satisfaction received from consuming an additional unit of a given product or service.

marginal utility analysis A theoretical framework underlying consumer decision making. This approach assumes that satisfaction can be measured and that consumers maximize satisfaction when the marginal utilities per dollar are equal for all products and services.

market cap The market value of a firm determined by the current price per share of its stock mul-

tiplied by the total number of shares issued.

market failure When markets fail to provide the socially optimal level of output, and will provide output at too high or low a price.

market period Time period so short that the output and the number of firms are fixed. Agricultural products at harvest time face market periods. Products that unexpectedly become instant hits face market periods (there is a lag between when the firm realizes it has a hit on its hands and when inventory can be replaced).

market power A firm's ability to set prices for goods and services in a market.

market segmentation A strategy of making a single good in different versions to target different consumer markets with varying prices.

market structure analysis By observing a few industry characteristics such as number of firms in the industry or the level of barriers to entry, economists can use this information to predict pricing and output behavior of the firm in the industry.

market-based policies Environmental policies that use charges, taxes, subsidies, deposit-refund systems, or tradable emission permits to achieve environmental goals.

markets Institutions that bring buyers and sellers together so they can interact and transact with each other.

maturity The date on which the face value of the bond must be repaid.

medium of exchange Money is a medium of exchange because goods and services are sold for money, then the money is used to purchase other goods and services.

microeconomics The decision making by individuals, businesses, industries, and governments.

misallocation of resources Occurs when a good or service is not consumed by the person who values it the most, and typically results when a price ceiling creates an artificial shortage in the market.

monetary rule Keeps the growth of money stocks such as M1 or M2 on a steady path, following the equation of exchange (or quantity theory), to set a long-run path for the economy that keeps inflation in check.

monetized debt Occurs when debt is reduced by increasing the money supply, thereby making each dollar less valuable through inflation.

money Anything that is accepted in exchange for goods and services or for the payment of debt.

money multiplier Measures the *potential* or *maximum* amount the money supply can increase (or decrease) when new deposits enter (exit) the system and is defined as 1 divided by the reserve requirement. The actual money multiplier will be less, because some banks hold excess reserves.

monopolistic competition A market structure with a large number of firms producing differentiated products. This differentiation is either real or imagined by consumers and involves innovations, advertising, location, or other ways of making one firm's product different from that of its competitors.

monopolistic exploitation of labor Occurs when workers are paid less than the value of their marginal product because the firm has monopoly power in the product market.

monopoly A one-firm industry with no close product substitutes and with substantial barriers to entry.

monopsonistic exploitation of labor Occurs when workers are paid less than the value of their marginal product because the firm is a monopsonist in the labor market.

monopsony A labor market with one employer.

multiplier Spending changes alter equilibrium income by the spending change times the multiplier. One person's spending becomes another's income, and that second person spends some (the MPC), which becomes income for another person, and so on, until income has changed by $1/(1 - MPC) = 1/MPS$. The multiplier operates in both directions.

mutual interdependence When only a few firms constitute an industry, each firm must consider the reactions of its competitors to its decisions.

Nash equilibrium An outcome that occurs when all players choose their optimal strategy in response to all other players' potential moves. At a Nash equilibrium, no player can be better off by unilaterally deviating from the noncooperative outcome.

national income All income, including wages, salaries and benefits, profits (for sole proprietors, partnerships, and corporations), rental income, and interest.

natural monopoly An industry exhibiting large economies of scale such that the minimum efficient scale of operations is roughly equal to market demand.

natural rate of unemployment That level of unemployment at which price and wage decisions are consistent; a level at which the actual inflation rate is equal to people's inflationary expectations and where cyclical unemployment is zero.

net domestic product Gross domestic product minus depreciation, or the capital consumption allowance.

net exports Exports minus imports for the current period. Exports include all the items we sell overseas such as agricultural products, movies, and technology products. Imports are all those items we bring into the country, such as vegetables from Mexico, wine from Italy, and cars from Germany.

network A structure that connects various entities with one another. A network can be physical, virtual, or social.

network demand curve A demand curve for a good or service that experiences a network effect, causing it to slope upward at lower quantities before sloping downward once the market matures.

network effect An external benefit generated from the consumption of a network good that is taken into account by individuals and firms in their decision making. It increases the value of a good as more people use or subscribe to a good.

network externality An external benefit generated from the consumption of a network good.

network good A good or service that requires the existence of a physical, virtual, or social network to exist.

nominal exchange rate The rate at which one currency can be exchanged for another.

nonexcludability Once a good or service is provided, it is not possible to exclude others from enjoying that good or service.

nonrivalry The consumption of a good or service by one person does not reduce the utility of that good or service to others.

normal goods Goods that have positive income elasticities of less than 1. When consumer income grows, quantity demanded rises for normal goods, but less than the rise in income.

normal profits The return on capital necessary to keep investors satisfied and keep capital in the business over the long run. Equal to zero economic profits; where P = ATC.

normative question A question that is based on societal beliefs on what should or should not take place.

oligopoly A market with just a few firms dominating the industry, where (1) each firm recognizes that it must consider its competitors' reactions when making its own decisions (mutual interdependence), and (2) there are significant barriers to entry into the market.

on-the-job training Training typically done by employers, ranging from suggestions at work to intensive workshops and seminars.

open market operations The buying and selling of U.S. government securities, such as Treasury bills and bonds, to adjust reserves in the banking system.

opportunity cost The value of the next best alternative; what you give up to do something or purchase something.

paradox of thrift When investment is positively related to income and households *intend* to save more, they reduce consumption, income, and output, reducing investment so that the result is that consumers *actually* end up saving less.

partnership Similar to a sole proprietorship, but involves more than one owner who share the management of the business. Partnerships are also subject to unlimited liability.

peak-load pricing A versioning strategy of pricing a product higher during periods of higher demand, and lower during periods of lower demand.

pensions A retirement program into which an employer pays a monthly amount to retired employees until they die.

perfect competition A market structure with many relatively small buyers and sellers who take the price as given, a standardized product, full information to both buyers and sellers, and no barriers to entry or exit.

perfect (first-degree) price discrimination Charging each customer the maximum price each is willing to pay, thereby expropriating all consumer surplus.

personal consumption expenditures Goods and services purchased by residents of the United States, whether individuals or businesses; they include durable goods, nondurable goods, and services.

personal income All income, including wages, salaries, and other labor income; proprietors' income; rental income; personal interest and dividend income; and transfer payments (welfare and Social Security payments) received, with personal contributions for social insurance subtracted out.

personal or family distribution of income The distribution of income to individuals or family groups (typically quintiles, or fifths, of the population).

Phillips curve The original curve posited a negative relationship between wages and unemployment, but later versions related unemployment to inflation rates.

physical capital All manufactured products that are used to produce goods and services.

physical network A network connected by a physical structure such as fiber optics, transportation routes, or satellites.

Pigouvian tax A tax that is placed on an activity generating negative externalities in order to achieve a socially efficient outcome.

positive question A question that can be answered using available information or facts.

poverty thresholds Income levels for various household sizes, below which people are considered to be living in poverty.

present value The value of an investment (future stream of income) today. The higher the discount rate, the lower the present value today, and vice versa.

price caps Maximum price at which a regulated firm can sell its product. They are often flexible enough to allow for changing cost conditions.

price ceiling A government-set maximum price that can be charged for a product or service. When the price ceiling is set below equilibrium, it leads to shortages.

price discrimination Charging different consumer groups different prices for the same product.

price elasticity of demand A measure of the responsiveness of quantity demanded to a change in price, equal to the percentage change in quantity demanded divided by the percentage change in price.

price elasticity of supply A measure of the responsiveness of quantity supplied to changes in price. An elastic supply curve has elasticity greater than 1, whereas inelastic supplies have elasticities less than 1. Time is the most important determinant of the elasticity of supply.

price floor A government-set minimum price that can be charged for a product or service. When the price floor is set above equilibrium, it leads to surpluses.

price level The absolute level of a price index, whether the consumer price index (CPI; retail prices), the producer price index (PPI; wholesale prices), or the GDP deflator (average price of all items in GDP).

price system A name given to the market economy because prices provide considerable information to both buyers and sellers.

price taker Individual firms in perfectly competitive markets get their prices from the market because they are so small they cannot influence market price. For this reason, perfectly competitive firms are price takers and can produce and sell all the output they produce at market-determined prices.

Prisoner's Dilemma A noncooperative game in which players cannot communicate or collaborate in making their decisions, which results in inferior outcomes for both players. Many oligopoly decisions can be framed as a Prisoner's Dilemma.

producer price index (PPI) A measure of the average changes in the prices received by domestic producers for their output.

producer surplus The difference between market price and the price at which firms are willing to supply the product. It is equal to the area below market price and above the supply curve.

product differentiation One firm's product is distinguished from another's through advertising, innovation, location, and so on.

production The process of converting resources (factors of production)—land, labor, capital, and entrepreneurial ability—into goods and services.

production efficiency Goods and services are produced at their lowest resource (opportunity) cost.

production function Measures the output that is produced using various combinations of inputs and a fixed level of technology.

production possibilities frontier (PPF) Shows the combinations of two goods that are possible for a society to produce at full employment. Points on or inside the PPF are attainable, and those outside of the frontier are unattainable.

productivity How effectively inputs are converted into outputs. Labor productivity is the ratio of the output of goods and services to the labor hours devoted to the production of that output. Higher productivity and higher living standards are closely related.

profit Equal to the difference between total revenue and total cost.

profit maximizing rule Firms maximize profit by producing output where MR = MC. No other level of output produces higher profits.

progressive tax A tax that rises in percentage of income as income increases.

public choice theory The economic analysis of public and political decision making, looking at issues such as voting, the impact of election incentives on politicians, the influence of special interest groups, and rent-seeking behaviors.

public debt The total accumulation of past deficits less surpluses; it includes Treasury bills, notes, and bonds, and U.S. Savings Bonds.

public goods Goods in which one person's consumption does not diminish the benefit to others from consuming the good (i.e., nonrivalry), and once provided, no one person can be excluded from consuming (i.e., nonexclusion).

purchasing power parity The rate of exchange that allows a specific amount of currency in one country to purchase the same quantity of goods in another country.

quota A government set limit on the quantity of imports into a country.

rate of return Uses the present value formula, but subtracts costs, then finds the interest rate (discount rate) at which this investment would break even.

rate of return regulation Permits product pricing that allows the firm to earn a normal return on capital invested in the firm.

ratio of income to poverty The ratio of family income to the poverty threshold. Families with ratios below 0.5 are considered severely poor, families with ratios between 0.5 and 1.0 are considered poor, and those families with ratios between 1.0 and 1.25 are considered near poor.

rational expectations Rational economic agents are assumed to make the best possible use of all publicly available information, then make informed, rational judgments on what the future holds. Any errors in their forecasts will be randomly distributed.

real exchange rate The price of one country's currency for another when the price levels of both countries are taken into account; important when inflation is an issue in one country; it is equal to the nominal exchange rate multiplied by the ratio of the price levels of the two countries.

real GDP The total value of final goods and services produced in a country in a year measured using prices in a base year.

real GDP per capita Real GDP divided by population. Provides a rough estimate of a country's standard of living.

recessionary gap The increase in aggregate spending needed to bring a depressed economy back to full employment; equal to the GDP gap divided by the multiplier.

recognition lag The time it takes for policymakers to confirm that the economy is in a recession or a recovery. Short-term variations in key economic indicators are typical and sometimes represent nothing more than randomness in the data.

regressive tax A tax that falls in percentage of income as income increases.

rent The return to land as a factor of production. Sometimes called economic rent.

rent seeking Resources expended to protect a monopoly position. These are used for such activities as lobbying, extending patents, and restricting the number of licenses permitted.

reserve ratio The percentage of a bank's total deposits that are held in reserves, either as cash in the vault or as deposits at the regional Federal Reserve Bank.

reserve requirement The required ratio of funds that commercial banks and other depository institutions must hold in reserve against deposits.

resources Productive resources include land (land and natural resources), labor (mental and physical talents of people), capital (manufactured products used to produce other products), and entrepreneurial ability (the combining of the other factors to produce products and assume the risk of the business).

return on investment The earnings, such as interest or capital gains, that a saver receives for making funds available to others. It is calculated as earnings divided by the amount invested.

right-to-work laws Laws created by the Taft-Hartley Act that permitted states to outlaw union shops.

Rule of 70 Provides an estimate of the number of years for a value to double, and is calculated as 70 divided by the annual growth rate.

saving The difference between income and consumption; the amount of disposable income not spent.

scarcity Our unlimited wants clash with limited resources, leading to scarcity. Everyone (rich and poor) faces scarcity because, at a minimum, our time on earth is limited. Economics focuses on the allocation of scarce resources to satisfy unlimited wants.

screening or signaling The use of higher education as a way to let employers know that the prospective employee is intelligent and trainable and potentially has the discipline to be a good employee.

second-degree price discrimination Charging different customers different prices based on the quantities of the product they purchase.

segmented labor markets Labor markets split into separate parts. This leads to different wages paid to different sectors even though both markets are highly competitive.

sequential-move games Games in which players make moves one at a time, allowing players to view the progression of the game and to make decisions based on previous moves.

share of stock A unit of ownership in a business that entitles the shareholder to one vote at shareholder meetings and one share of any dividends paid.

short run A period of time over which at least one factor of production (resource) is fixed, or cannot be changed. Firms can employ more people, have existing employees work overtime, or hire part-time employees to produce more, but this is done in an existing plant.

shortage Occurs when the price is below market equilibrium, and quantity demanded exceeds quantity supplied.

short-run aggregate supply (SRAS) curve The short-run aggregate supply curve is positively sloped because many input costs are slow to change (*sticky*) in the short run.

short-run supply curve The marginal cost curve above the minimum point on the average variable cost curve.

shutdown point When price in the short run falls below the minimum point on the AVC curve, the firm will minimize losses by closing its doors and stopping production. Because P < AVC, the firm's variable costs are not covered, therefore by shutting the plant, losses are reduced to fixed costs only.

simultaneous-move games Games in which players' actions occur at the same time, forcing players to make decisions without knowing how the other players will act. These games are analyzed using diagrams called game tables.

social network A network that combines elements of physical and virtual networks by describing groups of people using the same product or service who also are connected more directly (for business or entertainment purposes) within the network.

sole proprietorship A type of business structure composed of a single owner who supervises and manages the business and is subject to unlimited liability.

solvency crisis A situation when a bank's liabilities exceed its assets.

stagflation Simultaneous occurrence of rising inflation and rising unemployment.

store of value The function that enables people to save the money they earn today and use it to buy the goods and services they want tomorrow.

structural unemployment Unemployment caused by changes in the structure of consumer demands or technology. It means that demand for some products declines and the skills of this industry's workers often become obsolete as well. This results in an extended bout of unemployment while new skills are developed.

subprime mortgage Mortgages that are given to borrowers who are a poor credit risk. These higher-risk loans charge a higher interest rate, which can be profitable to lenders if borrowers make their payments on time.

substitute goods Goods consumers will substitute for one another depending on their relative prices. When the *price* of one good rises and the *demand* for another good increases, they are substitute goods, and vice versa. Substitutes have a positive cross elasticity of demand.

substitution effect (labor) Higher wages mean that the value of work has increased, and the opportunity costs of leisure are higher, hence work is substituted for leisure.

substitution effect When the price of one good rises, consumers will substitute other goods for that good, therefore the quantity demanded for the higher priced good falls.

sunk cost A cost that has been paid and cannot be recovered; therefore, it should not enter into decision making affecting the present or future.

sunk cost fallacy Occurs when people make decisions based on how much was already spent rather than how the decision might affect their current well-being.

supply The maximum amount of a product that sellers are willing and able to provide for sale over some time period at various prices, holding all other relevant factors constant (the *ceteris paribus* condition).

supply curve A graphical illustration of the law of supply, which shows the relationship between the price of a good and the quantity supplied.

supply of labor The amount of time an individual is willing to work at various wage rates.

supply-side fiscal policies Policies that focus on shifting the long-run aggregate supply curve to the right, expanding the economy without increasing inflationary pressures. Unlike policies to increase aggregate demand, supply-side policies take longer to have an impact on the economy.

surplus The amount by which annual tax revenues exceed government expenditures.

switching cost A cost imposed on consumers when they change products or subscribe to a new network.

tariff A tax on imported products. When a country taxes imported products, it drives a wedge between the product's domestic price and its price on the world market.

Taylor rule A rule for the federal funds target that suggests that the target is equal to 2% + Current Inflation Rate + 1/2(Inflation Gap) + 1/2(Output Gap). Alternatively, it is equal to 2% plus the current inflation rate plus 1/2 times the difference between the current inflation rate and the Fed's inflation target rate plus 1/2 times the output gap (current GDP minus potential GDP).

teaser rates Promotional low-interest rates offered by lenders for a short period of time to attract new customers and to encourage spending.

teaser strategies Attractive up-front deals used as an incentive to entice new customers into a network.

terms of trade The ratio of the price of exported goods to the price of imported goods (P_x/P_m).

third-degree price discrimination Charging different groups of people different prices based on varying elasticities of demand.

tight money or **restrictive monetary policy** Fed actions designed to decrease excess reserves and the money supply to shrink income and employment, usually to fight inflation. *See also* contractionary monetary policy.

tipping point (or critical mass) The quantity from which network effects are strong enough to support the network.

tit-for-tat strategies A trigger strategy that rewards cooperation and punishes defections. If your opponent lowers its price, you do the same. If your opponent returns to a cooperative strategy, you do the same.

total cost The sum of all costs to run a business. To an economist, this includes out-of-pocket expenses and opportunity costs.

total factor productivity The portion of output produced that is not explained by the number of inputs used in production.

total revenue Price × quantity demanded (sold). If demand is elastic and price rises, quantity demanded falls off significantly and total revenue declines, and vice versa. If demand is inelastic and price rises, quantity demanded does not decline much and total revenue rises, and vice versa.

total surplus The sum of consumer surplus and producer surplus, and a measure of the overall net benefit gained from a market.

total utility The total satisfaction that a person receives from consuming a given amount of goods and services.

tradeoff between risk and return The pattern of higher risk assets offering higher average annual returns on investment than lower risk assets.

tragedy of the commons Resources that are owned by the community at large (e.g., parks, ocean fish, and the atmosphere) and therefore tend to be overexploited because individuals have little incentive to use them in a sustainable fashion.

trigger strategies Action is taken contingent on your opponent's past decisions.

union shop Nonunion hires must join the union within a specified period of time.

unit of account Money provides a yardstick for measuring and comparing the values of a wide variety of goods and services. It eliminates the problem of double coincidence of wants associated with barter.

unitary elastic supply Price elasticity of supply is equal to 1. The percentage change in quantity supplied is equal to the percentage change in price.

unitary elasticity of demand The absolute value of the price elasticity of demand is equal to 1. The percentage change in quantity demanded is just equal to the percentage change in price.

utility A hypothetical measure of consumer satisfaction.

utility maximizing rule Utility is maximized where the marginal utility per dollar is equal for all products, or $MU_a/P_a = MU_b/P_b = \ldots = MU_n/P_n$.

value of the marginal product The value of the marginal product of labor (VMP_L) is equal to marginal physical product of labor times price, or $MPP_L \times P$.

variable costs Costs that vary with output fluctuations, including expenses such as labor and material costs.

versioning A pricing strategy that involves differentiating a good by way of packaging into multiple products for people with different demands.

vesting period The minimum number of years a worker must be employed before the company's contribution to a retirement account becomes permanent.

vicious cycle When a network good does not reach its tipping point, and therefore does not increase in value enough to retain its customers, customers leave the network, thereby further diminishing the value of the good until all customers leave the network.

virtual network A network connected by groups of people using the same type or brand of good.

virtuous cycle The point at which a network good reaches its tipping point, when network effects cause demand for the good to increase on its own. As more people buy or subscribe to a good or service, it generates even more external benefits and more demand.

wealth A stock measure of an individual's or family's assets, net of liabilities, at a given point in time.

wealth effect Households usually hold some of their wealth in financial assets such as savings accounts, bonds, and cash, and a rising aggregate price level means that the purchasing power of this monetary wealth declines, reducing output demanded.

willingness-to-pay An individual's valuation of a good or service, equal to the most an individual is willing and able to pay.

withdrawals Activities that remove spending from the economy, including saving, taxes, and imports.

x-inefficiency Protected from competitive pressures, monopolies do not have to act efficiently. Spending on corporate jets, travel, and other perks of business represents x-inefficiency.

yield The annual return to a bond measured as the coupon payment as a percentage of the current price of a bond.

yield curve Shows the relationship between the interest rate earned on a bond (measured on the vertical axis) and the length of time until the bond's maturity date (shown on the horizontal axis).

Credits for Chapter Opening Photographs

Index

Note: Page numbers followed by f indicate figures; those followed by n indicate notes; those followed by t indicate tables.